LATIN AMERICAN NEWSPAPERS
IN UNITED STATES LIBRARIES

A Union List

Publication Number Two

Conference on Latin American History

LATIN AMERICAN NEWSPAPERS
IN UNITED STATES LIBRARIES

A Union List

Compiled in the Serial Division, Library of Congress
by STEVEN M. CHARNO

Published for the Conference on Latin American History by the

UNIVERSITY OF TEXAS PRESS, AUSTIN AND LONDON

Conference on Latin American History Publications

This series is issued under an arrangement between the Conference on Latin American History, Inc., and the University of Texas Press. It includes works approved by the Publications Committee of the Conference and the Faculty Board of the Press. Publication funds are furnished by the Conference from a Ford Foundation grant.

Standard Book Number 292-78403-1
Library of Congress Catalog Card No. 69-63004
Copyright © 1968 by the Conference on
Latin American History
All Rights Reserved

Type set by WOS Company, Austin, Texas
Printed by LithoCrafters, Inc., Ann Arbor, Michigan
Bound by Universal Bookbindery, Inc., San Antonio, Texas

PREFACE

This second title in the Conference on Latin American History Publications should be welcomed by researchers and the libraries which serve them. As explained in the Introduction which follows, this volume presents detailed data on approximately 5,500 Latin American newspapers in libraries of the United States, providing a firm base for individual research and at the same time establishing a necessary factual foundation for possible future cooperative plans among libraries to develop further the national resource of Latin American newspapers.

In its discussions of this program, the Committee on Activities and Projects of the Conference on Latin American History developed a general plan, of which the present work represents a first step. The Committee agreed that it was essential to have an inventory of present resources, and authorized expenditure of Ford Foundation grant funds to permit the Serial Division of the Library of Congress to obtain and present such information. The present volume is the tangible result of that decision.

A second phase in the plan will enlist the specialized knowledge of the Conference membership. The Committee on Activities and Projects expects to elicit from specialists in CLAH their views and opinions on the relative importance of various newspapers in the countries on which they have done extensive research. They will also be asked to indicate omissions from the present work, as well as to advise the Committee on the existence of files or runs of papers which the union list indicates are lacking or deficient in United States repositories taken as a whole. In short, the Conference membership will provide priorities and possible sources in order that obvious lacunae can be identified, and steps taken to fill them.

The third phase, contingent on future funding, is the development of a cooperative plan among interested libraries to obtain on microfilm the missing issues and runs of papers, with first attention to those in the highest priorities. The minimum goal of such a continuing program would be to have in the United States, from each of the Latin American republics and Puerto Rico, newspaper coverage of at least one paper for each year following the establishment of the periodical press in that country. Hopefully, for some of the larger and more complex nations, more than a single newspaper for a given time span would be included in a cooperative work plan.

Further developments of the Conference Newspaper Program will appear in the *Newsletter* which is issued by the CLAH Secretariat in the Hispanic Foundation in the Library of Congress. Interested scholars and individuals should write to the director of the Hispanic Foundation; their comments and suggestions will be welcomed by the Committee on Activities and Projects of the Conference.

The Conference is extremely grateful to the Serial Division of the Library of Congress for this excellent and highly professional union list. On behalf of the Conference, I should also like to reiterate its appreciation of the support from the Ford Foundation, which made possible the preparation and publication of this work.

HOWARD F. CLINE
*Chairman, Committee on
Activities and Projects*

CONTENTS

INTRODUCTION

This union list provides a record of some 5,500 Latin American newspapers owned by seventy reporting libraries. The reports range from a single, usually unique, issue of a newspaper title up to extensive files of titles published for several decades, including those currently published. In providing an up-to-date record of Latin American newspaper resources within the United States of America, the objective has been not only the traditional provision of a key to the researcher in need of specific material, but also, for the longer range and, perhaps more importantly, because of the physical deterioration of the pulp newspaper files, the identification of the holdings of specific titles so that a composite of such holdings could be merged in the preparation of master negative microfilms.

The bibliographic data included in this publication provide a detailed record of holdings of the seventy reporting libraries out of some eighty-six known to have Latin American collections or area studies programs. Each institution was invited to furnish a current report on newspaper holdings. In the original questionnaire a rather specific definition, taken from UNESCO's *Statistics of Newspapers and Other Periodicals* (1959), was offered as a guideline to the reporting libraries. As reports were received, however, it became evident that the basis of selection should be broadened beyond the somewhat rigid definition originally suggested, in order to provide more comprehensive historical coverage. For example, official gazettes before 1900 were included, since many carried general news, as indeed some still do today. Specifically excluded were specialized periodicals, such as legal, medical, religious, and labor newspapers, but only if their special nature was clearly evident in the title. Undoubtedly, some specialized and general literary titles appear in this list. Their inclusion should in no way diminish the usefulness of the publication as a reference aid. The list includes over 5,500 titles, a total which represents a 10 percent increase over those reported in Arthur E. Gropp's *Union List of Latin American Newspapers in Libraries in the United States*, published by the Pan American Union in 1953.

The arrangement of the publications in this volume is based on place of publication, first by country, then by city. Within each city the arrangement is alphabetical by title. In determining alphabetical arrangement, the initial article of a title has been ignored. Contrariwise, an initial article as part of a geographical name is not ignored in the alphabetical arrangement. El Salvador, for example, follows the Dominican Republic in this listing, but the title *El Tiempo* is included in the *T*'s rather than the *E*'s. Newspapers bearing identical main titles and variant subtitles are arranged by date of establishment. In such instances the subtitle is ignored in arranging the entries. Throughout the list, the English rather than the Latin American system of alphabetization has been followed.

The bibliographic entry for each title includes, wherever such data were available, the title, periodicity, and date of establishment. The "Note" adds supplemental data concerning title and periodicity changes, dates of suspension and cessation, mergers and successions, language of publication if other than the native language of the country of publication, changes in the place of publication, references to related titles, and other pertinent information. Reporting libraries are identified by the National Union Catalog symbol list following this Introduction.

The citation of holdings, whenever possible, is by the date of the newspaper rather than by volume and number. Space-saving considerations have been disregarded in favor of more detailed reporting. The format for listing the holdings has been adopted in order to eliminate confusion. Microfilm holdings are listed immediately following the bound material, and an indication of negative film, positive film, or both, is presented.

In addition to reporting newspaper holdings of the twenty Latin American republics, the newspaper publications of Puerto Rico, because of its historical and cultural relationship to Latin America, have been included as a supplement.

It would not have been possible to compile these data without the cooperation of the seventy reporting institutions. Their reports were generally in excellent form, lessening to some extent the tedious editorial tasks. To these institutions we express our appreciation. We are especially grateful to the following institutions for their extensive reports: The American Antiquarian Society, the University of California at Berkeley, The University of Texas at Austin, and Yale University.

To the many individuals, too numerous to mention by name, who rendered advice and assistance during the preparation of this publication, we express our appreciation. In addition to the loyal staff who assisted Mr. Charno in this effort — Mary Kay McCarvel and Judith Hinz Ho — we must also mention Bernard A. Bernier and Carolyn G. Stoakes, of the regular Serial Division Staff, who provided a substantial service in reading copy and preparing the Bibliography.

Finally, we have a special note of appreciation to the Conference on Latin American History, which through the Hispanic Foundation made Ford Foundation funds available for preparation and publication of this work.

CHARLES G. LaHOOD, JR.
Chief, Serial Division
Library of Congress

SYMBOLS USED
IN THIS VOLUME

AU   University of Alabama, University, Alabama 35486

AzU   University of Arizona, Tucson, Arizona 85721

CLCM   Los Angeles County Museum Library, Exposition Park, Los Angeles, California 90007

CLSU   University of Southern California, Los Angeles, California 90007

CLU   University of California at Los Angeles, Los Angeles, California 90024

CSt   Stanford University Libraries, Stanford, California 94305

CSt – H Hoover Institution on War, Revolution, and Peace, Stanford University, Stanford, California 94305

CU   University of California at Berkeley, Berkeley, California 94720

CU – B University of California at Berkeley, Bancroft Library, Berkeley, California 94720

CoDU   University of Denver, Denver, Colorado 80202

CtY   Yale University, New Haven, Connecticut 06520

DCU   Catholic University of America, Washington, D.C. 20017

DLC   United States Library of Congress, Washington, D.C. 20540

DPU   Pan American Union Library, Washington, D. C. 20006

DeU   University of Delaware, Newark, Delaware 19711

FMU   University of Miami, Coral Gables, Florida 33124

FU   University of Florida, Gainesville, Florida 32601

ICN   Newberry Library, Chicago, Illinois 60610

ICRL   Center for Research Libraries, Chicago, Illinois 60637 (Formerly Midwest Inter-Library Center)

ICU   University of Chicago, Chicago, Illinois 60637

IEN   Northwestern University, Evanston, Illinois 60201

IU   University of Illinois, Urbana, Illinois 61803

IaAs   Iowa State University of Science and Technology, Ames, Iowa 50010

InU   Indiana University, Bloomington, Indiana 47405

KHi   Kansas State Historical Society, Topeka, Kansas 66612

KU   University of Kansas, Lawrence, Kansas 66044

LNHT   Tulane University, New Orleans, Louisiana 70118

LNT–MA Tulane University, Latin American Library, New Orleans, Louisiana 70118 (Formerly Middle American Research Institute)

LU   Louisiana State University, Baton Rouge, Louisiana 70803

MB   Boston Public Library, Boston, Massachusetts 02117

MBAt	Boston Athenaeum, Boston, Massachusetts 02108
MH	Harvard University, Cambridge, Massachusetts 02138
MWA	American Antiquarian Society, Worcester, Massachusetts 01609
MiEM	Michigan State University, East Lansing, Michigan 48823
MiU	University of Michigan, Ann Arbor, Michigan 48104
MnU	University of Minnesota, Minneapolis, Minnesota 55455
MoSU	St. Louis University, St. Louis, Missouri 63108
MoU	University of Missouri, Columbia, Missouri 65201
NBuU	State University of New York at Buffalo, Buffalo, New York 14214 (Formerly University of Buffalo)
NHi	New York Historical Society, New York, New York 10024
NIC	Cornell University, Ithaca, New York 14850
NN	New York Public Library, New York, New York 10018
NNC	Columbia University, New York, New York 10027
NPV	Vassar College, Poughkeepsie, New York 12601
NSyU	Syracuse University, Syracuse, New York 13210
NbU	University of Nebraska, Lincoln, Nebraska 65808
NcD	Duke University, Durham, North Carolina 27706
NcU	University of North Carolina, Chapel Hill, North Carolina 27515
NhD	Dartmouth College, Hanover, New Hampshire 03755
NjP	Princeton University, Princeton, New Jersey 08540
NmU	University of New Mexico, Albuquerque, New Mexico 87106
OCl	Cleveland Public Library, Cleveland, Ohio 44114
OU	Ohio State University, Columbus, Ohio 43210
OkU	University of Oklahoma, Norman, Oklahoma 73069
OrU	University of Oregon, Eugene, Oregon 94703
PPAmP	American Philosophical Society, Philadelphia, Pennsylvania 19106
PPiU	University of Pittsburgh, Pittsburgh, Pennsylvania 15213
PSt	Pennsylvania State University, University Park, Pennsylvania 16802
PU	University of Pennsylvania, Philadelphia, Pennsylvania 19104
PrU	University of Puerto Rico, Rio Piedras, Puerto Rico 00931
RPB	Brown University, Providence, Rhode Island 02912
TNJ	Joint University Libraries (Vanderbilt University, George Peabody College for Teachers, and Scarritt College), Nashville, Tennessee 37203
Tx	Texas State Library and Historical Commission, Austin, Texas 78711
TxSjM	San Jacinto Museum of History Association, San Jacinto Monument, Texas 77584
TxFTC	Texas Christian University, Fort Worth, Texas 76129
TxLT	Texas Technological College, Lubbock, Texas 79409
TxU	University of Texas at Austin, Austin, Texas 78712
ViU	University of Virginia, Charlottesville, Virginia 22903
WU	University of Wisconsin, Madison, Wisconsin 53706
WaU	University of Washington, Seattle, Washington 98105

ABBREVIATIONS USED
IN THIS VOLUME

d.	daily
sw.	twice a week
3w.	three times a week
w.	weekly
3m.	three times a month
bw.	every two weeks
irr.	irregular
m.	monthly
Micro	microfilm
(P)	positive
(N)	negative
est.	established
n.d.	no date
No.	number
Vol.	volume

Material within brackets "[   ]" is uncertain bibliographic data or incomplete holdings.

LATIN AMERICAN NEWSPAPERS
IN UNITED STATES LIBRARIES

A Union List

THE UNION LIST

ARGENTINA

Azul

EL CIUDADANO. d. est. Sept. 17, 1907.
DLC
  1955 Nov. 21.

DIARIO DEL PUEBLO. d. est. Sept. 8,
1918.
DLC
  1955 Nov. 18.

EL TIEMPO. d. est. July 9, 1933.
DLC
  1955 Nov. 26.

Bahía Blanca

LA NUEVA PROVINCIA. d. est. Aug. 1,
1898.
DLC
  1955 Oct. 31.

NUEVOS TIEMPOS. w. est. Oct. 1,
1913.
DLC
  1937 Sept. 3 – Dec. 31.
  1938 Jan. 1 – 6, 22 – Apr. 28, 30 –
       Dec. 29, 31.
  1939 Jan. 1 – Feb. 11, 13 – Mar. 4,
       6 – 18, 20 – May 6, 8 – June 17,
       19 – July 1, 3 – 15, Aug. 7 –
       Sept. 26, Nov. 6 – Dec. 31.
  1940 Jan. 1 – Feb. 22, 24 – Aug. 29,
       Nov. 2 – Dec. 31.
  1941 Jan. 1 – Feb. 13, 15 – 27, Mar.
       1 – 13, 15 – Apr. 3, 26 – May 15,
       17 – Aug. 28, 30 – Nov. 6, 8 –

       13, 15 – Dec. 4, 6 – 11, 13 – 31.
  1942 Jan. 1, 3 – 22, 24 – 29, 31 – May
       7, 9 – July 23, 25 – Sept. 17,
       19 – 24, 26 – Oct. 22, 24 – Nov.
       5, 7 – 12, 14 – Dec. 31.
  1943 Jan. 1 – 14, 16 – Feb. 4, 6,
       June 24, 26 – Aug. 19, 21 –
       Sept. 2, 4 – 16, 18 – Oct. 28,
       30 – Nov. 18, 20 – Dec. 9.

Bernal

CRONICA. w. est. Jan. 10, 1922.
DLC
  1956 May 12.

Bolívar

LA VERDAD. d. est. Nov. 4, 1911.
DLC
  1941 Dec. 4.

Buenos Aires

ACCION ARGENTINA. w. est. Aug. 21,
1940.
DLC
  1940 Sept. 11.
  1941 Nov. 26, Dec. 3.

ACCION LIBERTARIA.
CSt
  1944 Sept. 1-30.

ALBORADA DEL PLATA. w.
MWA
  1877 Dec. 2 – 23.

ALBUM DEL HOGAR. w.
　MWA
　　1885　Mar. 15.

AMERICAN. [w.]
　Note: In English.
　MWA
　　1827　Aug. 18.

ANTON PERULERO. w.
　MWA
　　1876　Mar. 23 – Apr. 6.

LA ANTORCHA. w.
　CSt
　　1924　Sept. 12.

ANTORCHA.
　DLC
　　1956　Apr. 2.

ARCHIVO AMERICANO Y ESPIRITU
DE LA PRENSA DEL MUNDO. irr.
est. June 12, 1843.
　Note: In Spanish, English and French.
　MWA
　　1846　Aug. 3.
　TxU
　　1843　Prospecto.
　　　　　June 12 – Nov. 30.
　　1844　Feb. 24 – Dec. 11.
　　1845　Feb. 28 – Nov. 5.
　　　　　Extraordinario: Nov. 5, 30.
　　1846　Feb. 28 – Nov. 5.
　　1847　Mar. 1 – Sept. 31.
　　1848　Feb. 1 – Nov. 30.
　　1849　Feb. 1 – Dec. 31.
　　1850　May 1 – Dec. 31.
　　1851　Jan. 1 – Dec. 31.

LA ARGENTINA. d. est. Apr. 4, 1901.
　CSt
　　1915　Oct. 25, Nov. 15, Dec. 24, 29.
　DLC
　　1942　Dec. 6, 9.
　IU
　　1910　July 11, 21.

ARGENTINA LIBRE. w., irr. est. 1940.
　Note: Suspended publication Feb.
　19 – 26, Aug. 6 – 27, Sept. 10 – Oct.
　29, 1942.

　CSt
　　1942　Mar. 19, Apr. 16.
　　1947　Sept. 22, Oct. 2.
　　1949　Feb. 25.
　CU
　　1941　June 5 – July 24, Aug. 7 – Dec.
　　　　　25.
　　1942　Jan. 1 – Dec. 31.
　　1943　Jan. 14 – Feb. 4, Apr. 1 – 8.
　ICRL
　　1941　June 5 – Dec. 31.
　　1942　Jan. 1 – Dec. 31.
　　1943　Jan. 1 – Apr. 8.
　TxU
　　1941　June 12 – July 10, 24 – Dec. 25.
　　1942　Jan. 8 – May 14, June 4 – 18,
　　　　　July 2 – Dec. 24.

THE ARGENTINE WEEKLY. w.
　Note: In English. Title *Buenos Aires
　Weekly Herald*, 1876 – Apr. 27, 1917;
　The River Plate Observer, May 4,
　1917 – May 25, 1923; *The Argentine
　Weekly*, after May 25, 1923. See also
　Buenos Aires Herald.
　IU
　　1910　Jan. 7.
　　1913　Aug. 29.
　　1914-1931　Jan. 1 – Dec. 31.
　　1932　Jan. 1 – June 30.
　MWA
　　1899　Dec. 15.
　　1901　Jan. 25.

ARGENTINISCHES TAGEBLATT. d. est.
Apr. 29, 1889.
　Note: In German. Suspended publica-
　tion Jan. 11 – Mar. 8, 1950.
　CU
　　1964　Apr. 29.
　DLC
　　1942　Sept. 20, 27, Oct. 4, 11, 25,
　　　　　Nov. 1, 8, 15, 29, Dec. 6, 13,
　　　　　27.
　　1943　Jan. 3, 17, 24, Feb. 7, 14, 21,
　　　　　28, Mar. 7, 14, 28, Apr. 4, 11,
　　　　　25, May 2, 9, 16, 23, 30, July
　　　　　1 – Dec. 31.
　　1944　Jan. 1 – Dec. 31.

1945　Jan. 1 – Mar. 16, 18 – Sept.
29, Oct. 1 – Dec. 31.
1946　July 1 – Dec. 31.
1947 – 1951　Jan. 1 – Dec. 31.
1952　Jan. 1 – June 21, 23, 24, 26 –
Dec. 31.
1953　Jan. 1 – Dec. 31.
1954　Jan. 1 – Mar. 10, 12 – Apr. 15,
18 – Sept. 8, 10 – Dec. 31.
1955　Jan. 1 – Dec. 31.
1956　Jan. 1 – Sept. 10, 12 – Dec. 31.
1957　Jan. 1 – Mar. 1, 3 – May 10,
12 – Nov. 19, 21 – Dec. 31.
1958　Jan. 1 – Mar. 7, 9 – Aug. 3, 5,
7 – Dec. 31.
1959　Jan. 1 – Apr. 7, 9 – Sept. 16,
18 – 20, 22 – Dec. 31.
1960　Jan. 1 – Dec. 31.
1961　Jan. 1 – July 12, 14 – Dec. 31.
Micro　(P) & (N)
1962　Jan. 1+.

ARGENTINISCHES WOCHENBLATT.
w. est. Mar. 2, 1878.
Note: In German.
CSt – H
1943　Oct. 23.
1944　Mar. 4 – 18, Apr. 8 – 15, May
27.
DLC
1940　Nov. 9 – Dec. 31.
1941　Jan. 1 – Dec. 31.
1942　Jan. 1 – June 26, 28 – July 3,
5 – Aug. 8.
1943　Dec. 18.
1944　Mar. 25, May 20.

ARGENTINOS LIETUVIU BALSAS. bw.
est. 1927.
Note: In Lithuanian.
DLC
1954　Nov. 4 – 18.
1955　Jan. 20, Sept. 1 – Dec. 15.
1956　Jan. 5 – Dec. 20.
1957　Jan. 3 – Feb. 28, Apr. 25 – Dec.
19.
1958　Jan. 16 – Dec. 31.
1959　Jan. 1 – Dec. 17.

ARGENTINSKE NOVINE. w. est. Mar.
21, 1934.
Note: In Croatian.

DLC
1942　Feb. 27, Mar. 27, Apr. 3, May
22, July 3, 17, 24, Sept. 10 – 24,
Oct. 15, 22, Nov. 5, 12, 26 –
Dec. 10, 22.
1943　Jan. 7 – July 22.
1944　Jan. 20.

**EL ARGOS DE BUENOS AYRES Y
AVISADOR UNIVERSAL.** est. May
12, 1821.
Note: Title *El Argos de Buenos Ayres*,
Aug. 20, 1823; *El Argos de Buenos
Ayres y avisador universal*, Jan. 17 –
Dec. 1, 1824. Ceased publication Dec.
3, 1825.
DLC
1821　May 26, June 16 – July 24, 31 –
Aug. 4, 11 – Oct. 6.
1823　Aug. 20.
1824　Jan. 17, 31, Feb. 11, July 14 –
Aug. 25, Oct. 20, 27 – 30, Nov.
3, 10 – 13, 20 – 27, Dec. 1.
1825　Mar. 19, Apr. 2 – Oct. 19.
MWA
1824　Jan. 24.
1825　May 6, 14, 25.
TxU
1821　May 12 – Dec. 31.
1822 – 1824　Jan. 1 – Dec. 31.
1825　Jan. 1 – Sept. 3.
WU
1821　May 12 – Dec. 31.
1822 – 1824　Jan. 1 – Dec. 31.
1825　Jan. 1 – Sept. 3.

ARMENIA. 3w. est. Apr. 24, 1931.
Note: In Armenian.
DLC
1942　Dec. 8, 28.
1943　Apr. 22 – 24, May 4 – 8, 20 –
25, 29, June 1.
Micro　(P) & (N)
1957　Jan. 1+.

ASSALAM. irr. est. Nov. 17, 1902.
Note: In Spanish and Arabic.
DLC
1943　Apr. 17 – May 4, 13 – June 12.

ASUNTOS AGRARIOS. w.
OrU
  1956   Feb. 1 – Dec. 31.

AYUDA AL PUEBLO ESPAÑOL. w. est.
July 1, 1939.
  Note: Title *La Defensa*, July 1,
  1939 – May 17, 1941; *Ayuda al pueblo
  español*, after May 18, 1941.
NN
  Micro (P) & (N)
  1939   July 1 – Sept. 1, 3 – 15, 24 –
      Dec. 31.
  1940   Jan. 1 – Dec. 31.
  1941   Jan. 1 – Mar. 8, 22 – Aug. 23.

AZZAUBAHA. bw. est. 1941.
  Note: In Spanish and Arabic.
DLC
  1942   June 1 – July 1, Aug. 15 – Sept.
      15.
  1943   Jan. 1, June 15, July 1, Sept. 1.

LA BANDERA ARABE. w. est. Feb. 1,
1934.
  Note: In Arabic.
DLC
  1940   Nov. 27.

BANDERA ARGENTINA. d. est. Aug. 1,
1932.
DLC
  1942   Aug. 11, 12.

¡BASTA! w. est. June 20, 1940.
DLC
  1942   Oct. 10, 31.

BOLETIN GERMANICO. est. 1914.
MH
  1914   Oct. 20.

BOLETIN INFORMATIVO DE LA
SITUACION ARGENTINA.
  Note: In Spanish and English.
CSt
  Spanish edition:
  1948   Jan. 6, 24, Mar. 6, Apr. 13,
      June 10, July 19, Aug. 10, Oct.
      18, Dec. 1.
  1949   Apr. 25.
  1950   June 4.
  English edition:

  1948   Apr. 13, 27, June 10, July 19,
      Aug. 10, Sept. 8.
  1949   Mar. 16, Apr. 25, May 25,
      Sept. 20, Oct. 29.

BOLETIN OFICIAL DE LA NACION. d.
CU – B
  Micro (N)
  1871   Jan. 5 – Dec. 31.
  1872 – 1873   Jan. 1 – Dec. 31.
  1874   Jan. 1 – Sept. 25.

THE BRITISH PACKET AND ARGEN-
TINE NEWS. w., irr. est. Sept. 25,
1826.
  Note: In English. *The British Packet,
  and Argentine News*, May 17, 1828 –
  Aug. 11, 1832; *The British Packet and
  Argentine News*, Aug. 12, 1832 –
  Sept. 25, 1859. Ceased publication
  Sept. 25, 1859.
CU – B
  Micro (P)
  1826   Aug. 4 – Oct. 14.
  1827   Aug. 11 – Dec. 29.
  1828 – 1829   Jan. 1 – Dec. 31.
  1830   Jan. 2, 16 – Apr. 17, May 1 –
      Dec. 25.
  1831 – 1832   Jan. 1 – Dec. 31.
  1833   Jan. 5 – Aug. 31, Sept. 14, 28 –
      Dec. 28.
  1834   Jan. 4 – Sept. 6, Oct. 18, Nov.
      1 – 8, 22 – Dec. 13, 27.
  1838   Sept. 22 – Dec. 15.
  1839   Jan. 1 – Dec. 31.
  1840   Jan. 4 – June 20, July 4 – Dec.
      26.
  1841 – 1844 Jan. 1 – Dec. 31.
  1845   Jan. 4 – July 26.
CtY
  1832   Feb. 25.
  1843   Nov. 11 – 18.
  1848   Jan. 1 – Dec. 31.
  1849   Jan. 1 – Dec. 23.
  1850 – 1851   Jan. 1 – Dec. 31.
DLC
  1828   May 17 – July 5.
  1829   Jan. 17, Apr. 11, Aug. 8 – Nov.
      7.

1830 Mar. 6, Apr. 10 — May 15, 29,
   July 12 — 17.
1831 Apr. 2 — 30, May 14 — 28.
1832 Feb. 11, 18, Mar. 10, July 21 —
   Aug. 11, Dec. 22.
1833 Jan. 19, 26, Feb. 9, Sept. 7, 28.
1837 Apr. 22 — May 6.
1838 Jan. 6 — 20, Aug. 18, 25, Sept.
   8 — Oct. 13.
1845 Feb. 15, Nov. 29, Dec. 13.
 MB
1835 Nov. 14 — Dec. 26.
1836 Jan. 2 — Dec. 31.
1837 Jan. 1 — Dec. 31.
1838 Jan. 1 — Dec. 25.
1839 Jan. 5 — 26.
 MH
1846 Aug. 22.
 MWA
1829 Aug. 29.
1832 Jan. 21 — 28.
1833 Sept. 21.
1835 July 11.
1837 Dec. 16.
1850 May 18.
NHi
1832 Oct. 27.
NN
1829 Oct. 17.

BUENOS AIRES HERALD. d. est. Sept.
15, 1876.
 Note: In English. Absorbed *The*
 Times of Argentina. Title *Buenos*
 Aires Herald and Times, [Jan. 3] —
 Feb. 1, 1900; *The Buenos Aires*
 Herald, Feb. 2, 1900 — July 9, 1904.
 See also *The Argentine Weekly.*
CSt
1915 Oct. 29, 30.
CSt — H
1963 Oct. 1 — 11, 15 — 29, Nov. 5 —
   11, 30 — Dec. 2, 10 — 13, 21 —
   28, 31.
CU
1925 Feb. 18.
1939 Oct. 15 — Dec. 12.
1940 Apr. 3, 4, 6 — 9.

DLC
 Micro (P) & (N)
1900 — 1905 Jan. 3 — Dec. 31.
1906 Jan. 1 — Oct. 12, 14 — Dec. 31.
1907 Jan. 1 — Nov. 26, 28 — Dec. 31.
1908 Jan. 1 — Dec. 31.
1909 Jan. 1 — 6, 8 — Apr. 1, 3 — 9, 11-
   May 11, 13 — June 26, 28 — July
   1, 3 — Aug. 22, 24 — Dec. 31.
1910 Jan. 1 — Apr. 30.
1912 June 1 — Dec. 31.
1913 Jan. 1 — Dec. 15, 17 — 31.
1914 Jan. 1 — 21, 23 — 27, 29 — Nov.
   12, 14 — Dec. 31.
1915 — 1918 Jan. 1 — Dec. 31.
1919 Jan. 1 — Nov. 10, 12 — Dec. 31.
1920 — 1921 Jan. 1 — Dec. 31.
1922 Jan. 1 — June 8, 10 — Dec. 31.
1923 Jan. 1 — Dec. 31.
1925 Jan. 1 — Mar. 5, 7 — Dec. 31.
1926 Jan. 1 — June 8, 10 — July 5, 7 —
   Dec. 31.
1927 Jan. 1 — Dec. 31.
1928 Jan. 1 — Sept. 20, 22 — Dec. 13,
   15 — 31.
1929 Jan. 1 — 19, 21 — Mar. 20, 22 —
   Oct. 2, 4, 6 — Nov. 11, 13 — Dec. 31.
1930 Jan. 1 — Feb. 14, 16 — Mar. 19,
   21 — Aug. 22, 24 — Nov. 20, 22 —
   Dec. 31.
1931 Jan. 1 — 28, 30 — Feb. 27, Mar.
   1 — 21, 23 — May 28, 30 — Dec. 31.
1932 Jan. 1 — May 11, 13 — 16, 18 —
   Sept. 25, 27 — Oct. 16, 18 — 23,
   25 — Dec. 31.
1933 Jan. 1 — May 25, 27 — Dec. 31.
1934 — 1937 Jan. 1 — Dec. 31.
1938 Jan. 1 — Mar. 12, 14 — Apr. 26,
   28 — Dec. 31.
1939 Jan. 1 — Dec. 31.
1940 Jan. 1 — Feb. 2, 4 — Dec. 31.
1941 Jan. 1 — Dec. 31.
1942 Jan. 1 — June 23, 27, 28, July
   2, 4 — 31, Aug. 2 — Dec. 31.
1943 Jan. 1 — Dec. 31.
1944 Jan. 1 — Mar. 1, 3 — Dec. 31.
1945 Jan. 1 — June 25, 27 — Oct. 11,
   13 — Dec. 31.

1946   Jan. 1 – Aug. 31, Sept. 2 – Dec. 31.

1947   Jan. 1 – Dec. 31.

1948   Jan. 1 – Sept. 18, 20 – Oct. 8, 10 – Dec. 31.

1949   Jan. 1 – Dec. 31.

1950   Jan. 1 – 9, 11 – 22, 24 – Apr. 8, 10 – Dec. 15, 17 – 31.

1951   Jan. 1 – 15, 18 – Dec. 10, 12 – 31.

1952   Jan. 1 – 7, 9 – Feb. 22, 24 – 26, Mar. 1 – Apr. 14, 16 – June 6, 8 – July 27, 29 – Sept. 23, 25 – 30, Oct. 2 – Dec. 31.

1953   Jan. 1 – 4, 6 – 26, 28, 29, 31 – Dec. 31.

1954   Jan. 1 – May 10, 12 – 24, 26 – July 23, 26, Aug. 2, 9, 16, 22, 30, Sept. 6, 13, 20, 27, Oct. 3, 11, 18, 25, Nov. 1, 6, 8, 14, 28, 29, Dec. 6, 13, 26, 31.

1955   Jan. 3, Feb. 5, 6, 9 – 12, 14 – 16, 18 – Mar. 17, 19 – 22, 28, Apr. 2, 4, 6 – Sept. 6, 8 – Dec. 7, 9 – 31.

1956   Jan. 1 – 27, 29 – Feb. 4, 6 – July 18, 20 – Aug. 25, 27, 28, Sept. 2, 3, 5, 9 – 13, 16 – 19, 21 – 24, 26, 29 – Oct. 2, 4 – 9, 11 – 17, 19 – Dec. 1, 3 – 20, 22 – 31.

1957   Jan. 1 – 3, 5 – Apr. 16, 18 – July 1, 3 – Oct. 8, 10 – Nov. 17, 19 – Dec. 31.

1958   Jan. 1 – July 9, 11 – Dec. 13, 15 – 31.

1959   Jan. 1 – 5, 7 – Apr. 29, May 1 – Dec. 31.

1960   Jan. 1 – Aug. 8, 10, Oct. 7, 9 – Dec. 31.

1961   Jan. 1+.

ICRL

1932   [July 3 – Dec. 31].

1933   [Jan. 1 – Oct. 25].

MWA

1926   July 4.
            Suplemento: July 4.

1949   Feb. 1.

NHi

1946   Feb. 25, 26.

NN

1916   n.d. (special centenary issue).

1919   Jan. 1, n.d. (special peace issue).

1941   June 28 – Dec. 31.

1942   Jan. 1.

1943 – 1945   Jan. 1 – Dec. 31.

1946   Jan. 1 – 17, 19 – Sept. 30, Nov. 1 – Dec. 31.

1947 – 1948   Jan. 1 – Dec. 31.

1949   Jan. 2 – Feb. 7, Mar. 1 – Dec. 31.

1950 – 1952   Jan. 1 – Dec. 31.

1953   Jan. 1 – June 16, 18, 20 – 24, 26 – 29, July 1 – 8, 10 – Aug. 7, 9 – Oct. 6, 8 – 16, 18, 19, 21 – 28, 30 – Nov. 17, 19 – 21, 23 – Dec. 3, 6, 7, 13, 16, 18 – 29, 31.

1954 – 1961   Jan. 1 – Dec. 31.

1962   Jan. 2 – Dec. 31.

1963   Jan. 1 – Apr. 30, May 2 – 30, June 1 – Dec. 31.

1964   Jan. 1+.

BUENOS AIRES WEEKLY HERALD. See *The Argentine Weekly*.

CABILDO. d. est. Sept. 1942.

CSt

1944   July 9, 10, 16, 27, 29, 31, Sept. 21, 24, 30, Oct. 2, 3, Dec. 15, 16.

DLC

1942   Oct. 13, 14.

LA CACHIPORRA. w.

CSt

1944   Sept. 20 – 27, Oct. 4, 11, 25.

CARTAS DE LA LIBERTAD.

CSt

1944   Nov. 6.

1945   Jan. 10.

CARTEL. w.

CSt

1946   May 2.

TxU

1946   May 2.

EL CENSOR. w. est. Jan. 7, 1812.
  Note: Continuous pagination.
  NN
    1812   Jan. 21 – Mar. 10.
           Suplemento: Jan. 29.
  TxU
    1812   Jan. 7 – Mar. 24.

EL CENSOR. bw., w. est. Aug. 15, 1815.
  Note: Ceased publication Feb. 6,
  1819.
  DLC
    1815   Aug. 15 – Dec. 31.
    1816   Jan. 1 – Dec. 31.
    1817   Jan. 1 – 30.
  TxU
    1815   Aug. 15 – Dec. 31.
    1816 – 1818   Jan. 1 – Dec. 31.
    1819   Jan. 1 – Feb. 6.

EL CENTINELA. est. July 22, 1822.
  Note: Ceased publication 1823.
  MH
    1823   June 29.
  TxU
    1822   July 22 – Dec. 31.
    1823   Jan. 1 – Dec. 7.

CHOQUE. w. est. Dec. 27, 1940.
  DLC
    1940   Dec. 27.

EL CIUDADANO. d. est. Feb. 1956.
  DLC
    1956   Feb. 23.

CLARIN. d. est. Aug. 28, 1945.
  DLC
    Micro (P) & (N)
    1962   Sept. 1 – 19, 21 – Dec. 31.
    1963   Jan. 1 – Apr. 16, 18 – Dec. 31.
    1964   Jan. 1+.
  MWA
    1949   Feb. 1.

CODZIENNY NIEZALEZNY KURJER
  POLSKI. D. Est. Feb. 22, 1928.
  Note: In Polish.
  DLC
    1943   Sept. 24, 28, Nov. 4.
    1944   Jan. 6, 7, 14, 21.

EL COMBATE. w.
  CSt
    1915   July 15, Sept. 2.

EL COMERCIO DEL PLATA. w. est.
  1872.
  MWA
    1888   May 13, 27, Sept. 16.

COMPAÑERO. w.
  CSt – H
    1964   Aug. 1 – Dec. 31.
    1965   Jan. 1 – Feb. 28.

CONCLUSION DE LA GAZETA DEL
  GOBIERNO.
  MWA
    1809   Oct. 12, Nov. 14.

CORREO DE ASTURIAS. w. est. Jan. 1,
  1932.
  DLC
    1937   Sept. 11 – 17, 19 – 24, 26 – Oct.
           1, 3 – Dec. 3, 5 – 31.
    1938   Jan. 1 – Feb. 11, 13 – Mar. 4,
           6 – 18, 20 – May 6, 8 – June 17,
           19 – July 1, 3 – 15, 17 – 22, 24 –
           29, 31 – Aug. 5, 7 – 26, 28 –
           Sept. 2, Nov. 6 – 12.
    1942   Oct. 24.

CORREO DE COMERCIO. w. est. Mar.
  3, 1810.
  Note: Ceased publication Apr. 6,
  1811.
  CtY
    1810   Mar. 3 – Dec. 29.
    1811   Jan. 5 – Apr. 6.
  DLC
    1810   Mar. 3 – Dec. 31.
    1811   Jan. 1 – Apr. 6.

CORREO DE LA NOCHE. d.
  CSt
    1915   Sept. 18, 22.

EL CORREO DE LAS PROVINCIAS. bw.
  est. Nov. 19, 1822.
  TxU
    1822   Nov. 19 – Dec. 31.
    1823   Jan. 1 – Apr. 10.

EL CORREO NACIONAL. d. est. Mar.
29, 1826.
>   Note: Ceased publication Mar. 30,
>   1827.
>   DLC
>   1827   Mar. 5.

CORRIERE DEGLI ITALIANI. d. est.
1948.
>   Note: In Italian.
>   DLC
>   1956   May 19.

COSMOPOLITAN. w.
>   NHi
>   1832   July 11 – Aug. 1, 29, Oct. 17 –
>   Nov. 7.

LE COURRIER DE LA PLATA. d. est.
July 1, 1865.
>   Note: In French.
>   CSt
>   1914   Feb. 13.

CRISOL. d. est. Feb. 1, 1932.
>   DLC
>   1941   Dec. 13, 16 – 19, 21 – 25.
>   1942   Jan. 1 – 3, 8, 9, 31, Feb. 7, 8, 11,
>   12, 19, 27, Mar. 10, 19, Apr. 2,
>   8, 10, 12, 16, 17, 19 – 22, 24, 30,
>   May 5, 6, 8, 9, 12, June 3, 4, 9,
>   July 15, 17, 23 – 25, Aug. 6, 8,
>   10 – 13, 18 – 22, 26 – Sept. 3, 5,
>   9 – 22, 24 – 29, Oct. 1 – 4, 7 – 9,
>   11, 14 – 21, 23 – Nov. 1, 4 – 29,
>   Dec. 2 – 22, 24 – 30.
>   1943   Jan. 1 – 10, 13 – Feb. 12, 14 –
>   20, 23 – 25, 28, Mar. 4 – 27,
>   30 – Apr. 7, 9, 11 – 22, 28 –
>   May 18, 20 – June 9, 11 – Aug.
>   1, 10, 12 – Sept. 11, 21 – 24,
>   28 – 30, Oct. 8 – 12, Nov. 5 – 9,
>   11, 14 – 18, 20 – 25, 28 – Dec. 4.
>   1944   Jan. 4 – 11.

CRITICA. d. est. Sept. 15, 1913.
>   CU
>   1941   [Oct. 15 – Dec. 31.]
>   1942 – 1946   [Jan. 1 – Dec. 31.]
>   1947   Jan. 2 – 26, 28 – Feb. 28, Mar.
>   2, 4 – 19, 21 – 26, 28 – Apr. 10,

>   12 – May 9, 11 – 31.
>   1948   May 10 – 29, 31 – July 14, 16 –
>   Dec. 31.
>   1949   Jan. 2 – 23, 25 – 28, 30, Mar.
>   5 – 16, 18 – 27, 31 – Apr. 28,
>   May 2 – 4, 8 – June 17, 19, 21 –
>   29, July 1 – 5, 7 – 31, Aug. 2 –
>   24, 26 – 28, Sept. 5 – 11,
>   13 – 25, 27 – Oct. 30, Nov. 1 –
>   18, 20 – 27, Dec. 2, 4 – 26, 28 –
>   31.
>   DLC
>   1936   Dec. 17, 19.
>   1941   Aug. 14.
>   1942   Sept. 14, 18.
>   1943   Sept. 22, Nov. 26.
>   MWA
>   1949   Feb. 1.

LA CRONICA ARGENTINA. w. est. Aug.
30, 1816.
>   Note: Ceased publication Feb. 8,
>   1817.
>   TxU
>   1816   Aug. 30 – Dec. 31.
>   1817   Jan. 1 – Feb. 8.

LA CRONICA POLITICA Y LITERARIA
DE BUENOS AIRES. d. est. Mar. 3,
1827.
>   Note: Ceased publication Oct. 6,
>   1827.
>   DLC
>   1827   Aug. 6, 7, 9 – 19, 22 – 27.

EL CRONISTA COMERCIAL. d. est.
Nov. 1, 1908.
>   DLC
>   1947   Nov. 1.

LOS DEBATES. d. est. Apr. 1, 1852.
>   Note: Ceased publication June 25,
>   1852.
>   NIC
>   1852   Apr. 1 – June 25.
>   WU
>   1852   Apr. 1 – June 25.

LA DEFENSA.
>   See *Ayuda al pueblo español*.

DEMOCRACIA. d. est. Dec. 12, 1945.
  DLC
    1952   Dec. 1 — 15, 17 — 28, 30, 31.
    1953   Jan. 1 — 25, 27, 28, 30 — May 14,
            16 — June 4, 6 — Sept. 4, 6 — 17,
            19 — 23, 25 — 28, 30 — Oct. 25,
            27, 28, 30 — Nov. 2, 4 — 30, Dec.
            2 — 14, 16 — 31.
    1954   Jan. 1 — Feb. 8, 10 — 18, 20 —
            Apr. 7, 9 — Aug. 23, 26 — 31,
            Sept. 5, 16, 24, 29, Oct. 25 —
            29, 31 — Nov. 10, 13 — 15, 18 —
            24, 27 — 29, Dec. 1 — 9, 15, 17,
            29.
    1955   Jan. 2 — 7, 9 — Feb. 1, 3 — 15,
            17 — Apr. 27, May 1 — 26, 28 —
            June 27, 29 — Sept. 15, 18 — 22,
            24, 27 — Dec. 31.
    1956   Jan. 1 — Feb. 1, 4 — Mar. 5, 8 —
            June 7, 9 — Aug. 15, 18 — Sept.
            5, 7 — Oct. 30, Nov. 1, 3 — Dec.
            31.
    1957   Jan. 1 — Feb. 7, 9 — Mar. 2, 5 —
            10, 12 — Apr. 14, 16 — 22, 24 —
            May 12, 14 — 29, 31 — June 7,
            9 — 11, 13 — 18, 21 — 23, 26 —
            July 3, 5 — 14, 16 — Aug. 3, 5 —
            17, 19 — 29, 31 — Sept. 4, 6, 7,
            9 — 19, 21 — 29, Oct. 1 — Nov.
            22, 24 — Dec. 31.
    1958   Jan. 1 — 10, 12 — 19, 21 — 24, 26,
            28 — Feb. 15, 19 — Mar. 21, 23 —
            30, Apr. 1, 2, 6, 8 — 26, 28 — May
            3, 5 — 11, 15 — 17, 19 — June 10,
            12 — 14, 16 — July 7, 9 — Aug.
            29, Sept. 1, 3 — 27, 29 — Oct. 12,
            14 — Nov. 4, 6 — 14, 16 — 23,
            25 — Dec. 15, 17 — 27, 29 — 31.
    1959   Jan. 2 — Apr. 2, 4 — 19, 21 —
            30, May 2 — July 4, 6 — 15, 17 —
            Aug. 31, Sept. 2, 4 — 22, 25 —
            Oct. 20, 23 — 29, 31 — Nov. 3,
            6 — Dec. 31.
    1960   Jan. 1 — 4, 6 — 13, 15 — 25, 28 —
            Mar. 3, 5 — May 18, 21 — June 3,
            5 — 7, 9 — 30, July 6 — 22, Sept.
            7 — Oct. 4, 6 — Dec. 3, 5 — 8,
            10 — 16.

    1961   Mar. 1 — 4, 6 — Dec. 31.
  FU
    1950   ₁Nov. 1 — 30₁.
    1951   ₁Feb. 1 — Mar. 31₁.
  MWA
    1949   Feb. 1.

EL DESPERTADOR TEO-FILAN-
  TROPICO MISTICO-POLITICO. w.,
  irr. est. Apr. 1820.
    Note: Suplemento published 1820 —
    Sept. 18, 1822. Ceased publication
    Oct. 12, 1822.
  CtY
    1820   May 14, Sept. 2, 6, 16, 23, 30,
            Oct. 12, 14, 19, 21, 28.
            Suplemento: Sept. 4, 11, 18,
            25, Oct. 2, 26, Nov. 2.

DEUTSCHE LA PLATA ZEITUNG. d.
  est. Apr. 1, 1868.
    Note: In Spanish and German. See
    also *La Plata Post*.
  CSt
    1915   Jan. 17.
  CSt — H
    1942   Nov. 19.
    1943   Feb. 17, May 6 — Dec. 31.
    1944   Jan. 1 — June 27.
  DLC
  German edition:
    1940   Mar. 10.
    1941   Jan. 3, 4, 9, 10, 23, 28, Mar. 21,
            22, 25 — 31, Apr. 1 — June 18,
            20 — Aug. 3, 6 — Sept. 7, 9 —
            15, 17 — Oct. 1, 3, 5 — 10, 12,
            27 — June 30, July 11 — Aug. 18,
            Sept. 9 — Oct. 18, 20, 21, 23 —
    1942   Jan. 1 — 28, 30 — Mar, 16, 19 —
            Apr. 26, 29 — May 6, 8 — 25,
            27 — June 30, July 11 — Aug. 18,
            Sept. 9 — Oct. 18, 20, 21, 23 —
            Nov. 10, 20 — Dec. 6, 8 — 10.
    1943   Feb. 4 — 16, Mar. 11 — 24, Apr.
            8 — 21, 29 — May 1, 3 — 5, June
            10.
  Spanish edition:
    1942   June 30.
    1943   Apr. 19.

1944   Jan. 11.

EL DIA. d.
  CSt
    1915   Sept. 8, Oct. 7, 13.

EL DIARIO. est. [1882].
  MH
    1913   Aug. 29.

DIARIO DE LA TARDE, COMERCIAL,
  POLITICO Y LITERARIO. d. est. May
  16, 1831.
    Note: Succeeded by *El Nacional*.
    Ceased publication Oct. 1852.
  CU−B
    Micro (N)
    1839   Sept. 2.
    1840   Feb. 5.
  DLC
    1838   Jan. 16−19, 22, May 28−June
            1.
  MWA
    1841   Apr. 15, 22.
  NHi
    1832   Aug. 7.

EL DIARIO ESPAÑOL. d. est. May 2,
  1913.
    Note: Succeeded *El Correo español*.
  CSt
    1915   Jan. 19.
  CU
    1925   Extraordinario: Oct. 12.
  DLC
    1941   Dec. 5.
    1942   Feb. 7, Oct. 12.
    1943   Mar. 29.

DIARIO UNIVERSAL.
  See *El Universal*.

EL 16. bw. est. Nov. 1, 1956.
  DLC
    1956   Nov. 1.

EL DIARIO ISRAELITA.
  See *Die Yiddishe Tsaitung*.

DON QUIJOTE. w. est. 1857.
  CtY
    1898   Aug. 7−14, Nov. 27−Dec. 31.
    1899   Jan 1−Feb. 19.

EL ECO. w.
  Note: In Russian.
  DLC
    1942   Apr. 4−June 20, July 11−Oct.
            31, Nov. 8−Dec. 20.
    1943   Jan. 1−Sept. 25.

EL ECO DE FLORES.
  CSt
    1914   Nov. 20.

EL ECONOMISTA. w. est. Jan. 17, 1877.
  CU
    1961−1964   Jan. 1−Dec. 31.
  LNHT
    1955   Aug. 12−Dec. 31.
    1956−1957   Jan. 1−Dec. 31.
    1958   Jan. 1−Oct. 10.

ECONOMISTA DEL PLATA. w.
  MWA
    1881   June 8, July 1−8.

LA EPOCA. d. est. Dec. 15, 1915.
  CU
    1917   [Nov. 13−Dec. 31.]
    1918   [Jan. 1−Dec. 31.]
    1919   Jan. 1−June 30.
    1947   Nov. 19, 29, Dec. 3, 4, 7−9, 14,
            17, 18, 21, 24−31.
    1948   Jan. 2−13, 15−Feb. 18, 20−
            29, Mar. 2−18, 20−25, 27−
            Apr. 28.
  DLC
    1946   Apr. 3−30, May 2−June 30,
            Sept. 1−Nov. 11, 13−18, 20−
            Dec. 28, 30.
    1947   Jan. 2−18, 20−27, 29−Feb. 1,
            3−21, 23−Mar. 9, 11−27,
            30−Dec. 31.
    1948   Jan. 1−Apr. 30, May 3−Oct.
            25, 29−Dec. 31.
    1949   Jan. 1−9, 11−30, Feb. 1−3,
            8−28, Mar. 5−24, 26−30,
            Apr. 1, 2, 4−30, May 3−Dec.
            31.
    1950   Jan. 1−June 12, 14, 15, 18−
            26, 29−July 3, 6, 7, 10−Aug. 6,
            8−Sept. 25, 27−29, Oct. 1−
            11, 13−23, 25−Nov. 1, 3−18,
            20−23, 27−Dec. 9, 11−31.

1951 Jan. 2 — Apr. 5, 7 — June 27,
29 — July 5, 7 — 15, 18 — 22,
24 — Aug. 13, 15 — 23, 25 — Oct.
4, 6 — 9, 11, 13 — 15, 18 — Nov.
14, 16 — Dec. 27, 29 — 31.

1952 Jan. 2 — Apr. 23, May 1 — July 2,
7 — Aug. 12, 18 — Nov. 5, 8 — 28,
30 — Dec. 31.

1953 Jan. 1 — Feb. 15, 17 — Apr. 29,
May 2 — June 15, 17 — 29, July
1 — 12, 14 — 19, 21 — Aug. 3, 5 —
Dec. 5, 7 — 31.

1954 Jan. 2 — 4, 6 — 19, 21 — Feb. 21,
23 — Apr. 30, May 2 — Aug. 25,
27 — Dec. 30.

MWA
1949 Feb. 1.

ESPAÑA INDEPENDIENTE.
CSt
1948 June 2.

ESPAÑA LIBRE. bw.
CSt — H
1945 Aug. 21 — Oct. 10.

**ESPAÑA REPUBLICANA. w. est. Oct.
10, 1918.**
CSt
1948 July 3.
CSt — H
1938 July 30.
1941 Aug. 16, 30, Oct. 25 — Nov. 8,
22 — Dec. 27.
1942 Jan. 3, 17 — Feb. 7, Apr. 25,
May 23, Sept. 5.
1944 June 5, July 3 — 10, 24, Dec. 30
1945 Mar. 24.
1947 Dec. 20 — 27.
1948 — 1951 Jan. 1 — Dec. 31.
DLC
1943 Mar. 20.

**EL ESPAÑOL PATRIOTA EN BUENOS-
AYRES. m. est. Jan. 1, 1818.**
Note: Ceased publication Feb. 1. 1818.
CtY
1818 Jan., Feb.

**LA ESTRELLA DEL SUD. est. Sept. 9,
1820.**

Note: Ceased publication Oct. 16,
1820.
TxU
1820 Prospecto.
Sept. 9 — Oct. 16.

EL FEDERAL. d. est. Feb. 8, 1944.
Note: Published during suppression
of *El Pampero.* Ceased publication
Jan. 17, 1945.
CSt
1944 Feb. 8 — May 10, 12 — June 2, 4,
5, 7 — July 4, 6, 8, 13, 28, Aug. 6,
10 — 12, 18, 19, 22, 24, 30, 31,
Sept. 3, 15 — 17, 20, 23, 26, Oct.
1, 16, 17, 19, 20, 24, 25, 28 —
30, Nov. 1, 4, 5, 9, 13, 18, 19,
26, 27, 30, Dec. 10, 18, 20, 21,
26, 27, Mar. 11.
1945 Jan. 4, 6.
DLC
1944 Feb. 8 — May 31.
NN
Micro (P) & (N)
1944 Feb. 8 — Dec. 31.
1945 Jan. 2 — 17.

**FRANCE-JOURNAL. d. est. Sept. 15,
1941.**
Note: In French.
DLC
1955 Nov. 16.
MWA
1949 Feb. 1.

**LA FRANCE NOUVELLE. LA NUEVA
FRANCIA. w.**
Note: In Spanish and French.
CSt — H
1944 July 7, Aug. 25, Sept. 1.
CU
1943 Jan. 29 — Feb. 5, 26, Apr. 9 —
July 9, Sept. 24 — Dec. 17.
1944 Feb. 11 — Apr. 14, 28 — Dec. 29.
1945 Jan. 1 — Dec. 31.
1946 Jan. 4 — Oct. 11.

FREIE PRESSE. d. est. Dec. 1, 1945.
Note: In German.
DLC
1945 Dec. 6 — 18, 20 — 31.

1946   Jan. 1—15, 19—21, 23, 24, 27,
        28—Mar. 8, 10—May 3, 5—
        June 24, July 4—25, Aug. 10—
        13, 17—Sept. 9, 21—Oct. 24,
        Nov. 21, 23—29, 31—Dec. 19,
        21—31.
1947   Jan. 1—3, Feb. 5, 28—Mar. 6,
        18—28, Apr. 26—May 28, 30—
        Aug. 21, 23—31, Sept. 4—Dec.
        31.
1948   Jan. 1—Mar. 23, 25, 27—Apr. 7.
MWA
1949   Feb. 1.

LA FRONDA. d. est. Oct. 1, 1919.
  CSt
    1944   July 13, 14, Aug. 9, Sept. 1,
            Nov. 26.
  DLC
    1944   Mar. 20—Apr. 4, 19—Dec. 31.
    1945   Jan. 1—Mar. 29, Apr. 2—Sept.
            13.
  NN
    Micro (P) & (N)
    1944   Oct. 1—Dec. 31.
    1945   Jan. 1—24, 26—Feb. 3, 5—
            Mar. 24, 26, 27, 29—31, Apr. 2,
            4—10, 13, 14, 16, 17, 19, 20,
            25—27, 30, May 5, 7, 9, 11, 16,
            19, 21, 22, June 11, 13, 15, 16,
            18, July 2, 9, 13, 15, 21, 25, 26,
            30, 31, Aug. 7, 9, 15, 21.
    1947   Apr. 9, 13, 19, 22, 24, 25, 29,
            30, May 3, 5, 7, 8, 20—22, 27,
            30, 31, June 4, 7, 13, 14, 24, 25,
            28, 30, July 1, 3, 4, 8—19, 24—
            29, 31, Aug. 2—8, 10—12, 14,
            16—19, 21—23, 25—31, Sept.
            2, 3, 12.
    1948   Apr. 3.

GACETA DE BUENOS AIRES. w., sw., w.
  est. June 7, 1810.
    Note: Title *Gazeta de Buenos
    Ayres*, June 7, 1810—Mar. 27, 1812;
    *Gazeta ministerial del gobierno de
    Buenos Ayres*, Apr. 3, 1812—Apr.
    28, 1815; *Gazeta de Buenos Ayres*,

Apr. 29, 1815—Oct. 27, 1819; *Gaceta
de Buenos Ayres*, Nov. 3, 1819—
Mar. 7, 1820; *Gaceta de Buenos
Aires*, Mar. 15, 1820—Sept. 12, 1821.
Periodicity June 7, 1810—Oct. 1811,
weekly; Nov.—Dec. 1811, semiweekly; after 1811, weekly. An un-
numbered *Gazeta extraordinaria de
Buenos Ayres*, which underwent the
same title changes, was published
irregularly at about the same fre-
quency as the *Ordinaria*. Ceased
publication Sept. 12, 1821.
  CtY
    1810   Jun. 7—Dec. 27.
    1811   Jan. 3—Aug. 8.
    1813   Jan. 1—Dec. 29.
    1814   Jan. 5—Dec. 14.
    1817   Jun. 21, July 12—Sept. 20, Oct.
            4—Oct. 25, Dec. 6.
    1818   Jan. 31, June 3—24.
    1819   Jan. 27, Mar. 31—Nov. 10.
    1820   Mar. 7—15, Apr. 19, May 10—
            June 14, June 28—July 5, Aug.
            16—Sept. 13, Sept. 27—Oct. 4,
            Oct. 18—25, Nov. 8—22.
  DLC
    1810   June 7—Dec. 31.
    1811—1820   Jan. 1—Dec. 31.
    1821   Jan. 1—Sept. 12.
  FU
    Micro (N)
    1910—1915   Jan. 1—Dec. 31.
  ICN
    1810   June 7—Dec. 31.
    1811—1820   Jan. 1—Dec. 31.
    1821   Jan. 1—Sept. 12.
  IU
    1810   June 7—Dec. 31.
    1811—1819   Jan. 1—Dec. 31.
  MWA
    1818   Apr. 22.
  TxU
    1810   June 7—Dec. 31.
            Extraordinario: June 8, 23, July
            3, 10, 16, 23, Aug. 7, 11, 21,
            Sept. 10, 17, 25, Oct. 2, 15, 23,
            Nov. 6, 13, 20, 25, Dec. 3, 8, 26.

Suplemento: June 7, 8, Oct. 4.
1811   Jan. 1 – Dec. 31.
Extraordinario: Jan. 2, 22, Feb.
4, 12, 18, 25, Mar. 5, 8, Apr. 1,
8, 15, 22, May 4, 21, 24, 29,
June 15, 18, 26, July 5, 9, 22,
30, Sept. 10, 25, Oct. 14, 19, 26,
27.
Suplemento: Feb. 7, 18, May 2,
9, June 26, July 25, Nov. 5, 29,
Dec. 17.
1812   Jan. 1 – Dec. 31.
Extraordinario: Jan. 4, 23, Feb.
8, 15, Apr. 5, 6, 30, May 27,
Oct. 13, 22, Nov. 10, 21.
Suplemento: Jan. 3, 10, 31,
May 1, 15, 29, June 12, July 10,
17, 24, Aug. 21.
1813   Jan. 1 – Dec. 31.
Extraordinario: Jan. 8, 12, Feb.
9, Mar. 4, 16, May 14, June 19,
Oct. 21, Nov. 5, 13.
Suplemento: Jan. 1, June 30,
Aug. 11, Nov. 10, Dec. 22.
1814   Jan. 1 – Dec. 31.
Extraordinario: May 23, July
4, 25, Nov. 23.
1815   Jan 1 – Dec. 31.
Extraordinario: Apr. 15, 29, 30,
May 14, 24, June 3, 18, July 24,
Aug. 2, Sept. 12, 14, Oct. 19,
Nov. 1, 20.
Suplemento: Dec. 23, 30.
1816   Jan. 1 – Dec. 31.
Extraordinario: Jan. 24, Mar.
31, May 24, July 5, Sept. 4, 5,
25, Oct. 3, 9, 16, 24, Nov. 11,
26, Dec. 1, 7
Suplemento: Apr. 6, Oct. 19,
Nov. 26.
1817   Jan. 1 – Dec. 31.
Extraordinario: Jan. 17, Feb. 5,
18, 20, 21, 27, Mar. 6, 11, May
7, 14, 22, June 17, Nov. 6.
Suplemento: Feb. 15, Mar. 1,
13, 22, 29, Aug. 16, Sept. 27,
Oct. 18, Nov. 1, 15, 22.
1818   Jan. 1 – Dec. 31.

Extraordinario: Jan. 13, Mar.
5, 27, Aug. 14, Oct. 9, 16, 22,
Dec. 3, 12, 24, 28.
Suplemento: Feb. 28, Apr. 8.
1819   Jan. 1 – Dec. 31.
Extraordinario: Feb. 10, 22,
Apr. 17, May 3, 24, June 3, 10,
30, July 24, Aug. 5.
1820   Jan. 1 – Dec. 31.
Extraordinario: Jan. 8, Feb. 4,
7, 15 – 19, 22, 23, Mar. 2, 6, 10,
11, 24, Apr. 2, 6, 13, 18, May
21, 25, Sept. 22, Nov. 26, Dec.
7, 14, 21.
Suplemento: Dec. 7.
1821   Jan. 1 – Sept. 12.
Extraordinario: Jan. 11, 24, 25,
28, Feb. 20, Mar. 10, Apr. 21,
26, June 11, July 2, 19.
Suplemento: Apr. 26, June 13,
23.

LA GACETA MERCANTIL. d. est. Oct. 1,
1823.
    Note: Ceased publication Feb. 3, 1852.
CU – B
    Micro (N)
    1839   Sept. 19.
DLC
    1824   Aug. 24 – 26, Nov. 5, 25, 26.
    1825   Apr. 22, May 3, 7.
    1826   Feb. 17.
    1828   Apr. 2 – 9, 15, 17, 18, 20, 21, 23,
            25 – 27, 29 – May 1, 3, 4, 6 – 9,
            14, 16 – 29, 31, June 1, 4, 6 – 8,
            10 – 15, 17 – 20, 22 – 27.
    1829   May 4, June 23, 26, 30, July
            15 – 27, 31 – Oct. 28, 31 – Nov.
            18, 20, 22, 23, 27 – 29, 31, Dec.
            1, 3 – 9, 12 – 31.
    1830   Jan. 2 – Feb. 14, 17 – 25, 27 –
            Mar. 19, 21 – 26, 28, 29, Apr.
            4, 5, 7, 15 – 22, 24 – 28, 30 –
            May 9, 11 – June 1, 3 – 13, 15 –
            28, 30 – July 6.
    1831   Mar. 21 – Apr. 23.
    1832   Feb. 15 – 25.
    1833   Jan. 18, 24.
    1835   Nov. 14.

1836	Sept. 28 – 30, Oct. 3 – 7, 11.
1838	May 30, 31, June 2, Aug. 13 – 26, 28 – Sept. 6, 12, 13, 17, 18, 20 – 26, 28, Oct. 2 – 4, 15, 16.
1840	Mar. 21 – Apr. 23.
1844	Mar. 15, 18 – 30, Apr. 8, 10, 13 – 19, July 19, 22 – 24, Aug. 6 – 8.
1845	Dec. 13, 15 – 19.
1846	Apr. 25, 28 – 30, May 1 – 5, 14.
1851	Feb. 13.

MH
1849	Oct. 30, Nov. 21, Dec. 13, 18.
1850	Jan. 7.

MWA
1841	Apr. 15, 17.

LA GACETA PAZ.
DeU
Current (three months).

GALICIA. w., bw., 3m. est. Dec. 4, 1922.
Note: Periodicity [Dec. 4, 1922] – Aug. 18, 1948, weekly; Aug. 28, 1948 – Sept. 10, 1949, biweekly; after Sept. 20, 1949, three times a month.
DLC
1937	Jan. 10 – 31.
1938	Dec. 11.
1940	Nov. 2.
1941	Feb. 1 – 7, 9 – Mar. 14, 16 – Dec. 31.
1942	Jan. 1 – Mar. 27, 29 – June 26, 28 – July 3, 5 – Nov. 6, 8 – 20, 22 – 27, 29 – Dec. 11, 13 – 31.
1943	Jan. 1 – Dec. 11.
1944	Aug. 5 – 11, 13 – Dec. 31.
1945	Jan. 1 – Oct. 19, 21 – Nov. 9, 11 – 16, 18 – Dec. 31.
1946	Jan. 1 – Feb. 8, 10 – Apr. 5, 7 – 12, 14 – May 10, 12 – July 19, 21 – Dec. 6, 8 – 20, 22 – 31.
1947	Jan. 1 – 24, 26 – Dec. 31.
1948	Jan. 1 – May 21, 30 – Dec. 31.
1949	Jan. 1 – July 15, 24 – Nov. 29, Dec. 1 – 31.
1950	Jan. 1 – Mar. 9, 11 – 29, 31 – Apr. 29, May 31 – June 29, July

	1 – 29, 31 – Aug. 29, 31 – Sept. 29, Oct. 1 – 29, 31 – Nov. 29, Dec. 1 – 29.
1951	Jan. 11 – Feb. 26, 28 – June 9, 11 – Sept. 29, Oct. 1 – Nov. 9, 11 – Dec. 30.
1953	Aug. 30 – Oct. 15, Nov. 15, Dec. 15.
1954	Jan. 15, Feb. 15, Mar. 15, Apr. 15 – May 15, June 30 – July 30, Oct. 15 – Dec. 15.
1955	Jan. 15 – 30, Aug. 15 – 30, Sept. 30.
1956	Mar. 15 – 30, Apr. 30, May 30, Aug. 15 – 30.
1957	May 15, June 30, July 30, Aug. 30, Sept. 30, Oct. 30, Nov. 30, Dec. 30.
1958	Jan. 30, Feb. 28, Mar. 30, Apr. 20 – May 25, Oct. 31 – Nov. 30.

GAZETA DE BUENOS AYRES.
See *Gaceta de Buenos Aires*.

GAZETA MINISTERIAL DE SEVILLA.
MWA
1808	[June 18 – July 6.]

GAZETA MINISTERIAL DEL GOBIER-NO DE BUENOS AYRES.
See *Gaceta de Buenos Aires*.

GAZETA EXTRAORDINARIA DE BUENOS AYRES.
See *Gaceta de Buenos Aires*.

GAZETAS EXTRAORDINARIAS DE MADRID.
MWA
1808	Apr. 9, Aug. 16, 26. Extraordinario: Nov. 30. Suplemento: Aug. 16, 19, Nov. 15.

GAZETTA EXTRAORDINARIA DE SEVILLA.
MWA
1808	June 19.
1809	Jan. 4.

GIORNALE D'ITALIA. d. est. 1906.
Note: In Spanish and Italian.

DLC
  1942   Jan. 29, Mar. 11.

EL GORILA. w. est. Oct. 11, 1956.
DLC
  1956   Oct. 11.

EL HERALDO DEL PACIFICO. d. est.
Apr. 19, 1879.
MWA
  1879   Apr. 19—29.

EL HIMNO NACIONAL.
CSt
  1944   Aug. 15.

LA HORA. d. est. Jan. 12, 1940.
  Note: Suspended publication 1950—
  May 2, 1958.
CSt
  1940   Apr. 9.
  1942   Mar. 25, 26.
  1948   Jan. 2—6, 8—11, 13—Feb. 8,
          10—Aug. 18, 20—23, Oct. 1—
          Nov. 30.
DLC
  1941   Dec. 1—31.
  1942   Jan. 1—Mar. 24, 26—Apr. 28,
          30, May 3—Aug. 29, Sept. 1—7,
          27—Dec. 31.
  1943   Jan. 1—May 23, 25, 27—June
          6.
  1945   Dec. 22—31.
  1946   Jan. 1—Feb. 18, 20—Mar. 19,
          21—Apr. 27, May 25—27, June
          1—July 8, 10—16, 18—20, 22—
          Sept. 15, 17—Oct. 16, 18—Dec.
          13, 15—31.
  1947   Jan. 1—16, 18—Feb. 25, 27—
          Mar. 26, 29—Apr. 2, 4—27,
          29—May 28, 30—Aug. 16, 18—
          Sept. 6, 8—20, 22—29, Oct. 1,
          2, 4—16, 18—24, 26—31, Nov.
          2—6, 8—10, 12—14, 16—28,
          Dec. 2—5, 7—12, 14—19, 21—
          31.
  1948   Jan. 1—9, 11—23, 25—30, Feb.
          1—8, 10—Mar. 5, 7—12, 14—
          25, 27—Apr. 2, 4—9, 11—16,
          18, 19, 30, May 2—4, 7—21,

          24—28, June 1—11, 13—19,
          21—30.
  1958   May 2—31, June 2—Oct. 6, 8—
          Nov. 2, 4, 5, 8—18, 20—Dec. 3,
          5—30.
NN
  Micro (P) & (N)
  1940   Jan. 13—Aug. 31, Sept. 24—
          Dec. 31.
  1941   Jan. 1—Dec. 31.
  1942   Jan. 1—June 22, July 8—Dec.
          31.
  1943   Jan. 1—June 6.
  1945   Nov. 10, 11, Dec. 9—14, 18, 19,
          22—31.
  1946   Jan. 1—Dec. 31.
  1947   Jan. 1—Aug. 26.

HRVATSKI DOMOBRAN. w., irr. est.
May 12, 1931.
  Note: In Spanish and Croatian.
DLC
  1941   July 24, Sept. 26, Dec. 12.
  1942   Jan. 9, 16, Apr. 10, May 7—21,
          June 4—13, July 9—Aug. 20,
          Sept. 10, Oct. 22, 28, Nov. 5—
          Dec. 24.
  1943   Jan. 7—Oct. 28, Nov. 25—Dec.
          2.

EL INDEPENDIENTE. est. Sept. 15,
1816.
  Note: Ceased publication Jan. 7, 1817.
TxU
  1816   Sept. 15—Dec. 31.
  1817   Jan. 1—5.

ITALIA LIBRE. w., d., w. est. 1940.
  Note: In Spanish and Italian. Title
  Italia libre, 1940—Nov. 23, 1943;
  Italia libera, Nov. 24, 1943—Dec. 30,
  1944; *Italia libre* after Dec. 30, 1944.
  Periodicity 1940—Nov. 23, 1943,
  weekly; Nov. 24, 1943—Dec. 30,
  1944, daily; after Dec. 30, 1944,
  weekly.
CSt
  1942   Dec. 26.
  1943   Jan. 2, Oct. 9.
NN
  Micro (P) & (N)

1941   Feb. 1, Apr. 19 – Dec. 27.
1942   Jan 3 – Dec. 26.
1943   Jan. 2 – Nov. 23, Dec. 2, 3, 16 –
        31.
1944   Jan. 1 – Dec. 30.
1945   Jan. 6 – Dec. 31.
1946   Jan. 1 – Dec. 31.
1947   Jan. 1 – Dec. 27.

INTERALIADO. w. est. May 29, 1941.
  DLC
    1942   Feb. 5.
    1943   Nov. 18.

JUEDISCHE WOCHENSCHAU.
    Note: In German.
  NN
    Micro (N)
    1948   Jan. 3 – Dec. 31.
    1949   Jan. 1+.

LA LIBERTAD.
  CSt
    1913   Nov. 16.

LIBRE EXPRESION.
  CSt
    1947   Oct. 6.

LIBRE PALABRA. d. est. Aug. 19, 1940.
  DLC
    1940   Aug. 19 – Dec. 31.
    1941   Jan. 1 – May 1, 3 – Dec. 31.
    1942   Jan. 1 – Feb. 16, 18 – 28.
    1943   Jan. 1 – Feb. 28, Mar. 2 – Dec.
            31.
    1944   Jan. 1 – Dec. 31.
    1945   Jan. 1 – Mar. 31.

EL LUCERO. d. est. Sept. 7, 1829.
    Note: Ceased publication July 31,
    1833.
  DLC
    1829   Sept. 7 – Oct. 5, 7 – 29, 31 –
            Nov. 13, 15 – 20, 22 – 24, 27 –
            29, Dec. 2 – 10, 13 – 31.
    1830   Jan. 1 – 4, 6 – 18, 21 – 24, Feb.
            1 – 8, 10, 11, 13 – 17, 19 – Mar.
            2, 4, 6 – 21, 23 – 31, Apr. 2 –
            May 28, 30 – June 4, 6 – July
            11, 14 – 29, Dec. 16 – 31.

1831   Jan. 1 – Mar. 10, 12 – 14, 16,
        20 – 24, 26 – Apr. 23.
1832   Feb. 16, 17, 20 – Mar. 15, 17 –
        21, May 11, 13, 14, 27 – 29,
        June 3 – 12, 14 – 17, 19 – 26,
        28 – 30, July 3 – 20, 22 – 24,
        26 – 29, Aug. 8 – 10, 12 – 18.

MARTIR O LIBRE. w. est. Mar. 29, 1812.
  TxU
    1812   Mar. 29 – May 25.

IL MATTINO D'ITALIA. d. est. May 21,
1930.
    Note: In Spanish and Italian.
  CSt
    1942   Nov. 19 – Dec. 31.
    1943   Jan. 1 – Dec. 7.
  DLC
    1941   Dec. 30.
    1942   Jan. 4, 9, 15, 16, Mar. 10, Sept.
            6, Oct. 23, 24, 26 – 29, Nov.
            20 – 30, Dec. 1 – 6, 8 – 10.
    1943   Feb. 4 – 16, Mar. 11 – 24, Apr.
            8 – 21, 29 – May 5, June 4, 6.

MAYO.
  CSt
    1945   July 5.

EL MOMENTO ARGENTINO. d. est.
Nov. 23, 1933.
  DLC
    1942   Aug. 13, 20, 21, Sept. 14, 18 –
            21, 23, Oct. 8.
    1943   Jan. 22.

EL MUNDO. d. est. May 14, 1928.
  DLC
    1936   Dec. 1.
    1941   Aug. 22.
    1942   June 17.
    1943   May 2.
    1949   Jan. 1 – Mar. 31, May 22, 23,
            25 – June 1, 3 – 16, 18, 21 – 30,
            July 2 – 11, 13 – 16, 18 – 27, 29,
            Aug. 1 – 3, 5 – 20, 22 – Sept.
            4, 6, 8 – 14, 16 – 20, 22 – Oct.
            10, 12 – Dec. 31.
    1950   Jan. 1 – Mar. 28, 30 – Apr. 8,
            10 – Sept. 15, 17 – Oct. 9, 11 –

Nov. 17, 19 — Dec. 22, 24 — 31.
1951 Jan. 1 — 25, 27 — Apr. 15, 17 —
Aug. 8, 10 — Dec. 31.
1952 Jan. 1 — Feb. 1, 3 — 8, 10 — 22,
24 — 26, 28 — Mar. 4, 6 — 8, 10 —
16, 18 — June 18, 20 — July 25,
27 — Sept. 19, 21 — Oct. 16,
19 — Dec. 2, 5, 6, 8 — 31.
1953 Jan. 1 — 20, 22 — May 8, 10 — 12,
14, 16 — 27, 29 — July 24, 26 —
Oct. 14, 16 — Dec. 31.
1954 Jan. 1 — Feb. 9, 11 — May 10,
12 — Aug. 7, 9 — 15, 18 — Dec.
31.
1955 Jan. 1 — Apr. 3, 5 — 10, 12 —
July 10, 12, 13, 15 — 17, 19 —
Aug. 10, 12 — 25, 27 — Dec. 31.
1956 Jan. 1 — Mar. 27, 29 — Apr. 1,
3 — May 26, 28 — Oct. 30, Nov.
1 — Dec. 31.
1957 Jan. 2 — 6, 8 — 11, 13 — Mar. 7,
9 — 28, 30 — Apr. 30, May 2 — 6,
8 — 20, 22 — June 29, July 1 — 5,
7 — Sept. 1, 3, 4, 6 — 19, 22,
24 — 26, 28 — Oct. 28, 30, 31.

LA NACION. d. est. Jan. 4, 1870.
Note: Suspended publication Feb.
8 — Mar. 3, 1949. Succeeded *La Nación argentina*. See also weekly edition.
  CLU
    1927 — 1939 Jan. 1 — Dec. 31.
    1940 Jan. 1 — June 30.
    1941 — 1942 Jan. 1 — Dec. 31.
    1943 Apr. 1 — Dec. 31.
    1944 — 1948 Jan. 1 — Dec. 31.
    1949 July 1 — Dec. 31.
    1950 Jan. 1 — Dec. 31.
    1951 Mar. 1 — Dec. 31.
    1952 Jan. 1 — Dec. 31.
    1953 Jan. 1 — Nov. 30.
    1954 Jan. 1 — Mar. 31, May 1 — Dec.
31.
    1955 Jan. 1+.
  CSt
    1915 Jan. 1, Oct. 1, 11, Nov. 23, 24.
  Micro (N)
    1908 July 9.

1909 May 25, July 9.
CU
  1917 — 1941 Jan. 1 — Dec. 31.
  1942 Jan. 1 — Aug. 31.
  1943 May 1 — Dec. 31.
  1944 — 1945 Jan. 1 — Dec. 31.
  1946 Jan. 1 — Dec. 20, 22 — 31.
  1947 Jan. 2 — May 9, 14.
  1948 May 6 — July 6, 8 — Dec. 28, 30,
31.
  1949 Jan. 2 — Apr. 7, 9 — Aug. 14, 18,
21, 26.
  1957 Jan. 21 — Feb. 7, 14 — 16, 18,
20 — 22, Mar. 6, 8, 9, 12 — 31,
Apr. 2 — 12, 24.
CU — B
  Micro (N)
  1872 Apr. 13, May 1, 3, 9,
June 7, 18.
  1882 Jan. 29.
CtY
  Micro (P)
  1951 — 1956 Jan. 1 — Dec. 31.
DLC
  1870 Jan. 4.
  1891 May 28 — June 14, 25, 27 — July
4, 6 — 8, 10 — 25, 27 — Aug. 18,
21 — Nov. 23, 25 — Dec. 31.
  1892 Jan. 1 — 28, 30 — Feb. 12, 16 —
22, 24 — July 11, 13 — 31, Aug.
2 — 31.
  1902 Jan. 1.
  1939 July 1, 2, 4 — 7, 15 — Aug. 18,
26 — 28, 30 — Sept. 1, 16 — 26,
28 — Nov. 3, 5 — 24, Dec. 8 — 17,
19 — 31.
  1940 Jan. 1 — 5, 7 — June 5, 7 — 22,
24 — July 5, 20 — Aug. 1, 3 — 9,
11 — 31, Sept. 5 — 7, 10 — Dec.
31.
  1941 Jan. 1 — 22, 24 — 31, Feb. 11,
18 — Aug. 2, 4 — Sept. 13, 15 —
18, 20 — Oct. 11, 13 — Dec. 16,
19 — 23, 25, 26, 28 — 31.
  1942 Jan. 1 — Apr. 4, 8, 9, 11, 13 —
18, 20 — 26, May 1 — June 23,
27, 28, July 2, 4 — Dec. 31.
  1943 Jan. 1 — Dec. 31.

1944   Jan. 1 – Mar. 26, 28 – Dec. 31.
1945   Jan. 1 – Dec. 31.
1946   Jan. 1 – June 1, 3 – Dec. 31.
1947 – 1948   Jan. 1 – Dec. 31.
1949   Jan. 1 – Apr. 1, 3 – Aug. 10,
        12 – Sept. 28, 30 – Dec. 31.
1950   Jan. 1 – Aug. 24, 26 – 30, Sept.
        1 – Dec. 31.
Micro (P)
1951   Jan. 1+.
DPU
Current (six months).
Micro (P)
1950   Aug. 1 – Dec. 31.
1951 – 1955   Jan. 1 – Dec. 31.
ICRL
1923   Sept. 4 – Dec. 31.
1924 – 1950   Jan. 1 – Dec. 31.
Micro (N)
1951   Jan. 1+.
ICU
Micro (P)
1951 – 1955   Jan. 1 – Dec. 31.
IEN
1950   Oct. 1 – 8, 10 – 15, 18 – 23, 25 –
        Nov. 6, 8 – 18, 21, 25, 27 – 30.
1951   June 14 – Sept. 30, Nov. 22 –
        Dec. 31.
1952   Jan. 1+.
IU
1951 – 1954   Jan. 1 – Dec. 31.
1955   Jan. 1 – Feb. 28.
Micro (P)
1923   Sept. 4 – Dec. 31.
1924   Jan. 1+.
KHi
1908   Jan. 31.
MH
1920   Jan. 4.
1929   Feb. 3.
Micro (P)
1951 – 1955   Jan. 1 – Dec. 31.
1956   Jan. 1 – Sept. 30.
MWA
1892   Nov. 28, Dec. 3.
MnU
1929   Apr. 16 – Dec. 31.
1930 – 1933   Jan. 1 – Dec. 31.

1934   Jan. 1 – July 15.
1935 – 1939   Jan. 1 – Dec. 31.
1940   Jan. 1 – Sept. 15, Oct. 1 – Nov.
        30.
1941   Jan. 1 – Apr. 30.
Current (one year).
Micro (P)
1951 – 1955   Jan. 1 – Dec. 31.
MoSU
Current (two years).
NBuU
Current (three months).
NNC
1965   May 9, 11 – 12, 14 – 17, 19 – 20,
        22 – 31, June 2 – 7, 10 – 19, 21 –
        25, 29, July 1 – 4, 6 – 9, 11 – 15,
        17 – 31, Aug. 1 – 5, 7, 9 – 10, 12,
        14 – 15, 18 – 20, 22 – 25, 28 –
        31, Sept. 1 – 9, 11 – 12, 14 –
        24, 26 – 30, Oct. 1 – 4, 6, 10 –
        11, 13 – 18, 20 – 25, 28 – 29,
        31, Nov. 1 – 5, 8 – 10, 13 – 23,
        25, 27 – 28, 30, Dec. 1 – 9, 11 –
        12, 15 – 20, 22 – 23, 26 – 29.
1966   Jan. 4 – 5, 7.
NPV
1919   Sept. 1 – 8, 10 – Nov. 8, 10 –
        Dec. 1.
1920   Feb. 1 – 16, 18 – Mar. 11, 13 –
        May 25, 27 – June 13, 15 – Dec.
        31.
1921   Jan. 1, 3 – 31.
1922   Jan. 1 – May 25, 27 – Oct. 29,
        31 – Dec. 31.
1923   Jan. 1, 3.
1934   Aug. 25 – Dec. 31.
1935   Jan. 1 – Mar. 11, Oct. 13 – Dec.
        31.
1936   Jan. 1 – June 12.
1937   July 11 – Dec. 31.
1938   Jan. 1 – Apr. 11, 21, Aug. 28 –
        Dec. 31.
1939   Jan. 1 – Apr. 29, Dec. 23 – 31.
1940   Jan. 1 – Dec. 31.
1941   Jan. 1, 3 – 17, 22 – 24, 26, 27.
1942   Sept. 1 – 8, 14 – 17, 26 – 28,
        30 – Dec. 31.
1943   Jan. 1 – 4, 6 – June 25, 27, 29,

30, July 4, 11, 18, 25, Aug. 1 –
8, 15, 22, 29, Sept. 5, 12, 19,
26, Oct. 3, 10, 17, 24, 31, Nov.
7, 14, 21, 28, Dec. 5, 12, 19, 26.
1944 – 1945   Jan. 1 – Dec. 31.
1946   Jan. 1 – Mar. 31.
1947   Aug. 1 – Dec. 31.

NSyU
1957   Jan. 1+.

NcD
1928   Apr. 5 – 12, 17 – 21, 29, May
15 – 18, 20 – 29, Oct. 8, 10 –
13, 18 – 20, 22 – 31, Nov. 1 –
Dec. 31.
1929   Jan. 1 – July 12, 14, 17 – Sept.
3, 6 – Dec. 31.
1930   Jan. 1 – June 26, 28 – Aug. 11,
16 – Nov. 13, 15 – Dec. 31.
1931   Jan. 1 – Nov. 5, 7 – Dec. 31.
1932   Jan. 1 – May 25, 27 – July 19,
21 – Dec. 31.
1933   Jan. 1 – Dec. 31.
1934   Jan. 1 – Apr. 16, 18 – June 30.
1935 – 1936   Jan. 1 – Dec. 31.
1937   Jan. 1 – Oct. 12, 14 – Dec. 31.
1938   Jan. 1 – Nov. 8, 10 – Dec. 31.
1939 – 1941   Jan. 1 – Dec. 31.
1942   Feb. 1 – May 31, Aug. 1 – Dec.
31.
1943   Jan. 1 – Mar. 31, May 1 –
Sept. 30, Nov. 1 – Dec. 31.
1944 – 1950   Jan. 1 – Dec. 31.
Micro (P)
1942   Jan. 15, 16, 20 – 24.
1943   Apr. 6.
1951   Jan. 1+.

NhD
1929   Nov. 1 – Dec. 31.
1930   Jan. 1 – Oct. 31.
1931   June 1 – Dec. 31.
1932 – 1933   Jan. 1 – Dec. 31.
1934   Jan. 1 – Apr. 16, 18 – June 30.
1935 – 1941   Jan. 1 – Dec. 31.
1942   Jan. 1 – June 23, 26 – 29, July
2 – Dec. 31.
1943 – 1944   Jan. 1 – Dec. 31.
1945   Jan. 1 – 28, 30 – July 28, 30 –
Dec. 31.

1946   Jan. 1 – Mar. 18, 20 – 27, 29 –
Dec. 31.
1947   Jan. 1 – 20, Feb. 1 – 14, 20,
22 – Oct. 16, 18 – Nov. 6, 8 –
Dec. 31.
1948   Jan. 1 – Aug. 16, 18 – Oct. 5,
7 – Dec. 31.
1949   Jan. 2 – 21, July 6 – 30, Aug.
1 – Dec. 31.
1950   Jan. 1 – Dec. 31.
Micro (P)
1951   Jan. 1+.

NjP
1945   Jan. 4.
Micro (P)
1951   Jan 1+.

OkU
1965   Jan. 12 – Dec. 31.
1966   Jan. 1+.

OrU
1960   Aug. 29, Sept. 5, 12, 19.

PSt
Current (six months).

PU
1908   June 11 – Dec. 31.
1909   Jan. 1 – Apr. 9, 11 – May 25,
27 – July 9, 11 – Dec. 31.
1910   Jan. 3 – Feb. 8, 10 – Mar. 12,
27 – Apr. 16, 18 – 23, 25 – May
1, June 1 – July 1, 8, 21 – Sept.
13, 16, 17, 21, 25, Oct. 1 – 18,
26 – Dec. 31.
1911 – 1916   Jan 1 – Dec. 31.
Micro (P)
1951 – 1955   Jan. 1 – Dec. 31.

TxU
1938   July 1 – 8, 10 – 31, Sept. 1 – 12,
Dec. 16 – 31.
1939   Jan. 1, 3 – Mar. 22, 24 – June
21, July 1 – 8, 10 – Aug. 16,
18 – 31.
1941   July 11 – 31, Aug. 2 – 19, 21 –
27, 29 – Dec. 31.
1942   Jan. 1 – May 31, June 24 – July
31, Oct. 1 – Dec. 31.
1943   Jan. 1 – Aug. 31, Sept. 18 – 20.
1944   Aug. 1 – Dec. 31.
1945   Jan. 1 – Apr. 22, 24 – 26, 28 –

Sept. 11, 13 – 23, 25 – Nov. 4,
6 – 18, 20 – 22, 24 – Dec. 31.
1946   Jan. 1 – June 12, 14 – July 13,
15 – 23, 25 – Nov. 17, 19, 20,
22 – Dec. 21, 25 – 31.
1947   Jan. 1 – 11, 13 – 20, Feb. 13,
14, 20, 22 – Mar. 10, 12 – May
19, 21 – 24, 26 – Dec. 31.
1948   Jan. 1 – 3, 5 – 31, Feb. 2 – June
9, 11 – 22, 24 – July 18, 20 –
28, 30 – Sept. 13, 15 – Oct. 3,
5 – Dec. 31.
1949   Jan. 1 – 21, July 6 – 17, 19 –
Dec. 31.
1950   Jan. 1 – May 24, 26 – Dec. 31.
1951 – 1952   Jan. 1 – Dec. 31.
Micro (P)
1953 – 1955   Jan. 1 – Dec. 31.
WU
Micro (P)
1941 – 1952   Jan. 1 – Dec. 31.
1953   Jan. 1 – June 30.

LA NACION. EDICION AREA INTER-
NACIONAL. w. est. 1960.
Note: International edition.
CSt – H
1962   July 2 – Nov. 19.
1963   Oct. 14 – 21, Nov. 25 – Dec. 31.
1964   Jan. 1 – July 27, Aug. 10 – 24.
1965   Aug. 9 – Dec. 31.
1966   Jan. 1+.
CU
1960   Sept. 5 – 19.
1961   May 2 – Dec. 26.
1962 – 1965   Jan. 1 – Dec. 31.
FU
1963   Sept. 2 – Dec. 31.
1964   Jan. 1+.
TxLT
Current (one month).

LA NACION. WEEKLY EDITION.
FU
1963   Sept. 1 – Dec. 31.
1964   Jan. 1+.
CSt
1933   Oct. 28 – Nov. 26.
1934   Oct. 7 – Dec. 31.

1935   Jan. 1 – Dec. 31.
1936   Jan. 1 – Mar. 8.
1942   Feb. 1 – 15.
NPV
1948 – 1951   Jan. 1 – Dec. 31.
1952   Jan. 1 – Aug. 3.
1953   Jan. 1 – Dec. 31.
1954   Jan. 1 – Oct. 16, 18 – 31, Nov.
2 – 7, 9 – Dec. 31.
1955   Jan. 1 – Oct. 1, 3 – Dec. 31.
1956   Jan. 1+.
NmU
1941 – 1942   Jan. 1 – Dec. 31.
1943   Jan. 3 – 17, Apr. 11 – Dec. 26.
1944   Jan. 1 – 23, May 7 – Dec. 31.
1945   Jan. 4 – 28, Mar. 11 – Dec. 30.
1946   Jan. 1 – Dec. 31.
1947   Jan. 5 – Apr. 6, July 6 – Dec.
28.
1948   Jan. 1 – Dec. 31.
1949   Jan. 2 – Feb. 6, Mar. 6 – Dec.
25.
1950   Jan. 1 – Mar. 12, June 4 – Dec.
31.
1951   Jan. 1 – Dec. 31.
1952   Jan. 6 – 13, July 20 – Dec. 28.
1953 – 1954   Jan. 1 – Dec. 31.
1955   Jan. 2 – 9, Mar. 13 – Dec. 24.
1956 – 1961   Jan. 1 – Dec. 31.
1962   Jan. 7 – Mar. 4, Apr. 1 – Aug.
5, Sept. 23 – Dec. 30.
1963 – 1964   Jan. 1 – Dec. 31.
1965   Jan. 10 – Nov. 28.
Micro (P)
1934   Feb. 1 – Dec. 31.
1935   Jan. 1 – 24, Mar. 1 – Dec. 31.
1936 – 1937   Jan. 1 – Dec. 31.
1938   Jan. 1 – Feb. 27.
PrU
1948   Jan. 1 – June 27, July 11 – Sept.
26, Oct. 10, 24 – 31, Nov. 7,
21 – Dec. 31.
1949   Jan. 2 – 9, Feb. 18, Mar. 20,
July 3 – Dec. 31.
1950   Jan. 1 – Apr. 16, 30 – Aug. 6,
20 – Dec. 17.
1951   Aug. 1 – Dec. 16, 30.
1952   Jan. 1 – Mar. 16, 30 – July 6,

20 — Aug. 10, Sept. 7 — Dec. 31.
1953   Jan. 4 — 18, Feb. 1 — Apr. 19,
       May 3 — Dec. 31.
1954   Jan. 1 — Oct. 10, 24 — 31, Nov.
       14 — Dec. 31.
1955   Jan. 1 — Sept. 25, Oct. 9 — Dec.
       24.
1956 — 1957   Jan. 1 — Dec. 31.
1958   Jan. 5 — 12, Mar. 1, Aug. 1 —
       Dec. 31.
1959   Jan. 1 — Dec. 20.
1960   Jan. 1 — Aug. 7, 21 — Dec. 31.
1961   Jan. 1 — Mar. 25, Apr. 30, May
       7, 21 — Dec. 31.
1962   Jan. 1 — June 21, Aug. 26 —
       Sept. 16, Oct. 1 — Dec. 31.
1963   Jan. 1 — Apr. 30, July 21 — Dec.
       31.
1964 — 1965   Jan. 1 — Dec. 31.

NACION CATALANA. w., bw., 3m. est.
  1923.
    Note: Periodicity 1923 — 1929, weekly;
    Jan. 1930, biweekly; after Feb. 5,
    1930, three times a month.
  DLC
    1927   Oct. 8 — Dec. 31.
    1928   Jan. 1 — Dec. 31.
    1929   Jan. 1 — Feb. 1, 3 — Nov. 9, 11 —
           Dec. 31.
    1930   Jan. 1 — Feb. 24, 26 — Mar. 24,
           26 — May 15.

NACION Y PUEBLO. sw. est. June 28,
  1953.
  DLC
    1958   June 23.

EL NACIONAL. w. est. Dec. 23, 1824.
    Note: Suspended publication June
    23 — Oct. 1825.
  CtY
    1824   Dec. 23, 30.
    1825   Jan. 6 — June 23.
  TxU
    1824   Dec. 23 — 31.
    1825   Jan. 1 — Dec. 31.
    1826   Jan. 1 — Apr. 6.

EL NACIONAL. d. est. May 1, 1852.
    Note: Succeeded *El Diario de la*

tarde, comercial, político y literario.
    Ceased publication Aug. 28, 1893.
  CU — B
    Micro (N)
    1872   May 6, June 7.
  DLC
    1852   July 8.
    1859   Nov. 25.

EL NACIONAL. d. est. Aug. 12, 1958.
  DLC
    1958   Aug. 12 — Oct. 26, 31 — Nov. 17,
           Dec. 18 — 31.
    1959   Jan. 2 — Apr. 2, 4 — 19, 21 —
           May 6, 8 — 29.

EL NACIONAL DE LA SEMANA. w. est.
  Oct. 25, 1868.
  CU — B
    Micro (N)
    1868   Oct. 25 — Dec. 31.
    1869 — 1870   Jan. 1 — Dec. 31.
    1871   Jan. 1.

NASA SLOGA. w. est. Feb. 17, 1938.
    Note: In Croatian.
  DLC
    1942   Feb. 12 — Mar. 4, 6 — Apr. 1,
           15 — June 18, Dec. 10.
    1943   Mar. 4, June 3.

NASH KLYCH. w., irr.
    Note: In Ukrainian.
  IEN
    1959   Jan. 1 — Apr. 23, May 3 — Aug.
           6, Aug. 20 — Dec. 3, 17 — 24.
    1960   Jan. 7 — Oct. 27, Nov. 24, Dec.
           8 — 15.
    1961   Jan. 12 — 26, Feb. 23 — Mar. 2,
           16 — May 4, 15 — 25, Oct. 19.
    1962   Feb. 22, May 3.

NASHA STRANA. w.
    Note: In Russian.
  MH
    1950   Apr. 15 — Dec. 23.
    1951   Jan. 6 — Nov. 3, Dec. 22, 29.
    1952   Jan. 5 — June 7, Aug. 23, Sept.
           13 — 20, Oct. 11 — 18, Nov. 1 —
           Dec. 6.

1953   Jan. 17, Feb. 7, 14, July 18—
        Dec. 26.
1954   Jan. 2—Dec. 23.
1955   Jan. 1—June 2, 16.
1956   Feb. 2, Mar. 1—Oct. 4, Dec. 20.
1957   Jan. 10—31, Feb. 21—Dec. 26.
1958   Jan. 2—Dec. 25.
1959   Jan. 1—July 2, 16, 23, Aug.
        13—Oct. 29, Nov. 19—Dec. 31.
1960   Jan. 7—14, 28, Feb. 4—Dec. 27.
1961   Jan. 3—Oct. 10, 31, Nov. 7,
        21—Dec. 26.
1962   Jan. 2—Mar. 20, Apr. 3—Dec.
        25.
1963   Jan. 1—May 7, 21—Dec. 24.
1964   Jan. 1—Dec. 31.
1965   Jan. 5—Nov. 2, 30.

NOTICIAS GRAFICAS. d. est. June 10,
1931.
    CSt
    1943   Jan. 2—19, 21—27, 29—31,
            Feb. 2, 3, 5, 7—10, 12—19,
            20—25, 27—Apr. 2, 4—30, May
            2—June 2, 4, 7—July 1, 4—7,
            9—11, 14—22, 24—Aug. 6, 8—
            10, 12, 15—20, 23, 26, 30, Sept.
            1, 2, 5, 16, 17, 19, 26, Oct. 1—
            3, 5—8, 14, 19, 23, 25, 31, Nov.
            12, 13, 23, 25, 28, 30, Dec. 1, 6,
            10, 11, 18, 19, 21, 23—25, 27,
            30.
    1944   Jan. 5, 6, 8, 12, 15—21, 23, 26,
            28, Feb. 2, 3, 8—11, 18—20, 22,
            23, 28, Mar. 4, 11—15, 19, 21—
            23, 25, 26, Apr. 2, 4, 6—8, 11,
            13, 16, 18, 19, 21, 23, May 16,
            Nov. 29, Dec. 1, 31.
    1945   Jan. 15, Feb. 4, 9, Apr. 9, 10, 12,
            29, May 11, 15, 20—27, 29,
            June 22, July 3, 6, 10, 18, 22, 23,
            25, 29, Aug. 3, 9, 10, 16, 27,
            Sept. 5, 12, 16, 21.
    1947   Jan. 20, 22, Feb. 1—6, 8—13,
            18—Mar. 12, 15—18, 20—26,
            28—Apr. 8, 14, 20, 27, 29, May
            1—5, 7—12, 14, 16—26, June
            1—3, 5—8, 11—17, 19, 20, 22—
            24, 26, July 1—6, 8—20, 22—

            24, 26—30, Aug. 1—30, Sept.
            1—7, 13, 17—19, 25, 26, Oct.
            5, 10—16, 18—Nov. 6, 9, 10, 12,
            13, 16—19, 21—26, Dec. 2, 3, 8,
            9, 11, 12, 18—20, 22—24, 26,
            28, 30.
    DLC
    1942   Jan. 9, 19.
    1943   June 7.
    1944   Apr. 24.
    MWA
    1949   Feb. 1.

LA NOVELA SEMANAL. w. est. 1920.
    CU
    1928   May 14—21, June 11, Aug. 20,
            Sept. 17—24.

NUESTRA PALABRA. w.
    CSt—H
    1965   Feb. 3—Dec. 31.
    1966   Jan. 1+.

LA NUEVA ERA. bw.
    TxU
    1846   Feb. 11—Mar. 8.

LA NUEVA ESPAÑA. sw. est. July 3,
1936.
    DLC
    1937   Feb. 16—24, 26—Mar. 6, Sept.
            6—11, Oct. 1—6, 18—27, 29—
            Nov. 24, 26—Dec. 4, 6—26.
    1938   Jan. 27—Mar. 12, 14—Apr. 27,
            29—May 7, 9—June 15, 17—
            July 12, 14—Aug. 6, 8—16,
            18—23, 25—27, 29—Sept. 2,
            18—27, Oct. 2—7, Nov. 28, 30.
    NN
    1939   Feb. 4—7, 9—21, 23—Mar. 1,
            18, Apr. 1—11, 16—30, June
            15—21.

LA NUEVA FRANCIA.
    See *La France Nouvelle. La Nueva
    Francia*.

LA NUEVA PROVINCIA.
    KHi
    1908   Jan. 7.

LA OBRA.
    CSt
    1939   Feb. 1—28.

EL OBRERO. w. est. [1890].
  CU—B
    Micro (N)
    1891   Feb. 7.

EL OBSERVADOR AMERICANO. w.
  est. 1816.
  TxU
    1816   Prospecto.
            Aug. 19—Nov. 4.

¡OIGA! d. est. Feb. 3, 1941.
  DLC
    1941   Mar. 18.
    1942   Feb. 5, 19, Mar. 5, May 4, July
            18—22, 24, Aug. 6, 7, 9—14,
            16—19, 21—28, 30, 31, Sept.
            8—15, 18, 24—26, 29, Oct. 1, 2,
            4, 9, 11—15, 17, 19, 22, 30.

ORIENTACION. w. est. Sept. 17, 1936.
  CSt
    1948   Jan. 6—June 9, 11—July 5, 7—
            Aug. 25.

EL PAMPERO. d. est. Nov. 4, 1939.
    Note: Suppressed Jan. 27, 1944—
    Feb. 8, 1945. *El Federal* published
    during suspension. Ceased publica-
    tion Feb. 15, 1945.
  DLC
    1939   Nov. 4.
    1940   Dec. 7—19.
    1941   Feb. 17—Mar. 11, 13—24, 26—
            Apr. 4, 7—21, 23—May 1, 3—
            12, 14—19, 22—24, 26—June
            17, 19—July 4, 6—12, 14, 16—
            18, 20, 22, 23, 25, 27, 28, 30—
            Aug. 2, 4, 5, 8—17, 19, 20, 22—
            24, 27—Sept. 5, 8, 9, 11—14,
            16, 18—Oct. 15, 17—Dec. 31.
    1942   Jan. 2—19, 21—24, 27—Mar.
            21, 26, 30—Apr. 9, 13—19, 21,
            23, 24, 26—May 3, 7—9, 11, 12,
            14—19, 21—24, 26, 27, 30,
            June 1—7, 18—20, 22, 24—
            Aug. 1, 3—Sept. 9, 11—Dec.
            31.
    1943   Jan. 1—July 27, Aug. 2, 3, 5, 7,

            9—Sept. 12, 14—16, 19—23,
            Oct. 5—26, 31—Dec. 30.
  NN
    Micro (P) & (N)
    1943   June 21—Aug. 1, 4, 6, 8, 15,
            Sept. 5, 7, 13, 14, 17, 18, 20—
            24, 26—29, Oct. 2—7, 9—20,
            23—29, Nov. 1—Dec. 1, 3, 13,
            15—19, 21—31.
    1944   Jan. 2—5, 7—9, 11—26.
    1945   Feb. 11—14.
  ViU
    Micro (P)
    1943   Jan. 9, 11—21, 23—26.

PATRIA. w. est. Oct. 11, 1924.
    Note: In Greek.
  DLC
    1942   Oct. 11.
    1943   July 9.

LA PLATA POST. w. est. July 10, 1884.
    Note: In Spanish and German. Week-
    ly edition of *Deutsche La Plata Zei-
    tung.*
  DLC
    1942   Feb. 18, July 15, Sept. 9, 30,
            Oct. 7, 21, Dec. 2—16.
    1943   Feb. 3, 17, 24, Apr. 14, May 5,
            12, June 2, 16.

LA PRENSA. d. est. Oct. 18, 1869.
    Note: Suspended publication Apr.
    26—30, 1944; Feb. 8—Mar. 3, 1949;
    suppressed Jan. 25, 1951—Feb. 2,
    1956.
  AU
    1944   June 18, July 30, Aug. 27.
    1945   Feb. 4, June 17, 24, Aug. 5,
            Dec. 23.
    1946   Mar. 10, May 5, 12.
    1948   Apr. 11.
  AzU
    1943   Jan. 1, 3—Feb. 1, 3—8, 9—
            Mar. 17, 19—June 27, 30—
            Sept. 20, 22—Oct. 14, 16—
            Dec. 16, 18—31.
    1944   Jan. 1—31, Feb. 2—Apr. 25,
            May 1—22, 23—June 2, 4—

July 11, 13 – Aug. 9, 11 – Dec.
31.

1945 Jan. 1, 3 – 13, Feb. 1 – 28, Mar.
2 – 14, 16 – Oct. 8, 10 – Dec.
31.

1946 Jan. 1, 3 – Mar. 31, Apr. 2 –
May 1, 3 – 15, 17 – July 31, Aug.
2 – Nov. 15, 17 – Dec. 11, 13 –
31.

1947 Jan. 1 – Feb. 16, 18 – Apr. 3,
5 – 30, May 2 – June 19, 21 –
24, 26 – July 12, 14 – Oct. 16,
18 – Dec. 31.

1948 Jan. 1 – Feb. 8, 10 – Mar. 17,
19 – 25, 27 – Apr. 30, May 2 –
June 19, 21 – Aug. 16, 18 – Oct.
16, 18 – Nov. 5, 7 – Dec. 31.

1949 Jan. 2 – Feb. 7, 9 – Mar. 2, 4 –
26, 28 – Apr. 14, 16 – 30, May
2 – June 19, 21 – 23, 25 – Aug.
16, 18 – Sept. 14, 16 – Oct. 16,
18 – Nov. 6, 8 – Dec. 29, 31.

1950 Jan. 1 – Feb. 16, 18, 19, 21 –
Mar. 20, 22 – Apr. 30, May 2 –
June 19, 21 – Aug. 16, 18 –
Sept. 3, 5 – Oct. 16, 18 – Nov.
6, 8 – Dec. 29, 31.

1951 Jan. 2 – 25.

1956 Feb. 3, 4, 5, 6, 16 – 23, Mar. 1 –
June 20, 22 – July 16, 18 – Aug.
16, 18 – Oct. 11, 13 – 20, 22 –
Nov. 6, 8 – 12, 25 – Nov. 30,
Dec. 2 – 4, 6 – 23, 25 – 31.

1957 Jan. 1 – Mar. 3, 5 – Apr. 18,
20 – 30, May 2 – June 19, 21 –
28, July 1, 3 – Aug. 9, 11 – 16,
18 – Oct. 11, 13 – 20, 22, 24 –
Nov. 2, 4 – 6, 8 – Dec. 31.

1958 Jan. 1 – Feb. 16, 18 – Apr. 3,
5 – May 3, 4 – June 7, 9 – 19, 21,
22, 24 – July 20, 22 – Aug. 16,
18 – Sept. 22, 24 – Oct. 11, 13 –
Nov. 6, 8 – Dec. 1, 3 – 23, 25 –
31.

1959 Jan. 1 – 18, 21, 22, 24 – Feb. 4,
6 – 8, 10 – Mar. 26, 28 – Apr.
30, May 2 – June 7, 9 – 19, 21 –
Aug. 16, 18 – Sept. 22, 25, 27 –
29, Oct. 1 – 6, 8 – Nov. 18, 20 –

24, 26 – Dec. 24, 26 – 31.

1960 Jan. 1 – 17, 19 – Apr. 14, 16 –
22, 24 – 30, May 2 – 11, 15 –
June 7, 9, 10, 12 – 19, 21 – 30,
July 2 – 31, Aug. 2 – 16, 18 –
Sept. 18, 20 – Oct. 6, 8 – Nov.
6, 8 – 13, 15 – Dec. 23, 29

1961 Jan. 2 – 14, 16 – Feb. 12, 14 –
18, 20 – Mar. 4, 6 – June 7, 9 –
19, 21 – 25, 27 – July 4, 6 – 17,
19 – 31, Aug. 2 – 16, 18 – 20,
22 – Sept. 16, 18 – Oct. 5, 6 –
16, 18 – Nov. 6, 8 – 24, 26 –
Dec. 7, 9, 11 – 24, 26, 29 – 31

1962 Jan., Feb., Mar., Apr. 1 – 19,
21 – 30, May 2 – June 7, 13 –
July 31, Aug. 3 – 16, 18 – 24,
26 – Nov. 6, 8 – Dec. 24, 26,
28 – 31.

1963 Jan. 1 – Feb. 11, 13 – 24, 26 –
Apr. 5, 7 – 11, 13 – 30, May 2 –
22, 24 – 29, June 1 – 7, 9 – 18,
21 – July 15, 17 – Aug. 16, 18 –
21, 23 – Sept. 24, 26 – Oct. 13,
16 – Nov. 5, 8 – Dec. 12, 15 –
24, 26, 27, 29 – 31.

1964 Jan. 2 – Feb. 9, 11 – 14, 16 –
Mar. 1, 3, 4, 6 – 19, 21 – 26,
28 – Apr. 30, May 2 – 22, 24 –
June 2, 4 – 7, 9 – 14, 16 – 19,
21 – July 19, 21 – 25, 27 – Aug.
16, 18 – Oct. 10, 13 – Nov. 6,
8 – 28, 30, Dec. 2 – 17, 19 – 24,
26 – 31.

1965 Jan. 2, 3, 5 – 21, 24 – 27, 29 –
Feb. 2, 4 – 8, 10 – 22, 24 – 28,
Mar. 2 – 11, 13 – Apr. 13, 17 –
30, May 2 – 31, June 2, 3, 5 –
7, 9 – 19, 21 – Aug. 9, 11 – 14,
16, 18 – 20, 22 – Sept. 13, 15 –
30, Oct. 2 – 10, 12 – Nov. 5, 8 –
25, 27 – Dec. 18, 20 – 24, 26 –
30.

1966 Jan. 2 – 8, 11 – Dec. 31.

1967 Jan. 1+.

CLSU
  Micro (P)
  1938 July 1 – Dec. 31.

1939–1950   Jan. 1–Dec. 31.
1951   Jan. 1–25.
1956   Feb. 3–Dec. 31.
1957   Jan. 1+.
CLU
  1926   Mar. 1–Dec. 31.
  1927   Jan. 1–Feb. 28, Oct. 1–Dec.
       31.
  1938–1940   Jan. 1–Dec. 31.
  1941   July 1–Dec. 31.
  1942–1946   Jan. 1–Dec. 31.
  1947   Jan. 1–Nov. 30.
  1948–1950   Jan. 1–Dec. 31.
  1951   Jan. 1–25.
  1956   Feb. 3–Dec. 31.
  1957   Jan. 1+.
  Micro (P)
  1928–1937   Jan. 1–Dec. 31.
CSt
  1869   Oct. 18.
  1915   Aug. 1–Oct. 31.
  1944   Nov. 26.
  1946–1950   Jan. 1–Dec. 31.
  1951   Jan. 1–25.
  Micro (N)
  1910   Jan. 1–Sept. 30.
CU
  1927   July 24.
  1930   Dec. 21.
  1931   Jan. 1.
  1937   Jan. 9–Feb. 11, 13–June 30,
       July 2–Aug. 27, 30–Dec. 31.
  1938   Jan. 30, Mar. 13, 20, 27, Apr. 3,
       10, 17, May 8, 15, 22, 29, June
       5, 12, 19, 26, July 3, Sept. 11,
       Oct. 16.
  1939   Oct. 29, Nov. 5, 12, 19, 26.
  1940   Jan. 7, 14, 21, 28, Feb. 4, 11, 18,
       25, Mar. 3, 10, 17, 24, 31, Apr.
       7.
  1945   Jan. 5–Nov. 29.
  1947   Oct. 1–Dec. 31.
  1956   Apr. 21–Dec. 31.
  1957   Jan. 2–May 27, 29–Dec. 31.
  1958   Jan. 2–Apr. 30, May 3–Aug.
       19, 21–Dec. 31.
  1959   Jan. 2–Feb. 19, 21–Aug. 10,
       12–Oct. 21, 23–Dec. 7, 9–31.

1960   Jan 2–May 11, 15–27, July
     19–29, 31–Aug. 16, 19–Oct.
     19, 21–Dec. 31.
1961   Jan. 2–Nov. 24, 26–Dec. 31.
1962   Jan. 2–June 19, 21–28, 30–
     Aug. 14, 16–Sept. 6, 8–Dec.
     31.
1963   Jan. 2–June 19, 21–Dec. 31.
1964   Jan. 1–Dec. 31.
Micro (P)
1948   Jan. 1–Dec. 31.
1949   Jan. 2–May, 18, 20–Dec. 31.
1950   Jan. 1–Dec. 31.
1951   Jan. 1–25.
CU–B
Micro (N)
1872   June 8.
CtY
  1911   Sept. 1–Dec. 31.
  1912   Jan.–June 1.
  1914   Mar. 30–July 30, Aug. 15–
       Dec. 31.
  1916   Jan. 1–31.
  1919–1927   Jan. 1–Dec. 31.
Micro (P)
  1928–1950   Jan. 1–Dec. 31.
  1951   Jan. 1–25.
  1956   Feb. 3–Dec. 31.
  1957   Jan. 1+.
DLC
  1908   July 1–8, 12–Aug. 15, 18–
       Sept. 7, 9–Nov. 15, 18–Dec.
       31.
  1909   Jan. 1–Feb. 12, 15–July 1, 3–
       7, 10–Aug. 21, 23–Dec. 31.
  1910   Jan. 1–May 22, 24–June 2,
       4–15, July 20–Sept. 24, 26–
       Dec. 31.
  1911   Jan. 1–Mar. 30, Apr. 1–May
       21, 23–Dec. 31.
  1912   Jan. 1–Dec. 31.
  1913   Jan. 1–Mar. 14, 16–Sept. 2,
       4–Nov. 20, 22–Dec. 31.
  1914   Jan. 1–6, June 1–7, 9–21,
       23–Sept. 6, 8–18, 20–Dec.
       31.
  1938–1939   Jan. 1–Dec. 31.
  1940   Jan. 1–21, 23–June 2, 5–
       Dec. 31.

1941   Jan. 1 – Feb. 19, 21 – May 15,
17 – Aug. 16, 18 – Sept. 13,
15 – Dec. 31.
1942 – 1943   Jan. 1 – Dec. 31.
1944   Jan. 1 – Apr. 25, May 1 – Dec.
31.
1945   Jan. 1 – May 19, 21 – Nov. 15,
17 – Dec. 31.
1946 – 1948   Jan. 1 – Dec. 31.
Micro (N)
1847   July 1 – Dec. 31.
1869   Oct. 18 – Dec. 31.
1870 – 1907   Jan. 1 – Dec. 31.
1908   Jan. 1 – June 30.
Micro (P) & (N)
1915   Jan. 1 – 7, 9 – June 2, 4, 5, 7 –
9, 11 – 21, 23 – July 10, 12 – 17,
19 – Aug. 8, 10 – 29, 31 – Sept.
10, 12 – 17, 19 – Dec. 6, 8 –
15, 17, 18, 20 – 31.
1916   Jan. 1 – 7, 9 – 11, 13 – 27, 29 –
Feb. 3, 5 – 12, 14 – July 28, 30 –
Aug. 15, 17 – 26, 28 – Sept. 11,
13 – 17, 19 – Oct. 29, 31 – Nov.
4, 6 – 13, 15 – Dec. 26, 28 – 31.
1917   Jan. 1 – 24, 26 – May 5, 7 – July
27, 29 – Dec. 31.
1918   Jan. 1 – 21, 23 – Feb. 5, 7 –
Mar. 11, 13 – Dec. 31.
1919   Jan. 1 – Apr. 29, May 8 – 28,
June 12 – July 20, 22 – Aug. 4,
7 – Oct. 1, 3 – Nov. 22, 24 –
Dec. 31.
1920   Jan. 1 – Feb. 10, 12 – May 17,
19 – Aug. 1, 3 – Sept. 2, 5 –
Oct. 12, 14 – 17, 19 – Nov. 4,
6 – Dec. 31.
1921   Jan. 1 – Feb. 3, 5 – 15, 17 –
May 30, June 1 – Dec. 31.
1922   Jan. 1 – Dec. 31.
1923   Jan. 1 – Mar. 29, 31 – Sept. 2,
4 – Dec. 31.
1924 – 1925   Jan. 1 – Dec. 31.
1926   Jan. 1 – Apr. 17, 19 – Dec. 31.
1927 – 1928   Jan. 1 – Dec. 31.
1929   Jan. 1 – June 28, 30 – July 13,
15 – 31, Aug. 2 – Dec. 31.
1930   Jan. 1 – Apr. 12, 14 – Dec. 31.

1931   Jan. 1 – Mar. 2, 4 – July 8, 10 –
Nov. 20, 22 – Dec. 31.
1932   Jan. 1 – Aug. 21, 23 – Nov. 6,
8 – Dec. 31.
1933   Jan. 1 – 21, 23 – July 3, 5 –
Dec. 31.
1934   Jan. 1 – Apr. 5, Sept. 5, 7, 9 –
Dec. 10, 12 – 28, 30, 31.
1935   Jan. 1 – 27, 29 – Dec. 31.
1936   Jan. 1 – Feb. 9, 11 – Mar. 29,
31 – June 10, 12 – Oct. 31,
Nov. 2 – 16, 18 – Dec. 31.
1937   Jan. 1 – Dec. 31.
Micro (P)
1949   Jan. 1 – Feb. 7, Mar. 4 – June
30.
1950   Jan. 1 – Dec. 31.
1951   Jan. 1 – 25.
1956   Feb. 3 – Dec. 31.
1957   Jan. 1+.
DPU
Micro (P) & (N)
1938   Jan. 31 – Dec. 31.
1939 – 1943   Jan. 1 – Dec. 31.
Micro (N)
1944   Mar. 7 – Apr. 10, June 15 –
Dec. 31.
Micro (P)
1945 – 1950   Jan. 1 – Dec. 31.
1951   Jan. 1 – 25.
FU
1962   Jan. 2 – Dec. 31.
1963   Jan. 1+.
Micro (N)
1909   Nov. 1 – 5, 9 – 13, 15 – Dec.
10, 12 – 31.
1910   Jan. 1 – Feb. 28, July 1 – 13,
15 – Aug. 12, 14 – 25, 27 – 31.
1911   Aug. 1 – 15, 17 – Oct. 1, 3 –
31.
1912   Jan. 1 – 31, Apr. 1 – 30, Nov.
1 – 30.
1913   Feb. 1 – 12, 14, 15, 17, 18, 20 –
Mar. 6, 8 – Apr. 7, 9 – 20, 22,
24 – 30, June 1, 2, 4 – 8, 10 –
19, 21 – 29.
1915   Dec. 1 – 7, 9 – 23, 26 – 31.
1916   Jan. 1 – Apr. 19, 21 – May 7,

9 – 18, 20 – June 30, Sept. 1 –
Nov. 1, 3 – Dec. 31.
1919   Sept. 1, Oct. 1, 3 – 31, Dec. 1 –
18, 20 – 31.
1920   Oct. 1 – Nov. 25, 27 – Dec. 31.
1921   Dec. 1 – 31.
ICRL
1913   Feb. 23 – Dec. 31.
1914 – 1918   Jan. 1 – Dec. 31.
1928   Sept. 30 – Dec. 31.
1929 – 1950   Jan. 1 – Dec. 31.
1951   Jan. 1 – 25.
Micro (P) & (N)
1956   Feb. 3 – Dec. 31.
1957   Jan. 1+.
ICU
Micro (P)
1938   July 11 – Dec. 31.
1939 – 1950   Jan. 1 – Dec. 31.
1951   Jan. 1 – 25.
IU
1950   Jan 2 – Dec. 31.
1951   Jan. 1 – 25.
1956   Feb. 3 – Dec. 31.
1957 – 1958   Jan. 1 – Dec. 31.
1965   Jan. 1 – Dec. 31.
Micro (P)
1959   Oct. 1 – Dec. 31.
1960 – 1964   Jan. 1 – Dec. 31.
1965   Jan. 1 – Aug. 31.
IaAS
Current (one year).
InU
1946   Oct. 1 – Dec. 31.
1947 – 1950   Jan. 1 – Dec. 31.
1956   Mar. 1 – Dec. 31.
1957 – 1959   Jan. 1 – Dec. 31.
1966   Jan. 1+.
LU
Micro (P)
1946 – 1950   Jan. 1 – Dec. 31.
1951   Jan. 1 – 25.
1956   Feb. 3 – Dec. 31.
1957   Jan. 1+.
MB
Current (one month).
MH
1911   Dec. 31.

1912   Jan. 1 – 31, Mar. 1 – Apr. 16, 18 – 28, 30, June 1 – Dec. 31.
1913   Jan. 1, 3 – 6, Apr. 26 – May 24, 27 – June 28, 30, July 1 – Oct. 31, Nov. 3 – Dec. 31.
1914   Jan. 1 – 18, 20 – Feb. 24, Mar. 1 – 25, 28, Apr. 10, 12 – May 12, 15 – 19, 21, 23 – 25, 27 – June 15, 17 – 28, 30 – Oct. 6, 8 – Nov. 5, 7 – Dec. 31.
1915   Mar. 1 – 30, July 1 – Nov. 11, 13, 16, 18 – Dec. 21.
1916   Jan. 1 – 6, 11, 12, 14 – 29, Feb. 1 – May 20, 22 – July 23, 25 – Nov. 17, 19 – Dec. 31.
1917   Jan. 1 – 9, Apr. 24 – 30, July 1 – Oct. 25, 27, 29, Nov. 1 – 26, 28, 30 – Dec. 25, 27 – 30.
1918   Jan. 1 – 11, Feb. 20 – Apr. 25, 27 – June 25, 27 – Oct. 30, Nov. 1 – Dec. 31.
1919   Jan. 1 – Apr. 29, May 8 – 28, June 12 – Oct. 1, 3 – 9, 11 – Nov. 3, 5 – Dec. 4, 6 – 31.
1920   Jan. 1 – July 13, 18 – Sept. 10, 15 – Nov. 10, 12 – 29, Dec. 1 – 31.
1921   Jan. 1 – Mar. 30, Apr. 1 – 8, July 14 – 17, 20 – Aug. 25, 27 – Dec. 31.
1922   Jan. 1 – May 24, 31 – Dec. 31.
1923   Jan. 1 – Dec. 31.
1924   Jan. 1 – Dec. 1, 3 – 31.
1925   Jan. 1 – 18.
1926   July 30.
1927   June 2.
1928   Jan. 8, 11, 14 – 21, 24 – 26, Feb. 10 – Mar. 28, Apr. 1, 8, 15, 22, 29, May 6, 13, 20, 27, July 8, 15, 22, Sept. 9, 16, Nov. 18.
1929   Jan. 16, 20, 27, Feb. 3, 10, 17, 24, May 25, June 2, 9, 16, 23, 30, July 7, 9, 14, 21, 28, Aug. 11, 18, Sept. 15, 26, Nov. 3.
1930   Feb. 6, Oct. 28, Nov. 5.
1937   Apr. 13 – Dec. 26, 28 – 31.
1938   Jan. 1, 3 – 8.

Micro (P)
1938 – 1948   Jan. 1 – Dec. 31.
1949   Jan. 1 – 31, Apr. 1 – Dec. 31.
1950   Jan. 1 – Dec. 31.
1951   Jan. 1 – 25.
MWA
1891   Aug. 5.
1919   Oct. 18.
1949   Feb. 3.
1956   Feb. 3.
MiEM
1965   Jan. 1+.
MnU
1938   July 1 – Dec. 31.
1939 – 1950   Jan. 1 – Dec. 31.
1951   Jan. 1 – 25.
Micro (P)
1938   July 1 – Dec. 31.
1939 – 1950   Jan. 1 – Dec. 31.
1951   Jan. 1 – 25.
MoSU
Current (one year).
MoU
Micro (P)
1938   July 1 – Dec. 31.
1939 – 1950   Jan. 1 – Dec. 31.
1951   Jan. 1 – 25.
NBuU
Micro (P)
1963   Jan. 1+.
NIC
Micro (P)
1956   Feb. 3 – Dec. 31.
1959   Jan. 1+.
NN
1916   Mar. 3, 5 – 19, 21 – Apr. 9, 11 –
15, 17, 19, 21, 23 – May 22,
24 – 31, June 2 – 10, 12 – 16,
18 – 22, 24 – 30, July 3 – 14,
16 – 23, 25 – 30, Aug. 1 – 11,
13 – 15, 17 – 25, 27, 29 – Sept.
2, 4 – 9, 11 – 15, 17 – 19, 21 –
23, 26 – Oct. 4, 6, 8 – 25, 27,
29 – Nov. 12, 14 – 17, 19 – 28,
30 – Dec. 13, 15 – 31.
1917   Jan. 2 – 25, 28, 29, 31, Feb, 4,
6 – 8, 12 – 23, 25, 27, 28, Mar. 2,
9 – 12, 14 – 17, 19 – 22, 25, 27,

29, 30, Apr. 2, 10, 11, 14 – 16,
18 – 22, 28 – May 1, 3, 5 – 7, 11
– 13, 16, 19, 22, 23, 25, 27,
June 2, 6, 8, 9, 12, 17, 19 – 22.
1941   Feb. 1 – Dec. 31.
1942   Jan. 1 – Aug. 25, 27 – Dec. 31.
1943   Jan. 1 – 28, 30 – Dec. 31.
1944 – 1948   Jan. 1 – Dec. 31.
1949   Jan. 1 – Feb. 7, Mar. 1 – Dec.
31.
1950   Jan. 1 – Dec. 31.
Micro (P)
1928 – 1937   Jan. 1 – Dec. 31.
1938   July 1 – Dec. 31.
1939 – 1943   Jan. 1 – Dec. 31.
1956   Feb. 3 – 25.
1957   Jan. 1+.
NNC
1965   June 4 – 7, 10, 12 – 19, 21, 22,
24 – 30, July 2 – 31, Aug. 2, 3,
5 – 13, 15, 16, 19 – Sept. 6, 8, 9,
11 – Oct. 11, 12 – 22, 24 – Nov.
2, 4 – 6, 8 – Dec. 24, 26 – 31.
1966   Jan. 2, 4 – 9.
Micro (P)
1938   July 1 – Dec. 31.
1939 – 1950   Jan. 1 – Dec. 31.
1951   Jan. 2 – 25.
1956   Feb. 3 – Dec. 31.
1957 – 1963   Jan. 1 – Dec. 31.
1964   Jan. 1 – Oct. 31, Dec. 1 – 31.
NPV
1902   Jan. 29.
1931   Dec. 26 – 31.
1932   Jan. 1 – July 28, 30 – Nov. 9.
1933   Apr. 4 – July 14.
1934   Aug. 1 – 5, 7 – 21, 23 – Dec. 1,
3.
1939   Dec. 9 – 11.
1943   Sept. 5 – Oct. 17, 24 – Dec. 31.
1944   Jan. 1 – Sept. 3.
1945   Feb. 10 – Dec. 30.
1946   Jan. 1 – Dec. 29.
1947 – 1950   Jan. 1 – Dec. 31.
1951   Jan. 1 – 25.
1956   Feb. 3 – July 31.
1957 – 1961   Jan. 1 – Dec. 31.
1962   Jan. 7 – 14, 28 – Feb. 4, 18 – 25,
Mar. 18.

1963   Jan. 1 – June 30.
NcU
    1905 – 1907   ₁Jan. 1 – Dec. 31₁.
    1908   Jan. 1 – Dec. 31.
    1909 – 1913   ₁Jan. 1 – Dec. 31.₁
    1914   Jan. 1 – Dec. 31.
    1922 – 1930   Jan. 1 – Dec. 31.
    1931   ₁Jan. 1 – Dec. 31₁.
    1932 – 1933   Jan. 1 – Dec. 31.
    1934   ₁Jan. 1 – Dec. 31₁.
    1935 – 1937   Jan. 1 – Dec. 31.
    1945   Jan. 1 – Dec. 31.
    1946   ₁Jan. 1 – Dec. 31₁.
    1958 – 1965   ₁Jan. 1 – Dec. 31₁.
    1966   Jan. 1+.
NjP
    1956   Feb. 3.
NmU
    1921   Oct. 25.
    1922   Jan. 14, 19, 25, 28, Feb. 1, 6 – 8,
                13, 28, Mar. 2 – 25, Sept. 2, 25,
                Oct. 11 – 31, Nov. 1 – Dec. 31.
    1940   One issue per week.
    1950   Nov. 1 – Dec. 31.
    1951   Jan. 2 – 25.
    1956   Mar. 17 – Dec. 31.
    1957 – 1959   Jan. 1 – Dec. 31.
    1960   Jan. 2 – July 15, Sept. 13 – Dec.
                31.
    1961   Jan. 1 – Dec. 31.
    1962   Jan. 2 – July 24.
    1963 – 1964   Jan. 1 – Dec. 31.
    1965   Jan. 2 – Feb. 3.
    Micro (P)
    1920   Jan. 1 – July 8.
    1932 – 1939   Jan. 1 – Dec. 31.
OCl
    1942   July 1 – Aug. 7.
    1944   Jan. 1 – Dec. 31.
    1945   Jan. 1 – June 30, Sept. 1 – Dec.
                31.
    1946   Jan. 1 – Feb. 28, Dec. 1 – 31.
    1947   Jan. 1 – Nov. 30.
    1948   Jan. 1 – Dec. 31.
    1949   Jan. 1 – 31, Feb. 8 – Dec. 31.
    1950   Jan. 1 – Dec. 31.
    1951   Jan. 1 – 23.
    1956   June 2 – Dec. 31.

1957 – 1958   Jan. 1 – Dec. 31.
1959   Jan. 1 – Aug. 16.
OU
    1930   May 1 – Dec. 31.
    1931 – 1950   Jan. 1 – Dec. 31.
    1951   Jan. 1 – 25.
    1956   May 1 – Dec. 31.
    Micro (P)
    1957   Jan. 1+.
OkU
    1964   May 2 – Dec. 31.
    1965   Jan. 1+.
OrU
    1928   May 1 – July 31.
    1930   Feb. 9, 23, Mar. 2, 9, 16, 23, 30,
                Apr. 6, 13, 20, 27, May 4, 11,
                18, 25, June 1, 8.
    1960   Feb. 28 – Dec. 31.
    1961   Jan. 2 – 11, 13, 14, 16 – Mar. 4,
                6 – June 27, 30 – Oct. 11, 13 –
                Dec. 31.
    1962   Jan. 1 – July 15, 17 – Dec. 31.
    1963   Jan. 1 – Feb. 2, 4 – 8, 10, 11,
                13 – 28, Mar. 2 – 18, 20 – 30,
                Apr. 1 – 3, 27, 28, 30 – May 3,
                5 – June 4, 6 – July 3, 5 – 12,
                14 – 28, 30 – Oct. 25, 27 – Nov.
                26, 28 – Dec. 31.
    1964   Jan. 1 – 12, 14, 15, 17 – 19, 21 –
                Feb. 9, 11 – 27, 29, Mar. 2 –
                July 25, 27 – Sept. 8, 19 – Oct.
                10, 13 – Nov. 1, 3 – 30, Dec. 2 –
                20, 22 – 24, 26 – 31.
    1965   Jan. 1 – Feb. 2, 4 – 9, 11 – 28,
                Mar. 2 – Apr. 15, 17 – 30, May
                2 – 11, 13 – June 23, 25 – July
                28, 30, 31 – Aug. 18, 20 – Sept.
                30 – Dec. 31.
    1966   Jan. 1+.
PPiU
    Current (one month).
PSt
    1966   Feb. 1 – Dec. 31.
    1967   Jan. 1+.
PrU
    1963   July 18 – Dec. 31.
    1964   Jan. 1 – 27, 30 – Feb. 8, 11 –
                29, Mar. 2 – 26, Apr. 1 – Oct.

27, 30 – Dec. 31.
1965   Jan. 1+
RPB
1965   Apr. 1 – Dec. 31.
1966   Jan. 1+.
TxU
1919   Aug. 17 – Oct. 1, 3 – Nov. 1,
3 – Dec. 31.
1920 – 1921   Jan. 1 – Dec. 31.
1922   Jan. 1 – 13, Mar. 1 – Dec. 31.
1923   Jan. 1 – Dec. 31.
1924   Feb. 29, Aug. 5 – Nov. 11, 13 –
Dec. 31.
1925   Jan. 1 – Dec. 31.
1938   May 1 – Dec. 31. (Sunday
only).
1939 – 1940   Jan. 1 – Dec. 31. (Sunday only).
1941   Jan. 1 – Aug. 31. (Sunday only),
Sept. 1 – 11, 13 – Nov. 12, 14 –
Dec. 27.
1942   Jan. 1 – June 23, July 2 – 5, 7 –
Aug. 22, 27 – Sept. 14.
1943   Jan. 1 – Apr. 15, 17 – Dec. 31.
1944   Jan. 1 – Apr. 25, May 1 – July
4, 6.
1945   Feb. 1 – Dec. 31.
1946 – 1947   Jan. 1 – Dec. 31.
1948   Jan. 1 – Oct. 25, 27 – Dec. 31.
1949   Jan. 1 – Apr. 14, 17 – Dec. 31.
1950   Jan. 1 – June 2, 4 – Oct. 23,
25 – Dec. 31.
1951   Jan. 1 – 12, 14 – 25.
WU
Micro (P)
1941 – 1950   Jan. 1 – Dec. 31.
1951   Jan. 1 – 26.
WaU
1943 – 1950   Jan. 1 – Dec. 31.
1951   Jan. 1 – 25.
1956   Feb. 3 – Dec. 31.
1957 – 1960   Jan. 1 – Dec. 31.
1961   Jan. 1 – 22, Mar. 17 – Dec. 31.
1962   Jan. 1 – Feb. 6.
1964   Sept. 24 – Dec. 31.
1965   Jan. 1+.

LA PRENSA. d. est. 1952.
Note: This paper is a government sub-

stitute for the *La Prensa* which was
suppressed Jan. 25, 1951 – Feb. 2,
1956.
CLU
1953   Oct. 1 – Dec. 31.
1954 – 1955   Jan. 1 – Dec. 31.
CSt
1952   Feb. 17.
DLC
1952   July 15 – 19, 21 – 25, Sept. 6 –
16, 18 – 22, Oct. 16, Nov. 5 – 8,
10, 11, 13, 16, 18 – 29, Dec. 1,
6 – 20, 22 – 27, 29 – 31.
1953   Jan. 2 – 10, 12 – 17, 19 – 22,
24 – Mar. 10, 12 – 28, 30 – July
30, Aug. 1 – 18, 20 – Sept. 8,
10 – 14, 17 – 29, Oct. 1, 2, 15,
16, 20, 21, 24, 26 – 30, Nov. 1 –
19, 21 – Dec. 28, 30, 31.
1954   Jan. 1 – Nov. 24, 26 – Dec. 30.
1955   Jan. 1 – Feb. 3, 5 – Dec. 5.
LA PRENSA ARGENTINA. est. Sept. 12,
1815.
Note: Ceased publication Nov. 12,
1816.
TxU
1815   Prospecto: Sept. 5.
Sept. 12 – Dec. 31.
1816   Jan. 1 – Nov. 12.
PRENSA CONTINENTAL. d. est. May
24, 1927.
DLC
1941   July 19.
DIE PRESSE. LA PRENSA ISRAELITA.
d. est. Jan. 1, 1918.
Note: In Spanish and Yiddish.
MH
1943   Sept. 4, 6 – 9, 11.
1945   Nov. 18 – 23.
1946   Jan. 3 – 7, 14 – 21, 23 – 30, Feb.
3, 5 – 7, 14, 15, 17 – 19, 26, 27,
Mar. 2, 3, 5, 8 – 28, Apr. 3 – 7,
14 – 18, May 3, 10 – 16, 29 – 31,
June 17 – 30, July 1 – 3, Aug.
13 – 18.
NN
Micro (P) & (N)
1926 – 1960   Jan. 1 – Dec. 31.

LA PRODUCCION. w. est. Aug. 17, 1935.
  DLC
    1940   Jan. 13.
    1941   Aug. 30.
    1942   July 4.
    1945   Apr. 14.

LA PRODUCCION ARGENTINA. w.
  CU–B
    Micro (N)
    1898   Aug. 31.

LA PROTESTA. d., w., 3w. est. June 13,
  1897.
    Note: Periodicity June 13, 1897–
    June 13, 1932, daily; June 14–Aug.
    16, 1932, weekly; after Aug. 17, 1932,
    three times a week.
  NN
    1932   Feb. 4, 27, Mar. 9, 12, 15, 19,
            22–31, Apr. 1–Sept. 10.

EL PUEBLO. d. est. Apr. 1, 1900.
    Note: Suppressed Dec. 31, 1954–Oct.
    2, 1956; Oct. 13–24, 1956; Dec. 22,
    1959–May 20, 1960; discontinued
    publication July 22, 1960.
  DLC
    1941   Dec. 21–24.
    1942   Feb. 1–4, Aug. 30, Sept. 1–3,
            17, 18, 24–26, Oct. 1–4, 8,
            11–17, 22–24, 29–Nov. 1, 4,
            8, 10, 11, 13, 14, 22, 24, 25, Dec.
            1, 2, 24, 25.
    1943   Jan. 1–Dec. 28, 30, 31.
    1944   Jan. 1–Mar. 4, 6, 9–Dec. 31.
    1945   Jan. 1–Dec. 31.
    1946   Jan. 1–July 25, 29–Aug. 15,
            19–Sept. 5, 9–16, 20–Dec.
            31.
    1947   Jan. 1–Apr. 18, 20–May 5,
            9–Nov. 1, 3–Dec. 8, 10–31.
    1948   Jan. 1–May 9, June 30–Dec.
            31.
    1949   Jan. 1–Dec. 31.
    1950   Jan. 1–May 26, 28–June 17,
            19, 21–27, 29, 30, July 2–Oct.
            2, 4–21, 23–Nov. 18, 20–
            Dec. 30.

    1951   Jan. 1–Mar. 9, 12, 14–31,
            Apr. 2–30, May 2–June 30,
            July 2–7, 9–Aug. 1, 3–24,
            26–30, Sept. 15, 17–Nov. 22,
            24–30, Dec. 2–7, 9–31.
    1952   Jan. 1–23, 25–Dec. 31.
    1953   Jan. 1–Dec. 31.
    1954   Jan. 1–Mar. 17, 19–Dec. 31.
    1956   Oct. 3–Nov. 12, 25–Dec. 12,
            18–31.
    1957   Jan. 1–5, 8–23, 25–July 12,
            14–Dec. 31.
    1958   Jan. 1–19, 21–Dec. 31.
    1959   Jan. 1, 2, 4–Mar. 26, 28–Dec.
            22.
    1960   May 21–July 5, 7–22.

EL PUEBLO. sw.
  CSt
    1915   Apr. 29.

LE QUOTIDIEN. d.
    Note: In French.
  MWA
    1949   Feb. 1.

RADICAL. w.
  CU
    1945   Dec. 22–29.
    1946   Jan. 5–May 18.

LA RAZON. d. est. Mar. 1, 1905.
  CSt
    1915   May 21, 23, Sept. 4, 6, 30.
    1941   Oct. 16, 17, 21–31, Nov. 1–27,
            Dec. 1–31.
    1942   Jan. 2–Apr. 25.
  CSt–H
    1966   Jan. 2–Dec. 31.
    1967   Jan. 1+.
  DLC
    1940   Sept. 19–Oct. 2.
    1944   Mar. 4.
    1957   Jan. 2–Mar. 2, 5, 8–Apr. 12,
            14–July 14, 16–27, 29–Sept.
            27, 29–Oct. 10, 13–22, 24–
            Dec. 31.
    1958   Jan. 1–6, 8–Feb. 8, 10–Mar.
            20, 22–Apr. 12, 14–June 6,
            9–Dec. 31.
    1959   Jan. 1–Dec. 8, 10–31.

1960   Jan. 1 – July 9, 11 – Aug. 5,
       8 – Sept. 4, 6 – Dec. 31.
1961   Jan. 1 – 31, Feb. 2 – Apr. 29,
       May 2 – June 30, July 2 – Oct.
       13, 15 – Dec. 31.
Micro (P) & (N)
1962   Jan. 1+.
MH
1920   Sept. 1 – Dec. 31.
1921 – 1924   Jan. 1 – Dec. 31.
1925   Jan. 1 – Oct. 31.
1926   Jan. 1 – Dec. 31.
1929   Jan. 2 – Feb. 28, Mar. 2 – Dec.
       31.
1930   Jan. 2 – Dec. 31.
1931   Jan. 3 – Dec. 31.
1932   Jan. 2 – Dec. 31.
1933   Jan. 2 – 31, Feb. 2 – Mar. 6,
       8 – 29, Apr. 4 – Dec. 31.
1934   Jan. 2 – Mar. 31, Apr. 2, 4 –
       May 5, 7 – July 7, 9, 10, 12 – 16,
       Aug. 25 – Dec. 31.
1935 – 1937   Jan. 1 – Dec. 31.
1938   Jan. 1 – 19, 21 – 23, 25 – Feb.
       23, 25 – Apr. 26, 28 – 30, May
       3 – 18, 20 – 26, 28 – June 3, 5 –
       13, 16, 18 – 26, 28 – Dec. 31.
1939   Jan. 1 – Apr. 12, 14 – 30, May
       2 – Dec. 31.
1940   Jan. 1 – Apr. 15, 17, 20 – Dec.
       31.
1941   Jan. 3 – 29, 31 – Apr. 30, May
       2 – Nov. 25, 27 – Dec. 31.
1942   Jan. 2 – Apr. 30, May 2 – 9,
       11 – 27, 29 – June 25, 27, 30,
       July 1, 3, 5, 8, 10, 12 – Nov. 3,
       5 – 10, 12 – Dec. 31.
1943   Jan. 2, 5 – Apr. 9, 11 – 26, 28,
       30, May, 2 – 18, 20 – June 2,
       4 – 17, 20 – July 17, 19, 21, 25,
       27 – Aug. 11, 13 – Oct. 6, 8,
       10 – 16, 18 – Dec. 31.
1944   Jan. 1 – 7, 9 – 29, 31 – June 16,
       18, 20 – 25, 27 – July 2, 4, 5, 7 –
       17, 19 – 25, 27, 29 – Aug. 11,
       13 – 27, 29 – Sept. 8, 10 – 12,
       15 – Oct. 2, 4 – 10, 12 – 16, 19 –
       Nov. 27, 29, Dec. 1 – 7, 10 – 12,
       14, 15, 18 – 31.

1945   Jan. 1, 2, 4, 9 – 14, 18 – 30, Feb.
       1 – 7, 9 – Mar. 5, 7 – 13, 15 – 18,
       20 – 25, 29, Apr. 5, 6, 10 – 12,
       14 – 19, 21 – 30, May 2 – 19,
       July 30, 31, Aug. 2 – 8, 11 – 17,
       19 – 30, Sept. 1 – Oct. 9, 13 –
       17, 19 – Nov. 19, 21, 22, 25 – 28,
       30 – Dec. 6, 8 – 15, 17 – 20, 25,
       27, 30.
1946   Feb. 1 – 4, 21 – 28, Mar. 2, 3, 5,
       7 – 25, 27 – Apr. 6, 8 – 17.
MWA
1949   Feb. 1.
NN
1920   Dec. 1 – 31.
1921   Jan. 1 – Feb. 28.
TxU
1920   Jan. 24 – Feb. 3, 5 – Apr. 26,
       29 – Dec. 31.
1921   Jan. 1 – Dec. 31.
1922   Jan. 1 – Mar. 15.

RECONQUISTA. d. est. Nov. 15, 1939.
DLC
1939   Nov. 15.

LA REPRESENTACION DE LOS
   LIBRES.
CSt
1944   Oct. 1.

LA REPUBLICA. d. est. 1867.
   Note: Ceased publication 1881.
CU – B
   Micro (N)
   1872   May 14, 15, June 7.

LA REPUBLICA. d. est. 1913.
CSt
1915   Mar. 2.

THE REVIEW OF THE RIVER PLATE. w.

   Note: In English.
CU – B
   Micro (N)
   1892   July 2 – Dec. 31.
   1893   Jan. 1 – Dec. 31.
   1894   Jan. 1 – Apr. 28.

RISORGIMENTO. w., sw., d. est. 1945.
   Note: In Italian.

CSt
    1948   May 7.
DLC
    1955   Nov. 2.
MWA
    1949   Feb. 1.

THE RIVER PLATE OBSERVER.
    See *The Argentine Weekly.*

RUSSKII V ARGENTINE. w. est. June 1,
1930.
    Note: In Russian.
DLC
    1941   May 17, 24, June 7.

SEMANA RURAL. w.
MH
    1911   June 20.

SEMANARIO DE AGRICULTURA,
    INDUSTRIA Y COMERCIO. w. est.
Sept. 1, 1802.
    Note: Ceased publication Feb. 11,
    1807.
CtY
    1802   Sept. 1 – Dec. 31.
    1803   Jan. 1 – Aug. 5.

EL SEMINARIO.
CSt
    1914   Mar. 26.

EL SIGLO. d.
CSt
    1915   Jan. 27, 28.

SLOVO VERBO. w.
NIC
    Micro (P) & (N)
    1949   Jan. 13 – Dec. 31.
    1950   Jan. 1 – 19.

EL SOCIALISTA.
CSt
    1948   May 1, 18, June 1, 15.

THE STANDARD. w., d. est. May 1, 1861.
    Note: In English. Title varies, *The
    Standard and River Plate News.*
    Periodicity May 1 – Dec. 2, 1861,
    weekly; after Dec. 2, 1861, daily.

CSt
    1915   Sept. 26, Oct. 22, 25, 28, 31.
CU
    1939   Oct. 10 – Dec. 12.
    1940   Apr. 3 – 9.
CU – B
    Micro (N)
    1870   Feb. 1 – July 13.
    1871   July 1.
    1872   Jan. 1 – June 22.
    1873   Feb. 6 – 12.
    1874   Mar. 1 – Dec. 31.
    1875 – 1905   Jan. 1 – Dec. 31.
DLC
    1868   Sept. 29.
    1920   May 1.
    1921   Mar. 10 – Oct. 26, 28 – Dec. 31.
    1922 – 1923   Jan. 1 – Dec. 31.
    1924   Jan. 1 – June 11, 13 – Dec. 31.
    1925   Jan. 1 – June 3, 5 – Dec. 31.
    1926   Jan. 1 – Dec. 25, 27 – 31.
    1927   Jan. 1 – Dec. 31.
    1928   Jan. 1 – June 2, 4 – July 11,
           13 – Dec. 31.
    1929   Jan. 1 – 5, 7 – 12, 14 – May 25,
           27 – Dec. 31.
    1930   Jan. 1, 3, 4, 6 – 8, 10 – Dec. 31.
    1931   Jan. 1 – Apr. 8, 10 – Mar. 21,
           23 – Dec. 31.
    1932   Jan. 1 – July 11, 13 – Sept. 7,
           9 – Dec. 14, 16 – 21, 23 – 31.
    1933   Jan. 1 – 7, 9 – Feb. 15, 17 –
           Mar. 16, Aug. 2 – 31, Sept. 5 –
           Dec. 17, 19 – 31.
    1934   Jan. 1 – Mar. 31, Apr. 2 – Dec.
           24, 27 – 31.
    1935   Jan. 1 – Nov. 4, 6 – Dec. 31.
    1936   Jan. 1 – 8, 10 – 12, 14 – 23, 25 –
           Dec. 31.
    1937   Jan. 1 – Dec. 19, 21 – 31.
    1938   Jan. 1 – 28, 30 – Feb. 8, 10 –
           Mar. 16, 18 – 23, 25 – Apr. 3,
           5 – June 20, 22 – July 3, 5 – 17,
           19 – 26, 29 – 31, Aug. 2 – 31,
           Nov. 1, 9, 12, 13, 15 – 20, 22,
           24 – 26, 28, Dec. 1, 4, 7 – 9, 12,
           13, 15, 19, 20, 22, 23, 27, 29 –
           31.
    1939   Jan. 5 – 8, 10, 12 – Feb. 12,

14 – 26, 28 – Mar. 15, 17 – Apr.
4, 6 – May 3, 5, 6, 15, 16, 18,
June 10, 11, 13, 14, 16 – 26,
28 – Dec. 31.

1940   Jan. 1 – May 22, 24 – Dec. 31.
1941   Jan. 1 – Dec. 31.
1942   Jan. 1 – Mar. 13, 16 – 18, 23 –
May 19, 21 – June 23, 27, 28,
July 2, 4 – Aug. 23, 28 – Sept.
24, 26 – Oct. 12, 14 – 21.
1943   Mar. 30, Dec. 2.
1947   July 1 – Aug. 6, 8 – Sept. 8, 10 –
Oct. 15, 18, 19, 21 – Nov. 7,
10 – 21, 23 – 25, 27, 28, 30,
Dec. 1, 3 – 23, 25 – 31.
1948   Jan. 1 – 4, 6 – 15, 17 – 19, 21 –
Feb. 29, Mar. 2 – Apr. 29, May
2 – June 27, 29, 30, July 9 – 13,
15 – Aug. 26, 28 – Sept. 18, 20.
1949   July 17, Nov. 13, 20, Dec. 11.
1950   Oct. 29, Nov. 5, 12, 19, 26,
Dec. 3, 24, 31.
1951   Jan. 14, 28, Feb. 4, 11, 18, 25,
Mar. 4, 11, 25, Apr. 1, 15, 29,
May 6, June 3, 24, July 1, 15,
Aug. 19, 26, Sept. 2, 9, 23, Dec.
9, 16.
1952   Mar. 9, 16, 23.
ICRL
1908 – 1923 [Jan. 1 – Dec. 31.]
MB
1866   Feb. 4, Apr. 6, May 12, Aug. 25.
1867   July 26.
1868   July 12.
1869   Feb. 24, Mar. 11, 25, Apr. 11,
25, May 25, June 11, 25, July
11, 25, Aug. 11, 25, Sept. 11, 25,
Oct. 9, 26, Nov. 13, 28, Dec. 14,
30.
1870   Jan. 29, Mar. 17, Apr. 13, May
24, June 14, 29, July 14, Aug.
13, 28, 29, Sept. 13, Oct. 14,
29, Nov. 14, 29, Dec. 29.

MH
1871   Oct. 30.
1875   Feb. 15, Sept. 1, Oct. 1.
1881   Feb. 6, 23, Mar. 11, Apr. 20,
May 7, 14, 22, June 4, 14, 28,

Aug. 7, 28, Sept. 7, 14, 23, 28,
Oct. 4, 28, Nov. 13, Dec. 4, 18.
MWA
1949   Feb. 1.
NHi
1863   Jan. 15, 25.

THE STANDARD. (MAIL SUPPLE-
MENT). w. est. May 1, 1861.
Note: In English. Title *The Weekly
Standard*, May 1 – Nov. 27, 1861.
CU – B
Micro (N)
1870   Jan. 5 – Dec. 31.
1871   Jan. 1 – June 28, Aug. 2 – Dec.
31.
1872 – 1873   Jan. 1 – Dec. 31.
1874   Jan. 1 – June 17.
1882   Jan. 25.
CtY
1908 – 1911   Jan. 1 – Dec. 31.
DLC
1921   Mar. 10 – Dec. 31.
1922   Jan. 1 – May 31, June 2 – Dec.
31.
1923   Jan. 1 – June 20, 22 – Dec. 5,
7 – 31.
1924   Jan. 1 – Dec. 31.
1925   Jan. 1 – June 17, 19 – Dec. 31.
1926   Jan. 1 – June 2, 4 – Dec. 31.
1927   Jan. 1 – Feb. 16, 18 – Dec. 31.
1928   Jan. 1 – July 18, 20 – Dec. 31.
1929   Jan. 1 – June 26, 28 – Dec. 31.
1932   Jan. 1 – Sept. 14, 16 – 21, 23 –
Dec. 31.
1933   Jan. 1 – Feb. 9.
MB
1867   Jan. 2 – Dec. 18.
1868   Jan. 1 – Nov. 18.
1869   Jan. 6 – Dec. 22.
1871   Jan. 13, Feb. 13, 27, Mar. 16,
Apr. 30, May 15, 29.
1875   Feb. 15, Mar. 1, 15, Apr. 1,
Sept. 1, Nov. 15.
1876   Jan. 14.
1878   Dec. 31.
1879   Feb. 1, May 1.
MH
1865   July 12.

1866 July 4.
1871 Nov. 1.
MWA
1867 [Aug. 28 – Dec. 31.]
1868 [Jan. 1 – Nov. 18.]
1869 [Jan. 6 – Aug. 25.]

THE STANDARD AND RIVER PLATE
NEWS.
See *The Standard*.

SVITLO. sw. est. July 23, 1935.
Note: In Ukranian.
DLC
1942 Apr. 10 – June 22, July 4 – Dec.
31.
1943 Jan. 8 – 14, 16 – 21, 23 – 25,
27 – Aug. 30. Sept. 4 – 24.

LA TARDE.
CSt
1914 Nov. 30.

EL TELEGRAFO DEL COMERCIO. d.
est. 1832.
DLC
1832 May 28, July 4, 11, 17 – 19,
23 – 28.

TELEGRAFO MERCANTIL. sw., w. est.
Apr. 1, 1801.
Note: Periodicity Apr. 1 – Dec. 31,
1801, semiweekly: Jan. 1 – Oct. 17,
1802, weekly. Ceased publication
Oct. 17, 1802.
CtY
1801 Apr. 1 – Dec. 31.
1802 Jan. 1 – Oct. 17.

TIEMPO. d. est. 1894.
MWA
1895 Feb. 27 – Mar. 5.
1903 Nov. 18 – 20, 23, 24.

EL TIEMPO, DIARIO POLITICO,
LITERARIO Y MERCANTIL. d. est.
1828.
Note: Ceased publication 1829.
DLC
1828 Aug. 1, 2, 4, 8 – 14, 16, 18 – 29,
Sept. 1 – 6, 9 – 26, 30, Oct. 1 –
3, 6, 10, Nov. 13 – 15, 17, 19 –

21, 24 – 26, 29, Dec. 1, 3, 4, 6,
9 – 12, 15 – 20, 22 – 24, 27,
29 – 31.
1829 Jan. 2 – 5, 7 – 23, 26 – 31, Feb.
4 – 16, 20, 21, 23, 27, 28,
Mar. 4, 5, 7 – 10, 13 – 16, 23,
27 – Apr. 8, 21 – 25, May 5, 6, 8,
12, 16, 18, 19, 21, 22, June 4, 9,
16, 30, July 1.

THE TIMES OF ARGENTINA.
See *Buenos Aires Herald*.

TRIBUNA. d. est. July 17, 1945.
DLC
1945 July 17 – Dec. 29, 31.
1946 Jan. 1 – 7, 9, 12 – Aug. 4, 6 –
Nov. 29, Dec. 1 – 19, 21 – 31.
1947 Jan. 1 – 28, 30 – Feb. 5,
7 – 10, 12 – 24, 26 – June 30.

LA TRIBUNA. d. est. Aug. 7, 1853.
Note: Ceased publication Sept. 27,
1880.
CU – B
Micro (N)
1872 May 2, 3, 10, 11, 14, 15, June 8,
20.
MWA
1876 Nov. 6 – 7.

TRIBUNA DEL NORTE. w. est. Apr. 15,
1938.
DLC
1942 Feb. 8.

EL TRIBUNAL. d. est. 1944.
DLC
1955 Nov. 15.

EL TRIBUNAL DE COMERCIO. d. est.
July 29, 1895.
CSt
1915 July 28, Aug. 11, Oct. 1.

ULTIMA HORA. d.
CSt
1914 Apr. 22.

UNIDAD NACIONAL.
CSt
1944 Aug. 4.

LA UNION. d. est. 1853.
  CU–B
    Micro (N)
    1872   May 1.

LA UNION.
  CSt
    1914   Dec. 31.

LA UNION. est. 1915.
  MH
    1917   Jan. 18.

EL UNIVERSAL. d. est. Oct. 1, 1829.
    Note: Title *Diario universal*, Oct. 1,
    1829 – Jan. 27, 1830; *El Universal*
    Jan. 28 – Feb. 9, 1830. Ceased publica-
    tion Feb. 9, 1830.
  DLC
    1829   Oct. 1 – 5, 7 – 29, 31 – Nov. 24,
            29, 30, Dec. 2 – 6, 10 – 31.
    1830   Jan. 1 – 13, 15 – 27, Feb. 9.

LA V DE LA VICTORIA. w. est. July 1,
  1941.
  DLC
    1942   June 18.
  MH
    1941   July 1 – Dec. 25.
    1942   Jan. 2 – Dec. 31.
    1943   Jan. 7 – Apr. 28, May 5, 19 –
            Aug. 11.

LA VANGUARDIA. d. est. Apr. 7, 1894.
  CSt
    1915   May 5, 8, 9.
    1945   Mar. 13, 20, Apr. 17, 24, June
            26, July 3, 10, 17.
    1947   Oct. 21.
  DLC
    1938   Sept. 30.
    1941   Aug. 21, 22.
    1942   Sept. 15, 17, 25, 27 – 29, Oct.
            1, 2, Dec. 1, 23.
    1943   Jan. 22, Mar. 14, 21 – 23, 27 –
            29, 31.
    1944   Jan. 7.
  NN
    1945 – 1946   Jan. 1 – Dec. 31.
    Micro (P) & (N)
    1922   July 1 – Dec. 31.

    1923   Jan. 1 – June 30, Oct. 1 – Dec.
            31.
    1924   Jan. 1 – Mar. 31, July 1 – Dec.
            31.
    1925   Oct. 1 – Dec. 31.
    1926   Feb. 1 – Sept. 30, Nov. 1 – 30.
    1927   Jan. 1 – May 31, Aug. 1 – Sept.
            30.
    1928   Jan. 1 – June 30, Aug. 1 – Dec.
            31.
    1929   Jan. 1 – Mar. 31.

LA VANGUARDIA; VOCERO DEL PAR-
  TIDO SOCIALISTA DEMOCRATICO.
  w.
  CSt – H
    1964   Oct. 7, Nov. 4, 18, 25, Dec. 2, 9,
            16, 23.
    1965   Jan. 13 – Dec. 31.
    1966   Jan. 1+.

LA VERDAD. d. est. 1869.
    Note: Ceased publication 1873.
  CU – B
    Micro (N)
    1872   May 1, 2, 4, 10, 11, 15, June 7.

LA VERDAD DESNUDA. irr. est. Sept.
  24, 1822.
    Note: Removed to Montevideo Aug.
    1823.
  NN
    1822   Oct. 26.

LA VOZ DEL CONTINENTE. d. est.
  Sept. 1, 1940.
  DLC
    1940   Sept. 1.

VOZ PROLETARIA. w.
  CSt – H
    1964   July 31 – Dec. 31.
    1965   Jan. 1+.

VOZ RADICAL. sw.
  CSt
    1944   Sept. 21, Oct. n.d.

THE WEEKLY STANDARD.
    See *The Standard (Mail Supplement)*.

DIE YIDDISHE TSAITUNG. EL
  DIARIO ISRAELITA. d.
    Note: In Spanish and Yiddish.

NN
  Micro (P) & (N)
  1923   Oct. 7 – Dec. 31.
  1924 – 1961   Jan. 1 – Dec. 31.

DIE ZEITUNG. d. est. Dec. 18, 1944.
  Note: In German.
  DLC
  1944   Dec. 18 – 23, 25 – 27, 29, 30.
  1945   Jan. 1 – 6, 8 – 13, 15 – Feb. 10,
          12 – 16, 18 – Mar. 6, 11 – Apr.
          29, May 1 – June 16, 18 – July
          2, 4 – Aug. 14, 23 – 25, 28 – 30,
          Sept. 4 – 7.

EL ZONDA.
  CSt
  1944   Sept. 4, 5, Dec. 10, 11.

Casilda

LA NOTA DE CASEROS. w. est. Mar. 5,
  1923.
  DLC
  1955   Nov. 17.

Catamarca

LA UNION. d. est. Aug. 30, 1928.
  DLC
  1955   Nov. 18.

Chivilcoy

EL TIEMPO. d. est. 1952.
  DLC
  1955   Nov. 17.

Colón

DIARIO DEL PUEBLO. d. est. Aug. 1,
  1918.
  DLC
  1940   Mar. 29.
  1941   Mar. 20.

EL INDUSTRIAL. w.
  DLC
  1882   Aug. 13, Sept. 3.

Córdoba

COMERCIO Y JUSTICIA. d. est. Oct. 2,
  1939.
  DLC
  1955   Nov. 17.

CORDOBA. d. est. Oct. 22, 1928.
  DLC
  1955   Nov. 16.

EL ECO DE CORDOBA. d. est. 1862.
  DLC
  1889   July 16.
  MB
  1875   Feb. 17 – 28, Mar. 1 – 3, 5 – 10,
          12 – 24, 29 – 31, Apr. 1 – 17,
          20 – 24, 26 – 30, May 1 – 15,
          17 – June 29, July 1 – 19, 21 –
          26, 28 – Nov. 30, Dec. 1 – 3,
          5 – 31.
  1876   Jan. 1 – 23, 25 – Feb. 17, 19 –
          Mar. 21, Apr. 1 – May 3, 5 – 30,
          Oct. 12 – Nov. 3, 5 – 16, 18, 30,
          Dec. 1 – 21, 23 – 27, 29 – 31.
  1877   Jan. 1 – 5, 7 – Feb. 23, 25 –
          June 9, 11 – July 26, 28 – Sept.
          2, 4 – Dec. 31.
  1878   Jan. 1, 3 – Feb. 2, 4 – Mar. 4, 7 –
          14, 16 – 25, 27 – Apr. 2, 4 –
          13, 15 – 19, 22 – May 25, 27 –
          June 20, 22 – 24, 26 – Oct. 23,
          25 – Dec. 31.
  1879   Jan. 1 – 27, 29, 30, Feb. 2 –
          Mar. 23, Apr. 8 – 9, May 7, 27,
          June 6, 8, 9, 11 – 16, 18 – 20,
          22 – 24, 26 – 27, 29, 30, July 1 –
          29, 31 – Sept. 19, 21, 30, Oct.
          2 – 20, 22 – 31, Nov. 2 – Dec.
          31.
  1880   Jan. 1 – Feb. 26.

EL INTERIOR. d. est. 1881.
  Note: Ceased publication 1890.
  DLC
  1888   Oct. 24.

LA LIBERTAD. d. est. 1890.
  DLC
  1892   Nov. 2.

LOS PRINCIPIOS. d. est. Apr. 22, 1894.
  CSt
  1915   Oct. 13 – 15.

LOS PRINCIPIOS.
DLC
Micro (P) & (N)
1942 Feb. 8, 9, 15, 16, 22, 23, Mar. 1,
2, 8, 9, 15, 16.
1943 Jan. 1 — Dec. 31.
1944 Jan. 1 — Mar. 14, 16, 18, 22,
24 — 26, 28 — June 22, 24 — 28,
July 1 — Sept. 9, 11 — 27, 29 —
Oct. 5, 7 — 21, 23 — Dec. 31.
1945 Jan. 1 — 24, 26 — Oct. 3, 5 —
Dec. 31.
1946 Jan. 1 — 31, Feb. 2 — Mar. 5, 7 —
June 4, 6 — July 22, 24 —
Aug. 18, 20 — Sept. 8, 10 — 15,
18 — 21, 23, 24, 26 — Oct. 31,
Nov. 2 — Dec. 8, 10 — 31.
1947 Jan. 1 — Feb. 4, 6 — 24, 26 —
Apr. 14, 16 — Aug. 12, 14 — Oct.
12, 14 — 30, Nov. 2 — 10, 12 —
Dec. 31.
1948 Jan. 1 — Feb. 20, 22 — May 5,
7 — Sept. 22, 24 — Dec. 31.
1949 Jan. 1 — Feb. 5, 7 — Dec. 28, 31.
1950 Jan. 1 — Aug. 23, 25 — Dec. 31.
1951 Jan. 1 — June 13, 15 — July 6,
8 — 31, Aug. 2 — Sept. 5, 7 —
Dec. 31.

LA VOZ DEL INTERIOR. d. est. Mar. 15,
1904.
DLC
1942 Feb. 8, 9, 15, 16, 22, 23, Mar. 1,
2, 8, 9, 15, 16.

Corrientes

LA CALLE. d. est. 1953.
DLC
1955 Nov. 24.

Dolores

JORNADA. est. June 3, 1943.
DLC
1956 Mar. 1.

EL NACIONAL. d. est. May 16, 1903.
CSt
1914 Sept. 6, Oct. 2.
1915 Mar. 24, 25.

EL TRIBUNO. d. est. May 25, 1926.
DLC
1955 Nov. 11.

Eldorado

ALTO PARANA. est. Apr. 28, 1943.
DLC
1960 Dec. 3.

Esperanza

EL COLONO. 3w. est. Nov. 1, 1909.
DLC
1955 Nov. 15.

Formosa

VOZ FORMOSENA. d. est. Aug. 15, 1951.
DLC
1955 Nov. 11.

General Villegas

EL COMENTARIO. sw.
CSt
1912 Feb. 18.

Goya

LA HORA.
CSt
1915 July 8.

LA PATRIA.
CSt
1915 Feb. 14.

Jujui

CONFRATERNIDAD. est. 1861.
MWA
1861 June 9.

La Plata

EL ARGENTINO. d. est. 1905.
NN
Micro (P) & (N)
1943 Mar. 11, 12, July 1 — Aug. 4, 6 —
Oct. 24, 26 — 31, Nov. 2 — 4, 6 —
18, 20 — Dec. 1, 4 — 21, 23 — 30.

1944   [Jan. 1 – Dec. 31.]
1945   [Jan. 1 – June 30.]
1946 – 1947   [Jan. 1 – Dec. 31.]

DEMOCRACIA. d. est. Jan. 2, 1928.
  DLC
   1941   June 2.

NUEVOS RUMBOS. d. est. Oct. 1, 1925.
  DLC
   1955   Nov. 17.

Lomas de Zamora

LA UNION. d. est. 1897.
  CSt
   1915   Mar. 23.

Lucas González

DER RUSSLANDDEUTSCHE. w. est. 1929.
   Note: In German.
  DLC
   1941   Feb. 7, Apr. 4, 11, May 2 – 23,
       June 6, 13, 27 – July 18, Aug.
       15, 22, Sept. 5, 19 – Oct. 3, 24,
       Nov. 14 – Dec. 5.
   1942   Jan. 2 – Feb. 6, 20 – Apr. 3,
       May 15.

Mar del Plata

EL ATLANTICO. d. est. Feb. 1, 1938.
  DLC
   1955   Nov. 28.

LA CAPITAL. d. est. 1905.
  CSt
   1915   May 4, Oct. 26, 30.

LA MAÑANA. d. est. 1948.
  DLC
   1955   Nov. 18.

Mendoza

LOS ANDES. d. est. Oct. 20, 1882.
  CSt
   1915   Sept. 17 – 19.
  DLC
   1940   Dec. 15.

1954   July 9, 25 – Sept. 25, 27 – Oct.
       16, 18 – Nov. 11, 13 – 28, 30 –
       Dec. 20, 29 – 31.
1955   Jan. 1 – 26, Feb. 3 – Mar. 25,
       27 – Apr. 30, May 2 – 16, 24 –
       Oct. 4, 13 – Dec. 31.
1956   Jan. 1 – 19, 21 – Feb. 21, Mar.
       2 – Dec. 31.
1957   Jan. 2 – Feb. 7, 9 – Mar. 22, 30,
       31, Apr. 2 – 30, May 2 – Dec.
       31.
1958   Jan. 2 – Apr. 30, May 2 – Dec.
       31.
1959   Jan. 1 – Dec. 31.
1960   Jan. 2 – Mar. 22, 30 – Dec. 31.
1961   Jan. 2 – Mar. 7, 9 – Nov. 5, 16 –
       Dec. 31.
Micro   (P) & (N)
1962   Jan. 1+.
  MWA
   1892   Dec. 7.

EL ECO DE LOS ANDES. w. est. Sept. 23, 1824.
   Note: Suspended publication Sept.
     12 – Oct. 8, 15 – Dec. 25, 1825.
   Ceased publication Dec. 25, 1825.
  CtY
   1824   Sept. 23 – Dec. 31.
   1825   Jan. 1 – Sept. 5.
  IU
   1824   [Sept. 23 – Dec. 31].
   1825   [Jan. 1 – Dec. 25]. `
  WU
   1824   Sept. 23 – Dec. 31.
   1825   Jan. 1 – Dec. 25.

LA LIBERTAD. d. est. Feb. 8, 1924.
  DLC
   1955   Nov. 23.

LA PALABRA. d. est. Sept. 11, 1916.
  DLC
   1955   Nov. 18.

EL TIEMPO DE CUYO. d. est. 1956.
  DLC
   1960   May 25.
   1961   Mar.

Mercedes

OESTE. d.
  MWA
    1905   Sept. 16.

LA RAZON. bw. est. Apr. 1, 1898.
  DLC
    1955   Dec. 3.

Moreno

EL ORDEN. d. est. July 10, 1910.
  CSt
    1915   Feb. 10.

Paraná

LA ACCION. d. est. May 1, 1912.
  CSt
    1915   Sept. 25, 26, 28, 29.

EL ARGENTINO. est. 1866.
  CU – B
    Micro (N)
    1880   Oct. 9 – Dec. 31.
    1882 – 1883   Jan. 1 – Dec. 31.
    1884   Jan. 1 – Mar. 29.

EL PARANENSE INDUSTRIAL. w. est.
  1864.
  CU – B
    Micro (N)
    1880   Oct. 11 – Dec. 31.
    1881   Jan. 1 – Dec. 31.
    1882   Jan. 2.

Posadas

EL ECO DE MISIONES. d. est. 1903.
  CSt
    1915   Feb. 27.

EL PUEBLO. d. est. 1906.
  CSt
    1915   Mar. 1, 2.

EL TERRITORIO. d. est. June 2, 1925.
  CtY
    1943 – 1946   Jan. 1 – Dec. 31.

EL TERRITORIO.
  DLC
    1956   May 12.

Rosario

LA ACCION. d. est. June 1, 1938.
  NHi
    1946   Mar. 16.

LA CAPITAL. d. est. Nov. 15, 1867.
  CSt
    1915   Nov. 15, 18, 22.
  CU
    Micro (P)
    1951 – 1952   Jan. 1 – Dec. 31.
  DLC
    1940   Sept. 20 – Oct. 7, 11 – Nov. 18,
            22 – 25, Dec. 3 – 16, 20 – 31.
    1941   Jan. 1 – Apr. 17, 22 – June 4, 6,
            7, 10 – 12, 15, 16, 20 – Aug. 25,
            27, 29 – Oct. 27, Nov. 4 – 17,
            21 – 31.
    1942   Jan. 1 – 5, 9 – 12, 20 – Feb. 2,
            6 – 23, 27 – Mar. 2, 6 – 19, 24 –
            Apr. 13, 17 – June 8, 12 – 22,
            July 7 – 30, Aug. 4 – 6, 14 – 17,
            21 – Sept. 7, 15 – 17, Oct. 2 –
            19, 30 – Nov. 16, 18, 24 – Dec.
            31.
    1943   Jan. 1 – 18, 26 – Feb. 4, 9 – 11,
            23 – Mar. 4, 9 – 11, 16 – 18,
            26 – Apr. 2, 4, 5, 9 – 12, 20 – 22,
            27 – May 3, 11 – 13, 21 – 24,
            28 – June 3, 8 – 14, 23, 25 –
            July 26, 30 – Aug. 5, 13 – 19,
            31 – Sept. 6, 10 – Oct. 7, 12 –
            18, 22 – 28, Nov. 2 – 8, 16 – 18,
            23 – Dec. 16, 21 – 23, 28 – 31.
    1944   Jan. 1 – 24, 28 – Dec. 31.
    1945   Jan. 1 – Feb. 15, 20 – Apr. 9,
            13 – May 3, 5 – Sept. 3, 7 – 10,
            12, 14 – Nov. 27, 29 – Dec. 1,
            4 – 13, 18 – 20, 22, 23, 25 – 27.
    1946   May 2, 18 – 21, 23 – June 4, 6,
            8 – 11, 14, 15, 18, 20 – 25, 28 –
            July 1, 3, 4, 6 – 9, 11 – 13, 15,
            17, 19 – 24, 26 – 28, 30, 31, Aug.
            2, 3, 6 – 12, 14 – 21, 23 – 25, 28,
            31, Sept. 2, 5 – 14, 16, 17, 21,
            26, 28 – Oct. 1, 3, 4, 7 – 10, 13,
            15 – 24, 27, 30, Nov. 2 – 4, 6, 8,
            10, 12, 14 – 16, 21, 24 – 26, 28,

30, Dec. 2 – 5, 7 – 11, 13 – 22,
25 – 27, 29 – 31.

1947 Jan. 1 – 4, 6, 7, 9 – 12, 14 – 16,
18, 19, 22 – 26, 29, 30, Feb. 2 –
5, 7, 9 – 16, 18, 21, 22, 25 – 27,
Mar. 1, 3, 4, 6 – 9, 11 – 15, 17 –
20, 22 – 30, Apr. 1, 2, 5, 6, 8 –
14, 17 – 21, 23, 26 – May 12,
14 – 25, 27, 28, 30, June 1, 4,
6 – 8, 10 – 13, 15 – 17, 21 – 23,
25 – July 10, 12 – 22, 25, 27 –
Aug. 6, 9, 10, 12 – 15, 18, 20 –
22, 25 – 27, 29 – Oct. 4, 6, 8 –
15, 18, 24 – 26, 28, 30 – Nov. 2,
4, 6, 8 – 12, 14, 15, 18 – 26, 29,
Dec. 2 – 6, 9 – 15, 17 – 19, 22 –
31.

1948 Jan. 1, 2, 4, 5, 7 – 10, 14, 15, 18,
19, 21, 23 – 28, Feb. 2 – 29,
Mar. 1 – 4, 6, 7, 9 – 14, 16 – 25,
28 – 31, Apr. 3 – 10, 13 – May 3,
5, 6, 8 – June 1, 4 – 10, 12, 14,
17 – 19, 21 – 23, 25 – 29, July
1 – 10, 12 – 16, 19 – 26, 28 –
Aug. 19, 21, 24 – 26, 28, 30, 31,
Sept. 2, 3, 5, 7 – 15, 17, 18, 20,
25, 26, 28 – Oct. 3, 5 – 8, 11 –
16, 19 – 22, 24 – 26, 28 – Nov.
17, 19, 22, 24 – 29, Dec. 2 – 15,
18 – 27, 31.

1949 Apr. 1 – 10, 13, 14, 16, 17, 20 –
22, 24 – 26, 28, 29.

1950 Mar. 1, 3 – 6, 10, 12, 14 – 16, 19,
24, 25, 29, 30, Apr. 12 – 14, 17 –
20, 22, 24 – 30, May 5 – 17, 19,
21, 23 – June 12, 14, 15, 17 – 19,
22, 24, 25, Nov. 17.

Micro (P) & (N)
1949 Jan. 1 – Mar. 31, May 1 – Dec.
31.
1950 Jan. 1 – Feb. 28, July 1 – Oct.
31.
1951 – 1953 Jan. 1 – June 30.
1966 Jan. 1+.

ICRL
1939 Mar. 1 – 31.
1940 Jan. 1 – Mar. 31.
Micro (N)

1945 – 1952 Jan. 1 – Dec. 31.
1953 Jan. 1 – June 30.
MH
Micro (P)
1951 – 1952 Jan. 1 – Dec. 31.
1953 Jan. 1 – June 30.

CRONICA. d. est. May 14, 1913.
DLC
1956 May 24.

EL DEBER. w. est. Sept. 8, 1901.
DLC
1942 Feb. 7.

DEMOCRACIA. d. est. Aug. 30, 1924.
DLC
1942 July 27 – Aug. 8, 10 – 13, 15 –
19, 21, 23 – 25, 28, 30 – Sept. 3,
5, 6, 9, 10, 12, 13, 15 – 17, 19 –
Oct. 6, 13, 15 – 17, 20, 22, 27,
29, 31, Nov. 2, 3, 5, 7, 10, 12,
13, 16 – 19, 21 – 25, 27 – 29,
Dec. 2, 6, 13, 14, 19, 29.
1943 Jan. 2, 12, 14, Feb. 1, 17, 18, 20,
22, 24, 25, 27 – Mar. 4, 5 – 8, 10,
11, 13 – 16, 18 – 20, 22 – 27, 29,
31, Apr. 6 – 8, 10, 13, 14, 18, 20,
24, 28, 30, May 2, 5, 7, 12, 15,
20, 26, June 1, 10 – 12, 17, 26,
28.

LA TIERRA. sw. est. Sept. 21, 1912.
DLC
1942 May 19, July 7, Oct. 2 – 13,
Nov. 24 – Dec. 8.
1943 Jan. 5 – 12, Feb. 19 – 26, Mar.
16 – 19, 26 – Apr. 20.

TRIBUNA. d. est. Oct. 12, 1928.
DLC
1943 Nov. 29.

Salta

CIVICO. d.
MWA
1892 Oct. 31.

DIARIO POPULAR. d. est. May 11, 1885.
MWA
1887 July 31, Aug. 10.

1888   Nov. 11.

INTERESES AMERICANOS. w. est.
Mar. 20, 1879.
MWA
    1879   Mar. 20.

LIBERTAD EN EL ORDEN. sw. est. Feb.
16, 1859.
    Note: Ceased publication Nov. 17,
    1860.
MWA
    1860   Apr. 21.

EL TRIBUNO. d. est. 1949.
DLC
    1955   Nov. 21.

LA UNION. d.
MWA
    1892 Oct. 31.

Salto

See Uruguay. Salto.

San Antonio de Areco

LA REFORMA. sw. est. 1902.
CSt
    1915   Mar. 21.

San Fernando

LA RAZON. w. est. 1898.
CSt
    1915   Aug. 15, Sept. 19.

San Isidro

REPORTER. w.
MWA
    1892   Nov. 13.

San Juan

DIARIO DE CUYO. d. est. July 5, 1947.
DLC
    1958   Nov. 1 – 23, 25, 26, 28 – Dec.
            31.
    1959   Jan. 1 – Feb. 12, 14 – 22, 24 –
            Mar. 7, 9 – 13, 15 – 30, Apr. 1,

            2, 4 – 6, 8 – 25, 27 – 29, May 3 –
            7, 18, 20 – Aug. 8, 10 – Oct. 8,
            10 – Nov. 23, 25, 27 – Dec. 2,
            4 – 14, 16 – 19, 21 – 31.
    1960   Jan. 3 – 19, 21 – 28, 30 – Feb. 2,
            4 – 12, 14 – Mar. 17, 19 – May
            6, 8 – June 16, 18 – July 6, 8 –
            Aug. 5, 7 – Nov. 10, 12 – 15, 17,
            19 – Dec. 22, 24 – 28, 30, 31.
    1961   Jan. 1 – 6, 8 – Feb. 18, 20 –
            Mar. 30, Apr. 2 – 8, 10 – 24,
            26 – July 10, 12 – Sept. 9, 11 –
            30.
    Micro (P) & (N)
    1961   Oct. 1 – Dec. 31.
    1962   Jan. 1+.

EL PORVENIR. w. est. Apr. 30, 1899.
DLC
    1942   Sept. 12, 19, Oct. 3 – Dec. 5.
    1943   Jan. 23.

SAN JUAN.
CSt
    1915   Jan. 26.

TRIBUNA. d. est. May 1, 1931.
DLC
    1955   Dec. 4.

San Nicolás

EL PROGRESO. d. est. 1872.
CSt
    1915   Mar. 29, Apr. 17.

Santa Fé

EL LITORAL. d. est. Aug. 7, 1918.
DLC
    1942   Feb. 8, 9, 15, 16, 23, Mar. 1, 2,
            8, 9, 15, 16.

LA MAÑANA DE SANTA FE. d., w. est.
Sept. 10, 1937.
    Note: Periodicity Sept. 10, 1937 – Oct.
    31, 1952, daily; after Dec. 7, 1952,
    weekly. Suspended publication Nov.
    1 – Dec. 6, 1952.
DLC
    1943   Jan. 1 – Apr. 20, 26 – June 19,

21 — July 1, 3 — Aug. 8, 10 — 31,
Sept. 2 — 21, 23 — Dec. 31.
1944 Jan. 1 — Dec. 31.
1945 Jan. 1 — 27, 29 — July 29, 31 —
Aug. 2, 4, 6 — Dec. 5.
1946 Jan. 1 — 21, 24 — June 29, July
1 — 16, 18 — Aug. 9, 11 — Sept.
30.
1947 Jan. 2 — 27, 29 — Mar. 15, 17 —
Sept. 30.
1949 Feb. 10, 12, 14 — 16, 18 — Mar.
8, 10 — Apr. 20, 22, 25 — May 22,
24 — July 7, 9 — 22, 24 — 30, Aug.
1 — 8, 10 — Sept. 5, 12, 14 — 29,
Oct. 1 — 5, 8 — 22, 24 — Nov. 13,
15 — 20, 22 — 27, 29 — Dec. 3,
6 — 11, 13 — 18, 20 — 31.
1950 Jan. 1 — Feb. 12, 14 — Mar. 10,
12 — May 9, 11 — 30, June 1 — 8,
10 — Oct. 16, 18 — Dec. 24, 27 —
31.
1951 Jan. 2 — 4, 8 — Feb. 7, 9 — Sept.
12, 14 — Dec. 9, 11 — 19, 21,
23 — 31.
1952 Jan. 1 — 16, 18 — 21, 23 — Feb. 6,
8 — 23, 27, 28, Mar. 1 — 6, 8,
10 — Apr. 8, 10 — 21, 23 — May 9,
11 — 21, 23 — 26, 28 — June 15,
17 — 29, July 1 — 7, 9 — 13, 15 —
Aug. 26, 28, 31 — Oct. 9, 11,
14 — 31, Dec. 7 — 28.
1953 Jan. 11 — May 3, 17, 31 — Aug.
23, Sept. 6, 27, Oct. 24.
1954 Apr. 10, May 8 — Dec. 31.
1955 Jan. 8 — Apr. 16, 30 — June 18,
July 30, Aug. 6, 20 — Sept. 10,
Oct. 1 — Dec. 31.
1956 Jan. 7 — Nov. 10, Dec. 1 — 22.
1957 Jan. 5 — Feb. 15, 17 — June 1,
15, 29 — Dec. 28.

LA NUEVA EPOCA. d. est. 1896.
CSt
1915 July 31, Nov. 25, 26.

EL ORDEN. d. est. Nov. 3, 1927.
DLC
1942 Feb. 8, 9, 15, 16, 25, 26, Mar. 1,
5, 9, 12, 15, 17.
1943 Sept. 8, 9.

Santiago del Estero

EL LIBERAL. d. est. Nov. 3, 1898.
CSt
1915 Feb. 23.

Tandil

EL ECO DE TANDIL. d. est. June 31,
1882.
CSt
1915 Jan. 28.

Tucumán

CULTURA.
CSt
1948 June 13, 26, July 4, 11, Aug. 8.

EL DIARIO DEL NORTE. d.
CSt
1914 Sept. 5.

LA GACETA. d. est. Aug. 4, 1912.
DLC
1958 June 29.

EL ORDEN. d. est. Sept. 14, 1882.
DLC
1942 July 4.

TROPICO. d.
CU
1947 Sept. 20, 24, 28, 30, Oct. 3, 8, 9,
14, 22 — 25, 28, Nov. 4 — 6, 8,
Dec. 18, 21.
MH
1947 Apr. 1 — 3, 5 — 19, 21 — 30, May
2 — 6, 10 — 14, 18 — 22, 25, 27 —
June 13, 15 — 17, 19, 21 — 26,
July 1 — 6, 9, 11, 12, 14 — 26,
28 — 31, Aug. 2 — 7, 9 — 13, 16,
18 — 30, Sept. 10, 17 — 27, 29 —
Oct. 3, 5, 7, 8, 11 — 14, 23 — 28,
30 — Nov. 5, 8, 13 — 15, 17 — 22,
24 — 27, 29, 30, Dec. 3 — 7, 10 —
14, 17 — 21, 24 — 31.
1948 Jan. 2 — 6, 8 — 11, 13 — 15, 17 —
22, 25.

Victoria

LA COALICION.
CSt
  1915   May 15.

BOLIVIA

Antofagasta

See Chile. Antofagasta.

Aroma

ECO DE AROMA. irr. est. May 28, 1887.
MWA
  1887   May 28, July 9, Aug. 28 – Dec.
         31.
  1888   Jan. 1 – 21, Feb. 4.

Caracoles

ECO DE CARACOLES. w. est. Oct. 31,
  1875.
  MWA
  1875   Oct. 31 – Nov. 9, 24 – Dec. 1,
         22 – 31.
  1876   Jan. 1 – 6, Dec. 9, 29.

LA VERDAD. sw. est. Apr. 16, 1874.
CtY
  1875   Sept. 12, 17.
MWA
  1875   July 29 – Aug. 1, 8, 22, Sept.
         12 – 30.

Chuquisaca

AMIGO DE LA CONCORDIA. w. est.
  July 24, 1830.
  MWA
  1830   July 24 – Sept. 25.

BOLIVIANO. w., sw. est. Aug. 9, 1829.
  Note: Periodicity Aug. 9, 1829 – July
  19, 1835, weekly; after July 19, 1835,
  semiweekly. Ceased publication
  [1841].
  MWA
  1832   Apr. 12, Sept. 6, Nov. 8 – 15.
  1834   Nov. 30.
  1835   Mar. 1 – 22, Apr. 19, May 17 –
         July 19.

1838   June 14, July 5, 19 – 26, Aug.
       12, 19, 26, Sept. 2.
1839   Feb. 10.
1841   June 17.
       Suplemento: July 7.

CENTINELA DEL YLLIMANI. w. est.
  Oct. 25, 1829.
  MWA
  1829   Oct. 25 – Nov. 29.

CONCORDE DE BOLIVIA.
  MWA
  1826   Suplemento: Oct. 28.

CONDOR DE BOLIVIA. w. est. Nov. 12,
  1825.
  Note: Ceased publication June 26,
  1828.
  MWA
  1827   Mar. 22 – 29, Apr. 26.

RESTAURADOR. w. est. Apr. 4, 1839.
  Note: Removed to Sucre, Nov. 18,
  1842.
  MWA
  1839   Apr. 4 – 11, 25.

VEINTICINCO DE MAYO. [w.] est. May
  25, 1826.
  MWA
  1826   May 25, June 10.

Ciudad Natal de Murillo

ALERTADOR. irr.
  MWA
  1881   July 21.

Cobija

GACETA MUNICIPAL. irr.
  MWA
  1874   Aug. 27.
  1876   Jan. 28.

Cochabamba

ACTUALIDAD. irr. est. Jan. 25, 1861.
  MWA
  1861   Jan. 25 – Mar. 5.

ALIANZA NACIONAL. bw. est. Sept. 3,
1875.
MWA
    1875   Sept. 3 – Dec. 31.
    1876   Jan. 1 – Feb. 11, 26 – Mar. 24.
            Extraordinario: Feb. 25.

ARTESANO. irr. est. Apr. 29, 1872.
MWA
    1873   Apr. 18.
    1887   July 15, Dec. 25.
    1888   Apr. 30.

EL AVISADOR. w. est. 1877.
MWA
    1877   Dec. 13.

BANDERA BLANCA. est. Nov. 7, 1865.
MWA
    1865   Nov. 7.

BANDERA NACIONAL. w.
MWA
    1888   Feb. 11.

BOLETIN DE INSTRUCCION. bw.
MWA
    1875   June 30.
    1888   May 15.

BOLETIN OFICIAL. irr.
MWA
    1857   Oct. 2.
    1858   Nov. 22.
    1859   Jan. 28 – May 12.

EL 14 DE SEPTIEMBRE. w. est. Sept.
25, 1882.
CtY
    1882   Sept. 29, Oct. 27 – Dec. 29.
    1883   Jan. 5 – Feb. 23, Mar. 16, 30,
            Apr. 13, May 7 – Dec. 28.
    1884   Jan. 18 – Mar. 14, Apr. 16.
MWA
    1882   Sept. 25 – Dec. 31.
    1883   Jan. 1 – Dec. 31.
    1884   Jan. 1 – Apr. 24, June 28.
    1885   Jan. 14 – Mar. 5, 22 – 30, Apr.
            20 – 29, June 26 – Sept. 7, Oct.
            9, 23 – Dec. 31.
    1886   Jan. 1 – Dec. 31.

    1887   Jan. 1 – June 22, Aug. 23 –
            Sept. 14.
    1888   Jan. 31.
NcD
    1883   Jan. 19.

CENTINELA DEL PUEBLO. irr.
MWA
    1879   Jan. 31.

CLAMOR DEL PUEBLO. irr. est. Oct. 2,
1874.
MWA
    1874   Oct. 2.

CLUB REPUBLICANO. irr.
MWA
    1880   Mar. 5.

COLERA. w.
MWA
    1887   Dec. 8.

COMERCIO. d. est. Aug. 5, 1892.
MWA
    1893   Dec. 27 – 31.
    1894   Jan. 1, 2.
    1898   May 17.
    1900   Jan. 26, 27.

EL CONSTITUCIONAL. irr., w. est. Feb.
22, 1861.
DLC
    1862   July 12.
MWA
    1861   Feb. 22.
    1862   July 2 – 12.

CORREO. irr. est. [1865].
MWA
    1865   July 1 – 9, Aug. 14 – 31.

CORREO POLITICO. irr.
MWA

    1870   Feb. 1, 17, May 3, 30, June 20.

CORRESPONDENCIA. w., sw. est. Nov.
8, 1879.
    Note: Periodicity Nov. 8 – Dec. 15,
    1879, weekly; after Dec. 15, 1879,
    semiweekly.

CtY
1880   Jan. 12—Feb. 24, Mar. 19, 23, Apr. 10, 16.
MWA
1879   Nov. 8, 20, Dec. 15—31.
        Suplemento: Nov. 15.
1880   Jan. 1—May 15.

CREPUSCULO. irr. est. Aug. 12, 1891.
MWA
1891   Aug. 12.

DEMOCRACIA PACIFICA. w. est. May 25, 1862.
MWA
1862   May 26, June 20—July 12.
NcD
1862   June 20.

DISCUSION. irr. est. Jan. 12, 1864.
MWA
1864   Jan. 12.

ECO DE LA DEMOCRACIA. irr.
MWA
1888   Mar. 29—Apr. 13.

ECO LIBERAL. w. est. Nov. 8, 1903.
MWA
1904   Jan. 6, 30, Mar. 17, Apr. 14—May 18.

ELECTOR. w., irr. est. Dec. 27, 1872.
CtY
1872   Dec. 27.
1873   Jan. 3—Feb. 20.
MWA
1872   Dec. 27—31.
1873   Jan. 1—Feb. 6, 20.

ELECTOR; ORGANO DEL PARTIDO LIBERAL. w. est. Feb. 27, 1892.
MWA
1892   Feb. 27—Mar. 11, Apr. 3—May 17.

ESTANDARTE. irr.
MWA
1871   Mar. 9.

ESTUDIANTE. irr.
MWA
1884   Apr. 29.

FEDERALISTA. irr. est. Mar. 31, 1871.
MWA
1871   Apr. 28—May 7.

FUSIONISTA. irr.
MWA
1884   Feb. 12.

GACETA DEL GOBIERNO. irr. est. Mar. 1858.
    Note: Removed from La Paz to Cochabamba, Jan. 24, 1859; removed to Sucre, Apr. 26, 1859; returned to La Paz, [Nov.] 1859.
MWA
1859   Jan. 24—Feb. 11, Apr. 12—26.

GARROTE. w.
MWA
1892   July 12.

GERMEN DEL PROGRESO. irr. est. Aug. 21, 1874.
MWA
1874   Aug. 21, Sept. 16.

GOLONDRINA. bw.
MWA
1887   Sept. 14—Oct. 6.

HERALDO. w., sw., 3w., d. est. Apr. 13, 1877.
    Note: Periodicity Apr. 13, 1877—Feb. 15, 1878, weekly; Mar. 14, 1878—Jan. 4, 1879, semiweekly; May 18, 1879—1892, three times a week; after 1892, daily. Ceased publication [1908].
MWA
1877   Apr. 13—26.
1878   Jan. 25, Feb. 8—15, Mar. 14, June 7.
1879   Jan. 4, May 18—21, Sept. 9—12.
1880   Jan. 26—28, Mar. 15—18, [Apr. 13—Sept. 13], 23—Dec. 31.
1881   Jan. 1—Dec. 16.
1882   Feb. 14, 23, Mar. 5—15, July 21, Oct. 2, 9.
1883   [Aug. 20—Nov. 14], Dec. 17, 31.
1884   Jan. 1, 10—31, Feb. 8—13,

Mar. 4, May 3 — 8, July 5 — 11.
1885 — 1887   [Jan. 1 — Dec. 31].
1888   [Jan. 1 — July 12, Oct. 1 — Dec. 19].
1890   July 5 — 10, 15.
1891   Aug. 8.
1892   June 2 — 14, July 2, 7 — 12.
1903   Jan. 15.
1908   Oct. 27, Nov. 3.

EL IMPARCIAL. d. est. Dec. 10, 1930.
Note: Suspended publication June 15 — July 8, 1946.
DLC
1945   Sept. 1, 3 — 16, 18 — Oct. 14, 16 — Dec. 31.
1946   Jan. 3 — Apr. 28, May 1 — 5, 7 — July 21, 23 — Dec. 1, 6 — 22, 24 — 29.
1947   Jan. 1 — Feb. 7, 9 — Apr. 18, 20 — June 27, 29, July 1 — 4, 6 — Dec. 31.
1948   Jan. 1 — Mar. 5, 12 — Apr. 10, 12 — May 17, 19 — 27, 31 — June 10, 13 — 27, 29 — Aug. 6, Sept. 1 — 30.

INDEPENDIENTE. irr. est. May 16, 1862.
MWA
1862   May 16 — July 31.

EL INDEPENDIENTE; PERIODICO POLITICO, LITERARIO Y COMERCIAL. w. est. Jan. 20, 1889.
CtY
1889   Feb. 3, Mar. 3.
MWA
1889   Jan. 20, Feb. 17 — Mar. 3, Apr. 17, Aug. 14.
NcD
1889   Mar. 3.

INDUSTRIA. sw.
MWA
1889   Jan. 7.

INTERPRETE DEL PUEBLO. irr.
MWA
1862   May 27 — June 15.
Suplemento: May 27.

EL IRIS. irr. est. Mar. 10, 1876.
DLC
1876   Mar. 31.
MWA
1876   Mar. 10 — 31, Apr. 21 — 28.

LA LEY. irr. est. Jan. 1, 1873.
MWA
1873   Feb. 7.
Suplemento: Apr. 25.

LIBERAL. irr.
MWA
1884   Jan. 21 — May 10.

MEJILLONES. irr. est. July 1, 1863.
MWA
1863   July 1 — Sept. 19.

MOSQUITO. irr.
MWA
1892   Apr. 6, 27.

NACION. irr. est. [Feb. 4, 1881].
MWA
1881   [Feb. 4,]

NACIONAL. est. July 4, 1883.
MWA
1883   July 4.

OBRERO. w. est. Apr. 1, 1892.
MWA
1892   Apr. 1 — 18.

ORDEN. irr.
MWA
1853   Apr. 24 — 27, July 22, Sept. 4 — 25.
1854   Mar. 29 — Apr. 2, June 20, July 12, Dec. 14.

ORDEN. d.
MWA
1909   Apr. 1.

PABELLON NACIONAL. irr. est. Feb. 14, 1873.
MWA
1873   Feb. 14 — Apr. 3.

EL PAIS. d. est. 1937.
DLC
1945   Aug. 11 — Nov. 1, 4 — Dec. 10, 12 — 31.

1946   Jan. 1 – 18, 20 – Apr. 1, 3 –
        18, 22 – 27, 29, May 1 – June
        22, 24 – July 29, 31 – Aug. 5,
        9 – 16, 18 – Dec. 29.
1947   Jan. 1 – Apr. 1, 3 – 25, 27 –
        June 2, 5 – 20, 22 – 27, 29, July
        1 – 4, 6 – Aug. 22, 24 – Dec. 31.
1948   Jan. 1 – May 28, 30 – June 10,
        12 – Aug. 4, Sept. 4 – 30.

LA PATRIA. sw. est. Aug. 20, 1875.
MWA
    1875   Aug. 20 – 26, Sept. 29 – Dec.
            31.
    1876   Jan. 1 – Feb. 23.

PATRIOTA. w.
MWA
    1881   Jan. 21.
    1883   Dec. 28.
    1884   May 16.

PORVENIR. bw.
MWA
    1909   Apr. 1.

PORVENIR; ORGANO DE LA SOCIE-
DAD DE "EL PORVENIR." bw.
MWA
    1887   Aug. 23 – Dec. 18.
    1888   Feb. 11 – June 24.

PRENSA. irr. est. Aug. 16, 1860.
MWA
    1860   Aug. 16 – Nov. 27.

PRENSA. irr.
MWA
    1874   Aug. 21.

PRENSA. irr.
MWA
    1892   June 4, 20 – July 5.

PRENSA. w. est. Jan. 3, 1879.
    1879   Jan. 3.
            Boletín: Mar. 1.

PRENSA. d.
MWA
    1908   Oct. 26.

EL PROGRESO. w., irr. est. 1883.
CtY
    1885   Sept. 21 – 28, Oct. 16, Nov. 2,
            20 – Dec. 31.
    1886   Jan. 15 – July 23.
    1887   Jan. 22, Feb. 18, May 13.
MWA
    1883   Sept. 21.
    1884   Mar. 7, Apr. 10, May 2, Sept.
            4 – 19, Nov. 14 – Dec. 31.
    1885 – 1886   Jan. 1 – Dec. 31.
    1887   Jan. 1 – Mar. 8, Apr. 27 – June
            3, [July 1 – Dec. 24.]
    1888   Jan. 6, Feb. 10 – 29, May 30 –
            June 21, July 24.
    1892   June 27 – July 27.
NcD
    1885   Sept. 21, Oct. 16, Nov. 2, 20,
            Dec. 11, 21, 31.
    1886   Jan. 15, 26, Feb. 10, Mar. 7,
            24, Apr. 2, 8, 16, 29, May 4, 10,
            June 20, 30, July 9, 16, 23.
    1887   May 13, June 3.

PUEBLO CONSTITUYENTE. w.
MWA
    1876   June 16 – Sept. 29.

RAZON. w. est. Jan. 2, 1874.
MWA
    1874   Feb. 6, 27, Apr. 10 – 17.
    1878   June 7.

REFORMA. irr.
MWA
    1879   Jan. 3, Mar. 9.

TIEMPO. irr. est. Apr. 4, 1860.
MWA
    1860   Apr. 4, 20 – July 11, Sept. 19 –
            27, Oct. 18, Nov. 10 – Dec. 31.
    1861 Jan. 1 – May 4.

LOS TIEMPOS. d. est. Sept. 1944.
    Note: Suspended publication June
    4 – Aug. 3, 1950. Plant destroyed by
    fire, Nov. 9, 1953.
DLC
    1945   Aug. 5 – 18, 22 – Sept. 26,
            28 – Dec. 29.
    1946   Jan. 1 – 5, 7 – 18, 21 – May 10,

14—July 18, 20—26, 28, Aug.
1—6, 9—Sept. 1, 3—Nov. 15,
19—Dec. 31.
1947   Jan. 1—Feb. 7, 9, 10, 12—14,
16—27, Mar. 1—5, 7—26, 28—
May 1, 3, 5—Nov. 15, 17—Dec.
16, 18—31.
1948   Jan. 1—Feb. 3, 5—May 27,
29—June 12, 14—Aug. 10,
Sept. 8—Oct. 28, 31—Dec. 31.
1949   Jan. 1—Mar. 21, 23—May 25,
30, June 4—Aug. 31, Sept. 2—
Dec. 7, 9—12, 16—20, 22—31.
1950   Jan. 3—July 3, Aug. 4, 10—
Sept. 4, 8—Dec. 18, 22—31.
1951   Jan. 13—Mar. 12, 19, 26—Dec.
13, 15—21, 23—29.
1952   Jan. 1—6, 8—24, Feb. 17—
Mar. 29, 31—Apr. 9, 19—Aug.
31, Sept. 2—30, Oct. 2—7, 11—
Dec. 20, 22—31.
1953   Jan. 1—9, 11—17, 19—Feb. 2,
4—16, 21—Mar. 30, Apr. 1—23,
25—June 1, 3—15, 17—20,
22—25, 27—July 1, 3—6, 8—
11, 13—Oct. 23, 25.
FU
1948   Nov. 4.
1952   [Jan. 1—Dec. 31].
1953   [Jan. 1—Oct. 31].

TRASMISION LEGAL. w. est. 1855.
MWA
1855   Sept. 26—Dec. 31.
1856   Jan. 1—Dec. 31.
1857   Jan. 1—June 12.

TRIBUNO DEL PUEBLO. irr. est. Mar.
8, 1872.
MWA
1872   Apr. 8, May 1, Dec. 17—31.
1873   Jan. 1—Dec. 31.
1874   Jan. 1—May 1, 29.

TUNARI. w.
MWA
1887   May 27, Aug. 10—Oct. 29.
1888   Apr. 19.

LA UNION. irr.
CtY
1875   Dec. 24.

UNION.
MWA
1875   Feb. 20—Dec. 31.
1876   Jan. 1—Feb. 24.

VAPOR. irr. est. Sept. 5, 1873.
MWA
1874   July 17.

VERDAD. bw.
MWA
1887   Apr. 29—May 13, July 15, Aug.
19.

VIGIA. irr. est. Jan. 20, 1862.
MWA
1862   Jan. 20.

VOLANTE. irr.
MWA
1887   Mar. 30, June 23—Sept. 30.

LA VOZ DE BOLIVIA. 3w., irr. est. Oct.
30, 1862.
Note: Removed from La Paz to Oruro,
Jan. 3, 1863; removed to Cochabam-
ba, Oct. 25, 1863; removed to Oruro,
May 1, 1864; returned to Cochabamba,
June 23, 1864.
CtY
1863   Oct. 25—Dec. 23.
1864   Jan. 1—26, Feb. 7, 20—27,
Mar. 12, 23, Apr. 4—11, Aug. 6.
MWA
1863   Oct. 25—Dec. 31.
1864   Jan. 1—Oct. 29.

VOZ DEL PUEBLO. w. est. [1848].
MWA
1848   Sept. 16.

VOZ DEL PUEBLO; ORGANO DEL
PARTIDO LIBERAL. w.
MWA
1891   Sept. 16.

Colquechaca

INDUSTRIAL. w.
MWA
    1891   Jan. 29, Apr. 2, 20, July 2, Aug.
          6, Sept. 28 — Oct. 15.
    1892   Jan. 11 — 17, 29.

Corocoro

IDEA. irr. est. July 16, 1877.
MWA
    1877   July 16 — 28, Oct. 20 — 30.
    1878   June 28.
    1883   Mar. 4, Dec. 10.
    1884   Jan. 25, Feb. 15, Mar. 15, Apr.
          20, May 26.
    1885   Mar. 2 — 12, Apr. 3 — 12.

OBRERO. w.
MWA
    1884   Jan. 28.

Lamar

VOZ DEL LITORAL. irr.
MWA
    1874   Sept. 23 — Nov. 19.

La Paz

LA ACTUALIDAD. sw. est. Apr. 13, 1872.
CtY
    1872   Apr. 13.
MWA
    1872   Apr. 13 — 20, May 1.

AMERICA LIBRE; ORGANO DEL
PARTIDO LIBERAL. irr. est. Oct. 13,
1887.
MWA
    1887   Oct. 13 — Nov.
    1888   Jan. 1, Feb. 6 — 10, Mar. 3 — 10,
          May 11 — 23, June 5.

AMERICA LIBRE; ORGANO QUE
DEFIENDE EL PARTIDO "CON-
STITUCIONAL." sw.
MWA
    1888   May 13.

AMERICANO. d.
MWA
    1896   Jan. 14 — Mar. 20, 27, Apr. 21 —
          May 18.

AMIGO DEL PUEBLO. w.
MWA
    1888   Aug. 15.

AMIGO DEL SABER. irr.
MWA
    1887   July 3.

ANTORCHA. irr.
MWA
    1862   May 12.

ARTESANO; PAPEL EVENTUAL,
POLITICO, LITERARIO, INDUS-
TRIAL Y RELIGIOSO. irr.
MWA
    1862   Apr. 20.

ARTESANO; ORGANO DE LA CLASE
OBRERA. [w.] est. Oct. 4, 1883.
MWA
    1883   Oct. 4, 29.

ARTESANO; ORGANO DE LOS ARTE-
SANOS LIBERALES. irr.
MWA
    1894   Feb. 25, Sept. 8, Dec. 1.
    1895   June 1, Sept. 30.
    1896   Apr. 21.

ARTESANO HONRADO. irr. est. June
21, 1887.
MWA
    1887   June 21, July 12, Sept. 8.
    1888   Feb. 3, Mar. 1, 24, Apr. 18, 28.

BANDERA FEDERAL. irr. est. Feb. 13,
1876.
MWA
    1876   Feb. 13 — Mar. 11.

BANDERA LIBERAL. 3w. est. Sept. 19,
1907.
MWA
    1907   [Sept. 19 — Dec. 31.]
    1908   [Jan. 1 — May 30.]

BANDERA NACIONAL. irr. est. June 8,
1883.
MWA
    1883   June 8, Aug. 6, Oct. 5.

BANDO.
  MWA
    1862   [Jan. 1 — May 30.]
BIEN PUBLICO. irr. est. Apr. 1, 1871.
  MWA
    1872   Jan. 12 — Feb. 5.
BIEN PUBLICO.
  MWA
    1891   June 18 — 21, [Nov. 1.]
    1892   [Feb. 1.]

BOLETIN.
  MWA
    1865   [Jan. 8, 9, 15.]

BOLETIN; PUBLICACION OFFICIAL.
  irr. est. June 12, 1865.
  MWA
    1865   June 12 — Dec. 14.

BOLETIN. irr. est. Dec. 28, 1874.
  MWA
    1874   Dec. 28 — 31.
    1875   Jan. 1 — 12.

BOLETIN.
  MWA
    1890   Aug. 1.

BOLETIN DE ACTUALIDAD.
  MWA
    1902   Aug. 31, Oct. 2.

BOLETIN DE INSTRUCCION. irr.
  MWA
    1872   Aug. 29 — Dec. 31.
    1873   Jan. 1 — Apr. 1.

BOLETIN DEL AYUNTAMIENTO DE
  LA PAZ. irr.
  MWA
    1904   Oct. 3.

BOLETIN ELECTORAL DEL PARTIDO
  NACIONAL.
  MWA
    1888   May 12.

BOLETIN LIBERAL. 3w. est. 1888.
  DLC
    1888   May 3, 13.
  MWA
    1888   Apr. 26, 30, May 3, 10 — 13, 25.

BOLETIN NACIONAL.
  MWA
    1895   Dec. 6.

BOLETIN OFICIAL. irr. est. Dec. 27,
  1857.
  MWA
    1858   May 26.

BOLETIN OFICIAL. [3w.] est. May 7,
  1876.
  MWA
    1876   May 7 — June 30.

BOLETIN OFICIAL. irr. est. Nov. 28,
  1870.
    Note: Removed from La Paz to Co-
    chabamba, May 3, 1871; removed to
    Sucre, June 13, 1871; removed to
    Potosí, Nov. 25, 1871; returned to La
    Paz, Jan. 12, 1872.
  MWA
    1871   Feb. 1, 28, Mar. 14, Apr. 28.
    1872   Feb. 1 — 17, Mar. 17 — 30, Sept.
           23 — Oct. 8, Nov. 20.
           Suplemento: Dec. 18.
    1873   Jan. 3 — 7.

BOLETIN OFICIAL. irr. est. Dec. 14,
  1898.
  MWA
    1899   Mar. 2.

BOLIVIA. bw. est. [1960].
    Note: Succeeded *Boletín de la Direc-
    ción de Informaciones*.
  PPiU
    1960   Jan. 1 — Dec. 31.
    1961   Jan. 1 — July 31, Sept. 1 — Dec.
           31.
    1962   Jan. 1+.

BOLIVIANO. sw.
  MWA
    1861   Nov. 20.

LA CALLE. d. est. 1936.
  DLC
    1941   June 8, 12, 15, 17, 20 — 22, 24,
           26, Dec. 24, 25, 28, 30, 31.
    1942   Jan. 1, 3, 4, 24, Feb. 7, 27, 28,

Mar. 3, 5, 15, 17 – 19, May 3,
Oct. 14 – 16.
1944   Oct. 29 – Nov. 1, 6, 7, 9 – Dec.
6, 8 – 27, 29 – 31.
1945   Jan. 1 – 27, 29 – Feb. 9, 11 –
Mar. 20, 22 – Apr. 7, 9 – 11, 13,
16 – May 3, 5, 7 – 10, 12 – 16,
18 – 29, 31 – June 16, 18 – July
10, 12 – 14, 16, 23, 30, Aug. 1 –
Sept. 9, 14, 15, 17, 24, 30 – Oct.
19, 22 – 25, 29, Nov. 1 – Dec.
30.

CAUSA DE DICIEMBRE; PUBLICA-
CION OFICIAL. [sw.]
MWA
1866   Feb. 3 – 9.

CELAJES. bw.
MWA
1905   Apr. 30 – May 14, Aug. 20, Oct.
1.

CHOLO. irr. est. July 7, 1849.
MWA
1849   July 7.

CIUDADANO. d., 3w. est. May 10, 1877.
Note: Periodicity May 10 – 12, 1877,
daily; after May 12, 1877, three times
a week.
MWA
1877   May 10 – Oct. 27.

CIVILISTA. sw.
MWA
1880   Feb. 18.

COMERCIO. 3w., d. est. Jan. 13, 1878.
Note: Periodicity Jan. 13, 1878 – Dec.
28, 1880, three times a week; after
Dec. 28, 1880, daily. Ceased publication. [1910].
MWA
1878   Jan. 13 – Dec. 31.
1879 – 1887   [Jan. 1 – Dec. 31.]
1888   Jan 12, May 7, 12, July 2 – 4,
Nov. 7 – Dec. 5, 22 – 24, 29.
1890   June 4, Sept. 13, 23 – Nov. 20,
24, Dec. 1 – 15, 17 – 31.
1891 – 1892   [Jan. 1 – Dec. 31.]

1893   Jan. 5, Mar. 15 – 18, Dec. 26.
1894   Jan. 8, Apr. 19 – 21, 24 – May
5, 25 – June 5, 8, 16, July 31,
Aug. 8.
1895   Mar. 14, May 27, 30 – June 4, 7,
8, 11 – 18, 21, 25.
1896 – 1902   Jan. 1 – Dec. 31.
1903   Jan. 3 – 31, Feb. 4 – 13, Mar.
3 – 20.
1904   Mar. 4, Apr. 5 – 11, June 22.
1906   July 7, Aug. 11 – Dec. 22.
1907   [Jan. 3 – Dec. 23.]
1908   [Jan. 2 – Sept. 12.]
1909   Feb. 16.
1910   July 28.

EL COMERCIO.
NcD
1878   Jan. 19.
1888   July 3.
1907   May 7.

COMERCIO DE BOLIVIA. 3w., d. est.
June 3, 1899.
Note: Periodicity June 3, 1899 – Feb.
28, 1901, three times a week; after
Feb. 28, 1901, daily. Ceased publication [1920].
MWA
1899   June 3 – July 14, 25 – 29, Aug.
3, 16, 29.
1900   June 3, 21, Dec. 15, 20 – 22, 27.
1901   Feb. 22, Apr. 25, June 4, Aug.
23, 31 – Oct. 5, 9 – Dec. 31.
1902   Jan. 1 – Dec. 31.
1903   Jan. 1 – July 31, Aug. 22, 27,
Oct. 3, 23, 25, 28, Dec. 8, 31.
1904   Jan.1 – Dec. 31.
Boletín: Feb. 12, 18.
1905   Jan. 1 – Feb. 11, Mar. 11, 26 –
Apr. 14, 23 – Dec. 31.
1906   [Jan. 1 – Dec. 31].
Boletín: May 7.
1907   [Jan. 1 – Dec. 31].
Boletín: Oct. 10.
1908   [Jan. 1 – Dec. 31].
1909   Jan. 24, Mar. 13, Dec. 5.
1910   Feb. 3.
1913   Oct. 7.

CONCORDIA. irr. est. [1861].
  MWA
    1862   May 3.

LA CONCORDIA. irr. est. July 8, 1874.
  DLC
    1874   Prospecto: July 3.
    1875   Mar. 10.
  MWA
    1874   Prospecto: July 3.
            July 8 — Dec. 31.
    1875   Jan. 1 — Dec. 31.
    1876   Jan. 1 — Apr. 7.

CONCORDIA. [w.] est. Mar. 10, 1907.
  MWA
    1907   Mar. 10, Apr. 6.

CONFEDERACION. irr. est. May 2, 1880.
  MWA
    1880   May 2 — June 18.

CONSTITUCIONAL. irr. est. Feb. 19,
  1835.
  MWA
    1835   Feb. 19 — May 4.

EL CONSTITUCIONAL. w., irr. est. Feb.
  19, 1839.
  CtY
    1839   Oct. 23, Nov. 13 — 27.
    1840   June 24, July 15, Sept. 2, Oct.
            7.
    1841   Mar. 4 — Apr. 8, May 20, Oct.
            23.
  MWA
    1839   Feb. 26 — Apr. 23, June 4, Aug.
            27, Sept. 17 — Dec. 31.
    1840   Jan. 1, May 27 — Sept. 30, Oct.
            14 — Dec. 31.
    1841   Jan. 1 — 6, Mar. 4 — June 10.

EL CONSTITUCIONAL. irr. est. 1860.
  CtY
    1862   Jan. 19, Feb. 7, 18 — 23, Apr.
            11, Nov. 20.
    1869   Jan. 30.
  DLC
    1862   Feb. 7.
  MWA
    1861   Dec. 2.

Suplemento: Dec. 11.
    1862   Jan. 8 — 27, Feb. 7 — 27, Mar.
            27, Apr. 11 — May 19, Nov. 2 —
            20.

CONSTITUCIONAL.
  See *Situación*.

EL CORREO. irr. est. 1875.
  MWA
    1875   Boletín: n.d. (Nov.).

CRISALIDA. w. est. Apr. 9, 1871.
  MWA
    1871   Apr. 9 — May 7.

CRUZROJA. [bw.]
  MWA
    1881   Mar. 30 — Apr. 29.

CUQUITO. w.
  MWA
    1902   Dec. 7 — 14.

EL DANTE. irr. est. Oct. 15, 1882.
  DLC
    1888   June 22.
  MWA
    1888   June 22.
    1890   Aug. 22.
    1892   July 16.
    1895   July 10, Oct. 30.
    1902   Sept. 15.
    1903   Aug. 12.

DEBATES. 3w. est. Mar. 5, 1899.
  MWA
    1899   Mar. 5 — Nov. 1, 17.

DEBER. d., 3w. est. June 22, 1883.
  Note: Periodicity June 22, 1883 —
  Sept. 27, 1884, daily; after Sept. 27,
  1884, three times a week.
  MWA
    1883   June 22 — Dec. 31.
    1884   Jan. 1 — Oct. 10.

DECALOGO. 3w. est. June 1, 1901.
  MWA
    1901   June 1 — Oct. 31, Dec. 3 — 31.
    1902   Jan. 1 — Dec. 31.
    1903   Jan. 1 — 3.

DEFENSA. w., sw.
    Note: Periodicity Apr. 6, 1905 – Mar.
    13, 1907, weekly; after May 13, 1907,
    semiweekly.
    MWA
        1904   Dec. 20.
        1905   [Jan. 1 – Dec. 31.]
        1906   Jan. 1 – 17, 31 – May 23, June
                7 – 20, July 5 – Dec. 31.
        1907   Jan. 1 – 10, Feb. 6, 28, Mar. 13.
        1908   June 3 – 6, July 4 – 8, Aug. 12 –
                19.

DEFENSOR DEL PUEBLO. [sw.] est.
    June 2, 1865.
    MWA
        1865   June 2 – 5.

DEMOCRACIA. irr. est. Mar. 7, 1858.
    MWA
        1858   Mar. 7.

LA DEMOCRACIA. irr., w., sw. est Aug.
    6, 1875.
    CtY
        1875   Sept. 23.
        1877   July 5 – Dec. 31.
        1878   Jan. 3 – Sept. 28.
        1879   Feb. 13 – Dec. 31.
        1888   Jan. 28.
    MWA
        1875   Aug. 6 – Dec. 31.
        1876 – 1878   Jan. 1 – Dec. 31.
        1879   Jan. 1 – June 19, July 28 – Dec.
                27.

DEMOCRACIA. irr. est. Aug. 25, 1887.
    MWA
        1887   Aug. 25, Sept. 8 – 23, Oct. 20 –
                Dec. 2, 16 – 31.
        1888   Jan. 1 – 28.

DEMOCRATA. irr.
    MWA
        1861   Dec. 27.

DEMOCRATA. irr., sw. est. May 13, 1881.
    Note: Periodicity May 13, 1881 – Oct.
    1, 1886, irregular; after Oct. 1, 1886,
    semiweekly.
    MWA
        1881   May 13 – Sept. 12.

1884   Apr. 12, 20 – May 10.
1885   Dec. 13 – 30.
1886   Apr. 22, Sept. 28 – Oct. 1.
1887   Jan. 12 – Dec. 17.
1888   Feb. 8 – May 13, June 9 – July
        12.

DEMOCRATA. irr.
    MWA
        1891   Oct. 2, Dec. 19.
                Boletín: Dec. 12, 14.
        1892   Jan. 24.

DERECHO. irr.
    MWA
        1908   May 22 – June 8, July 1 – 11.
    NcD
        1908   June 8.

DEUTSCHE WOCHENSCHRIFT FÜR
    BOLIVIEN. w. est. June 1, 1934.
    Note: In German.
    DLC
        1934   June 1.

DIARIO. d. est. Oct. 1, 1883.
    MWA
        1883   Oct. 1 – Dec. 31.
        1884   Jan. 1 – 7, 10, Mar. 19 – June 3,
                Aug. 8 – Nov. 2.

EL DIARIO. d. est. Apr. 5, 1904.
    CLU
        1965   Apr. 5, 13 – 16, 18, May 7 – 12,
                June 18 – July 3, 9 – 30, Aug.
                5, 6, 9 – 28, Oct. 1 – 5, 12 – 18,
                20 – 27, Nov. 16 – 26, Dec. 3,
                28 – 31.
        1966   Jan. 1+.
    DLC
        1905   Apr. 8, 9, 13 – May 19, 23 –
                June 16, 18 – July 25, 27 – Aug.
                4, 6, 10 – Sept. 16, 18 – Dec.
                31.
        1941   June 4 – 10, 26 – July 9, Oct.
                4 – 8, Dec. 24 – 28.
        1942   Jan. 23 – 29, Feb. 13 – 15, 27,
                28, Mar. 2 – 4, 7, 15 – 19, May
                3, 4, June 18 – 25.
        1943   Apr. 5.

1944   Nov. 20 – Dec. 6, 8 – 27, 29 –
        31.
1946   Sept. 4 – 6, 9 – 26, 28 – Oct. 5,
        7 – 11, 14, 19 – 22, 24 – 29, Nov.
        3 – 5, 7 – 18, 20 – 26, 28 – Dec.
        2, 4 – 16, 18 – 31.
1947   Jan. 1 – Apr. 16, 18 – 30, May
        3 – Dec. 31.
1948   Jan. 1 – Nov. 1, 4 – Dec. 31.
1949   Jan. 1, 3 – Dec. 31.
1950   Jan. 1 – Dec. 31.
1951   Jan. 1 – Oct. 19, 21 – Nov. 11,
        14 – Dec. 22, 24 – 31.
1952   Jan. 1 – July 20, 22 – Oct. 2,
        4 – Dec. 4, 6 – 16, 18 – 31.
1953   Jan. 1 – May 25, 27 – Dec. 31.
1954   Jan. 1 – 25, 27 – Feb. 19, 21 –
        Dec. 6, 8 – 31.
1955   Jan. 1 – Feb. 21, 25 – May 30,
        June – Aug. 6, 8 – Dec. 31.
Micro (P)
1956   Jan. 1+.
DPU
Current (six months).
FU
Current (two years).
ICRL
Micro (P) & (N)
1956   Jan. 1+.
MWA
1904   Apr. 16, June 17 – Dec. 26.
1905   Jan. 3 – Feb. 8, [Mar. 26 – Dec.
        31].
1906 – 1907   [Jan. 1 – Dec. 31].
1908   [Jan. 1 – Dec. 17].
1909   Jan. 23, 24, Feb. 10, 20, Apr. 7,
        July 11, Nov. 24, Dec. 5.
1910   Jan. 21.
1914   Mar. 26, Apr. 29, 30.
NcU
1941   Jan. 1 – June 30.

DISCUSION. irr. est. May 25, 1855.
MWA
1855   May 25, June 8.

LOS DOMINGOS DE "EL LIBERAL." d.
est. 1892.
DLC
1892   May 22.

DUENDE. w. est. Mar. 11, 1839.
MWA
1839   Mar. 11 – Apr. 10, 27.

ECO DE BOLIVIA. irr.
Note: Removed to and returned from
Sucre during 1868.
MWA
1867   Oct. 9, Nov. 8.
1868   Dec. 9, 30.
1869   Jan. 8, 26.

ECO DE LA JUVENTUD. w., sw. est. June
10, 1874.
Note: Periodicity June 10 – Oct. 1,
1874, weekly.
MWA
1874   June 10 – July 12, Aug. 18, Oct.
        1, Dec. 18.

EL ECO DE LA PAZ. sw. est. July 9,
1864.
CtY
1864   July 9 – Sept. 14.
1865   Feb. 12, Mar. 9, Apr. 2.
MWA
1864   July 9 – Dec. 31.
1865   Jan. 1 – May 2.

EL ECO DEL EJERCITO. irr. est. Mar. 9,
1861.
CtY
1861   Mar. 15.
MWA
1861   Mar. 9 – 19.

ECO DEL NORTE. 3w. est. Aug. 20,
1862.
MWA
1862   Aug. 20, 28 – Oct. 12.

ECO NACIONAL. 3w.
MWA
1847   Nov. 2, 18, 27.

ECOS FEDERALES. sw. est. 1899.
MWA
1899   Aug. 20 – 26, Sept. 10.

ECOS LIBERALES. irr., sw. est. Mar. 11,
1894.
Note: Periodicity Mar. 11 – June 13,

1894, irregular; after June 13, 1894,
semiweekly.
MWA
1894   [Mar. 11 – Oct. 16.]

ELECTOR. d. est. Mar. 15, 1892.
MWA
1892   Mar. 15, 29, May 4, 21.

LA EPOCA. d. est. May 1, 1845.
Note: Suspended publication Sept.
19, 1857 – Feb. 17, 1866; ceased regular publication Nov. 6, 1867. See also
La Nueva época.
CtY
1845   [Aug. 20 – Dec. 31.]
1846   [Jan. 2 – Dec. 4].
1847   [Jan. 2 – Nov. 30].
1848   [June 12 – Dec. 23].
1849   [Mar. 1 – Dec. 31].
1850   [Jan. 3 – Nov. 25].
1851   Aug. 25.
1852   [Jan. 5 – Dec. 21].
1853   [Apr. 19 – Dec. 10].
1854   [Jan. 30 – Dec. 20].
1855   [Jan. 4 – Dec. 4].
1856   [Jan. 26 – Sept. 12].
1866   [Mar. 5 – Oct. 19].
1867   [Jan. 2 – Aug. 8].
DLC
1845   Nov. 5.
1846   Jan. 3, 5, 8, 10, 14, 17, 24, 27,
        28, Feb. 6, Mar. 13, 16, 17, 19,
        20, 28, 30, June 2, 6, 8, 9, 10, 12,
        13, 15, July 28 – 31, Oct. 28.
1848   Aug. 25.
1866   June 16.
MH
Micro (P)
1845   May 24 – Nov. 29, Dec. 1 – 31.
1846   Jan. 1 – Dec. 31.
1847   Jan. 1 – Aug. 7, 9 – Dec. 14.
MWA
1845   May 24 – Dec. 31.
1846   Jan. 1 – Oct. 31, Dec. 1 – 31.
1847   Jan. 1 – Sept., [Oct. – Dec.]
1848   Jan. 31, June 10 – Dec. 30.
1849   [Jan. 1 – Dec. 31.]
1850   Jan. 1 – July 31, [Sept. 4 –
        Dec. 31.]

1851   [Jan. 1 – Dec.]
1852 – 1855   Jan. 1 – Dec. 31.
1856   Jan. 1 – Sept. 29, Oct. 31, Nov.
        22, 28, 29, Dec. 13, 23.
1857   [Jan. 2 – Sept. 19.]
1866   [Feb. 17 – Dec. 31.]
1867   [Jan. 1 – Oct. 13.]
1868   July 2 – 9.
NcD
1845   Nov. 14, 26.
1846   Jan. 2 – Feb. 6, 11, 16 – 26,
        Mar. 1 – Apr. 2, 4 – 20, 24 –
        Aug. 5, 31, June 1 – 30, July 4,
        7 – 22, 24 – 31, Aug. 1 – 5, 31,
        Sept. 1 – 24, Oct. 1 – 31.
1847   May 8, 17, Aug. 30 – 31, Sept.
        1, 2, 13 – 15.
1848   Aug. 2 – 31, Oct. 7, 9 – 14, 17 –
        21, 26, Dec. 1 – 19.
1851   Oct. 19.
1852   Jan. 17, 28, Apr. 16, July 27.
1854   June 7, 8, 10, Aug. 23.
1866   June 16, July 9, 14 – 17, 19, 23,
        24, 31, Aug. 22.
1867   Jan. 2, Feb. 21.

LA EPOCA. d. est. Mar. 28, 1891.
CtY
1891   Mar. 28 – May 2, 19 – 23, June
        2 – 4.
MWA
1891   Mar. 28 – May 2, 19 – 23, June
        2 – 4.

LA EPOCA. d. est. Jan. 1, 1909.
CtY
1909   [Jan. 8 – Sept. 20].
1910   Jan. 21.
MWA
1908   Prospecto: Dec. 31.
1909   [Jan. 1 – Dec. 29.]
1910   [Jan. 13 – Feb. 11.]

LA ESPERANZA. d. est. Nov. 16, 1857.
Note: Ceased publication [Dec. 31,
1857].
CtY
1857   Dec. 2, 5, 11, 17, 19, 30.
DLC
1857   Nov. 26, 28, Dec. 1 – 18.

MWA

　1857　Nov. 16 – Dec. 31.
NcD
　1857　Dec. 30.

ESPIRITISTA. w. est. Aug. 5, 1900.
MWA
　1900　Aug. 5.

EL ESTADO. d. est. July 5, 1900.
MWA
　1902　Boletín: Nov. 3.
　1903　Boletín: Feb. 2.
NcD
　1900　Nov. 24.
　1902　Aug. 10, 13, 16, 19, 21, 23, 26,
　　　　28, 30, Oct. 3.

EL ESTANDARTE. sw., irr. est. Mar. 18,
1852.
CtY
　1852　[Mar. 18 – Oct. 9].
MWA
　1852　Mar. 18 – Nov. 7.
NcD
　1852　Mar. 18, 24, 31, Apr. 3, 7, 13,
　　　　17, 21, 24, 28, July 6, Sept. 27.

ESTRELLA DEL NORTE. w. est. Apr.
30, 1876.
MWA
　1876　Apr. 30.

ESTUDIANTE. w., bw. est. Apr. 1, 1897.
MWA
　1897　July 30 – Aug. 30, Sept. 30.
　1898　Mar. 15 – Apr. 30, May 31.

FANTASMA. w.
MWA
　1902　Nov. 1.

FEDERACION. w. est. June 19, 1899.
MWA
　1899　June 19.

EL FEDERAL. est. July 15, 1894.
MWA
　1894　July 15.

FERROCARRIL. d. est. Mar. 1, 1877.
MWA
　1877　Mar. 1 – June 9.

LA FUSION. irr est. Jan. 24, 1873.
DLC
　1873　Jan. 24.
MWA
　1873　Jan. 24 – Feb. 10.

GACETA DEL GOBIERNO. w., sw., 3w.,
sw. est. Nov. 25, 1841.
　Note: Periodicity Nov. 25, 1841 – May
　3, 1843, weekly; May 4 – Aug. 16,
　1843, semiweekly; Aug. 16, 1843 –
　Apr. 18, 1846, three times a week;
　after Apr. 18, 1846, semiweekly.
CtY
　1841　Nov. 25, Dec. 11 – 25.
　1842　Jan. 22 – Feb. 26, Mar. 12, Apr.
　　　　9, 23 – July 19, Oct. 8 – Nov.
　　　　26, Dec. 10.
　1843　Feb. 4, Mar. 4, Apr. 15, July 29,
　　　　Aug. 12, 16, Sept. 21, 23, Oct.
　　　　3, 7, Nov. 28, Dec. 19.
　1844　Mar. 12, Apr. 9 – 16, May 11,
　　　　16, 18, June 8 – 18, 22, 29 –
　　　　July 18, Aug. 10, 22 – 27, 31 –
　　　　Sept. 21, 26 – Oct. 3, 10 – 29,
　　　　Nov. 5 – Dec. 14.
MWA
　1841　Nov. 25 – Dec. 31.
　1842 – 1843　Jan. 1 – Dec. 31.
　1844　Jan. 1 – Dec. 19.
　1845　Jan. 7 – Apr. 19.
　1846　Jan. 4 – Apr. 26, June 11 – Aug.
　　　　13, Dec. 19 – 31.
　1847　Jan. 1 – 6, 20 – Mar. 6, 27, July
　　　　28, Aug. 4 – 7, Nov. 3 – Dec. 1.

GACETA DEL GOBIERNO. irr. est. Mar.
1858.
　Note: Removed from La Paz to Cocha-
　bamba, Jan. 24, 1859; removed to
　Sucre, Apr. 26, 1859; returned to La
　Paz, [Nov.] 1859.
CtY
　1859　Nov. 26.
　1862　Jan. 18.
MWA
　1859　Nov. 26 – Dec. 31.
　1860　Jan. 1 – Feb. 3, July 4 – 19,
　　　　Nov. 26, 27.

1861   Mar. 15.
1862   Jan. 18, 31.

GACETA MUNICIPAL. irr. est. 1872.
MWA
    1874   July 14.
    1875   Mar. 9.

GACETA MUNICIPAL. est. Apr. 20,
1886.
MWA
    1886   Apr. 20.

GACETA MUNICIPAL. w. est. Mar. 29,
1895.
MWA
    1895   Mar. 29 – June 26, Aug. 24 –
            Dec. 31.
    1896   Jan. 1 – Feb. 6, Mar. 6 – Apr.
            10, May 4 – 25, June 12, 25 –
            July 31, Aug. 15, Sept. 5 – 12,
            22 – 26.
    1897   Jan. 25 – Apr. 8, June 21 – 28.

EL GRITO DE LA LIBERTAD. sw. est.
Oct. 20, 1847.
CtY
    1848   Jan. 3, 20, Feb. 14, Apr. 12.
MWA
    1847   Dec. 22 – 31.
    1848   Jan. 1 – Apr. 22.

HERALDO. d. est. Apr. 19, 1894.
MWA
    1894   Apr. 19 – May 8.

EL ILLIMANI. est. Sept. 7, 1829.
    Note: Suspended publication 1830 –
    Apr. 22, 1839.
MWA
    1839   Apr. 22 – May 20.

EL ILLIMANI. irr. est. Jan. 1, 1868.
CtY
    1868   Jan. 1, Feb. 21.
MWA
    1868   Jan. 1 – May 3.

ILLIMANI. irr. est. Sept. 25, 1871.
MWA
    1871   Sept. 25 – Dec. 31.
    1872   Jan. 1 – Nov. 24.

ILUSTRACION. w.
MWA
    1889   Prospecto.

IMPARCIAL. irr. est. Oct. 27, 1863.
MWA
    1863   Oct. 27, Nov. 28 – Dec. 31.
    1864   Jan. 17.

EL IMPARCIAL. d., sw., 3w. est. July 1,
1888.
    Note: Periodicity July 1, 1888 – Aug.
    6, 1892, daily; Dec. 1894 – Mar. 29,
    1895, semiweekly; after Mar. 29,
    1895, three times a week. Suspended
    publication Aug. 7, 1892 – Jan. 14,
    1893; [June 26, 1893 – Dec. 17, 1894].
CtY
    1888   July 27 – Aug. 2, 10 – 17, 29 –
            Sept. 6, 10, 22, Oct. 2.
    1889   Jan. 6 – 16, 18 – Feb. 9, 22 – 26,
            28 – Mar. 19, 22 – 28, 30, 31,
            Apr. 3 – 6, 11, 14, 17 – 25, 27,
            30 – May 8, 30 – June 9, 18, 22,
            26, July 1 – 9, 11 – 21, 24 – Aug.
            3, 9 – 16, 22, Sept. 10 – 18, 21,
            22, 26 – Nov. 17, 28 – Dec. 1,
            5 – 7, 10 – 17, 19 – 22, 27.
    1890   Jan. 4 – 12, 15 – Feb. 9, 14, 25,
            Mar. 2, 12 – 16, Apr. 22 – May
            1, 3, 8, 11, 27.
    1891   May 12 – 16, 20 – June 12, 16 –
            27, July 1, 3, 10 – 14, 23, 24, 28,
            29, 31 – Aug. 9. 12 – 22, 26,
            30 – Oct. 13, 15 – 23, 25, Nov.
            29, Dec. 18.
    1892   Jan. 6, 9 – 16, 20 – 27, 30 – Feb.
            12, 16 – Mar. 8, 10 – 19, 23 –
            31, Apr. 2 – June 24, July 1 –
            23, 28, 30, Aug. 2 – 6.
    1893   Jan. 15 – 21, Feb. 2 – Mar. 18,
            24, Apr. 6, 21 – June 9, 15, 18.
    1896   June 24, Sept. 23, Oct. 6.
    1898   Jan. 7, Apr. 29, May 13, Sept.
            16.
    1899   Mar. 8.
MWA
    1888   July 1 – Oct. 23, Nov. 9 – Dec.
            31.

1889 – 1891   Jan. 1 – Dec. 31.
1892   Jan. 1 – Aug. 6.
1893   Jan. 15 – June 25.
1894   Dec. 18 – 31.
1895   Jan. 1 – Mar. 29, July 25 – Dec. 31.
1896   Jan. 1 – Dec. 31.
1897   Jan. 1 – June 4, Oct. 6, Nov. 19, Dec. 6 – 24, 31.
 NcD
1888   Aug. 1.
1889   Jan. 31, June 18, July 13, 24, Oct. 2, 15, 18, 29, 30, Nov. 1, 5, 7 – 17.
1890   Jan. 4, 15, 21, Feb. 2, Apr. 24.
1891   June 12, 16, July 1, 3, 31, Aug. 14, Sept. 1 – 12, 16 – 20, Oct. 7, 15 – 18.
1892   Feb. 17, May 10, June 21, July 22, 23.
1893   Jan. 15, 19, Mar. 18.

IMPARCIAL 2°. 3w. est. 1897.
 MWA
1898   Jan. 7, 21, 28, [Mar. 30 – Dec. 31].
1899   Jan. 1 – Dec. 31.
1900   Jan. 1 – Feb. 23.

INDEPENDIENTE. irr. est. Dec. 20, 1870.
 MWA
1870   Dec. 20 – 31.
1871   Jan. 1 – 21, Mar. 11.

INDEPENDIENTE. sw.
 MWA
1888   Apr. 11.

INDICADOR. irr. est. Jan. 21, 1844.
 MWA
1844   Feb. 24, Apr. 18.
1845   Jan. 31.

INDUSTRIA; DIARIO OFICIAL. d.
 MWA
1889   [Jan. 29 – Aug. 20.]

LA INSTRUCCION. irr. est. Jan. 1, 1887.
 DLC
1887   Mar. 26, June 16.
 MWA
1887   Mar. 12, 26 – Apr. 8, June 16.

INTEGRIDAD NACIONAL. sw. est. Apr. 28, 1894.
 MWA
1894   [Apr. 28 – Oct. 24].

INTI. d. est. 1941.
 DLC
1941   June 11, 12.

INVESTIGADOR. sw., w. est. Sept. 12, 1839.
  Note: Periodicity Nov. 21, 1839 – Jan. 6, 1840, semiweekly; after Jan. 6, 1840, weekly.
 MWA
1839   Sept. 26, Nov. 21.
1840   Jan. 6, Mar. 12, May 7, 21.
    Extraordinario: Feb. 9, May 4.

EL IRIS DE LA PAZ. w. est. July 11, 1829.
  Note: Official publication. Ceased publication Feb. 9, 1839.
 CU – B
 Micro (N)
1829   July 25 – Aug. 1.
1830   May 1 – Aug. 21.
 DLC
1838   [Jan. 1 – Dec. 31].
 MWA
1836   Sept. 25.
1839   Feb. 3.

JUICIO PUBLICO. irr. est. Nov. 29, 1861.
  Note: Ceased publication Mar. 20, 1862.
 MWA
1861   [Nov. 29 – Dec. 31].
1862   [Jan. 1 – Mar. 15].

JUSTICIA DEL PUEBLO. irr.
 MWA
1873   Feb. 21.

LABARO. d. est. May 17, 1888.
 MWA
1888   May 17 – 29, June 1 – 7, 12 – 21, 27, 30 – July 6, 11 – 13.

LATIGO. irr. est. 1848.
 MWA
1848   Sept. 23.

LIBERAL. d., 3w. est. Dec. 4, 1891.
  Note: Periodicity Dec. 4, 1891 — July
  16, 1892, daily; after July 16, 1892,
  three times a week.
  MWA
    1891   Dec. 4 — 31.
    1892   Jan. 1 — Dec. 31.
    1893   Jan. 1 — Sept. 22.
  NcD
    1891   Dec. 5 — 15, 19 — 31.
    1892   Jan. 1 — 5, 13, 15, 29, Feb. 1,
            3 — 6, 9, 10, 12, 13, 16, 17, 19,
            20, 25, Mar. 4, 5, 8 — 12, 15 — 17,
            21 — 24, 29 — 31, Apr. 1 — 22, 26,
            28 — 30, May 3 — 7, 11 — 13,
            18 — 22, 25, 26, 29, June 1 — 5,
            8, 10 — 12, 22 — 24, 26, 30, July
            1, 2, 7, 9, 10, 16.
    1893   Aug. 5, 10, 13, 17, 24, 27, Sept.
            12, 15.

LIBERTAD. d. est. Dec. 21, 1870.
  MWA
    1870   Dec. 21.

LIBERTAD. irr. est. Mar. 25, 1871.
  MWA
    1871   Mar. 25 — Dec. 31.
    1872   Jan. 1 — June 7.

MERCURIO. d. est. 1904.
  MWA
    1904   May 17, June 22.

LA NACION. d. est. Apr. 1, 1890.
  DLC
    1890   May 14.
  MWA
    1890   Apr. 1 — May 27.

NACION. irr. est. Jan. 1, 1901.
  MWA
    1901   Jan. 1 — July 27, Dec. 24.
    1902   Jan. 11.
    1903   Apr. 4.
    1904   Feb. 9, 17, 27 — Apr. 13, May
            17, June 5, 25, July 30 — Oct.
            15, Nov. 16 — Dec. 23.
  NcD
    1902   Jan. 11.

LA NACION. d. est. 1939.
  DLC
    1939   Oct. 14 — 25.

LA NACION. d. est. Oct. 12, 1952.
  Note: Suspended publication Sept.
  22 — Nov. 27, 1956.
  DLC
    1952   Oct. 12, 31, Nov. 2, 3.
    1953   Feb. 12, 14, 15, 20, 22, 23, 25 —
            Mar. 12, 14, 17 — 28, 30 — Apr.
            8, 13 — 15, 17 — 20, May 21,
            31 — June 23, 28, 30 — July 2,
            6 — 16, 19, 20, 22 — 29, 31, Aug.
            1, 12, 13, 18 — 20, 22 — 24, 27 —
            31, Sept. 2, 14, 17, 18, 24 — 29,
            Oct. 1, 24 — 29, Nov. 10 — Dec.
            31.
    1954   Jan. 1 — Sept. 25, 27 — Dec. 31.
    1955   Jan. 1 — Dec. 31.
    1956   Jan. 1 — Sept. 22, Nov. 27 —
            Dec. 31.
    1957 — 1958   Jan. 1 — Dec. 31.
    1959   Jan. 3 — Mar. 25, 31 — Dec. 31.
    1960 — 1961   Jan. 1 — Dec. 31.
  Micro (N) & (P)
    1962   Jan. 1+.
  FU
    1952   [Oct. 12 — Dec. 31].
    1953   [Jan. 1 — Dec. 31].
    1962   May 16 — Dec. 31.
    1963   Jan. 1 — Dec. 31.
    1964   Jan. 1 — Nov. 1.

NACIONAL. irr. est. Sept. 17, 1867.
  Note: Ceased publication Dec. 16,
  1867.
  MWA
    1867   Sept. 22 — Dec. 16.

NACIONAL. irr. est. Jan. 17, 1873.
  MWA
    1873   Jan. 17 — Apr. 9.
    1874   Apr. 24.
  NcD
    1873   Jan. 22, 28, Feb. 7.

NACIONAL. d. est. Jan. 1, 1885.
  MWA
    1885   Jan. 1 — Dec. 31.
    1886   Jan. 1 — Sept. 2.

1887 Mar. 17, Apr. 9, 21 – 23, 28,
   June 14, 16, 21, 23, 27, 28, July
   2, 7 – 11, 14.
1888 Jan. 12, Mar. 14.
1889 Boletín: Oct. 24.
1890 Feb. 21, July 23.
1892 Feb. 27, Apr. 6, July 16, Sept. 5,
   Oct. 1.
1893 Sept. 7.
1895 May 30, July 6.
1898 May 3, 17.
1901 Jan. 22, Feb. 2, 23.

LA NOCHE. d. est. 1936.
 DLC
  1941 June 4, 7, 9 – 11, 14, 19 – 21, 23,
     25 – 28, 30 – July 5, 7.
  1942 Jan. 15, 17, Feb. 9, 19, 27, 28,
     Mar. 14, 16 – 18, Apr. 30, May
     2, June 17 – 20, July 4.

EL NORTE. d. est. Apr. 1, 1913.
 DLC
  1927 Oct. 2 – 4, 6 – 20, 22 – Nov. 1,
     6 – 18, 21 – 24, 27, 28, Dec. 1,
     7, 11 – 14.
  1928 June 1 – 7, 12 – 26, 28 – July 9,
     14 – 20, 22 – 28, 30 – Aug. 3,
     9 – 15, 17, 18, 20 – 25, 27 – 30,
     Sept. 1, 3 – 12, 14 – 16, 18 –
     20, 23 – 25, 27, 28, 30 – Oct. 10,
     14, 16 – 19, 21, 25, 27 – Nov. 15,
     23 – 29, Dec. 21, 22, 24 – 28, 30,
     31.
  1929 Jan. 1, 4, 5, 10 – 17, 19, 21, 22,
     24, Feb. 10, 11, 15 – 18, 20 – 25,
     27 – Mar. 21, 31, Apr. 1, 3, 4,
     7 – 12, 14, 15, 17, 18, 29, 30,
     May 4 – 6, 8 – 29, June 1, 3 –
     13, 28 – July 4, Aug. 10 – 12,
     15 – 28, 31 – Sept. 30, Oct. 2 –
     Nov. 1, 3, 4, 6, 8, 9, 11 – 14,
     16 – 28, 30 – Dec. 25, 27 – 30.
  1930 Jan. 3 – 22, 24 – Feb. 12, 14 –
     19, 24 – 26, Mar. 2, 3, 9 – 12,
     17 – Apr. 16, 20, 21, 23 – 28,
     May 1, 3 – 14, 22 – June 2, 12 –
     19, 21 – 23.

NORTE.
 MWA
  1914 Apr. 7, 9, 14, 18, 25, 27, 29.

EL NOTICIOSO. d., irr. est. Dec. 21, 1870.
 Note: Periodicity Dec. 21, 1870 – Jan.
 21, 1871, daily; after Jan. 21, 1871, irregular. Ceased publication [Feb. 14],
 1871.
 CtY
  1870 Dec. 31.
  1871 Jan. 1, 6, 12, 18.
 MWA
  1870 Dec. 24 – 31.
  1871 Jan. 1 – Feb. 14.

LA NUEVA EPOCA. d. est. Jan. 2, 1858.
 Note: Continuation of *La Época* during its suspension by one of its publisher; the other publisher resumed
 La Época, Feb. 17, 1866. *La Nueva*
 época ceased publication Jan. 16,
 1858.
 DLC
  1858 Jan. 9.
 MWA
  1858 Jan. 7 – 9, 14.

NUEVA ERA. d. est. 1892.
 MWA
  1892 May 29, July 5, 27.

OBRERO. w. est. July 15, 1883.
 MWA
  1883 July 15.

OBSERVADOR. irr. est. Jan. 18, 1842.
 MWA
  1842 Jan. 18 – July 12.

OPINION. irr. est. Apr. 9, 1872.
 MWA
  1872 May 2.

OPINION. irr., d. est. 1902.
 Note: Periodicity 1902 – Feb. 12,
 1903, irregular; after Feb. 12, 1903,
 daily.
 MWA
  1902 Jan. 18, Feb. 5, 18, Mar. 27,

July 5 — Aug. 31, Nov. 1 — Dec.
30.
1903   Feb. 1 — 12, Oct. 20, 21, 23,
27 — 30.

OPINION NACIONAL; ORGANO DEL
CLUB PROGRESISTA DE LA JUVEN-
TUD. irr.
MWA
1895   Feb. 9 — Sept. 25.

OPINION NACIONAL. irr.
MWA
1908   [Aug. 28 — Sept. 25.]

ORIENTE. irr. est. Dec. 19, 1863.
MWA
1863   Prospecto.
Dec. 19 — 31.
1864   Jan. 1 — Nov. 8.

PAIS. irr. est. July 16, 1885.
MWA
1885   July 16 — Aug. 7, 25 — Sept. 11,
19.

EL PAIS. sw. est. Sept. 24, 1903.
DLC
1903   Oct. 20.
MWA
1903   Sept. 24 — Oct. 10, 20 — Nov.
12, 26.

PALABRA. w.
MWA
1895   July 6.

LA PATRIA; DIARIO DE LA PAZ. d. est.
Apr. 16, 1880.
CtY
1880   [Apr. 16 — Dec. 31].
1881   [Jan. 4 — Apr. 12].
MWA
1880   Apr. 16 — Dec. 31.
1881   Jan. 1 — Dec. 31.
1882   Jan. 1 — Apr. 15.
1883   May 10, [Aug. 17 — Dec. 30.]
1884   [Jan. 2 — July 10,] Dec. 4.
1885   [Jan. 29 — Dec. 31.]
1886   Jan. 5 — May 23.
NcD
1880   Apr. 16 — 23, 26, 28 — 30, May

4, 5, 12, 15, 21, 29, June 3, 4,
21, July 5, 23, 27, Aug. 13, 20 —
24, Sept. 20, 22, Oct. 6, 18, 22,
27, Nov. 12.
1881   Jan. 13, 14.

PATRIA. w. est. 1897.
MWA
1897   Dec. 23.

LA PATRIA. irr. est. Dec. 22, 1904.
CtY
1905   Jan. 20 — 31.
MWA
1904   Dec. 22 — 31.
1905   Jan. 1 — 31.
NcD
1905   Jan. 20, 31.

PEDAGOGO. d.
MWA
1901   Aug. 29.

LA POLEMICA. irr. est. Feb. 19, 1860.
MWA
1860   Mar. 4, 28, Sept. 8.

POLICIA. bw.
MWA
1887   July 29.

POPULAR. sw.
MWA
1849   Jan. 8, 20.

PORVENIR. sw. est. Apr. 9, 1892.
MWA
1892   Apr. 9 — 19.

POSTRIMERIAS DEL SIGLO. bw. est.
Apr. 25, 1897.
MWA
1897   Apr. 25 — June 4.

PRENSA. irr.
MWA
1858   Mar. 23, 26, 29, 30.

PRENSA. d.
MWA
1883   Sept. 8, Oct. 27.
1884   July 18.

PRESENCIA. w., d. est. 1952.
DLC
1956   Mar. 16, 29 – May 17, June 7 –
14, July 5 – 19, Aug. 2, 16 – 30,
Sept. 13 – Oct. 25.
1957   Jan. 12, Feb. 16 – Mar. 2, 14 –
21, Apr. 4 – 25, May 9 – Aug. 1,
15 – Sept. 19, Oct. 10 – 24,
Nov. 7 – 24.
1959   Jan. 3 – 12, 14 – 16, 18 – 21, 23,
25 – 28, 30 – Feb. 6, 8 – 13, 15 –
18, 21 – 27, Mar. 12, 15 – 19,
21 – 23, 26 – Apr. 12, 14 – 17,
22 – 24, 26 – 30, May 3 – 6, 8 –
27, 30, 31, June 1, 3 – 17, 20 –
23, 25, 26, 28 – July 1, 8, 9, 11,
12, 14, 18 – 26, 28, 29, 31, Aug.
2 – 4, 11, 13, 15 – 24, 26, 27,
31, Sept. 1, 3, 4, 6 – 9, 12 – 16,
19 – Oct. 12, 15 – 29, 31 – Nov.
4, Dec. 6 – 9, 12 – 14, 16 – 22,
24 – 29.
1960   Jan. 1 – 7, 9 – Feb. 1, 3 – 18,
20 – Mar. 6, 8 – 21, Apr. 1, 3 –
7, 9, 10, 13 – 20, 22 – May 1, 3 –
5, 7 – 10, 14 – 17, 21 – 31, June
2, 3, 5 – 8, 10 – 15, 18, 19, 21 –
23, 25 – 28, 30 – July 6, 8 – 12,
15 – 17, 20 – 23, 27 – Aug. 3,
5 – 10, 12 – 14, 16 – 30, Sept.
1 – 8, 11 – 16, 18 – 20, 23 – 30,
Oct. 2, 3, 5 – 7, 9, 17, 18, 20, 23,
25, 27, 28, 30, 31, Nov. 5 – 7,
9 – 16, 18 – Dec. 31.
1961   Jan. 1 – 5, 7 – 12, 14 – 17, 21 –
29, 31, Feb. 2, 4 – 7, 10 – 12,
17 – Mar. 2, 4, 5, 7, 8, 10 – 12,
18, 19, 21, 25 – 27, 30, Apr. 4,
6 – 13, 15 – 20, 22 – May 12,
15 – 17, 19 – 23, 25, 28 – 31,
June 3, 5 – 13, 15 – 17, 19 –
23, 25 – July 2, 4 – 9, 11 – 16,
18 – 21, 23 – 25, 28 – 31.

PRESENCIA.
FU
1952   Dec. 1 – 31.
1953   Jan. 1 – July 31.

PROGRESO. irr. est. Mar. 16, 1885.
MWA
1885   [Mar. 16 – Dec. 31.]
1886   [Jan. 1 – Apr. 23,] Dec. 9.
1887   Mar. 28 – Sept. 28.
1888   Feb. 7.
PROGRESO DE BOLIVIA. [3w.] est. May
21, 1906.
MWA
1906   [May 21 – Dec. 31.]
1907   [Jan. 1 – Dec. 31.]
1908   Jan. 5, 21, Apr. 2, [May 10 –
Dec. 1.]
1909   Jan. 5 – 7, 10 – 12, Apr. 4.
PROGRESO SOCIAL. sw. est. Dec. 29,
1866.
MWA
1866   Dec. 29.
1867   Feb. 20.
PUEBLO. sw. est. 1869.
Note: Ceased publication [May 3],
1870.
MWA
1869   Dec. 4, 14 – 17, 23.
1870   Jan. 19, Feb. 19, Mar. 17, 23,
Apr. 3 – 9, 27.
PUEBLO. sw.
Note: Suspended publication [Aug.
7 – Sept. 3, 1881.]
MWA
1881   Apr. 5 – Aug. 6, Sept. 4 – 17,
Oct. 8 – 12, 26 – 29.
PUEBLO.
MWA
1908   Apr. 30.
EL PUEBLO. w. est. 1931.
LNT – MA
1931   Oct. 19.
EL PUEBLO. w. est. 1950.
CSt – H
1965   Jan. 1+.
CU
1963   Apr. 6 – June 8, 22 – Dec. 14,
28.
1964   Jan. 4, 17 – Feb. 15, Mar. 7,
Apr. 4, 18 – 25, May 9, 16, 30 –
June 17, July 4, 18 – Aug. 1,
22 – Nov. 21, Dec. 5 – 19.

DLC
  1955   Jan. 1 – Dec. 31.
  1956   Jan. 1 – Aug. 3, 12 – Dec. 31.
  1957   Jan. 1 – May 17, 26 – July 26,
         28 – Oct. 4, 6 – Dec. 31.
  1958   Jan. 1 – June 28.

PUEBLO BOLIVIANO. irr.
  MWA
  1879   Feb. 20.

QUINCE DE ENERO. 3w. est. Mar. 9,
1871.
  MWA
  1871   Mar. 9 – Apr. 12.

RADICAL. sw. est. 1900.
  MWA
  1900   Feb. 12, 22, June 2 – 13, 20 –
         July 4, 11 – Oct. 3, 10 – 28, Nov.
         8 – 21, 28 – Dec. 5, 12 – 23.
         Boletín: Mar. 25.
  1901   Jan. 5.
  1903   May 20.

RAYO. irr. est. Jan. 15, 1861.
  MWA
  1861   Jan. 15.

LA RAZON. d., irr. est. 1883.
  CtY
    Micro (N)
    1884   Oct. 29.
    1885   Jan. 1, 12, Feb. 5 – Apr. 30,
           May 7 – Dec. 26.
    1886   Jan. 1 – Mar. 23, 28, Apr. 1 –
           18, 28 – June 16, July 7 – Sept.
           23, Oct. 7, 14, Nov. 8, 15, 25 –
           Dec. 11, 30.
    1887   Jan. 1 – 7, 14 – Feb. 11, 17 –
           May 5, 20 – Aug. 26, Sept. 4 –
           Dec. 30.
    1888   Jan. 6 – June 14, 24, July 1, 15
           – Aug. 24.
  MWA
    1884   [Oct. 8 – Dec. 30.]
    1885   Jan. 1, 8 – 12, Feb. 4 – Dec. 31.
    1886 – 1887   Jan. 1 – Dec. 31.
    1888   Jan. 1 – Sept. 7.
  NcD
    1888   May 6, Aug. 3.

LA RAZON. d. est. Feb. 7, 1917.
  Note: Ceased publication Apr. 9,
  1952.
  CU
  1941   July 4.
  DLC
  1941   June 16 – 19, 26 – July 9, Sept.
         30 – Oct. 8, Dec. 24 – 30.
  1942   Jan. 16, 17, 21, 26, Feb. 9, 12,
         13, 27 – Mar. 2, 5, 7, 15 – 19,
         May 3, 4, June 18 – 22, Oct. 31.
  1943   Jan. 1 – 6, 8 – 25, 27 – 30, Feb.
         1, 2, 5, 6, 9 – 21, 23 – 26, Mar.
         1 – 7, 12 – Apr. 30.
  1946   June 1 – July 16, 22 – Dec. 31.
  1947   Jan. 1 – 20, 22, 23, 30 – Dec. 31.
  1948 – 1951   Jan. 1 – Dec. 31.
  1952   Jan. 1 – Apr. 9.

  FU
  1951   May 11 – 23.
  NIC
  1942   Oct. 31.
  TxU
    Sunday editions only:
    1948   Oct. 3 – Dec. 19.
    1949   Jan. 2 – Apr. 10, May 29 – Dec.
           31.
    1950   Jan. 1 – July 31.

REDACTOR. irr. est. Aug. 9, 1868.
  MWA
  1868   Aug. 9 – Oct. 6.

REDACTOR DE LA ASAMBLEA CON-
STITUCIONAL. irr. est. Aug. 6, 1872.
  MWA
  1872   Aug. 27.
         Extraordinario: Dec. 13.

REDACTOR DE LA ASAMBLEA EX-
TRAORDINARIA. irr. est. May 5,
1873.
  MWA
  1873   May 5 – 25.

REDACTOR DE LA ASAMBLEA NA-
CIONAL DE BOLIVIA EN 1864. irr.
est Aug. 6, 1864.
  MWA
  1864   Aug. 21, 24.

REDACTOR DE LA CONVENCION NACIONAL DE BOLIVIA. irr. est. July 20, 1851.
MWA
  1851 July 24.

LA REFORMA. irr., sw., 3w. est. Feb. 26, 1871.
  Note: Periodicity Feb. 26, 1871 – May 20, 1873, irregular; May 23 – Aug. 22, 1873, semiweekly; after Aug. 26, 1873, three times a week. Suspended publication Dec. 25, 1874 – Jan. 23, 1875; ceased publication Jan. 13, 1913.
DLC
  1871 Feb. 26 – Dec. 31.
  1872 Jan. 1 – Dec. 31.
  1873 Jan. 1 – Oct. 1, 3 – Dec. 31.
  1874 Jan. 1 – 26, 28 – 30, Feb. 1 – Mar. 27, 29 – May 29, 31 – Dec. 31.
  1875 Jan. 1 – Aug. 12.
  1876 Jan. 1 – 27, Mar. 28 – May 2, Aug. 9, Sept. 23, Dec. 3, 5.
MWA
  1871 Feb. 26 – Dec. 31.
  1872 – 1876 Jan. 1 – Dec. 31.
  1877 Jan. 1 – May 11.
NcD
  1872 Aug. 2.
  1873 Mar. 19, Apr. 27, May 1, 6, 9, 12, 14, 16, 18, 20, 23, 26, June 1, 12, 15, July 9, Sept. 13.

REJENERADOR. w. est. June 18, 1841.
MWA
  1841 June 18 – Aug. 27.

REJIMEN LEGAL. irr. est. Oct. 8, 1873.
  Note: Removed from Sucre to La Paz after Dec. 31, 1874.
MWA
  1875 Aug. 27 – Sept. 24.
  1876 Feb. 1, Mar. 12, Apr. 7 – 23.

REPUBLICA. 3w. est. Apr. 27, 1861.
MWA
  1861 July 11 – 20.

REPUBLICA. irr. est. Dec. 7, 1872.
MWA
  1872 Dec. 7, 16 – 31.
  1873 Jan. 1 – Mar. 21, [28 – Dec. 25.]
  1874 [Jan. 1 – Aug. 9.]

LA REPUBLICA. d. est. 1920.
DLC
  1941 Dec. 25, 27, 28, 30.
  1942 Jan. 16, Mar. 4, 7, 15, 17 – 19, May 3.

REPUBLICA BOLIVIANA. w. est. Oct. 2, 1831.
MWA
  1831 Oct. 2 – Nov. 27.

REPUBLICANO. irr., sw. est. Nov. 29, 1870.
  Note: Periodicity Nov. 29, 1870 – Mar. 8, 1871, irregular; after Mar. 8, 1871, semiweekly.
MWA
  1870 Nov. 29 – Dec. 31.
  1871 Jan. 1 – Dec. 31.
  1872 Jan. 1 – Feb. 23.

REVISTA DEL NORTE. sw., 3w. est. Nov. 13, 1900.
  Note: Periodicity Nov. 13, 1900 – Mar. 30, 1901, semiweekly; after Mar. 30, 1901, three times a week.
MWA
  1900 [Nov. 13 – Dec. 31.]
  1901 [Jan. 1 – July 4.]
NcD
  1900 Nov. 24.

REVISTA LIBERAL. irr. est. Oct. 26, 1902.
MWA
  1902 Oct. 26 – Dec. 3, 11 – 24, 31.

REVISTA MILITAR. irr. est. July 16, 1885.
MWA
  1885 July 16 – Aug. 6, Oct. 15.

REVISTA PARLAMENTARIA. irr. est. Aug. 17, 1900.
MWA
  1900 Aug. 17 – 23.

LA REVOLUCION; DIARIO POPULAR.
d. est. Sept. 22, 1857.
Note: Ceased publication Nov. 14,
1857.
CtY
1857   Oct. 3, 16, 21, 23, 29, Nov. 12.
MWA
1857   Sept. 26 — Nov. 14.
REVOLUCION.
MWA
1888   July 16.
1890   July 16.
RIO. w.
MWA
1883   Jan. 1, Apr. 14, 26.
RUNDSCHAU VOM ILLIMANI. d.
Note: In German.
MH
1941   Nov. 17 — Dec. 29.
1942   Jan. 5 — Mar. 30, Apr. 13 — May
        25, June 15 — Aug. 31, Sept. 8,
        22, 28, Oct. 1 — Dec. 31.
1943   Jan. 1 — Dec. 31.
1944   June 1 — Nov. 30.
1945   Jan. 1 — Mar. 31.
SEMANARIO CATOLICO. w.
MWA
1879   Sept. 11, Nov. 27.
1880   Aug. 19, Oct. 14.
1881   Sept. 22 — 29.
1882   Mar. 27, June 1 — 8.
1883   Aug. 2, 31, Sept. 13, 27 — Oct.
        16, Nov. 9, 29.
SIGLO INDUSTRIAL. 3w., w., sw. est.
Nov. 27, 1883.
Note: Periodicity Nov. 27, 1883 — June
30, 1885, three times a week; July 1,
1885 — Aug. 7, 1888, weekly; after
Aug. 7, 1888, semiweekly.
MWA
1883   Nov. 27 — Dec. 31.
1884   Jan. 1 — Dec. 20.
1885   Jan. 27 — June 30.
1887   Jan. 15 — Dec. 31.
1888   Jan. 1 — Aug. 7.
1892   Oct. 26 — 29, Nov. 9, 19, 26,
        Dec. 3, 24, 31.
1893   Jan. 1 — Nov. 19.

1896   June 2.
NcD
1893   Feb. 5.
SITUACION. w., irr. est. Nov. 8, 1868.
Note: Title *Constitucional*, Nov. 8,
1868 — Feb. 5, 1869; *Situación*, after
Feb. 15, 1869. Periodicity Nov. 8,
1868 — Feb. 5, 1869, weekly; after
Feb. 15, 1869, irregular.
DLC
1870   Apr. 1.
MWA
1868   Nov. 8 — Dec. 31.
1869   Jan. 1 — Feb. 5, 16 — Dec. 31.
1870   Jan. 1 — Mar. 20.
SOBERANIA. irr. est. Feb. 4, 1862.
MWA
1862   Apr. 25.

TARDE. d. est. Dec. 1, 1908.
MWA
1908   Dec. 1.
1909   Feb. 2, Mar 11, July 14 — 16.

EL TELEGRAFO. sw., 3w., d. est. Oct. 16,
1858.
Note: Ceased publication Dec. 31,
1864.
CtY
1858   Prospecto: Oct. 4.
        Dec. 8.
1859   June 16, Nov. 24, 26.
        Suplemento.
1860   Jan. 26, Mar. 8, 24 — 31, Apr.
        17, 24, June 21, 23, July 12, 21,
        28, Aug. 13.
1861   Jan. 9, 12, 26, Feb. 6 — 25, Mar.
        17, 27 — 31.
1862   Mar. 28, July 22.
1863   Feb. 13, Apr. 14 — 17, May 28 —
        June 20, 29 — July 20.
1864   Feb. 17, 25 — 29, June 18, Nov.
        4.
DLC
1861   Oct. 27.
MWA
1858   Oct. 16 — Dec. 31.
        Suplemento: Oct. 4.

1859 — 1864   [Jan. 1 — Dec. 31.]
NcD
    1860	July 12.
    1861	Feb. 6, 16, 20.
    1863	July 20.

TELEGRAFO. est. Jan. 15, 1873.
MWA
    1873	Jan. 15.

EL TELEGRAFO. 3w., d.
    Note: Periodicity prior to Apr. 24,
    1894, three times a week; after Apr.
    24, 1894, daily.
MWA
    1893	Feb. 21, Aug. 10, 18 — 26, Sept.
        8 — 16, Nov. 30, Dec. 15, 22.
    1894	Jan. 23 — 27, Feb. 20, Mar. 6,
        Apr. 21 — 24, Oct. 10, 13.
    1895	Mar. 30, May 31, June 4, 19 —
        Dec. 31.
    1896	Jan. 1 — Dec. 31.
    1897	Jan. 1 — July 24, Aug. 16 — Nov.
        26, Dec. 10.
    1898	Apr. 4, 20.
        Boletín: May 2.
    1899	May 30.

TIEMPO. 3w. est. Nov. 30, 1880.
MWA
    1880	Nov. 30 — Dec. 31.
    1881	Jan. 1 — Feb. 4.

TIEMPO. d. est. 1904.
MWA
    1905	Apr. 12, 29 — May 12.
    1909	Dec. 5.
    1914	Apr. 19, 25.

TIERRA. d. est. Jan. 1, 1942.
DLC
    1942	Jan. 3, Feb. 11, 12, 27, Mar. 2,
        14, 16, 17, 18, May 2.

TIJERA. w. est. Aug. 8, 1897.
MWA
    1897	Dec. 12, 26 — 31.
    1898	Jan. 1 — 9, Feb. 5 — Mar. 13,
        27 — Apr. 7.

LA TITICACA. d., w., irr. est. Oct. 3,
1876.
CtY
    1877	[Mar. 6 — Nov. 23]
DLC
    1877	May 17, 19, 21, 24.
MWA
    1876	Oct. 3 — Dec. 31.
    1877 — 1879	Jan. 1 — Dec. 31.
    1880	Jan. 1 — 3.
NcD
    1877	Nov. 8.

EL TRABAJO; ORGANO DE LA JUVEN-
TUD. sw., 3w. est. June 15, 1883.
    Note: Periodicity June 15, 1883 — Mar.
    4, 1884, semiweekly; after Mar. 4,
    1884, three times a week.
CtY
    1883	June 15 — July 24, 31 — Sept. 18,
        25, Oct. 2, 16 — Nov. 13, 27, 30,
        Dec. 28.
    1884	Jan. 1 — 11, 18 — Feb. 5, 12, 14.
MWA
    1883	June 15 — Dec. 31.
    1884	Jan. 1 — Feb. 21, [Mar. 1 —
        May 22.]

TRABAJO; ORGANO DE LA SOCIEDAD
"UNION GRAFICA NACIONAL." w.
est. Feb. 12, 1906.
MWA
    1906	Feb. 26.

TRAVESURA. w.
MWA
    1881	Aug. 25, Sept. 8.

TRIBUNA. sw., 3w., d. est. Feb. 21, 1880.
    Note: Periodicity Feb. 21 — Mar. 26,
    1880, semiweekly; Mar. 28 — Apr. 24,
    1880, three times a week; after Apr.
    24, 1880, daily.
MWA
    1880	Feb. 21 — Dec. 31.
    1881	Jan. 1 — 23.
    1893	May 15 — Dec. 31.
    1894	Jan. 1 — Mar. 6.

ULTIMA HORA. d. est. Apr. 30, 1929.
  DLC
    1941   June 7, 9, 10, 11, 14, 18−21, 23,
            25.
    1942   Feb. 28, Mar. 2, 4, 6, 14, 16, 17,
            18.
    1951   May 2−Sept. 25, 27−Oct. 17,
            20−Nov. 20, 22−Dec. 27, 29−
            31.
    1952   Jan. 1−Mar. 14, 16−Apr. 24,
            26−30, May 2−21, 24−June 9,
            11, 14−July 17, 19−31, Aug.
            2−19, 21−30, Sept. 1−15,
            17−26, 28, 30, Oct. 2−Nov.
            25, 27−Dec. 31.
    1953   Jan. 2−Feb. 3, 5−Mar. 16,
            20−Apr. 22, 24−30, May 2−4,
            7−12, 14, 15, 20−26, 28, 29,
            31−June 3, 5−10.
    1954   Jan. 2−Feb. 11, 14, 19−Apr. 1,
            3−13, 18−21, 24−June 3, 7−
            Aug. 12, 14−19, 26−Sept. 15,
            17−Dec. 31.

UNION.
  MWA
    1865   Dec. 31.
    1866   Jan. 21.

UNION. irr.
  MWA
    1874   Apr. 24.

UNION. sw. est. Oct. 27, 1896.
  MWA
    1896   Oct. 27−Dec. 31.
    1897−1898   Jan. 1−Dec. 31.
    1899   Jan. 1−Oct. 27.
    1900   Dec. 28.
    1901   Oct. 8−11, Dec. 11, 31.
    1902   May 2.

UNION MEDICA.
  MWA
    1887   Apr. 1−15.

UNION NACIONAL. irr. est. Dec. 1, 1864.
  MWA
    1864   Dec. 1, 25.

UNION NACIONAL. irr. est. June 22,
  1883.
  MWA
    1883   June 22−29, July 13, Aug. 3−
            Dec. 15.

LA UNION NACIONAL.
  NcD
    1883   Nov. 4.

VERDAD. irr. est. Apr. 7, 1876.
  MWA
    1876   Apr. 7−20.

VERDAD CONSTITUCIONAL. irr. est.
  Apr. 8, 1862.
  MWA
    1862   Apr. 12, n.d.

VERDADERO ARTESANO. irr.
  MWA
    1862   July 4.

VERDADERO BOLIVIANO. sw. est. Nov.
  16, 1862.
  MWA
    1862   Nov. 16.

VERDADES. sw.
  MWA
    1882   Aug. 31−Sept. 9.
    1883   Dec. 2−31.
    1884   Jan. 1−Feb. 15, Apr. 8.

VIOLETA. irr. est. Aug. 20, 1874.
  MWA
    1874   Aug. 20−Dec. 31.
    1875   Jan. 1−Oct. 21.

VIOLETA. bw. est. Mar. 11, 1888.
  MWA
    1888   Mar. 11.

VOTO DEL PUEBLO. irr. est. Apr. 24,
  1872.
  MWA
    1872   Apr. 24.

LA VOZ DE BOLIVIA. 3w. est. Oct. 30,
  1862.
        Note: Removed from La Paz to Oruro,
        Jan. 3, 1863; removed to Cochabamba,

Oct. 25, 1863; removed to Oruro, May
1, 1864; returned to Cochabamba,
June 23, 1864.
CtY
    1862   Oct. 30, Nov. 7, 10, 14 — 27.
MWA
    1862   Oct. 30 — Dec. 5.

VOZ DE LA JUVENTUD. irr. est. Mar. 5,
1861.
MWA
    1861   Mar. 5.

VOZ DE LA PATRIA. est. Nov. 15, 1864.
MWA
    1864   Nov. 15.

VOZ DEL PUEBLO. est. May 16, 1901.
MWA
    1901   May 16.

LA VOZ DEL PUEBLO. sw. est. Feb. 2,
1904.
DLC
    1904   Feb. 2 — June 25, Aug. 13.

THE WEST COAST LEADER.
    Note: This special number of the Li-
    ma, Perú, newspaper was printed in
    La Paz, Bolivia.
DLC
    1924   March.

Liberalta

EL COMERCIO. d. est. [1879.]
    LNT — MA
    1921   July 4, 28, Aug. 24, Sept. 2.

Loreto

LIBERAL LORETANO. irr. est. Apr. 22,
1888.
MWA
    1888   Apr. 22.

Macha

VOZ DE LOS LIBRES. irr. est. May 15,
1866.
MWA
    1866   Sept. 15.

Melgarejo

PRENSA. w., bw. est. 1869.
MWA
    1869   Aug. 17, Sept. 1 — 9.
    1870   [Feb. 17 — Nov. 9.]

Moquequa

ASPIRANTE. w.
MWA
    1888   Mar. 30.

Orton

GACETA DEL NORTE. irr.
MWA
    1887   Nov. 9.
    1888   Mar. 9.

SERINGUERITO. est. Dec. 11, 1887.
MWA
    1887   Dec. 11.

Oruro

ALIANZA. irr., w.
    Note: Periodicity before Apr. 11, 1880,
    irregular.
MWA
    1880   Feb. 1, Mar. 21 — July 5, 18,
        Aug. 1, 22, Sept. 12 — 19, Oct.
        10 — 21.
        Suplemento: Feb. 1.

AMERICANO. sw. est. Nov. 25, 1893.
MWA
    1893   Nov. 25 — 28, Dec. 12 — 15.

ARTESANO LIBERAL. irr. est. Mar. 25,
1883.
MWA
    1883   Mar. 25 — June 7.

BANDERA NACIONAL. irr.
MWA
    1884   Jan. 20 — Feb. 11, May 5 — 14.
    1885   Feb. 24, May 26.

BOLETIN DEPARTAMENTAL. irr. est.
June 14, 1874.
MWA
    1874   June 14.

1880   May 9.
1884   Jan. 28, Apr. 17.
1887   July 24−31.
1888   Jan. 22.

CALVERIO. w.
MWA
1887   Nov. 13−20.

EL CONSTITUCIONAL; PERIODICO
OFICIAL. irr. est. 1861.
CtY
1861   Dec. 28.

CONSTITUCIONAL; PERIODICO OFI-
CIAL.
MWA
1861   Dec. 13−28.
        Suplemento: Dec. 28.
1862   Sept. 26.

DEFENSA NACIONAL. [w.]
MWA
1881   Apr. 24, June 5.

DEFENSOR DEL ORDEN. irr.
MWA
1865   Apr. 16.

DEMOCRACIA. irr. est. Feb. 21, 1892.
MWA
1892   Feb. 21, May 5.

DEMOCRATA.
MWA
1888   Apr. 22.

10 DE FEBRERO. irr.
MWA
1887   June 16, July 16−30, Sept. 4−
        Nov. 19.
1888   Feb. 10.

EVOLUCION. [sw.] est. July 1897.
MWA
1901   Apr. 11.
1902   Apr. 2−25, 30, May 4−8, 24−
        28, June 3−6, July 5−10, Aug.
        2−6.
1903   Jan. 2, June 20, 24.

FERROCARRIL.
MWA
1888   Apr. 22.

FERROCARRIL; ORGANO DEL PAR-
TIDO LIBERAL. irr.
MWA
1891   Aug. 14−21, 26, Sept. 16−21,
        28, Oct. 9−26, 30−Nov. 13,
        Dec. 7−11.
1892   Feb. 6, Mar. 19, Apr. 18−24,
        May 7.

GACETA MUNICIPAL. irr. est. Jan. 31,
1883.
MWA
1883   Jan. 31.

GACETA MUNICIPAL. irr. est. Feb. 10,
1885.
MWA
1885   Feb. 10, Mar. 28, June 30−
        Dec. 31.
1886   Jan. 1−3.

GACETA MUNICIPAL. irr.
MWA
1887   Sept. 14−Nov. 19.

GACETA MUNICIPAL DE ORURO. irr.
MWA
1876   [Sept. 30.]
1877   Feb. 1.

HERALDO CONSTITUCIONAL. w. est.
Mar. 30, 1863.
MWA
1863   Mar. 30, May 10.

IGUALDAD. irr.
MWA
1884   Mar. 23.

INDUSTRIAL. d. est. Mar. 1, 1907.
MWA
1908   Mar. 25.

JUSTICIA.
MWA
1892   Jan. 10.

LEY. irr. est. Jan. 20, 1873.
MWA
1873   Jan. 20−Feb. 23.

LIBERTAD. irr.
MWA
1884   Jan. 27−Apr. 13.

MONITOR. w.
  MWA
    1895   Jan. 18.

NACION. irr. est. Apr. 18, 1887.
  MWA
    1887   Apr. 18 – May 3, 12 – July 16,
            24 – Nov. 29, Dec. 18 – 31.
    1888   Jan. 1 – Apr. 29.
  NcD
    1887   May 22.

OBRERO. w. est. Aug. 1, 1901.
  MWA
    1901   Nov. 11.

EL ORDEN. w. est. 1883.
  CtY
    1884   Jan. 17.
  MWA
    1884   Jan. 17.

ORUREÑO. bw. est. Dec. 5, 1887
  MWA
    1887   Dec. 5.

PAIS. w., irr., d. est. May 12, 1887.
    Note: Periodicity May 12, 1887 – Apr.
    13, 1890, weekly; Apr. 14, 1890 –
    July 17, 1892, irregular; after July 17,
    1892, daily.
  MWA
    1887   May 12 – 19, July 28, Aug. 13 –
            Sept. 1, 22 – Dec. 14.
    1888   Feb. 5 – 17, May 9, 20 – July
            22.
    1889   Jan. 13 – Feb. 3, Mar. 4 – 31.
    1890   Apr. 13.
    1891   Sept. 4 – 10.
    1892   June 7, July 17, Aug. 22, Oct.
            19, 22, Nov. 1, 9, 10, 16, 20.

PORVENIR. w. est. Feb. 5, 1852.
  MWA
    1852   Feb. 5 – Dec. 31.
    1853   Jan. 1 – Dec. 31.
    1854   Jan. 1 – Apr. 13.

PORVENIR. w.
  MWA
    1883   Jan. 8, 21, Feb. 4 – Mar. 18.
    1885   Apr. 18, May 30, July 4.

PRENSA. d.
  MWA
    1909   May 21.

RAZON. d.
  MWA
    1893   Apr. 28 – June 9, 27 – July 9,
            Aug. 13 – Sept. 22, Oct. 21.

EL REDACTOR. est. 1863.
  CtY
    1863   Sept. 20.

REPUBLICANO. w., sw., w., irr. est. Feb.
    10, 1849.
    Note: Periodicity Feb. 10 – Mar. 28,
    1849, weekly; Mar. 30 – July 18, 1849,
    semiweekly; Oct. 15, 1849 – Jan. 27,
    1850, weekly; after 1850, irregular.
  MWA
    1849   Feb. 10 – July 18, Oct. 15 –
            Dec. 31.
    1850   Jan. 1 – 27, Sept. 14 – Dec. 31.
    1851   Jan. 1 – Dec. 17.

TAGARETE. w. est. Jan. 24, 1886.
  CtY
    1886   Mar. 28.
    1887   Apr. 17, May 9.
  MWA
    1886   Jan. 24 – Dec. 31.
    1887   Jan. 1 – July 24.

TELÉGRAFO.
  MWA
    1823   Extraordinario: Oct. 21.

TRIBUNO.
  MWA
    1891   Jan. 17, Aug. 16.

TRIBUNO. d. est. Aug. 2, 1902.
  MWA
    1902   Aug. 2.

VAPOR. w. est. Jan. 6, 1884.
  MWA
    1884   Jan. 6, 27 – Feb. 3, 17 – 24,
            Mar. 25 – 29, Apr. 20.

VAPOR. d., w. irr. est. 1899.
    Note: Periodicity before Dec. 4, 1903,

daily; Dec. 5, 1903 — Mar. 12, 1904,
weekly; after Mar. 13, 1904, irregular.
MWA

1900	Oct. 23, Nov. 13 — 18, 20, 22, 30.
1903	Mar. 1 — May 13, Oct. 2, Nov. 23 — Dec. 4.
1904	Jan. 9 — Mar. 12, May 8 — 19.

VERDAD. w. est. Feb. 23, 1883.
MWA

| 1883 | Feb. 23, Mar. 8 — 16. |

LA VOZ DE BOLIVIA. irr. est. Oct. 30,
1862.

Note: Removed from La Paz to Oruro,
Jan. 3, 1863; removed to Cochabamba,
Oct. 25, 1863; removed to Oruro, May
1, 1864; returned to Cochabamba,
June 23, 1864.

CtY

| 1863 | Jan. 9, 11, Feb. 24, Mar. 7 — Apr. 9, 15 — 24, May 25, 29, July 15 — Aug. 12, 27 — Sept. 14, 29 — Oct. 8. |
| 1864 | June 2. |

MWA

| 1863 | Jan. 3 — Mar. 5, 31 — Oct. 8. |

VOZ DEL PUEBLO. irr. est. Apr. 5, 1888.
MWA

| 1888 | Apr. 5, 29 — July 8. |

Potosí

ACTUALIDAD. w., irr. est. Jan. 1869.
MWA

| 1869 | Jan. 31, Aug. 23, Nov. 19, Dec. 7. |
| 1870 | Jan. 19 — 24, Feb. 4 — Mar. 30, May 1, June 14, July 23. Suplemento: July 23. |

AMETRALLADORA. w. est. Feb. 16,
1873.
MWA

| 1873 | Feb. 16 — 23. |

AMIGO DEL PUEBLO. irr. est. Apr. 5,
1871.
MWA

| 1871 | Oct. 15. |
| 1872 | Sept. 1 — 6, 19, 27. |

BOLETIN DE PEDIMENTOS MINEROS.
irr.
MWA

| 1888 | Mar. 8 — 20, Apr. 30 — May 10. |

BOLETIN OFICIAL. irr. est. May 9, 1876.
MWA

| 1876 | May 9, 28 — 31, July 11, Aug. 15. |

BOLETIN OFICIAL DEL SUD. est. Feb.
20, 1880.
MWA

| 1880 | Feb. 20. |
| 1884 | Feb. 7. |

EL CELAGE. w. est. July 30, 1849.
CtY

| 1849 | Sept. 24. |

MWA

1849	July 30 — Dec. 31.
1850	Jan. 1 — Feb. 4, 18 — Mar. 4, Apr. 4 — 15, July 15, Sept. 23 — Oct. 14, 28 — Nov. 4, 25, Dec. 23.
1851	Jan. 6 — 13, Feb. 10, 24 — Mar. 17, Apr. 7 — 21, May 19, June 16, Aug. 11 — Sept. 22. Extraordinario: May 31 — June 2.
1852	Feb. 16, Mar. 10, 24, Apr. 7 — 25, May 9, 23 — June 16, Aug. 4, 23, Sept. 9.
1853	Apr. 17.
1854	[June 19 — Sept. 21.]

CERRO DE POTOSI. bw., w. est. Mar. 1,
1886.

Note: Periodicity Mar. 1 — Dec. 31,
1886, biweekly; after Dec. 31, 1886,
weekly.

MWA

| 1886 | Mar. 1 — 15. |
| 1887 | Jan. 2, Feb. 13, Mar. 6. |

CLARIN. irr. est. May 3, 1872.
MWA

| 1872 | May 3. |

CONCILIADOR. w. est. 1848.
MWA

| 1849 | June 9, 23 — July 15. |

CONCORDIA. irr. est. Mar. 15, 1858.
MWA
    1858   Mar. 15 — Sept. 25.

CONSTITUCIONAL. irr.
MWA
    1886   Nov. 3 — 17, Dec. 6 — 31.
    1887   Jan. 1 — 15, Feb. 5 — 18, Apr.
          8 — 20, May 7, 24 — June 23.

DEBATE DE LAS ELECCIONES. [sw.]
est. Feb. 11, 1873.
MWA
    1873   Feb. 11 — 14.

EL DEBATE DE LAS ELECCIONES. est.
1876.
CtY
    1876   Mar. 22, May 2.
MWA
    1876   Mar. 22 — May 4.

DEBER. w. est. Sept. 3, 1880.
MWA
    1880   Sept. 3 — Oct. 1, 15 — Dec. 31.
    1881   Jan. 1 — June 17.

DEMOCRATA. irr. est. Mar. 15, 1871.
MWA
    1873   Jan. 10.

10 DE NOVIEMBRE. 3m.
MWA
    1887   Nov. 20, Dec. 10.
    1888   Mar. 26, Apr. 7 — 21.

LA DISCUSION. w., irr. est. Mar. 4, 1874.
CtY
    1874   Aug. 5 — Sept. 2, 16.
    1875   Mar. 10, 31, June 2, Sept. 29.
    1876   Feb. 27, Mar. 15, 24.
MWA
    1874   Apr. 2 — 23, July 1 — 15, Aug.
          5 — Sept. 16, Oct. 14, Nov. 7 —
          Dec. 2.
    1875   Jan. 1, 15, Feb. 1, 16, Mar. 10 —
          Dec. 31.
    1876   Jan. 1 — 21, Feb. 9 — Apr. 12.
    1880   Apr. 27.
          Suplemento: Jan. 9.

ECO DEL SUD. irr.
MWA
    1855   June 9.

ELECTOR POPULAR; PUBLICACION
OFICIAL. [w.] est. May 14, 1868.
MWA
    1868   May 14, June 16.

ESTANDARTE CIVIL. irr. est. Oct. 16,
1874.
MWA
    1874   Oct. 16.

EVOLUCION. [w.]
MWA
    1892   Apr. 27 — May 1.

FE CATOLICA. bw. est. Feb. 1, 1885.
MWA
    1885   Feb. 1 — 15, June 15 — Dec. 1.
    1886   Jan. 1, Feb. 1.

FE SOCIAL, POLITICO Y LITERARIO.
w. est. [1897].
MWA
    1903   Oct. 25 — Nov. 1, 28.

FERRO-CARRIL. irr.
MWA
    1873   Feb. 21 — Mar. 28.

FUSION. irr.
MWA
    1876   Mar. 31 — Apr. 21.

GACETA COMERCIAL. 3w. est. 1903.
MWA
    1904   Mar. 13.

GACETA DEL SUD. [w.]
MWA
    1877   Mar. 29.
          Suplemento: [Apr. 12.]

GACETA MUNICIPAL. [bw.]
MWA
    1887   July 1, Aug. 6, Nov. 9 — Dec. 7.
    1888   June 7.
    1900   Extraordinario: Nov. 12.

LAS GARANTIAS. w., irr. est. Feb. 2,
1882.
    Note: Periodicity Feb. 2, 1882 —
    June 18, 1883, weekly; after June 18,
    1883, irregular.
CtY
    1882   July 20 — Aug. 3, 17 — Sept. 7.

MWA
  1882   Feb. 2—Sept. 14, 28—Dec. 31.
  1883   Jan. 1—4, 25—Apr. 5, 20—
          July 18, Aug. 18—Dec. 31.
  1884   Jan. 1—28, Mar. 15—21, Apr.
          10, July 4, Sept. 30.

HONOR POTOSINO. irr. est. Apr. 30,
  1872.
  MWA
  1872   Apr. 30.

HONRA POLITICA; ORGANO DE LA
  JUVENTUD LIBERAL. w. est. Jan. 13,
  1887.
  MWA
  1887   Jan. 13—27, Feb. 10, Mar. 1—
          Apr. 6, May 4—Dec. 11.
  1888   Jan. 11—Feb. 9, Apr. 10.
  NcD
  1887   July 24.

HONRA POLITICA; ORGANO DEL
  PARTIDO LIBERAL. [w.]
  MWA
  1892   Mar. 11, June 12, July 9.

KRUPP.
  MWA
  1873   Mar. 14.

LIBERAL. bw. est. July 12, 1883.
  MWA
  1883   July 12, Nov. 9.
  1884   Jan. 4, Apr. 11.

MINERO. bw. est. Aug. 25, 1855.
  MWA
  1855   Aug. 25—Nov. 1, Dec. 1.
  1856   Jan. 1—Feb. 1, Mar. 1—16.

OPINION. w. est. July 17, 1887.
  MWA
  1887   July 17, Aug. 7, 28, Sept. 25—
          Dec. 15, 29—31.
          Extraordinario: Aug. 9.
  1888   Jan. 1—3, 17, 31—May 30.
          Suplemento: June 1.
  1892   June 10, July 8.

ORDEN Y PROGRESO. w. est. 1853.
  MWA
  1853   May 23—30, June 27—July

25, Sept. 7, Oct. 17, Dec. 12.
  1854   Jan. 2, 23—Feb. 13, Mar. 20—
          27, Apr. 10—17, May 1.

PAIS. w.
  MWA
  1881   Mar. 3, 16—23, Apr. 13, 27—
          May 11.

PALABRA. w. est. July 14, 1897.
  MWA
  1898   June 11.

EL PENSAMIENTO DE LA REVOLU-
  CION. irr. est. Oct. 27, 1857.
  CtY
  1857   Nov. 3.
  MWA
  1857   Oct. 27—Dec. 12.

POTOSI; ORGANO DEL "CLUB DE LA
  JUVENTUD." irr. est. Mar. 22, 1876.
  MWA
  1876   Mar. 22—Apr. 26.

POTOSI. irr.
  MWA
  1881   July 28, Aug. 20—Sept. 3.

POTOSI LIBRE. w. est. Feb. 17, 1839.
  MWA
  1839   Mar. 17—25, May 5.

LA PRENSA.
  MWA
  1902   Boletín: Nov. 4.

PROGRESO. w. est. Aug. 23, 1903.
  MWA
  1903   Aug. 23.

REACCION. [w.]
  MWA
  1909   Sept. 7—20.

REPRODUCCION.
  MWA
  1863   Mar. 24.

REPUBLICA. irr.
  MWA
  1873   Jan. 20.

REVISTA DEL SUD. 3m.
  MWA
  1879   Dec. 24.

SACERDOTE. w. est. Mar. 8, 1860.
MWA
    1860   Mar. 8, 29.

SENDA LEGAL. w. est. July 6, 1885.
MWA
    1885   July 6 — Oct. 2, Nov. 12.

TIEMPO. w. est. Jan. 1, 1885.
MWA
    1885   Jan. 24, June 13, July 4, Aug.
        22, Oct. 17.
    1886   Dec. 4.
    1887   [Jan. 1 — Aug. 27,] Sept. 10 —
        Dec. 31.
    1888   Jan. 1 — Feb. 18, [Mar. 3 —
        Aug. 18,] Sept. 20, Dec. 31.
    1889   Apr. 13, May 4, Sept. 7.
    1892   June 11, July 2, Aug. 20 — 27.

22 DE OCTUBRE. irr.
MWA
    1873   Feb. 28.
        Suplemento.

VERDAD. irr., w.
MWA
    1884   Jan. 25 — 31, Mar. 11 — 18,
        May 13.
        Suplemento: May 13.
    1885   Jan. 10 — 20.
    1886   [July 6 — 28.]

Punata

ECO DE PUNATA. irr. est. May 16, 1888.
MWA
    1888   May 16.

Riberalta

GACETA DEL NORTE. bw.
MWA
    1905   July 15.

MANUTATA. bw. est. Mar. 15, 1895.
MWA
    1895   Mar. 15 — Apr. 15.

LA REPUBLICA. est. [1921].
LNT — MA
    1921   Dec. 8.

Santa Cruz

ALBUM LITERARIO. bw. est. Jan 26,
1887.
MWA
    1887   Jan. 26 — Feb. 15, Mar. 16 —
        Apr. 1, 16 — July 15, Dec. 19 —
        31.
    1888   Jan. 1 — 5, Mar. 2 — Apr. 14,
        Dec. 21.
    1889   Jan. 26.

BOLETIN DE INSTRUCCION. irr.
MWA
    1887   Dec. 21.
    1888   Mar. 7, June 27.

CLAMOR PUBLICO. irr. est. Jan. 13,
1876.
MWA
    1876   Jan. 13 — Feb. 20.

CORREO DEL PLATA. w.
MWA
    1884   Feb. 14 — Mar. 26.

DEMOCRATA. w. est. Apr. 21, 1888.
MWA
    1888   Apr. 21.

ECO DE LA JUVENTUD. w. est. Apr. 2,
1884.
MWA
    1884   Apr. 2 — 24.

ELECTOR CONSTITUCIONAL. 5m. est.
Jan. 25, 1884.
MWA
    1884   Jan. 25, Feb. 10 — 15, 23 — Mar.
        25, Apr. 19.

ESTANDARTE CATOLICO. irr. est. Mar.
16, 1887.
MWA
    1887   Mar. 16 — Apr. 1.

ESTRELLA DEL ORIENTE. bw. est.
[1863].
MWA
    1864   May 8.

LA ESTRELLA DEL ORIENTE. 3w., irr.
est. Apr. 6, 1879.
CtY
    1887   Oct. 27.

1888   June 19, 22, 23, Nov. 5, 6, 8, 10.
1889   Jan. 2, 3, 5.
MWA
1879   May 9, June 23 — July 5.
1880   [Mar. 3 — Dec. 31.]
1881   [Jan. 1 — Dec. 31.]
1882   [Jan. 1 — Mar. 23.]
1883   Feb. 24, Apr. 29, Nov. 7, 25,
        Dec. 13.
1884   [Jan. 7 — Apr. 14.]
1885   [Mar. 14 — Dec. 31.]
1886   [Jan. 1 — June 13], Oct. 30 —
        Nov. 13, Dec. 18.
1887   Jan. 3 — 8, [July 19 — Dec. 31.]
1888   [Jan. 11 — July 12, Oct. 23 —
        Dec. 29.]
1889   Jan. 2 — 5, 22-26.
1892   Apr. 27, May 25 — 28, June 8 —
        11, 22, 29 — July 2.
NcD
1889   Jan. 2.

FEDERALISTA. w. est. Mar. 8, 1884.
MWA
1884   Mar. 8 — Apr. 15.

FRANKLIN. w. est. May 6, 1888.
MWA
1888   May 6, 20 — 27, June 10.

GACETA MUNICIPAL.
MWA
1888   Nov. 28.

IGUALIDAD.
MWA
1892   Apr. 27.

IMAGINACION.
MWA
1890   July 24.

INDEPENDIENTE. irr.
MWA
1884   Mar. 28.

LABARO ORIENTAL.
MWA
1883   Dec. 31.
1884   Feb. 20 — Apr. 19.

LEY. irr. est. 1884.
MWA
1884   Jan. 19.
1885   Nov. 7.
1886   Dec. 2 — 8, 16 — 31.
1887   Jan. 1 — 5, [6 — Dec. 31.]
1888   [Jan. 1 — May 9], June 22 — 28,
        Dec. 19 — 27.
1889   Jan. 4, Apr. 4.
1890   Feb. 23.
1892   May 28, June 28.
1893   Apr. 29.
1906   Aug. 5.

LA NACION. d.
LNT — MA
1940   Apr. 3, 6, 8, 9.

PUEBLO CRUCENO. bw. est. May 16,
1887.
MWA
1887   May 16 — July 12.
1888   Apr. 10.

REPUBLICANO. irr.
MWA
1883   Nov. 24 — Dec. 4.
1884   Mar. 12 — Apr. 22.

SEMANARIO. w. est. Sept. 7, 1873.
MWA
1873   Oct. 28.
1875   Apr. 2.

UNION NACIONAL. bw.
MWA
1888   June 18.

VOZ DEL PUEBLO. irr. est. Feb. 6, 1880.
MWA
1880   Feb. 6 — 19, June 4.

Sorota

EL ECO DEL ILLAMPU. w. est. Sept. 22,
1892.
MWA
1892   Sept. 22.

Sucre

LA ACTUALIDAD. w. est. Aug. 23, 1874.
CtY
1874   Oct. 1.

DLC
  1874   Sept. 11.

MWA
  1874   Aug. 23 — Oct. 1.

ACTUALIDAD. w. est. 1906.
MWA
  1908   Mar. 22.

ACTUALIDAD.
  See *Actualidad de Sucre*.

ACTUALIDAD DE SUCRE. w., irr. est.
  June 24, 1865.
    Note: Title *Actualidad*, June 24,
    1865 — Sept. 5, 1866; *Actualidad de
    Sucre*, after Sept. 6, 1866. Ceased
    publication [Oct. 24], 1870.
  MWA
    1866   [Jan. 29], Apr. 16, 30, May 31,
            July 13 — 16, 31, Aug. 17.
            Suplemento: July 17.
    1868   Mar. 14 — 24, May 2, June 5,
            Sept. 30 — Oct. 16, Nov. 6, 28 —
            Dec. 16.
    1869   Jan. 16, 27 — Feb. 14, Mar. 2.
    1870   Jan. 25, Feb. 5, 16, 23, Mar. 17,
            Apr. 30 — May 17, June 30,
            July 24 — Aug. 7, Sept. 8 — 23.

ALBORADA. irr. est. May 20, 1875.
MWA
  1875   May 20 — July 5.

ALIANZA. bw.
MWA
  1880   Apr. 19 — 30.

AMERICA. irr. est. Jan. 1, 1889.
MWA
  1889   Jan. 1 — 24, Mar. 8, 28, May 10.

AMIGO DEL PUEBLO. irr. est. Nov. 17,
  1857.
MWA
  1857   Prospecto: Nov. 5.

ARTESANO DE SUCRE. irr. est. Mar. 27,
  1858.
MWA
  1858   Mar. 27.

ARTESANO DE SUCRE. irr. est. Aug. 20,
  1858.
MWA
  1858   Aug. 20.

ARTESANO DE SUCRE. irr. est. June 1,
  1872.
MWA
  1872   June 1 — Aug. 22.

ARTESANO DE SUCRE. irr. est. Apr.
  14, 1876.
MWA
  1876   Apr. 14 — 30.
  1880   Mar. 16.

ARTESANO DE SUCRE. bw.
MWA
  1884   Jan. 18 — Feb. 20.
          Suplemento.

ARTESANO HONRADO. w. est. June 21,
  1887.
MWA
  1887   June 21.
  1888   Mar. 8.

AUTONOMIA. w., irr. est. Apr. 12, 1889.
  Note: Periodicity Apr. 12 — July 14,
  1889, weekly; after July 14, 1889, irregular.
MWA
  1889   Apr. 12, July 14.
  1890   Jan. 7.

BANDERA DEL ORDEN. est. Sept. 1875.
MWA
  1875   Oct. 8.

BANDERA FEDERAL. irr., w. est. [1883].
  Note: Periodicity after May 1, 1884,
  weekly.
MWA
  1884   Feb. 5 — 22, Mar. 18, Apr. 9 —
          11, May 2 — 16.

BARRA EN 1871. irr. est. July 24, 1871.
MWA
  1871   Aug. 2.

BATALLA. irr. est. Mar. 25, 1888.
MWA
  1888   Mar. 25 — May 15.

BOLETIN. irr. est. Jan. 8, 1875.
MWA
  1875   May 25.

BOLETIN.
MWA
  1879   ₁Mar. 9.₁

BOLETIN DE JURISPRUDENCIA Y
ALGO DE TODO. w.
MWA
  1857   Aug. 1.

BOLETIN DE LA EMPRESA NACION-
AL DE BOLIVIA. irr.
MWA
  1888   June 16.

BOLETIN DE LA GUERRA. w. est. Mar.
22, 1879.
MWA
  1879   Mar. 22, Apr. 10, May 9.

BOLETIN DEPARTAMENTAL. bw. est.
1873.
    Note: Periodicity before July 15,
    1873, biweekly.
MWA
  1873   June 1, July 1 – 15.
  1875   Apr. 9.

BOLETIN DEPARTAMENTAL. irr.
MWA
  1886   June 26.
  1887   Dec. 28.
  1888   Jan. 20, Feb. 4 – May 4.

BOLETIN ELECTORAL.
MWA
  1892   Mar. 31.

BOLETIN LIBERAL.
MWA
  1892   Apr. 9.

BOLETIN OFICIAL. irr. est. Nov. 28,
1870.
    Note: Removed from La Paz to Cocha-
    bamba, May 3, 1871; removed to
    Sucre, June 13, 1871; removed to
    Potosí, Nov. 25, 1871; returned to
    La Paz, Jan. 12, 1872.

MWA
  1871   Aug. 17, Oct. 23 – 28, Nov. 10.
          Nov. 10.

BOLETIN OFICIAL DE LA REVOLU-
CION. est. Sept. 13, 1888.
MWA
  1888   Sept. 13.

BOLETIN REPUBLICANO. irr. est. 1857.
DLC
  1857   Nov. 10.
MWA
  1857   Oct. 4 – Dec. 31.
  1858   Jan. 1 – 4.

BOLIVIANO. sw. est. ₁1847₁.
MWA
  1848   Mar. 18 – May 31, June 7 – Oct.
          4, Nov. 1 – 4, 29.

LA CAPITAL. sw., 3w., sw., 3w. est.
₁1889₁.
    Note: Periodicity before Dec. 1903,
    semiweekly; Dec. 5, 1903 – June 22,
    1904, three times a week; June 23 –
    Dec. 3, 1904, semiweekly; after Dec.
    3, 1904, three times a week.
DLC
  1924   Aug. 12 – Dec. 31.
  1925   Jan. 1 – 24, Feb. 25 – Mar. 11.
MWA
  1892   Apr. 11, 29, May 7, 22.
  1902   Oct. 4.
  1903   Sept. 11 – 13, 25 – 27, Oct. 9 –
          11, Nov. 12 – 22, Dec. 4.
  1904   ₁Mar. 1 – Dec. 3.₁
  1905   Oct. 3, 7, 28 – 31, Nov. 7, 14 –
          25.
  1906   ₁Jan. 16 – Sept. 1.₁
  1908   ₁Mar. 17 – Dec. 12.₁
  1909   ₁Feb. 4 – Dec. 24.₁
  1910   Jan. 12, 26, Feb. 10, July 20.

CATOLICO. irr. est. Jan. 30, 1860.
MWA
  1860   Jan. 30 – May 7.

CAUSA DE LOS PUEBLOS. irr. est. Mar.
14, 1861.
MWA
  1861   Apr. 12 – May 4.

CAUSA NACIONAL. irr. est. Dec. 1861.
MWA
    1861   Dec. 5.
    1864   Apr. 19.

CENSOR. 3m. est. [1891].
MWA
    1891   July 26.
    1892   May 5.

CENTINELA DE LA REVOLUCION DE
SEPTIEMBRE. irr. est. [1860].
MWA
    1861   Feb. 21, Mar. 8, Apr. 11 – 13,
          May 21.

CIRCULAR DE 10 DE FEBRERO.
MWA
    1887   Apr. 24.

CLUB NACIONAL. 3m., irr. est. July 18,
1873.
MWA
    1874   Extraordinario: Feb. 14.

CLUB NACIONAL. irr. est. July 18, 1875.
MWA
    1875   July 18 – Oct. 19.

COLUMNA DE INGAVI. 3w. est. Nov. 18,
1842.
MWA
    1842   Nov. 18 – Dec. 31.

COMETA. irr.
MWA
    1842   Aug. 30.

COMETA. w. est. Jan. 21, 1848.
MWA
    1848   Apr. 13 – Aug. 10.

COMETA. irr.
MWA
    1855   May 25, Sept. 1 – 7, 19.

CONCIENCIA NACIONAL. w. est. Mar.
21, 1884.
MWA
    1884   Mar. 21.

CONCILIADOR. irr.
MWA
    1855   June 26.

CONSERVADOR. irr.
MWA
    1849   Apr. 6 – May 20, June 4, 29,
          July 9, 17 – 20, 27 – 31.

CONSTITUCIONAL. irr. est. Oct. 26,
1861.
CtY
    1862   Aug. 22.
MWA
    1861   Oct. 26 – Nov. 13.
    1862   Aug. 14 – 22.

CONSTITUCIONAL. w., irr. est. 1872.
MWA
    1872   Apr. 1 – July 9, Dec. 12.
    1873   Feb. 6, Mar. 14 – May 9.

EL CORREO DE BOLIVIA. sw., irr. est.
Aug. 6, 1876.
CtY
    1876   Aug. 6, Sept. 22, Oct. 27.
    1877   Jan. 12, Mar. 29.
MWA
    1876   Aug. 6 – Dec. 31.
    1877   Jan. 1 – Mar. 29.

CRISIS. irr. est. June 7, 1857.
MWA
    1857   June 7.

CRONICA. d. est. Sept. 3, 1874.
MWA
    1874   Sept. 3 – Nov. 18.

CRUZADO. bw. est. Sept. 15, 1868.
MWA
    1868   Sept. 15 – Dec. 31.
    1869 – 1870   Jan. 1 – Dec. 31.
    1871   Jan. 1 – Feb. 28.
    1873   Mar. 13, Dec. 8.
    1874   July 10.
    1875   Jan. 6 – Feb. 26, Apr. 19, May
          20 – June 12, July 8 – Nov. 17.
    1876   Jan. 19 – Dec. 31.
    1877   Jan. 1 – Mar. 9, Apr. 6 – June
          15, Sept. 14 – Dec. 29.
    1878   Jan. 18 – Sept. 27.
    1880   Suplemento: July 23.
          Extraordinario: Aug. 19.

CUCHILLA. bw. est. Apr. 7, 1890.
  MWA
    1890   Apr. 7.

CUESTION QUESADA.
  MWA
    1880   [Dec. 2.]

DEBATES. sw.
  MWA
    1886   Nov. 17.
    1887   Jan. 12−20, 26−29, Feb. 6−
            Apr. 7, 17−May 29, June 8−
            July 30, Aug. 25, Sept. 9−Dec.
            31.
    1888   Jan. 1−Feb. 22.
            Extraordinario: Aug. 14.

DEBER. w.
  MWA
    1889   Mar. 10−31, Apr. 28, July 21,
            Aug. 25, Sept. 15, Oct. 6−13,
            Dec. 15.
    1890   Jan. 26, Feb. 9−16.

DERECHO. sw. est. [1889].
  MWA
    1892   July 3.

DIA. d.
  MWA
    1884   Nov. 14.
    1888   Aug. 14, 17−Sept. 2, 5, 6.
    1890   Jan. 11−17.
    1891   Aug. 13, Oct. 2.
    1892   July 1−6, 20, 21, 24−27, 30
            Aug. 24, Sept. 17−22, 28.
    1893   Jan. 7−10, Apr. 7−May 17,
            June 8−July 10, 15−26, Aug.
            19.

DIA. d. est. July 3, 1908.
  MWA
    1908   [July 3−31.]

DINAMITA. w. est. Aug. 11, 1886.
  MWA
    1886   Aug. 11−Sept. 16, Oct. 1−22,
            Nov. 12−Dec. 31.
    1887   Jan. 1−May 15, 29−June 12,
            July 1, 30, Aug. 31−Oct. 23.

DUENDE. w. est. 1897.
  MWA
    1897   Nov. 7.

ECO DE BOLIVIA.
    Note: Removed from La Paz to Sucre,
    Dec. 1867; returned to La Paz, Dec.
    1868.
  MWA
    1868   Feb. 10−Mar. 31.

EL ECO DE LA JUVENTUD. irr. est. Apr.
  11, 1872.
  CtY
    1874   June 12.
    1876   Feb. 26.
  MWA
    1872   Apr. 11−Dec. 31.
    1873−1875   Jan. 1−Dec. 31.
    1876   Jan. 1−Feb. 26.
            Suplemento: Apr. 21.

ECO DE LA OPINION. irr. est. June 4,
  1850.
  MWA
    1852   Apr. 3.
    1854   Sept. 6.

ECO DE LOS PUEBLOS. w., sw., irr. est.
  Nov. 6, 1847.
    Note: Periodicity Nov. 6, 1847−
    Feb 26, 1848, weekly; after Feb. 27,
    1848, semiweekly. Succeeded by *La
    Guardia nacional* Feb. 27, 1848.
  MWA
    1847   Nov. 6.
    1848   Jan. 8.

ECO DE MAYO. w., bw. est. [1877].
    Note: Periodicity before Dec. 21,
    1877, weekly; after Dec. 21, 1877, bi-
    weekly.
  MWA
    1877   Nov. 23, Dec. 21.
    1878   Nov. 15.

EL ECO DE SUCRE. irr. est. Feb. 16,
  1871.
  CtY
    1871   Feb. 16−Sept. 16.
    1872   Jan. 13−Dec. 28.

1873   Jan. 2 – Dec. 26.
1874   Jan. 9 – Nov. 17.
1875   Oct. 17, 21.
MWA
  1871   Feb. 16 – Dec. 31.
  1872 – 1873   Jan. 1 – Dec. 31.
  1874   Jan. 1 – Mar. 13, Apr. 9 – July
          3, 10 – 24, Oct. 2 – 16, 29 – Nov.
          17.
  1875   Apr. 17 – June 11, 22 – Aug. 6,
          Oct. 17 – 21, Nov. 19 – Dec. 31.
  1876   Jan. 1 – 6.
NcD
  1871   July 22.
  1872   Sept. 19, 25.
  1873   Aug. 7.

ECO DEL SUD. irr. est. Dec. 14, 1848.
MWA
  1849   Mar. 7.

ENTUSIASTA. irr. est. Aug. 8, 1871.
MWA
  1871   Aug. 25.

ESTRELLA. w., irr. est. June 25, 1872.
CtY
  1873   Feb. 20, Mar. 8.
MWA
  1872   June 25, Oct. 25, Dec. 31.
          Extraordinario: Dec. 5.
  1873   Jan. 8 – 24, Feb. 14 – Mar. 8,
          Apr. 9.

GACETA DEL GOBIERNO. irr. est. Mar.
1858.
  Note: Removed from La Paz to Cocha-
  bamba, Jan. 24, 1859; removed to
  Sucre, Apr. 26, 1859; returned to La
  Paz, [Nov.] 1859.
MWA
  1859   July 27, Aug. 24 – 27.

GACETA JUDICIAL. irr. est. May 10,
1858.
MWA
  1874   Dec. 1.
  1875   Aug. 15.
  1887   Extraordinario: Aug. 26.
          Suplemento: Aug. 26.

GACETA MUNICIPAL. bw.
MWA
  1874   June 10.
  1875   Aug. 23 – Nov. 8.
  1877   Jan. 10.
  1879   Apr. 4, Oct. 24.
  1880   Apr. 1, 20.
  1884   Mar. 14.
  1885   Apr. 27, May 30.
          Extraordinario: n.d.
  1886   Mar. 24 – Sept. 20, Nov. 4 – 9.
  1887   Feb. 5, Mar. 7 – May 18, July
          23 – Aug. 12, 20, Sept. 13, 24 –
          Oct. 29, Nov. 9 – Dec. 29.
  1888   Jan. 10 – 27, Feb. 7 – 22, Mar.
          26, Apr. 20, May 24 – June 2,
          30 – July 9, Nov. 15, Dec. 19 –
          31.
  1889   Jan. 1 – 12, 21.

GUARDIA NACIONAL. irr. est. May 25,
1847.
  Note: Succeeded by *Éco de los pueblos*,
  Feb. 27, 1848.
MWA
  1847   May 25, June 23, July 28, Aug.
          7, Oct. 23, Nov. 11 – 17.

IDEA.
MWA
  1887   Aug. 4.

IMPARCIAL. irr. est. Aug. 26, 1875.
MWA
  1875   Aug. 26 – Oct. 15.

INDEPENDIENTE. sw.
MWA
  1894   May 30, June 22, 29, July 17 –
          Aug. 13.

LA INDUSTRIA. d., 3w., sw. est. 1881.
  Note: Periodicity before Feb. 1, 1884,
  daily; Feb. 2, 1884 – Sept. 21, 1886,
  semiweekly; Sept. 22 – Nov. 10, 1886,
  daily; Nov. 11, 1887 – Oct. 28, 1888,
  semiweekly; Oct. 29 – Dec. 18, 1888,
  daily; Dec. 19, 1888 – Jan. 16, 1891,
  semiweekly; Jan. 17, 1891 – July 12,
  1892, three times a week; after July
  13, 1892, semiweekly.

MWA
- 1881 [Feb. 4—Dec. 31].
- 1882 [Jan. 1—Dec. 31].
- 1883 [Jan. 1—Dec. 28].
- 1884 Jan. 5—Mar. 27, Apr. 4—June 14, Oct. 4.
- 1885 Jan. 17—Apr. 3, 14—21, May 1—22, June 2—26, July 3, 10, 17—21, Aug. 4, Sept. 4—Oct. 6, 16—Nov. 3, 10, 20—Dec. 31.
- 1886 Jan. 1—Dec. 31.
- 1887 Jan. 1—Feb. 16, Mar. 5—July 20, Aug. 27, Sept. 14, 21—Nov. 23, Dec. 3—31.
- 1888 Jan. 1—Feb. 22, Mar. 10—July 25, Oct. 29—Dec. 18.
- 1891 Jan. 17.
- 1892 June 2—14, July 2—12.
- 1894 Sept. 4.
- 1908 Mar. 19, Nov. 29—Dec. 4, 10.

INDUSTRIAL. irr. est. Apr. 9, 1878.
MWA
- 1878 Apr. 9—Dec. 31.
- 1879 Jan. 1—24, Mar. 10.

JUSTICIA. irr. est. Mar. 27, 1886.
MWA
- 1886 Mar. 27—June 23, July 10—Sept. 17, Oct. 10—Dec. 7.
- 1887 Apr. 19, May 6, June 3.

JUVENTUD. w. est. Feb. 12, 1860.
MWA
- 1860 Feb. 12—Apr. 28.

JUVENTUD. bw. est. July 2, 1875.
MWA
- 1875 July 2, Aug. 6.

JUVENTUD IMPARCIAL. irr. est. Oct. 14, 1875.
MWA
- 1875 Oct. 14—Nov. 19, Dec. 31.
- 1876 Jan. 1—May 4.

EL LIBERAL. w. est. Feb. 9, 1862.
MWA
- 1862 Feb. 13—Aug. 3.

EL LIBERAL. bw. est. Jan. 10, 1885.
CtY
- 1885 Jan. 10, Feb. 6, 27.

MWA
- 1885 Jan. 10—Feb. 27.
NcD
- 1885 Jan. 10, Feb. 6, 27.

LIBERTAD. w., irr., w. est. June 3, 1887. Note: Periodicity June 3—Oct. 6, 1887, weekly; Oct. 7, 1887—Sept. 6, 1888, irregular; after Sept. 6, 1888, weekly.
MWA
- 1887 June 3—Dec. 31.
- 1888 Jan. 1—Sept. 6.
NcD
- 1888 Mar. 9, May 25, July 1, Sept. 4, 6.

MUNICIPAL DE SUCRE. irr. est. [1862].
MWA
- 1862 Dec. 19.

NACION. w. est. [1881].
MWA
- 1881 Suplemento: Jan. 30.

NACION. w. est. Jan. 1, 1881.
MWA
- 1881 Jan. 1—Nov. 17.
- 1882 Sept. 22, Oct. 27, Nov. 24, Dec. 29—31.
- 1883 Jan. 1—Feb. 11, Mar. 9, Apr. 13, May 12, 26, Oct. 12.
- 1884 Jan. 12—26.

EL NACIONAL. sw., w., irr. est. Aug. 1849.
CtY
- 1850 Aug. 24.
- 1851 May 31.
- 1853 Feb. 3, 26, 27, Oct. 6, Nov. 18, 19.
- 1854 May 6.

NACIONAL. w. est. [1883].
MWA
- 1883 Sept. 28.
- 1884 Jan. 30, May 6.

NUEVA ERA. sw. est. Aug. 26, 1855.
MWA
- 1855 Aug. 26—Dec. 31.

1856   Jan. 1 – Dec. 31.
1857   Jan. 1 – Sept. 23.

NUEVE DE FEBRERO. w. est. Mar. 1840.
MWA
1840   Apr. 30.

EL OBRERO. bw., w. est. July 11, 1875.
Note: Periodicity July 11, 1875 – Jan.
25, 1875, biweekly; after Feb. 4, 1876,
weekly.
CtY
1875   July 21, Aug. 12, Nov. 18.
1876   Jan. 25, Feb. 4, 16, Mar. 2 –
Apr. 7, 21 – 30.
MWA
1875   July 11 – Aug. 12, Sept. 20,
Nov. 6 – 18, Dec. 30.
1876   Jan. 25 – June 10, July 3 – 29.

OPINION. d. est. Feb. 20, 1883.
MWA
1883   Feb. 20.

EL ORDEN. est. Aug. 14, 1864.
CtY
1864   Aug. 14.
MWA
1864   Aug. 14.

PATRIA. w. est. Aug. 1, 1871.
MWA
1871   Aug. 15.
1905   Sept. 14.

PATRIA EN PELIGRO. irr. est. Mar. 11,
1879.
MWA
1879   Mar. 11, 21 – 27.

PATRIOTA. irr. est. Jan. 13, 1873.
MWA
1873   Jan. 24.

PENSAMIENTO. bw. est. Feb. 26, 1877.
MWA
1877   Feb. 26.

PENSAMIENTO DE LA JUVENTUD. irr.
est. Apr. 26, 1862.
MWA
1862   Apr. 26 – May 22.

PINTOR. irr. est. May 6, 1865.
MWA
1865   May 6.

PORVENIR. irr. est. Apr. 20, 1855.
MWA
1855   Apr. 30 – June 18.

PORVENIR. bw., w. est. [1883].
MWA
1884   Apr. 19.

PORVENIR DEL SUD. irr. est. June 30,
1867.
MWA
1867   June 30.

PRECURSOR. irr. est. Sept. 17, 1864.
MWA
1864   Oct. 25.

PRENSA. irr.
MWA
1881   June 11.

PRENSA. w. est. Mar. 26, 1886.
MWA
1886   Mar. 26 – Sept. 24, Oct. 15 –
22, Nov. 5 – Dec. 31.
1887   Jan. 1 – 15.
NcD
1886   Apr. 2, 9, Nov. 5, 26, Dec. 3, 10.
1887   Jan. 15.

PRENSA. d. est. [1893].
MWA
1893   Aug. 22, Sept. 2, 3, 14 – 20.

PRENSA LIBRE. w. est. Mar. 29, 1902.
MWA
1903   Jan. 25.

PROGRESO. bw. est. Apr. 30, 1878.
MWA
1878   Apr. 30 – May 18, June 28, Aug.
23 – Oct. 2.

PROPAGANDA. irr. est. Apr. 16, 1885.
MWA
1885   Apr. 16, May 23 – June 10, July
29 – Oct. 27, Dec. 19.

PUEBLO. irr.
MWA
1883   Dec. 27.

1884   Jan. 18 – 26, Feb. 22 – Apr. 7,
        23 – May 10.
1885   May 3, 25.
1886   Jan. 1, 22, Sept. 11, Nov. 11.
1887   Apr. 29, June 14, July 2 – Dec.
        31.
1888   Jan. 1 – May 3.

RAYO. irr. est. Jan. 4, 1865.
  MWA
    1865   Jan. 4 – 11.

RAYON. irr. est. Jan. 15, 1861.
  MWA
    1861   Jan. 15.

RECREO LITERARIO. w.
  MWA
    1881   Dec. 15 – 31.
    1882   Jan. 1 – Feb. 15.

REDACTOR. irr.
  MWA
    1871   July 5 – 24, Aug. 5 – 9, Sept. 20.

REDACTOR. w. est. Oct. 17, 1873.
  MWA
    1873   Oct. 17 – Nov. 26.

REDACTOR DEL CONGRESO EXTRA-
ORDINARIA DE BOLIVIA.
  MWA
    1848   Sept. 7, Oct. 7.

LA REFORMA. w. est. Nov. 1891.
  MWA
    1892   Feb. 13, 21 – Mar. 12, June 14.

REGIMEN LEGAL. irr. est. Oct. 8, 1873.
  MWA
    1873   Oct. 8 – Dec. 31.
    1874   Jan. 1 – Dec. 31.
    1875   Jan. 1 – Apr. 18.

REPUBLICA. w. est. May 28, 1880.
  MWA
    1880   May 28, July 23.
    1883   Sept. 28, Nov. 22.
    1884   Jan. 17, Feb. 8 – 21, May 1.

REPUBLICA. d. est. [1881].
  MWA
    1884   Oct. 5.

REPUBLICA. 3w. est. [1908].
  MWA
    1908   June 12.

REPUBLICANO. w.
  MWA
    1891   Oct. 29 – Nov. 6, Dec. 3.
    1892   Jan. 15, Mar. 13, Apr. 14.

RESTAURADOR. w., 3w., d. est. Apr. 4,
1839
  MWA
    1843   Mar. 20, 21.
    1844   Oct. 12.
    1846   July 8.

REVISTA. irr. est. Oct. 18, 1860.
  MWA
    1860   Oct. 18.

REVOLUCION. irr. est. Jan. 1, 1871.
  MWA
    1871   Jan. 10, Mar. 17 – Apr. 9.

EL REVOLUCIONARIO. irr. est. Sept.
16, 1855.
  MWA
    1857   Nov. 5 – Dec. 19.
    1858   Jan. 11 – Feb. 26.

REVOLUCIONARIO. irr. est. May 25,
1864.
  MWA
    1864   May 25 – Aug. 22.

EL SIGLO. irr. est. Dec. 10, 1859.
  CtY
    1860   Jan. 19.
  MWA
    1859   Dec. 10 – 31.
    1860   Jan. 1 – 12.

SIGLO XIX. irr.
  MWA
    1889   Mar. 22.

SINAPISMO. irr.
  MWA
    1874   Oct. 13, Dec. 10.
    1875   July 9.
    1876   Jan. 24, Mar. 10, Oct. 16.
            Suplemento: Oct. 20.

SOCIEDAD LITERARIA. bw. est. July 13,
1877.
CtY
1877 July 13.
MWA
1877 July 13.
1878 Aug. 1.

TIEMPO. irr. est. Mar. 8, 1872.
MWA
1874 [May 1.]

TREN. irr.
MWA
1876 May 12—Dec. 21.

EL 3 DE JUNIO. irr., w.
Note: Periodicity Jan. 9, 1885—June
4, 1886, irregular; after June 4, 1886,
weekly.
DLC
1887 May 15.
1888 Jan. 28.
MWA
1885 Jan. 9, Mar. 9—Apr. 4, June 3—
27, Aug. 28.
1886 Jan. 23, Apr. 6—June 25, July
23—30, Aug. 6, Sept. 19, Nov.
15—29.
1887 Jan. 7—15, Feb. 5—Mar. 16,
May 15—Aug. 1, Dec. 18.
1888 Jan. 15—28.

UNION. bw. est. Jan. 17, 1885.
MWA
1885 Jan. 17—28, Feb. 5—Apr. 15.

UNION MEDICA. irr. est. Apr. 6, 1876.
MWA
1876 Apr. 6.

UNION NACIONAL. irr. est. May 4, 1876.
MWA
1876 May 4.

VERDAD. irr. est. Jan. 15, 1865.
MWA
1865 Jan. 15—Apr. 26.

VERDAD. bw., irr. est. Apr. 16, 1874.
Note: Periodicity Apr. 16, 1874—
July 18, 1874, biweekly; after July 19,
1874, irregular.

MWA
1874 Apr. 16—Dec. 31.
1875 Jan. 1—Mar. 4.

EL 25 DE MAYO. w.
MWA
1891 Aug. 28, Sept. 29.

VOZ DE SUCRE. w. est. July 18, 1789.
MWA
1789 July 18.

Tacna

See Chile. Tacna.

Tarata

COMETA. irr. est. Mar. 14, 1884.
MWA
1884 Mar. 14, Apr. 24.

GACETA MUNICIPAL DE PUNATA. irr.
MWA
1874 Mar. 28.
1875 Sept. 2.

PRIMAVERA. irr. Oct. 28, 1887.
MWA
1887 Oct. 28—Nov. 24.

UNION. irr.
MWA
1875 Jan. 22—24.

Tarija

EL ALBUM.
See *La Estrella de Tarija*.

BOLETIN DE INSTRUCCION. irr.
MWA
1887 June 19—July 23, Dec. 6—31.
1888 Jan. 1—June 20, Aug. 30—Oct.
6.

BOLETIN OFICIAL.
MWA
1888 Apr. 23.

CLUB. irr. est. Dec. 23, 1875.
MWA
1875 Dec. 23—31.
1876 Jan. 1—Apr. 22.

CONSTITUCIONAL. w. est. Mar. 25, 1886.
MWA
1886   Mar. 25, Apr. 18 – 25, May 19.

CREENCIA.
MWA
1885   Mar. 18.

DEMOCRACIA. w. est. Dec. 23, 1880.
MWA
1880   Dec. 23 – 31.
1881   Jan. 1 – 22, Feb. 5.

ESTRELLA DE TARIJA. irr.
Note: Published biweekly supplement, *El Album*.
MWA
1876   Oct. 5 – Dec. 31.
1877   Jan. 1 – May 4.
1878   May 19, Nov. 27.
1879   June 19, July 19, Oct. 12 – 16, 30.
1880   Jan. 20, Mar. 10, Apr. 13, May 9, July 7 – Dec. 31.
1882   Feb. 3 – Aug. 31, Oct. 15, Dec. 10.
1883   Mar. 28 – Apr. 5, Aug. 2, Oct. 24, Dec. 6.
1884   Feb. 20, Mar. 14.
1885   [Jan. 5 – Nov. 13.]
1886   Mar. 17, Sept. 21, Nov. 30, Dec. 11.
1887   Jan. 1 – 4, 15 – Feb. 8, 19 – Apr. 19, May 4 – 10, 27 – June 7, July 5 – 26, Sept. 3 – 14, Oct. 8 – 21, Dec. 20.
1888   Jan. 7, 18, 28, Feb. 10, Mar. 24, May 12 – July 11.
        Album: Feb. 29.
1892   June 7, 25 – July 5.

FEDERALIST. sw. est. Apr. 18, 1886.
MWA
1886   Apr. 18 – May 1.

FIGARO.
MWA
1888   July 15.

LIBERAL. irr.
MWA
1886   Apr. 2 – Oct. 7.

LIBERAL. w.
MWA
1908   Apr. 1 – 8, 25.

PENSAMIENTO. irr.
MWA
1886   Sept. 20 – Oct. 10, Nov. 17 – Dec. 31.
1887   Jan. 1 – Feb. 18, Apr. 10 – May 7, Dec. 21 – 31.
1888   Jan. 1 – May 18.
1891   Aug. 7, Sept. 13, Oct. 13 – 16, 24 – 31, Nov. 14 – 19.
1892   June 28.

PILCOMAYO. sw.
MWA
1892   Feb. 18, May 29 – June 6, 29.

PORVENIR. irr. est. Apr. 13, 1885.
MWA
1885   Apr. 13, 26, May 26, June 28 – Aug. 6.

EL PUEBLO. bw., w., irr. est. [1875].
CtY
1875   Nov. 18.
1876   Jan. 1, Feb. 1, Mar. 20, Apr. 15.
1878   Jan. 31, Mar. 28 – May 10, 25 – July 23, Aug. 6 – Sept. 26, Oct. 10 – 26.

MWA
1876   May 21, July 19 – Apr. 15, May 15 – June 1, Oct. 19, Dec. 19.
1877   Apr. 4, Aug. 24, Nov. 21.
1878   Jan. 1, 31, Feb. 28 – Dec. 10.
1879   Mar. 6, July 23.
1880   May 6 – 13, June 14 – 17, July 2 – 27, Aug. 26 – Sept. 2, 20 – Dec. 30.

PUEBLO TARIJENO.
MWA
1886   [Apr. 6.]

SOLDADO. bw.
MWA
1876   Aug. 30.

TRABAJO. irr.
MWA
1882   Oct. 9.
1883   Aug. 6, Nov. 27, Dec. 24 – 27.

1884   Jan. 4 – 8, 21 – 24, Feb. 18 – 21,
        Mar. 8 – 18, Apr. 8 – 10, 19 –
        May 6.
1885   Jan. 6 – Apr. 24, May 25 – Dec.
        31.
1886 – 1887   Jan. 1 – Dec. 31.
1888   Jan. 1 – July 6, Sept. 27 – Dec.
        31.
1889   Jan. 1 – 17, Mar. 14.
1892   May 28 – July 5, Sept. 30.

TRIBUNA. sw. est. 1942.
  DLC
  1942   June 3, 6, 10, 13.

UNION. irr.
  MWA
  1875   Dec. 16.

Trinidad

BENIANO. bw. est. July 15, 1884.
  MWA
  1884   July 15 – Dec. 31.
  1885   Jan. 1 – Feb. 28, Apr. 15 – June
          16.

ECO DEL ORIENTE. bw.
  MWA
  1883   Feb. 28.

ECO LIBERAL. 3m. est. Apr. 20, 1898.
  MWA
  1898   Apr. 20.

INDEPENDIENTE. irr. est. Mar. 7, 1886.
  MWA
  1886   Mar. 7 – Apr. 10, May 13 – June
          15, July 31 – Sept. 20.

LIBERAL. irr. est. Apr. 2, 1886.
  MWA
  1886   Apr. 2.

MAMORE. bw., w. est. Jan. 15, 1888.
  Note: Periodicity Jan. 15 – Mar. 15,
  1888, biweekly; after Mar. 15, 1888,
  weekly.
  MWA
  1888   Jan. 15 – Apr. 15.

Tupiza

CHOROLQUE. w. est. Apr. 28, 1876.
  MWA
  1876   Apr. 28 – May 5, Oct. 13.

1879   Oct. 24.
1880   Jan. 22, Apr. 22.
1883   July 16.

ECO DE BOLIVIA. w.
  MWA
  1909   Mar. 4.

LA FE POLITICA. 3m.
  MWA
  1883   Dec. 28 – 31.
  1884   Jan. 1 – 17, Mar. 28.

Uncia

INDUSTRIAL. w., irr. est. [1906].
  MWA
  1908   Feb. 29, Mar. 31, Apr. 15,
          May 3 – July 10.
  1909   May 11 – 20.

Uyuni

COMERCIO. sw.
  MWA
  1909   Mar. 24.

Viacha

OFRENDA. est. July 16, 1887.
  MWA
  1887   July 16.

PORVENIR DE PACAJES. est. Apr. 29,
1900.
  MWA
  1900   Apr. 29.

BRAZIL

Aracaty

O ARACATY.
  CU
  1909   Jan. 13.

Bahia

BAHIANO. 3w.
  MWA
  1828   Sept. 30, Oct. 16.

CORREIO DA BAHIA. 3w.
  MWA
  1828   Sept. 22, Oct. 8 – 15.

NN
 1828   Oct. 18.

DIARIO DA BAHIA. d. est. Jan. 1, 1856.
 DLC
  1941   Apr. 1−5, 8−10, 15−18, 22,
          24, 25, 29−May 3, 6, 8−11,
          13−17, 20−23, 28−31, June 4,
          5, 7, 10−14, 17−19, 26, 28,
          July 1, 2, 5, 8, 12, 15, 19, 25, 26,
          29, 30, Aug. 15, 20, 23, 28−30,
          Sept. 2, 3, 9, 11−13, 16−20,
          23, 25−27, 30−Oct. 4, 7−9,
          12, 14, 16−18, 28, Nov. 1, 2, 6,
          8, Dec. 2, 3, 5, 16, 18, 19, 31.
  1942   Feb. 4−6, 10−12, 14, 19−21,
          24, 25, Mar. 1, 3, 4, 6, 8, 10, 11,
          13, 15, 17, 18, 20, 25, 26, 28.
 LNT−MA
  1941   Apr. 1−30.
 MH
  1910   Aug. 24−Oct. 22.

DIARIO DE NOTICIAS. d.
 CLCM
  1905   Aug. 1, 3.
 MWA
  1884   Dec. 3.

ESTADO DA BAHIA. d. est. 1932.
 DLC
  1941   Apr. 2−9, 13−May 3, 5−28,
          30−July 24, 26−Aug. 7, 9−22,
          24−Sept. 16, 18−22, 24−Oct.
          2, 5, 7−20, 25−29, Nov. 1−3,
          5−14, 16−23, 25−Dec. 5, 7−
          18, 20−31.
  1942   Feb. 1−13, 15−22, 24, 25, 27−
          Mar. 3, 5−9, 12−16, 18−22,
          24−26, Apr. 28.

O FAROL BAHIA.
 PPAmP
  1827   Aug. 17.

GAZETA COMMERCIAL DO BAHIA.
 3w.
 CU−B
  Micro (N)
  1839   Nov. 27.

GAZETA DO BAHIA. sw. est. 1828.
 CtY
  1828   June 28.
 MWA
  1828   Sept. 27, Oct. 18.
 NN
  1828   Oct. 11.

O IMPARCIAL. d. est. 1918.
 DLC
  1941   Apr. 1−10, 12−May 22, 24,
          26−31, June 2−10, 12, 13,
          16−21, 23, 26−July 19, 21−
          24, 28−Aug. 23, 25−28, 30−
          Sept. 6, 8−27, 29−Oct. 15, 17,
          18, 20, 23−25, 27−Dec. 23,
          25−31.
  1942   Feb. 1−14, 16, 20−Mar. 6, 8,
          9, 11−13, 15−25, 27.

RELACÃO DA RECEITA, E DESPESA,
QUE TEVA ESTA CASA DA SANTA
MISERICORDIA DA BAHIA.
 MWA
  1818   July 2.

O SETE DE NOVEMBRO. d. est. Nov. 21,
1837.
 DLC
  1837   Nov. 21−Dec. 5.

A TARDE. d. est. 1915.
 DLC
  1941   Apr. 1, 3, 5−10, 12−14, 16, 18,
          22−26, 28−30, May 2, 5−10,
          15, 16, 19−21, 23, 26, 27, 29−
          June 12, 14−17, 20−23, 25,
          26, 28, July 1, 3, 5−26, 28−
          Aug. 30, Sept. 2−4, 6−11, 13,
          16−18, 20, 24, 25, 27−Oct. 7,
          10, 11, 15−21, 24−Nov. 7,
          11−17, 19−24, 27−29, Dec.
          3, 5, 9−11, 13−17, 19−24,
          26−31.
  1942   Feb. 2, 4−16, 18−Mar. 3, 5−
          11, 13, 14, 18−23, 25, 28−30,
          Apr. 22, 24.

Barretos

O CORREIO.
 CU
  1933   Jan. 7.

Bebedouro

O BEBEDOURENSE.
  CU
    1933   Jan. 12.

Belém

CORREIO DE BELEM. d. est. Dec. 17,
  1907.
  KHi
    1914   Nov. 23.

DIARIO DO GRAM-PARA. d. est. Apr.
  10, 1853.
  MWA
    1885   July 30.

FOLHA DO NORTE. d. est. Jan. 1, 1896.
  DLC
    1950   Feb. 12 — Mar. 31, May 3 —
            Dec. 31.
    1951   Jan. 1, 3 — Feb. 6, 8 — Apr. 16,
            18 — 21, 23 — Dec. 31.
    1952   Jan. 1 — 4, 7, 12 — May 5, 7 — 13,
            15, 17 — 22, 24 — Aug. 29, 31,
            Sept. 1, 3 — 26, 28 — Nov. 15,
            17 — Dec. 31.
    1953   Jan. 1 — Feb. 17, 19 — May 7,
            9 — 14, 17 — Sept. 4, 6 — 14, 17 —
            Oct. 1, 3 — Nov. 29, Dec. 1 — 8,
            10 — 28.
    1954   Jan. 1 — May 1, 3 — 27, 29 — Oct.
            9, 11 — Dec. 28.
    1955   Jan. 1 — May 13, 15 — June 29,
            July 1 — 7, 10 — Oct. 27, 30 —
            Dec. 1, 4 — 31.
    1956   Jan. 1 — Mar. 30, Apr. 1 — June
            29, July 1 — Sept. 30, Oct. 2 —
            19, 22 — 25, 27 — Dec. 4, 7 —
            21, 23 — 28.
    1957   Jan. 1 — Feb. 1, 3 — 28, Mar. 3 —
            21, 25 — 31, Apr. 2, 4 — 12, 14 —
            19, 21 — 25, 29, May 1, 3 — 18,
            20, 22, 23, 26 — 30, June 1 — 6,
            9 — 20, 23 — 29, July 1 — 8, 11 —
            17, 20 — 25, 29, Aug. 1 — 8, 11 —
            27, Sept. 1 — 7, 9 — 19, 22 — Oct.
            3, 6 — 12, 14 — Nov. 2, 4 — 6,
            10 — 15, 17 — 20, 23 — Dec. 5, 8,
            9, 16, 22 — 25, 29, 30.

    1958   Jan. 1, 3 — 16, 19 — 23, 26 — Feb.
            13, 16 — 18, 20 — Mar. 5, 7 — 20,
            24, 26, 27, 30, Apr. 1, 2, 6, 8 —
            11, 15, 16, 19, 20, 23 — 27, May
            3, 4, 20 — 25, 27 — 29, 31, June 1,
            3 — 5, 7, 8, 10, 15, 17 — 22, 24 —
            28, July 6, 8 — 13, 15 — 20, 22 —
            27, Aug. 6 — 10, 13 — 15, 24, 26 —
            31, Sept. 3 — 7, 11 — 14, 16 —
            21, 24, 25, 27, 28, 30 — Oct. 3, 5,
            9, 10, 12, 15 — 19, 21 — 26, 28 —
            30, Nov. 1, 2, 4, 5, 7 — 9, 11 — 15,
            25 — 28, Dec. 4 — 7, 14, 19 — 21,
            25, 27, 28.
    1959   Jan. 1 — Feb. 10, 14 — 17, 21 —
            28, Mar. 2, 4 — 10, 15 — June 3,
            5 — 17, 20 — 26, July 1 — 5, 7 —
            12, 14 — 16, 18, 21 — 26, 28 —
            Aug. 2, 4 — 9, 11, 15 — 21, 25 —
            30, Sept. 1, 3, 4, 9 — 13, 15 — 17,
            20, 22 — 24, 26, 27, 29, 30, Oct.
            2 — 16, 19 — 21, 26, 28 — Nov. 2,
            4 — Dec. 31.
    1960   Jan. 1 — 18, 21 — 29, Feb. 1, 5 —
            Mar. 10, 12, 14, 16 — Apr. 3, 7 —
            10, 12 — 15, 20, 21, 23, 24, 26 —
            May 1, 3 — 8, 13 — 15, 17 — 22,
            24, 31 — June 3, 5, 7 — 12, 14 —
            16, 21 — 25, 28, 29, July 3 — 16,
            26 — Aug. 5, 9 — 21, 24 — 27, 30,
            31, Sept. 3 — Oct. 1, 9, 11 — 16,
            18 — 23, 28 — 30, Nov. 1 — 15, 19,
            20, 22 — 27, 29 — Dec. 2, 4 — 7,
            13 — 18, 20 — 29.
    1961   Jan. 1 — 6, 9 — 13, 16 — 20, 22 —
            26, 30, Feb. 1 — 28, Mar. 5 — 7,
            13 — 27, Apr. 3, 6 — 19, 21, 23 —
            May 10, 14 — 26, June 11 — 22,
            28, 29, July 1 — 4, 16 — 18, 22 —
            Aug. 4, 15 — 22, 26 — 29, Sept.
            1 — 5, 12 — 15, Oct. 10, 11, 14 —
            17, 20, 24 — 27, Nov. 1, 2, 4 — 15,
            17 — Dec. 3, 12, 17 — 19, 24 — 27.

A PROVINCIA DO PARA. d. est. Mar. 25,
  1876.
  DLC
    1907   July 22 — Sept. 14, 23 — Oct. 22,
            24, 25, 28 — Nov. 1, 9 — Dec. 17,
            19 — 31.

1908   Jan. 1 – Apr. 22, 24 – Aug. 30,
        Sept. 1 – Nov. 3, 5 – Dec. 4, 6 –
        25, 27 – 31.
1909   Jan. 1 – 10, 12 – 25, 27 – Feb. 7,
        9 – 28, Mar. 3 – Apr. 25, 27 –
        Dec. 31.
1910   Jan. 1 – Apr. 30, May 4 – July
        20, 22 – Aug. 2, 4 – 24, Sept.
        3 – 7, 9 – Dec. 31.
1911   Jan. 1 – 12, 14 – May 13, 15 –
        June 28, 30 – July 12, 14 – Aug.
        1, 3 – Nov. 1, 14 – Dec. 31.

Belo Horizonte

ESTADO DE MINAS. d. est. 1927.
DLC
    1942   Feb. 4.

FOLHA DE MINAS. d. est. 1934.
DLC
    1941   June 20 – 22, 24 – 29, July 1 – 3,
            17 – 20, 22 – 27, 29 – 31, Aug.
            1 – 31, Sept. 2 – 7, 9 – 14, 16 –
            21, 23 – 28, 30, Oct. 1 – 5, 7 –
            12, 21 – 26, 28 – 31, Nov. 1, 2,
            4 – 9, 11 – 16, 18 – 23, 25 – 30,
            Dec. 2 – 7, 9 – 20, 23 – 25, 27,
            28, 30, 31.
    1942   Jan. 1 – 4, 6 – 11, 13 – 18, 20 –
            25, 27 – 31, Feb. 1, 3 – 8, 10 –
            15, 17, 19 – 22, 24 – 28, Mar. 1,
            3 – 8, 10 – 15, 17 – 22, 24 – 29,
            31, Apr. 1 – 3, 5, 7 – 12, 14 – 19,
            21 – 26, May 17.

O PROPAGADOR MINEIRO. d. est. Apr.
21, 1907.
MH
    1907   Apr. 21.

Blumenau

CORREIO DA MATA ANTIGO DER UR-
WALDSBOTE. sw.
    Note: Continuation of *Der Urwalds-
    bote*, beginning Sept. 2, 1941; contin-
    ued as *Der Urwaldsbote mensageiro
    da mata*, beginning Sept. 12, 1941.
DLC
    1941   Sept. 2 – 9.

DER URWALDSBOTE. sw.
    Note: In Portuguese and German.
    Continued as *Correio da mata antigo
    der urwaldsbote*.
DLC
    1940   Apr. 26 – Oct. 4, 10 – Dec. 31.
    1941   Jan. 1 – Aug. 29.

DER URWALDSBOTE MENSAGEIRO
DA MATA. sw.
    Note: In Portuguese. Continuation of
    *Correio da mata antigo der urwalds-
    bote*, beginning Sept. 12, 1941.
DLC
    1941   Sept. 12 – 30.

Bragança

CIDADE DE BRAGANÇA. est. [1896.]
NN
    1915   Jan. 17.

Cachoeiro de Itapemirim

FOLHA DA CIDADE.
DLC
    1958   Aug. 9.

Campinas

DIARIO DO POVO. d. est. Jan. 20, 1912.
DLC
    1958   Apr. 13.

Campo Belo

FOLHA EXPEDICIONARIA. w.
CSt
    1946   Apr. 28 – Aug. 30.

Caxias do Sul

VOZ DO POVO. w.
CSt
    1946   Jan. 27, Mar. 24 – May 26.

Ceará

See Fortaleza.

Cerqueira César

A SEMANA. w.
  DLC
    1941   July 4.

Cuiabá

O ESTADO DE MATO GROSSO. d.
  DLC
    1940   Apr. 24, 28.
    1941   May 21 – 25, 27, 28.

Curitiba

DER BEOBACHTER. sw.
    Note: In German.
  DLC
    1904   Dec. 24.

O DIA. d. est. 1923.
  DLC
    1942   June 4.

ESTADO DE PARANA. d. est. 1951.
  DLC
    1967   Jan. 1+.

GAZETA DO POVO. d. est. 1919.
  DLC
    1936   Nov. 18.

Diamantina

A IDEA NOVA. w. est. 1906.
  MH
    1907   Apr. 14, 21.

Feira de Santa Anna

FOLHA DO NORTE. w.
  CSt
    1951   Jan. 6 – Sept. 15, Sept. 21 –
            Nov. 23, 25 – Dec. 29.
  Micro (N)
    1913 – 1950   Jan. 1 – Dec. 31.

Fortaleza

CORREIO DO CEARA. d. est. 1915.
  DLC
    1941   May 19, 26, 28, Dec. 5.
    1942   Jan. 9, 10.

O ESTADO. d. est. 1936.
  DLC
    1941   Apr. 17, May 24, 29.
    1942   Jan. 11.

GAZETA DE NOTICIAS. d. est. July 10,
  1927.
  DLC
    1941   Apr. 22, May 30.

O NORDESTE. d. est. 1922.
  DLC
    1941   May 19.

PEDRIOL.
  MH
    1860   Sept. 24.

O POVO. d. est. Jan. 1928.
  DLC
    1941   May 19, 30, Dec. 3, 15.
    1942   Jan. 7, 10.

UNITARIO. d. est. 1903.
  DLC
    1941   Apr. 8, 24, May 29, June 4.

França

O FRANÇANO.
  CU
    1933   Jan. 5.

Guará

A VOZ DE POVO ORGÃO DE AÇÃO
  SOCIAL.
  CSt
    1946   Apr. 15.

Igarapava

TRIBUNA DE IGARAPAVA. est. 1908.
  MWA
    1931   Jan. 4.

Ijuí

DIE SERRA – POST. sw.
    Note: In German and Portuguese.
  DLC
    1941   Aug. 5, 8, 26, 29.

João Pessoa

A UNIÃO. d. est. Feb. 2, 1893.
> Note: *A União* was the official organ
> of the state until Aug. 16, 1941 when
> the *Diario oficial* was issued as the
> second section of *A União.*
> DLC
> 1941   Aug. 16 — Sept. 4, 8, 11 — Dec.
> 31.
> 1942   Jan. 1 — 5, 11 — 16, 18 — 24, 26,
> 29 — Feb. 9, 12 — Mar. 7, 9, 12 —
> May 4, 8 — 16, 19 — July 25, 27,
> Aug. 3, 10, 13 — 22, 24, 27 —
> Sept. 2, 7, 13 — 18, 20 — Oct. 3,
> 5, 8 — 14, 16 — 22, 26 — 29, Nov.
> 2, 4 — 18, 21 — 24, 29 — Dec. 31.
> 1943   Jan. 1 — 16, 18, 22 — Feb. 2, 8 —
> 20, 22, 26 — Apr. 15, 19 — 21, 25,
> 26, May 3, 10 — 18, 24, 31, June
> 7, 12 — 21, 26 — July 2, 4, 5, 8, 9,
> 12, 19, 26, 30, Aug. 1 — 21, 23,
> 27 — 31, Sept. 6, 10, 13 — 17, 20,
> 23 — 27, 29 — Oct. 1, 4, 11, 17 —
> 20, 25, 28 — Nov. 5, 8, 15, 22, 29,
> Dec. 6, 12 — 25.
> 1944   Jan. 1 — 21, 24, 27 — May 26,
> 28 — June 29.
> 1945   Jan. 3 — 6, 13 — Feb. 23, Mar.
> 1 — 14, 16 — Apr. 7, 9 — 13, 19 —
> May 8, 16 — 24, 30 — June 4, 9 —
> July 3, 5 — Oct. 19, 25 — Nov. 11,
> 13 — Dec. 29.
> 1947   Jan. 1 — 3, 10 — 31, Feb. 7 — Mar.
> 13, 21 — Apr. 11, 19 — May 28,
> June 4 — Aug. 20, 22 — Dec. 15,
> 17 — 29, 31.
> 1948   Jan. 1 — Feb. 17, 24 — Mar. 1,
> 28, 29, 31 — June 24, 26 — Aug.
> 16, 18 — Sept. 20, 26 — 28, 30 —
> Oct. 18, 24 — 29, 31 — Nov. 29,
> Dec. 1 — 10, 16 — 31.
> 1949   Jan. 1 — 10, 12, 14, 16 — 19, 25 —
> Feb. 7, 9 — Mar. 4, 6 — June 2,
> 12 — July 25, 28 — Aug. 29, Sept.
> 2 — Nov. 26, Dec. 2 — 7, 21 — 31.
> 1950   Jan. 8 — 14.

Joinville

CORREIO DE DONA FRANCISCA. sw.
est. 1941.
> Note: Continuation of *Kolonie-Zei-*
> *tung.*
> DLC
> 1941   Sept 23 — Oct. 2, Nov. 4, 6.

KOLONIE-ZEITUNG. sw. est. 1862.
> Note: In German. Continued as *Cor-*
> *reio de Dona Francisca.*
> DLC
> 1904   Aug. 18.
> 1941   June 17 — July 17, Aug. 12 — 28.

Juiz de Fora

CORREIO DE MINAS. d. est. 1894.
> DLC
> 1942   June 21.

La Plata

EL ECO HISPANO-AMERICANO.
CLCM
> 1859   Feb. 26, 28.

Maceió

O EVOLUCIONISTA. w., d. est. Sept. 1,
1902.
> Note: Ceased publication Dec. 1906.
> DLC
> 1903   May 4 — 20, 22 — June 25, 27 —
> Oct. 8, 13 — 15, 21 — Nov. 13,
> 17 — Dec. 31.
> 1904   Jan. 1 — 4, 9 — Mar. 27, Apr. 7,
> 8, 17 — 26, 28 — May 27, 29 —
> June 10, 12 — Aug. 1.

Manaus

DIARIO DA TARDE. d.
> Note: Evening edition of *O Jornal.*
> DLC
> 1937   Mar. 25 — 27.

Maranhão

DIARIO DO MARANHÃO. d. est. Aug. 1,
1873.
MWA
    1885   July 27.

Minas

O ITAMBE. est. Dec. 15, 1901.
MH
    1901   Dec. 15.

O NORTE. est. 1907.
MH
    1907   Mar. 21, Apr. 2, 25.

Olinda

OLINDENSE. 3w. est. May 2, 1831.
    Note: Ceased publication [Apr. 21,
    1832].
DLC
    1831   Sept. 20 – 30.

Ourinhos

A VOZ DO POVO. w. est. 1927.
DLC
    1942   June 13, 20, 27.

Pará

See Belém.

Paraíba

A ORDEM. sw. est. May 19, 1894.
CU – B
    Micro (N)
    1895   [May 11 – June 23.]

Pernambuco

See Recife.

Pôrto Alegre

CORREIO DO POVO. d. est. Oct. 1, 1895.
DLC
    1941   Apr. 1, May 15.
    1944   Jan. 1 – 12, 14 – Feb. 10, 12 –

            Apr. 18, 20 – 29, May 1 – 3, 5 –
            13, 15 – June 30, Sept. 1, 2, 5 –
            9, 12 – 15, 19 – 23, 26 – Oct. 31.
    1945   July 1, 3 – Sept. 1, 3 – Oct. 31.
    1947   June 10 – Dec. 31.
    1948   Jan. 1 – Mar. 26, 28 – Dec. 31.
    1949   Jan. 1 – Apr. 27, May 4, 5, 7 –
            10, 12 – 31, July 1 – Dec. 31.
    1950   Jan. 1 – June 29, July 1 – Sept.
            20, 22 – Dec. 31.
    1951   Jan. 3 – Feb. 22, 24 – Oct. 31,
            Nov. 20 – 26, 28 – Dec. 28, 30,
            31.
    1952   Jan. 3 – 11, 13 – 30, Feb. 2 – 15,
            29 – Sept. 11, 15, 17 – Dec. 31.
    1953   Jan. 1 – Mar. 16, 18 – June 4,
            6 – Dec. 24, 27 – 31.
    1954   Jan. 1 – Mar. 15, 17 – Apr. 12,
            14 – 29, May 4 – June 8, 10 – 29,
            July 1 – Aug. 16, 18 – Sept. 20,
            22 – Oct. 11, 13 – Dec. 31.
    1955   Jan. 1 – 20, 22 – Mar. 17, 19 –
            Apr. 19, 21 – May 12, 14 – June
            15, 18 – 29, July 1 – 6, 8 – 20,
            22 – 29, 31 – Aug. 22, 28 – Sept.
            12, 14 – Dec. 5, 10 – 12, 14 – 31.
    1956   Jan. 1 – 25, 27 – Mar. 21, 23 –
            Apr. 11, 13 – 25, 27 – May 12,
            14 – 23, 29 – June 20, 22 – 29,
            July 1 – 4, 6 – 23, 27 – Oct. 18,
            22 – Nov. 1, 5 – Dec. 31.
    1957   Jan. 1 – 10, 14 – 31, Feb. 4 –
            Mar. 7, 11 – Apr. 9, 11 – 29,
            May 1 – 16, 20 – July 1, 5 – Oct.
            14, 18 – Nov. 25, 29 – Dec. 31.
    1958   Jan. 1 – 8, 10 – Feb. 3, 7 – 10,
            14 – 24, 28 – Apr. 23, 25 – June
            18, 20 – July 2, 4 – Aug. 4, 8 –
            Oct. 22, 24 – Nov. 1, 7 – 26,
            28 – Dec. 6, 8 – 31.
    1959   Jan. 1 – 5, 9 – 28, 30 – Mar. 2,
            6 – 11, 13 – Apr. 8, 10 – May 20,
            22 – June 27, 29 – July 29, 31 –
            Aug. 19, 21 – 24, 28 – 30, Sept.
            1 – 16, 18 – Oct. 9, 12 – Nov. 16,
            20 – Dec. 10, 14 – 30.
    1960   Jan. 1 – 11, 15 – Feb. 25, 29 –
            Mar. 25, 27.

FU
    1954   Jan. 1+.

DEUTSCHES VOLKSBLATT. w., sw.
    est. Mar. 10, 1871.
    Note: In German. Periodicity Apr.
    13 — Nov. 9, 1940, weekly; Nov. 13,
    1940, semiweekly; Nov. 16 — Dec. 13,
    1940, weekly; Dec. 17, 1940 — July 25,
    1941, semiweekly; July 30 — Aug. 27,
    1941, weekly.
    DLC
    1940   Apr. 13 — 26, Sept. 1 — Nov. 15,
            17 — Dec. 6, 8 — 31.
    1941   Jan. 1 — 13, 15 — Apr. 28, 30 —
            May 5, 7 — June 9, 11 — Aug. 27.

DIARIO DE NOTICIAS. d. est. Mar. 1,
    1925.
    DLC
    1941   Apr. 1, May 15.
    1944   Jan. 1 — 20, 22, 24 — Feb. 10,
            12 — Mar. 17, 19 — Apr. 29.
    1945   July 3 — Aug. 24, 26 — 31.

GAZETA DE PORTO ALEGRE. d.
    DLC
    1880   July 6.

A NAÇÃO. d. est. 1938.
    DLC
    1941   Apr. 1, May 14.

Recife

O CLARIM DA FAMA. est. 1863.
    DCU
    1863   Dec. 1 — 6.

CORREIO DA TARDE. d. est. Jan. 3,
    1876.
    CU — B
    Micro (N)
    1876   [Feb. 11 — 25.]

DIARIO DA MANHÃ. d. est. 1927.
    DLC
    1942   Feb. 26.

DIARIO DE PERNAMBUCO. d. est. Nov.
    7, 1825.
    CSt
    1925   n.d. (centenario).

CU
    1951   July 18 — Dec. 30.
    1952   Jan. 1 — Feb. 10.
CtY
    1826   Nov. 20.
    1828   May 22.
DLC
    1925   Nov. 7.
    1950   May 3, 5 — June 2, 4 — 8, 11 — 24,
            26 — July 28, 30 — Sept. 4, 6, 9 —
            14, 17 — 20, 22, 24, 25, 27, Oct.
            5, 6, 8 — 10, 15, 16, 21, 30 — Nov.
            1, 4, 10, 14, 19, 20, 28, 29.
    1951   Mar. 1 — 16, 18 — 20, 22 — 31,
            May 3 — 5, 8, 11 — 24, 26 — June
            23, 26 — 29, July 3 — Aug. 8,
            10 — Sept. 19, Dec. 1 — 4, 6, 7,
            11, 13 — 18, 20 — 31.
    1952   Jan. 1 — 13, 16, 17, 19 — 27, 31,
            Feb. 5, 8, 17, 20, 22, 26, 29 —
            Mar. 11, 14 — Apr. 13, June
            18 — 26, 28 — July 16, 19, 20,
            25 — Aug. 19.

A ESMERALDA. est. Sept. 6, 1850.
    DCU
    1850   Sept. 6.

FOLHA DO POVO. d. est. 1935.
    DLC
    1957   Jan. 16 — Mar. 1, 9 — Apr. 12,
            16, 18 — May 11, 16, 18 — 21,
            23 — 28, 30, 31, June 2, 5, 6, 8 —
            12, 14 — 20, 26, 28, July 2 — 10,
            12 — 23, 26 — Aug. 4, 7 — 9, 14 —
            30, Sept. 3 — 7, 13 — 19, 24 — 26,
            Oct. 1 — 4.

O FRADE. w. est. Mar. 13, 1876.
    Note: Ceased publication May 6, 1876.
    CU — B
    Micro (N)
    1876   Mar. 13.

O FUTURO. bw. est. June 1, 1878.
    Note: Ceased publication Sept. 1,
    1878.
    DCU
    1878   June 1 — July 1.

JORNAL DO COMMERCIO. d. est. 1919.
DLC
1953   July 1–24, Aug. 1–Sept. 17,
          Nov. 1–12, 16, 20–Dec. 31.
1954   Jan. 1–12, 14, 22–27, 29–
          Feb. 28, Mar. 4–Apr. 7, Nov.
          13–Dec. 31.
1955   Jan. 1–Dec. 31.
1956   Jan. 1–Apr. 7, 9–29, May 1–
          June 29, July 1–Dec. 30.
1957   Jan. 1–Apr. 25, June 1–29,
          July 2–Oct. 10, 12–Dec. 31.
1958   Jan. 1–Dec. 31.
1959   Jan. 1–Feb. 28.

JORNAL DO RECIFE. w., d. est. Jan. 1,
1859.
Note: Periodicity Jan. 1, 1859–Dec.
31, 1861, weekly; after Jan. 1, 1861,
daily.
DCU
1859–1860   Jan. 1–Dec. 31.
1861   Jan. 1–Dec. 28.

O LIDADOR ACADEMICO. 3m.
DCU
1861   June 10–Dec. 31.

O LIDADOR MONSTRO.
DCU
1845   [Apr. 1–Dec. 31.]
1846   [Jan. 1–Dec. 31.]
1847   [Jan. 1–Mar. 14.]

A LUCTA. irr. est. May 10, 1869.
Note: Ceased publication July 1869.
DCU
1869   May 10–July (n.d.).

O PHILEIDEMON. irr. est. June 1, 1846.
Note: Ceased publication Aug. 1,
1847.
DCU
1846   June 1–Dec. 31.
1847   Jan. 1–July 31.

O POSTILHÃO. w. est. Mar. 1, 1882.
Note: Ceased publication 1884.
DCU
1883   Jan. 2–Oct. 16.

A PROVINCIA. d. est. Sept. 6, 1872.
CU–B
Micro (N)
1874   [Aug. 4–Dec. 31.]
1875   [Jan. 1–Dec. 31.]
1876   [Jan. 1–July 10.]

O TRIBUNO. w. est. Sept. 5, 1866.
Note: Suspended publication Dec. 23,
1867–Mar. 30, 1869; ceased publication Dec. 11, 1869.
DCU
1866   Oct. 11–Dec. 17.
1867   Jan. 1–Dec. 31.
1869   Mar. 30–Dec. 11.

A UNIÃO. est. Aug. 14, 1848.
Note: Ceased publication Dec. 22,
1855.
DCU
1848   Aug. 14–Oct. 27.

A VIOLETA. est. Oct. 28, 1849.
Note: Ceased publication Mar. 16,
1850.
DCU
1850   Jan. 19–Feb. 23.

A VOZ DA VERDADE. est. Oct. 26, 1863.
Note: Ceased publication Dec. 7, 1863.
DCU
1863   Oct. 26–Nov. 24.

Rio de Janeiro

A. B. C. w.
CSt
1948   Apr. 8, 22.

ACÃO DIRETA. w.
CSt–H
1946   July 6, Sept. 20.

A ACTUALIDADE. d.
CU–B
Micro (N)
1863   Aug. 23–Dec. 22.

THE AMERICAN MAIL.
See *The British and American Mail*.

THE ANGLO-BRAZILIAN TIMES. bw.
est. 1865.
  Note: In English. Ceased publication
  1881.
  CU—B
  Micro (N)
  1865   Oct. 24.
  1874   July 7—Dec. 31.
  1875   Jan. 1—May 22, June 2—July
          23.
  MH
  1873   May 23.

ARARA PERNAMBUCANA.
  PPAmP
  1823   June—July (n.d.).

ASTREA. 3w. est. June 17, 1826.
  Note: Ceased publication Aug. 1832.
  CtY
  1827   July 19, Aug. 4, Oct. 6.
  1828   July 12, Dec. 11, 13, 16.
  DLC
  1827   Feb. 13, May 5.
  1831   Mar. 1—4, 6—Apr. 2, 26, May
          5—16, 18—31, June 7—Aug. 6,
          20—23, Sept. 29—Oct. 6, 20—
          Nov. 10.
  1832   Jan. 7—Mar. 16, 18—Apr. 19,
          28—May 9, 11—18, 20—June
          15, 17—19, 30—July 4, 6—21,
          28—Aug. 25.
  MWA
  1827   Feb. 13.
  1828   Feb. 26.
  PPAmP
  1826   June 17—July 20, 27—Dec. 31.
  1827   Jan. 1—Mar. 1, 15—Sept. 30.

ATALAIA. irr.
  PPAmP
  1823   May 31, June 7, 17, 22, 28, July
          7, 16, 23, 28, Aug. 6, 13, 18, 21,
          Sept. 2.

ATALAIA DA LIBERDADE. est. 1826.
  DLC
  1826   Feb. 15.
  PPAmP
  1826   Feb. 22, 24, 27, Mar. 1, 3, 6, 8,

10, 13, 15, 17.
  Extraordinario: Feb. 15.

AURORA FLUMINENSE. 3w. est. Dec.
21, 1827.
  Note: Ceased publication Dec. 30,
  1835.
  DLC
  1831   Mar. 2—31, Apr. 16—23, May
          16—19, 28—June 5, 7—16, 18—
          21, 25—July 14, 16—Aug. 4,
          Sept. 29—Nov. 3, 5—13, Dec.
          1—31.
  1832   Jan. 1—Apr. 17, 19—24, 26—
          May 3, 5—Aug. 28, 30—Sept.
          16, 18—Nov. 20, 27—Dec. 2,
          4—23, 25—31.
  1833   Jan. 1—15, 17—Feb. 10, 12—
          Mar. 3, 5—28, Apr. 3, 9—Aug.
          6, 8—11, 29—Sept. 26, 28—
          Nov. 28, 30—Dec. 13.
  1835   Apr. 1—7, 28—May 17, 21—26,
          28—June 16, 18—July 9, 11—
          26, 30—Aug. 4, 6—25, 29—Oct.
          11, 13—Nov. 8, Dec. 15—30.
  IU
  Micro (N)
  1827   Dec. 21, 24, 28, 31.
  1828—1830   Jan. 1—Dec. 31.

AUTORES E LIBROS.
  See *A Manhã*.

A BATALHA. d. est. 1929.
  DLC
  1940   July 27.

O BEIJA FLOR. est. Apr. 7, 1848.
  DCU
  1848   Apr. 7—Dec. 31.
  1849   Jan. 1—Dec. 31.
  1850   Jan. 1—Mar. 31, Apr. 13—Sept.
          28.

BENDEGO. est. 1889.
  DLC
  1889   May 30.

O BRASIL DE AMANHÃ.
  CSt
  1946   Mar. 1.

BRASIL-PORTUGAL. d. est. 1944.
  DLC
    1946   Apr. 2−6, 8−30, May 2−23,
            25−Sept. 26, Oct. 1−27, 29−
            Dec. 31.
    1947   Jan. 1−23, 25−May 3, 5−23,
            25−Aug. 13, 15−Dec. 24, 27−
            31.
    1948   Jan. 1−June 20, 22−July 27,
            29−Oct. 4, 6−Dec. 5.
BRAZIL DE HOJE. bw. est. Jan. 15, 1936.
  MWA
    1936   Jan. 15.
BRAZIL HERALD. d. est. Feb. 1, 1946.
    Note: In English.
  DLC
    1946   Apr. 25−Aug. 19, 21−Sept. 13,
            15−Dec. 8, 10−31.
    1947   Jan. 1−Dec. 31.
    1948   Jan. 1−July 31, Aug. 2−Dec.
            4, 6−31.
    1949   Jan. 1−Dec. 31.
    1950   Jan. 1−20, 23−Feb. 6, 8−
            15, 17−23, 25−Mar. 6, 8−24,
            27−Apr. 17, 22−30, May 3−
            July 1, 3, 6−31, Aug. 2−Sept.
            9, 11−Nov. 20, 22−Dec. 12, 18,
            21−24.
    1951   Jan. 28−Mar. 29, Apr. 1−9,
            11−May 8, 10−23, 25, June
            24−26, July 16−26, 29, 30,
            Aug. 1−10, 12−21, 23, 24,
            26−Sept. 13, 15−18, 21−24,
            27, 29, Oct. 1, 3−6, 8, 10, 24−
            Nov. 5, 8, 9, 12−14, 17−19,
            28, Dec. 2−4, 6, 7, 10−13, 15,
            23.
    1952   Jan. 1, 7−9, 25−31, Feb. 3, 4,
            6, 7, 9, 11, 14, 18−29, Mar. 2−
            19, 24−29, 31, Apr. 1, 7−10,
            13−16, 18−22, 24, 25, 27−29,
            May 2−5, 7, 12−16.
    1953   Feb. 1, 28, Nov. 8−Dec. 31.
    1954   Jan. 1−July 21, 23−Dec. 31.
    1955   Jan. 1−May 7, 9−Dec. 13,
            15−19, 21−31.
    1956   Jan. 1−Feb. 2, 4−23, 25−Apr.
            29, May 1−3, 5−22, June 8,
            11−21, 23−July 3, 5−Sept. 5,

            7−Dec. 30.
    1957   Jan. 1−June 19, 22−July 9,
            11−13, 15−Sept. 3, 5−Oct. 9,
            12−Nov. 5, 8−Dec. 11, 13−17,
            19−31.
    1958   Jan. 1−7, 9−14, 16−May 8,
            10−July 17, 20−25, 27, 28,
            Aug. 1−Sept. 26, 28−30, Oct.
            2−7, 10−25, 27−Nov. 19,
            21−27, 29−Dec. 23, 26, 27,
            29−31.
    1959   Jan. 1−15, 17−22, 24−Feb.
            14, 16−26, 28−Apr. 2, 4−13,
            15−22, 24−27, 29−May 6, 8,
            10−13, 15−June 23, 25−July
            9, 11, 12, 16−21, 23−31.
BRAZILIAN AMERICAN. w. est. 1918.
    Note: In English.
  CtY
    1921   Aug. 27.
    1926   Jan. 30, Feb. 27, Mar. 27, June
            26, Oct. 30, Dec. 25.
    1927   Jan. 29.
    1928   Mar. 17.
    1937   July 3−10, 24−Aug. 7, Sept.
            11, Dec. 18.
    1938   Jan. 29−Feb. 5, 19−26, Mar.
            12, 26−Apr. 16, 30, May 21−
            July 30.
LE BRESIL. w. est. 1863.
    Note: In French.
  CU−B
    Micro (N)
    1863   ₁Feb. 25−May 24₁.
LE BRESIL REPUBLICAIN. sw. est.
  1890.
    Note: In French. Ceased publication
    1898.
  CU−B
    Micro (N)
    1893   Oct. 11, 25.
THE BRITISH AND AMERICAN MAIL.
  bw. est. 1873.
    Note: In English. Title *The American
    Mail*, 1873; *South American Mail*,
    1874−1877; *The British and Ameri-
    can Mail*, Aug. 17, 1877−Jan. 8, 1879.
    Ceased publication Jan. 8, 1879.

NHi
1874   Jan. 26.
CAMPEÃO LUSITANO. irr. est. Jan. 2,
1883.
DLC
1883   Dec. 22 – 31.
1884   Jan. 1 – Mar. 31, May 1 – Dec.
13.
O CARAPUCEIRO. est. 1835.
DCU
1836   Jan. 3 – Aug. 29.
A CLASSE OPERARIA. w.
CSt
1946   Mar. 9 – Aug. 3, 17 – Sept. 21,
Oct. 5 – Nov. 2, 16, 23, Dec. 7,
21 – 28.
1947   Jan. 18 – Feb. 8, Mar. 15, 26,
Apr. 25.
1948   Apr. 30 – May 31, June 28, July
12 – Oct. 2, 16 – 23, Nov. 6.
1949   Jan. 22, Feb. 5.
CONSTITUCIONAL BRASILEIRO. sw.
est. Aug. 14, 1826.
PPAmP
1826   Aug. 14 – Oct. 23, Nov. 2 – 9.

CORREIO DA MANHÃ. d. est. June 15,
1901.
CLU
1959   Oct. 3 – Dec. 31. (Saturday
only).
1960   Jan. 1+. (Saturday only).
CSt
1942   Jan. 28.
1949   Jan. 30.
DLC
1941   Apr. 16, 18, 19, 21 – 24, 26, 28,
29, May 1, 3, 5, 6, 8, 9, 12, 13,
15 – 17, 19 – 21, 23, 25 – 27,
June 1 – Sept. 13, 21 – Nov. 15,
17, 18, 23 – Dec. 31.
1942   Jan. 1 – 7, 9 – Feb. 7, 15 – Mar.
5, 8, 12 – Apr. 12, 16, 19, 23, 26,
30, May 3 – June 3, 5 – 8, 10 –
14, 16 – Oct. 21, 23 – 27, 29 –
Dec. 31.
1943   Jan. 1 – May 30, Dec. 1 – 31.

1944   Jan. 1 – Aug. 9, 11 – 31.
1946   Jan. 1 – Feb. 6, 8 – Mar. 9, 11 –
June 27, 29 – Sept. 9, 11 – Oct.
21, 23, 24, 26 – Nov. 9, 11 – 29,
Dec. 1 – 31.
1950   Apr. 1 – 30, May 3, 4, 6 – 19,
21 – June 21, 23 – July 3, 6 – 28,
30 – Aug. 3, 5, 7 – 10, 12 – 14,
17 – Sept. 27, 29 – Nov. 24,
26 – Dec. 12, 14 – 31.
1951   Jan. 3 – Mar. 30, Apr. 1 – Oct.
18, 20 – Dec. 31.
1952   Jan. 1 – Mar. 15, 17, 19, 20, 25,
26, Apr. 4 – 7, 18 – 21, 23, 30 –
May 2, 6, 9, 20, 21, 23, 27 –
June 6, 9 – 18, 20 – Aug. 29,
31 – Sept. 11, 13 – 26, 29 – Oct.
30, Nov. 1 – 18, 22 – 25, 27 –
Dec. 31.
1953   Jan. 1 – 17, 19 – 24, 26 – Mar.
13, 15, 16, 18 – Apr. 9, 11 –
June 22, 24 – Aug. 31, Sept. 3 –
10, 12 – Oct. 29, 31 – Nov. 5,
7 – Dec. 1, 3 – 11, 13 – 25, 28 –
31.
1954 – 1955   Jan. 1 – Dec. 31.
1956   Jan. 1 – May 28, 30 – Oct. 1,
3 – Dec. 31.
1957   Jan. 1 – Mar. 11, 13 – Sept. 21,
23 – Nov. 7, 9 – Dec. 31.
1958   Jan. 1 – Sept. 2, 4 – 19, 21 –
Dec. 31.
1959   Jan. 1 – Dec. 31.
1960   Jan. 1 – May 27, 29 – June 9,
13 – Dec. 31.
1961   Jan. 1 – Mar. 23, 25 – Aug. 28,
31 – Dec. 31.
Micro (N) & (P)
1962   Jan. 1 – Feb. 24, 26, 28 – Apr.
14, 16, 18 – Dec. 31.
1963   Jan. 1+.

FU
1965   Jan. 1 – Aug. 10.
Micro (N)
1962   June 27 – Dec. 31.
1963   Jan. 1 – Dec. 31.
1964   Jan. 1 – Nov. 30.

ICRL
  1943   Sept. 29—Dec. 31.
  1944   Jan. 1—Oct. 4, Dec. 22—31.
  1945—1960   Jan. 1—Dec. 31.
InU
  1966   Jan. 1+.
LU
  1946   Sept. 19, 28, Oct. 4—8, 15—20,
            27—31, Nov. 2—25, 27—30,
            Dec. 7—11, 13, 22—29.
  1947   Jan. 2—4, Feb. 9—15, Mar. 2,
            9, 16, Apr. 6, 10—13, 15—30,
            May 1—31, June 1, 3—8, 10—
            14, 16—20, 22, 24—29, July 1—
            6, 8—13, 16—20, 22—27, 29—
            31, Aug. 1—3, 5—9, 11—31.
NN
  1944   July 13—Aug. 3, Sept. 1—Dec.
            31.
NNC
  1966   Jan. 2, 4—8, 11, 12, Feb. 3—5,
            9, 13.
NSyU
  1961   Dec. 6—31.
  1962   Jan. 1+.
NjP
  Micro (P)
  1962   Jan. 1+.
TxU
  1920   Jan. 26—Apr. 23, 25—Aug. 19.
  1921   Mar. 14—May 1, 3—June 22,
            24—Aug. 1, 3—Oct. 2, 4—21,
            31—Dec. 31.
  1922   Jan. 1—Feb. 28, Mar. 2—Apr.
            30, May 2—June 8, 10—Aug.
            27, 29—Sept. 6, 8—Dec. 31.
  1923   Jan. 2—4, 6—24.
  1948   May 9—Nov. 13, 15, 17, 21—
            Dec. 31.
  1949   Jan. 1—May 20, Nov. 25—Dec.
            31.
  1950—1952   Jan. 1—Dec. 31.
CORREIO DA NOITE. d. est. 1935.
  DLC
  1940   July 27.
CORREIO DO BRASIL. w.
  DLC
  1940   Nov. 7.

CORREIO DO RIO DE JANEIRO. d. est.
  Apr. 10, 1822.
    Note: Ceased publication 1823.
  PPAmP
  1822   Oct. 1—15, 17, 18.
            Extraordinario: Oct. 17.
  1823   Aug. 1—Nov. 24.
            Extraordinario: May 24—July
            31, Aug. 30.
CORREIO ESTUDANTIL.
  CSt
  1946   May 7.
CORREIO MERCANTIL. est. 1848.
    Note: Ceased publication 1868.
  CU—B
  Micro (N)
  1858   Jan. 17.
CORREIO PORTUGUES. d.
  DLC
  1942   July 12.
COURRIER DU BRESIL: FEUILLE
POLITIQUE, COMMERCIALE ET
LITTERAIRE. sw. est. 1828.
    Note: In French.
  MWA
  1829   July 4.
COURRIER DU BRESIL. w. est. Oct. 7,
1854.
    Note: In French. Ceased publication
    1862.
  CU—B
  Micro (N)
  1854   Oct. 7—Dec. 31.
  1855—1856   Jan. 1—Dec. 31.
  1857   Jan. 1—Sept. 26, 28—Dec. 31.
  1858—1861   Jan. 1—Dec. 31.
  1862   Jan. 1—Oct. 19.
O DESPERTADOR COMMERCIAL E
POLITICO. est. 1838.
    Note: Ceased publication 1841.
  DLC
  1841   Apr. 8.
DESPERTADOR CONSTITUCIONAL w.
est. 1824.
  PPAmP
  1824   June 26—July 24.

1825   Extraordinario: Feb. 1, 25.
1826   Extraordinario: Jan. 7, 25, Aug.
        17, 29.
1827   Extraordinario: May 12.

DEUTSCHE RIO-ZEITUNG. DIARIO
ALEMÃO DO RIO. d.
    Note: In Portuguese and German.
    DLC
    1941   July 20 – 26, Sept. 7 – 13, 21 –
            27.

O DIA. d. est. 1889.
    Note: Ceased publication 1890.
    CU – B
        Micro (N)
        1889   Nov. 16.
    DLC
        1889   June 11.

DIARIO ALEMÃO DO RIO.
    See *Deutsche Rio-Zeitung. Diario
    alemão do Rio.*

DIARIO CARIOCA. d. est. July 17, 1928.
    DLC
    1941   Apr. 19, 29, May 3, 6, 7, 11, 13,
            17, 20, 27 – June 1, 6, 7, 10, 14,
            17, 19, 27, July 1, 5, 6, 10, 12,
            15 – 17, 24, 26, 31, Aug. 1, 5, 6,
            8, 14, 19 – 22, 26 – 29, Nov. 15.
    1942   Dec. 6.
    1944   Jan. 1 – Apr. 16, 18 – July 15,
            17 – Dec. 22, 24 – 31.
    1945   Jan. 1 – Dec. 31.
    1946   Jan. 1 – May 23, 25 – June 10,
            12 – Nov. 25, 27 – Dec. 31.
    1947   Jan. 1 – Apr. 12, 14 – May 17,
            19 – 22, 24 – July 15, 17 – Aug.
            14, 16 – Dec. 31.
    1948   Jan. 1 – Feb. 10, 12 – Apr. 1,
            3 – Nov. 18, 20 – 26, 28 – Dec.
            31.
    1949   Jan. 1 – 5, 7 – 27, 29 – Feb. 14,
            21 – Mar. 28, 30 – Nov. 27.
    1950   Jan. 1 – Apr. 14, 16 – May 30,
            June 1 – Sept. 19, 21 – Oct. 24,
            26 – Nov. 8, 10 – Dec. 31.
    1951   Jan. 1 – Mar. 17, 19 – Apr. 17,
            19 – May 24, 26 – July 6, 8 –

        Aug. 10, 12 – Oct. 24, 26 – Dec.
        31.
    1952   Jan. 1 – Sept. 18, 20 – Oct. 24,
            26 – Dec. 31.
    1953   Jan. 1 – Sept. 15, 17 – Dec. 31.
    1954   Jan. 1 – May 24, 26 – Dec. 31.
    1955   Jan. 1 – Dec. 31.
    1956   Jan. 1 – Mar. 30, Apr. 1 – May
            8, 10 – June 6, 10 – Sept. 30,
            Oct. 2 – Dec. 30.
    1957   Jan. 1 – 12, Feb. 8 – 27, Mar.
            2 – 31, Apr. 2 – 16, 18 – May 7,
            11 – June 24, 26 – Sept 29, Oct.
            1 – 16, 18 – Dec. 12, 15 – 31.
    1958   Jan. 4 – 31, Feb. 2 – 7, 9 – May
            27, 29 – June 4, 6 – 21, 24 –
            Sept. 4, 6 – 10, 18 – 28, Oct. 1 –
            8, 10, 11, 14 – 16, 18 – Nov. 3, 5,
            6, 8 – 17, 19 – 21, 23 – Dec. 9,
            11 – 20, 23 – 27, 30, 31.
    1959   Jan. 1, 4 – 7, 9 – 13, 15 – 18,
            20 – Feb. 12, 14 – Mar. 13, 15 –
            26, 29 – Apr. 11, 14 – May 16,
            19 – 22, 26 – 28, 30 – July 15,
            17 – 29, 31, Aug. 1, 4 – Sept.
            21, 23 – 30.

DIARIO DA NOITE. d. est. 1929.
    DLC
    1942   Aug. 10.

DIARIO DE NOTICIAS. d. est. Aug. 2,
1870.
    Note: Ceased publication 1872.
    DLC
    1870   Nov. 27 – Dec. 1, 3, 6, 7.

DIARIO DE NOTICIAS. d. est. 1885.
    Note: In Spanish. Ceased publication
    1895.
    CU – B
        Micro (N)
        1889   Nov. 16.
    DLC
        1885   Sept. 7.
    MWA
        1887   Jan. 19.

DIARIO DE NOTICIAS. d. est. 1930.
    CLU
    1959   Sept. 1 – Dec. 31.

1960 – 1962   Jan. 1 – Dec. 31.
1963   Jan. 1 – May 31.
DLC
1938   July 5.
1941   May 9, June 24, July 10, 11,
Sept. 21, 28, Oct. 5, 12, 19, 26,
Nov. 2, 9, 16, 19, 23, 30, Dec. 7,
14, 21, 28.
1942   Jan. 4, 11, 18, 25, Feb. 1, 8, 15,
22, Mar. 1, 8, 15, 22, 29, Apr. 5,
12, 19, 26, May 3, 10, 17, 24, 31,
June 7, 14, 21, 28, July 5, 12, 19,
26, Aug. 2, 9, 16, 30, Sept. 6, 13,
20, 27, Oct. 4, 11, 18, 25, Nov. 1,
8, 15, 22, Dec. 6, 13, 27.
1943   Jan. 10, 24, Mar. 21, 28, May 9,
16, Aug. 8, 29, Sept. 5, 12, 19,
26, Oct. 3, 10, 17, 24 – 31, Nov.
7, 14, 21, 28, Dec. 5, 12, 19, 25.
1944   Jan. 1 – June 10, 12 – 25, Nov.
5, 6, 12 – Dec. 31.
1945   Jan. 1 – Feb. 28, July 1 – 11,
13 – 25, 27 – Oct. 18, 20 – 31.
1947   Jan. 1 – 30, Feb. 1 – 10, 14 – 28.
1951   Nov. 1 – 9, 11 – 19.
1952   Dec. 9, 14 – 24, 27 – 31.
1953   Jan. 1 – 16, 18 – Feb. 10, Mar.
4, 6, 31 – Apr. 2, 5 – June 10,
12 – 17, 20 – 23, 25, 30 – July 2,
17 – Aug. 30, Sept. 3 – Oct. 14,
16 – 22, 28 – Nov. 18, 24 – Dec.
31.
1954   Jan. 1 – 28, 31 – Feb. 3, 7 – 9,
13 – 24, 27 – Oct. 31, Nov. 2 –
Dec. 31.
1955   Jan. 1 – Sept. 30, Oct. 12 – 30,
Nov. 1 – Dec. 27, 29 – 31.
1956   Jan. 1 – July 5, 7 – Oct. 8, 10,
11, 16 – 20, 31 – Nov. 6, 13 – 23.
1957   Jan. 1 – Sept. 12, 18 – Dec. 18,
24 – 31.

DIARIO DE RIO DE JANEIRO. d. est.
June 1, 1821.
Note: In Spanish. Suspended publication 1859 – Mar. 25, 1860; ceased publication Oct. 31, 1878.
CU – B
Micro (N)

1825   May 18 – June 30.
PPAmP
1822   Sept. 24, 30, Oct. 11, Nov. 5.
1823   July 1 – 24, 26, 28 – Aug. 14, 16,
18 – Dec. 24, 27, 29 – 31.
1824   Jan. 2, 3, 5, 7 – 17, 19, 21 – 31,
Feb. 3 – Mar. 18, 20, 22 – 24,
26 – Apr. 15, 17 – May 26, 28 –
June 16, 18 – 23, 26, 28, 30 –
Sept. 7, 9 – Oct. 30, Nov. 2 –
Dec. 7, 9 – 24, 27 – 31.
1825   Jan. 3 – 5, 7 – 19, 21 – Feb. 1,
3 – Mar. 18, 22 – 24, 26, 28 –
May 11, 13 – June 1, 3 – 9, 11,
15 – 23, 25 – 28, 30 – Aug. 21,
23 – Sept. 3, 5 – 7, 9 – Oct. 25,
27 – 31, Nov. 2 – Dec. 2, 5 – 7,
9 – 16, 19 – 31.
1826   Jan. 1 – 16, 18, 21 – Feb. 1, 3 –
Mar. 23, 25 – May 3, 5 – 24,
26 – June 1, 3 – 12, 14 – 23,
26 – 28, 30 – July 17, 19 – 24,
26 – Aug. 14, 16 – Sept. 7, 9 –
Dec. 7, 9 – 31.
1827   Jan. 2 – 5, 8 – 15, 17 – 19, 22 –
Feb. 1, 3 – Apr. 12, 14.

DIARIO DO COMMERCIO. d. est. 1888.
Note: Ceased publication 1892.
CU – B
Micro (N)
1889   Nov. 16.

DIARIO DO GOVERNO.
See *Diario fluminense.*

DIARIO DOS ESTADOS.
CSt
1946   July 7.

DIARIO FLUMINENSE. 3w., sw., d. est.
Sept. 10, 1808.
Note: Title *Gaceta do Rio de Janeiro*,
Sept. 10, 1808 – 1822; *Gaceta do Rio*,
1822 – Jan. 2, 1823; *Diario do govêrno*,
Jan. 2, 1823 – May 20, 1824; *Diario
fluminense*, May 21, 1824 – Apr. 25,
1831.
PPAmP
1821   Feb. 28.

1822   Jan. 1 – Apr. 30, May 4 – 9,
16 – Sept. 3, 7 – Oct. 3, 8, 12 –
Dec. 31.

1823 – 1826   Jan. 1 – Dec. 31.

1827   Jan. 2 – Apr. 14, 20, May 4, 10,
15 – 17, 21, 22, May 30 – Sept.
19, Nov. 17.

DIARIO MERCANTIL. d. est. Nov. 3, 1824.

Note: Title *Diario mercantil do Rio de Janeiro*, Nov. 3, 1824 – Apr. 30, 1827; *Diario mercantil*, Apr. 30 – Oct. 31, 1827. Ceased publication Oct. 31, 1827.

CtY

1827   Jan. 2 – June 30, July 2 – Oct. 31.

DIRETRIZES. d. est. 1938.

CSt

1946   May 24, 29.

DLC

1945   May 29 – Dec. 31.

1946   Jan. 1 – Mar. 27, 30 – June 28,
July 1 – Aug. 30, Sept. 1 – 17,
19 – Nov. 8, 10 – Dec. 12, 14 – 31.

1947   Jan. 1 – 11, 13 – Feb. 2, 4 – Dec. 31.

1948   Jan. 1 – Nov. 12, 16 – 23, 25 – Dec. 31.

1949   Jan. 1 – Dec. 19, 21 – 31.

1950   Jan. 1 – 14, 16 – 31, Feb. 2 – 17,
28, Mar. 2 – 7, 13 – 20, 22 – Apr. 5.

DOM CASMURRO. w.

CLU

Micro (P)

1940   [Jan. 27 – Dec. 31].

1941 – 1943   Jan. 1 – Dec. 31.

1944   [Jan. 1 – Dec. 9].

ICRL

1937   [June 3 – Dec. 31].

1938 – 1945   [Jan. 1 – Dec. 31].

1946   [Jan. 1 – Oct. 26].

L'ECHO DE L'AMERIQUE DU SUD. sw. est. 1827.

Note: In French. Ceased publication 1828.

MWA

1828   Feb. 23.

PPAmP

1827   Aug. 1 – 8.

A EMANCIPACÃO. est. Feb. 2, 1879.

DCU

1879   Feb. 2 – Dec. 31.

1880   Jan. 1 – 23.

O ESPELHO. sw. est. 1821.

Note: Ceased publication 1823.

PPAmP

1822   Oct. 15.

1823   Mar. 14, May 6.

A ESTRELLA BRASILEIRA. 3w. est. 1823.

Note: Ceased publication 1824.

CU – B

Micro (N)

1824   [July 9 – 30.]

DLC

1824   Jan. 26, Feb. 4, 20 – 25.

PPAmP

1823 – 1824   Jan. 1 – Dec. 31.

FOLHA ACADEMICA.

CU

1929   June 6.

FOLHA DA SEMANA. w.

CSt – H

1965   Sept. 2 – Dec. 31.

1966   Jan. 1+.

FOLHA DO POVO. d.

CSt

1946   Mar. 21 – May 28, Aug. 20 – Dec. 31.

1947   Mar. 28.

1948   Oct. 18, 19, 26, 27, Nov. 1, 2, 4, 5, 8, 11, 12.

GACETA DO RIO.

See *Diario fluminense*.

GACETA DO RIO DE JANEIRO.

See *Diario fluminense*.

GACETA EXTRAORDINARIA DO RIO
DE JANEIRO.
   Note: See also *Diario fluminense*.
   CU – B
   Micro (N)
   1821   May 21.

GAZETA DE NOTICIAS. w., d. est. 1875.
   DLC
   1880   June 10.
   1940   July 30.
   1941   Dec. 6.
   MWA
   1891   Apr. 19.
   TxU
   1920   Apr. 1 – Aug. 2, 4 – Sept. 10,
           12, 13, 15 – 21 – Nov. 18, 20 –
           Dec. 27.
   1921   Jan. 6 – Dec. 31.

O GLOBO. d. est. 1925.
   CSt
   1946   May 24.
   CU
   1940   June 29.
   DLC
   1942   Sept. 9.
   Micro (P) & (N)
   1962   Jan. 1+.

O GRITO DA RAZÃO NA CORTE DO
RIO JANEIRO. sw. est. 1825.
   PPAmP
   1825   Feb. 23 – Mar. 22, 29, Apr. 8 –
           26.

O GUARANY. est. Aug. 8, 1853.
   DCU
   1853   Aug. 8 – Sept. 8.

O IMPARCIAL. d. est. 1934.
   DLC
   1941   May 31.

IMPRENSA POPULAR. d. est. 1947.
   Note: Suspended publication Aug. 3,
   1958.
   DLC
   1953   Jan. 3 – 30, Feb. 2 – Mar. 14,
           16 – Apr. 9, 11 – June 17, 19 –
           Aug. 5, 7, 10, 12 – Nov. 2, 4 –
           Dec. 31.

1954   Jan. 1 – 20, 22 – June 12, 14 –
        Sept. 5, 7 – Dec. 31.
1955   Jan. 1 – Feb. 2, 9, Mar. 30 –
        Apr. 27, May 12, 28, 29, 31 –
        June 3, 15 – 18, 21 – 23, 29, 30,
        July 2 – 5, 8, 16 – 22, 30, 31,
        Aug. 2 – 12, 14 – 20, Sept. 1 – 7
        15, 17 – 30, Oct. 4, 5, 8 – Nov.
        13, 15 – Dec. 31.
1956   Jan. 1 – Mar. 22, 24 – Nov. 21,
        23 – Dec. 30.
1957   Jan. 1 – 31, Feb. 2 – 5, 7 – Dec.
        31.
1958   Jan. 1 – Aug. 3.

O INDEPENDENTE. est. 1821.
   DCU
   1821 – 1822   Jan. 1 – Dec. 31.
   1831   May 3 – Dec. 31.
   1832   Jan. 1 – Dec. 31.
   1833   Jan. 1 – Apr. 22.

A INFORMACÃO. d.
   CSt
   1946   Aug. 17.

O JORNAL. w., d. est. 1919.
   CLU
   1959   Oct. 1 – Dec. 31.
   1960   Jan. 1 – Dec. 31.
   1961   Jan. 1 – Sept. 30.
   DLC
   1928   Nov. 1 – Dec. 17, 19 – 30.
   1929   Jan. 1 – 13, 15 – Mar. 16, 18 –
           Sept. 12, 20 – Oct. 21, 23 – Dec
           30.
   1930   Jan. 1, 3 – 10, 12 – Feb. 25,
           Mar. 3 – 10, 15 – Aug. 19, 21 –
           23, 25 – 29.
   1941   Apr. 17 – 26, 28 – May 9, 11 –
           13, 15 – 17, 19, 20, 23 – 26, 28,
           30, 31, June 2, 6, 9 – 17, 19, 21,
           23, 25 – 29, July 2, 5, 7 – 11,
           14 – 19, 21 – 25, 28, 29, Aug. 4,
           5, 7, 11, 14, 18, 20, 22, 23, 25 –
           30.
   1942   Jan. 11, 18, 21, 25, Feb. 22, 25,
           Mar. 1, 4, 8, 15, 22, 25, 26, 29,
           Apr. 8, 12, 15, 19, 22, 26, May 3,
           6, 13, 17, 20, 24, June 3, 7, 10,

14, 17, 21, 24, 28, July 5, 8, 12,
15, 19, 22, 26, 29, Aug. 2, 5, 9,
12, 16, 19, 23, 30, Sept. 2, 6, 9,
13, 16, 27, Oct. 4, 7, 11, 14, 18,
21, 28, Nov. 1, 4, 8, 11, 15, 18,
22, 25, 29, Dec. 2, 6, 9, 13, 16,
20, 23, 27, 30.
- 1943   Nov. 16.

MH
- 1924   Oct. 26.
- 1953   Jan. 1 – Feb. 15, 19 – Apr. 21,
23 – 30, May 3 – June 3, 11 –
Dec. 31.
- 1954   Jan. 1 – Feb. 28, Mar. 4 – Dec.
31.
- 1955 – 1957   Jan. 1 – Dec. 31.
- 1958   Jan. 1 – Mar. 13.
- 1964   Feb. 27 – Dec. 31.
- 1965   Jan. 1 – Feb. 13, 18 – 22, 25 –
27.

NN
Micro (P) & (N)
- 1943   [Oct. 1 – Dec. 31.]
- 1951   [Mar. 1 – Dec. 31.]
- 1952 – 1957   [Jan. 1 – Dec. 31.]
- 1958   [Jan. 1 – Feb. 28.]

JORNAL DO BRASIL. d. est. Apr. 9, 1891.
CSt – H
- 1966   June 1.

DLC
- 1908   Sept. 2 – 14, 16 – Oct. 27, 29 –
Dec. 31.
- 1909   Sept. 15 – Oct. 8, 10 – 15, 17 –
Dec. 16, 18 – 31.
- 1910   Jan. 1 – Mar. 18.
- 1940   July 2, Aug. 6.
- 1941   Apr. 29, 30, May 7, 15, 28, June
28, July 5, 30, Aug. 12.
- 1954   June 13 – Sept. 6, 11, 14 – 23,
25 – Dec. 31.
- 1955   Jan. 1 – Mar. 28, 30 – June 18,
25, 28 – Sept. 12, 17, 20 – Dec.
31.
- 1956   Jan. 1 – Feb. 13, 16 – Oct. 31.

DPU
Current (six months).
Micro (P)
- 1938   July 1 – Dec. 31.

- 1939 – 1943   Jan. 1 – Dec. 31.

FU
Micro (N)
- 1965   July 1 – 12, 14 – 24, 27 – Aug. 2,
5 – Dec. 31.
- 1966   Jan. 1+.

ICRL
- 1945 – 1947   Jan. 1 – Dec. 31.
Micro (N)
- 1938 – 1943   Jan. 1 – Dec. 31.

MH
- 1910   Nov. 6 – Dec. 17.
- 1964   Feb. 27 – May 11, June 23, 26 –
Dec. 8, 27.
- 1965   Jan. 21, Feb. 5, 14, 15, 17, 23,
24, 28, Mar. 4 – 7, 10 – 30, Apr.
3, 14 – 16, 19, 29, May 3 – 18,
Aug. 17 – 23.

NN
- 1939   Nov. 24, 25.
- 1940   Mar. 16 – 27, May 25 – June 30.

NNC
- 1965   May 15, 16, 23, 25, 26, June 1 –
6, 8, 9, 12, 13, 16 – 20, 22 – 24,
26, 27, 29, 30, July 1 – 4, 6 – 11,
13 – 18, 20 – 24, 27 – 31, Aug. 1,
5 – 8, 10 – 15, 17 – 22, 24 – 29,
31 – Sept. 5, 7 – 12, 14 – 19,
21 – 26, 28 – Oct. 3, 5 – 10, 12 –
17, 19 – 24, 26 – 31, Nov. 5 – 7,
9 – 11, 13, 14, 16 – 18, 23 – 28,
30, Dec. 2 – 5, 7, 8, 10 – 12, 14 –
19, 22 – 25, 31.
- 1966   Jan. 2, 15, 16, 18 – 23, 25 – 30,
Feb. 1 – 3, 5, 6, 10+.

OrU
- 1964   Sept. 1 – 25, 29 – Nov. 2, 4 –
Dec. 25, 27 – 31.
- 1965   Jan. 1+.

ViU
- 1965   Jan. 1+ .

JORNAL DOS DEBATES. sw. est. May 3,
1837.
DLC
- 1837   May 3 – 20.

LETRAS E ARTES. w.
CSt
- 1948   Oct. 10.

1949   Feb. 13—20, Mar. 3, 20, May
        15.

LIBERTACÃO.
  CSt
    1947   Apr. 14, May 25.

LIGA.
  NjP
    Micro (N)
    1962   Oct. 9—Dec. 31.
    1963   Jan. 1—Dec. 31.
    1964   Jan. 1—Feb. 19.

LUTA.
  CSt
    1946   Oct. 29.

MALAGUETA EXTRAORDINARIA. irr.
  est. Dec. 1821.
    Note: Title *A Malagueta*, Dec. 1821—
    July 31, 1822; *Malagueta extraordi-
    naria*, July 31, 1822—1832. Ceased
    publication 1832.
  ICN
    1821   Dec. (two issues).
    1822—1823   Jan. 1—Dec. 31.
    1824   Jan. 1—July 10.
  PPAmP
    1823   June 5.
    1824   May 28—July 10.

A MANHÃ. w., bw., m. est. Aug. 10, 1941.
    Note: Periodicity Aug. 10, 1941—Mar.
    11, 1945, weekly; June 6, 1948—Apr.
    1, 1949, biweekly; May 1949—Dec.
    1950, monthly. Published biweekly
    literary supplement *Autores & libros*.
  CSt
    1946   Sept. 1, Oct. 10.
    Autores & libros:
    1948   Sept. 26.
    1949   Feb. 1—Mar. 15.
  CU
    1941   Aug. 10, 31, Sept. 14—Dec. 28.
    1942   Jan. 1—Dec. 31.
    1943   Jan. 3—Feb. 21, Mar. 14—Apr.
            11, May 5—23, June 6—Dec.
            12.
    1944   Jan. 1, 16—May 7, 21—June 4,

        25, July 9—Sept. 17, Oct. 8—
        15, Nov. 5—Dec. 19.
    1945   Jan. 14—21, Feb. 18, Mar. 11.
    1948   June 6—Dec. 25.
    1949   Jan. 1—Dec.
    1950   Jan.—Dec.
  DLC
    1942   Sept. 6—Dec. 19, 21—27.
    1945   July 1—Oct. 31, Nov. 2—Dec.
            17, 19—Dec. 31.
    1946   Jan. 1—Apr. 17, 19, 21—June
            30, July 2—Aug. 10, 12—23,
            25—30, Sept. 1—12, 14—Oct.
            18, 20, 21, 23, 24, 26—Nov. 8,
            10—12, 14—19, 21—27, 29—
            Dec. 12, 14—31.
    1947   Jan. 3—6, 8—17, 19—25, 27—
            Feb. 14, 16—Mar. 11, 13—May
            2, 4—7, 10—Aug. 29, 31—Oct.
            7, 9—14, 16—22, 24—Dec. 10,
            13—31.
    1948   Apr. 1—28, June 1—30.
    1949   Sept. 24—Oct. 17, 21—28.
    1950   Mar. 1—May 1, 3—June 21,
            23—Dec. 31.
    1951   Jan. 1, 3—Mar. 30, Apr. 1—30,
            May 7, 9—Oct. 13, 15—18, 20—
            Nov. 15, 18—Dec. 30.

MEIO-DIA. d.
  DLC
    1940   July 26.

O MERCURIO. est. Oct. 25, 1823.
  PPAmP
    1823   Oct. 25—27.

O MOSQUITO. est. Sept. 19, 1869.
    Note: Ceased publication May 26,
    1877.
  DCU
    1873   Jan. 4—Dec. 31.
    1874   Jan. 1—Dec. 31.
    1875   Jan. 1—Dec. 18.

O MUNDO. d. est. 1947.
  DLC
    1953   Jan. 2, 4—6, 8, 9, 11—28, 30—
            Feb. 13, 15, 19, 22—Mar. 5, 7—
            9, 11—May 1, 3—24, 26—June
            10, 12—July 6, 8—Aug. 31.

THE NEWS. d. est. Sept. 19, 1939.
  Note: In English.
  DLC
    1939   Sept. 19.

A NOITE. d. est. 1911.
  Note: Ceased publication Dec. 27,
  1957.
  DLC
    1940   Jan. 2—Feb. 26, 28—Apr. 19,
            21—May 27, 29—Dec. 31.
    1941   Jan. 1—Apr. 2, 4—May 29,
            31—Sept. 28, 30—Dec. 31.
    1942   Jan. 1—Dec. 31.
    1943   Jan. 1—9, 11—Oct. 19, 28—
            Dec. 31.
    1944   Jan. 1—Oct. 27, Nov. 1—Dec.
            31.
    1945   Jan. 1—Apr. 18, 22, 24—28,
            30—May 10, 12—Nov. 26, 28—
            Dec. 31.
    1946   Jan. 1—May 1, 3—Dec. 29.
    1947   Jan. 2—Apr. 15, 17—Dec. 31.
    1948—1951   Jan. 1—Dec. 31.
    1952   Jan. 1—Feb. 19, 21—Mar. 2, 4,
            6—Dec. 31.
    1953   Jan. 1—Dec. 31.
    1954   Jan. 1—5, 10—Sept. 6, 8—Dec.
            31.
    1955   Jan. 1—July 11, 16—Dec. 31.
    1956   Jan. 1—Dec. 31.
    1957   Jan. 1—Mar. 3, 7—May 4, 6—
            25, 27—June 8, 11—Dec. 27.
  ICRL
    1944   Nov. 1—Dec. 31.
    1945   Jan. 1—Dec. 31.
    1946   Apr. 1—Aug. 31, Oct. 1—Dec.
            31.
    1947—1954   Jan. 1—Dec. 31.
    1955   Jan. 1—Feb. 28.
  TxU
    1936   Dec. 21—31.
    1937   Jan. 1—Apr. 30, May 3—July
            31.

NORTH AMERICA.
  Note: In English.
  MH
    1865   Supplement: Dec. 2.

LE NOUVELLISTE. sw. est. Sept. 2, 1836.
  Note: In French. Ceased publication
  1848.
  DLC
    1836   Sept. 24—Oct. 7, 9—18, 20—
            25, 27—Nov. 1, 3—25, 27—
            Dec. 5, 7—30.

NOVIDADES. est. 1887.
  Note: Ceased publication 1892.
  CU—B
    Micro (N)
    1889   Nov. 16.

NOVOS RUMOS. w. est. Feb. 28, 1959.
  Note: Ceased publication Mar. 27,
  1964.
  CLU
    Micro (P)
    1959   Feb. 28—Dec. 31.
    1960—1962   Jan. 1—Dec. 31.
    1963   Jan. 1—3.
  DLC
    1959   Feb. 28—Oct. 15, 30—Nov. 12,
            20—Dec. 3, 11—31.
    1960   Jan. 1—21, 29—Feb. 4, 26—
            June 30, July 8—Dec. 30.
    Micro (P) & (N)
    1959   Feb. 28—Dec. 31.
    1960—1963   Jan. 1—Dec. 31.
    1964   Jan. 1—Mar. 27.

ORGÃO DOS DIARIOS ASSOCIADOS.
  d.
  CSt
    1946   July 7, Aug. 11, Sept. 22.

OSTENSOR BRASILEIRO. est. 1845.
  DCU
    1845   Jan. 1—Dec. 31.
    1846   [Jan. 1—Dec. 31].

PAGINAS DE COMBATE.
  CSt
    1946   Aug. 8.
    1947   Jan. 9.

O PAIZ. d. est. Oct. 1, 1884.
  Note: Ceased publication 1930.
  CU—B
    Micro (N)

1893 [Oct. 5 — Dec. 13.]
DLC
  1929 Nov. 17 — Dec. 31.
  1930 Jan. 1 — 17, 19 — Feb. 1, 9 —
     Apr. 10, 12 — July 26, Aug. 3 —
     30, Sept. 7 — 19, 28 — Oct. 11.
ICRL
  1915 Apr. 15 — Dec. 31.
  1916 — 1920 Jan. 1 — Dec. 31.
  1921 Jan. 1 — June 17.
MH
  1908 Dec. 18.
  1909 Jan. 17, 24, 28, Feb. 5 — 10.
  1910 May 19 — 21, June 13, July 9,
     Oct. 23 — 26, Nov. 11, 12.
MWA
  1885 July 18.

O PAQUETE DE RIO, FOLHA COM-
MERCIAL, POLITICA, E LITTERA-
RIA. d. est. Jan. 1, 1836.
  Note: Ceased publication 1837.
DLC
  1836 Jan 2 — 7, 9, 13, 15, 30 — May 5,
     7 — 9, 11 — 13, 16 — 18, 20 — 24,
     26 — 29, 31 — June 5, 7 — 12, 15 —
     22, 25 — 30, July 2 — 6, 8 — 17,
     19 — 26, 28 — Aug. 11, 13 — 18,
     20 — 26, 29, 31 — Sept. 4, 6 — 14,
     16, Oct. 17 — 21, Nov. 2, 3, 9,
     14 — Dec. 27, 29 — 31.
  1837 Jan. 3 — 16.

PARA TODAS. bw., irr. est. 1920.
IU
  1957 Dec. 1 — 31.
  1958 Jan. 1 — Aug. 3.
WaU
  1956 May 10 — Dec. 31.
  1957 Jan. 1 — Dec. 31.
  1958 Jan. 1 — July 7.

O PETIZ JORNAL. d. est. Sept. 19, 1888.
DLC
  1888 Sept. 21 — 26.

POLITICA E LETRAS.
CSt
  1948 Sept. 23, Oct. 21.

PORTUGAL MODERNO. sw. est. 1899.
DLC
  1912 June 12.

O PROPUGNADOR. est. July 1824.
PPAmP
  1824 n.d. (July), July 13.

A RAZÃO. d.
MH
  1916 Dec. 19 — 29.

REGENERACÃO. est. Aug. 1840.
  Note: Succeeded *O Cronista*. Ceased
  publication 1852.
DCU
  1840 Aug. 1 — Dec. 31.
  1841 Jan. 1 — Mar. 31.

RELIGIÃO. est. June 1848.
  Note: Ceased publication 1850.
DCU
  1848 June 1 — May 31.
  1850 July 1 — Nov. 30.

A REPUBLICA. d. est. Dec. 3, 1870.
  Note: Resulted from the merger of
  Correio nacional and *Opinião liberal*.
CU — B
  Micro (N)
  1871 Nov. 8 — Dec. 31.
  1872 Jan. 1 — Nov. 6.
CtY
  1897 Oct. 22 — 31.

RESISTENCIA. d.
IEN
  1945 Nov. 1, 10 — 11, 17 — 20, 22 — 23,
     27 — Dec. 19, 28 — 29.
  1946 Jan. 1 — 8, 10, 12, 15 — Feb. 10,
     13 — 15, 17 — 20, 22 — 28, Mar.
     8 — Apr. 21, May 14 — 18, 21 —
     23, 25 — 29, June 2 — 8.

REVISTA ILUSTRADA. est. 1876.
  Note: Ceased publication 1898.
CU — B
  Micro (N)
  1889 Nov. 16.

RIO MERCANTILE JOURNAL. m. est.
1849.
  Note: In English.
DLC
  1856 July 12 — Nov. 12.

THE RIO NEWS. bw., 3m, w. est. 1874.
  Note: In English. Suspended publica-

tion Dec. 5, 1893 – Jan. 1, 1895; Sept.
24 – Dec. 3, 1901.
  CU – B
    Micro (N)
    1893   [Sept. 14 – Dec. 5].
  CtY
    1892   Aug. 9 – Dec. 27.
    1893   Jan. 3 – Nov. 28.
  DLC
    1883   Jan. 5 – Dec. 4, 6 – 31.
    1884   Jan. 1 – May 14, 16 – 23, 25 –
        Dec. 31.
    1885 – 1889   Jan. 1 – Dec. 31.
    1890   Jan. 1 – July 6, 8 – Dec. 31.
    1891   Jan. 1 – Aug. 17, 19 – Dec. 31.
    1892   Jan. 1 – Mar. 21, 23 – Dec. 31.
    1893   Jan. 1 – Dec. 5.
    1895 – 1897   Jan. 1 – Dec. 31.
    1898   Jan. 1 – Dec. 26, 28 – 31.
    1899 – 1901   Jan. 1 – Dec. 31.
  FU
    Micro (N)
    1883   Jan. 5 – Dec. 31.
    1884 – 1896   Jan. 1 – Dec. 31.
    1897   Jan. 1 – Dec. 28.
  MH
    1881   May 24.
    1883   Apr. 24 – May 15.
  NIC
    1879   Jan. 8 – Dec. 31.
    1880 – 1887   Jan. 1 – Dec. 31.
    1888   Jan. 1 – Dec. 24.
    1891   Jan. 6 – Dec. 31.
    1892   Jan. 1 – Dec. 31.
    1893   Jan. 1 – Dec. 5.
    1895 – 1899   Jan. 1 – Dec. 31.
    1900   Jan. 1 – Dec. 25.

JORNAL DO COMMERCIO. d. est. Oct.
1, 1827.
  CLU
    1940   Apr. 1 – Dec. 31.
    1941 – 1943   Jan. 1 – Dec. 31.
    1944   Jan. 1 – June 30.
    1945   Apr. 1 – Nov. 30.
    1946 – 1953   Jan. 1 – Dec. 31.
    1954   Jan. 1 – 31, Mar. 1 – 31.
    1955   Feb. 1 – Dec. 31.
    1956 – 1957   Jan. 1 – Dec. 31.

    1958   Jan. 1 – Sept. 30.
  CU
    1922   Sept. 7.
    Micro (P)
    1950 – 1955   Jan. 1 – Dec. 31.
  CU – B
    Micro (N)
    1889   Nov. 16.
  CtY
    1827   Nov. 2 – 21, 23 – Dec. 24.
    1828   Jan. 2 – 26, 28 – Apr. 16, 18 –
        21, 23 – May 13, 19 – June 10,
        12 – 14, 17 – Aug. 4, 13, 16 –
        Oct. 27, 29, 30, Nov. 3 – Dec.
        24, 29 – 31.
  DLC
    1827   Nov. 24.
    1832   Aug. 4, 24, Sept. 10, Oct. 22, 29.
    1833   Sept. 26 – Oct. 11, 13 – Dec. 13,
        15, 18 – 31.
    1834   Jan. 1 – 12, 14 – Feb. 28, Mar.
        21 – 28.
    1835   Jan. 5, 19 – 26, 30 – Feb. 12,
        Mar. 2 – 30, Apr. 1 – 4, 8 – 29,
        May 1 – 30, June 1 – 6, 9 – 12,
        15 – 27, 30 – Dec. 20, 22 – 31.
    1836   Jan. 1 – 7, 9 – Sept. 9, 11 – 14,
        16 – Dec. 31.
    1837   Jan. 1, 2, 4 – 30, Feb. 1 – 6, 8 –
        14, 16 – Mar. 6, 8 – Apr. 16,
        18 – 24, 26 – May 22, 24 – June
        21, 23 – Aug. 13, 16 – Sept. 26,
        29 – Oct. 1, 3, 5, 7, 8, 10 – 12,
        18, 20, 24, 26, 29, 30, Nov. 4 – 7,
        9 – 15, 19 – 23, 26 – 28, Dec. 1 –
        7, 10 – 13, 15 – 21, 23 – 25, 27 –
        31.
    1838   Jan. 2, 3, 5, 10 – 18, 20 – Feb.
        18, 20 – 23, 25 – 28, Mar. 2 – 7,
        9 – 15, 17 – Apr. 17, 19 – June
        26, 28 – July 19, 21 – Aug. 8,
        10 – Nov. 2, 4, 5, 8, 9, 11 – 26,
        28 – Dec. 12, 16 – 31.
    1839   Jan. 2 – 23, 29, Feb. 1 – 15, 17 –
        20, 22, Mar. 3 – 11, 17 – 25,
        Apr. 1 – 8, 10 – 19, 21 – 30, May
        16, 18, 25 – June 3, 5 – 8, 12,
        16 – 20, 22, 24 – 26, 28, July 2 –
        Aug. 16, 18 – 23, 27 – 30, Sept.

2 – 14, 16, 18 – 21, 23 – 29, Nov.
1 – 5, 8 – 18, 21, 22, 25 – 27,
29 – Dec. 3, 5, 6, 8, 10, 12, 14 –
22, 24 – 31.

1840　Jan. 3, 12 – 18, 20 – 28, 30, 31,
Feb. 6 – 22, 25, 26, Mar. 4, 6 – 8,
10 – 24, 28 – May 1, 3, 4, 6 – 13,
July 20 – 27, 30, Aug. 2 – 8, 10 –
13, 16 – 30, Sept. 1, 2, 4 – 13,
15 – 18, 20, 22, Nov. 16 – 21,
23, 24, 26 – 28, Dec. 11 – 31.

1841　Jan. 1 – Feb. 22, 24 – Mar. 5,
7 – Apr. 21, 23 – May 12, 14,
20 – 23, 25 – 27, 29 – June 19,
21 – 23, 25 – July 19, 21 – Aug.
6, 8 – 20, 22 – Sept. 2, 4 – 17,
19 – 22, 24, Oct. 29 – Nov. 6,
8 – 12, 14 – 18, 20, 21, 24, 26,
28, 29, Dec. 1 – 3, 8 – 11, 13 –
31.

1842　Jan. 1, 2, 4 – 7, 9 – 17, 19, 20,
22, 24, 26, 29 – Feb. 4, 6 – 22,
25 – Mar. 17, 22 – Apr. 12, June
1 – 4, 6, 8 – July 3, 5 – 17, 20 –
29, Aug. 2.

1932 – 1943　Jan. 1 – Dec. 31.
1944　Jan. 1 – Mar. 16, 18 – Dec. 31.
1945　Jan. 1 – Dec. 31.
1946　Jan. 1 – Mar. 20, 22 – Dec. 31.
1947 – 1948　Jan. 1 – Dec. 31.
1949　Feb. 28, Mar. 3 – June 30.

Micro　(P) & (N)
1902 – 1905　July 1 – Dec. 31.
1906　Jan. 1 – Dec. 29.
1907　Jan. 6 – Dec. 31.
1908　Jan. 1 – June 9, 11, 12, 15 – Oct.
14, 16 – Dec. 25.
1909 – 1912　Jan. 1 – Dec. 31.
1913　Jan. 1 – June 3, 5 – Dec. 31.
1914　Jan. 1 – Oct. 21, Nov. 11, 23 –
Dec. 4, 18 – 23, 30, 31.
1915　Jan. 1 – 14, 21 – Feb. 10, 12,
15 – 25, Mar. 2 – Apr. 3, 5 –
Dec. 31.
1916　Jan. 1 – June 30, July 2 – Oct.
30, Nov. 1 – Dec. 31.

Micro　(P) & (N)
1917　Jan. 1 – Dec. 17.

1918　Jan. 8 – 14, Feb. 5 – 13, 15 – 18,
23, 24, 26 – 28, Nov. 10 – Dec.
16.
1919　Jan. 9 – 20, Feb. 4 – 24, Mar.
1 – June 30.
1925　May 1 – 7, 13 – Aug. 8, 11, 13 –
23, 26, 28 – Dec. 31.
1926　Jan. 1 – Mar. 13, 15 – Apr. 16,
18 – May 10, 16 – 30, June 3 –
Aug. 11, 14, 16 – 18, 21, 23 –
Nov. 17, 20, 25 – Dec. 31.

Micro　(P)
1949　Jan. 1+.

DPU
Micro　(P)
1944 – 1955　Jan. 1 – Dec. 31.
Micro　(N)
1947　June 1 – Dec. 31.

ICRL
1899　Oct. 1 – Dec. 31.
1900 – 1902　Jan. 1 – Dec. 31.
1905 – 1906　Jan. 1 – Dec. 31.
1908　July 1 – Dec. 31.
1909 – 1912　Jan. 1 – Dec. 31.
1943　Oct. 1 – Dec. 31.
1944 – 1949　[Jan. 1 – Dec. 31.]
1950　Jan. 1 – Oct. 31.
Micro　(N)
1939 – 1940　Jan. 1 – Dec. 31.
1941　Jan. 1 – Mar. 12, 16 – Apr. 30,
May 16 – Dec. 31.
1942　Jan. 1+.

IU
Micro　(P)
1950 – 1954　Jan. 1 – Dec. 31.
1955　Jan. 1 – Aug. 31.

KHi
1909　Sept. 8.

LU
Micro　(P)
1946　Jan. 3 – Dec. 31.
1947　Jan. 1+.

MH
1911 – 1913　Jan. 1 – Dec. 31.
1914　Mar. 1 – Dec. 31.
1915　Jan. 10 – Aug. 14, 23, 25 – Dec.
31.
1916　July 1 – Dec. 19, 25, 28 – 31.

1917   Jan. 1 – Feb. 1, 6, 8 – May 7,
       13 – July 30, Aug. 2 – 14, 17, 26,
       Sept. 1 – 19, 21 – 26, 29, Oct.
       1 – Nov. 28, 30, Dec. 1 – 17.
1918   Jan. 8 – 14, Feb. 12 – Apr. 15,
       21, 23 – July 8, 14, 16 – Aug. 19,
       25, Sept. 1 – Nov. 25, Dec. 3 –
       30.
Micro (P)
1939 – 1940   Jan. 1 – Dec. 31.
1941   Jan. 1 – Apr. 30, May 16 – Dec.
       31.
1942 – 1943   Jan. 1 – Dec. 31.
1944   Jan. 1 – July 31.
1945   May 1 – July 31, Aug. 16 – Dec.
       31.
1946 – 1955   Jan. 1 – Dec. 31.
MWA
1829   July 3, Oct. 24 – 28, Nov. 4.
1842   June 9 – 12.
1844   Nov. 29.
1876   June 2.
NN
1915   Aug. 6 – Dec. 31.
1916   July 1 – 4, 6 – 15, 17, 19 – Aug.
       29, Sept. 1 – 17, 22, 24, 25, 27 –
       Oct. 24, 29, 31 – Dec. 19, 25,
       28 – 31.
1917   Jan. 1 – Feb. 7, 12 – June 30.
OrU
1922   June 4.
TxU
1921   Jan. 1 – 7, 9 – 19, 21, 22, 24 –
       Feb. 1, 3 – 8, 11, 12, 14 – 19, 21,
       27 – Mar. 2, 4 – 26, 28 – Apr. 11,
       17, 19 – May 2, 4 – 9, 11 – 16,
       18 – 30, June 5, 7 – 12, 14 – 19,
       21 – 26, 28 – Dec. 4, 6 – 12, 20 –
       31.
1923   Jan. 2 – 22, 30 – Feb. 5, 7 – 13,
       15 – Apr. 16, 22 – May 7, 13,
       15 – 21, 27, 29 – Nov. 4, 6 –
       Dec. 31.
ViU
1842   Sept. 19.
WU
Micro (P)
1949 – 1952   Jan. 1 – Dec. 31.
1953   Jan. 1 – Oct. 31.

SEMANARIO MERCANTIL. w. est. 1823.
   Note: Ceased publication 1824.
PPAmP
   1823   Prospecto.
          June 4 – July 30.

SENTINELLA DA LIBERDADE A'
   BEIRA DO MAR DA PRAIA GRANDE.
   irr. est. Aug. 5, 1823.
   Note: Title *Sentinella da liberdade a
   Beira do Mar da Praia Grande*, Aug.
   5 – 9, 1823; *Sentinella da liberdade a'
   Beira do Mar da Praia Grande* after
   Aug. 14, 1823.
PPAmP
   1823   Aug. 5 – Nov. 8.

A SENTINELLA DA MONARCHIA. d.
   est. Apr. 2, 1840.
   Note: Ceased publication 1847.
ViU
   1842   Apr. 23.

O SETE D'ABRIL. sw. est. 1833.
   Note: Suspended publication Mar. 20,
   1839.
DLC
   1836   Jan. 9 – 15, 17 – Feb. 23, 28 –
          Apr. 8, 10 – May 21, 23 – July
          22, 24 – Sept. 16, Oct. 16 – Nov.
          8, 10 – Dec. 31.
   1837   Jan. 1 – 6, 8 – Feb. 24, 26 – Mar.
          10, 12 – Apr. 25, 30 – May 10,
          11 – June 3, 5 – 13, 15 – 20,
          22 – July 16, 18 – Aug. 2, 11 –
          Sept. 5, 10 – 19, 21 – 30, Oct.
          1 – 14.

SOUTH AMERICAN MAIL.
   See *The British and American Mail.*

O SPECTADOR BRASILEIRO. 3w. est.
   July 1, 1824.
   Note: Ceased publication [May 23],
   1827.
CU – B
   Micro (N)
   1824   [Aug. 2 – Dec. 31.]
   1825   [Jan. 1 – July 13.]
DLC
   1826   Nov. 20.
   1827   May 7.

PPAmP
- 1824 Prospecto: June 28.
  July 1—Dec. 31.
- 1825 Jan. 3—Dec. 30.
- 1826 Jan. 9, Mar. 13, Apr. 7, 10, June 14, July 24.
- 1827 Apr. 2—11, May 7.

O SYLPHO. sw. est. 1823.
PPAmP
- 1823 Aug. 6—Nov. 1.
  Extraordinario: Aug. 22.

O TAMOYO. 3w. est. Aug. 12, 1823.
Note: Ceased publication Nov. 11, 1823.
CtY
- 1823 Aug. 12—Nov. 11.
PPAmP
- 1823 Aug. 12, 19, 22, 26, Sept. 2— Nov. 11.
  Suplemento: Nov. 11.

A TARDE. d.
DLC
- 1939 Apr. 19. (Special edition in English)

O TEMPO. est. 1891.
Note: Ceased publication 1894.
CU—B
Micro (N)
- 1893 Nov. 23.

A TRIBUNA CATOLICA. est. Feb. 1, 1851.
Note: Suspended publication 1853— 1857; ceased publication 1861.
DCU
- 1851 Feb. 1—Dec. 31.
- 1852 Jan. 1—Dec. 31.
- 1853 Jan. 1.

TRIBUNA DA IMPRENSA. d. est. 1949.
DLC
- 1954 Aug. 16—31, Nov. 16—Dec. 30.
- 1955 Jan. 10, 11, 13—Apr. 18, 20, 23—28, 30—July 12, 14—Nov. 25, 29—Dec. 4, 6, 8—31.

TRIBUNA POPULAR. d.
DLC
- 1945 Sept. 1—Oct. 12, 14—29, Nov.

2—Dec. 18, 20—30.
- 1946 Sept. 1—3, 6, 8—10, 12—Oct. 21, 23, 24, 26—Nov. 8, 11—27, 29—Dec. 25, 27, 29.
- 1947 Jan. 1—3, 5—16, 20, 23—Apr. 3, 7, 8, 10, 12, 14, 28—May 9, 11—16, 19—22, 25—27, 29— June 5, 7—10, 12—July 11, 13—Sept. 20, 22—28.

TRIUMPHO DA LEGITIMIDADE CON-TRA FACÇÃO DE ANARQUISTAS. irr.
PPAmP
- 1825 Dec. 9, 15, 16, 19, 21, 22, 28, 30.
- 1826 Jan. 10, 14, 21, 24, 27, 28.

ULTIMA HORA. d. est. 1951.
DLC
- 1955 Jan. 7—17, 20—31, Feb. 2— Mar. 27, 30, Apr. 1—6, 10—15, 17—19, 21—28, May 1, 3, 5, 6, 9, 11—26, 29, 31, June 3—5, 8, 10, 12, 13, July 3—11, 13—18, 20—27, 29—31, Aug. 2—12, 14, 15, 17—21, 23—Sept. 4, 6, 8— 28, 30—Oct. 11, 13—23, 25— 31, Nov. 2—10, 12—18, 20—24, 26—Dec. 12, 14—18, 20—22, 24, 26, 27, 29, 30.
- 1959 July 1—Dec. 31.
- 1960 Jan. 4—Feb. 9, 11, 12, 14— Apr. 1, 3—30, May 7—July 13, 16—Nov. 2, 4—Dec. 31.
- 1961 Jan. 1—Apr. 29, May 2—June 26, 28—Sept. 17, 19—Nov. 28, 30—Dec. 30.
Micro (P) &(N)
- 1962 Jan. 1+.

VANGUARDA SOCIALISTA. w.
CSt
- 1945 Aug. 31—Dec. 31.
- 1946—1947 Jan. 1—Dec. 31.
- 1948 July 13.

O VERDADEIRO LIBERAL. 3w. est. 1826.
PPAmP
- 1826 Mar. 2, 7—Apr. 6.
  Suplemento: Mar. 21.

VIDA FLUMINENSE. w. est. 1889.
  Note: Ceased publication 1890.
  CU—B
  Micro (N)
  1889   Nov. 24.
  DCU
  1889   [Sept. 15—Oct. 6].

VITRINE. d.
  DLC
  1941   Oct. 24.

O YTORORO. est. Sept. 1, 1859.
  DCU
  1859   Sept. 1—Dec. 31.
  1860   Jan. 1—May 1.

Rio Grande

MERCANTIL DO RIO GRANDE.
  MWA
  1840   Aug. 26.

O TEMPO. d. est. 1906.
  CU
  1927   Apr. 1.

VOZ DO POVO. w.
  CSt
  1946   Apr. 20.

Rio Preto

NOTICIA. [d.]
  MWA
  1930   Oct. 25, Nov. 15.

Santa Cruz

JORNAL DE SANTA CRUZ. sw.
  DLC
  1941   Sept. 23, 26.

Santos

O DIARIO. d. est. 1936.
  DLC
  1941   July 19.

A TRIBUNA. d. est. Mar. 26, 1894.
  DLC
  1941   July 19.

A TRIBUNA.
  MH
  1911   Mar. 3—5, 22.
  1917   Nov. 8, 11.

São Lourenço

O ARAUTO. w.
  DLC
  1942   Nov. 8.

São Luiz

O IMPARCIAL. d. est. 1926.
  DLC
  1942   June 14.

São Paulo

AURORA ALEMA. w.
  DLC
  1941   Oct. 3, 24.

BRASIL ASAHI. d.
  Note: In Portuguese and Japanese.
  DLC
  1941   June 25, 27, 28.

CORREIO PAULISTANO. d. est. June
  26, 1854.
  DLC
  1945   Nov. 4, 6, 7, 9—Dec. 30.
  1946   Jan. 1—Feb. 28, Mar. 2—5, 7—
          31, Apr. 2—May 30, June 1—
          30, July 2—5, 7—Sept. 7, 9—12,
          14—26, 28, 30—Nov. 18, 20—
          26, 28—Dec. 3, 5—11, 13—31.
  1947   Jan. 1—6, 8—21, 24—27, 29—
          Feb. 14, 16—28, Mar. 3—8,
          10—20, 24—Apr. 16, 18—25,
          27, 28, May 1—3, 5—27, 29—
          Aug. 8, 10—14, 17—Sept. 25,
          27—30.
  Micro (P) & (N)
  1962   Jan. 1+.
  MH
  1913   Aug. 13.

DEUTSCHE ZEITUNG. DIARIO ALE-
  MÃO. w., sw., 3w., d. est. 1896.
  Note: In Portuguese and German.

Commenced daily publication Apr. 1, 1903.
DLC
1941   Aug. 23.

DEUTSCHER MORGEN AURORA ALLEMÃ. w.
Note: In Portuguese and German.
DLC
1941   Apr. 4, May 9, June 20.

DIARIO ALEMÃO.
See *Deutsche Zeitung. Diario alemão.*

DIARIO DA NOITE. d. est. 1925.
MWA
1930   Nov. 14, 25.

DIARIO DE SÃO PAULO. d. est. Jan. 5, 1929.
DLC
1942   Jan. 1, 8, 11, 18, 22, 25, Feb. 1, 5, Mar. 1, 5, 8, 15, 19, 22, 26, 29, Apr. 5, 12, 19, 23, 30, May 3, 10, 21, 24, 28, 31, June 4, 7, 11, 14, 18, 21, 28, July 5, 9, 12, 16, 19, 23, 26, 30, Aug. 2, 6, 9, 13, 16, 20, 23, 27, 30, Sept. 3, 6, 9, 10, 13, 27, Oct. 4, 8, 11, 15, 18, 22, Nov. 1, 5, 8, 12, 15, 19, 22, 26, 29, Dec. 3, 6, 10, 13, 17, 20, 24, 27, 31.
MWA
1930   Oct. 25, 26.
TxU
1947   Jan. 16.

DIARIO NACIONAL. d.
MWA
1930   Nov. 16, 25, 30, Dec. 5, 7, 19, 20, 27, 28.
1931   Jan. 24, Feb. 3, 4.

DIARIO POPULAR. d. est. Oct. 8, 1884.
DLC
1941   Feb. 3 − 8, May 6 − 12, 20 − 26, July 15, 24 − 30, Aug. 6 − 11, Nov. 21 − 24, 26 − 28.
MH
1908   Dec. 11.
1909   Jan. 21, Feb. 9, 10, 22, Apr. 10.

O ESTADO DE SÃO PAULO. d. est. Jan. 4, 1874.
Note: Title *Provincia de São Paulo*, Jan. 4, 1874 − [1890]; *O Estado São Paulo*, after [1890].
CLU
1959   Sept. 26 − Dec. 31.
1960   Jan. 1+.
CSt − H
1965   Feb. 6 − Dec. 31.
1966   Jan. 1+.
CU
1936   Sept. 8 − Nov. 20.
CtY
1966   Jan. 30 − Feb. 15, 17 − 22, 24 − Mar. 19, 21, 25.
Micro (P)
1962   Jan. 2 − Dec. 30.
1963 − 1964   Jan. 1 − Dec. 31.
1965   Jan. 1 − 15, June 2 − 14, Dec. 1 − 15.
1966   Jan. 2 − 15, Feb. 1 − 15.
DLC
1927   June 1 − Nov. 19, 21 − Dec. 31.
1928 − 1931   Jan. 1 − Dec. 31.
1932   Jan. 1 − Mar. 31, May 1 − 31.
1939   May 2 − June 6.
1940 − 1941   Jan. 1 − Dec. 31.
1942   Jan. 1 − Apr. 20, 22, 27, 29, May 3 − July 23, 25 − Dec. 31.
1943   Jan. 1 − Feb. 1, 3 − July 14, 16 − 28, 30 − Dec. 31.
1944   Jan. 1 − Dec. 31.
1945   Jan. 1 − 3, 5 − Mar. 22, 26 − Dec. 31.
1946   Jan. 1 − Dec. 31.
1947   Jan. 1 − 14, 16 − 18, 20, 21, 23 − Mar. 6, 10 − Dec. 31.
1948 − 1950   Jan. 1 − Dec. 31.
1951   Jan. 1 − July 3, 5 − 10, 12, 14 − 24, 26 − Dec. 31.
1952   Jan. 1 − May 10, 12 − July 25, 27 − Aug. 5, 7 − Dec. 31.
1953   Jan. 1 − Feb. 4, 7 − 23, 25 − May 1, 4 − June 17, 19 − Aug. 7, 9 − 24, 26 − Dec. 31.
1954   Jan. 1 − Dec. 31.
1955   Jan. 1 − Feb. 28, Mar. 2, 4 − 8, 10 − Dec. 31.

1956   Jan. 1 – July 14, 16 – Nov. 30.
Micro (P)
1956   Sept. 1 – Dec. 31.
1957   Jan. 1+.
DPU
Current (six months).
FU
1962   Feb. 1 – Dec. 31.
1963   Jan. 1+
ICRL
Micro (P) & (N)
1956   Sept. 1 – Dec. 31.
1957   Jan. 1+.
InU
1966   Jan. 1+.
KHi
1914   Nov. 9 – Dec. 31.
1915   Jan. 1 – 25.
LNHT
1963   Aug. 1 – Dec. 31.
1964   Jan. 1 – May 31, Sept. 1 – Dec.
        31.
1965   Jan. 1 – Mar. 31, May 1 – Dec.
        31.
1966   Jan. 1+.
MH
1909   May 6 – 8.
1910   Aug. 30, Oct. 31.
1917   Nov. 1.
1964   Feb. 22 – Dec. 31.
1965   Jan. 1.
MWA
1930   Oct. 12, 24 – 26, Nov. 3, 25.
NNC
1965   May 16, 18 – 23, 25 – 30, June
        1 – 6, 8 – 13, 15, 16, 18, 19, 22 –
        27, 29, 30 – July 4, 6 – 11, 13 –
        18, 20 – 25, 27 – 30, Aug. 3 – 8,
        10 – 14, 17 – 22, 24 – 29, 31 –
        Sept. 5, 7 – 12, 14 – 19, 21 – 26,
        28 – 30, Oct. 1 – 3, 5 – 7, 9, 10,
        12 – 17, 19 – 21, 23, 24, 26 – 31,
        Nov. 2, 4 – 7, 9 – 14, 16 – 21, 23,
        24, 27, 28, Dec. 1 – 5, 7, 8, 10 –
        12, 14 – 19, 21 – 24, 26, 28 – 31.
1966   Jan. 2, 4.
NIC
Micro (P)

1956   Sept. 1 – Dec. 31.
1957   Jan. 1+.
PSt
Current (six months).
TxU
1921   Mar. 16 – 24, 26, 27, 29 – May
        1, 3 – Sept. 27, Oct. 1 – 31, Nov.
        2 – Dec. 31.
ViU
1965   Jan. 1+.

O FAROL PAULISTANO. w. est. Feb. 7,
1827.
    Note: Ceased publication 1833.
PPAmP
    1827   Feb. 14 – Apr. 11, May 9.

FOLHA DE SÃO PAULO. d. est. 1931.
    Note: Title *Fôlha da manhã*, [Mar.
    21, 1942] – Dec. 31, 1959, *Fôlha de
    São Paulo* after Dec. 31, 1959.
DLC
    1942   Mar. 21.
    1944   Nov. 1 – 8, 10 – 21, 24 – Dec.
            18, 20 – 31.
    1945   Jan. 1, 2, 4 – Feb. 28, July 1 –
            30, Aug. 1 – 31.
    1958   July 17 – Oct. 29, 31 – Dec. 3,
            5 – 17, 19 – 31.
    1959   Jan. 1 – 26, 28 – May 19, 21,
            23 – June 5, 7 – Dec. 31.
    1960   Jan. 1 – Feb. 25, 27 – Apr. 30,
            May 4 – June 3, 5 – 15, 23 – 28,
            30 – July 31, Aug. 2 – 6, 8 – 30,
            Sept. 1 – 23, 25 – 27, 29 – Dec.
            31.
    1961   Jan. 1 – Mar. 4, 6 – 22, 24 – 31,
            Apr. 2 – 8, 10 – 30, May 2 –
            June 1, 3 – July 30, Aug. 1 – 21,
            23 – Sept. 2, 4 – 7, 9 – Nov. 4,
            6 – 28, 30, Dec. 1, 5 – 31.

A GAZETA. d. est. May 16, 1906.
DLC
    1941   Sept. 12, 14 – 16, 19 – 28, Oct.
            1 – 19, 26 – 29, Nov. 28 – Dec.
            21, 24 – 28, 31.
    1942   Jan. 17 – 31.
    1943   Jan. 30, Apr. 27 – 30, May 12,
            13, 20, 21, 29, 31, June 11, 16,

Aug. 3, 4, 16, Oct. 1, 19, 20, 28, 29.

1944 Jan. 19 – 28, 30 – Mar. 9, 11 – 14, 16, 17, 19 – 31, Apr. 2 – 11, 13 – 24, 26 – 29, May 1 – 23, 25, 26, 29 – 31, June 2 – 5, 7 – 26, July 3 – 11, 14 – 19, 22 – 26, 28 – Aug. 10, 14 – 16, 18 – 21, 24 – 31, Sept. 2 – 5, 6, 9 – 25, 27, 28, 30 – Oct. 2, 4 – 17, 19 – 24, 26 – 31, Nov. 4 – 16, 18 – 22, 24 – Dec. 15, 18 – 23.

1945 Jan. 12 – 15, Feb. 20 – Mar. 1, 3 – 5, 20, 27 – Apr. 4, 6 – 20, 23, 24.

GERMANIA. 3w. est. 1878.
Note: In German.
DLC
1906 Mar. 15.

HOJE.
CSt
1946 Aug. 29.

JORNAL TRABALHISTA.
CSt
1946 Dec. 1.

MLADOROSSOE SLOVO. w.
Note: In Russian.
CtY
1934 Dec. 1 – 8, 22 – 29.

NOTICIAS DE HOJE. d. est. 1948.
DLC
1955 June 12.

ORIENTACÃO SOCIALISTA.
CSt
1946 Nov. 5.

A PLATEA. w., sw., d. est. Apr. 1, 1888.
DLC
1942 Apr. 16.

A PLEBE.
DLC
1935 Oct. 26.

PROVINCIA DE SÃO PAULO.
See *O Estado de São Paulo.*

SÃO PAULO-SHIMBRA. est. 1946.
Note: In Portuguese and Japanese.
CSt
1947 Feb. 19.

SÃO PAULO JOURNAL. d.
Note: In English.
MWA
1930 Oct. 15, 21.

ULTIMA HORA. d.
DLC
Micro (P) & (N)
1962 Jan. 1+.

São Salvador

See Bahia.

Timbaúba

A SERRA. sw.
Note: Ceased publication Oct. 4, 1930.
DLC
1926 Sept. 8 – 10, Oct. 24 – Nov. 26, Dec. 9 – 28.
1927 Jan. 2 – 7, 13 – 21, 30 – Feb. 4, 6 – 11, 17 – Mar. 22, 27 – Apr. 19, 21 – May 24, 26 – 31, June 2 – Aug. 16, 18 – Sept. 8, 16 – 18, 23 – 25, Oct. 1 – 9, 23 – 28, Nov. 9 – 15, 24 – Dec. 31.
1928 Jan. 1 – Apr. 3, 5 – June 26, 28 – July 6, 8 – 31, Aug. 2 – Nov. 10, 12 – 23, 25 – Dec. 4, 6 – 31.
1929 Jan. 2 – Mar. 31, Apr. 6, 13, 20, 27, May 4, 11, 18, 25, June 1, 8, 15, 22, 29, July 6, 13, 20, 27, Aug. 3, 10, 17, 24, 31, Sept. 7, 14, 21, 28, Oct. 5, 12, 19, 26, Nov. 2, 9, 16, 23, 30, Dec. 7, 14, 21, 28.
1930 Jan. 4, 11, 18, 25, Feb. 1, 8, 15, 22, Mar. 1, 8, 15, 22, 29, Apr. 5, 12, 19, 26, May 3, 10, 17, 24, 31, June 7, 14, 21, 28, July 5, 12, 19, 26, Aug. 2, 9, 16, 23, 30, Sept. 6, 13, 20, 27.

Uberlân

O ESTADO DE GOIAZ. sw.
  CSt
    1946   Mar. 23, Apr. 3—30, May 4—
            29, June 8.

Victoria

A GAZETA. d. est. Sept. 11, 1928.
  DLC
    1941   Jan. 3—9, 14, 26—Feb. 24,27—
            Mar. 27, 29, 30.

CHILE

Antofagasta

EL ABECE. d. est. Oct. 14, 1920.
  DLC
    1937   June 13.
    1941   May 14—July 6, 8—Sept. 7, 9—
            Oct. 25, 27—Dec. 31.
    1942   Jan. 1—30, Feb. 2—Apr. 18,
            20—May 16, 18—July 11, 13—
            Aug. 13, 15—Sept. 16, 18—Oct.
            12, 17—31, Nov. 2—21, 23—
            Dec. 11, 13—31.
    1943   Jan. 1—Mar. 20, 22—Aug, 16,
            18, 20, 22—Oct. 3, 5—Dec. 26,
            28—31.
    1944   Jan. 1—13, 15—21, 23—Mar.
            27, 29—June 30.
    1946   Jan. 1—May 10, 12—Sept. 1,
            3—26, 28—Oct. 20, 22—Dec.
            31.
    1947   Jan. 1—25, 27—Feb. 4, 6—16,
            19—Mar. 2, 5—8, 10—12, 16—
            21, 23, 24, 26—29, 31.

ACTUALIDAD. w.
  MWA
    1875   Feb. 23.

CARACOLINO. w., sw., 3w.
  Note: Periodicity Nov. 6, 1874—May
  6, 1876, weekly; 1877—Feb. 9, 1878,
  semiweekly; after Feb. 10, 1878, three
  times a week.
  MWA
    1872   Sept. 27, Dec. 13.

1873   Jan. 10, 24, June 10—July 1,
        29—Aug. 1, 8.
1874   Mar. 27, Apr. 17, 24, May 5,
        Aug. 28, Nov. 6—Dec. 4, 18.
1875   Jan. 8—29, Feb. 19—Mar. 27,
        Apr. 13, May 12—June 2, 10,
        July 7—Aug. 27, Sept. 24—
        Nov. 5, 19—Dec. 11.
        Extraordinario: Aug. 28.
1876   Jan. 22, May 6.
1877   May 14, Oct. 17, Nov. 14.
1878   Jan. 10—16, 23, Feb. 2—9,
        July 18—20, 25—27.

DIARIO. d. est. Dec. 8, 1903.
  MWA
    1906   Apr. 27.

EL INDUSTRIAL. d. est. Aug. 1, 1881.
  Note: Ceased publication Jan. 31,
  1938.
  DLC
    1903   Aug. 18.
  MWA
    1892   June 2, 3, 8, 11—13, 24—July
            2, 8, 9.

LITORAL. w., sw. est. Oct. 9, 1875.
  Note: Periodicity Oct. 9, 1875—1876,
  weekly; after 1876, semiweekly.
  MWA
    1875   Oct. 9—Dec. 4, 25—31.
    1876   Jan. 1—19, Feb. 5, Mar. 4—18,
            Apr. 3—12.
    1877   Jan. 9—12, Dec. 20.
    1878   Jan. 27, Feb. 3—17.

EL MERCURIO DE ANTOFAGASTA. d.
  est. Dec. 16, 1906.
  DLC
    1941   May 13—31, June 2—Aug. 20,
            22—Dec. 6, 8—31.
    1942   Jan. 1—Mar. 30, Apr. 1—May
            31, June 2—11, 13—19, 21—
            July 3, 5—25, 27—Aug. 31,
            Sept. 2—11, 13—20, 22—Oct.
            12, 17—Dec. 31.
    1943   Jan. 1—Feb. 13, 15—20, 23—
            26, 28—Mar. 20, 22—29, 31,
            Apr. 1, 3—30, May 3—Dec. 26,
            28—31.

1944 Jan. 1–10, 13–Feb. 10, 12–
28, Mar. 1–25, 29–Apr. 4, 6–
30.
1946 Jan. 1, 3–Apr. 9, 11–May 26,
28–31, Sept. 1–Nov. 16, 18–
Dec. 31.
1947 Jan. 1–20, 22–Feb. 6, 8–
Mar. 1, 3, 5–10, 13, 15–28, 30.

LA OPINION DE ANTOFAGASTA. d.
est. July 4, 1942.
DLC
1942 Dec. 15, 17–31.
1943 Jan. 6–May 7, 9–16, 18–29,
31–July 14, 19–Nov. 25, 27–
Dec. 30.

EL POPULAR. d. est. Oct. 4, 1938.
DLC
1942 Oct. 14, 16–Dec. 31.
1943 Jan. 1–13, 15–Mar. 1, 3–Apr.
5, 7–16, 18, 19, 22, 25–29,
May 3, 4, 7–24, 26–June 10,
12–Aug. 20, 22–31, Oct. 15,
18, 25, 26, 28–Dec. 31.
1944 Jan. 1–6, 8–29, 31–Feb. 17,
19–24, 26–28, Mar. 1, 4–10,
12–17, 20–30, Apr. 1, 3–12,
14–28, 30–May 5, 7–20, 22–
June 22, 25–30.
1945 Jan. 1–5, 7–13, 15, 19–Feb.
3, 5–9, 11–13, 17, 18, 20–23,
26–28, Mar. 2–10, 12–17, 19,
20, 22, 24, 26–28, 30–Apr. 17,
20, 22–30, May 19, 21–29,
July 1–10, 12–17, 19, 20, 22–
31, Aug. 2–12, 14–Sept. 14,
16–30. Nov. 1–Dec. 31.
1946 Jan. 1–27, 29–Feb. 2, 4–
Sept. 3, 5–Nov. 14, 16–Dec.
31.
1947 Jan. 1–21, 23–Feb. 2, 4, 6–
Mar. 24, 26–29, 31.

EL PUEBLO CHILENO. d. est. Mar. 1,
1879.
DLC
1879 Mar. 1–18, 21–31, Apr. 5–8,
12–15, 18–21, 23, 28, 30–
Dec. 31.

Boletín: May 25.
Extraordinario: Nov. 24.
Suplemento: Nov. 6, Dec. 29.
1880 Jan. 1–18, 20–Feb. 15, 17–
June 6, 8–Nov. 11, Dec. 10,
16–18, 22, 24–30.
Extraordinario: Jan. 5, Mar. 25.
Suplemento: Feb. 10.
MWA
1879 Mar. 11, 26.

Arica

El AJICITO. irr. est. Aug. 1925.
DLC
1925 Nov. 1, Dec. 10, 17.

LA AURORA DE ARICA. d. est. Nov.
1914.
MH
1926 Feb. 16.

BOLETIN DE LA GUERRA. sw.
MWA
1880 Feb. 15.

EL MORRO. sw. est. Aug. 1925.
DLC
1925 Oct. 10, 24.

EL PACIFICO ARICA. d. est. Nov. 22,
1927.
Note: See *El Pacíficio*, Tacna.
DLC
1927 Dec. 3–6, 10–31.
1928 Jan. 13, 15, 17, 19–Feb. 5, 7–
15, 17–Mar. 22, 24–Apr. 9,
11–June 21, 23, Nov. 27–Dec.
31.

EL PLEBISCITO. irr. est. 1925.
DLC
1926 Feb. 22.

LA VOZ DEL SUR. d. est. Aug. 9, 1925.
DLC
1925 Aug. 10, 13, 17–Nov. 8, 10–
Dec. 31.
1926 Jan. 1, Feb. 4–6, 20–Apr. 24,
28–June 22.

Cobija

See Bolivia. Cobija.

Cochabamba

See Bolivia. Cochabamba.

Concepción

LA PATRIA. d. est. Nov. 1923.
DLC
   1955   Oct. 9.

EL SUR. d. est. Nov. 15, 1882.
DLC
   1953   Feb. 1 – 8, 10 – 12, 14 – 18, 20 –
           27, Mar. 1 – Apr. 1, 3 – June 29,
           July 1 – Aug. 24, 26, 28 – Oct.
           22, 24 – Nov. 9, 11 – Dec. 6, 8 –
           18, 21, 23 – 28, 31.
   1954   Jan. 1, 3 – 19, 21 – Apr. 25, 27 –
           29, May 1 – 5, 7 – 24, 26 – June
           9, 11 – 22, 24 – July 1, 3, 4, 6 –
           15, 17 – 20, 23, 26 – Aug. 1, 5 –
           Sept. 11, 13, 14, 17 – 23, 25 –
           Oct. 18, 20 – Nov. 9, 11, 13, 14,
           16 – 24, 26 – Dec. 5, 7 – 28, 30,
           31.
   1955   Jan. 1 – 16, 20 – Feb. 1, 3 – 13,
           15 – 21, 24 – 27, 29 – Mar. 25,
           28 – Apr. 6, 8, 10 – May 16,
           18 – 27, 30 – June 8, 10 – 15,
           17 – July 7, 9 – 24, 26 – Aug. 16,
           19 – Sept. 26, 28 – Oct. 7, 9 –
           28, 30 – Dec. 1, 3 – 8, 17 – 19,
           21 – 31.

SUR.
MWA
   1883   Dec. 7.

TELEGRAFO. sw. est. Dec. 15, 1842.
   Note: Title *Telégrafo de Concepción*,
   Dec. 15, 1842 – Dec. 1843; *Telégrafo*,
   after Dec. 1843.
MWA
   1842   Dec. 15 – 31.
   1843   Jan. 1 – Dec. 13.
   1845   Jan. 25.

Copiapó

EL AMIGO DEL PAIS. d. est. Aug. 2,
   1872.
DLC
   1945   Oct. 1 – Nov. 23, 25 – Dec. 23,
           25, 27 – 31.
   1946   Jan. 1, 3 – 16, 18 – Mar. 22,
           24 – Apr. 1, 3 – 23, 25 – May 21,
           23 – June 2, 4, 6 – Aug. 2, 4 – 7,
           9 – Sept. 3, 5 – 15, 17 – Nov. 11,
           13 – 18, 20 – Dec. 1, 3 – 9, 17 –
           25, 27 – 31.
   1947   Jan. 1 – 10, 12, 13, 15 – 17, 19 –
           Feb. 4, 6, 8 – 12, 14 – 17, 27,
           28, Mar. 2 – 5, 7 – 10, 12 – 27,
           29 – Apr. 14, 16 – 21, 23 – 30.

CONSTITUCIONAL. d.
MWA
   1892   July 26.

Coquimbo

AVISADOR IMPARCIAL. est. Jan. 26,
   1830.
   Note: Published only two numbers.
MWA
   1830   Jan. 26.

EL PROGRESO. d. May 8, 1923.
DLC
   1942   July 27, 28.

Curicó

LA PRENSA. d. est. Nov. 13, 1898.
DLC
   1944   Jan. 1 – Feb. 22, 24 – 29, Mar.
           2, 4 – 8, 10 – 31.

Iquique

NACIONAL. d. est. Jan. 1, 1890.
MWA
   1892   June 8, 10 – 14, 16 – 19.
   1906   June 19.

PATRIA. d.
MWA
   1894   Feb. 7.

PUEBLO. 3w. est. Dec. 20, 1898.
  MWA
    1906   June 19.

EL TARAPACA. d. est. Mar. 1, 1894.
  DLC
    1941   June 1 – Dec. 31.
    1942   Jan. 1 – Mar. 10, 14 – 23, 25 –
           May 15, 20 – Oct. 9, 11 – Dec.
           31.
    1943   Jan. 1 – Apr. 20, 22 – May 21,
           26 – June 15, 17 – July 30, Aug.
           1 – Dec. 16, 18 – 26.
    1946   June 7 – Aug. 30, Sept. 1 – 17,
           20 – Oct. 17, 22 – Nov. 12, 14 –
           Dec. 31.
  MH
    1911   Apr. 5.
  MWA
    1906   June 16 – 19, 21, Oct. 31, Nov.
           6.

TIEMPO. est. Oct. 1, 1875.
  MWA
    1875   Oct. 1.

Linares

EL HERALDO. d. est. Aug. 29, 1937.
  DLC
    1955   Aug. 29.

Osorno

LA PRENSA. d. est. Dec. 2, 1917.
  DLC
    1942   Jan. 31, Feb. 1, 3 – 22.

Ovalle

LA PROVINCIA. d. est. 1936.
  DLC
    1954   Sept. 18.

San Fernando

NOTICIAS. d.
  MWA
    1910   Nov. 19.

Santiago

ACTUALIDAD. d. est. Feb. 1, 1858.
  MWA
    1858   Feb. 1 – Dec. 11.

ALMIREZ. irr. est. May 13, 1828.
    Note: Published only two numbers.
    Ceased publication May 27, 1828.
  MWA
    1828   May 13, 27.

AMIGO DE LA CONSTITUCION. irr.
  est. Jan. 26, 1830.
  MWA
    1830   Jan. 26 – Feb. 4.

AMIGO DEL PUEBLO. d. est. Apr. 1,
  1850.
    Note: Ceased publication [June 3,
    1850.]
  MWA
    1850   Apr. 1 – June 3.

ANTORCHA. irr. est. Sept. 26, 1839.
  MWA
    1839   Sept. 26 – Dec. 31.
    1840   Jan. 1 – Feb. 10, Mar. 5 – 24.

ANTORCHA DE LOS PUEBLOS. irr.
  est. Jan. 1, 1831.
  MWA
    1831   Jan. 1 – Mar. 6.

EL ARAUCANO. w., sw., 3w. est. Sept. 17,
  1830.
    Note: Periodicity 1830 – 1849, weekly;
    1849 – 1850, semiweekly; 1850 – 1877,
    three times a week. Succeeded *Gaze-
    ta ministerial de Chile* as official ga-
    zette; succeeded by *Diario oficial*.
    Ceased publication Feb. 1877.
  CSt
    1861   Oct. 13 – Dec. 28.
    1863   Nov. 1 – Dec. 31.
    1864   Jan. 1 – Dec. 31.
  CU – B
    1833   Jan. 4 – Sept. 13, 27 – Dec. 27.
    1834 – 1836   Jan. 1 – Dec. 31.
    1837   Jan. 7 – Mar. 3, 17 – Dec. 1,
           15 – 22.
    1838   Jan. 12 – Feb. 16, Mar. 2 – July
           27, Aug. 10 – Dec. 28.

1839   Jan. 4 — Mar. 26, Apr. 5 — Nov.
           15, 29 — Dec. 27.
1840   Jan. 10 — Dec. 25.
1841   Jan. 1 — May 14, 28 — Dec. 31.
1842   Jan. 1 — Dec. 31.
1843   Jan. 6 — Dec. 8, 22 — 29.
1844   Jan. 5 — Mar. 1, 15 — May 10,
           31 — Dec. 27.
Micro (N)
1830   Sept. 17 — Dec. 31.
1831 — 1850   Jan. 1 — Dec. 31.
1852 — 1864   Jan. 1 — Dec. 31.
1867   July 1 — Dec. 31.
1869 — 1872   Jan. 1 — Dec. 31.
1873   Jan. 1 — July 30.
CtY
   1834   Nov. 13 — Dec. 31.
   1835 — 1838   Jan. 1 — Dec. 31.
   1839   Jan. 1 — Aug. 16.
DLC
   1830   Sept. 17 — Dec. 31.
   1831 — 1875   Jan. 1 — Dec. 31.
   1876   Jan. 1 — Dec. 30.
MnU
   Micro (P)
   1830   Sept. 17 — Dec. 31.
   1831 — 1876   Jan. 1 — Dec. 31.

EL ARGOS DE CHILE. est. May 28, 1818.
   Note: Ceased publication Nov. 19,
   1818.
   DLC
   1818   May 28 — Nov. 19.

ASIES. d. est. Mar. 21, 1938.
   DLC
   1942   Oct. 13 — 17, Dec. 15 — 19.
   1943   June 23.

AUGIJON. irr. est. May 15, 1838.
   MWA
   1838   May 15 — June 6.

EL AUGURIO FELIZ. est. 1813.
   Note: Ceased publication 1817.
   WU
   1814   n.d. (July).

LA AURORA. 6m., irr. est. June 16, 1827.
   Note: Ceased publication Feb. 22,
   1828.

CtY
   1827   July 7, 13, Aug. 8, 11, 17.
DLC
   1827   June 21.

AURORA DE CHILE. w. est. Feb. 13,
1812.
   Note: Succeeded by *El Monitor araucano* as official gazette, Apr. 6, 1813.
   Ceased publication Apr. 1, 1813.
   CU — B
   Micro (P)
   1812   Feb. 13, 20, Mar. 5 — 26.
   CtY
   1812   Feb. 13 — Dec. 24.
   1813   Jan. 7 — Apr. 1
   DLC
   1813   Feb. 13.
   DPU
   1812   Feb. 13 — Dec. 31.
   1813   Jan. 1 — Apr. 1.
   IU
   1812   Feb. 13 — Dec. 31.
   1813   Jan. 1 — Apr. 1.
   MB
   1812   Feb. 13 — Dec. 31.
   1813   Jan. 7 — Mar. 25.
   NN
   1812   Prospecto.
            Feb. 13.
   WU
   Micro (P) & (N)
   1812   Feb. 13 — Dec. 31.
   1813   Jan. 1 — Apr. 1.

CANTARO CONTRA LA PIEDRA. sw.
est. Mar. 7, 1835.
   Note: Ceased publication Apr. 18,
   1835.
   MWA
   1835   Mar. 7 — Apr. 18.

CARTAS PEHUENCHES. est. 1819.
   WU
   1819 — 1920   Jan. 1 — Dec. 31.

CEFIRO DE CHILE. irr. est. Aug. 26,
1829.
   Note: Published only two numbers.
   Ceased publication Sept. 4, 1829.

MWA
1829   Aug. 26, Sept. 4.

CELADOR. irr. est. Sept. 14, 1832.
MWA
1832   Sept. 14 – Nov. 30.

AVISOS. d. est. Apr. 21, 1851.
Note: Ceased publication June 30,
1851.
MWA
1851   June 17, 18, 21, 24.

BALAS A LOS TRAIDORES. irr. est.
Jan. 26, 1838.
MWA
1838   Jan. 26 – Feb. 8.

BOLETIN DE LA GUERRA DEL PACI-
FICO. w. est. Apr. 14, 1879.
CU – B
Micro (N)
1879   Apr. 14 – Dec. 29.
1880   Jan. 14 – Dec. 31.
1881   Jan. 1 – May 16.

BOLETIN OFICIAL. d. est. June 6, 1837.
MWA
1837   June 6, 7.

BULLETIN DE LA GUERRE DES PACI-
FIC.
Note: In French.
MH
1881   Jan. 24.

CAMPANA. irr. est. July 5, 1870.
MWA
1870   July 5 – Aug. 30, Sept. 28.

CENSOR DEL AÑO DE 28. irr. est. Jan.
28, 1828.
Note: Ceased publication Sept. 11,
1828.
MWA
1828   Jan. 28 – Sept. 11.

CENTINELA. w. est. Dec. 3, 1828.
Note: Ceased publication July 28,
1829.
MWA
1828   Dec. 3 – 31.
1829   Jan. 1 – July 28.

CHILENO. irr. est. Aug. 20, 1835.
Note: Ceased publication Sept. 5,
1835.
MWA
1835   Aug. 20 – Sept. 5.

EL CHILENO. d. est. Dec. 8, 1938.
DLC
1941   Aug. 7 – 9, 11, 14, 16, 18 – 21,
25 – 28, 30, Sept. 1, 3 – 6, 8 –
13, 15 – 17, 22 – 26, 29, 30, Oct.
2 – 4, 6, 9, 10, 14, 16, 17, 20 –
25, 27 – 29, Nov. 4, 5, 7, 10, 11,
13 – 15, 17, Dec. 2, 9, 12, 13, 17,
22, 26, 30.
1942   Jan. 3, 5, 6, 10, 12 – 14, 20, 22,
27, 29, 30, Feb. 3, 11, 12, 20, 21,
23, 25, 26, Sept. 1 – 5, 7, 9 – 15,
18, 20 – Oct. 9, 11 – 16, 19 –
Dec. 31.
1943   Jan. 1 – Mar. 30, Apr. 1 – Oct.
22, 24 – Dec. 31.
1944   Jan. 1 – May 31, Sept. 2 – 30.
1945   Nov. 1 – 5, 7, 8, 10 – Dec. 31.
1946   Jan. 1, 3 – Feb. 13, 15, 17, 21,
22, 24 – 26.

CHILOTE. w. est. July 4, 1826.
MWA
1826   July 4 – Aug. 1.

EL CLAMOR DEL PUEBLO CHILENO.
sw. est. Dec. 11, 1827.
Note: Ceased publication Jan. 19,
1828.
DLC
1827   Dec. 11.
MWA
1827   Dec. 11 – 31.
1828   Jan. 1 – 19.

CLARIN. d.
DLC
1955   Oct. 14.

LA CLAVE DE CHILE. w., 3w. est. June
21, 1827.
Note: Periodicity June 21, 1827 – Jan.
1828, weekly; Feb. 1828 – Oct. 29,
1829, three times a week. Ceased publication Oct. 29, 1829.

CtY
    1827   July 12, Aug. 9, 16, 18.
    1828   Oct. 2 – Dec. 31.
    1829   Jan. 1 – Aug. 27.
DLC
    1827   June 21 – Dec. 31.
    1828   Jan. 1 – Dec. 20.
    1829   Jan. 3 – 31, Apr. 2 – 16.
            Suplemento: Apr. 11.
MWA
    1827   June 21 – Dec. 31.
    1828   Jan. 1 – Dec. 31.
    1829   Jan. 1 – Oct. 29.
            Suplemento: Nov. 1, 28.

LA COLA DEL COMETA. bw.
    Note: See also *El Cometa.*
CtY
    1827   Mar. 15 – Apr. 11.
MWA
    1827   Feb. 22 – May 10.

COLEJIAL. w. est. July 30, 1865.
MWA
    1865   Prospecto.
            July 30 – Sept. 18.

EL COMETA. irr. est. Feb. 16, 1827.
    Note: Ceased publication June 11,
    1827. See also *La Cola del cometa.*
DLC
    1827   May 31.
            Suplemento: May 31.
MWA
    1827   Feb. 16 – June 11.

COMILON. irr. est. Mar. 16, 1841.
MWA
    1841   Mar. 16 – Apr. 17.

CONDOR. w. est. June 15, 1863.
MWA
    1863   June 15 – Aug. 2.

CONSERVADOR. irr. est. Jan. 30, 1840.
MWA
    1840   Jan. 30 – June 12, July 30, Sept.
            30.

CONSTITUCIONAL. sw., w. est. July 15,
    1833.
    Note: Periodicity July 15 – Aug. 14,

1833, semiweekly; Aug. 14 – Sept. 14,
    1833, weekly; ceased publication Sept.
    14, 1833.
MWA
    1833   July 15 – Sept. 14.

CONSTITUCIONAL. w. est. Aug. 24,
    1839.
MWA
    1839   Aug. 24 – Sept. 23.

CONSTITUYENTE. sw. est. June 3, 1828.
    Note: Ceased publication July 5, 1828.
MWA
    1828   June 3 – July 5.

EL CORREO DE ARAUCO. irr. est. Jan.
    30, 1824.
    Note: Ceased publication June 22,
    1825.
DLC
    1824   July 3 – 16, 30 – Aug. 27, Oct.
            23 – Nov. 20, Dec. 11 – 16.
    1825   Jan. 8 – 26, Feb. 21, Apr. 13 –
            May 20.
            Suplemento: Mar., June.
MWA
    1824   Jan. 30 – Dec. 31.
    1825   Jan. 1 – June 22.
            Suplemento: June.

CORREO DEL DOMINGO. w. est. Apr.
    20, 1862.
MWA
    1862   Apr. 20 – Oct. 12.

EL CORREO LITERARIO. w. est. July
    18, 1858.
TxU
    1858   July 18, Aug. 14 – Dec. 11.

CORREO MERCANTIL-POLITICO-
    LITERARIO. 3w. est. Apr. 20, 1826.
    Note: Title *Correo mercantil y indus-
    trial*, Apr. 20 – Aug. 17, 1826; *Correo
    mercantil-político-literario*, Aug.
    18 – Oct. 17, 1826. Ceased publica-
    tion Oct. 17, 1826.
DLC
    1826   May 30, Sept. 5 – 12, 19 – 30,
            Oct. 3 – 17.
MWA
    1826   Apr. 20 – Oct. 17.

CORSARIO. d. est. Apr. 17, 1849.
  Note: Ceased publication Sept. 4,
  1849.
  MWA
    1849   Apr. 17—May 7, 28—June 16,
        July 4—Sept. 4.

CREPUSCULO. w., irr. est. Sept. 19, 1829.
  Note: Periodicity Sept. 19—Oct. 3,
  1829, weekly; Oct. 3—Dec. 26, 1829,
  irregular. Ceased publication Dec. 26,
  1829.
  MWA
    1829   Sept. 19—Dec. 26.

LA CRITICA. d.
  DLC
    1941   Aug. 7—9, 12—17, 19—21, 24,
        26—30, Sept. 1—27, Oct. 2—5,
        7—12, 14—19, 21, 23, 25—29,
        31—Nov. 8, 10—19, 21, 24—
        27, 30—Dec. 2, 4—6, 10, 11,
        13—20, 22—31.
    1942   Jan. 1—6, 10, 13, 14, 18—20,
        22, 24, 28—30, Feb. 4—9, 11,
        12, 18, 19, 21, 23, 25, 27, 28,
        Oct. 14, 15, 17—20, 22, 24, 26.

CRITICON MEDICO. w. est. June 5, 1830.
  Note: Ceased publication June 26,
  1830.
  MWA
    1830   June 5—26.

EL DEBATE. d. est. Nov. 16, 1950.
  DLC
    1955   Oct. 14.

DEFENSA. d. est. June 26, 1940.
  DLC
    1941   Mar. 3—22, 26—28, 31, Aug.
        8—11, 13, 14, 18, 20, 27—29,
        Sept. 1, 2, 4, 10—16, 23, 24,
        29—Oct. 15, 18—24, 29, 30,
        Nov. 3, 6—14, 17—21, 24, 25,
        27, 28, Dec. 1—6, 9—13, 16,
        18, 19, 22, 24, 26, 27, 29, 30.
    1942   Jan. 5, 6, 8—10, 13, 14, 16, 20,
        21, 23—28, 30—Feb. 2, 4, 5, 10,
        12, 16, 24, 26, 27, June 8, 9, 16,
        19, 22, 23, 26, 27, 30, July 8—

        17, 22, 23, 27, 29, Aug. 1—4, 6,
        7, 10—12, 14, 17—19, 21, 24,
        26, 28, Sept. 15, 24, 25, 29,
        Oct. 16—19, 24.
  MH
    1940   June 26—Dec. 31.
    1941   Jan. 1—Feb. 26.

DEMOCRACIA. [w.]
  MWA
    1892   Dec. 10.

DEMOCRACIA. d.
  Note: Published during suspension of
  El Siglo. Ceased publication Oct. 24,
  1952.
  DLC
    1951   Aug. 26, Sept. 2—6, 8—12,
        29—Oct. 4, 7—21, 23—29,
        Nov. 1, 5, 6, 8—22, 24—26,
        28—Dec. 7, 9—18, 20—22, 26,
        28.
    1952   Jan. 1—21, 23, 24, 26—Aug.
        29, Sept. 3—Oct. 20, 22—24.

DESCAMIZADO. est. May 2, 1827.
  Note: Published only one number.
  MWA
    1827   May 2.

DESPEDAZADO. irr. est. July 5, 1844.
  MWA
    1844   July 5—18.

DEUTSCHE PRESSE. d.
  Note: In German.
  DLC
    1915   Apr. 3.

DEUTSCHE ZEITUNG FÜR CHILE. d.
  est. Mar. 1910.
  Note: In German. Succeeded
  Deutsche Nachrichten (Valparaíso).
  Supplement in Spanish.
  DLC
    1915   Apr. 15.
    1941   Dec. 5—15.
    1942   Jan. 30—Feb. 2.
        Suplemento: *Diario alemán
        para Chile.*
    1940   Aug. 5.

1942   Jan. 6, Feb. 16, 17, 19 – 24,
Mar. 3, May 25 – 29, June 1 – 3,
11, 16, Sept. 14, Nov. 20, Dec.
5 – 7.

MH
  1941   Jan. 15 – Feb. 4, 6 – 11, 14 –
Mar. 11, 13 – Apr. 10, 13 – 30,
May 2 – 20, 23 – June 11, 13 –
July 3, 5 – Aug. 15, Oct. 16 –
Dec. 31.
  1942   Jan. 2 – 26, 28 – Apr. 2, 5 –
May 13, 15 – 20, 22 – 29, 31 –
June 2, 4 – 28, 30 – Aug. 4, 6 –
14, 16 – Sept. 4.
        Suplemento: *Diario alemán*
para Chile.
  1940   Nov. 22.
  1941   Feb. 21 – Oct. 24, 26 – Nov. 14,
16 – 27, 29 – Dec. 18.

EL DIARIO ILUSTRADO. d. est. Mar. 31,
1902.
  DLC
  1928   Dec. 12.
  1941   Mar. 1 – 6, 8, 9, 11, 12, 15 – 17,
20, 23 – 26, 28 – 31, June 8, 9,
16, 22, 23, 26, 28 – 30, Aug. 8, 9,
11 – 16, 18 – 21, 24 – 27, 29, 30,
Sept. 2 – 5, 8, 9, 12 – 26, 28, 29,
Oct. 2 – 6, 8, 9, 11, 12, 14 – 16,
18, 20, 21, 24, 26, 28, 29, 31 –
Nov. 2, 4, 6, 9 – 11, 14, 23, 26,
30, Dec. 1, 5, 8, 10, 11, 14, 15,
17 – 19, 21, 24 – 28, 30, 31.
  1942   Jan. 1, 3 – 9, 11 – 14, 16, 18, 23,
24, 26, 28 – Feb. 2, 4, 5, 7 – 9,
11, 12, 15 – 18, 20 – 28, May 28,
30, June 1, 8, 15, 17 – 19, 21, 26,
27, 29, 30, July 2, 10, 11, 13, 14,
18 – 20, 22, 23, Aug. 3, 4, 6, 9,
12, 15, 17, 20 – 22, 24, 29, Sept.
1 – 16, 19 – 21, 23 – Oct. 31,
Nov. 2 – Dec. 31.
  1943   Jan. 1, 3 – 11, 13 – 30, Feb. 1 –
7, 9 – May 21, 23 – June 14,
16 – July 31, Sept. 1 – 30, Dec.
1 – 31.
  1944   Feb. 1 – Mar. 31, Oct. 1 – Dec.
31.

1945   Jan. 1 – 25, 27 – Feb. 28.
1946   May 9 – June 5, 8, Oct. 3 – Nov.
16, Dec. 9 – 29.
1947   Sept. 11, 13 – 15, 18 – Dec. 10,
12 – 31.
1948   Jan. 1 – Mar. 8, 10 – Dec. 26,
28 – 31.
1949   Jan. 1 – Dec. 31.
1950   Jan. 1 – Feb. 3, 5 – Dec. 7, 9 –
31.
1951   Jan. 1 – Sept. 9, 11 – Dec. 31.
1952   Jan. 1 – Nov. 18, 20 – Dec. 31.
1953   Jan. 1 – Apr. 30, May 2 – July
20, 22 – Sept. 12, 14 – Oct. 2,
5 – Nov. 6, 10 – 12, 16 – 21,
23 – 28, 30 – Dec. 11, 14 – 31.
1954   Jan. 1 – Apr. 16, 19 – 29, May
2 – 22, 24 – June 6, 8 – 26, 29 –
July 2, 6 – 10, 12 – 17, 19 – 31,
Aug. 2, 3, 5 – Sept. 8, 10, 11,
13 – 20, 22 – 25, 27 – 29, Oct. 1,
3 – 9, 11 – Dec. 31.
1955   Jan. 1 – 8, 10 – Feb. 12, 14 –
Nov. 20, 22, 23, 25 – Dec. 23.

MH
  1919   Nov. 12 – 15.
  1939   Jan. 28, 29, Feb. 4, 7.
  MWA
  1906   Oct. 21, 23.

DOCE DE FEBRERO. est. Feb. 12, 1838.
  MWA
  1838   Feb. 12.

EPOCA. d. est. Nov. 15, 1881.
    Note: Ceased publication Jan. 28,
1892.
  MWA
  1886   Dec. 26.

ERCILLA. w.
  CU
  1964   Feb. 5 – Dec. 30.

ESTAFETA DE SANTIAGO. est. Feb. 9,
1830.
    Note: Published only one number.
  MWA
  1830   Feb. 9.

EL ESTANDARTE CATOLICO. d. est.
July 20, 1874.
> Note: Succeeded *La Revista catolica*
> which was established Apr. 1, 1843;
> succeeded by *El Porvenir*, Aug. 31,
> 1891. Ceased publication Jan. 8, 1891.

DLC
> 1883   July 27, Aug. 2.

ICRL
> 1874   July 20 – Dec. 31.
> 1875 – 1879   Jan. 1 – Dec. 31.

MWA
> 1889   Apr. 7.

ESTUDIANTE. est. Aug. 15, 1863.

MWA
> 1863   Aug. 15.

LA ESTRELLA DE CHILE. w. est. Aug.
31, 1826.
> Note: Ceased publication Apr. 23,
> 1827.

CtY
> 1826   Dec. 30.

DLC
> 1826   Sept. 9, Oct. 28, Nov. 4, Dec. 2,
>   30.
>   Extraordinario: Nov. 6.
> 1827   Feb. 24 – Mar. 16.
>   Suplemento: Feb. 24.

FERROCARRIL. d. est. Dec. 22, 1855.
> Note: Ceased publication [1911].

MWA
> 1868   May 9.
> 1872   June 15.
> 1888   May 20.
> 1890   Feb. 2, Nov. 20.
> 1892   Dec. 11.
> 1906   Apr. 4, 6, June 8, 9, Oct. 28 –
>   30.

GACETA MERCANTIL Y DE ANUNCIO
DE SANTIAGO. sw. est. Apr. 26, 1827.
> Note: Published only prospectus and
> one number.

MWA
> 1827   Prospecto.
>   Apr. 26.

GAZETA DE SANTIAGO DE CHILE.
> See *Gazeta ministerial de Chile.*

GAZETA DEL SUPREMO GOBIERNO
DE CHILE. w. est. Feb. 26, 1817.
> Note: Title *Viva la patria+ gazeta*
> *del gobierno de Chile* on prospectus
> only. Succeeded *Gazeta ministerial*
> *del gobierno de Chile*; succeeded by
> *Gazeta ministerial de Chile.* Ceased
> publication June 11, 1817.

WU
> 1817   Feb. 26 – June 11.

GAZETA MINISTERIAL DE CHILE. w.
est. June 18, 1817.
> Note: Title *Gazeta de Santiago de*
> *Chile*, June 18, 1817 – Mar. 21, 1818;
> *Gazeta ministerial de Chile*, May 2,
> 1818 – Feb. 5, 1823. Succeeded *Ga-*
> *zeta del supremo gobierno de Chile*;
> succeeded by *El Araucano.* Ceased
> publication Feb. 5, 1823.

CU – B
> Micro (N)
> 1818   Jan. 17 – Mar. 14, May 2 – Dec.
>   31.
> 1819   Jan. 1 – Dec. 31.
> 1820   Jan. 1.

CtY
> 1817   June 18 – Aug. 9, Sept. 6 – 20,
>   Oct. 25 – Nov. 22, Dec. 6, 20,
>   27.
> 1818   Jan. 17 – 31, Feb. 21, Mar. 7,
>   May 2 – Dec. 26.
> 1819   Jan. 2 – Apr. 24, May 8 – Nov.
>   27, Dec. 11 – 25.
> 1820   Jan. 1 – 22, Feb. 5 – Apr. 29,
>   May 13 – Aug. 12, 26 – Dec. 30.
> 1821   Jan. 13 – Dec. 21.
> 1822   Jan. 5 – Dec. 27.
> 1823   Jan. 15 – Feb. 5.

DLC
> 1817   [June 18 – Dec. 31].
> 1818 – 1822   [Jan. 1 – Dec. 31].
> 1823   [Jan. 1 – Feb. 5].

MWA
> 1819   Jan. 2 – Feb. 6.

NN
> 1818   June 13.

WU
　1817　June 18 – Dec. 31.
　1818　Jan. 1 – Mar. 21, May 2 – Dec.
　　　　31.
　1819　Jan. 1 – Dec. 31.
　1820　Jan. 1 – Dec. 30.

GAZETA MINISTERIAL DEL GOBIER-
NO DE CHILE. w. est. Nov. 17, 1814.
　Note: Title *Viva el rey*; *gazeta del
　gobierno de Chile*, on the prospectus,
　Nov. 11, 1814, and one extra, Nov. 14,
　1814; *Gaceta ministerial del gobier-
　no de Chile*, Nov. 17, 1814 – Feb. 11,
　1817. Succeeded *El Monitor arau-
　cano*; succeeded by *Gazeta del su-
　premo gobierno de Chile*. Ceased
　publication Feb. 11, 1817.
　WU
　1814　Prospecto: Nov. 11.
　　　　Nov. 17 – Dec. 31.
　　　　Extraordinario: Nov. 14.
　1815 – 1816　Jan. 1 – Dec. 31.
　1817　Jan. 1 – Feb. 11.

GAZETA MINISTERIAL EXTRAORDI-
NARIA DE CHILE. 3w., irr. est. 1818.
　Note: Ceased publication 1823.
　CtY
　1820　Nov. 8 – 18.
　1821　May 10, Aug. 15, 29.
　DLC
　1818　[Aug. 11 – Dec. 31].
　1819 – 1822　[Jan. 1 – Dec. 31].
　1823　Jan. 1 – 29.

HERALDO. bw.
　MWA
　1886　Mar. 25, Sept. 23, Dec. 2.
　　　　Suplemento.
　1887　Jan. 13, June 30 – July 14.
　1888　Dec. 27.
　1889　Jan. 24, July 25 – Aug. 8, Sept.
　　　　19 – Oct. 31, Dec. 12 – 26.

EL HERALDO YUGOESLAVO.
　See *Jugoslovenski glasnik. El Heraldo
　yugoeslavo*.

LA HORA. d. est. June 25, 1935.
　Note: Ceased publication Oct. 18,
　1951. See also *La Tercera de la hora*.

DLC
　1939　June 25.
　1941　Mar. 2 – 12, 15 – 18, 20, 29,
　　　　Aug. 7 – 11, 13, 16, 18 – 21,
　　　　24 – 27, 29, 30, Sept. 1 – 13,
　　　　15 – 19, 22 – 29, Oct. 2 – 10,
　　　　14 – 16, 18 – 25, 28, 29, 31 –
　　　　Nov. 3, 6 – 12, 14 – 16, 18, 19,
　　　　21, 23, 24, 26 – 29, Dec. 1, 4 –
　　　　6, 11 – 21, 24, 25, 27 – 31.
　1942　Jan. 1, 2, 4 – 8, 10, 12 – 15, 18,
　　　　20, 22 – 24, 26 – Feb. 9, 11, 12,
　　　　14, 17, 20, 21, 23 – 28, June 4,
　　　　5, 8, 10, 16, 17, 23, July 1, 9, 13,
　　　　14, 16, 18 – 20, 22, 23, 27, Aug.
　　　　7, 9, 17, 20, 21, 26, 29, Sept. 23,
　　　　26, 28, Oct. 8, 12, 15, 16, 19,
　　　　22, 24, 25, Dec. 1 – 7, 9 – 31.
　1943　Jan. 1, 2, 4, 10, 11, 18, 19, 23,
　　　　27, 29, Feb. 1 – Mar. 4, 9 – 11,
　　　　13, 16 – 31, Apr. 2 – May 1, 3 –
　　　　June 13, 16 – Aug. 16, 18 –
　　　　Sept. 30.
　1944　Feb. 1 – Mar. 31.
　1946　Sept. 1 – Dec. 31.
　1947　Mar. 1 – 3, 5 – 19, 21 – 29, 31 –
　　　　Apr. 5, 7 – 30, Oct. 1 – Dec. 4,
　　　　6, 8 – 31.
　1948　Jan. 1 – Feb. 29, Mar. 10 – Dec.
　　　　31.
　1949　Jan. 1 – Feb. 22, 24 – Dec. 31.
　1950　Jan. 1 – Feb. 3, 5 – Apr. 7, 9 –
　　　　Dec. 31.
　1951　Jan. 1 – June 8, 10 – 15, 17 –
　　　　July 7, Aug. 12 – 27, 29 – Sept.
　　　　11, 13 – 17, 21 – 25, 27 – Oct. 4,
　　　　6 – 18, 20 – 25.

ILUSTRACION ARAUCANA. est. Sept.
6, 1813.
　Note: Ceased publication Sept. 13,
　1813.
　WU
　1813　Sept. 6 – 13.

IMPARCIAL. est. Mar. 8, 1830.
　Note: Published only one number.
　MWA
　1830　Mar. 8.

EL IMPARCIAL. d. est. Nov. 6, 1926.
Note: Ceased publication Nov. 30,
1953.
DLC
1941　Feb. 27, Mar. 1, 3, 4, 6 — 13,
16 — 26, 28 — 30, May 1 — 4, 6, 8,
10 — 12, 14, 16, 18, 19, 21 — 24,
26, 27, 29, June 3 — 7, 10, 15, 17,
21 — 24, 26 — 30, Aug. 7, 9, 10,
12 — 14, 16 — 19, 23, 24, 26 — 29,
31 — Sept. 2, 4, 6, 8, 9, 11 — 13,
17, 18, 20, 22 — 24, 26 — 28, Oct.
1 — 4, 6 — 10, 15, 17 — 19, 22 —
24, 27, 29 — 31, Nov. 3 — 6, 8 —
10, 12, 13, 15, 16, 20 — 26, 30 —
Dec. 2, 4, 9 — 12, 15 — 19, 23 —
30.
1942　Jan. 1, 4 — 6, 9, 12, 14 — 19, 21 —
23, 25, 29, Feb. 4 — 9, 11, 13, 19,
20, 23 — 26, May 20, 27, 28,
June 8, 17, 19, 20, 22, 23, 26 —
30, July 2, 8, 11, 19, 23, 27,
30, Aug. 2, 10, 11, 13 — 17, 19 —
22, 27, Sept. 1 — 3, 5, 6, 8 — Oct.
20, 22 — Dec. 30.
1943 — 1944　Jan. 1 — Dec. 31.
1945　Jan. 1 — Mar. 23, 25 — Apr. 27,
30 — June 12, 14 — 16, 18 — July
29, 31, Aug. 2 — 26, 28 — Sept.
19, 21 — Nov. 25, 28 — Dec. 3,
5 — 31.
1946　Jan. 1 — Feb. 20, 22 — Mar. 24,
26, 28 — June 18, 21 — July 5,
7 — 17, 19 — 21, 23 — Sept. 8, 10,
11, 13 — Nov. 7, 9 — Dec. 3, 6 —
21, 23 — 25, 27 — 30.
1947　Jan. 1 — Apr. 29, May 1 — June
2, 4 — 20, 23 — Dec. 31.
1948　Jan. 1 — Dec. 31.
1951　Jan. 1 — Feb. 12, 14 — 24, 26 —
Apr. 12, 16 — 29, May 1 — June
22, 24 — Oct. 13, 15 — 17, 19 —
Dec. 31.
1952　Jan. 1 — 17, 19 — 23, 25 — Feb.
15, 17, 18, 28, 29, Mar. 3 — 14,
16 — 28, 30 — Apr. 30, May 5 —
16, 18 — 20, 23 — June 17, 19 —
July 19, 21 — Aug. 1, 5 — 8, 12 —

Sept. 29, Oct. 1 — 4, 6 — 17, 21 —
24, 28 — Nov. 8, 10 — 28, 30 —
Dec. 4, 7, 9 — 12, 14 — 19, 21 —
26, 28 — 31.
1953　Jan. 2 — 9, 11 — 23, 25 — Feb. 6,
8 — 13, 15 — Mar. 27, 29, 30.

INDEPENDIENTE. d. est. Mar. 1, 1864.
Note: Ceased publication Jan. 7, 1891.
MWA
1889　Oct. 25, Dec. 26, 27, 31.

EL INDICADOR. irr. est. Jan. 10, 1827.
Note: Ceased publication Mar. 31,
1827.
DLC
1827　Feb. 21, Mar. 1.

LA INFORMACION. d. est. 1915.
DLC
1926　Jan. 18 — 29, 31 — Feb. 12, 16 —
20, Mar. 8 — 12, Apr. 1, 5 — 7, 9,
10, 19 — 30, May 2 — 21, 23 —
July 10, Aug. 1 — 15, 17 — Sept.
23, 25 — Oct. 14, 16 — 31, Dec.
21, 23 — 31.
1927　Jan. 1 — 5, 8 — Feb. 5, 14 — Mar.
5, 7 — Apr. 26, 28 — June 3, 9 —
July 8, 10 — Aug. 24, 26 — Sept.
26, 28 — Oct. 15, 17 — 21, Nov.
13 — 26.

JUGOSLOVENSKI GLASNIK. EL HER-
ALDO YUGOESLAVO. irr. est. Feb.
1935.
Note: In Spanish and Croatian.
DLC
1942　Apr. 15.
1947　July 9.

JUICIO. irr. est. Aug. 27, 1830.
Note: Ceased publication Oct. 11,
1830.
MWA
1830　Aug. 27 — Oct. 11.

JUSTICIA. irr. est. Feb. 10, 1841.
MWA
1841　Feb. 10, Mar. 18.

JUVENTUD. w. est. Apr. 25, 1867.
MWA
1867　Apr. 25 — July 25.

EL LIBERAL. irr. est. July 28, 1823.
  Note: Ceased publication Feb. 4, 1825.
  DLC
    1824   Aug. 17, Sept. 4, Oct. 14 — Dec.
            24.

LIBERAL. w. est. Jan. 22, 1840.
  MWA
    1840   Jan. 22 — Feb. 8.
            Suplemento.

LINCOLN. w. est. June 11, 1865.
  MWA
    1865   June 11 — 25.

LINCOLN. w. est. Aug. 5, 1865.
  MWA
    1865   Aug. 5 — Sept. 28.

LUCERNA. w. est. July 11, 1832.
  Note: Ceased publication Jan. 31,
  1833.
  MWA
    1832   July 11 — Dec. 31.
    1833   Jan. 1 — 31.

LUNES. w. est. Sept. 4, 1882.
  MWA
    1882   Sept. 4 — Oct. 16, Nov. 13 —
            Dec. 31.
    1883   Jan. 1 — May 7, 21 — Aug. 27,
            Oct. 8 — 22, Nov. 5 — 13.

EL MERCURIO. d. est. June 1, 1900.
  Note: Established by *El Mercurio* of
  Valparaíso but became a separate
  newspaper. See also *Las Ultimas no-*
  ticias.
  CLU
    1942   June 1 — Dec. 31.
    1943   Jan. 1 — Dec. 31.
    1944   Jan. 1 — Mar. 31.
    1945 — 1954   Jan. 1 — Dec. 31.
    Micro (P)
    1955   Jan. 1+.
  CSt — H
    1964   Dec. 20 — 31.
    1965   Jan. 1+.
  CU
    1919   Sept. 16, Dec. 23, 24 — 31.
    1920 — 1926   Jan. 1 — Dec. 31.

    1927   Jan. 1 — Oct. 12, Nov. 10 — Dec.
            31.
    1928   Jan. 1 — Oct. 3.
  CtY
    1965   Aug. 1 — Dec. 31.
    1966   Jan. 1+.
  Micro (P)
    1962 — 1964   Jan. 1 — Dec. 31.
    1965   Jan. 1 — July 31.
  DLC
    1941 — 1942   Jan. 1 — Dec. 31.
    1943   Jan. 1 — Aug. 29, 31 — Sept. 15,
            17, 19 — Dec. 31.
    1944   Jan. 1 — 31, Mar. 1 — June 30,
            Oct. 1 — Nov. 30.
    1945   Apr. 1 — Aug. 30, Sept. 1 — Dec.
            31.
    1946   Jan. 1 — Mar. 16, 18 — Aug. 1,
            3 — 27, 29 — Dec. 31.
    1947   Jan. 1 — Dec. 31.
    1948   Jan. 1 — Oct. 30, Nov. 1 — 28,
            30 — Dec. 31.
    1949   Jan. 2 — Sept. 20, 22 — Dec. 31.
    1950 — 1951   Jan. 1 — Dec. 31.
    1952   Jan. 1 — Nov. 10, 22 — Dec.
            16.
    1953   Jan. 1 — 8, 10 — May 10, 12 —
            July 16, 18 — Aug. 31.
    1954   Jan. 1 — Dec. 31.
    1955   Jan. 1 — Feb. 26, 28 — June 30.
  Micro (P) & (N)
    1914 — 1940   June 1 — Dec. 31.
    1953   Jan. 1+.
  DPU
    Current (six months).
    Micro (P)
    1938 — 1943   Jan. 1 — Dec. 31.
    1946 — 1947   Jan. 1 — Dec. 31.
    1953 — 1954   Jan. 1 — Dec. 31.
    1955   Jan. 1 — Dec. 30.
    Micro (N)
    1948   Jan. 30 — Dec. 31.
    1949   Jan. 1 — July 31.
    1950   Jan. 1 — Feb. 10, July 1 — Aug.
            31, Dec. 5 — 31.
  ICRL
    1927   Feb. 1 — Dec. 31.
    1929   Nov. 1 — Dec. 31.

1942   Apr. 16 – Dec. 31.
1943 – 1952   Jan. 1 – Dec. 31.
1953   Jan. 1 – June 31.
1954   Mar. 1 – Dec. 31.
Micro (N)
1938 – 1943   Jan. 1 – Dec. 31.
1946 – 1947   Jan. 1 – Dec. 31.
IU
  Micro (P)
  1953 – 1955   Jan. 1 – Dec. 31.
LNT – MA
  1934   Dec. 24.
  1941   May 30.
MB
  Current (one month).
MH
  1945   July 4 – 6, 8, 9, 11 – Sept. 9,
          11 – Oct. 10, 12 – Nov. 16,
          18 – 30, Dec. 2 – 25, 27 – 31.
  1946   Jan. 1 – May 25, 27 – July 23.
  1947   Jan. 4 – 6, 21, Feb. 4, 5, 8, 9,
          11 – 13, 18 – 20, Mar. 13 – 15,
          17, Apr. 12, 13, 15, 24, 25, 27,
          28, May 5, 6, 8 – June 9, 13, 14,
          24 – July 31, Aug. 4 – 25, 27 –
          30, Sept. 1 – 17, 19 – 27, 29,
          Oct. 1 – 19, 21 – Nov. 4, 7, 9 –
          12, 14 – 19, 21, 22, 24, 26 – Dec.
          3, 5, 7 – 10, 12 – 31.
  1948   Jan. 1 – 25, 27, 28, Apr. 1 – 12,
          14 – 24, 26 – June 10, 12 – July
          23, 25 – Nov. 30, Dec. 2 – 31.
MWA
  1904   May 24.
MnU
  Current (two years).
NIC
  Micro (P)
  1964   Jan. 1 – Dec. 31.
  1965   Feb. 1 – Dec. 31.
  1966   Jan. 1+.
NN
  1915   Nov. 1 – 23, 25 – Dec. 31.
  1916   Jan. 1 – Dec. 31.
  1917   Mar. 1 – July 31.
  1944   Mar. 1 – 21, 23 – Aug. 1, 9 – 23,
          25 – Sept. 16, 18 – Oct. 19, 21 –
          Dec. 31.

1945   Jan. 1 – Mar. 20, 22 – Dec. 31.
1946   Apr. 1 – Aug. 1, 3 – 19, 21 –
        Sept. 18, 20 – 25, 27 – Dec. 31.
1947   Jan. 1 – Mar. 6, 8 – 11, 13 – 31.
NNC
  1965   May 29 – 31, June 8 – 15, 17 –
          27, 29 – July 8, 11 – 15, 17 – 22,
          24, 25, 27 – Aug. 9, 11 – 16, 18,
          20 – Sept. 1, 3 – 30, Oct. 2 – 4,
          6 – 14, 17 – 19, 21 – 31, Nov.
          2 – 4, 6, 9 – 23, 26 – Dec. 5, 8 –
          12, 16.
NcD
  1928   Jan. 2 – 21, 23 – Feb. 14, 16 –
          Mar. 17, 19 – Apr. 7, 9 – May
          24, 26 – July 19, 21 – Dec. 31.
  1929 – 1933   Jan. 1 – Dec. 31.
  1934   Feb. 1 – 28, July 1 – Dec. 31.
NjP
  Micro (P)
  1962 – 1964   Jan. 1 – Dec. 31.
  1965   Feb. 1 – Dec. 31.
  1966   Jan. 1+.
PU
  1909   July 1 – Dec. 31.
  1910   Jan. 1 – Apr. 30, June 1 – Dec.
          31.
  1911 – 1914   Jan. 1 – Dec. 31.
  1915   Mar. 1 – Dec. 31.
  1916   Jan. 1 – Dec. 31.
TxU
  1920   Jan. 1 – 7, 9 – 16, 27 – Dec. 31.
  1921 – 1924   Jan. 1 – Dec. 31.
  1941   July 9 – Dec. 31.
  1942   Jan. 1 – July 20, 22 – Dec. 31.
  1943   Jan. 1 – 24, 26, 27, 29 – Dec.
          31.
  1944   Jan. 1 – Feb. 29.
  1945   Mar. 1 – 21, 23 – June 21, 24 –
          30, Aug. 1 – Oct. 21, 23 – Nov.
          18, 20 – Dec. 31.
  1946   Jan. 1 – Mar. 29.
  1947   June 1 – Dec. 31.
  1948   Jan. 1 – Dec. 31.
  1949   Jan. 1 – Nov. 9, 11 – Dec. 31.
  1950   Jan. 1 – Feb. 3, 5 – Dec. 31.
  1951 – 1952   Jan. 1 – Dec. 31.
  1956   July 1 – Sept. 30.

1958   Apr. 1 – Dec. 31.
1959   Jan. 1 – Feb. 28.
Micro (P)
1953 – 1955   Jan. 1 – Dec. 31.

MICROSCOPIO. est. Jan. 31, 1838.
  MWA
    1838   Jan. 31.

MOCION. irr. est. June 27, 1840.
  MWA
    1840   June 27 – Aug. 13.

EL MONITOR ARAUCANO. 3w., sw.
  est. Apr. 6, 1813.
    Note: Periodicity Apr. 6 – Nov. 30,
    1813, three times a week; Dec. 2,
    1813 – Sept. 30, 1814, semiweekly.
    Succeeded *Aurora de Chile* as offi-
    cial gazette; succeeded by *Gazeta
    ministerial del gobierno de Chile*.
    Ceased publication Sept. 30, 1814.
  CtY
    1813   Apr. 8 – Dec. 31.
    1814   Jan. 1 – Sept. 30.
  DLC
    1813   Apr. 8 – Dec. 31.
    1814   Jan. 1 – Sept. 30.

EL MONITOR IMPARCIAL. w. est.
  Aug. 18, 1827.
    Note: Ceased publication Mar. 21,
    1828.
  DLC
    1828   Mar. 21.

MUNDO.
  MWA
    1840   Feb. 15.

MUNDO JUDIO. w. est. Jan. 1935.
  DLC
    1942   July 24, Oct. 16.

MUNDO LIBRE. d. est. Mar. 1, 1956.
  DLC
    1956   Mar. 1 – Apr. 19, 21 – May 23,
            25 – 30, June 1 – 3, 8 – 16, 18 –
            23, 25 – 30.

EL MUSEO. w. est. June 11, 1853.
    Note: Ceased publication Dec. 17,
    1853.

TxU
  1853   June 11 – Dec. 17.

LA NACION. d. est. Jan. 14, 1917.
  CSt
    1941   Oct. 21 – Dec. 31.
    1942 – 1943   Jan. 1 – Dec. 31.
    1944   Jan. 1 – May 20, 22 – July 31,
            Aug. 8 – Oct. 28, Nov. 5 –
            Dec. 9.
    1945   Jan. 1 – Aug. 31, Oct. 1 – 31,
            Nov. 6 – 28, Dec. 1 – 31.
    1946 – 1947   Jan. 1 – Dec. 31.
    1948   Feb. 1 – Dec. 31.
    1949   Jan. 1 – Sept. 30, Nov. 1 –
            Dec. 31.
    1950 – 1953   Jan. 1 – Dec. 31.
    1954   Jan. 1 – July 31.
  CU
    1929   June 23, July 13 – 19, 24 – 26,
            Aug. 17 – 20, Dec. 4 – 6, 18 –
            24.
    1930   Apr. 30 – May 9.
  DLC
    1928   Dec. 12.
    1939   Jan. 1 – Aug. 4, 11 – 16, 18 –
            Oct. 9, 12 – Nov. 2, 4 – Dec. 31.
    1940   July 1 – Oct. 10, 12 – 30, Nov. 1
            – Dec. 22, 24 – 31.
    1941   Jan. 1 – May 7, 9 – July 27, 29 –
            Aug. 2, 4, 5, 8 – Sept. 2, 4 – 7,
            9 – 20, 22 – Oct. 4, 6 – 9, 11 –
            15, 17 – 25, 27 – Dec. 31.
    1942   Jan. 1 – Dec. 31.
    1943   Jan. 1 – Sept. 9, 11 – Dec. 31.
    1944   Jan. 1 – July 30, Aug. 1 – Dec.
            31.
    1945   Jan. 1 – Apr. 14, 16 – June 19,
            July 14 – Dec. 31.
    1946   Jan. 1 – Mar. 31, Apr. 2 – Sept.
            12, 15, 16, 18, 19, 21 – 26, 28 –
            Oct. 15, 17 – Dec. 31.
    1947 – 1948   Jan. 1 – Dec. 31.
    1949   Jan. 1 – Mar. 11, 14 – June 28,
            30 – July 3, 5 – Oct. 27, 29 –
            Nov. 20, 22 – Dec. 18.
    1950   Jan. 1 – Dec. 31.
    1954   Jan. 6 – 10, 12 – 15, 17 – 22, 24,
            26 – 29, 31 – Feb. 22, 24 – Mar.

1, 3−21, 27−30, Apr. 1, 2, 5−
7, 9, 10, 12−15, 18, 20, 22−26,
29, May 1−13, 15, 17, 22−25,
28−30, June 1−7, 9−16, 19,
20, 22, 24−July 2, 6−10, 12−
17, 19−31, Aug. 2, 3, 5−25,
27−Sept, 27, 29−Oct, 1, 3, 5−
9, 11−19, 22−Nov. 17, 19−25,
27, 28, 30−Dec. 7, 9−23, 25−
31.

1955   Jan. 1−8, 10−Feb. 12, 14−19,
21−Oct. 18, 20−Dec. 20, 22−
25, 28−31.

1956   Jan. 3−23, 25−Mar. 29, 31−
Apr. 29, May 1−29, June 1−
26, 28−Aug. 4, 6−24, 26−
31, Sept. 2−23, 25−29, Oct.
1−28, 30−Nov. 22, Dec. 3−
31.

1957   Jan. 1−Feb. 5, 7−Mar. 10,
13−15, 17−Apr. 4, 6−11,
14−25, 28−May 7, 14−24,
28−June 13, 15−19, 22−30,
July 2, 3, 5, 10−15, 18, 20, 22,
24, 28−30, Aug. 2−14, 16, 17,
19, 21−23, 25−Sept. 2, 4−14,
16, 18−Oct. 10, 12−14, 16,
19−24, 26−Nov. 10, 12−30,
Dec. 2−8, 10−13, 15−31.

1958   Jan. 1−29, 31−Mar. 19, 21−
May 14, 27−Aug. 11, 13−
Sept. 23, Oct. 1−Dec. 31.

1959   Jan. 1−Feb. 9, 18−May 29,
July 1−Aug. 30, Sept. 1−Dec.
31.

1960   Jan. 1−July 19, 22−25, 28−
Oct. 22, 28−Dec. 1, 9−20,
23−31.

1961   Jan. 1−29, Feb. 1, 2, 4−25,
28−Mar. 10, 13−Apr. 7, 15−
Dec. 31.

Micro   (P) & (N)
1962   Jan. 1+.
ICRL
1927   Apr. 8, 10, 11.
1960   June 29−Dec. 31.
MH
1920   Oct. 22−26.

1937   Jan. 1−14, 19−21, 29−Mar. 4,
12−18, 23−29, Apr. 2−5,
13−19, 23−May 21, 23−June
4, 11−July 22, 24−Dec. 27.

1938   Jan. 4−10, 14−Feb. 7, 11−
Apr. 14, 16−May 16, 18, 20−
June 7, 9−13, July 5, 7, 8, 10−
12, 14, 15, 18−20, 23−27, 29,
30, Aug. 1−2, 4, 6, 7, 10−12,
14, 15, 17, 18, 20, 21, 23, 27−
Sept. 1, 6, 7, 23, 25−27, 29, 30,
Oct. 2, 3, 5−12, 14, 15, 17−22,
24−27, 29−Nov. 1, 3, 8, 10,
15−17, 25, 27, 28, Dec. 3−7,
10−14, 17−20, 22−24, 27−
31.

1939   Jan. 2, 3, 5−8, 11−18, 20, 21,
23, 25−29, 31, Feb. 2−5, 7,
8, 11−13, 14−16, 18−20, 22−
25, 27−Mar. 1, 4−7, 9−11,
13−15, 18−21, 23, 25−28,
30, Apr. 1−4, 6−10, 12−16,
19, 20, May 5, 6, 8, 10, 12, 15,
18, 19, 21, 22, 24, 25, 27, 28, 30,
June 2, 6, 8−10, 12−15, 17,
21−26, 28−30, July 4, 5, 10−
12, 15−24, 26, 27.

NOTICIAS DE LA SEMANA. w.
DLC
1942   Feb. 13, 20, June 5, Aug. 21.
MH
1940   Oct. 12−Nov. 9, 23−Dec. 31.
Extraordinario: Oct. 1−Nov.
30, Dec. 7, 21.

1941   Jan. 1−Apr. 4, 10−Nov. 28,
Dec. 12−26.
Extraordinario: Jan. 6, 18, Feb.
1, 15, Mar. 1, 15, Apr. 12, 26,
May 10, 24, June 6, 23, July 9,
23, Aug. 6, 20, Sept. 3, Oct. 1−
29, Nov. 7, 26, Dec. 24.

1942   Jan. 1−Mar. 27, Apr. 2−Aug.
21, Sept. 4−Dec. 11, 25−31.
Extraordinario: Jan. 7, 21, Feb.
4, 17, 18, Mar. 4, 18, Apr. 1, 15,
May 13, 27, 29, June 10, 24,
July 8, 22, Aug. 5, 19, Sept. 2,

16, 30, Oct. 14, 28, Nov. 11,
25, Dec. 21, 23.
1943   Jan. 1 – 8, 15 – Mar. 5, 19 –
Dec. 31.
Extraordinario: Jan. 6, 20,
Feb. 3, 17, Mar. 3, 17, Apr. 13,
May 12.
Suplemento: Mar. 31, Apr. 28,
May 26, June 7, 23, July 7, 21,
Aug. 4, 18, Sept. 1, 15, 27, Oct.
20, 27, Nov. 10, 24, Dec. 8, 22.
1944   Jan. 1 – July 28, Aug. 11 – Sept.
1, 8 – Dec. 31.
Suplemento: Jan. 19, Feb. 2,
16, Mar. 1, 15, 29, Apr. 12, 26,
May 10, 24, June 7, 21, July 5,
19, Aug. 16, 30, Sept. 13, 27,
Oct. 11, 25, Nov. 8, 22, Dec. 6,
20.
1945   Jan. 1 – May 18.

LAS NOTICIAS DE LA ULTIMA HORA.
d. est. Oct. 15, 1943.
CSt – H
1966   May 24, 26, 28 – June 5, 7, 15,
16, 21+.
DLC
1943   Oct. 18 – Dec. 31.
ICRL
1960   July 1 – Dec. 31.
1961   Jan. 1 – 31.

LAS NOTICIAS GRAFICAS. d. est. Feb.
8, 1944.
DLC
1944   Feb. 8 – Mar. 6, 8, 9, 11 – Apr.
11, 13, 15 – 23, 26 – June 29,
July 1 – 4, 6 – Oct. 11, 13, 15 –
17, 21 – 23, 28 – 31.
Oct. 11, 13, 15 – 17, 21 – 23,
28 – 31.

NOTICIAS ORBIS DE ULTIMA HORA.
d.
Note: Title *Servicio informativo
orbis* before Mar. 1, 1942.
DLC
1942   Feb. 19, 24, 26, Mar. 6, 12, 14,
17, Apr. 1.

NOTICIERO ESPAÑOL. w.
MWA
1896   June 11.

NUEVO MAQUIAVELO. irr. est. June 23,
1840.
MWA
1840   June 23 – July 30, Sept. 30 –
Oct. 17.

NUNCIO DE LA GUERRA. w. est. Dec.
30, 1837.
Note: Published only two numbers.
Ceased publication Jan. 9, 1838.
MWA
1837   Dec. 30.
1838   Jan. 9.

EL O'HIGGINISTA. bw. est. Jan. 18, 1831.
Note: Ceased publication Feb. 12,
1831.
CU – B
Micro (N)
1831   Jan. 18 – Feb. 12.

OPINION. irr. est. May 8, 1830.
MWA
1830   May 8 – Dec. 31.
1831   Jan. 1 – Dec. 31.
1832   Jan. 1 – Apr. 12.

LA OPINION. d. est. Mar. 21, 1932.
Note: Ceased publication Nov. 21,
1951.
DLC
1937   Feb. 8
1939   Mar. 21.
1941   Mar. 1 – 4, 6 – 11, 15, 18 – 22,
25 – 28, 30, Aug. 5 – 12, 15, 17,
18, 20, 21, 25, 30, Sept. 1 – 3,
8, 12, 24, Oct. 8, 16, 21, 22, 26,
29, 30, Nov. 3, 6, 8, 10, 11, 13,
15 – 17, 22, 25, 28, 29, Dec. 1,
6, 8 – 10, 15, 18, 29.
1942   Jan. 9, 12, 21, 29, 31, Feb. 14 –
16, 23, 25, 26, May 29, June 1,
13, 16 – 18, 23, July 17, 22, 23,
29 – 31, Aug. 2, 6, 9, 20 – 23,
Sept. 19, 26 – 28, Oct. 6, 8, 11 –
15, 18, 19, 24, Dec. 7 – 16, 19 –
31.

1943 Jan. 1 – Feb. 26, 28, Apr. 1 –
July 3, 5 – 31, Sept. 1 – Dec.
31.

1944 Jan. 1 – Feb. 29, May 1 – 31,
Aug. 1 – Sept. 30.

1947 June 2 – July 20, 28 – 30, Aug.
1 – 4, 6 – 18, 26 – 31.

1948 Jan. 1 – 16, 18 – Feb. 22, Mar.
1 – Oct. 31, Nov. 9 – 21, 25 –
Dec. 17, 20 – 31.

1949 Jan. 1 – Dec. 31.

1950 Jan. 1 – Mar. 29, Apr. 2 – Nov.
23, Dec. 1 – 31.

1951 Jan. 1 – 23, 25 – July 4, 6 – Nov.
21.

PATRIOTA. est. Feb. 5, 1840.
 MWA
  1840 Feb. 5.

PATRIOTA CHILENO. irr., sw. est. Dec.
19, 1825.
 Note: Ceased publication Jan. 31,
 1827.
 CtY
  1826 Apr. 12, Sept. 2.
 DLC
  1826 Apr. 12, 19, May 6 – 10, 17,
   24 – June 10, 21, 28 – July 5,
   12 – Aug. 12, 19 – 26, Sept. 2 –
   Nov. 11, 20, 29 – Dec. 6, 23 –
   30.

PENQUISTO. w. est. Apr. 1, 1829.
 Note: Ceased publication Apr. 28,
 1829.
 MWA
  1829 Apr. 1 – 28.

PERRERO. bw. est. July 19, 1837.
 MWA
  1837 July 19 – Oct. 1.

EL PIPIOLO. est Mar. 10, 1827.
 Note: Ceased publication July 6,
 1827.
 DLC
  1827 May 26.

POLITICO REFUTADOR DE LA
 ANTORCHA. est. Feb. 7, 1831.

Note: Published only one number.
MWA
 1831 Feb. 7.

EL PORVENIR. d. est. Aug. 31, 1891.
 Note: Succeeded *El Estandarte
 católico*. Ceased publication Sept. 30,
 1906.
 MWA
  1891 Sept. 5.

PRIMERA PELUCADO. est. Nov. 27,
1838.
 MWA
  1838 Nov. 27.

PROGRESO. d. est. Nov. 10, 1842.
 Note: Suspended publication Nov. 8 –
 Dec. 22, 1850; Apr. 20 – June 2, 1851;
 Sept. 14, 1851 – [Nov. 1852.]
 MWA
  1842 Nov. 10 – Dec. 31.
  1843 Jan. 1 – Dec. 31.
  1844 Jan. 1 – Dec. 31.
   Suplemento: June 11 – Dec. 5.
  1845 – 1850 Jan. 1 – Dec. 31.
  1851 Jan. 1 – Sept. 31.
  1852 Dec. 1 – 31.
  1853 Jan. 1 – Mar. 11.

¿QUIEN VIVE? est. July 31, 1833.
 Note: Published only one number.
 MWA
  1833 July 31.

EL RADIO-EXPRESO. d. est. Apr. 10,
1941.
 DLC
  1941 Apr. 10 – July 23, 25 – Aug. 12,
   14, 15, 17 – Sept. 5, 7 – Nov. 2,
   4 – Dec. 9, 11 – 31.
  1942 Jan. 1 – 5, 7, 8, 10 – Apr. 13,
   15 – June 16, 18, 20, 21, 23 –
   July 10, 12 – 15, 17 – Aug. 7,
   9 – Oct. 11, 13 – Dec. 31.
  1943 Jan. 4 – 18, 20 – 22.

RECUERDOS DE COLOCOLO. irr. est
Jan. 5, 1838.
 MWA
  1838 Jan. 5 – 20.

REDACTOR DE LAS NULIDADES DE
LAS ULTIMAS ELECCIONES. [w.]
est. June 10, 1840.
MWA
 1840 June 10 – 20.

LA REFORMA. w. est 1931.
 Note: In Spanish and Arabic.
DLC
 1942 Mar. 7, 14.

REFUTADOR. est. Oct. 17, 1829.
 Note: Published only one number.
MWA
 1829 Oct. 17.

REGISTRO MUNICIPAL. w., irr. est.
Mar. 15, 1828.
 Note: Periodicity Mar. 15 – June 14,
 1828, weekly; after June 14, 1828, irregular. Ceased publication Feb. 27,
 1830.
MWA
 1828 Mar. 15, Apr. 12 – May 10, 24,
   June 14 – Sept. 27, Oct. 13,
   Nov. 21 – Dec. 31.
 1829 Jan. 1 – Aug. 19.
 1830 Jan. 30 – Feb. 9.

REPUBLICA. d. est. June 7, 1866.
 Note: Ceased publication Nov. 15,
 1878.
MWA
 1872 May 30.

REPUBLICANO. est. Aug. 21, 1829.
 Note: Published only one number.
MWA
 1829 Aug. 21.

REPUBLICANO. irr. est. June 4, 1836.
 Note: Published only two numbers.
 Ceased publication June 18, 1836.
MWA
 1836 June 4 – 18.

REVISTA AMERICANA. w. est. Aug. 29,
1869.
 Note: Ceased publication Nov. 19,
 1869.
MWA
 1869 Aug. 29 – Nov. 19.

ROL DE POLICIA. w. est. Apr. 28, 1827.
 Note: Ceased publication July 23,
 1827.
CtY
 1827 July 9.
MWA
 1827 Apr. 28 – May 7, 21 – June 25.

SACA-PICA. w. est. [May 16, 1942].
DLC
 1942 June 27, July 27.

LA SEGUNDA DE LAS ULTIMAS NO-
TICIAS. d. est. July 1931.
DLC
 1942 Jan. 14, Feb. 26, June 3, Aug.
   10, 13, Sept. 1 – 3, 5, 15 – 17,
   21 – 26, 28 – Oct. 2, 5 – 8, 10,
   12 – 17, 19, 20, 22, 24, 27 – 31,
   Nov. 2 – 7, 9 – 14, 16 – 21, 23 –
   28, 30 – Dec. 5, 7, 9 – 12, 14 –
   19, 21 – 24, 26, 28 – 31.
 1943 Jan. 2, 29, 30, Feb. 1 – 6, 8 –
   13, 15 – 20, 22 – 27, Mar. 1 – 6,
   8 – 13, 15 – 20, 22 – 27, 29 –
   Apr. 3, 5 – 10, 12 – 22, 25 –
   30, May 3 – 8, 10 – 15, 17 – 20,
   22, 24 – 29, 31 – June 2, 4, 5,
   7 – 12, 14 – 19, 21 – 23, 25, 26,
   28, 30.
 1955 Oct. 14.

LAS SEIS. est. Dec. 11, 1941.
DLC
 1941 Dec. 11.

SEMANARIO DE POLICIA. w., irr. est.
Sept. 3, 1817.
 Note: Ceased publication May 20,
 1818.
WU
 1817 Sept. 3 – Dec. 31.
 1818 Jan. 1 – May 20.

SERVICIO INFORMATIVO ORBIS.
 See *Noticias orbis de última hora.*

EL SIGLO. d. est. Aug. 31, 1940.
 Note: Suspended publication Dec. 12,
 1948; succeeded by *Democracia*
 which ceased publication Oct. 24,

1952: *El Siglo* resumed publication Oct. 25, 1952.

CSt–H
1964   Aug. 1–Dec. 31.
1965   Jan. 1+.

DLC
1941   Jan. 13, 14, Mar. 2, 7, 9, 10, 16, Aug. 7–21, 25, 26, 28, Sept. 2, 7, 10–12, 14, 16, 21, 24, 26, 27, Oct. 2–4, 7–9, 11–14, 16–18, 20, 23, 24, 30, Nov. 4, 5, 7, 8, 11–13, 15–19, 21–24, 26, Dec. 1, 2, 4, 6, 9–11, 15, 16, 18, 20, 23, 28–30.
1942   Jan. 4, 5, 7, 10–12, 20, 21, 25, 26, Feb. 6, 7, 11, 23–25, June 23, July 5, 14, 17–19, 29, 31, Aug. 2, 5, 7, 9, 10, 12, 14, 18, 21, 22, 26, 27, Sept. 1–14, 17–28, 30–Oct. 24, 26–Dec. 31.
1943   Jan. 1, 5–8, 13, 15–21, 24–26, 28–June 30, Aug. 1–Dec. 31.
1944   Jan. 1–Apr. 6, 8–12, 14, 15, May 1–July 9, 12, 14–23, 26, 27, 29–Sept. 5, 7–25, 27–Oct. 3, 5–10, 14–16, 18, 19, 21–24, 26, 27, Nov. 3–9, 11–Dec. 28, 31.
1945   Jan. 1, 6–8, 10–Mar. 14, 16–21, 23–27, Apr. 2–6, 8, 10–19, May 11–15, 17–25, 28, 29, June 4, 5, 7, 8, 12–14, 16–18, 20–24, 27–30, Oct. 1–21, 23, 24, 26, 27, 29–Dec. 31.
1946   Apr. 1–27, May 2–June 30.
1952   Oct. 25–Dec. 31.
1953   Jan. 1–Apr. 28, May 9–Aug. 10, 14–17, 20, Sept. 5–9, 12–23, 25–28, Oct. 6, 7, 9–16, 18–24, 27–Nov. 3, 5–10, 13–Dec. 14, 16, 18–24, 29, 31.
1954   Jan. 1–4, 6–31, Feb. 2, 9–23, 26–Mar. 24, 27, 30–Apr. 30, July 20–31, Aug. 2–6, 8, 9, 11–17, 19–28, 30–Nov. 1,

3–15, 17–Dec. 31.
1955   Jan. 1–Feb. 15, 18–23, 25–28, Mar. 2–Apr. 30, May 2–July 6, 8–Dec. 31.
1956   Jan. 1–Apr. 18, 20–29, May 1–17, 20–23, June 4–Dec. 31.
1957   Jan. 1–Mar. 31, May 2–Dec. 31.
1958   Jan. 1–Mar. 19, 21–May 14, 16–June 20, 22–July 14, 18, 21, 22, 25–30, Aug. 1–Oct. 30, Nov. 1–Dec. 31.
1959   Jan. 1–Feb. 7, 18–20, 22–27, Mar. 1–Aug. 14, 16–Nov. 26, 28–Dec. 31.
1960   Jan. 1–Apr. 5, June 1–10, 12, 16–Aug. 12, 14–Sept. 7, 9–13, 16–Dec. 14, 18–31.
1961   Jan. 1–Apr. 29, May 1–July 21, 23–Nov. 29, Dec. 1, 5–31.

Micro (P) & (N)
1962   Jan. 1–Dec. 7, 9–31.
1963   Jan. 1+.

NN
Micro (P) & (N)
1953   July 30–Aug. 1, 11–16, 18–Sept. 2, 5–10, 13–24, 26, Oct. 6–Nov. 22, 24–Dec. 9, 11–25, 27–31.
1954   Jan. 1–Mar. 21, 24–26, 28–Apr. 8, 11, 15–June 7, 9–30.

NjP
Micro (P)
1962   May 1–Dec. 31.
1963   Jan. 1–June 30.

EL SOL. w. est. July 3, 1818.
    Note: Title *El Sol de Chile* on prospectus only. Ceased publication [Jan. 8,] 1819.

DLC
1818   Prospecto.
        July 3–17, Aug. 14, Oct. 9, Nov. 20, Dec. 18–31.
1819   Jan. 1–8.

SOUTH PACIFIC MAIL. w. est. Nov. 6, 1909.
>Note: In English. Removed from Valparaíso, June 2, 1950.

CSt
>1950 June 2 – Dec. 31.
>1951 July 1 – Dec. 31.
>1953 July 1 – Dec. 31.
>1954 Jan. 1+.

DLC
>1950 June 2 – 30, July 7 – Dec. 29.
>1951 – 1952 Jan. 1 – Dec. 31.
>1953 Jan. 1 – June 26, July 3 – Aug. 27, 29 – Sept. 24, 26 – Nov. 12, 28 – Dec. 31.
>1954 Jan. 1 – 28, 30 – Feb. 11, 13 – May 13, 15 – July 22, 24 – 29, 31 – Aug. 19, 21 – Sept. 30, Oct. 2 – Nov. 4, 6 – Dec. 16, 18 – 31.

TARDE. d.
MWA
>1898 Apr. 28.

EL TELEGRAFO. est. May 4, 1819.
CU – B
>Micro (N)
>1819 Nov. 19, 23.

WU
>1819 May 4 – Dec. 31.
>1820 Jan. 1 – Dec. 31.

LA TERCERA DE LA HORA. d. est. July 7, 1950.
>Note: Afternoon edition of *La Hora*.

DLC
>1955 Oct. 14.

FU
>Micro (N)
>1962 Oct. 1 – Dec. 31.
>1963 Jan. 1 – June 30.

TIEMPO. 3w. est. May 28, 1845.
MWA
>1845 ₁May 28 – Nov. 29.₁

TRIBUNA. d. est. May 1, 1849.
>Note: Ceased publication Sept. 13, 1851.

MWA
>1849 May 1 – Dec. 31.

>1850 Jan. 1 – Dec. 31.
>1851 Jan. 1 – Sept. 13.

TRIBUNA NACIONAL. est. Feb. 1, 1840.
MWA
>1840 Feb. 1.

TRIBUNO. irr. est. Mar. 5, 1841.
MWA
>1841 Mar. 5 – 17.

EL TROMPETA. w., sw. est. Dec. 11, 1830.
>Note: Ceased publication Feb. 25, 1831.

CU – B
>Micro (N)
>1830 Dec. 11 – 28.
>1831 Jan. 7 – Feb. 25.

LAS ULTIMAS NOTICIAS. d. est. Nov. 15, 1902.
>Note: Established as the afternoon edition of *El Mercurio*, but became independent.

DLC
>1941 Aug. 1, Oct. 1, 10, 16, Dec. 18.
>1942 Feb. 14, 16, May 29, June 8, Aug. 11, 29, 31, Oct. 21, Nov. 19 – Dec. 31.
>1943 Jan. 1 – 3, 6 – 11, 14, 15, 18 – 21, 27 – 29, Feb. 5, 7 – 15, 20 – 25, 27, 28, Mar. 2 – 31, Apr. 3 – 20, 22, 24 – 27, 29, 30, May 4 – 26, June 1 – 11, 13 – 15, 17 – 30, Aug. 1 – Oct. 9, 11 – Nov. 11, 13 – Dec. 31.
>1944 Jan. 1 – June 7, 10 – Sept. 18, 20 – 30, Nov. 2 – Dec. 31.

ICRL
>1927 Oct. 15 – 21.

MH
>1913 Sept. 9.

PU
>1909 July 1 – Dec. 31.
>1910 Jan. 1 – Apr. 30, June 13 – Dec. 31.
>1911 Jan. 1 – Dec. 31.
>1912 Jan. 1 – Mar. 31.

EL VALDIVIANO FEDERAL. bw. est.
Dec. 1, 1827.
  Note: Ceased publication Apr. 20,
  1844.
  CtY
  1838   Apr. 15.

VENGADOR. est. Oct. 30, 1829.
  MWA
  1829   Oct. 30.

EL VERDADERO LIBERAL. sw. est. Jan.
4, 1827.
  CtY
  1827   July 3 – 13.
  DLC
  1827   Prospecto.
          Jan. 4, 9, 12, Feb. 7, 9, May
          15 – 29, June 8, 22, 28, July 6 –
          17, 31, Aug. 14.

EL VIJIA POLITICO.
  Note: Published only Prospecto.
  MWA
  1830   Prospecto: July 24.

VISTAZO. w.
  DLC
  1955   Mar. 11.

VIVA EL REY; GAZETA DEL
GOBIERNO DE CHILE.
  See *Gazeta ministerial del gobierno
  de Chile.*

VIVA LA PATRIA; GAZETA DEL
GOBIERNO DE CHILE.
  See *Gazeta del supremo gobierno de
  Chile.*

VOTO LIBERAL. irr. est. May 20, 1841.
  MWA
  1841   May 20 – June 10.

VOTO PUBLICO. w. est. Oct. 17, 1835.
  Note: Ceased publication Dec. 5,
  1835.
  MWA
  1835   Oct. 17 – Dec. 5.

VOZ DE LA JUSTICIA. est. Aug. 27, 1829.
  Note: Published only one number.

MWA
  1829   Aug. 27.

VOZ DEL COMERCIO. est. Aug. 17,
1829.
  Note: Published only one number.
  MWA
  1829   Aug. 17.

Serena

CORREO DE LA SERENA. w. est. Mar. 4,
1854.
  MWA
  1854   Mar. 4 – Dec. 31.
  1855   Jan. 1 – Dec. 31.
  1856   Jan. 1 – Dec. 27.

REFORMA. 3w. est. June 1, 1869.
  Note: Ceased publication Mar. 3,
  1915.
  MWA
  1887   June 11.
  1892   Dec. 14.

Tacna

BOLETIN DE GUERRA DEL EJERCITO
BOLIVIANO. irr.
  MWA
  1879   June 15, July 9, 26 – Aug. 2,
          Sept. 4 – 10.
  1880   Jan. 3 – Feb. 1, 19 – 22, 29 –
          May 20.

BOLETIN DE LA GUERRA. sw.
  MWA
  1880   Apr. 19, May 9.
          Extraordinario: Apr. 17.

BOLETIN DE "LA REVISTA DEL
SUR."
  MWA
  1879   Aug. 1.

EL CORVO. sw. est. Oct. 14, 1925.
  DLC
  1925   Oct. 14, 24 – 28, Nov. 4, 11,
          21 – 25, Dec. 9 – 12.

CRUZ ROJA. irr.
MWA
  1880   Apr. 25.

DEBER. d.
MWA
  1888   Mar. 28.
  1890   Nov. 20, Dec. 3.

FENIX; PERIODICO OFICIAL. w.
MWA
  1844   Dec. 7.
  1845   Jan. 4 – 25.

MOQUEGUANO. w.
MWA
  1845   Oct. 1.

EL PACIFICO. d. est. Nov. 19, 1901.
  Note: Established with a Tacna imprint as *El Pacífico*; removed to
  or newly established in Arica as *El
  Pacífico* (*Arica*) with new volume
  numbering, Nov. 22, 1927; removed to
  Tacna as *El Pacifico* under the double
  imprint Tacna-Arica, June 24, 1928;
  removed to Arica resuming the single
  imprint Arica, Nov. 27, 1928; title
  changed to *El Pacífico* Arica, Nov.
  28, 1928; removed to Tacna as *El
  Pacífico*, Jan. 1, 1929; resumed
  original volume numbering, Apr. 24,
  1929; suspended publication, Aug.
  25, 1929; Tacna ceded to Peru,
  Aug. 28, 1929.
  DLC
  1925 – 1926   Aug. 1 – Dec. 31.
  1927   Jan. 1 – May 25, 27 – 31, July
          1 – 7, 9 – Aug. 12, 14, 17 – 21,
          23, 24, 26, 28.
  1928   June 24 – July 7, 9 – 18, 20 –
          Nov. 26.
  1929   Jan. 1 – Apr. 16, 18 – July 6,
          8 – 10, 12, 13, 15 – 18, 20 –
          Aug. 25.
  MH
  1925   Nov. 27, 28, 30, Dec. 3, 19.
  1926   Jan. 4.
  MWA
  1909   May 24, 25.

PROGRESISTA. w.
MWA
  1888   Apr. 10.
  1892   May 28.

PROGRESO. 3w.
MWA
  1869   Jan. 13.
  1871   Jan. 21.

RAZON. w. est. Nov. 28, 1872.
MWA
  1872   Nov. 28.

REGISTRO OFICIAL. [w.]
MWA
  1854   May 27, June. 10.

EL TACNEÑO. w. est. Feb. 1, 1845.
  Note: Ceased publication Feb. 22,
  1845.
  CtY
  1845   Feb. 1 – 22.

TACORA. d.
MWA
  1884   Suplemento: Apr. 9.
  1886   Dec. 30.
  1890   Mar. 27.
  1896   July 1.
  1900   Feb. 25.

VOZ DEL SUR. d. est. 1893.
MWA
  1905   Oct. 28.
  1909   May 21.

Valdivia

EL CORREO DE VALDIVIA. d. est.
  Oct. 1, 1895.
  DLC
  1942   Oct. 18.

Valparaíso

ACTUALIDAD. d. est. Dec. 12, 1892.
MWA
  1892   Dec. 12, 13.

THE AMERICAN WORLD.
  Note: In English.
  MH
  1919   Jan. 1 – Dec. 13.

CENSOR IMPARCIAL. irr. est. July 10, 1840.
MWA
   1840   July 10 — Sept. 7.

CHILEAN TIMES
   See *South Pacific Mail.*

EL COMERCIO DE VALPARAISO. d. est. Nov. 20, 1847.
   Note: Ceased publication Apr. 24, 1851.
MWA
   1847   Nov. 20 — Dec. 31.
   1848   Jan. 1 — Dec. 30.

EL COSMOPOLITA. d. est. Apr. 30, 1833.
   Note: Ceased publication June 1, 1833.
DLC
   1833   May 1, 8 — 31.
MWA
   1833   Apr. 30, June 1.

CRISOL. irr. est. Aug. 1, 1829.
MWA
   1829   Aug. 1 — Oct. 31.

DEBER. d. est. Aug. 5, 1875.
   Note: Ceased publication Jan. 11, 1879.
MWA
   1875   Oct. 26, Nov. 4, 8.

DEUTSCHE NACHRICHTEN. 3w., bw. est. Nov. 15, 1870.
   Note: In German. Succeeded by *Deutsche Zeitung für Chile* (Santiago).
DLC
   1893   Aug. 1 — 19, 24, 26, 31 — Oct. 12, Nov. 2 — 7, 11, 14, 18 — 23, Dec. 16, 28.
   1900   Feb. 1.

DIABLO POLITICO. irr.
   Note: Removed to Santiago.
MWA
   1840   July 23 — Aug. 13, Sept. 18.

LA ESTRELLA. d.
MH
   1848   May 9.

LA ESTRELLA; DIARIO DE LA TARDE. d. est. Jan. 1, 1921.
DLC
   1921   Jan. 1 — Apr. 30.
   1922   Oct. 2 — Dec. 30.
   1939   July 1 — Dec. 31.
   1940   Jan. 2 — Mar. 14.
MH
   1921   Jan. 1 — Aug. 26.
   1922   June 27, 30.

FERMOMETRO DE LA OPINION. w.
MWA
   1839   Feb. 2 — 21.

GACETA DEL COMERCIO. d.
DLC
   1846   Mar. 2 — 5, 10, 12 — 24, 27, 28, 31 — Apr. 2.
MWA
   1842   Apr. 28, May 9, 10, 14 — 16, 19, 20, June 21, 22, July 30.

LA GUERRA ENTRE ESPAÑA Y CHILE.
MH
   1865   Sept. 28.

L'ITALIA. d. est. Sept. 1890.
DLC
   1942   Feb. 21, 23, 25.

EL MERCURIO. sw., d. est. Sept. 12, 1827.
   Note: Title *Mercurio de Valparaíso*, Sept. 12, 1827 — May 4, 1830; *El Mercurio*, May 7, 1830 — Aug. 28, 1832; *El Mercurio de Valparaíso*, Sept. 3, 1832 — Dec. 31, 1842; *El Mercurio*, after Jan. 1, 1843. Periodicity Sept. 12, 1827 — Apr. 29, 1829, semiweekly; after May 5, 1829, daily. Suspended publication Jan. 8 — Aug. 31, 1891. Began publishing a separate newspaper in Santiago June 1, 1900.
CU — B
   Micro (P)
   1827   Sept. 12 — Dec. 29.

1828   Jan. 2 – June 14, 28 – Sept. 27, Oct. 4 – Dec. 31.

1829   Jan. 3 – Apr. 29, May 5 – June 1, 3, 4, 6 – July 10, 13 – Dec. 31.

1830   Jan. 2 – 8, 12 – 25, 28, Feb. 1 – 3, 5 – 12, 15 – 17, 19, 22 – Mar. 3, 5 – Apr. 30, May 4, 7 – July 2, 5 – 8, 10 – 13, 15 – Oct. 23, 26 – Dec. 31.

1831   Jan. 3 – Apr. 4, 6 – July 2, 5 – Sept. 16, 19 – Dec. 31.

1832   Jan. 2 – Aug. 28, Sept. 3 – 28, Oct. 2 – Dec. 31.

1833   Jan. 2 – Mar. 2, 8 – June 28, July 4 – 6, 10 – Aug. 2, 6 – Dec. 14, 16 – 31.

1834   Jan. 2 – Sept. 1, 3 – 5, 9 – Dec. 31.

1835   Jan. 2 – Mar. 3, 5 – May 26, 29 – Aug. 10, 12 – Oct. 16, 19 – 28, 30 – Nov. 16, 18, 19, 21 – 23, 25 – Dec. 31.

1836   Jan. 2 – Mar. 28, 30 – Apr. 16, 19 – June 28, July 1 – Sept. 26, 28, 29, Oct. 1 – 11, 13 – Nov. 24, 28 – Dec. 2, 7 – 16, 19 – 31.

1837   Jan. 2 – 10, 16, 24, 26, 28 – May 13, 16 – June 10, 13, 17 – July 17, 19 – Aug. 14, 17 – Sept. 12, 14 – Nov. 3, 6 – Dec. 31.

1838   Jan. 2 – 27, 30 – June 8, 11, 12, 14 – Aug. 8, 10, 11, 14 – 28, 30 – Oct. 10, 12 – 26, 29, 30, Nov. 5 – 30, Dec. 3 – 31.

1839   Jan. 3 – 19, 22 – Feb. 13, 15 – Apr. 7, 9 – 14, 16 – June 13, 15 – Dec. 14, 17 – 31.

1840   Jan. 2 – Feb. 1, 4 – Sept. 7, 9 – Oct. 7, 9 – 13, 15 – 19, 21 – Dec. 31.

1841   Jan. 2 – Mar. 10, 12 – Dec. 31.

1842   Jan. 1 – Feb. 2, 4 – 9, 14 – 20, 28 – Mar. 31, Apr. 2 – 10, 12 – 25, 28 – May 11, 13 – June 28, July 1 – Aug. 31, Sept. 2, 3, 5 – 10, 12 – Oct. 29, 31 – Nov. 4, 5 – Dec. 8, 10 – 31.

1843   Jan. 1 – 3, 5, 7 – Mar. 15, June 2 – 11, 13 – Aug. 3, 5 – Sept. 17, 20 – 26, 28 – Oct. 16, 18 – Dec. 13, 15 – 31.

1844   Jan. 1 – Mar. 9, 11 – Apr. 30, May 2 – 27, 29 – June 3, 6 – 16, 18 – 20, 22 – July 8, 10, 12, 15 – 24, 26 – 28, Aug. 1 – 14, 16 – 19, 21 – 27, 29, 31 – Sept. 12, 14, 16 – 18, 21 – Oct. 15, 17 – 22, 24, 25, 27 – Nov. 11, 14, 16 – 23, 25 – Dec. 31.

1845   Jan. 1 – 8, 10 – 23, 25 – Feb. 3, 5 – 13, 15 – Mar. 14, 16 – May 31, June 2 – 14, 17, 18, 20 – July 1, Aug. 19 – Dec. 31.

1846   Jan. 1 – Apr. 16, 18 – 26, 28 – May 1, 3 – 11, 13 – June 8, 12 – 14, 16 – 19, 21, 23 – July 1, 3 – 14, 18 – Aug. 1, 3 – Sept. 1, 3 – 13, 15 – 21, 23 – Nov. 21, 23 – Dec. 23, 25 – 31.

1847   Jan. 1 – 27, 29 – Feb. 1, 3 – 12, 15 – Mar. 22, 24 – May 18, 20 – Aug. 2, 4 – Sept. 11.

Micro (N)

1839   July 6.

CtY

1836   Sept. 23, 24, Oct. 24.

1837   June 10, 12, Nov. 2, Dec. 2. Extraordinario: June 1, 7.

1838   July 7, Sept. 27, 29, Oct. 26.

1839   Mar. 19.

DLC

1840   Jan. 1 – Mar. 16, 18 – July 2. Suplemento: Jan. 20.

1845   Sept. 15 – 18, 21 – Dec. 31.

1846   Jan. 6 – Apr. 4, July 30.

1908   July 1 – 17, 19 – Dec. 31.

1909   Jan. 1 – Feb. 23, 25 – Dec. 31.

1910 – 1913   Jan. 1 – Dec. 31.

1914   Jan. 1 – Aug. 31.

1943   Mar. 2, 4 – 9, 14 – 20, 22 – Apr. 10, 14, 17, 18, 20 – 22, 29, May 1 – 12, 15 – 20, 22, 26, 28 – June 2, 5, 9 – 20, 22, 25, 27 – 29.

1944   Sept. 1 – Oct. 31.

Micro (P) & (N)

1827   Sept. 12 — Dec. 31.
1828 — 1938   Jan. 1 — Dec. 31.
1939   Jan. 1 — Feb. 14.
InU
    1966   Jan. 1+.
MH
    1911   Dec. 13 — 31.
    1912   Jan. 1 — Sept. 6, 11 — Dec. 31.
    1913 — 1915   Jan. 1 — Dec. 31.
    1916   Jan. 1, 10 — 19, 24, Dec. 31.
    1917   Jan. 1 — 22, 24 — Feb. 28, Apr. 1 — Sept. 30, Oct. 3 — Dec. 18, 24 — 31.
    1918   Jan. 1 — 29, Feb. 6 — Dec. 31.
    1919 — 1920   Jan. 1 — Dec. 31.
    1921   Oct. 30.
    1922   Feb. 1 — June 21, July 1 — 29.
    1923   Feb. 1 — Dec. 31.
    1924   Jan. 1 — Apr. 30, July 1 — Dec. 30.
MWA
    1827   Oct. 24.
    1828   Jan. 23.
    1829   Sept. 15 — 17.
    1831   [June 6 — 27.]
    1832   May 15, [Sept. 1 — Dec. 31.]
    1833   [Jan. 1 — Mar. 3], June 3.
    1836   Nov. 25.
    1837   Aug. 10.
    1838   [May 21 — Sept. 11.]
    1840   [Aug. 22 — Oct. 16.]
    1841   [Jan. 7 — Sept. 27.]
    1842   [Jan. 1 — Nov. 13.]
    1843   June 19.
    1844   May 12.
    1845   Dec. 21.
    1847   July 24.
    1879   Apr. 4.
    1883   [Oct. 2 — Dec. 31.]
    1884   [Jan. 1 — Dec. 31.]
    1885   [Jan. 1 — Oct. 24.]
    1892   Mar. 1.
NcU
    1950   Apr. 1 — 9, 13 — May 20.
ViU
    1827   Sept. 12.

EL MERCURIO DEL VAPOR. bw.
    Note: In Spanish and English.
CU — B
Micro (N)
    1858   Mar. 15.
DLC
    1855   Jan. 14 — Mar. 30.
MH
    1881   Jan. 26.
MWA
    1862   Jan. 17.

THE NEIGHBOUR. m., w. est. Jan. 27, 1847.
    Note: In English.
DLC
    1849   July 28.
MWA
    1848   Jan. 27 — Feb. 28.
NHi
    1851   Jan. 2, Feb. 14.
NN
    1847   Jan. 27.

EL OBSERVADOR DE VALPARAISO. irr. est. Apr. 14, 1827.
    Note: Ceased publication July 31, 1827.
DLC
    1827   Apr. 29 — July 31.

SAN MARTIN. sw. est. Aug. 29, 1864.
    Note: Suspended publication Dec. 21, 1864 — Nov. 27, 1865. Ceased publication Mar. 28, 1866.
MWA
    1864   Aug. 29 — Dec. 21.
    1865   Nov. 27 — Dec. 31.
    1866   Jan. 1 — Mar. 10.

SOUTH AMERICAN GAZETTE. w. est. 1828.
    Note: In English.
DLC
    1828   Dec. 5.

SOUTH PACIFIC MAIL. w. est. Aug. 1, 1801.
    Note: In English. Title *Chilean*

Times, Aug. 1, 1801 — Nov. 5, 1909;
The South Pacific Mail, Nov. 6,
1909 — Jan. 15, 1931; *South Pacific
Mail*, after Jan. 16, 1931. Removed
to Santiago June 2, 1950.
CLCM
  1891   June 27.
CSt
  1940 — 1949   Jan. 1 — Dec. 31.
  1950   Jan. 1 — June 1.
CU
  1937   July 1 — Dec. 30.
  1938   Jan. 1 — Dec. 31.
DLC
  Micro (P) & (N)
  1924   Jan. 4 — Dec. 31.
  1925 — 1949   Jan. 1 — Dec. 31.
  1950   Jan. 1 — June 1.
DPU
  1913   Jan. 1 — Feb. 28.
  1914 — 1937   Jan. 1 — Dec. 31.
LNT — MA
  1941   June 6.
MH
  1920   May 20.
MWA
  1883   Oct. 6, Dec. 15.
  1897   May 12 — 15.
NN
  Micro (P) & (N)
  1918   [Jan. 24 — Dec. 31.]
  1919 — 1947 [Jan. 1 — Dec. 31.]

NcD
  1906   Aug. 21.
  1923   Sept. 14.
ViU
  Micro (P)
  1942   Nov. 5.

TELEGRAFO MERCANTIL. 3w. est.
  Oct. 3, 1826.
  Note: Title *El Telégrafo mercantil
  y político*, Nov. 9, 1826 — Mar. 31,
  1827.
CtY
  1826   Dec. 23.
  1827   Feb. 20, Mar. 22.

DLC
  1826   Oct. 10, 21, Nov. 9 — 24, Dec.
          26, 28.
  1827   Jan. 4, 11, 18, Feb. 14 — 28,
          Mar. 2, 6 — 20, Apr. 19, 23, 30,
          May 7, 10, 17, 24.
MWA
  1826   Nov. 14, 25.

EL TELEGRAFO MERCANTIL Y
  POLITICO.
  See *Telégrafo mercantil*.

EL TRABAJO. d.
  Note: Paged continuously.
DLC
  1882   June 3 — 6.

LA UNION. d. est. Jan. 23, 1885.
DLC
  1941   July 1 — 4, 6 — 31, Aug. 2 —
          Dec. 20, 22 — 31.
  1942   Jan. 1 — Dec. 31.
  1943   Jan. 1 — Apr. 30, Nov. 1 — 6,
          8 — 19, 21 — Dec. 31.
  Micro (P) & (N)
  1962   Jan. 1+.

VALPARAISO & WEST COAST MAIL.
  w. est. Aug. 17, 1867.
  Note: In English. Ceased publication
  Nov. 27, 1875.
CU — B
  Micro (N)
  1873   Jan. 4 — Nov. 21, 28 — Dec. 31.
  1874   [Jan. 1 — Dec. 24].
  1875   [Mar. 20 — Nov. 20].

THE WEEKLY MERCANTILE RE-
  PORTER. w. est. Oct. 6, 1849.
  Note: In English.
NN
  1849   Oct. 6.

COLOMBIA

Angostura
See Venezuela. Ciudad Bolívar.

Aspinwall

See Panamá. Aspinwall.

Barranquilla

LA COSTA ATLANTICA.
  CU – B
    Micro (P)
    1883   June 15.
  MWA
    1883   July 24.

DIARIO DEL COMERCIO. d. est. 1922.
  DLC
    1933   Oct. 5.
  LNT – MA
    1929   July 13 – 26, Aug. 21 – Nov. 22,
            Dec. 21 – 31.
    1930   Jan. 2 – 4, 6 – 10, 18, 20 – 24,
            Apr. 26, 28 – 30, May. 2.

EL LIBERAL. d. est. 1910.
  DLC
    1926   May 18 – 24.

LA NACION. d. est. 1914.
  ICRL
    1927   Oct. 24 – 29.

LA PRENSA. d. est. Feb. 17, 1928.
    Note: Ceased publication Oct. 4,
    1960.
  CU
    1953   Aug. 13, 14, 19 – Dec. 30.
    1954   Jan. 1 – Dec. 31.
    1955   Jan. 3 – Apr. 15.
  DLC
    1939   Dec. 30.
    1941   Jan. 2, Mar. 12 – 15, 17, 19 –
            21, Apr. 22, Sept. 25 – 27, 29 –
            Oct. 1.
    1953   Aug. 13 – Oct. 31, Nov. 2 – 10,
            15, 18 – Dec. 30.
    1954   Jan. 1 – Aug. 13, 15, 21 – Nov.
            26, 28, Dec. 4 – 31.
    1955   Jan. 3 – Apr. 16.
  FU

    1954 – 1959   Jan. 1 – Dec. 31.
    1960   Jan. 1 – Oct. 4.
  ICRL
    1953   Aug. 1 – Dec. 31.
    1954 – 1958   Jan. 1 – Dec. 31.
    1959   Jan. 1 – Sept. 30.
  IEN
    1942   Apr. 1 – Dec. 31.
    1943 – 1950   Jan. 1 – Dec. 31.
    1951   Jan. 1 – 25.
    1953   Aug. 13 – Dec. 31.
    1954   Jan. 1 – Dec. 31.
    1955   Jan. 1 – Apr. 15.
  KHi
    1953   Aug. 15, 17, 18.
  NHi
    1953   Aug. 15 – Dec. 31.
    1954 – 1955   Jan. 1 – Dec. 31.
  ViU
    1954   Jan. 16, 18 – 23, 25 – 30, Feb.
            1 – 6, 8 – 13, 15 – 20, 22 – 27,
            Mar. 3 – 6, 8 – 13, 15 – 18, 20,
            22 – 27, 29 – Apr. 3, 5 – 10,
            12 – 15, 19 – 24, 26 – May 8,
            10 – 15, 17 – 22, 24 – 29, 31 –
            June 5, 7 – 12, 14 – 19, 21 –
            26, 28 – July 3, 5 – 10, 12 – 17,
            19, 21 – 24, 26 – 31, Aug. 2 – 6,
            9 – 14, 16 – 21, 23 – 27, Sept.
            11, 13 – 15, 17, 18, 20 – 25,
            27 – Oct. 2, 4 – 9, 11, 13 – 16,
            18 – 23, 25 – 30, Nov. 1 – 6, 8 –
            10, 12, 20, 22, 24, 26, 27, 29 –
            Dec. 4, 6 – 9, 11, 13, 14, 16 – 18,
            20 – 24, 27 – 31.
    1955   Jan. 3 – 8, 10 – 15, 17 – 22, 24 –
            29, 31 – Feb. 5, 7 – 12, 14 – 19,
            23 – 25, Mar. 5, 7 – 12, 14 – 19,
            21 – 26, 28 – Apr. 2, 4 – 6, 9,
            11 – 15.

PROMOTOR. w.
  MWA
    1872   Sept. 21 – 28.
    1883   July 24.

LA TARDE. d.
  DLC
    1941   May 26.

Bogotá

ABEJA. bw.
  MWA
    1883   July 24.

EL ARGOS. w. est. Nov. 26, 1837.
    Note: Ceased publication May 19,
    1839.
  CU
    Micro (N)
    1837   Nov. 26.
    1838   Jan. 21 – Feb. 18, Mar. 4, 18,
            Apr. 4 – 15, June 10 – 17, July
            4 – 8, 22 – 29, Aug. 12 – 19,
            Sept. 2 – 16, 30 – Oct. 14, Nov.
            11, 25.
    1839   Jan. 6, Feb. 24, Mar. 10, Apr.
            14 – 28, May 19.
  DLC
    1838   Feb. 26 – May 20, Dec. 23.

EL ATALAYA. bw.
  CU
    Micro (P) & (N)
    1824   Jan. 1 – Dec. 31.

EL ATALAYA. w. est. Nov. 1831.
  DLC
    1831   Nov. 27.

LA AURORA. est. 1830.
    Note: Paged continuously.
  DLC
    1830   May 16.

LA BAGATELA. w. est. Sept. 15, 1852.
  CU – B
    Micro (N)
    1852   Sept. 15 – Dec. 31.
    1853   [Jan. 1 – Oct. 1.]

LA BANDERA NACIONAL. w. est. Oct.
  1837.
    Note: Ceased publication 1839.
  DLC
    1838   Apr. 1 – Dec. 31.
    1839   Jan. 1 – Feb. 2, 4 – 10.

EL CATOLICISMO. bw., w.
    Note: Periodicity Nov. 10, 1849 – May
    1853, biweekly; June 4, 1853 – 1860,

weekly. Suspended publication July
15, 1851 – Jan. 24, 1852; Apr. 23,
1854 – Jan. 7, 1855. Ceased publication Apr. 4, 1861. Resumed publication Aug., 1942.
  CSt – H
    1964   June 4, 25 – July 2, 16 – Sept.
            10, 24 – Oct. 1, 22 – 29.
    1965   Feb. 11 – Mar. 3, 5 – Aug. 24,
            26 – Oct. 7.
  CU – B
    Micro (P)
    1849   Nov. 10 – Dec. 15.
    1850   Jan. 1 – Dec. 31.
    1851   Jan. 1 – July 15.
    1852   Jan. 25 – Dec. 31.
    1853   Jan. 1 – Aug. 13, 27 – Dec. 24.
    1854   Jan. 1 – Apr. 23.
    1855   Jan. 8 – Dec. 31.
    1856 – 1860   Jan. 1 – Dec. 31.

LA CIVILIZACION. w. est. Aug. 9, 1849.
  CU – B
    Micro (N)
    1849   [Aug. 9 – Dec. 31.]
    1850   [Jan. 1 – Dec. 31.]
    1851   Jan. 1 – July 12.
  CtY
    1849   Aug. 9 – Dec. 27.
    1850   Jan. 3 – Dec. 26.
    1851   Jan. 2 – Feb. 20.

EL COLOMBIANO. w. est. Sept. 7, 1861.
    Note: Ceased publication [June 30,
    1864].
  DLC
    1861   Sept. 7, 14, 28, Oct. 12, Nov. 9,
            16.
    1863   Nov. 6 – 12, 14 – Dec. 31.
    1864   Jan. 1 – Mar. 9, 11 – 24, 26 –
            May 19, 21 – June 9, 11 – 19.

EL COMERCIO. sw. est. June 15, 1873.
  CtY
    1883   Apr. 4 – Dec. 24.
    1884   Jan. 3 – Feb. 29, Mar. 9 – Dec.
            29.
    1885   Jan. 3 – 31.
    1887   July 4 – 14, 21 – Sept. 12, 19 –
            Oct. 6, 13 – 20.

COMERCIO-BOLETIN INDUSTRIAL.
w.
MWA
1883   July 24.

CONDOR. w.
MWA
1841   Mar. 18.

EL CONDUCTOR. sw. est. Feb. 2, 1827.
DLC
1827   Feb. 2 – Aug. 1.

EL CONSERVADOR. sw., 3w. est. June
16, 1881.
    Note: Periodicity June 16, 1881 – Jan.
    17, 1882, semiweekly; after Jan. 20,
    1882, three times a week.
CU – B
    Micro (P)
    1883   July 3.
CtY
    1881   June 16 – Dec. 30.
    1882   Jan. 3 – 17, 20 – June 24, July
            1 – Dec. 30.
    1883   Jan. 2 – Oct. 9, 13 – Dec. 22.
    1884   Jan. 5 – Dec. 23.

CONTRAPUNTO. w.
FU
    Micro (N)
    1965   June 3 – Oct. 7.

CORREO DE LAS ALDEAS. w., irr. est.
July 20, 1887.
    Note: Succeeded *La Caridad.*
CtY
    1887   July 20 – Dec. 22.
    1888   Jan. 12 – May 12.

CORREO MERCANTIL. w.
MWA
    1883   July 24.
    1884   Apr. 26 – May 17.

EL CORREO NACIONAL. d. est. Sept.
1, 1890.
CLU
    Micro (P)
    1890   [Sept. 22 – Dec. 31.]
    1891   [Jan. 1 – June 12.]

CtY
    1890   Sept. 1 – Dec. 28.
    1891   Jan. 4 – Dec. 24.
    1892   Jan. 2 – Dec. 23.
    1893   Jan. 13 – Dec. 23.
    1894   Jan. 23 – Nov. 17.
DLC
    Micro (P)
    1890   Sept. 22 – Dec. 31.
    1891   Jan. 1 – Apr. 28, 30 – May 19,
            21 – June 9, 11, 12.
MH
    1907   Apr. 30.
MWA
    1904   Sept. 26, 28, Oct. 11.
NN
    Micro (P)
    1890   [Sept. 22 – Dec. 31.]
    1891   [Jan. 1 – June 12.]

EL CRITERIO. d. est. Mar. 16, 1892.
    Note: Ceased publication Oct. 10,
    1892.
CU – B
    Micro (N)
    1892   [Mar. 16 – July 30.]
CtY
    1892   Mar. 16 – Oct. 10.

EL CULTIVADOR CUNDINAMAR-
QUES. bw. est. 1832.
CU
    Micro (N)
    1832   Jan. 1 – July 15.

LA DEFENSA. sw. est. Apr. 1, 1880.
CtY
    1880   Apr. 1 – Sept. 13, 23 – Dec. 23.

EL DIA. w., sw., w. est. Aug. 23, 1840.
    Note: Ceased publication July 15,
    1851.
CU
    Micro (P)
    1840   Aug. 23 – Sept. 6, 20 – Oct. 4,
            Nov. 1, 15 – Dec. 27.
    1841   Jan. 3 – 6, 17 – 21, 31 – Dec. 30.
    1842   Jan. 2 – Sept. 25, Oct. 9 – Dec.
            29.
    1843   Jan. 8 – Dec. 10.
    1844   Jan. 1 – Dec. 29.

1845   Jan. 5 – Nov. 16, 27, Dec. 4 –
        31.
1846   Jan. 18 – Oct. 29, Nov. 5 – Dec.
        6, 20 – 27.
1847   Jan. 3, 31, Feb. 14 – July 6,
        20 – Dec. 25.
CU – B
  Micro (N)
1840   [Sept. 20 – Dec. 31.]
1841 – 1843   [Jan. 1 – Dec. 31.]
1844   Jan. 1 – Dec. 31.
1845   Jan. 1 – Dec. 28.
1846   Jan. 4.
1847 – 1848   Jan. 1 – Dec. 31.
1849   Jan. 1 – Dec. 12.
1850   Jan. 2.
1851   Jan. 1 – July 15.
DLC
1843   Oct. 8, 29, Nov. 19, Dec. 3, 10.
1845   Dec. 28 – 31.
1846   Jan. 1 – Mar. 21, 23 – 28, 30 –
        May 23, 25 – 27, 29 – July 1,
        3 – 8, 10 – Dec. 13.

EL DIA. d.
  CU
1939   Aug. 18, Sept. 29, Dec. 15, 21.
1940   Feb. 3, 15, Mar. 6, June 22, July
        13, Sept. 10, Dec. 10.
1941   Jan. 29, Mar. 13, May 12, Sept.
        8, Dec. 11.
  DLC
1941   May 10.

DIARIO DE COLOMBIA. d.
  DLC
1953   Aug. 3 – Sept. 21, 23 – Oct. 11,
        13, 15 – Dec. 31.
1954   Jan. 1 – Feb. 15, 17 – June 6,
        8 – Dec. 31.
1955   Jan. 1 – Dec. 31.
1956   Jan. 3 – June 19, 21 – Aug. 10,
        12 – Oct. 17, 19 – Dec. 26, 28 –
        31.
1957   Jan. 3 – 29, 31 – Feb. 12, 14 –
        27, Mar. 1 – 5, 7 – May 8.

DIARIO DE CUNDINAMARCA. d., 3w.,
  4w. est. Oct. 1, 1869.

Note: Periodicity Oct. 1, 1869 – Aug.
21, 1876, daily; Aug. 22, 1876 – Dec.
31, 1877, three times a week; after Jan.
1, 1878, four times a week. Ceased
publication Dec. 20, 1884.
CtY
1869   Oct. 1 – Dec. 31.
1870 – 1871   Jan. 1 – Dec. 31.
1872   Jan. 1 – Oct. 31.
1875   Nov. 2 – Dec. 31.
1876   Jan. 1 – Oct. 11.
1877   Nov. 1 – Dec. 31.
1878 – 1883   Jan. 1 – Dec. 31.
1884   Apr. 15 – Dec. 20.
MWA
1883   July 24.

EL DIARIO NACIONAL. d. est. 1915.
  TxU
1921   Jan. 1 – Sept. 10, 19 – Dec. 17,
        26 – 31.
1922   Jan. 1 – Feb. 4, 13 – 25, Mar.
        1 – July 5, 10 – 15, 24 – Aug.
        27, Sept. 1 – 10, 14 – Dec. 3,
        5 – 28.
1923   Jan. 1 – Apr. 7, 9 – June 28,
        July 2 – 21, 23 – Sept. 25, 27 –
        Oct. 3, 5 – 22, 24 – 28, 30 –
        Nov. 18, 22 – 26, 28 – Dec. 23.
1924   Jan. 4 – Feb. 3, 8 – 19, 22 –
        25, 28, 29, Mar. 2 – 25, 27 –
        30, May 26 – June 1, 17 – 22,
        Sept. 15 – Oct. 5.

DIARIO OFICIAL. d. est. Apr. 30, 1864.
  Note: Succeeded *Rejistro oficial*
  as official gazette.
  CSt
1896   Feb. 5 – June 30.
  CU
  Micro (P)
1872   Aug. 6 – Dec. 31.
1873   Jan. 1 – June 14.
1874   Jan. 1 – Oct. 31.
1875   Apr. 1 – Dec. 24.
1876   Jan. 17 – Dec. 6.
1877   Jan. 19 – May 7.
1878   May 28 – June 26.
1879   Jan. 18 – Feb. 28.

CU—B
  Micro (P)
  1883   July 20, 23, 24.
  1884   Oct. 30.
CtY
  1864   Apr. 30—Dec. 31.
  1865—1900   Jan. 1—Dec. 31.
DLC
  1864   ₁Apr. 30—Dec.₁.
  1865—1900   ₁Jan. 1—Dec. 31₁.
IU
  1864   Apr. 30—Dec. 31.
  1865—1900   Jan. 1—Dec. 31.
MWA
  1869   Apr. 12, June 12.
  1892   June 13.
NHi
  1887   Feb. 23.

LA DISCUSION. w. est. May 22, 1852.
  Note: Ceased publication May 21,
  1853.
CtY
  1852   May 22—Dec. 25.
  1853   Jan. 1—May 21.
MWA
  1853   Jan. 22.

EL ECO DE LOS ANDES. w. est. Jan. 5,
1852.
  Note: Ceased publication Jan. 4,
  1853.
CU—B
  Micro (N)
  1852   Jan. 5—Dec. 31.
  1853   Jan. 1—4.

EL ESPECTADOR. d. est. Mar. 22, 1887.
  CSt
  1948   Apr. 13—15, 17.
  1949   Sept. 8, Nov. 9—12, 24, 28, 29.
  CSt—H
  1964   Oct. 1, 5, 8, 10, 15, 22, 26, Nov.
         2, 5, 9, 12, 16, 19, 23.
  DLC
  1926   July 19—Aug. 1, 25—28, 30—
         Sept. 23, 25—Oct. 2, 4—17,
         Dec. 22—25, 28—31.
  1927   Jan. 1—9, Feb. 7—Mar. 9, 11—
         19, 28—Apr. 2, 4—20, 22—

         30, May 2—8, 23, 25—June 6,
         8—30, Aug. 13—Sept. 11, 26—
         Oct. 2, 10—31, Nov. 15—Dec.
         31.
  1928   Jan. 1—Mar. 4, 6—29, Apr. 1,
         2, 4, 9—22, 24—30, May 2—
         10, 13—July 5, 8—14, 18—
         Aug. 26, Sept. 26—Oct. 7,
         18—20, 22—Dec. 31.
  1929   Jan. 1—Mar. 24, 26—Apr. 29,
         May 2—27, 29—June 6, 8—
         July 7, 9, 10, 13—18, 20—Dec.
         20, 22—28, 30, 31.
  1930   Jan. 1—3, 5—19, 21—Feb. 2,
         4—27, Mar. 1—3.
  1941   Apr. 19, 21, 25, 26, May 9.
  MWA
  1937   Feb. 5.

EL ESTANDARTE.
  CU—B
  Micro (P)
  1883   June 27.

FERROCARRIL. w.
  MWA
  1883   July 24.

GACETA DE COLOMBIA. w. est. Sept.
  6, 1821.
  Note: Succeeded by *Gaceta de la
  Nueva Granada*. Ceased publication
  Dec. 29, 1831.
  CU—B
  1823   July 20—Dec. 31.
  1824   June 1—Dec. 31.
  1825   Extraordinario: Apr. 27.
  1825—1826   Jan. 1—Dec. 31.
  1827   Jan. 1—Dec. 31.
         Extraordinario: May 23.
  1828—1829   Jan. 1—Dec. 31.
  1830   Jan. 1—Dec. 31.
         Extraordinario: June 28, Aug.
         12, Oct. 17.
  1831   Jan. 1—Oct. 13.
         Extraordinario: Jan. 12, Apr.
         7, May 18, June 7, Aug. 20.
  Micro (N)
  1822   Jan. 13—Dec. 29.
  CtY

1821   Sept. 9 – 30, Oct. 11 – 14.
1822   Sept. 15.
1827   July 29, Oct. 21.
1828   July 24 – 27, Oct. 23.
1829   Sept. 6 – 13, Oct. 25 – Nov. 22,
        Dec. 6 – 27.
1830   Jan. 3, 24 – Feb. 7, 21 – 28,
        Apr. 18.
DLC
    1821   Sept. 6 – Oct. 14.
    1822 – 1830   Jan. 1 – Dec. 31.
    1831   Jan. 1 – Dec. 29.
            Extraordinario: Jan. 12.
MWA
    1828   Feb. 3 – 24.

GACETA DE CUNDINAMARCA. irr. est.
Oct. 20, 1857.
    CtY
        1857   Oct. 20 – Dec. 30.
        1858   Jan. 7 – July 24, Aug. 21 –
                Dec. 30.

GACETA DE LA NUEVA GRANADA. w.,
sw. est. Jan. 1, 1832.
    Note: Succeeded *Gaceta de Colom-
    bia+* succeeded by *Gaceta oficial.*
    Ceased publication Dec. 30, 1847.
    CU – B
        Micro (P)
        1843   May 4.
        1846   Jan. 18 – May 24.
        1847   Apr. 1, Oct. 3 – 7.
    CtY
        1832   Feb. 12, Mar. 11, 22, July 15,
                Aug. 5 – 12.
        1833   Feb. 10, Oct. 6 – 27.
        1835   Oct. 18.
        1836   Aug. 14, Sept. 25.
        1837   Mar. 26.
        1840   Dec. 6, 20.
        1841   Jan. 3 – Dec. 26.
        1842   Jan. 25, Apr. 3 – May 15, 29,
                June 12, July 8, Dec. 4 – 15.
        1843   Feb. 5.
        1844   Jan. 7, Mar. 8.
        1845   July 6, Dec. 21.
        1846   July 2, 19, Dec. 15.

1847   July 11, 18 – Aug. 1, 8 – Dec.
        30.
DLC
    1832 – 1837   Jan. 1 – Dec. 31.

GACETA OFICIAL. sw. est. Jan. 2, 1848.
    Note: Succeeded *Gaceta de la Nueva
    Granada*; succeeded by *Rejistro
    oficial.* Suspended publication Apr.
    16 – Dec. 9, 1854; ceased publication
    July 9, 1861.
    CU – B
        Micro (P)
        1848   Jan. 2 – Dec. 31.
        1853   Feb. 22 – Dec. 31.
        1854 – 1855   Jan. 1 – Dec. 31.
    CtY
        1848   Jan. 20, Feb. 20, Mar. 5 – 30,
                Apr. 9 – May 21, 28 – June 1,
                8 – Dec. 31.
        1849   Jan. 7 – Dec. 30.
        1854   Jan. 1 – Dec. 28.
        1855   Jan. 1 – Dec. 30.
        1857   Oct. 24 – Dec. 29.
        1858   Jan. 7 – Dec. 29.
        1859   Jan. 3 – Dec. 28.
    DLC
        1848 – 1860   [Jan. 1 – Dec. 31].
        1861   [Jan. 1 – July 9].

EL GLOBO. 3w. est. Jan. 18, 1899.
    CU – B
        Micro (N)
        1899   [Jan. 18 – July 20.]

LOS HECHOS. d. est. Jan. 18, 1894.
    CtY
        1894   [Jan. 18 – Dec. 31.]

EL HERALDO. w.
    DLC
        1861   Jan. 4 – 25.

EL HERALDO. w., sw., 3w. est. July 4,
1889.
    Note: Periodicity July 4, 1889 – June
    24, 1891, weekly; July 1, 1891 – Feb.
    25, 1894, semiweekly; Mar. 1 – Dec.
    23, 1894, three times a week. Ceased
    publication Dec. 23, 1894.

CU – B
  Micro (P)
  1889 July 4 – Dec. 31.
  1890 Jan. 1 – Sept. 3, 17 – Dec. 10.
  1891 Jan. 28.
CtY
  1889 July 4 – Dec. 18.
  1890 Jan. 1 – Dec. 10.
  1891 Jan. 7 – Dec. 19.
  1892 Jan. 2 – Dec. 17.
  1893 Jan. 4 – Dec. 23.
  1894 Jan. 5 – Feb. 25, Mar. 1 – Dec. 23.
DLC
  Micro (P)
  1889 July 4 – Dec. 31.
  1890 Jan. 1 – [Dec. 16].
  1891 Jan. 1 – 6, 22 – 28.
FU
  Micro (P)
  1889 July 4 – Dec. 31.
  1890 Jan. 1 – Sept. 9, 11 – Dec. 10.
  1891 Jan. 28.
MoU
  Micro (P)
  1889 July 4 – Dec. 31.
  1890 Jan. 1 – Dec. 31.
  1891 Jan. 1 – 28.
NN
  Micro (P)
  1889 July 4 – Dec. 31.
  1890 Jan. 1 – Sept. 9, 11 – Dec. 16.
  1891 Jan. 28.

HOY. d. est. Aug. 15, 1954.
  DLC
  1954 Aug. 15.

EL IMPARCIAL.
  CU – B
  Micro (P)
  1883 May 17.

INTERMEDIO. d. est. Feb. 21, 1956.
  Note: Published during the suspension of *El Tiempo*. Ceased publication June 7, 1957.
  CLU
  1956 Apr. 1 – Dec. 31.
  1957 Jan. 1 – June 6.

DLC
  1956 Feb. 21 – Mar. 12, 14 – Apr. 6, 8 – Aug. 8, 10 – Dec. 31.
  1957 Jan. 1 – May 1, 3, 4, 11 – June 7.
FU
  1956 Apr. 1 – Dec. 31.
  1957 Jan. 1 – June 7.

EL LIBERAL. d. est. Apr. 17, 1911.
  Note: Ceased publication Dec. 4, 1951.
  CSt
  1948 Apr. 14.
  1949 Aug. 17, 30, Oct. 29, Nov. 9, 11, 13, 20, 29.
  1950 Jan. 26.
  DLC
  1941 Apr. 22, 25 – 28, Oct. 4, Dec. 6, 7, 23, 24, 30, 31.
  1942 Jan. 2 – Mar. 21, 24 – Apr. 11, 13 – May 30, June 1 – 11, 13 – Aug. 5, 7 – Sept. 7, 9 – Dec. 31.
  1943 Jan. 1 – 10, 12 – 17, 19 – 30, Feb. 2 – Mar. 30, Apr. 1 – 13, 15 – 17, 20, 22 – 26, 28 – May 6, 8 – 11, 13 – 24, 26 – June 1, 3, 5, 16 – 18, 20 – 30.
  1944 Jan. 2 – 15, Feb. 1 – Mar. 5, 7 – 18, 20 – May 13, 15 – 17, 19, 22, 23, 26 – June 30.
  1946 July 1 – 4, 16 – Oct. 5, 8 – Dec. 31.
  1947 Jan. 1 – Apr. 2, 6 – Dec. 24, 26 – 31.
  1948 Jan. 1 – Apr. 9, 14 – Dec. 24, 26 – 31.
  1949 Jan. 1 – Nov. 13, 15 – 20, 22 – Dec. 12, 16 – 30.
  1950 Jan. 1 – 5, 7 – 10, 12 – Sept. 13, 15 – Dec. 31.
  1951 Jan. 1 – Feb. 8, 10 – May 6, 8 – June 1, 3 – 27, 29 – July 5, 7 – Aug. 18, 20 – 25, 27 – Sept. 26, 28 – Dec. 4.

LIBERTAD Y ORDEN. w.
  CU
  Micro (N)
  1846 May 3 – Dec. 27.

1847   Jan. 2 – May 30.

LA LUZ. w., sw. est. Feb. 15, 1881.
　　Note: Periodicity Feb. 15 – 22, 1881,
　　weekly; after Mar. 1, 1881, semiweek-
　　ly. Ceased publication 1884.
　CtY
　　1881   Feb. 15 – 22, Mar. 1 – Dec. 22.
　　1882   Jan. 3 – Dec. 23.
　　1883   Jan. 3 – Dec. 22.
　　1884   Jan. 2 – Dec. 17.

EL MENSAJERO. d. est. Nov. 1, 1866.
　　Note: Ceased publication Mar. 15,
　　1867.
　CtY
　　1866   Nov. 1 – Dec. 31.
　　1867   Jan. 1 – Mar. 15.

LA NACION. w.
　CSt
　　1951   Dec. 1 – 31.
　　1952   Jan. 1 – Feb. 29, May 1 – 31.
　　1953   May 1 – June 30.
　ICRL
　　1951   [Aug. 1 – Dec. 31].
　　1952   [Jan. 1 – Dec. 31].
　　1953   [Jan. 1 – June 30].

EL NEO-GRANADINO. w., irr. est. Aug.
4, 1848.
　　Note: Ceased publication [July 1857].
　CU
　　Micro (P)
　　1851   Jan. 3 – Feb. 14, 28, Mar. 14 –
　　　　　　Oct. 17, 31 – Nov. 28, Dec. 12 –
　　　　　　26.
　　1852   Jan. 16 – Feb. 20, Mar. 5 – 26,
　　　　　　Apr. 9, July 15 – Dec. 31.
　　1853   Jan. 7 – Nov. 17, Dec. 1 – 29.
　　　　　　Extraordinario: Nov. 26.
　CU – B
　　Micro (N)
　　1848   Aug. 4 – Dec. 31.
　　1849 – 1850   Jan. 1 – Dec. 31.
　　1851   Jan. 1 – Dec. 26.

NUEVA ERA. [w.]
　MWA
　　1883   July 24.

EL NUEVO TIEMPO. d. est. May 16,
1902.
　MWA
　　1905   Apr. 14.
　　1923   Oct. 25.
　NcU
　　1917   Jan. 28 – Feb. 3, 18 – 24, 26 –
　　　　　　Apr. 6, 8 – 10, 12 – 15, 17 –
　　　　　　June 24, 26 – July 8, 10 – 14,
　　　　　　16 – 21, 24 – Oct. 1, 5 – 15, 17 –
　　　　　　25, 27 – Dec. 8, 10 – 22, 30, 31.

　　1918   Jan. 1 – 12, 20 – Mar. 5, 8 – 11,
　　　　　　13 – 28, 31 – June 30, July 4,
　　　　　　6 – 10, 12 – 15, 17 – Sept. 2, 4,
　　　　　　6 – 10, 12 – 17, 20 – Oct. 2, 4 –
　　　　　　9, 11 – 19, 27 – Nov. 7, 9 – 15,
　　　　　　23 – 29, Dec. 8 – 13, 15, 16,
　　　　　　18 – 21.

　　1919   Jan. 3, 4, 12, 16 – 21, 23, 25 –
　　　　　　Feb. 8, 17 – Mar. 1, 3 – 16, 18 –
　　　　　　Apr. 6, 8 – 17, 20 – June 7, 15 –
　　　　　　24, 26 – July 6, 8 – 16, 18 – 31,
　　　　　　Aug. 2 – Oct. 11, 19 – Nov. 19,
　　　　　　21 – Dec. 11, 13 – 31.

　　1920   Jan. 1 – 17, 25 – 27, 29 – 31,
　　　　　　Feb. 8 – 18, 20, 21, 23 – 28,
　　　　　　Mar. 1 – 15, 22, 23, 27, Apr.
　　　　　　11 – 14, 16, 28, May 1 – 10, 12 –
　　　　　　16, 18 – 25, 27 – 29, June 20,
　　　　　　21, 24 – 29, July 1, 2, 4 – 31,
　　　　　　Aug. 15 – 31, Oct. 1 – 24, 26 –
　　　　　　31, Dec. 1 – 20, 22 – 25, 28, 29.

　　1921   Jan. 1, 3 – 31, Feb. 2 – Apr.
　　　　　　10, 15, 16, 24 – May 1, 3 – 16,
　　　　　　18, 20, 21, 29 – June 1 – 4, 12 –
　　　　　　Aug. 2, 4 – 6, 14 – 18, 20, 28 –
　　　　　　31, Sept. 1 – 17, Oct. 2 – 13,
　　　　　　15 – 22, 24 – Nov. 1, 3 – 5, 13 –
　　　　　　26, 28, 29, Dec. 17, 26 – 31.

　　1922   Jan. 1 – 7, 29 – Feb. 4, 12, 14 –
　　　　　　18, 26 – Apr. 13, 16 – 21, May
　　　　　　7 – 16, 18 – 24, 27 – June 9, 11,
　　　　　　13 – July 17, 19 – Aug. 6, 8 –
　　　　　　Sept. 3, 5 – 9, 17 – Oct. 7, 15,
　　　　　　16, 18 – 21, 23 – 27, 29 – Nov.
　　　　　　1 – 26, 28 – Dec. 3, 5 – 16, 31.

1923   Jan. 1 – Apr. 30, May 2 – 14,
        16 – June 3, 5 – July 20, 22,
        24 – Aug. 9, 11 – 19, 24 – Dec.
        8, 10 – 13, 15 – 21, 30, 31.
1924   Jan. 1 – 6, 8 – 10, 12, 13, 15 –
        Feb. 23, Mar. 11 – Apr. 28,
        30, May 1, 3 – 5, 7 – July 12,
        20 – 26, Aug. 3, 4, 6 – 30, Sept.
        3, 7 – 13, 21 – Nov. 1, 3 – 8, 24,
        25, 27, 29 – Dec. 31.
1925   Jan. 5, 7 – 26, 28 – Feb. 15,
        17 – Mar. 2, 4, 5, 8 – Apr. 17,
        19 – 29, May 1 – July 18, 20 –
        Sept. 26, 31, Oct. 11 – Nov. 2,
        10 – Dec. 28.
1926   Jan. 5 – Mar. 21, Apr. 5, 6, 8,
        14 – 19, 27 – Oct. 12, 14 – Nov.
        29, Dec. 7 – 31.
1927   Jan. 1 – Apr. 5, 7 – June 9, 11 –
        July 28, 30 – Nov. 14, 16 – Dec.
        31.
1928   Jan. 1 – Feb. 8, 10 – Aug. 17,
        19 – 22, 24 – Nov. 1, 3 – Dec.
        31.
1929   Jan. 1 – Feb. 4, 13 – Mar. 11,
        13 – June 2, 4, 6 – Aug. 21, 23 –
        Oct. 2, 4 – Nov. 12, 14 – 21,
        23 – Dec. 2, 10 – 24, 26 – 31.
1930   Jan. 1, 3 – 13, 21, 22, 24, 25,
        27, 29 – Feb. 3, 12 – 18, 20 –
        24, Mar. 4 – 18, 20, 22 – Apr.
        15, 17, 20 – May 1, 3 – June 17,
        19 – July 29, 31 – Sept. 4, 6 –
        23, 25 – Oct. 7, 9 – Nov. 3, 5 –
        Dec. 4, 6 – 8, 17 – 30.
1931   Jan. 1 – 5, 7 – 12, 20 – 22, 25 –
        28, 30 – Feb. 4, 6 – Mar. 23,
        31 – May 13, 15 – Aug. 14, 16 –
        Oct. 6, 8 – 15, Dec. 15 – 28.
1932 – 1945   Jan. 1 – Dec. 31.
1948   Mar. 1 – Apr. 30.

LA OPINION; PERIODICO OFICIAL.
  est. Aug. 20, 1900.
  CtY
    1900   Aug. 20 – Dec. 24.
    1901   Jan. 2 – Dec. 26.
    1902   Jan. 3 – Mar. 17.

EL ORDEN. w. est. Nov. 14, 1852.
    Note: Ceased publication May 22,
    1853.
  CtY
    1852   Nov. 14 – Dec. 26.
    1853   Jan. 2 – May 22.

EL ORDEN; POLITICA, RELIGION,
  FILOSOFIA Y LITERATURA. w. est.
  Jan. 1, 1887.
    Note: Ceased publication Dec. 7,
    1892.
  CtY
    1887   Jan. 1 – 31.
    1888 – 1891   Jan. 1 – Dec. 31.
    1892   Jan. 1 – Dec. 7.

EL ORDEN PUBLICO. d. est. Nov. 14,
  1899.
  CtY
    1899   Nov. 14 – Dec. 30.
    1900   Jan. 1 – July 31.

EL PASATIEMPO. w. est. Sept. 1, 1851.
    Note: Ceased publication Apr. 1854.
  CU – B
    Micro (N)
    1851   [Sept. 14 – Dec. 31.]
    1852   [Jan. 1 – Sept. 29, Oct. 6 – Dec.
            31.]
    1853   [Jan. 1 – Dec. 31.]
    1854   [Jan. 1 – Apr. 12.]

PATRIOTA.
  MWA
    1883   July 24.

LA PAZ. sw. est. Mar. 26, 1868.
    Note: Ceased publication Feb. 23,
    1869.
  DLC
    1869   Jan. 5 – 8.

PAZ Y TRABAJO. w.
  MWA
    1904   Oct. 16.

EL PORVENIR. sw. est. 1855.
    Note: Ceased publication [May, 1861].
  DLC
    1859   July 15 – 17, 19 – 21, 23 – Aug.

21, 23 — 28, 30 — Sept. 8, 10 —
Oct. 6, 8 — Dec. 30.
1860   Jan. 1 — Mar. 22, 24 — 26, 28 —
May 24, 26 — 31, June 2 — 4, 6,
7, 9 — 11, 13 — July 12, 14 — 16,
18, 19, 21 — 23, 25, 26, 28 —
Sept. 6, Oct. 1 — 4, Nov. 1 —
Dec. 6.
1861   Jan. 1 — 31, Feb. 16 — Apr. 1,
3 — 18, 20 — 22, 24, 25, 27 — May
17.

LA PRENSA. bw. est. July 9, 1866.
Note: Ceased publication Dec. 3,
1869.
DLC
1869   Alcance: Jan. 8.

RECONCILIADOR BOGOTANO. w. est.
May 6, 1827.
MWA
1827   May 6 — July 15.

REJISTRO OFICIAL. w. est. July 26,
1861.
Note: Succeeded *Gaceta oficial*;
succeeded by *Diario oficial*. Ceased
publication Apr. 27, 1864.
CU — B
Micro
1861   July 26 — Dec. 31.
1862 — 1863 Jan. 1 — Dec. 31.
1864   Jan. 1 — Apr. 27.
DLC
1861   July 26 — Dec. 31.
1862 — 1863   Jan. 1 — Dec. 31.
1864   Jan. 1 — Apr. 27.
MWA
1861   July 26 — Dec. 31.
1862   Jan. 1 — Dec. 23.

EL REPORTER. d. est. Oct. 6, 1898.
CtY
1898   Oct. 6 — Dec. 31.
1899   Jan. 2 — Feb. 27, Mar. 1 — 24.

LA REPUBLICA. sw., d. est. June [14],
1893.
Note: Ceased publication Apr. 30,
1894.

CtY
1893   June 21 — Sept. 9, 30 — Nov.
22, 29 — Dec. 16.
1894   Jan. 24 — Apr. 30.

LA REPUBLICA. d. est. 1953.
CSt — H
1964   Oct. 1, 5, 8, 10, 15, 22, 26, Nov.
2, 5, 9, 16, 19, 23.
DLC
1955   Apr. 12 — 26, 30 — June 1, 3 —
8, 10 — 24, 29 — July 5, 8 — 14,
19 — 28, 31 — Aug. 5, 9 — 18,
20 — 23, 26 — 30, Sept. 3 — Dec.
9, 13 — 31.
1956   Jan. 2 — 5, June 4 — July 18,
20 — Nov. 22, 24 — Dec. 31.
1957   Jan. 1 — Feb. 23, 26 — May 4,
12 — Dec. 31.
1958   Jan. 1 — Feb. 24, 26 — June 27,
July 1 — 18, 20 — Sept. 10, 12 —
19, 24 — 26, Oct. 1 — Dec. 3, 5 —
31.
1959   Jan. 3 — July 4, 6 — 31, Aug.
18 — 28, Sept. 1 — 8, 10 — Nov.
14, 16, 18 — Dec. 31.

EL REPUBLICANO. w.
CU
Micro (P)
1849   Jan. 14 — Apr. 8
MH
1910   Nov. 12.

SABADO. w.
CSt
1951   Nov. 24 — Dec. 15.
1952   Feb. 16.
MH
1943   Dec. 4 — 31.
1944   Jan. 1 — May 13.
OrU
1952   June 21.

EL SIGLO. d. est. Feb. 1, 1936.
CSt
1949   Nov. 9, 11, 13, 20, 26 — 28.
CSt — H
1964   Oct. 1, 5, 8, 10, 15, 22, 26, Nov.
2, 5, 9, 12, 16, 19, 23.

DLC
  1941 May 7, 8, 11, 12, 14, Dec. 16 –
        31.
  1942 Jan. 1 – Mar. 11, 13 – Apr. 2,
        6 – 21, May 13 – June 27, July
        1 – 25, 27 – Aug. 2, 4 – Oct.
        16, 21 – Nov. 6, 8 – 11, 13 –
        Dec. 3, 5 – 14, 16 – 31.
  1943 Jan. 1 – 3, 5 – 26, 28 – Feb. 10,
        12 – Apr. 11, 13 – 21, 25, 27 –
        June 6, 8, 9, 14 – 20.
  1944 Jan. 2 – 15, 17 – 22, 26 – Feb.
        8, 11 – 17, 23 – Mar. 11, 13 –
        May 26, June 1 – 14, 16 – 18,
        20 – 29.
  1946 July 1 – Dec. 31.
  1947 Jan. 1 – Dec. 31.
  1948 Jan. 1 – Apr. 9, 28 – 30, May
        3 – 9, 12 – 16, June 11, 16 – 18,
        21 – 28, July 1, 3, 5 – Sept. 4,
        6 – 20, 26 – Nov. 18, 20 – Dec.
        31.
  1949 Jan. 1 – May 26, 28 – Dec. 31.
  1950 Jan. 1 – June 19, 21 – Dec. 31.
  1951 Jan. 2 – June 11, 14 – Dec. 31.
  1952 Jan. 2 – Aug. 17, 21 – Sept. 29,
        Oct. 1 – Dec. 31.
  1953 Jan. 2 – July 13, 15 – Aug. 4,
        10 – Sept. 9, 11 – 22, 24.
  1960 Jan. 2 – 13, 15 – Mar. 7, 9 –
        Apr. 3, 5 – 12, 14 – Sept. 28,
        Oct. 1 – 26, 28 – Dec. 19, 21 –
        31.
  1961 Jan. 2 – 23, 25 – Nov. 22, 24 –
        Dec. 24.
  Micro (P) & (N)
  1962 Jan. 1+.
FU
  1951 [Jan. 1 – Dec. 31].
MWA
  1937 Feb. 7.
TxU
  1947 May 24.

EL SUR-AMERICANO. w.
  CU
    Micro (N)

  1849 Aug. 23 – Dec. 9.
  1850 Jan. 20 – Apr. 14.

EL TALLER. irr. est. June 24, 1884.
  Note: Paged continuously.
  CU – B
    Micro (P)
    1888 Apr. 28 – Dec. 31.
    1889 Jan. 1 – Mar. 10, Apr. 1 –
          Sept. 25, Oct. 22 – Dec. 31.
    1890 Jan. 1 – Feb. 26, Oct. 2.
  DLC
    Micro (P)
    1888 Apr. 28 – Dec. 31.
    1889 Jan. 1 – Mar. 9, Apr. 2 – May 3,
          25 – Sept. 25, Oct. 22 – Dec.
          31.
    1890 Jan. 1 – Feb. 26, Oct. 2.
  FU
    Micro (P)
    1888 Apr. 1 – Dec. 31.
    1889 Jan. 1 – Dec. 31.
    1890 Jan. 1 – Feb. 28, Oct. 2.
  MoU
    Micro (P)
    1888 Apr. 28 – Dec. 31.
    1889 Jan. 1 – Dec. 31.
    1890 Jan. 1 – Oct. 2.
  NN
    Micro (P)
    1888 Apr. 28 – Dec. 31.
    1889 Jan. 1 – Mar. 10, Apr. 1 – Sept.
          25, Oct. 22 – Dec. 31.
    1890 Jan. 1 – Feb. 26, Oct. 2.

EL TIEMPO. w. est. Jan. 1, 1855.
  Note: Suspended publication Aug.
  28, 1860 – Sept. 3, 1861; Dec. 31,
  1861 – Jan. 6, 1864; Oct. 5, 1866 –
  Feb. 11, 1871; ceased publication
  Feb. 1, 1872.
  CU
    Micro (N)
    1855 Jan. 1 – Mar. 6, 20 – July 10,
          24 – Dec. 11.
    1856 Jan. 22 – Feb. 26, Mar. 18 –
          Apr. 22, May 6 – 13, 27 – June

10, 24 – Aug. 19, Sept. 2 – 9,
23, Oct. 7, 28 – Dec. 30.
1857   Jan. 6 – Feb. 10, 24, Mar. 10 –
Apr. 7, 21 – June 16, 30 – Dec.
8, 22 – 29.
1858   Jan. 5 – July 13, 27 – Dec. 28.
1859   Jan. 4 – 25, Feb. 8 – Apr. 12,
26 – Sept. 13, 27 – Dec. 27.
1860   Jan. 3 – Apr. 3, 17 – Aug. 28.
1861   Sept. 10 – Oct. 22, Nov. 5 –
Dec. 31.
1864   Jan. 6 – Mar. 2, 16 – 23, Apr.
6 – 27, May 11 – Aug. 10, 24 –
Dec. 28.
1865   Jan. 4 – Sept. 13, Oct. 4 – Dec.
27.
1866   Jan. 3 – Aug. 29, Sept. 21 – 28.
DLC
1859   July 12 – Aug. 15, 17 – Nov. 7,
9 – Dec. 26, 28 – 31.
1860   Jan. 1, 2, 4 – 30, Mar. 1 – 12,
14 – 19, 21 – Apr. 16, 18 –
May 21, 23 – 28, 30 – June
4, 6 – 11, 13 – 18, 20 – July 2,
4 – 9, 11 – 16, 18 – 23, 25 –
Aug. 28.
1861   Sept. 3, 10, Oct. 15, 22, Nov.
5, 12.
1864   Feb. 10.
MWA
1855   Apr. 24.

EL TIEMPO. d. est. Jan. 15, 1911.
Note: Suspended publication Aug. 3,
1955 – June 8, 1957. *Intermedio*
published during suspension.
CLSU
Micro (P)
1954   Mar. 1 – May 31.
CLU
1938 – 1954   Jan. 1 – Dec. 31.
1955   Jan. 1 – July 31.
1956   June 8 – Dec. 31.
1957   Jan. 1+
CSt
1938   July 17 – Sept. 15.
CSt – H
1964   Nov. 30 – Dec. 5, 7, 9 – 16.
1965   Feb. 11 – Mar. 10, 15 – May 1,

3 – 5, 8 – 22, 24 – June 14, 16 –
21, 23 – 28, 30 – July 5, 7 – 19,
21 – 25, 27 – Dec. 31.
1966   Jan. 1+.
CU
1929   Suplemento: June 2, Aug. 4.
Micro (P)
1950 – 1954   Jan. 1 – Dec. 31.
1955   Jan. 2 – Aug. 3.
CtY
1965   Jan. 1 – Dec. 31.
1966   Jan. 1 – Mar. 31.
Micro (P)
1962 – 1964   Jan. 1 – Dec. 31.
1965   Jan. 1 – Mar. 31, May 1 – June
30.
DLC
Micro (P) & (N)
1930   July 1 – 26, 28 – 30, Aug. 2 –
24, 26 – Sept. 15, 17 – 21, Oct.
3 – 6, 16 – 20, 22, Nov. 6 – 27,
Dec. 1 – 18, 20 – 26, 28 – 31.
1931   Jan. 1 – 24, 26 – 28, 30 – Feb. 4,
6 – Mar. 8, 10 – 27, 29, 30, May
1, 3 – Aug. 7, 9 – Oct. 31, Nov.
3 – Dec. 31.
1932   Jan. 1 – Feb. 12, 14 – Dec. 31.
1933   Jan. 1 – May 9, 11 – July 17,
19 – Oct. 30, Nov. 5, 16 – Dec.
30.
1934   Jan. 1 – May 16, 18, 20 – 22,
26 – 28, 31 – Dec. 31.
1935   Jan. 2 – Dec. 31.
1936   Jan. 1 – Dec. 31.
1937   Jan. 1 – 30, Feb. 1 – May 21,
24 – Dec. 31.
1938   Jan. 1 – 12, 14 – June 30.
1942   Jan. 1 – Apr. 20, 22, 23, 25 –
29.
Micro (P)
1938   July 1 – Dec. 31.
1939 – 1954   Jan. 1 – Dec. 31.
1955   Jan. 1 – Aug. 3.
1957   June 8 – Dec. 31.
1958   Jan. 1+.
DPU
Current (six months).
Micro (P)
1938 – 1954   Jan. 1 – Dec. 31.

1955   Jan. 1 – July 31.
Micro (N)
1938   July 6 – Dec. 31.
1937 – 1943   Jan. 1 – Dec. 31.
FMU
  Micro (P)
  1953 – 1954   Jan. 1 – Dec. 31.
  1955   Jan. 1 – Aug. 3.
FU
  1951 – 1954   Jan. 1 – Dec. 31.
  1955   Jan. 1 – Aug. 3.
  1957   June 8 – Dec. 31.
  1958   Jan. 1+.
ICRL
  1938   July 1 – Dec. 31.
  1939 – 1949   Jan. 1 – Dec. 31.
  1950   Jan. 1 – Sept. 30.
  Micro (N)
  1938   July 1 – Dec. 31.
  1939 – 1954   Jan. 1 – Dec. 31.
  1955   Jan. 1 – Aug. 3.
  1957   June 8 – Dec. 31.
  1958   Jan. 1+.
ICU
  Micro (P)
  1938   July 1 – Dec. 31.
  1939 – 1954   Jan 1 – Dec. 31.
  1954   Jan. 1 – Aug. 3.
IU
  Micro (P)
  1950 – 1954   Jan. 1 – Dec. 31.
  1955   Jan. 1 – July 31.
InU
  1966   Jan. 1+.
LU
  1946   Jan. 2 – Dec. 31.
  1947 – 1954   Jan. 1 – Dec. 31.
  1955   Jan. 1 – Aug. 3.
MB
  Current (one month).
MH
  1963   Oct. 20, Nov. 3, 10, 17, 24, Dec. 1, 8, 15, 29.
  1964   Jan. 5, 26, Feb. 2, 9, Mar. 8, 15, 22, 29, Apr. 5, 12, 19, 26, May 3, 10, 17, 24, 31, June 7,

21, 28, July 5, 12, Aug. 2, 9, 16, 23, 30, Sept. 6, 20, Oct. 11, 18.
  1965   June 17, 18, 26, July 1 – Oct. 14, 16 – 20, 22 – Dec. 12.
Micro (P)
  1938   July 1 – Dec. 31.
  1939 – 1944   Jan. 1 – Dec. 31.
  1945   Jan. 1 – Mar. 15, Apr. 1 – Dec. 31.
  1946 – 1954   Jan. 1 – Dec. 31.
  1955   Jan. 1 – Aug. 3.
MiEM
  1965   Jan. 1+.
NBuU
  Current (three months).
NNC
  1965   May 15, June 4, 12 – 15, 17 – July 7, 9 – Aug. 23, 25 – Sept. 25, 27 – Oct. 11, 13 – Nov. 6, 8 – 13, 18 – 20, 23, 25 – Dec. 31.
  Micro (P)
  1938   Aug. 1 – Dec. 31.
  1939 – 1941   Jan. 1 – Dec. 31.
  1942   Jan. 1 – 31, Mar. 1 – 31, May 1 – Dec. 31.
  1943 – 1954   Jan. 1 – Dec. 31.
  1955   Jan. 1 – Aug. 3.
  1957   June 8 – Dec. 31.
  1958 – 1964   Jan. 1 – Dec. 31.
NSyU
  1960   May 13 – Dec. 31.
  1961   Jan. 1+.
OrU
  1964   June 13.
PrU
  1961   Mar. 11 – 30, Apr. 1 – Oct. 4.
  1962   Apr. 9 – 19, 22 – Nov. 27, 30 – Dec. 31.
  1963   Jan. 1 – Apr. 11, 14 – Dec. 31.
  1964   Jan. 1 – Mar. 26, 29 – May 13, 16 – July 6.
  1965   Jan. 24 – Dec. 7, 18 – 21, 30.
  1966·   Jan. 1+.
TxU
  1939   Dec. 1 – 28.
  1941   June 29 – Aug. 26, 29 – Oct. 20, 22 – Nov. 7, 9 – Dec. 31.

1942   Jan. 1 – Mar. 13, 15 – Apr. 2,
        5 – 25, May 1, 2, 4 – 31.
1943   Jan. 1 – May 2, 5, 6, 8 – June
        10, 12, 14 – 16, 18 – 28, 30 –
        July 7, 9 – 13, 15 – 17, 19 – Dec.
        30.
1944   Jan. 2 – Mar. 15, 17 – 31, Apr.
        2 – 6, 9 – June 19, 23, 26 –
        Sept. 3, 6 – 26, 28 – Oct. 6, 8 –
        20, 22 – 24, 27 – 29, Nov. 1 – 5,
        7, Dec. 2 – 15, 17 – 31.
1945   Jan. 2 – 15, 17 – Dec. 31.
1946   Jan. 1 – July 26, 28 – Aug. 18,
        20 – 28, 30 – Nov. 12, 14, 16 –
        Dec. 31.
1947   Jan. 1 – July 31, Aug. 2 – 13,
        15 – Sept. 12, 14 – Dec. 31.
Micro (P)
1953 – 1954   Jan. 1 – Dec. 31.
1955   Jan. 1 – Aug. 3.

LA TIRA. w. est. Jan. 31, 1881.
  CtY
    1881   Jan. 31 – Dec. 31.
    1882   Jan. 1 – Mar. 14.

TOLERANTE. bw.
  MWA
    1872   Dec. 1.
    1873   Jan. 1 – 15.

EL TRADICIONALISTA. w., 3w., sw.
  est. Nov. 7, 1871.
    Note: Periodicity Nov. 7, 1871 – May
    7, 1872, weekly; May 9, 1872 – June
    25, 1874, three times a week; July
    7 – Dec. 29, 1874, weekly; after Dec.
    30, 1874, semiweekly.
  MB
    1874   Jan. 1, 4, 6, 8, 10, 13, 15, 17, 20,
            22, 24, 27, 29, 31, Feb. 3, 5, 7,
            10, 12, 14, 28, Mar. 3, 5, 7, 10,
            12, 14, 19, 21, 24, 28, Apr. 3, 7,
            9, 11, 14, 16, 18, 21, 23, 25, 28,
            30, May 2, 5, 7, 9, 12, 14, 16, 19,
            21, 23, 26, June 10, 12, 14, July
            14.
  MWA
    1871   Nov. 7 – Dec. 31.
    1872   Jan. 1 – Dec. 31.

1873   Jan. 1 – Feb. 6.
1874   Jan. 1 – Dec. 31.
1875   Jan. 1 – June 29.

LA TRIBUNA. w. est. Sept. 1, 1861.
  DLC
    1861   Sept. 1, 8, 15, Oct. 6.
            Alcance: Sept. 15.

VOZ PROLETARIA. w.
  CSt – H
    1965   Sept. 2, 16 – 23, Oct. 14, Nov.
            4 – 11, 25, Dec. 16 – 23.

Bucaramanga

DIARIO DEL ORIENTE.
  CSt
    1949   Nov. 22.

VANGUARDIA LIBERAL. d. est. 1919.
  DLC
    1940   Dec. 17.
    1941   Apr. 5 – 7, 26.

Cali

AVANCE. irr.
  DLC
    1942   Nov. 12, Dec. 31.

BALUARTE. bw.
  CU
    Micro (N)
    1849   Dec. 1 – 15.
    1850   Jan. 15 – Mar. 10.

DIARIO DEL PACIFICO. d. est. 1925.
    Note: Ceased publication Aug. 30,
    1956.
  DLC
    1940   Dec. 2, 3, 28, 30.
    1941   Jan. 8, 9, 11, 13 – 15, 17, 24,
            25, 27 – Feb. 3, 19 – 28, Mar.
            3, 5 – 7, 10, 11, 14, Apr. 2, 4,
            21, 23 – 25, May 7 – 27.

EL HERALDO. w. est. 1930.
  DLC
    1940   July 6 – 13, Sept. 12, 28.
    1941   Apr. 29.

RELATOR. d. est. Oct. 15, 1916.
DLC
1940   July 16.
1941   Jan. 21, Apr. 7, 8, 19, 21, 22,
           May 19, 23.
LNT—MA
1929   [July 1—Dec. 31.]
1930   [Jan. 2—Dec. 31.]
1931   [Jan. 7—Mar. 11.]

EL UNIVERSAL. w.
DLC
1941   Feb. 7.

Caracas

See Venezuela. Caracas.

Cartagena

BARRA.
MWA
1850   Sept. 18.

COMETA DE CARTAGENA. w., bw. est
[1826].
CtY
1827   Jan. 11—Feb. 8, Mar. 1, Apr.
           5—19.

DIARIO DE LA COSTA. d. est. Dec. 1,
1916.
DLC
1941   Apr. 4, 6, 9, 10, 13, 15, 18, 22—
           24, 26, 27, May 1, 3, 4, 6, 8, 10,
           11, 13, 14, 21—23, 25, 27, 28,
           30, 31.
1944   Apr. 12—May 31, June 2—5,
           7—9, 11—24, 26—July 2, 6—
           Nov. 30.
MWA
1937   Feb. 9.

EL FANAL. w.
CU
Micro (N)
1849   Jan. 4, 18—Mar. 15, 29, Apr.
           19—May 3, 17, June 7—14.

EL FIGARO. d. est. 1936.
DLC
1941   Apr. 7, 8, 15, 16, 25, 26, 28, 29,
           May 1, 7, 8, 12, 13, 23, 24, 26,
           31.
MWA
1937   Feb. 9.

GACETA DE CARTAGENA DE
COLOMBIA. w.
CtY
1822   Feb. 16—Sept. 14.
1824   Oct. 2—Nov. 13, 27—Dec. 25.
1825   Jan. 1—8, Apr. 23—May 7, 21,
           July 23, Sept. 10—Oct. 1, Nov.
           26—Dec. 17.
1826   Jan. 14—Feb. 4, 19—Mar. 5,
           26—Apr. 16, Aug. 27—Sept.
           24, Oct. 15, Nov. 5—Dec. 10.
1827   Jan. 7—Mar. 4, 25—Apr. 8.
DLC
1830   May 30.

MUNDO. d.
MWA
1937   Feb. 9.

EL SEMANARIO DE LA PROVINCIA
DE CARTAGENA. w.
CU
Micro (N)
1845   Apr. 20, May 4, Aug. 17, Oct.
           12.
1846   Sept. 20, Oct. 11, Nov. 8.

Cucutá

COMENTARIOS. d. est. June 24, 1922.
DLC
1941   Apr. 2, June 5—7, 9, 10, 12,
           14, 16—20.

Funza

EL CUNDINAMARQUES. w. est. Aug. 7,
1861.
CtY
1861   Aug. 7—Dec. 31.

1862   Jan. 8 – Dec. 31.
1863   Jan. 1 – Apr. 18.

Honda

EL VAPOR. w.
CU
Micro (N)
1857   Aug. 27 – Oct. 4, 18 – Dec. 23.
1858   Jan. 12 – Feb. 10, Apr. 28 –
        May 19, June 16 – July 20.

Manizales

LA PATRIA. d. est. June 21, 1921.
DLC
1941   Jan. 27 – Feb. 2, 19 – 22, 24 –
        27, Mar. 5 – 8, 10, 14, 21, 22,
        Apr. 3, 4, 17, 23, 26, 28, May
        7 – 12, 14 – 26.

Medellín

ANGLO-AMERICA. w. est. July 5,
1941.
DLC
1941   July 5.

ANTIOQUIA NUEVA.
DLC
1941   April 13.

COLOMBIA. d. est. Sept. 1906.
DLC
1925   May 4 – Dec. 31.
1926   Jan. 1 – Dec. 31.
1927   Jan. 4 – 22, 31 – Apr. 13, 24 –
        May 1, 3 – 13, 15 – 18, 20 –
        June 17, 19 – 22, 24 – 28, July
        1 – 30, Aug. 1 – 22, 24 – Sept.
        7, 9 – Oct. 29, 31, Nov. 2 – 26,
        28 – Dec. 22.

COLOMBIA NACIONALISTA. m. est.
1930.
DLC
1941   July 10.

EL COLOMBIANO. d. est. Feb. 6, 1912.
DLC
1941   Mar. 21, 22, 26, 27, Apr. 21,
        May 7 – 17, 23 – 28, 30 – June
        22, 24 – 26, 28, 29, July 1 – 3,
        5, 7, 10, 11, 13 – 16, 19 – 21,
        23, 28, 30, Aug. 2 – 5, 9 – 29,
        31, Sept. 6, 8, 10, 14, 15, 18,
        20 – Oct. 3, 5 – 21, 23 – 25,
        28, 29, Nov. 5 – 9, 11, 13 – 15,
        17, 19 – 22, 24, 26, 27, Dec. 1 –
        3, 5 – 10, 12 – 24.
1956   Jan. 6 – 8, 11 – 17, 19, 21 – Feb.
        13, 17, 20 – Apr. 22, 24 – May
        4, 6, 8 – June 19, 21 – July 2,
        4 – 28, 31 – Sept. 28, 30 – Oct.
        17, 20 – Dec. 31.
1957   Jan. 1 – 8, 10 – Feb. 23, 25,
        27 – Apr. 1, 3 – May 5, 11 – July
        20, 22 – 26, 28, 29, 31 – Aug.
        26, 28 – Sept. 1, 3 – 5, 7 – 9,
        11, 13 – Dec. 24.

EL CORREO. d. est. 1913.
DLC
1956   Jan. 5 – Feb. 4, 6 – 8, 11 – Mar.
        1, 3 – 6, 26 – 28, Apr. 3 – 5, 7 –
        13, 17 – 23, 25 – 28, May 4 –
        10, 13, 15 – 26, 28, 29, 31 –
        June 7, 10, 12, 14, 16, 18, 19,
        21 – July 6, 8 – 17, 19 – 22, 24,
        26, 29 – Aug. 5, 7 – 11, 13 –
        Sept. 9, 11 – 22, 27 – Oct. 4,
        6 – 11, 13, 21 – 24, 27 – 30, Nov.
        1, 3 – 7, 9 – 15, 17 – 21, 23, 24,
        26 – Dec. 1, 3, 5, 7 – 10, 16 – 23.
1957   Jan. 8, 18, 22, 25 – Feb. 19, 21,
        23 – Mar. 1, 3, 5 – 7, 9 – 25,
        27 – 30, Apr. 1 – 26, 28 – May
        3, 5, 11 – June 8, 10 – 30, July
        2 – 21, 23 – 26, 28 – Aug. 14,
        16 – Oct. 10, 12 – Nov. 26,
        28 – 30, Dec. 2 – 24.

LA DEFENSA. d. est. 1919.
DLC
1941   Apr. 30 – May 2, 5 – 7, 10 – 14,

17—21, 26—28, 30, June 3, 5,
7, 9—13, 18—23, July 5—12,
18, 22, 23, 25, 31, Aug. 5, 9—
11, 13, 14, 27—Sept. 2, 4, 11,
15, 19—22, 24, 26—Oct. 2, 4—
20, 22, 24, 25, 28, 29, Nov. 8—
21, 24, 26, 27, Dec. 1, 3—11,
19—22.

EL DIARIO. d. est. Feb. 13, 1930.
DLC
1941   Apr. 30—May 6, 8—20, 23—
June 4, 6, 7, 10, 17, 18, 20—
25, 27—30, July 3, 5—18, 21—
25, 28, 29, 31—Aug. 4, 8, 9,
14—18, 28, Sept. 1—6, 11, 15,
19, 24—Oct. 4, 7—10, 15—18,
24, 25, 28, Nov. 4, 5, 7, 14, 21,
24, Dec. 2, 4, 6, 11, 13—15, 17.

EL HERALDO DE ANTIOQUIA. d. est.
June 10, 1927.
CU
1933   Mar. 30—Apr. 1.
DLC
1929   Nov. 18—25, 27—Dec. 8, 12—
31.
1930   Jan. 1—24, 26, Feb. 2—10,
12—June 2, 4—10, 12—15,
18—July 13, 15—Sept. 29, Oct.
1—6, 14—Nov. 10, 18—24,
26—Dec. 1, 7, 9—15, 30, 31.
1931   Jan. 1—6, 8—11, 14—31, Feb.
10—18, 20—26, Mar. 1, 2, 6—
9, 11—16, 19—July 17, 19—
Sept. 10, 15—Oct. 26, 29—
Nov. 15, 17, 19—22, 24—26,
28, 29, Dec. 1—8, 10, 12—31.
1932   Jan. 1—8, 10—15, 23, 25—
Feb. 1, 3, 5—8, 10—17, 19—
21, 23—25, 27—29, Apr. 1—
Sept. 17, 19—24, 26—Dec. 23,
25—31.
1933   Jan. 1—14, 16—31, Feb. 2—20.
1941   May 28, June 18, 23, July 2—
4, 6—10, 12—16, 18—26, 28—
Aug. 6, 8—Sept. 2, 7, 12, 14—
16, 20, 22, 24—Oct. 3, 5—26,
28—30, Nov. 6—22, 24—Dec.

22, 27, 28.
1942   Nov. 22.

EL HERALDO DE ANTIOQUIA.
ViU
Micro (P)
1942   Nov. 22.

EL OBRERO CATOLICO. w. est. 1924.
DLC
1941   June 14, 28, July 26.

LA POLIANTEA. w. est. July 1896.
Note: Paged continuously.
DLC
1896   Nov. 25.

EL PUEBLO; PERIODICA COM-
MERCIAL, INDUSTRIAL, LITERARIO
I POLITICO DEL ESTADO DE
ANTIOQUIA. w., sw.
CU
Micro (N)
1858   Feb. 1—June 8, July 12—Dec.
31.
1859   Jan. 14—Feb. 8.

EL PUEBLO. w., d. est. 1934.
DLC
1941   June 23, July 14, 18, 24, Dec.
11.

REPERTORIO ECLESIASTICO.
MWA
1883   July 24.

Mompos

LA PALESTRA. bw.
CU
Micro (N)
1869   June 8, Oct. 15, Dec. 15.
1870   Feb. 15, July 30, Aug. 30—
Sept. 15, Oct. 20—Dec. 20.
1871   Jan. 5—Oct. 5, Nov. 5—Dec.
20.
1872   Jan. 5—Mar. 20, Apr. 21—June
7, July 7—Aug. 21, Oct. 7—
Dec. 21.
1873   Jan. 7—Feb. 7, Apr. 7—July
7, Aug. 7—Nov. 23, Dec. 23.

1874   Jan. 9 – May 23, June 23 – Oct.
        5.
1875   Jan. 20.
1878   Feb. 28 – May 23, June 23,
        July 23 – Sept. 23, Oct. 23 –
        Dec. 23.
1879   Jan. 7 – 23, Feb. 23 – June 7,
        July 7 – Sept. 7, Oct. 15 – 30,
        Nov. 30 – Dec. 15.
1880   Jan. 8 – Apr. 24, May 24 –
        Sept. 24, Nov. 12 – Dec. 12.
1881   Jan. 12 – July 9, Aug. 13 –
        Sept. 28, Nov. 10 – Dec. 18.
1882   Jan. 11, Feb. 11 – 25, Mar. 26 –
        May 12, June 10 – July 12, Aug.
        14 – 28, Sept. 28 – Oct. 13,
        Nov. 15, Dec. 19 – 30.
1883   Jan. 15 – July 14, Aug. 31 –
        Sept. 15, Oct. 17 – Nov. 17,
        Dec. 15 – 31.
1884   Jan. 16, Feb. 16 – July 30.
CU – B
  Micro (P)
  1883   July 24.

Neiva

ESTRELLA DEL TOLIMA. [w.]
  MWA
    1883   July 24.

Panama City
See Panama. Panama City.

Pasto

CIUDAD DE PASTO.
  LNT – MA
    1841   June 28.

Popayán

EL FOSFORO DE POPAYAN. w. est.
  1823.
  CU
    Micro (N)
    1823   Jan. 19 – July 24.

EL INDEPENDIENTE. bw. est. 1838.
    Note: Ceased publication 1839.
  CU
    Micro (N)
    1838   Nov. 10 – Dec. 10.
    1839   Jan. 10 – 25, Apr. 10.

EL LIBERAL. d. est. 1938.
  DLC
    1941   Apr. 26.

EL TRABAJO. w., d., 3w. est. 1887.
  CU
    Micro (N)
    1887   May 21 – Dec. 31.
    1888   Jan. 14 – May 5.
    1889   Jan. 19 – Dec. 28.
    1890   Apr. 19 – Dec. 20.
    1891   Jan. 24 – Oct. 1.
  MH
    1911   July 22, 29, Sept. 30.
    1912   Jan. 27, Feb. 3, Mar. 9, 16,
            May 11, 18, June 9, 15, July 6,
            13, 20, 27, Aug. 3, 10, 17, 24,
            Oct. 5, 12, Nov. 2, 9, 16, 23,
            30, Dec. 7, 14, 21, 28.
    1913   Jan. 11, 18, 25, Feb. 1, 8, 15,
            22, Mar. 1, 8, 15, 29, Apr. 5,
            12, June 7, 14, 21, 28, July 5,
            12, 19, 26, Aug. 2, 9, 16, 23,
            Oct. 4, Nov. 1, 8, 15, 22, 29,
            Dec. 6, 13, 20, 27.
    1914   Jan. 22, 29, Feb. 26, Mar. 5,
            12, 19, Apr. 30, May 7, 14, 21,
            28, June 4, 11, 18, 25, July 2,
            9, 16, 23, 30, Aug. 6, 13,
            Sept. 3, 10, 17, 24, Oct. 15, 31,
            Nov. 7, 14, Dec. 19, 26.
    1916   May 20, 27, June 3, 10, July
            15, 22, Nov. 18, Dec. 9.

Santa Marta

AMIGO DEL PUEBLO.
  MWA
    1883   Extraordinario: July 24.

Sincelejo

EL ANUNCIADOR. sw. est. 1911.
DLC
1942 Oct. 1–31.

Socorro

INTEGRIDAD.
MWA
1883 July 24.

Tunja

EL CONSTITUCIONAL DE BOYACA.
w. est. [1825].
CtY
1825 Aug. 12–Sept. 9, Nov. 4–11,
Dec. 23.
1826 Jan. 13.
MWA
1826 July 7–14.

EL ORIENTE. irr.
CU
1959 Apr. 10, May 6–10, June 6–
16, 25, July 3–10, 25–Aug.
7, 21–28, Sept. 2–Oct. 7, 16–
27, Nov. 6, 24–Dec. 25.
1960 Jan. 1, 8, 16–19, 28, Feb. 12,
July 26–Aug. 7, 19, Oct. 14.
1961 Sept. 14–20, Oct. 12, Nov. 1,
11, 17, Dec. 6, 13, 29.
1962 Jan. 1–12, Feb. 8, Aug. 11–
26, Sept. 7–18, Oct. 10–Nov.
9, 23–Dec. 4.
1963 Jan. 15, Feb. 4, 27–Apr. 2,
13–19, 29, May 7–June 8,
18–25, July 6–12,
Sept. 13–Oct. 25, Nov. 8, 16,
28–Dec. 4, 16–25.
1964 Jan. 1–Feb. 1, 10–Mar. 13,
Apr. 13, 23–May 13, 23–July
14, 24–Aug. 7, 14–20, Sept.
4–18, 29–Dec. 4.

COSTA RICA

Alajuela

NOTICIOSO UNIVERSAL. est. Jan. 4,
1833.
Note: Removed to San José, Mar. 7,
1835.
LNT–MA
Micro (P)
1834 Dec. 27.
1835 Jan. 3.

Limón

LA VOZ DEL ATLANTICO. w. est. 1933.
Note: In Spanish and English.
DPU
1941 July 12, 26, Aug. 9, Sept. 20–
27, Oct. 18–Dec. 27.
1942 Jan. 10–Apr. 25.
LNT–MA
1937 July 17, Aug. 21, 28, Oct.
2.

Puntarenas

EL PACIFICO. sw., 3w. est. 1896.
Note: Periodicity before Feb. 23,
1897, semiweekly; after Apr. 16, 1898,
three times a week. Suspended publication Feb. 23, 1897–Apr. 16, 1898.
DLC
1896 Dec. 6, 7, 10–31.
1897 Jan. 1–Feb. 22.
1898 Apr. 16–Oct. 20, 22–Dec. 31.
1899 Jan. 1–June 19, 21–July 23.
1900 Jan. 3–Mar. 7, 18–May 16,
June 22–July 4.
1901 Aug. 16–Dec. 12, 14–31.
1902 Jan. 1–Feb. 1, 14–May 23,
June 22–July 9, 16–19, 21–
Aug. 23, 25–31.
1903 Oct. 21–Dec. 31.
1904 Jan. 1–11, 13–20, 22–Feb.
26, 28–June 29, July 1–Dec.
31.
1905 Jan. 1–Feb. 10, 12–17, 19–
May 31, June 2–Aug. 1, 3–
Dec. 31.

1906   Jan. 1 – Feb. 26, 28 – Oct. 28,
        30 – Dec. 29.
1908   Jan. 2 – Dec. 31.
1909   Jan. 1 – Apr. 7, 9 – 21, 23 –
        Dec. 30.

San José

ACCION DEMOCRATA. w. est. Feb. 26,
1944.
  CtY
    1944   Feb. 26 – Dec. 31.
    1945   Jan. 1 – Apr. 28.

ALBUM SEMANAL. WEEKLY ALBUM.
w.
    Note: In Spanish and English.
    CU – B
    1856   Sept. 12 – Oct. 3.

EL ANUNCIADOR COSTARRICENSE.
bw. est. 1887.
    CU – B
    Micro (P) & (N)
    1890   May 16 – June 1.

BOLETIN JUDICIAL. d. est. July 19,
1861.
    Note: Suspended publication 1865 –
    1895. Combined with *La Gazeta*
    Jan. 17 – Feb. 5, 1919; Nov. 4, 5,
    Dec. 7, 1920.
    LNT – MA
    1934   Oct. 2 – Dec. 18.
    1940   Dec. 31.
    1949   Apr. 1.
    1951   Feb. 1 – 7, Mar. 28, June 7 – 9,
            Aug. 8 – 12, 14, Dec. 22.
    1952   Apr. 3 – 6, 8, 9, May. 1.
    1955   Jan. 22, Mar. 6, June 4, Aug.
            4, 5, 7, 9, 10.
    1956   May 20.
    1957   May 30, 31, June 1, 2, 4, Aug.
            22, 28 – 30, Sept. 4, 6 – 12, 24,
            25.
    1958   May 1, 3, 4, 7, 10, 13 – 16, 18,
            20 – 31, July 1 – Aug. 1, 7, 14,
            15, 17, 20, 22, 23, Sept. 2, 4 – 7,
            9 – 13, 19 – 28, Oct. 1 – 31.

1959   Oct. 5 – 8, 11, 12, 14, 16, 18 –
        23, 25 – 30, Dec. 1 – 4, 6, 7, 11,
        14 – 18, 20 – 22, 25, 28, 29.
1961   Feb. 1 – May 31.
MWA
    1897   July 18, Oct. 1, 31, Nov. 14 –
            Dec. 29.
    1898   Jan. 8, July 2 – Dec.
    1899   July 1 – Dec. 31.
    1900 – 1901   Jan. 1 – Dec. 31.
    1903   July 1 – Aug. 1, Oct. 11 – Dec.
    1904   Feb. 20, [Apr. 17 – Dec. 18.]
    1905   [Feb. 19 – Apr. 29.]
    1906   Nov. 8 – 13.
    1907   [Apr. 17 – Dec. 14.]
    1908   [Jan. 1 – Oct. 21.]
    1909   Mar. 6, 10, Nov. 24, 27, 30.
    1910   Jan. 1, 6, [Apr. 8 – Dec. 31.]
    1911   [Jan. 1 – Dec. 31.]
    1912   [Jan. 1 – June 30,] Nov. 22 –
            Dec. 20, 25 – 29.
    1913   [Jan. 1 – May 7], July 2, Oct. 9.
    1914   Mar. 5, [Apr. 8 – July 29], Oct.
            4, 6, 11.
    1916   Feb. 19 – 27, Mar. 2 – 7, Oct.
            6.
    1917   Sept. 5.
    1918   June 1, 7 – 11, 15, 16, 20.
    1919   Jan. 19, 29 – 31, Feb. 5, 11,
            Mar. 19, Dec. 6, 7, 11, 16 – 18,
            20 – 24.
    1920   [Nov. 6 – Dec. 31.]
    1921   [Jan. 1 – 26.]

BOLETIN OFICIAL. irr. est. 1853.
    CU – B
    1853   Dec. 8 – 31.
    1854   Jan. 1 – 5, Feb. 9 – Mar. 30,
            Apr. 20 – May 4, June 22 –
            Sept. 21, Dec. 23 – 31.
    1855   Jan. 1 – Mar. 7, 14 – 21.
    Micro (P)
    1885   Mar. 13 – 15, 17 – Apr. 9.

EL COSTARRICENSE. w. est. Nov. 14,
1846.
    Note: Succeeded *La Gaceta oficial*
    as official gazette; succeeded by

La Gaceta del gobierno. Ceased
publication Dec. 15, 1849.
CU−B
   1849   Nov. 10−Dec. 31.
           Suplemento:Nov. 18.
CtY
   1848   Jan. 15, Feb. 5, Apr. 22−
           May 13, June. 3.
   1849   Jan. 6−Feb. 3, May 26−June
           2.

LA CRONICA DE COSTA RICA. w., sw.
est. Apr. 1, 1857.
   Note: Semi-official publication suc-
   ceeding *Boletín oficial*; succeeded
   by *La Gaceta oficial.* Ceased publication Aug. 17, 1859.
CU−B
Micro (P)
   1857   July 18−22.

DIARIO COSTARRICENSE.
CU−B
Micro (P)
   1888   Aug. 21.

DIARIO DE COSTA RICA. d. est. July 1,
1919.
CLCM
   1927   Sept, 4, 24, Oct. 11, Dec. 23.
DLC
   1928   Mar. 1−Apr. 12, 15−22, 24,
           26−29, May 1−17, 19, 20, 22−
           June 3, 5−7, 9−14, 16−24,
           27−July 6, 14−18, 20, 28−
           Oct. 17, 26−Dec. 21.
   1929   Jan. 3, 4, 7−23, 25, 28, Feb.
           2−9, 11, 13−27, Mar. 1, 4, 9−
           23, 25−27, Apr. 1−3, 5, 8,
           13−19, 22, 27−May 4, 6−
           24, 27, June 1−11, 13−July
           4, 6−Aug. 3, 5−7, 9−14, 17,
           19−Sept. 21, 23−Oct. 4, 7−
           Dec. 31.
   1930   Jan. 1−Mar. 19, 21−28, 31,
           Apr. 1, 5−14, 16, 17, 21−28,
           30−May 12, 29−June 18,
           20−28, 30−July 4, 6−11,
           13−24, 27−Aug. 4, 6−11,

           13−19, 20−28, Sept. 1, 8, 13,
           15, 17−Oct. 7, 9−31, Nov. 8−
           Dec. 3, 5−11, 20, 21, 23−31.
   1931   Jan. 1−30, Feb. 1, 2, 4−6, 8−
           Mar. 19, 21−May 10, 12−23,
           25−July 3, 5−Aug. 12, 14−28,
           30, Sept. 2, 3, 5−12, 21−25,
           27−Oct. 16, 18−Nov. 6, 8−
           10, 12−14, 22−24, 26−Dec.
           1, 3−12, 14−31.
   1932   Jan. 1−Mar. 11, 13−18, 20−
           Apr. 1, 9−16, 18−22, 24−
           May 31, June 2−July 31, Aug.
           2−Oct. 3, 5−Dec. 31.
   1933   Jan. 1−Feb. 11, 13, 19−Mar.
           4, 6−July 13, 15−Aug. 16,
           18−Sept. 15, 17−Oct. 12, 14−
           17, 19−Dec. 31.
   1934   Jan. 1−24, 26−Mar. 25, 27−
           29, Apr. 1−22, 24−26, 28−
           Aug. 11, 13−21, 23−Sept. 10,
           12−Oct. 11, 13−Dec. 3, 5, 7−
           22, 24−29, 31.
   1935   Jan. 1−9, 11−Mar. 12, 14−
           May 4, 6−17, 26−June 19,
           21−July 2, 4−12, 14, 15, 17−
           26, 28−31, Aug. 2, 6−24, 28−
           Sept. 4, 6−8, 10−14, 17−19,
           22, 24−Oct. 3, 5−14, 16−22,
           24−Nov. 17, 20−Dec. 6, 8−
           12, 14, 15, 18−25, 28, 29.
   1936   Jan. 3, 4, 15, 17, 19−24, 26−
           31, Feb. 3−7, 9−23, 27−Mar.
           1, 5−8, 11−13, 28, 29, 31, Apr.
           2−8, 19−22, 24−May 17, 20,
           23−31, June 3−July 1, 3−
           10, 19, 22−Aug. 12, 14−22,
           24, 25, 27, 28, 30−Sept. 5,
           15−Oct. 17, 19−Nov. 1, 3−
           7, 9−12, 20, 25, 27−29, Dec.
           1−7, 11, 12, 15−18, 20, 22−
           25, 29, 31.
   1937   Jan. 5−8, 17, 21. 24−30, Oct.
           12.
   1938   Apr. 10.
   1941   Apr. 20, 22−27, 29−May 1,
           3, 4, 6−11, 13−18, 20−25,
           27−June 1, 3−7, 11, 12, 14,

15, 17 – 22, 24 – 29, July 1, 2,
4 – 6, 8, 10, 13, 16 – 20, 22 –
26, 29 – 31, Aug. 2, 3, 5 – 10,
13, 14, 17, 19 – 24, 26, 28 – 31,
Sept. 2 – 6, 9, 11, 12, 18, 19,
23, 25, 27, 28, 30 – Oct. 5, 7,
9, 11, 14 – 18, 22 – 26, 29 – 31,
Nov. 2, 4 – 6, 8, 9, 11 – 13, 15,
16, 18 – 20, 25 – 27, 29, 30, Dec.
2, 4 – 7, 9 – 21, 23, 24, 26 – 30.
1942   Jan. 6 – 18, 20 – 25, 27 – Feb.
1, 3, 5 – 7, 10 – 15, 17, 19 – 22,
24 – Mar. 1, 3 – 8, 10 – 12, 14,
15, 17 – 19, 21, 22, 24 – 29,
31 – Apr. 2, 8 – 12.
1943   Jan. 5.
1944   Jan. 16 – 30, Feb. 6, 21, 26 –
29, Mar. 2 – 16, 18 – 26, 29,
31 – Apr. 6, 11 – 13, 18, 20 –
25, 27, May 3, 5, 11 – 14, 17,
21, 31 – June 2.
1946   Mar. 1 – 5, 7 – 10, 12 – 15, May
1 – June 8, 13 – 16, 26 – 29, July
2 – 5, 7 – Dec. 20, 22 – 31.
1947   Jan. 1 – 4, 6 – Feb. 20, 22 –
May 23, 25 – July 3, 5 – Aug. 2,
4 – 8, 10 – 22, 25 – Sept. 11,
15, 17 – Oct. 4, 6 – 11, 13, 14,
16 – 18, 20 – 24, 27 – 30, Nov.
3 – 8, 10 – 21, 23 – 29, Dec. 1 –
19, 22 – 27, 29 – 31.
1948   Jan. 1 – Feb. 3, 5 – Mar. 8,
10 – 12, Apr. 14 – May 17, 19 –
Aug. 14, 16 – Sept. 4, 6 – Oct.
29, 31 – Nov. 5, 7 – 18, 20 –
Dec. 31.
1949   Jan. 1 – Apr. 30, May 2 – 9,
11 – Dec. 31.
1950   Jan. 1 – Aug. 2, 4 – Dec. 8,
11 – 31.
1951   Jan. 1 – Apr. 13, 15 – Sept. 30,
Oct. 10, Nov. 1 – 24, 26 – Dec.
31.
1952   Jan. 1 – 14, 16 – Feb. 29, Mar.
3 – 28, 31 – May 4, 6 – 20, 22 –
June 19, 21 – 25, 27, July 1 –
Dec. 31.
1953   Jan. 1 – Mar. 13, 16 – June 28,

Oct. 1 – Nov. 11, 13 – Dec. 8,
10 – 31.
1954   Jan. 1 – Apr. 1, 3 – May 7, 9 –
June 11, 13 – July 2, 5, 7 – 23,
25 – 30, Aug. 1, 2, 4 – 10, 12 –
Dec. 31.
1955   Jan. 1 – Apr. 16, 18 – July 12,
14 – Dec. 29.
Micro (P)
1956   Jan. 1+.
ICRL
Micro (P) & (N)
1956   Jan. 1+.
LNHT
1937   July 27, 29, 31, Aug. 1, 5, 6, 8,
10, 11, 14, Nov. 5 – 7, 10, 11,
14.
1953   Oct. 31.
Micro (N)
1925 – 1935   [Jan. 1 – Dec. 31.]
(P)
1956   Jan. 1+.
TxU
1941   June 21 – Aug. 8, 16 – Sept.
12, 20 – Nov. 21, 29 – Dec. 18,
20 – 25, 27 – 30.
1942   Jan. 3 – 22, 30 – Feb. 15, 18 –
Mar. 15, 18 – 26, May 8 – 14,
July 18 – 22, 24 – 28, 31.
1944   May 16 – June 16, Sept. 1 –
Oct. 31, Nov. 2 – 30.
1945   Feb. 16 – 23, 25 – Mar. 29, June
2 – 16, July 1 – 31, Oct. 5 –
31, Nov. 2 – 24, Dec. 16 – 28.
1946   Jan. 3 – Feb. 15, Mar. 1 – 5,
7 – 15, May 1 – June 8, Aug.
1 – 9, 11 – Sept. 2, 4 – 6, 8 –
Oct. 1, 4 – Nov. 8, 10 – Dec. 4.
1947   Jan. 10 – Feb. 5, Apr. 1 – 3, 8 –
9, 11 – 13, 16 – May 8, June
13 – July 15, 22 – Aug. 13,
Sept. 11 – Oct. 12, 15 – 28, Dec.
25 – 28.
1948   Jan. 6 – 15, July 1 – Aug. 1,
4 – Sept. 17, Oct. 3 – Nov. 28,
Dec. 21 – 30.
1949   Jan. 4 – 8, 12 – 16, 19 – Mar.
29, June 23 – 30, July 2 – 16,

19 – 22, 29 – Aug. 2, 5 – 11.
1950　Jan. 4 – 8, 11 – July 25, Nov.
　　　1 – 18, Dec. 29 – 31.
1951　Jan. 3 – 5, 7 – Mar. 9, May 24 –
　　　Aug. 17, 25 – Sept. 15, 18 – 28,
　　　30 – Oct. 14, 17, 19 – 26, Nov.
　　　3 – 30.
1952 – 1953　Jan. 1 – Dec. 31.

DIARIO DEL COMERCIO. d.
LNHT
　Micro (N)
　1920 – 1923　[Jan. 1 – Dec. 31.]

DIARIO NACIONAL. d. est. [1889].
LNT – MA
　1954　[Mar. 25 – Dec. 8.]
　1955　[Jan. 5 – Aug. 31, Oct. 1 – 31.]

DOMINICAL. w.
LNT – MA
　1937　Aug. 8.

LA EPOCA. w.
DLC
　1941　Apr. 27.

EL FERROCARRIL. w. est. Mar. 17, 1872.
CtY
　1876　Apr. 12.

LA GACETA. w. est. 1846.
Note: Title *La Gaceta oficial*, 1846 –
Feb. 1853; *La Gaceta*, after Feb.
1853. Succeeded *La Gaceta del
gobierno*; succeeded by *Boletín
oficial*.
CU – B
　1850　Oct. 26, Nov. 16 – 23.
　1853　July 16 – Sept. 10, Dec. 12 – 31.
　1854　Jan. 1 – May 8, June 10 –
　　　　Sept. 23, Oct. 14 – 21.
　Micro (P) & (N)
　1952　Aug. 14 – Oct. 2.
NHi
　1854　Jan. 7, Feb. 13, 18, 27, Mar. 4,
　　　　13, 18, June 24, July 15, 22.

LA GACETA; DIARIO OFICIAL. d. est.
Feb. 23, 1878.
Note: Succeeded *El Costarricense*

as the official publication.
CU – B
　Micro (P)
　1883　Jan. 20.
　1885　Feb. 3 – Mar. 12, Apr. 30 –
　　　　Sept. 30, Nov. 1 – 29.
　1888　Aug. 21.
DLC
　1878　Feb. 23 – Dec. 31.
　1879 – 1900　Jan. 1 – Dec. 31.
MWA
　1897　July 18, Oct. 1, 31, Nov. 14 –
　　　　Dec. 31.
　1898　Jan. 1 – Sept. 29.
　1899　June 10, [July 1 – Dec. 31.]

GACETA OFICIAL. w. est. Aug. 15, 1859.
Note: Succeeded *La Crónica de
Costa Rica* as official publication.
CU – B
　Micro (P)
　1864　July 23, Aug. 27 – Sept. 3, 25,
　　　　Oct. 29, Nov. 12, Dec. 3 – 10.
CtY
　1863　July 12.

EL GRITO DEL PUEBLO.
LNT – MA
　1937　Aug. 1.

EL GUERRILLERO. est. Mar. 28, 1850.
Note: Ceased publication June 17,
1850.
CU – B
　1850　Apr. 18, May 9, June 17.

LA HORA. d. est. 1932.
LNT – MA
　1937　Aug. 5, 12.

LA INFORMACION. d. est. Apr. 1, 1908.
LNT – MA
　1914　[Jan. 1 – Dec. 31.]
　1916 – 1918　[Jan. 1 – Dec. 31.]
　Micro (N)
　1915　[Jan. 1 – Dec. 31.]

LEALTAD.
　LNT – MA
　　1937　Aug. 2.
MENTOR COSTARRICENSE. irr. est.
　Dec. 31, 1842.
　　Note: Succeeded by *La Gaceta*
　　oficial as the official publication.
　　Ceased publication Aug. 8, 1846.
　CtY
　　1845　Sept. 20 – Dec. 27.
　　1846　Jan. 3 – 17, Feb. 7 – 28, Mar.
　　　　　21 – 28, Apr. 18 – May 2, June
　　　　　20 – July 11.
　DLC
　　1845　Aug. 9 – Dec. 31.
　　1846　Jan. 1 – Apr. 10, 12 – Aug. 8.

MUJER Y HOGAR. w.
　TxU
　　1948　Feb. 26, Mar. 11.

LA NACION. d. est. Oct. 12, 1946.
　CLU
　　1965　Jan. 7 – 12, Feb. 4 – 11, 14 –
　　　　　19, 21 – 25, 28, Mar. 2 – 4, 26 –
　　　　　28, Apr. 1 – 6, 15, 20 – May 5,
　　　　　13 – 20, 23 – 27, June 16 – 21,
　　　　　July 1, 2, 4 – Aug. 4, 6 – 13,
　　　　　15 – 19, 26 – Sept. 1, 3, 5 – 8,
　　　　　17 – 19, 22 – 25, 27 – 30, Oct.
　　　　　1 – 3, 5, 6, 21 – 27, 29, 31 – Nov.
　　　　　7, 9 – 12, 14 – 17, 26 – Dec. 6,
　　　　　8 – 31.
　　1966　Jan. 1+.
　CSt – H
　　1964　Oct. 8 – 16, 18 – 28, Nov. 5 –
　　　　　10, 26 – Dec. 2.
　　1965　Jan. 7 – 12, Feb. 4 – 7, 9 – 10,
　　　　　25, 28, Mar. 2 – 4, 19, 21 – 28,
　　　　　Apr. 1 – 6.
　DLC
　　1955　Feb. 15, 17 – 22, 25 – Apr. 19,
　　　　　21 – May 6, 8 – 24, June 2 – 4,
　　　　　6 – July 5, 7 – 11, 15 – 30, Aug.
　　　　　1, 4 – 15, 17 – 30, Sept. 1, 2,
　　　　　4 – 7, 10, 14, 17, 19, 21 – 24,
　　　　　26, 28 – 30, Oct. 2 – 4, Nov.
　　　　　2, 10, 16, 28 – Dec. 8, 11, 12,
　　　　　14 – 31.

　　1956　Jan. 1 – 21, 23, 24, 26, Feb. 10,
　　　　　12, 13, 28, Mar. 1, 2, 11, 12,
　　　　　16 – 29, 31 – Apr. 7, 9 – May
　　　　　25, 27 – June 18, 20 – 29, July
　　　　　1 – 9, 11, 13 – Aug. 6, 10,11,
　　　　　13 – 31, Sept. 2 – 28, Oct. 3 –
　　　　　9, 11 – Nov. 7, Dec. 5 – 28.
　　1957　Jan. 3 – 17, 19 – 23, 31, Feb. 1,
　　　　　Mar. 1 – 31, Apr. 2 – 7, Dec. 17.
　　1958　Jan. 3 – 21, 23, 24, 27 – Apr.
　　　　　30, May 3 – Aug. 8, 11 – Sept.
　　　　　15, 18 – Dec. 31.
　　1959　Jan. 1, 2, 4 – 13, 15 – 17, 19 –
　　　　　Apr. 22, 25 – May 11, 13 – 23,
　　　　　25 – June 1, 3, 6 – 8, 10, 13 –
　　　　　Sept. 27, Oct. 1 – Nov. 4, 6 –
　　　　　Dec. 31.
　　1960　Jan. 1 – 22, 26, 27, 29 – Feb. 13,
　　　　　15 – 20, 22, 23, Mar. 1 – 14,
　　　　　16 – 31, Apr. 2 – 5, 7 – 25, 27,
　　　　　May 3, 7 – 9, 13, 18, 25 – June
　　　　　3, 5 – 7, 9 – 13, 15, 17, 21 – 24,
　　　　　July 1 – 14, 16 – Sept. 22, 24 –
　　　　　Dec. 20, 22 – 31.
　　1961　Jan. 1 – Mar. 30, Apr. 3 – May
　　　　　15, 17 – 24, 26 – Dec. 31.
　Micro　(P) & (N)
　　1962　Jan. 1 – 23, 25 – June 1, 3 –
　　　　　29, July 1 – Oct. 10, 12 – Dec.
　　　　　31.
　　1963　Jan. 1+.
　KU

　　Current (two months).

　LNT – MA
　　1957　Feb. 12 – Apr. 14, 23 – June 9,
　　　　　16 – Nov. 24, Dec. 10 – 28.
　　1958　Jan. 3 – Feb. 23, Mar. 4 – Oct.
　　　　　12, 21 – Nov. 2, 18 – Dec. 7,
　　　　　16 – 27.
　　1959　Jan. 3 – Mar. 15, 23 – Apr. 28,
　　　　　May 4 – June 7, 15 – 26, 28 –
　　　　　July 5, 13 – 20, 23 – Aug. 20,
　　　　　23 – 25, 27 – Sept. 20, Oct. 5,
　　　　　7 – 18, 26 – Nov. 15, 23 – Dec.
　　　　　31.
　　1960　Jan. 1, 3, 4, Oct. 10.
　　1962　Aug. 5 – 21, 23 – 25, 28.

NOTICIOSO UNIVERSAL.
   See Costa Rica. Alajuela.

NOVEDADES.
  LNT — MA
    1937   July 27.

LA NUEVA PRENSA. d. est. 1921.
  CSt
    1925   Feb. 2.

LA PATRIA. w. est. Aug. 1, 1882.
  DLC
    1882   Sept. 21 — Oct. 9.

LA PATRIA. d. est. 1895.
  CU — B
    Micro (P) & (N)
    1896   June 3 — 20, 23 — 26.

PATRIA NUEVA. bw
  TxU
    1923   Dec. 15 — 31.
    1924   Jan. 1 — Feb. 15, 29.

LA PRENSA. d. est. 1818.
  DLC
    1927   Mar. 17, 18, 22, 24 — Apr. 10,
           12 — May 4, 6 — 13, 15 — 22, 24,
           26 — 29, 31 — June 2, 4 — 30.

LA PRENSA LIBRE. d. est. 1889.
  CLU
    Micro (P)
    1955   Jan. 1 — Dec. 31.
  DLC
    1941   May 1.
    1942   Mar. 5.
    1959   Feb. 24.
  DPU
    Micro (P)
    1953   Jan. 2 — Dec. 31.
    1954 — 1955   Jan. 1 — Dec. 31.
    Micro (N)
    1945   Jan. 2 — Dec. 31.
    1946 — 1949   Jan. 1 — Dec. 31.
    1950   Jan. 1 — Dec. 28.
    1952   Jan. 2 — Dec. 11.
  ICRL
    Micro (P)
    1945   July 1 — Dec. 31.

    1946 — 1950   Jan. 1 — Dec. 31.
    1952   Jan. 1 — Sept. 2.
  KU
    1961   Jan. 2 — Dec. 31.
    1962   Jan. 1+.
  LNT — MA
    1951   [Mar. 1 — Aug. 27.]
    1952   Apr. 1 — July 8, 16 — Aug. 14,
           16 — Oct. 31, Nov. 5 — Dec. 27.
    1953 — 1954   [Jan. 1 — Dec. 31.]
    1955   [Jan. 3 — Dec. 27.]
    1956   [Jan. 3 — Dec. 21.]
    1957   [Jan. 2 — Dec. 18.]
    1959   [Jan. 16 — Dec. 31.]
    1960   [Jan. 4 — Dec. 28.]
    1961   Jan. 1 — June 10, 19 — July 8,
           17 — Dec. 9.
    1962 — 1964   [Jan. 1 — Dec. 31.]
    1965   [Jan. 1+.]
    Micro (N)
    1937 — 1945   [Jan. 1 — Dec. 31.]

REPERTORIO AMERICANO. bw., 3m.
  est. Sept. 1, 1919.
  CU
    1919   Sept. 1 — 11, Oct. 15 — Dec. 15.
    1920   Jan. 1 — Feb. 1, Mar. 15 — Dec.
           15.
    1921   Jan. 1 — Feb. 1, Mar. 15 — June
           30.
  LNT — MA
    1953   June 15, Aug. 15.
    1954   May 15, June 15.
    1955   Feb. 15, Dec. 15.
    1956   Jan. 20.
  TNJ
    1947   May 1 — Dec. 31.
    1948 — 1950   Jan. 1 — Dec. 31.

LA REPUBLICA. d. est. 1886.
  CU — B
    Micro (P)
    1888   Aug. 21.

LA REPUBLICA. d. est. 1950.
  DLC
    1955   May 15.
    1956   May 1 — 11, 13 — Oct. 1, 3 —
           15, 20 — Nov. 1, 3 — Dec. 28.

1957   Jan. 3 – 30, Feb. 2 – 21, 23 –
        May 11, 13 – 23, 25 – June 10,
        12 – 20, 22 – 29, July 1 – Aug.
        14, 17 – Sept. 26, 28 – Oct. 5,
        7 – Dec. 24, 27 – 31.
1958   Jan. 1 – Feb. 7, 9 – 19, 21 –
        Mar. 1, 3, 4, 6 – 25, 27, 29 –
        May 22, 24 – June 29, July 1 –
        Sept. 17, 19 – Dec. 28.
1959   Jan. 3 – 12, 15, 16, 21 – Feb.
        10, 12 – 19, 21 – Mar. 16, 18 –
        Apr. 3, 5 – 22, 25 – May 14, 16,
        18 – 23, 25, 26, 28 – June 1, 3,
        6 – 29, July 1 – Aug. 15, 17 –
        Sept. 14, 17 – 27, Oct. 1 – Nov.
        4, 6 – Dec. 18, 20 – 30.
1960   Jan. 5 – 22, 26 – Feb. 8, 11 –
        16, 18 – 20, Mar. 1 – 14, 16 –
        28, 30, 31, Apr. 2 – 5, 8 – 12,
        19, 21 – 25, 27, 29, May 12, 13,
        15, 16, 18, 25 – June 3, 5, 6, 9,
        11 – 15, 18 – 24, July 1, 2, 4 –
        6, 8, 10 – 13, 16 – 18, 21, 27,
        29 – Aug. 11, 13 – Sept. 2, 7,
        9 – Nov. 29, Dec. 2 – 28.
1961   Jan. 3 – 30, Feb. 1 – 5, 7 – Mar.
        30, Apr. 4 – May 24, 26 – June
        29, July 1 – Aug. 29, 31 – Dec.
        28.
Micro (P) & (N)
1962   Jan. 1+.
FU
1965   Jan. 1+.
Micro (N)
1962   July 1 – Dec. 29, 31.
1963   Jan. 3 – Aug. 2, 4 – Sept. 28,
        30 – Nov. 27, 29 – Dec. 31.
1964   Jan. 1 – Nov. 14, 16 – Dec. 31.
LNT – MA
1953   Oct. 31.
1962   [Aug. 7 – Dec. 29.]
1963   [Jan. 3 – Dec. 31.]
1964   [Jan. 3 – Dec. 29.]
1965   [Jan. 3 – Oct. 31.]
RUMBOS.
LNT – MA
1956   Apr. 9, May 9.

EL SEMANARIO. w., irr. est. Aug. 26,
1939.
LNT – MA
1940   Feb. 24.
NN
1939   Aug. 26 – Dec. 23.
EL SHEIK.
LNT – MA
1954   Apr. 1 – June 30.
EL SOL.
LNT – MA
1955   Nov. 14, 28, Dec. 26.
1956   Jan. 23, Mar. 26, Aug. 13, Dec.
        3.
1958   Feb. 10.
1959   Sept. 21, Dec. 21.
1960   Feb. 29, Mar. 31, May 31, Aug.
        31.

TRABAYO. w.
CSt
1938   July 30, Aug. 13, Sept. 24.
LA TRIBUNA. est. 1920.
CLCM
1927   Oct. 14, Nov. 13.
DLC
1926   Jan. 17 – Feb. 16, 20 – 26, 28 –
        Apr. 5, 7 – 11, 13 – 15, 17 –
        23, June 27 – July 13, 15, Aug.
        7 – 13, 15 – Sept. 6, 8 – Oct. 1,
        9 – 21, 23 – Nov. 1, 3 – 5, Dec.
        27 – 30.
1927   Jan. 3 – Feb. 5, 20 – Mar. 12,
        14 – 23, 25 – Apr. 10, 12 – 14,
        19 – 21, 23 – May 26, 28 – June
        20, 22, 23, 25 – Sept. 1, 3 –
        Oct. 4, 6, 7, 14 – 21.
1939   Dec. 17.
1941   Apr. 22 – June 2, 4 – 7, 9, 10,
        12 – 30, July 7, 10, 11, 14, 16,
        18 – 21, 23, 24, 26, 28 – Aug. 1,
        3 – 7, 9 – 20, 23 – 25, 27, 28,
        30 – Sept. 6, 8, 9, 11, 15, 18,
        20, 22, 27 – Oct. 13, 15 – 23, 26,
        27, 29, Nov. 3, 5, 6, 8, 9, 11, 12,
        14 – 19, 22 – 30, Dec. 4, 8 – 19,

21—23, 25, 26, 29.
1942 Jan. 1—3, 5, 7—23, 25—28,
31—Feb. 6, 8, 9, 12—17, 19—
Mar. 3, 7—12, 14—18, 20—24,
27, 29, 30, Apr. 1, 2, 6, 11, 12.
1943 Oct. 16.
LNHT
1937 Aug. 4.
Micro (N)
1936 Dec. 20—31.
TxU
1923 Dec. 28.
1924 Jan. 30—31.

WEEKLY ALBUM.
See *Album semanal. Weekly Album.*

CUBA
Banes

CORREO SEMANAL. w.
MWA
1914 Mar. 5.

EL PUEBLO. d. est. 1915.
DLC
1954 May 11.

VERDAD Y JUSTICIA.
MWA
1914 Feb. 28.

Bayamo

BAYAMO. d.
MWA
1914 Mar. 2.

HATUEY. w. est. 1938.
DLC
1942 Oct. 22, Nov. 1, 10, 21.

EL CUBANO LIBRE.
See Cuba. Camaguey.

Camagüey

EL CAMAGÜEYANO. d. est. 1900.
DLC
1954 Nov. 10.

LNT—MA
1929 July 23—Aug. 5.
MWA
1914 Feb. 4.

EL CUBANO LIBRE. est. Oct. 17, 1868.
Note: Removed from Bayamo to
Camagüey Jan. 12, 1869. Suspended
publication Jan. 12—July 4, 1869;
1871—Aug. 3, 1895. See also com-
memorative *2ª época* published in
Santiago.
LNT—MA
1870 Apr. 21, 27, May 2, 25.

GACETA DE PUERTO-PRINCIPE. sw.,
3w.
NN
1838 Jan. 10, June 13—23, Oct. 3—
10, 20, Nov. 24, Dec. 5, 15.
1839 Jan. 26, Feb. 2—9, 20—27,
Mar. 6, 13, Apr. 10, 20, May 4,
8, 25, June 5, 15, 19, July 3, 27,
Aug. 17, 21, Sept. 18, 25, Oct.
2, 5, 30, Nov. 9, 13.
1840 May 21, June 2, 16, July 4, 11,
16, 21—28, Aug. 13, 29, Sept.
1, 26, Oct. 13.
1841 Mar. 2, 4, May 27, June 1, July
3, 6, 15, Dec. 2.
1842 Jan. 15, July 26, Aug. 2, Sept.
22, Nov. 15—17.
1843 Mar. 2.

IMPARCIAL. d.
MWA
1914 Feb. 4.

LA VERDAD. est. 1870.
DLC
1870 July 31.

Cayo Hueso

EL REPUBLICANO. w. est. 1869.
DLC
1870 Jan. 16—29, Feb. 12, 26—Apr.
2, 23—June 14, 28, Sept. 3.

Cienfuegos

EL COMERCIO. d. est. Nov. 2, 1902.
DLC
1941 Sept. 30.
1942 Feb. 7.

LA CORRESPONDENCIA. d. est. Oct.
31, 1898.
DLC
1941 Apr. 2 – 6, 8 – 10, 13 – May 5,
7 – Sept. 22, 27, 28, 30 – Nov.
13, 15 – Dec. 9, 11 – 18, 20 –
31.
1942 Jan. 1 – Mar. 13, 15 – 23, 26,
27, 29 – Apr. 2, 4 – 17, 19 – 21,
23, 24, 26, 27, 29, 30, May 2 –
15, 17 – June 5, 7 – Aug. 19,
21 – Sept. 10, 12 – 15, 17, 20,
22 – Oct. 5, 7 – 11, 13 – 18, 20 –
23, 25, 26, 29, 30, Nov. 1, 2, 4 –
9, 15 – 19, 22 – Dec. 2, 4 – 10,
12 – 17, 19 – 25, 27, 28, 30, 31.
1943 Jan. 1, 3, 4, 6 – 10, 12, 13, 15 –
21, 23 – 26, 28, 30 – Feb. 7, 9,
10, 12, 14 – 19, 21 – 28, Mar.
5, 7 – 10, 12 – 21, 23, 24, 26,
28, 30 – Apr. 13, 15, 17 – 19,
21 – Nov. 5, 7 – 23, 25 – 28,
30 – Dec. 12, 16, 17, 19 – 31.
1944 Jan. 1 – Mar. 26, 28 – Apr. 2,
4, 6 – June 11, 13 – July 23,
25 – Aug. 28, 31 – Oct. 27, 29 –
Nov. 11, 13 – 20, 22 – Dec. 10,
12 – 22.

LIBERACION. d. est. 1959.
FU
Micro (N)
1960 May 13, 14, 23 – 27, 30 – July
25, 27 – Aug. 8, 10 – Sept. 1, 3,
5, 7, 8, 11 – 13, 15 – 19, 22,
24 – Oct. 6, 10, 13, 14, 16 – 26,
29, 31 – Nov. 16, 18 – 20, 22,
23, 26, 27, 29, Dec. 1 – 12, 15,
17 – 19, 21 – 26, 28 – 31.
1961 Jan. 1 – Feb. 12, 14 – Mar. 8,
10 – Apr. 14, 16 – 19, 21 – May
23, 25 – 27, 29 – June 1, 3 –

July, 11 – 16, 19, 20, 22, 24, 25,
28 – Aug. 4, 6 – 14, 16 – 19, 21,
22, 24, 26, 28 – Sept. 14, 16,
18 – Oct. 2, 5 – 10, 12 – 25,
27 – Nov. 13, 15 – 17, 20 – 24,
Dec. 1 – 8, 10 – 14, 16 – 31.
1962 Jan. 1, 2, 4 – 14, 16 – 22, 24 –
26, 29 – Feb. 27, Mar. 1, 2, 4 –
6, 8 – 24, 26 – 31.

Gibara

EL GIBAREÑO. irr.
DLC
1942 Apr. 2 – May 8, June 9, 30,
July 18, Sept. 1, Nov. 10, 20 –
28.

EL PROGRESO. d. est. 1898.
MWA
1914 [Feb. 1 – 28].

TRIUNFO. est. 1898.
MWA
1914 Mar. 3.

Guantánamo

DEMOCRACIA. d.
DLC
1942 May 19.

ECO DE GUANTANAMO. d.
MWA
1914 Mar. 4.

HERALDO. d.
MWA
1914 Feb. 5.

NATIONALISTA. d.
MWA
1914 Mar. 4.

EL NACIONALISTA. d. est. 1931.
DLC
1942 Mar. 30, Nov. 11.

LA RAZON. w. est. June 8, 1942.
DLC
1942 June 8.

RESUMEN. d.
   MWA
      1914   Feb. 28.

LA VOZ DEL GUASO. sw.
   DLC
      1889   Jan. 17, Feb. 1, 8, 11, Mar. 5,
              Oct. 27.

VOZ DEL PUEBLO. d. est. 1899.
   MWA
      1914   Mar. 4.

Havana

ACCION.
   See *Cuba nueva en acción.*

AHORA. d. est. Jan. 1931.
   Note: Published by staff of *El Mundo*
   Jan. [11]−31, 1931 and 1933−1935.
   Began *2ª época* 1933.
   DLC
      1933   Oct. 18, 20, 21, Nov. 8, 9,
              14−20, 22−Dec. 9, 11−31.

¡ALERTA! d. est. Sept. 1935.
   CLU
      1943   Aug. 1−Dec. 31.
      1944−1945   Jan. 1−Dec. 31.
      1946   Jan. 1−31.
   CSt   (Monday issues only)
      1941   Nov. 10−Dec. 31.
      1942   Jan. 1−Apr. 13.
   DLC   (Monday issues only)
      1940   Mar. 11−Apr. 14, 16−Oct.
              6, 8−Dec. 31.
      1941   Jan. 1−Oct. 27, Nov. 3−Dec.
              31.
      1942−1943   Jan. 1−Dec. 31.
      1944   Jan. 1−Apr. 30, May 2−Dec.
              24, 26−31.
      1945   Jan. 1−Mar. 18, 20−May 20,
              22−27, 29−Dec. 31.
   ICRL   (Monday issues only)
      1942   Jan. 5−Dec. 31.
      1943−1945   Jan. 1−Dec. 31.
      1946   Jan. 1−21.
      1947   Jan. 27.

MWA
      1937   Feb. 14.
   TxU   (Monday issues only)
      1941   June 23−Oct. 6, 20−Dec. 31.
      1942   Jan. 1−June 15.
      1943   Jan. 11−July 26, Aug. 9−Dec.
              27.
      1945   Jan. 29, Feb. 12, 26, Mar. 12,
              26, Apr. 9−May 14, 28−Dec.
              31.
      1946   Jan. 1−21.

ALMA MATER. d.
   DLC
      1933   Sept. 30−Oct. 12, 24, Nov. 4,
              8, 28, Dec. 1−19, 21, 22, 24−
              28, 30, 31.

EL AMIGO DE LA CONSTITUCION. d.
   est. 1821.
   DLC
      1821   Nov. 21, 29, Dec. 9.
      1822   Jan. 12.

AURORA. w. est. 1800.
   Note: Paged continuously.
   DLC
      1802   Jan. 6−Dec. 1.
              Extraordinario: Jan. 9, Apr. 10,
              May 22, June 5, July 17, 24,
              Aug. 14.
              Supplement: Jan. 9.
      1804   Apr. 25.
   MWA
      1810   June 22.

EL AVANCE CRIOLLO.
   See *El Avance revolucionario.*

EL AVANCE REVOLUCIONARIO. d.
   est. Oct. 17, 1934.
   Note: Title *El Avance criollo*, Oct.
   17, 1934−Jan. 21, 1960; *El Avance
   revolucionario*, after Jan. 22, 1960.
   Removed to Miami, Florida, June
   1962.
   DLC
      1941   Mar. 1−3, 7−10, 14−16, 18,
              19, 21, 23, 25, 28−30, Apr. 1,

2, 4, 6, 8 – 10, 12, 13, 16, 19 –
26.
1942   June 27.
1960   Jan. 18 – 25, 27 – Feb. 28, Mar.
1 – 4, 6 – Apr. 6, 9 – 30.
MWA
1937   Feb. 16.

AVISADOR COMERCIAL. d. est. 1869.
DLC
1903   Jan. 2 – Aug. 25, Sept. 3 – Oct.
23, Nov. 1 – Dec. 31.
1904   Jan. 1 – Apr. 29, May 1 – June
6, 8 – 30, Sept. 1 – Oct. 14,
16 – 24, 27 – Dec. 27, 29 – 31.
1906   Jan. 2 – Dec. 31.
1908   Jan. 2 – 15, 18 – Apr. 6, 8 –
Oct. 16, 20 – Dec. 23, 26 – 31.

EL AVISO.
See *Gaceta de la Habana.*

AVISO DE LA HABANA.
See *Gaceta de la Habana.*

BOLETIN COMERCIAL. d.
MB
1864   June 24.
1867   Jan. 2, 4 – 10, 19, 21 – 26, 28 –
May 29, 31 – July 24, 26 – Oct.
26, Nov. 2 – Dec. 10.
1868   Jan. 1 – Dec. 31.

BOLETIN DE LA PRENSA.
DLC
1869   Feb. 11.

LA CALLE.
See *Diario de la tarde.*

LA CAMPAÑA.
DLC
1908   Aug. 5.

LA CAMPAÑA CUBANA. d. est. 1926.
DLC
1955   Mar. 3.

LA CARICATURA. w.
KHi
1895   Sept. 22.

LA CENA. d. est. [1812]
DLC
1813   Sept. 6 – Oct. 30, Nov. 2 –

Dec. 6, 9, 17 – 31.
Alcance: Oct. 28, Nov. 11, 14,
Dec. 21.
Supplement: Oct. 13, 26.
La Lancha; no. 12.
1814   Jan. 2 – Feb. 8, 10 – 28, Mar.
2 – Apr. 30, May 2 – July 2, 4, 5,
8 – 30.

LAS CLARIDADES. sw. est. Dec. 18,
1898.
NN
1898   Dec. 18.

COMBATE; DIARIO REPUBLICANO,
DE LA TARDE. d.
MWA
1883   July 6.

EL COMBATE. w. est. Sept. 9, 1907.
DLC
1907   Sept. 9.

COMBATE; UN ARMA DE LA REVOLU-
CION AL SERVICIO DEL PUEBLO. d.
FU
Micro (N)
1961   Jan. 1 – 3, 5 – 8, 10 – 16, 19 –
24, 27 – 29, 31 – Sept. 22, 24 –
28.
1964   [Jan. 1 – 31].

EL COMERCIO. d. est. 1886.
DLC
1899   Nov. 30.
MWA
1914   Mar. 8.

EL CRISOL. d. est. 1934.
DLC
1941   Nov. 14 – Dec. 6, 10, 11, 13 –
20, 23 – 31.
1942   Jan. 1 – 8, 10 – 12, 15 – 17, 20,
23, 24, 27 – Feb. 5, 7, 17 –
Mar. 9, 11 – 28, Apr. 8, 9, May
7 – 22, 25 – June 9, 12, 15 – 19,
23 – 27, July 2, 10, 11, 15, 17,
20, 21, 23, Aug. 5 – 7, 10 – 13,
15 – 18, 25, 27, 28.
MWA
1937   Feb. 16.

CUBA. d.
  MWA
    1914   Mar. 8.
  TxU
    1913   July 23.

THE CUBA NEWS. w. est. [1912].
    Note: In English.
  CtY
    1912   Nov. 23 – Dec. 28.
    1913   Jan. 4 – 11, Feb. 1 – Mar. 8,
            22 – Apr. 5, 19 – May 10, Aug.
            9, Sept. 7, 20 – Dec. 6, 20.
    1914   Jan. 3, 24 – Aug. 15, 29 – Dec.
            26.
    1915   Jan. 2 – Dec. 25.
    1916   Jan. 5, 23.
  NN
    Micro (P) & (N)
    1913   Mar. 8 – Dec. 31.
    1914   Jan. 1 – Dec. 31.
    1915   Jan. 1 – Mar. 26, 28 – Oct. 15,
            17 – Nov. 12, 14 – Dec. 18.

CUBA NUEVA EN ACCION. d. est. 1934.
    Note: Title *Acción*, 1934 – July 9,
    1939; *Cuba nueva en acción*, after
    July 10, 1939.
  DLC
    1939   Oct. 14, Nov. 6 – 10, 13, 14.
    1940   Jan. 8, 9, 17, 18, Feb. 22, Mar.
            6, 7, 28, Apr. 22 – 27, June 17,
            July 17 – 20, 23 – 29, 31 – Aug.
            13, 17 – 31, Sept. 3 – 24, 27 –
            Oct. 1, 6 – 8, 18 – 20, 27 –
            Dec. 31.
    1941   Jan. 1, 2, 4 – 17, 19, 21 – Mar.
            3, 5 – 9, 12 – 25, 27 – Apr. 18,
            22 – May 18, 23, 25 – July 28,
            30 – Sept. 14, 19 – 22, Oct. 7 –
            12, 15 – 28, 31, Nov. 1, 3 – 17,
            19 – 25, 27 – Dec. 15, 17 – 31.
    1942   Jan. 1 – 12, 14, 15, 18 – 24,
            26 – Feb. 14, 16 – 23, 25 – 28,
            Mar. 2 – 5, 7 – 14, 16 – 19, Apr.
            12 – 21, 23 – June 5, 7, 8, 10 –
            13, 15, 17, 18, 21 – 26, 29, 30,
            July 2 – 4, 6 – 8, 10, 13 – 20,
            22 – 28, Aug. 2 – 5, 8, 11 – 13,

            15 – 19, 21 – 23, 29, 30, Sept.
            1, 3, 4, 6.

THE CUBAN MESSENGER. EL MEN-
  SAGERO CUBANO. w.
    Note: In English; beginning Spring
    1861, in Spanish and English.
  DLC
    1861   Jan. 20, Feb. 10, Mar. 24, June
            9, 16.
            Supplement: Jan 20, Feb. 10.

EL CUBANO. d. est. 1887.
  DLC
    1888   Mar. 16.

DAILY AMERICAN AND HAVANA
  JOURNAL. d.
    Note: In English.
  NcD
    1899   May 5.

DIARIO CONSTITUCIONAL DE LA
  HABANA.
    See *Gaceta de la Habana.*

DIARIO DE LA HABANA. d. est. Dec.
  4, 1933.
  DLC
    1933   Dec. 4 – 9.

DIARIO DE LA HABANA.
    See *Gaceta de la Habana.*

DIARIO DE LA MARINA. d. est. Sept. 16,
  1832.
    Note: *El Noticioso y lucero de la
    Habana*, Sept. 16, 1832 – [Aug.],
    1844; *Diario de la marina*, after
    [Aug.], 1844. Suspended publication
    Nov. 13 – 27, 1930; Dec. 19 – 24,
    1930; Jan. 10 – 29, 1931; Aug. 5 –
    12, 1933; Sept. 24 – Oct. 27, 1933; and
    Dec. 20, 1933 – Jan. 12, 1934; ceased
    publication May 12, 1960.
  CLU
    1943   May 1 – Dec. 31.
    1944   Jan. 1 – Apr. 30, July 1 –
            Dec. 31.
    1945 – 1954   Jan. 1 – Dec. 31.
    Micro (P)

1955 Jan. 1+.
CSt
1928 Jan. 16 – 29.
1941 Nov. 1 – Dec. 31.
1942 Jan. 1 – Apr. 30.
CSt – H
1956 Nov. 6 – 9, 13, 15 – Dec. 4, 6 –
20, 22 – 30.
1957 Jan. 1 – Mar. 27, 29 – Apr. 19,
21 – May 3, 5 – Dec. 5, 7 – 14,
17, 18, 20 – 24, 26 – 31.
1958 Jan. 15, Feb. 14, 15, 18, 21, 22,
27, 28, Mar. 1 – 18, Mar. 20,
22 – July 30.

Micro (P)
1949 Jan. 1 – Apr. 1, 3 – 30, Oct. 1 –
30.
1951 Oct. 2 – Dec. 30.
1952 Jan. 1 – 31, Apr. 1 – May 31.
DLC
1832 Dec. 1 – 7, 9 – 31.
1833 Jan. 1 – Feb. 24, 26 – 28.
1835 Jan. 1 – Feb. 3, 6 – 8, 10 – July
23, 25 – Aug. 8, 10 – Oct. 17,
19 – Dec. 31.
Alcance: May 16, June 7, Oct.
9, 23.
1836 Jan. 1 – 16, 18 – Sept. 10, 26 –
Nov. 29, Dec. 1 – 31.
Parte judicial y económ.: Oct.
21, 23 – 29.
1837 Jan. 8 – Feb. 4, 6 – 22, 24 –
Mar. 15, 17 – Aug. 2, 4 – 18,
20 – 25, 27 – Dec. 31.
1838 Jan. 1 – Feb. 17, 25 – Apr. 28,
May 6 – 28, 30 – June 23,
25 – Aug. 25, Sept. 2 – 8, 13,
23 – Nov. 3, 6 – Dec. 13, 15 –
29.
1839 Jan. 2 – 12, 14 – 19, 27 – Mar.
28, 30 – Apr. 12, 14 – Aug. 7,
9 – Sept. 3, 5 – 12, 14 – Oct.
22, 24, 25, 29 – Dec. 31.
1840 Jan. 1 – 21, 27 – Feb. 18, 20 –
23, 25, Mar. 3, 8 – 11, 14, 16,
18, 20, 24 – Apr. 5, 8 – 10, 12,
13, 15 – 19, 23, 24, 27, May 1,
2, 4 – 7, 9 – 16, 19, 21 – 23, 29,

30, June 1 – 3, 5 – 7, 10 – 12,
15, 18, 21 – 25, 27 – 30, July
2, 4 – 11, 14, 28 – Aug. 6, 9 –
14, 27, 30 – Sept. 1, 4, 5, 7, 8,
23, Oct. 1, 4, 5, 8, 10, 12, 13,
16 – 31, Nov. 5 – 8, 12, 21, 23,
27, 29, Dec. 2, 4, 6, 8 – 13, 18,
20, 26 – 28, 31.
1841 Jan. 1, 2, 4 – 14, 16 – 19, 21 –
Feb. 2, 5 – Mar. 13, 16, 18 –
20, 28 – Apr. 1, 3 – 11, 13 – 15,
19 – 29, May 1 – 3, 5 – 15, 17 –
29, 31 – June 2, 4 – 6, 9 – 22,
24 – 30, July 2 – 23, 25 – 31,
Aug. 2 – 13, 22, 23, 25 – 30,
Sept. 3, 4, 9 – 12, 15, 19, 22 –
25, 27 – Oct. 3, 7, 8, 10, 27, 28,
31 – Nov. 4, 8, 9, 11, 12, 16 –
20, 22, 24 – 30, Dec. 3, 8, 10 –
17, 26 – 31.
1842 Jan. 1 – Feb. 10, 13 – 19, 21,
25 – Mar. 9, 11 – 13, 15 – 28,
30 – Apr. 14, 16, 18 – 26, 28 –
30, May 8, 10 – 14, 16 – 18,
20 – 25, 27 – June 11, 13 – 20,
22 – July 9, 11 – 15, 17 – 24,
26 – Aug. 15, 17 – 27, 29 – Sept.
5, 7 – 28, 30, Oct. 1, 4, 5, 8 –
16, 18 – 25, Nov. 20, Dec. 2 –
9, 11, 13 – 21, 24 – 26, 28 – 30.
1843 Jan. 2, 4 – 6, 8, 9, 15 – 29, Feb.
1 – 9, 12 – 24, 28 – Mar. 3, 5 –
7, 10 – 13, 15 – 20, 23 – 25, 27,
30, 31, Apr. 8, 11, 12, 18, 20 –
22, 24, 25, May 1, 3, 4, 6 – 31,
July 1 – 3, 5 – 7, 9, 11, 12, 14 –
19, 21 – 27, 29 – Aug. 3, 5 –
7, 9 – 12, 20, 21, 23 – 28, 30 –
Sept. 1, 3, 5, 7, 11 – 13, 15, 16
18, 19, 21, 22, 28, 30 – Oct. 5,
7, 8, 10, 12 – 27, 29 – Nov. 7,
9 – 14, 18, 20 – 27, 29, 30, Dec.
2 – 21, 24 – 31.
1844 Jan. 21, 22, 25 – 27, Feb. 9 –
13, 15 – Mar. 3, 5 – 12, 14 –
Apr. 1, 3 – 15, 17 – 29, May 1 –
13, 15 – 17, 19 – 23, 25 – 28,
31, June 2 – 5, 7 – 18, 20 – 27,

29 – July 3, 5 – 12, 14 – 31,
Sept. 3 – 10, 12 – 18, 20 – 26,
28, 29, Oct. 1 – 5, 7 – 24, 27 –
Nov. 6, 10 – 18, 21 – Dec. 3,
5 – 19, 22 – 30.
Suplemento: Dec. 10.

1845 Jan. 2, 3, 5 – 9, 11 – Feb. 3,
5 – 7, 9 – 15, 22 – 28, Mar. 2 –
5, 9 – 11, 15 – 19, 22, 23, 25 –
Apr. 26, 29 – May 6, 8, 9, 11 –
19, 21 – 27, 29 – June 7, 9, 10,
12 – 14, 19, 20, 23 – 27, 29,
July 2, 3, 7 – 9, 12, 17 – 31,
Aug. 3 – 9, 11, 15 – Oct. 19,
21 – 25, 27, 28, 30 – Nov. 1, 3 –
Dec. 21.

1846 Jan. 1 – 7, 10, 13 – 15, 17 – 26,
29, 30, Feb. 1 – 10, 15 – 18,
21 – 26, Mar. 3 – Apr. 8, 11 –
22, 24 – May 13, 15 – 29, 31 –
July 9, 11 – 18, 20 – Aug. 25,
31 – Sept. 12, Oct. 11 – Nov.
6, 10 – 18, 20 – Dec. 10, 12 –
14, 16 – 28, 30.

1847 Feb. 2 – 5, 28 – Mar. 2, 17 –
July 31, Aug. 8 – Sept. 11,
13 – Nov. 13, 15 – 20, 22 – Dec.
31.

1848 Jan. 1 – 8, 10, 12 – 25, Feb. 11,
12, 14 – Mar. 9, 11 – 23, 26 –
Apr. 20, 22 – June 4, 6 – 8, 10 –
Aug. 12, 14 – Sept. 9, 11, 13 –
15, 17, 18, 20 – Nov. 20, 22 –
Dec. 31.

1849 Jan. 1 – Mar. 25, 27 – Apr. 10,
12 – 23, 25 – May 13, 15 – June
10, 12 – Aug. 5, 7 – 12, 14 –
19, 21 – Sept. 2, 4 – 9, 11 – Oct.
24, 26 – Nov. 9, 11 – Dec. 31.

1850 Jan. 1 – July 1, 3 – 18, 25 –
Sept. 14, 16 – Dec. 22.

1851 Jan. 1 – 18, Feb. 3 – 7, 17 –
Mar. 3, 6 – Apr. 28, 30 – May
12, 17 – Aug. 15, 17 – Sept. 1,
5 – 11, 14 – 27, 29 – Nov. 7,
9 – Dec. 31.

1852 Jan. 1 – Feb. 23, 25 – Apr. 7,
21 – May 15, 17 – Sept. 30,

Oct. 2 – Dec. 29.

1853 Jan. 5 – 25, 27 – Feb. 21, 23 –
Mar. 13, 17 – Apr. 2, 4 – May
10, 12 – 21, June 2 – 21, 24 –
July 7, 11 – Nov. 24, 26 – 30,
Dec. 2 – 31.

1854 Jan. 1 – 7, 9 – Feb. 14, 16 –
Mar. 16, 18 – 30, Apr. 2 – Sept.
27, 29 – Oct. 5, 7 – Dec. 27.

1855 Jan. 1 – 30, Feb. 8 – Mar. 30,
Apr. 1 – 3, 5, 7 – 9, 11 – Sept.
11, 13 – Oct. 15, 17 – Dec. 31.

1856 Jan. 1 – 30, Feb. 1 – Apr. 29,
May 1, Oct. 25, 27 – 29, 31 –
Dec. 28, 31.

1857 Jan. 1 – June 12, 14 – July 22,
24 – Aug. 28, Sept. 7 – Nov. 14,
16 – Dec. 10, 12 – 31.

1858 Jan. 1 – 28, 30 – Feb. 2, 4 –
June 3, 5 – 16, 20 – 30, July 3 –
27, 29 – Sept. 9, 11 – 13, 15,
16, 18 – Oct. 19, 21 – Dec. 8,
10, 12 – 17, 19 – 23, 26 – 30.

1859 Jan. 1 – 3, 5 – 10, 12 – 22, 26 –
Apr. 1, 3 – 11, 14 – June 6, 8 –
10, 12 – 24, 26 – Aug. 8, 10,
12 – Sept. 13, 15 – 23, 25 – Dec.
10, 12 – 16, 18 – 31.

1860 Jan. 1 – Feb. 9, 11 – 23, 25 –
29, Mar. 2, 4 – 12, 14 – 26, 28 –
June 28, 30 – July 2, 4 – 6, 8 –
20, 23 – 31, Aug. 2 – 24, 26 –
Sept. 13, 15 – 28, 30, Oct. 1,
3 – 8, 10, 11, 14 – 27, 29, 31,
Nov. 1, 3 – 5, 11 – Dec. 13,
15 – 28, 31.

1861 Jan. 1 – 18, 20 – 26, 28 – Feb.
1, 3, 4, 8 – 16, 18 – Mar. 5, 8 –
13, 16 – 22, 24 – Apr. 4, 6 – 24,
26 – 29, May 2 – 6, 12 – 28,
30 – June 10, 12 – 14, 16, 17,
19 – July 1, 3, 4, 6 – 12, 14 – 17,
19, 21 – 29, 31 – Aug. 5, 7 –
9, 11 – 14, 16 – 31, Sept. 2 – 5,
7 – Oct. 2, 4 – 7, 9 – 12, 14 –
16, 18 – 26, 28 – Nov. 21, 23 –
25, 27 – 30, Dec. 2, 3, 5 – 23,
26, 28 – 31.

1862   Jan. 1, 2, 4 – 13, 15 – 21, 23 –
       Feb. 4, 6 – 10, 12 – Mar. 3, 5 –
       11, 13 – 28, 31 – Apr. 3, 5 –
       16, 19 – 24, 26 – 28, May 2 –
       13, 15 – 20, 23 – Sept. 8, 10 –
       Oct. 8, 10 – 16, 18 – 22, 24 –
       Nov. 7, 9 – 15, 17 – Dec. 3, 5,
       6, 8 – 10, 12 – 30.
1863   Jan. 1 – Feb. 6, 8 – Apr. 27, 29,
       30, May 2, 3, 5 – 18, 20 – June
       3, 5 – 20, 22 – Sept. 1, 3 – 25,
       27 – 30, Oct. 2, 3, 5 – 7, 11 – 14,
       16 – 27, 31 – Nov. 3, 5, 8 – 17,
       19 – Dec. 5.
1864   Jan. 23 – Mar. 7, 9 – May 1,
       5 – Aug. 26, 28 – Oct. 21, 23 –
       Nov. 15, 17 – 19, 21 – Dec. 6,
       9, 10, 12, 14 – 29, 31.
1865   Jan. 1 – Mar. 16, 18 – 20, 22,
       24, 25, 27 – Apr. 4, 6 – 11, 15,
       17, 18, 20 – May 1, 3 – 8, 11 –
       24, 26 – 29, June 1 – 14, 17 –
       24, 26 – Aug. 17, 19 – 21, 23 –
       Oct. 7, 18, 19, 21 – 30, Nov. 1 –
       9, 18 – Dec. 18, 20 – 25, 27 –
       30.
1866   Jan. 1 – 12, 14 – 27, 29 – Feb.
       10, 12 – May 7, 9 – June 2, 4 –
       July 7, 9 – Aug. 4, 6 – Sept. 6,
       8 – 29, Oct. 1 – 4, 6 – 13, 15,
       17 – 27, 29 – Nov. 2, 7 – 17, 19,
       20, 22, 28, Dec. 1, 3 – 8, 10 –
       18, 20 – 22, 26 – 31.
1867   Jan. 1, 2, 4 – 11, 13 – 19, 31,
       Feb. 3 – 11, 13 – 15, 17 – 23,
       25 – Mar. 8, 10 – 12, 14, 15,
       17 – 27, 29, 30, Apr. 1 – 15, 18,
       21 – 27, May 5 – June 25, 27 –
       July 15, 17, 19 – Aug. 24, 26 –
       Sept. 12, 14 – 16, 18, 19, 21 –
       Dec. 21, 23 – 30.
1868   Jan. 1 – 4, 6 – 9, 11 – 15, 17 –
       Feb. 5, 8 – 14, 16 – 21, 23 –
       Mar. 5, 7 – 10, 12, 14 – 26, 28,
       30 – Apr. 1, 4, 5, 11, 13, 14, 18,
       20 – May 5, 7, 9, 17 – 22, 24 –
       27, 30, June 1, 7 – 11, 13 – 27,
       29 – July 1, 3, 5 – 18, 20 – Aug.

       11, 13 – 27, 29 – Sept. 4, 9 –
       12, 14 – 30, Oct. 2 – 6, 8 – 21,
       23 – Nov. 14, 16 – Dec. 1, 3 –
       19, 21 – 23, 25 – 31.
1869   Jan. 2 – 9, 11 – Apr. 13, 15 –
       June 19, 21 – 26, 28 – July 1,
       3 – 10, 15, 20 – Nov. 6, 8 –
       Dec. 23, 25 – 28, 30, 31.
1870   Jan. 1 – 29, Mar. 6 – 10, 12 –
       17, 19 – 21, 23 – Apr. 8, 10 –
       13, 16 – July 2, 4 – Nov. 26,
       28 – Dec. 31.
1871   Jan. 1 – 31, Feb. 2 – 25, 27 –
       Mar. 9, 11 – Oct. 30, Nov. 1 –
       20, 22 – Dec. 31.
1872   Jan. 1, 3 – Mar. 30, Apr. 1 –
       27, 29, May 1 – 8, 10 – Aug.
       10, 12 – Sept. 28, 30 – Oct. 12,
       14 – Dec. 21, 23 – 31.
1873   Jan. 1 – 4, 9 – 28, 30, Feb. 1 –
       28, Mar. 2 – 8, 10 – 13, 15 –
       Apr. 24, 26, 28 – June 16, 18 –
       25, 27 – Aug. 23, 25 – Nov. 29,
       Dec. 1 – 31.
1874   Jan. 1 – 16, 18 – Mar. 20, 22 –
       Apr. 7, 9 – 21, 23 – May 13,
       15 – July 20, 22 – Nov. 10,
       12 – Dec. 31.
1875   Jan. 1 – Feb. 6, 8 – Aug. 9, 11 –
       17, 19 – 25, 27, 29 – Dec. 2, 4 –
       31.
1876   Jan. 1 – May 18, 21 – June 4,
       6 – Dec. 31.
1877   Jan. 1 – Dec. 31.
       Suplemento: Jan. 8.
1878   Jan. 2 – 14, 16 – June 14, 17 –
       Dec. 28, 30.
1879   Jan. 1 – Nov. 8, 13, 14, 16 –
       Dec. 31.
       Suplemento: July 26, Aug. 4.
1880   Jan. 1 – Oct. 16, 24 – Dec. 11,
       19 – 31.
       Suplemento: Jan. 9, 12, Feb.
       22, Mar. 7, 17, 19, 29, Apr. 25,
       July 10, 18, 19.
1881   Jan. 1 – June 18, 20 – 30, July
       2 – Aug. 2, 4 – Nov. 4, 6 – Dec.
       30.

1882   Jan. 1 – May 13, 15 – Dec. 31.
        Suplemento: July 15.
Micro (P) & (N)
1899   Sept. 1 – 20, 23 – 30, Oct. 4 –
        14, 21 – Nov. 29, Dec. 10 – 31.
1900 – 1916   Jan. 1 – Dec. 31.
1917   Jan. 1 – June 16, 18 – Dec. 31.
1918   Jan. 1 – Aug. 31, Sept. 3 –
        Dec. 31.
1919   Jan. 1 – Apr. 30, May 2 – 24,
        27 – Dec. 31.
1920   Jan. 1 – Apr. 30, May 4 – Dec.
        31.
1921 – 1925   Jan. 1 – Dec. 31.
1926   Jan. 1 – Apr. 30, May 2 – Aug.
        14, 16 – Dec. 31.
1927   Jan. 1 – Dec. 31.
1928   Jan. 1 – Apr. 30, May 2 –
        Dec. 31.
1929 – 1936   Jan. 1 – Dec. 31.
1937   Jan. 1 – 19, 21 – 26, 29 – Mar.
        2, 4 – 10, 12 – 17, 19 –
        Apr. 30, May 2 – July 4, 7 –
        13, 15 – 18, 20, 22 – Aug. 1, 3 –
        8, 10 – 13, 15, 17 – 21, 24 –
        Sept. 12, 14 – Oct. 12, 14 –
        Nov. 12, 15, 17 – Dec. 9, 11,
        13 – 24, 26 – 31.
1938   Jan. 1 – Nov. 4, 7, 8, 10, 12, 16,
        18, 20 – 22, 25, Dec. 5, 6, 13,
        18, 19.
1939   Jan. 1, 5, 6, 17, 20, 21, 31, Feb.
        3, 8, 11, 14, 17 – 19, 21, 23, 25,
        26, 28, Mar. 1, 3, 10 – 13, 15,
        16, 21, 24, 26, 27, 29, 31, Apr.
        2 – 4, 7, 9 – 11, 13, 15 – 18, 22,
        24, 30, May 4, 7, 10, 11, 14, 21,
        25, 28, 29, June 4, 6, 8, 9, 12,
        13, 17, 18, 25 – 27, 29 – Dec. 31.
1940 – 1943   Jan. 1 – Dec. 31.
1944   Jan. 1 – Aug. 30, Sept. 1 –
        Dec. 31.
1945   Jan. 1 – 22, 24 – Apr. 5, 7 –
        June 7, 9 – Sept. 27, 29 – Dec.
        30.
1946   Jan. 1 – 5, 7 – May 17, 19 –
        Dec. 31.
1947 – 1954   Jan. 1 – Dec. 31.

1955   Jan. 1 – June 30.
1960   Jan. 2 – May 12.
        (P)
1955   July 1 – Dec. 31.
1956 – 1959   Jan. 1 – Dec. 31.
FMU
   Micro (P)
   1953 – 1959   Jan. 1 – Dec. 31.
FU
   1929 – 1931   Jan. 1 – Dec. 31.
   1942 – 1946   Jan. 1 – Dec. 31.
   1949 – 1953   Jan. 1 – Dec. 31.
   Micro (P)
   1956   Apr. 1 – Dec. 31.
   1957 – 1959   Jan. 1 – Dec. 31.
   1960   Dec. 31.
   1961   Jan. 1 – May 6.
   Micro (N)
   1947 – 1948   Jan. 1 – Dec. 31.
   1949   Jan. 1 – 30.
   1951   Oct. 1 – Dec. 31.
   1952   Jan. 1 – 31, Apr. 1 – May 31.
   1953   Jan. 1 – Feb. 28, Apr. 1 –
           Dec. 31.
   1954 – 1955   Jan. 1 – Dec. 31.
   1956   Jan. 1 – Nov. 31.
ICRL
   1942 – 1943   Jan. 1 – Dec. 31.
   1944   Jan. 1 – 31.
   1945   Jan. 1 – Dec. 31.
   1946   Jan. 1 – Mar. 31.
   1947   [Feb. 1 – Dec. 31].
   1948 – 1952   [Jan. 1 – Dec. 31].
   1953   [Jan. 1 – 31].
   1954   [Jan. 1 – June 30], July 1 –
           Dec. 31.
   1955 – 1959   Jan. 1 – Dec. 31.
   1960   Jan. 1 – Apr. 30.
IU
   Micro (P)
   1953   Jan. 1 – Feb. 28, Apr. 1 –
           Dec. 31.
LNT – MA
   1931   June 5.
MB
   1833   Aug. 1.
   1836   Apr. 12, 17, July 9, 10.
   1839   Aug. 3.

1841   Sept. 29.
1842   Oct. 15.
MH
  1869   Dec. 4, 8 – 10.
      Suplemento: Dec. 13.
MWA
  1841   Apr. 19.
  1842   Mar. 12.
  1844   Apr. 16, 18, 19.
  1846   May 27.
  1860   Nov. 28.
  1903   Feb. 6.
  1905   Apr. 14.
  1914   Mar. 8.
  1937   Feb. 14.
NN
  1832   Sept. 16.
  1935 – 1938   Jan. 1 – Dec. 31.
  1939   Jan. 1 – 3, 5 – 20, 22 – Dec. 22,
      24 – 31.
  1940   Jan. 1 – July 18, 20 – Dec. 31.
  1941   Jan. 1 – Dec. 31.
  1942   Jan. 1 – Mar. 1, 3 – July 20,
      22 – Dec. 31.
  1943   Jan. 1 – Dec. 31.
  1944   Jan. 1 – June 1, 3 – Aug. 12,
      14 – Oct. 31, Nov. 3 – Dec. 31.
  1945   Jan. 1 – Mar. 17, 20 – June
      7, 10 – Dec. 31.
  1946   Jan. 1 – Feb. 23, 25 – Dec. 31.
  1947   Jan. 1 – 15, 17 – Feb. 6, 9 –
      11, 17, 20 – Mar. 14, 16 – May
      16, 18 – Dec. 31.
  1948   Jan. 1 – Feb. 6, 8 – Aug. 8,
      10 – Dec. 16, 18 – 31.
  1949   Jan. 1 – 16, 18 – June 2, 4 –
      Sept. 28, 30 – Oct. 9, 10 – 16,
      19 – Dec. 31.
  1950   Jan. 1 – Feb. 12, 14 – Dec. 31.
  1951   Jan. 1, 3 – 13, 15 – Feb. 9, 12 –
      Apr. 30, May 2 – 13, 15 – 31,
      June 2, 4 – Aug. 18, 20 – Nov.
      28, 30 – Dec. 12, 14 – 17, 19 –
      28, 30, 31.
  1952   Jan. 1 – 14, 16 – Mar. 8, 10 –
      21, 23 – July 27, 29 – Sept. 28,
      30 – Dec. 31.
Micro (P)

1953   Jan. 1 – Feb. 28, Apr. 1 – Dec.
      31.
1954 – 1959   Jan. 1 – Dec. 31.
NPV
  1940   Mar. 14 – Dec. 31.
  1941 – 1942   Jan. 1 – Dec. 31.
  1943   Jan. 1 – Feb. 28.
  1945   Jan. 1 – Dec. 31.
  1946   Jan. 1 – Mar. 31.
  1947   Feb. 1 – Dec. 31.
  1948   Jan. 4 – Mar. 21.
  1949   Jan. 9 – Dec. 25.
  1950   Jan. 1 – Dec. 31.
TxU
  1941   June 13 – Dec. 13.
  1942   Jan. 1 – Apr. 30, May 2 – June
      26.
  1943   Jan. 5 – 7, 9 – 19, 21 – 24, 27,
      29 – Feb. 2, 4 – 14, 17 – 20,
      23 – Mar. 10, 12 – 19, 21 – Apr.
      30, May 2 – Dec. 5, 9 – 31.
  1944   Jan. 1 – 6, 8 – 25.
  1945   Jan. 25 – Apr. 5, 7 – 29, May
      2 – 21, 23, 24, 26 – June 7, 10 –
      Dec. 31.
  1946   Jan. 1 – Feb. 8, 12 – 17, 25 –
      Mar. 31.
  1947   Jan. 1 – Feb. 18, 20 – May 7,
      9 – July 11, 13 – Nov. 10, 12 –
      Dec. 31.
  1948   Jan. 1 – Feb. 21, 23 – Dec. 31.
  1949   Jan. 1 – Dec. 31.
  1950   Jan. 1 – July 31, Aug. 3 – Dec.
      31.
1951 – 1952   Jan. 1 – Dec. 31.
Micro (P)
1953 – 1955   Jan. 1 – Dec. 31.

DIARIO DE LA TARDE. d.
  Note: Title *La Calle* before Nov.
  25, 1961; *Diario de la tarde*, after
  Nov. 25, 1961.
  DLC
    1961   Jan. 1, 18, 24 – 26, 31, Feb. 1,
        10, 12, Mar. 8, 10 – 15, 18, 19,
        Nov. 2 – 11, 14 – 23.
  LNT – MA
    1961   [Nov. 6 – Dec. 31.]

1962 — 1964   [Jan. 1 — Dec. 31.]
1965   Jan. 1 — 31.

DIARIO DEL GOBIERNO CONSTITU-
CIONAL DE LA HABANA.
See *Gaceta de la Habana.*

DIARIO DEL GOBIERNO DE LA
HABANA.
See *Gaceta de la Habana.*

LA DISCUSION. d. est. 1887.
DLC
1900   Mar. 29 — 31, Apr. 2 — 4, 6 — 11,
13 — 18, 22 — 25, May 3 — 23,
31, June 3, 4, 13 — 18, 23 —
July 14, 16, 21, 23, 28, 30,
Aug. 7 — 10, 28 — 31, Sept. 4,
5, Oct. 27, 29, Nov. 23, Dec.
24, 26 — 28.
1901   Jan. 3 — 5, 9 — 11, 15, 21, 28 —
30, Feb. 1, 4 — 9, 15, 22, 23, 28,
Mar. 8, 9, 14 — 18, 20, 27, Apr.
2 — 4, 12, May 3, 4, 8, 9, 11, 17,
20, 21, 24, 27, 28, June 24, 25,
27, 29, July 2, 8, 9, 16, 18, 19,
30, Aug. 12, 23, Sept. 2, 3, 23,
24, 27, 30, Oct. 28, 29, Nov.
23, Dec. 2, 3, 19, 23.
1902   Jan. 4, 22 — 25, Mar. 14, 25,
Apr. 29, May 14, 26, 28, 31,
June 3, 4, 6 — 17, 19 — 22, 24,
25, 27 — July 11, 13, 15 — 18,
20, 22 — 25, Aug. 20, 21, 23,
25 — 28, Sept. 3 — 6, 12, 13, 15,
16, 20, 24 — 27, 30, Oct. 15, 16,
Nov. 11 — Dec. 31.
1903   Jan. 1 — Nov. 12, 15 — Dec. 31.
1904 — 1905   Jan. 1 — Dec. 31.
1906   Jan. 1 — Mar. 4, 6 — 8, 11, 12,
14 — Dec. 31.
1907 — 1909   Jan. 1 — Dec. 31.
FU
Micro (N)
1924   Jan. 1 — 4, 6, 8 — 13, 19 — 23,
25, 28 — Feb. 7, 9 — Apr. 21, 24,
29 — Aug. 4, 8 — Oct. 18, 20 —
Dec. 31.
1925   Jan. 3, 4, 8 — 27, 29 — Mar. 19,

21 — 31, Apr. 2 — 9, 11 — 13,
15 — 20, 22 — 26, 28 — 30, May
2 — 16, 18 — 21, 23 — 25, 28 —
June 22, 24 — 30.
KHi
1895   Oct. 16.
1900   Dec. 7, 17.
1911   Sept. 9.
MH
1906   Apr. 25.
MWA
1901   May 21 — Aug. 10.
1914   Mar. 8.
1937   Feb. 16.

EL ESPAÑOL LIBRE. 3w. est. Sept.
15, 1822.
Note: Ceased publication Feb. 25,
1823.
TxU
1822   Nov. 12 — Dec. 31.

EL ESPECTADOR.
NHi
1871   Feb. 7.

EL ESPECTADOR LIBERAL. d.
DLC
1869   Jan. 9, 12.

EXCELSIOR. d. est. 1921.
FU
1951   May 8 — June 21.
ICRL
1940   Nov. 1 — Dec. 31.
1941   Jan. 1 — June 30.

FARO INDUSTRIAL DE LA HABANA.
d. est. [1840].
DLC
1842   Jan. 18 — 21.
MB
1848   Jan. 22 — 25.
1849   Dec. 14.
1850   Mar. 1 — June 30, Sept. 1 —
Dec. 31.
1851   Jan. 1 — Aug. 30.
MWA
1848   Jan. 4.

EL FIGARO.
  NcD
    1900   July 1.

FINANZAS. d. est. 1933.
  DLC
    1936   July 14.
    1941   May 23.
    1942   Mar. 21.
    1952   Oct. 10.

FLASH. w., m. est. June 1, 1939.
  DLC
    1941   Mar. 8.

FRENTE. d.
  DLC
    1938   Dec. 8.

GACETA DE LA HABANA. w., sw., d.
  est. 1782.
    Note: Title *La Gaceta de la Havana.*
    1782 – Oct. 30, 1790; *Papel periódico
    de la Havana*, Oct. 31, 1790 – May
    1805; *El Aviso*, June 1805 – 1808;
    Aviso de la Habana, 1809 – 1810;
    Diario de la Habana, 1810 – 1812;
    Diario del gobierno de la Habana,
    1812 – 1820; *Diario constitucional
    de la Habana*, 1820; *Diario del
    gobierno constitucional de la Habana*,
    1820 – 1823; *Diario del gobierno de
    la Habana*, 1823 – 1825; *Diario de
    la Habana*, Feb. 1, 1825 – Feb. 2,
    1848; *Gaceta de la Habana*, Feb. 3,
    1848 – May 20, 1902. Continued as
    *Gaceta oficial de la República de
    Cuba*. Periodicity before Dec. 31,
    1790, weekly; Jan. 1, 1791 – 1805,
    semiweekly; after 1806, daily.
  CU – B
    Micro (P)
    1782   Nov. 22.
  CtY
    1791   July 28, Oct. 16, 23, 30, Dec.
            15.
    1792   Oct. 4.
            Suplemento.
    1793   Mar. 24 – 28, Apr. 21, June
            30 – July 18.

    1820   Jan. 30, 31, Feb. 7.
    1900   Apr. 24, June 22, Nov. 15, Dec.
            11.
  DLC
    1800   Sept. 4 – 6, 8 – Dec. 6, 8 – 31.
    1801   Jan. 1 – Feb. 7, 9 – Aug. 8,
            10 – Oct. 10, 12 – Dec. 31.
            Suplemento: Dec. 10.
    1802   Jan. 1 – Feb. 6, 8 – 10, 12 –
            Mar. 3, 5 – Apr. 10, 12 – 21,
            23 – May 19, 21 – July 3, 5 –
            21, 23, 24, 26 – Aug. 4, 16 –
            28, Sept. 6 – 15, 17 – 25, 27 –
            29, Oct. 1 – 13, 15, 16, 18 –
            Nov. 3, 5 – Dec. 1, 3 – 31.
            Suplemento: May 13.
    1803   Jan. 1 – Dec. 30.
    1804   Jan. 1 – 4, 6 – 21, 23 – 25, 27 –
            Feb. 15, 17 – Mar. 3, 5, 6, 8 –
            13, 15 – Apr. 4, 6 – 28, 30 –
            June 9, 11 – 13, 15 – July 4, 6 –
            18, 20 – 28, 30 – Nov. 7, 9 –
            21, 23 – Dec. 12, 14 – 31.
            Suplemento: Feb. 26, Mar. 1,
            14, Apr. 26, June 3, 7.
    1805   Jan. 1 – 19, 21 – Mar. 13, 15,
            16, 18 – Apr. 13, 15 – May 8,
            10 – 19.
    1841   Feb. 14.
    1842   Mar. 30, Apr. 1, 6, 20, 22, 24,
            May 4 – 6, 12 – 15, 19, 21, 22,
            25, 31, June 2 – 9, 13 – 18,
            20, 21, July 3, Sept. 9, 10,
            21, 22, 27, Oct. 2, 3, 9, 14, Nov.
            2, 4, 5, 7, 8, 11, 13 – 30, Dec.
            3, 6 – 11, 13 – 19, 28.
    1845   Jan. 2.
  FMU
    1849 – 1852   Jan. 1 – Dec. 31.
    1866 – 1868   Jan. 1 – Dec. 31.
    1870 – 1872   Jan. 1 – Dec. 31.
    1874   Jan. 1 – Dec. 31.
    1876 – 1897   Jan. 1 – Dec. 31.
  LNHT
    1790   Oct. 24.
  MB
    1850   Feb. 22, Apr. 19, May 21, 22.
    1851   Aug. 1, 2, 17, Sept. 6.

1853   Jan. 1.
1869   July 20.
MH
    1846   Nov. 29, 30.
    1847   Jan. 12, May 7, 23.
MWA
    1810   June 19, Sept. 28, Nov. 10.
    1819   Apr. 2.
    1828   Feb. 24.
    1841   Nov. 3.
    1842   Jan. 29, 30, Feb. 1, Mar. 6 — 9,
            13 — 15, May 26, 27, Dec. 4 — 6.
    1843   Nov. 27, 28.
    1844   Feb. 22 — 26.
    1846   Sept. 11 — 15.
NN
    1790   Oct. 24.

EL GORRO FRIGIO. d. est [1873]
  DLC
    1873   Oct. 1, Nov. 29, Dec. 2, 3, 5.

GRANMA. d. est. Oct. 4, 1965.
    Note: Succeeded *Hoy* and
    Revolución.
  CSt — H
    1965   Oct. 4 — Dec. 31.
    1966   Jan. 1+.
  DLC
    Micro (P) & (N)
    1966   Jan. 1+.
  FMU
    1965   Oct. 4 — Dec. 14, 16 — 27.
  FU
    1965   Oct. 5 — Dec. 31.
    1966   Jan. 1+.
  PrU
    1965   Prospecto: Sept. 30.
            Oct. 1, 3 — 15, 17 — 22, 24 — Dec.
            31.
    1966   Jan. 1+.

GRANMA. WEEKLY REVIEW. w. est.
[Feb. 20], 1966.
  CSt — H
    1966   May 1+.

HAVANA ADVERTISER & DAILY
  GAZETTE.
    See *The Havana Daily Advertiser.*

HAVANA ADVERTISER AND WEEKLY
  GAZETTE. w.
    Note: In English. See also *The*
    Havana Daily Advertiser.
  MB
    1898   Nov. 13 — 27.

THE HAVANA ADVERTISER.
    See *The Havana Daily Advertiser.*

THE HAVANA AMERICAN.
    See *The Havana-American News.*

THE HAVANA-AMERICAN NEWS. d.
  est. Mar. 1, 1920.
    Note: In English. Title *The Havana*
    American, Mar. 1, 1920 — Jan. 8,
    1930; *The Havana American News*,
    after Jan. 9, 1930. Absorbed *The*
    Evening News, Jan. 9, 1930.
  CU
    1929   Dec. 8, 11, 13, 14, 16, 19, 20,
            22, 24, 28 — Dec. 31.
    1930   Jan. 1, 2, 4 — 10, 12 — July 21,
            23 — 29, Aug. 1, 3 — 13, 15 —
            20, 22 — Sept. 6, 8 — Oct. 2,
            6 — 8, 10, 11, 13, 15 — 17, 19 —
            24, 27, 28, 30, Nov. 1, 4 — 7, 10,
            11, 13, 16, 19, 21, 27 — 30, Dec.
            2, 3, 5, 6, 9, 11, 13, 15, 17 — 19,
            21 — 24, 26 — 28.
    1931   Jan. 2 — 9.
    1932   Jan. 1 — Dec. 31.
    1933   Jan. 1 — 21, 23 — 28, 30 — Feb.
            4, 6 — 11, 13 — 18, 20 — 25,
            27 — Mar. 4, 6 — 11, 13 — 18,
            20 — 25, 27 — Oct. 24, 27, 30 —
            Nov. 3, 6, 8 — 10, 13, 14, 17, 18,
            24 — 28, Dec. 1, 4, 5, 9, 12, 14,
            23, 29.
  DLC
    1920   Mar. 1 — Apr. 15.
    1932   Mar. 25.

THE HAVANA DAILY ADVERTISER. d.
  est. Oct. 30, 1898.
    Note: In English. Title *Havana*
    Advertiser & Daily Gazette, Oct.
    30 — Dec. 22, 1898; *The Havana*

Advertiser, Dec. 28, 1898 – Mar. 24,
1899; *The Havana Daily Advertiser*,
after Mar. 25, 1899. See also *Havana
Advertiser and Weekly Gazette.*

DLC
  1898   Dec. 3, 5 – 15, 20 – 31.
  1899   Jan. 9 – Mar. 24, 28 – Apr. 9,
          11 – 14, 19 – May 4.
MB
  1898   Dec. 1 – 31.
  1899   Jan. 2 – 31, Feb. 2 – Mar. 24,
          27 – Apr. 15, 18, May 4, 5.

THE HAVANA DAILY TELEGRAPH. d.
  est. 1905.
    Note: In English.
  DLC
    1906   Aug. 22, 29, 30, Sept. 1, 15,
            21, Oct. 14, 21 – 28, 30, 31 –
            Dec. 22, 25, 27 – 31.
    1907   Jan. 1 – 18, 20 – Mar. 6, 8, 10,
            11, 13, 15 – 20, 22 – Apr. 29,
            May 1 – Oct. 2, 5, 7, 8, 10, 12,
            14 – 16.
    1908   Jan. 21 – 25, 27 – 29, 31 – Feb.
            20, 22 – 24, 27 – Mar. 23, 25 –
            31.

THE HAVANA EVENING TELEGRAM.
  w., d. est. Jan. 2, 1922.
    Note: In English. Title *The Havana
    Telegram*, Jan. 2, 1922 – [1930]; *The
    Havana Evening Telegram*, [1930] –
    Aug. 22, 1938. Ceased publication
    Aug. 22, 1938.
  CU
    1925   Mar. 5.
    1934   Nov. 12.
    1937   Sept. 27.
  DLC
    1936   Mar. 30 – May 24, 26 – Sept.
            20, 22 – 27, 29 – Dec. 31.
    1937   Jan. 1 – Nov. 7, 9 – Dec. 31.
    1938   Jan. 1 – Aug. 22.

THE HAVANA HERALD. EL HERALDO
  HABAÑERO. d. est. 1898.
    Note: In Spanish and English.

DLC
  1899   June 7, Sept. 2, 12, 13, 17 –
          22, Oct. 15 – 18, 20, Nov. 9, 10.
KHi
  1900   Apr. 3.
NN
  1899   Apr. 26.
NcD
  1899   Aug. 8.

HAVANA JOURNAL. w.
    Note: In English.
  CtY
    1867   Oct. 19.
    1868   June 13.

HAVANA MORNING AMERICAN. d.
    Note: In English.
  KHi
    1901   Jan. 12 – 20.

HAVANA P.M. d.
  DLC
    1940   July 10, 14, 15, 17 – 19, 21,
            23 – 26, 28 – Aug. 16, 18 –
            Sept. 23, 26 – 29, Oct. 9, 28 –
            Dec. 31.
    1941   Jan. 1 – Mar. 25, 27 – May 20,
            22 – 30, June 1, 5 – 13, 27 –
            July 4, 15 – Aug. 21.

HAVANA POST. d. est. May 1, 1900.
    Note: In English. Suspended pub-
    lication Oct. 16 – Nov. 2, 1954; Nov.
    4, 1954 – Jan. 22, 1955; ceased pub-
    lication Sept. 7, 1960.
  CLCM
    1912   Mar. 24.
  CU
    1924   June 14 – Aug. 19, 21 – Sept.
            5, 14 – Oct. 26, 28, 29, 31 –
            Nov. 7, 10 – Dec. 22, 25 – 29,
            31.
    1925   Jan. 2 – 29, 31 – Mar. 26, 28 –
            May 20, June 3 – Aug. 4, 6 – 9,
            11 – 22, 24 – 30, Oct. 2 – 14,
            16 – Nov. 2, 4 – 7, 9 – 18, 20.
  1926 – 1933   Jan. 1 – Dec. 31.
    1934   Jan. 1 – Feb. 6, 8 – Mar. 5,
            13 – Apr. 2, 4 – 30, May 2,
            July 10, 12 – 24, 26 – Aug. 6,

8 – 16, 18 – Sept. 2, 4 – 9, 11 –
16, 18 – 23, 25 – 30, Oct. 2 –
7, 9 – 14, 16 – 21, 23 – 28, 30 –
Nov. 4, 6 – Dec. 18, 20.

1935　Jan. 1 – Feb. 17, 19 – Mar. 8,
14 – 28, 30 – May 19, 21.

1936　Jan. 2 – 26, 28.

1937 – 1947　[Jan. 1 – Dec. 31.]

1948　Jan. 1 – Nov. 13, 16 – Dec. 31.

1949　Jan. 1 – 28, 30, Feb. 1 – Oct.
30, Nov. 1 – Dec. 31.

1950　Jan. 1 – Feb. 24, 26.

DLC

1900　May 26, 30, June 13, 14, 28,
29, July 18 – 21, 28, Aug. 7, 9,
10, 18, 21, 22, Nov. 15 – 18.

1901　Feb. 5, June 23, 25 – 30, July
2 – 4, 6, 7, 9 – 14, 16, 17, 19 –
21, 23 – 27, 30, 31, Aug. 2 – 4,
6 – 18, 21 – 30, Sept. 3 – 6, 8,
10, 14 – Oct. 2, 5 – 15, 19 – 25,
27 – Nov. 8, 13 – 25, 27 – Dec.
31.

1902　Jan. 1 – Feb. 6, 8 – 14, 16 –
26, 28 – Mar. 5, 7 – 10, 12 –
15, 17 – 21, 23 – 28, 30 – Apr.
5, 7 – 11, 13 – 17, 19 – May 2,
4 – 6, 9 – 16, 19, 20, 23 – 26, 28.

1903　Aug. 28, 29.

1906　Sept. 2, 18, Oct. 29 – Nov. 8,
10 – 20, 22 – Dec. 13, 15 – 31.

1907　Jan. 1 – Feb. 17, 19 – 28, Mar.
3 – Apr. 4, 7 – 9, June 10, 14,
15, July 22, Aug. 14 – 19, Dec.
17.

1908　Apr. 16.

Micro (P) & (N)

1913 – 1917　Jan. 2 – Dec. 31.

1918　Jan. 1 – Dec. 11, 13 – 31.

1919　Jan. 1 – Dec. 31.

1920　Jan. 1 – Oct. 10, 12, 13, 15 –
22, 24 – 28, 30 – Nov. 1, 3, 4, 6,
7, 9 – 14, 16 – 21, 23, 25 – Dec.
31.

1921　Jan. 1 – 6, 8 – Feb. 11, 13 –
Dec. 31.

1922　Jan. 1 – Apr. 30, May 2 – Dec.
31.

1923　Jan. 1 – Dec. 31.

1924　Jan. 1 – June 25, 27 –
Dec. 31.

1925　Jan. 1 – May 13, 28 – June 11,
13 – 20, 23 – 26, 28 – July 7, 9 –
Sept. 14, 16 – 30, Oct. 2, 4 –
11, 13 – Dec. 31.

1926 – 1928　Jan. 1 – Dec. 31.

1929　Jan. 1 – Mar. 5, 7 – May 25,
27 – Oct. 19, 21 – Dec. 21,
23 – 31.

1930　Jan. 1 – 4, 6 – Mar. 10, 12 –
Apr. 30, May 2 – Aug. 20,
22 – Oct. 1, 3 – 31, Nov. 2 –
Dec. 31.

1931 – 1932　Jan. 1 – Dec. 31.

1933　Jan. 1 – Apr. 30, May 2 – 9,
11 – Aug. 4, 13 – Oct. 31, Nov.
2 – 19, 21 – Dec. 5, 7, 9 – 11,
13 – 31.

1934　Jan. 1, 3 – Feb. 6, 8 – Mar. 5,
13 – Apr. 30, May 2 – July 10,
12 – Oct. 26, 28 – Dec. 31.

1935　Jan. 1 – Mar. 7, 14 – Apr. 3,
5 – 30, May 11 – June 30,
July 2 – 7, 11 – 14, 16 – 21,
23 – 28, 30 – Aug. 4, 6 – 11,
13 – 18, 20 – 25, 27 – Sept. 1,
3 – 8, 10 – 15, 17, 18, 20 – 22,
24 – Oct. 20, 22 – Nov. 3, 5 –
Dec. 29, 31.

1936　Jan. 1 – May 24, 26 – 28, 30 –
Sept. 20, 22 – Dec. 31.

1937　Jan. 1 – May 1, 3 – June 25,
27 – Dec. 31.

1938　Jan. 1 – Apr. 30, May 2 – Dec.
9, 11 – 31.

1939　Jan. 1 – Feb. 25, 27 – Mar. 6,
8 – Apr. 22, 24 – May 16, 18 –
July 8, 10 – 25, 27 – Oct. 6, 8 –
18, 20 – Dec. 22, 24 – 31.

1940　Jan. 1 – 12, 14 – Apr. 20, 22 –
Dec. 31.

1941　Jan. 1 – 20, 22, 24 – July 7, 9 –
24, 26 – Dec. 24, 26 – 31.

1942 – 1943　Jan. 1 – Dec. 31.

1944　Jan. 1 – June 19, 21 – 28, July
1 – Dec. 25, 27 – 31.

1945   Jan. 1 – May 2, 4 – Dec. 31.
1946 – 1949   Jan. 1 – Dec. 31.
1950   Jan. 1 – Apr. 24, 26 – Dec. 31.
1951 – 1957   Jan. 1 – Dec. 31.
1958   Jan. 1 – June 26, 28 – Dec. 31.
1959   Jan. 1, 7 – Mar. 3, 5 – Dec. 31.
1960   Jan. 1 – Aug. 17, 19 – Sept. 7.
FU
1952   Dec. 1 – 31.
1953 – 1959   Jan. 1 – Dec. 31.
1960   Jan. 1 – Sept. 7.
ICRL
1926   Dec. 26 – 31.
1927 – 1940   Jan. 1 – Dec. 31.
1947 – 1950   Jan. 1 – Dec. 31.
KHi
1900   May 1 – Aug. 19.
1906   Aug. 29 – Oct. 11.
LNT – MA
1937   Oct. 1.
MH
1909   July 4.
MWA
1913   Feb. 11, 12.
1937   Feb. 16.
NbU
1942 – 1953   Jan. 1 – Dec. 31.
OCL
1949   Mar. 3 – Dec. 31.
1950 – 1959   Jan. 1 – Dec. 31.
1960   Jan. 1 – Sept. 7.
OrU
1943   Sept. 1 – 20, 22 – Dec. 31.
1945   July 1 – Aug. 2, 4 – Nov. 13,
        14 – Dec. 19, 22 – 28, 30.
1946   Jan. 1 – 13, 15 – 25.
TxU
1946 – 1951   Jan. 1 – Dec. 31.
1952   Jan. 1 – Apr. 30.

THE HAVANA SUN. d. est. Dec. 15,
1901.
    Note: In English.
DLC
1901   Dec. 15 – 31.
1902   Jan. 1, 3, Mar. 7, 8.

THE HAVANA TELEGRAM.
    See *The Havana Evening Telegram.*

HAVANA WEEKLY REPORT. w. est.
1823.
    Note: In English.
DLC
1890   Jan. 4 – Mar. 21, 23 – Dec. 31.
1891   Jan. 1 – May 8, 10 – Sept. 4,
        6 – 25, 27 – Dec. 31.
1892   Jan. 1 – 29, Feb. 28 – Dec. 31.
MB
1864   Jan. 2 – May 28, June 11 –
        Sept. 17, Oct. 1 – Dec. 31.
1865   Jan. 7 – Dec. 30.
1866   Jan. 6.

EL HERALDO. d. est. 1908.
DLC
1908   Sept. 18, 21, 22.

HERALDO COMERCIAL. d. est. Oct. 18
1917.
DLC
1941   Apr. 13, Oct. 18.

HERALDO DE CUBA. d. est. 1913.
CU
1927   Apr. 13 – May 3, 5 – 20, 22 –
        Aug. 1, 3 – 23, 25 – Sept. 9,
        11 – Dec. 31.
1928   Jan. 1 – Dec. 31.
1929   Jan. 1 – Mar. 10, 12 – 21, 23,
        24, 26 – 31, Apr. 2 – 10, 12 –
        14, 16 – 18, 20 – May 12, 14 –
        June 1, 4 – 9, 11, 13, 14, 16,
        19 – 28, 30 – July 14, 16 – Aug.
        5, 7, 8, 10, 13 – 16, 18 – 22,
        24 – 30, Sept. 2 – 7, 9, 11 – 17,
        20, 22, 24 – 29, Oct. 2 – 4, 6,
        8 – 10, 12, 13, 15, 16, 18, 20 –
        27, 29 – Nov. 6, 8 – 16, 18 – 21,
        24 – 28, 30 – Dec. 3, 5 – 7, 9,
        10, 12 – 15, 17 – 19, 21, 22, 24,
        25, 27, 29 – 31.
1930   Jan. 1 – Dec. 31.
1931   Jan. 1 – 23, 26 – 28, 30 – June
        7, 9 – 13, 15 – Aug. 29, Nov.
        16 – Dec. 31.
1932   Jan. 1 – Sept. 3, 5, 6, 14 –
        Oct. 6.

DLC
  1927 May 20.
  1928 May 20.
  1929 May 20.
  1932 Aug. 18 — Dec. 31.
  1933 Jan. 1 — Mar. 2, 4 — 12,
         14 — 22, 24 — Apr. 30, May 2 —
         Aug. 4.
FU
  Micro (N)
  1932 Mar. 1 — 16, 18 — Apr. 30, July
         1 — Sept. 6, 14 — Nov. 2, 4 —
         Dec. 31.
MWA
  1914 Mar. 8.
NcU
  1932 Jan. 1 — May 2, June 30.

EL HERALDO HABANERO.
  See *The Havana Herald. El Heraldo
  habanero.*

HERALDO LIBERAL. w.
MWA
  1937 Feb. 5.

EL HIJO DE LA VERDAD. est. Feb. 9,
  1869.
DLC
  1869 Feb. 9.
MWA
  1869 Feb. 9.

HOMBRE FUERTE. w.
MWA
  1914 Mar. 5.

HOY. d. est. May 16, 1938.
  Note: Title *Notícias de hoy*, May 16,
  1938 — Dec. 31, 1963; *Hoy*, Jan. 1,
  1964 — Oct. 3, 1965. Succeeded by
  Granma. Suspended publication
  Sept. 14 — [Nov. 16], 1951; ceased
  publication Oct. 3, 1965.
CLU
  1961 Nov. 3 — Dec. 31.
  1962 — 1964 Jan. 1 — Dec. 31.
  1965 Jan. 1 — Oct. 3.
CSt — H
  1962 Aug. 8 — Nov. 1, 11 — 24, Dec.
         1 — 4, 6 — 11, 13, 14, 16 — 30.

1963 Jan. 2, 3, 6 — 8, 10 — 28, 30 —
         Feb. 26, 28 — June 4, 6 — 24,
         26 — July 2, 10, 15 — Aug. 29,
         31 — Sept. 2, 4 — Oct. 6, 8, 10 —
         13, 16 — 29, Nov. 1 — 28, 30 —
         Dec. 31.
1964 Jan. 2 — Feb. 19, 21 — May 20,
         26, 27, 30 — June 28, Aug. 1 —
         Sept. 30, Oct. 2 — 4, 6 — 8, 10 —
         Dec. 9, 11 — 13, 15.
Micro (P)
1962 Jan. 3 — July 8, 10 — Aug. 9,
         11 — Nov. 4, 6 — 15, 18 — Dec.
         19, 21 — 31.
1963 Jan. 1 — Mar. 17, 19 — July 9,
         12 — Dec. 31.
CU
1938 May 16, 19, 20, 24 — 26, 28 —
         June 1, 3, 4, 8, 16 — 21, 23 —
         July 12, 14, Oct. 3.
1939 Apr. 7 — 11, 16, 20, 25 — May
         4, 12 — 16, 19 — 24, June 1 —
         14, 17, 18, 24 — 27, 29 — July
         12, 18, 19, 22, 23, Aug. 2 — 10,
         12 — 19, 24 — Sept. 8.
DLC
1938 June 2, 8, 14, 15, 17, 22, 23,
         25 — 30, July 2 — 12, 14 — 30,
         Aug. 1, 2, 4 — 11, 16, 17, 22 —
         Sept. 3, 5 — 22, 27, 28, 30 —
         Nov. 5, 8 — 12, 27, 29, Dec. 1,
         7 — 18, 22 — 25, 29 — 31.
1939 Feb. 17 — Mar. 4, 14 — Apr. 23,
         May 16 — 27, June 3 — 7, 9 —
         Nov. 27, 29 — Dec. 25, 28 — 31.
1940 Jan. 1 — May 7, 9 — June 10,
         12 — Sept. 5, 7 — Oct. 28, 30 —
         Dec. 31.
1941 Jan. 1 — June 22, 24 — Dec. 31.
1942 Jan. 1 — June 30, July 6, 9 —
         13, 16, 17, 19 — 21, 23 — 28,
         30 — Oct. 27, 29 — Dec. 31.
1943 Jan. 1 — Oct. 21, 23 — Dec. 31.
1944 Jan. 1 — Dec. 31.
1945 Jan. 1 — 17, 19 — Apr. 20, 22 —
         29, May 2 — 31, June 6, 8, 10,
         12, 14, 15, 17, 20, July 1 — Sept.
         13, 15 — Dec. 31.

1946 Jan. 1 – Mar. 12, 14 – May 14, 16 – Dec. 31.
1947 Jan. 1 – Dec. 31.
1948 Jan. 1 – Oct. 4, 6 – Nov. 6, 8 – Dec. 31.
1949 Jan. 1 – 29, 31 – Mar. 4, 6 – Apr. 7, 9 – Dec. 31.
1950 Jan. 1 – Aug. 24.
1951 Nov. 17, 18, 21 – 29, Dec. 4.
1952 Jan. 8 – 22, 25 – Feb. 15, 17 – 23, 25 – Mar. 8, 10, 11, 13 – 20, Apr. 16 – May 21, 23 – July 2, 4 – 23, 25 – 29, 31 – Aug. 19, 21 – 25, 28 – Sept. 6, 8 – 17, 19 – Nov. 5, 7 – 26, 28 – Dec. 31.
1953 Jan. 1 – Feb. 3, 5 – 23, 26 – Mar. 7, 9 – 11, 13, 14, 16 – 20, 22, 23, 25, 27, 28, 30, 31, Apr. 2 – 6, 8 – June 1, 3 – 16, 18 – 27.
1959 Jan. 6 – 9, 11, 12, 15, 16, 18 – Feb. 17, 19 – Apr. 21, 28 – May 29, June 3 – 17, 19 – July 23, 25 – Aug. 3, 5 – 21, 23 – Sept. 25, 27 – Oct. 26, 28 – Dec. 30.
1960 Jan. 1 – Feb. 12, 14 – Apr. 14, 16 – June 18, 20 – Sept. 22, 24 – 26, 28 – Dec. 31.
1961 Jan. 1 – 4, 12, 14, 15, 18 – 20, Feb. 3, 5 – 21, 23 – Mar. 10, 12 – 25, 28, 31, Apr. 6, 16 – 18, 20, 21, 23 – 29, May 4, 6, 7, 24, 31, June 1, 3, 6, 7, 10 – July 14, 19 – 25, 27 – Aug. 6, 8 – 10, 13 – 15, 17 – 29, 31, Sept. 2, 5 – 8, 12, 14 – 17, 19, 20, 23, 26, 28, 30 – Oct. 4, 6 – 25, 27 – Dec. 31.
Micro (P) & (N)
1962 – 1964 Jan. 1 – Dec. 31.
FU
1965 Jan. 2 – Oct. 3.
NN
Micro (P) & (N)
1938 May 16 – June 8.
1941 Dec. 16 – 31.
1942 Jan. 1 – 29, Feb. 8 – June 10,

12 – Dec. 3, 5 – 10.
1943 Feb. 28 – June 26.
1945 Sept. 23 – Oct. 31.
1946 Aug. 1 – Dec. 31.
1947 – 1948 Jan. 1 – Dec. 31.
1949 Jan. 1 – Feb. 26.
NjP
Micro (P)
1938 May 16 – Dec. 31.
1939 – 1942 Jan. 1 – Dec. 31.
1943 Jan. 1 – Apr. 11, May 16 – Dec. 31.
1944 – 1948 Jan. 1 – Dec. 31.
1949 Jan. 1 – Feb. 26.
PrU
1961 Apr. 8, 22.
1963 Feb. 21 – 24, 26 – Mar. 31 – Apr. 3 – Dec. 31.
1964 Jan. 1 – 5, 9 – Mar. 31 – Aug. 1 – Oct. 2, 6 – Dec. 20, 23, 24, 27, 29 – 31.
1965 Jan. 1 – Feb. 19, 23 – Apr. 15, 18 – May 23, 26 – 30, June 1 – 4, July 1 – Sept. 30, Oct. 2.

EL INDICADOR CONSTITUCIONAL REINADO DE LA LEY. d. est. 1820.
DLC
1821 Aug. 28, Nov. 20.
1823 Mar. 14, 16, 19, 20, 24 – Apr. 6, Nov. 14.

INFORMATIVO OBRERO INTER-AMERICANO.
CSt
1949 Aug. 5.
1950 July 1.

INFORMACION. d. est. Jan. 8, 1931.
DLC
1931 Jan. 8 – May 2, 4 – July 19, 21 – 31, Aug. 2 – Dec. 31.
1932 Jan. 1 – Aug. 2.
MWA
1937 Feb. 16.

JUVENTUD REBELDE. d. est. Oct. 22, 1965.
CSt – H
1965 Oct. 22 – Dec. 31.
1966 Jan. 1+.

KUANG HUA PAO. d.
  Note: In Chinese.
  CSt—H
    1966   Jan. 4+.

L.P.V. w.
  Note: *Listos para vencer.*
  PrU
    1961   Nov. 7—28, Dec. 5—26.
    1962   Jan. 2—30, Feb. 6—27, Mar.
            6—27, Apr. 3—24, June 12—
            26, July 3—24, Sept. 4—25,
            Oct. 2—16, Dec. 18—25.
    1963   Jan. 1—29, Feb. 5—26, Mar.
            4—25, Apr. 1—29, May 6—
            27, July 1—29, Aug. 5—26,
            Oct. 7—28, Nov. 5—26, Dec.
            3—31.
    1964   Jan. 7—28, Feb. 4—25, Mar.
            3—31, Apr. 7—28, May 5—
            26, June 2—30, July 7—28,
            Aug. 4—25, Sept. 1—29, Dec.
            1—29.
    1965   Jan. 5—26, Feb. 2—23, Mar.
            1—22, Apr. 5—26, May 3—31,
            June 7—28, July 5—26, Aug.
            2—30.+.

LABOR. w.
  MWA
    1937   Feb. 12.

LA LINTERNA. w. est. Jan. 24, 1869.
  DLC
    1869   Jan. 31.

LORO. d.
  MWA
    1914   Mar. 8.

LA LUCHA. d. est. 1885.
  Note: English section published
  1899—Aug. 4, 1925. Ceased pub-
  lication 1931.
  CU
    1911   Nov. 17, 19—Dec. 31.
    1912   Jan. 1—Mar. 7, 10—Dec. 26.
  DLC
    1888   Mar. 16, 17.

    1899   Sept. 1—Nov. 2, 4—27, 29—
            Dec. 30.
    1901   Mar. 15, 16, 18, 19.
    1902—1908   Mar. 20—Dec. 31.
    1909   Jan. 1—Aug. 24, 26—Dec. 31.
    1910—1919   Jan. 1—Dec. 31.
    1920   Jan. 1—Apr. 30, May 2—8,
            10—July 8, 10, 12—Aug. 10,
            12—Dec. 25, 27, 29—31.
    1921   Jan. 1, 3—Dec. 31.
    1922   Jan. 1—Mar. 6, 8—Apr. 12,
            15—June 15, 17—Dec. 31.
    1923   Jan. 1—Dec. 31.
    1924   Jan. 1—Nov. 25, 27—Dec. 31.
    1925—1927   Jan. 1—Dec. 31.
    1928   Jan. 1—Apr. 5, 7—Sept. 20,
            23, 24, 26—Nov. 29, Dec. 1—31.
    1929   Jan. 1—May 18, 20—Dec. 31.
    1930   Jan. 1—Dec. 8, 10—14, 16—
            24, 26—31.
    1931   Jan. 1—5, 7—Apr. 25.
  FU
    1907   May 1—Dec. 31.
    1908—1911   Jan. 1—Dec. 31.
    1912   Jan. 1—Feb. 28, May 1—Oct.
            31.
    1913   Jan. 1—Dec. 31.
    1914   Mar. 1—Dec. 31.
    1916   Nov. 1—Dec. 31.
    1917   Jan. 1—Aug. 31.
    1918   Jan. 1—31, Mar. 1—Aug. 31,
            Nov. 1—Dec. 31.
    1919   Jan. 1—Aug. 31.
    1920—1921   [Jan. 1—Dec. 31].
    1922—1923   Jan. 1—Dec. 31.
  MWA
    1910   Oct. 20.
    1914   Mar. 8.
  MiU
    1903—1904   Jan. 1—Dec. 31.
    1905   Jan. 1—June 30.
  NN
    Micro (P) & (N)
    1898   Apr. 22—Dec. 29.
    1901—1909   Jan. 1—Dec. 31.
    1910   Jan. 1—Aug. 31, Oct. 1—
            Dec. 31.
    1911   Jan. 1—Dec. 31.

1912   Jan. 1 – June 1, 30 – Oct.
        31, Dec. 1 – 31.
NcD
    1929   July 1 – Aug. 16, 18 – Sept. 13,
            16 – Oct. 5, 7 – Nov. 5, 7 –
            Dec. 6, 8 – 22, 24 – 31.
    1930   Jan. 2 – 16, 18 – Apr. 17, 19 –
            May 9, 11 – Nov. 23, 25 – Dec.
            14, 16 – 24, 26 – 31.
    1931   Jan. 1 – Apr. 30.
NcU
    1912   Mar. 6 – Apr. 11, 25 – Nov. 14,
            16 – 21, 23, 24, 26 – Dec. 10,
            12 – 21, 23 – 31.
    1913   Jan. 1 – Dec. 31.
    1914   Jan. 2, 3, 7 – Feb. 9, 11 – Dec.
            31.
    1915 – 1916   Jan. 1 – Dec. 31.
    1917   Jan. 1 – Sept. 2, 4, 7 – Oct. 6,
            8 – 12, 14 – 27, 29 – 31, Nov.
            2 – Dec. 5, 7 – 28, 30, 31.
    1918   Jan. 1 – Feb. 10, 12 – Oct. 5,
            7, 9 – 18, 20 – Dec. 31.
    1919   Jan. 1 – Sept. 8, 11 – 23, 26 –
            Oct. 21, 23, 26 – Nov. 2, 4 – 9,
            11 – Dec. 8, 13 – 15, 19 – 29.
WaU
    1898   Apr. 1 – Aug. 31.

LUZ. d. est. Dec. 29, 1933.
    DLC
        1933   Dec. 29.

EL MENSAGERO CUBANO.
        See *The Cuban Messenger. El
        Mensagero cubano.*

LOS MERCADOS. w. est. Mar. 6, 1908.
    DLC
        1908   Mar. 6 – 16, 30.

MERCANTILE WEEKLY REPORT. w.
    Note: In English.
    MWA
        1845   Dec. 27.
        1846   Jan. 31, May 30.
        1855   May 5 – 26, June 16 – July 21.

EL MERCURIO. d. est. 1912.
    LNT – MA
        1929   ₁July 18 – Aug. 3, Oct. 9 –

        Dec. 31.₁
    1930   ₁Jan. 4 – Feb. 29, Apr. 1 –
            Dec. 31.₁
    1931   ₁Jan. 1 – Dec. 31.₁
    1932   ₁Jan. 1 – June 30.₁
    1934   Dec. 23.

EL MUNDO. d. est. Apr. 11, 1901.
        Note: Suspended publication Nov.
        13 – Dec. 1930; Jan. 9 – Feb. 1, 1931;
        Aug. 4 – 11, 1933; Nov. 15, 1933 –
        May 20, 1934; Mar. 6 – Apr. 14, 1935.
        During periods of suspension in 1931
        and 1933 – 1935, the staff of *El Mundo*
        published *Ahora*. Published sepa-
        rate section entitled *Nuevo Mundo*
        1939 – 1949.

    CU
        1911   Nov. 20 – Dec. 31.
        1912 – 1913   Jan. 1 – Dec. 31.
        1914   Jan. 1 – Aug. 3, 5, 7 – 16, 31,
                Sept. 1 – 13, 21 – Oct. 4, 25 –
                Dec. 31.
        1915   Jan. 1 – Dec. 31.
        1916   Jan. 1 – Nov. 12, 27 – Dec. 3,
                11 – 17.
        1917   Jan. 22 – 28, Feb. 6 – Sept.
                29, Oct. 1 – Dec. 31.
        1918   Jan. 1 – Mar. 30, Apr. 1 – May
                18, 20 – June 13, 15 – 29, July
                1 – Nov. 9, 11 – Dec. 31.
        1919   Jan. 1 – 20, 22 – 30, Mar. 1 –
                11, 14 – Dec. 31.
        1920 – 1923   Jan. 1 – Dec. 31.
        1924   Jan. 1 – Nov. 25.

    CSt – H
        1961   Mar. 5, 7.
        1962   June 23, 24, 26, 27, 30 – July
                7, 11, 13 – 25, 28, 31, Aug. 5,
                8, 12, 17, 22, 23, 25, 26, 28, 29,
                Oct. 2, 6, 7, Dec. 2, 5, 9, 13 –
                15, 19 – 21, 27.
        1963   Jan. 18, 19, 29, Feb. 6, 10, 13,
                15, 24, Mar. 1, 9, 12, Apr. 9,
                10, 24 – 30, May 2, 4, 9, 10,
                12 – 16, 22, 24, 25, 29 – 31.
        1965   Jan. 2 – Dec. 31.

1966 Jan. 1+.
CtY
  Micro (P)
  1962 Jan. 1 – Dec. 31.
  1963 May 1 – June 30.
  1964 Jan. 1 – Feb. 28.
DLC
  1905 Sept. 30.
  1906 Aug. 29, 30, Sept. 1, 6, 7, 12,
       16, Oct. 14, 21, 24, 25, 28 –
       31, Nov. 2 – Dec. 17, 19 – 31.
  1907 Jan. 1 – 4, 6 – 29, 31, Feb. 3 –
       5, 7 – 19, 21 – Mar. 16, 19 –
       Apr. 11, 17 – May 10, 12 – June
       1, 4 – 6, 8 – 29, July 2 – 25,
       27 – Aug. 22, 24, 27 – Sept. 12,
       14 – 26, 28 – 30, Oct. 11, Nov.
       1 – 6, 8 – 10, 12 – Dec. 6, 8 –
       15, 17 – 23, 25 – 31.
  1908 Jan. 1, 3 – 6, 8 – 23, 25, 28 –
       Mar. 6, 8 – 10, 12, 14 – 19, 21,
       22, 24 – 31, May 1 – 16, 18 –
       June 9, 11 – 22, 24 – July 1, 3 –
       16, 18 – Aug. 7, 9 – 24, 28 –
       Sept. 7, 9 – 13, 16, 18 – 30.
  1941 Mar. 4 – 8, 10 – 18, 20, 22, 24,
       25, 27, 31 – Apr. 10, 12, 14, 15,
       18 – 21, 23 – May 10, 12 – 19,
       21, 22, 26, 29 – June 9, 11, 12,
       15 – 17, 19, 21 – 23, 25 – 28,
       Dec. 31.
  1942 Jan. 2 – 13, 15, 16, 18 – 20, 22,
       24 – 30, Feb. 25, Mar. 4, 8, 11,
       18, 25.
  1943 Feb. 23 – 25, Aug. 15.
  1944 Feb. 8, 17, 22, 23, 29, Mar.
       2 – 4, 10, 15, 17, 22 – 28, 30 –
       Apr. 1, 5 – 9, 12, 14 – 19, 21 –
       25, 27, 28, 30, May 4, 7, 17, 19,
       20, 25, 26, 28, 30 – June 3, 8,
       9, 11, 14 – 16, 18, 21, 23, 24,
       27, 28, 30, July 4 – 7, 12, 14,
       16 – Aug. 3, 5 – 12, 17 – Sept.
       10, 13, 14, 16 – Oct. 5, 7 – 18,
       20 – Nov. 7, 9 – Dec. 2, 5, 8,
       12 – 14, 19 – 27, 29 – 31.
  1945 Jan. 2 – Feb. 6, 8 – 10, 12 –
       Mar. 10, 12 – Apr. 1, 3, 5 –

       30, May 2 – 15, 17 – June 9,
       12 – 23, 25 – July 24, 26 –
       Aug. 8, 10 – 21, 23, 24, 26 –
       Sept. 1, 3 – Oct. 20, 22 – 24,
       26 – Nov. 12, 19, 26, Dec. 1 –
       15, 17 – 25, 28 – 31.
  1946 Jan. 1 – 7, 10, 14, 15, 21, 27 –
       Feb. 23, 25, Mar. 1, 3 – 5, 8 –
       16, 18 – Apr. 11, 13 – 18, 20 –
       30, May 2 – Dec. 31.
  1947 Jan. 1 – 3, 5 – May 19, 23 –
       Sept. 12, 14 – Dec. 31.
  1948 Jan. 1 – Feb. 12, 14 – May 18,
       20 – July 8, 10 – 13, 15, 17 –
       Sept. 20, 22 – Nov. 2, 8 –
       Dec. 31.
  1949 Jan. 1 – Apr. 9, 11, 12, 17 –
       23, 25, May 2 – Dec. 31.
  1950 Jan. 1 – Feb. 21, 23 – Sept. 19,
       21 – Dec. 31.
  1951 Jan. 1 – Dec. 31.
  1952 Jan. 1 – July 2, 4 – Dec. 31.
  1953 Jan. 1 – Dec. 31.
  1954 Jan. 1 – Dec. 25, 27 – 31.
  1955 Jan. 1 – Dec. 31.
  1956 Jan. 1 – Dec. 19, 21 – 30.
  Micro (P) & (N)
  1901 Apr. 11 – Nov. 2.
DPU
  Micro (P)
  1938 – 1943 Jan. 1 – Dec. 31.
  1946 – 1947 Jan. 1 – Dec. 31.
FMU
  1961 July 18 – 20, 23 – 26.
  1963 Oct. 29 – Nov. 1, 3 – 24, Dec.
       1 – 22.
  1964 Jan. 2 – 11, 14 – Feb. 2, 5 –
       Apr. 9, 11 – 24, 26, 29, 30,
       May 7 – 28, 30 – June 6, 9 –
       23, 28, 29, July 1 – Oct. 11, 20,
       25, Nov. 12 – Dec. 30.
  1965 Jan. 2 – 16, 19 – 21, 23 – Feb.
       20, 23 – June 20, 23 – Dec. 23,
       26.
FU
  1952 [Dec. 1 – 31].
  1953 Jan. 1 – Dec. 31.
  1961 Jan. 1 – June 14.

ICRL
  Micro (N)
  1938–1943   Jan. 1–Dec. 31.
  1946–1947   Jan. 1–Dec. 31.
  Micro (P) & (N)
  1956   Jan. 1+.
IU
  1959   Nov. 27.
MH
  1915   Mar. 1–Apr. 30.
MWA
  1906   Aug. 5.
  1914   Mar. 8.
  1937   Feb. 14.
NSyU
  1961   Jan. 27–Dec. 31.
  1962   Jan. 1+.
NcD
  1925   June 23.
NcU
  1936   May 2–Aug. 2, 4–Dec. 31.
  1937   Mar. 1–3, 5–July 8, 10–14,
          16–24, 29–Aug. 4, 6–30.
  1944   May 1–19, 21–June 22, 24–
          Aug. 23, 25–Oct. 8, 12–17,
          20–31.
  1945   Apr. 1–12, 18, 20, 21, 23–
          June 1, 3–5, 7–18, 23–26.
NmU
  1920–1958   Jan. 1–Dec. 31.
  1959   Jan. 1–Dec. 1, 30, 31.
  1960   Jan. 2–Mar. 3, 12, 22, 25–
          27, 29, Apr. 3, 12, 24.
  1964   Jan. 2–Dec. 12, 16, 22, 29–31.
  1965   Jan. 2–13, 21, Feb. 6, 21–
          28, Mar. 2–Nov. 27.
TxU
  1915   Jan. 1–Feb. 2, 4–20, 22–
          Mar. 10, 13–Apr. 5, 7–June
          26, 28, 30–Sept. 9, 11–Dec.
          28.
  1916   Jan. 2–14, 16–Mar. 5, 7–
          16, 20, 21, 23–28, 30–Dec. 31.
  1917   Jan. 1–31, Feb. 4–22, 24–
          Mar. 6, 11–31, Apr. 2–May
          15, 17–Aug. 5, 7–19, 22–
          30, Sept. 1–27, 29, Oct. 1–
          11, 13–Nov. 30, Dec. 3, 4, 6–

          8, 10–31.
  1918   Jan. 1–12, 14–Feb. 2, 4, 5,
          7–14, 16–Mar. 11, 13–25,
          27–May 12, 14–18, 20–Aug.
          14, 16–22, 24–Sept. 25, 27–
          30, Oct. 2–10, 12–26, 28–
          Nov. 12, 14–Dec. 11, 13–31.
  1919   Jan. 1–Feb. 5, 13–May 24,
          28–Sept. 8, 11–Dec. 31.
  1920   Jan. 1, 5–Apr. 30, May 4–
          June 24, 26–July 8, 10–Dec.
          31.
  1921   Jan. 1–Apr. 30, May 2–
          Dec. 31.
  1922   Jan. 1–3, 5, 6, 8, 9, 11, 27–
          Feb. 1, 3, 4, 6–9, 13, 16, 20,
          25–28, Mar. 3, 6, 8, 10, 13, 15,
          17, 20–22, 24, 25, 27–Apr. 1,
          3–12, 15–22, 24, 25, 29–
          May 2, 4, 5, 8, 11–13, 15–17,
          19–21, 23, 25, 27, 29–June
          3, 5, 6, 8, 14, 15, 17, 20, 23, 27,
          29, July 4, 11, 14, 18, 21, 24,
          31, Aug. 1, 3–5, 8, 9, 11, 14,
          Sept. 7, 20, Nov. 14.
  1924   Sept. 22.
  1946   Sept. 22.

EL MUNDO ILUSTRADO.
  NHi
  1905   June 11.

NOCHE DE LA HABANA. d. est. 1912.
  MWA
  1914   Mar. 8.

NOTICIAS DE HOY.
  See *Hoy*.

NOTICIERO DEL LUNES. w. est. Oct. 1,
1934.
  Note: Supersedes Monday issue of
  Diario de la marina. Ceased publication Feb. 26, 1940.
  DLC
  1934   Oct. 1, 8, 22, 29.
  1935   July 29.
  1937   Nov. 1–Dec. 27.
  1938   Jan. 3–Oct. 31.
  1939   Feb. 13, Mar. 6, 13, Apr. 10–

24, May 29, June 12, July 3 —
Dec. 25.
1940   Jan. 1, 8, 22 — Feb. 26.
MWA
1937   Feb. 15.
NN
Micro (P) & (N)
1934   [Oct. 1 — Dec. 31.]
1935 — 1939 [Jan. 1 — Dec. 31.]
1940   [Jan. 1 — Feb. 26.]

NOTICIERO MERCANTIL. d. est. 1935.
DLC
1939   Feb. 4, Oct. 14, 15, Nov. 7 —
10, 14.
1940   Jan. 3, 9, 17, 18, Feb. 21, 22,
Mar. 6, 7, 22, 28, Apr. 23 — 27,
July 17 — Aug. 9, 13, 17 — 25,
27 — Sept. 24, 27 — Oct. 4, 8,
18 — 20, 29 — Nov. 1, 3 — Dec. 1,
4 — 6, 10 — 13, 18 — 27, 29, 31.
1941   Jan. 4 — 19, 22 — Feb. 9, 12 —
22, 27 — Mar. 1, 3 — 8, 12, 15,
18, 19 — 21, 23 — 30.

NOTICIOSO MERCANTIL. d.
MWA
1828   Feb. 24, 25.

EL NOTICIOSO Y LUCHERO DE LA
HABANA.
See *Diario de la marina*.

NUEVO MUNDO.
See *El Mundo*.

LA OPINION. d.
NN
Micro (P) & (N)
1919   [July 30 — Dec. 31.]
1920   [Jan. 1 — Dec. 31.]
1921   [Jan. 1 — Aug. 27.]

LA OPINION NACIONAL.
NcD
1919   Feb. 3.

EL PAIS. d.
DLC
1888   Mar. 17, 21, 23.

EL PAIS. d. est. 1921.
DLC
1931   Aug. 1 — 31.

1933   Sept. 5, Nov. 8 — 10.
1939   Dec. 12, 13.
1940   Jan. 2, 31, Mar. 6, 8, 9, 11.
1942   Sept. 20.
FU
Micro (N)
1934   Jan. 9 — Feb. 5, 9 — 15, 20 —
May 7, 9 — 28, 30 — June 8,
10 — 22, 24 — Oct. 13, 15 — 20,
22 — 27, 29 — Nov. 3, 5 — 10,
12 — 23, 25 — Dec. 5, 7 — 23,
26 — 31.
1935   Jan. 1 — 15, 17 — Feb. 5, 7 —
14, 16 — Mar. 6, 15 — 17, 19 —
25.
MWA
1937   Feb. 16.
NcD
1937   Aug. 24.

PALANTE. w.
CSt — H
1966   May 26+.

PALENQUE. d.
MWA
1883   Aug. 17.

PAPEL PERIODICO DE LA HAVANA.
See *Gaceta de la Habana*.

EL PARTIDO LIBERAL. d. est. 1906.
DLC
1906   Dec. 8.

PATRIA. d. est. 1899.
DLC
1901   Mar. 16 — 19, 28 — Apr. 2, 6 —
13, 16.
Supplement: Apr. 6, 13.
MH
1901   Apr. 17 — 19.

LA PATRIA LIBRE. w. est. Jan. 23, 1869.
DLC
1869   Jan. 23.

LA PRENSA. sw., 3w., d. est. July 1,
1841.
Note: Title *La Prensa*, July 1, 1841 —
May 15, 1843; *La Prensa*; *diario*

mercantil, económico y literario,
July 11, 1845 – June 30, 1852; *La
Prensa de la Habana*, July 1, 1852 –
[Dec. 29, 1856]; *La Prensa de la
Habana; periódico político, mercantil,
literario y económico,* [Dec. 30,
1856] – June 22, 1858; *La Prensa de
la Habana; periódico político,
literario, mercantil y económico,*
Jan. 4, 1859 – [Apr. 14, 1869]; *La
Prensa; periódico conservador de
las Antillas españolas,* Apr. 15,
1869 – May 29, 1870. Ceased publication May 29, 1870.

DLC
    1843   May 17 – 19, 21, 23, 25 – 28,
            30 – June 2, Sept. 16.
    1855   Jan. 2 – 8, 10 – 22, 24 – Mar.
            30, Apr. 1 – May 7, 9 – Oct.
            15, 17 – Dec. 15, 17, 19 – 31.
    1856   Jan. 1 – Sept. 15, 17 – Oct. 25,
            27 – Dec. 5, 8 – 10, 13 – 31.
    1857   Jan. 1 – Aug. 28, Sept. 8 –
            Dec. 31.
    1858   Jan. 3 – 13, 15 – 23, 25 – 28,
            30, Feb. 1 – Mar. 24, 26 – June
            9, 12 – Aug. 5, 8 – Sept. 4, 6 –
            24, 26 – Oct. 4, 6 – 21, 23 –
            Dec. 31.
    1859   Jan. 1 – 26, 29, 31 – Apr. 4, 6 –
            May 16, 18, 20 – June 4, 6 –
            20, 22 – 24, 27 – Sept. 29, Oct.
            1 – Nov. 7, 9 – Dec. 6, 8 – 31.
            Suplemento: Nov. 16.
    1860   Jan. 1 – 23, 25 – Feb. 1, 3 –
            11, 13 – 16, 18 – 21, 23, 25 –
            Mar. 1, 4 – 19, 21, 22, 24 – 26,
            28 – Apr. 5, 7 – May 14, 16 –
            June 13, 15 – 20, 22 – 30, July
            2 – 10, 12 – 24, 27 – 30, Aug. 1,
            6 – 8, 10 – 20, 23 – 29, 31, Sept.
            2 – 7, 9 – 12, 15 – 19, 22 – 28,
            30, Oct. 1, 3, 5 – 10, 12 – 25,
            27, 29, 30, Nov. 1 – 6, 10 – 21,
            24 – 30, Dec. 2 – 28.
    1861   Jan. 1 – 25, 27 – Feb. 1, 9, 11 –
            Mar. 5, 8, 10 – 28, 30 – Apr. 4,
            6 – 16, 18 – 25, 27 – 29, May 1,

            3 – 6, 8, 9, 12 – June 6, 8 – 17,
            19 – July 2, 4 – 15, 17 – 29,
            Aug. 1 – 3, 5 – Sept. 4, 6 –
            Oct. 5, 7 – 16, 18 – 21, 23 –
            Nov. 21, 23 – Dec. 26, 28 – 31.
    1862   Jan. 1 – 9, 12 – 21, 23, 25 – 31,
            Feb. 2 – 7, 9 – Mar. 3, 5 – 7,
            9 – Apr. 4, 6 – 16, 19 – 29, May
            2 – June 27, 29 – Oct. 8, 10 –
            21, 23 – Dec. 31.
    1863   Jan. 1 – Mar. 28, 30 – Apr. 2,
            4 – 29, May 1, 2, 4 – June 20,
            22 – Aug. 13, 15 – Sept. 30,
            Oct. 2 – 7, 10 – 29, 31 – Dec. 5.
    1864   Jan. 23 – Feb. 16, 19 – Mar.
            24, 26 – July 23, 25 – 29, 31 –
            Sept. 20, 22 – Dec. 24, 26, 27,
            29 – 31.
    1865   Jan. 1 – 3, 5 – Feb. 17, Mar.
            4 – 16, 18 – 25, 27 – 30.

MH
    1845   Feb. 1, 27.
    1869   Dec. 8, 9.

LA PRENSA. d. est. 1908.
CU
    1927   May 10, July 5.
DLC
    1938   Apr. 27.
FU
    1916   Jan. 1 – June 30, Sept. 1 –
            Oct. 31.
NN
    Micro (P) & (N)
    1913   [Oct. 3 – Dec. 31.]
    1914 – 1919   [Jan. 1 – Dec. 31.]
    1920   [Jan. 1 – Mar. 31.]

PRENSA LIBRE. d. est. Apr. 13, 1941.
DLC
    1941   Apr. 14, May 6, 16, July 28,
            Aug. 4, 6.
    1942   May 12.
    1951   June 1 – 15, 18 – July 6, 8 –
            21, 23 – 31, Aug. 3, 5 – Oct. 2,
            5 – 9, 12 – Nov. 9, 11, 12, 14 –
            Dec. 21, 23 – 31.
    1952   Jan. 1 – Apr. 30, May 3 – July
            2, 4 – 18, 20 – Aug. 19, 23 – 25,

28 — Sept. 1, 3 — Oct. 21, 23 —
Dec. 31.

1953 Jan. 1 — 12, 14 — Apr. 10, 12 —
18, 20 — June 8, 14 — July 4, 6 —
30, Aug. 1 — Sept. 4, 6 — Oct.
22, 24 — 27, 29 — Dec. 31.

1954 Jan. 1 — 18, 20 — Mar. 26, 29 —
Apr. 19, 22, 23, 26 — 28, 30, May
2 — 7, 9 — 11, 13 — June 16, 18 —
23, 25 — 28, July 1 — 12, 14, 15,
17 — 27, Aug. 3 — 19, 21 — 24,
26, 27, Sept. 1 — 8, 10 — 13,
15 — 22, 24 — Oct. 19, 21 — 29,
31, Nov. 3, 4, 7 — 10, 14 — 24,
26 — Dec. 1, 3, 5 — 7, 9 — 31.

1955 Jan. 1 — 17, 20, 21, 24, 25, 27,
28, 31 — Feb. 4, 10 — 18, 21 —
28, Mar. 2 — 4, 8 — 14, 23, 25 —
Apr. 5, 8 — 18, 27 — May 9,
13 — 20, 22 — 24, 27, 29 — June
8, 10 — July 7, 9 — 12, 14 — Aug.
18, 20 — 31, Sept. 2 — 13, 15,
16, 19 — Oct. 21, 23, 24, 26 —
Nov. 4, 6 — 22, 24 — Dec. 6, 9 —
17, 19 — 30.

1956 Jan. 3 — 24, 26 — Feb. 9, Mar.
17 — Aug. 11, 13 — 24, 26 —
Sept. 27, Oct. 1 — Nov. 2, 24,
29 — Dec. 13, 15 — 30.

1957 Apr. 6 — 17, 19 — 30, May 2 —
22, 24, 25, 27, 31, June 1, 3 —
15, 17, 19 — 30, July 2 — 25,
27 — Aug. 6, 8 — Sept. 29, Oct.
1 — 4, 8 — 25, 29 — Nov. 24, 26 —
Dec. 7, 9 — 31.

1958 Jan. 1 — 15, 17 — 24, 26 — Feb.
25, 28, Mar. 5 — 9, 11 — 16.

1961 Jan. 4, 5, 8, 14 — 24, 26, 28 —
Feb. 10, June 21 — July 13, 15 —
26, 29 — 31, Aug. 2, 4 — Sept. 13,
15 — 27, 29, Oct. 1 — 10, 12 — 31.

LNHT

1960 Dec. 2.
1961 Jan. 25, 28, 29, 31, Feb. 2 —
28, Mar. 1 — 29, Apr. 2 — 6, 8,
12, Oct. 20, 21, 25, 27.

PRENSA LIBRE; SEMANARIO IN-
DEPENDIENTE. w.
MWA
1937 Feb. 13.

EL PROGRESO. w.
MH
1858 June 6, 20, July 4 — 18, Aug.
1, 15 — Sept. 26, Oct. 10 —
Nov. 28, Dec. 26.
1859 Jan. 23 — 30, Mar. 6 — May 1,
15, July 3.
1862 July 20 — Aug. 3, 17 — Sept. 28,
Oct. 5.

PUEBLO. d. est. 1937.
DLC
1941 Jan. 31.
1942 Mar. 19.
1943 June 18.
1944 Feb. 26.

LA REALIDAD. d. est. Mar. 1901.
DLC
1901 June 19 — July 5, 7 — Aug. 14,
16 — 31.

¡REBELION! w. est. Oct. 14, 1908.
DLC
1908 Oct. 14.

EL REGAÑON DE LA HAVANA. w. est.
Sept. 30, 1800.
Note: Ceased publication Apr. 27,
1802.
TxU
1800 Sept. 30 — Oct. 7, 21 — Nov. 30.
1801 Jan. 15 — Feb. 24, Apr. 28 —
Sept. 22, Oct. 6 — Dec. 29.
1802 Feb. 14 — Mar. 2, 16 — Apr. 27.

EL REVISOR. 3w. est. Mar. 3, 1823.
Note: Ceased publication Aug. 30,
1823.
TxU
1823 Mar. 3 — Aug. 30.

REVOLUCION. d. est. 1958.
CSt — H
1959 Sept. 15.
1960 June 11, 20, 21, 25, 29, July 7,
14, 19 — 21, 25, 27 — 30, Aug.
1, 3 — 6, 8 — 13, 15 — 19, 22 —

26, 29 – 31, Sept. 1 – 3, 6 – 9,
13 – 15, 19, 27, Oct. 3, 6, 7, 10,
12, 20, 24, 29, 31, Nov. 2, 4,
7 – 9, Dec. 1, 2.

1961   Mar. 7 – 11, 17 – 20, 22 – 24,
27, 30, Apr. 3, 5 – 7, 13, 19,
21, 29 – May 8, 11, 12, 15 – 26,
29, 31 – June 1, 3 – 9, 12 – 21,
23 – 26, 28 – 30, July 3 – 5, 8,
10 – 14, 17 – 19, 21, 25 – Aug.
5, 8 – 16, 18 – 24, 26, 29, Sept.
2 – 7, 9 – 25, 27 – Oct. 3, 5, 7 –
19, 21 – 31, Nov. 2 – 3, 6 – 20,
22, 29, 30, Dec. 2 – 14, 18 – 30.

1962   Jan. 2 – 4, 9, 12, 15 – 17, 19,
20, Feb. 1, 3 – 9, 13, 15 – 17,
20, 21, 24, 27 – Mar. 1, 7, 9 –
12, 15 – 19, 21 – 23, 27 – 28,
30 – Apr. 2, 5 – 9, 11 – 17, 19,
23, 25, 26, 28, 30 – May 7, 9,
11 – 14, 16, 19 – 26, June 1, 4,
5, 7, 9 – 11, 14, 16 – 19, 21 –
25, 28, July 2, 4, 5, 7 – 9, 11, 12,
14 – 17, 19, 21 – 23, 26 – Aug.
1, 3, 6, 8, 9, 11 – 13, 15, 18, 20,
21, 23, 25 – 28, 30, Sept. 1 – 3,
5, 8 – 10, 12, 15 – 17, 19, 21 –
24, 28, Oct. 6 – 8, 11, 13, 17,
19, 20, 25, Dec. 21, 26.

1963   Jan. 8, 9, 12, 15, 17 – 19, 23 –
25, 30 – Feb. 1, 4, 6, 9 – 13, 15,
18, 21, Mar. 5 – 7, 9 – 11, 14,
16 – 18, 20, 22 – 26, Apr. 1,
5 – 10, 20 – 22, 24, 25, 27 – 29,
May 3, 4, 7 – 14, 16 – 24, 27 –
June 6, 10, 11, 14 – 17, 19, 21,
22, 26, 28, 29, July 15, 17, Aug.
1, 6, 9, 12 – 30.

1964   Oct. 27 – Dec. 31.

1965   Jan. 2 – 28, 30 – Mar. 21, 23 –
Sept. 9, 11 – 18, 21 – 23, 25 –
30.

DLC
    Micro (P) & (N)
    1959   Jan. 2 – Dec. 31.
    1960   Jan. 1+.

DPU
    Micro (P)

1959   Jan. 2 – Dec. 31.
1960 – 1962   Jan. 1 – Dec. 31.
1963   Jan. 1 – June 29, Oct. 1 –
Dec. 31.
1964   Jan. 2 – Mar. 31.

FMU
    1960   Nov. 29 – Dec. 2, 5 – 10, 13 –
27, 29 – 31.
    1961   Jan. 1, 4 – 10, 13, 16 – 19, 21 –
26, 28 – Feb. 3, 6 – 13, 15 –
17, 20 – 22, 24, July 20, 24.
    1965   Jan. 2 – Mar. 31, July 6, 23 –
Aug. 19, Sept. 28 – Oct. 2.
    Micro (P)
    1959   Jan. 2 – Dec. 31.
    1960 – 1964   Jan. 1 – Dec. 31.

FU
    Micro (P)
    1959   Jan. 2 – Dec. 31.
    1960   Jan. 1+.

MH
    Micro (P)
    1959   Jan. 2 – Apr. 6, May 2 – June
9, July 1 – Oct. 31, Nov. 2 –
Dec. 31.
    1960 – 1962   Jan. 1 – Dec. 31.

NIC
    Micro (P)
    1959   Jan. 2 – Dec. 31.
    1960   Jan. 1+.

NN
    1959   Oct. 1 – Dec. 31.
    1960   Jan. 1 – Oct. 13, 15 – 31.
    1961   Jan. 1 – Apr. 3, 5 – 13, 21, 26,
27, 29, 30, May 5 – 8, 10 – 15,
18 – 25, 27 – 31, June 2 – 19,
28 – July 4, 6, 10 – Aug. 4, 8 –
Sept. 15.
    Micro (P)
    1959   Jan. 2 – Dec. 31.
    1960   Jan. 1+.

NjP
    Micro (P)
    1959   Jan. 2 – Dec. 31.
    1960   Jan. 1+.

OrU
    1962   July 26, 28.

PrU
　1959　Jan. 2 – Aug. 31, Nov. 2 –
　　　　Dec. 31.
　1960　Jan. 1+.
ViU
　1959　Dec. 30.

LA SATIRA.
　MH
　1907　Nov. 17.

EL SIGLO. d. est. 1862.
　Note: Ceased publication 1868.
　DLC
　1865　Mar. 19 – Apr. 11, 13 – May
　　　　23, 25 – 27, 29, 31 – June 2,
　　　　4 – 8, 11 – 15, 18 – July 17,
　　　　19 – Aug. 5, 7 – 10, 12, 14 –
　　　　Sept. 28, 30 – Oct. 26, 28 –
　　　　Nov. 16, 18 – Dec. 4, 6 – 9,
　　　　11 – 31.
　1866　Jan. 3 – 6, 8 – Feb. 10, 12 –
　　　　Mar. 29, 31 – Apr. 12, 14 – May
　　　　11, 13 – June 28, 30 – July 3,
　　　　5 – Oct. 27, 29 – Nov. 7, 9 –
　　　　17, 19, 20, 22, 24, 26 – Dec. 10,
　　　　12 – 15, 20 – 24, 26 – 28, 31.
　1867　Jan. 1 – 5, 7 – 19, 27 – Mar. 6,
　　　　9 – 16, 18 – Apr. 12, 17, 18,
　　　　20 – May 6, 9 – 11, 13 – 24,
　　　　26 – June 14, 16 – July 6, 8,
　　　　10 – 25, 27 – Aug. 5, 7 – 16,
　　　　25 – Sept. 19, 21 – 24, 26 – Oct.
　　　　2, 4 – 14, 16 – 19, 21 – 24, 27,
　　　　28, 30, Nov. 1 – 7, 9 – 13, 15,
　　　　17 – 19, 21 – Dec. 7, 9 – 21,
　　　　23 – 29.
　　　　Suplemento: June 8.

EL SIGLO. w. est. 1937.
　CU
　1943　July 14 – Dec. 29.
　1944 – 1945　Jan. 1 – Dec. 31.
　1946　Jan. 2 – Apr. 3, 17 – May 15,
　　　　29 – July 3, 17 – Aug. 14, Sept.
　　　　4 – 25, Oct. 9 – Dec. 25.
　1947　Jan. 1 – Mar. 12, 26 – June 18,
　　　　July 2 – 9, 23 – Aug. 20, Sept.
　　　　3 – Nov. 12, Dec. 3 – 31.
　1948　Jan. 7 – 14, 28 – Apr. 21, May
　　　　12 – June 30, July 14, 28 – Oct.

　　　　5, 20 – 27, Nov. 10 – Dec. 1,
　　　　15 – 29.
　1949　Jan. 5 – 26.

LA TARDE. d.
　CSt – H
　1965　May 6 – July 1, 3 – Aug. 4, 6 –
　　　　Oct. 1, 3 – 21.

TIEMPO. d. est. Jan. 14, 1945.
　Note: Title *Tiempo en Cuba*, Jan. 14,
　1945 – Apr. 10, 1950; *Tiempo*, after
　May 2, 1950. Periodicity Jan. 14,
　1945 – Apr. 10, 1950, weekly; after
　May 2, 1950, daily.

　DLC
　1950　June 20 – Aug. 12, 14, 16 – 21,
　　　　23 – Sept. 21, 23 – 30, Oct. 2 –
　　　　14, 16 – 21, 23 – Nov. 4, 6 –
　　　　11, 13 – 18, 20 – 25, 27 – Dec.
　　　　2, 4 – 7, 9, 11 – 13, 15, 17 –
　　　　23, 25 – 29.
　1951　Jan. 3 – Sept. 23, 27 – Dec. 31.
　1952　Jan. 1 – Mar. 20, 22 – Oct. 11,
　　　　13 – 23, 27 – Dec. 31.
　1953　Jan. 1 – Apr. 2, 5 – 7, 9 – 14,
　　　　16 – Oct. 7, 9 – 20, 22 – Dec. 31.
　1954　Jan. 1 – Feb. 15, 17 – Mar. 31,
　　　　Apr. 2 – 6, 8 – 12, 14 – 23,
　　　　26 – June 12, 14, 18 – July 31,
　　　　Aug. 2 – 10, 12 – 26, 28 –
　　　　Dec. 9, 11 – 16, 18 – 24, 28 – 31.
　1955　Jan. 1 – 12, 15 – Feb. 21, 23,
　　　　24, 28 – Mar. 7, 9, 13 – 19, 21 –
　　　　Apr. 6, 8 – 30, May 8 – June
　　　　8, 10, 11, 13 – 18, 20 – 23,
　　　　25 – 27, 29 – July 14, 17, 18,
　　　　21 – 26, 28 – 30, Aug. 1, 2, 5 –
　　　　11, 13 – 17, 20 – 31, Sept. 2 –
　　　　26, 28 – Dec. 31.
　1956　Jan. 1 – Mar. 29, Apr. 1 – 25,
　　　　27 – June 2, 4 – July 2, 4 – 30,
　　　　Aug. 1 – 4, 6 – 23, 25 – Sept. 3,
　　　　5 – Dec. 30.
　1957　Jan. 1 – 16, 18 – 22, 24 – Feb.
　　　　12, 14 – Mar. 1, 3 – 5, 7 – 31,
　　　　Apr. 2 – May 11, 13 – 20, 22 –
　　　　29, 31 – June 30, July 2 – 15,
　　　　17 – Aug. 1, 3 – 24, 26 – Sept.

12, 14 – 29, Oct. 1 – 7, 9 – Nov.
1, 3 – 9, 11 – 20, 22 – 26, 28 –
Dec. 31.
1958   Jan. 1 – Mar. 4, 6 – 28, 30 –
Apr. 1, 6 – May 8, 10 – 14,
17 – 23, 25 – 27, 29 – 31, June
2, 4, 5, 7 – July 15, 17 – 30,
Aug. 1 – 11, 13 – Sept. 24,
26 – Oct. 5, 7 – Nov. 8, 10 –
12, 14 – 22, 24, 26 – Dec. 1, 5.

TIEMPO NUEVO. d., w. est. 1940.
Note: Periodicity [Nov.] 1940 – Apr.
9, 1941, daily; after Apr. 26, 1941,
weekly.
DLC
1940   Dec. 31.
1941   Jan. 1, 2, 5 – Mar. 3, 5 – 7, 9,
11 – 17, 19 – Apr. 3, 5 – 9.

THE TIMES OF CUBA. d. est. Aug. 1,
1898.
Note: In Spanish and English. Removed from Santiago de Cuba, Fall
1898.
DLC
1898   Dec. 28.

THE TIMES OF HAVANA. sw. est. Feb.
4, 1957.
Note: In Spanish and English.
Removed to Miami, Florida, Nov. 3,
1960.
FMU
Micro (P)
1957   Feb. 4 – Dec. 31.
1958 – 1959   Jan. 1 – Dec. 31.
1960   Jan. 1 – Nov. 3.
LNHT
Micro (P)
1957   Feb. 4 – Dec. 31.
1958 – 1959   Jan. 1 – Dec. 31.
1960   Jan. 1 – Nov. 3.
NIC
Micro (P)
1957   Feb. 4 – Dec. 31.
1958 – 1959   Jan. 1 – Dec. 31.
1960   Jan. 1 – Nov. 3.
NNC
Micro (P)

1957   Feb. 4 – Dec. 31.
1958 – 1959   Jan. 1 – Dec. 31.
1960   Jan. 1 – Nov. 3.
NmU
Micro (N)
1957   July 1 – Dec. 31.
1958 – 1959   Jan. 1 – Dec. 31.
1960   Jan. 1 – Nov. 3.

EL TRIUNFO. d.
DLC
1878   Dec. 21.
1880   July 11, Dec. 5, 7.
1881   Jan. 1 – May 11, 13 – Dec.
26, 28 – 31.
1882   Jan. 1 – Apr. 6, 9 – 13, 16 –
Sept. 12, 18 – Dec. 14, 17 –
25, 27 – 31.
Suplemento: Dec. 24.
1883   Jan. 1 – 4.

EL TRIUNFO. d. est. [1906].
CU
1911   Nov. 17 – 22, 24 – Dec. 31.
1912   Jan. 1 – Dec. 31.
1913   Jan. 1 – Mar. 5, 7 – Dec. 31.
1914 – 1916   Jan. 1 – Dec. 31.
1917   Jan. 1 – 31, Feb. 2, 6 – 8, 11 –
14, Nov. 15 – 23, Dec. 26 – 30.
1918   Jan. 2 – 18, 20 – Dec. 31.
1919   Jan. 1 – Dec. 31.
1920   Jan. 1 – Apr. 30, May 2 –
Dec. 30.
1921   Jan. 1 – Feb. 6, 9 – Mar. 20,
23 – 30, Apr. 1 – 5, 7, 10, 13 –
15, 17 – 29, May 1, 4, 7, 8, 11,
12, 14, 15, 18, 20 – 26, 28 –
June 9, 11 – 21, 23, 25, 29, 30,
July 2, 5, 6, 8, 10, 15, 16, 22,
24, 27, 29, 31, Aug. 2, 5, 11, 14,
21, 31, Sept. 4, 7, 14, 17, 21,
22, Oct. 2, 5, 9, 14, 16, 21, 30,
Nov. 6, 10, 13, 20, 27, Dec. 4,
11, 18, 25.
1922   Jan. 21 – 26, 28 – Feb. 1, 3 –
Dec. 31.
1923   Jan. 1 – Dec. 30.
1924   Jan. 1 – Dec. 31.
1925   Jan. 1 – Mar. 24, Apr. 1 – June
29.

MWA
  1914   Mar. 8.

LA UNION ESPAÑOLA. d. est. 1898.
  DLC
    1899   Aug. 31 – Dec. 31.
    1900   Jan. 3 – Feb. 28, Apr. 5 – 11,
            15, 22 – 26, 28 – May 26, 31,
            June 1 – 23, 28 – July 28, 30,
            Aug. 2 – 7, 12 – Nov. 22, 24 –
            29, Dec. 1 – 29, 31.
    1901   Jan. 1 – 9, 13 – 19.
    Edición de la tarde.
    1899   Aug. 30 – Sept. 2, 5 – Dec. 12,
            14 – 18, 20 – 30.
    1900   Jan. 2 – Feb. 28, Apr. 2, 4, 5,
            7, 10, 21, 23, 25 – May 7, 10 –
            14, 16 – 22, 24, 25, 30, 31, June
            1 – 14, 16 – 20, 22, 27 – July 27,
            Aug. 1 – 7, 11 – 17, 20 – Sept.
            3, 10, 26 – Oct. 5, 9 – 12, 15 –
            19, 22 – Nov. 9, 17, 19, 23, 26,
            28, Dec. 1 – 4, 8 – 12, 14 – 17,
            19 – 21, 24, 26 – 28.

VANGUARDIA OBRERA. bw.
  CSt – H
    1966   Jan. 1+.

LA VOTICIA. d.
  CSt
    1952   Jan. 31.

LA VOZ DE CUBA. d. est. 1868.
  DLC
    1869   Nov. 1, 3 – 5.
    1870   July 24 – Aug. 5, 7 – Nov. 26,
            28 – Dec. 31.
    1871   Jan. 1 – May 13, 15 – 31, June
            2 – Nov. 4, 6 – Dec. 30.
    1872   Jan. 1, 3 – Apr. 1, 4 – 19, 21 –
            27, 29, May 2 – 6, 8 – July 13,
            15 – Sept. 28, 30 – Oct. 12,
            14 – Nov. 15, 17 – Dec. 21, 23 –
            31.
    1873   Jan. 1 – 4, 9 – 31, Feb. 2, 3, 5 –
            27, Mar. 1 – 6, 8 – 29, 31 – Apr.
            24, 26 – July 26, 28 – Nov. 29,
            Dec. 1 – 16, 18 – 31.
    1874   Jan. 1 – 29, 31 – Feb. 10, 12 –

            Mar. 10, 12 – May 6, 8 – July
            20, 22 – Aug. 8, 10 – Dec. 31.
    1875   Jan. 1 – Feb. 6, 8 – Aug. 9, 11 –
            27, 29 – Nov. 2, 4 – 11, 13 –
            27, 29 – Dec. 31.
    1876   Jan. 1 – May 18, 21 – Dec. 31.
    1877   Jan. 1 – Oct. 27, 29 – Dec. 31.
    1878   Jan. 1 – June 14, 17 – July 6,
            8 – 11, 13 – Dec. 28, 30.
    1879   Jan. 1, 2, 4 – Dec. 5, 7 – 27.
    1880   Jan. 1 – Mar. 25, 28 – Dec. 11,
            19 – 31.
    1881   Jan. 1 – 29, 31, Feb. 2 – Apr.
            28, 30 – Oct. 20, 22 – Dec. 26,
            28 – 31.
    1882   Jan. 1 – 20, 22 – Mar. 30, Apr.
            1 – July 1, 7 – Nov. 4, 16 –
            Dec. 31.
  MH
    1869   Dec. 3, 8, 9.

LA VOZ DE LA RAZON. w. est. 1892.
  TxU
    1923   [Dec. 29].
    1924   Jan. 26 – Feb. 2, [Mar. 8 – 15].

Holguín

CORREO DE ORIENTE. [w.]
  MWA
    1914   Mar. 3.

ECO DE HOLGUIN. sw., w. est. 1884.
  MWA
    1914   Mar. 4.

Manzanillo

DEBATE. d. est. 1901.
  MWA
    1914   Mar. 3.

LA DEFENSA. d. est. 1904.
  MWA
    1914   Feb. 4.

MANZANILLO. d.
  MWA
    1914   Mar. 2.

Marianao

LA REPUBLICA DE MARIANAO. w. est.
Sept. 7, 1927.
DLC
    1927   Sept. 7 – Oct. 20.

EL SOL. w., d. est. 1908.
DLC
    1939   Feb. 25, Mar. 11, Apr. 8, 15,
            Dec. 2, 23.
    1940   June 1 – 29.

Matanzas

LA AURORA DE MATANZAS.
    See *Aurora del Yumurí.*

AURORA DEL YUMURI. 3w., d. est.
Sept. 2, 1828.
    Note: Title *La Aurora de Matanzas*,
    Sept. 2, 1828 – Jan. 28, 1831; *La*
    Aurora, Feb. 1831 – Mar. 28, 1833;
    Boletín de la aurora, Mar. 29, 30,
    1833; *La Aurora*, Mar. 31 – Apr. 2,
    1833; *Boletín a la aurora*, Apr. 3 – 16,
    1833; *La Aurora*, Apr. 17, 1833 –
    [1840]; *Aurora de Matanzas*, [1840] –
    July 31, 1857; *Aurora del Yumurí*,
    Aug. 1, 1857 – 1900. Periodicity Sept.
    2, 1828 – Jan. 28, 1831, three
    times a week; Feb., 1831 – 1900,
    daily. Absorbed *El Yumurí*, Aug. 1,
    1857. Ceased publication 1900.
DLC
    1829   Sept. 21, Dec. 5.
    1833   Feb. 11 – 16, 18 – Mar. 4, 6 –
            15, 17 – 20, 22 – Apr. 3, 5 –
            May 9, 29 – June 6, 8 – 15,
            17 – 30.
    1846   Feb. 4.
    1869   Jan. 8, 9, 12, 14, Apr. 23.
MWA
    1829   Mar. 19 – 21, 26.
    1845   May 4 – 8.
    1846   July 14 – 18.

BOLETIN DE LA AURORA.
    See *Aurora del Yumurí.*

EL CORREO DE MATANZAS. d. est.
[1880].
    CU – B
      Micro (P)
      1889   Aug. 31 – Sept. 6.

ECO DE ESPAÑA.
DLC
    1869   Supplement: Feb. 14.

REPUBLICANO CONSERVADOR. d.
est. 1904.
MWA
    1914   Feb. 3.

EL YUMURI. d. est. Feb. 1, 1842.
    Note: Absorbed by *Aurora de*
    Matanzas Aug. 1, 1857 and then
    began publishing under the title
    Aurora del Yumurí.
DLC
    1842   Feb. 1 – Apr. 26.

Nueva Gerona

ISLE OF PINES APPEAL. w. est. Apr.
14, 1904.
    Note: In English. Removed from
    Santa Fe, before Dec. 28, 1912.
DLC
    1906   Oct. 14.
    1912   Dec. 28.
    1913   Jan. 4.

ISLE OF PINES POST.
    Note: In English.
KHi
    1930   Oct. 25.
MWA
    1932   June 10.

PATRIA. d.
KHi
    1900   Apr. 5.

Pinar del Río

DEFENSA SOCIAL. [w.] est. 1940.
DLC
    1941   Apr. 18.

Sagua la Grande

EL COMERCIO. 3w. est. Feb. 1871.
  DLC
    1877   Feb. 13 – Mar. 19, 21 – Apr.
           2, 4 – 28, 30 – June 26.

Sancti-Spíritus

COMERCIO. d. est. Mar. 3, 1913.
  MWA
    1914   Mar. 6.

EL FENIX. 3w., d. est. May 1894.
  MWA
    1914   Feb. 3.

GUZMAN DE ALFARACHE. w., d. est.
  1877.
    Note: Ceased publication 1893.
  CU – B
    Micro (P)
    1880   Sept. 5.

EL SUFRAGIO. d. est. Jan. 5, 1914.
    Note: Ceased publication Mar. 1914.
  MWA
    1914   Feb. 3.

EL TRABAJO. 3w. est. June 4, 1899.
    Note: Ceased publication Oct. 1,
    1905.
  DLC
    1900   Feb. 23.

Santa Clara

LA MAÑANA. d.
  MWA
    1914   Mar. 6.

LA PUBLICIDAD. w. est. Oct. 3, 1904.
  CU
    1943   June 21.

Santa Fe

ISLE OF PINES APPEAL.
    See Nueva Gerona. *Isle of Pines
    Appeal.*

Siboney

NEW YORK JOURNAL AND ADVER-
  TISER. EL JORNAL DE NUEVA
  YORK. d.
    Note: In Spanish and English.
  MWA
    1898   July 10.

Santiago

CO. F ENTERPRISE.
    Note: In English.
  DLC
    1898   July 26.

EL CUBANO LIBRE. w., bw., w., bw.,
  d. est. Aug. 3, 1895.
    Note: Began publishing with *2ª
    época* in commemoration of a revolu-
    tionary journal of the same name
    published in Bayamo and Camagüey.
    Periodicity Aug. 3 – Sept. 7, 1895,
    weekly; Sept. 1, 1895 – Nov. 30,
    1896, biweekly; Dec. 1 – 31, 1897,
    weekly; Jan. 1, 1897 – May 31,
    1898; biweekly; after May 31, 1898,
    daily.
  DLC
    1903   Jan. 2 – Apr. 14, 21 – July 24,
           26, 27, 29 – Dec. 1, 3 – 31.
    1904 – 1905   Jan. 1 – Dec. 31.
    1906   Jan. 1 – Dec. 22, 24 – 31.
    1907   July 1 – Dec. 31.
    1908   Jan. 1 – Dec. 31.
    1909   Jan. 1 – Aug. 24, 26 – Sept. 9,
           12 – 30.
  MH
    1901   Jan. 9 – 15, 30, 31.
  MWA
    1914   Mar. 9.

DERECHO. d.
  MWA
    1914   Mar. 9.

DIARIO CONSTITUCIONAL DE
  SANTIAGO DE CUBA.
  CU – B
    1836   Suplemento: Sept. 29, Oct. 22.

DIARIO DE CUBA. d. est. 1917.
  MWA
    1937   Feb. 14.

EL DIARIO REDACTOR.
  MH
    1849   Oct. 6.

EL FERROCARRIL.
  MH
    1859   Sept. 6.

INDEPENDENCIA. d. est. 1871.
  MWA
    1914   Mar. 9.

ORIENTE. d. est. 1937.
  DLC
    1940   Aug. 1, Dec. 19, 20.

PARTIDO LIBERAL. d.
  MWA
    1914   Mar. 9.

THE SANTIAGO HERALD. est. Nov. 13,
  1898.
    Note: In English.
  DLC
    1898   Nov. 13.

 SIERRA MAESTRA. d. est. 1959.
  DLC
    1961   June 13 – July 20, 22 – Aug.
            19, 21 – 31, Sept. 2 – Oct. 16,
            18 – 25, 27, 28, Nov. 1 – 16.

LA TARDE. d.
  MWA
    1914   Mar. 5.

THE TIMES OF CUBA. d. est. Aug. 1,
  1898.
    Note: In Spanish and English.
    Removed to Havana in Fall, 1898.
  DLC
    1898   Aug. 1, 11.
  MH
    1898   Aug. 1 – Sept. 5.
  NcD
    1898   Aug. 23.

Trinidad

CORREO DE TRINIDAD. sw.
  MWA
    1844   Feb. 22.

Victoria de las Tunas

EL ECO DE TUNAS. sw. est. Nov. 3,
  1909.
  DLC
    1942   Jan. 3, 10, 21, 24.
  LNT – MA
    1940   June 2.

DOMINICAN REPUBLIC

Azúa de Compostela

LA HORA. w. est. Apr. 9, 1944.
  DLC
    1945   July 1 – 14, 16 – Dec. 31.
    1946   Jan. 1 – 19, 21 – Apr. 20, 29 –
            May 25, 27 – Oct. 12, 14 –
            Nov. 9, 11 – 23.
    1947   Jan. 1 – 4, 27 – Feb. 9.

Ciudad Trujillo
See Santo Domingo.

La Ramón

LA TARDE. w. est May 5, 1918.
  TxU
    1924   Jan. 24.

Monte Cristi

LA UNION DEL N.O.E. irr.
  CU – B
    Micro (P)
    1880   Aug. 7 – Sept. 16.

Puerto Plata

LA NUEVA ERA. w. est. 1877.
  CU – B
    Micro (P)
    1877   Apr. 4 – 18, May 2, 23 – June
            23.

EL PORVENIR. w. est. Jan. 1, 1872.
  CU
    1942   Feb. 7 – 14, Mar. 7, 21 – Apr.

4, 18 — June 20, July 11 — Aug. 1, 15, 29, Oct. 3, 17, 31, Nov. 28, Dec. 26.

1943   Jan. 30 — Feb. 6, 20 — Apr. 24, May 8 — June 5, 8 — 29, Aug. 11 — 19, Sept. 2 — Nov. 20, Dec. 15 — 20.

1944   Jan. 8 — 28, Feb. 25 — Aug. 21, Sept. 6, 28, Oct. 11 — 18, Nov. 18, Dec. 2 — 30.

1945   Jan. 8 — 16, 31, Feb. 9, Apr. 9, June 5.

CU — B

Micro (P)

1875   [Dec. 15.]

1877   Feb. 11, Apr. 22.

1878   Oct. 12 — Nov. 4.

1880   Jan. 31.

LNT — MA

1942   June 27, Aug. 1, 8, 29.

TxU

1942   Aug. 29.

1943   Nov. 27.

San Pedro de Macorís

DIARIO DE MACORIS. d. est. Oct. 16, 1922.

DLC

1953   Jan. 21.

Santiago de los Caballeros

EL BIEN PUBLICO. w. est. 1877.

CU — B

Micro (P)

1877   Feb. 4 — 11, 25, Apr. 8, 29.

EL DIARIO. d. est. Aug. 12, 1902.

DLC

1927   July 1 — Nov. 24, 26, 27, 29, Dec. 1 — 15, 17 — Dec. 31.

1928   Jan. 1, 2, 4 — 9, 11 — Feb. 8, 10 — Mar. 13, 16 — Apr. 5, 7 — 13, 15 — May 13, 20 — 23, 25 — June 28, 30, July 31 — Aug. 29.

LA INFORMACION. d. est. Nov. 16, 1915.

DLC

1926   Jan. 18 — 29, 31 — Feb. 12, 16 —

20, Mar. 8 — 12, Apr. 1, 5 — 7, 9, 10, 19 — 30, May 2 — 21, 23 — July 10, Aug. 1 — 15, 17 — Sept. 23, 25 — Oct. 14, 16 — 31, Dec. 21, 23 — 31.

1927   Jan. 1 — 5, 8 — Feb. 5, 14 — Mar. 5, 7 — Apr. 26, 28 — June 3, 9 — July 8, 10 — Aug. 24, 26 — Sept. 26, 28 — Oct. 15, 17 — 21, Nov. 13 — 26.

1928   Feb. 13 — Apr. 18, 20 — May 1, 3, 4.

1929   Jan. 2 — 23, 25 — 27, 29 — Feb. 12, 14, 16, 17, 19 — Mar. 8, 10, 12 — 25, 28 — June 30, July 2 — 5, 7 — 14, 16 — Aug. 7, 9 — 18, 20 — 28, 30, Sept. 1, 3 — 13, 15, 17 — 25, 28 — Oct. 1, 3 — 10, 13 — 25, 27 — Nov. 1, 3, 10, 11, 13 — 15, 17, 18, 20, 22 — 28, 30, Dec. 1, 3, 5 — 13, 15, 17 — 30.

1930   Jan. 1 — 10, 12 — 28, 30 — Feb. 13, 16 — 19, 21 — Mar. 2, 4 — 27, 29 — Apr. 20, 22 — 27, 29 — May 6, 8, 10 — June 1, 3 — 9, 11 — 23, 25 — 29, July 6 — 9, 11 — 17, 19 — 21, 23 — Aug. 6, 8 — 13, 15 — Sept. 3, 5 — 15, 17 — Oct. 12, 14 — 26, 28 — Nov. 4, 7 — 19, 21 — Dec. 3, 5 — 10, 12 — 31.

1931   Jan. 1 — 15, 17, 19 — 27, 29 — Feb. 6, 8 — Mar. 2, 4, 6 — 10, 12 — 17, 19 — 31, Apr. 2 — 19, 21 — May 1, 3 — 11, 14 — 30, Nov. 2 — 4, 6 — 8, 16 — 22, 24 — Dec. 3, 5 — 31.

1932   Jan. 1 — 14, 16 — 26, 28 — Feb. 5, 7 — Apr. 8, 10 — 15, 17 — May 17, 19 — 24, 27 — 29, 31 — June 4, Oct. 10 — 14, 16 — Nov. 19.

1939   Nov. 20.

1942   Feb. 25, Mar. 4, 6, 13, May. 12.

1945   Jan. 16 — 19, 24 — Feb. 7, 15, 16, Mar. 3, Apr. 2 — 30, May 3 — June 4, 6 — Aug. 3, 5 — 19,

21 — Sept. 19, 21 — Oct. 31,
Nov. 2 — 18, 20 — Dec. 30.

1946   Jan. 2 — Feb. 1, 3 — 7, 9 — Mar.
1, 3 — 10, 12 — May 8, 12 — July
24, 26 — Aug. 22, 24 — Sept. 25,
28, 29, Oct. 1 — 11, 13, 15 — 18,
20 — Nov. 4, 6 — 11, 13 — 17,
21 — 26, 28 — Dec. 31.

1948   Jan. 7.

1951   July 27 — Sept. 27, 29, Oct. 1 —
5, 12, 13, 19 — Dec. 31.

1952   Jan. 2 — 7, 9 — June 3, 5 — Aug.
31, Sept. 2 — 10, 13 — 25, 27 —
Dec. 31.

1953   Jan. 2 — 11, 13 — Apr. 5, 11 —
15, 17 — 28, 30 — May 19, 21, 22,
24 — June 26, 28 — July 3, 5 —
13, 15 — Aug. 7, 9 — 13, 16 —
Nov. 9, 11 — Dec. 31.

1954   Jan. 2 — 25, 27 — Feb. 2, 4 —
26, 28 — Mar. 28, Apr. 1, 3 —
8, 10 — 20, 22 — 27, 29, 30, May
4 — July 15, 17 — Sept. 12, 14 —
Oct. 17, 19 — Nov. 17, 19 — Dec.
12, 14 — 31.

1955   Jan. 3 — Mar. 28, 31 — Apr.
30, May 2 — July 6, 8 — 20, 22 —
Aug. 24, 26 — 29, 31 — Sept. 14,
16 — Oct. 7, 9 — 26, 28 — Dec.
13, 15 — 31.

1956   Jan. 3 — June 26.

1957   Jan. 2, 3, 5 — 14, 16 — 29, Feb.
1 — 3, 5, 7, 10, 11, 13 — 17,
20 — 22, 29 — Mar. 1, 3 — 17, 20,
21, 23 — Apr. 9, 12 — 26, May
2, 4, 5, 7 — 9, 11 — 16, 18 — 27.

1958   July 1 — Aug. 4, 14 — 21, 23,
25 — 28, Sept. 12 — 16, 18 — 28,
30, 31, Oct. 6 — Nov. 5, 7, 9 —
Dec. 4, 9 — 31.

1959   Jan. 7, 8, 10 — 18, 20 — Feb. 17,
19 — Mar. 20, 22 — Apr. 9, 11 —
15, 17, 19 — May 22, 24 — 31,
June 4, 10, 11, 13 — 16, 18,
24 — July 16, 19 — 26, 28, 29,
Aug. 1 — 9, Sept. 16, 25 — 29,
Oct. 7, 8, 10, 11, 14, 15, 23, 29,
31, Nov. 1, 3 — 10, 12 — Dec. 29,
31.

LA INFORMACION.
FU

Micro (N)

1946   Jan. 1 — 4, 6 — 29, 31 — Feb. 3,
5 — 18, 20 — 26, 28 — May 7, 9 —
Aug. 4, 6, 8 — 30, Sept. 1 — 9,
11 — Oct. 8, 10 — 13, 15, 17 —
31, Nov. 2 — 10, 18 — 29, Dec.
1 — 6, 8 — 15, 17 — 27, 29, 31.

1947   Jan. 1 — 10, 12, 14 — 19, 22 —
26, 28 — Mar. 28, 30 — Apr. 17,
19 — 24, 26 — 29, May 1 — 15,
17 — 21, 23 — 27, 31.

1949   Apr. 1 — 15, 17 — May 11, 13 —
16, 18 — June 19, 26 — July 10,
12, 13, 15 — Aug. 2, 4 — 23,
25 — Sept. 9, 11 — Oct. 9, 11,
12, 14, 16 — Dec. 31.

1950   Jan. 1 — Mar. 14, 16 — Apr. 2,
4 — July 7, 9 — 14, 16, 18 — 23,
25, 26, 28 — 30, Aug. 6, 13 — 29.

LA INFORMACION.
NN

Micro (P) & (N)

1940   Jan. 7 — 21, 23 — Feb. 7, 9 —
27, Mar. 2, 4 — 9, Apr. 1 — 7,
14 — 19, 21 — 24, 26 — 30, May
2 — 22, 25 — June 2, 9 — 12, 14 —
19, 21 — 27, 29 — July 7, 14 —
Aug. 25, Sept. 1 — 8, 15 — Nov.
3, 10 — 17, 19 — 22, 24 — Dec.
8, 15 — 31.

1941   Jan. 1 — 20, 22 — Feb. 15, 24 —
26, 28 — Apr. 10, 12 — May 22,
24 — 31, June 10, 11, 13 — July
13, 15 — 26, Sept. 2 — 15, 17 —
23, 25 — Oct. 8, 10, 11, 27 —
Nov. 9, 11 — Dec. 9, 11 — 15,
17 — 31.

1942   Jan. 1 — Feb. 10, 12 — 20, 22 —
26, 28 — Mar. 29, 31 — Apr. 2,
4 — 17, 19 — 30.

Santo Domingo

EL CARIBE. d. est. Apr. 14, 1948.
Note: Suspended publication Apr.
28 — Nov. 1, 1965.

CLU
1965 Feb. 18 – Mar. 7, 9 – Apr. 15,
17 – 28, Nov. 2 – 20, 22, 30 –
Dec. 31.
1966 Jan. 1+.
CSt – H
1966 Jan. 29+.
Micro (N)
1964 Dec. 14.
1965 Jan. 6 – 9, Feb. 18, Mar. 1,
Apr. 10, 11, 13 – 15, 17, 22, 23,
Nov. 2 – 4, 6, 7, 13, 18, 20,
22 – 27, 29, Dec. 2, 6 – 9, 13,
14, 16, 18, 21 – 25, 27, 28, 30,
31.
1966 Jan. 1, 3 – 8, 10 – 14, 17 – 21,
24, 26, 27, 31, Feb. 8 – 11.
DLC
Micro (P)
1948 Apr. 14 – May 14, 16 – June 5,
7 – Dec. 31.
1950 Jan. 1 – July 30, Aug. 1 – Oct.
21, 23 – Dec. 31.
1951 Jan. 1 – Mar. 26, 28 – Dec. 31.
1952 – 1953 Jan. 1 – Dec. 31.
1954 Jan. 1 – May 21, 24 – 28, 31 –
Aug. 7, 9 – Oct. 2, 4 – 8, 10 –
15, 17, 19 – 22, 25, 26, 28, 29,
Nov. 1 – Dec. 10, 12 – 17,
19 – 31.
1955 Jan. 1 – 12, 14 – 28, 30, Feb. 1,
2, 4 – 12, 14 – 26, 28 – Mar. 20,
22 – 28, 30 – Apr. 1, 3 – 7, 9 –
16, 18 – 29, May 1 – 6, 8, 10 –
July 28, 30 – Aug. 1, 5, 6, 7, 9,
11, 13, 16, 17, 19 – Oct. 14, 16,
18, 20 – 28, 30, 31, Nov. 2 –
9, 11 – 26, 28, 30 – Dec. 10,
12 – 16, 18, 19, 21 – 26, 31.
1956 Jan. 1+.
FU
Micro (P)
1948 Nov. 1 – Dec. 31.
1960 July 1 – Dec. 31.
1961 Jan. 1+.
Micro (N)
1948 Apr. 14 – Dec. 31.
1949 – 1952 Jan. 1 – Dec. 31.
1953 Jan. 1 – June 28, 30 – Dec. 31.

1954 – 1959 Jan. 1 – Dec. 31.
1960 Jan. 1 – Oct. 7, 9 – Dec. 31.
1961 – 1964 Jan. 1 – Dec. 31.
1965 Jan. 1 – Feb. 24, 26 – Mar. 7,
9 – Apr. 19, 31.
ICRL
Micro (P)
1948 Apr. 14 – Dec. 31.
1949 – 1955 Jan. 1 – Dec. 31.
(P) & (N)
1956 Jan. 1+.
PrU
1962 Sept. 13 – Oct. 7, Nov. 3 –
Dec. 31.
1963 Jan. 1 – Mar. 8, 26 – June 18,
24 – July 22, 24 – 28, 30 – Sept.
25, 27, 29 – Oct. 7, 15 – Nov.
4, 11, 13 – Dec. 31.
1964 Jan. 1 – Mar. 26, 28 – Apr. 20,
May 1 – 30, June 1 – July 30,
Aug. 1 – Oct. 30, Nov. 1 – Dec.
31.
1965 Jan. 1 – Mar. 7, 9 – Apr. 14,
16 – 26, Nov. 2 – 13, 15 – 20,
22, 30 – Dec. 4, 6 – 11, 13 –
18, 20 – 31.
1966 Jan. 1+.

DIALOGO. w. est. July 18, 1965.
CSt – H
Micro (N)
1965 July 18 – Aug. 29.

DIARIO DEL COMERCIO. d. est. June 2,
1930.
DLC
1938 May 13, June 21, 23, 24, 27 –
30, July 1 – 15, 17 – 22, 24,
26 – 29, 31 – Aug. 19, 21 – 26,
28 – Sept. 4, 6 – 11, 15 – Oct.
3, 5, 7 – 13, 15 – Nov. 8, 10 –
23, 25 – Dec. 22, 24 – 31.
1939 Jan. 1 – 26, 28 – Feb. 14, 16 –
Mar. 5, 7 – 9, 12 – 23, 25 – Apr.
14, 16 – 23, 26 – May 7, 14 –
23, 25 – 29, 31, June 1, 3, 4, 6,
8 – July 13, 15 – 25, 27 – 31,
Aug. 3 – Sept. 21, 23, 24, 28 –
Oct. 1, 3 – Nov. 22, 25 – 29,

Dec. 1−5, 8−17, 19−21,
23−26, 28−31.

1940   Jan. 1−31, Feb. 2, 4−6, 8,
10−22, 24−Mar. 3, 5−20,
26−Apr. 4, 6−14, 16, 17, 19−
22, 24−26, 28, 29, May 1, 2,
4−9, 12−22, 25−27, 29, June
1, 2, 4, 5, 7, 26−July 3, 5−14,
17−29, 31−Aug. 6, 9−11,
13−15, 18−26, 28, 30−Sept.
30, Oct. 3, 5−17, 20, 23−25,
27, 29, 31−Nov. 7, 10−12, 14,
16−20, 22−25, 27−Dec. 5,
7−25, 27−29, 31.

1941   Jan. 2−8, 10−12, 15−29,
31, Feb. 2−6, Mar. 3−11, 13,
14, 16−25, 27−Apr. 7, 9−
28, 30−May 19, 21−June 19,
21−July 18, 20−Aug. 21, 23,
24, 26−28, 30−Sept. 23,
26−Oct. 22, 25−31, Nov.
2−17, 20, 21.

EL DOMINGO.
See *Nuevo domingo*.

DOMINICAN HERALD; THE CARIBBEAN COURIER. w. est. May 4, 1958.
Note: In English.
FU
1958   May 4−11.

EL ECO DE LA OPINION. w., d. est. Mar. 19, 1879.
Note: Periodicity Mar. 19, 1879−
1885, weekly; after 1885, daily.
CU−B
Micro (P)
1883   June 8.

JUVENTUD. w., bw. est. Dec. 12, 1940.
CtY
1940   Dec. 19.
1941   Jan. 2−Mar. 28, Apr. 18−June
6, 22−27, July 11−Dec. 26.
1942   Jan. 2−Feb. 27, Mar. 13−27,
Apr. 10, May 29, July 31, Sept.
25−Oct. 23, Dec. 12−31.
1943   Jan. 22, Mar. 26−June 22,
Aug. 16−27, Oct. 24−Dec. 12.

1944   Jan. 28−May 31, Oct. 24.
1945   Sept. 28.

LISTIN DIARIO. d. est. Aug. 1, 1889.
Note: Title *Listín diario marítimo*,
Aug. 1, 1889−[1925]; *Listín diario*,
after 1926. Suspended publication
Sept. 4−9, 1930; June 14, 1942−
1963; Apr. 26−Nov. 1, 1965.
CLU
1963   Aug. 30−Dec. 31.
1964   Jan. 1−Dec. 31.
1965   Jan. 2−Apr. 24, Nov. 3−
Dec. 31.
1966   Jan. 1+.
CSt−H
1964   Nov. 3−Dec. 31.
1965   Jan. 2−29, 31−Feb. 8, 10−
Mar. 22, 24, 25, 27−Apr. 24,
Nov. 3−5, 23−Dec. 24, 27,
29, 31.
1966   Jan. 1+.
Micro (N)
1965   Jan. 30, Apr. 26, Nov. 2−8,
13−15, 22−24, 26, 29, 30,
Dec. 8, 18, 25, 28, 30.
1966   Jan. 14, 17−21, 24−28, 31,
Feb. 1, 3, 4, 7−11, 18.
DLC
1926   Jan. 2−July 6, 8−Sept. 18,
20−25, 27−Dec. 31.
1927   Jan. 1−15, 17, 19−May 4,
6−8, 10−Aug. 22, 28, 30−
Sept. 6, 8, 9, 11−13, 15−18,
20−Nov. 2, 4−Dec. 8, 10−31.
1928   Jan. 1−Apr. 5, 7−16, 18−
Oct. 3, 5, 7−18, 20−Dec. 31.
1929   Jan. 1−Oct. 17, 19−Dec. 31.
1930   Jan. 1−Aug. 26, 28−Dec. 31.
1931   Jan. 1−Dec. 31.
1932   Jan. 1−19, 27−Sept. 4, 6−
Dec. 8, 10−31.
1933   Jan. 1−4, 6−Feb. 21, Mar. 1,
8−Apr. 30, May 2−July 9,
11−Dec. 31.
1934   Jan. 1−Nov. 26, 28−Dec. 31.
1935   Jan. 1−15, 23−Dec. 31.
1936   Jan. 1−7, 15−Dec. 31.

1937 – 1938   Jan. 1 – Dec. 31.
1939   Jan. 1 – May 6, 8 – 13, 15, 16,
18, 19, 22 – 26, 29 – June 6, 8 –
10, 12, 13, 21 – 24, 26 – 28,
30, July 1, 3 – 7, 10 – 12, 14,
15, 17 – 19, 21, 22, 24, 25, 27 –
29, 31 – Aug. 5, 7 – 12, 14 – 19,
21 – 26, 28 – Sept. 1, 4 – 9, 11,
12, 14 – 16, 18 – 23, 25 – 30,
Oct. 2, 3, 5, 6, 9 – 13, 16 – 21,
23 – 28, 30 – Nov. 6, 9 – 11,
14 – 18, 20 – 25, 27 – Dec. 2,
4 – 9, 11 – 16, 18 – 22, 25 – 27,
29, 30.
1940   Jan. 2 – 8, 10 – 16, 18, 20 –
30, Feb. 4, 7, 9 – 23, 25 –
Mar. 10, 14 – Apr. 4, 7, 11, 12,
14 – 19, 21 – 30, May 2, 3, 5 –
Nov. 26, 28, Dec. 1, 5 – 31.
1941   Jan. 1 – 9, 11 – 22, 24 – Apr.
20, 22 – July 13, 15 – Sept. 2,
4 – 11, 13 – Dec. 31.
1942   Jan. 2 – June 2, 7, 11 – 15, 21,
28.
Micro (P)
1966   Jan. 1+.
FU
Micro (N)
1909   Dec. 23 – 31.
1910   Jan. – Apr. 17, 19 – 21, 23 –
May 10, 12, 14, 15, 19 – 24,
26 – June 24, July 1, 3, 5 – 8,
10 – 22, 24 – Nov. 1, 3 – 7, 9 –
21, 23, 25 – Dec. 8, 10 – 15, 17,
18, 20 – 26.
1911   Jan. 5 – 30, Feb. 1 – Apr. 10,
12 – 17, 19 – May 17, 19 – 21,
23 – July 10, 13 – 17, 20 – Aug.
8, 10 – Sept. 20, 22 – Oct. 19,
21 – Nov. 19, 21 – Dec. 31.
1912   Jan. 1, 2, 4 – Feb. 29, Mar.
2 – 5, 7, 9 – 15, 17 – May 23,
25 – July 26, 31 – Aug. 8, 10 –
12, 14 – Sept. 23, 25 – Oct. 6,
8 – Nov. 10, 13 – Dec. 31.
1913   Jan. 1 – 17, 19 – 26, 28 – Feb. 9,
13 – 28, Mar. 2, 3, 5 – July 18,
20 – Nov. 4, 7 – Dec. 31.

1914   Jan. 1 – 13, 15 – 26, 28 – Feb.
23, 25 – Apr. 13, 15 – 26, 28 –
May 31, June 2 – July 19, 21 –
Oct. 27, 29 – Nov. 26, 28 – Dec.
17, 19 – 31.
1915   Jan. 1 – 3, 29 – Feb. 11, 13 –
21, 23 – June 6, 8 – Aug. 12,
14 – 19, 21 – Sept. 8, 10 – Oct.
4, 6 – 14, 16 – 21, 23 – 28,
30 – Dec. 8, 27 – 31.
1916   Jan. 1 – 9, 11 – 25, 27 – 30,
Feb. 1 – 4, 6 – 13, 15 – Mar. 6,
8 – 16, 18 – 29, Apr. 1 – 4, 6 –
16, 19 – May 13, 15 – 28, 30,
June 1, 3 – 5, 7 – 13, 15 – 29,
July 1 – 27, Aug. 10 – 29, 31,
Oct. 8, 10 – 18, 21 – 26, 28 –
Nov. 9, 11 – Dec. 31.
1917   Jan. 1 – 21, 23 – May 6, 8 –
July 12, 14 – Nov. 2, 4 – 27,
29 – Dec. 16, 18 – 28, 30, 31.
1918   Jan. 1 – 31, Mar. 14 – 17, 19,
21, 23 – May 8, 16 – 28, June
6, 8 – July 10, 25 – 28, 30, 31,
Aug. 22 – 27, 29 – Sept. 4,
13 – 29, Oct. 2, 4 – 11, 13 – 24,
26 – Nov. 6, 8 – 24, 26 – Dec.
8, 10 – 26, 29, 30.
1919   Jan. 1, 2, 4 – 8, 11 – 30, Feb.
1 – 18, 20, 26, 28 – Apr. 4, 6 –
13, 16 – 24, 26 – 28, May 1 – 4,
7, 8, 10 – 14, 17 – June 1, 4 –
12, 14 – 18, 20 – 29, July 2 –
6, 10 – Aug. 19, 21 – Sept. 3,
5 – 15, 17 – Oct. 2, 4 – 7, 10,
14 – 30, Nov. 2, 4 – 21, 23, 24,
26, 28 – 30, Dec. 4, 6, 18 – 28,
30, 31.
1920   Jan. 8, 10 – 12, 16, 18, 19, 21,
22, 24 – 29, 31, Feb. 1, 3, 5,
12 – 25, 27 – Mar. 10, 12 – 15,
17 – 22, 25 – Apr. 2, 4 – 12, 14 –
20, 22 – May 2, 4 – 12, 14 – 17,
19 – 21, 23 – June 13, 15 – 28,
July 2 – 4, 7, 10, 11, 13, 15, 16,
18, 20 – 29, 31 – Sept. 26, 28,
30 – Oct. 3, 5 – 10, 12, Nov. 2,
3, 5 – 12, 14 – 28, 30 – Dec. 2,

4−6, 8−27, 29−31.

1921   Jan. 7−30, Feb. 1−24, 26−
Mar. 22, 24−May 1, 3−10,
12, 14−June 19, 21−Aug. 16,
18−Sept. 11, 13−18, 20−Oct.
10, 12−Dec. 11, 13, 15, 17−31.

1922   Jan. 1−June 9, 11−Nov. 6,
14−Dec. 31.

1923   Jan. 1−Apr. 9, 17−May 6, 8−
14, 22−June 4, 6−Sept. 25,
29−Oct. 29, 31−Dec. 31.

1924   Jan. 1−Feb. 24, 26−Mar. 21,
23−June 26, 28−30, Nov. 2,
4−16, 25−Dec. 12, 14, 15,
17−21, 23−31.

1925   Jan. 1, 3, 5−10, 12−17, 19−
24, 26−31, Feb. 2, 10−14,
16−28, Mar. 2−7, 9−14, 16,
18−21, 23−28, 30−Apr. 4,
6−11, 13−18, 20−25, 27−
May 2, 4−9, 11−16, 18−23,
25, 27−30, June 1−6, 8−13,
15−20, 22−27, 29−July 4,
6−11, 14−16, 18, 20, 22−25,
27−Aug. 8, 11−15, 17−22,
24−29, 31−Sept. 5, 7−12,
14−19, 21−26, 28−Oct. 3,
5−10, 12−17, 19−24, 26,
Nov. 3−5, 7, 9, 17−21, 23−
28, 30−Dec. 5, 7−12, 14−19,
21−26, 28−31.

1926   Jan. 2, 4−9, 11−16, 18−23,
25−30, Feb. 1−6, 8−13,
15−20, 22−27, Mar. 1−6,
8−20, 22−27, 29−Apr. 3,
5−7, 9, 12−17, 19−22, 24,
26−May 1, 3−8, 10−15, 17−
22, 24−June 5, 7−12, 14−
19, 21−26, 28−July 3, 5−
10, 12−17, 19−24, 26−29,
31, Aug. 2−7, 9−14, 16−21,
23−28, 30−Sept. 4, 6−11,
13−18, 20−25, 27−31, Oct.
2, 5−9, 11−16, 18−23, 25−
30, Nov. 1−6, 8−13, 15−20,
22−27, 29−Dec. 4, 6−11,
13−17, 21−25, 27−31.

1927   Jan. 3−8, 10−15, 17−22,

24−29, 31−Feb. 5, 7−12,
14−19, 21−26, 28−Mar. 5.
7−12, 14−19, 21−26, 28−
Apr. 2, 4−9, 11−16, 18−23,
25−30, May 2−4, 6, 7, 10−
14, 16−21, 23−28, 30−June
4, 6−11, 13−18, 20−25, 27−
29, July 1, 2, 4−9, 11−16,
18−23, 25−30, Aug. 1−6,
8−13, 15−20, 22, 30−Sept.
3, 5, 6, 8, 9, 12, 13, 15−17,
20−24, 26−Oct. 1, 3−8,
10−15, 17−22, 24−29, 31−
Nov. 5, 7−12, 14−26, 28, 29,
Dec. 7−10, 12−17, 19−24,
26−31.

1928   Jan. 2−7, 9−14, 16−21, 23−
28, 30−Feb. 4, 6−11, 13−
18, 20−25, 27−Mar. 3, 5−
10, 12−17, 19−24, 27−31,
Apr. 2−5, 7, 9−14, 16, 18−
21, 23−28, 30−May 5, 7−12,
14−19, 21−26, 28−June 2,
4−9, 11−16, 18−23, 25−30,
July 2−7, 9−14, 16−21, 23−
28, 30−Aug. 4, 6−11, 13−18,
20−25, 27−Sept. 1, 3−8, 10−
15, 17−22, 24−29, 31−Oct.
5, 8−13, 15−20, 22−27, 29−
Nov. 3, 5−10, 12−17, 19−24,
26−Dec. 1, 3−8, 10−15, 17−
22, 24−29, 31.

1929   Jan. 1−5, 7−12, 14−19, 21−
26, 28−Feb. 2, 4−9, 11−16,
18−23, 25−Mar. 2, 4−9, 11−
16, 18−23, 25−Apr. 6, 8−
13, 15−20, 22−27, 29−May
4, 6−11, 13−18, 20−25, 27−
June 1, 3−8, 10−15, 17−22,
24−29, July 1−6, 8−13, 15−
20, 22−27, 29−Aug. 3, 5−
10, 12−24, 26−31, Sept. 2−7,
9−14, 16−28, 30−Oct. 5,
7−12, 14−19, 21−26, 28−
Nov. 2, 4−9, 11−16, 18−23,
26−30, Dec. 2−7, 9−14, 16−
21, 23, 24, 26−31.

1930   Jan. 1−4, 6−11, 13−18, 20−

25, 27 — Feb. 1, 3 — 8, 10 — 15,
17 — 22, 24 — Mar. 1, 3 — 8, 10 —
15, 17 — 22, 24 — 29, 31 — Apr. 5,
7 — 12, 14 — 26, 28 — May 3,
5 — 10, 12 — 17, 19 — 24, 26 —
31, June 2 — 7, 9 — 14, 16 — 21,
23 — 28, 30 — July 5, 7 — 12,
14 — 19, 21 — 26, 28 — Aug. 2,
4 — 9, 11 — 16, 18 — 23, 25 — 30,
Sept. 1 — 3, 10 — 27, 29 — Oct.
4, 6 — 11, 13 — 18, 20 — 25,
27 — Nov. 1, 3 — 8, 10 — 15,
17 — 22, 24 — 29, Dec. 1 — 6,
8 — 13, 15 — 20, 22 — 27, 29 — 31.

1931　Jan. 1 — 3, 5 — 10, 12 — 17, 19 —
24, 26 — 31, Feb. 2 — 7, 9, 10,
12 — 14, 16 — 21, 23 — 28, Mar.
2 — 7, 9 — 14, 16 — 21, 23 — 28,
30 — Apr. 4, 6 — 11, 13 — 18,
20 — 25, 27 — May 2, 4 — 9, 11 —
16, 18 — 23, 25 — 30, June 1 — 6,
8 — 13, 15 — 20, 22 — 27, 29, 30,
July 8 — 11, 13 — 18, 20 — 25,
27 — Aug. 1, 3 — 8, 10 — 15, 17 —
22, 24 — 29, 31 — Sept. 5, 7 — 12,
14 — 19, 21 — 26, 28 — Oct. 3,
5 — 10, 12 — 17, 19 — 24, 26 —
31, Nov. 2 — 7, 9 — 14, 16 — 21,
23 — Dec. 5, 7, 8, 16 — 19, 21 —
26, 28 — 31.

1932　Jan. 1, 2, 4 — 9, 11 — 16, 18 —
23, 25 — 30, Feb. 1 — 6, 8 — 13,
15 — 20, 22 — 27, 29 — Mar. 5,
7 — 12, 14 — 19, 21 — 26, 28 —
Apr. 2, 4 — 9, 11 — 16, 18 — 23,
25 — 30, May 2 — 4, 6, 7, 11 —
14, 16 — 21, 23 — 28, 30 — June
4, 6 — 11, 13 — 18, 20 — 22, 24,
26, 27, 29 — July 2, 4 — 9, 11 —
16, 18 — 23, 25 — 30, Aug. 1 — 6,
8 — 13, 15 — 20, 22 — 27, 29 —
Sept. 3, 5 — 10, 12 — 17, 19 —
24, 26 — Oct. 1, 3 — 8, 10 — 15,
17 — 22, 24 — 29, 31 — Nov. 5,
7 — 12, 14 — 19, 21 — 26, 28 —
Dec. 3, 5 — 10, 12 — 17, 19 — 24,
26 — 31.

1933　Jan. 1 — 7, 9 — 14, 16 — 21, 23 —

28, 30 — Feb. 4, 6 — 11, 13 —
18, 20 — 25, 27 — Mar. 4, 6 —
11, 13 — 18, 20 — 25, 27 — Apr.
1, 3 — 8, 10 — 15, 17 — 22, 24 —
29, May 1 — 6, 8 — 13, 15 — 20,
22 — 27, 29 — June 3, 5 — 10,
12 — 17, 19 — 24, 26 — July 1,
3 — 8, 10 — 15, 17 — 22, 24 — 29,
31 — Aug. 5, 7 — 9, 12, 14 — 19,
21 — 26, 28 — Sept. 6, 8, 9,11 —
16, 18 — 23, 25 — 31, Oct. 2 —
7, 9 — 14, 16 — 21, 23 — 28, 30 —
Nov. 4, 6 — 11, 13, 15 — 18,
20 — 25, 27 — Dec. 2, 4 — 9, 11 —
16, 18 — 23, 25 — 30.

1934　Jan. 1 — 6, 8 — 13, 15 — 20, 22 —
27, 29 — Feb. 10, 12 — 17, 19 —
24, 26 — Mar. 3, 5 — 10, 12 — 14,
16, 17, 19, 21 — 24, 26 — 31,
Apr. 2 — 7, 9, 10, 18 — 21, 23 —
28, 30 — May 5, 7 — 12, 14 — 19,
21 — 26, 28 — June 2, 4 — 9,
11 — 16, 18 — 23, 25 — 30.

1935　Jan. 1 — 5, 7 — 12, 14 — 19, 21 —
26, 28 — Feb. 9, 11 — 16, 18 —
23, 25 — Mar. 2, 4 — 9, 11 — 16,
18 — 23, 25 — Apr. 6, 8 — 13.
15 — 20, 22 — 27, 29 — May 4,
6 — 11, 13 — 18, 20 — 25, 27 —
June 1, 3 — 8, 10 — 15, 17 — 22,
24 — 29, July 1 — 6, 8 — 13, 15 —
20, 22 — 27, 29 — Aug. 3, 5 —
10, 12 — 17, 19 — 24, 26 — 31,
Sept. 2 — 7, 9 — 14, 16 — 21,
23 — 28, 30 — Oct. 5, 7 — 12,
14 — 19, 21 — 26, 28 — Nov. 2,
4 — 9, 11 — 16, 18 — 23, 25 — 30,
Dec. 2 — 7, 9, 10, 12 — 16, 18 —
21, 23 — 28, 30, 31.

1936　Jan. 1 — 4, 7 — 11, 13 — 17, 20 —
Feb. 1, 3 — 8, 10 — 15, 17 — 21,
24, 25, 27, Mar. 2 — 5, 7, 9 —
14, 16 — 21, 23 — 27, 30 — Apr.
4, 6 — 11, 13 — 18, 20, 22 — 25,
27 — May 2, 4 — 9, 11 — 16, 18 —
23, 25 — 30, June 1 — 6, 8 — 13,
15, 16, 24 — 27, 29 — July 4, 6 —
11, 13 — 18, 20 — 25, 27 — Aug. 1,

3–8, 10–15, 17–Sept. 5, 7–
12, 14–19, 21, 22, 24, 25, 28,
29, 31–Oct. 3, 5–10, 12–14,
16, 17, 19–29, Nov. 2–7, 9–
14, 16–21, 23–28, 30–Dec.
5, 7–12, 14–19, 21–26, 28–
31.

1937   Jan. 1, 2, 4–9, 11–16, 18–
23, 25–27, 29, 30, Feb. 1–6,
8–13, 15–20, 22–27, Mar.
1–6, 8, 9, 13, 15–20, 22–27,
29–Apr. 3, 5–10, 12–17,
19–24, 26–May 1, 3–8, 10–
15, 17–22, 24–29, 31–June
5, 7–12, 14–19, 21–26, 28–
July 2, 5–10, 12–17, 19–24,
26–31, Aug. 2–7, 9–14, 16–
21, 23–28, 30, Sept. 1–4, 6–
10, 14–18, 20–25, 27–Oct. 2,
4–9, 11–16, 18–23, 25–30,
Nov. 1–6, 8–13, 15–20, 22–
27, 29–Dec. 3, 6–11, 13–
18, 20–23, 25, 27–31.

1938   Jan. 1, 3–8, 10–15, 17–20,
22, 24–29, 31–Feb. 5, 8–
12, 14–16, 18, 19, 22–26,
28–Mar. 2, 4, 5, 7–11, 14–19,
21–26, 28, 29, Apr. 4, 6–19,
11–14, 18–22, 25–30, May
2–7, 9, 10, 18–21, 23–June
4, 6–11, 13–18, 20–25, 27–
July 2, 4–9, 12–16, 18–23,
25–Aug. 6, 8–13, 15–20,
22–Sept. 1, 3, 5–10, 12–17,
19–24, 26, 28–Oct. 1, 3, 4,
12–15, 17–29, 31–Nov. 4,
7–12, 14, 15, 17, 18, 21–26,
28, 29, Dec. 21, 24, 26, 27.

1939   Jan. 11–14, 16–21, 23–28,
30–Feb. 4, 6, 7, 15–-18, 20–
25, 27, 28, Mar. 2–4, 6–11,
14–18, 20, 21, 23–25, 27–
Apr. 1, 3–5, 7, 8, 10, 11, 13–
15, 17, 18, 21, 22, 24–29, May
1–5, 8–11, 13, 15, 16, 18, 19,
22–26, 29–June 5, 8–10, 12,
13, 21–24, 26–28, 30, July 1,
3–7, 10, 11, 13–15, 17–19,

21, 22, 24, 25, 27–29, Aug. 1–
5, 7–19, 22–28, 30–Sept. 1,
4–9, 11, 12, 14–16, 18–23,
25–31, Oct. 2, 3, 11–13, 16–
19, 21, 23–27, 30–Nov. 2, 4,
5, 9–11, 14–18, 20, 21, 29–
Dec. 2, 4–9, 11–16, 18–22,
25–27, 29, 30.

1940   Jan. 2, 3, 10–13, 16, 18–20,
22–26, 29, Feb. 7, 9, 10, 12–
17, 19–23, 26–Mar. 2, 4, 6–
8, 11, 12, 14–17, 19–25, 27–
30, Apr. 1–8, 11, 12, 15–19,
22–30, May 2, 3, 5–11, 13–
25, 27–June 1, 3–8, 10–15,
17–19, 21, 22, 24–29, July
1–6, 8–13, 15–20, 23–27,
29, 30, Aug. 1–3, 5–10, 12–
17, 19–24, 26–31, Sept. 2–7,
9–14, 16–21, 23–28, 30–
Oct. 4, 6–13, 15–19, 21–
26, 28–Nov. 2, 4–9, 11–16,
18, 20–23, 25–30, Dec. 2, 3,
5–14, 16–21, 23–28, 30, 31.

1941   Jan. 1–4, 6–9, 11, 13–17,
20–25, 27–Feb. 1, 3, 5–8,
10–15, 17–22, 24–Mar. 1,
3–8, 10–15, 17, 18, 26–29,
31, Apr. 1, 9–12, 14–19, 22–
26, 28, 30–May 10, 12, 13,
21–24, 26–June 7, 9–14,
16–21, 23–27, 30–July 5,
7–12, 15, 16, 18–19, 21–23,
25, 26, 28–Aug. 8, 11–16,
18–23, 26–30, Sept. 1–6, 8,
10, 11, 13, 15–19, 21–23,
25–27, 29, Oct. 2, 4, 6–11,
13, 14, 17–25, 27, 28, 30, 31,
Nov. 3–7, 9, 10, 12–15, 17–
22, 24–29, Dec. 1–6, 8–13,
15–20, 22–27, 29, 30.

1942   Jan. 14–17, 19–24, 26–Feb.
3, 11–14, 16–21, 23–28, Mar.
2, 4–9, 12–14, 17, 18, 20–
25, 27–Apr. 11, 13–15, 17,
18, 20–25, 27–May 2, 4–9,
11–16, 18–23, 25–30, June
1–6, 8–13, 15.

LNT—MA
  1938   Apr. 18, 19, 21, 22, 24.
MWA
  1936   Oct. 25.
NcD
  1930   Feb. 2, Mar. 8, 20, 28, Apr. 1, 2.
  1931   July 6, 13, 20.
PrU
  1963   Oct. 7, 10−21, 29, Nov. 1−20,
         26−30, Dec. 2−12, 19.
  1964   Jan. 7, 8, 11, 14, 15, 19, 20, 22,
         25−28, 31−Feb. 2, 8−10,
         14−18, 21−26, Mar. 7−17,
         22−26, 28, Apr. 2−6, 8−24,
         27, May 14, June 6, 10−17,
         July 1−8, Aug. 8, 13−26,
         Sept. 17−29, Oct. 8, 9.

LA NACION. d. est. Feb. 14, 1940.
    Note: Suspended publication 1960.
  CSt
  1946   Dec. 23.
  CSt−H
    Micro (N)
  1965   Jan. 1+.
  CtY
  1944   Feb. 23, 26−Apr. 27, 29−May
         7, 9−19, 21−June 8, 10−July
         1, 3, Aug. 10, 12−Dec. 31.
  1945   Jan. 1−16, 19−Feb. 19, May
         10−11, 13−17, Aug. 4, 6,
         Sept. 3, Oct. 1.
  1946   Jan. 7, 8, Dec. 28.
  1949   June 23.
  DLC
  1940   July 1−28, 30−Aug. 4, 6−
         11, 13−18, 20−Sept. 1, 3−8,
         10−15, 17−22, 24−29, Oct.
         1−6, 8−20, 22−27, 29−Nov.
         10, 12−17, 19−24, 26−Dec.
         3, 5, 6, 14, 15, 17−22, 24−
         29, 31.
  1941   Jan. 1−5, 7−19, 21−Feb. 2,
         4−Sept. 30, Oct. 8−Dec. 31.
         Special edition: Feb. 19.
  1942   Jan. 1−Mar. 17, Apr. 7−
         July 6.
  1945   Apr. 1−May 9, 11, 12, 14, 15,

         17−28, 30−June 1, 3−July
         28, 30−Oct. 25, Nov. 1−8,
         10−Dec. 31.
  1946   Jan. 1−Mar. 7, 10−19, 21,
         23, 25−Apr. 28, 30−May 30,
         June 1, 3−22, 24−Dec. 31.
  1947   Jan. 1−Apr. 11, 13−28, May
         10−22, 24−June 30.
  1948   Jan. 1−11, 13−Dec. 31.
  1949−1953   Jan. 1−Dec. 31.
  1954   Jan. 1−May 2, 6−June 1, 3−
         8, 10−11, 13−July 10, 12−
         18, 21, 22, 24−26, 29, 30, Aug.
         1−23, 30−Sept. 21, 23−Oct.
         11, 13, 15−Nov. 12, 14−29,
         Dec. 1−31.
  1955   Jan. 1, 3−14, 16−21, 23−27,
         30−Feb. 28, Mar. 3−20, 22−
         29, 31, Apr. 1, 3−6, 8−15,
         17−25, 27−May 2, 4, 5, 7−
         12, 14−25, 29−June 6, 8−
         19, 23−July 4, 7−27, 29−
         Aug. 3, 5, 6, 21−Sept. 12,
         15−27, 29−Oct. 10, 12, 13,
         15−18, 22−Nov. 11, 14−23,
         25, 27−Dec. 13, 15, 16, 24−
         27, 29, 30.
  1956   Jan. 1, 2, 5−13, 15−25, 27,
         29−31, Feb. 2−7, 9−11, 13−
         18, 21−Oct. 5, 9−Dec. 2,
         4−31.
  1957   Jan. 1−18, 20−24, 30−Feb.
         1, 5−Mar. 4, 6, 8−24, 26−30.
  1960   Sept. 1−13, 15, 16 18−28,
         30, Oct. 1, 3−7, 9−Oct. 31.
  FU
  1944   Jan. 1−Feb. 3, 5−13, 15−
         Mar. 2, 4−Apr. 10, 12−19, 21,
         22, 24−June 28, 30−Aug. 1,
         3−Sept. 15, 17−Oct. 12, 14−
         24, 26−Nov. 5, 7, 8, 10, 11,
         13−Dec. 31.
  1945   Mar. 1−3, 11, 15−17, 19−
         25, 27−Apr. 30, May 4−11,
         14−19, July 1−15, 17−30,
         Aug. 7−15, 18, 21, 23, 26−
         Sept. 3, 5−14, 17−23, 25−30.
  1946   Jan. 1, 2, 5, 7, 9−11, 13, 19,

22 — 26, 28, 30 — Feb. 2, 7, 11 —
16, 18, 19, 23 — 25.

1950   June 26 — Oct. 23, 29 — Dec. 31.
1951   Jan. 1 — Feb. 25, Dec. 24 — 30.
1952   Jan. 1 — May 17, 19 — June 1,
        8 — Oct. 1, 3 — Dec. 11, 13 — 31.
1953   Jan. 1 — Mar. 9.
1954   Jan. 1 — 18, 20 — 26, 28, 30, 31,
        Feb. 3 — 8, 10, 15 — Mar. 8,
        10 — 12, 14 — 26, 28 — Apr. 2,
        4 — 15, 18 — 26, 28, 30 — May 10,
        12 — 31, June 2 — 6, 8 — 14,
        21 — Dec. 31.
1955   Jan. 1 — Feb. 27, Mar. 1 —
        Dec. 31.
1956   Jan. 1 — Mar. 18, 26 — Apr. 9,
        11 — July 15, 23 — 31, [Aug. 1 —
        31], [Oct. 1 — 31].
1957   Jan. 1 — 3, 5 — Feb. 15, 17 —
        26, Mar. 1 — 6, 8, 9, 11 — 21, 23,
        24, 26, 28 — 31, Apr. 3, 11 — 14,
        16 — 24, 26, 28 — 30, [May 1 —
        31], June 2, 3, 5, 8 — 22, 24 —
        28, July 6, 8 — 10, 13, 18, 21 —
        23, 25, 29, Aug. 1 — 3, 5 — 30,
        Sept. 1 — 13, 15 — 17, 20 — Nov.
        14, 22 — Dec. 31.
1958   Jan. 1 — Mar. 7, 13 — Oct. 15,
        18 — 23, 25 — 31, Nov. 2, 4 —
        Dec. 31.
1961   Jan. 1 — Sept. 21, 23 — Nov. 9,
        Dec. 1 — 31.
1962   Jan. 1 — 27, 29 — Feb. 16, 18 —
        July 10, 12 — Dec. 19, 21 — 31.
1963   Jan. 2, 4 — 23, 25 — Feb. 5, 10,
        11, 17 — June 30.

LNT — MA

1941   Feb. 19.

NN

Micro (P) & (N)
1942   Nov. 2, 3, 6 — 30.
1943   Mar. 20 — Apr. 22, 24 — June 11,
        15 — 27, 29 — July 3, 11, 13 — 17,
        Aug. 9 — 15, 23 — 27, 29 — Sept.
        10, 12 — 16, 18 — 28, Oct. 7 —
        Dec. 31.
1944 — 1945   Jan. 1 — Dec. 31.

EL NACIONAL. w. est. Jan. 10, 1874.
    CU — B
    Micro (P)
    1876   July 6.

NUEVO DOMINGO. w. est. 1924.
    Note: Succeeded *El Domingo*.
    DLC
    1952   Jan. 20 — Feb. 3, 17 — Apr. 13,
            Aug. 31 — Sept. 21, Oct. 5,
            26 — Dec. 31.
    1953   Jan. 1 — May 17, July 26, Aug.
            9, 23 — Sept. 13, 27 — Dec.
    1954   Jan. 4 — 18, Feb. 28 — Mar. 28,
            Oct. 17 — 21, Nov. 14 — Dec. 5.

LA OPINION. d. est. Nov. 25, 1923.
    DLC
    1940   June 3 — 15, July 22 — Aug. 3,
            Oct. 7 — 12, 21 — 23, 24 — Dec.
            7, 15 — 31.
    1941   Jan. 1 — 19, 26 — Feb. 16, 23,
            25 — 27, Apr. 1 — 14, 16 — May
            13, 15 — 26, 28 — Dec. 3, 5 — 31.
    1942   Jan. 1 — 4, 11 — 18, 25 — Feb.
            26, 28 — Mar. 3, 5 — 30, Apr.
            1 — 18.
    1946   July 1 — 15, 17 — Dec. 31.
    LNT — MA
    1938   [Aug. 15 — Dec. 31.]
    1939   [Jan. 1 — Dec. 31.]
    1940   [Jan. 1 — Sept. 28.]
    NcD
    1929   Dec. 26.
    1930   Jan. 28, Mar. 1, 5, 8, 26, July
            6.

PRENSA LIBRE. d.
    CSt — H
    1964   Oct. 27, 28, Nov. 3 — 5, 14 —
            21, 23, Dec. 3 — 9, 12 — 18,
            21 — 30.
    1965   Jan. 2 — 4, 7, 8, 11, 12, 14 — Mar.
            20, 22 — Apr. 15, 19 — 23.

SOL. w. est. 1868.
    MWA
    1870   Jan. 6.

EL SUFRAGIO. w. est. Sept. 19, 1878.
    CU — B
    Micro (P)
    1878   Oct. 14.

LA TRIBUNA. d. est. Aug. 23, 1932.
DLC
    1941   Apr. 29.

ECUADOR

Ambato

NUEVO RUMBO. w. est. Aug. 25, 1935.
    Note: Succeeded *El Tungurahua.*
DLC
    1935   Aug. 25 – Sept. 22.

EL TUNGURAHUA. w. est. Apr. 13,
1935.
    Note: Succeeded by *Nuevo rumbo.*
DLC
    1935   Apr. 13 – Aug. 11.

Bahía de Caráquez

EL GLOBO. d. est. Apr. 1, 1911.
DLC
    1941   July 3, Dec. 18, 19, 21.
    1942   Jan. 1, 2, 4 – 9, 12, 19 – Feb. 10,
          12 – 27, Apr. 1 – 3, 5 – 17, 20,
          27, 29 – May 13, 15 – June 22,
          24 – 29, July 1 – 13, 16 – Aug.
          1, 3 – 10, 12 – 29, 31 – Sept.
          4, 6 – 11, 14, 16, 17, 19 – 22, 27.

Cuenca

EL MERCURIO. d. est. Oct. 22, 1924.
DLC
    1940   Nov. 3.
    1942   Feb. 5.

Guayaquil

EL ARIETE. w. est. May 12, 1838.
CtY
    1838   May 12 – June 1.

LA AURORA. w. est. May 4, 1826.
    Note: Ceased publication Feb. 1,
    1827.
CtY
    1827   Feb. 1.

LA BALANZA. w. est. Oct. 5, 1839.
    Note: Removed to Quito, Jan. 23,
    1841; returned to Guayaquil, May 27,
    1841. Ceased publication Sept.
    25, 1841.
CtY
    1839   Oct. 5 – Dec. 28.
    1840   Jan. 4 – Dec. 26.
    1841   Jan. 2 – 22, May 28 – Sept. 25.

EL CHANDUY. irr. est. June 19, 1839.
CtY
    1839   June 19 – Oct. 23.

EL COLOMBIANO. w. est. Aug. 10.
1829.
    Note: Suspended publication Nov.
    25 – Dec. 9, 1830.
DLC
    1832   Sept. 27.
    1833   Mar. 28.

CORREO DEL PERU. w. est. Feb. 11,
1899.
MWA
    1899   Feb. 25.

DIARIO DEL PUEBLO. d. est. 1928.
DLC
    1928   Nov. 30 – Dec. 3.

DIARIO ILUSTRADO. d. est. May 24,
1913.
DLC
    1918   Jan. 1 – Mar. 30.
    1920   Jan. 2 – Mar. 31, July 1 – Sept.
          30.

EL ECUATORIANO. w., d. est. July 4,
1903.
    Note: Periodicity July 4, 1903 –
    Sept. 30, 1904, weekly; Oct. 1,
    1904 – Oct. 15, 1917, daily. Ceased
    publication Oct. 15, 1917.
CtY
    1912   Feb. 27, Mar. 21 – 23, 26,
          Apr. 6, 9, 15, 16, June 5, 10,
          12, 19.
MWA
    1905   July 19.

ECUATORIANO DEL GUAYAS. est.
  Nov. 28, 1833.
    Note: Ceased publication Sept. 21,
    1838.
  MWA
    1836   Dec. 13.
GACETA DEL GOBIERNO DEL
  ECUADOR. w. est. Sept. 6, 1834.
    Note: Succeeded by *El 21 de junio*.
  DLC
    1835   [June 1 – Dec. 31].
    1836   [Feb. 20 – Nov. 7].
    1837   Oct. 14 – Dec. 30.
    1838 – 1839   Jan. 1 – Dec. 31.
    1840   [Jan. 5 – Dec. 27].
    1841   [Jan. 3 – Dec. 26].
    1842 – 1844   Jan. 1 – Dec. 31.
    1845   Jan. 1 – May 18.
  MWA
    1835   May 23.
EL GRITO DEL PUEBLO.
    See *El Grito del pueblo auténtico*.
EL GRITO DEL PUEBLO AUTENTICO.
  d. est. Jan. 22, 1895.
    Note: Title *El Grito del pueblo*; *diario
    de la mañana- órgano del partido
    radical*, Jan. 22 – Aug. 2, 1895;
    El Grito del pueblo; *diario radical
    de la mañana*, Aug. 3, 1895 – June
    30, 1911; *El Grito del pueblo
    ecuatoriano*, July 1, 1911 – Dec.
    1914; *El Grito del pueblo auténtico*,
    Jan. 1, 1917 – Feb. 23, 1918. Sus-
    pended publication Oct. 5 – 8, 1896;
    and Dec. 1914 – Dec. 31, 1916;
    ceased publication Feb. 23, 1918.
  CtY
    1911   Dec. 27, 29.
    1912   Jan. 19, Feb. 6, 9, 24 – 26,
            Mar. 2, 5 – 7, 25, 29, Apr. 1,
            12, 15, 16, June 5, 12, 19.
  DLC
    1895   Nov. 7, Dec. 17, 20.
    1900   Jan. 1 – Feb. 16, 20 – Mar. 24,
            26 – May 15, 17 – June 17,
            19 – 30.
  MH
    1916   Dec. 24, 30.

EL GUANTE. bw., d. est. Aug. 28, 1910.
    Note: Periodicity Aug. 28, 1910 –
    Feb. 25, 1912, biweekly; after Mar. 1,
    1912, daily. Suspended publication
    Dec. 28, 1911; removed to Riobamba
    Jan. 9, 1912; returned to Guayaquil
    Feb. 5, 1912.
  DLC
    1920   Jan. 1 – Feb. 25, 27, 29 – Mar.
            31.
    1921   July 7, 10 – 29, 31 – Aug. 27,
            29 – Sept. 9, 12 – 30.
    1922   July 1 – Oct. 2, 4 – 13, 15 –
            Nov. 17, 19 – Dec. 31.

LA NACION. 3w., d. est. Mar. 1, 1879.
    Note: Title *La Nación*, Mar. 1, 1879 –
    Apr. 16, 1899; *La Nación*; *diario
    radical*, Apr. 17, 1899 – Mar. 5, 1900;
    La Nación; *diario demócrata,
    industrial, literario y comercial*,
    Mar. 6 – Sept. 1900; *La Nación*,
    Sept. 1900 – Sept. 18, 1906.
    Periodicity Mar. 1, 1879 –
    Jan. 2, 1881, three times a week;
    Jan. 3, 1881 – Sept. 16, 1906, daily.
    Suspended publication Apr. 24 –
    June 6, 1895; Oct. 5 – 13, 1896; and
    Dec. 28, 1900 – July 1, 1901; ceased
    publication Sept. 18, 1906.
  DLC
    1885   Dec. 17.

LA NACION. d. est. 1940.
  DLC
    1950   Sept. 2 – Oct. 21, 23 – 31,
            Nov. 2 – 14, 16 – 24, 26 –
            Dec. 31.
    1951   Jan. 1 – 24, 26 – 29, 31 – Mar.
            8, 10 – May 4, 6 – Aug. 1, 3 –
            Dec. 31.
    1952   Jan. 1 – Mar. 9, 11 – Apr. 15,
            17 – 21, 23 – 27, 29 – June 13,
            15 – July 3, 5 – 20, 22, 29, 31 –
            Sept. 16, 18 – Nov. 27, 29 –
            Dec. 30.
    1953   Jan. 1 – Feb. 20, 22 – Apr. 25,
            Oct. 1 – 7, 9 – Nov. 8, 10 – 12,
            14 – Dec. 10, 13, 15 – 30.

1954   Jan. 1 – 26, Feb. 2, 5 – 7, 9 –
        14, 16 – Mar. 4, 6 – 9, 11, 13,
        15 – 19, 21, 25 – 28, 30.
1955   Apr. 1, 2, 5, 6, 10 – 12, 14 –
        18, 20, 21, 23 – 25, 27 – May 7,
        11, 13 – 23, 26, 28 – June 24,
        26 – 30, July 10, Aug. 16 –
        27, 29 – Sept. 1, 3 – Oct. 3,
        5 – 15, 27 – Nov. 2, 4 – 24,
        27 – Dec. 16, 18 – 31.
1956   Jan. 1, 3 – 20, 22 – Feb. 3, 5 –
        10, 14 – 16, 19 – 22, 24 – Apr.
        18, 20 – June 14, July 13 – Sept.
        5, 8 – Nov. 6, 8 – 19, 21 – Dec.
        16, 19 – 30.
1957   Jan. 1, 3 – 31, Feb. 16 – 28,
        May 16 – July 25, Aug. 15 –
        Sept. 30, Nov. 1 – 14, Dec. 1 –
        29, 31.
1958   Jan. 1 – Feb. 15.

PATRIA. bw. est. May 1, 1917.
  CU
    1917   July 16.
    1918   Aug. 1 – Dec. 15.

EL PATRIOTA DE GUAYAQUIL. w., irr.
  est. May 26, 1821.
    Note: Periodicity May 26, 1821 –
    1826, weekly; 1826 – July 1829,
    irregular. Ceased publication July
    1829.
  CtY
    1821   May 26 – July 28, Aug. 11.
  DLC
    1826   July 29 – Aug. 12.
    1827   Extraordinario: July 8.
  MWA
    1825   Dec. 24.

LA PRENSA. d. est. Aug. 1, 1923.
  DLC
    1928   Dec. 1.
    1942   Mar. 2 – 27, 29 – Apr. 19, 21,
            22, 24 – 29, June 1 – 30, Sept.
            1, 4 – 9, 13 – 30, Dec. 15.
  TxU
    1938   Apr. 5.

PUBLICO.
  MWA
    1826   Dec. 16.
LA RIQUEZA AGRICOLA. est. Jan. 1931.
  LNT – MA
    1932   Apr. 1 – June 30.
    1933   Mar. 1 – Aug. 31.
    1934   Mar. 1 – 31, Sept. 1 – 30, Dec.
            1 – 31.
EL TELEGRAFO. d. est. Feb. 16, 1884.
    Note: Suspended publication July 3,
    1886 – Oct. 13, 1896; July 16 – 26,
    1902; Nov. 8, 1902 – June 30, 1903;
    Sept. 17, 1906 – 1908.
  CU
    1938   Apr. 5.
    1942   Dec. 15.
  DLC
    1920   Jan. 1 – Feb. 12, 14 – Mar. 31.
    1923   Jan. 1 – Mar. 31.
    1924   Feb. 16.
    1939   Jan. 1 – 26, 28 – Apr. 20, 22 –
            May 27, 29 – June 10, 12 –
            Aug. 9, 11 – 16, 18 – Oct. 5,
            8 – Dec. 31.
    1957   Sept. 1 – 18, 20 – 25.
  Micro (P)
    1938 – 1939   Jan. 1 – Dec. 31.
  Micro (P) & (N)
    1927   June 1 – Sept. 22, 24 – Oct. 7,
            9 – Nov. 10, 12 – Dec. 31.
    1928   Jan. 1 – May 16, 25 – June 19,
            29 – Sept. 3, 5 – Nov. 16, 18 –
            Dec. 28, 30, 31.
    1929   Jan. 1 – 11, 13 – 29, 31 – Apr.
            30, May 2 – 26, 28 – July 8,
            10 – Nov. 3, 5 – Dec. 31.
    1930   Jan. 1 – 20, 22 – Feb. 21, 23 –
            Mar. 8, 10, 11, 13 – Aug. 25,
            27 – Dec. 31.
    1931   Jan. 1 – 13, 15 – Feb. 15, 17 –
            19, 21 – Mar. 3, 5 – 22, 24 –
            Sept. 15, 17 – Oct. 8, 10 – Nov.
            2, 4 – 12, 15 – 30, Dec. 2 – 24,
            26 – 30.
    1932   Jan. 1 – Mar. 31.
    1940   Jan. 1 – 29, 31 – Feb. 12, 17 –
            19, 22 – 26, Mar. 1, 3 – Apr.

17, 20 – 22, 24, 27 – May 3, 7 –
17, 23, 24, 30, 31, June 4 – 7,
11 – 21, 29 – Aug. 6, 8 – Nov.
6, 14 – Dec. 6.

1941   Jan. 1 – 15, 17 – Apr. 25, 30 –
June 3, 21, Dec. 31.

1942   Jan. 6 – 9, Feb. 5, 6, Mar. 14 –
Apr. 18, 21 – 27, May 7 – 17,
19 – 27, 30 – June 1, 13 –
July 27, 30 – Aug. 15, 19 – 30,
Sept. 1 – 9, 12 – 18, 20, 22 –
Oct. 5, 7 – 12, 14 – Nov. 26,
28 – Dec. 8, 10 – 22, 30, 31.

1943   Jan. 1 – 5, 13 – 29, 31 – Feb.
2, 10 – 16, 18 – 20, 22 – Mar.
9, 17 – 23, Apr. 1 – 30, May
5 – 11, 13 – 18, 20 – June 1, 4,
16 – 23, 25 – July 23, 25 – 27,
Aug. 4 – 17, 25 – Sept. 1, 3 –
12, 14 – Nov. 23, Dec. 8 – 14,
17, 22, 23, 25 – 31.

1944   Jan. 1 – 4, 6 – 8, 10 – Feb. 1,
3 – Mar. 11, 13 – July 4, 12 –
25, Aug. 3 – Sept. 19, Oct. 5 –
24, Nov. 15 – 28, Dec. 6 – 19,
27 – 31.

1945   Jan. 1 – 5, 7 – 15, 17 – Feb. 21,
23 – Apr. 6, 8 – May 27, 29 –
June 14, 16 – July 18, 20 – 26,
28 – Aug. 14, 22 – Sept. 1, 3 –
11, 19 – 29, Oct. 1 – 3, 5 – Nov.
20, 28 – Dec. 31.

1946   Jan. 1 – Dec. 31.

1947   Jan. 1 – Sept. 21, 23 – Nov. 16,
25 – Dec. 31.

1948   Jan. 1 – Nov. 1, 3 – Dec. 31.

1949   Jan. 1 – Nov. 18, 20 – Dec. 31.

1950   Jan. 1 – 16, 18 – June 20, 22 –
July 14, 16 – Sept. 27, 29 – Nov.
6, 12, 15, 18 – Dec. 19, 24.

1951   Jan. 1 – Mar. 15, 17 – Sept. 25,
Oct. 3 – 9, 17 – Dec. 31.

1952   Jan. 1, 3 – Feb. 17, 19 – Apr.
1, 3 – June 29, July 1 – Nov.
16, 18 – Dec. 31.

1953   Jan. 1 – Nov. 1, 3 – Dec. 31.

1954   Jan. 1 – Feb. 22, 24 – Mar. 9,

11 – 24, 26 – 29, 31 – Apr. 6,
8 – 14, 16 – June 16, 18 – July
3, 5 – Oct. 4, 6 – 26, 28 – Nov.
2, 5, 6, 8 – Dec. 8, 10 – 31.

1955   Jan. 1 – 5, 7 – 19, 21 – Feb. 1,
3 – 15, 17 – 24, 27 – Mar. 8,
10 – 26, 28 – Apr. 2, 4 – 13,
15 – Aug. 2, 4 – 18, 20 – 24,
26 – Sept. 2, 4 – 7, 9, 11 – 20,
22 – 24, 26 – Oct. 15, 17 – Dec.
31.

1956   Jan. 1 – Apr. 11, 13 – July 22,
24 – Sept. 9, 11 – 28, 30 –
Oct. 6, 8 – 22, 25 – Nov. 16,
18, 19, 21, 22, 24 – Dec. 11,
14 – 22, 24 – 31.

1957   Jan. 1 – 14, 16 – 23, 31 – Feb.
6, 19 – 26, 28 – Mar. 2, 4 – 7,
12 – 14, 21 – Apr. 10, 18 – 24,
May 9, 10, 12 – June 8, 10 – 23,
25 – July 17, 25, 29 – Aug. 31.

1958   May 22 – 28, June 1 – 17, 19 –
July 2, 10 – 19, 21 – 23, 30 –
Aug. 25, 27 – Sept. 1, 3 – Oct.
9, 11 – 15, 23 – Nov. 8, 11, 12,
14 – Dec. 22, 24.

1959   Jan. 8 – 21, 29 – Feb. 16, 18 –
23, 26 – 28, Mar. 7 – 11, 19 –
25, Apr. 2 – 6, 11, 16 – May 6,
8 – 23, 25 – 29, 31 – June 22,
24 – 29, July 1, 9 – 20, 22, 30 –
Aug. 2, 4 – 19, 27 – Sept. 2, 4,
7 – Oct. 7, 9 – 19, 23 – 27, 29 –
Nov. 3, 12 – Dec. 8, 10 – 31.

1960   Jan. 1 – Mar. 6, 8 – Apr. 1, 3 –
12, 14 – June 4, 6, 8 – July 8,
10 – 13, 26, 28 – 30, Aug. 3, 12,
13, Sept. 1, 4 – 22, 24 – 28,
Oct. 6 – 12, 14, Nov. 4 – 27,
29 – Dec. 11, 13, 15 – 31.

1961   Jan. 1 – 15, 17 – Feb. 1, 7, 9 –
Mar. 9, 11 – 22, 30 – June 18,
20 – Aug. 4, 6 – 31, Nov. 1 –
Dec. 27, 30, 31.

1962   Jan. 1+.

DPU

  Micro (P)

  1938 – 1939   Jan. 1 – Dec. 31.

ICRL
  Micro (N)
  1938 – 1939   Jan. 1 – Dec. 31.
MH
  1910   Dec. 24.
OrU
  1956   Apr. 3, 4.
TxU
  1938   Apr. 5.
ViU
  Micro (P)
  1943   Feb. 13 – 24.

EL TIEMPO. d. est. Jan. 23, 1899.
  CtY
    1911   Dec. 28.
    1912   Jan. 2, 3, 10 – 13, 15, 16, 18,
           20, Feb. 20, 27, Mar. 27, Apr.
           12, 13, 16, May 28, June 5,
           8, 12, 14.
  MH
    1910   Dec. 26.

EL UNIVERSO. d. est. Sept. 16, 1921.
  CSt – H
    1944   May 29, 30.
    1964   May 31.
  DLC
    1951 – 1952   Jan. 1 – Dec. 31.
    1953   Jan. 1 – Aug. 31, Sept. 3, 6 –
           26, Oct. 4 – Dec. 31.
    1954   Jan. 1 – Dec. 14, 16 – 28, 30,
           31.
    1955   July 1 – 30, Aug. 16 – Oct. 3,
           5 – 15, 26 – Nov. 3, 5, 7, 9, 11 –
           13, 15 – 23, 25 – Dec. 25, 28 –
           31.
    1956   Jan. 1 – 20, 22, 24 – Feb. 10,
           14 – 16, 19 – 22, 24 – Apr. 5,
           7 – 18, 20 – May 26, 28 – June
           14, July 13 – Sept. 6, 8 – Oct.
           31, Nov. 2 – Dec. 10, 12 – 16,
           18 – 22, 24 – 30.
    1957   Jan. 1 – Feb. 28, May 16 –
           June 16, 18 – July 4, 6 – 25,
           Aug. 15 – Sept. 30, Nov. 1 – 8,
           10 – 12, 14, Dec. 1 – 28, 30, 31.
    1958   Jan. 1 – Apr. 6, 8 – May 2, 4 –
           June 11, 13 – July 21, 23 – 30,

Aug. 2 – 9, 11, 13 – Sept. 3, 5,
           6, 12 – Oct. 9, 11 – Dec. 31.
    1959   Jan. 1 – May 29, 31 – June 2,
           6 – July 21, 23 – Aug. 12, 14 –
           Nov. 30, Dec. 2 – 31.
    1960   Jan. 1 – Feb. 29, Apr. 1 – May
           25, 27 – June 28, 30 – Aug. 1,
           3, 5 – Sept. 3, 5 – Oct. 7, 9,
           11 – Dec. 31.
    1961   Jan. 1 – 24, 26 – Apr. 7, 9 –
           11, 13 – 19, 21 – 25, 27 – July
           22, 25 – Aug. 4, 6 – Sept. 30,
           Nov. 15 – Dec. 11, 13 – 21,
           23 – 31.
  Micro (P) & (N)
    1941   Apr. 1 – Dec. 31.
    1942   Jan. 1 – Oct. 3, 5 – Dec. 16,
           18 – 31.
    1943   Jan. 1 – Dec. 31.
    1944   Jan. 1 – Apr. 20, June 1 – Nov.
           4, 6 – Dec. 31.
    1945   Jan. 1 – 25, 27 – Oct. 5, 7 –
           Dec. 31.
    1946   Jan. 1 – Dec. 28, 30, 31.
    1947   Jan. 1 – Aug. 30, Sept. 1 –
           Dec. 30.
    1948   Jan. 1 – 30, Feb. 1 – Dec. 31.
    1949   Jan. 1 – Dec. 31.
    1950   Jan. 1 – Nov. 28, 30 – Dec. 31.
    1962   Jan. 1 – Aug. 31, Sept. 2 –
           Dec. 31.
    1963   Jan. 1+.
  FU
    1962   Oct. 12 – 17.
  TxU
    1938   Apr. 5.
  ViU
    Micro (P)
    1943   Jan. 8 – 15.

LA VERDAD DESNUDA. bw., 3m. est.
June 1, 1839.
  Note: Ceased publication May 21,
  1840.
  CtY
    1839   June 1 – Oct. 16, Dec. 1 – 21.
    1840   Jan. 1 – May 21.

EL 21 DE JUNIO; PERIODICO OFI-
CIAL. est. July 13, 1845.
Note: Succeeded *Gaceta del gobi-
erna del Ecuador*; succeeded by
El Nacional; *periódico oficial*. Ceased
publication Mar. 1846.
DLC
1845 [July 13 – Dec. 31].
1846 Jan. 1 – Feb. 23.

Machala

LA PALABRA. w. est. Feb. 27, 1912.
CtY
1912 Feb. 27 – Mar. 11.

Portoviejo

EL CRONISTA. 3w. est. Dec. 6, 1913.
DLC
1942 May 3 – 8.
DIARIO MANABITA. d. est. Mar. 13,
1934.
DLC
1942 Apr. 11 – 20, May 3 – 22, 25 –
July 27, Aug. 1 – Oct. 2.

Quito

LA BALANZA. w. est. Oct. 5, 1839.
Note: Established in Guayaquil;
removed to Quito, Jan. 23, 1841;
returned to Guayaquil May 27, 1841.
CtY
1841 Jan. 23 – May 27.

COLOMBIANO DEL ECUADOR. est.
1825.
MWA
1826 Extraordinario: Nov. 21.

COMBATE. d. est. Feb. 12, 1953.
DLC
1953 July 1 – Aug. 13, 15 – 31, Nov.
6.
1954 Jan. 1 – 5, 7 – 10, 12, 13, 15,
19 – 23, 25 – 29, Feb. 2 – 5, 9,
11, 12, 15 – 21, 23 – 26, 28 –
Mar. 15, 17 – Apr. 2, 4 – 12,
14 – 28, May 1 – June 3, 5 – 29,
July 1 – Dec. 2, 4 – 6, 11 – 16,
18 – 31.

1955 Jan. 1 – 3, 5 – 10, 12 – July 14,
16 – 25, 27 – Oct. 22, 24, 25,
27 – Nov. 20, 22 – Dec. 31.
1956 Jan. 1 – 20, 22 – Feb. 12, 14 –
Mar. 22, 24, 25, 27 – Aug. 6,
8 – 26, 28.

EL COMERCIO. d. est. Jan. 1, 1906.
Note: Suspended publication Nov.
13 – Dec. 26, 1953.
CLU
1943 Dec. 1 – 31.
1944 Jan. 1 – Dec. 31.
1945 Jan. 1 – Oct. 31.
1948 – 1949 Jan. 1 – Dec. 31.
1965 Jan. 22 – 29, 31 – Feb. 1, 3 – 6,
8, 10 – 15, 17, 19 – 22, 24, 25,
28 – Mar. 1, 3, 4, 6, 9 – 13, 18,
20, 23 – 26, 28 – 30, Apr. 1 – 8,
11, 12, 14 – 19, 21, 23 – May 9,
11 – 16, 19, 20, 21 – 24, 27, 28,
30 – June 6, 8, 10, 11, 13 – 20,
21 – July 3, 5 – 9, 11, 13 – 25,
29 – Aug. 9, 11 – 19, 21 – Sept.
1, 3 – 7, 9 – 21, 24 – 26, 29, Oct.
1 – 5, 8, 10 – 12, 14 – Dec. 31.
DLC
1931 Jan. 19 – 30, Feb. 1 – Mar. 30,
Apr. 1 – 9, 11 – May 2, 4 – 15,
17 – June 3, 5 – 27, 29 – July
18, 20 – Aug. 24, 26 – Sept. 14,
16 – Dec. 31.
1932 – 1933 Jan. 1 – Dec. 31.
1934 Jan. 1 – June 17, 19 – July 8,
16 – Dec. 23.
1936 Jan. 13 – 19, 27 – Mar. 1, 9 –
Apr. 12, 20 – 26, May 1 – Sept.
5, 28 – Dec. 31.
1937 Jan. 1 – Dec. 31.
1938 Jan. 1 – Apr. 2, 10 – May 22,
30 – July 8, 10, 11, 13 – 16,
18 – 29, 31 – Aug. 14, 26 – Dec.
31.
1939 Jan. 5 – 14, 16 – 21, 24 – Feb.
12, 17 – 19, May 23, 24, 26, 27,
June 5, 7, 8, July 26, Aug. 13,
Sept. 1 – Dec. 31.
1940 Jan. 1 – Dec. 31.
1941 Jan. 1 – Sept. 19, 21, 23 – 29,

Oct. 1 – Dec. 31.
1942 Jan. 1 – Mar. 19, 23 – May 21, 27 – 31, June 3 – 18, 20 – July 19, 22 – Sept. 29, Oct. 2 – Nov. 20, 22 – Dec. 31.
1943 Jan. 1 – Dec. 31.
1944 Jan. 1 – Sept. 29, Oct. 1 – Nov. 23, 25, 27 – Dec. 15, 18 – 31.
1945 Jan. 1 – June 27, 29 – Aug. 20, 22 – Sept. 6, 8 – Nov. 30, Dec. 4 – 31.
1946 Jan. 1 – Mar. 15, 17 – Apr. 3, 5 – June 25, 27 – July 18, 20 – Aug. 15, 17 – Sept. 13, 17 – 30, Oct. 3 – Nov. 29, Dec. 3 – 23, 26 – 31.
1947 Jan. 1 – Dec. 31.
1948 Jan. 1 – Feb. 27, Mar. 1 – Dec. 31.
1949 Jan. 1 – Apr. 21, 23 – Sept. 4, 6 – Dec. 31.
1950 Jan. 1 – Feb. 23, 26, 28 – Dec. 31.
1951 Jan. 1 – June 12, 15 – 19, 22 – Dec. 31.
1952 Jan. 1 – Dec. 31.
1953 Jan. 1 – 12, 14 – Dec. 31.
1954 – 1955 Jan. 1 – Dec. 31.
Micro (P)
1956 Jan. 1+.
DPU
Current (six months).
Micro (P)
1940 – 1944 Jan. 1 – Dec. 31.
1945 Jan. 1 – Apr. 20.
1946 Apr. 1 – Dec. 31.
1947 Jan. 1 – Dec. 31.
ICRL
Micro (N)
1940 Feb. 23 – Dec. 31.
1941 – 1944 Jan. 1 – Dec. 31.
1945 Jan. 1 – Apr. 30.
(P) & (N)
1956 Jan. 1+.
IU
1965 [Jan. 1 – Dec. 31].
LNT – MA
1941 Jan. 7.

1946 Jan. 1.
MH
1910 Dec. 30.
NN
1940 Feb. 25 – Sept. 1, 3 – 27, 29 – Dec. 4, 6 – 16, 20 – 31.
1941 Jan. 1 – May 23, 25 – June 11, 13 – 16, 18 – July 12, 14 – Aug. 8, 13 – 15, 17 – Sept. 1, 4 – 26, 28 – Oct. 5, 7, 8, 10 – Dec. 31.
1942 Jan. 1 – June 30.
1945 Apr. 1, 13, 19, 21 – Dec. 31.
1946 – 1948 Jan. 1 – Dec. 31.
1949 Jan. 1 – Feb. 28.

EL DEBATE. d. est. Aug. 24, 1929.
DLC
1940 Nov. 2, 20, 23, 26, 30 – Dec. 4, 6 – 11, 16, 19 – 23.
1941 Jan. 1, 2, 5 – 14, 16 – 26, 29 – Feb. 8, 10 – 12, 14 – 22, 24 – 26, 28 – Mar. 8, 10, 11, 13, 14, 16 – 22, 24 – 30, Apr. 1, 2, 4, 5, 7, 9, 10, 13 – 21, 24 – May 3, 5 – 10, 12, 13, 15 – June 15, 17 – July 12, 14, 16 – 25, 27 – Aug. 3, 5, 6, 8 – 14, 17 – 19, 21 – 25, 27 – Sept. 1, 3 – 10, 12 – Oct. 3, 6, 7, 13, 15, 17, 19 – 21, 23, 26 – 28, 30, 31, Nov. 3, 4, 7, 9 – 19, 21, 23 – 25, Dec. 6 – 10, 12 – 31.
1942 Jan. 1 – 31, Feb. 2 – 7, 9 – 16, 18 – 25, Apr. 1 – 10, 12 – May 4, 7 – 12, 16 – 22, 24, 25.
1947 July 1 – 13, 15 – Aug. 22, 24 – Dec. 31.
1948 Jan. 1 – May 30, June 1 – 30.

EL DIA. d. est. Aug. 1, 1913.
DLC
1940 Nov. 2, 30.
1941 Jan. 19, 23 – Feb. 12, 14 – 16, 21 – June 12, 14 – 27, July 1 – Aug. 15, 17 – Sept. 21, 23, 24, 26 – 28, 30 – Oct. 1, 3, 4, 7, 8, 10, 12 – 18, 20 – Nov. 1, 3 – 11, 13 – 17, 19 – 22, 24 – Dec. 1, 3 – 10, 12 – 16, 18 – 31.
1942 Jan. 1 – Feb. 7, 9 – 26, 28 –

Apr. 27, 29 — May 11, 13 — July
15, 17 — Aug. 9, 11 — 13, 15 —
Sept. 17, 19 — 30, Nov. 1, 4, 6 —
8, 15 — 17, 21 — Dec. 1, 3 — 6,
8 — 17, 19 — 25, 27, 29, 30.
1953   Jan. 1 — 22, 24 — May 1, 4 — 16,
18 — 31, Nov. 21 — Dec. 31.

DIARIO DEL ECUADOR. d. est. [1955].
DLC
1955   Dec. 20 — 31.
1956   Jan. 1 — 20, 23 — Feb. 3, 7 — 10,
16, 17, 20, 21, 23 — Apr. 19,
21 — May 10, 12 — June 15, 29,
July 14 — Sept. 5, 7 — 17, 19 —
30, Nov. 2 — 27, 29 — Dec. 27,
29, 31.
1957   Jan. 1 — 12, 14 — 28, Feb. 16 —
28, May 18 — June 2, 4 — July 5,
7 — 25, Aug. 16 — 26, 28 — Sept.
2, 4 — 26, 28 — 30, Nov. 1 — 14,
Dec. 1 — 18, 21 — 30.

INFORMACIONES. [w.] est. Mar. 23,
1929
MWA
1929   Apr. 17.

LA LEY. 3w., d. est. Sept. 25, 1895.
Note: Periodicity before May 10,
1904, three times a week; after May
17, 1904, daily.
DLC
1903   July 2 — Sept. 7, 11 — Oct. 30,
Nov. 1, 2, 6 — 11, 13 — 16, 18 —
27, 29 — Dec. 31.
1904   Jan. 1 — Mar. 21, 23 — June 21,
23 — 26, 28 — July 3, 5 — Nov. 24,
27 — Dec. 31.
1905   Jan. 1 — 27, 29 — June 2.

EL MERIDIANO. d. est. Dec. 25, 1903.
DLC
1904   May 27, June 16, 17.

EL NACIONAL; PERIODICO OFICIAL.
3w., d. est. Mar. 16, 1846.
Note: Succeeded *El 21 de junio*;
periódico oficial (Guayaquil);
succeeded by *El Ocho de setiembre*.
Suspended publication Dec. 12,

1858 — May 8, 1859; ceased publication Dec. 1876.
CtY
1867   Sept. 14.
DLC
1846   Mar. 16 — Dec. 31.
1847 — 1851   Jan. 1 — Dec. 31.
1852   Jan. 1 — Feb. 24, [Aug. 5 —
Dec. 31].
1853 — 1857   Jan. 1 — Dec. 31.
1858   Jan. 1 — Dec. 11.
1859   May 9 — Dec. 31.
1860 — 1876   Jan. 1 — Dec. 31.
MH
1850   Jan. 4 — May 3.
TxU
1871   Jan. 8 — Dec. 29.
1872   Jan. 3 — Dec. 30.
1873   Jan. 3 — Apr. 16, 30 — Sept.
12.
EL NACIONAL. d. est. Sept. 24, 1947.
DLC
1947   Sept. 24 — Oct. 1, 3 — 26, 28 —
Dec. 31.
1948   Apr. 8, 12 — 21, 23 — May 1, 3 —
30, June 1 — July 4, 6, 8 — Aug.
19, 21 — 29, 31 — Sept. 16, 18 —
30, Oct. 2 — Dec. 18, 20 — 31.
1950   Mar. 1, 3 — Apr. 30, May 2 —
July 30, Aug. 1 — Oct. 4, 6 —
Dec. 21, 23 — 31.
1951   Jan. 1 — 14, Feb. 1 — May 7, 9 —
July 5, 7 — 23, 25, 26, 28 — Aug.
2, 4 — Dec. 30.
1952   Jan. 1 — Feb. 23, 25 — May 11,
16 — 27, 29 — 31, June 2 — 13,
15 — July 1, 3 — Aug. 6, 8 — Sept.
24, 27 — Nov. 2, 4 — 6, 8 — 13,
15 — Dec. 31.
1953   Jan. 1 — Feb. 12, 14, 15, 17 —
May 17, 19 — June 6, 8 — 19,
21 — 26, 28, 29.

LA PRENSA. est. Aug. 10. 1909.
MH
1910   Dec. 27.

EL SOL. d. est. Jan. 21, 1951.
DLC
1951   Jan. 21, 23 — 31, Apr. 5, July

21, 22, 24 — Aug. 2, 4 — 8, 10 —
Oct. 30, Nov. 2 — 25, 27 — 29,
Dec. 1 — 4, 6 — 31.

1952   Jan. 1 — Feb. 21, 23 — 28, Mar.
1, 2, 4 — Apr. 8, 10 — May 25,
27 — June 13, 15, 17 — July 12,
15 — Sept. 20, 22 — Dec. 18,
20 — 31.

1953   Jan. 1 — Mar. 31, Apr. 2 — 9,
11 — 15, 17 — 30, May 2 — 7, 9 —
14, 16 — June 24, 26 — Aug. 19,
Nov. 11, 16 — Dec. 23, 25 — 30.

EL TIEMPO. d. est. Oct. 11, 1901.
    Note: Ceased publication Aug. 1911.
  DLC
  1904   Jan. 2 — June 30.

LA TIERRA. d. est. [1945.]
  DLC
  1947   July 1 — Sept. 18, 20 — Oct. 31,
Nov. 6 — Dec. 25, 27 — 31.'
  1948   Jan. 1 — Feb. 7, 9 — 20, 23 —
June 5, 8 — Aug. 16, 18 — Dec. 4,
6 — 23, 25 — 31.
  1949   Jan. 1, 2, 5 — 10, 18 — 24, Apr.
18 — 20, 22 — May 1, 3 — 27, 30 —
June 9, 11, 13, 15 — 27, 29 —
July 5, 7 — 22, 24 — Aug. 12,
17, 18, 20, 22 — 31, Oct. 6 —
14, 16 — 28, 30 — Nov. 3, 5 — 8,
30 — Dec. 23, 25 — 27, 29, 30.
  1950   May 1 — 19, 23, 24, 26 — June 2,
July 21, Sept. 5 — 17, 20 — 26,
28 — Oct. 1, 11, 12, 15 — 29.
  1951   Sept. 4 — 11, 13 — 20, 25, 26,
28 — Oct. 11, 28 — 31, Nov. 6, 7,
9 — 21, 23 — 30, Dec. 4 — 28.
  1952   Jan. 1 — Feb. 4, 6 — 29, Mar.
2 — Apr. 24, 26 — June 2, 4 — 29.
  1953   Jan. 1 — 4, 6 — 13, 29 — 31, Feb.
5, 7 — 23, 25 — Mar. 4, 7 — 13,
15 — Apr. 30, May 3 — 7, 9 —
June 30, July 2 — 31, Aug. 2 —
12, 14 — Dec. 31.
  1954   Jan. 1 — 16, 18 — 25, 27, 29 — 31,
Feb. 2, 3, 5 — 18, 20 — Mar. 16,
18 — 23, 28, 29, 31.

1955   Apr. 13 — 20, 22 — May 10, 12 —
June 1, 4 — 6, 8, 9, 11 — 13, 15 —
22, 24 — 30, July 11, 12, 16, 17,
19, 23, 24, 26 — Aug. 1, 4, 6,
12 — 16, 22, Sept. 12, 13, 15,
24 — 27, Oct. 1 — 3, 6 — 10, 12 —
18, 22, 23, 25, 26, 29 — Nov. 1,
6 — 10, 13, 14, 17, 18, 20 — 24,
29 — Dec. 6, 8 — 14, 16, 19 — 28.
1956   Jan. 1 — 6, 9, 10, 12 — 20, 22 —
27, 29 — Feb. 4, 6 — 11, 13 — 24,
27 — Mar. 16, 19 — Apr. 6, 9 —
May 22, 26 — June 12, 14 — 22,
25 — July 7, 9 — 14, 16 — Aug. 7,
9 — Sept. 12, 14 — 24, Nov. 1, 2,
4 — 25, 28 — 30.
1957   Apr. 23 — 26, 29 — May 6, 9 —
25, 27 — June 19, 21 — 27, 30 —
July 12, 15 — 23, 25 — Aug. 15,
18 — 31, Sept. 2 — 25, 27, Oct.
3 — Nov. 2, 4 — 26, 28 — 30, Dec.
2 — 5, 8 — 18, 27 — 29.
1958   Jan. 1, 6 — 16, 18 — 28, 31 — Feb.
15, 17 — May 1, 3 — 9, 11 — June
30, July 2 — 11, 13 — Sept. 6, 8 —
Oct. 9, 13 — 25, 27 — 31, Nov.
6 — 20, 24 — Dec. 12, 19, 20.
1959   Jan. 6 — 14, 17 — 20, 22, 24 — 28,
30 — Mar. 20, Apr. 7 — 15, 17,
21 — 30.

ULTIMAS NOTICIAS. d. est. June 8,
1938.
    Note: Suspended publication Nov.
13 — Dec. 27, 1953.
  CSt
  1944   Aug. 10.
  CU
  1940   Oct. 2.
  DLC
  1942   July 4.
  1950   Feb. 18 — Mar. 4, Apr. 1 — 26,
28 — May 17, 19, 21 — June 7,
9 — 12, 14 — Aug. 24, 26 — Oct.
23, 25 — Dec. 3, 5 — 30.
  1951   Jan. 2, 4 — Feb. 11, 13 — Mar.
12, 14, 16 — Apr. 1, 3 — Mar. 7,
9 — June 12, 14 — 27, 29 — Aug.
15, 17 — 20, 22 — 31, Sept. 4 —

Nov. 6, 8—18, 20—23, 25, 27—
Dec. 5, 7—30.
1952   Jan. 2—13, 15—25, 27—Feb. 6,
8—11, 13—15, 17—28, Apr. 1,
2, 4—16, 18—23, 25—30, May
2—12, 14—28, 31, June 3, 4,
6—10, 17—July 11, 13—26.

Victoria

SEMANARIO POPULAR ECUATO-
RIANO. sw.
CSt
1944   Aug. 10.

EL SALVADOR.
Ahuachapán.

LA NUEVA TRIBUNA. d. est. 1928.
LNT—MA
1935   Sept. 15.
1941   Sept. 21.

Cojutepeque

GACETA DEL SALVADOR. w. est. Mar.
23, 1847.
Note: Succeeded *El Boletín oficial*
as the official gazette; succeeded
by *El Constitucional*. Removed from
San Salvador June 1, 1855; returned
to San Salvador Apr. 17, 1858. Ceased
publication Mar. 28, 1863.
CU—B
1856   Apr. 3—24.
DLC
1855   June 21—Dec. 31.
1856—1857   Jan. 1—Dec. 31.
1858   [Jan. 1—Apr. 14].

MWA
1857   Feb. 26, Apr. 15.

San Miguel

DIARIO DE ORIENTE. d. est. Mar. 1906.
LNHT
1937   May 17.

DIARIO DEL PUEBLO. sw.
DLC
1957   July 11.

LA NACION. d. est. Mar. 24, 1924.
Note: Merged with *El Gran diario*
(San Salvador) to become *El Gran
diario. La Nación* July 30, 1945.
CU
1944   Oct. 18—22, Dec. 28—31.
ICRL
1938—1939   Jan. 1—Dec. 31.

VIDA NUEVA. w. est. Jan. 1, 1941.
DLC
1943   July 31.

San Salvador

LA AMERICA CENTRAL. d. est. 1874.
CtY
1875   Dec. 22—24.

EL AMIGO DEL PUEBLO. est. 1843.
LNHT
Micro (P)
1843   July 20.

EL ANOTADOR. est. [1845].
LNHT
Micro (P)
1845   Oct. 8.

ARGOS DE CENTRO-AMERICA.
MWA
1826   Feb. 20.

EL ATLETA. est. Dec. 10, 1839.
LNHT
Micro (P)
1839   Dec. 25.

AVANCE. d.
Note: Morning edition of *Diario
latino*.
DLC
1941   Dec. 9.

EL BIEN COMUN. bw. est. Jan. 15,
1838.
LNHT
Micro (P)
1838   Jan. 15—31.
TxU
1838   Jan. 15.

BOLETIN DE NOTICIAS. irr. est. Jan.
8, 1851.
CU−B
1851   Jan. 8, 17, 28, 29, Feb. 14−
17, 24−28.

BOLETIN DEL EJERCITO. est. [1844].
LNHT
Micro (P)
1844   Feb. 1.

BOLETIN OFICIAL. est. Apr. 26, 1871.
Note: Succeeded *El Constitucional* as
the offical gazette; succeeded by
Diario oficial.
CU−B
Micro (P)
1875   Jan. 9.

EL CENTROAMERICANO. d. est. 1903.
DLC
1903   Aug. 22.

EL COMBATE. bw., w. est. Nov. 7, 1953.
Note: Periodicity Nov. 7, 1953−Feb.
22, 1954, biweekly; after Mar. 2, 1954,
weekly.
DLC
1953   Nov. 7−Dec. 31.
1954   Jan. 1−June 30.

EL CONSTITUCIONAL; PERIODICO
OFICIAL DEL GOBIERNO. w. est.
Nov. 7, 1863.
Note: Succeeded *Gaceta del Salvador* as the official gazette; succeeded by *Boletín oficial*.
DLC
1864−1865   [Jan. 1−Dec. 31].
MWA
1863   Nov. 28−Dec. 11.
1864   Jan. 14−Dec. 31.
1865−1866   Jan. 1−Dec. 31.
1867   Jan. 1−Sept. 19.

CORREO NACIONAL. d. est. July 1891.
MWA
1891   [Oct. 1−31].

CORREO SEMANARIO DEL SAL-
VADOR. sw., w. est. May 1, 1840.
Note: Succeeded *La Gaceta*; suc-
ceeded by *El Salvador regénerado*.

CtY
1841   Mar. 22, Aug. 19.
Suplemento: Dec. 4.
1842   Jan. 5, 20−Feb. 5, Apr. 18−
22, May 24−June 3, 17, July
15−26.
1843   Apr. 21, May 19−June 2, 3,
July 21, Oct. 2.
1844   Mar. 15−29, Apr. 26, Aug. 31,
Nov. 9.

EL CRISOL. est. [1845].
LNHT
Micro (P)
1845   June 6.

LOS DEBATES. w.
MWA
1889   Mar. 16, May 18.

DEFENSA.
LNHT
1957   May 1−Dec. 31.
1958−1959   Jan. 1−Dec. 31.
1960   Jan. 1−Nov. 18.

EL DIARIO DE HOY. d. est. May 2,
1936.
CSt
1937   Apr. 17.
1950   Sept. 15.
CU
1942   Oct. 25−Nov. 15, 22, Dec. 6−
20.
1943   Jan. 3, 10−17, 24−Aug. 15.
DLC
1939   May 30.
1941   Sept. 21−27.
1942   Dec. 6, 13.
1943   Jan. 4−7, 9, 10, Mar. 1−5, 7,
Apr. 12−18, Sept. 6−12.
1944   Mar. 27−Apr. 2, May 9−13,
15−June 4, July 24−Aug. 4,
8−13, 21−Sept. 10, 18−22.
1945   July 10−15.
1947   July 9, 12, 14−16, 26, 28−Aug.
2, 8, 9, 11, 12, 15, 17, 18, 23, 24,
28, 29, Sept. 1, 4−11, 15−29,
Oct. 4, 6−9, 12, 13, 15−18, 20,
21, 24−28, Nov. 1, 3−5, 7−11,
14−17, 19, 20, 22−25, 27−

Dec. 4, 6 – 11, 13 – 16, 19 – 25.
1948   Jan. 3 – 9, 11, 13, 15, 16, 18 –
21, 31, Feb. 3, 5, 6, 9, 10, 13,
16 – 19, 21, 24 – 28, Mar. 2, 3, 5,
6, 9, 11, 16, 17, 20, 23 – 25, 30 –
Apr. 1, 3, 5 – 10, 12, 14, 16 –
22, 24 – May 5, 7, 8, 10, 11, 13,
16 – 21, 24, 26, 28, 30 – June 8,
10, 11, 13 – 16, 18, 21 – 23, 25 –
July 5, 7, 8, 10 – 14, 16, 17, 19,
21, 23, 25 – 29, Aug. 13, 14, 20,
21, Sept. 3, 8 – 13, 16 – 20, 22 –
28, Oct. 1, 18, 24 – 27, 30, 31,
Nov. 3, 7, 14, 16, 17, 19, 22 – 24,
27, 29, Dec. 1 – 3, 5, 6, 8.
1949   Jan. 13, 14, 17 – 19, 24, 29, Feb.
1, Apr. 2 – 6, 8 – 22, 24, 25, 27,
28, June 17 – 24, 27.
1950   Mar. 1 – 3, 5 – 8, 10, 12 – 14,
16, 17, 19 – 24, 26, 28 – 31, Apr.
2 – 4, 6, 9 – 20, 23, 25, 27 – 30,
May 2 – 10, 12 – 15, 18 – 23,
26 – 29, 31, June 18, 25, July
1, 2, 4, 5, 7 – 9, 11, 12, 14, 16 –
21, 23, 27 – Aug. 3, 6 – 13, 16,
17, 19, 21, 23 – Sept. 1, 6 – 8,
10 – 14, 20 – 22, 25, 26, 28 – 30,
Oct. 11 – 14, 16 – 19, 21, 22, 26,
27, 29 – 31, Dec. 2, 4 – 6, 9, 12,
20, 24, 25, 27 – 31.
1951   Jan. 2, 10 – 17, 21, 23 – 26, 28,
29, 31 – Feb. 8, 10, 11, 13 – 16,
18, 19, 23, 24, Mar. 2, 11, 12, 16,
18 – 21, 25 – 31.
1952   Sept. 1 – 14, 17 – Oct. 12, 14 –
Nov. 10, 18 – 28, Dec. 1 – 3, 5 –
8, 22.
1953   Jan. 7 – 11, 27 – Mar. 16, 18 –
30, Apr. 14 – May 11, 19 – 25,
June 2 – 8, July 7 – Aug. 4.
DPU
  Current (six months).
ICRL
  Micro (P) & (N)
  1956   Jan. 1+.
LNT – MA
  1937   Feb. 10, 13, Mar. 30.
  1938   Mar. 4.

1942   Oct. 25 – Nov. 22, Dec. 20.
1943   Jan. 3 – Feb. 7, May 16 – Aug.
15.
1950   Sept. 15.
1953   Feb. 1 – Oct. 1, 3 – 31, Nov. 3 –
Dec. 31.
Micro (P)
1956   Jan. 1+.
PrU
  1961   Jan. 23 – Mar. 22, 24 – 29, Apr.
3 – 15, 17 – 23, 25 – 30, May 1 –
July 11, 13, 14, 17 – Oct. 30,
Nov. 1 – Dec. 31.
  1962   Jan. 1 – Feb. 29, Mar. 1 – 10,
13 – 31, Apr. 1 – 19, 22 – Oct. 5,
7 – 31, Nov. 1 – 24, 27 – Dec.
22 – 27 – 31.
  1963   Jan. 1 – Feb. 17, 21 – Apr. 10,
14 – May 9, 12 – Oct. 24, 27 –
Dec. 31.
  1964   Jan. 1 – Mar. 26, 30 – Apr. 11,
16 – June 23, 26 – Dec. 31.
  1965   Jan. 1, 4 – Apr. 14, 18 – July 30,
Aug. 2 – 31, Sept. 2 – 11, 14 –
29, Oct. 1 – 31, Nov. 2 – Dec.
31.
  1966   Jan. 1+.
TxU
  1950   Sept. 15, 16.

DIARIO DEL SALVADOR. d. est. July
22, 1895.
  Note: Ceased publication 1943.
CU
  1912   Jan. 8 – 25, 27 – June 15, 18 –
Oct. 26, 29 – Dec. 31.
  1913   Jan. 1 – 23, 25 – Mar. 19, 24 –
Apr. 29, May 1 – Dec. 31.
  1914   Jan. 1 – May 2, 4 – Dec. 5, 14 –
31.
  1915   Jan. 1 – Aug. 31, Oct. 6 – Dec.
12, 20 – 31.
  1916   Jan. 1 – Apr. 30.
DLC
  1900   Jan. 1 – Apr. 29, May 6 – June
22, 24 – Aug. 19, 21 – Sept. 26,
28 – Nov. 24, 26 – Dec. 30.
  1901   Jan. 1, 3 – 6, 8 – June 23, 25,

26, 28 — July 2, 4 — 27, 29 —
Sept. 2, 4 — Nov. 2, 11 — 30.
1902   July 1 — Sept. 28, Oct. 6, 8 — 25,
Nov. 10 — 14, 17 — 22, 24 — Dec.
31.
1903 — 1908   Jan. 1 — Dec. 31.
1909   Jan. 1 — May 6, 12 — Dec. 31.
1910   Jan. 1 — Feb. 23, 25 — July 2,
5 — Aug. 12, 14 — Dec. 31.
1911 — 1912   Jan. 1 — Dec. 31.
1913   Jan. 1 — Aug. 3, 9, 12 — Sept. 7,
10 — 13, 16 — 28, Oct. 2 — 4, 6 —
Dec. 31.
1914   Jan. 1 — Apr. 7, 12 — June 30.
1926   Jan. 7 — Feb. 22, 25 — Apr. 26,
29 — June 23, July 20 — Aug. 19,
22 — Sept. 6, 8 — 24, 26, 28 —
Oct. 19, Nov. 27 — 29, Dec. 13,
14, 24 — 31.
1927   Jan. 1 — 20, Feb. 4 — 6, 10 — 14,
17 — Apr. 28, May 1, 4 — 8, 11 —
July 14, 17 — Sept. 1, 4 — 11,
14 — Oct. 10, 17 — Nov. 7, 9 —
Dec. 5, 8 — 14, 16 — 31.
1928   Jan. 1 — 8, 10 — 15, 18 — 20, 22 —
31, Feb. 3 — 10, 12, 14 — 23,
28 — Mar. 1.
1931   Aug. 3 — Dec. 31.
1932 — 1933   Jan. 1 — Dec. 31.
1934   Jan. 1 — 9, 11 — Feb. 4.
LNT — MA
1906   Jan. 1 — June 30.
1907   July 1 — Dec. 31.
1908   July 1 — Dec. 31.
1909 — 1915   Jan. 1 — Dec. 31.
1916   Jan. 1 — Aug. 31, Oct. 1 — Dec.
31.
1917 — 1918   Jan. 1 — Dec. 31.
1919   Feb. 10 — Dec. 31.
1920 — 1932   Jan. 1 — Dec. 31.

DIARIO LATINO. d. est. Nov. 5, 1890.
Note: Title *El Siglo XX*, Nov. 5,
1890 — 1896; *Latinoamericana*, 1896 —
Nov. 6, 1903; *Diario latino*, after Nov.
7, 1903. Publishes morning edition,
Avance.
CU
1943   Sept. 1 — 11, 14 — 18, 20 — 25,

27 — Oct. 2, 4 — 9, 11 — 16, 18 —
23, 27 — 30, Nov. 1 — 5, 17 — 20,
22 — Dec. 3, 6 — 11, 27 — 31.
1944   Jan. 3, 4, 9, 16, 23 — 27, Feb. 4,
5, 7 — 9, 17, 18, 25, 26, 28, Mar.
8, 9, 29, 30.
DLC
1908 — 1910   Oct. 21 — Dec. 30.
1939   May 29.
1941   Apr. 1 — 8, 16 — June 20, 22 —
July 20, 22 — 30, Aug. 1 — Sept.
19, 21 — Oct. 23, Nov. 21 — 24,
26 — 28, 30, Dec. 2 — 31.
Avance: Dec. 9.
1942   Jan. 26 — 28, 31 — Feb. 6, 8 — 10,
12 — Mar. 24, 26 — Apr. 1, 5 —
May 14, 16 — 22, 24, 25.
1946   June 1 — July 31.
1956   Jan. 2 — 24, 28 — Feb. 3, 5, 7 —
10, 12 — 24, 26 — Mar. 9, 11,
14 — 23, 25, 27, Apr. 1 — 6, 8,
12 — June 15, 17 — July 24, 26 —
Aug. 17, 19 — Oct. 30, Nov. 1 —
20, 22 — 30.
LNT — MA
1937   Feb. 7 — 12, May 17 — Dec. 31.
1938   Mar. 28 — Dec. 31.
1939   Jan. 1 — Dec. 31.
1940   [Jan. 1 — Dec. 31.]
1941   Jan. 2 — 20.
1949   Mar. 1 — July 27.
1956   [Mar. 16 — Dec. 31.]
1957 — 1958   Jan. 1 — Dec. 31.
1959   Jan. 2 — 31.

DIARIO NUEVO.
See *Tribuna libre*.

DIARIO OFICIAL. d. est. 1875.
Note: Succeeded *Boletín oficial* as
the official gazette.
CU — B
Micro
1875   Jan. 15 — 20, 22, 24 — 28, 30 —
Feb. 24, 27 — Dec. 28, 30, 31.
1876   Jan. 1 — 9, 11 — 27, 29 — Feb.
26, Mar. 2 — 9, 14 — 19, 22 — 30,
Apr. 1 — May 9.
Extraordinario: Jan. 10.

1878   Jan. 1 — Apr. 12, May 15 — Sept.
        29, Oct. 1 — Dec. 31.
1879   Jan. 1 — Feb. 1, 28 — Apr. 15,
        17 — May 9, 11 — 20, 22 — June
        1, 4 — 29, July 1 — Aug. 16, 19 —
        Sept. 14, 16 — Oct. 3, 5 — Dec.
        18.
        Extraordinario: May 15.
1880   Jan. 10 — 17.
1899   Mar. 1 — 27, 29 — Apr. 15.
CtY
1875   Dec. 21 — 25.
DLC
1876 — 1896   [Jan. 1 — Dec. 31].
1897   [Jan. 1 — June 30].
1899 — 1900   [Jan. 1 — Dec. 31].

LA EPOCA. d. est. June 4, 1930.
    DLC
    1930   June 4 — 9, 11 — July 1, 3 — 7,
            9 — 13, 15, 16, 18 — 21, 25, 27 —
            Aug. 11, 13, 15 — 18, 20 — 25,
            27, 29 — Sept. 3, 5, 7 — 12, 14 —
            17, 19 — 21, 23 — Oct. 2, 4 — 26,
            28 — Nov. 4, 7 — 20, 23 — 26,
            28 — Dec. 10, 12 — 31.
    1931   Jan. 1 — 21, 24 — 27, 29 — Feb. 4,
            6 — 20, 22 — Mar. 8, 10 — 19, 21,
            22, 24 — 26, 28, 29, Apr. 10,
            12 — 15, 17 — 19, 23, 25 — May 5,
            7 — 26, 28, 30 — June 8, 11 — 20.

FARO SALVADOREÑO. w. est. Nov. 14,
    1864.
    CtY
    1866   Dec. 10.
    1867   Jan. 21, May 13.
    MWA
    1864   Nov. 21 — 28.
    1865   Apr. 25 — May 1, June 19 — Dec.
            31.
    1866   [Jan. 1 — Sept. 3.]

LA GACETA. w. est. Mar. 1839.
    Note: Succeeded *El Nacional*;
    succeeded by *Correo semanario
    del Salvador*.
    CtY
    1839   Mar. 31.

GACETA DEL GOBIERNO DEL ES-
TADO DE EL SALVADOR. est. Apr.
2, 1827.
    Note: Succeeded by *El Revisor
    oficial* as the official gazette.
    LNHT
    Micro (P)
    1831   Mar. 19, June 3, July 16.

GACETA DEL SALVADOR. w. est. Mar.
23, 1847.
    Note: Succeeded *El Boletín oficial*
    as the official gazette; succeeded
    by *El Constitucional*. Removed to
    Cojutepeque June 1, 1855; returned
    to San Salvador Apr. 17, 1858. Ceased
    publication Mar. 28, 1863.
    CU — B
    1849   Aug. 3, Dec. 7 — 21.
    1850   Jan. 4, 26 — Mar. 22, Apr. 5 —
            May 17, Aug. 23, Sept. 6.
    1851   Sept. 12, 26, Oct. 31.
    1853   July 15 — Aug. 12, Sept. 9, Oct.
            28 — Nov. 25, Dec. 30.
    1854   Jan. 13 — Feb. 3, 17, Mar. 3 —
            10, 24, May 26, Oct. 12.
    CtY
    1851   May 9.
    DLC
    1847   [Mar. 23 — Dec. 31].
    1848 — 1848   [Jan. 1 — Dec. 31].
    1849 — 1854   Jan. 1 — Dec. 31.
    1855   Jan. 1 — June 14.
    1858   [Apr. 17 — Dec. 31].
    1859 — 1862   Jan. 1 — Dec. 31.
    1863   Jan. 1 — Mar. 28.
    NHi
    1850   May 17, Aug. 23.
    1851   Jan. 3, Sept. 26, Oct. 31.
    1854   Mar. 3 — 10.

GACETA OFICIAL. irr., d. est. 1876.
    CU — B
    Micro (P)
    1876   May 11 — June 10, 21 — 25, 28 —
            Dec. 31.
    1877   Jan. 2 — Sept. 30, Oct. 3 — 12,
            Nov. 8 — Dec. 30.

GAZETA DEL GOBIERNO FEDERAL.
irr. est. Aug. 17, 1834.
MWA
1834   Aug. 17 – Dec. 31.
1835   Jan. 1 – Aug. 8.

EL GRAN DIARIO.
See *El Gran diario. La Nación.*

EL GRAN DIARIO. LA NACION. d. est.
June 3, 1939.
Note: Title *El Gran diario*, June 3,
1939 – July 29, 1945; *El Gran diario.
La Nación*, after July 30, 1945.
Merged with *La Nación* (San Miguel)
July 30, 1945.
CU
1944   July 11, 13 – 25, Oct. 19 – Nov.
3, 10 – 14, 16, 17, 29 – Dec. 31.
1945   Jan. 2 – 31.
DLC
1941   Mar. 15, Dec. 10.
1942   Nov. 24.
1946   Feb. 5 – 8.
1947   July 14, 15, 24 – Aug. 3, 6, 12,
14 – 19, 21 – 26, 28 – Sept. 22,
24 – 28, 30, Oct. 1, 3 – 7, 9, 11,
12, 14, 15, 17 – 22, 24, 26 – 29,
31, Nov. 2, 4 – 8, 14 – 25, 27,
28, 30, Dec. 1, 3, 4, 7, 8, 11 – 24,
27 – 30.
1948   Jan. 1, 4, 5, 7 – 10, 12 – 14,
16 – 20, 29 – Feb. 5, 8 – 18,
20 – 24, 26 – Mar. 5, 8 – 12,
15 – 31, Apr. 2 – 10, 16, 18 –
24, 26, 28 – May 1, 4, 6, 7, 12,
15 – 18, 20, 22, 28, 31, June 5 –
7, 9, 10, 12 – 17, 19 – 23, 25, 26,
30, July 2 – 4, 7 – 23, 26, Aug.
11, 12, 19, 21, Sept. 1, 7, 10 –
13, 18 – 20, Oct. 19, 21, Nov. 5,
9, 12, 15, 18, 22 – 25, 27 – Dec.
3, 5 – 7.

EL IMPARCIAL. est. [1829.]
LNHT
Micro (P)
1829   Nov. 30.

INFORMACIONES DE EL SALVADOR.
LNT – MA
1957   Sept. 10.

LATINOAMERICANA.
See *Diario latino.*

LA LINTERNA. w. est. Feb. 1880.
CU – B
Micro (P)
1882   Dec. 24.
LNHT
1881   July 24, Sept. 10.

EL MONITOR. irr. est. July 1835.
TxU
1835   n.d. (Nos. 5 – 7).

EL MUNDO LIBRE. w. est. Mar. 30,
1941.
DLC
1941   Mar. 30.
1942   June 8.

EL NACIONAL. d. est. 1944.
Note: Succeeded by *Patria libre*,
Dec. 1948.
CU
1945   June 4 – 9, 12 – 14, 16 – 19,
21 – July 28, 31 – Aug. 9, 15 –
20, 22 – Sept. 24, 26, 28 – Oct.
3, 6 – Nov. 9, 12 – 29, Dec. 1 –
6, 10 – 17, 19 – 22.
1946   Jan. 3 – 5, 10 – Feb. 9, 13, 15 –
Mar. 15, 18, 19, Apr. 24, 25, 29,
May 7, 25, 28 – June 8, 11, 28,
July 5, Aug. 15, Oct. 10, 14 –
Dec. 19, 23.
1947   Jan. 3 – May 7, 9 – Dec. 23.
1948   Jan. 5 – Dec. 13.
DLC
1947   July 8, 9, 12 – 14, 19, 26 – 30,
Aug. 8, 11 – 19, 22, 23, 26, 28,
Sept. 3, 11 – 16, 19 – 25, 27 –
Oct. 1, 15, 16, 20, 23, 25 – Nov.
6, 8 – 24, 26, 27, 29, Dec. 2 – 6,
9 – 23.
1948   Jan. 5, 8, 12 – 21, 29 – Feb. 12,
14 – 24, 26 – Mar. 4, 6 – July
31, Aug. 10 – 31, Sept. 2 – Nov.
3, 6 – Dec. 8.

LNT—MA
  1947   Oct. 28, Nov. 17—24, Dec. 22, 23.
  1948   [Jan. 1—July 31,] Oct. 25—Dec. 1.

EL NOTICIERO. d. est. Nov. 13, 1944.
  CU
  1944   Nov. 13, 14, 25, Dec. 25.
  1945   Jan. 1, 6, 9—12, 15—18, 22, 24—31, Feb. 6, Mar. 24, Apr. 5, 12, 14—23, 25.
  DLC
  1944   Nov. 13—Dec. 1, 3—31.
  1945   Jan. 1—Feb. 28.

EL PAIS. w.
  CtY
  1856   May 31—June 14.

LA PALABRA. bw.
  DLC
  1942   Feb. 25.

LA PALABRA DE DIOS. est. [1845].
  LNHT
    Micro (P)
  1845   Aug. 20, Sept. 22, Nov. 30.

PATRIA. d. est. Apr. 27, 1928.
  LNT—MA
  1938   Mar. 4

PATRIA LIBRE. d. est. Dec. 1948.
    Note: Succeeded *El Nacional.*
  CU
  1948   Dec. 23—31.
  1949   Jan. 4—6, 8—12, 14—Feb. 14, 16—26.

PAZ Y ORDEN. est. Nov. 18, 1835.
    Note: Ceased publication 1837.
  LNHT
    Micro (P)
  1835   Nov. 18—Dec. 2.

LA PRENSA GRAFICA. d. est. May 10, 1915.
    Note: Title *La Prensa*, May 10, 1915—Aug. 9, 1939; *La Prensa gráfica*, after Aug. 10, 1939.
  CLU
  1964   [Dec. 11—31].

1965   Jan. 1—4, 6—Dec. 31.
1966   Jan. 1+.
CSt
  1942   Feb. 1, 3—7, 10—15, 17—21, 24—Mar. 1, 3—8, 10—15, 17—22, 24—28, 31—Apr. 2, 7—12, 14—19, 21—26, 28—30.
CSt—H
  1964   Mar. 31—Apr. 6, 10, 12, 14—16.
  1965   May 27—June 1, 5, Oct. 16—Nov. 25.
DLC
  1946   July 4.
  1947   July 10, 12, 13, 15, 16, 25—30, Aug. 1, 3—12, 15—30, Sept. 1, 3—5, 7, 8, 10—24, 26—30, Oct. 2, 4—8, 10—20, 22—Nov. 6, 11, 13, 14, 16—20, 22—25, 27, 28, Dec. 1—8, 10, 11, 14—17, 19, 21—25, 28, 29.
  1948   Jan. 1—3, 5—7, 9, 12—21, 30—Feb. 6, 11, 13—16, 18, 20—24, 26—29, Mar. 11, 13—25, 31—Apr. 5, 8—19, 21, 23—May 1, 3—13, 15—18, 21, 23, 24, 26, 27, 29—31, June 2, 3, 5—8, 10, 11, 13—17, 20—July 7, 9—22, 24, 26, 27, 29, Aug. 13—17, 20—23, 30, Sept. 3—11, 13—28, Oct. 8, 11—15, 17—19, 22—27, 29, 30, Nov. 1, 3—5, 8—10, 12—15, 17—20, 22, 24, 27—Dec. 1, 3—7.
  1949   Jan. 15, 18, 21, 25, 26, 30—Feb. 2, 17, 18, 20, 22, 24, Mar. 31—Apr. 3, 9, 19, 20, 22, 24—28.
  1950   Mar. 1—3, 5—9, 12, 13, 15—17, 19, 22—24, 26—31, Apr. 3—13, 17—23, 25, 27—May 16, 19—21, 23—26, 28, 30, 31, July 1—10, 12—21, 26—Aug. 2, 9, 11, 13—16, 18, 21, 24—26, 28, 29, 31, Sept. 1, 5—14, 16—22, 26, 29, 30, Oct. 9—11, 13—18, 21, 26—31, Nov. 4, 6, 7, 10, 12—14, 16—18, 23—25, 27, 28, 30, Dec. 2, 5—9, 11, 13, 17, 20—23, 25—27, 29—31.

1951   Jan. 10−14, 16, 19, 21, 23, 24,
26−28, 30, Feb. 1−3, 9−11,
13, 14, 16, 18−22, 25, 26, Mar.
1, 2, 5, 8, 11, 14, 18−21, 28, 30,
31.

1952   Jan. 1−3, 5−Mar. 7, 9−29,
31−Apr. 5, 7−9, 15−May 24,
26−29, June 2, 3, 5−13, 15−
18, 20, 22−30, July 2, 3, 5, 8,
10, 11, 13−19, 21−Aug. 4, 8, 9,
11−16, 18−Nov. 1, 3−Dec.
31.

1953   Jan. 1−Apr. 1, 7−June 27,
29−July 16, 18−20, 22−26,
28−Sept. 14, 16−Oct. 17, 21−
Nov. 25, 27−Dec. 29.

1954   Jan. 1−Feb. 15, 17−19, 22−
Mar. 2, 4−11, 13−Apr. 14,
19−24, 26−May 1, 3−15, 17−
June 9, Aug. 5−13, 15−20,
23−31, Sept. 11−22, Oct. 6−
15, 17−Nov. 5, 7−Dec. 30.

1955   Jan. 1−Feb. 26, 28−Mar. 19,
21−25, 28−Apr. 1, 3−Sept. 2,
4−Dec. 31.

1956   Jan. 1−Mar. 2, 4−Aug. 18,
20−Oct. 12, 14−Nov. 2, 4−6,
8, 11−13, 15−Dec. 21, 24−31.

1957   Jan. 1−29, Feb. 2−8, 10−23,
25−Mar. 11, 13−Apr. 2, 4−
June 4, 6−July 5, 7−Oct. 22,
24−30, Nov. 1−Dec. 31.

1958   Jan. 1−15, 18, 20−29, 31−
Feb. 18, 20−May 5, 7−13,
16−June 29, July 3−7, 9−
16, 18−Sept. 16, 18, 20, 23−
27, 30−Oct. 2, 4−13, 16−Dec.
17, 19−31.

1959   Jan. 1−Mar. 18, 20−Apr. 8,
10, 11, 13−May 9, 11−22, 24−
Aug. 2, 4−11, 13−Sept. 26,
28−Dec. 15, 17−31.

1960   Jan. 1−Mar. 3, 5, 7−16, 18,
19, 21−Nov. 18, 20−Dec. 31.

1961   Jan. 1−Feb. 1, 3−24, Mar.
1−30, Apr. 3−May 5, 7−July
4, 6−Sept. 22, 24−Oct. 25,
27−Dec. 31.

Micro (P) & (N)
   1962   Jan. 1+.
FU
   1965   Jan. 1+.
Micro (N)
   1962   Aug. 1−Sept. 8, 10, 12, 14−
           Dec. 31.
   1963   Jan. 1−Apr. 6, 9−21, 23−
           May 21, 23−Aug. 14.
   1964   Feb. 13−Dec. 31.
LNT−MA
   1937   Feb. 8−10, May 3, 29.
   1941   Sept. 15, Dec. 4−11.
   1943   Feb. 3, 4.
   1951   Feb. 1−Oct. 12.
TxU
   1946   Sept. 21.

EL PROGRESO. w. est. Apr. 11, 1850.
  CU−B
   1850   Apr. 11−Oct. 10.
  NHi
   1850   June 27, July 11.

LA REGENERACION. sw., w.
  CU−B
  Micro (P)
   1876   May 16−27, June 7, July 3−
           Aug. 21, Sept. 18, Oct. 9.
   1877   May 24−June 7.

EL SALVADOR REGENERADO. irr. est.
Feb. 7, 1845.
  Note: Succeeded *Correo semanario
  del Salvador*.
  CtY
   1845   Feb. 7, Apr. 30−July 4, Aug.
           1−Nov. 7, Dec. 5.
   1846   May 31−June 12, Aug. 13−
           Sept. 25, Oct. 5−Nov. 6, Dec.
           11−31.
   1847   Jan. 21−Mar. 11.
           Suplemento: Mar. 11.

SEMANARIO POLITICO MERCANTIL
DE SAN SALVADOR. w. est. 1824.
  Note: Ceased publication 1826.
  LNHT
  Micro (P)
   1824   July 31−Oct. 23.

EL SIGLO. irr. est. Jan. 1851.
  CU – B
    1851   Jan. 10, Feb. 15 – 27, Mar. 20,
            Apr. 22, May 16 – June 12, 30,
            July 6 – Aug. 14, 26 – Oct. 25,
            Nov. 10 – 28, Dec. 13 – 25.
            Suplemento: May 5.
    1852   Jan. 1, 13 – 31, Feb. 12 – 21,
            Mar. 4 – May 21, June 2 – July
            8, 14 – Dec. 28.
    1853   Jan. 1 – 7.
  CtY
    1851   Feb. 9 – Mar. 8, 26 – Apr. 13,
            22 – June 6, 15, 27 – Aug. 11,
            20 – 26.

  NHi
    1851   Apr. 22 – Dec. 25.
    1852   Jan. 1 – Dec. 22.

EL SIGLO XX.
  See *Diario latino*.

TELEGRAFO DEL SALVADOR. bw.
  MWA
    1889   July 15.

LA TIJERETA. est. 1838.
  LNHT
    Micro (P)
    1838   Mar. 16.

TRIBUNA LIBRE. d. est. Nov. 25, 1933.
  Note: Title *Diario nuevo*, Nov. 25,
  1933 – June 25, 1944; *La Tribuna*,
  June 26, 1944 – Dec. 14, 1948;
  Tribuna libre, after 1949. Suspend-
  ed publication Jan. 2, Apr. 10 – 13,
  Aug. 5 – 7, 1952; Jan. 2, Apr. 15 – 19,
  Aug. 6 – 9, Dec. 15, 26, 1954.
  CU
    1944   Feb. 15 – 19, 22, 24 – Mar. 22,
            25 – Apr. 1, 10 – May 4, [18 –
            Sept. 9], 12 – 29, Oct. 2 – Nov.
            14, 17.
  DLC
    1935   Feb. 16, 17, 19, 20, 22 – Mar.
            1, 3 – 14, Apr. 27 – 29, May 2 –
            7, 16 – 18.
    1939   May 30.
    1940   June 3.

1941   Apr. 1 – 8, 16 – May 26, 28 –
        June 2, 4 – 23, 25 – July 1, 3 –
        Aug. 4, 7 – Sept. 18, 20 – Oct.
        9, Nov. 21 – 25, 27, 28, Dec.
        2 – 14, 17 – 19, 22 – 24.
1942   Jan. 28, Feb. 3, 4, 7, 10, 11, 13,
        14, 17, 20 – 28, Mar. 3, 5, 7, 11,
        12, 14 – 20, 23 – 31, Apr. 9,
        11 – 13, 15 – 22, 24 – 28, 30 –
        May 6, 8, 9, 12, 14 – 19, 21 – 25.
1943   Apr. 29, Sept. 30, Oct. 1 – 6,
        8 – 10, 12 – 18, 20 – Nov. 5, 7,
        9 – Dec. 26, 28 – 31.
1944   Jan. 1 – 3, 6 – 9, 11 – Feb. 9,
        12 – Mar. 31.
1946   Apr. 2 – 8, 10 – Aug. 26, 29 –
        31.
1950   Aug. 1, 2, 8 – 17, 23, 25 – 29,
        31, Nov. 9 – 11.
1951   Jan. 3, 4, 7 – 10, 12 – Feb. 27,
        Mar. 1 – June 26, 29 – July 5,
        7 – Aug. 18, 20 – Dec. 25, 27 –
        30.
1952   Jan. 1 – Mar. 20, 22, 24 – Apr.
        25, 27 – 30, May 3 – June 29,
        July 1 – Sept. 5, 8, 11 – Dec.
        29.
1953   Jan. 1 – 3, 5 – 23, 26 – Feb. 20,
        22 – Mar. 26, 28 – May 6, 8,
        11 – Aug. 20, 22, 24 – Sept. 8,
        10 – Oct. 30, Nov. 1 – 18, 20 –
        Dec. 31.
1954   Jan. 1 – July 2, 8 – Aug. 4, 11 –
        Oct. 5, 7 – 28, 30 – Nov. 3, 5 –
        Dec. 6, 9 – 31.
1955   Jan. 1 – 10, 13 – Feb. 16, 18,
        21 – Sept. 9, 11 – Oct. 31, Nov.
        7 – Dec. 31.
1956   Jan. 1 – Mar. 29, Apr. 3 –
        Sept. 30, Oct. 2 – Dec. 30.
FU
1950 – 1952   [Jan. 1 – Dec. 31].
1953 – 1956   Jan. 1 – Dec. 31.
1957   Jan. 1 – Feb. 5.
IEN
1950   Aug. 31, Sept. 8 – 12, 14 – 19,
        22 – Oct. 13, 16, Nov. 17, 19 –
        21, 24, 26 – Dec. 5, 7, 12, 14 –
        17, 20 – 31.

1951–1956   [Jan. 1–Dec. 31].
LNT–MA
1947   Jan. 1–Feb. 5.
1948   Dec. 1–11.
1949–1956   Jan. 1–Dec. 31.
Micro (N)
1934–1943   Jan. 1–Dec. 31.
TxU
1950   June 9, 13–15, Aug. 25, 27–
       Sept. 2, 6–19, 21–23, 27–
       Oct. 8, 11–28, 31–Nov. 7,
       9–16, 18–Dec. 9, 12–31.
1951   Jan. 1–Feb. 14, 16–Mar. 16,
       27–Dec. 31.
1952   Jan. 1–18, 21–Apr. 26, 28–
       Sept. 12, 15–22, 24, 25, 28–
       Oct. 2, 6–31, Nov. 3–7, 10–
       Dec. 3, 13–18, 20–22, 24, 25,
       27–31.
1953   Jan. 1–Apr. 2, 6–28, 30, May
       3–July 2, 4–Aug. 5, 8–Sept.
       30, Oct. 3–5, 7–12, 16–Dec.
       31.
1954   Jan. 1, 3–Feb. 15, 17–Sept.
       15, 17–27, Oct. 1–31, Nov. 2,
       3, 8–Dec. 31.

ViU
1950   June 1–4, 6–8, 10, 11, 13, 14,
       Aug. 25–27, 29–Sept. 3, 5–
       10, 12, 14, 17, 19–Oct. 1, 3–8,
       10–12, 15, 17–22, 24–Nov. 5,
       7–13, 17–30, Dec. 1–14,
       17–25, 27–31.
1951   Jan. 3–7, 9–14, 16–21, 23–
       28, 30–Feb. 4, 6, 8–11, 13–
       18, 20–24, 27–Mar. 4, 6–11,
       13, 14, 17, 18, 20–22, 27–Apr.
       1, 3–8, 10–15, 17–22, 24–
       29, May 1, 4–6, 8–13, 15–
       17, 19, 20, 22, 24–27, 29–June
       3, 5–7, 9, 10, 12–17, 19–24,
       30, July 1, 3, 4, 6–8, 10–15,
       17–22, 24–29, 31–Aug. 4,
       8–12, 14–18, 21, 25, 28–
       Sept. 2, 4–9, 11–15, 18–23,
       25–29, Oct. 2–7, 9–12, 14,
       16–19, 24–28, 30–Nov. 4,
       6–11, 13, 14, 16–18, 20–25,

27, 28, 30–Dec. 2, 4–9, 11–
13, 16, 18–23, 25, 27–30.
1952   Jan. 1, 3–6, 8–20, 22–27,
       29–Feb. 3, 5–10, 12–17,
       19–24, 26–Mar. 2, 4–9, 11–
       16, 21–23, 25–30, Apr. 1–6,
       8, 9, 30–May 1, 3, 4, 6–11,
       13–18, 20, 21, 24, 25, 27, 29–
       June 1, 3, 4, 5–8, 10–13, 15,
       17–29, July 1–6, 8–13, 15–
       20, 22–27, Aug. 1–3, 8–10,
       12–23, 26–28, 30–Sept. 7,
       9–14, 17–21, 23–27, Oct. 1–
       5, 7–12, 14–19, 21–26, 28–
       Nov. 2, 5, 7–9, 11–15, 17–
       23, 25–Dec. 8, 10–13, 17, 20,
       21, 23–25, 27, 28, 30, 31.
1953   Jan. 1, 3, 4, 8–11, 13–20, 22,
       23, 25, 27–Feb. 1, 3–8, 10–
       15, 17–20, 24–Mar. 1, 3–8,
       10–15, 17–22, 24–29, 31–
       Apr. 2, 7–12, 14–19, 21–26,
       28–May 1, 3, 5–10, 12–17,
       19–24, 26–31, June 2, 3, 5–
       7, 9–14, 16–19, 23–25, 27,
       28, 30, July 2–5, 7, 9–12, 14–
       16, 18, 19, 21–26, 28–Aug. 2,
       4, 5, 8, 9, 11–16, 18–23, 25–
       29, Sept. 1–6, 8–13, 17–20,
       22–27, 29–Oct. 3, 6–11, 13–
       18, 20–25, 27–Nov. 1, 3–8,
       10–15, 17–22, 24, 26–29,
       Dec. 2–4, 8–13, 15–20, 23,
       25–27, 29–31.
1954   Jan. 1, 3, 6–8, 10, 13, 15–17,
       19–23, 26–Feb. 7, 9–14,
       16–21, 23–26, Mar. 3–7, 9,
       10, 12–14, 16–19, 21, 23–
       28, 30–Apr. 4, 6–9, 14, 15,
       20–25, 27–May 2, 4–9, 11–
       16, 18–23, 25–June 6, 8–13,
       15–20, 22–27, 29–July 4, 6–
       9, 13–18, 20–25, 27–Aug. 1,
       3–5, 10–15, 17–22, 25–29,
       31–Sept. 5, 7, 8, 10–12, 15–
       18, 21–26, 29, Oct. 1, 2, 5–
       10, 12–17, 19–24, 26–31,
       Nov. 3, 5–7, 9–14, 16–21,

23—28, 30—Dec. 5, 7—12, 14,
16—19, 21—25, 28—31.
1955   Jan. 1, 4—9, 11—16, 18—20,
22, 23, 25, 26, 28—30, Feb. 1—
6, 9—13, 15—20, 22—27, Mar.
1—6, 8—13, 15—20, 22—27,
29—Apr. 3, 5—7, 12—17, 19—
24, 26—May 1, 3—8, 10—15,
17—22, 24—29, 31—June 5,
7—12, 14—19, 21—26, 28—
July 3, 5—10, 12—17, 19—24,
26—Aug. 5, 9—14, 16—21,
23—28, 30—Sept. 4, 6—9, 11,
13—15, 17, 18, 20—25, 27—
Oct. 2, 4—9, 11—16, 18, 21—
23, 25—30, Nov. 8—13, 15—
20, 24—27, 29—Dec. 4, 6—11,
13, 14, 16—18, 20—25, 27—31.
1956   Jan. 1, 3—8, 10, 11, 14, 15, 17—
22, 24—29, 31—Feb. 5, 7—19,
21—26, 28—Mar. 4, 6—18,
20—25, 27—29, Apr. 3—5, 7, 8,
10—15, 17—22, 24—29, May 1,
3—6, 8—13, 15—20, 22—27,
29—June 3, 5—10, 12—17,
19—24, 26—July 1, 3—8, 10—
15, 17—22, 24—29, 31—Aug. 5,
8—12, 14—19, 21—26, 28—
Sept. 2, 4—9, 11—15, 18—23,
25—30, Oct. 2—7, 10—14, 16—
21, 23—28, 30—Nov. 4, 6—12,
14—18, 20—23, 25, 27—Dec. 2,
4—9, 11—16, 18—23, 25, 27—
30.
1957   Jan. 1, 3—6, 8—13, 15—20,
22—27, 29—Feb. 3.

LA UNION. bw. est. June 15, 1849.
  CU—B
    1849   June 15—Sept. 1, Oct. 1, Nov.
            15—Dec. 15.
    1850   Jan. 1—15.
EL UNIONISTA.
  LNT—MA
    1956   Nov. 1—Dec. 31.
    1957   Jan. 1—May 31.
EL UNIVERSO. d.
  CtY
    1875   Dec. 22.

LA VOZ DE LA NACION. bw. est. 1927.
  DLC
    1927   June 25—Aug. 31.

San Vicente

EL ROL. w. est. 1854.
  CU—B
    1854   Sept. 29—Dec. 15.
    1855   Jan. 19—Mar. 21.

Santa Ana

BOLETIN DEL EJERCITO. est. Jan.
  16, 1851.
  CU—B
    1851   Jan. 16.

DIARIO DE OCCIDENTE. d. est. Sept.
  1, 1910.
  DLC
    1928   May 1—12, July 16—29, Aug.
            7—31, Sept. 2—Oct. 25, Nov.
            6, 26, 28—Dec. 31.
    1929   Jan. 1—Feb. 1, 3, 4, 6—Apr.
            30.
  LNT—MA
    1937   May 21.

LA LINTERNA.
  LNHT
    1908   Feb. 8.

EL UNIVERSAL. d.
  CU
    1944   Nov. 7—9.

Santiago de María

PRISMA. est. 1938.
  LNT—MA
    1944   Jan. 23.

Sonsonate

HERALDO DE SONSONATE. sw., d.
  est. 1918.
  LNT—MA
    1937   Feb. 8.

GUATEMALA

Antigua

EL ECO DEL VALLE. bw., w. est. 1882.
  CU–B
    Micro (P)
    1882   Dec. 8–31.
    1883   Jan. 7, Feb. 4.

Ciudad Flores

EL IMPULSO. w. est. [1927].
  LNT–MA
    1928   June 3.

Cobán

RUTA.
  LNHT
    1948   Apr. 1–Dec. 31.
    1949   Jan. 1–Oct. 31.

Guatemala City

ACCION. d. est. [1938].
  DLC
    1940   Sept. 17.
    1941   July 22.

ACTUALIDAD. w. est. [1940].
  DLC
    1941   Oct. 11, 18.
            Suplemento: n.d. (Nos. 30, 32,
            35).

EL ALBUM REPUBLICANO. w. est. 1848.
  LNT–MA
    Micro (P)
    1848   Mar. 1–May 11, Aug. 28–
            Nov. 24.

EL AMIGO DE GUATEMALA. irr. est.
  Mar. 29, 1838.
  DLC
    1838   Mar. 29–July 2.
  LNT–MA
    Micro (P)
    1838   Mar. 29–Apr. 24.

EL AMIGO DE LA PATRIA. w. est. Oct.
  16, 1820.

CtY
  1820   Nov. 24–Dec. 2.
  1821   Jan. 27, May 29.
  1822   Jan. 25.
TxU
  1820   Oct. 16–Dec. 31.
  1821   Jan. 1–12, 27–Dec. 31.
  1822   Jan. 1–Apr. 1.

LA ANOMALIA. est. Mar. 17, 1838.
  LNT–MA
    Micro (P)
    1838   Mar. 22, Apr. 2.
  MWA
    1838   Mar. 22, Apr. 2.

EL APENDICE. irr. est. Mar. 23, 1838.
  CtY
    1838   Apr. 6–17, May 5, 19–31,
            June 9, 27–July 18.
            Suplemento: May 31.
  DLC
    1838   Mar. 23–July 18.
            Alcance: May 19, June 7.
            Suplemento: June 7.
  LNT–MA
    Micro (P)
    1838   Mar. 23, 27, May 25, June 7,
            July 12.

EL APOSTOL.
  LNT–MA
    1937   Mar. 21.

LA AURORA. bw. est. Jan. 19, 1845.
  MWA
    1845   Prospecto: Jan. 1.
            Jan. 19–Dec. 11.

AVE DE MINERVA.
  MWA
    1829   n.d., Oct. 28, Nov. 23.

BOLETIN DE NOTICIAS. sw. est. 1850.
  CU–B
    1850   Jan. 5, 16.
    1851   Mar. 1.
    1853   July 12, Sept. 3, 5.
  LNT–MA
    Micro (P)
    1850   Jan. 5, 12, 16, 19, 23.
    1855   July 16, 17, 18.

BOLETIN DE NOTICIAS. est. Feb. 1867.
  MWA
    1868   Apr. 29.

BOLETIN OFICIAL. bw. est. Apr. 1, 1831
    Note: Established Part 3 in 1836. Suc-
    ceeded *La Gaceta*; succeeded by *El
    Tiempo*. Ceased publication Feb.
    1839.
  CU – B
    Part 1.
    1831   Apr. 15.
    1833   May 14, July 1 – 31.
    1834   Feb. 27 – Oct. 29.
    1835   Aug. 17, 27, Oct. 13, Nov. 19.
    1836   Aug. 20, Oct. 26.
    1837   Sept. 13.
    Part 2.
    1832   Mar. 1 – 3, May 19, 26, July
            15.
    1834   Jan. 7 – 18, Feb. 25 – May 1,
            June 1, July 15, Oct. 15.
    1835   June 22.·
    1837   June 26.
    Part 3.
    1837   Nov. 16.
    1838   Aug. 13, Oct. 22.
  CtY
    1831   Apr. 1 – Dec. 15.
    1832   July 15 – Aug. 15.
    1834   May 26.
    1838   Jan. 16.
  DLC
    Part 1.
    1831   [Apr. 1 – Dec. 31].
    1832 – 1838   [Jan. 1 – Dec. 31].
    1939   [Jan. 1 – Feb. 28].

    Part 2
    1831   [Apr. 1 – Dec. 31].
    1832 – 1838   [Jan. 1 – Dec. 31].
    Part 3.
    1836 – 1838   [Jan. 1 – Dec. 31].
    1839   [Jan. 1 – Feb. 28].
  LNT – MA
    Part 1.
    1831   Apr. 1 – July 31, Sept. 1, Oct.
            14 – Nov. 12, Dec. 9.
    1832   Feb. 1 – Dec. 31.

    1833   Jan. 1 – Dec. 31.
    1834   Feb. 27 – May 29, Aug. 22 –
            Dec. 9.
    1835   Feb. 13, 18, 26, 28, Mar. 3, 10,
            14, Apr. 7, 10, May 4, 7, 8, 15,
            25, Aug. 18, 25, Sept. 27, Oct.
            13, Nov. 13, 19, Dec. 9, 11, 21.
    1836   Feb. 11, Mar. 14, May 12, 13,
            Sept. 8, Oct. 6, 26.
    1837   Feb. 28, Mar. 15, 29, Apr.
            19 – Oct. 30.
    1838   Feb. 8 – Aug. 9, Dec. 24.
    Part 2.
    1831   May 1 – July 31, Sept. 1 – 30,
            Nov. 15, Dec. 1.
    1833   Jan. 1 – 31, May 6 – Oct. 10,
            Dec. 22.
            Extraordinario: Jan. 4, Mar.
            18, May 18, July 1 – 31, Aug.
            22, Sept. 1 – 30, Dec. 1 – 31.
    1834   Feb. 1, 28, Mar. 31, Aug. 26,
            Sept. 1, 30.
            Extraordinario: Jan. 28, Feb. 1,
            Mar. 15, Oct. 4, Nov. 14, Dec.
            22.
    1835   Jan. 17, Mar. 14, Aug. 1.
            Extraordinario: Jan. 17, Apr.
            11, May 21, Aug. 1.
    1836   June 4, Aug. 1, 23.
    1837   Jan. 27 – May 26.
    1838   Oct. 31.
    Part 3.
    1836   Nov. 30.
            Extraordinario: Jan. 26, May
            13, Sept. 24.
    1837   Jan. 21, 23, Feb. 15 – June 23,
            July 12 – Oct. 1, Dec. 23.
    1838   Jan. 15 – May 25, Aug. 22.
  MWA
    1831   Apr. 15 – Dec. 31.
    1832   Jan. 1 – Dec. 31.
    1833   Jan. 1 – July 15.

BOLETIN OFICIAL. est. July 11, 1871.
    Note: Succeeded *Gaceta de Guate-
    mala*; succeeded by *El Guatemal-
    teco*. Ceased publication Feb. 13,
    1873.

LNHT
   1871   [July 11 – Dec. 31].
   1872   Jan. 1 – Dec. 31.
   1873   Jan. 1 – Feb. 13.

EL CAFE. est. Aug. 1, 1839.
  LNT – MA
   Micro (P)
   1839   Aug. 1 – Sept. 8.

EL CAPICULTOZ.
  LNT – MA
   1958   Mar. 15, Apr. 15, July 31.

EL CENTRO-AMERICANO. w., irr. est.
  May 22, 1833.
   Note: Ceased publication [Jan. 19,
   1834].
  CtY
   1833   Sept. 27, Oct. 18, Dec. 12.
  MWA
   1833   May 22 – Sept. 21.

EL COLERA.
  LNT – MA
   1887   Dec. 29.
   1888   Jan. 6.

COMETA. est. May 1, 1847.
  MWA
   1847   May 1 – 25.

CONTINUACION DE LAS NOTICIAS
  DE ESPAÑA, SACADAS DE GAZE-
  TAS DE MADRID.
  MWA
   1808   n.d., [July 17, Aug. 20.]

EL CORREO DE LA TARDE. d. est. Dec.
  8, 1890.
   Note: Published by Rubén Darío,
   famous Latin American poet, while
   living in exile in Guatemala. Ceased
   publication June 5, 1891.
  DLC
   1890   Dec. 8 – 31.
   1891   Jan. 1 – June 5.

CORREO DE LOS POBRES DE
  CENTRO-AMERICA. est. Oct. 11,
  1834.
  MWA
   1834   Oct. 25.

EL CRONISTA. d.
  CU
   1914   Feb. 9, Apr. 20.

CURATORIO POLITICO Y MORAL.
  est. Sept. 26, 1832.
  MWA
   1832   Sept. 26.

EL DEMOCRATA. irr. est. Apr. 3, 1838.
  CtY
   1838   Apr. 3, 20.
  DLC
   1838   Apr. 3 – 29.

DIARIO DE CENTRO AMÉRICA. d. est.
  Aug. 13, 1880.
   Note: On Mar. 21, 1931 superseded
   El Guatemalteco (1886+) as the official publication with two sections:
   official and informative. The first
   number of the official publication
   bears the imprint "2a. época, año
   L" as well as "fundado en 1880."
   The official section was superseded
   on Feb. 1, 1950 by *El Guatemalteco*.
   Only the official section ceased publication on Jan. 31, 1950. From 1931 –
   Jan. 31, 1950, *Diario de Centro América* is classified as a periodical
   (Official Gazette) under the call
   number J5.G73.
  CU – B
   1930   Mar. 20 – Dec. 31.
   1931   Jan. 1 – July 17, 19 – Dec. 31.
   1932   Jan. 1 – Dec. 31.
   1933   Jan. 1 – June 16, 18 – Dec. 31.
   1934 – 1936   Jan. 1 – Dec. 31.
   1937   Jan. 1 – Nov. 28, Dec. 12 – 31.
   1938 – 1939   Jan. 1 – Dec. 31.
   1940   Jan. 1 – Dec. 29.
   1941 – 1942   Jan. 1 – Dec. 31.
   1943   Jan. 1 – Oct. 26, 28 – Dec. 30.
   1944 – 1945   Jan. 1 – Dec. 31.
   1946   Jan. 1 – July 1, Sept. 13 – Dec.
     31.
   1947 – 1953   Jan. 1 – Dec. 31.
   1954   Jan. 1 – Feb. 14, Apr. 26 –
     July 22, 27 – Nov. 8, 14 – Dec.
     31.

1955   Jan. 1 – Mar. 13, 20 – May 24,
   25 – June ₁30₁.
Micro (P)
1880   Dec. 15, 17 – 29.

CtY
1882   Oct. 2.
1940   Feb. 22 – Dec. 31.
1941 – 1945   Jan. 1 – Dec. 31.
1946   Jan. 1 – July 1, Sept. 13 – Oct.
   8, 18, Nov. 19 – Dec. 31.
1947   [Jan. 1 – Dec. 31].
1948   Jan. 1 – Dec. 31.
1949   Jan. 1 – Aug. 2.

DLC
1931   Mar. 21+.

DPU
Current (six months).

ICRL
1950   Apr. 1 – Dec. 31.
1951 – 1952   Jan. 1 – Dec. 31.
1953   Jan. 1 – Apr. 30.
Micro (P) & (N)
1956   Jan. 1+.

IU
1935   Oct. 31, Dec. 10, 12, 14.
1936   Mar. 2, June 15 – July 3, 13 –
   25, Aug. 1 – 7, 14 – 28, 31 –
   Dec. 31.
 1937   Jan. 1 – 9, 18 – Mar. 5, 15 –
   June 19, 28 – Dec. 31.
 1938   Jan. 18 – 22, Mar. 2 – July 9.

KHi
1886   May 10.

LNHT
1931 – 1944   Jan. 1 – Dec. 31.
1951   Mar. 30 – Sept. 8, 17 – Dec. 31.
1952   ₁Jan. 1 – Dec. 31.₁
1953   Jan. 1 – Dec. 31.
1954   Jan. 1 – Feb. 28, Apr. 1 –
   Dec. 31.
1955   Jan. 1 – June 30.
Micro (N)
1908 – 1931   Jan. 1 – Dec. 31.
Micro (P)
1956   Jan. 1+.

NN
Micro (N)

1949   Aug. 3 – 15, 17 – Nov. 17, 19 –
   Dec. 31.
1950   Jan. 1 – Apr. 26, 28 – Oct. 15,
   17 – Dec. 31.
1951   Jan. 1 – Feb. 4, 11 – 16, 18 –
   25, 27 – Sept. 9, 16 – Nov. 18,
   25 – Dec. 31.
1952   Jan. 1 – Oct. 16, 19, 26 – Nov.
   15, 26 – Dec. 13, 22 – 31.
   Suplemento: May 29.
1953   Jan. 1 – 10, 19 – May 23, June
   1 – 6, 15 – Aug. 22, 31 – Sept. 8,
   10 – Oct. 24, Nov. 2 – Dec. 26,
   28 – 31.
1954   Jan. 1 – 4, 6 – Feb. 13, 15 –
   May 29, June 14 – July 22, 27 –
   Dec. 31.
1955   Jan. 1 – 23, 30 – May 24, 26 –
   Dec. 31.
Micro (P)
1956   Jan. 1+.

PrU
1963   Nov. 8 – 30, Dec. 1 – 7, 10 – 23,
   26 – 30.
1964   Jan. 8 – Feb. 19, 21 – 29, Mar.
   2, 4 – 11, 13 – 25, 30 – Apr. 3,
   5 – 17, 19 – 22, 24 – 30, May 2 –
   7, 9 – 12, 14 – 30, June 1 – 28,
   30, July 1 – Aug. 1, 4 – 8, 10 –
   14, 17 – 22, 24 – 29, 31 – Sept.
   5, 7 – 10, 17, 19, 21 – 26, 28, 29,
   Oct. 1, 5 – 10, 13 – 17, 19 – 24,
   26 – 31, Nov. 2 – 22, 24 – 30,
   Dec. 1 – 5, 7 – 23, 27 – 31.
1965   Jan. 4 – 9, 11, 13, 15, 16, 18 –
   20, 22, 23, 25 – 30, Feb. 1 – 18,
   20 – 25, 27, Mar. 1 – 8, 10 – 31,
   Apr. 1 – 14, 18 – 30, May 3 – 6,
   8 – 11, 15 – June 5, 7 – 28, July
   1 – 5, 6 – 12, 14, 17 – 19, 21, 22,
   24 – 31, Aug. 3, 5 – 7, 9, 11 –
   14, 16, 17, 19 – 21, 23 – 25, 27,
   28, 30 – Oct. 21, 26, 29 – 30,
   Nov. 2 – 16, 24, 26 – 30, Dec.
   1 – 31.

WaU
1965   Mar. 18 – Dec. 31.
1966   Jan. 1+.

DIARIO DE GUATEMALA. d. est. Jan. 24, 1828.
> Note: Ceased publication Mar. 3, 1828.
> FU
>> 1828   Jan. 24 – Mar. 2.
>
> LNT – MA
>> Micro (P)
>> 1828   Feb. 1, 28, Mar. 3.

DIARIO DE GUATEMALA. d. est. Sept. 1, 1924.
> DLC
>> 1930   Dec. 6 – 18, 27, 28, 30.
>> 1931   Jan. 1 – 10, 15, 16, 18 – 20, 22 – Feb. 10, 19 – 26, Mar. 21, 22, 24 – Apr. 1, 7 – 9, 11 – 29, May 1, 3 – June 15, 18 – 26.
>
> ICRL
>> 1927   Oct. 31.
>
> TxU
>> 1924   Dec. 19, 20, 23.

DIARIO DEL PUEBLO. d. est. 1953.
> DLC
>> 1954   Feb. 4, 6, 9, 10, 12 – 15, 17 – 26, May 1 – 8, 11 – 22, 25 – 27, 29.

EL EDITOR. irr. est. Feb. 8, 1837.
> Note: Ceased publication Dec. 28, 1837.
> DLC
>> 1837   Feb. 8 – Mar. 16, 25 – June 24, July 13 – Dec. 28.
>>   Alcance: July 20.
>
> LNHT
>> Micro (P)
>> 1837   Mar. 1 – Dec. 28.

EDITOR CONSTITUCIONAL.
> See *Genio de la libertad.*

LA EPOCA.
> LNT – MA
>> 1955   Nov. 20, Dec. 25.
>> 1956   Jan. 8, Apr. 29, May 13, Dec. 23.
>> 1958   May 13, July 6, Oct. 19.
>> 1959   Jan. 10, Apr. 19, Sept. 27, Nov. 1.

>> 1960   Jan. 17, May 8, Sept. 18.

EL ESPECTADOR. d. est. [1953].
> DLC
>> 1954   Jan. 5, 12 – 15, 19, 20, Feb. 24, Mar. 18, 23, 25, Apr. 23, 27, May 3, 5 – 7, 11, 14, 17, 19 – 21, 24 – 26, 28 – June 10, 12, July 1, 3, 9 – 12, 16 – 20, 26, 30, Aug. 3 – 6, 19, 24, 30, Sept. 2.
>> 1956   Jan. 2 – 20, 25, 27 – 29, Feb. 1, 11, Mar. 8 – 28, Apr. 1 – June 17, 20 – Nov. 6, Dec. 6 – 31.
>
> LNT – MA
>> 1955   June 16, 17, 20.

LA ESTAFETA. est. Oct. 17, 1832.
> LNT – MA
>> Micro (P)
>> 1832   Oct. 17, 27, Nov. 3, 9.

LA ESTRELLA DE GUATEMALA. w., d. est. June 20, 1885.
> Note: Ceased publication [1888]. See also the *Guatemala Star.*
> CU – B
>> Micro (P)
>> 1885   June 27 – July 4, Aug. 1.
>> 1886   Jan. 28, May 4 – 16, June 8 – 20, Sept. 1 – Oct. 27, 29 – Nov. 6, 9 – 17, 19, 20, 23 – Dec. 31.
>> 1887   Jan. 1 – 19, 21 – 26, 28 – Feb. 6, 9 – 13, 18 – 20, 26, 27.

EXCELSIOR. d. est. [1918].
> Note: Ceased publication [1930].
> DLC
>> 1926   Jan. 6 – 19, Feb. 19, 20, Apr. 22 – 24, June 18 – 30, July 12, 14 – 19, 21 – 24, Aug. 3, 4, 17 – 24, Sept. 9 – 20, 22 – Dec. 5, 7 – 31.
>> 1927   Jan. 1 – Feb. 22, 24 – Mar. 29, Apr. 1 – 29, May 1 – 23, 25 – Nov. 30.
>>   Extraordinario: Aug. 14.
>> 1928   Jan. 3 – 24, 26 – Feb. 8, 10 – 27, 29 – Mar. 4, 6 – Apr. 4, 8, 10 – 20, 22 – 27, 29 – May 18, 20 – 22, 24 – June 24, 26 – Oct.

7, 9, 11−14, Nov. 4, 6, 7, 9−24.
1929   Jan. 1−Apr. 23, 25−June 9,
16, 21−Aug. 11, 18−Dec. 31.
1930   Jan. 1−Feb. 27, Mar. 1−Aug.
9.

EL FEDERALISTA. irr. est. Aug. 7, 1833.
CtY
1833   Oct. 17.
TxU
1833   Aug. 7−14.
1834   Jan. 9.

EL FERROCARRIL. d. est. Mar. 5, 1894.
NN
Micro (P) & (N)
1894   Mar. 5−July 9.

FRENTE POPULAR LIBERTADOR. w.
CSt
1947   June 28, July 19.

LA GACETA. irr. est. Feb. 9, 1830.
Note: Title *Gaceta federal*, Feb. 8,
1830−June 4, 1833; *Gaceta*, after
June 5, 1833. Succeeded *El Boletín*;
succeeded by *Boletín oficial*. Ceased
publication 1834.
CtY
1833   June 5, July 17−30, Oct. 16.
LNHT
1830   Mar. 26.
1831   Jan. 18.
1832   July 12, Sept. 3.
Micro (P)
1833   Oct. 1−Nov. 30.
MWA
1830   Feb. 8−Dec. 31.
1831   Jan. 1−Dec. 31.
1832   Jan. 1−Sept. 18.
1833   June 5−Dec. 31.
1834   Jan. 1−12.
TxU
1830   Sept. 3, Oct. 19−Dec. 22.
1831   Aug. 22, Dec. 3.
1832   Sept. 3.

GACETA DE GUATEMALA. w. est. Mar.
4, 1841.
Note: Title *Gaceta oficial*, Mar. 4,
1841−Mar. 29, 1847; *Gaceta de*

Guatemala, Apr. 8, 1847−June 25,
1871. Succeeded *El Tiempo*, succeeded
by *Boletín oficial*. Ceased publication June 29, 1871.
CU−B
1849   June 18, Aug. 23, Nov. 30.
1850   Feb. 21−Mar. 7, May 3.
1851   July 19.
1853   May 13−20, July 29−Aug. 5,
26, Sept. 9−Dec. 30.
1854   Jan. 6−Mar. 10, Apr. 9−Dec.
31.
1855−1859   Jan. 1−Dec. 31.
1860   Jan. 1−Apr. 19.
Micro (P)
1850   June 28−Dec. 31.
1851   Jan. 1−Dec. 31.
1852   Jan. 1−Oct. 1.
1858   Mar. 7.
CtY
1841   Mar. 4−20, May 28, July 16,
Sept. 1, Nov. 19.
1842   May 17−June 23, July 3, Aug.
18, 30, Sept. 17, Oct. 12, 28.
1843   Dec. 9.
1844   Aug. 7, Sept. 7−Oct. 12, Nov.
15.
1845   Jan. 17−Dec. 6.
1846   Jan. 14−Dec. 25.
1847   Jan. 11−Mar. 29, Apr. 8−Dec.
22.
1848   Jan. 5−Mar. 22.
1849   Mar. 16.
1854   May 19.
1858   Nov. 27, Dec. 29.
1862   Nov. 8.
1865   Apr. 8.
DLC
1841   Mar. 4−Dec. 31.
1842−1868   Jan. 1−Dec. 31.
1869   Jan. 2.
1870   Jan. 6−Dec. 31.
1871   Jan. 1−June 18.
LNHT
1841   Mar. 4−Dec. 31.
1842−1844   Jan. 1−Dec. 31.
1850   June 1−Dec. 31.
1851−1871   Jan. 1−Dec. 31.

Micro (P)
1845 – 1849   Jan. 1 – Dec. 31.
1850   Jan. 1 – June 30.
MWA
1841   Mar. 4 – Dec. 31.
1842 – 1843   Jan. 1 – Dec. 31.
1844   Jan. 1 – Dec. 18.
1845   Jan. 17 – Dec. 31.
1846 – 1853   Jan. 1 – Dec. 31.
1854   Jan. 1 – Apr. 21 [May 5 – Nov. 17.]
1855   Jan. 1 – Apr. 27, [May 18 – Dec. 31.]
1856 – 1870   Jan. 1 – Dec. 31.
1871   Jan. 1 – June 29.
NHi
1853   Sept. 16, Dec. 30.
1854   Jan. 6, 27, Feb. 3, Mar. 3, Apr. 12, 28, May 5, 12.

GACETA DEL GOBIERNO. irr. est. Mar. 1, 1824.
    Note: Title *Gaceta del gobierno supremo de Guatemala*, Mar. 1, 1824 – Aug. 24, 1826; *Gaceta del gobierno*, Aug. 25, 1826 – Apr. 1829. Succeeded *La Tribuna*; succeeded by *El Boletín*. Ceased publication Apr. 1829.
CU – B
    Micro (P)
    1824   Mar. 1 – Dec. 31.
    1825   Jan. 1 – Apr. 28, Nov. 10 – Dec. 31.
    1826   Jan. 1 – Aug. 24, Sept. 30 – Dec. 31.
    1827 – 1828   Jan. 1 – Dec. 31.
    1829   Jan. 1 – Mar. 13.
CtY
    1828   Extraordinario: May 5.
DLC
    1824   Apr. 14, May 1, 14, Aug. 19.
    1827   Apr. 17.
LNHT
    Micro (P)
    1826   Sept. 30 – Dec. 31.
    1827   May 2.
    1828   Mar. 2, Apr. 15, Aug. 30, Nov. 13.

1829   Feb. 5, 17, 21, 24, Mar. 7, 13.
MWA
    1824   Prospecto.
            Mar. 1 – Dec. 31.
    1825 – 1828   Jan. 1 – Dec. 31.
    1829   Jan. 1 – Mar. 13.

GACETA DEL GOBIERNO DE GUATE-
MALA. m., w., irr. est. Nov. 1, 1729.
    Note: Title *Gazeta de Guatemala*, Nov. 1, 1789 – Sept. 1811; *Gaceta del gobierno de Guatemala*, Oct. 1811 – 1822. Periodicity Nov. 1, 1729 – Feb. 12, 1797, monthly; Feb. 13, 1797 – Jan. 1, 1798, weekly; Jan. 1, 1798 – 1822, irregular.
CU – B
    1807   May 19 – Dec. 31.
    1808 – 1809   Jan. 1 – Dec. 31.
    1810   Jan. 1 – Dec. 13.
    Micro (P)
    1797   Feb. 13 – Dec. 31.
    1798 – 1806   Jan. 1 – Dec. 31.
    1807   Jan. 1 – May 18.
    1821   Nov. 21 – Dec. 31.
    1822   Jan. 1 – Feb. 6.
CtY
    1803   Aug. 29.
ICN
    1797   Feb. 13 – Dec. 31.
            Suplemento: Sept. 25, Oct. 23.
    1798   Jan. 1 – Feb. 19 – Dec. 31.
    1799   Jan. 1 – 14, Feb. 11 – Mar. 11, Apr. 29 – Dec. 31.
            Suplemento: July 15, Oct. 28, Nov. 18.
    1800   Jan. 1 – Dec. 15.
    1801   Jan. 12 – Feb. 9, Mar. 2 – Nov. 14.
            Suplemento: May 2.
    1802   Jan. 11 – Dec. 9.
            Suplemento: June 14, Oct. 2.
    1803   Jan. 31 – Apr. 4, 18 – Dec. 31.
    1804   Jan. 9.
LNHT
    1813   June 18.
    1814   Apr. 2, 19, 23.
    1815   Apr. 2, 23.
    Micro (P)

1802   May 31.
1805   May 3.
MWA
　1797   Prospecto.
　　　　　Feb. 13 — Dec. 31.
　1798 — 1799   Jan. 1 — Dec. 31.
　1800   Jan. 1 — Mar. 12, Apr. 8 — Dec.
　　　　　31.
　1801 — 1806   Jan. 1 — Apr. 14.
　1808   Sept. 19 — Dec. 31.
　1809   Jan. 1 — Apr. 10, Oct. 7 — Dec.
　　　　　31.
　1810 — 1814   Jan. 1 — May 25.

GACETA DEL GOBIERNO SUPREMO
DE GUATEMALA.
　See *Gaceta del gobierno*.

GACETA FEDERAL.
　See *La Gaceta*.

GACETA OFICIAL.
　See *Gaceta de Guatemala*.

GAZETA DE GUATEMALA.
　See *Gaceta del gobierno de Guate-
　mala*.

GENIO DE LA LIBERTAD. w., irr. est.
May 28, 1820.
　Note: Title *Editor constitucional*,
　May 28 — Aug. 20, 1820; *Genio de la
　libertad*, Aug. 27 — Dec. 10, 1821.
　Periodicity May 28 — Aug. 20, 1821,
　weekly; Aug. 27 — Dec. 10, 1821,
　irregular. Ceased publication Dec.
　10, 1821.
　DLC
　　1820   May 28 — June 4, Aug. 1 — Dec.
　　　　　 31.
　　　　　 Extraordinario: Sept. 11.
　　　　　 Suplemento: Aug. 21, Sept. 4,
　　　　　 18, 25, Oct. 9, 16, Nov. 13.
　　1821   Jan. 1 — Feb. 11, 13 — May 21,
　　　　　 Aug. 20.
　MWA
　　1821   Jan. 1 — 8, 22 — Feb. 5, 19 —
　　　　　 Mar. 19, May 28 — Aug. 20,
　　　　　 27 — Nov. 5, 19, Dec. 10.

THE GUATEMALA HERALD.
　Note: In English.

LNT — MA
　1955   July 16.

THE GUATEMALA POST. d.
　Note: In English.
　MH
　　1909   Oct. 24, 31, Nov. 6, 28, Dec.
　　　　　 5.

GUATEMALA STAR. w. est. 1888.
　Note: English edition of *Estrella
　de Guatemala*.
　M WA
　　1888   Sept. 15.

GUATEMALA TIDINGS. w.
　Note: In Spanish and English.
　CSt
　　1924   July 5, 14, 24, 31.
　CU
　　1923   Mar. 11 — June 23, July 7, 21 —
　　　　　 Oct. 27, Nov. 10 — Dec. 29.
　　1924   Jan. 5 — Apr. 24, May 15 — 29,
　　　　　 July 5 — 21.
　MH
　　1924   June 21.

EL GUATEMALTECO. d. est. Feb. 18,
1873.
　Note: Succeeded *Boletín oficial*;
　superseded by *Diario de Centro
　América*, Mar. 31, 1931 — Feb. 1,
　1950; began publishing again as
　official publication, Feb. 2, 1950.
　CU — B
　　1886   Jan. 1 — July 7, Nov. 18 — Dec.
　　　　　 31.
　　1887   Jan. 1 — Mar. 22.
　　Micro (P)
　　1876   Apr. 25.
　　1884   Jan. 1 — July 19, Aug. 16 — Dec.
　　　　　 24.
　CtY
　　1879   Sept. 7.
　DLC
　　1873   Feb. 18 — Dec. 31.
　　1874 — 1900   Jan. 1 — Dec. 31.
　ICN
　　1907   Oct. 2, 4, 5, 7 — 12, 14 — 19, 21 —
　　　　　 24, 26, 30 — Nov. 2, 4 — 9, 11 —
　　　　　 16, 18, 19, 21 — 23, 25 — 30,

Dec. 2 – 7, 9 – 14, 16 – 21, 23,
24, 26, 27.
1908   Jan. 2 – 4, 6 – 11, 13, 14, 17, 19,
20, 23, Feb. 3 – 6, 10, 12, 14,
15, 17 – 22, 25, 26.
KU
Micro (P)
1959   Jan. 1+.
LNT – MA
1882 – 1885   Jan. 1 – Dec. 31.
1886 – 1931   [Jan. 1 – Dec. 31].
1950   Jan. 1 – June 7.
Micro (P)
1827   Dec. 1.
1950   June 8 – Dec. 31.
1951   Jan. 1+.
MB
Micro (P)
1957   Apr. 5 – Dec. 31.
1958 – 1959   Jan. 1 – Dec. 31.
1960   Jan. 1 – 9.
PrU
1964   Apr. 11, 13 – 15, 17, 20, 22 –
25, 27, 28, May 28, June 1 – 5,
8 – 13, 15 – 20, 22 – 27, 29, July
1 – 4, 6 – 11, 13 – 18, 20 – 25,
27 – 31, Aug. 4 – 8, 10 – 14,
17 – 22, 24 – 29, 31 – Sept. 5,
7 – 10, 17, 19, 21 – 26, 28, 29,
Oct. 1, 5 – 7, 9, 10, 13, 14, 16,
19, 27 – 31, Nov. 2 – 7, 9, 11, 17,
19 – 21, 23 – 28, 30 – Dec. 5,
8 – 12, 14, 15, 17 – 19, 22 – 24,
28 – 31.
1965   Jan. 4 – 9, 10, 12, 14 – 16, 18 –
23, 25 – 30, Feb. 1 – 6, 8, 9,
11 – 13, 15 – 17, 19, 20, 22 – 27,
30 – Apr. 3, 5 – 10, 12 – 14,
19 – 24, 26 – 30, May 3 – 6, 8,
10 – 12, 14, 15, 17 – 22, 24 –
29, 31, June 2, 3, 5, 7 – 12,
14 – 19, 21, 26, 28, 29, July 1 –
3, 5 – 10, 12 – 17, 19 – 24, 28,
29, Aug. 3 – 7, 9 – 14, 16 – 21,
23 – 28, 30 – Sept. 4, 6, 7, 9 –
11, 13 – 15, 17, 18, 20 – 25, 27 –
Oct. 2, 4 – 9, 13 – 16, 18 – 22,
26 – 30, Nov. 2 – 6, 8 – 13, 15 –

20, 22 – 24, 26, 27, 29 – Dec. 4,
6 – 11, 13 – 15, 18, 20, 22, 28 –
31.

EL HERALDO. w. est. Sept. 26, 1909.
CU
1909   Nov. 21 – Dec. 24.
1910   Jan. 1 – June 5, July 10 – 31.
1911   July 9, 23 – 30, Sept. 3.
CtY
1909   Nov. 7 – Dec. 24.
1910   Jan. 1 – June 5, July 10 – 31.

LA HORA. d. est. 1926.
DLC
1950   Jan. 3 – May 12, 14 – June 11,
13 – July 23, 25 – Aug. 2, 4 – 9,
13, 17 – Dec. 31.
1951   Jan. 1 – July 3, 5 – Dec. 24, 28,
30.
1952   Jan. 2 – Dec. 12, 14 – 31.
1953   Jan. 2 – 5, 7 – Feb. 12, 14 –
July 5, 7 – 9, 11 – Dec. 8, 10 –
30.
1954   Apr. 1, 3 – 7, 9 – 21, 23 – 30,
May 3, 4, 6 – June 10, 12 – 27,
30, July 3 – 5, 7 – 18, 20, 22 –
Aug. 3, 5, 6, 25, 31.
Micro (P) & (N)
1962   Jan. 1 – May 13, 15 – Dec. 31.
1963   Jan. 1+.
LNT – MA
1951   [July 23 – Sept. 22.]
1952   May 24.
1953   June 12, 15.
1954   Oct. 11 – 16, Nov. 8 – 13.
1955   June 12, 13, 16, 20, 21, July 7,
8, 16.

LA HORA DOMINICAL. d. est. 1944.
LNT – MA
1952   May 11, 25.

EL HORIZONTE. w. est. Jan. 19, 1879.
CtY
1881   Aug. 6.
TxU
1881   July 16.

IMPACTO. d. est. Aug. 13, 1951.
Note: Ceased publication [1955].

DLC
1951 Aug. 13−17, 20−25, 28−30,
Sept. 1, Nov. 2−9, 12, 14−22,
24−28, Dec. 1−26, 28−31.
1952 Jan. 2, 3, 5−22, 24−26, 29−
Feb. 29, Apr. 1−14, 16−May
21, 23−June 25, 27−July 1,
Sept. 1−11, 13−Oct. 10, 12−
30, Nov. 2−6, 8−10, 12−27,
29−Dec. 31.
1953 Jan. 1−16, 18−Feb. 11, 13−
16, 19−July 1, 6−Dec. 31.
1954 Feb. 2−4, 6−25, 27−Apr. 2,
4, 5, 7−May 1, 5−8, 10−25,
27−June 26, 30, July 14−21,
23−26, 28−30, Aug. 1, 2, 4, 6,
9, 10, 15, 16, 19, 22, Sept. 2,
22, Oct. 29.
1955 Mar. 1−May 29, 31−July 2,
19−Sept. 25.
LNT−MA
1951 Aug. 13, 14.
1952 May 10, 15, 16, 19−23, 26−
29.
1953 June 13, 15.

EL IMPARCIAL; PERIODICO PARA
EL PUEBLO. w. est. Aug. 9, 1872.
LNHT
1872 Aug. 9−Dec. 21.
1873 Jan. 4−11.
MWA
1872 Aug. 9−Dec. 31.
1873 Jan. 1−11.

EL IMPARCIAL; DIARIO INDEPEN-
DIENTE. d. est. June 16, 1922.
Note: Suspended publication July
19−30, 1949.
CSt
1941 Aug. 1−Dec. 31.
1942 Jan. 1−Feb. 28.
CSt−H
1964 June 8−July 25, Oct. 19−31.
CU
1948 Dec. 20−24, 27.
DLC
1941 Feb. 1−13, 15−Apr. 2, 4, 6−
10, 12−May 1, 3−7, 9−16,

18−23, 25−29, Aug. 1−6, 9−
28, 30, 31, Sept. 2−7, 10, 12−
Oct. 1, 3−12, 14−16, 18−26,
28−30, Nov. 1−27, 29, 30,
Dec. 2.
1943 Jan. 2−Feb. 13, 15−Dec. 31.
1944−1948 Jan. 1−Dec. 31.
1949 Jan. 1−July 17, 19−Dec. 22,
24−30.
1950 Jan. 1−Dec. 31.
1951 Jan. 2−June 30, July 2−Dec.
31.
1952 Jan. 2−Oct. 19, 21−Dec. 31.
1953 Jan. 2−Dec. 31.
1954 Jan. 2−Dec. 31.
1955 Jan. 3−Dec. 31.
1956 Jan. 2−June 30, July 2−Dec.
31.
1957 Jan. 2−June 29, July 1−Dec.
31.
1958 Jan. 2−July 2, 4−Dec. 31.
1959 Jan. 2−Dec. 31.
1960 Jan. 2−Apr. 30, May 2,−Aug.
14, 16−Oct. 31, Nov. 2−Dec.
31.
1961 Jan. 2−Dec. 30.
Micro (P) & (N)
1962 Jan. 1+.
ICRL
1954 [June 8−Dec. 31].
1955 [Jan. 1−Dec. 31].
1956 [Jan. 1−May 30].
LNT−MA
1930 Dec. 22−31.
1931 Jan. 1−Dec. 31.
1932 Jan. 1−Feb. 29, Apr. 1−July
31, Dec. 26−30.
1933 Jan. 1−Dec. 31.
1934 [Jan. 1−Dec. 31.]
1935 Sept. 27, Dec. 16.
1936 [Jan. 1−Dec. 31.]
1937−1938 Jan. 1−Dec. 31.
1939 [Jan. 1−Dec. 31.]
1940−1941 Jan. 1−Dec. 31.
1942 Jan. 1−Mar. 11.
1951 Apr. 1−Dec. 31.
1952 Jan. 1−Dec. 31.
1955 Aug. 1−Dec. 31.

1956   Jan. 1+.
OrU
1959   Mar. 1 – June 23, 25 – Dec. 31.
1960   Jan. 1 – Feb. 27.
TxU
1941   June 21 – Dec. 24, 26 – 31.
1942   Jan. 2 – Apr. 1, 5 – 29, May 7 –
        Sept. 23, 25 – Oct. 14.
1945   Feb. 7 – Apr. 4, 12 – 30, May
        2 – 16, June 7 – Sept. 26.
1946   Dec. 19.
1947   May 8 – Dec. 31.
1948   Jan. 1 – Dec. 31.
1949   Jan. 1 – July 19, 30 – Dec. 31.
1950 – 1951   Jan. 1 – Dec. 31.
1952   Jan. 2 – Sept. 14, 16 – Oct. 4,
        7 – 18, 20 – Nov. 20, 24 – Dec.
        24, 26 – 31.
1953   Jan. 2 – Feb. 10, 12 – Apr. 1,
        6 – 15, 17 – 30, May 2 – 12, 14 –
        Aug. 14, 16 – Sept. 14, 16 –
        Oct. 21 – Nov. 9, 24 – Dec. 26 –
        31.
1954   Jan. 2 – 29, Feb. 1 – Apr. 14,
        19 – July 24, 27 – Sept. 14, 17 –
        Nov. 30, Dec. 23, 26 – 31.
1955   Jan. 3 – Mar. 21, 29 – Apr. 11 –
        May 14 – July 30, Aug. 2 – 13,
        16 – Sept. 14, 16 – Oct. 31,
        Nov. 2 – Dec. 30.
1956   Jan. 1 – June 30.
1958   Apr. 7 – 26.

EL IMPARCIAL EN LAS PROVINCIAS.
w.
LNT – MA
1938   [Jan. 1 – Dec. 31.]

1939   Jan. 1 – Mar. 31.
1941   Apr. 19, May 3.

EL INDICADOR. w. est. Oct. 11, 1824.
LNHT
    Micro (P)
1824   Oct. 11 – Dec. 31.
1825 – 1827   Jan. 1 – Dec. 31.

EL LIBERAL. w. est. 1824.
CtY
1825   Sept. 14, 28.

EL LIBERAL. d. est. 1825.
LNHT
    Micro (P)
1826   Feb. 1 – July 31, Nov. 21, Dec.
        22.

EL LIBERAL. d. est. 1926.
DLC
1927   Mar. 19 – 26.

EL LIBERAL PROGRESISTA. d. est.
1931.
    Note: In Spanish and French.
CSt
1942   Feb. 1 – Mar. 31.
DLC
1940   Mar. 25 – 30.
1941   Feb. 1 – 13, 15 – Mar. 16, 18 –
        Apr. 28, 30 – May 31, Aug. 2 –
        6, 8 – 25, 27 – 31, Sept. 2 – 7,
        9 – 14, 16 – 19, 21 – 30, Oct. 3,
        5 – 9, 11 – Nov. 12, 14 – 16,
        20 – 29.
LNHT
    Micro (N)
1933   [May 8 – Dec. 31.]
1934 – 1942   [Jan. 1 – Dec. 31.]
NN
    Micro (P) & (N)
1942   [May 2 – Dec. 31.]
1943   [Jan. 1 – Dec. 31.]
1944   [Jan. 1 – July 4.]

EL LIBERTADOR. d.
CSt – H
1944   July 23 – Aug. 24, Oct. 10, 25,
        27, 28, Nov. 10, 24, 27 – 29.

LA LOCA. w. est. Sept. 6, 1885.
LNHT
1885   Sept. 6, 12.

EL LOCO. w. est. 1885.
LNHT
1885 – 1886   Jan. 1 – Dec. 31.

LUZ. w. est. 1940.
DLC
1941   Mar. 2 – May 25, June 8 – 22,
        July 20, Oct. 12.

MEDIODIA. d.
  CU
    1946   Nov. 23 – Dec. 31.
    1947   Jan. 2 – Feb. 21.

EL MOMO. bw.
  MWA
    1830   May 16 – 30.

LA NACION. d. est. 1943.
  CU
    1943   Aug. 23 – Oct. 30, Nov. 2 –
            Dec. 31.
    1944   Jan. 1 – 14, 17 – June 30, July
            4 – Oct. 14.
  NN
    Micro (P) & (N)
    1944   July 5 – Oct. 14.

EL NACIONAL. d. est. Feb. 9, 1910.
  MH
    1910   July 7, 8, 11, 13 – 16, 18 – 23,
            25, Aug. 7, 21, Sept. 8 – 10,
            12 – Nov. 27, Dec. 10 – 14, 16.
    1911   Jan. 24 – 26, 28.

EL NACIONALISTA. d. est. [1955].
  DLC
    1956   Mar. 12 – Apr. 18, 20 – May 30,
            June 1 – 24, 27 – July 3, 6 – 11,
            13 – Oct. 31, Nov. 3 – Dec. 13,
            15 – 31.
    1957   Jan. 1 – 31, Feb. 2, 3, 5 – 7, 9,
            10, Apr. 1 – May 23, 25 – June
            26, July 7 – 26, 31 – Aug. 7, 9 –
            12, 16 – Oct. 19.

EL NORTE.
  LNHT
    1937   Jan. 1, Feb. 13, 20.

NOTICIOSO GUATEMALTECO. irr. est.
  Feb. 9, 1838.
  CtY
    1838   Feb. 23.
  DLC
    1838   Feb. 20, Mar. 2 – July 8.
            Alcance: Mar. 29, Apr. 10, May
            1.
  LNHT
    Micro (P)
    1838   Mar. 2, 17.

MWA
    1838   Feb. 9, 20 – Aug. 16.

NUESTRO DIARIO. d. est. Nov. 12, 1922.
  Note: Ceased publication [1958].
  DLC
    1941   Feb. 1 – 13, 15 – 25, 27 – Mar.
            16, 18 – Apr. 4, 6 – 9, 13 – 25,
            27 – May 1, 3 – 7, 9 – 11, 13 –
            16, 18 – 29, 31, Aug. 1 – 3, 5 –
            28, 30 – Sept. 7, 9 – 29, Oct.
            3 – 7, 9 – 16, 18 – 31, 4 – 16, 18,
            19, 21, 23 – 26, 28.
    1947   Mar. 1 – 19, 23, 27 – 30, Apr.
            6, 10 – Dec. 31.
    1948   Jan. 1 – Dec. 31.
    1949   Jan. 1 – June 25, Aug. 5 – 10,
            19 – Dec. 31.
    1950   Jan. 1 – 22, 27 – Dec. 31.
    1951 – 1952 Jan. 1 – Dec. 31.
    1953   Jan. 2 – Apr. 30, May 2 – Dec.
            31.
    1954   Jan. 4 – Feb. 1, 3 – Apr. 30,
            May 4 – 9, 11 – 14, 16 – 18, 20,
            22 – 30, June 1 – 14, 16 – 27,
            29 – July 9, 11 – 22, 24, 25, 27 –
            Aug. 13, 15, 16, 19, 20, 22 –
            31, Sept. 2, 5 – 8, 12 – 17, 19 –
            21, 26, 29 – Oct. 1, 3 – Nov. 16,
            18, 19, 21 – 30, Dec. 2 – 16, 18,
            19, 21 – 24.
    1955   Jan. 2 – 9, 15 – 17, 19 – Feb. 10,
            12 – 24, 26 – Mar. 22, 24 – May
            20, 22 – June 30, July 2 – Aug.
            5, 7 – Oct. 28, 30 – Dec. 2, 4 –
            7, 11 – 19, 22, 25, 27, 28, 30,
            31.
    1956   Jan. 1 – 10, 12 – June 6, 8 – 17,
            19 – July 5, 7 – 26, 28 – Aug. 1,
            4 – 6, 8 – 23, 25 – 30, Sept. 1 –
            12, 14, 16, 18 – 23, 25 – Nov. 30,
            Dec. 2 – 13, 15 – 18, 20 – 31.
    1957   Jan. 1 – 4, 6 – Feb. 3, 5 – 8, 10,
            11, 13 – Apr. 9, 11 – May 9,
            11 – 22, 24 – 28, 30 – June 14,
            16 – 20, 22 – 28, 30, July 2 – 25,
            27 – Aug. 1, 3 – 11, 13, 14, 17 –
            Sept. 11, 13 – 26, 29, Oct. 1 –
            22, 24 – Nov. 1, 5 – 25, 27 –

Dec. 18, 20 — 24, 27 — 31.
1958   Jan. 2 — Feb. 3, 5 — 28.
LNT — MA
1937   Jan. 18, Feb. 13.
1939   Aug. 23, 26.
1953   June 12, 13, 15.
1955   July 18, 20.

LA NUEVA ERA. sw. est. Dec. 22, 1837.
Note: Ceased publication Jan. 16, 1838.
CtY
1837   Dec. 22 — 29.
1838   Jan. 2 — 16.
DLC
1837   Dec. 22 — 31.
1838   Jan. 1 — 16.
LNHT
Micro (P)
1837   Dec. 22, 29.
1838   Jan. 2.
MWA
1837   Dec. 26.
1838   Jan. 2 — 9.

EL OBSERVADOR. irr. est. Feb. 15, 1838.
DLC
1838   Feb. 15 — May 16.
LNHT
Micro (P)
1838   Feb. 15, 22, 24, Mar. 1, 10, 16, 19, 24, Apr. 12, May 16.
MWA
1838   Feb. 22 — May 16.

OCTUBRE.
See *Tribuna popular*.

EL OFICIOSO. est. [1833].
LNHT
1833   Jan. 20.

EL OJO. irr. est. 1885.
LNHT
1885   July 19, 23, 27, Aug. 15, 21, 27, Sept. 8, 11.

LA OPOSICION. irr. est. Sept. 1, 1837.
DLC
1837   Sept. 1 — Nov. 5, 25 — Dec. 31.

1838   Jan. 1 — 13.
Alcance: Jan. 13.
LNHT
Micro (P)
1837   Sept. 5, 11, 23, Nov. 5, 26.
1838   Jan. 4, 9, 13.

EL PAPAGAYO. est. Aug. 13, 1885.
LNHT
1885   Aug. 13, Sept. 2, 6.

PAPEL NUEVO. est. 1837.
Note: Published only four numbers.
Ceased publication 1837.
MWA
1837   n.d. (Nos. 1 — 4).
LNHT
Micro (P)
1837   n.d. (No. 4).

EL PERIODISTA.
LNHT
1956   Sept. 30, Oct. 30.
1958   Jan. 1 — 31.

LA PRENSA. d. est. May 7, 1942.
DLC
1942   May 7, 9.

PRENSA LIBRE. d. est. [1951].
DLC
1951   Oct. 1, 2, 4 — 12, 14 — 28, 30 — Nov. 15, 17 — 22, 24 — Dec. 7, 9 — 18, 20 — 23, 25 — 31.
1952   Jan. 1 — 27, 29 — Feb. 1, 3, 4, 7, 9 — Apr. 8, 10 — May 11, 14 — 27, 29 — June 9, 11 — July 9, 11 — 20, 23 — 25, 27, 29 — Aug. 30.
1953   Feb. 7, 10, 12, 17, 21, 24, 25, Mar. 4, 25, 31, Apr. 7, 9, 13, 21, 22, 24, May 5, 8, 9, 15, 29, June 9, 23, 25, July 1, 13, 22, 25, 27 — Aug. 1, 6, 11, 12, 25 — 31, Sept. 2, 3, 5, 22, 25, Oct. 6, 8 — 10, 23, 24, 26, Nov. 2 — 5, 8, 9, 14, 16, 24, 25, 27, 28.
1954   Jan. 16, 22, 23, 27 — 29, Feb. 2 — 9, 25 — Mar. 1, 28, 29, 31, Apr. 23, 25 — 28, May 2 — 4, 6 — 9, 12, 13, 17 — June 13, July 1, 2,

10 – 13, 17 – 22, 24 – Aug. 1, 4,
5, 14, 15, 19, 23, 25, 26, 29 –
Sept. 4, 8, 22.

1957   Jan. 3 – 22, 24 – 31, Feb. 2 – 26,
Mar. 1 – 10, 12 – July 12, 14 –
28, 30, 31, Aug. 2 – Sept. 19,
21 – Dec. 31.

1958   Jan. 1 – Apr. 11, 13 – 27, 29 –
May 22, 24 – July 14, 16 – Aug.
10, 12 – 22, 24 – Sept. 28, 30 –
Dec. 14, 16 – 29.

1959   Jan. 3 – Mar. 18, 20 – Apr. 16,
18 – May 1, 3 – 26, 28 – July 3,
5 – 20, 22 – Aug. 13, 15 – Sept.
21, 23 – 25, 27, 29 – Oct. 5, 7 –
9, 11 – 16, 18 – 26, 28 – Nov. 4,
6 – Dec. 24, 29.

1960   Jan. 5 – 27, 29 – Feb. 2, 4 – 10,
12 – Apr. 30, May 2 – 12, 27 –
29, 21, 23 – 30, June 1, 2, July
7 – Aug. 6, 8, 9, 11, 13, 14, 17,
24 – Sept. 9, 11 – 21, 23 – 25,
27 – Dec. 12, 14 – 31.

1961   Jan. 3 – 11, 13 – Mar. 8, 10 –
July 3, 5 – Aug. 17, 20 – Oct.
19, 22 – Dec. 31.

LNT – MA
1953   June 12 – 14, 16, 29.
1955   June 14, 15, 17, 21, 22, July 2,
6 – 9, 11 – 13, 16, Sept. 7.

EL PROCURADOR DE LA LEY. est.
[1830].
LNHT
Micro (P)
1830   Dec. 15, 23.
1831   Jan. 27.

EL PROCURADOR DE LOS PUEBLOS.
w. est. Sept. 12, 1840.
LNHT
Micro (P)
1840   Sept. 12 – 26.

EL PROGRESO NACIONAL. irr. est.
Aug. 14, 1894.
LNHT
1894   Aug. 14 – Dec. 31.
1895   Jan. 1 – Oct. 31.

EL PUEBLO. d.
CU – B
Micro (P)
1885   July 26.

REDACTOR GENERAL. est. 1825.
LNHT
Micro (P)
1825   June 1 – Dec. 31.
1826   Sept. 1 – Oct. 31.

REDACTOR LEJISLATIVO. w. est. May
21, 1838.
DLC
1838   May 21 – July 19.
LNHT
1838   June 1 – Aug. 31.
Micro (P)
1838   May 21 – 31.

EL RENACIMIENTO. d. est. July 13,
1885.
CU – B
Micro (P)
1885   July 18 – 20, 24, Aug. 18, Sept.
11.
LNHT
1885   July 13 – Sept. 12.

LA REPUBLICA. d. est. 1891.
LNT – MA
1891   Nov. 7, 9, 10.
MWA
1913   Feb. 20.

LA REVISTA. bw.
CU – B
Micro (P)
1886   July 22.

**REVISTA; PERIODICO SEMANARIO
DE LA SOCIEDAD ECONOMICA DE
AMIGOS DE GUATEMALA.** w. est.
Dec. 3, 1846.
Note: Suspended publication May
20 – June 26, 1847.
MWA
1846   Dec. 3 – 31.
1847   Jan. 1 – May 13, July 3 – 16,
Oct. 1 – Dec. 31.
1848   Jan. 1 – May 26.

LA SEMANA. w. est. Jan. 1, 1865.
 CtY
  1866   Dec. 31.
  1867   Jan. 13, Apr. 17, May 14.
 MWA
  1865 – 1866   Jan. 1 – Dec. 31.
  1867   Jan. 1 – 13.
  1869   [June 5 – Dec. 31.]
  1870   [Jan. 1 – Dec. 18].
  1871   Jan. 15 – 22, Feb. 5, 19 – Mar.
       5, 26, Apr. 16 – 30, June 7.

SEMANARIO DE GUATEMALA. w. est.
 Apr. 3, 1836.
  Note: Ceased publication Jan. 1837.
 CtY
  1836   Sept. 15, 23, Oct. 6 – Dec. 22.
 DLC
  1836   Apr. 3 – July 15, Aug. 12 – Oct.
       12, 28 – Nov. 30, Dec. 2 – 14,
       16 – 31.
       Alcance: June 21, Dec. 20.
  1837   Jan. 5.
 LNHT
  Micro (P)
  1836   May 7 – Dec. 29.
  1837   Jan. 5, 12.

SEMI-DIARIO DE LOS LIBRES. 3w.
 est. Nov. 8, 1837.
 LNHT
  Micro (P)
  1837   Nov. 8 – 22.
  1838   Jan. 3, 23.
 TxU
  1837   Nov. 8 – Dec. 27.

EL SIGLO DE LAFAYETTE. w. est. Oct.
 6, 1831.
 LNHT
  1831   Oct. 6 – Dec. 31.
  Micro (P)
  1831   Oct. 6 – Dec. 31.
  1832   Jan. 4, 14, Aug. 15 – Nov. 2.

SUCESOS. sw.
 CSt
  1950   Dec. 23.
  1951   Jan. 13, 27, Feb. 3, 17.

EL TAMBOR. w. est. May 27, 1843.
 LNHT
  Micro (P)
  1843   May 27, June 10.

LA TERTULIA. est. Jan. 1, 1838.
 LNHT
  Micro (P)
  1838   Jan. 1.

TERTULIA PATRIOTICA. bw. est. 1825.
 MWA
  1825   Nov. 24 – Dec. 7.

EL TIEMPO. sw. est. Mar. 9, 1839.
  Note: Continuous pagination. Succeeded *Boletín oficial*; succeeded by
  Gaceta oficial. Ceased publication
  Jan. 30, 1841.
 DLC
  1839   May 3 – June 8, 10 – Dec. 31.
       Suplemento: May 3, 14, Nov.
       3.
  1840   Jan. 1, 2, 4 – 6, 8 – Feb. 11.
 LNHT
  Micro (P)
  1839   Mar. 9 – Dec. 31.
  1840   Jan. 1 – Dec. 31.
  1841   Jan. 1 – 30.
 MWA
  1839   Apr. 23.
  1840   Nov. 24 – Dec. 21.
  1841   Jan. 7 – 30.
 NN
  1839   Mar. 9 – Dec. 28.
  1840   Jan. 1 – Dec. 28.
  1841   Jan. 7 – 30.

TIJERETA. [w.]
 MWA
  1829   Aug. 12 – 14, 28 – Sept. 11, 18,
       Oct. 2.
       Suplemento: Sept. 27.

EL 30 DE JUNIO.
 CU
  1916   June 30.

TRIBUNA POPULAR. w., d. est. June
 21, 1950.
  Note: Title *Octubre*, June 21, 1950 –

Aug. 14, 1953; *Tribuna popular*, after
Aug. 15, 1953. Periodicity June 21,
1950 – Aug. 14, 1953, weekly; after
Aug. 15, 1953, daily.
DLC
    1951   June 29 – Dec. 31.
    1952   Jan. 1 – Dec. 31.
    1953   Jan. 1 – Aug. 13, 15 – Dec. 31.
    1954   Jan. 1 – June 27.
LNHT
  Micro (P)
    1950   June 21 – Nov. 30.
    1951 – 1952   Jan. 1 – Dec. 31.
    1953   Jan. 1 – May 31.

VERBUM. bw., w. est. Mar. 8, 1942.
  DLC
    1942   Mar. 8.
    1954   May 2 – 30.

LA VERDAD. irr. est. Oct. 5, 1837.
  DLC
    1837   Oct. 5, 19 – Nov. 29.
             Alcance: Nov. 14, Dec. 7.
  LNHT
  Micro (P)
    1837   Oct. 5 – 27, Nov. 14, 29.

Quenzaltenango

EL BIEN PUBLICO. 3w. est. 1877.
  Note: Ceased publication [1897].
  CU – B
  Micro (P)
    1894   Jan. 4 – 7, 23 – 30, Feb. 4, 13 –
             18, Mar. 20, 27 – Apr. 29, May
             3 – 13, 22 – June 3, 12 – July
             1, 24 – Aug. 5, Sept. 11 – 30,
             Oct. 16 – Nov. 18, Dec. 4, 8 –
             15, 27 – 29.
    1895   Jan. 1, 8 – 12, 22 – 26, Feb. 5 –
             16, Mar. 5 – 9, Apr. 9, 23 – 27,
             May 7 – 11, 21 – June 1, 11 –
             Aug. 31, Sept. 10 – 12, 24 –
             Oct. 19, Nov. 12 – 16, 26 – Dec.
             7, 17 – 21, 31.
    1896   Jan. 4 – 25, Feb. 4 – 15, 25 –
             Mar. 7, 31, May 19 – 23, June
             9 – 13, 23 – July 4, 14 – 18.

MWA
    1881   Apr. 10, Aug. 11 – 14.
    1896   Aug. 18.
    1897   Jan. 2.

EL CIUDADANO.
  LNT – MA
  Micro (P)
    1836   Mar. 5 – May 21.

EL COMETA DE 1839.
  LNT – MA
  Micro (P)
    1839   Apr. 27 – May 11.

CORREO DE OCCIDENTE. d. est.
  July 2, 1950.
    Note: Succeeded by *Diario de Quezal-
    tenango*. Ceased publication Dec.
    24, 1953.
  DLC
    1950   Aug. 3, 4, 6, 10, 13, 20, 26 –
             Sept. 22, 24 – 26, 29, Oct. 1 – 3,
             5 – Nov. 15, 18 – Dec. 3, 7, 10,
             17, 23 – 31.
    1951   Jan. 1 – 18, 21 – 24, 26, 27,
             June 2 – 17, 21, 23 – 25, 28, July
             1, 3 – 6, 8, 10 – 27, 29, 31 – Aug.
             5, 7, 8, 10 – 14, 16 – 26, 29 –
             31, Oct. 1 – Nov. 4, 6 – Dec.
             29.
    1952   Jan. 2 – 6, 9 – 29, Feb. 1, 3 –
             20, 23 – Mar. 9, 11 – 18, 20 –
             28, 30 – Apr. 6, 8 – July 9, 11,
             13, 15 – Aug. 12, 14 – Sept. 11,
             19 – Dec. 31.
    1953   Jan. 2 – 28, 30, Feb. 1 – 25,
             27 – Mar. 4, 6 – 8, 11 – 31, May
             1 – 28, 31, June 2 – 21, 23 –
             July 1, 3 – 15, 17 – Sept. 11,
             17 – Oct. 25, 27 – Nov. 13, 15 –
             29, Dec. 1 – 15, 17 – 24.
  LNT – MA
    1952   Feb. 20 – 29, Mar. 1, 4, 13, 18 –
             Dec. 31.
    1953   Jan. 2 – Dec. 21.

CRONOS. d. est. 1932.
  LNT – MA
    1937   Mar. 6, 8 – 10, 20, May 1 – 31.

DIARIO DE QUEZALTENANGO. d. est.
Jan. 7, 1954.
    Note: Succeeded *Correo de occidente*.
    DLC
        1954   Jan. 7−13, 16−30, Feb. 3−10,
                12−16, 18−26, Mar. 1, 3−8,
                11−25, 27−31.
    LNT−MA
        1954   Jan. 7−Dec. 31.
        1955   Jan. 1−31.

LA EPOCA. d. est. 1923.
    LNT−MA
        1931   Jan. 5.
        1932   Nov. 3, 9, 20, 21, Dec. 2−12,
                21.
        1934   Jan. 13.

GACETA DEL GOBIERNO DE LOS
    ALTOS.
    LNHT
        Micro (P)
        1839   Aug. 27, 31, Sept. 11, Oct. 7,
                9, 19, Nov. 7.

LA INFORMACION.
    LNT−MA
        1930   Dec. 23.

EL POPULAR. irr. est. 1839.
    LNHT
        Micro (P)
        1839   Aug. 3, 7, 11, 27, Sept. 14, Dec.
                4, 30.

PROA. w. est. 1941.
    Note: Suspended publication July
    30−Sept. 6, 1949.
    DLC
        1954   May 8−29.
    LNT−MA
        1941   Sept. 1−Dec. 31.
        1942−1950   Jan. 1−Dec. 31.
        1951   Jan. 1−Feb. 28.

Rabinal

PROVINCIA Y CULTURA. est. 1959.
    LNT−MA
        1959   Aug. 1−31.

RABINAL ACHI. est. 1959.
    LNT−MA
        1959   Sept. 1−30.

Salamá

LA VOZ DEL NORTE. 3m. est. Feb. 15,
    1883.
    LNHT
        1884   [Jan. 31−Dec. 27.]

HAITI
Cap-Français

See Cap-Haïtien.

Cap-Haïtien

L'ARENIR. est. 1859.
    MH
        1859   June 5, 19, 26, Aug. 21.

BULLETIN OFFICIEL DE SAINT-
    DOMINGUE. w. est. Jan. 1797.
    Note: Ceased publication Aug. 1799.
    MWA
        1797   July 7, Aug. 11−16, 26.
        1798   [Jan. 18−Sept. 5].
        1799   Mar. 14, 24, Apr. 3−June 22,
                July 27, Aug. 26.

GAZETTE DE SAINT-DOMINGUE.
    See *Gazette officielle de Saint-Dom-*
    ingue.

GAZETTE OFFICIELLE DE L'ETAT
    D'HAYTI.
    See *Gazette royale d'Hayti*.

GAZETTE OFFICIELLE DE SAINT-
    DOMINGUE. sw., w. est. Jan. 1, 1791.
    Note: Title *Gazette de Saint-Dom-*
    ingue, 1791−1804; *Gazette offi-*
    cielle de Saint-Domingue, 1806.
    Removed from Port-au-Prince to Cap-
    Haïtien where it was published for a
    short period in 1806.
    DLC
        1791   Aug. 20, 31.

GAZETTE ROYALE D'HAYTI. w., irr.
est. Jan. 1808.
  Note: Title *Gazette officielle de L'État
  d'Hayti* 1808–1812; *Gazette royale
  d'Hayti*, 1812–1820. Ceased publication 1820. Succeeded by *Le Moniteur; journal officiel de la République
  d'Haiti.*
CtY
  1809   Sept. 28, Oct. 12–Dec. 7.
  1810   June 14.
  1811   Jan. 3–17.
MWA
  1813   July 22–26.
  1814   Aug. 16–Nov. 19.
  1818   Sept. 27–Nov. 5.

LA LANTERNE. w. est. 1936.
  Note: Ceased publication ₍Dec. 6,
  1947₎.
  DLC
  1939   May 27–June 30, July 2–14,
          Aug. 20–Sept. 1, 10–22, Oct.
          1–Nov. 3, 5–24, 26–Dec. 15,
          24–31.
  1940   Jan. 6–Apr. 26, 28–May 3,
          July 1–Aug. 31.

MONITEUR GENERAL DE LA PARTIE
  FRANCAISE DE SAINT-DOMINGUE.
  d. est. Nov. 15, 1791.
  Note: Ceased publication 1795.
  MWA
  1793   ₍Feb. 1–Mar. 25,₎ June 17, 18.

LE NOUVEAU MONDE. w. est. Jan. 19,
  1958.
  FU
  Micro (N)
  1962   Jan. 28–Dec. 31.
  1963   Jan. 1–Dec. 31.
  1964   Jan. 1–Nov. 22.

Cap-Henri

See Cap-Haïtien

Gonaïves

COURRIER DE L'ARTIBONITE. w. est.
  1875.

  Note: Ceased publication ₍1902₎.
DLC
  1875   Oct. 9.

Port-au-Prince

L'ACTION. sw., d. est. May 28, 1929.
  Note: Periodicity May 28, 1929–Dec.
  1945, semiweekly; after Jan. 1946,
  daily.
NN
  Micro (P) & (N)
  1929   Oct. 1–26.
  1930   Jan. 1–Mar. 22.
  1947   May 26–Aug. 14, Dec. 10–31.
  1948   Sept. 6–Dec. 31.
  1949   Jan. 1–Mar. 11.
  1950   May 18–31, July 13–Dec. 31.
  1951   Jan. 1–6, May 9–June 21.

L'ACTION NATIONALE. w., d. est. Oct.
  30, 1931.
  Note: Periodicity Oct. 30–Dec. 28,
  1931, weekly; after Dec. 28, 1931,
  daily.
NN
  Micro (P) & (N)
  1931   Oct. 30, Nov. 20, Dec. 15,
          28–31.
  1932   Jan. 4, 7–22, 25–Feb. 4, 6–
          Mar. 3, 7–15, 17–29, 31–
          May 11, 14–June 2, 4–30,
          ₍July 1–Dec. 31.₎
  1933   ₍Jan. 1–Dec. 31.₎
  1934   ₍Jan. 1–June 19.₎

BULLETIN OFFICIEL. GAZETTE DU
  PORT-AU-PRINCE. w.
  MWA
  1809   Sept. 9, Nov. 18, Dec. 9.

LE CIVILISATEUR. w. est. Mar. 10, 1870.
  MH
  1871   Feb. 2, 16, 23.

LE COURRIER HAÏTiEN. d. est. 1920.
  TxU
  1924   Oct. 10, 11, 16, 17.

L'ECHO DE L'EVANGILE E L'AVANT
  COURRIER DU NOUVEL AGE. est.
  June 1, 1871.
  MH
  1871   June 1–Dec. 31.

1872 Jan. 1—May 31.

L'ECLAIREUR. sw. est. Sept. 1911.
DLC
1914 Mar. 11.
MWA
1914 Mar. 11.

FEUILLE DU COMMERCE. w. est. 1824.
Note: Ceased publication 1866.
MWA
1834 May 11—18.
NN
1829 Jan. 4—May 3, 17—31, June
14—July 12, 26—Nov. 29, Dec.
18—27.

LA GAZETTE DU PEUPLE. w. est. 1870.
Note: Ceased publication 1871.
MH
1871 Mar. 16—Apr. 6.

THE HAITI HERALD. w. est. 1956.
Note: In English. Title *Haiti Herald*,
1956—May 1957; *The Haiti Herald*,
after June 1957.
DLC
1956 Dec. 23—31.
1957 Jan. 1—Feb. 9, 18—Mar. 9,
11—Apr. 20, 27—June 1, 17—
Aug. 3, 5—24, 26—Sept. 21,
23—Dec. 29.

FU
Micro (N)
1956 Sept. 2—Dec. 23.
1958—1963 [Jan. 1—Dec. 31].

HAITI-JOURNAL. d. est. Jan. 20, 1930.
Note: Suspended publication Sept.
10—Oct. 1, 1952.
DLC
1938 July 7.
1939 Sept. 26—Dec. 3, 5—8, 10—
12, 14—31.
1940 Jan. 1—June 2, 4—Dec. 31.
1941 Jan. 1—Apr. 9, 11—May 29,
31—June 2, 8, 10—23, 26—
Sept. 22, 28, 30—Dec. 4, 7—
21, 24—28, 30, 31.

1942 Jan. 1—12, 18, 25, 27—Feb.
8, 10—Mar. 22, 24—29, 31—
July 26, Aug. 2—9, 16—Oct. 4,
6—Dec. 28, 30, 31.
1943 Jan. 1—17, 20—Feb. 1, 3—
18, 10—12, 14, 17—19, 21, 24—
28, Mar. 3—Apr. 18, 20—Aug.
17, 19—Oct. 3, 5—Nov. 5, 7,
9—Dec. 19, 21—31.
1949 May 28—June 2.
1950 Jan. 3—5, 9—29, May 2—6,
July 1—Oct. 23, 25—Nov. 8,
11—Dec. 31.
1951 Jan. 1—Apr. 12, 16—Sept. 3,
5—Dec. 31.
1952 Jan. 1—Feb. 8, 10—Mar. 4, 6—
Oct. 12, 15—Dec. 31.
1953 Jan. 1—Sept. 3, 5—27, 29—
Dec. 31.
1954 Jan. 1—5, 7—May 2, 4—Aug.
5, 10—Dec. 23, 25—31.
1955 Jan. 1—Apr. 13, 18—22, 25—
June 10, 14—July 1, 5—Nov.
17, 25—Dec. 30.
1956 Jan. 16—Feb. 4, 7—Aug. 3, 7—
31, Sept. 4—Oct. 20, 23—Dec.
29.
1957 Jan. 3—Sept. 6, 9—Dec. 31.
1958 Jan. 1—Dec. 10, 12—31.
1959 Jan. 9—Apr. 11, 23—May 12,
14—June 9, 12, 13, 24—July 7,
9—30, Aug. 3—5, 7—20, 22—
Sept. 6, 8—10, 12—24, 26—
Oct. 1, 3, 4, 6—13, 15—21, 23,
24, 27—29, 31—Nov. 4, 6—9,
12—16, 18, 19, 26, 30, Dec. 31.
1960 Jan. 4—Oct. 6, 9—20, 23—27,
29—Nov. 3, 5—18, 20—22, 24,
26—Dec. 1, 5—21, 26, 27, 29—
31.
1961 Jan. 5, 9—19, 23—26, 28—Feb.
16, 18—Mar. 6, 8—Apr. 25,
27—May 6, 10—16, 18—24, 29,
30, June 1, 2, 15—20, 22, 28—
July 7, 10—13, 15—20, 22—27,
29—Aug. 1, 3, 4, 7, 8, 10, 12—
17, 21—Sept. 5, 7, 8, 11, 12,
14—19, 25, 26, 28—Oct. 3, 5,

7 – 10, 12 – 24, 26 – 30, Nov.
1 – 7, 10 – 21, 23 – Dec. 12,
14 – 20, 23 – 30.
FU
  Micro (N)
  1930 Jan. 20 – Dec. 31.
  1931 – 1935 Jan. 1 – Dec. 31.
  1937 Jan. 1 – Dec. 31.
  1942 – 1945 [Jan. 1 – Dec. 31].
  Micro (P)
  1937 Jan. 1 – Dec. 31.
LNT – MA
  1938 Apr. 5 – 9, 13.

HAITI SUN. w. est. 1951.
  Note: In English.
  DLC
    1952 May 11 – Nov. 8, 10 – Dec. 24.
    1953 Jan. 1 – 31, Feb. 9 – Mar. 28,
        31 – Apr. 18, May 11 – June 6,
        8 – Dec. 5, 7 – 31.
    1954 Jan. 1 – Aug. 14, 16 – Nov. 6,
        8 – Dec. 19.
  FU
    1957 Mar. 1 – Dec. 31.
    1958 Jan. 1 – Feb. 28.
    1960 June 1 – Nov. 30.
    1961 Mar. 5.

L'ILLUSTRATION ANTILLAISE. bw.,
w. est. June 15, 1942.
  CU
    1942 June 15 – Dec. 23.
    1943 Jan. 9 – Feb. 6, 20 – Dec. 23.
    1944 – 1945 Jan. 1 – Dec. 31.
    1946 Jan. 8 – Apr. 12.
  DPU
    1942 June 27, July 1, Nov. 5 – 12.
    1943 Jan. 9 – 16, 30, Feb. 1 – 28,
        Mar. 6, 20, 27 – Apr. 17, May
        1 – 8, 22, June 19 – July 17,
        Aug. 3, 14 – 21, Sept. 8, 18 –
        Oct. 22, Nov. 9 – 23, Dec. 6,
        15 – 23.
    1944 Jan. 15, 29, Feb. 5 – 19, Mar.
        4 – 18, Apr. 1 – 15, 26, May 3,
        13 – 23, June 3, 13 – 20, July 4,
        18, Aug. 4 – 11, 24, Sept. 9, 30,
        Oct. 11, 19 – 25, Nov. 9, 16, 28,
        Dec. 7, 21.

1945 Jan. 8 – 15, 24 – Feb. 7, 19,
    Mar. 1, 12, 20, Apr. 2 – 16, May
    1, 15, June 1, 18, 21, July 3, 22,
    30, Aug. 6, 15, Sept. 1, 15, 24,
    Oct. 2, 12, 24, Nov. 10, 19, Dec.
    3, 12, 19.
1946 Jan. 8, 16, 27, Feb. 3, 17, 27.
    Mar. 24.

L'IMPARTIAL. d. est. Aug. 28, 1890.
  MWA
    1910 Jan. 12, 14.

LE JOUR. d. est. ₁1950₎.
  DLC
    1957 Apr. 10 – 17, 19 – May 2, 10 –
        June 16, 18 – July 25, 28 – Aug.
        12, 16 – Sept. 6, 8 – 10, 18 –
        25, 30 – Oct. 9, 11 – 17, 19 – 23,
        25 – 28, 30 – Dec. 31.
    1958 Jan. 3 – 14, 16 – 22, 24 – Mar.
        14, 16, 17, 19 – Apr. 28, 30 –
        Aug. 28, Sept. 1 – Nov. 10, 12 –
        25, 27 – Dec. 3, 6 – 31.
    1959 Jan. 1 – 8, 10 – Mar. 18, 21 –
        May 21, 25 – July 1, 3 – 30,
        Aug. 2 – 6, 9 – 19, 21 – 24, 26,
        27, 29, 30, Sept. 1 – Oct. 1, 4 –
        Nov. 5, 8, 9, 12 – 16, 19, 24, 26,
        Dec. 1, 8, 9, 11 – 21, 28 – 31.
    1960 Jan. 4 – 7, 18 – 20, 22 – 27, Feb.
        1 – 3, 5 – 10, 15 – 18, 22 – 24,
        26 – Mar. 3, 8, 9, 11 – 16, 21 –
        Apr. 7, 11 – 17, 21, 26 – May
        16, 19 – June 20, 22, 23, 27, 28,
        30, July 4, 6 – 21, 25 – 28, Aug.
        1 – 24, 29 – Sept. 1, 5 – 29, Oct.
        3 – 27, 30 – Nov. 22, 24 – 28,
        30 – Dec. 7, 16, 17.
    1961 Mar. 2 – 9, 14 – 20, 22, 24 – 30,
        Apr. 4 – 11, May 8 – 15, 17 –
        25, June 2 – 29, July 3 – 5, 10 –
        25, 27 – 31, Aug. 2 – 9, 11 – 16,
        18 – 23, 27, 28, 31 – Sept. 7,
        12 – 14, 18, 19, 21 – Oct. 11,
        13 – 19, 25, 26, Nov. 6 – 21, 23,
        27 – Dec. 9, 12 – 20, 26 – 30.
  DPU
  Current (six months).

LE MANIFESTE. w. est. Apr. 4, 1841.
  DLC
    1841   Apr. 18 – June 27, July 11 –
            Sept. 12, 26 – Nov. 14, 28, Dec.
            12, 19.
    1842   Jan. 16 – 30, Feb. 20.
    1843   Mar. 26.
  FU
    Micro (N)
    1841   Apr. 4 – Dec. 31.
    1842 – 1843 Jan. 1 – Dec. 31.
    1844   Jan. 1 – May 26.
  NN
    1841   Apr. 4, 18, May 2, 23 – June
            27, July 11 – Aug. 22, Sept. 5 –
            Dec. 26.
    1842   Jan. 2 – Mar. 27, June 26 – July
            31.

LE MATIN; JOURNAL QUOTIDIEN. d.
  est. 1898.
  FU
    Micro (N)
    1898   May 1 – Dec. 31.
    1899   Jan. 1 – Apr. 29.

LE MATIN. d. est. Apr. 1, 1907.
  DLC
    1930   Dec. 8.
    1931   Apr. 9, May 2, 7 – 11, 13, 15 –
            23, June 10, 15 – 26, 29, July 1,
            2, 4, 6, 8 – 16.
    1937   Aug. 28.
    1939   Sept. 13 – Oct. 31, Nov. 2 – 22,
            24, 25, 28 – Dec. 31.
    1940   Jan. 1 – Dec. 31.
    1941   Jan. 1 – May 19, 21 – 26, June
            3 – 5, 7 – Oct. 6, 8 – Nov. 7, 9 –
            Dec. 26, 28 – 31.
    1942   Jan. 1 – 27, 31 – Apr. 16, 18,
            19, 21 – June 13, 16 – 30, July
            2 – 13.
    1943   Feb. 2, 4, 5, 7 – 10.
    1944   Feb. 1 – July 7, 9 – 11, 13 – 24,
            27 – Aug. 3, 5 – 26, 30, Sept.
            1 – 13, 15, 16, 21, 23 – 30, Oct.
            3 – Dec. 31.
    1945   Jan. 1 – 17, 19 – 27, 30 – Feb.
            17, 20 – Mar. 8, 11 – 17, 20, 21,

            23 – 28, Apr. 1 – May 29, 31,
            June 1, 3 – July 17, 19 – 21,
            26 – Aug. 22, 24, 25, 30 – Oct.
            23, 26 – 29, 31 – Nov. 13, Dec.
            24, 25, 29 – 31.
    1946   Jan. 4, 5, 9, Apr. 1 – 8, May 4,
            22 – 29, June 1 – 3, 6 – 13, 26 –
            29, Sept. 3, 6 – 12, 19 – 28, Oct.
            1, 2, 5.
    1947   Jan. 4, Feb. 1 – 6, June 28, July
            2 – Aug. 2, 6 – 11, 17, 18, 21, 22,
            24 – Sept. 22, 26 – 29, Nov.
            30 – Dec. 5, 7, 8, 10, 12 – 29.
    1848   Jan. 1 – 8, 10 – 29, 31 – Feb.
            28, July 16 – Aug. 4, 6 – 23,
            25 – Sept. 9, 11 – 28, Oct. 3, 4,
            26 – Dec. 22, 29, 31.
    1949   Jan. 4 – 26, 29 – 31, May 28 –
            31, June 2 – 4.
    1950   July 1 – 24, 27 – Sept. 20, 22 –
            Nov. 9, 12 – Dec. 31.
    1951   Jan. 4 – Apr. 2, 4 – June 9, 12 –
            Dec. 31.
    1952   Jan. 1 – June 23, 25 – Oct. 14,
            16 – 30, Nov. 1 – Dec. 31.
    1953   Jan. 1 – July 31, Aug. 2 – Sept.
            25, 27 – Dec. 25, 29, 31.
    1954   Jan. 1 – May 2, 5 – July 11, 13 –
            Dec. 31.
    1955   Jan. 1 – Apr. 23, 26 – Aug. 2,
            4 – 6, 9 – Sept. 15, 17 – Dec.
            29, 31.
    1956   Jan. 1 – Oct. 23, 26 – Dec. 31.
    1957   Jan. 1 – Feb. 7, 9 – Apr. 17,
            21 – June 29, July 1 – Dec. 31.
  DPU
    Current (six months).
  FU
    Micro (N)
    1907   Apr. 1 – Dec. 31.
    1908   Jan. 1+.
  LNT – MA
    1938   Dec. 8 – 11, 13
  MWA
    1914   Mar. 10.

LE MONITEUR HAÏTIEN. w., sw. est.
  Feb. 8, 1845.
        Note: Suspended publication Apr.

16 — July 7, 1848. Succeeded *La Telegraphe*.
DLC
1845   Apr. 19.
MH
1859   Feb. 19 — Dec. 26.
1860 — 1861   Jan. 1 — Dec. 31.
1862   Jan. 1 — Aug. 26.
1870   Nov. 12 — 19, Dec. 24.
1871   Jan. 14 — 21, Feb. 4, 25, Mar. 25, Apr. 8, Sept. 2.

LA NATION. d. est. [1944].
DLC
1946   July 1 — 26, 28 — 30, Aug. 1 — 9, 13 — Sept. 13, 15 — 20, 22, 27 — Oct. 3, 5 — 23, 25 — 30, Nov. 3 — 7, 9 — Dec. 10, 12 — 31.
1947   Jan. 1 — Apr. 16, 18 — 29, May 1 — Sept. 30, Oct. 2 — 28, 30 — Dec. 31.
1948   Jan. 1 — Feb. 2, 4 — Mar. 9, 11 — 23, 28 — Apr. 5, 9 — 22, 24 — May 16, 19 — Dec. 31.
1949   Jan. 1 — Sept. 23, 28, 30 — Nov. 14.
1950   July 19 — Oct. 29, 31 — Dec. 29.
NN
Micro (P) & (N)
1946   Jan. 23, 26, 30, 31, Feb. 2, 7 — 9, 12 — 15, 19 — Mar. 6, 15, 16, 25, 27, Apr. 5, 8, 10 — 15, 22 — 24, 26, 27, May 9 — 11, 15 — 24, 28 — June 3, 13 — 15, 18, 21 — July 11, 22 — Sept. 17, 23 — 25, 27, 28, Oct. 2 — 11, 14 — 17, 21, 23 — Nov. 6, 9, 12 — Dec. 20, 26 — 30.
1947   Jan. 3 — 30, Feb. 1, May 10 — 13, 16 — 31, June 2 — 16, 18 — 21, 25 — July 9, 22 — 26, 29 — Aug. 2, 13, Nov. 24.
1948   May 31.
1949   Feb. 9, Aug. 22, 23.
1950   Oct. 11, 12.

LE NATIONAL. d. est. July 19, 1953.
DLC
1953   July 19 — 23, 26 — Oct. 4, 6 — 17.

1954   Sept. 6 — 11.
1955   July 6, 7, 9.
1956   Dec. 11, 12.

LE NOUVELLISTE. d. est. May 1, 1896.
CLU
1965   June 14 — Dec. 31.
1966   Jan. 1+.
DLC
1930   Nov. 24 — 26, 28, 29, Dec. 2 — 20.
1931   Apr. 9, 13 — 20, 22 — June 6, 9 — 29, July 1 — 29, Aug. 14, 18 — 27, 29 — Sept. 5, 8, 10 — 14.
1941   May 2 — 14, July 1 — 3, 5 — 19, 28, 29, 31, Aug. 2, Oct. 29.
1942   Jan. 31.
1943   Feb. 24, Mar. 13, July 15 — Aug. 4, Dec. 24.
1945   July 3, 6, 10, 12 — 18, 20, 21, 24 — Aug. 10, 12, 13, 20, 21, 23, 24, 29, Sept. 3, 7, 8, 12, 13, 15 — 20, 22 — 25, 28 — Oct. 6, 10, 12, 16, 20, 22, 23, 25 — 29, 31 — Nov. 5, 7 — 14, 16 — 20, 22 — Dec. 21, 23 — 31.
1946   Jan. 1, 4 — 19, 21 — Feb. 27, Mar. 1 — 13, 15 — June 29, July 1 — 31, Aug. 2 — Oct. 9, 11 — Dec. 31.
1947   Jan. 1 — Oct. 28, 30 — Dec. 31.
1948   Jan. 1 — Mar. 5, 7 — May 16, 18 — Dec. 31.
1953   Jan. 1 — Sept. 25, Oct. 2 — Dec. 31.
1954   Jan. 5 — June 4, 6 — Sept. 16, 18 — Dec. 31.
1955   Jan. 1 — Dec. 28.
Micro (P)
1956   Jan. 1+.
DPU
Current (six months).
FU
Micro (N)
1899   [Aug. 1 — Dec. 31].
1890 — 1912   [Jan. 1 — Dec. 31].
1913   [Jan. 1 — Sept. 5].

1925—1950   [Jan. 1—Dec. 31].
ICRL
Micro (P) & (N)
1956   Jan. 1+.
MWA
1914   Mar. 10.

L'OPINION NATIONALE. est. Jan. 5,
1861.
Note: Ceased publication 1867.
MH
1861   Jan. 5—Dec. 31.
1862   Jan. 1—Sept. 6.

PANORAMA. d. est. [1961].
DPU
Current (six months).
LNT—MA
1961   Sept. 18.
1962   Jan. 22, Feb. 12, 19, 26, Mar.
12, Oct. 3, 5.
1963   May 30.
WaU
1963   Feb. 22.

LE PASSE-TEMPS UTILE. est. 1861.
MH
1861   Aug. 14, Sept. 4, 11.

LA PATRIE. d. est. Dec. 24, 1940.
Note: Suspended publication Dec. 25,
1940—Jan. 2, 1941. Ceased publication [Apr. 10], 1941.
DLC
1940   Dec. 24.
1941   Jan. 3—6, 10—Feb. 18, 23,
26—Apr. 7.

LE PATRIOTE. w. est. Mar. 2, 1842.
DLC
1842   Mar. 9—June 14, July 7—Aug.
16, Oct. 13—Nov. 1, 10—22,
Dec. 22—31.
1843   Jan. 18.

LE PAYS. d. est. 1930.
NN
Micro (P) & (N)
1930   Oct. 28.
Boletin: Nov. 10.
1931   Jan. 6—17, 22, Feb. 19—24,

Apr. 7—9, Sept. 29, Dec. 15.
1932   Jan. 7, 12—21, 26—Mar. 19,
21—May 10, 14—31, June 4—
July 16, Aug. 2, 4, 9—13.

LE PETIT PORT-AU-PRINCIEN. w. est.
July 10, 1936.
DLC
1940   Dec. 30.

LE PEUPLE. w. est. May 24, 1871.
DLC
1875   Sept. 25.

LA PHALANGE. w., sw., d. est. Mar. 18,
1939.
Note: Periodicity Mar. 18—Sept. 16,
1939, weekly; Sept. 20—Nov. 18, 1939,
semiweekly; after Nov. 20, 1939, daily.
DLC
1939   June 24—30, Aug. 6—18, Sept.
3—19, 28—Oct. 17, 19—Nov.
7, 9—14, 16—Dec. 6, 8—22,
24—26, 28—31.
1940   Jan. 1—4, 6—June 12, 14—
July 31, Aug. 2—Nov. 24, 26—
Dec. 22, 24—31.
1941   Jan. 1—Mar. 16, 18—Apr. 28,
Sept. 16, 19—Oct. 16, 21—25,
Nov. 3—8, 11—26, Dec. 2—4,
6, 10—12, 15, 16, 29—31.
1957   Jan. 1, 2, 8—10, 12, 16—Feb.
9, 12—26, 28—Mar. 26, 28—
May 2, 5—9, 11—17, 20—31,
June 7—July 26, 28—Aug. 31,
Sept. 3—12, 15—20, 23—Oct.
14, 17—29, 31—Nov. 7, 9—
Dec. 31.
1958   Jan. 1—Feb. 1, 4—Mar. 4, 6—
Apr. 30, May 3—June 30.
MiU
1939   Mar. 18—Dec. 31.
1940   Jan. 1—Dec. 31.
1941   Jan. 1—June 30.

LA PLUME. w., irr. est. May 2, 1914.
Note: Periodicity May 2—Dec. 31,
1914, weekly; Aug. 25—Nov. 27,
1915, irregular. Suspended publication Jan. 1—Aug. 24, 1915; ceased
publication Nov. 27, 1915.

NN
  Micro (P) & (N)
  1914 May 2 – Dec. 31.
  1915 Aug. 25 – Nov. 27.

LA PRESSE. d. est. Aug. 1929.
  DLC
  1930 Nov. 25 – Dec. 22.
  1931 Apr. 12 – 20, 22, 23, 25 – June
        8, 10 – Aug. 3, 19 – 21, 23 –
        Sept. 9, 11 – 15.
  MH
  1929 Sept. 4 – Oct. 1, 4 – 7, 9 – 11,
        14, 15, 17 – 22, 28, Nov. 4, 5,
        7, 8, 11.
  NN
  Micro (P) & (N)
  1929 Sept. 21 – 25, 27, Oct. 15 – 18,
        22, 24, 29 – Nov. 8, 11, 19 –
        Dec. 31.
  1930 Jan. 3 – Feb. 26, 28 – Mar. 4,
        6 – 19, 21 – June 7, 10 – 16,
        20 – 24, 26 – Aug. 14, 19 – Oct.
        29, 31 – Nov. 11, 13 – 26, 28 –
        Dec. 9, 11 – 12, 26 – 31.
  1931 Jan. 5 – 24, 27 – Mar. 30, Apr.
        4 – 30, May 4 – July 15, 17 –
        Aug. 19, 22 – Oct. 10, 12 – Nov.
        25.

LE PROGRES. w. est. Jan. 1, 1860.
  MH
  1860 Jan. 1 – May 12, 26 – June 23,
        July 6 – Oct. 20, Nov. 3 – 24.

LE REPUBLIQUE. w. est. Feb. 20, 1859.
  MH
  1859 Prospecto: Feb. 10.
        Dec. 29.
  1860 Jan. 5 – Sept. 20.
  1861 Jan. 10 – 17, Apr. 11, June 6 –
        Nov. 21.
  1862 Jan. 30, Feb. 13 – Apr. 3, May
        1 – June 5, Aug. 14 – Sept. 4.

REVUE DU COMMERCE ET DES
  TRIBUNAUX. w. est. 1852.
  Note: Succeeded *Revue des tri-
  bunaux*.
  MH
  1858 Dec. 24.

1859 Aug. 6 – 27.
      Supplément: Aug. 6.
1860 Aug. 18.
      Supplément: Aug. 25.
1861 July 13, Aug. 31, Sept. 7.
      Supplément: July 13, Aug. 31.

LE SOIR. d. est. Dec. 26, 1941.
  DLC
  1941 Dec. 26, 29 – 31.
  1942 Jan. 30, Mar. 3, Apr. 6 – 11,
        15 – 18, 24 – 27.
  NN
  Micro (P) & (N)
  1944 Sept. 5, 6, 8 – 14, 20 – 23, 26 –
        28, 30, Oct. 2 – 6, 9 – 11, 13,
        18 – Dec. 14.
  1945 Feb. 3 – Mar. 6, 8 – 24, Apr.
        7 – May 5, 15 – 25, June 4 – 25,
        28 – 30, July 2 – 21, Aug. 8 – 14,
        17, 21 – Sept. 18, 26 – Oct. 26.
  1946 Jan. 22, 24 – Feb. 1, 6 – Mar. 2,
        8, 14, 15, 19, 25, 26, Apr. 1, 5, 6,
        9, 10, 12 – 15, 22 – 30, May 2 –
        6, 9 – 31.

LE SPECTATEUR. w. est. Nov. 1876.
  CU – B
  Micro (P)
  1877 Oct. 31 – Nov. 7.

LE TELEGRAPHE. w. est. Jan. 6, 1821.
  Note: Succeeded by *Le Moniteur
  Häitien*.
  NN
  1829 Jan. 11 – Feb. 15, Mar. 1 – Aug.
        9, 30 – Sept. 20, Oct. 4, 18 –
        Nov. 8, 22 – Dec. 6, 20 – 27.
  1837 Nov. 12.
  1838 Mar. 4, May 27.
  1841 Aug. 1 – 29, Sept. 19, Oct. 4,
        17, Dec. 19.
  1842 Jan. 2, 30, Feb. 20, Mar. 6, 24,
        Apr. 3 – 24, May 8 – 15, 29,
        June 19.

LE TEMPS; FEUILLE POLITIQUE
AGRICOLE ET COMMERCIALE. w. est.
  Feb. 10, 1842.
  DLC
  1842 Feb. 17 – Apr. 27, 29 – June 8,

July 8 – 20, 22 – Aug. 24, Sept.
16 – Oct. 5, 7 – Nov. 23, Dec.
16 – 31.
Supplémente: Sept. 29.
1843   Jan. 1 – 18, 20 – Feb. 9.
NN
1842   June 30, July 14 – Aug. 4.

LE TEMPS. d. est. Dec. 1, 1922.
Note: Suspended publication June
1932; resumed publication 1941.
Ceased publication shortly thereafter. During periods of suspension
the staff published *Le Temps-Revue.*
DLC
1930   Jan. 4 – 7, 15 – Feb. 24, 26,
Mar. 18 – Apr. 14, 30 – May 13,
June 12 – 24, July 9 – 11, 13 –
22, Aug. 10 – 19, Sept. 3, 4, 7 –
17, Oct. 31, Nov. 2, 4 – 16, 20,
22 – 25, 30 – Dec. 31.
1931   Apr. 20, 23, 26 – 28, 30, May 5,
6, 8, 10, 11, 13, 24 – 26, 30 –
June 16, 18 – 22, 24 – 28, 30 –
Aug. 2, 18 – Sept. 4, 6, 7, 10 –
14.
NN
Micro (P) & (N)
1929   Apr. 6, Oct. 21, 23.
1930   Jan. 28, Feb. 10, 12, 24, 25,
Mar. 1 – 4, 7, 8, Apr. 12 – 15,
29, Sept. 3, Nov. 22 – 25, 27 –
Dec. 1, 23 – 31.
1931   Jan. 5, 8 – 19, 21, 23, 24, Mar.
21 – 24, Dec. 2, 3.

LE TEMPS-REVUE. w., sw. est. July
1932.
Note: Periodicity July 1932 – Oct. 7,
1933, weekly; after Oct. 1933, semiweekly. Published by staff of *Le
Temps* during its suspension. Ceased
publication [1941].
DLC
1932   July 15 – Dec. 31.
1933   Jan. 1 – 19, 28 – Dec. 29.
1934   Jan. 1 – Mar. 23, 25 – July 3,
8 – Aug. 3, 5 – Sept. 14, 16 –
25, 27 – Nov. 20, 22 – Dec. 31.

1935   Jan. 1 – Mar. 5, 10 – 15, 24 –
May 7, 9 – Aug. 13, 15 – Dec.
31.
1936   Jan. 1 – Dec. 25.
1937   Jan. 3 – Mar. 23, 28 – Apr. 20,
22 – June 22, 24 – July 30,
Aug. 1 – 10, 19 – Sept. 24, 26 –
Nov. 16, 18 – Dec. 14, 23 – 31.
1938   Jan. 1 – Feb. 18, 20 – June 24,
26 – Nov. 25, 27 – Dec. 31.
1939   Jan. 1 – Apr. 4, 20 – June 2,
4 – Sept. 1, 3 – Dec. 31.
1940   Jan. 1 – Mar. 19, 24 – July 6.

L'UNION. w. est. 1836.
FU
Micro (P) & (N)
1837   June 2 – Dec. 31.
1838   Jan. 1 – Dec. 31.
1839   Jan. 1 – Sept. 15.
NN
1837   Apr. 20 – Dec. 28.
1838   Jan. 4 – Aug. 9.

Port Republican

See Port-au-Prince.

HONDURAS

Amapala

EL PACIFICO. w. est. May 11, 1918.
LNT – MA
1918   May 25.

LA VOZ DEL GOLFO. w. est. [1919].
LNT – MA
1919   Feb. 16.

Catacamas

EL COMETA. bw. est. Apr. 17, 1897.
LNT – MA
1897   May 17.

Choluteca

MOSQUITO. w. est. Apr. 26, 1917.
LNT – MA
1917   May 10 – June 7.

Comayagua

BOLETIN DEL EJERCITO DE HON-
DURAS. est. May 28, 1853.
  CU – B
    1853   Prospecto.
             May 28.

BOLETIN OFICIAL. est. 1872.
    Note: Supplement to *La Gaceta*.
  LNT – MA
    1872   Sept. 24 – Dec. 6.

BOLETIN OFICIAL DEL GOBIERNO
DE HONDURAS. est. Jan. 16, 1851.
  CU – B
    1851   Mar. 27.
    1853   Sept. 21, 29, Oct. 13, Nov. 11,
             Dec. 5, 13, 25.
    1854   Jan. 31.
  DLC
    1851   [Jan. 16 – Aug. 15].
  NHi
    1854   Jan. 31.

CLARIN OFICIAL. est. 1871.
  LNT – MA
    1871   June 7 – 11.

GACETA OFICIAL DE HONDURAS.
  3m.
  LNT – MA
    1869   [Feb. 10 – Sept. 30.]

EL INFIERNO. est. [1902].
  LNT – MA
    1902   Aug. 11.

EL NACIONAL. w., irr. est. 1874.
  LNT – MA
    1875   [Mar. 20 – Nov. 27].

EL PATRIOTISMO. w. est. 1911.
  LNT – MA
    1911   Oct. 17.

EL PORVENIR. est. June 22, 1905.
  LNT – MA
    1905   June 22, 29.

EL REDACTOR OFICIAL DE HON-
DURAS. est. Sept. 15, 1840.
    Note: Succeeded *Termómetro*

político oficial; succeeded by
Gaceta oficial de Honduras. Ceased
publication 1848.
  CtY
    1847   Jan. 30.
  LNT – MA
    1840   Oct. 15, Nov. 15, Dec. 15.
    1844   Dec. 30.
    1845   Jan. 1 – Nov. 30.
    1846   Dec. 15.

EL TAQUIGRAFO DE LA DIETA
NACIONAL. est. June 18, 1847.
  CtY
    1847   June 18.

Comayagüela

EL BATIDOR. w. est. 1922.
  LNT – MA
    1922   Mar. 5.

Juticalpa

EL CLARIN. w. est. June 19, 1902.
  LNT – MA
    1902   June 26.

EL COMBATE. w. est. June 3, 1902.
  LNT – MA
    1902   June 3.

LA PAZ. w. est. 1898.
  CU – B
    Micro (P)
    1900   July 14.
  LNT – MA
    1898   Jan. 14.

LA VOZ DEL PUEBLO. w. est. 1902.
  LNT – MA
    1902   Apr. 5 – 12.

La Ceiba

EL ATLANTICO. 3w. est. Nov. 4, 1926.
  DLC
    1942   Mar. 11.

EL CENTINELA. w., sw. est. 1907.
  LNT – MA
    1907   Dec. 17, 23.
    1908   Jan. 1 – Mar. 31.

DIARIO DEL NORTE. d. est. May 4, 1922.
 DLC
  1941   Apr. 1, 12, May 17, 24, 31, June 7, 17, 30.

 TxU
  1924   Dec. 20—24.

EL ESPECTADOR. est. 1930.
 LNT—MA
  1931   July 4, 18.

EL HERALDO. [3w.], d. est. Dec. 1, 1936.
 DLC
  1941   Apr. 14, 22—25, May 5—10, 12—14, 17, 19, 21—24, 26—30, June 14, 16—21, 25, 26, 28, 30.
  1942   Mar. 4, 16.

HERALDO DE LA CEIBA. sw. est. Mar. 18, 1924.
 LNT—MA
  1924   July 9, Aug. 27.
 NN
  1924   Mar. 18.

INTER AMERICA. w. est. 1922.
 LNT—MA
  1922   Nov. 5—Dec. 3.

NUEVAS IDEAS. w. est. 1922.
 LNT—MA
  1922   Oct. 26, Dec. 7.
  1923   Mar. 22.

EL PAIS. sw. est. June 8, 1929.
 DLC
  1941   Apr. 2, May 4, 14, 21, 25, 28, June 1, 4, 11, 18.

LA TRIBUNA. sw.
 DLC
  1947   July 2—9, 16—Aug. 27, 30, Sept. 10—Dec. 31.
  1948   Jan. 1—21, 28—31, Feb. 7—18, 25—29, Mar. 6—13, Apr. 14, May 15—19, 29, June 5—30, July 7, 14—Oct. 6.

Progreso

PROGRESO. est. 1930.
 LNT—MA
  1931   Feb. 7, 15.

Puerto Cortés

BLANCO Y ROJO. est. 1923.
 LNT—MA
  1923   May 26.

EL DEBATE.
 CU
  1923   July 19.

NEW LOUISIANA LOTTERY.
 Note: In English.
 NHi
  1819   Dec. 29.

Puerto de Amapala

See Amapala.

Roatán

EL CARIBE. bw. est. June 1, 1918.
 LNT—MA
  1918   June 1—Dec. 31.
  1919   Jan. 1—June 30.

CINCO ESTRELLAS. w. est. 1918.
 LNHT
  1918   Jan. 1, 15.

San Pedro Sula

EL ANUNCIDOR DE CORTES. w. est. May 2, 1915.
 CU
  1915   Suplemento: Sept. 14.

EL AVISADOR. w. est. [1901].
 LNT—MA
  1901   Oct. 26.

EL CENTINELA. w. est. Sept. 8, 1902.
 LNT—MA
  1902   Sept. 22.

EL COMERCIO; PERIODICO INDE-PENDIENTE. est. May 28, 1899.
 LNT—MA
  1899   May 28.

EL COMERCIO. [sw.] est. 1908.
 LNT—MA
  1917 Dec. 17—21.

EL COMETA. bw. est. 1906.
 LNT—MA
  1906 Oct. 15.

EL DERECHO. w. est. June 18, 1903.
 LNT—MA
  1903 June 18—July 2.

DIARIO COMERCIAL. d. est. Feb. 1, 1933.
 Note: Ceased publication May 15, 1954.
 DLC
  1941 Feb. 28—Apr. 8, 11—29, May
    1—8, 10—June 25, 27—July 2,
    4—Oct. 9, 11—26, 28—Dec. 23,
    25—31.
  1942 Jan. 1—6, 8—25, 27—Feb. 11,
    13—23, 25—Mar. 15, 17—May
    8, 10, 11, 13—June 5, 7, 9—28,
    30, July 1, 3—12, 16—Aug. 4,
    8—11, 15—18, 20, 22—24, 27—
    30, Sept. 2—9, 11—14, 24, 27,
    28, Oct. 1, 2, 4, 10, 11, 18—20.
  1947 July 1—Aug. 17, 19—Oct. 28,
    30—Dec. 23, 25—31.
  1948 Jan. 1—Feb. 27, Mar. 1—July
    9, 11, 13—Dec. 30.
  1949 Jan. 2—24, 26—Feb. 24, 26—
    Mar. 2, 4—21, 23, 25, 27, 29—
    May 2, 4, 5, 7—29, June 1—
    Aug. 22, 24—Sept. 26, 28—
    Nov. 4, 6, 8, 9, 12, 13, 15, 18—
    21, 23—Dec. 2, 4—16, 18—31.
  1950 Jan. 1, 3—11, 13—23, 25—30,
    Feb. 1—19, 21—Mar. 13, 15—
    26, 28—Apr. 21, 23—27, 29,
    30, May 3, 5—14, 16—24, 26—
    28, June 1—6, 9—25, 27—29,
    July 1—3, 5, 7—11, 13—18,
    20—23, 25, 26, 28—30, Aug. 2,
    4—8, 10, 13—17, 20, 21, 23, 24,
    27, 28, Sept. 1—7, 9—18, 21—
    24, 26—Oct. 2, 6—9, 13—17,
    22, 24, 26, 29, Nov. 1, 5, 8—15,

17—Dec. 12, 16, 17, 19, 20, 22—
    25, 27, 28, 30, 31.
  1951 Jan. 1, 3—11, 14, 15, 17—22,
    25, 28—31, Feb. 3—9, 28, Mar.
    1, 3—28, 30—Apr. 1, 3—12, 17,
    19, 20, 22, 23, 25—27, 29—May
    1, 3, 5—7, 13—22, 24—29, 31—
    June 5, 7—10, 12, 14—17, 19—
    July 2, 4—8, 10—15, 19—26,
    28—30, Aug. 1—13, 16—23,
    25, 26, 28—Sept. 6, 8—23, 26—
    Oct. 19, 21—31, Nov. 2—Dec.
    11, 13, 14, 16—18, 20—27, 30.
  1952 Jan. 1—29, Feb. 16, 17, 19, 20,
    22—26, Mar. 1—4, 20—25,
    Apr. 6—8, 15, 30—May 6, 7, 8,
    10—13, 16—19, 21, 22, 29—
    June 12, 20—24, 27—July 24,
    Aug. 1, 6—10, 12—21, 24, 25,
    29, Sept. 3, 4, 6—22, 24—Oct.
    2, 4—8, 10—27, 29—Nov. 11,
    14—27, 29—31, Dec. 3, 5—10,
    12—25, 27, 28, 30, 31.
  1953 Jan. 1—11, 14, 15, 17, 18, 21—
    30, Feb. 1—Mar. 2, 7—10, 13—
    15, 18—26, 28—June 29, July
    1—Dec. 20.
  1954 Jan. 3—Mar. 28, Apr. 4—24,
    May 2—15.
 LNT—MA
  1933 [Feb. 1—May 23].
  1935 [Feb. 21—Mar. 22].
  1937 July 8—Dec. 31.
  1938 Jan. 1—Dec. 31.
  1949 [Jan. 1—Dec. 31].
  1951 July 1—Dec. 31.
 NN
  Micro (P) & (N)
  1945 [Dec. 15—31].
  1946—1948 [Jan. 1—Dec. 31].

ENSAYOS. w. est. Sept. 22, 1917.
 LNT—MA
  1917 Nov. 10—24.

LA ESTRELLA DEL NORTE. w. est. Jan.
 27, 1900.
 LNT—MA
  1900 Jan. 27.

EL FERROCARRIL. sw. est. Oct. 9, 1898.
LNT–MA
1898 Oct. 9–13.

EL HERALDO. w.
LNHT
1921 Sept. 15.

EL LATIGO. w. est. Feb. 5, 1900.
LNT–MA
1900 Feb. 5.

EL NACIONAL. d. est. June 2, 1926.
LNT–MA
1932 Dec. 1, 2, 6.

EL NORTE. w., d. est. Feb. 17, 1921.
DLC
1940 July 29, Aug. 5.
1941 Jan. 5, 9, 16, 30, Feb. 28–Mar.
14, 17–20, 22–25, 27, 28, 31,
Apr. 3–9, 13–30, May 3–22,
24–June 8, 10–17, 19–23, 25,
26, 28–30, July 6, 8–10, 12–
16, 18–22, 24–28, 30–Aug. 4,
6–13, 17, 18, 20, 23–26, 29,
31–Oct. 5, 7–16, 19–29,
Nov. 1–16, 18–20, 22–24,
29–Dec. 2, 6, 7, 11–17, 19–
31.
1942 Jan. 1–4, 7, 8, 10–15, 18–23,
25–29, 31, Feb. 1, 6–Mar. 31,
Apr. 5–28, May 2, 6, 7, 10, 13,
Aug. 26–28, Sept. 5, 11–19,
30–Oct. 2, 6, 7, 10–16, 19, 23.
1944 Mar. 29, Oct. 24.
1946 Mar. 17, 20–23, 29, Apr. 3, 5,
10, 11, 14, June 5, 11, 12.
1947 June 20, 30, July 2–12, 15–23,
25, Aug. 8, 10–29.
1948 June 1–3, 5–7, 9, 12–14,
16–19, 23–July 3, 7, 8, 12–
15, 19–23, 27–Aug. 11, 14–
19, 21–27, 30, 31, Sept. 8–27.
LNT–MA
1932 Nov. 17, 21, 25.
1933 Feb. 7.

LAS NOTICIAS. sw. est. Mar. 22, 1902.
LNT–MA
1902 Mar. 22.

NUESTRO CRITERIO. d., w. est. Nov. 4,
1927.
LNT–MA
1931 Aug. 1, 15.
1932 Nov. 16.
1933 May 22.

LA OPINION DEL PUEBLO. w. est. May
20, 1903.
LNT–MA
1903 May 20.

EL PERIODICO DEL NORTE. est. 1903.
LNT–MA
1903 June 14.

EL PROGRESO. w. est. Aug, 8, 1904.
LNT–MA
1904 Sept. 16.

LA RAZON. w. est. Aug. 30, 1902.
LNT–MA
1902 Oct. 4.

EL ZANCUDO. irr. est. June 10, 1917.
LNT–MA
1917 June 10, 17, 24, July 1, 15.

Santa Barbara

LA EPOCA. bw. est. 1903.
LNT–MA
1903 Nov. 8.

LA LUZ.
LNT–MA
1915 Jan. 1–Dec. 31.
1923 June 23.

LA VERDAD. bw. est. [1898].
LNT–MA
1898 Apr. 15.

Santa Rosa de Copán

EL COMERCIO. w. est. Nov. 14, 1931.
LNT–MA
1932 Jan. 23–30, Feb. 13–Mar. 5,
Apr. 16–23, May 7–21, June
4–July 2.

Tegucigalpa

EL ALFILER. irr., sw., w. est. Sept. 10,
1916.
  LNT—MA
    1916   Sept. 10—Nov. 30.
    1917   Jan. 1—May 6.
    1918   July 21—Aug. 18.
    1919   May 4—June 15.

ALMA INCAICA. est. June 28, 1923.
  LNT—MA
    1923   June 28.

AMERICA CENTRAL. sw. est. Sept. 19,
1917.
  CU
    1917   Sept. 19—25, Oct. 2.
  MWA
    1917   Sept. 19—22.

EL ARPON. w. est. Apr. 27, 1919.
  LNT—MA
    1919   Apr. 27—July 19.

AZUL Y BLANCO. w. est. 1914.
  CU
    1915   May 7—21, June 25, July 9,
            Aug. 13—Oct. 1, 22—Nov. 12,
            26—Dec. 17.
    1916   Jan. 1—7, 28—Feb. 11.

LA BANDERA LIBERAL. 3w. est. 1907.
    Note: Ceased publication [1908].
  CU—B
    Micro (N)
    1907   Apr. 15—Aug. 8, 26—Oct. 24,
            30—Dec. 27.
    1908   Feb. 4—27.

EL BIEN PUBLICO. est. 1928.
  CU
    1928   July 4.

BLANCO Y ROJO. w. est. 1918.
  LNT—MA
    1919   May 15.

BOLETIN DEL EJERCITO. est. Sept. 15,
1913.
  LNT—MA
    1913   Sept. 15.

1915   Dec. 1—31.
1916   Jan. 1—31.

EL BUEN PASTOR. w. est. Nov. 8, 1911.
  LNT—MA
    1923   July 15.

EL CIUDADANO. d.
  DLC
    1948   July 1, 2, 5—8, 12—16, 19—22,
            24—29, 31—Aug. 5, 10—12,
            14—16, 18, 19, 21—23, 25—
            Sept. 8, 10—17, 20—Oct. 1, 4—
            6.

EL CLARIN. irr. est. Aug. 14, 1923.
  LNT—MA
    1923   Aug. 14, 23, Sept. 7, 14, 26.

EL COMELENGUAS. w. est. May 6, 1923.
  LNT—MA
    1923   May 6—Sept. 2.

EL COMERCIO. w.
  PrU
    1962   May 5, June 2—30, July 7—28,
            Aug. 4—25, Sept. 1—29, Oct.
            6—27, Nov. 3—24, Dec. 1.
    1963   Jan. 5—26, Feb. 2—23, Mar.
            2—30, Apr. 6—27, May 4—25,
            June 1—29, July 6—27, Aug.
            3—31, Sept. 7—21, Oct. 5—19,
            Nov. 2—30, Dec. 7—14, 28.
    1964   Jan. 3—10, 31, Feb. 7—28,
            Mar. 6—27, Apr. 3—24, May 1,
            15—29, June 5—26, July 3—24,
            Aug. 7—28, Sept. 3—24, Oct.
            1—29, Nov. 6—27, Dec. 4—25.
    1965   Jan. 1—22, Feb. 5—12, Mar.
            12—26, Apr. 2—30, May 7—28,
            June 4, 18—25, July 2—30,
            Aug. 13—27, Sept. 3—24, Oct.
            1—29, Nov. 6—Dec. 31.
    1966   Jan. 1+.

EL CONSTITUCIONAL. w. est. 1903.
  CU—B
    Micro (P) & (N)
    1903   Mar. 6—21.

EL CONSTITUCIONAL; DIARIO DE LA
TARDE. d. est. [1923].
  LNT—MA
    1924   Jan. 14.

EL CRONISTA. sw., d. est. Apr. 10. 1912.
Note: Periodicity Apr. 10, 1912 – Dec.
15, 1913, semiweekly; after Dec. 16,
1913, daily. Suspended publication
Dec. 28, 1943 – Apr. 9, 1953.

CU
Micro (P) & (N)
1912 Oct. 26.
1917 Sept. 25 – Oct. 26, 29 – Nov. 8,
10 – 15, 17 – 27, 29, Dec. 1 – 13,
18 – 26.
1918 Jan. 4 – 11, Feb. 16 – 20, 26 –
28.
1943 Aug. 2 – Dec. 23.
DLC
1925 Dec. 26 – 31.
1926 Jan. 1 – 11, 13 – 15, 17 – Feb.
28, Mar. 2 – 16, 19, 28 – Apr. 7,
9 – July 2, 7 – 18, 20 – 23, 25,
26, 28 – Aug. 6, 14 – 22, 25 –
Sept. 8, 10 – 19, 21 – Oct. 8, 10,
11, 13 – 15, 23 – 29, 31 – Nov.
10, 12 – 26, 28 – Dec. 1, 3 – 10,
25 – 31.
1927 Jan. 1 – 17, 19 – Feb. 27, Mar.
1 – 4, 6 – 11, 30.
1930 Sept. 22 – Dec. 31.
1931 Jan. 1 – May 4, 6 – June 11,
13 – July 10, 12, 18 – Aug. 7,
9 – Nov. 6, 8 – Dec. 31.
1932 Jan. 2 – June 29, July 1 – Dec.
31.
1933 Jan. 1 – Dec. 31.
1934 Jan. 1 – 31, Feb. 2 – Apr. 30,
May 2 – 7, 11 – July 6, 9 – Aug.
9, 12 – 16, 31 – Oct. 4, 12 – Nov.
1, 9 – Dec. 20, 28 – 31.
1935 Jan. 1 – Dec. 31.
1936 Jan. 1 – Oct. 2, 10 – Nov. 20,
28 – Dec. 31.
1937 Jan. 1 – Oct. 6, 21 – Dec. 10,
18 – 31.
1938 – 1941 Jan. 1 – Dec. 31.
1942 Jan. 2 – Dec. 31.
1943 Jan. 1 – Apr. 21, 25 – June 15,
17 – Dec. 17.

1959 Jan. 2 – 9, 11 – 16, 18 – 23, 25 –
June 12, 14 – 25, 27 – 30, Aug.
1 – 7, 9 – Dec. 31.
1960 Jan. 1 – Apr. 22, 24 – 29, May
28 – June 10, 12, 18 – Nov. 10,
12 – Dec. 31.
1961 Jan. 3 – Dec. 30.
Micro (P) & (N)
1962 Jan. 1 – June 24, 26 – Dec. 31.
1963 Jan. 1+.
FU
Micro (N)
1929 July 1 – Sept. 30.
LNT – MA
Micro (N)
1925 [Feb. 4 – Dec. 31.]
1926 – 1942 [Jan. 1 – Dec. 31.]
1943 [Jan. 1 – Dec. 23.]
OrU
1964 Feb. 29.

LA CRUZ DE LORENA. bw. est. [1942].
DLC
1942 Mar. 15.

EL DEMOCRATA; DIARIO DE LA TAR-
DE, INDEPENDIENTE, Y DE IN-
TERESES GENERALES. d. est. Mar. 4,
1926.
DLC
1927 May 18 – 23, 30, 31, June 4, 6,
8, 9, 13, 20 – 22, 30, July 1, 6,
11, 12, 14, 15, 26, 28 – 30, Aug.
2 – 5, 8 – 12, 15 – 31, Oct. 11 –
20.

EL DEMOCRATA; ORGANO DEL
COMITE CENTRAL DEL PARTIDO
NACIONAL DEMOCRATICO. w. est.
1919.
LNT – MA
1919 Nov. 8.

EL DIA. d. est. May 19, 1903.
DLC
1903 May 19 – Dec. 30.

EL DIA. d. est. June 11, 1948.
CLU
1964 Nov. 25.
1965 Jan. 4 – 7, 9, 12, 13, 16, 19, 21,

23, 25 — 28, 30, Feb. 1, 2, 6, 8 —
10, 13, 17, 18, 20, 23 — 25, 27,
Mar. 1 — 6, 10, 11, 15 — 20, 22,
24 — 27, 30 — Apr. 3, 6 — 9, 11,
13, 20 — 24, 26, 27, 29, 30, May
3 — 9, 11 — 13, 18 — 20, 22, 24,
26 — 29, 31 — June 3, 7 — 10, 12,
15, 16, 19, 20 — 23, 26, 28 — 30,
July 3, 5, 6, 10 — 12, 14, 17, 19,
21, 23, 24, 26, 27, 29, 30, Aug.
1, 3, 8 — 11, 14, 16, 17, 21, 24,
25, 28, 30, Sept. 1, 2, 4, 6 — 11,
13, 14, 16 — 18, 20, 21, 23 — 25,
27 — 30, Oct. 2, 5 — 16, 18, 19,
23, 25 — Nov. 2, 4, 10, 14 — 18,
23 — 26, 29, Dec. 1, 2, 4, 6, 8 —
11, 13, 15 — 17, 22 — 24, 27 — 31.

DLC
1948   June 12 — July 8, 11 — Aug. 3,
        5 — Dec. 6, 8 — 31.
1949   Jan. 1, 2, 4 — 11, 13, 14, 16, 18 —
        Feb. 13, 15, 18, 20 — Mar. 3, 5,
        6, 10 — 16, 18, 20, 21, 23, 25, 27,
        29 — Apr. 6, 9 — 20, 22 — May 13,
        15 — Nov. 29, Dec. 1 — 5, 8 — 19,
        21 — 30.
1950   Jan. 1 — 9, 11 — 30, Feb. 1 —
        Mar. 17, 19 — 21, 23 — May 23,
        25 — June 12, 15 — Dec. 30.
1951   Jan. 1 — Dec. 29.
1952   Jan. 1 — Apr. 18, 20 — June 29,
        July 1 — 28, 30 — Sept. 12, 14 —
        27, 29 — Nov. 15, 17 — 20, 22 —
        Dec. 12, 15 — 23, 25 — 31.
1953   Jan. 1 — Mar. 23, 25 — July 7,
        9 — Aug. 25, 28, 30 — Sept. 5,
        7 — 19, 21 — Dec. 17, 19 — 31.
1955   Mar. 1 — Apr. 13, 15 — 23, 25,
        26, 29 — July 30, Aug. 1 — Oct.
        7, 10 — 13, Dec. 5 — 31.
1956   Jan. 3, 4, 6 — 19, Feb. 5, 6, 8, 21,
        23 — June 12, 14 — Oct. 3, 6 —
        Nov. 28, Dec. 3 — 29.
1960   May 1 — 16, 25 — Sept. 13, 15 —
        30.
1961   Jan. 10 — Mar. 23, Apr. 1 — 7,
        24 — 28, Oct. 1 — Nov. 5, 7 —
        Dec. 16, 18 — 22, 24 — 30.

Micro (P) & (N)
1962   Jan. 1+.
LNT — MA
1952   Nov. 1 — Dec. 31.
1953   Jan. 1 — Dec. 31.
1954   [Jan. 1 — Dec. 31].
1955   Jan. 1 — Mar. 22.
MoSU
Current (one year).

DIARIO DE HONDURAS. d. est. Oct. 15,
1897.
CU — B
Micro (P) & (N)
1902   Oct. 11, Dec. 8, 9.
DLC
1897   Oct. 15 — Dec. 31.
1898   Jan. 1 — May 1, 3 — Dec. 31.
1899   Jan. 1 — Apr. 11.
LNT — MA
1900   Nov. 29.

EL DIARITO DE LA GUERRA. d. est.
1896.
LNT — MA
1896   Apr. 18, 19, 25, 26, May 9 — 19.

LA EPOCA. d. est. July 1, 1933.
Note: Ceased publication Jan. 18,
1958.
CU
1947   Mar. 18 — 27, Apr. 11 — 28, May
        10 — 30, July 8 — 19, Aug. 16 —
        27, Sept. 1 — Oct. 17, 20 — Nov.
        14, 17 — Dec. 12, 15 — 31.
1948   Jan. 2 — 6, 8 — Feb. 12, Mar.
        1 — 24, 29 — Nov. 9, 20 — Dec.
        31.
1949   Jan. 3, 29 — Apr. 6, 20 — May 3,
        5, 7, June 15 — July 2, 5 — 7,
        9 — Aug. 5, 23 — 31, Sept. 2, 5,
        12 — Nov. 5, 10 — 19, 26, Dec.
        1 — 5, 7, 10 — 12, 14 — 24.

DLC
1936   Extraordinario: Feb. 1.
1937   Oct. 6 — 9, 13, 23, 25 — 30, Nov.
        2, 3, 5, 6, 8, 10, 11, 13, 15, 27,
        Dec. 21, 23, 24, 27 — 31.
1938   Jan. 3 — 5, 13, 14, 16 — 20, Feb.
        6 — 13, 19 — Mar. 2, 10 — 14,

16−28, 30−Apr. 13, 24−May
26, June 3−7, 9−July 17, Aug.
11−14, 16−19, 21−Sept. 30,
Nov. 10−14, 16−18.
1939   July 17, 19, 24−31, Aug. 2, 3,
11−14, 16−19, 22, 23, 28−
Sept. 1, 4−8, 12, 19, 22, 28−
Oct. 13, 23, 25, 27, 30−Nov. 1,
3, 4, 7, 9−22, 24−27, 29, 30,
Dec. 12−18, 20, 22−28, 31.
1940   Jan. 1, 3−5, 7−10, 12−18,
21−25, 27, 28, 31, Feb. 2−6,
8−11, 13−15, 18, 20−29, Mar.
3, 5−13, 16−18, 20, 24, 27−
Apr. 5, 7−10, 14, 16−22, 24−
May 5, 7−9, 11−16, 19, 21−
24, 26−28, 30, 31, June 2−5,
8−13, 16, 18−23, 25, 29−July
1, 3−5, 7, 10−12, 14−16, 18−
21, 23−26, 28, Aug. 1−6, 9−
14, 17−22, 25−28, 30−Sept.
1, 4, 5, 7−10, 12−15, 17, 18,
22, 27−Oct. 2, 4−9, 13, 20,
26−28, 30, 31, Nov. 2−7, 10,
17, 24, 27−Dec. 6, 8−31.
1941   Jan. 1−18, 25, 27, 29, 30, Feb.
1−7, 15−20, Mar. 1−18, 21−
31, Apr. 3, 5−May 17, 20−27,
29−June 3, 5−9, 11−17, 19,
21−25, July 1, 2, 5−8, 14, 21,
Aug. 26, Sept. 10, 11, Oct. 1, 3,
15, 18, 20, 31, Nov. 6, 15, 21, 24,
25, Dec. 1.
1942   Apr. 1, 7, June 2, 11, 23, 26,
July 22, 27, Aug. 1, 4−11, 22,
27, Sept. 1, 3−5, 8, 10, 12, 14,
17−22, 29, 30, Oct. 3, 10−15,
19, 21, 23, 28.
1944   Sept. 18, 19, 21, Oct. 21−Nov.
15, 17−30.
1945   Jan. 29−Feb. 3, 16, 17, 20−
Mar. 6, 8, 9, 12−14, 16, 17,
20−22, May 15−21.
1947   May 31−June 13, July 1−7,
9−Sept. 5, 8−27, 30, Oct. 30,
31, Nov. 3.
1948   Mar. 24−Apr. 11, 13−June 22,
27, July 1, 3−8, 11−Aug. 30,

Sept. 1−28, 30−Nov. 11, 13−
Dec. 31.
1949   Jan. 1−Dec. 4, 6−31.
1950   Jan. 1, 3−23, 25−Apr. 30,
May 2−Dec. 20, 22−31.
1951   Jan. 1−Feb. 5, 11, 14−Mar.
19, 21−Apr. 1, 3−May 15, 18,
20−June 3, 5−Dec. 21, 23, 26,
27, 30, 31.
1952   Jan. 4−24, 27−31, Feb. 3, 8−
20, 22, 24−Mar. 13, 16, 22, 23,
30, 31, Apr. 2−6, 18, 24−May
1, 9−Oct. 14, 16, 19, 21−Dec.
31.
1953   Jan. 1−26, 29−Sept. 4, 6, 8−
18, 20, 22−Dec. 31.
Micro (P)
1956−1957   Jan. 1−Dec. 31.
1958   Jan. 1−18.
ICRL
Micro (P) & (N)
1956−1967   Jan. 1−Dec. 31.
1958   Jan. 1−8.
LNHT
1937   Nov. 29, 30, Dec. 2−6, 20.
1951−1955   [Jan. 1−Dec. 31].
Micro (N)
1944   [Mar. 17−Dec. 31].
1945   [Jan. 1−June 6].
(P)
1956−1957   Jan. 1−Dec. 31.
1958   Jan. 1−18.

LA ESPERANZA. bw. est. 1897.
LNT−MA
1897   Mar. 2.

EL ESTADO. 3w. est. July 1, 1904.
Note: Ceased publication [1907].
CU
1906   Jan. 6, 13.
CU−B
Micro (P)
1904   [July 1−Dec. 31].
1905   [Jan. 1−Dec. 31.].
1906   [Jan. 1−Mar. 31].
Micro (N)
1904   July 1−Dec. 31.
1905−1906 Jan. 1−Dec. 31.

1907　Jan. 1 – Mar. 21.
DLC
1904　July 1 – Dec. 31.
LNT – MA
1906　Jan. 2.
1907　Feb. 2 – 28.

EXCELSIOR. d. est. Apr. 15, 1921.
CU
1921　Aug. 2 – Nov. 15, Dec. 1 – 31.
1922　Mar. 9, May 31, July 1 – Oct. 6, 9 – 30, Nov. 1 – 13, 15 – Dec. 30.
1923　Jan. 2 – 18, 22, 23, 25, Feb. 3 – 23, 26 – 28, Mar. 20 – July 25.
LNT – MA
Micro (N)
1922　[Feb. 17 – Dec. 31].
1923　[Jan. 1 – Dec. 29].

LA FARANDULA. w. est. Nov. 12, 1916.
LNT – MA
1916　Nov. 12 – Dec. 31.
1917　Jan. 7 – 14.

LA GACETA; DIARIO OFICIAL DE LA REPUBLICA DE HONDURAS. d. est. Oct. 25, 1876.
CU – B
1887　Jan. 22 – Dec. 29.
DLC
1876　Oct. 25 – Dec. 31.
1877　Jan. 1 – 18.
1880　Jan. 1 – Dec. 31.
1881　Feb. 1 – Dec. 31.
1882 – 1900　Jan. 1 – Dec. 31.
LNHT
1887 – 1895　[Jan. 1 – Dec. 31].
1898 – 1900　[Jan. 1 – Dec. 31].
Micro (P)
1954　Jan. 1+.
LNT – MA
1876　Oct. 25 – Dec. 30.

GACETA DE HONDURAS. bw., 3m. est. Oct. 15, 1848.
Note: Title *Gaceta oficial del gobierno de Honduras*, Oct. 15, 1848 – May 19, 1853; *Gaceta de Honduras*, May 20, 1853 – 1857; *Gaceta de Honduras*, 1857 – 1864. Succeeded *El Redactor*

oficial de Honduras; succeeded by *Gaceta oficial de Honduras*. Ceased publication 1864.
CU – B
1849　Aug. 5, Oct. 19, Nov. 30.
1850　Aug. 31.
1851　Nov. 26.
1852　Jan. 15, Mar. 15, Apr. 30, May 15 – Dec. 15.
1853　Jan. 10, 20, 24, 30 – Dec. 31.
1854　Jan. 1 – May 30, July 30.
1855　Jan. 20, Feb. 10.
1856　Oct. 20.
1861　Feb. 20.
CtY
1848　Oct. 15 – Nov. 15.
1849　Feb. 15, July 20, Oct. 19, Dec. 15.
NHi
1852　Mar. 15, May 30, July 31, Aug. 15.
1853　Jan. 20, Feb. 20, 28, May 20, June 20, 30.
1854　Feb. 28, Mar. 10, 30, Apr. 20, May 10.

LA GACETA DEL GOBIERNO. bw. est. Apr. 27, 1829.
DLC
1829　Apr. 27 – Dec. 31.
1830　Jan. 1 – Dec. 31.
1831　Jan. 1 – July 25.

GACETA OFICIAL DEL GOBIERNO DE HONDURAS.
See *Gaceta de Honduras*.

EL GESTO. w. est. Mar. 14, 1915.
LNT – MA
1915　Mar. 14 – May 30.
1917　Jan. 28.

EL GRAFICO; SEMANARIO NACIONAL. w. est. May 16, 1931.
LNHT
1931　June 13.

EL GRAFICO. w., irr. est. Oct. 21, 1933.
LNT – MA
1933　Oct. 21 – Dec. 31.
1934　Jan. 1 – Dec. 31.
1935　Jan. 1 – Feb. 23.

EL HERALDO. w. est. 1917.
  LNT—MA
    1917　Feb. 25.

EL HERALDO LITERARIO. w. est. Aug.
  1909.
  LNHT
    1909　Sept. 12, 19.

HISPANO-AMERICA. est. Nov. 1, 1922.
  LNT—MA
    1923　Mar. 1.

HONDURAS. w. est. July 9, 1921.
  LNT—MA
    1921　July 9.

HONDURAS INDUSTRIAL. bw.
  LNT—MA
    1884　June 1.

HONDURAS NUEVA. d.
  CU
    1947　Jan. 11—Feb. 9, 12, 13, 15—
          Mar. 23, Apr. 1—19, May 22—
          June 3, 5—7, 10—14, 17—20,
          27—July 1, 8—11, 13—22.

  DLC
    1947　July 1—12, 14—23, 25—Aug.
          20, 22—Sept. 5, 7—Oct. 6,
          9—17, 19—30, Nov. 1—29,
          Dec. 1—6, 8—20, 22—30.
    1948　Jan. 1—11, 14—23, 27—Feb.
          6, 8—12, 14—20, 22—29, Mar.
          3, 5, 9—12, 23—29, 31, Apr.
          6, 9, 13—16, 20—24, 27, 29,
          May 6, 8, 11, 14, 18—26, June
          1—27, July 1, 7—9, 13—16,
          21—24, 27, 29, 31.

HONDURAS PROGRESS. w. est. Jan.
  12, 1888.
    Note: In English.
  CU—B
    Micro (P)
    1889　May 2.
    1893　June 23.
  LNHT
    1888　Jan. 12—Dec. 31.
    1889—1892　Jan. 1—Dec. 31.

MH
    1888　Mar. 1—15, Apr. 5—26, May
          17, June 21, July 5, Sept. 20—
          Oct. 11.

LA HORA. est. 1955.
  LNT—MA
    1955　Oct. 15, 29.

EL IMPARCIAL. w. est. Nov. 4, 1955.
  LNT—MA
    1955　Nov. 4—26.
    1956　Jan. 21, 28, Oct. 20, Nov. 17,
          Dec. 22.

JUVENTUD LIBERAL. w. est. Mar. 1919.
  DLC
    1919　Apr. 24.

EL LATIGO. w. est. 1926.
  DLC
    1927　Jan. 16, 23.

MR. X. w.
  LNHT
    1924　June 15, 22, Aug. 17, Sept. 7,
          20, Oct. 4.

EL MONITOR. 3w., w. est. 1908.
  CU
    Micro (P)
    1908　Mar. 7—Apr. 7, 11—June 20,
          23—Aug. 3.

LA NACION. 3w. est. Feb. 1919.
  CU
    1919　Feb. 18—27, Mar. 20—24.
    1928　June 6.

EL NACIONAL. w. est. 1873.
  LNT—MA
    1873　Dec. 22.
    1874　Jan. 5, 9.

EL NACIONAL. w. est. [1946].
  DLC
    1947　July 13—19, 28—Sept. 6, 29—
          Oct. 11, 13—Nov. 1, Dec. 15—
          31.
    1948　Jan. 1—Feb. 1.

EL NOTICIOSO DEL EJERCITO LIBER-
  TADOR. w. est. [1848].
  CtY
    1849　Jan. 4—12.

EL NUEVO TIEMPO. d. est. Apr. 11,
1911.
 Note: Ceased publication [1919].
 CU
  1915 May 10 – June 19, 28 – July 3,
    6 – 17, Aug. 16 – Oct. 23, Nov.
    1 – 20, 29 – Dec. 31.
  1916 Jan. 3 – Mar. 21, 28, 29, 31,
    Apr. 3 – 7, 10 – 13, 17, 18, 25 –
    May 12, 15 – July 14, 17 – Oct.
    25, 27 – Dec. 30.
  1917 Jan. 2 – June 6, 8 – Dec. 31.
  1918 Jan. 2 – Mar. 27, 30 – May 25,
    28 – Dec. 31.
  1919 Jan. 2 – July 31, Sept. 1 – 6,
    10 – 16, 19 – 30.
 CU – B
  Micro (N)
  1911 [May 10 – Dec. 31].
  1912 [Jan. 2 – May 4].
 LNT – MA
  Micro (N)
  1911 June 1 – Dec. 31.
  1912 – 1918 [Jan. 1 – Dec. 31].

EL PABELLON DE HONDURAS. w.
 CU – B
  Micro (N)
  1900 Feb. 10 – Mar. 3, June 2 – Dec.
    20 – 31.
  1901 Feb. 2 – Mar. 9, 23 – Dec. 31.
  1902 Jan. 1 – May 24, June 7 – Aug.
    30, Sept. 20 – Dec. 31.
  1903 Jan. 1 – 24.

PATRIA; PERIODICO DE TRANSI-
CION. est. July 1898.
 LNT – MA
  1898 Aug. 28.

PATRIA. irr. est. Aug. 28, 1917.
 CU
  1917 Aug. 28 – Dec. 17.
  1918 Jan. 10 – Feb. 6.

LA PAZ. est. 1902.
 LNT – MA
  1902 Oct. 6.

PAZ Y UNION. w. est. Oct. 31, 1914.
 CU
  1915 June 5, July 10, Aug. 21, Sept.
    3 – 18, Oct. 9 – 16.
  1916 Feb. 1.
 LNT – MA
  1915 Sept. 18.

EL PENSAMIENTO. w. est. 1894.
 LNT – MA
  1894 Aug. 4, 25, Sept. 8, 15.

EL PORVENIR. irr. est. July 13, 1852.
 CU – B
  1852 July 13 – Nov. 5.
 NHi
  1852 July 13, 23, Oct. 20.

LA PRENSA. d. est. Apr. 9. 1907.
 Note: Ceased publication [1909].
 CU – B
  Micro (N)
  1908 Aug. 7 – Dec. 10, 12 – 18, 21 –
    Dec. 31.
  1909 Jan. 1 – Mar. 31.
 DLC
  1908 Aug. 7 – Oct. 31, Nov. 2 – Dec.
    10, 12 – 31.
  1909 Jan. 1 – Mar. 31.

EL PUEBLO. d. est. Oct. 1949.
 DLC
  1949 Oct. 17, 19, 20, 22 – 24, 27 –
    29, 31.
  1956 Jan. 3 – Dec. 31.
  1957 Jan. 1 – Aug. 15, Sept. 17 –
    Dec. 31.
  1958 Jan. 2 – Sept. 12, 14 – 26, 28 –
    Nov. 7, 9 – Dec. 31.
  1959 Jan. 2 – 7, 9 – 15, 17 – 23, 25 –
    June 12, 14 – 21, 27 – 30, Aug.
    1 – Oct. 15, 17 – 20, 22 – Dec. 3,
    5 – 31.
  1960 Jan. 1 – 21, 23 – Apr. 22, 24 –
    Sept. 8, 10 – Oct. 25, 27 – Dec.
    31.
  1961 Jan. 3 – 8, 11 – Mar. 6, 8 – Apr.
    30, May 3 – Sept. 8, 10 – Dec.
    30.
 Micro (P) & (N)
  1962 Jan. 1+.

FU
    1951−1952   [Jan. 1−Dec. 31].
LNT−MA
    1952 ₁Oct. 27−Dec. 19₎.
    1953 ₁Jan. 1−Dec. 31₎.
    1954 Jan. 28.

EL RAYO. w. est. July 8, 1919.
  LNT−MA
    1919 July 8, 15.

RECONCILIACION. d. est. 1924.
  CSt
    1925 Feb. 1−Dec. 31.
    1926 Jan. 1−Dec. 31.
    1928 Jan. 1−Mar. 31.
  CU
    1924 June 17−27, Aug. 15−19, 21−
          Sept. 4, 30−Oct. 18, 30−Nov.
          4, 6−Dec. 26.
    1925 Feb. 9−Dec. 31.
    1926 Jan. 1−Dec. 31.
    1927 Jan. 3−May 9, 11−Dec. 31.
    1928 Jan. 2−Mar. 15.
  DLC
    1925 Nov. 3−Dec. 31.
    1926−1928 Jan. 1−Dec. 31.
  LNT−MA
    1925 June 4−10.
  Micro (N)
    1924 ₁June 17−Dec. 26₎.

EL RENACIMIENTO. w., bw. est. 1913.
  CU
    1915 Aug. 15−Nov. 1.
  LNT−MA
    1915 Mar. 21.

LA REGENERACION. sw., 3w., d. est.
  Mar. 5, 1894.
    Note: Periodicity Mar. 5−Apr. 19,
    1894, semiweekly; Apr. 23−Aug. 31,
    1894, three times a week; Sept. 1,
    1894−Sept. 3, 1895, daily. Ceased
    publication Sept. 3, 1895.
  DLC
    1894 Mar. 5−Dec. 31.
    1895 Jan. 1−Sept. 3.
  RENOVACION. est. 1926.
  LNHT
    Micro (N)

1926 ₁Apr. 11−Dec. 31₎.
1927 ₁Jan. 1−Sept. 18₎.

EL REPUBLICANO. 3w. est. Apr. 25,
  1903.
  CU−B
  Micro (N)
    1903 May 2−Dec. 31.
    1904 Jan. 1−June 13.

LA SEMANA; PERIODICO GENERAL.
  w. est. 1895.
  LNT−MA
    1895 May 18.

LA SEMANA. w. est. 1908.
  CU
    1915 Dec. 5.
    1916 Jan. 2−Apr. 16, 30−May 28,
          Dec. 3−10, 24.
    1917 Jan. 7−21, Feb. 4.

SEMANA POLICIACA. w. est. July 10,
  1920.
  LNT−MA
    1920 July 10−31.

EL SOLDADO.
  CU−B
  Micro (P)
    1892 Aug. 19, Sept. 3.

SUFRAGIO LIBRE. w. est. 1922.
  LNT−MA
    1923 May 26.

EL TIEMPO. d. est. July 6, 1904.
  LNT−MA
    1905 Sept. 26.

LA TRIBUNA. d. est. Jan. 15, 1927.
  DLC
    1927 Jan. 15−Mar. 29, 31−Dec.
          31.
    1928 Jan. 1, 2, 7−Apr. 2, 4−June 6,
          9−30.

EL TRIUNFO. irr. est. 1919.
  LNT−MA
    1919 June 7, 14, 21, July 1, 19.

EL UNIONISTA. w. est. 1920.
  LNT−MA
    1920 Oct. 3.

Tela

EL CRISOL. w. est. 1935.
  DLC
    1942   Feb. 28.

PLUS ULTRA. w. est. [1941].
  DLC
    1942   Feb. 26.

LA SEMANA. w.
  LNT – MA
    1924   Nov. 30.

 SOCIAL. w. est. Jan. 1, 1932.
  DLC
    1942   Mar. 5.

Trujillo

EL ECO DE TRUJILLO. w. est. June 30,
  1901.
  LNT – MA
    1901   Nov. 10.

LA NACION. 3w., w. est. 1919.
  LNT – MA
    1924   July 5.

EL PRECURSOR. w. est. 1923.
  LNT – MA
    1923   Oct. 6.

MEXICO
Acapulco

EL GUERRERENSE. w. est. 1915.
  CU
    1915   July 25, Aug. 8 – Oct. 10, 24 –
            Nov. 7.

EL PROGRESO DE GUERRERO. irr.
  CU – B
    Micro (P)
    1868   Apr. 28, May 8, 15 – 29, June
            16 – July 21, Sept. 15 – 18.

TROPICO. w., d. est. 1939.
  DLC
    1942   Sept. 20.

LA ESTRELLA DEL ISTMO. w.
  TxU
    1887   June 5, 12 – Aug. 7.

Aguascalientes

LA EPOCA. d.
  KHi
    1914   Apr. 23, June 15, 16, 18, 26,
            27, July 3.

THE MEXICAN TIMES. w. est. 1883.
  Note: In English.
  CU – B
    Micro (P)
    1884   Dec. 14.

EL PATRIOTA.
  CU – B
    Micro (P)
    1847   Suplemento: July 2.

PROVINCIA. w. est. [1943].
  DLC
    1943   Feb. 13.

EL QUIJOTE. irr. est. [1936].
  CU
    1939   Aug. 6 – Dec. 12.
    1940   Mar. 11 – 18, Apr. 3 – July 20,
            Sept. 19 – 29.
    1941   Feb. 9, Mar. 30.

EL REPUBLICANO; PERIODICO
  OFICIAL. sw., w.
  CU – B
    Micro (P)
    1877   May 27.
    1878   Oct. 27.
  TxU
    1862   Nov. 13, 28.
    1880   Aug. 8, 15, Oct. 18, Nov. 14.

30 – 30. w.
  TxU
    1911   Sept. 3.

Ajusco

BOLETIN DE NOTICIAS. est. 1860.
  CtY
    1860   July 5, 8, 12, 13, 16, 23, 27, 29,
            Aug. 1, 3, 5, 6, 9, 11, 17, 20, 23,
            27, 29, Sept. 1, Oct. 10.

Álamos

BOLETIN OFICIAL. sw.
　CU – B
　　Micro (P)
　　1876　Feb. 26 – 29.

EL DEMOCRATA. w. est. Apr. 7, 1877.
　CU – B
　　Micro (P)
　　1877　May 5.
　　1878　May 25 – June 22, July 6 – 20,
　　　　　Aug. 4.

EL ELECTOR. w. est. 1875.
　CU – B
　　Micro (P)
　　1875　Feb. 24.

EL FANTASMA. w. est. 1874.
　CU – B
　　Micro (P)
　　1875　July 16, 30.

OPINION PUBLICA DE OCCIDENTE.
　est. July 9, 1829.
　CU – B
　　1829　July 9 – 30.

EL PERICO. irr. est. 1876.
　CU – B
　　Micro (P)
　　1878　July 17.

EL PUEBLO. irr. est. 1877.
　CU – B
　　Micro (P)
　　1877　Apr. 28.
　　1878　June 21 – 28, July 19 – Aug. 2,
　　　　　16 – 25, Oct. 22.

LA VOZ DE ALAMOS. w. est. 1874.
　CU – B
　　Micro (P)
　　1876　Apr. 8.
　　1877　Feb. 27 – Mar. 13.
　　1878　May 29 – June 11, 25, July 9 –
　　　　　23, Aug. 13 – 29.

　TxU
　　1881　Mar. 30, Apr. 6, 28, May 5, 12,
　　　　　19, 26, June 16, 23, July 7,
　　　　　Aug. 11.

Arizpe

EL RESTAURADOR FEDERAL. w. est.
　Sept. 1837.
　CU – B
　　Micro (P)
　　1838　Jan. 16, 30 – Mar. 13, May 1,
　　　　　June 26 – July 3, 17, 31, Aug.
　　　　　28.
　　　　　Suplemento: Jan. 23, Apr. 17.

Arriaga

LA OPINION. bw. est. [1943].
　DLC
　　1943　Aug. 1.

Atlántico

EL CORREO.
　Tx
　　1835　Apr. 1 – Dec. 31.
　　1836　Jan. 1 – Aug. 31.

Bravos

BOLETIN OFICIAL.
　CU – B
　　Micro (P)
　　1854　June 9.

Cádiz

TELEGRAFO AMERICANO.
　CU – B
　　Micro (N)
　　1811　Oct. 10 – Dec. 31.
　　1812　Jan. 1 – Mar. 31.

Camargo

EL COLEGA. est. Jan. 1903.
　NN
　　1909　May 23.

DEMOCRATA. d. est. Mar. 30, 1884.
　MWA
　　1884　Mar. 30.

Campeche

DIARIO DE CAMPECHE. d. est. Aug.
　22, 1926.
　TxU
　　1926　Aug. 22 – 24, 26 – Sept. 7.

LA ESPERANZA. w. est. 1870.
  CU – B
    Micro (P)
    1878   May 5 – 19.

EL ESPIRITU PUBLICO. sw. est. July
  4, 1857.
    Note: 4*a. epocá* established July
    5, 1867 and ceased publication Jan. 4,
    1870. Succeeded by *La Restauración*
    as official publication of the state.
    Ceased publication 1943.
  CU – B
    Micro (P)
    1869   Jan. 26.

EL FENIX. sw. est. 1848.
    Note: Ceased publication 1851.
  CU – B
    Micro (P) & (N)
    1848   Nov. 1 – Dec. 25.
    1849 – 1850   Jan. 1 – Dec. 31.
    1851   Jan. 1 – Oct. 25.

EL HURACAN. sw. est. Nov. 1831.
  DLC
    1831   Dec. 7 – 28.
    1832   Jan. 12, 16, May 22, June 2 –
            July 3.

IDEA. d. est. 1909.
    Note: Ceased publication 1910.
  MWA
    1910   Sept. 11 – 16, Oct. 2 – 16,
            Nov. 6.

EL INVESTIGADOR. w. est. 1833.
  DLC
    1833   Mar. 2 – June 22.

EL INVESTIGADOR O EL AMANTE DE
  LA RAZON. w. est. 1823.
    Note: Ceased publication 1833.
  DLC
    1828   Feb. 2 – May 3, 5 – June 30,
            July 2 – Dec. 30.
            Suplemento: Feb. 9, 26.
  TxU
    1824   July 15.

LA NUEVA ERA. sw. est. May 1, 1877.
    Note: Succeeded *El Voto libre* as the
    official publication of the state; suc-
    ceeded by *Periódico oficial*. Ceased
    publication Apr. 27, 1883.
  CU – B
    Micro (P)
    1878   July 23 – Aug. 2.
  MWA
    1881   [July 15 – Dec. 30].
    1882   [Jan. 6 – Sept. 8].
    1883   Jan. 19, Apr. 6 – 17, 27.
  TxU
    1880   Dec. 27, 31.
    1881   Jan. 11.

EL PACIFISTA. w. est. Apr. 13, 1913.
  TxU
    1913   Apr. 13.

EL PELICANO. w. est. [1828].
  DLC
    1828   Dec. 11 – 25.

PERIODICO OFICIAL DEL GOBIERNO
  DEL ESTADO LIBRE Y SOBERANO
  DE CAMPECHE. sw. est. May 1, 1883.
    Note: Succeeded *Nueva era*.
  MWA
    1883   May 1 – July 24.
    1886   Nov. 26.

Cananea

EL TIEMPO. d. est. Oct. 1918.
  DLC
    1919   Aug. 21.

Carmen

EL MONITOR DE CARMEN. w.
  LNT – MA
    1931   Nov. 29.

PERLA DEL GOLFO.
    See *Semanario del partido del Carmen*.

LA RAZON. est. Dec. 6, 1931.
  LNT – MA
    1931   Dec. 6 – 31.
    1932   Jan. 1 – 31.

SEMANARIO OFICIAL DEL PARTIDO DEL CARMEN. w.
Note: Title *Perla del golfo*, before May 6, 1883; *Semanario oficial del partido del Carmen*, after May 13, 1883.
MWA
1878   Oct. 20 – 27.
1881   Jan. 16, Feb. 6, July 10 – Oct. 2, Nov. 27 – Dec. 4.
1882   [Jan. 1 – Dec. 31].
1883   Apr. 29 – May 6, 13 – June 10, July 22.

Celaya

EL INFORMADOR. w. est. 1925.
DLC
1942   Sept. 19.

LA PALABRA. w., d. est. 1939.
DLC
1943   July 2.

Chalco

LA AURORA POLITICA. w. est. Oct. 22, 1880.
LNT – MA
1880   Oct. 22 – Dec. 31.
1881   Jan. 7 – May 13.
TxU
1880   Nov. 12.

Chetumal

EN MARCHA. bw.
CU
1943   Oct. 15.

Chiapa

EL BALUARTE DE LA LIBERTAD. w., irr. est. July 5, 1867.
LNT – MA
1867   [July 5 – Dec. 21].
1868   Jan. 3, Mar. 20, Apr. 17, May 1, 29, July 17.

1869   [May 21 – Dec. 31].
1870   [Jan. 7 – Nov. 17].

BOLETIN OFICIAL DE NOTICIAS. est. Sept. 24, 1871.
LNHT
1871   [Sept. 24 – Dec. 28].

EL PUEBLO LIBRE.
TxU
1881   Jan. 12, Feb. 9, Apr. 20, May 4 – 11, 25 – July 27.

Chihuahua

ACTUALIDADES. sw. est. Oct. 11, 1917.
DLC
1918   Apr. 25 – May 2, June 2.
NN
1917   Oct. 18.

LA ALIANZA DE LA FRONTERA. est. 1860.
CU – B
Micro (P)
1864   Apr. 2.

THE ANGLO SAXON. est. Mar. 18, 1847.
Note: In English.
DLC
1847   Mar. 18.

ANTORCHA. 3w.
CU
1943   Aug. 4 – 6, 25 – 27, 30 – Sept. 3, 8 – Oct. 8, 13 – Nov. 24, Dec. 6, 10, 24, 28.
1944   Jan. 1 – 7, 13 – Mar. 31, Apr. 3 – May 17, 22 – Aug. 10, 14 – 21, 25 – Sept. 29, Oct. 4 – 13, 18, 23 – 25, [29 – Nov. 1,] 10 – 13, 17 – Dec. 4, 8 – 15, 20, 25 – 27.
1945   Jan. 1, 6 – 19, 24, 29 – Feb. 9, 16 – 28, Mar. 5 – 14, 19 – Apr. 25, 30 – May 9, 14 – 30, June 6 – July 4, 9, 13 – 19, 24 – Aug. 1, 6 – 22, 27, 31 – Sept. 11, 16 – Oct. 12, 17 – 26, 31 – Dec. 29.

1946   Jan. 1 — Feb. 2, 9 — Mar. 27,
        Apr. 3 — 17, 24 — May 4, 15 —
        18, 25 — July 19, 25 — Aug. 24,
        30 — Sept. 10, 16 — Oct. 8, 12 —
        19, 24 — 26, 31 — Nov. 3, 12,
        16 — 19, 23, 30 — Dec. 3, 7 —
        14, 21 — 28.
1947   Jan. 1, 8, 11, 18 — 30, Feb. 18 —
        22, 27, Mar. 6 — 27, Apr. 5 —
        15, 29, May 1, 6 — 27, June 5 —
        14, 28, July 5, 12 — 26, Aug.
        2 — 5, 14, 20, 21, 28, Sept. 6 —
        9, 24, Oct. 1 — 8, 18 — 25, Nov.
        15, 22, Dec. 10 — 17, 24 — 27.
1948 — 1949   Jan. 1 — Dec. 31.

EL BALUARTE. d.
  TxU
    1912   Sept. 21.

EL CENTINELA. sw. est. 1853.
  CU — B
    Micro (P)
    1855   Aug. 18, Sept. 11 — 18, 29, Oct.
            20, Nov. 10 — 13.

CHIHUAHUA ENTERPRISE. m., w.
    Note: In English.
  CU — B
    Micro (P)
    1882   Dec. 15.
    1883   Jan. 15 — June 15, Aug. 15 —
            Nov. 15.
    1884   Jan. 15.
  TxU
    1912   Oct. 5.

THE CHIHUAHUA MAIL. w. est. July 18,
  1882.
    Note: In Spanish and English.
  CU — B
    Micro (P)
    1882   Sept. 12.
    1883   Mar. 10 — Apr. 14, May 5, 19,
            Oct. 22 — 29, Nov. 12, Dec. 3,
            17.
  KHi
    1883   May 12, 19.
  MWA
    1882   Oct. 17.

CHIHUAHUENSE. w.
  MWA
    1884   Aug. 24.

EL CLARIN. d. est. Mar. 12, 1912.
  TxU
    1912   Mar. 12.

LA COALICION. w. est. 1858.
  CU — B
    Micro (P)
    1859   Dec. 20.

EL CORREO. d.
  TxU
    1911   Mar. 23.

EL CORREO DE CHIHUAHUA.
  CU — B
    Micro (P) & (N)
    1902 — 1925   [Jan. 1 — Dec. 31].

EL DEFENSOR DEL PUEBLO. d. est.
  Sept. 27, 1911.
  TxU
    1911   Sept. 27.

EL DIARIO. d.
  TxU
    1924   Oct. 25.
    1925   Mar. 5.

EL ECO DE LA FRONTERA. est. 1856.
  CU — B
    Micro (P)
    1857   Jan. 8.

EL ECO DEL PUEBLO. d. est. May 5,
  1913.
  TxU
    1913   May 5.

EL EVANGELISTA MEXICANO. bw.
  TxU
    1921   Aug. 1.

EL FANAL DE CHIHUAHUA. est.
  [1835].
  CU — B
    Micro (P)
    1835   Mar. 10.

EL FANTASMA. d. est. May 3, 1913.
  TxU
    1913   May 3.

EL FARO.
  CU – B
    Micro (P)
    1849   Suplemento: June 21.

EL HERALDO. d. est. 1927.
  DLC
    1941   Apr. 14, 16 – May 3, 5 – 11,
            13 – 30.
    1942   Nov. 13.
    1943   Jan. 11.
    1952   Jan. 30, 31, Feb. 4, 5, 7 – 16,
            19 – Mar. 16, 18 – Apr. 3, 6,
            8 – 11, 13 – 18, 20, 21, 24, 27 –
            29, May 1 – 7, 9 – 17, 20 – 24,
            26 – June 13, 16 – 22, 24 – 27,
            29 – July 6, 8 – 12, 14 – 20, 22 –
            Aug. 3, 5, 6, 8 – Sept. 12, 14,
            16, 17, 19 – 28, 30, Oct. 2 – 8,
            10 – 13, 15 – 23, 25 – 27, 30,
            31, Nov. 6 – Dec. 31.
    1953   Apr. 1 – 30, May 2 – June 30,
            Aug. 6, 19 – 21, 23, 24, 26 –
            Sept. 20, 22 – 25, 27, 29, 30 –
            Oct. 18, 20 – Nov. 3, 5 – 17,
            19 – Dec. 29, 31.
    1954   Jan. 1 – 31, Feb. 2 – 4, 27 –
            Apr. 14, 16, 18 – May 9, 11 –
            June 1, 3 – 11, 13 – July 2, 4 –
            25, 27 – Aug. 25, 27, 29 – Sept.
            26, 28 – Oct. 22, Nov. 4 – Dec.
            27, 29 – 31.
    1955   Jan. 1 – 10, 12 – 15, 17 – 30,
            Feb. 1 – 4, 6 – 11, 13 – Mar. 6,
            9 – 16, 18 – Apr. 5, 7 – 21, 23 –
            May 5, 7 – June 30, July 2 –
            24, 26 – Aug. 7, 9 – 19, 21 –
            Sept. 28, 30 – Oct. 12, 14 – 22,
            Nov. 3 – 30, Dec. 3 – 5, 7 – 9,
            14 – 28, 30, 31.
    1956   Jan. 1, 2, 4 – 11, 13 – 29, 31 –
            Mar. 16, 18 – Apr. 20, 22 –
            May 8, 10, 12 – 15, 17 – 24,
            26 – June 2, 5 – 10, 12 – July
            26, 28 – Aug. 25, 27, 29 – Sept.

            3, 5, 6, 8 – 19, 21, 23 – Oct. 3,
            5, 6, 8 – 24, 26 – Nov. 20, 23 –
            Dec. 1, 3 – 24, 27.

EL LIBERAL. d. est. 1912.
  TxU
    1912   Mar. 26.

EL MONITOR CHIHUAHUENSE.
  CLCM
    1889   July 19.

NO-REELECCION. d.
  TxU
    1911   July 14.

NORTE. sw. est. 1891.
  MWA
    1904   June 26.

NOTICIAS DE TIERRA-FUERA.
  CtY
    1852   Jan. 6.
    1853   Jan. 10, Apr. 20, 23.
    1855   Sept. 13.

EL NOTICIOSO DE CHIHUAHUA.
  [w.] est. 1833.
  CU – B
    Micro (P)
    1835   Suplemento: Aug. 31.
    1838   Suplemento: May 31.

EL PADRE PADILLA. d.
  TxU
    1912   Sept. 21.

PERIODICO OFICIAL. w.
  CU – B
    Micro (P)
    1878   July 21 – 28.
    1884   Apr. 19.
  TxU
    1880   July 10, 17, Aug. 12, Sept. 25,
            Oct. 2, 9, 16, Nov. 6, 27, Dec.
            4, 11, 18.

LA REPUBLICA. w. est. 1867.
  CU – B
    Micro (P)
    1872   May 3.

SEMANARIO OFICIAL. w.
  CU – B
    Micro (P)
    1876   Oct. 27 – Nov. 3.

EL SUFRAGIO EFECTIVO. 3w. est.
  June 29, 1911.
  TxU
    1911   June 29.

TOMOCHIC. d., w. est. 1922.
    Note: Periodicity before 1942, daily;
    after 1942, weekly.
  DLC
    1942   May 30, June 27, Aug. 8, Sept.
            13, Nov. 14, Dec. 12 – 19.

VERDAD Y LUZ. d. est. Apr. 6, 1913.
  TxU
    1913   Apr. 6.

VIDA NUEVA. d. est. 1914.
  DLC
    1915   Mar. 25.

LA VOZ DE CHIHUAHUA. d. est. 1920.
  DLC
    1941   Apr. 13, Dec. 28.
    1943   Jan. 17, Feb. 8.
  TxU
    1924   Oct. 15.
    1925   Mar. 5.

Chilpancingo

EL FENIX; PERIODICO OFICIAL DEL
  ESTADO LIBRE Y SOBERANO DE
  GUERRERO. sw. est. Jan. 3, 1824.
  CU
    Micro (N)
    1874   Jan. 3 – Nov. 28, Dec. 5 – 26.
    1875   Jan. 6 – 27, Feb. 3 – Mar. 6,
            May 1 – 26, June 2 – 5, 19 –
            July 3, 10 – 17, 31 – Aug. 28,
            Sept. 18, Oct. 2, 16, Nov. 3 –
            Dec. 11.
    1876   Jan. 1 – Feb. 26, Mar. 8 – May
            3, 17 – Dec. 16.

GUERRERO; PERIODICO OFICIAL.
  TxU
    1880   June 2, 9, 19, July 1, 8, 16,

                Aug. 26, Sept. 5, 13, 22, Dec. 3.

LA OPINION DEL SUR. w. est. 1879.
  TxU
    1880   July 6, Sept. 8.

ORIENTACION GUERRERENSE. bw.
  CU
    1943   Nov. 30, Dec. 15.

LA PAZ; PERIODICO OFICIAL DEL
  ESTADO DE GUERRERO. sw.
  CU – B
    Micro (P) & (N)
    1870   Oct. 26.
    1871   Feb. 17 – Mar. 4, Apr. 4.
    1872   Dec. 7.
    1873   Jan. 1 – June 11, 18 – Sept. 6,
            20 – Dec. 31.

PERIODICO OFICIAL DEL GOBIERNO
  CONSTITUCIONAL DEL ESTADO
  LIBRE Y SOBERANO DE GUERRE-
  RO. sw.
  CU – B
    Micro (P)
    1877   June 2, 13 – July 4, 18 – Oct.
            3, 27, Nov. 3, 10 – 28, Dec. 15 –
            29.
    1878   Jan. 5 – 19, 30, Feb. 13 – 27,
            Mar. 6 – Apr. 13, 24 – May 11,
            18 – 29, June 22 – July 10, 17 –
            Sept. 21, 28 – Oct. 5, 12, 19 –
            Dec. 11, 18 – 28.
    1879   Jan. 4 – Apr. 30, May 14 – Aug.
            30, Oct. 15.

EL REGENERADOR. sw., w. est. 1876.
  CU – B
    Micro (P)
    1877   Jan. 5 – Feb. 27, Mar. 13 –
            Apr. 24.

Cieneguita

BOLETIN OFICIAL DE LA DIVISION
  DE SONORA. sw.
  CU – B
    Micro (P)
    1865   May 9 – 13.

Ciénagas

EL NORTE. w. est. Feb. 2, 1913.
TxU
  1913   Feb. 2.

Ciudad de Victoria

See Durango.

Ciudad Juárez

EL ALACRAN. w., sw. est. Aug. 1932.
  DLC
  1942   Dec. 17.
  1943   Jan. 10, 24.

EL MEXICANO. d. est. [1933].
  DLC
  1939   Aug. 26.
  1943   Jan. 1, 28, Mar. 17, 18.

NUEVA ERA. NEW ERA. 3w. est. 1884.
  Note: In Spanish and English.
  CU−B
  Micro (P)
  1885   Mar. 16−18, 30−Apr. 13, 17,
         June 19.
  MWA
  1885   Apr. 20−24.

PERIODICO OFICIAL.
  NHi
  1865   Sept. 21.

VOZ DEL NORTE. est. [1932].
  LNT−MA
  1932   Jan. 10.

Ciudad Obregón

HERALDO DEL YAQUI. d. est. 1929.
  DLC
  1941   Mar. 27, 28, Apr. 1, 5, 6, 8, 9,
         13, 15, 16.
  1943   May 31.

Ciudad Victoria

EL CENTINELA DE TAMAULIPAS. w.
  est. 1839.

TxU
  1839   Jan. 10−17, 31−Feb. 21.
         Alcance: Mar. 28.

EL CONSTITUCIONAL; PERIODICO
  DEL ESTADO DE LAS TAMAULIPAS.
  LNHT
  1951   Oct. 6.

EL DEFENSOR DE TAMAULIPAS. w.
  est. 1846.
  Note: Removed from Tula to Ciudad
  Victoria, Jan. 1848.
  CtY
  1848   Nos. 11, 14, 16−18, 20, 34.
  TxU
  1848   Jan. 16, Feb. 6−20, Mar. 12−
         19, May 7, June 11−July 2,
         20−Aug. 17, Oct. 6−20, Nov.
         6.
  1849   Mar. 11−18, Apr. 15, 29,
         June 9−Sept. 7, Nov. 3, 17.
  1850   Jan. 5−26.

DESPERATOR DE TAMAULIPAS. w.
  est. Sept. 1, 1831.
  TxU
  1831   Sept. 1, Oct. 20, Nov. 10−17,
         Dec. 1−22.
  1832   Jan. 5−26, Feb. 2−Mar. 8,
         22−26, May 3, 31, June 14,
         July 5−26.

LA OLIVA. w. est. Apr. 1, 1841.
  CtY
  1841   Nos. 2−5, 7, 9, 11−16, 18, 19,
         22.
  DLC
  1841   Apr. 1−June 9, 11−23, 25−
         Aug. 4, 6−26.

LA OPINION.
  TxU
  1919   Alcance: June 23.

LA PALENQUETA.
  CtY
  1850   Jan. 14.

PERIÓDICO OFICIAL DEL GOBIERNO
LIBRE Y SOBERANO DE TAMAULI-
PAS. 3w.
TxU
   1897   July 6 – 8, 15, 20 – 22.
   1898   July 21, Aug. 2, 13.

EL PROGRESISTA. w.
TxU
   1902   Jan. 19, Feb. 2, 16 – 23, Mar.
           2, Oct. 12, Nov. 2.
   1903   Mar. 8, 22, June 28, July 5, 19.
   1904   Feb. 7, 28, July 17 – Sept. 4,
           18 – Oct. 2.
   1906   Feb. 11.
   1908   Jan. 5 – Feb. 2, 16 – 23, Mar.
           1 – 8.

LA RECONSTRUCCION.
CU – B
   Micro (P)
   1878   Oct. 10.

EL RESTAURADOR DE TAMAULIPAS.
bw. est. Aug. 1, 1832.
TxU
   1832   Aug. 1 – 21, 28 – 31, Sept. 11 –
           14, 25, Oct. 2 – 5, 16 – 26, Nov.
           9, 21 – Dec. 11, 18 – 31.
   1833   Jan. 1, 15 – Feb. 20, Mar. 14 –
           Apr. 4, 18 – May 16, 30, June
           13 – 20, July 18 – 25, Aug. 15 –
           Sept. 12, 26 – Oct. 10, 24 –
           Dec. 19.

EL RIFLE DE TAMAULIPAS. w.
TxU
   1858   May 22 – 27, June 10, July 31,
           Aug. 12.
   1859   Aug. 27, Sept. 3, Oct. 1.

EL TELESCOPIO DE TAMAULIPAS. w.
TxU
   1837   Jan. 5 – 12, 26 – Feb. 2, 16 –
           Mar. 30.

LA VOZ DE TAMAULIPAS. bw.
TxU
   1844   Dec. 25.
   1845   Jan. 2 – 16, 23 – Feb. 9, June
           12 – 16.

Colima

EL ADALID. w. est. Nov. 24, 1912.
TxU
   1912   Nov. 24.

LA AURORA. w.
TxU
   1877   Mar. 3.

BOLETIN OFICIAL DEL CONGRESO Y
DE LOS TRIBUNALES DEL ESTADO.
w.
CU – B
   1878   July 11.

LA CRUZ. w. est. 1888.
DLC
   1899   Dec. 10, 24 – 31.
   1900   Jan. 1 – Feb. 11, Mar. 4 – 25,
           Apr. 8 – May 13, 27, June 17 –
           July 22, Aug. 26 – Sept. 9,
           Oct. 28.

EL ESTADO DE COLIMA. w., sw.
CU – B
   Micro (P)
   1875   Mar. 19.
   1876   Aug. 25.
   1878   June 21 – July 2.
   1883   Mar. 2 – 9, 30 – Apr. 6, 20 –
           May 18.

EL FILOSOFO. bw. est. Jan. 15, 1910.
TxU
   1910   Jan. 15.

EL IMPULSO DE LA JUVENTUD. sw.
est. Mar. 23, 1913.
TxU
   1913   Mar. 23.

EL INTRANSIGENTE. w. est. Sept. 29,
1912.
TxU
   1912   Sept. 29.

IRIS COLIMENSE. d. est. Aug. 17, 1917.
DLC
   1918   Aug. 7, 8.

JUAN SIN MIEDO. w.
KHi
   1883   Apr. 22.

EL MUTUALISTA. w. est. Mar. 30, 1913.
TxU
1913   Mar. 30.

LA RECONQUISTA. w.
TxU
1923   Dec. 16−23.
1925   Mar. 1.

LA UNION LIBERAL. irr. est. June 23, 1878.
CU−B
Micro (P)
1878   June 23−July 12.

LA VOLUNTAD DEL PUEBLO.
TxU
1880   Aug. 28.

LA VOZ DEL PACIFICO. w. est. July 3, 1880.
CU−B
Micro (P) & (N)
1880   July 10, 24−Dec. 25.
1881   Jan. 1−Feb. 5, 19−June 25.

Comitán

EL CENTINELA DE LA FRONTERA. w., irr. est. May 13, 1872.
LNT−MA
1872   May 20−July 30.

EL CLAVEL ROJO. irr. est. 1901.
LNT−MA
1901   Aug. 11, 25, Sept. 16, Oct. 13, Nov. 10, 25, Dec. 8.

LA VOZ DE COMITAN. bw. est. 1950.
LNT−MA
1950   July 1.

Coyoacán

EL MOSQUITO. w. est. 1910.
TxU
1910   July 17.

TABASCO. bw.
CU
1936   May 15−June 15.

Cuajimalpa

EL ECO DEL DESIERTO. bw. est. 1906.
TxU
1907   Jan. 15.

Cuautitlán

LA IDEA LOCAL. w. est. 1880.
TxU
1880   Oct. 29, Nov. 21.

Cuernavaca

LA CONVENCION.
DLC
1915   Mar. 12.

EL ECO DEL SUR. bw. est. [1914].
DLC
1915   Apr. 20, May 6.
Boletín: Apr. 4.

PERIODICO OFICIAL DEL GOBIERNO DEL ESTADO DE MORELOS. irr.
CU−B
Micro (P)
1870   Jan. 4−21, 28, Feb. 4, 11−Apr. 8, 22, 29−June 10, July 8.
1871   June 9−Aug. 18, Sept. 19−22, Oct. 6, 13−Dec. 29.
1872   Jan. 2−Feb. 23, Mar. 1−Sept. 13, 24−Oct. 4, 11−18, 25, Nov. 5−8, 19−27.
1874   Jan. 2−9, 20−May 22, June 16−July 17, 24−Aug. 25, Oct. 6−Dec. 18, 25−29.
1875−1876   Jan. 1−Dec. 31.
1877   Jan. 5−Apr. 6.
1878   June 18−21.

PERIODICO OFICIAL; ORGANO DEL GOBIERNO DEL ESTADO LIBRE SOBERANO DE MORELOS.
CU−B
1877   Apr. 13−Dec. 31.
1878−1888   Jan. 1−Dec. 31.

TxU
  1880   May 28, July 2, 9, Aug. 17,
          Sept. 11, 14, Oct. 1, 19, 29,
          Nov. 2, 5, 16, 23, 26, 30, Dec.
          3, 21, 24, 28.
LA REVISTA DEL SUR. w.
  CU
  1936   Jan. 1 — Mar. 22.
VESPER. est. 1901.
  DLC
  1915   Apr. 11, May 9, 25.
LA VOZ DE JUAREZ. sw.
  TxU
  1914   Nov. 29.
LA VOZ DE LA REVOLUCION. est.
  June 1915.
  DLC
  1915   June 24.

Culiacán

LA BANDERA DE AYUTLA; PERIO-
DICO OFICIAL DEL ESTADO SOBE-
RANO, LIBRE E INDEPENDIENTE
DE SINALOA. w., irr. est. Dec. 28,
1855.
  Note: Succeeded *El Reformador* as
  official publication; succeeded by
  El Progreso. Ceased publication
  1857.
  CU — B
  Micro (P) & (N)
  1856   Jan. 12 — Apr. 26, May 17 —
          July 19, Aug. 30, Sept. 13 —
          Oct. 4, 18 — Nov. 1, 29 — Dec.
          29.
  1857   Jan. 3 — Feb. 7, Mar. 28 — Apr.
          18.
  TxU
  1856   Feb. 9 — 16, Mar. 22 — Apr. 12.

BOLETIN OFICIAL DEL ESTADO DE
SINALOA. irr. est. 1873.
  Note: Succeeded *El Fénix* as official
  publication.
  CU — B
  Micro (P)
  1873   Feb. 17 — Dec. 31.

EL CLAMOR PUBLICO. w. est. Nov. 16,
1872.
  CU — B
  Micro (P)
  1872   Nov. 16 — Dec. 14.
  1873   Jan. 4.

EL CONTINENTAL. irr. est. Mar. 1881.
  CU — B
  Micro (P)
  1881   Apr. 9, May 2, 22 — 30, June 14,
          July 17, Sept. 7, Nov. 10, Dec.
          30.
  1882   Mar. 13, June 24, July 22 —
          Aug. 22.

EL CORREO DE OCCIDENTE. w. est.
Aug. 1, 1882.
  CU — B
  Micro (P)
  1882   Aug. 16, 30.
  1883   Apr. 5 — 26.
  1884   Apr. 10.
  KHi
  1883   Apr. 19.

EL ESTADO DE SINALOA. irr. est. Jan.
10, 1873.
  CU — B
  Micro (P) & (N)
  1873   Jan. 10 — Feb. 14, 28 — Dec. 31.
  1874   Jan. 26 — Nov. 30.
  1878   June 13 — Aug. 1, Sept. 1 — 27,
          Oct. 18.
  1881   Aug. 6 — 13, 27 — Sept. 11, Oct.
          7, 22 — Nov. 28, Dec. 19 — 31.
  1882 — 1883   Jan. 1 — Dec. 31.
  1884   Jan. 7 — Apr. 7.
  TxU
  1875   Jan. 14 — Dec. 31.
  1880   June 19, July 17, 26, Aug. 5, 25,
          Sept. 6, 17, 24, Nov. 6, 20, 27,
          Dec. 4, 12, 19, 25.

EL LUCERO SINALOENSE. w. est. Nov.
3, 1837.
  CU — B
  Micro (P)
  1837   Nov. 24.

LA OPINION. d. est. 1924.
TxU
1924   Dec. 25, 26.

EL PROGRESO. irr. est. May 2, 1857.
Note: Succeeded *La Bandera de
Ayutla* as official publication; suc-
ceeded by *La Integridad nacional*
(Mazatlán) in 1858.
CU − B
Micro (P)
1857   May 9 − 23, June 6 − July 18,
Aug. 22 − Sept. 26, Oct. 31 −
Nov. 7, 28 − Dec. 19.

EL REGIONAL. d. est. 1903.
DLC
1943   Jan. 17, Mar. 4, June 3, Aug.
12, 27.

Cunduacán

EL ECO DE LA CHONTALPA. w. est.
1930.
CU
1930   Mar. 2 − 9.

Durango

EL AMIGO DEL PUEBLO. est. Feb. 1,
1912.
TxU
1912   Feb. 1.

EL AMIGO DEL PUEBLO. w. est. Feb.
18, 1912.
TxU
1912   Feb. 18.

LA CONVENCION LIBERAL. w. est.
1912.
TxU
1912   Jan. 15.

DIARIO DE DURANGO. d. est. Jan. 6,
1920.
DLC
1942   Mar. 6, 7, 10, 13 − 15, 19 − 22,
24, 25, 29, 31, Apr. 1, 3, 6 − 11,
14 − 17, 19, 23 − 26, 29 − May 1,
3, 8 − 10, 12 − 17, 27, June 3, 6,
7, 9, 10, 13, 19, 21, 23, 25 − 28,

July 3 − 5, 8, 9, 11, 12, 17 − 19,
21, 24 − 26, 28, 29, Aug. 1, 4 − 6,
14, 15, 18 − 20, 22, 23, 25 − 27,
30, Sept. 2, 5, 6, 8 − 13, 15, 16,
18, 19, 22, 24, 26, 27, 30 − Oct.
4, 6, 8 − 10, 13, 15, 18, 21, 24,
25, 29 − Nov. 1, 4, 6 − 8, 10 − 14,
18 − 20, 22, 24, 25, 27 − 29, Dec.
2 − 5, 8, 10, 12, 16, 17, 19, 22,
24, 27, 29.
1943   Jan. 6, 10 − 13, 15, 16, 20, 21,
24 − 31, Feb. 3, 6 − 13, 18 − 27,
Mar. 2, 4, 9 − 21, 23 − 27, 30,
Apr. 7 − 10, 13, 15, 16, 20, 21,
29, May 6, 8, 9, 16 − 25, 27, 29,
June 5 − 8, 10, 11, 13, 16, 17, 25,
26, July 1, 3, 11, 17, 20 − 22, 29,
30, Aug. 3 − 5, 10 − 12, 17, 18,
20, 22, 25 − 27, 29, Sept. 2, 4 −
7, 9, 16, 19 − 21, 25, 29, Oct. 1,
8, 10, 15, 17, 19, 21, 27, Nov. 13,
18, 25, 28 − 30, Dec. 8, 9, 14, 15,
21, 28.
1944   Jan. 4, 11 − 18, 21, 23, 27, 28,
Feb. 8 − 12, 17 − 23, 25 − 27,
Mar. 1, 17, 18, 23, 25 − 28, 31.

EL DOMINGO. w.
TxU
1887   Jan. 16.

DURANGO COMICO. w.
TxU
1912   Apr. 14.

GACETA DEL GOBIERNO DE DURANGO.
CU − B
Micro (P)
1833   Aug. 1.
CtY
1834   June 15.
1836   Aug. 18.
1837   Mar. 19, Apr. 9.

IMPERIO DE LA LEY. w. est. May 12,
1831.
CtY
1831   Sept. 22 − Dec. 29.
1832   Jan. 5 − July 19.

DLC
   1831   May 12, 26 – Oct. 12, 27 – Nov.
           9.
TxU
   1831   May 12 – 26, June 9 – 30, July
           14 – Nov. 10, 24 – 31.
   1832   Jan. 1 – July 19.

EL MENSAJERO DEL PUEBLO. sw. est.
  1885.
  CU – B
    Micro (P)
    1886   Aug. 1.

EL OBSERVADOR DURANGUERO. w.
  est. Oct. 1840.
  DLC
    1840   Nov. 15 – 29, Dec. 13, 20.
    1841   Jan. 3 – Mar. 7, 21, 28.
            Suplemento: Mar. 7.

PERIODICO OFICIAL DEL GOBIERNO
DEL ESTADO DE DURANGO. sw.
  CU – B
    Micro (P)
    1890   May 25.
  TxU
    1880   Sept. 26, 30, Oct. 10, 14, 31,
           Nov. 4, 7, 11, 14, 18, Dec. 23,
           26.
    1881   Feb. 10, June 30.

EL PIGMEO. w. est. Dec. 3, 1840.
  DLC
    1840   Dec. 3 – 31.
    1841   Jan. 1 – Aug. 30.
            Suplemento: Jan. 21, Feb. 25,
           Mar. 4, 11, 25, Apr. 1, 8, 29,
           June 16.

EL REGISTRO OFICIAL. sw.
  CU – B
    Micro (P)
    1846   June 21.
    1852   Aug. 22.
    1854   Aug. 27, Dec. 8.
    1855   Aug. 4.

EL TELEGRAFO. 3w. est. 1911.
  TxU
    1911   July 27.

EL TRIBUNO DEL PUEBLO. w. est
  [1845].
  CtY
    1845   Apr. 5.
  TxSjM
    1845   Apr. 19, 26, May 17, June 14,
           21.

El Oro

EL BARRETERO. bw. est. Nov. 1, 1912.
  TxU
    1912   Nov. 1.

EL MINERO. w. est. June 2, 1912.
  TxU
    1912   June 2.

Enseñada

THE LOWER CALIFORNIAN. w. est.
  Jan. 1, 1886.
    Note: In English. Ceased publication
    Oct. 1, 1898.
  CLCM
    1887   Aug. 9, Oct. 6, 13, Dec. 1.
    1888   May 31, Nov. 29.
    1889   Feb. 21 – Dec. 19.
    1890   Jan. 10 – Dec. 31.
    1891   Jan. 1 – July 31, Aug. 14 – Dec.
           31.
    1892   Jan. 1 – 22, Aug. 12 – 26, Sept.
           16 – Oct. 7, 29 – Dec. 31.
    1893   Jan. 21 – 28, Feb. 11 – June 16,
           July 7, 21, Aug. 11 – 25, Sept.
           8 – Oct. 31, Nov. 18, Dec. 2 –
           23.
    1894   Jan. 4, 6, 20 – Mar. 17, Apr. 1 –
           June 30, July 20 – Nov. 30, Dec.
           14 – 31.
    1895   Jan. 11 – May 3, 17 – Aug. 9,
           30 – Oct. 11, Nov. 1 – Dec. 31.
    1896   Jan. 1 – Mar. 20, Apr. 1 – June
           19, July 1 – Aug. 21, Sept. 18 –
           Dec. 3, 24.
    1897   Jan. 1 – Mar. 31, Apr. 9 – 16,
           May 7 – June 30, July 9 – Aug.
           31.

1898   Jan. 7 — Feb. 4.
CU — B
  Micro (P) & (N)
  1887   Aug. 9 — Dec. 29.
  1888   Jan. 5 — July 26, Aug. 9 — Dec.
          27.
  1889   Jan. 1 — Dec. 31.
  1890   Jan. 10 — Dec. 25.
  1891   Jan. 1 — Mar. 19, Apr. 2 — Dec.
          25.
  1892   Jan. 1 — Oct. 7.

PERIODICO OFICIAL.
  CLCM
  1890   Apr. 12.

LA VOZ DE LA FRONTERA DE LA
  BAJA CALIFORNIA. w. est. Nov. 1886.
  Note: In Spanish and English. Ceased
  publication Mar. 1889.
  CLCM
  1887   Oct. 1 — 15, Nov. 5.
  CU — B
  Micro (P)
  1887   May 14 — 21, Oct. 8.

Espita

DEMOCRATA. [w.] est. Feb. 11, 1888.
  MWA
  1888   Feb. 11.
  1889   Mar. 15.

Etzatlán

SATANAS. w.
  TxU
  1912   June 2.

Fresnillo

EL IMPIRANCA. w.
  TxU
  1911   Oct. 15.

Frontera

EQUILIBRIO SOCIAL. sw. est. 1923.
  LNT — MA
  1924   May 29, June 1, 8, 10 — 15.

Fuerte

EL PROGRESO. w. est. Oct. 12, 1911.
  TxU
  1911   Oct. 12.

Galeana

BOLETIN. irr. est. [1871].
  CtY
  1871   Nov. 17 — 29.

Gómez Palacio

EL LAGUNERO. w. est. [1934].
  DLC
  1943   Jan. 1, May 1.

Guadalajara

BOLETIN MILITAR. d. est. July 15, 1914.
  TxU
  1914   July 15 — 17, 25, 26, Aug. 2 — 5,
          8, 9, 13, 16.

BOLETIN REPUBLICANO DE JALISCO.
  bw. est. May 22, 1846.
  Note: Ceased publication Aug. 18,
  1846.
  CtY
  1846   May 22 — June 5.
  TxU
  1846   May 22 — Aug. 18.

LAS CLASES PRODUCTORAS. w. est.
  1877.
  CU — B
  Micro (P)
  1878   July 14, Aug. 4, 18 — Sept. 15,
          29 — Oct. 6.

LA CONVENCION. [w.] est. 1879.
  LNT — MA
  1880   Sept. 15.

EL CORREO DE JALISCO. d. est. Apr.
  7, 1895.
  Note: Ceased publication June 7,
  1914.
  TxU
  1914   Jan. 12, 13.

CULTURA PSIQUICA. w. est. Apr. 4,
1912.
TxU
   1912   Apr. 4.

DEFENSA. w.
   CtY
   1907   Sept. 15.

EL DEFENSOR DE LA RELIGION. sw.
est. Jan. 1827.
   CtY
   1827   Jan. 19—30, Feb. 6—Apr. 6,
           17—July 20, 27, Aug. 3—Oct.
           12, 23—Nov. 23, 30—Dec. 28.
   1828   Jan. 4—25, Feb. 5—8, 19, Mar.
           7, 25, Apr. 15—29, May 6—July
           8, 15—29, Aug. 5, 12—22, 29—
           Sept. 16, 26—Oct. 10, 17—Nov.
           7, 14, 28—Dec. 12, 19—26.
   1829   Jan. 2—16.

LA DEMOCRACIA. bw. est. 1885.
   CU—B
   Micro (P)
   1886   July 27.

EL DESPERTADOR AMERICANO. est.
Dec. 20, 1810.
   Note: Ceased publication Jan. 17,
   1811.
   IU
   1810   Dec. 20, 27, 29.
   1811   Jan. 3, 10, 11.

EL DIA. d.
   TxU
   1912   Sept. 25.

DIARIO DE LA REVOLUCION. irr. est.
1833.
   LNT—MA
   1833   Oct. 13.

EL ECO DE LA OPINION. w. est. 1880.
   TxU
   1880   Mar. 1.

LA ESCOBA. w. est. June 16, 1912.
   TxU
   1912   June 16.

EL ESPIRITU NACIONAL. w. est. Nov.
21, 1862.
   TxU
   1862   Nov. 21—28.

EL ESTADO DE JALISCO; ORGANO
OFICIAL DE GOBIERNO. sw., 3w.
est. May 11, 1872.
   CU—B
   Micro (P)
   1874   Sept. 11.
   1877   Jan. 21.
   1878   May 26—28, June 18, 27,
           July 2, 16, Sept. 8—12, Nov.
           19—28.

   TxU
   1872   May 11—31, June 1—25, 27—
           Aug. 16, 23—Dec. 31.
   1873   Jan. 1—Aug. 3, 5—Oct. 25,
           Nov. 1—Dec. 31.
   1874   Jan. 1—June 28, 30—Sept. 7.
   1876   Feb. 22—Dec. 18, 20—31.
   1877   Jan. 1—5, 7—Nov. 4.
   1879   Mar. 20—Dec. 31.
   1880   Jan. 3—Dec. 29.
   1881   Jan. 1—Feb. 12.

GACETA DEL GOBIERNO DE GUADA-
LAJARA. sw. est. June 23, 1821.
   Note: Ceased publication 1824.
   CU—B
   1821   June 23—Dec. 31.
   1822   Jan. 1—June 29.
   CtY
   1821   June 23—Dec. 29.
   1823   Aug. 15—22.
   1824   Nov. 23.
           Extraordinario: May 30.

GACETA DEL GOBIERNO DEL ESTA-
DO LIBRE DE JALISCO. est. 1824.
   CU—B
   1826   Apr. 25, July 28.
   1827   Jan. 2.

EL GATO. sw. est. Nov. 2, 1910.
   TxU
   1913   Nov. 27.
   1914   Feb. 15, Mar. 15—19.

EL HERALDO. d. est. Jan. 1, 1927.
  DLC
    1927   Jan. 2 – 5, 7 – 11, 13 – Feb. 8,
            10 – 28, Mar. 4.

EL IMPARCIAL. d. est. 1891.
  CU – B
    Micro (P)
    1892   Feb. 23.

EL IMPERIO. bw. est. July 9, 1864.
  TxU
    1864   July 9 – Aug. 10, 17 – Dec. 31.
    1865   Jan. 1 – July 22.

EL INDEPENDIENTE. [w]. est. 1927.
  CU
    1929   July 21.

EL INFORMADOR. d. est. 1917.
  CSt – H
    1964   July 5, 7, 10 – 15, 19 – 25, 27 –
            Sept. 15, 17 – 30, Oct. 11 – Nov.
            8, 11 – Dec. 23, 26 – 31.
    1965   Jan. 1 – Apr. 4, 6 – May 26,
            28 – June 30, July 2 – 7, 9 –
            Dec. 31.
    1966   Jan. 1+.
  CU
    1929   July 23.
    1936   Jan. 1 – Mar. 29, 31 – Apr. 24,
            26 – May 1, 3 – 29, 31 – Sept.
            16, 18 – Dec. 31.
    1937   Jan. 1 – Apr. 2, 4 – July 6.
    1946   Dec. 15.
    1947   Sept. 19 – Nov. 22, 24 – Dec.
            31.
    1948   Jan. 1 – Dec. 31.
    1949   Jan. 1 – 24, 26 – Apr. 14, 16 –
            June 21, 23 – July 1, 3 – Dec.
            31.
  DLC
    1941   Apr. 4, 6 – 8, 10, 11, 14 – 25, 27,
            28, 30 – May 2, 4, 6 – 26, 28 –
            June 1, 3 – 25, 27 – July 26,
            28 – Aug. 11, 13 – 31.
  MWA
    1918   [Jan. 3 – Sept. 9.]
    1937   Aug. 9.

TxU
    1924   Oct. 18, Dec. 31.
    1925   Jan. 2, May 12 – 15, 17 – June
            8, 10 – Sept. 12, 14 – Dec. 15,
            17 – 31.
    1926   Jan. 1, 2, 4 – 8, 10 – May 17,
            19 – Aug. 7, 9 – 23, 25 – 28,
            30 – Oct. 18, 22 – Dec. 31.
    1927   Jan. 1 – Dec. 31.
    1928   Jan. 1 – 13, 15 – 27, 29 – Sept.
            14, 16 – Dec. 31.
    1929   Jan. 1 – Oct. 26, 28 – Dec. 31.
    1930   Jan. 1 – June 20, 22 – July 22,
            24 – Dec. 31.
    1931   Jan. 1 – Dec. 31.
    1932   Jan. 1 – 7.

EL JALISCIENSE. bw. est. June 25, 1844.
  Note: Ceased publication May 19,
  1846.
  TxU
    1844   Nov. 1 – 8, 15 – 19, Dec. 3 – 24.

EL JALISCIENSE. w. est. 1875.
  CU – B
    Micro (P)
    1876   Nov. 1.
    1886   Aug. 1.

JALISCO LIBRE. d. est. 1901.
  CtY
    1907   Sept. 15.
  TxU
    1908   July 30.

JALISCO MERCANTIL.
  CtY
    1907   Sept. 15.

EL JOCOTE. sw. est. July 9, 1911.
  TxU
    1911   July 9.

JUAN PANADERO. w., sw. est. Apr. 28,
  1871.
  CU – B
    Micro (P) & (N)
    1871   July 10, Sept. 7, 28, Nov. 12, 26.
    1872   Jan. 11, Aug. 8 – Dec. 22, 29.
    1873   Jan. 2, 9 – 16, 23, Feb. 2 – Mar.
            9, May 1 – June 5, 12 – Aug. 7.
    1874   Jan. 1 – 22, 29 – Feb. 15, 22 –

Mar. 1, 8 – 19, 26 – May 21,
June [8] – 11, 25 – July 19, 26 –
Aug. 9, Oct. 11 – 22, Nov. 22 –
Dec. 31.

1875   Jan. 7 – 21, Apr. 4, 15, 25 – May
2, 9 – 27, June 3 – 10.

1878   Nov. 17, Dec. 1 – 8, 26.

1879   Jan. 5 – 9, 16 – 23, Feb. 13,
20 – 27, Mar. 6 – 20, 27 – Apr.
3, 13 – 17, 24, May 1 – 4, 11 –
15, July 3 – 6, Dec. 14.

1880   Jan. 15 – Mar. 28, Apr. 8 – July
1, 8 – Sept. 30, Oct. 7.

CtY

1877   May 27 – June 21, 28 – July 1,
12, 26 – Aug. 5, 16 – 23, 30,
Sept. 13 – 16, 27 – Oct. 7, 14 –
18, Nov. 1, 11, 18 – 22, Dec. 2,
16.

1878   Jan. 3 – 13, 20, Feb. 14, 24,
Mar. 3, 7, 14, 24, 31, Apr. 14 –
28, May 5 – 12, 19 – 23, June
6 – 23, 30 – July 18, 25, Aug.
1 – 4, 11 – 18, 25 – Sept. 12, 22,
Oct. 3 – 27, Nov. 3 – 11, 17 – 21,
28 – Dec. 26.

1879   Jan. 2, 9 – 16, Feb. 2 – 13, 20,
Mar. 2, 9 – 13, 23, Apr. 6, 13,
June 12, 29 – July 10, 20 – 24,
31 – Aug. 3, 10 – 17, 24, 31 –
Sept. 21, Oct. 2 – 12, Nov. 30 –
Dec. 4, 18, 28.

1880   Jan. 1, 8 – 11, 18, 25 – Feb. 5,
15, 22 – Mar. 4, 11 – 21, 28 –
Apr. 29, May 6 – 9, 16 – 23, 29,
June 6 – 10, 17 – Sept. 9, 16 –
Oct. 7.

TxU

1874   July 23 – 26, Aug. 2 – 6, 16 – 23,
30, Sept. 3 – 6, 13 – 17, 27, Oct.
4 – 29, Nov. 5 – 12, 19 – 26,
Dec. 3 – 16, 20, 27.

1875   Jan. 28 – 31, Feb. 7 – 14, 21,
Mar. 4, May 9 – 16, 22, 31.

1890   Oct. 9.

EL KASKABEL. w. est. 1906.
    CU
        1913   Dec. 25.

1914   Jan. 8 – May 14, 21 – June 4,
28.

DLC

1914   Mar. 22, Apr. 5, 9, 26 – May 7,
17, July 2.

LA LANZA DE SAN BALTAZAR. est.
1873.
    Note: Ceased publication [1883].
    LNT – MA
        1874   Sept. 2, Dec. 9.

EL LIBERAL. sw. est. Jan. 1, 1856.
    Note: Title *El Liberal verdadero*,
    Jan. 1 – Sept. 23, 1856; *El Liberal*,
    after Sept. 23, 1856.
    CtY
        1856   Jan. 1, 8 – 25, Feb. 8 – Mar. 7,
        14 – Apr. 4, 11 – 22, May 9 – 30,
        June 10 – 27, July 8, 22, Aug.
        15, Sept. 2, 19 – 30, Oct. 21, 28,
        Dec. 5.

        1857   Feb. 17 – Mar. 3 – 6, 17 – 20,
        Apr. 1, May 30 – June 13, 20 –
        Aug. 5, 10 – 22, Oct. 7 – 10,
        21 – 28, Nov. 4 – 18, 25 – Dec.
        12.

        1858   July 21, Aug. 25.

        1859   July 16 – Aug. 6, 22 – 27, Sept.
        3 – Nov. 9, 19.

        1860   May 2 – June 30, July 11 – Aug.
        4, 15 – 18, 25 – Sept. 1, 8 – Oct.
        6, 17, 24.

EL LITIGANTE. w. est. May 26, 1881.
    LNT – MA
        1888   May 8.

LA LUZ. sw. est. Feb. 23, 1913.
    TxU
        1913   Feb. 23.

EL NIVEL. sw. est. Aug. 1, 1824.
    CU – B
        1826   Jan. 3, 5, 10, Apr. 20.
    TxU
        1826   Feb. 9.

LAS NOTICIAS DE LA MAÑANA. d. est.
1928.
    Note: Title *Las Noticias*, Sept. 23,

1941 – May 1942; *Las Notícias de la mañana*, after May 1942.
CU
    1929   July 22, 23.
DLC
    1941   Sept. 23, 24, 26, 30 – Oct. 8, 11 – 23, 25 – Nov. 12, 14 – 21, 24, 25, 27, 29 – Dec. 3, 5 – 7, 9 – 31.
    1942   Jan. 1 – 13, 16 – 19, 21 – 26, 28 – Feb. 14, 17 – 19, 22 – 28, Mar. 3 – 5, 7 – 9, 11 – 16, 19 – 22, 24 – 29, Apr. 1, June 1 – 3, 5, 6, 14 – 18, 23, 25 – 29.

NOTICIAS DE LA TARDE. d. est. Jan. 6, 1942.
DLC
    1942   Jan. 6 – 12, 19, 20, Mar. 24 – 28, 31.

EL OCCIDENTAL. w. est. Apr. 18, 1886.
TxU
    1886   Oct. 28.

LA OPINION. w. est. 1832.
CtY
    1832   June 29.

EL PABELLON NACIONAL. w. est. Feb. 10, 1878.
    Note: Title *El Pabellón mexicano*, Feb. 10, 1878 – 1885; *El Pabellón nacional*, after 1885.
CU – B
Micro (P)
    1878   Sept. 29.
    1881   July 17, Aug. 28 – Sept. 11, Oct. 9, 30 – Dec. 4.

EL PAIS. 3w. est. Jan. 6, 1856.
    Note: Succeeded *La Voz de Jalisco*. Ceased publication Mar. 8, 1871.
CU – B
Micro (P)
    1868   July 21.

PALADION.
CU – B
Micro (P)
    1833   Aug. 19.

LA PALANCA. est. June 15, 1826.
    Note: Ceased publication Feb. 29, 1828.
CU – B
    1826   June 15 – Dec. 31.
    1827   Jan. 1 – July 16.

LA PALMERA DEL VALLE. bw. est. Feb. 5, 1888.
CtY
    1888   Feb. 5 – Dec. 16.
    1889   Jan. 6 – June 16.

PERIODICO OFICIAL DEL GOBIERNO DEL ESTADO DE JALISCO. sw. est. Feb. 9, 1882.
    Note: Succeeded *El Estado de Jalisco*; succeeded by *Diario oficial del gobierno del estado de Jalisco*. Ceased publication Dec. 4, 1888.
CU – B
Micro (P)
    1884   Jan. 10 – 17, 31 – Feb. 21, 28 – Mar. 27, Apr. 10 – July 6, 13 – Aug. 28, Sept. 7 – 11, 21 – Oct. 23.

PLUS ULTRA. w. est. July 24, 1910.
TxU
    1910   July 24 – Nov. 20, Dec. 11 – 31.
    1911   Jan. 1 – 8.

EL PORVENIR, w. est. Mar. 27, 1851.
CtY
    1851   Mar. 27 – May 8, 22 – July 10, Aug. 7 – Sept. 25, Oct. 18.

LA PRIMAVERA. w. est. Jan. 21, 1833.
LNHT
    1834   Jan. 28, Feb. 4.

EL RAYO. irr. est. Dec. 25, 1830.
CtY
    1830   Dec. 25.
    1831   Jan. 4 – Feb. 15, Mar. 11.

EL REPUBLICANO JALISCIENSE; PERIODICO OFICIAL DEL GOBIERNO DEL ESTADO. bw. est. Aug. 10, 1846.
    Note: Ceased publication Dec. 29, 1848.

TxU
1847   Aug. 10 — Dec. 31.
1848   Jan. 1 — July 21.

RESTAURACION. w. est. ₁1934₁.
DLC
1943   Oct. 24.

SINOPSIS. w.
TxU
1913   Apr. 6.

TELEGRAFO. sw. est. 1891.
MWA
1891   Apr. 19.

LA TRIBUNA. w. est. 1886.
CU — B
Micro (P)
1886   Aug. 10.

LA UNION LIBERAL. w. est. 1867.
CU — B
Micro (P)
1869   Feb. 26.

EL VIGIA CATOLICO. w. est. 1873.
CU — B
Micro (P)
1873   July 2 — Dec. 17, 31.
1874   Jan. 7 — Mar. 25, Apr. 8 — Aug.
19.

Guadalupe Hidalgo

LA AVISPA. w. Mar. 15, 1908.
TxU
1908   Mar. 15.

BOLETIN GUADALUPANO. sw. est.
Jan. 1, 1910.
TxU
1910   Jan. 1.

EL CENTINELA CATOLICA. bw. est.
May 1, 1908.
TxU
1908   May 1.

Guanajuato

BARRETERO.
MWA
1904   July 16.

LA FARSA. w.
TxU
1912   May 5.

EL HERALDO GUANAJUATENSE. w.
est. Aug. 6, 1911.
TxU
1911   Aug. 6.

EL JURADO. w.
TxU
1880   Nov. 4.

EL MERCURIO. w.
NHi
1855   Aug. 9.

LA NACIONALIDAD. bw. est. 1855.
TxU
1855   Oct. 11 — Dec. 31.
1856   Jan. 1 — Dec. 7.

OPINION LIBRE. w.
MWA
1904   June 19, July 10 — 17.

PERIODICO OFICIAL DEL GOBIERNO
DEL ESTADO GUANAJUATO.
TxU
1880   July 4, 22 — 29, Aug. 1 — 8, 19 —
31, Sept. 2 — 5, 30, Oct. 3, 31,
Nov. 4 — 7, Dec. 2 — 5, 16 — 26.
1881   June 30.

LA PRUDENCIA. sw.
CU — B
Micro (P)
1845   Dec. 24.

LA REPUBLICA. irr. est. 1868.
CU — B
Micro (P)
1874   Sept. 6.
1875   Apr. 4.

RESURRECCION. w.
TxU
1912   Feb. 15.

EL TRIUNFO DE LA JUSTICIA. w. est.
Oct. 13, 1911.
TxU
1911   Oct. 13.

VOZ DE GUANAJUATO. w.
CtY
1891   Sept. 6.

LA VOZ DE ITURBIDE. bw. est. Dec. 14,
1856.
Note: Ceased publication Oct. 4, 1857.
TxU
1856   Dec. 14, 28 – 31.
1857   Jan. 1 – Oct. 4.

Guaymas

LA ASOCIACION DEL PUEBLO. w.
est. July 15, 1870.
CU – B
Micro (P)
1870   Sept. 9.
1871   Feb. 17.

LAS CINCO VOCALES. bw. est. June
10, 1876.
CU – B
Micro (P)
1876   June 10, July 25 – Aug. 10,
Dec. 10.

EL CONCILIADOR. w. est. Apr. 7, 1845.
CU – B
Micro (P)
1845   June 23, July 21 – 28.
Suplemento: Aug. 14.

EL CONVENCIONAL. w. est. May 28,
1875.
CU – B
Micro (P)
1875   June 4.
Suplemento: June 13.

EL DEFENSOR DEL PUEBLO. w.
CU – B
Micro (P)
1875   June 18.

EL DIARIO. d. est. 1930.
DLC
1941   Mar. 31, Apr. 16.

EL ECO DE OCCIDENTE. w. est. May 2,
1878.

CU – B
Micro (P)
1878   May 2, 15 – June 19, July 3 –
Oct. 23, Nov. 6.

LA GACETA. d. est. 1915.
DLC
1919   Oct. 15.
1941   Mar. 26, 31, Apr. 7, 8, 16.
1943   Nov. 1 – 5, 8 – 11, 15, 18 – 26,
30 – Dec. 4, 8 – 31.
1944   Jan. 3 – 6, 15, 19 – 25, 27 –
Feb. 1, 3 – 8, 10, 12 – 15, 18,
19, 24 – Mar. 6, 8 – 14, 18, Apr.
1 – May 2, 5, 6, 9 – 18, 20 –
June 7, 9 – 15, 17 – 21, 23 –
30, July 3 – 9, 11 – Sept. 26,
29 – Dec. 30.
1945   Jan. 2 – Apr. 4, 6 – Oct. 10,
13 – 16, 18 – Dec. 16, 18 – 29.
LNT – MA
1933   Jan. 27.

GARANTIAS INDIVIDUALES. w. est.
Mar. 4, 1876.
CU – B
Micro (P)
1876   Mar. 18, 31, Apr. 14 – May 5.

EL GOLFO DE CORTES. w. est. June 12,
1872.
CU – B
Micro (P)
1872   July 10, Sept. 18 – 25, Oct. 9.
1873   Jan. 16, 29, Feb. 26, Mar. 19,
Sept. 10.
1874   Feb. 4, Mar. 25.
MWA
1874   Jan. 21.

EL INDEPENDIENTE. w. est. Feb. 18,
1877.
CU – B
Micro (P) & (N)
1877   Mar. 18, Apr. 15 – 29, May 13 –
20, June 17, Sept. 30 – Nov.
25, Dec. 9 – 26.
1878   Jan. 2 – Apr. 10, 26 – June 10,
July 10 – 24, Aug. 7 – Oct. 28,
Nov. 11.

EL LATIGO. w. est. July 4, 1873.
  CU—B
    Micro (P)
    1873   July 11.

LA LEY. irr. est. Nov. 2, 1878.
  CU—B
    Micro (P)
    1878   Nov. 2—10, Dec. 10.

LA LINEA RECTA. w. est. 1894.
  MH
    1894   May 8, June 19, Sept. 18,
           Oct. 2.
    1895   Jan. 15, 29, Feb. 12, Mar. 26.

EL MUNICIPIO. bw. est. Feb. 1, 1878.
  CU—B
    Micro (P)
    1878   Feb. 1—Oct. 17.

LA PAZ. w. est. May 17, 1876.
  CU—B
    Micro (P)
    1876   May 17.

EL PLAN DE TUXTEPEC. irr. est. Jan.
  28, 1877.
  CU—B
    Micro (P)
    1877   Feb. 4, May 11—18, June 8,
           July 1—23.

LA PRENSA. w. est. July 24, 1876.
  CU—B
    Micro (P)
    1876   July 24—31, Aug. 14.
    1877   Jan. 1, 15, 26—Feb. 22, Mar.
           9—28, May 6, July 23—Aug.
           29.
           Suplemento: Jan. 13.

EL SONORENSE. w. est. 1881.
  CU—B
    Micro (P)
    1883   Dec. 12.

EL SUSURRO. w. est. May 26, 1877.
  CU—B
    Micro (P)
    1877   Aug. 1—8, n.d. (Sept.), Sept.

28.
Suplemento: July 28.

EL TORITO. w. est. May 18, 1878.
  CU—B
    Micro (P)
    1878   May 18—Sept. 27.

EL TRAFICO. d. est. [1889].
  DLC
    1899   Oct. 4, 7, 9—14, 16—18, 21,
           23—28, 30—Nov. 4, 6, 7, 10,
           11, 13, 15—18, 20—25, 27, 28,
           30—Dec. 2, 4, 5, 7, 8, 11, 12,
           14—16, 20, 21.

EL TRECE DE JULIO. w. est. Feb.
  1876.
  CU—B
    Micro (P)
    1877   Feb. 16—Mar. 16.

EL TRIUNFO DE SONORA. w. est.
  May 23, 1877.
  CU—B
    Micro (P)
    1877   May 23—June 9.

UNIÓN Y PROGRESO. m. est. Dec. 1,
  1876.
  CU—B
    Micro (P)
    1876   Dec.
    1877   Jan.—Mar., May.

Guerrero

LA NUEVA ERA; PERIODICO OFICIAL
DEL GOBIERNO DEL ESTADO DE
GUERRERO. sw. est. May 5, 1869.
CU—B
  Micro (P) & (N)
    1869   May 5—15, 21—July 16, 23—
           30, Aug. 10—17, 24—Nov. 26.
    1870   Jan. 4—Apr. 12, 19—May 6,
           June 21—July 12, 19, 26—Aug.
           5, 12—23.

EL REGENERADOR. sw. est. 1867.
  CU – B
    Micro (P)
    1868   Mar. 18, [25,] Apr. 15 – 18,
            29 – May 2, 9, 16 – 20, 30 –
            June 3, 10 – 13, July 11, 18, 25,
            Aug. 15.

Hermosillo

ALERTA. w. est. Dec. 20, 1942.
  DLC
    1942   Dec. 20.

LA BALANZA POPULAR. w. est. Feb. 14,
  1841.
  CU – B
    Micro (P)
    1871   Feb. 21.

EL CLUB DE LA REFORMA. w. est.
  Apr. 29, 1877.
  CU – B
    Micro (P)
    1877   Apr. 29 – June 3.

LA CONSTITUCION; PERIODICO
  OFICIAL DEL GOBIERNO DEL
  ESTADO LIBRE Y SOBERANO DE
  SONORA. sw., w. est. Apr. 4, 1878.
  CU – B
    Micro (P)
    1878   Apr. 4.
    1879   Apr. 11 – Dec. 25.
    1880   Jan. 1 – May 6, 20 – Oct. 28,
            Nov. 11 – Dec. 30.
    1881   Jan. 6 – Dec. 3, 15, 22 – 27.
    1882   Jan. 6 – Mar. 14, 18 – 29, Apr.
            8 – 12, 25 – 29, May 9 – 30,
            June 9 – 16, 30, July 14 – Aug.
            15, 24 – Dec. 29.
    1883   Jan. 5 – July 13, 27 – Dec. 28.
    1884   Jan. 4 – Apr. 25.
  LNT – MA
    1879   Dec. 25.
    1880   Jan. 1, Mar. 2.
  TxU
    1880   Oct. 7, 28, Nov. 11 – Dec. 2,
            16 – 23.
    1881   Apr. 7.

EL ECO DE SONORA. w. est. Aug. 8,
  1870.

CU – B
  Micro (P)
  1870   Dec. 12 – 19.
  1871   Jan. 2 – Mar. 6, 27, Apr. 10 –
          17.

LA ERA NUEVA. w. est. Nov. 25, 1877.
  CU – B
    Micro (P)
    1877   Nov. 25 – Dec. 30.
    1878   Jan. 6 – July 28.

LA ESTRELLA DE OCCIDENTE. est.
  1865.
  CU – B
    Micro (P)
    1866   Aug. 20.

EL GLADIADOR DE SONORA. est.
  Sept. 23, 1846.
  CU – B
    Micro (P)
    1846   Sept. 23.

EL IMPARCIAL. d. est. 1937.
  AzU
    1958   May 14 – June 16, 18 – Aug. 1,
            3 – Sept. 14, 16 – Oct. 21, 23 –
            30, Nov. 2 – 19, 21 – Dec. 12,
            14 – 24, 26 – 31.
  DLC
    1942   May 25, 27, 30, June 3 – 15,
            17, 18, 20 – 26, July 3 – 17,
            20 – 22, 24, 28, 30, Aug. 1, 3,
            Sept. 19, 29, Oct. 1, 2, 8 – 28,
            Nov. 3, 5, 6, 9, 10, 12, 16, 21 –
            23, 27, 30 – Dec. 1, 7, 9, 11 –
            19, 22, 24.

EL INDEPENDIENTE. irr. est. May 13,
  1875.
  CU – B
    Micro (P)
    1875   May 13 – June 2.

LA OPINION DEL PUEBLO. w. est.
  May 9, 1875.
  CU – B
    Micro (P)
    1875   June 6.

LA OPINION PUBLICA. w.
  CU – B
    Micro (P)
    1878   July 18, Aug. 1.

EL PUEBLO. d. est. 1925.
  DLC
    1942   June 2, July 1, Aug. 15, Oct. 8.
    1943   Jan. 2 – 4, 27, Feb. 12, Mar.
            10, May 8, June 14.

LA RECONSTRUCION. irr. est. Mar. 27,
  1877.
  CU – B
    Micro (P)
    1877   Mar. 27 – May 22, June 5 – 14.

LA REGENERACION. w. est. June 7,
  1876.
  CU – B
    Micro (P)
    1876   June 14 – July 5, 20.

EL REGIONAL. d. est. 1955.
  AzU
    1958   May 15 – 31, July 1 – 13, 15
            19, 22 – 27, 29 – Aug. 7, 10 –
            27, 29 – Sept. 8, 10 – Oct. 7,
            13, 17 – 25, 27 – Nov. 20, 22 –
            27, 29 – Dec. 20, 22 – 24, 29 –
            31.
    1959   Jan. 1 – Dec. 31.
    1960   Jan. 1 – Apr. 14, 18, 20 – May
            16, 18 – Oct. 22, 24 – 27, 30 –
            Dec. 6, 8 – 14, 17 – 27, 29 – 31.
    1961   Jan. 1 – June 30, Aug. 1 –
            Dec. 31.
    1962   Jan. 1, 3 – 9, 11 – 17, 19 – 22,
            24 – Mar. 21, 23 – 31, Apr. 2 –
            4, 7 – 19, 22 – May 1, 3 – 9,
            12 – June 11, 13 – Aug. 6, 8 –
            28, 30 – Oct. 18, 20 – Nov. 20,
            22 – Dec. 6, 8 – 15, 17 – 25.
    1963   Jan. 1, 3 – Feb. 21, 23 – Mar.
            21, 23 – Apr. 11, 14 – 30, May
            3 – Sept. 16, 18 – Nov. 15,
            17 – 19, 22 – Dec. 31.
    1964   Jan. 1, 3 – 5, 7 – 12, 14 – 19,
            22 – 26, 28 – 31, Feb. 2, 4, 6 –
            9, 11 – 16, 18 – 23, 25 – 29,

            Mar. 1, 3 – 8, 10 – 15, 17 – 21,
            24 – 26.
    1965   Jan. 1, 3, 6 – 10, 13 – 17, 19 –
            25, 27 – 31, Feb. 2 – 4, 6, 7, 9 –
            14, 16 – 21, 23 – 28, Mar. 3 –
            7, 10 – 21, 22 – 28, 30 – Apr. 4,
            6, 8 – 11, 14, 15, 18, 20 – 25,
            27 – May 1, 4 – 9, 11 – 16, 18 –
            21, 23, 25 – 30, June 1 – 3, 5, 6,
            8, 9, 11, 12, 15 – 20, 23 – 27,
            29 – July 4, 6 – 11, 13 – 18, 20
            21, 23 – 25, 27 – Aug. 1, 3 – 8,
            11, 13 – 15, 17 – 21, 24 – 29,
            31 – Sept. 4, 7 – 11, 14 – 16,
            18, 19, 21 – 26, 28, 29, Oct. 1 –
            3, 5 – 10, 12 – 17, 19, 21 – 24,
            26 – 31, Nov. 2 – 7, 9 – 14, 16 –
            20, 23 – 28, 30 – Dec. 5, 7 –
            12, 14 – 19, 21 – 25, 28 – 31.
    1966   Jan. 1, 4 – 9, 11 – 16, 18 – 23,
            25 – 29, Feb. 1 – 6, 8 – 13, 15.

LA VERDAD. w. est. Oct. 12, 1878.
  CU – B
    Micro (P)
    1878   Oct. 12 – Nov. 2.

Heróica

EL PROCURADOR DEL PUEBLO.
  LNHT
    1834   Apr. 5.

Hidalgo del Parral

See Parral.

Iguala

EL MEJICANO INDEPENDIENTE. w.
  TxU
    1821   Mar. 31 – Apr. 14, 28.

Ixtapán del Oro

EL HERALDO. irr.
  LNT – MA
    1880   Jan. 10, 25, Feb. 10, 25, Mar.
            5, Apr. 9, July 26, Sept. 22,
            Nov. 5.

Izamal de Díaz

INFANCIA. bw.
MWA
1878　June 15, Oct. 15.

Jalapa

THE AMERICAN STAR. sw. est. Apr. 25,
1847.
Note: Removed to Mexico City Sept.
20, 1847.
NHi
1847　Apr. 25, May 2−6, 13.

NcD
1847　Apr. 29, May 2.

EL AMIGO DE LA PAZ Y DEL ORDEN.
3w. est 1834.
Note: Official publication of Vera
Cruz.
DLC
1835　Feb. 3−Mar. 3, 10−12, 21,
Apr. 9, 16, 18, 23−30, May 5−
7, Oct. 27−31, Nov. 5,
10−12, 17−Dec. 15.

BOLETIN DE JALAPA. 3w. est. 1859.
DLC
1859　Nov. 30−Dec. 22, 31.
1860　Jan. 1, 4−8.

EL CLARIN. w. est. May 5, 1912.
TxU
1912　May 5.

EL CONCILIADOR. sw., w. est. [1839].
Note: Official publication of Vera
Cruz.
CU−B
Micro (P)
1840　June 16.
DLC
1841　Jan. 1−Aug. 30, Sept. 1−16,
21−24.
MWA
1841　Aug. 10, Sept. 7.
1842　Feb. 26, Mar. 26.

EL CONSTITUCIONAL. d., 3w.
Note: Periodicity before June 15,
1832, daily; after June 17, 1832, three
times a week.
DLC
1832　May 18−July 20.

DIARIO DE XALAPA. d. est. Sept. 1943.
CU
1943　Sept. 14, 15.
1944　Sept. 20, 23, 25, Oct. 1, 15, 17,
22, Nov. 7, 30, Dec. 18, 20, 24,
29, 31.
1945　Jan. 8, 16, 17, 23, 27, 29, 30,
Feb. 1, 3, 11, 13, 28, Mar. 3−5,
10, Apr. 7, 19, May 5, 6, 11, 16,
18−28, June 2−5, 12, 20, 26−
30, July 1−5, 7, 14, 17, 19, 21,
29−31, Aug. 1, 2, 8, 15, 19, 26,
Sept. 4−14, 18, 23, 28, Oct. 7,
12−18, 21, 29, Nov. 25, Dec.
6, 20.
Extraordinario: Dec. 20.
1946　Jan. 10, 20−22, 25, 27, 29,
Feb. 3, 9, 12−17, 20, 22, 24−
26, 28, Mar. 5−8, 12, 15, 22,
Apr. 1, 22, May 12, 25, 27, 28,
June 6, 11, 14, 16, 22, 27, July
3, 4, 12, 14, 16, 21, 23, 28−30,
Aug. 13, Nov. 10.

EL ESTADO DE VERACRUZ. 3w.
TxU
1912　Aug. 11−13.

EL IRIS VERACRUZANO. w.
CtY
1907　Sept. 15.
TxU
1908　Nov. 1.

NACIONAL. w.
MWA
1841　July 15−Aug. 19.

EL ORDEN. w.
TxU
1908　Apr. 12.

EL ORIENTE. d. est. 1824.
  Note: Paged continuously.
  DLC
    1825   July 1 — Sept. 16, 23 — Oct. 6,
            8 — Dec. 31.
    1826   Feb. 3 — 9, Apr. 1 — 4, 7 — Dec.
            31.
            Suplemento: Feb. 16.
    1827   May 1 — Oct. 30, Nov. 2 — Dec.
            3, 5 — 31.
    1828   Jan. 1 — Mar. 18, 21 — 31, Apr.
            2 — 15.
  LNT — MA
    1828   Jan. 5, 6.
  TxU
    1824   Sept. 1 — Dec. 30.

EL ORIENTE. w. est. Nov. 1, 1887.
  TxU
    1887   Nov. 1 — Dec. 31.
    1888   Jan. 1 — 22, Feb. 8 — June 1,
            15 — July 22, Nov. 8 — 15, Dec.
            8 — 22.

THE WATCH TOWER. w. est. Feb. 12,
  1848.
  Note: In Spanish and English.
  CLU
    1848   May 4.
  DLC
    1848   Feb. 12.

Lagos

EL COBATE. w. est. Apr. 28, 1912.
  TxU
    1912   Apr. 28.

La Paz

ACCION. 3w., d. est. [1934].
  CU
    1943   Aug. 9 — 11, 18 — Sept. 9, 21,
            28 — 30, Oct. 6 — 11, 18 — Nov.
            8, 13 — Dec. 1, 6 — 28.
    1944   Jan. 1, 12 — 31, Aug. 23 — 28,
            Sept. 11 — 29, Oct. 6 — 19, 24 — 26.
    1945   Feb. 17, May 2, 9, 17, Dec.
            4 — 8.

DLC
  1941   Feb. 10, Apr. 7, 11, May 2, 5,
          7, 9, 12, 14, 16, 28.

LA BAJA CALIFORNIA. w. est. Feb. 16,
  1867.
  CU — B
    Micro (P)
    1867   June 15 — 22.
    1869   Sept. 25.
    1871   June 3.
  DLC
    1870   July 16 — Dec. 31.
    1871   Jan. 1 — 7.

BAJA CALIFORNIA. 3w., d. est. 1910.
  CU
    1943   Apr. 28 — June 18, July 1 — 9,
            11 — 25, 28 — Aug. 3.
  DLC
    1941   Feb. 11, 22, Apr. 1, 3, May 1,
            3, 8, 10, 13, 15, 17, 27, 29.

BOLETIN OFICIAL DEL GOBIERNO
DE LA BAJA CALIFORNIA. irr.
  CU — B
    Micro (P)
    1878   Mar. 1 — 15, Apr. 15 — May 15,
            July 15 — Aug. 1, Sept. 1 — Oct.
            15, Nov. 15 — Dec. 31.
    1879   Jan. 15, Feb. 25 — Mar. 8,
            Apr. 1 — 8, May 8, June 1 —
            July 8, 31 — Aug. 7, Oct. 15.
    1880   Mar. 1 — 10, 'pr. 21 — Dec. 31.
    1881   Jan. 1 — Dec. 31.
    1882   Jan. 8 — 16, Feb. 7 — Mar. 12,
            May 30 — June [10,] July 10 —
            Sept. 30, Oct. 31 — Nov. 20,
            Dec. 10 — 30.
    1883   Jan. 10 — 20, Feb. 10 — Aug.
            30, Sept. 30 — Dec. 30.
    1884   Jan. 10 — 30.

EL CENTINELA.
  CU — B
    Micro (P)
    1855   Mar. 15.

EL ECO DE CALIFORNIA. sw. est.
June 14, 1912.
TxU
1912 June 14.

LA EQUIDAD; PERIODICO OFICIAL
DEL TERRITORIO DE LA BAJA-
CALIFORNIA. w.
CU — B
Micro (P)
1875 July 4, Oct. 18 — Dec. 27.
1876 Jan. 4 — 11, 25 — Apr. 11, May
3 — Oct. 14, 28 — Dec. 20.
1877 Jan. 6 — 20.
TxU
1881 Apr. 10.

EL MEXICANO. w.
CtY
1869 Nov. 20.

LA ORQUESTA. sw.
LNT — MA
1861 Mar. 1 — Dec. 31.
1862 Jan. 1 — Dec. 31.
1863 Jan. 1 — May 31.
1864 Dec. 1 — 31.
1865 Jan. 1 — Dec. 31.
1866 Jan. 1 — July 31.
1867 June 26 — Dec. 31.
1868 — 1873 Jan. 1 — Dec. 31.

LA PAZ. irr. est. Feb. 9, 1884.
CU — B
Micro (P)
1884 Feb. 9 — Apr. 16.

EL PENINSULAR. w. est. 1870.
CU — B
Micro (P)
1871 June 9.

LA VOZ DE CALIFORNIA. irr. est. 1881.
CU — B
Micro (P)
1884 May 21 — Sept. 11.

La Piedad

ARGOS. w.
DLC
1943 Oct. 10.

EL OBRERO CATOLICO. w. est. Mar.
17, 1912.
TxU
1912 Mar. 17.

Leona-Vicario

GACETA DEL GOBIERNO DEPART-
MENTAL DE COAHUILA. w.
CU — B
Micro (P)
1838 Mar. 17.

Los Mochis

LAS NOTICIAS. sw.
DLC
1942 June 17, Dec. 24.
1943 May 31 — June 3.

UNIFICACION. w.
DLC
1943 Jan. 23.

Magdalena

THE LOWER CALIFORNIAN. irr. est.
[1870].
Note: In English.
CLU
1870 Nov. 10.
DLC
1871 Jan. 18.

Mapimí

ARTERIA COMERCIAL. w. est. Dec. 16,
1911.
TxU
1911 Dec. 16.

LIBERTAD. w. est. 1911.
TxU
1911 [July 9].

Matamoros

EL AGUILA DEL NORTE. w. est. Jan.
21, 1846.
> Note: Title *El Águila mexicana*,
> Jan. 21, 1846; *El Águila del
> norte*, after Jan. 28, 1846.
> CtY
> > 1846   Jan. 21, Feb. 25, Mar. 4, 18,
> >   25, Apr. 8, 15.
> TxU
> > 1846   Jan. 21 – 28, Feb. 11 – 18,
> >   Mar. 18.

AMERICAN FLAG. sw., irr., 3w., sw. est.
June 1846.
> Note: In Spanish and English. Title
> *Republic of Rio Grande and Friend of
> the People* (in English) and *República
> de Río Grande y amiga de los
> pueblos* (in English and Spanish),
> June – July 3, 1846; *The American
> Flag*, July 4, 1846 – Jan. 12, 1847;
> *American Flag*, after Jan. 13, 1847.
> CU – B
> > Micro (P)
> > 1847   Sept. 25.
> CtY
> > 1846   June 6, 27.
> DLC
> > English edition:
> > 1846   June 6, 16, 30.
> > English and Spanish edition:
> > 1846   June 6, 16, July 1.
> > Combined edition:
> > 1846   July 4, 7, 16 – Nov. 28, Dec.
> >   5 – 30.
> >   Extra: Sept. 29.
> > 1847   Jan. 4 – Feb. 6, 13 – May
> >   8, 15 – Dec. 30.
> >   Extra: Mar. 10.
> > 1848   Jan. 3 – July 29.
> >   Extra: Apr. 3.
> MWA
> > 1846   Sept. 26, Oct. 4 – 14, 21, 31,
> >   Nov. 7, 14.
> > 1847   Jan. 20, Apr. 24, May 15, 22.

NHi
> 1846   [June 6 – Dec. 31].
> 1847   [Jan. 1 – Dec. 31].
> 1848   [Jan. 1 – July 29], Nov. 22, 29,
>   Dec. 6.
Micro (P)
> 1846   June 6 – Dec. 31.
> 1847   Jan. 1 – Dec. 31.
> 1848   Jan. 1 – July 29, [30 – Oct. 31],
>   Nov. 22, 29, Dec. 6.
TxU
> English edition:
> 1846   June 6 – 12, 27.
> English and Spanish edition:
> 1846   June 6 – 12, 27.
> Combined edition:
> 1846   Oct. 1.
> 1847   Aug. 28.

EL ANCLA. w. est. Oct. 7, 1837.
> CtY
> > 1837   Prospecto: Oct. 6.
> >   Oct. 7 – Dec. 29.
> > 1838   Jan. 5 – Mar. 16, 30 – May 18,
> >   June 1 – July 20, Aug. 3 – Oct.
> >   26, Nov. 9 – Dec. 28.
> > 1841   Apr. 19, May 24, June 7, 21 –
> >   28, July 19 – Aug. 2, 16, 30.
> DLC
> > 1837   Prospecto: Sept. 29.
> > 1839   Jan. 5 – May 17, July 19, Aug.
> >   23 – 30.
> > 1840   Jan. 3, Mar. 6.
> > 1841   Jan. 4 – 25, Mar. 8 – Aug. 30,
> >   Nov. 30 – Dec. 28.

EL ARGOS DE MATAMOROS.
> TxU
> > 1833   Apr. 4, July 14.

LA BANDERA MEXICANA. w. est.
[Dec. 1849].
> CtY
> > 1850   Jan. 19, Feb. 16 – 23.
> >   Suplemento: Feb. 27.

LA BANDERA NACIONAL. w. est. 1864.
> TxU
> > 1864   May 14, June 22 – 29, July 6 –
> >   16, 27, Aug. 3 – 6.

EL BIEN PUBLICO. w.
  CtY
    1848   Oct. 23, Dec. 11.
    1849   Jan. 8, Aug. 22, Oct. 10 – 17,
            31 – Nov. 21.
            Suplemento: Aug. 11, Sept.
            25.
    1851   Apr. 16.

BOLETIN DE LA DIVISION DEL
  NORTE.
  CtY
    1846   Tom. 1, Nos. 1, 5, 8 – 11.
  TxSjM
    1846   Apr. 13, 28.

BOLETIN EXTRAORDINARIO.
  MWA
    1865   Nov. 3, 5.

BOLETIN OFICIAL DE LA COMAN-
  DANCIA MILITAR DE LA LINEA
  DEL BRAVO Y DEL DISTRITO DEL
  NORTE DE TAMAULIPAS.
  CU – B
    Micro (P)
    1867   Aug. 21.

LA BRISA. w. est. Aug. 30, 1839.
  CtY
    1839   Aug. 30 – Sept. 27, Oct. 11,
            Nov. 2 – 14.
  DLC
    1839   Oct. 4 – 31, Nov. 2 – 14, 16 –
            22.
            Suplemento: Nov. 8.
  TxU
    1839   Aug. 30, Sept. 1 – 30, Oct. 4 –
            25.

EL CRONISTA. 3w.
  TxU
    1895   Jan. 9.

DAILY RANCHER.
    See *Ranchero diario. Daily Rancher.*

LA DIANA DE MATAMOROS. sw. est.
  June 24, 1846.
    Note: Supplemented by *Matamoros
    Reveille.*

CtY
    1846   June 24 – 27.
  TxU
    1846   June 24 – 27.

ECO DEL NORTE DE TAMAULIPAS.
  sw., w. est. Mar. 3, 1845.
    Note: Periodicity Mar. 3 – Aug. 31,
    1845, semiweekly; after Sept. 1,
    1845, weekly.
  CtY
    1845   Vol. 3, No. 60.
    1846   Tomo 2, No. 73.
  DLC
    1845   Mar. 3 – Apr. 6, 8, 9, 11 – May
            4, 6 – June 8, 10 – July 12,
            Aug. 1 – 10, 30 – Sept. 14,
            Oct. 16 – Nov. 11, Dec. 5 – 24.
            Suplemento: May 15, July 3.

EL HONOR NACIONAL.
  TxU
    1841   Dec. 27.

EL JUSTO MEDIO. w. est. 1843.
  CtY
    1844   Jan. 26 – Feb. 2, Mar. 1, 29,
            Apr. 12 – May 3, 17, 31 – June
            7.
  TxU
    1844   Jan. 26 – Feb. 2, Mar. 1, 29,
            Apr. 12 – May 3, 17, 31 – June
            7.

EL LATIGO DE TEJAS. sw.
  TxU
    1843   Oct. 9 – 12, 23 – Nov. 20, 30,
            Dec. 4 – 7.
    1844   Jan. 1, 11 – Feb. 8, 15 – Mar.
            11, 18 – 25, Apr. 1 – 18, 25 –
            May 2, 9 – 16, 23, 30 – June
            3, 10 – 20, 28, July 4 – 18, 25 –
            29, Aug. 5, 12 – 22, 29 – Nov.
            4, 11 – Dec. 30.

MATAMOROS REVEILLE. sw. est.
  June 24, 1846.
    Note: Supplement to *La Diana de
    Matamoros.*
  CtY
    1846   June 24 – 27.

TxU
　　1846　　June 24－27.

MERCURIO DEL PUERTO DE
　MATAMOROS. w. est. Nov. 11, 1834.
　CtY
　　1834　　Nov. 27.
　　1835　　[Feb. 26－Mar. 5, Apr. 30－
　　　　　　June 4, 18－July 2, 16－30],
　　　　　　Aug. 20－27, Sept. 10, 24－
　　　　　　Oct. 15, Nov. 19－26.
　　　　　　Suplemento: Jan. 15, Apr. 9,
　　　　　　Oct. 15, Dec. 3.
　　1836　　Mar. 18, Apr. 8－29, May 27－
　　　　　　June 17, July 8－22, Aug. 5－
　　　　　　19, Sept. 2, 16, 30－Oct. 14,
　　　　　　28－Nov. 25, Dec. 9－31.
　　1837　　Jan. 1－6, Mar. 24, Apr. 21－
　　　　　　May 5, Dec. 1.
　　1838　　Jan. 12.
　MWA
　　1836　　Jan. 22, Feb. 26, Mar. 4.
　TxSjM
　　1835　　May 29, Aug. 20.

EL PROCURADOR DEL PUEBLA. w.
　CtY
　　1832　　July 28－Aug. 18.
　　1834　　July 14.

PROGRESO. 3w.
　MWA
　　1881　　May 15－17, June 14.

EL RANCHERO. w. est. Feb. 25, 1857.
　TxU
　　1857　　Feb. 25.

RANCHERO DIARIO. DAILY RANCH-
　ER. d. est. 1865.
　　Note: In Spanish and English.
　MWA
　　1865　　July 5.
　　1866　　Feb. 23.
　NHi
　　1865　　Nov. 2－5, 8－12.
　TxU
　　1865　　Oct. 12, 17－24, 27－Nov. 7, 9.

RECONSTRUCCION; ORGANO
　OFICIAL DEL GOBIERNO DE
　TAMAULIPAS. sw.
　MWA
　　1881　　June 16－19.
　TxU
　　1880　　July 15, Sept. 2－5, 19－Oct.
　　　　　　10, 21－24, Nov. 4－7, 18－
　　　　　　Dec. 5, 30.
　　1881　　June 30.

REPUBLIC OF RIO GRANDE AND
　FRIEND OF THE PEOPLE.
　　See *American Flag.*

REPUBLICA DE RIO GRANDE Y
　AMIGA DE LOS PUEBLOS.
　　See *American Flag.*

SOL DE MAYO. 3w. est. 1890.
　MWA
　　1898　　Aug. 3.

Matehuala

EL BARRETERO. w. est. 1905.
　　Note: Ceased publication 1910.
　NN
　　1909　　Oct. 3, 10.

SUFRAGIO LIBRE. w. est. June 25,
　1911.
　TxU
　　1911　　June 25.

Mazatlán

EL ALACRAN. w.
　DLC
　　1942　　Jan. 30.

BOLETIN OFICIAL. bw.
　TxU
　　1862　　May 10－26.

BOLETIN OFICIAL DEL ESTADO DE
　SINALOA. irr.
　CU－B
　　Micro (P) & (N)
　　1870－1871　　Jan. 1－Dec. 31.
　　1872　　May 8－June 18, 22, July 3－
　　　　　　Aug. 10, 16－Sept. 12.
　　　　　　Suplemento: Aug. 14.

UNA CONTESTACION DEL
"OCCIDENTAL." est. 1869.
CU – B
1869   Apr. 1.

EL CORREO DE LA TARDE. d. est.
July 15, 1885.
CU
1910   Nov. 1 – Dec. 31.
1911   Jan. 1 – 12, 14 – 28, 30, Feb.
1 – June 9, 11 – Oct. 31, Nov.
14 – Dec. 31.
1912   Jan. 1 – Feb. 13, 17 – Apr. 13,
20 – May 15, 18, 21 – 26, 30 –
Dec. 11, 16 – 31.
1913   Jan. 1 – May 16, 18 – Oct. 4,
6 – Dec. 31.
1914   Jan. 1 – Apr. 16, 20 – May 9,
13, 14, 16 – 27, 29, 30, June
16, July 2.
1920   Sept. 20, 21, 24, 29, Oct. 1, 2,
5 – 8, 13, 15.
1929   July 25 – 27.
DLC
1942   July 22, Oct. 28, Dec. 16.
1943   Mar. 22, Apr. 13.
TxU
1925   Jan. 2.

EL CORREO DE MAZATLÁN. irr. est.
1865.
CU – B
Micro (P).
1865   Dec. 25.

EL CORREO DEL PACIFICO. w. est.
Feb. 24, 1868.
CU – B
1868   Feb. 24 – Oct. 10.

CRONOS. d.
CU
1929   July 24, 25.

EL DEMOCRATA SINALOENSE. sw.,
d. est. Sept. 14, 1919.
Note: Periodicity before 1920,
semiweekly; after 1920, daily.
CU
1927   June 21.
1929   July 25 – 27.

1935   Dec. 27.
1936   Jan. 5.
1937   Oct. 28, 29.
DLC
1941   Sept. 24, 25, Oct. 22, 23.
1942   June 3, Oct. 13, Nov. 27.
1943   Jan. 26, June 17.

EL ECO DE OCCIDENTE. w. est. Apr.
13, 1859.
CU – B
Micro (P)
1859   Apr. 13 – June 1.

EL ECO DEL PUEBLO. w. est. July 17,
1869.
CU – B
1869   July 17 – 31.

EL ESTADO DE SINALOA; PERIO-
DICO OFICIAL DEL GOBIERNO.
sw., w.
CU – B
Micro (P)
1867   May 13, 27, June 10 – July 22,
Aug. 6 – 16, 23, Sept. 13 – 17,
Oct. 4 – 15, Nov. 8 – 19, 29 –
Dec. 27.
1868   Jan. 1 – Mar. 25.
TxU
1868   Jan. 1 – Mar. 31.

EL ESTADO DE SINALOA; ORGANO
OFICIAL DEL GOBIERNO. w., irr.
est. Jan. 10, 1873.
CU – B
Micro (P)
1877   Feb. 1.
TxU
1873   Jan. 10 – Mar. 27, Apr. 24 –
Dec. 31.
1874   Jan. 26 – Oct. 8, 22 – Dec. 14.

EL ESTADO DE SITIO. w., sw. est.
July 29, 1876.
Note: Official organ of the Co-
mandancia Militar de la Plaza.
CU – B
Micro (P)
1876   Sept. 30, Dec. 22 – 27.

EL FENIX; PERIODICO OFICIAL DEL
GOBIERNO DEL ESTADO DE
SINALOA. w. est. Oct. 17, 1872.
  CU–B
  Micro (P)
  1872   Oct. 17–Dec. 28.
  1873   Jan. 4.
  TxU
  1872   Oct. 17–Dec. 13, 29.

EL IMPULSOR. d. est [1942].
  DLC
  1942   June 28.

LA INTEGRIDAD NACIONAL. w. est.
Jan. 10, 1858.
  CU–B
  Micro (P)
  1858   Apr. 18.

JUAN SIN MIEDO. w. est. Mar. 27,
1869.
  CU–B
  1869   Mar. 27–June 19.
          Alcance: Apr. 22.

LA LEGALIDAD. w. est. Apr. 20, 1876.
  CU–B
  Micro (P)
  1876   Oct. 26, Dec. 31.

MAZATLAN TIMES. w. est. May 12,
1863.
  Note: In English.
  CU–B
  1865   July 8.
  DLC
  1864   June 21.

EL MONITOR DEL PACIFICO. w. est.
1877.
  CU–B
  Micro (P)
  1878   Oct. 17.

EL OCCIDENTAL. w. est. Mar. 24,
1869.
  CU–B
  1869   Mar. 24–Dec. 31.
  1870   Jan. 1–Feb. 16, Mar. 2–
          Aug. 27, Sept. 10–Dec. 31.

1871   Jan. 1–Mar. 7, July 15.
1878   June 6, July 25, Aug. 31, Oct. 8.

LA OPINION DE SINALOA; PERIO-
DICO OFICIAL DEL ESTADO. w.
  Note: Ceased publication Nov. 1864.
  CU–B
  Micro (P)
  1863   May 15.
          Suplemento: July 1.
  TxU
  1860   Nov. 7–Dec. 22.
  1862   Jan. 10–July 29, Aug. 16–
          29, Sept. 12–Dec. 9.
  1863   Feb. 3–Mar. 3, 20–May 8,
          22–Aug. 14, Sept. 4–Dec. 11.

PACIFICO. sw. est. 1861.
  MWA
  1881   Aug. 11, 18.

LA REGENERACION DE SINALOA;
PERIODICO OFICIAL DEL
GOBIERNO. bw., irr. est. Apr. 18,
1868.
  CU–B
  Micro (P) & (N)
  1868   May 9–Dec. 2, 9–12, 22–31.
  1869   Jan. 8–Feb. 2, 10–Mar. 3,
          10–31, Apr. 7–10, 17–Dec.
          28.
  TxU
  1868   Apr. 18–Dec. 31.

EL SUFRAGIO LIBRE. w. est. 1871.
  TxU
  1871   Dec. 15–31.
  1872   Jan. 1–Feb. 16, Sept. 18–
          Oct. 5.

LA VOZ DE MAZATLAN. w. est. 1883.
  CU–B
  Micro (P)
  1886   June 20.

LA VOZ DEL PUEBLO. w. est. 1871.
  CU–B
  Micro (P)
  1871   June 13.

LA VOZ DEL PUEBLO. w. est. 1931.
  DLC
    1942   Mar. 30.
    1943   Feb. 1, Mar. 1, Apr. 19—May
            10, 24, 31—June 14, 28—
            Sept. 13, 20, Oct. 25.
    1944   June 5, 12.

Mérida

EL AGUARRAS. w. est. 1917.
  LNT—MA
    1917   July 9.

ALBORADA. w. est. July 19, 1917.
  LNT—MA
    1917   July 19, 26.

AMIGO DEL PAIS. d. est. 1885.
  MWA
    1885   Suplemento (June).
    1889   Mar. 9.

ARTESANO. w.
  MWA
    1884   Sept. 15.

EL BALUARTE DE LA LIBERTAD. 3w.,
  w., sw. est. [1832].
    Note: Periodicity before Apr. 30,
    1833, three times a week; May 4—
    July 20, 1833, weekly; after Sept. 7,
    1833, semiweekly.
  DLC
    1833   Mar. 2—July 26, Sept.
            4—16, 18—Oct. 25, 27—Nov.
            30.
            Suplemento: June 22, 29.
  MWA
    1833   Mar. 2—28, Apr. 2—25, 30—
            May 4, 18—July 20, Sept. 7—
            14, 28—Oct. 22, 29—Nov. 19,
            26—30.

BANDERA DE ANAHUAC. sw. est.
  1827.
  DLC
    1828   May 6—30.

BANDERA TUXTEPECANA. w.
  MWA
    1877   Aug. 19.

BOLETIN DEL GOBIERNO DE
  YUCATAN. d., 3w.
    Note: Periodicity before Dec. 27,
    1863, daily; after [Dec. 28, 1863,]
    three times a week.
  MWA
    1863   Suplemento: Nov. 29, Dec. 4,
            8, 17—27, 31.
    1864   Suplemento: Jan. 1, 2, 7—21.

BOLETIN DIARIO DE SANIDAD, DEL
  AMIGO DEL PUEBLO. d. est. July 6,
  1833.
  DLC
    1833   July 6—8, 11, 12, 15—20, 22,
            24—26, 31, Aug. 1.

EL CONSTITUCIONAL. est. 1838.
  CU—B
    Micro (P)
    1838   Feb. 3.

EL CORREO. d. est. May 1918.
  LNT—MA
    1918   [Oct. 4—Nov. 23].

EL CUARTO PODER. w. est. 1898.
  LNT—MA
    1899   Mar. 5.

CUBA. irr. est. July 8, 1869.
  CtY
    1869   July 8—Dec. 18.
    1870   Jan. 9—Dec. 16.
    1871   Jan. 1—Dec. 11.
    1872   Jan. 1—20.

LA DEFENSA NACIONAL. sw.
  LNT—MA
    1911   July 6.

EL DEMOCRATA. d. est. 1905.
  LNT—MA
    1915   Apr. 5.

EL DEMOCRATA. w. est. Apr. 8, 1917.
  LNT—MA
    1917   Apr. 8—Nov. 4.

HOJA DE ANUNCIOS DE EL LIBRE
  EXAMEN. sw.
  MWA
    1880   May 12.

EL DIARIO DE YUCATAN. d. est. May
31, 1925.
  Note: Suspended publication Jan.
  20 — Mar. 21, 1959.
  CLU
    1943   July 1 — Dec. 31.
    1944 — 1945   Jan. 1 — Dec. 31.
    1946   Jan. 1+.
  DLC
    1941   Mar. 30, Apr. 24 — June 7, 9 —
           Dec. 31.
    1942   Jan. 1 — Mar. 29, 31 — Apr. 12,
           14 — Oct. 31, Nov. 2 — Dec. 31.
    1943 — 1947   Jan. 1 — Dec. 31.
    1948   Jan. 1 — Oct. 15, 17 — 26, 30 —
           Dec. 31.
    1949   Jan. 1 — Feb. 3, 5 — 9, 11 — Dec.
           31.
    1950 — 1958   Jan. 1 — Dec. 31.
    1959   Jan. 1 — May 29, 31 — Dec. 31.
    1960   Jan. 1 — Dec. 31.
    1961   Jan. 1 — 20, Mar. 1 — 29, Apr.
           1 — Aug. 16, 18 — 29, Sept. 6 —
           28, 30 — Nov. 21, 23 — Dec. 31.
  Micro (P) & (N)
    1962   Jan. 1+.
  LNT — MA
    1930   Jan. 23, Sept. 8.
    1935   July 26, Oct. 9, 12.
    1941   [Mar. 1 — July 31, Oct. 11 —
           Dec. 31.]
    1942 — 1943   [Jan. 1 — Dec. 31.]
    1944   [Jan. 1 — Oct. 31.]
    1945   [Jan. 1 — 31, May 1 — 31, Aug.
           1 — Dec. 31.]
    1946 — 1958   [Jan. 1 — Dec. 31.]
    1959   Jan. 3 — 13.

DIARIO DEL SURESTE. d. est. 1931.
  DLC
    1941   Feb. 22, Mar. 1 — 31, Apr. 25 —
           Dec. 31.
    1942   Jan. 1, 2, 4 — Feb. 21, 23 — Apr.
           8, 10 — Oct. 31, Nov. 2 — Dec.
           25, 27 — 31.
    1943 — 1945   Jan. 1 — Dec. 31.
    1946   Jan. 1 — Aug. 22, 24 — Dec. 31.
    1947   Jan. 1 — Nov. 20, 22 — Dec. 31.

    1948   Jan. 1 — Dec. 25, 28 — 31.
    1949   Apr. 1 — Dec. 31.
    1950   Jan. 1 — Dec. 31.
    1951   Jan. 1 — Mar. 19, Apr. 1 —
           June 28, July 1 — Sept. 23, 25 —
           Oct. 20, 22 — Nov. 4, 6 — Dec.
           31.
    1952   Jan. 1 — Dec. 31.
    1953   Jan. 1 — Mar. 31, May 1 — June
           25, July 1 — Dec. 31.
    1954   Jan. 1 — 17, 19 — Dec. 31.
    1955   Jan. 1 — Dec. 31.
    1956   Jan. 1 — June 25, July 1 — 22,
           24, Sept. 29, Oct. 1 — 28,
           Nov. 1 — Dec. 31.
    1957   Jan. 1 — Aug. 7, 9 — Dec. 31.
    1958   Jan. 1 — June 2, 4 — 24, 26 —
           Dec. 31.
    1959   Jan. 1 — Nov. 30.
    1960   Jan. 1 — July 9, 11 — Dec. 1,
           3 — 31.
    1961   Jan. 1 — Mar. 10, 12 — Oct. 20,
           22 — Nov. 3, 5 — 29, Dec. 1 —
           16, 18 — 23, 25 — 31.
  Micro (P) & (N)
    1962   Jan. 1 — Sept. 24, 26 — Dec. 31.
    1963   Jan. 1+.
  LNT — MA
    1933   Jan. 1.
    1950   Feb. 22 — Apr. 2.

DIARIO MATUTINO. sw., d. est. May 2,
1917.
  Note: Title *El Hombre libre contra
  todas las farsas,* May 2 — Oct. 7,
  1917; *Diario matutino,* after Oct. 9,
  1917.
  LNT — MA
    1917   May 2 — 9, Aug. 15 — Nov. 18.

DIARIO YUCATECO. d. est. 1907.
  Note: Ceased publication 1912.
  MWA
    1911   Feb. 25, Apr. 23.
           Suplemento: Feb. 26, Apr. 23.

DOMINGUERO. w.
  MWA
    1884   Jan. 6.

EL 2 DE ABRIL. est. 1877.
MWA
1877   Feb. 7, 21.

EL ECO DEL COMERCIO. 3w., sw. est.
Jan. 17, 1880.
LNT—MA
1897   Jan. 2, Apr. 17, Dec. 9.
1899   Mar. 25, May 18, Nov. 9.
1900   Mar. 15, Apr. 12.
1901   June 30.
1906   Nov. 26.
MWA
1880   Jan. 17—Dec. 7.
1881   [Jan. 1—May 10], June 14—
Dec. 31.
1882—1884   [Jan. 1—May 31].
1886   Aug. 17, Nov. 23, Dec.
18—31.
1887—1893   Jan. 1—Dec. 31.
1895   Feb. 12.
TxU
1880   Oct. 19.

ECOS DE LA GUERRA. w.
LNT—MA
1917   Nov. 10—24.
1918   Aug. 24.

ESPIRITU NACIONAL; PERIODICO
OFICIAL DEL ESTADO DE YUCA-
TAN. sw.
MWA
1863   June 8—July 6.

ESTADO DE YUCATAN. w. est. 1877.
MWA
1877   July 15, Aug. 12, Sept. 23,
Oct. 7—14.

LA EVOLUCION. w. est. Sept. 2, 1917.
LNT—MA
1917   Sept. 2, 9.

EL FUERTE DE LOS PATRIOTAS Y
TERROR DE LOS TIRANOS. sw. est.
Jan. 1833.
DLC
1833   Jan. 24, 29, Mar. 2—19.

GACETA DEL GOBIERNO. est. 1838.
CU—B
1838   Mar. 17.

EL HISPANO-AMERICANO
CONSTITUCIONAL. 3w. est. 1820.
TxU
1820   June 13, 17, 20—July 1.

EL HOMBRE LIBRE CONTRA TODAS
LAS FARSAS.
See *Diario matutino*.

EL HONOR NACIONAL. est. 1881.
Note: Ceased publication 1901.
NHi
1881   Feb. 2.

IGUALDAD. w.
MWA
1887   Feb. 17, Mar. 17—24.

ILUSTRACION YUCATECA. est. [1897].
LNT—MA
1897   May 9, June 27.

EL INDEPENDIENTE. sw. est. [1843].
CtY
1843   Jan. 20, 27—Feb. 7, 17,
Mar. 10—Apr. 11, 18—21, May
12—June 30, July 21.

INDICADOR. sw. est. Jan. 6, 1864.
MWA
1864   Jan. 6, 14—17.

LEALTAD YUCATECA. est. [1820].
TxU
1820   June 23.

LETRA DE CAMBIO. d. est. 1886.
Note: Ceased publication 1888.
MWA
1886   Nov. 17.
1887   Nov. 24, 25.

MENSAJERO DE LA INFANCIA. w. est.
Sept. 21, 1879.
MWA
1879   Sept. 21.

MERIDA FESTIVO. w. est. Apr. 13, 1902.
  LNT—MA
    1902   May 25, June 8, Aug. 3, Sept.
          21.

EL MERIDANO IMPARCIAL. sw. est.
  Feb. 1832.
  DLC
    1832   Apr. 24—May 15, 26—July 3.

MONITOR. w. est. Nov. 10, 1864.
  MWA
    1864   Nov. 10—Dec. 31.
    1865   Jan. 1—21.

MONITOR PENINSULAR. w. est. 1882.
  MWA
    1883   Apr. 1.
    1884   Aug. 31, Sept. 16.
    1885   Mar. 1.

EL MOSQUITO. d. est. 1917.
  LNT—MA
    1917   Nov. 3.

EL NOTICIOSO. 3w. est. Apr. 1830.
  DLC
    1830   Nov. 11—15, 19, 23—27.

LA NUEVA EPOCA; PERIODICO DEL
  GOBIERNO DE YUCATAN. sw., 3w.
  CU—B
    Micro (P)
    1863   Sept. 11.
  MWA
    1863   July 22—27, Sept. 11, Oct.
          12—Nov. 20.
    1864   [Jan. 29—Sept. 30].

PAZ PENINSULAR. w. est. 1877.
  MWA
    1877   Feb. 18.

LA PENINSULA. d. est. Sept. 15, 1917.
  LNT—MA
    1917   Sept. 15, 18, 26, 27.

EL PENINSULAR. d. est. 1905.
  LNT—MA
    1906   Feb. 5, 7—9.

EL PENINSULAR. d. est. [Nov. 26, 1917].
  LNT—MA
    1917   Nov. 28, Dec. 4, 9.

PENSAMIENTO. w. est. 1874.
  MWA
    1876   Oct. 15, Nov. 26.
    1877   Feb. 25, Apr. 29, [July 8—
          Aug. 19.]
    1878   May 5.
    1884   Sept. 7—Nov. 9, 23—Dec. 3.

PERIODICO OFICIAL. 3w. est. Oct. 3,
  1864.
  CU—B
    Micro (P)
    1865   Mar. 6—8, 22.
  MWA
    1864   Oct. 3—24, 31—Nov. 11.
    1865   Jan. 6—20, Feb. 6—Mar. 1,
          6—22, June 23.
  NHi
    1865   Jan. 16—Feb. 10, 20—Mar. 17,
          27—Apr. 7, Aug. 14—18, Oct.
          2—Nov. 1, 6—10, 15—Dec. 29.
    1866   Jan. 3—26, May 7—14, 21—25.

PILDORA. sw. est. June 20, 1866.
  MWA
    1866   June 20—23.

PORFIRISTA. sw., w. est. Jan. 23, 1877.
  Note: Periodicity Jan. 23—Oct. 23,
  1877, semiweekly; after Oct. 24,
  1877, weekly.
  MWA
    1877   Jan. 23, Oct. 23, Nov. 29.
    1878   Jan. 10, Apr. 18, May 9, 30,
          June 13.

PORVENIR. w. est. 1883.
  MWA
    1883   Dec. 12.
    1885   Sept. 15—30.

PUEBLO YUCATECO. w.
  MWA
    1881   Nov. 19.

EL RADICAL. w. est. Sept. 1, 1917.
  LNT—MA
    1917   Sept. 29—Oct. 20.

LA RAZA. d. est. Apr. 16, 1916.
  LNT—MA
    1916   Apr. 16.

LA RAZON ABSOLUTAMENTE
INDEPENDIENTE. w.
  TxU
    1919   July 10, 31, Sept. 6.

RAZON CATOLICA. sw. est. 1891.
  MWA
    1891   June 25.

LA RAZON DEL PUEBLO; PERIODICO
OFICIAL DEL ESTADO LIBRE Y
SOBERANO DE YUCATAN. 3w.
    Note: Published solely under sub-
    title, Jan. 29, 1877—Mar. 1, 1878.
  CU—B
    Micro (P)
    1874   Jan. 14—21, 26.
    1890   July 4.
    1891   Jan. 5, July 3, Sept. 18.
    1892   Jan. 4.
  LNT—MA
    1897   Sept. 1—Nov. 29.
  MWA
    1876   Dec. 28.
    1877—1881   Jan. 1—Dec. 31.
    1882   Jan. 1—Feb. 1.
    1886   Feb. 12, May 17, 21, July 7—
            12.
    1887   Aug. 17.
    1889   Mar. 6, Sept. 16—18.
    1891   Feb. 2.

LA RAZON DEL PUEBLO, PERIODICO
OFICIAL DEL ESTADO DE YUCA-
TAN.
  TxU
    1880   June 23—July 5, Aug. 18—30,
            Sept. 1, 8—13, Oct. 1—Nov. 15,
            24—Dec. 13, 17—31.
    1881   Jan. 1—10, 19—Mar. 26, Apr.
            13—25, May 4—July 4, 8—
            Aug. 1.

EL REGENERADOR. est. 1850.
    Note: Official organ succeeded by
    Las Garantías sociales.
  CU—B
    Micro (P)
    1855   July 6.

REGULADOR YUCATECO. 3w. est.
  [1831].
  DLC
    1832   Apr. 24—May 18, 20—June 1,
            3—11, 13—28.

REORGANIZACION LIBERAL. 3w. est.
  Apr. 14, 1877.
  MWA
    1877   Apr. 14.

REPUBLICO. w.
  MWA
    1885   Sept. 18—Oct. 3.

REVISTA DE MERIDA. sw., d., 3w., d.
  est. Jan. 1, 1869.
  CLCM
    1902   Apr. 10, 11.
    1908   Dec. 31.
  LNT—MA
    1894   Jan. 7, May 24, Nov. 6, 29.
    1898   Nov. 9, Dec. 10.
    1899   Apr. 30, Sept. 2.
    1900   July 26.
    1901   July 10.
  MWA
    1877   [Jan. 21—Dec. 31].
    1878—1879   [Jan. 1—Dec. 25].
    1880   Jan. 15—29, Feb. 5—12, Oct.
            13.
    1881   May 6—18.
    1882   Jan. 20, Apr. 21, June 27, 29,
            July 2, 5, Oct. 19.
    1883   Jan. 1—June 9, [July 6—Dec.
            29].
    1884—1885   Jan. 1—Dec. 31.
    1886   Jan. 1—Oct. 3, Dec. 5.
    1887   [Jan. 1—Feb. 13], Aug. 25,
            Dec. 15, 29—31.
    1888   Jan. 1, 8—10, 15—19, Feb. 19,
            May 13, Nov. 6.
    1889   Jan. 6, Nov. 3.

1894   Jan. 25.
1911   Apr. 23.
TxU
1880   Sept. 16, Dec. 22.
1881   July 3.

LA REVISTA DE YUCATAN. d. est.
1912.
LNT—MA
1913   June 22.
1918   [Oct. 1—Nov. 23].
1919   Jan. 12, Apr. 21, Aug. 28.
MH
1921—1923 Jan. 1—Dec. 31.
TxU
1912   Aug. 19.
1924   Nov. 22—Dec. 8, 14—19, 21,
        25—29.
1925   Jan. 1—5, 7—11, 14—16, 18—
        23, 25, 26, 29—Feb. 18, 24—
        Mar. 7, 10—21, 24—Apr. 27,
        29—Oct. 23, 25—Dec. 5, 8—
        31.
1926   Jan. 1—Feb. 18, 21—Apr. 8,
        12—May 1, 5—29, 31, June
        2—15, 18—29.

LA REVISTA PENINSULAR. d.
LNT—MA
1913   Apr. 29.

SACAMANCHAS. sw. est. Sept. 1911.
LNT—MA
1911   Oct. 1.

SEMANARIO YUCATECO. w. est. 1878.
Note: Ceased publication 1882.
MWA
1878   May 4.
1879   Jan. 4, 18, Feb. 1, Dec. 13.
1880   May 22.
1882   Jan. 21, June 24, Nov. 18,
        Dec. 2.

SIGLO XIX; PERIODICO DEL
GOBIERNO DEL ESTADO LIBRE
Y SOBERANO DE YUCATAN.
MWA
1841   May 25.

LA SOMBRA DE CEPEDA. w. est. 1885.
Note: Ceased publication 1893.

MWA
1887   Mar. 20, Aug. 14, Sept. 4.
1888   Feb. 19, Sept. 16.

LOS SUCESOS. d. est. [1916].
LNHT
1917   Oct. 12—Nov. 3.

SUEÑO Y LA SOLTURA. est. [Sept. 25,
1887].
MWA
1887   Sept. 25.

TUNCURUCHU. sw. est. 1863.
MWA
1863   Nov. 29—Dec. 10, 20.

TUXTEPEC. w. est. Jan. 20, 1877.
MWA
1877   Jan. 20, Feb. 11.

UNION YUCATECA; PERIODICO
OFICIAL DEL ESTADO LIBRE Y
SOBERANO DE YUCATAN. 3w. est.
Feb. 6, 1882.
MWA
1882   Feb. 6—June 30.
1883   Apr. 4, Dec. 12—15.

LA VOZ DE LA REVOLUCION. d. est.
Mar. 25, 1915.
LNT—MA
1915   Apr. 4—Sept. 16, Oct. 1—
        Dec. 31.
1916   Jan. 1—9.

LA VOZ DEL ESTADO. w. est. [1916].
LNHT
1917   Sept. 30, Oct. 27, Nov. 3.

XTACAY. d. est. 1917.
LNT—MA
1917   July 28, Aug. 4, 6, 8—10.

EL YUCATECO; O, EL AMIGO DEL
PUEBLO. 3w. est. 1821.
Note: Continuous pagination.
Ceased publication 1830.
DLC
1828   Jan. 1—Dec. 30.

Mexicali

CRONOS. w. est. June 26, 1941.
DLC
  1941   July 10, Aug. 8, 15 – 29, Oct.
          10, Dec. 5.

PERIODICO OFICIAL. est. Apr. 2, 1888.
CU – B
  1888   Apr. 2 – Dec. 22.

EL REGIONAL. w. est. Feb. 23, 1923.
CU
  1943   May 8, 22 – 29, June 12 – 26,
          July 10, 24 – Dec. 25.
  1944   Jan. 1 – Mar. 18, Apr. 1 – May
          13, 27 – Dec. 30.
  1945   Jan. 6 – Sept. 29, Oct. 13 –
          Dec. 29.
  1946   Jan. 5 – Mar. 16, 30 – Apr. 20,
          May 11 – Aug. 24, Sept. 7 –
          14, 28 – Oct. 19, Nov. 2 – 30,
          Dec. 14 – 28.
  1947   Jan. 11 – 25, Feb. 8 – 22, Mar.
          8 – Sept. 27, Oct. 11 – Nov. 1,
          15 – Dec. 27.
  1948   Jan. 3 – Apr. 3, 17 – Dec. 25.
  1949   Jan. 1 – Dec. 31.
  1950   Jan. 7 – 21, Feb. 4 – Sept. 9,
          23 – Oct. 28, Nov. 11 – 25,
          Dec. 16 – 23.
DLC
  1941   May 17, Dec. 20.

EL TIEMPO. w. est. Nov. 11, 1933.
CU
  1944   Jan. 16, Mar. 12, Apr. 16.
DLC
  1941   Dec. 14.
  1942   May 31.

Mexico City

A.B.C. sw., d. est. 1917.
  Note: Ceased publication Sept. 14,
  1965.
CU
  1919   July 12.
DLC
  1919   Extraordinario: May 17.

TxU
  1917   Sept. 21, Nov. 3.
  1918   Feb. 16 – 23, Mar. 9, 30 – Apr.
          3, 10 – 13, June 19 – 26, July
          3 – 24, 31, Aug. 10 – Sept. 14,
          21 – Oct. 2, 9 – 12.

LA ABEJA. d. est. Oct. 1, 1844.
CU – B
  1844   Oct. 1 – Nov. 30.
DLC
  1844   Oct. 1 – 4, 6 – Nov. 30.

EL ABOGADO CRISTIANO. bw.
KHi
  1886   Dec. 1.

ACCION MUNDIAL. sw., w., d. est.
  Feb. 5, 1916.
  Note: Suspended publication Feb.
  9 – Apr. 11, 1916.
CU
  1916   Feb. 5 – May 20, June 3 –
          July 23.
          Extraordinario: May 31.
CtY
  1916   May 20 – June 10, July 1 – 23.
DLC
  1916   Feb. 5 – May 13, 15, 19, 22, 25,
          26, 30 – July 28.
MB
  1916   May 19, 22, June 16, 20, 21,
          26 – 30, July 3, 5, 8, 11, 12, 14,
          15, 17, 19, 21, 24, 28.
NN
  1916   May 19 – 22, 24 – 29, 31 – June
          8, 12 – July 3, 5 – 28.
TxU
  1916   May 4, 5, 11, 22, 24 – 26, June
          12, 17, 19, July 10.

ACCION. d. est. [1934].
DLC
  1941   Feb. 10, Apr. 7, 11, May 2, 5,
          7, 9, 12, 14, 16, 28.

LA ACTUALIDAD. d. est. June 1, 1911.
  Note: Ceased publication Sept. 1,
  1911.
TxU
  1911   June 1 – Sept. 1.

ACTUALIDADES. w.
  TxU
    1909   Mar. 26 — Apr. 19, 23 — 30,
            May 28.

LAS ACTUALIDADES. sw. est. 1912.
  TxU
    1912   Nov. 10.

ACUSACION. d. est. Nov. 22, 1917.
  DLC
    1917   Nov. 22 — Dec. 31.
            Extraordinario: Dec. 3, 12.
    1918   Jan. 2, 3.

LA AFICION. d. est. 1930.
  DLC
    1942   Apr. 15, July 22.

EL AGUILA. d. est. May 31, 1918.
  DLC
    1918   May 31 — June 15.

LA AGUILA MEXICANA. d., 3w. est.
  Apr. 15, 1823.
      Note: Title *La Águila mejicana*,
      Apr. 13 — Sept. 28, 1823; *La Águila
      mexicana*, Sept. 29, 1823 — Dec. 1,
      1828. Ceased publication Dec. 1,
      1828.
  CU — B
    Micro (P) & (N)
    1823   Apr. 15 — Dec. 31.
    1824 — 1826   Jan. 1 — Dec. 31.
  CtY
    1823   Nov. 25.
    1824   May 17, 18, Nov. 23, Dec. 2,
            6 — 12, 14, 20.
    1825   Jan. 2, 4, 6, 8, 9.
    1826   Mar. 16 — 22, 26 — May 17, 20 —
            31.
    1827   June 12.
    1828   Jan. 27, 28.
  DLC
    1823   Apr. 15 — May 3, 5 — 13, 15, 16,
            18 — Dec. 31.
    1824   Jan. 1 — Sept. 25, 27 — Oct. 19.
    1825   June 11 — Aug. 15, 17, 31,
            Sept. 25, 27, 28, Oct. 16, Nov.
            29.

    1826   Jan. 16 — 31, Feb. 16 — Mar.
            15, Nov. 9, 11 — 16, 18 — 21.
            Suplemento: Mar. 7.
  NN
    1827   Suplemento.
  LNT — MA
    1824   Apr. 11.
    1828   July 3.
  TxU
    1823   Apr. 15 — Dec. 31.
    1824   Jan. 1 — Oct, 2–24, 26 — 31, Nov.
            2, 5 — 7, 9 — Dec. 31.
    1825   Jan. 1 — Dec. 31.
    1826   Jan. 1 — Mar. 13, 15 — Apr. 15,
            May 1, 15 — June 1, 4 — Oct.
            4, 6 — 31.
    1827   Jan. 1 — Dec. 31.
    1828   Jan. 1 — Dec. 1.
  ViU
    Micro (P)
    1823   Apr. 15 — Dec. 31.
    1824 — 1826   Jan. 1 — Dec. 31.

AGUILA MEXICANA. d. est. Jan. 1,
  1843.
  CU — B
    Micro (P) & (N)
    1843   Jan. 1 — 30.

EL AGUILUCHO. d. est. June 17, 1918.
  DLC
    1918   June 17 — 30, Aug. 1 — 11, 13 —
            21, 23 — 31.

EL AHUIZOTE; SEMINARIO FEROZ. w.
  est. Feb. 5, 1874.
      Note: Suspended publication Oct.
      14 — Nov. 30, 1876; ceased publication
      Dec. 29, 1876. Succeeded by *El
      Hijo del ahuizote*.
  CU — B
    Micro (P)
    1874   Nov. 27.
    1875   Mar. 15.
  LNT — MA
    1874   [Feb. 5 — Dec. 25].
    1875   Jan. 1 — Dec. 31.
            Parte política: Mar. 15 —
            Aug. 30.

TxU
- 1874   Feb. 5, 20 — Dec. 31.
- 1875   Jan. 1 — Dec. 31.
- 1876   Jan. 1 — Dec. 29.

EL AHUIZOTE. w. est. 1911.
CU
- 1911   Dec. 2 — 23.
- 1912   Jan. 6 — Aug. 24, Sept. 7 — Dec. 28.
- 1913   Jan. 11 — 18.
- 1936   Feb. 26.
TxU
- 1911   July 22.

EL AHUIZOTE JACOBINO. w. est. Jan. 1, 1904.
Note: Published during suspension of *El Hijo del ahuizote*. Ceased publication Jan. 1, 1905.
CtY
- 1904   Jan. 1 — Dec. 25.
- 1905   Jan. 1.
LNT — MA
- 1904   Jan. 1 — Mar. 6.
TxU
- 1904   Jan. 24 — Mar. 6, 20 — Apr. 21.

EL AHUIZOTITO. w. est. Apr. 1906.
TxU
- 1906   Apr. 19, 26.
- 1908   Dec. 13.

EL ALACRAN. est. July 1911.
TxU
- 1911   Dec. 31.

ALBA OBRERA.
DLC
- 1918   Mar. 4.

ALEMANIA LIBRE. bw.
TxU
- 1942   Sept. 1.

LA ALIANZA LIBERAL.
TxU
- 1880   Nov. 1.

AMENIDADES. w. irr. est. Mar. 26, 1916.
Note: Illustrated edition for the Sunday number of *El Demócrata*.
DLC
- 1916   Mar. 26, Apr. 9, Aug. 27, Sept. 3, 11, 16.
TxU
- 1916   Mar. 26 — Sept. 3, 16.

AMERICA LATINA. d. est. [1941].
LNT — MA
- 1941   Aug. 1 — Sept. 30.
TxU
- 1941   Nov. 1 — Dec. 31.

THE AMERICAN STAR.
See *Daily American Star*.

AMERICAN STAR--NO. 2. sw., 3w. est. June 1847.
Note: In English.
MWA
- 1847   June 20, 27, July 4.

EL AMIGO DE LA JUVENTUD. irr. est. Jan. 1835.
Note: Ceased publication June 1835.
CtY
- 1835   Jan. 1 — 31, Feb. 1 — 28, June 1 — 30.

EL AMIGO DE LA PATRIA. w. est. Nov. 6, 1812.
Note: Ceased publication Apr. 30, 1813.
CtY
- 1812   Nov. 6, Dec. 18 — 31.
- 1813   Jan. 8, Apr. 30.
TxU
- 1912   Nov. 6 — Dec. 31.
- 1913   Jan. 1 — Apr. 30.

EL AMIGO DE LA VERDAD. w.
LNT — MA
- 1919   Aug. 23 — 30.

EL AMIGO DEL PUEBLO. 3w. est. June 24, 1845.
Note: Suspended publication Jan. 13, 1846.
CU — B
- 1845   June 24 — Dec. 23.
- 1846   Jan. 3 — 13.

CtY
  1845   Sept. 13, Oct. 28, Nov. 27.
DLC
  1845   June 24 – July 30, Aug. 3 – 6,
          8 – Sept. 17, Oct. 8 – 17, 31 –
          Nov. 24, 30 – Dec. 12, 19 – 23.

EL AMIGO DEL PUEBLO. 3w., w. est.
  Feb. 14, 1861.
  CU – B
    1861   Feb. 14 – Mar. 2, 4 – June 23.

EL AMIGO DEL PUEBLO; PERIODICO
  MEXICANA. w. est. Aug. 1, 1827.
    Note: Ceased publication [Sept. 3],
    1828.
  CU – B
    1827   [Aug. 1 – Dec. 31].
    1828   Jan. 1 – Aug. 6.
  CtY
    1827   Aug. 1 – Oct. 31, Nov. 7 –
            Dec. 26.
    1828   Jan. 2 – Mar. 26, Apr. 2 – June
            25, July 2 – Sept. 3.

EL AMIGO DEL PUEBLO; ORGANO
  OFICIAL DEL CLUB "LIBERTADOR
  FRANCISCO I. MADERO." irr. est.
  1911.
  TxU
    1911   July 5 – Oct. 13.

EL AMIGO DEL PUEBLO; SEMANARIO
  POLITICO Y DE INFORMACION
  DE LA LIGA DE AGRICULTORES
  DEL ESTADO DE TLAXCALA. w.
  est. 1912.
  TxU
    1912   May 23.

LOS AMIGOS DEL PUEBLO. sw. est.
  1831.
  CtY
    1832   July 4 – 7.
  DLC
    1832   Feb. 4 – Apr. 23, 25 – Sept. 1.

ANAHUAC. w. est. Jan. 1, 1910.
  TxU
    1910   Jan. 1 – Feb. 28, Mar. 17 –
            Apr. 21.

ANGLO AMERICAN.
  Note: In English.
  NN
    1893   Oct. 8.

EL ANTEOJO. 3w. est. Aug. 1, 1835.
  Note: Ceased publication Jan. 31,
  1836.
  CU – B
    Micro (P) & (N)
    1835   Aug. 1 – Dec. 30.
    1836   Jan. 1 – 31.
  DLC
    1835   Prospecto: July 19.
            Aug. 1 – Nov. 4.
            Suplemento: Aug. 18.
  MWA
    1835   Aug. 16 – 21, 28, Sept. 2 – 4,
            11.
  TxU
    1835   Sept. 11.

EL ANTEOJO DEL PACIFICO. bw. est.
  1871.
  LNT – MA
    1871   July 27.

ANTI-REELECCIONISTA. w., d. est.
  June 6, 1909.
    Note: Periodicity June 6 – Aug. 11,
    1909, weekly; after Aug. 12, 1909,
    daily.
  TxU
    1909   June 6 – July 18, Aug. 1 – Sept.
            28.

LA ANTORCHA. d. est. Apr. 1, 1833.
  Note: Ceased publication June 30,
  1833.
  CU – B
    Micro (P) & (N)
    1833   Apr. 1 – June 30.
  CtY
    1833   Apr. 1 – June 19, 21, 23, 25 –
            28, 30.
  DLC
    1833   Apr. 1 – June 30.
            Suplemento: Apr. 4, 21, 24,
            May 10, 25, June 19.

MWA
1833   Apr. 24 – 30, June 1 – 9,
        11 – 28.
ANUNCIADOR MEXICANO. sw. est.
Nov. 22, 1877.
MWA
1877   Nov. 22.
LA ARANA. w. est. July 31, 1904.
TxU
1904   July 31 – Sept. 8.
EL ARTESANO.
DLC
1913   Alcance: Feb. 16.
        Extraordinario: Feb. 17, 18.
TxU
1913   Extraordinario: Feb. 18.
ASISTENCIA SOCIAL. bw.
LNT – MA
1937   Sept. 15 – Dec. 15.
1938   Jan. 1 – Mar. 15, Apr. 15,
        May 15, Nov. 4.
1939   Mar. 15.
ASUNTOS VARIOS SOBRE CIENCIAS,
Y ARTES. w. est. Oct. 26, 1772.
MWA
1772   Oct. 26 – Dec. 28.
EL ATENEO MEXICANO.
CU – B
Micro (P)
1844 – 1845   Jan. 1 – Dec. 31.
EL ATLETA. d. est. Dec. 20, 1829.
Note: Ceased publication May 9,
1830.
CtY
1829   Dec. 21 – 31.
1830   Jan. 1 – Mar. 13, 15 – May 9.
TxU
Micro (P)
1829   Dec. 20 – 31.
1830   Jan. 1 – May 9.
LA AURORA; PERIODICO POLITICO
LITERARIO, DE BUEN HUMOR Y
CON ESTAMPAS. 3w. est. 1861.
NN
1861   Oct. 10.

LA AURORA. bw.
TxU
1908   Jan. 1.
AURORA DEMOCRATICA. w. est.
July 10, 1910.
TxU
1910   July 10 – 18.
AVANTE. w. est. Jan. 8, 1910.
TxU
1910   Jan. 8.
BALUARTE. w., irr. est. 1937.
CU
1937   Sept. 4 – Oct. 2, 16, 30 –
        Dec. 18.
1938   Jan. 1 – Dec. 4.
1939   Apr. 29 – July 22.
LA BANDERA DEL PUEBLO. 3w. est.
Sept. 23, 1846.
CU – B
Micro (N)
1846   Sept. 23 – 30.
BANDERA NEGRA; PERIODICO DE
SENSACION POLITICO-
INDUSTRIAL.
TxU
1878   Mar. 28.
BANDERA NEGRA. w.
TxU
1902   Sept. 26, Nov. 2, 19.
EL BASILICO. bw. est. June 19, 1834.
TxU
1834   June 19 – July 10.
LA BATALLA.
CSt
1937   Apr. 9.
EL BIOGRAFO. w. est. Aug. 31, 1886.
CU – B
Micro (P)
1886   Aug. 31.

LA BLUSA. d. est. Nov. 13, 1855.
  Note: Ceased publication Dec. 10,
  1855.
  CU—B
  Micro (N)
  1855   Nov. 13—Dec. 10.

LA BOHEMIA.
  TxU
  1908   Mar. 15.

EL BOLETIN; PUBLICADO POR LA
COMPAÑIA EDITORA MEXICANA.
  DLC
  1916   Aug. 1.
          Extraordinario: Aug. 1.

BOLETIN DE INFORMACION LOCAL
Y EXTRANJERA. d. est. Mar. 1, 1915.
  DLC
  1915   Mar. 2, 3.

BOLETIN DE LA CIUDADELA. irr.
est. Sept. 2, 1841.
  Note: Ceased publication Oct. 6,
  1841.
  CtY
  1841   [Sept. 3—Oct. 6].
  TxU
  1841   Sept. 3—Oct. 6.

BOLETIN DE LA DEMOCRACIA. d. est.
[Feb.] 1847.
  CtY
  1847   Nos. 1—50.
  NN
  1847   Feb. 28, Apr. 17.

BOLETIN DE LA GUERRA. w. est. 1838.
  MWA
  1838   Dec. 8.
  TxU
  1838   Dec. 1—8.

BOLETIN DE LA GUERRA. d. est. Aug.
5, 1914.
  Note: Suspended Oct. 26—Nov. 9,
  1914, Jan. 8—Feb. 16, 1916.
  TxU
  1914   Aug. 5—Dec. 31.
  1915   Jan. 1—Apr. 23, May 1—

        Sept. 15, 17—Oct. 29, Nov.
        1—Dec. 31.
  1916   Jan. 1—Mar. 30, Apr. 1—Sept.
          6, 8—Oct. 5, 7—Dec. 31.
  1917   Jan. 1—Oct. 2, 4—Nov. 7, 9—
          Dec. 31.
  1918   Jan. 1—Dec. 31.
  1919   Jan. 1—20.

BOLETIN DE LA HONRADEZ. est.
[1859].
  CLCM
  1859   Aug. 1.

EL BOLETIN DE LA SITUACION
POLITICA. d. est. Jan. 16, 1912.
  TxU
  1912   Jan. 16.

BOLETIN DE NOTICIAS. d. est. Aug.
30, 1841.
  Note: Ceased publication Sept. 5,
  1841.
  CtY
  1841   Aug. 30—Sept. 5.
  NN
  1841   Sept. 4, 5.
  TxU
  1841   Aug. 30, Sept. 1, 2, 4.

BOLETIN DE NOTICIAS; UNION,
JUSTICIA Y LEYES. d., 3w. est.
Dec. 19, 1844.
  Note: Ceased publication Apr. 11,
  1845.
  CU—B
  1844   Dec. 19—31.
  1845   Jan. 1—Apr. 11.
  CtY
  1844—1845 Nos. 1—50, 52—68.
  DLC
  1844   Dec. 19.
  1845   Jan. 26—28, 30—Feb. 4, 6—
          Apr. 11.
  TxU
  1844   Dec. 19—31.
  1845   Jan. 1—Apr. 11.

BOLETIN DE NOTICIAS. d. est. Aug. 4, 1846.
  CtY
    1846   Aug. 4 – 6.
BOLETIN DE NOTICIAS. d. est. Apr. 24, 1847.
    Note: Ceased publication [May] 1847.
  CtY
    1847   Apr. 24 – May 1, 3 – 7, 9 – 15.
  DLC
    1847   Apr. 24 – May 15.
BOLETIN DE NOTICIAS. d. est. Dec. 25, 1860.
  CU – B
    1860   Dec. 25 – 31.
    1861   Jan. 1 – Apr. 30.
  CtY
    1860   Dec. 25 – 31.
    1861   Jan. 1 – Mar. 2.
BOLETIN DE NOTICIAS DEL EJER-CITO REGENERADOR. est. Jan. 1, 1858.
  TxU
    1858   Jan. 1 – 19.
BOLETIN DE NOTICIAS DEL SUP-REMO GOBIERNO. d. est. Oct. 16, 1858.
    Note: Published during the suspension of *Diario oficial del supremo gobierno*. Ceased publication Oct. 20, 1858.
  CtY
    1858   Oct. 16 – 20.
            Suplemento: Oct. 20.
BOLETIN DE UNIDAD. w. est. Apr. 18, 1940.
  DLC
    1940   Apr. 18 – Nov. 7.
BOLETIN DEL CLUB POTOSINO PONCIANO ARRIAGA.
    See *El Independiente; semanario político*.
BOLETIN DEL GOBIERNO. d. est. July 16, 1840.
    Note: Published during the suspension of *Diario del gobierno de la*

República Mexicana. Ceased publication July 27, 1840.
  CtY
    1840   July 19 – 27.
BOLETIN DEL PARTIDO LIBERAL CONSTITUCIONALISTA. irr. est. Nov. 4, 1916.
  DLC
    1916   Nov. 4, 7.
BOLETIN DEL PRIMER PARTIDO LIBERAL CONSTITUCIONALISTA. irr. est. [1917].
  DLC
    1917   Jan. 24, Feb. 12, Mar. 10.
  TxU
    1917   Mar. 8.
BOLETIN FEDERAL. irr. est. Dec. 1, 1838.
  NN
    1838   Dec. 1 – 26.
    1839   Jan. 8 – Feb. 5.
BOLETIN FINANCIERO Y MINERO DE MEXICO. d.
  TxU
    1919   June 10 – 13, 16 – Aug. 6, 8 – Oct. 11, 14 – Nov. 6, 8 – Dec. 31.
    1920   Jan. 1 – Apr. 12, 14, 15, 17 – 19, 21, 22, 24 – June 30, July 2 – Oct. 11, 14 – 30, Nov. 4 – Dec. 20, 22 – 31.
    1921   Jan. 1 – 4, 7 – Dec. 31.
    1922   Jan. 1 – 5, 9 – Apr. 4, 6 – Aug. 6, 8 – 26, 28 – Sept. 2, 4 – Oct. 26, 28 – Nov. 25, 29 – Dec. 31.
    1923   Jan. 1 – June 13, 15 – 28, 31 – Dec. 31.
    1924   Jan. 1 – May 2, 6 – June 7, 10 – Dec. 27, 30, 31.
    1925   Jan. 1 – Mar. 10, 12, 13, 16 – May 16, 20, 22 – Dec. 31.
    1926   Jan. 1 – Dec. 31.
    1927   Jan. 1 – Feb. 2, 7 – Mar. 25, 28 – Apr. 19, 23, 26 – May 3, 6, 7, 11 – July 4, 6 – Sept. 14, 16 – Dec. 30.

1928   Jan. 1 – 31.
1929   Jan. 1 – Aug. 20, 22 – Sept. 4,
         6 – Dec. 31.
1930   Jan. 1 – Mar. 24, 26 – June 12,
         14 – Dec. 4, 6 – 31.
1931   Jan. 1 – Nov. 25, 27 – Dec. 31.
1932   Jan. 1 – June 30, July 5 – Aug.
         8, Oct. 3 – Dec. 31.
1933   Jan. 1 – Dec. 31.
1934   Jan. 1 – Dec. 11, 14 – 31.
1935   Jan. 1 – Dec. 31.
1936   Jan. 1 – July 15, 17 – Dec. 30.
1937   Jan. 4 – 6, 8 – Dec. 31.
1938 – 1943   Jan. 1 – Dec. 31.
1944   Jan. 1 – Aug. 20, 22 – Nov. 17,
         21 – Dec. 31.
1945   Jan. 1 – 8, 10 – Apr. 6, 9 – 13,
         16 – May 14, 16 – 18, 21 – Dec.
         31.
1946   Jan. 1 – 28, 30 – Feb. 13, 15 –
         Mar. 28, 30 – Apr. 2, 5 – 30,
         May 2 – 18, 20 – June 20, 24 –
         Dec. 31.
1947   Jan. 3 – 10, 12 – 24, 27 – 31,
         Feb. 3 – 7, 9 – 14, 17 – 21, 24 –
         28, Mar. 3, 4, 17 – 20, 22, 26 –
         28, 31 – Dec. 31.
1948 – 1952   Jan. 1 – Dec. 31.

BOLETIN INTERNACIONAL. sw. est.
   1937.
   DLC
      1937   Sept. 24.

BOLETIN MADERISTA.
   TxU
      1914   May 25.

EL BOLETIN OFICIAL. d., irr. est. 1829.
   Note: Ceased publication Nov. 19,
   1829.
   CU – B
      1829   n.d. (Aug.) – Nov. 19.
   CtY
      1829   [Aug. 16], 17, 23 – Sept. 16,
               18 – Nov. 3.
   DLC
      1829   Aug. 26 – 29, n.d. (No. 18) –
               Sept. 11, 21, Oct. 2.

BOLETIN OFICIAL. est. [Nov. 27], 1838.
   Note: Ceased publication Dec. 18,
   1838.
   CtY
      1838   n.d. [Nov. 27, Dec. 1, 18].

BOLETIN OFICIAL. d. est. Aug. 31,
   1841.
      Note: Published during interruption
      of publication of *Diario del gobierno
      de la República Mexicana.* Ceased
      publication Oct. 8, 1841.
   CtY
      1841   Aug. 31 – Oct. 3.
   DLC
      1841   Aug. 31 – Sept. 10.

BOLETIN OFICIAL. est. 1844.
   CU – B
      Micro (P)
      1845   Dec. 27.
   DLC
      1844   Dec. 13.

BOLETIN OFICIAL. d. est. Mar. 1, 1847.
      Note: Ceased publication Mar. 23,
      1847.
   CtY
      1847   Mar. 1 – 23.

BOLETIN OFICIAL. d. est. Dec. 22,
   1858.
      Note: Published during the suspen-
      sion of *Diario oficial del supremo
      gobierno.* Ceased publication Jan. 23,
      1859.
   CtY
      1858   Dec. 25 – 31.
      1859   Jan. 1 – 22.

EL BOLETIN OFICIAL.
      See *El Boletín oficial del supremo
      gobierno.*

BOLETIN OFICIAL. d. est. Mar. 20,
   1859.
      Note: Published during the suspen-
      sion of *Diario del supremo gobierno.*
      Ceased publication Apr. 2, 1859.

CtY
  1859   Mar. 20 – Apr. 2.

BOLETIN OFICIAL DE LA COMPAÑA.
  est. May 1, 1867.
  CtY
    1867   May 1 – June 18.

BOLETIN OFICIAL DEL EJERCITO. d.
  est. Nov. 18, 1860.
    Note: Succeeded *Diario oficial del
    supremo gobierno.*
  CU – B
  Micro (P)
    1860   Nov. 18 – Dec. 22.

EL BOLETIN OFICIAL DEL SUPREMO
  GOBIERNO. irr. est. Oct. 16, 1852.
    Note: Title *El Boletín oficial* Oct.
    16 – 27, 1852; *El Boletín oficial del
    supremo gobierno*, Oct. 27, 1852 –
    Jan. 1, 1853. Succeeded *El Con-
    stitucional; periódico oficial del
    gobierno de los Estados-Unidos
    Mexicanos*; succeeded by a publica-
    tion of the same title. Ceased pub-
    lication Jan. 1, 1853.
  CtY
    1852   Oct. 16 – Dec. 29.
    1853   Jan. 1.

BOLETIN OFICIAL DEL SUPREMO
  GOBIERNO. sw., irr. est. Jan. 20,
  1853.
    Note: Succeeded a publication of the
    same title. Ceased publication June 1,
    1853.
  CU – B
    1853   Feb. 5.
  CtY
    1853   Jan. 20 – June 1.

BOLETIN OFICIAL DEL SUPREMO
  GOBIERNO. irr. est. Jan. 22, 1856.
    Note: Succeeded *Diario del gobierno
    de la República Mexicana*; succeeded
    by *Diario oficial del supremo gob-
    ierno de la República Mexicana.*
    Ceased publication May 17, 1856.
  CtY
    1856   Jan. 22, 23, 31 – Apr. 23, May 5.

BOLETIN PETROLERO MEXICANO. d.
  TxU
    1916   Feb. 29.

BOLETIN REPUBLICANO. d. est. June
  21, 1867.
  CU – B
    1867   June 21 – Sept. 4.
  CtY
    1867   June 23 – 30, July 2 – Dec. 31.
    1868   Jan. 1 – May 2.

BOLETIN Y REVISTA. sw. est. Feb. 18,
  1842.
  CU – B
  Micro (P) & (N)
    1842   Feb. 18 – Mar. 12.

LA BRUJA. sw. est. Sept. 1, 1841.
    Note: Ceased publication Apr. 23,
    1842.
  CtY
    1841   Sept. 1 – Dec. 29.
    1842   Jan. 1 – Apr. 23.

EL BUEN SENTIDO. sw. est. [1841].
  DLC
    1842   Jan. 29 – May 5.
  MWA
    1842   Mar. 2, 19 – 26, Apr. 2 – 30.

EL BUSCAPIE. sw. est. Feb. 9, 1865.
  NN
    1865   Feb. 9 – 12.

EL CABEZON. w. est. 1917.
  TxU
    1917   Sept. 9.

CABLE. irr. est. May 1914.
  DLC
    1914   Extraordinario: May 4 – 9.
  TxU
    1914   Extraordinario: May 1, 8.

EL CALAVERA. sw. est. [1846].
  NHi
    1847   Jan. 5 – 8, 29, Feb. 16, Apr. 6,
           16 – 20.
  NN
    1847   Feb. 26, Apr. 13.

CALAVERITAS Y CALAVEROTAS. est.
Nov. 1, 1917.
  TxU
    1917   Nov. 1.

LA CAMPAÑA. sw. est. Jan. 8, 1862.
  NN
    1862   Jan. 8 – 10, 17, 31.

LA CAMPAÑA ELECTORAL.
  TxU
    1910   Aug. 9.

EL CAMPO LIBRE. w.
  TxU
    1907   Dec. 8.

DON CANDIDO. w. est. 1880.
  TxU
    1880   May 6 – June 20.

EL CANGREJO. sw. est. Jan. 9, 1848.
  CU – B
    Micro (N)
    1848   Jan. 9 – June 21.
  MWA
    1848   Jan. 16 – June 17.

CANTACLARO. w.
  TxU
    1910   Feb. 3.

CARAS Y CARETAS. w. est. Aug. 16,
1914.
  TxU
    1914   Aug. 16.

LA CARTA FUNDAMENTAL. w. est.
1880.
  TxU
    1880   Mar. 28 – Apr. 4, May 24,
            June 3, July 9.

EL CASCABEL. w. est. 1917.
  TxU
    1917   Sept. 9.

LA CASERA. w. est. June 1, 1879.
  CtY
    1879   June 1 – Dec. 28.
    1880   Jan. 4 – May 2, 16 – July 4,
            18 – Oct. 31.
  LNT – MA
    1880   [July 4 – Oct. 10].

CATALUNYA. bw.
  CSt
    1940   Mar. 5 – Dec. 31.
    1949   Jan. 1 – Feb. 13.

EL CATOLICO. w. est. Aug. 30, 1845.
  CtY
    1845   Aug. 30 – Dec. 27.
    1846   Jan. 3 – Dec. 26.
    1847   Jan. 2 – Feb. 27.

CAUTERIO. d. est. May 1, 1917.
    Note: Suspended Sept. 27 – Oct. 10,
    1917.
  DLC
    1917   May 2, 4, 7 – 10, 12, 16 – 30,
            June 1 – 16, 19 – 21, 26 – July
            20, 23 – 26, 28, 30 – Sept. 26,
            Oct. 11 – Dec. 31.
            Extraordinario: May 14, 21,
            July 14, Sept. 28, Oct. 29,
            Nov. 5, 19, Dec. 14.
    1918   Jan. 2 – 31, Feb. 2 – Apr. 19,
            21 – 23, 26 – May 4.
  TxU
    1917   May 8, 25.

EL CENSOR. w.
  CU
    1941   Jan. 5 – Mar. 8.

EL CENTINELA. bw. est. Jan. 3, 1824.
  TxU
    1824   Jan. 3 – Apr. 28.

CENTINELA ESPAÑOL. sw. est. 1880.
  MWA
    1881   Apr. 14 – May 1.
  TxU
    1880   Sept. 11, Nov. 25 – 27.

CETEME. w.
  CU
    1957   Jan. 5 – 12, 26 – May 18, June
            8 – July 13, 27 – Dec. 21.
    1958 – 1960   Jan. 1 – Dec. 31.
    1961   Jan. 7 – Feb. 4, 18 – May 6,
            20 – Oct. 14, 28 – Dec. 2, 16 –
            23.
    1962   Jan. 6 – Mar. 24, Apr. 15 –
            Dec. 22.
    1963   Jan. 5 – Apr. 13.

EL CHAMIZAL. w. est. Aug. 11, 1912.
TxU
  1912   Aug. 11 – Sept. 8, 22 – Oct. 14,
          Nov. 17.

EL CHAMUQUITO. w. est. Apr. 20,
1911.
TxU
  1911   Apr. 20 – 27.

EL CHANGO. w. est. 1912.
TxU
  1912   Oct. 4.

EL CHANGO. w. est. 1917.
TxU
  1917   Sept. 11.

CHAPULTEPEC. d. est. June, 1914.
DLC
  1914   July 10, 13, 14, 16, 20, 22.
TxU
  1914   July 5 – 7, 10 – 12, 14, 15, 20 –
          24.

EL CHARRITO. w. est. Oct. 9, 1911.
TxU
  1911   Oct. 9 – Nov. 13, 27 – Dec. 9.

CHIAPAS. 3m. est. Jan. 31, 1923.
LNT – MA
  1923   Jan. 31 – Feb. 20.

EL CHICOTE. w. est. July 1917.
TxU
  1917   Sept. 10.

EL CHILE PIQUIN. w. est. Jan. 12, 1905.
TxU
  1905   Jan. 12 – Mar. 9, 30 – Apr. 13,
          May 18, June 22, July 13 – 20.

CHIN CHUN CHAN. w. est. 1904.
TxU
  1904   Aug. 28.

LA CHINACA. bw. est. Apr. 16, 1862.
TxU
  1862   Apr. 16 – Oct. 21.
  1863   Mar. 12 – May 8.

EL CHINACO. w. est. [1909].
LNT – MA
  1909   Aug. 7 – 14.

TxU
  1909   Aug. 7.

EL CHISMITO. d. est. Aug. 9, 1914.
TxU
  1914   Aug. 9.

CHURUBUSCO. d. est. May 1, 1914.
DLC
  1914   May 1 – July 18.
MWA
  1914   May 11 – July 18.
TxU
  1914   May 1, 5, 7 – 11, 13 – 21, 23 –
          June 20, 27, July 1 – 3, 16, 18.

EL CLAMOR PUBLICO. w.
TxU
  1884   May 26.

LOS CLAMORES DE LOS PUEBLOS
POR SU LEY Y LIBERTAD. est. 1829.
LNT – MA
  1829   Dec. 16.

EL CLARIN. w. est. Apr. 17, 1910.
TxU
  1910   Apr. 17 – 25.

CLARIN DEL PUEBLO. d. est. May 6,
1914.
DLC
  1914   May 6.

LA CLASE MEDIA. w. est. 1908.
TxU
  1908   Sept. 15.
  1909   Apr. 1.

EL CLUB "DEMOCRACIA." est. Mar. 15,
1892.
TxU
  1892   Mar. 15.

EL COLMILLO. sw. est. June 12, 1917.
DLC
  1917   June 12.
TxU
  1917   July 25.

EL COLMILLO PUBLICO.
LNHT
  1905   July 23.

LA COLONIA ESPAÑOLA. d.
TxU
1879   Jan. 9.

LA COLUMNA DE LA CONSTITUCION
FEDERAL DE LA REPUBLICA
MEXICANA. 3w. est. June 4, 1832.
Note: Ceased publication Nov. 30,
1833.
CU−B
Micro (P) & (N)
1832   June 4−Dec. 31.
1833   Jan. 2−30, Feb. 4−June 22,
29−Nov. 30.
CtY
1832   Dec. 31.
1833   Jan. 2, Sept. 25, Oct. 5, Nov.
13.
TxU
1833   Apr. 24.

EL COMBATE. sw., d. est. 1876.
MWA
1878   May 12−16.
TxU
1876   July 20.
1879   July 6.
1880   June 17−Sept. 5, 26.

EL COMBATE; PERIODICO POLITICO
LIBERAL. w. est. 1887.
Note: Ceased publication 1897.
CU−B
Micro (P)
1889   Sept. 8.
LNT−MA
1887   [Oct. 9−Dec. 11].
1888   [July 29−Dec. 16].
TxU
1887   May 29, Aug. 14.

EL COMBATE; HOJA PERIODICA DE
POLITICA. est. 1910.
TxU
1910   June 19.

EL COMBATE. w. est. 1912.
TxU
1912   Dec. 19−26.
1913   Jan. 9−26.

EL COMBATE. d. est. June 15, 1915.
DLC
1915   June 16−July 9.
Extraordinario: July 9.
TxU
1915   June 18.

COMBATE; SEMANARIO POLITICO.
w. est. Jan. 6, 1941.
Note: Ceased publication Aug. 18,
1941.
CSt
1941   Jan. 1−Aug. 11.
CU
1941   Jan. 6−Mar. 17, 31−Aug. 11.
NjP
1941   July 21.

EL COMERCIO. sw., w. est. Apr. 15,
1843.
CU−B
Micro (P) & (N)
1843   Apr. 15−Dec. 28.
1844   Jan. 6−July 31.

EL COMERCIO. w.
CU−B
Micro (P) & (N)
1852   Mar. 11−May 6, 20−June 24.

EL COMERCIO. bw.
TxU
1874   Nov. 21−26.

EL COMERCIO DE LOS TEATROS.
Note: Title *El Comercio en los
teatros* before 1879.
TxU
1878   July 6, Nov. 23.
1879   May 31−June 14, 28.

EL COMERCIO DEL GOLFO. w. est.
Oct. 18, 1880.
TxU
1880   Oct. 18−Dec. 31.
1881   Jan. 1−Feb. 8, 24−Mar. 24.

EL COMETA. bw. est. May 1, 1910.
LNT−MA
1910   May 1−Nov. 1.

LA COMUNA. sw. est. Oct. 26, 1914.
DLC
1914   Oct. 26.

EL CONCILIADOR. w. est. Nov. 30,
1850.
CU—B
Micro (P) & (N)
1850   Nov. 30—Dec. 29.
1851   Jan. 5—19.

EL CONSERVADOR. d. est. Aug. 16,
1859.
CU—B
1859   Aug. 16—Sept. 3.

LA CONSTITUCION; PERIODICO
POLITICO Y LITERARIO. sw. est.
[Feb.] 1880.
CtY
1880   July 9.
LNT—MA
1880   Aug. 10.
TxU
1880   Apr. 13, 30, May 18, June 4—
July 13.

LA CONSTITUCION; ORGANO DE LA
AGRUPACION LIBERAL "MEL-
CHOR OCAMPO." [w.]
TxU
1913   Oct. 16—25.

EL CONSTITUCIONAL. sw. est. Jan. 16,
1844.
CU—B
1844   Jan. 16—Apr. 23, 30—May 21.
DLC
1844   Jan. 16—Mar. 29.

EL CONSTITUCIONAL; PERIODICO
OFICIAL DEL GOBIERNO DE LOS
ESTADOS - UNIDOS MEXICANOS.
d. est. Sept. 16, 1851.
Note: Succeeded *Periódico oficial
del supremo gobierno de los Estados-
Unidos Mexicanos*; succeeded by *El
Archivo mexicano* and *Boletín
oficial*. Ceased publication Oct. 15,
1852.

CU—B
Micro (P)
1851   Sept. 16—Dec. 31.
1852   Jan. 1—Oct. 15.
MWA
1851   Sept. 16—Dec. 31.
1852   [Jan. 1—Aug. 30].

EL CONSTITUCIONAL; PERIODICO
POLITICO Y LITERARIO, DE
ARTES, INDUSTRIA, TEATROS,
ANUNCIOS, &. d. est. 1860.
CU—B
1867   Sept. 22, 23, 25, 26, 29, Oct. 6,
13, 20, 27, 31—Dec. 31.
1868   Jan. 1—June 30.
1874   Mar. 19—28, 31—June 30.
NN
1861   Mar. 22, Oct. 22.
Suplemento: Jan. 29.
Alcance: Aug. 14.
1863   Feb. 7.

EL CONSTITUCIONAL; PERIODICO
DE LOS MUNICIPIOS DE LA
REPUBLICA, INDEPENDIENTE Y
UNIVERSAL. d.
TxU
1875   May 21, 22.

EL CONSTITUCIONAL; ORGANO DEL
CENTRO ANTI-REELECCIONISTA
DE MEXICO. sw., d. est. 1910.
TxU
1910   Mar. 12—Apr. 23, 27—May 3,
10—15, 22, 30, June 7—July
2, 5—19, Aug. 2—6, 10, 11, 17,
30—Nov. 23.

EL CONSTITUCIONAL. w. est. July 31,
1911.
TxU
1911   July 31, Aug. 14.

EL CONSTITUCIONALISTA; PERIO-
DICO LIBERAL NACIONALISTA.
TxU
1914   Extraordinario: Aug. 2.

EL CONTINENTE AMERICANO. d. est.
1895.
LNT—MA
   1899   Dec. 16, 24.

EL CONTINENTE MEXICANO. d. est.
1895.
TxU
   1899   June 16—23, 25—27, 29, 30,
           July 2—4, 14—20, 22, 23, 26—
           Aug. 5, 10—12, 17—Sept. 6,
           8, 10, 15, 19, 20, 22—26, 28—
           Oct. 27, 31—Nov. 16, 19, 23—
           29, Dec. 1—7, 9—13, 19, 20,
           22—24.
   1900   Jan. 5, 9, 10, 12—14.

EL CONTRA-TIEMPO. sw. est. Mar. 10,
1846.
CU—B
   1846   Mar. 10—May 20.

LA CONVENCION. sw. est. Aug. 24,
1911.
TxU
   1911   Aug. 24, Sept. 21.

LA CONVENCION. d. est. Dec. 1, 1914.
   Note: Issue of Mar. 12, 1915 published in Cuernavaca. Suspended
   publication Jan. 27—Feb. 11, Mar.
   13—23, 28—Apr. 22, 1915.
DLC
   1914   Dec. 16—31.
   1915   Jan. 1—26, Mar. 24—27, Apr.
           26, 27, 30, May 6, 12—17, 19—
           21, 23, 25—27, 29—31, June 2,
           3, 6—13, 16—25, 27—July 9.
           Boletín: July 22, 23.
           Extraordinario: May 4, July 20,
           21. Suplemento: June 3.
TxU
   1914   Dec. 16—31.
   1915   Jan. 1—July 8.

LA CONVENCION NACIONAL. est.
1899.
TxU
   1899   Dec. 24.

LA CONVENCION RADICAL OBRERA.
w. est. 1887.
CU—B
   Micro (P)
   1889   Dec. 15.

EL CORALILLO. w. est. 1911.
TxU
   1911   Sept. 28.

EL CORREO. d. est. 1851.
CU—B
   Micro (P) & (N)
   1852   Feb. 1—Apr. 15.

EL CORREO. w. est. 1885.
TxU
   1885   Nov. 30.
   1886   Jan. 11.

EL CORREO ATLANTICO. sw. est.
May 2, 1835.
   Note: Suspended publication in
   Mexico City, June 24, 1835; re-
   established in New Orleans, Louis-
   iana, Feb. 29, 1836.
CU—B
   Micro (P) & (N)
   1835   Prospecto: Apr. 1.
           May 2—June 24.
MWA
   1835   Prospecto: Apr. 1.
           May 2—June 24.
TxU
   1835   May 2—June 24.

CORREO DE ESPAÑA. sw. est. Sept. 2,
1854.
CU—B
   1854   Sept. 2—Dec. 31.
   1855   Jan. 1—June 23.

CORREO DE LA FEDERACION
MEXICANA. d. est. Nov. 1, 1826.
CU—B
   1826   Nov. 1—Dec. 31.
   1827   Jan. 1—Dec. 31.
   1828   Jan. 1—Oct. 28.
   1829   Sept. 1—Dec. 31.

CtY
  1827 July 1 – Oct. 31.
  1828 June 2 – Oct. 28.
DLC
  1828 Sept. 1 – 19.
        Suplemento: Sept. 6.
  1829 May 1, 3, 7 – 14, 16, 18 – 21, 23,
        25 – 30, June 1, 3 – 15, 17, 19 –
        21, 25, July 2, 7, 11, Aug. 18,
        22 – 25, 28 – 30, Sept. 1, 3, 8 –
        19, 21, 24, 26 – 28, Oct. 2,
        7 – 9.
        Suplemento: May 23, June 14,
        17, Aug. 19, Sept. 11.
MBAt
  1826 Nov. 1 – Dec. 31.
  1827 Jan. 1 – Mar. 31.
MWA
  1829 Mar. 26.

EL CORREO DE LAS DOCE. d. est.
  Jan. 15, 1882.
    Note: In Spanish and English.
    Ceased publication July 31, 1888.
  CU – B
    Micro (P)
    1882 Aug. 31, Oct. 29.
    1883 Sept. 15.
    1885 Feb. 5, 22.
  DLC
    1882 July 22, 29.
  TxU
    1884 May 28.

EL CORREO DE LAS SEÑORAS. irr.
  IU
    1886 June 27.
    1887 June 12 – Dec. 31.
    1888 Jan. 1 – May 13.

EL CORREO DE LOS NIÑOS. w.
  IU
    1877 July 1 – 8, 22 – Aug. 5, 26,
          Sept. 9 – Oct. 28, Nov. 11 –
          25, Dec. 9 – 31.
    1878 Jan. 1 – Mar. 3, 19 – Aug. 11,
          25 – Dec. 8, 22 – 31.
    1879 Jan. 1 – Feb. 9, 23 – Dec. 31.
    1880 Jan. 1 – 18.

EL CORREO DE MEXICO; PERIODICO
REPUBLICANO E INDEPENDIENTE.
  d. est. Sept. 1, 1867.
    Note: Ceased publication Dec. 14,
    1867.
  CtY
    1867 Sept. 1 – Dec. 14.
  MoU
    Micro (N)
    1867 Sept. 12 – Oct. 4, 7 – Dec. 14.

CORREO DE MEXICO; SEMINARIO
POLITICO INDEPENDIENTE.
  w. est. Oct. 8, 1897.
  LNT – MA
    1897 [Oct. 22 – Dec. 31].
    1898 [Jan. 9 – Dec. 20].
    1899 [Jan. 8 – Dec. 31].
    1900 [Jan. 8 – Dec. 23].
    1901 [Jan. 16 – Aug. 10].
    1902 [May 9 – Sept. 22].

EL CORREO DE MEXICO. MEXICAN
COURIER. w. est. 1938.
    Note: In Spanish and English.
  LNHT
    1938 Apr. 16, 23, 30, May 7, 14, 21,
          June 1.
  NcD
    1938 Mar. 25, Apr. 2, 16 – May 14.

EL CORREO DEL COMERCIO. d. est.
  1871.
  LNT – MA
    1874 June 13.

EL CORREO DEL LUNES. w. est. Sept.
  15, 1879.
  CU – B
    Micro (P)
    1884 Jan. 7, Nov. 24, Dec. 8.
    1885 Jan. 12, Feb. 2 – 23,
          June 8 – 15.
  MWA
    1883 Aug. 6.
    1884 Dec. 29.
  TxU
    1879 Sept. 15 – Oct. 27, Nov. 24 –
          Dec. 22.

1880   Jan. 12, Apr. 12, 26, June 14.
1884   May 5, Oct. 13, Dec. 15.
1885   Mar. 16, June 1, July 1,
        13, Nov. 9.
1886   Jan. 18.

EL CORREO ESPAÑOL. d. est. Nov. 9,
1889.
    Note: Ceased publication 1915.
    DLC
    1914   Apr. 28.
            Extraordinario: Apr. 24, 25.
    1915   Extraordinario: Sept. 26,
            Oct. 3.
    TxU
    1890   Oct. 9.
    1914   Nov. 28, Dec. 4.
            Extraordinario: Apr. 25.

EL CORREO EVANGELICO.
    TxU
    n.d. (Vol. 10, No. 11).

EL CORREO GERMANICO. sw. est. Aug.
1, 1876.
    Note: Ceased publication Oct. 14,
    1876.
    MoU
    Micro (P)
    1876   Aug. 1 – Oct. 14.
    TxU
    1876   Aug. 1 – Oct. 14.

EL CORREO MERCANTIL. bw.
    TxU
    1880   Nov. 7 – 11.

EL CORREO NACIONAL. irr. est. Oct.
18, 1847.
    Note: Succeeded *Diario del gobierno
    de la República Mexicana*; suc-
    ceeded by *Periódico oficial del
    supremo gobierno de los Estados-
    Unidos Mexicanos*. Sometimes pub-
    lished in Queretaro.
    CU – B
    1847   Oct. 18 – Dec. 31.
    1848   Jan. 1 – Dec. 31.
    1849   Jan. 1 – Feb. 2.
    CtY
    1848   Tomo 1, No. 42.

DLC
    1847   Oct. 18 – Dec. 31.
    1848   Jan. 1 – Dec. 31.
    1849   Jan. 1 – Feb. 2.
NN
    1849   Jan. 2, 3.

CORREO SEMANARIO POLITICO Y
MERCANTIL DE MEXICO. w. est.
July 8, 1809.
    Note: Ceased publication Oct. 30,
    1811.
    CtY
    1809   July 8 – Dec. 26.
    1810   Jan. 6 – Dec. 26.
    1811   Jan. 2 – Oct. 30.
    ICN
    1810   Nov. 14.
    1811   Jan. 2 – 30, Feb. 13 – Mar. 20,
            Apr. 24 – May 8, 22 – Aug. 7,
            Sept. 4 – Oct. 30.

CORRESPONDANCE MEXICAINE.
    TxU
    1880   July 30.

EL CORRESPONSAL DEL EJERCITO.
sw. est. Feb. 13, 1847.
    CtY
    1847   Apr. 21 – May 5.
    DLC
    1847   Feb. 13 – 26, Apr. 4 – 20, May
            20 – June 4, 6 – 15, 17 – July 3.
    TxU
    1847   Apr. 21 – May 5.

IL CORRIERE D'ITALIA. w.
    Note: In Spanish and Italian.
    TxU
    1911   Nov. 8.
    1919   Mar. 22.

EL COSMOPOLITA. sw. est. Dec. 16,
1835.
    Note: Ceased publication July 8,
    1843.
    CtY
    1835   Dec. 16 – Dec. 30.
    1836   Jan. 2 – Mar. 16, 26 – Dec. 31.
    1837   Jan. 4 – Apr. 19, 26 – June 5,
            9 – July 12, Sept. 27, Oct. 2,

16 – 18, 23, 27 – Nov. 1, 8, 13,
17 – 20, 29 – Dec. 1, 6 – 30.
1838   Jan. 3 – Nov. 7, 14 – Dec. 29.
1839   Jan. 2 – Apr. 13, Aug. 7 –
Dec. 28.
1840 – 1842   Jan. 1 – Dec. 31.
1843   Jan. 4 – June 28, July 5 – 8.
DLC
1836   Jan. 9 – Nov. 8, 10 – Dec. 31.
Suplemento: Nov. 9.
1837   Jan. 1 – 13, 15 – Feb. 21, 23 –
Oct. 28, 30 – Dec. 4.
Suplemento: Jan. 4, Feb. 25,
Mar. 29, Aug. 26, Nov. 17.
1838   Jan. 10 – 20, 27, Feb. 7 – Apr.
18, 25 – May 16, 23, June 2, 6,
13, 23, July 25, 28, Aug. 11, 15,
Sept. 1 – 8, 15, 19, 26 – Nov.
7, 28, Dec. 8, 19 – 26.
Suplemento: Jan. 10.
1839   Jan. 5, 12, 16, 23 – Feb. 2,
13 – 16, Aug. 7, 10, 17, 31,
Sept. 7 – Dec. 28.
1840   Jan. 1 – July 7, 9 – 14, 26 –
Dec. 31.
1841   Jan. 1 – Dec. 31.
Alcance: Sept. 1.
Suplemento: Feb. 11, 20, Mar.
20, 25, May 1, 22, Sept. 1, Oct.
9.
1842   Jan. 1 – June 3, 5 – 7, 9 – 24,
26 – Dec. 16, 18 – 31.
Suplemento: Mar. 2.
1843   Jan. 4 – July 8.
Suplemento: Jan. 7.
NN
1836   June 1.
1837   May 24.
TxU
1835   Dec. 16 – 31.
1836   Jan. 1 – Nov. 8, 10 – Dec. 31.
1837   Jan. 1 – Dec. 31.
1838   Jan. 1 – Nov. 9, 11 – 30, Dec.
2 – 31.
1839 – 1842   Jan. 1 – Dec. 31.
1843   Jan. 1 – July 8.
Micro (P)
1835   Dec. 6 – 31.

1836 – 1839   Jan. 1 – Dec. 31.
1840   Jan. 1 – Dec. 30.

EL COSMOPOLITA. est. 1873.
MH
1873   June 6.

EL COSMOPOLITA. w. est. 1880.
TxU
1880   May 9 – 16, 30 – June 30,
Sept. 16.

THE COSMOPOLITAN. w. est. May 30,
1880.
Note: In English.
TxU
1880   May 30 – June 30, July 8 –
Aug. 16.

LAS COSQUILLAS. sw. est. May 5,
1852.
CU – B
Micro (P) & (N)
1861   Jan. 16 – Apr. 27.
TxU
Micro (P)
1852   May 5 – June 9.
1861   Mar. 6 – Apr. 6, 13 – 27.

LE COURRIER DE BAYONNE.
Note: In French.
TxU
1881   Mar. 11.

LE COURRIER DES DEUX MONDES.
3w. est. July 13, 1838.
Note: In French.
DLC
1838   July 16 – 20, Aug. 6, 8, 13,
17 – 22.
1839   Aug. 3, 24, 29, Sept. 24, Oct.
24, Nov. 16 – Dec. 28.

COURRIER DU MEXIQUE. d. est. Feb.
7, 1867.
Note: In French.
MWA
1867   Feb. 7 – Apr. 30.

LE COURRIER DU MEXIQUE. w. est.
1888.
Note: In French.

CU−B
  Micro (P)
  1890   Jan. 6.
  1892   Apr. 18.

LE COURRIER DU MEXIQUE ET DE L'EUROPE. d.

  Note: In French. Succeeded *Le Trait d'union*; succeeded by *Journal français du Méxique*.
  DLC
  1914   Apr. 28, May 18.
  1918   July 24−30, Oct. 25−31, Nov. 13−19, 28, Dec. 5, 10, 11, 13−21, 24, 26−31.
  1919   Jan. 2−Feb. 21, 24, 25, Mar. 5−15, Apr. 2−14, 16−29, May 2−13, 21−27, June 4−8, 10.
  NN
  Micro (P) & (N)
  1919   Nov. 8−Dec. 31.
  1920   Jan. 2−Feb. 4, 6−15, 17− Apr. 1, 3−May 12, 14−June 25, July 25−29, 31−Aug. 18, 20−Sept. 14, 17−Oct. 6, 8− 11, 13−17, 20−Nov. 4, 6− 9, 12−16, 18−22, 24−30, Dec. 3−31.
  1921   Jan. 2−31, Feb. 2−4, 6−11, 13−15, 17−Mar. 24, 26−Apr. 10, 12−May 4, 6−25, 27− June 19, 21−Aug. 2, 4−Sept. 15, 17−26, 28−Oct. 11, 13− Nov. 1, 3−10, 12−Dec. 11, 13−31.
  1922   Jan. 1−Mar. 16, 18−22, 24− Apr. 13, 15−July 13, 15−19, 21−Sept. 15, 17−Oct. 14, 16−Nov. 1, 3−10, 12−Dec. 11, 13−31.
  1923   Jan. 3−8, 10−Apr. 15, 17− 21.
  TxU
  1914   July 1, 6, 11, 25, Nov. 3−14, Dec. 1−14.
  1915   Jan. 2, 6, 8, 9, 12−14, Feb. 8, 10, 12, 15, Mar. 2, 3, 6−18,

22−26, 29, 31−Apr. 1, 5−7, 9−17, 20−22, 26−28, May 1−4, 10, 12−14, 17−21, 28, 29, June 1−4, 7, 9, 10, 14−21, 23−25, 29, 30, Aug. 2, 3, 6−14, Sept. 2, Nov. 1, 3, 4, 6−9, 11− 22.
  1916   Apr. 17, 19, 24−26, May 15, Aug. 16−21, 23−31, Sept. 15, 18−21, 23−29, Nov. 1, 3− 27, 29, Dec. 1−11, 13−18, 20−31.
  1917   Jan. 17−June 26, 28−July 13, Sept. 1−15, Oct. 1−Dec. 1, 4−31.
  1918   Jan. 2−Mar. 28, 30−July 2, Aug. 1−Oct. 3, 5−7, 9−Dec. 31.
  1919   Jan. 1−Mar. 29, Apr. 23− July 3, 5−24, 26−Sept. 27, 30−Dec. 2, 4−31.
  1920   Jan. 2−Feb. 12, 14−28, Mar. 1−9, 11−Apr. 31.

LE COURRIER DE SOIR.

  Note: In French.
  TxU
  1881   Aug. 21.

LE COURRIER FRANÇAIS. sw.

  Note: In French. Ceased publication July 14, 1847.
  CtY
  1844   Feb. 21−24, Mar. 20−27, Apr. 3−10, 21, 27, May 15, 25−29, July 6, Aug. 7, 21.
  1845   July 5, Sept. 20, 27−Oct. 1, 8−29, Nov. 12−Dec. 31.
  1846   Jan. 3−21.
  DLC
  1844   Apr. 3−June 1, 7−26, July 3− 17, 24−27, Aug. 3−14, 21− 31, Sept. 7−11, 25−Dec. 28.
  1845   Apr. 19, 26−30.
  1846   Mar. 4−Apr. 3, 5−28, 30, July 26−Oct. 30, Nov. 30− Dec. 9.
            Extraordinario: Sept. 2.

1847   Jan. 9 – July 14.
MWA
1847   Jan. 9 – Mar. 17, 24 – July 14.

LE COURRIER FRANÇAIS; JOURNAL
UNIVERSAL. d. est. Jan. 26, 1858.
   Note: In French. Published during
   the suspension of *Le Trait d'union*
   and succeeded by *Les Deux mondes*.
   Ceased publication June 10, 1858.
CU – B
   Micro (P) & (N)
   1858   Jan. 26 – June 10.
DLC
   1858   Feb. 3, 5 – Mar. 15, Apr. 5,
           8 – 30, May 2 – June 10.

EL COYOTE. w. est. Mar. 7, 1880.
   Note: Ceased publication [Nov. 21],
   1880.
CtY
   1880   Mar. 7 – Nov. 21.
LNT – MA
   1880   Mar. 7 – Nov. 21.

EL CREPUSCULO. w. est. Nov. 13, 1875.
LNT – MA
   1875   Nov. 13, 20.
   1876   Dec. 1 – 31.

LA CRONICA. w.
   Note: Supplement to *El Álbum de la
   Mujer*.
DLC
   1887   Nov. 20, Dec. 11.

CRONICA OFICIAL. d. est. Oct. 5, 1857.
   Note: Succeeded *El Estandarte
   nacional*; succeeded by *Diario oficial
   del supremo gobierno*. Ceased publication 1858.
CU – B
   Micro (P)
   1857   Oct. 5 – Dec. 31.
   1858   Jan. 1 – 9.
DLC
   1857   [Oct. 19 – Dec. 17].

EL CRONISTA. d. est. [1861].
CU – B
   1864   Dec. 5 – 31.
   1865   Jan. 2 – 3.

EL CRONISTA DE MEXICO. d. est.
Jan. 13, 1862.
   Note: Ceased publication [1867].
CU – B
   Micro (P) & (N)
   1862   Jan. 13 – Dec. 31.
   1863   Jan. 1 – Mar. 20, June 3 –
           Dec. 31.
   1864 – 1865   Jan. 1 – Dec. 31.
   1866   Jan. 1 – June 30.
DLC
   Micro (P)
   1862   Jan. 13 – Dec. 31.
   1863 – 1865   Jan. 1 – Dec. 31.
   1866   Jan. 1 – June 30.

EL CRUSADO.
TxU
   1914   Jan. 4.

EL CUARTELAZO.
DLC
   1913   Feb. 13.
           Extraordinario: Feb. 13, 23.

EL CUARTO PODER. d. est. Sept. 10,
1917.
DLC
   1917   Sept. 10 – 25.

LA CUCHARA. 3w. est. 1864.
CtY
   1864   Nov. 6 – Dec. 30.
   1865   Jan. 2 – May 14.

CULTURA PROLETARIA.
CSt
   1934   Oct. 29.

DAILY AMERICAN STAR. 3w., d. est.
Sept. 20, 1847.
   Note: In Spanish and English.
   Previously published in Jalapa and
   Puebla. Title *The American Star*,
   Sept. 20 – Oct. 10, 1847; *Daily
   American Star*, Oct. 12, 1847 – May
   30, 1848. Periodicity Sept. 20 – Oct.
   10, 1847, three times a week; Oct. 12,
   1847 – May 30, 1848, daily.
CLCM
   1848   May 28.

CLU
  Micro (P)
  1847   Sept. 20 — Dec. 31.
  1848   Jan. 1 — May 30.
CU — B
  Micro (N)
  1847   Sept. 20 — Dec. 31.
  1848   Jan. 1 — May 30.
CtY
  1847   Sept. 20 — Dec. 31.
  1848   Jan. 1 — May 30.
DLC
  1847   Sept. 20 — Dec. 31.
          Extraordinario: Dec. 26.
  1848   Jan. 1 — May 30.
          Extraordinario: Jan. 17, Feb.
          28, Mar. 6.
LNT — MA
  1847   Oct. 27.
MB
  1848   Feb. 12 — Mar. 4, 6 — 13, 15 —
          Apr. 23.
NHi
  1847   Sept. 20 — Oct. 7, 15 — 26,
          Nov. 3, 12, 17, 20.
  1848   Apr. 20, 21, May 3.
  Micro (P)
  1847   Sept. 20 — Dec. 31.
  1848   Jan. 1 — May 30.
MWA
  1847   Sept. 20, 25, 30 — Oct. 2, 13 —
          Dec. 31.
  1848   [Jan. 4 — May 27].
MnU
  1848   Feb. 10.
NN
  1848   Mar. 25.
NcD
  1847   Dec. 9.

THE DAILY LIBERAL.
  See *El Liberal. The Daily Liberal.*

DAILY MEXICAN & MINING PRESS.
  d. est. 1911.
  Note: In English.
  KHi
  1912   Feb. 17.

EL DEBATE. sw., w. est. June 5, 1909.
        Note: Periodicity June 5, 1909 — Mar.
        5, 1910, semiweekly; Mar. 5 — Nov.
        12, 1910, weekly. Ceased publication
        [Nov. 12], 1910.
  CU
    Micro (P)
    1909   June 5 — Dec. 29.
    1910   Jan. 1 — Nov. 12.
  DLC
    1909   June 5 — Dec. 31.
    1910   Jan. 1 — Apr. 16.
  LNT — MA
    1910   [Apr. 23 — Nov. 12].
  TxU
    1909   June 5 — Dec. 31.
    1910   Jan. 1 — Nov. 12.

EL DEBER. 3w. est. May 24, 1911.
  TxU
    1911   May 24, 26.

LA DEFENSA; ECO DE LA SOCIEDAD
  Y DE COMERCIO HONRADO. w.
  est. Mar. 22, 1914.
  TxU
    1914   Mar. 22.

LA DEFENSA; DIARIO REFORMISTA.
  d. est. [1916].
  DLC
    1916   Extraordinario: Aug. 1, 2, Nov.
            4, 8, 10.
    1917   Extraordinario: Sept. 16.
  LNT — MA
    1917   [Sept. 28 — Nov. 17].
  TxU
    1916   Nov. 17, 21, Dec. 27.
    1917   Mar. 30, May 8.
            Extraordinario: Mar. 2.
    1918   June 21, July 21.

DEFENSA. w.
  CSt
    1933   Nov. 4.
    1934   Nov. 10, Dec. 10, 15.
    1935   Jan. 15, July 26, Sept. 30.

DEFENSA DEL HOGAR.
 TxU
  1912   Nov. 1.

LA DEFENSA NACIONAL. sw. est.
 May 17, 1912.
 TxU
  1912   May 17, June 15.

LA DEFENSA SOCIAL. d. est. Mar. 14,
 1915.
 DLC
  1915   Mar. 14, 18.

EL DEFENSOR CATOLICO. d. est.
 June 15, 1872.
 MWA
  1872   June 15--Sept. 29.

EL DEFENSOR DE LA INTEGRIDAD
 NACIONAL. sw. est. Aug. 7, 1844.
 CU—B
  1844   Aug. 7—Nov. 30.
 DLC
  1844   Aug. 7—Oct. 29, 31—Nov. 30.
 MWA
  1844   Aug. 7—Nov. 30.

DEFENSOR DE LA LEY. w. est. 1880.
 MWA
  1881   Mar. 12—19, Apr. 2—10.

EL DEFENSOR DE LA NACION. w.
 est. Mar. 12, 1839.
 CU—B
  Micro (N)
  1839   Mar. 12, 19.
 CtY
  1839   Mar. 12—Apr. 9.
       Suplemento: Mar. 12.
 DLC
  1839   Mar. 12—Apr. 2.

EL DEFENSOR DE LAS LEYES. sw.
 est. Feb. 15, 1845.
 CU—B
  Micro (P) & (N)
  1845   Feb. 15—Aug. 1, 14.

EL DEFENSOR DE MEXICO. est. 1847.
 CtY
  1847   n.d. (No. 4).

EL DEFENSOR DE TAMAULIPAS.
 est. 1847.
 CtY
  1847   Vol. 1, Nos. 4, 5, 39, 41, 43,
       45, 46.
  1848   Vol. 2, Nos. 11, 14, 16—18,
       20, 34.

LA DEMOCRACIA. d. est. Feb. 1847.
 DLC
  1847   Feb. 16—26.

EL DEMOCRATA; FEDERACION O
 MUERTE. d. est. Apr. 25, 1833.
 CU—B
  Micro (N)
  1833   Apr. 25—Aug. 21, 23—28,
       30—Oct. 8, 10—18, 20—25,
       27—Nov. 15, 17—Dec. 17,
       19—20, 22—31.
  1834   Jan. 1—6, 11—22, 24—29.
       Suplemento: Jan. 8.
 CtY
  1833   May 30, Dec. 27, 31.
 DLC
  1833   Apr. 27, 30, June 4—Aug. 6,
       8—21, 23—Sept. 1, 3, 4, 7—
       18, 20—24, 26—Oct. 31, Dec.
       16—31.
  1834   Jan. 4—18, 21, 23—30.
 TxU
  1833   June 7, 8.

EL DEMOCRATA. 3w., w. est. Mar. 12,
 1850.
  Note: Ceased publication Aug.
  8, 1850.
 CU—B
  Micro (P) & (N)
  1850   Mar. 12—Aug. 8.

EL DEMOCRATA. d. est. 1893.
 TxU
  1893   Apr. 5, 23.

EL DEMOCRATA. d. est. 1911.
 CU
  1911   Nov. 10—26, 28—Dec. 18,
       20—31.
  1912   Jan. 1—31.

EL DEMOCRATA; DIARIO LIBRE DE
MAÑANA. d. est. Sept. 15, 1914.
   Note: Published in Vera Cruz Dec.
   8, 1914 — Aug. 4, 1915. Began publishing Sunday supplement *Ameni-*
   dades Mar. 26, 1916. Suspended
   publication July 31 — Aug. 2, 1916;
   ceased publication May 9, 1926.
CU
   1917   Dec. 15 — 19, 21 — 31.
   1918   Jan. 1 — 7, 9, 10, 12, 14 — 19,
           22, 24, 27, 29 — 31, Feb. 3, 6,
           8, 10, 15, 16, 18, 20 — 25, 27,
           Mar. 2, 10, 12, 16, 21 — 26, 29,
           31, Apr. 2 — 5, 8, 9, 11, May 9,
           10, 16, 22, June 1, 5.
DLC
   1914   Sept. 15 — 20, 29, Oct. 2, 6, 10,
           14, 19, 22, 23, 26 — 28, Nov. 3 —
           7, 10 — 12.
           Extraordinario: Oct. 6, 7, 30,
           Nov. 3, 10.
   1915   Aug. 12 — 28, Sept. 1 — 18, 20,
           21, 23 — 26, 28 — Oct. 9, 11 —
           23, 25 — Dec. 31.
           Extraordinario: July 18, Aug.
           19, 21, 24 — Sept. 4, 6, 7, 9 —
           11, 13 — 15, 17 — 23, 25, 26,
           28 — Oct. 2, 4 — 12, 14 — 16,
           18 — 29, Dec. 10, 21.
   1916   Jan. 1 — Dec. 31.
           Boletín: Aug. 1.
           Extraordinario: Mar. 6, May
           31, Aug. 16, 18, 19, 21 — 26,
           28 — 31, Sept. 7, Nov. 7, 8.
           Suplemento: Mar. 19, Oct. 22,
           Nov. 1, 5.
   1917   Jan. 1 — Dec. 31.
           Extraordinario: Feb. 5, Apr.
           6, 7, May 28, 29, June 1, Aug.
           5, Sept. 1, Dec. 12.
           Suplemento: Feb. 18, May 24,
           31.
   1918 — 1920   Jan. 1 — Dec. 31.
   1921   Jan. 1 — Mar. 8, 10 — Apr. 6,
           8 — 16, 18 — Sept. 12, 14 — Oct.
           28.

   1922   Feb. 28 — Nov. 29, Dec. 1, 3 —
           31.
   1923   Jan. 1 — 3, 5 — 16, 18 — Apr. 30,
           May 2 — June 10, 12 — 17, 19 —
           Oct. 6, 8 — Dec. 31.
   1924   Jan. 1 — Dec. 31.
   1925   Jan. 1 — Sept. 15, 17, 19 — Dec.
           31.
   1926   Jan. 1 — 9, 11 — 30, Feb. 1 —
           May 9.
ICRL
   1917   Mar. 20, May 1 — Dec. 31.
   1918   Jan. 1 — Dec. 31.
   1919   Feb. 1 — July 31.
LNT — MA
   1918   Jan. 4, Dec. 25.
MB
   1916   May 12, 14 — 26, 28, 29, June
           19, 21, 22, 24, 28, 30, July 1,
           4, 6 — 10, 12 — 22, 26, 28, Aug.
           29 — Sept. 2, 5, 6, 8, 9, 12, 15 —
           23, 26, 28, 30 — Oct. 7, 13 — 17,
           19 — 23, 25 — 30, Nov. 1, 2, 7,
           15 — 18, 21, 22, 25, 28, Dec. 15,
           19, 21 — 23, 28, 30, 31.
   1917   Jan. 1, 3 — 6, 9 — 17, 19, 21, 22,
           24, 27, 29, 30, Feb. 1, 2, 7, 10,
           11, 14 — 19, 21, 23, 27, 28,
           Mar. 6, 8 — 11, 13 — 15, 21, 22,
           Apr. 8, 10 — 13, 15 — 18, 22 —
           25, 27 — May 2, 5, 12, 14 — 19,
           22 — 24, 26 — 31, June 1.
NN
   Micro (P) & (N)
   1917   Jan. 1 — July 19, 21 — Aug. 25,
           27 — Dec. 20, 22 — 31.
   1918   Jan. 1 — Feb. 5, 7 — Apr. 28, 30.
TxU
   1914   Sept. 15 — Oct. 7, 12, 13, 15 —
           Nov. 11.
   1915   Jan. 1, 4 — 6, 8 — 11, 14 — 17,
           20, 22 — 26, Mar. 6 — 15, 17, 18,
           22 — 31, Aug. 16, 17, 19, 21, 24,
           28, Oct. 5 — 8, 21, 30, 31, Nov.
           5 — 8, 10 — 12, 14 — 17, 19, 22,
           23, 25, 28, Dec. 1, 13 — 26, 29,
           31.

1916 Apr. 1, 2, 4 – May 31, June 2 –
Dec. 31.
1917 Jan. 1 – Oct. 30, Nov. 24.
1918 Jan. 1 – Dec. 30.
1919 Mar. 14, 31.
1920 Feb. 3, Mar. 1, Apr. 3, May 8.
1921 Sept. 25.
1924 Sept. 25, Oct. 5 – 8, 12, 13, 16 –
18, 26, Nov. 16, Dec. 1, 15.
1925 Jan. 30, 31.

EL DEMOCRATA MEXICANO. d. est.
Apr. 8, 1911.
Note: Ceased publication Jan. 31,
1912.
LNT – MA
1911 [July 12 – Dec. 31].
TxU
1911 Apr. 8, 10 – Oct. 8, 10 – 14, 17,
18, 20 – 28, 30 – Dec. 31.
1912 Jan. 1 – 31.

DEMOKRATISCHE POST. bw., m. est.
Aug. 15, 1943.
Note: In German. Succeeds *Alemania
Libre* and its supplement *El Germano-
mexicano.* Periodicity Aug. 15,
1943 – Mar. 15, 1949, biweekly;
after Apr. 1949, monthly.
CU
1943 Aug. 15 – Dec. 31.
1944 – 1950 Jan. 1 – Dec. 31.
1951 Feb – May, July – Aug.
DLC
1943 Aug. 15 – Sept. 15, Oct. 15.

EL DESPERTADOR AMERICANO.
est. May 8, 1905.
Note: Ceased publication [July 30,
1907].
TxU
1905 May 8, Sept. 16.
1906 July 30, Sept. 16.
1907 May 8, July 30.

DEUTSCHE ZEITUNG IN MEXICO. w.
est. Jan. 20, 1866.
NHi
1866 Jan. 20 – June 9, 23 – 30, Oct.
13 – 27.

DEUTSCHE ZEITUNG VON MEXIKO.
3w. est. 1883.
Note: In Spanish and German.
CU
1919 July 17.
DLC
1918 Aug. 27.
1919 Jan. 1 – 6, 8 – 10, 12 – 29, 31,
Feb. 2 – 5, 7, 9 – 12, 14 – 17,
19 – 21, 23 – Sept. 15, 17 – 22,
24 – Dec. 31.
1920 Jan. 1 – Apr. 19, 21 – May 17,
19 – June 21, 23 – 28, 30 – July
9, 11 – 16, 18 – Aug. 31.
1937 Dec. 24.
1941 Jan. 16, 23, Sept. 13, Oct.
14 – 25.
TxU
1914 Aug. 1 – Dec. 31.
1915 Jan. 1 – Dec. 31.
1916 Jan. 1 – Nov. 23.
1916 Sept. 13 – Oct. 18.

LES DEUX MONDES. d. est. June 11,
1858.
Note: In French. Published during
the suspension of *Le Trait d'union.*
Succeeded *Le Courrier francais.*
Ceased publication July 20, 1858.
CU – B
Micro (N)
1858 June 11 – July 20.
DLC
1858 June 11 – July 19.

EL DIA. d. est. May 15, 1914.
DLC
1914 May 15, 20.
TxU
1914 May 15 – 17, 19, 20.

EL DIA; VOCERO DEL PUEBLO
MEXICANO. d. est. 1962.
AzU
1966 Feb. 1 – 6, 9 – 12.
CSt – H
1963 Nov. 17, 18.
1964 Mar. 19 – 25, 27 – Apr. 5, 7 –
15, 17 – May 28, 30 – June 19,
21 – 26, 28 – 30, July 2, 4 – 16,

18—29, 31—Aug. 22, 24—Oct.
7, 9—18, 20—27, 29—Nov. 2,
4—23, 25, 26, 29, 30, Dec. 2,
5—9, 14—16, 18—23, 26—
28, 31.

1965   Jan. 1—17, 19—Feb. 27, Mar.
2—10, 12—14, 16—Apr. 5, 7—
13, 15—May 8, 10, 11, 13—17,
20—Aug. 27, Sept. 2—26,
28—Dec. 24, 27—31.

1966   Jan. 1+.

TxU

1963   Jan. 1+.

EL DIABLITO BROMISTA. w.
TxU

1903   Apr. 26, May 6, Aug. 9—30,
Sept. 20—Oct. 11, 25, Nov.
15—29, Dec. 20—22.

1904   Jan. 3—Mar. 13, July 3—Nov.
27.

1905   Sept. 24—Oct. 1, 8—Nov. 26.

1906   Feb. 3—11.

1907   Jan. 6, July 7—Dec. 22.

1908   Apr. 5—May 31.

1909   May 16—23, Nov. 21—Dec. 12.

EL DIABLITO ROJO. w. est. 1900.
TxU

1900   Apr. 2, May 7, June 4—July
9, Sept. 3, 17, 24, Oct. 8—22.

1901   Jan. 14—Apr. 1, 22—July 23,
Aug. 19, Sept. 31—Oct. 7,
Dec. 17, 31.

1908   Feb. 23, Mar. 9—Apr. 6, 27—
Nov. 16, 30—Dec. 28.

1909   Jan. 4—July 12, Aug. 2, 23—
Dec. 31.

1910   Jan. 1—17, 31—Mar. 14, 28—
June 6, 21—July 11, 25, Aug.
8—Sept. 9, Oct. 17—24, Nov.
7—28.

EL DIABLO AMARILLO. d.
CtY

1867   Sept. 7, 11.

EL DIABLO COJUELO. irr.
LNT—MA

1883   Sept. 16.

EL DIABLO VERDE. w. est. Nov. 29,
1849.
Note: Ceased publication [Apr. 11,
1850].
CtY

1849   Nov. 29—Dec. 27.

1850   Jan. 3—Apr. 11.

EL DIARIO. d. est. 1905.
DLC

1912   Extraordinario: Oct. 23.

1913   June 17—19, Sept. 15, 16, 20,
25, 26, 30, Oct. 1, 3, 7, 12, 24,
Dec. 1—31.
Extraordinario: Apr. 30.

1914   Jan. 1—Apr. 20.

LNT—MA

1911   [July 13—Dec. 31].

TxU

1908   Mar. 24, June 24, 29, Dec. 29.

1909   May 2, 23, Aug. 2, 31, Sept. 25.

1910   Jan. 1—9, 11—Feb. 2, 4—Mar.
7, 13, 18, 19, 22, 28, Apr. 1—
30, May 3, 7, 10, 16, June 1,
17, 20, 21, 27, 28, 30, July 11,
13, 16, 18—21, 23, 25, 28, Aug.
3, 4, 12, 14, 15, 19—21, 28,
Sept. 3.

1911   Jan. 13—15, 17, 21, 22, Feb.
1, 5, 15—17, 19, 24, 26, Mar.
1, 4—6, 8—13, 16—21, 23—
Apr. 4, 7—9, 12—14, 16—
May 3, 5—13, 15—18, 20, 21,
June 2—July 2, 4—18, 21—
Aug. 8, 10—Dec. 31.

1912   Jan. 1—Dec. 31.

1913   Jan. 19, 22, 23, 26—Feb. 11,
22—Oct. 31, Nov. 3, 4, Dec.
3, 6, 7, 9, 11, 14.

1914   Jan. 1, 3—Mar. 2, 4—Apr. 19.

EL DIARIO. d. est. Aug. 15, 1917.
Note: Afternoon edition entitled
El Nacionalista.
DLC

1917   Aug. 15—Sept. 29, Oct. 1—11.

DIARIO CONSTITUCIONAL. d.
  CtY
    1820   July 9, 22, Aug. 6.
            Suplemento: July 9.
    1821   Feb. 15, 16, 24.
            Suplemento: Jan. 11.
DIARIO DE AVISOS. d. est. Nov. 6,
  1856.
  CU−B
    1856   Nov. 6−Dec. 31.
    1857−1859   Jan. 1−Dec. 31.
    1860   Jan. 1−Dec. 22.
  CtY
    1858   Jan. 1−Apr. 10, 13−July 24,
            26−Dec. 27.
    1859   Nos. 28−53, 55−134, 136−
            153, 155−338.
  ICN
    1858   July 1−Dec. 31.
  MoU
    Micro (N)
    1856   Nov. 6−Dec. 31.
    1857   Jan. 1−Dec. 31.
    1858   Jan. 1−Nov. 30.
    1859   Jan. 1−Dec. 30.
    1860   Jan. 2−Dec. 22.
EL DIARIO DE IMPERIO.
  LNT−MA
    1865−1866   Jan. 1−Dec. 31.
    1867   Jan. 1−June 19.
DIARIO DE LA GUERRA. d. est. Feb.
  28, 1847.
  NN
    1847   Mar. 6.
  TxU
    1847   Feb. 28−Mar. 14, 19, 20.
EL DIARIO DE LA GUERRA. d. est.
  Apr. 21, 1914.
  DLC
    1914   Extraordinario: Apr. 23, 24,
            26, 28, May 6−8.
  TxU
    1914   Extraordinario: May 8.
DIARIO DE LA GUERRA. d. est. June 3,
  1940.
    Note: Title *Diario alemán*, June 3−
    14, 1940; *Diario de la guerra*, after
    June 15, 1940.

  CSt
    1940   July 25−Oct. 14.
  DLC
    1940   June 3−Oct. 25, 27−Nov. 1,
            3−Dec. 2, 4−23, 25−31.
    1941   Jan. 1−20, 22−24, 26, 27,
            29−Feb. 2, 4−10, 12−14,
            16−19, 21−25, 27−Mar. 2,
            5−21, 23−25, 27, 28.

DIARIO DE LA TARDE. d.
  DLC
    1961   June 27.

DIARIO DE LOS FORASTEROS.
  TxU
    1889   Prospecto: June 1.

DIARIO DE MEXICO. d. est. Oct. 1,
  1805.
    Note: Title *Diario de México*, Oct. 1,
    1805−June 30, 1812, Dec. 20, 1812−
    Jan. 4, 1817; *Diario de México,
    político, económico, literario y
    mercantil*, July 1−Dec. 19, 1812.
    Ceased publication Jan. 4, 1817.
  CU−B
    1805   Oct. 1−Dec. 31.
    1806−1810   Jan. 1−Dec. 31.
    1811   Jan. 14, May 29, July 1−Dec.
            31.
    1812   Dec. 20−31.
    1813   Jan. 1−June 30.
    Micro (P) & (N)
    1805   Oct. 1−Dec. 31.
    1806   Jan. 1−Dec. 31.
    1807   Jan. 1−Oct. 29, Nov. 1−
            Dec. 31.
    1808   Jan. 1−26, 28−June 20, 22−
            Dec. 31.
    1809   Jan. 1−Dec. 31.
    1810   Jan. 1−Oct. 10, 12−Dec. 31.
    1811   Jan. 1−Oct. 4, 6−15, 17−
            Dec. 31.
    1812   Jan. 1−Oct. 16, 18−Dec. 4,
            10−12, 19−31.
    1813   Jan. 1−July 21, 23−Oct. 8,
            10−28, 30−Dec. 31.
    1814   Jan. 1−Apr. 13, 15−June 28,

30 — Oct. 5, 7 — Dec. 31.
1815   Jan. 1 — Dec. 31.
1816   Jan. 1 — June 17, 19 — Dec. 31.
1817   Jan. 1 — 4.
CtY
1805   Oct. 1 — Dec. 31.
1806 — 1809   Jan. 1 — Dec. 31.
1810   Aug. 1 — 5, 7, 9, 12, 14, 18, 20,
25, 27 — 31, Sept. 5, 11, 16, 25,
28, Oct. 1, 2, 4, 6, 7, 10, 12, 13,
15, 17, 21, 23 — 25, Nov. 3, 7.
1811   Aug. 1 — 5, 7, 9, 12, 14, 18, 20,
25, 27 — 31, Sept. 5, 11, 16, 25,
28, Oct. 1, 2, 4, 6, 7, 10, 12, 13,
15, 17, 21, 23 — 25, Nov. 3, 7.
1812   Jan. 13, Feb. 15, 16, 20, Aug.
13, 29, Sept. 1, 8, 12, 19, 29,
Oct. 5, 13, 15, 19, 22, 25, 26,
27, 28, 31, Dec. 2.
1813   June 1.
Suplemento: July 27.
1814   Mar. 15, 28, May 17, July 1, 2,
Sept. 3, 4, 12, 16, Oct. 13, 22.
Suplemento: Mar. 11, May 12.
DLC
1805   Oct. 1 — Dec. 31.
1806 — 1811   Jan. 1 — Dec. 31.
1812   Jan. 1 — Nov. 30.
ICN
1805   Oct. 1 — Dec. 31.
Suplemento: Nov. 8, 14, Dec.
3 — 5.
1806   Jan. 1 — Dec. 15, 17 — 31.
Suplemento: May 10, Nov. 29.
1807   Jan. 1 — Apr. 30.
Suplemento: Feb. 20.
1809   Jan. 1 — June 3, 5, 7, 10 — Aug.
11, 15, 16, 18 — Dec. 31.
Suplemento: June 29, July 22,
Sept. 23.
1811   Jan. 1 — 22, 24 — Feb. 13, 15 —
May 23, 25 — June 30.
Suplemento: Apr. 6, May 15.
LNT — MA
1805   Oct. 1 — 12, 14 — Dec. 31.
1806   May 1 — Dec. 31.
NN
1806   Oct. 6.

TxSjM
1805   Oct. 1 — Dec. 31.
1813   July 1 — Dec. 31.
1814   Jan. 1 — Dec. 31.
TxU
1805   Oct. 1 — Dec. 31.
1806 — 1816   Jan. 1 — Dec. 31.
1817   Jan. 1 — 4.

DIARIO DEL GOBIERNO DE LA
REPUBLICA MEXICANA. d. est.
Feb. 10, 1835.
    Note: Suspended publication July
    16 — 27, 1840; Sept. 4 — Oct. 8, 1841.
    Boletín del gobierno published dur-
    ing former suspension and *Boletín
    oficial* during latter. Succeeded
    El Telégrafo; periódico oficial; suc-
    ceeded by a publication of the same
    name. Ceased publication Jan. 31,
    1846.
CU — B
    Micro (P)
    1835   Feb. 10 — Dec. 31.
    1836 — 1839   Jan. 1 — Dec. 31.
    1840   Jan. 1 — July 14, 28 — Dec. 31.
    1841   Jan. 1 — Sept. 3, Oct. 9 — Dec.
    31.
    1842   Jan. 1 — May 19, 21 — Dec. 31.
    1843 — 1845   Jan. 1 — Dec. 31.
    1846   Jan. 1 — 31.
CtY
    1835   May 1 — Aug. 31.
    1836   Jan. 1 — Nov. 23.
    1837   Feb. 21, Oct. 27.
    1838   Mar. 31 — June 2.
    1839   June 15.
    1840   Feb. 14, 15, Nov. 5.
    1842   Jan. 1 — June 30, No. 2746.
    1843   Jan. 8, Nos. 2757, 2759, 2762,
    2766, 2767, 2769, 2771, 2812,
    2819, 2830, 2836, 2837,
    2869 — 72, 2874, 2875, 2878,
    2880, 2881, 2885, 2886, 2888 —
    92, 2896, 2897, 2900, 2901,
    2903 — 05, 2911, 2912, 2914,
    2917, 2919, 2920, 2922 — 25,
    2927 — 29, 2931, 2932, 2934,
    2935, 2937, 2939, 2941, 2942,

2954, 2956, 2973, 2974, 2989,
3001, 3002, 3004, 3005, 3009,
3012, 3015, 3018, 3021, 3023,
3026, 3031—33, 3035, 3037,
3038, 3042, 3052, 3093, 3107,
3108.

DLC
1835 ₁Feb. 10—Dec. 31₁.
1836—1843 ₁Jan. 1—Dec. 31₁.
1844 Jan. 1—Dec. 2, 4—31.
1845 Jan. 1—Nov. 25, Dec.
1, 3, 4, 6, 7, 10, 18.
1846 ₁Jan. 1—31₁.
ICN
1841 Oct. 8—Dec. 31.
IU
1835 Feb. 15—20, 23—28.
LNT—MA
1836 June 30—Dec. 31.
1837 Jan. 1—31.
MB
1844 Dec. 12.
TxSjM
1838 June 25, July 5.

DIARIO DEL GOBIERNO DE LA
REPUBLICA MEXICANA. d. est.
Feb. 1, 1846.
Note: Succeeded *Diario del gobierno
de la República Mexicana*; succeeded by a publication of the same
title. Ceased publication Feb. 28,
1846.
CU—B
Micro (P)
1846 Feb. 1—28.

DIARIO DEL GOBIERNO DE LA
REPUBLICA MEXICANA. d. est.
Mar. 1, 1846.
Note: Suspended publication Feb.
27—Mar. 1, 8—15, 1847. Succeeded
a publication of the same title; succeeded by *El Correo nacional*.
CU—B
Micro (P)
1846 Mar. 1—Dec. 31.
1847 Jan. 1—Dec. 31.

DLC
1846 Mar. 1—Dec. 31.
1847 Jan. 1—Sept. 12.
ICN
1847 Aug. 22.

DIARIO DEL HOGAR. sw., 3w., d. est.
Sept. 16, 1881.
CU—B
Micro (P) & (N)
1883 Oct. 9.
1887 Apr. 17, June 28.
1888 Apr. 12.
CtY
1908 Sept. 1, 2.
1909 June 16, July 4, 9.
DLC
1913 Apr. 23, 26, May 3, 24—July
7, 9, 10, Oct. 10.
1914 Feb. 5, Sept. 1—4, 9, 11—16,
20, 21, 23, 24, 26.
1917 Mar. 9, 11.
LNT—MA
1883 Sept. 16.
1885 May 24.
1889 Nov. 29, Dec. 5.
1890 Nov. 15.
1891 Apr. 9, 30, Oct. 13, 22.
1899 Oct. 11.
1901 Mar. 15.
1911 ₁July 1—Dec. 31₁.
MWA
1881 Nov. 1.
1886 Oct. 6, 8.
TxU
1882 Mar. 1—Apr. 9, 12—29, May
2—20, 22—Aug. 11.
1884 Aug. 12.
1886 July 15, Aug. 3, 4, 22—24.
1887 Aug. 14.
1890 Mar. 13, May 31, July 24,
Nov. 11.
1891 Feb. 7.
1893 Sept. 3.
1901 Apr. 16, 19.
1902 Dec. 14.
1903 Nov. 14.

1904   Jan. 9, 19.
1905   May 19, 20, June 3, 23 – 25,
       30 – July 2.
1906   July 15, Aug. 29, Sept. 7, 10,
       12, 13, 15, 19 – 21, 23, 25 – 30,
       Oct. 2, 3, 6, 7, 9, 11 – 14, 16,
       18 – 20, 23, 25.
1907   May 18, June 6, 13, 23, July
       4, 6, 9, Sept. 28, Oct. 6, Nov. 6,
       7, 14, 15, 17, 19, 22 – 24, 26 –
       28, Dec. 3, 11 – 14, 17 – 20.
1908   Jan. 2, 4, 6, 7, 11, 15, 17, 21 –
       23, 28 – Feb. 2, 4 – 16, 18 –
       23, 25, 27 – Mar. 1, 4, 5, 7, 8,
       10, 12, 14, 15, 17 – 19, 21, 22,
       24, 25, Apr. 1, 2, 4, 8 – 11, 14,
       24, May 12 – 17, 19 – 21, 23,
       24, 26, 28 – June 1, 4 – 7, 9 –
       14, 18 – 21, 24 – 26, 28, July 1,
       2, 4, 5, 7, 8, 10 – 12, 14 – 18,
       21, 23 – 26, 28 – Aug. 2, 4 –
       9, 11, 13, 14, 16, 18, 26, Sept.
       1, 2, 8, 9, 11 – 13, 15, 16, 18 –
       20, 22 – 27, 29, 30, Oct. 3, 6 –
       10, 13, 14, 16 – 18, 20 – 25,
       27 – Nov. 1, 4, 6, 7, 10, 11, 13,
       14, 16 – 18, 21, 24, 26, 28, 29,
       Dec. 1 – 5, 9 – 13.
1909   Aug. 8, Oct. 3, 5, 6, 8, 9, 12,
       27, Dec. 3, 5, 8, 17, 18.
1910   Jan. 4, 14, Aug. 1, 2, 8, 9, 11,
       Sept. 10 – Nov. 18.
1911   Mar. 27 – 31, May 1 – Sept.
       16, 19 – Dec. 23, 25 – 31.
1912   Jan. 1 – July 22, 26 – Aug. 6.
1913   Apr. 20, 21, 23 – July 12, Oct.
       10.
1914   Sept. 1 – 16, 18 – Oct. 18, 20 –
       25, 27 – Nov. 15.

DIARIO DEL IMPERIO. d. est. Jan. 1,
1865.
    Note: Succeeded *Periódico oficial
    del Imperio Mexicano*; succeeded by
    *Diario oficial del gobierno de los
    Estados Unidos Mexicanos*. Ceased
    publication June 18, 1867.

CU – B
    1865 – 1866   Jan. 1 – Dec. 31.
DLC
    1865 – 1866   Jan. 1 – Dec. 31.
    1867   Jan. 1 – June 18.
MBAt
    1865 – 1866   Jan. 1 – Dec. 31.
    1867   Jan. 1 – May 29.
MoU
    Micro (N)
    1867   Jan. 2 – Mar. 21, 23 – 28, 30 –
           June 18.
NHi
    1865 – 1866   Jan. 1 – Dec. 31.
    1867   Jan. 2 – June 18.

EL DIARIO DEL PUEBLO. d. est. June
23, 1919.
DLC
    1919   June 23 – July 9.

EL DIARIO ESPAÑOL. d.
TxU
    1912   July 10.

DIARIO ESPAÑOL. sw., 3w., d. est.
[1934].
CSt
    1946   Oct. 1 – Dec. 31.
    1947 – 1952   Jan. 1 – Dec. 31.
    1953   Jan. 1 – June 30.
    1954   Jan. 1 – July 31.
DLC
    1941   Nov. 20 – Dec. 6.
    1943   Feb. 22.

DIARIO ILUSTRADO. w.
TxU
    1907   Feb. 3 – 10, Mar. 3 – 10, 24 –
           Apr. 14.

DIARIO INDEPENDIENTE. d.
TxU
    1821   Sept. 27.

DIARIO LIBERAL DE MEXICO. d.
TxU
    1823   May 10, Aug. 27, 28.

DIARIO LITERARIO DE MEXICO. irr.
est. Mar. 12, 1768.
    Note: Ceased publication May 10,
    1768.

CtY
1768   Mar. 12 – May 10.

DIARIO OFICIAL DEL GOBIERNO DE LA REPUBLICA MEJICANA. d. est. June 5, 1853.

Note: Succeeded *El Telégrafo*; *periódico oficial*; succeeded by *Boletín oficial del supremo gobierno*. Ceased publication Sept. 12, 1855.

CU – B
Micro (P)
1853   June 5 – Dec. 31.
1854   Jan. 1 – Dec. 31.
1855   Jan. 1 – Sept. 12.

DIARIO OFICIAL DEL GOBIERNO DE LOS ESTADOS-UNIDOS MEXICANOS. d. est. 1867.

Note: Title *Diario oficial del gobierno supremo*, Aug. 1867 – Nov. 1876; *Diario oficial del gobierno de la república*, Nov. – Dec. 3, 1876; *Diario oficial del gobierno de los Estados Unidos Mexicanos*, Dec. 4, 1876 – Aug. 15, 1914. Succeeded *Diario del imperio*. Ceased publication Aug. 15, 1914.

CU – B
1867   Aug. 20 – Dec. 31.
1868 – 1870   Jan. 1 – Dec. 31.
1871   Jan. 1 – Mar. 1, 3 – Dec. 31.
1872   Jan. 1, 2, 8 – 23, 28, 30, Feb. 1, 2, 6, 7, 12 – Apr. 2, 4, 6 – 11, 13 – 15, 17 – May 1, 4 – 13, 17 – 20, 23 – 30, June 1, 3 – 5, 8, 10 – 13, 15 – 20, 23, 25, 26, 30, July 3 – Dec. 31.
1873   Jan. 3 – 31, Feb. 2, 22, 24, 25, 28 – Mar. 28, 30, 31, Apr. 12, 14 – May 20, 22, 27, 31 – Dec. 31.
1874   Jan. 1, 3 – 12, 14 – Mar. 4, 6 – 8, 10 – Dec. 31.
1875   Jan. 1 – Dec. 31.
1876   Jan. 1 – 12, 14 – Feb. 29, Mar. 2 – 5, 7 – Apr. 23, 26 – June 4, 6 – July 1, 3 – Oct. 30, Nov. 1 – 9, 11 – Dec. 31.

Micro (P)
1871   Jan. 11, Feb. 10.
1875   Jan. 1 – 9, 11 – 31, Feb. 2 – 4, 6 – Mar. 31, Apr. 17 – June 30, July 6 – 30, Aug. 1 – Oct. 25, 27 – Dec. 20, 22, 23.

DLC
1867   [Aug. 1 – Dec. 31].
1868 – 1900   [Jan. 1 – Dec. 31].

MB
1871   Nov. 13.
1883   Aug. 30 – Sept. 1, 3 – 5, 7, 8, 10, 11, 13 – 15, 17 – 25, Oct. 2 – 4, 6, 8 – 11, 15 – 17, 26, 27.

MBAt
1877   Jan. 2 – Dec. 31.
1878 – 1900   Jan. 1 – Dec. 31.

MoU
1867   Sept. 12 – Oct. 9, 11 – Nov. 22, 24 – 30, Dec. 2 – 31.
1868   Jan. 1 – Mar. 11, 13, 14, 16 – May 12, 14 – Dec. 31.
1869 – 1870   Jan. 1 – Dec. 31.
1871   Jan. 1 – 30, Feb. 1 – 21, 23 – Apr. 1, 3 – May 25, 27 – July 30, Aug. 1 – 6, 8 – 29, 31 – Dec. 31.
1872   Jan. 1 – 23, 25 – July 30.

TxU
1877   Jan. 24, May 4, Nov. 6.
1878   Jan. 1, Feb. 22, Aug. 17, Nov. 18, 27.
1879   Jan. 11, 18, Feb. 8, May 22, June 12, 16, July 7, 14, 15, Oct. 17, Nov. 6, Dec. 6, 13, 20 – 22.
1880   Feb. 11 – 13, 19, Mar. 19 – Dec. 31.
1881   Jan. 1 – Mar. 15, 17 – June 2, 6 – Sept. 22, 24 – Oct. 20, Nov. 1, 9, 10, 15, 24, 26.
1882   June 1.
1884   Aug. 16 – 18, Sept. 19, Nov. 8.
1885   Apr. 9.
1890   Mar. 29, July 10.
Alcance: June 25.

DIARIO OFICIAL DEL SUPREMO GOBIERNO. d. est. Jan. 23, 1858.

Note: Suspended publication Oct.

16—20, 1858; Dec. 22, 1858—Jan. 23, 1859; Mar. 20—Apr. 2, 1859. *Boletín' de noticias del supremo gobierno* published during first suspension; *Boletín oficial* during the latter two. Succeeded *Crónica oficial*; succeeded by *Boletín oficial del ejército.* Ceased publication Nov. 17, 1860.
CU—B
  1858   Jan. 23—Dec. 31.
  1859   Jan. 1—Dec. 31.
  1860   Jan. 1—Nov. 17.
CtY
  1860   Jan. 1—20, 22—25, 29—Feb. 6, 8, 13—Mar. 22, 24—31.
DLC
  1858   [Feb. 1—Aug. 31].
MWA
  1859   Dec. 6.

DIARIO OFICIAL DEL SUPREMO GOBIERNO DE LA REPUBLICA MEXICANA. d. est. June 15, 1856.
  Note: Succeeded *Boletín oficial del supremo gobierno*; succeeded by *El Estandarte nacional.* Ceased publication Nov. 17, 1856.
CU—B
  Micro (P)
  1856   June 15—Nov. 17.

DIARIO REPUBLICANO. d.
TxU
  1911   May 24—30, June 2, 3.

LA DISCUSION. est. 1881.
TxU
  1881   Oct. 9.

LA DISCUSION. d. est. 1916.
TxU
  1916   June 5, 27.

LA DISCUSION. sw. est. May 9, 1917.
DLC
  1917   May 9—26, June 2, 6.
TxU
  1917   May 19, June 2, 12.

EL DISLOQUE. w.
TxU
  1912   Oct. 14.

EL DISTRITO FEDERAL. 3w. est. Apr. 1, 1871.
CU—B
  1872   June 15—July 13, 20—Dec. 5, 10—31.
TxU
  1871   Apr. 1—Dec. 31.
  1872   Jan. 1—Dec. 31.

EL DOMINGO; PERIODICO DEL PUEBLO. w. est. Nov. 17, 1861.
CtY
  1863   Mar. 8.
NN
  1861   Nov. 17—Dec. 1.

EL DOMINGO; SEMANARIO DE LITERATURA, CIENCIAS Y MEJORES MATERIALES. w.
  Note: Subtitle *Semanario político y literario*, Dec. 17, 1871—Mar. 3, 1872; *Semanario de literario, ciencias y mejores materiales*, after June 2, 1872.
CtY
  1871   Dec. 17—24.
  1872   Jan. 21, Feb. 4—Mar. 3, June 2—23, Aug. 25, Dec. 29.
  1873   Jan. 5—19, Feb. 2—16, Apr. 13, May 18, July 20—Sept. 7, 28.

EL DOMINGO; SEMANARIO INDEPENDIENTE. w. est. 1881.
TxU
  1881   Sept. 11.

EL DOMINGO. w. est. 1902.
TxU
  1908   July 19.

DON CUCUFATE. w. est. July 29, 1906.
TxU
  1906   July 29—Oct. 1.

DON FOLIAS. sw. est. Jan. 6, 1865.
NN
  1865   Jan. 6.

DON QUIJOTE. w. est. Mar. 2, 1877.
Note: Ceased publication Jan. 10,
1878.
CtY
1877   Mar. 2 – Dec. 27.
1878   Jan. 10.
LNT – MA
1877   Mar. 2 – Oct. 31, Dec. 1 – 31.
TxU
1877   Mar. 9, Apr. 6, 20 – 27, May
11 – 18, June 1, July 20 – 27,
Aug. 24 – Sept. 2, 27.

DON QUIJOTE. w. est. July 9, 1911.
TxU
1911   July 9 – 16, Aug. 6 – 27, Sept.
10, Oct. 15 – 29.

DON SIMPLICIO. sw. est. Dec. 1845.
Note: Suspended publication May
1 – June 30, 1846; ceased publication
Mar. 24, 1847.
CtY
1846   July 1 – Dec. 30.
1847   Jan. 2 – Apr. 24.
LNT – MA
1845   n.d. (Dec.).
1846   [Jan. 1 – Apr. 30, July 1 –
Dec. 31].
1847   [Jan. 1 – Feb. 28, Apr. 1 – 30].
TxU
1845   Dec. 1 – 31.
1846   Jan. 1 – Apr. 23.
Micro (P)
1846   July 1 – Dec. 31.
1847   Jan. 1 – Mar. 24.

DON TRINI. w. est. Apr. 11, 1912.
TxU
1912   Apr. 11, 25, May 16.

EL DUENDE. sw. est. Jan. 25, 1832.
Note: Continuous pagination. Ceased
publication [July 14,] 1832.
CtY
1832   Apr. 18, 25.
NN
1832   May 4.

EL DUENDE. w. est. [1839].
CtY
1840   Feb. 29 – Mar. 7.

EL DUENDE. bw. est. Jan. 1, 1903.
TxU
1903   Jan. 1, 12.

EL DUENDE. bw. est. Nov. 15, 1904.
TxU
1904   Nov. 15 – Dec. 31.
1905   Jan. 1 – 12.

L'ECHO FRANÇAIS. sw. est. 1902.
Note: In French.
CU
1921   Special number: July 14.
DLC
1902   Oct. 16 – Dec. 31.
1903   Jan. 1 – 17, 19 – Feb. 7, 9 –
Apr. 11, 13 – June 6, 8 – Aug.
19, 21 – Sept. 5, 7 – Nov. 7,
9 – Dec. 31.
Special number: July 14.
1904   Jan. 1 – 13, 15 – 23, 25 – Feb. 4.
TxU
1909   Mar. 7.
1915   Special number: Mar. 11
(in Spanish).

EL ECO. w. est. Feb. 4, 1834.
Note: Title *El Eco del pueblo*, Feb.
4 – Apr. 15, 1834; *El Eco*, after
Apr. 15, 1834.
DLC
1834   Feb. 4 – Apr. 29.

EL ECO; DIARIO POLITICO E INFOR-
MATIVO DE LA TARDE. d. est. July
23, 1914.
TxU
1914   July 23.

EL ECO DE AMBOS MUNDOS. w., 3w.
est. 1871.
Note: Periodicity before Sept. 3,
1872, weekly; after Sept. 3, 1872,
three times a week.
CU – B
1872   Mar. 3 – Aug. 25, Sept. 3 –
Dec. 28.

TxU
1875 July 10.

EL ECO DE DURANGO. w. est. Mar. 15, 1917.
DLC
1917 Mar. 15 – 22.

ECO DE ESPAÑA. sw. est. July 20, 1853.
CU – B
1853 July 20 – Dec. 31.
1854 Jan. 1 – Apr. 29.

EL ECO DE LA JUSTICIA. sw. est. Dec. 13, 1842.
DLC
1842 Dec. 13 – 31.
1843 Jan. 1 – 26, 28 – May 1, 31 –
June 29, July 1 – 31, Aug. 30 –
Dec. 29.
Suplemento: June 27.

MWA
1842 Dec. 13 – 31.
1843 Jan. 1 – 24, 31 – Mar. 7, Apr.
7 – May 26, June 2 – July 28,
Aug. 12 – Dec. 29.
NN
1843 Sept. 29.
TxU
1880 June 6, 27.

EL ECO DEL CIRCO.
CtY
1867 July 23.

EL ECO DEL COMERCIO. d. est. Jan. 10, 1848.
CU – B
Micro (P) & (N)
1848 Jan. 10 – Sept. 18, 20 – Oct. 11.

EL ECO DEL NORTE. w. est. June 5, 1841.
DLC
1841 Prospecto: May 29.
June 5 – Aug. 28.

EL ECO MERCANTIL. sw. est. Apr. 6, 1882.
CU – B
Micro (P)

1882 Apr. 6, 27 – May 2.

EL ECO NACIONAL. est. Jan. 1, 1857.
CU – B
1857 Jan. 1 – Dec. 31.
1858 Jan. 1 – Dec. 30.

EL ECO NACIONAL; SEMANARIO DE INFORMACION Y VARIEDADES. w. est. 1906.
TxU
1906 June 24.

EL ECO SOCIAL. w. est. 1910.
TxU
1910 Dec. 25.
1911 Jan. 1, 22.
1913 Sept. 14.

EL ECO UNIVERSAL.
CU – B
Micro (P)
1884 Nov. 29.

EL ECONOMISTA. est. July 3, 1847.
CU – B
1847 July 3 – 10.

EL ECONOMISTA. sw., irr. est. Apr. 6, 1849.
CU – B
1849 Apr. 6 – May 30.
MWA
1849 Apr. 14 – May 5, 12, 19 – June
6, 13, 23 – July 11, 25 – Dec.
31.
1850 Jan. 1 – July 6.

LOS ECOS. sw.
CSt
1939 Apr. 19 – Oct. 29.

EGO. sw. est. 1912.
TxU
1912 Mar. 30.

ELEKTRON. w. est. Sept. 1, 1911.
TxU
1911 Sept. 1.

LA ENCICLOPEDIA DE LOS SANS-
CULOTTES.
LNT—MA
1835   Mar. 22—May 31.

LA ENSEÑA. sw. est. Nov. 2, 1839.
DLC
1839   Nov. 2—Dec. 31.
Alcance: Nov. 27.
1840   Jan. 1—28, 30—Feb. 1.

LA ENSEÑANZA OBJETIVA. w.
CtY
1881   Jan. 1—Dec. 24.

EL ENTREACTO. sw.
TxU
1907   May 26, June 9, 16, 23.

LA EPOCA. est. 1845.
DLC
1846   Feb. 13.

LA EPOCA. d. est. 1877.
CU—B
Micro (P)
1877   Oct. 30.
TxU
1877   May 23, 24.

LA EPOCA; DIARIO POLITICO,
SERIO E IMPARCIAL. d. est. 1883.
CU—B
Micro (P)
1884   Dec. 7, 23.
1885   Apr. 7, May 5, Aug. 25.
TxU
1885   July 18.

LA EPOCA; BISEMANARIO INDE-
PENDIENTE. sw.
TxU
1911   Sept. 21.

LA EPOCA; BISEMANARIO POLITICO,
DE INFORMACION Y VARIEDADES.
sw. est. Feb. 22, 1912.
TxU
1912   Feb. 22—Mar. 3, 17—21,
Apr. 7—21, 28—May 2, 9—
16, 23—30, June 6.

LA EPOCA; BISEMANAL DE CRITICA
POLITICA Y SOCIAL. sw. est. Aug.
5, 1914.
DLC
1914   Aug. 5.
TxU
1914   Aug. 5—10.

LA EPOCA; DIARIO DE LA MAÑANA.
d. est. Dec. 6, 1914.
DLC
1914   Dec. 6.
TxU
1914   Dec. 6.

EL EQUILIBRIO. w., sw. est. Nov. 19,
1839.
Note: Ceased publication Feb. 14,
1840.
CtY
1840   Feb. 14.
DLC
1839   Nov. 19—Dec. 28.
Suplemento: Dec. 21.

L'ERE NOUVELLE. d. & bw. est. Oct.
15, 1864.
Note: In French. Published both
daily and biweekly editions.
DLC
1864   Oct. 15—Dec. 31.
1865   Jan. 1—Dec. 31.
1866   Jan. 1—Mar. 30.
NHi
1864   Oct. 15—Dec. 31.
1865—1867   Jan. 1—Dec. 31.
Biweekly edition:
1865   Apr. 21—27.
1866   June 28—July 4, 27, Aug. 9,
Sept. 9, Oct. 9, 11—Dec. 16.
TxU
1881   Oct. 31.

LA ESPADA DE DAMOCLES. sw. est.
Sept. 1, 1850.
CU—B
Micro (P) & (N)
1850   Sept. 1—28.

ESPAÑA; REVISTA IMPARCIAL
IBERO-AMERICANO. w. est. 1885.
MWA
1885   Oct. 19.

ESPAÑA; ORGANO DE LA JUNTA
ESPAÑOLA DE LIBERACION. w.
est. Jan. 29, 1944.
CSt—H
    1944   Jan. 29—Dec. 31.
    1945   Jan. 1—Sept. 8.

ESPAÑA NUEVA. w. est. Nov. 24, 1945.
CSt—H
    1945   Nov. 24—Dec. 31.
    1946—1951   Jan.—Dec.
CU
    1945   Nov. 24—Dec. 29.
    1946   Jan. 5—Mar. 2, 16—30, Apr.
            13—Dec. 28.
    1947   Jan. 1—Dec. 31.
    1948   Jan. 10—Oct. 23, Nov. 27—
            Dec. 31.
    1949   Jan. 1—Dec. 31.
    1950   Jan. 21—Dec. 3.

ESPAÑA POPULAR. w. est. Feb. 18,
1940.
CSt—H
    1940   Feb. 18, Mar. 13, 28, Nov. 9.
    1941   Jan. 21, Feb. 3, Aug. 15, Sept.
            12.
    1942   Feb. 17, May 1, Aug. 5—12,
            Oct. 23—30, Dec. 18—31.
    1943   Jan. 1, Mar. 12, May 21, July
            16.
    1944   Jan. 21, Feb. 25, Apr. 21, May
            19, Nov. 3.
    1945   Jan. 5.
    1947   May 7, June 7, July 26, Oct. 4.
    1948   Feb. 20.
CU
    1941   July 4.
    1944   Mar. 17.
MH
    1940   Feb. 18—Dec. 31.
    1941   Jan. 1—Feb. 25, Mar. 11—22,
            Apr. 14, May 1—22, June 3—
            14.
NjP
    1941   July 18.
    1942   Aug. 5.

EL ESPAÑOL. w., sw., 3w. est. Sept.
11, 1851.

CU—B
    1852   Jan. 3—Dec. 31.
    1853   Jan. 1—May 4.
Micro (N)
    1851   Sept. 11—Oct. 25, Nov. 1—
            Dec. 31.

EL ESPAÑOL. sw.
LNT—MA
    1899   Nov. 19.

EL ESPECTADOR. sw. est. Feb. 1, 1846.
    Note: Ceased publication Sept. 30,
    1846.
CU—B
    Micro (N)
    1846   Feb. 1—Sept. 30.
DLC
    1846   Mar. 4—Apr. 24, 26—28, 30—
            May 8, 10—June 2, July 30—
            Sept. 9.

ESPECULADOR PATRIOTICO. 3w. est.
Oct. 18, 1911.
    Note: Ceased publication Jan. 3,
    1812.
TxU
    1811   Oct. 18—Dec. 31.
    1812   Jan. 1—3.

LA ESPERANZA; PERIODICO POLI-
TICO Y LITERARIO DE MEXICO.
sw. est. Nov. 23, 1841.
CU—B
    Micro (N)
    1841   Nov. 23—Dec. 24, 31.
    1842   Jan. 1—Oct. 18, 25—Nov. 4.
CtY
    1841   Nov. 23.
DLC
    1842   Jan. 4—27, Feb. 5—17, 19—
            24, 26—Mar. 3, 12—May 9,
            11—16, 18, 19, 21—27.
MWA
    1842   Aug. 23.

LA ESPERANZA; SEMANARIO DE
VARIEDADES. w.
TxU
    1880   Nov. 14, 21.

EL ESPIRITU DEL SIGLO. 3w. est. May
16, 1848.
CU – B
Micro (N)
1848   May 16 – June 3, 8 – 10.

EL ESPIRITU PUBLICO. d. est. July
1828.
DLC
1828   Sept. 1 – 19, Nov. 20 – 29, Dec.
2 – 15, 17, 18, 20, 21, 24 – 28.
1829   Jan. 1 – 15, 17, 18, 20, Sept.
3 – 10, 12 – 23, 25 – 30, Oct.
2, 5.
NN
1829   Aug. 15.

EL ESPIRITU PUBLICO. d. est. Jan. 1,
1865.
Note: Ceased publication Feb. 9,
1865.
CU – B
Micro (N)
1865   Jan. 1 – Feb. 9.

L'ESTAFETTE. d.
MWA
1864   July 1 – Dec. 31.
1865   Jan. 1 – June.
1866   Jan. 1 – Dec. 11.
NHi
1863   Sept. 1, 3 – 21, 25 – Dec. 10,
24 – 31.
1864   Jan. 2 – 16, Feb. 18 – 23, May
28 – June 10, Sept. 10 – 12,
15 – 22, 24 – 27, 29 – Oct. 8.

EL ESTANDARTE JACOBINO. w. est.
Oct. 6, 1901.
TxU
1901   Oct. 6 – 21.

EL ESTANDARTE NACIONAL. sw.
Note: Ceased publication June 12,
1845.
CU – B
Micro (N)
1845   Apr. 5 – May 28, June 12.
CtY
1845   Tercera época. Nos. 17 – 19.

MB
1844   Dec. 12.

EL ESTANDARTE NACIONAL;
PERIODICO OFICIAL. d. est. Nov.
16, 1856.
Note: Succeeded *Diario oficial del
supremo gobierno de la República
Mexicana*; succeeded by *Crónica
oficial*. Ceased publication Sept. 30,
1857.
CU – B
Micro (P)
1856   Nov. 16 – Dec. 31.
1857   Jan. 1 – Sept. 30.
DLC
1856   Nov. 16.
1857   Mar. 16 – 20, 22 – Apr. 9, 11 –
17, 19, 21, 25 – May 1, 3 – 7,
9 – 13, 15 – June 3, 7, 9 – 12,
14 – 17, 21, July 2, 3, 5, 7 –
10, 12, 16, 17, 19, 22 – 25, 27,
28, 30 – Aug. 9, 11 – 13, Sept.
2 – 9, 11 – 22, 24 – 30.

EL ESTUDIANTE. bw. est. Feb. 1, 1880.
TxU
1880   Feb. 1 – Mar. 15.

EL ESTUDIANTE Y EL OBRERO. d.
est. 1911.
TxU
1911   May 14.

LOS ESTUDIANTES. w. est. Jan. 1885.
CU – B
Micro (P)
1885   Jan. 25, Feb. 8.

EUZKO DEYA. bw., m. est. Mar. 16,
1943.
Note: In Spanish and Basque. Periodicity Mar. 16, 1943 – Dec. 31, 1945,
biweekly; after Jan. 1, 1945,
monthly.
CSt – H
1943   Apr. 15, May 15, July 1, 15,
Dec. 15.
1944   Jan. 1, Feb. 1, Mar. 1 – July 1,
Aug. 1 – Dec. 15.

1945   Jan. 1 – Feb. 1, Mar. 1 – Dec.
        15.
1946   Feb. – Dec.
1947 – 1949   Jan. – Dec.
ICRL
1943   Nov. 15 – Dec. 31.
1944 – 1947   Jan. 1 – Dec. 31.
1948   Jan. 1+.
MH
1943   Apr. 15 – July 1, Aug. 1 –
        Dec. 15.
1944   Jan. 1 – Nov. 1.
1945   Jan. 1 – Feb. 1, Mar. 1 – May
        1, June 1 – 30, Aug. 15 – Dec.
        31.
1946   Jan. – Dec.

EVOLUCION. w. est. May 1, 1910.
TxU
1910   May 1 – 29.
        Alcance: June 12.

LA EVOLUCION. w. est. 1911.
TxU
1911   Sept. 18.
1912   Mar. 25, Apr. 24.

EVOLUCION; DIARIO LIBRE DE
COMBATE. d. est. Mar. 9, 1918.
DLC
1918   Mar. 9 – 13, 15 – June 30,
        Aug. 1, 2.
TxU
1918   Mar. 30.

EXCELSIOR. d. est. Mar. 18, 1917.
Note: Suspended publication June
15 – 25, 1931.
AzU
1966   Feb. 4, 7 – 9, 11, 12.
CLSU
        Current (three years).
CLU
1940   May 1 – Dec. 31.
1941   Jan. 1 – Oct. 31.
1956   May 1 – Dec. 31.
1957   Jan. 1+.
CSt
1929 – 1944   Jan. 1 – Dec. 31.
1945   Jan. 1 – Aug. 27, Sept. 10 –
        Dec. 31.

1946 – 1948   Jan. 1 – Dec. 31.
1949   Jan. 1 – Oct. 31.
1950   May 3 – Dec. 31.
1951   Jan. 1 – Feb. 16.
1952   Jan. 1 – Apr. 30, May 2 – 21,
        23, 25 – Dec. 31.
1953 – 1962   Jan. 1 – Dec. 31.
1963   Jan. 1 – Oct. 14, Nov. 9, 11,
        12, 14 – Dec. 31.
CSt – H
1963   Dec. 4 – 31.
1964   Jan. 1+.
CU
1920   July 12, 14, Sept. 2, Oct. 13,
        14, Dec. 9.
1921   Feb. 20, July 22, 26 – Aug. 17,
        19 – 27, 29 – Sept. 14, 16 – 24,
        26 – Oct. 6, 8 – 18, 20, 23 –
        Nov. 2, 4 – 15, 17 – Dec. 12,
        14 – 31.
1922   Jan. 1 – 21, 23 – Mar. 28, Apr.
        2 – 10, 12 – June 17, 19 – 24,
        26 – July 26, Aug. 19, 21 – Sept.
        15, 17 – 23, 25 – 28, 30 – Oct.
        28, 30 – Dec. 31.
1923   Jan. 1 – Apr. 14, 16 – 28, 30 –
        Aug. 17, 19, 20, Sept. 13 – Oct.
        31, Nov. 2 – Dec. 1, 4 – 29, 31.
1924   Jan. 1 – Feb. 14, 16 – Mar. 29,
        31 – Apr. 19, 21 – July 8, 10 –
        29, Aug. 1 – 13, 15 – 18, 20 –
        Sept. 11, 13, 24 – Oct. 14, 16 –
        Dec. 31.
1925   Jan. 1 – Mar. 1, 3 – June 15,
        17 – July 29, 31 – Oct. 28, 30 –
        Dec. 5, 7 – 31.
1926   Jan. 1 – Apr. 13, 15 – July 16,
        18 – 24, 26, 27, 29 – Oct. 30,
        Nov. 1 – 8, 10 – Dec. 31.
1927   Jan. 1 – 9, 12 – Apr. 30, May
        2 – Sept. 20, 22 – Nov. 1, 3 –
        Dec. 31.
1928   Jan. 1 – June 16, 18 – Dec. 31.
1929   Jan. 1 – Feb. 25, Mar. 1 – 31,
        Apr. 3 – 30, May 2 – 4, 6 –
        Oct. 7, 9 – Dec. 31.
1930   Jan. 1 – June 14, 17 – Dec. 31.
1931   Jan. 1 – 22, 24 – Oct. 18, 20 –
        Dec. 31.

1932   Jan. 1 – Dec. 31.
1933   Jan. 1 – Dec. 25, 27 – 31.
1934   Jan. 1 – Sept. 16, 18 – Dec. 31.
1935   Jan. 1 – Feb. 15, 17 – May 12,
        14 – Dec. 31.
1936 – 1947 [Jan. 1 – Dec. 31].
1948   Jan. 1 – Dec. 31.
1949   Jan. 1 – 13, 15 – Dec. 31.
1950   Jan. 1 – 26, 28 – Mar. 20, 22 –
        July 29, Aug. 1 – 15, Nov. 3 –
        Dec. 31.
1951   Jan. 1 – Feb. 7.
CtY
  Micro (P)
  1962 – 1963   Jan. 2 – Dec. 31.
  1964   Jan. 2 – June 30, Oct. 1 –
          Dec. 31.
  1965   Jan. 2 – Nov. 30.
DLC
  1917   Mar. 20, Apr. 2, 7, 15, May 1,
          3, 4, 8 – 13, 16, 18 – 20, 22 –
          June 17, 21 – Dec. 31.
          Boletín: Apr. 6, Aug. 14, Nov.
          8.
          Extraordinario: Sept. 1.
          Suplemento: Apr. 29.
  Micro (P) & (N)
  1918   Jan. 1 – June 30.
  1919   Jan. 1 – Dec. 31.
  1920   Jan. 1 – July 31.
  1921   Jan. 1 – Dec. 31.
  1922   Jan. 1 – July 14, Sept. 7 – 14,
          16 – Nov. 16, 18 – Dec. 31.
  1923   Jan. 1 – 28, 30 – Mar. 24, 26 –
          Apr. 28, 30 – May 12, 14 – Oct.
          13, 15 – Dec. 22, 24 – 31.
  1924   Jan. 1 – Dec. 13, 15 – 31.
  1925   Jan. 1 – May 29, 31 – Dec. 31.
  1926   Jan. 1 – Dec. 31.
  1927   Jan. 1 – Aug. 20, 22 – Oct. 13,
          15 – Dec. 31.
  1928   Jan. 1 – Dec. 12, 14 – 31.
  1929   Jan. 1 – Feb. 10, 12 – Dec. 31.
  1930   Jan. 1 – June 29, July 1 – Dec.
          31.
  1931   Jan. 1 – Dec. 31.
  1932   Jan. 1 – June 8, 10 – Aug. 13,
          15 – Nov. 5, 7 – Dec. 31.

1933   Jan. 1 – Nov. 12, 14 – Dec. 9,
        11 – 25, 27 – 31.
1934   Jan. 1 – Apr. 16, 18 – Sept. 1,
        4 – Dec. 31.
1935   Jan. 1 – Feb. 2, 4 – Dec. 31.
1936   Jan. 1 – July 4, 16 – Dec. 31.
1937   Jan. 1 – May 14, 16 – Dec. 31.
1938 – 1941   Jan. 1 – Dec. 31.
1942   Jan. 1 – May 1, 3 – June 16,
        18 – Dec. 31.
1943 – 1945   Jan. 1 – Dec. 31.
1946   Jan. 1 – Mar. 4, 6 – 8, 11 – 15,
        19 – 23, 25 – 30, Apr. 1 – 8,
        10 – 12, 15, 16, 20, 22, 24, 27,
        29, 30, May 4, 8 – 11, 17, 20 –
        25, 27 – June 5, 7 – 12, 14, 15,
        17 – 19, 21 – Aug. 26, 28 – 30,
        Sept. 1 – Dec. 31.
1947   Jan. 1 – Oct. 15, 17 – 21, 23 –
        Dec. 31.
1948   Jan. 1 – Apr. 3, 5 – Dec. 31.
1949 – 1953   Jan. 1 – Dec. 31.
1954   Jan. 1 – 17, 19 – Dec. 31.
1955   Jan. 1 – 3, 5 – Dec. 31.
1956   Jan. 1 – Dec. 31.
1957   Jan. 1 – Apr. 30, May 2 –
        Dec. 31.
1958 – 1959   Jan. 1 – Dec. 31.
1960   Jan. 1 – Nov. 4, 6 – Dec. 31.
1961   Feb. 1 – 10, 14 – Dec. 31.
1962   Jan. 1+.
DPU
  Current (six months).
ICRL
  1926   Mar. 1 – June 30.
  1943   Nov. 1 – Dec. 31.
  1944 – 1945   Jan. 1 – Dec.
  1946   Jan. 1 – Feb. 28.
  1947 – 1951   [Jan. 1 – Dec. 31].
  1952   [Jan. 1 – May 30].
  1953 – 1957   [Jan. 1 – Dec. 31].
  1958   Jan. 1 – Aug. 31, Oct. 1 –
          Nov. 30.
LNT – MA
  1918   Aug. 16, Sept. 2 – 4, 9 – 11.
  1919   Jan. 24.
  1930   Jan. 19, Sept. 16, Nov. 11.
  1931   July 26, Aug. 17.

1933   [Feb. 23 – Dec. 31].
1934 – 1945   [Jan. 1 – Dec. 31].
1946   [Jan. 1 – July 16].
1949   Apr. 1, 6, May 24, Oct. 26 –
       Dec. 31.
1950   Jan. 1 – May 10, Aug. 3 –
       Dec. 31.
1951 – 1961   [Jan. 1 – Dec. 31].
1962   Jan. 1+.
MB
1917   Apr. 3 – 13, 15, 16, 18 – 21, 23,
       24, 27, May 3 – 6, 10, 13 – 18,
       20 – 22, 24, 26, 28, 30, 31.
MoSU
Current (two years).
NN
1921 – 1926   Jan. 1 – Dec. 31.
NNC
1965   Aug. 27 – 29, Sept. 3 – 5, 8, 10,
       14, 15, 17 – 23, 25 – 30, Oct. 1,
       2, 4 – 6, 8 – Nov. 19, 21, 23 –
       Dec. 23, 26 – 31.
1966   Jan. 2 – 6, 8 – 29, Feb. 1, 2.
NcU
1956 – 1958   [Jan. 1 – Dec. 31].
1960 – 1962   [Jan. 1 – Dec. 31].
1964   [Jan. 1 – Dec. 31].
1966   Jan. 1+.
NjP
1942   Aug. 23.
Micro (P)
1963   Jan. 1+.
OrU
1961   Jan. 11.
1963   June 1 – Dec. 31 (Sunday only).
1964   Jan. 5, 12, June 1 – Dec. 31
       (Sunday only).
1965   Jan. 1+. (Sunday only).
TNJ
Current (one year).
TxFTC
1952   Jan. 1+.
TxLT
Current (two years).
TxU
1917   Mar. 19 – 27, 29 – Apr. 8, 10 –
       Dec. 31.
1918   Jan. 1 – Sept. 10, 12 – Dec. 31.

1919   Jan. 1 – May 18, 20 – June 10,
       12 – Dec. 31.
1920   Jan. 1 – Aug. 1, 3 – Dec. 31.
1921   Jan. 1 – Apr. 30, May 2 – Dec.
       31.
1922   Jan. 1 – Mar. 27, 29 – Aug. 2,
       4 – Oct. 17, 19 – 29, 31 – Dec.
       31.
1923   Jan. 1 – 4, 6 – Apr. 30, May 2 –
       Dec. 31.
1924   Jan. 1 – Apr. 2, 4 – 23, 25 –
       June 12, 14 – 28, 30 – July 13,
       15 – 19, 21 – Aug. 20, 22 –
       Sept. 6, 8 – Dec. 31.
1925   Jan. 1, 3 – Oct. 7, 9 – Dec. 31.
1926   Jan. 1 – 25, 27 – May 24, July
       1 – Aug. 18, 20 – Dec. 31.
1927   Jan. 1 – May 1, 3 – July 6, 8 –
       Aug. 4, 6 – 24, 26, 27, 29 –
       Dec. 31.
1928   Jan. 1 – 10, 12 – Apr. 30, May
       2 – July 5, 8 – Dec. 31.
1929   Jan. 1 – Feb. 20, 22 – Apr. 30,
       May 2, 3 – Dec. 31.
1930   Jan. 1 – Apr. 30, May 2 – Dec.
       31.
1931   Jan. 1 – Apr. 30, May 2 –
       Dec. 31.
1932   Jan. 1 – June 8, 10 – Aug. 13,
       15 – 17, 19 – 23, 25 – Sept. 12,
       14 – 16, 18 – Nov. 5, 7 – 11,
       13 – 28, 30 – Dec. 31.
1933   Feb. 1 – July 15, 17 – Sept. 15,
       17 – 30.
1940   July 11.
1952 – 1955   Jan. 1 – Dec. 31.
1956   Jan. 1 – Nov. 30.
1958   Aug. 15 – Nov. 15, 28 – Dec. 7,
       9 – 17, 19 – 24, 26 – 31.
1959   Jan. 1+.

EL EXPLORADOR MINERO. w.
TxU
1877   Mar. 10 – 17.

EXTRA DE HOY. d. est. Feb. 17, 1913.
DLC
1913   Feb. 17, 18.

FACTS AND FIGURES. bw.
  Note: In English.
  LNHT
    1938   Dec. 10.
    1939   Jan. 10, Feb. 30, Apr. 5, July 1,
            Aug. 6.
  MWA
    1938   Dec. 10.

LA FALANGE. sw. est. May 1, 1917.
  DLC
    1917   May 1.

EL FANDANGO. w. est. 1912.
  TxU
    1912   July 18.

EL FARO.
  CtY
    1885   Jan. 1 – Dec. 1.
    1886 – 1888   Jan. 1 – Dec. 15.
    1892   Feb. 15 – Dec. 15.
    1893   Jan. 1 – Dec. 15.
    1894   Jan. 1.

LA FEDERACION. w.
  TxU
    1886   Mar. 13.

EL FEDERALISTA. sw. est. June 24,
1823.
  Note: Ceased publication Oct. 14,
  1823.
  CU – B
  Micro (N)
    1823   June 24 – Oct. 14.

EL FEDERALISTA. sw. est. Feb. 13,
1847.
  CU – B
  Micro (N)
    1847   Feb. 13, 20 – 27.

EL FEDERALISTA. d. est. Jan. 2, 1871.
  CU – B
    1871   Jan. 2 – Mar. 31, Apr. 6 – May
            26, June 1 – Nov. 19, 21 – Dec.
            7, 9 – 17, 19 – 31.
    1872   Jan. 1 – 19, 23 – Mar 27, Apr.
            2 – 13, 16 – 18, 20 – May 18,
            22 – 28, 30 – Aug. 9, 13 – Sept.
            7, 11 – Oct. 19, 22 – Dec. 31.

    1873   Jan. 23 – Feb. 22, 25 – Apr. 18,
            22 – 26, 29 – May 4, 7 – 24,
            26 – June 1, 4 – 6, 10 – 29, July
            1 – Sept. 13, 16 – 24, 26 – Oct.
            17, 21 – Nov. 15, 18 – 30, Dec.
            3 – 31.
    1874   Jan. 1 – Feb. 10, 13 – Mar. 13,
            17 – May 21, 23 – Aug. 27, 29 –
            Sept. 1, 5 – 26, 30 – Oct. 1, 3 –
            14, 16 – 20, 22 – 29, 31 – Nov.
            17, 20, 24 – Dec. 12, 16 – 31.
    1875   July 23, Sept. 21.
    1876   Mar. 16.
  MH
    1871   Oct. 13, 14.
  TxU
    1875   Apr. 28.
    1877   Mar. 13, Oct. 28, Nov. 22.
    1878   Apr. 14.

EL FEDERALISTA. 3m., w. est. July
18, 1911.
  TxU
    1911   July 18, Aug. 6.

EL FEDERALISTA MEXICANA. sw. est.
July 21, 1838.
  Note: Ceased publication Sept. 5,
  1838.
  CU – B
  Micro (N)
    1838   July 21, Aug. 18 – Sept. 5.

EL FENIX. sw. est. Aug. 16, 1914.
  DLC
    1914   Aug. 30.
  TxU
    1914   Aug. 16.

EL FENIX DE LA LIBERTAD. sw., 3w.,
d. est. Dec. 7, 1831.
  Note: Periodicity Dec. 7, 1831 –
  July 14, 1832, semiweekly; July 16 –
  Dec. 29, 1832, three times a week;
  Jan. 7, 1833 – June 1834, daily.
  Suspended publication Oct. 18 –
  Dec. 28, 1832 and Dec. 30, 1832 –
  Jan. 6, 1833. Ceased publication
  [July 4], 1834.

CU – B
  1833   May 9.
  Micro (P)
  1833   Apr. 14, May 30.
CtY
  1831   Dec. 7 – 31.
  1832   Jan. 4 – Dec. 29.
  1833   Jan. 7 – Dec. 31.
  1834   Jan. 1 – May 13, June 4.
DLC
  1831   Dec. 7 – 31.
  1832   Jan. 1 – Feb. 7, 9 – Aug. 17,
           19 – Sept. 25, 27 – 29, Oct. 1 –
           Dec. 29.
           Alcance: Mar. 24, 31, Apr. 28,
           June 23.
           Suplemento: Jan. 7.
  1833   Jan. 1 – Mar. 17, 19 – 31, May
           1, 16, 20, 21, 29, 30, June 1 – 3,
           Sept. 1 – Dec. 31.
           Alcance: Mar. 3.
           Suplemento: Jan. 27, Feb. 24,
           25, Mar. 1, 6, 10.
  1834   Jan. 1 – Feb. 5, 7 – Apr. 13,
           15 – May 10, 12 – 20, 22 – June
           4.
           Extraordinario: May 12.
           Suplemento: Feb. 4.
LNT – MA
  1834   Apr. 5.
NjP
  1834   Jan. 1 – June 4.
TxU
  1831   Dec. 7 – 31.
  1832 – 1833   Jan. 1 – Dec. 31.
  1834   Jan. 1 – June 4.

EL FERROCARRILERO Y BOLETIN DE MEJORES MATERIALES. THE RAILROADER AND BULLETIN OF PUBLIC IMPROVEMENTS.
  See *La República*.

FIERABIAS. irr. est. May 17, 1918.
DLC
  1918   May 17 – 22, June 11 – 17.

FIERABRAS Y NADA MAS. sw.
TxU
  1918   May 31.

FIN DE SIGLO.
TxU
  1906   Apr. 22.

EL FINANCIERO MEXICANO. THE MEXICAN FINANCIER. w.
  Note: In Spanish and English.
CU – B
  Micro (P) & (N)
  1883   Oct. 13, Nov. 10, Dec. 1 – 15,
           29.
  1884   Jan. 12 – 26, Feb. 23, Mar. 8,
           Apr. 12 – June 28, July 26,
           Aug. 16 – Sept. 6, Oct. 11 –
           18, Dec. 13, 27.
  1885   Jan. 10, 24 – 31, Mar. 14 –
           May 2, 16 – 30, June 20, July
           4 – 11, Aug. 1.
  1888   Feb. 25, Mar. 31 – Apr. 7,
           May 19, June 30 – July 7, Aug.
           25, Sept. 22, Oct. 6, Nov. 24 –
           Dec. 1.
  1889   Jan. 5 – 19, Feb. 2 – Mar. 16,
           30 – Apr. 6, 20 – 27, May 11 –
           25, June 8 – 22, July 6, Aug. 10,
           Sept. 7 – Nov. 30, Dec. 14 – 28.
  1890   Jan. 4 – 18, Feb. 22, Mar. 8 –
           22, Apr. 5 – 19, May 3 – 24,
           June 7 – 14, 28, July 12, 26 –
           Aug. 9, 23 – Dec. 27.
  1891   Jan. 10 – 17, 31 – Mar. 14, Apr.
           4, 18, May 2 – 23, June 6 – 20,
           July 4 – Oct. 10, 24 – 31, Nov.
           14 – 28, Dec. 19 – 26.
  1892   Jan. 9 – 16, Feb. 6 – 27, Mar.
           12, 26 – Apr. 9, 30, Sept. 3,
           Oct. 22.

FINANZAS. w.
  Note: In Spanish and English.
TxU
  1916   Mar. 16.

LA FIRMEZA. w. est. 1874.
CU – B
  Micro (P)
  1875   Mar. 13.

EL FLAGELO. w. est. Jan. 27, 1918.
DLC
  1918   Jan. 27.

EL FORO. d. est. June 1, 1873.
  CU—B
    Micro (P)
    1878   Sept. 5.
  LNT—MA
    1873   [June 1—Dec. 31].
    1874   [Jan. 1—Dec. 31].
    1875—1878   Jan. 1—Dec. 31.
    1879   Jan. 1—June 30.
    1880   Jan. 1—June 30.
    1882   July 1—Aug. 30, Sept. 1—
        Dec. 31.
    1883   July 1—Dec. 31.
  NHi
    1874   Jan. 1—26, 28—Feb. 27, Mar.
        1—June 26, July 1—Dec. 27.
    1877   July 3—Dec. 29.
    1878   Jan. 4—31, Feb. 2—19, 22—
        25, 27—Apr. 22, 29—June 7,
        11—14, 17, 19—Aug. 15, 19—
        Dec. 25.
    1879   Jan. 1—June 24.
  TxU
    1873   June 1—Dec. 31.
    1874—1886   Jan. 1—Dec. 31.
    1887   Jan. 1—June 29.

FRAIWELT. w.
  Note: In Yiddish.
  MH
    1947   Feb. 21—28, Apr. 2, 25—May
        2, 16, June 6—13, Aug. 15.

FRANCE LIBRE. w. est. Nov. 6, 1940.
  CSt—H
    1940   Nov. 6—Dec. 31.
    1941—1943   Jan. 1—Dec. 31.
    1944   Jan. 1—Apr. 29.
  CU
    1944   Mar. 25.

FRAY TRAPALA. sw. est. 1862.
  NN
    1862   Jan. 22—Feb. 1.

FRENTE DEMOCRATICO.
  CSt
    1938   Sept. 27.

LA FUERZA OBRERA. w. est. May 31,
  1912.
  TxU
    1912   May 31—June 7.

LA GACETA.
  TxU
    1882   Oct. 22.

LA GACETA; DIARIO DE INFOR-
  MACION. d. est. Oct. 12, 1917.
  DLC
    1917   Oct. 12.

LA GACETA COMERCIAL. d. est. Oct.
  3, 1899.
  DLC
    1900   Jan. 2—17, 20—Feb. 9, 11—
        13, 17, 18, 28—Mar. 12, 14—
        25, 28—June 9, 12—Nov. 27,
        29, Dec. 1—7, 9—31.
    1901   Jan. 1—5, 7—Feb. 7, 9—
        May 30, June 1—Oct. 13, 15—
        20, 22, 24, 25, 27—30, Nov. 1—
        17, 20—Dec. 21.

GACETA DE CAYO-PUTO. est.
  [Aug.] 1820.
  CtY
    1820   Aug. 15—Sept. 30.
        Suplemento: Sept. 30.

GACETA DE LA GUERRA. w.
  Note: Originally published as
  a supplement to *Journal français
  du Méxique* and began as a separate
  series in [Nov.] 1940.
  CSt
    1940   Mar. 27—July 18, Sept. 12.
  DLC
    1940   Apr. 18, May 30, June 13, Aug.
        8—Oct. 10, 24, Dec. 12, 26.
    1941   Jan. 2—Mar. 20, Apr. 10—
        May 15, 29.
  NjP
    1941   July 10.

LA GACETA DE MEXICO. THE MEXI-
  CAN GAZETTE. w.
  Note: In Spanish and English.
  TxU
    1923   Nov. 11.

LA GACETA DE POLICIA. 3w. est.
Aug. 1868.
CU – B
1868 Oct. 1 – Dec. 27.
1869 Jan. 1 – Apr. 18, 22 – May 27,
July 1 – Aug. 1, 5 – Sept. 3, 9 –
30.
GACETA DEL GOBIERNO DE MEXICO.
irr. est. Jan. 2, 1810.
Note: Succeeded *Gazetas de México*;
*compendio de noticias de Nueva
España*; succeeded by *Gaceta del
gobierno imperial de México*. Ceased
publication Sept. 29, 1821.
CtY
1810 Nos. 1 – 117, 119 – 121, 122,
124 – 136, 148, 150, 158.
1811 Nos. 1 – 161.
1812 Nos. 162 – 338.
1813 Nos. 339 – 504.
1814 Nos. 505 – 677.
1815 Nos. 678 – 704, 718 – 808,
810 – 828, 831, 833, 834, 838 –
842.
1817 Nos. 1038, 1091, 1093, 1094,
1097, 1110, 1107, 1120, 1163,
1170, 1175, 1184.
1819 Nos. 82, 103, 105, 110, 116,
154.
1820 Nos. 27 – 92, 95 – 99, 104 – 111,
113 – 123, 125 – 177.
1821 Nos. 33, 34, 39, 46, 55 – 57, 59,
65, 78, 80, 93.
Suplemento: Aug. 18.
DLC
1810 [May 1 – June 30].
1811 – 1820 Jan. 1 – Dec. 31.
ICN
1810 Jan. 2, 5, 9, 12, 16, 19, 23, 26,
30, Feb. 2, 6, 9, 13, 16, 20, 23,
Mar. 2, 6, 9, 13, 17, 20, 23, 27,
30, Apr. 3, 6, 10, 13, 17, 20, 24,
27, May 1, 4, 8, 11, 13, 18, 22,
25, 29, June 1, 5, 8, 12, 15, 19,
22, 26, 29, July 3, 6, 10, 13, 17,
20, 24, 27, 31, Aug. 3, 7, 10, 14,
17, 21, 24, 28, 31, Sept. 4, 7, 11,
14, 18, 21, 25, 28, Oct. 2, 5, 9,
12, 16, 19, 23, 26, 30, Nov. 2, 6,
9, 13, 16, 20, 23, 27, 30, Dec. 4,

7, 11, 14, 18, 21, 25, 28.
Extraordinario: Jan. 10, Feb.
24, Apr. 1, 14, May 1, 23, 29,
June 2, 4, July 15, Sept. 3, 28,
Oct. 1, 5, 28, Nov. 4, 8, 25, 28,
29, Dec. 5, 8, 15, 17, 20.
Suplemento: Jan. 5, Feb. 16,
20, 27, Mar. 9, 23, Apr. 3, 17,
May 15, June 19, Aug. 14, 24,
31, Sept. 7, 14, 21, 23, 25, 28,
Oct. 2, 5, Nov. 20, 28, Dec. 7,
21.
1811 Jan. 1, 4, 8, 11, 15, 18, 22, 25,
29, Feb. 1, 5, 8, 12, 15, 19, 22,
24, 26, Mar. 1, 5, 8, 12, 15, 19,
22, 26, 29, Apr. 2, 5, 9, 12, 16,
19, 23, 26, 30, May 3, 7, 10, 14,
17, 21, 24, 28, 31, June 4, 7, 11,
14, 18, 21, July 2, 4, 9, 11, 13,
16, 18, 20, 23, 25, 27, 30, Aug.
1, 3, 6, 8, 10, 13, 15, 17, 20, 22,
24, 27, 29, 31, Sept. 3, 5, 7, 10,
12, 14, 17, 19, 21, 24, 26, 28,
Oct. 1, 3, 5, 8, 10, 12, 15, 17,
19, 22, 24, 26, 29, 31, Nov. 2, 5,
7, 9, 12, 14, 16, 19, 21, 23, 26,
28, 30, Dec. 3, 5, 7, 9, 12, 14,
16, 19, 21, 23, 26, 28, 31.
Extraordinario: Jan. 4, 9, 17,
23, 25, Feb. 10, 12, 24, Mar.
31, Apr. 9, 14, 20, 25, May 11,
18, 22, June 8, 13, July 4, 11,
12, Sept. 29, 30, Oct. 2, Dec. 10.
Suplemento: Feb. 5, 8, 15, May
3.
1812 Jan. 2, 4, 7, 9, 11, 14, 16, 18, 21,
23, 25, 28, 30, Feb. 1, 4, 6, 8,
11, 13, 15, 18, 20, 22, 25, 27,
29, Mar. 3, 5, 7, 10, 12, 14, 17,
19, 21, 24, 26, 28, 31, Apr. 2,
4, 7, 9, 11, 14, 16, 18, 21, 23, 25,
28, 30, May 2, 5, 7, 9, 12, 14,
16, 19, 21, 23, 28, 30, June 2, 4,
6, 9, 11, 13, 16, 18, 20, 21, 22,
25, 27, 30, July 2, 4, 7, 9, 11,
14, 16, 18, 21, 23, 25, 28, 30,
Aug. 1, 4, 6, 8, 11, 13, 15, 18,
20, 22, 25, 27, 29, Sept. 1, 3, 5,

8, 10, 12, 15, 17, 19, 22, 24, 26,
29, Oct. 1, 3, 6, 8, 10, 13, 15,
17, 20, 22, 24, 27, 29, 31, Nov. 3,
5, 7, 10, 12, 14, 17, 19, 21, 24,
26, 28, Dec. 1, 3, 5, 8, 10, 12,
15, 17, 19, 22, 24, 26, 29, 31.
Extraordinario: Jan. 5, 19, Feb.
15, Mar. 18, May 1, 2, 8, 11,
25, June 8, 18, 21, Aug. 16, 31,
Oct. 11, Nov. 2, 3, 21.
Suplemento: Feb. 9, May 30,
Oct. 30.

1814 Jan. 1, 4, 6, 8, 11, 13, 15, 18,
20, 22, 25, 27, 29, Feb. 1, 3, 5, 8,
10, 12, 15, 17, 19, 22, 24, 26,
Mar. 1, 3, 5, 8, 10, 12, 15, 17, 19,
22, 24, 26, 29, 31, Apr. 2, 5, 7, 9,
12, 14, 16, 19, 21, 23, 26, 28,
30, May 3, 5, 7, 10, 12, 14, 19,
21, 24, 26, 28, 31, June 2, 4, 7,
9, 11, 14, 16, 18, 21, 23, 25, 28,
30, July 2, 5, 7, 9, 12, 13 – 15,
19, 21, 23, 26, 28, 30, Aug. 2, 4,
6, 9, 11, 31, 16, 18, 20, 23, 25,
27, 30, Sept. 1, 3, 6, 8, 10, 13,
15, 17, 20, 22, 24, 27, 29, Oct.
1, 4, 6, 8, 11, 13, 15, 18, 20, 22,
25, 27, 29, Nov. 1, 31, 5, 8, 10,
12, 15, 17, 19, 22, 24, 26, 29,
Dec. 1, 3, 6, 8, 10, 13, 15, 17,
20, 22, 24, 27, 29, 31.
Extraordinario: Jan. 3, 29, 30,
Feb. 1, Mar. 20, Apr. 14, May
16, 21, 29, June 7, 14, July 13,
Aug. 7, Oct. 2, Nov. 11, 20.
Suplemento: May 12, 17, June
4, July 28, Aug. 16, 20, Nov. 8,
Dec. 15.

1815 Jan. 2, 4, 6, 9, 12, 14, 17, 18, 21,
24, 25, 27, Feb. 2, 4, 7, 9, 11,
14, 16, 18, 21, 23, 25, 28, Mar. 2,
4, 7, 9, 11, 14, 16, 18, 21, 23, 25,
28, 30, Apr. 1, 4, 6, 8, 11, 31,
15, 18, 20, 21, 25, 27, 29, May 2,
4, 6, 9, 11, 13, 16, 18, 20, 23, 25,
27, 30, June 1, 3, 6, 8, 10, 13,
15, 17, 20, 22, 24, 27, 29, July 1,
4, 6, 8, 11, 13, 15, 18, 20, 22, 25,

27, 29, Aug. 1, 3, 5, 8, 10, 12,
15, 17, 19, 22, 24, 26, 29, 31,
Sept. 2, 5, 7, 9, 12, 14, 16, 19,
21, 23, 26, 28, 30, Oct. 3, 5, 7,
10, 12, 14, 17, 19, 21, 24, 26,
28, 31, Nov. 2, 4, 7, 9, 11, 14,
16, 18, 21, 23, 25, 28, 30, Dec.
2, 5, 7, 9, 12, 14, 16, 19, 21, 23,
26, 28, 30.
Extraordinario: Feb. 8, May 14,
June 30, Sept. 15, Nov. 9,
Dec. 22.
Suplemento: Apr. 1, June 17,
July 6, 15, Dec. 7.

1816 Jan. 2, 4, 6, 9, 11, 13, 16, 18,
23, 25, 27, 30, Feb. 1, 3, 5, 8, 10,
13, 15, 17, 20, 22, 24, 27, 29,
Mar. 2, 5, 7, 9, 12, 14, 16, 19,
21, 23, 26, 28, 30, Apr. 2, 4, 6,
9, 11, 13, 16, 18, 20, 23, 25, 27,
30, May 2, 4, 7, 9, 11, 14, 16,
18, 21, 23, 25, 28, 30, June 1, 4,
6, 8, 11, 13, 15, 18, 20, 22, 25,
27, 29, July 2, 4, 6, 9, 11, 13, 16,
18, 20, 23, 25, 27, 30, Aug. 1, 3,
6, 8, 10, 13, 15, 17, 20, 22, 24,
27, 29, 31, Sept. 3, 5, 7, 10, 12,
14, 17, 19, 21, 24, 26, 28, Oct.
1, 3, 5, 8, 10, 12, 15, 17, 19, 22,
24, 26, 29, 31, Nov. 2, 5, 7, 9,
12, 14, 16, 19, 21, 23, 26, 28,
30, Dec. 3, 5, 7, 10, 12, 14, 17,
19, 21, 24, 26, 28, 31.
Extraordinario: Mar. 21, Dec.
8, 14, 15, 30.

1817 Jan. 2, 4, 7, 9, 11, 14, 16, 18,
21, 23, 25, 28, 30, Feb. 1, 4, 6,
8, 11, 13, 14, 18, 20, 22, 25, 27,
Mar. 1, 4, 6, 8, 11, 13, 15, 18,
20, 22, 25, 27, 29, Apr. 1, 3, 5,
8, 10, 12, 15, 17, 19, 22, 24, 26,
29, May 1, 3, 6, 8, 10, 13, 15,
17, 20, 22, 24, 27, 29, 31, June
3, 5, 7, 10, 12, 14, 17, 19, 21,
24, 26, 28, July 1, 3, 5, 8, 10,
12, 15, 17, 19, 22, 24, 26, 29,
31, Aug. 2, 5, 7, 9, 12, 14, 16,
19, 21, 23, 26, 28, 30, Sept. 2,

4, 6, 9, 11, 13, 16, 18, 20, 23,
25, 27, 30, Oct. 2, 4, 7, 9, 11,
14, 16, 18, 21, 23, 25, 28, 30,
Nov. 1, 4, 6, 8, 11, 13, 15, 18,
20, 22, 25, 27, 29, Dec. 2, 4, 6,
9, 11, 13, 16, 18, 20, 23, 25, 27,
30.
Extraordinario: Jan. 9, 24, 29,
Feb. 8, 27, Mar. 6, 8, 18, Apr.
7, 16, June 4, 12, 14, 20, 21, 23,
27, July 3, 16, Aug. 27, Sept.
6, 15, 21, 24, Oct. 23, 27, 31,
Nov. 1, 12, 19, Dec. 4, 7.
Suplemento: Dec. 18.

1818 Jan. 1, 3, 6, 8, 10, 13, 15, 17,
20, 22, 24, 27, 29, 31, Feb. 3, 5,
7, 10, 12, 14, 17, 19, 21, 24, 26,
28, Mar. 3, 5, 7, 10, 12, 14, 17,
19, 21, 24, 26, 28, 31, Apr. 2,
4, 7, 9, 11, 14, 16, 18, 21, 23,
25, 28, 30, June 2, 4, 6, 9, 11,
13, 16, 18, 20, 23, 25, 27, 30,
July 2, 4, 7, 9, 11, 14, 16, 18, 21,
23, 25, 28, 30, Aug. 1, 4, 6, 8,
11, 13, 15, 18, 20, 22, 25, 27,
29, Sept. 1, 3, 5, 8, 10, 12, 15,
17, 19, 22, 24, 26, 29, Oct. 1, 3,
6, 8, 10, 13, 15, 18, 20, 22, 24,
27, 29, 31, Nov. 3, 5, 7, 10, 12,
14, 17, 19, 21, 24, 26, 28, Dec.
1, 3, 5, 8, 10, 12, 15, 17, 19, 22,
24, 26, 29, 31.
Extraordinario: Jan. 6, 8, 10,
20, 23, 24, 25, 29, Feb. 12, Mar.
11, June 6, 24, Nov. 29.
Suplemento: July 30.

1819 Jan. 2, 5, 7, 9, 12, 14, 16, 19,
21, 23, 26, 28, 30, Feb. 2, 4, 6,
9, 11, 13, 16, 18, 20, 23, 25, 27,
Mar. 2, 4, 6, 9, 11, 13, 16, 18,
20, 23, 25, 27, 30, Apr. 1, 3, 6,
8, 10, 13, 15, 17, 20, 22, 24, 27,
29, May 1, 4, 6, 8, 11, 13, 15,
18, 20, 22, 25, 27, 29, June 1, 3,
5, 8, 10, 12, 15, 17, 19, 22, 24,
26, 29, July 1, 3, 6, 8, 10, 13,
15, 17, 20, 22, 24, 27, 29, 31,
Aug. 3, 5, 7, 10, 12, 14, 17, 19,

21, 24, 26, 28, 31, Sept. 2, 4, 7,
9, 11, 14, 16, 18, 21, 23, 25, 28,
30, Oct. 2, 5, 7, 9, 12, 14, 16,
19, 21, 23, 26, 28, 30, Nov. 2, 4,
6, 9, 11, 13, 16, 18, 20, 23, 25,
27, 30, Dec. 2, 4, 7, 9, 11, 14,
16, 18, 21, 23, 25, 28, 30.
Extraordinario: Jan. 21, Mar.
24, Apr. 20, May 19, July 8, 31,
Aug. 3, 6, 7, 11, 13, 17, 30, Oct.
9, 14, 27, 31, Nov. 15, 16, Dec.
8.
Suplemento: Aug. 24.

1820 Jan. 1, 4, 6, 8, 11, 13, 15, 18,
20, 22, 25, 27, 29, Feb. 1, 3, 5,
8, 10, 12, 15, 17, 19, 22, 24, 26,
29, Mar. 2, 4, 7, 9, 11, 14, 16,
18, 21, 23, 25, 28, 30, Apr. 1, 4,
6, 8, 11, 13, 15, 18, 20, 22, 25,
27, 29, May 2, 4, 6, 9, 11, 13, 16,
18, 20, 23, 25, 27, 30, June 1, 3,
6, 8, 10, 13, 15, 17, 20, 22, 24,
27, 29, July 1, 4, 6, 8, 11, 13,
15, 18, 20, 22, 25, 27, 29, Aug.
1, 3, 5, 8, 10, 12, 15, 17, 19, 22,
24, 26, 29, 31, Sept. 2, 5, 7, 16,
19, 21, 23, 26, 28, 30, Oct. 3,
5, 7, 10, 12, 14, 17, 19, 21, 24,
26, 28, 31, Nov. 2, 4, 7, 9, 11,
14, 16, 18, 21, 23, 25, 28, 30,
Dec. 2, 5, 7, 9, 12, 14, 16, 19,
21, 23, 26, 28, 30.
Extraordinario: Jan. 1, June 7,
13, 19, 20, 28, July 12, 26, Aug.
18, 29, Sept. 7, 15, 19, 25, Nov.
21, 24, 28, Dec. 1, 8.
Suplemento: Oct. 7.

1821 Jan. 2, 4, 6, 9, 1, 31, 16, 18, 20,
23, 25, 27, 30, Feb. 1, 3, 6, 8,
10, 13, 15, 17, 20, 22, 24, 27,
Mar. 1, 3, 6, 8, 10, 13, 15, 17, 20,
22, 24, 27, 29, 30, Apr. 3, 5, 7,
10, 12, 14, 17, 19, 21, 24, 26,
28, May 1, 3, 5, 8, 10, 12, 15,
17, 19, 22, 24, 26, 29, 31, June
2, 5, 7, 9, 12, 14, 16, 17, 21, 23,
26, 28, 30, July 3, 5, 7, 10, 14,
17, 19, 21, 24, 26, 28, 31, Aug.

25, 28, 30, Sept. 1, 4, 6, 8, 11,
13, 15, 18, 20, 22, 25, 27, 29.

15, 18, 20, 22, 25, 27, 29.

Extraordinario: Feb. 23, Mar.
26, Apr. 30, May 2, 4, 16, June
12, 16, 25, July 21, Aug. 14, 23.

IU
   1810   Jan. 2 – Dec. 31.
   1811 – 1820   Jan. 1 – Dec. 31.
   1821   Jan. 1 – Sept. 29.

LNHT
   1810   [Apr. 3 – Dec. 20].
   1811   [Jan. 9 – Dec. 26].
   1812   [Jan. 2 – Dec. 17].
   1813   [Jan. 7 – Dec. 7].
   1814   [Jan. 29 – June 30].
   1815   Jan. 26.
   1820   Jan. 25.

MoSU
   Micro (P)
   1810   Jan. 2 – Dec. 31.
   1811 – 1818   Jan. 1 – Dec. 31.
   1819   Jan. 1 – July 31.

TxH – SJ
   1810   Jan. 2 – Dec. 31.
   1811 – 1812   Jan. 1 – Dec. 31.

GACETA DEL GOBIERNO IMPERIAL DE MÉXICO. 3w. est. Oct. 2, 1821.
   Note: Title *Gaceta imperial de México*, Oct. 2, 1821 – Apr. 18, 1822; *Gaceta del gobierno imperial de México*, Apr. 19 – Dec. 31, 1822. Succeeded *Gaceta del gobierno de México*; succeeded by *Gaceta del supremo gobierno de la Federación Mexicana*. Ceased publication Dec. 31, 1822.

CU – B
   1821   Oct. 2 – Dec. 31.
   1822   Jan. 1 – Dec. 31.

CtY
   1821   Oct. 2 – Dec. 29.
   1822   Jan. 1 – Dec. 31.

DLC
   1821   [Oct. 2 – Dec. 31].
   1822   [Jan. 1 – Dec. 31].

ICN
   1821   Oct. 2, 4, 5, 9, 11, 13, 16, 18,

20, 23, 25, 27, 30, Nov. 1, 2, 3,
6, 8, 10, 13, 15, 17, 20, 22, 24,
27, 29, Dec. 1, 4, 6, 8, 11, 13,
15, 18, 20, 22, 25, 27, 29, Dec.
1, 4, 6, 8, 11, 13, 15, 18, 20, 22,
25, 27, 29.

Extraordinario: Oct. 17, 23,
Nov. 27, Dec. 13.

   1822   Jan. 1, 3, 5, 8, 10, 12, 15, 17,
19, 22, 23, 24, 26, 29, 31, Feb. 2,
5, 7, 9, 12, 14, 16, 19, 21, 23,
26, 28, Mar. 2, 5, 7, 9, 12, 14,
16, 19, 21, 23, 26, 28, 30, Apr.
2, 4, 6, 9, 10, 11, 13, 16, 18, 20,
23, 25, 27, 30, May 2, 4, 7, 9, 11,
14, 16, 18, 21, 23, 25, 28, 30,
June 1, 4, 6, 8, 11, 13, 15, 18, 20,
22, 25, 27, 29, July 2, 4, 6, 9, 11,
25, 27, 29, July 2, 4, 6, 9, 11,
13, 16, 18, 20, 23, 25, 27, 30,
Aug. 1, 3, 6, 8, 10, 13, 15, 17,
20, 22, 24, 27, 29, 31, Sept. 3,
5, 7, 10, 12, 14, 17, 19, 21, 24,
26, 28, Oct. 1, 3, 5, 8, 10, 12,
15, 17, 19, 22, 24, 26, 29, 31,
Nov. 2, 5, 7, 9, 12, 14, 16, 19, 21,
23, 26, 28, 30, Dec. 1, 3, 5, 7,
10, 12, 14, 17, 19, 24, 26, 28, 31.

Extraordinario: Apr. 13, 21,
May 1, 24, 26, June 26, Aug. 27,
Sept. 18, Oct. 20, 27, Nov. 1,
Dec. 8, 11, 17, 19, 23, 25.

IU
   1821   Oct. 2 – Dec. 31.
   1822   Jan. 1 – Dec. 31.

MWA
   1821   Oct. 2 – Dec. 31.
   1822   Jan. 1 – Dec. 31.

GACETA DEL GOBIERNO SUPREMO DE LA FEDERACION MEXICANA. 3w. est. May 2, 1826.
   Note Succeeded *Gaceta diaria de México*. Ceased publication May 31, 1827.

CU – B
   1826   May 2 – Dec. 31.
   1827   Jan. 1 – May 31.

CtY

1826   Sept. 12, Oct. 17–21, 26–28,
        Nov. 2–Dec. 26, 30.
1827   Jan. 2–18, 23–Feb. 3, 8, 13,
        20–Mar. 1.

DLC

1826   [May 2–Nov. 21].

GACETA DEL SUPREMO GOBIERNO DE LA FEDERACION MEXICANA.

2w. est. Jan. 2, 1823.
    Note: Title *Gaceta del gobierno
    imperial de México*, Jan. 2–Mar. 27,
    1823; *Gaceta del gobierno supremo
    de México*, May 23, 1823–Jan. 27,
    1824; *Gaceta del supremo gobierno
    de la Federación Mexicana*, Jan. 28,
    1824–May 31, 1825. Succeeded
    *Gaceta del gobierno imperial de
    México*; succeeded by *Gaceta diaria
    de México*. Ceased publication May
    31, 1825.

CU–B

1823   [Jan. 7–Dec. 31].
1824   [Jan. 1–Dec. 31].
1825   [Jan. 1–May 31].

Micro (P)

1823   Jan. 7–Dec. 31.
1824   Jan. 1–Dec. 31.
1825   Jan. 1–Mar. 10.

CtY

1823   Jan. 2–23, 28, Feb. 1–4, Mar.
        27, July 2, Aug. 29, Oct. 1, Nov.
        27, Dec. 31.
        Suplemento: Feb. 26, Mar. 5,
        May 23, 27.
1824   Jan. 23, 25–27, Mar. 30, Apr.
        6, 27, May 8, July 1, 26, Dec.
        28–30.
        Suplemento: May 28, Aug. 19.
1825   Mar. 1–8.
        Suplemento: Mar. 10.

DLC

1823   [Jan. 2–Dec. 31].
1824   [Jan. 1–Dec. 30].

TxH–SJ

1824   Jan. 1–Dec. 31.

GACETA DEL LUNES. w. est. June 21, 1880.

TxU

1880   June 21–Dec. 31.

1881   Jan. 1–Mar. 21.

GACETA DIARIA DE MEXICO. d. est. June 1, 1825.

    Note: Succeeded *Gaceta del gobierno
    de la Federación Mexicana*; suc-
    ceeded by *Gaceta del gobierno su-
    prema de la Federación Mexicana*.
    Ceased publication Apr. 1826.

CU–B

1825   [June 1–Dec. 31].
1826   [Jan. 1–Apr. 30].

Micro (P)

1825   June 1–Dec. 31.
1826   Jan. 1–Apr. 30.

CtY

1825   June 11, 21–23, 25–28,
        30–Dec. 17, 19–31.
        Suplemento: June 24.

DLC

1825   [June 1–Dec. 31].
1826   [Jan. 1–Apr. 26].

GACETA IMPERIAL DE MEXICO.

    See *Gaceta del gobierno imperial de
    México*.

GACETA INTERNACIONAL.

TxU

1881   June 24, July 7.

GACETA LIBRE. w. est. July 2, 1911.

TxU

1911   July 2.

GACETA MUSICAL. bw.

TxU

1910   July 15–Aug. 1.
1911   Mar. 15–Apr. 15, July 1,
        Nov. 1–Dec. 31.
1912   Jan. 1–15, Feb. 15, Apr. 1–
        May 15, June 15–July 15,
        Aug. 15–Dec. 31.
1913   Jan. 1, June 1–July 1, Nov. 1.
1914   Mar. 1, Apr. 1.

GACETA OFICIAL.

TxU

1890   Aug. 17, Oct. 5, 16.

GACETA PATRIOTICA DEL EJERCITO
NACIONAL.
LNT—MA
1820   Apr. 21.

LA GACETILLA. d., sw. est. Sept. 26,
1877.
CtY
1877   Sept. 26 — Dec. 28.
1878   Jan. 1 — June 29, July 4 — Dec.
29.
LNT—MA
1878   Jan. 1 — Mar. 31.

EL GALLO. w. est. Sept. 28, 1917.
DLC
1917   Sept. 28, Oct. 10.

GAZETA DE MEXICO. m. est. Jan. 1,
1722-
Note: Succeeded by *Gazetas de México*. Ceased publication Nov. 1739.
CU—B
1722   Jan. — June.
1728 — 1730   Jan. — Dec.
Micro (P)
1728 — 1730   Jan. — Dec.
DLC
1727 — 1730   Jan. — Dec.
1731   Jan., July, Aug.
1732   Jan. — June.
1734   Apr.
1735   Jan. — Mar., May — Sept.
1737   Jan. — Dec.
1738   Jan. — Mar., June — Dec.
1739   Jan. — June.
ICN
1728 — 1730   Jan. — Dec.
1731   Jan. — Aug, [Sept., Dec.]
1732   Jan., Apr. — Sept., Nov.
1733   Jan. — June, Aug, Nov., Dec.
1734   Jan., Mar. — May, July, Aug.,
Nov., Dec.
1735   Jan. — Apr., July, Sept., Oct.
IU
1728 — 1730   Jan. — Dec.
LNHT
1728   Jan. — Dec.
1729   Jan. — Mar.
1731   Sept., Oct.

MoSU
Micro (P)
1722   Jan. — June.
1728 — 1729   Jan. — Dec.
NN
1722   Jan., Mar. — June.
1728 — 1735   Jan. — Dec.
1736   Jan. — Apr., July — Dec.
1737   Jan. — Dec.
1738   Jan., Mar. — July, Sept. — Nov.
1739   Jan. — Nov.
TxSjM
1728   Jan. — Dec.
1732 — 1735   Jan. — Dec.

GAZETAS DE MEXICO; COMPENDIO
DE NOTICIAS DE NUEVA ESPAÑA.
irr. est. Jan. 14, 1784.
Note: Succeeded *Gazeta de México*;
succeeded by *Gaceta del gobierno
de México*. Ceased publication
Dec. 1809.
CU—B
1784   Jan. 14 — Dec. 31.
1785 — 1809   Jan. 1 — Dec. 31.
CtY
1784   Jan. 14 — Dec. 29.
1785   Jan. 4 — Dec. 27.
1786   Jan. 10 — Dec. 19.
1787   Jan. 3 — Dec. 18.
1788   Jan. 8 — Dec. 23.
1789   Jan. 6 — Dec. 22.
1790   Jan. 12 — Dec. 21.
1791   Jan. 11 — Dec. 27.
1792   Jan. 10 — Dec. 25.
1793   Jan. 8 — Dec. 30.
1794   Jan. 7 — Dec. 23.
1795   Jan. 13 — Dec. 29.
1797   Jan. 18 — Dec. 27.
1798   Jan. 12 — Dec. 14.
1799   Jan. 11 — Sept. 28, Oct. 23 —
Dec. 18.
Suplemento: Sept. 28.
1800   Jan. 18 — June 18, July 14 —
Dec. 31.
1801   Jan. 20 — Dec. 19.
DLC
1784   Jan. 14 — Dec. 31.
1785 — 1809   Jan. 1 — Dec. 31.

ICN
1784   Jan. 14, 28, Feb. 11, 25,
       Mar. 10, 24, Apr. 7, 21, May 5,
       19, June 2, 16, 30, July 14,
       28, Aug. 11, 25, Sept. 8, 22,
       Oct. 6, 20, Nov. 3, 17, Dec. 1,
       15, 29.
       Suplemento: Feb. 25, May 5,
       July 28, Aug. 11, Sept. 8, Oct.
       20, Nov. 17, Dec. 1, 29.
1785   Jan. 4, 18, 25, Feb. 8, 22,
       Mar. 8, 22, Apr. 5, 19, May 3,
       10, 24, June 7, 21, July 5, 12,
       26, Aug. 9, 23, Sept. 9, 20,
       Oct. 4, 18, Nov. 8, 22, Dec. 6,
       27.
       Suplemento: Jan. 4, 18, Mar.
       8, Oct. 18, Dec. 6.
1786   Jan. 10, 24, Feb. 4, 28, Mar.
       14, 28, Apr. 18, May 2, 16, 30,
       June 13, 27, July 11, 25, Aug. 8,
       22, Sept. 12, 26, Oct. 10, 24,
       Nov. 7, 21, Dec. 5, 19.
       Suplemento: Feb. 28, Aug. 22,
       Oct. 10.
1787   Jan. 3, 16, 30, Feb. 13, 27,
       Mar. 13, 27, Apr. 17, 24, May 1,
       22, June 5, 19, July 10, 26, Aug.
       21, Sept. 11, Oct. 2, 23, Nov 6,
       20, Dec. 4, 18.
       Suplemento: Oct. 23, Nov. 20.
1788   Jan. 8, 22, Feb. 12, 26, Mar.
       15, Apr. 8, 22, May 6, 27, June
       17, 24, July 15, Aug. 5, 18, 26,
       Sept. 16, 30, Oct. 14, 29, Nov.
       18, Dec. 2, 23.
       Suplemento: May 6, June 24,
       July 15.
1789   Jan. 6, 20, Feb. 3, 17, 24, Mar.
       10, 24, Apr. 14, May 5, 19, 26,
       June 9, 23, July 7, 28, Aug. 11,
       25, Sept. 8, 22, Oct. 6, 20, Nov.
       10, Dec. 1, 22.
       Suplemento: Mar. 24, Apr. 14.
1790   Jan. 12, 19, Feb. 2, 23, Mar. 9,
       23, Apr. 13, 27, May 4, 18, June
       1, 22, July 6, 20, Aug. 10, 24,
       Sept. 7, 21, Oct. 5, 19, Nov. 23,

Dec. 7, 21.
       Suplemento: Mar. 30, June 1,
       Sept. 21, Nov. 2.
1791   Jan. 11, 25, Feb. 8, Mar. 11,
       15, 29, Apr. 12, 26, May 10, 24,
       June 7, 21, July 12, 26, Aug. 2,
       16, 30, Sept. 13, 27, Oct. 11, 25,
       Nov. 15, 29, Dec. 13, 27.
1792   Jan. 10, 24, Feb. 7, 21, Mar. 6,
       20, Apr. 3, 24, May 8, 15, 29,
       June 12, 26 July 17, Aug. 7, 21,
       Sept. 4, 18, Oct. 2, 16, 30, Nov.
       13, 27, Dec. 11, 25.
       Suplemento: Apr. 3, Nov. 13.
1793   Jan. 8, 22, Feb. 5, 26, Mar. 27,
       Apr. 16, May 7, 14, 18, 21, 24,
       June 11, 18, 22, July 2, 9, 13, 23,
       Aug. 6, 31, Sept. 3, 7, 10, 14, 17,
       19, 24, 28, 30, Oct. 4, 8, 21, 24,
       29, Nov. 9, 16, 23, 26, 30, Dec.
       3, 7, 10, 14, 16, 18, 21, 23, 30.
       Suplemento: Jan. 22, Feb. 26,
       Aug. 6, 31, Dec. 3.
1794   Jan. 7, 21, Feb. 10, 12, 15, 17,
       18, Mar. 8, 10, 11, 15, 17, 20, 24,
       26, 29, 31, May 2, 6, 8, 10, 13,
       15, 17, 20, 22, 24, 27, June 16,
       July 5, 8, 9, 10, 15, 17, 21, 24,
       29, Aug. 2, 18, 22, 26, 30, Sept.
       3, 6, 9, 10, 12, 13, 15, 17, 19, 20,
       23, Oct. 4, 8, 11, 21, 27, 29, 31,
       [Nov. 4,] 6, 8, 11, 13, 19, Dec.
       6, 9, 11, 16, 18, 23.
       Suplemento: Nov. 19, Dec. 23.
1795   Jan. 13, 21, Feb. 3, 18, 21, 23,
       25, 27, Mar. 2, 6, 9, 13, 30, Apr.
       8, 10, 14, 17, 20, 25, 28, 30, May
       2, 5, 7, 11, 16, 19, 21, 30, June
       20, July 4, 8, 13, 15, 20, 24, 29,
       Aug. 10, 17, 21, Sept. 12, 16,
       18, 26, 30, Oct. 2, 7, 20, Nov.
       12, 19, 21, Dec. 11, 16, 19, 23.
       Suplemento: Feb. 3, 25, Apr.
       17, May 30, July 4, Sept. 18,
       Oct. 20, Dec. 29.
1796   Jan. 12, 29, Feb. 9, 20, Mar. 1,
       18, 22, 31, May 10, 20, June 4,
       25, July 13, 27, Aug. 17, Sept.

3, 17, Oct. 3, 21, 28, Nov. 11,
26, Dec. 7, 28.
Suplemento: Jan. 12, Nov. 11,
Dec. 7.

1797 Jan. 18, Feb. 8, Mar. 3, 22, Apr.
15, May 20, July 10, 22,
Aug. 19, Sept. 2, 23, Oct. 28,
Nov. 25, 29, Dec. 27.
Suplemento: Jan. 18, Aug. 19,
Sept. 23, Oct. 21.

1798 Jan. 12, Feb. 2, Mar. 23, May
21, June 30, July 28, Aug. 18,
Sept. 26, Oct. 8, 22, Nov. 16,
26, Dec. 14.
Suplemento: Aug. 18, Oct. 22,
Nov. 16, 26, Dec. 14.

1799 Jan. 11, 28, Feb. 11, Mar. 4,
18, Apr. 8, 15, May 8, 29, June
12, July 20, Aug. 3, 28, Sept.
14, 28, Oct. 23, Nov. 11, 30,
Dec. 7, 18.
Suplemento: Jan. 11, 28, Feb.
11, Mar 4, 18, Apr. 15, May 8,
29, June 12, July 20, Aug. 3, 28,
Sept. 14, 28, Nov. 11.

1800 Jan. 18, 25, Feb. 8, 22, Mar. 8,
19, Apr. 2, 23, May 14, 28, June
18, July 14, Aug. 6, 30, Sept. 22,
Nov. 4, 18, Dec. 31.
Suplemento: Jan. 25, June 18,
July 14, Sept. 22, Nov. 18.

1801 Jan. 20, Feb. 24, Mar. 10, Apr.
14, 21, May 20, July 8, 22, Aug.
29, Sept. 3, 19, Oct. 17, 24,
Nov. 28, Dec. 19.
Suplemento: Apr. 21, Aug. 29,
Dec. 19.

1802 Jan. 13, 30, Feb. 27, Mar. 13,
27, Apr. 17, 21, 29, May 5, 19,
June 9, July 21, Aug. 18, Sept.
10, 17, Oct. 8, 29, Nov. 12, Dec.
6, 27, 30.
Suplemento: June 9, July 21,
Aug. 18, Oct. 8, Nov. 12.

1803 Jan. 7, 28, Feb. 11, Mar. 11,
Apr. 1, 15, May 6, 21, June 11,
25, July 23, Aug. 20, 31, Sept.
13, 28, Oct. 26, Nov. 11, 28,

Dec. 16.
Suplemento: Feb. 11, May 6,
July 23, Sept. 13, Dec. 16.

1804 Jan. 7, 28, Feb. 18, 29, Apr. 4,
25, May 2, 23, 26, [May 26,]
June 30, Aug. 1, 15, 29, Sept.
19, Oct. 6, 27, Dec. 11.
Suplemento: Jan. 7, Feb. 18,
Apr. n.d., June 30, Oct. 6,
27.

1805 Jan. 8, Feb. 26, Apr. 9, May
14, June 4, July 16, Aug. 6, 27,
Sept. 17, Oct. 30, Nov. 2, 6, 9,
13, 16, 23, 27, 29, Dec. 3, 7, 11,
14, 18, 20, 25, 28.
Suplemento: Jan. 8, Feb. 26,
Apr. 9, June 4, Nov. 2, 29, Dec.
11.

1806 Jan. 1, 4, 8, 11, 15, 18, 22, 25,
29, Feb. 1, 5, 8, 12, 15, 19, 22,
26, Mar. 1, 5, 8, 12, 19, 22, 26,
29, Apr. 2, 5, 9, 12, 16, 19, 23,
26, 30, May 3, 7, 10, 14, 17, 21,
24, 28, 31, June 4, 7, 11, 14, 18,
21, 25, 28, July 2, 5, 9, 12, 16,
19, 23, 26, 30, Aug. 2, 6, 9, 13,
16, 20, 23, 27, 30, Sept. 6, 10,
13, 17, 20, 24, Oct. 1, 4, 8, 11,
15, 18, 22, 25, 29, Nov. 1, 5, 8,
12, 15, 18, 19, 22, 26, 29, Dec.
3, 6, 10, 13, 17, 20, 24, 27, 31.
Suplemento: July 2, Sept. n.d.,
Sept. n.d., Sept. n.d., Dec. 23.

1807 Jan. 3, 7, 10, 14, 17, 21, 24, 28,
31, Feb. 4, 7, 11, 14, 18, 21, 25,
28, Mar. 4, 7, 11, 14, 18, 21, 25,
28, Apr. 1, 4, 8, 11, 15, 18, 22,
25, 29, May 2, 6, 9, 13, 16, 20,
23, 27, June 3, 6, 10, 13, 17, 20,
24, 27, July 1, 4, 8, 11, 15, 18,
22, 25, 29, Aug. 1, 5, 8, 12, 15,
19, 22, 26, 29, Sept. 2, 5, 9, 12,
16, 19, 23, 26, 30, Oct. 7, 10,
14, 17, 21, 24, 31, Nov. 4, 7, 11,
14, 18, 21, 25, 28, Dec. 2, 5, 9,
12, 16, 19, 23, 26, 30.
Extraordinario: May 27, July
26, Oct. 24, 31, Dec. 6. 7.

1808   Jan. 2, 6, 9, 13, 16, 20, 23, 27,
30, Feb. 3, 6, 10, 13, 17, 20, 24,
27, Mar. 2, 5, 9, 12, 16, 23, 26,
30, Apr. 2, 6, 9, 13, 16, 20, 23,
27, 30, May 4, 7, 11, 13, 18, 21,
25, 28, June 1, 4, 8, 11, 15, 18,
22, 25, 29, July 2, 6, 9, 13, 16,
20, 23, 27, 30, Aug. 3, 6, 10, 12,
13, 17, 20, 24, 27, 31, Sept. 3, 7,
10, 14, 17, 21, 24, 28, Oct. 1, 5,
8, 12, 15, 19, 22, 26, 29, Nov. 2,
5, 9, 12, 16, 19, 23, 26, 30, Dec.
3, 7, 10, 14, 16, 17, 21, 23, 24,
28, 31.
Extraordinario: June 9, July 29,
31, Aug. 1–5, 29, Sept. 7, 9, 16,
19, Oct. 4, 7, 11, 15, Nov. 11,
14, 18, 21, 28, Dec. 6, 23, 24,
28.
Suplemento: Feb. 10, Aug. 3,
5, 6, 20, 31, Sept. 3, 10, 14, 28,
Oct. 15, Dec. 28.

1809   Jan. 4, 7, 11, 14, 18, 21, 25, 28,
Feb. 1, 8, 11, 15, 18, 22, 25,
Mar. 1, 4, 8, 11, 15, 18, 22, 25,
29, Apr. 1, 8, 12, 15, 19, 22, 26,
29, May 3, 6, 10, 13, 17, 20, 24,
27, 31, June 3, 7, 10, 14, 17, 21,
24, 28, July 1, 5, 8, 12, 15, 19,
22, 26, 29, Aug. 2, 5, 9, 12, 16,
19, 23, 26, 30, Sept. 2, 6, 9, 13,
16, 20, 23, 27, 30, Oct. 4, 7, 11,
14, 18, 20, 21, 25, 28, Nov. 1, 4,
8, 11, 15, 18, 22, 25, 29, Dec. 2,
6, 9, 13, 16, 20, 23.
Extraordinario: Jan. 6, 11, 20,
24, Feb. 7, 24, Mar. 9, 14, 16,
24, 28, 29, Apr. 1, 2, 6, 14, 15,
28, May 12, 16, 30, June 17, 24,
26, 29, July 7, 11, 15, 17, 18,
Aug. 1, 6, 11, Sept. 5, 21, 27,
Oct. 4, 5, Nov. 2, 3, 13, Dec. 26.
Suplemento: Jan. 7, 14, Feb.
22, Nov. 25, Dec. 6.

IU
  1784   Jan. 14–Dec. 31.
  1785–1809 Jan. 1–Dec. 31.

LNHT
  1784   Jan. 15–Dec. 29.
  1786   Aug. 22.
  1787   Oct. 23.
  1789   Mar. 24.
  1790–1791 Jan. 1–Dec. 31.
  1793   May 14–Dec. 3.
  1796   Oct. 3–Dec. 31.
  1797   Jan. 1–Aug. 19.
  1799   May 29.
  1800   June 18–Dec. 31.
  1801   Jan. 1–Oct. 17.
  1802   Jan. 13–Dec. 31.
  1803   Jan. 1–Nov. 28.
  1805   June 4–Nov. 29.
  1806   Apr. 19–June 25.
  1807   Mar. 7–June 27.
  1808   June 25–Dec. 10.
  1809   Jan. 11–Dec. 6.
MoSU
  Micro (P)
  1784   Jan. 14–Dec. 31.
  1785–1808 Jan. 1–Dec. 31.
  1809   Jan. 1–Dec. 30.
NN
  1784   Jan. 28–Mar. 24, Apr. 21–
Aug. 11, Sept. 8–Oct. 20, Dec.
1–29.
Suplemento: May 5, July 28,
Aug. 11, Sept. 8, Oct. 20, Nov.
17, Dec. 1, 29.
  1785   Jan. 4–May 10, July 5–Aug.
23, Sept. 20, Oct. 18–Nov. 22.
Suplemento: Jan. 18, Mar. 8.
  1788   Jan. 8–Dec. 23.
Suplemento: May 6, June 24,
July 15.
  1789   Jan. 6–May 19, July 7–Dec.
22.
Suplemento: Feb. 3, Mar. 24,
Apr. 14-
  1790   Jan. 12, Feb. 23–Apr. 13, May
4–Sept. 21, Nov. 2–Dec. 21.
Suplemento: Mar. 30, Nov. 2.
  1791   Jan. 11, 25, Mar. 29–Dec. 27.
  1792   Jan. 10–Aug. 7, Sept. 4–Nov.
27, Dec. 25.
Suplemento: Apr. 3, Nov. 13.
  1793   Jan. 8–May 24, Aug. 6–Dec. 30

Suplemento: Jan. 22, Feb. 26,
Aug. 6, 31, Dec. 3.

1794   Jan. 7 – May 2, July 5 – Dec. 27.

1796   Jan. 1 – Dec. 31.

1797   Jan. 18 – Feb. 8, Mar. 22 –
Aug. 19, Sept. 2 – Dec. 27.

1798   Jan. 12, Mar. 23, June 30 – Aug.
18, Sept. 26 – Oct. 22, Nov.
16 – Dec. 14.
Suplemento: Oct. 22, Nov. 16,
26, Dec. 14.

1799   Jan. 11 – Feb. 11, Mar. 18 –
May 8, Aug. 3, Nov. 30 – Dec.
18.
Continuación: Mar. 18.
Suplemento: Jan. 11, 28, Feb.
11, Mar. 4, 18, Apr. 15, May
8, Aug. 3, Sept. 28, Nov. 11.

1800   Jan. 18 – Dec. 31.
Suplemento: Jan. 25, June 18,
July 14, Sept. 22, Nov. 18.

1801   Jan. 20 – Mar. 10, Apr. 21 –
Dec. 19.
Continuación: [Sept. 19.]
Suplemento: Apr. 21. Aug. 29,
Dec. 19.

1802   Jan. 13 – Dec. 30.
Suplemento: June 9, July 21,
Aug. 18, Oct. 8, Nov. 12.

1803   Jan. 7 – Dec. 16.
Suplemento: Feb. 11, May 6,
July 23, Sept. 13, Dec. 16.

1804   Jan. 7 – June 30, Sept. 19 –
Dec. 11.
Suplemento: Jan. 7, Feb. 18,
May 26, June 30, Oct. 6, 27.

1805   Jan. 8 – Apr. 9.
Suplemento: Jan. 8, Feb. 26,
Apr. 9.

1806   Sept. 27 – Dec. 27.
Suplemento: Dec. 23.

1807   Jan. 3 – Dec. 26.
Suplemento: Jan 24,
Extraordinario: May 27, July
26, Oct. 24, Dec. 6, 7.

1808   Jan. 2 – Dec. 31.
Suplemento: Feb. 10, Aug. 3,

5, 6, 20, 31, Sept. 3, 10, 14, 28,
Oct. 15, Dec. 24, 28.
Extraordinario: June 9, July 29,
31, Aug. 1 – 5, 12, 29, Sept. 7, 9,
16, 17, 19, Oct. 4, 11, 15, 25,
Nov. 11, 14, 18, 21, 25, 28, Dec.
6, 16, 23.

1809   Jan. 4 – Dec. 30.
Suplemento: Jan. 7, 14, Feb.
22, Nov. 25, Dec. 6, 26.
Extraordinario: Jan. 6, 11, 20,
24, Feb. 7, 24, Mar. 9, 14, 16,
24, 28, 29, Apr. 1, 2, 6, 14, 15,
28, May 12, 16, 30, June 17, 24,
26, 29, July 7, 11, 15, 17, 18,
Aug. 1, 6, 11, Sept. 5, 21, 27, 28,
Oct. 4, 5, 20, Nov. 2, 13, Dec.
26.

TxSjM
1784   Jan. 14 – Dec. 31.
1786 – 1808   Jan. 1 – Dec. 31.
1809   Jan. 1 – Dec. 30.

GAZETTE OFFICIELLE DE L'EMPIRE
MEXICAIN. 3w. est. July 21, 2863.
Note: In French. Spanish edition published under title *Periódico oficial
del Imperio Mexicana*. Succeeded by
Diario del imperio. Ceased publication Dec. 31, 1864.
CtY
1863   July 21 – Sept. 12, 17 – Dec.
31.
1864   Jan. 2 – May 19, 24 – June 18.

EL GENIO. irr. est. May 1846.
Note: Continuous pagination.
DLC
1846   May 10 – 15, 30.

EL GENIO DE LA LIBERTAD. est.
[1832].
CtY
1832   July 3, 6, 10.

GENTE NUEVA. w., sw. est. May 11,
1911.
TxU
1911   May 11 – 25.

GIL BLAS. sw., 3w., d. est. [1895].
  DLC
    1911   Extraordinario: May 25.
    1912   Extraordinario: Oct. 17.
    1913   Mar. 31.
           Extraordinario: Feb 19, Mar.
           26, 27, Apr. 4.
    1914   Apr. 21.
           Extraordinario: Apr. 28, July
           27, Aug. 10.
  LNT – MA
    1911   ₁July 14 – Dec. 31₁.
  TxU
    1895   Mar. 16 – 19, 23 – Apr. 2, 4.
    1908   Dec. 5, 19, 26 – 31.
    1909   Jan. 1 – 9, 16 – Feb. 20, 27 –
           Mar. 3, 13 – 20, 31, Apr. 10 –
           24, May 4, June 15 – 22, 26 –
           July 3, 17, 31 – Aug. 24, 31,
           Sept. 4 – 7, 14 – 16, 21, 25 –
           Oct. 2, 14, 19.
    1910   Mar. 29, Sept. 13, Nov.
           14, 18, 19, 22, 24 – 26, Dec. 1.
    1911   Mar. 30, 31, Apr. 4, 5, 9, 14,
           15, June 22, July 10, Aug. 14,
           Sept. 4, 30, Nov. 2, Dec. 26.
    1912   July 6 – 8, 10, 15, 17 – 19, 23,
           26, 31 – Aug. 3, 6, 8, 9, 12, 14 –
           17, 20, 22, 23, 26, 28 – 30, Sept.
           2 – 4, 6 – 9, 11 – 18, 21, Oct. 10,
           17, Nov. 2, 20, Dec. 20, 24.
    1913   Jan. 15, 19 – 27, Mar. 4, 15, 26,
           27, 31, Apr. 15, 17 – 19, 22, 24,
           28, May 21, Aug. 19, Oct. 16,
           Nov. 6, 11 – 27, Dec 1, 3 – 5,
           8 – 12, 15 – 19, 22, 23, 26, 27.
    1914   Jan. 8, Apr. 17, July 27, Aug.
           4 – 6, 8, 11, 13, 15 – 20, 22, 24.

EL GLADIADOR. d. est. Mar. 27, 1830.
  Note: Succeeded by *El Verdadero*
  federal. Ceased publication Sept.
  30, 1830.
  CU – B
    Micro (N)
    1830   Sept. 7.
  CtY
    1830   Mar. 27 – Sept. 30.

TxU
    1830   Mar. 27 – Sept. 30.

EL GLADIADOR. bw. est. 1912.
  LNT – MA
    1912   Sept. 15 – Oct. 15.

GLADIADOR. d. est. Dec. 1, 1916.
  Note: Suspended publication Jan.
  7 – May 4, 1917.
  DLC
    1916   Dec. 1 – 31.
    1917   Jan. 1 – 6, May 5 – 20, 22 –
           June 30.
  TxU
    1916   Dec. 1 – 6, 8 – 31.
    1917   Jan. 1 – May 5, 9, 10, 12, June
           18 – 21.

EL GLOBO. d. est. June 28, 1867.
  Note: Ceased publication Oct. 31,
  1869.
  CtY
    1869   Jan. 11 – Oct. 31.
  DLC
    1867   June 28, 30 – Aug. 3, 5 – Sept.
           30, Oct. 9 – Dec. 7.
  MH
    1868   Apr. 30.

EL GLOBO. d. est. Jan. 26, 1925.
  Note: Ceased publication [Apr. 22],
  1925.
  LNT – MA
    1925   Apr. 18.
  TxU
    1925   Jan. 26 – Apr. 22.

EL GLOBO Y ESTANDARTE MEJI-
  CANO. d.
  Note: Ceased publication Jan. 22,
  1850.
  TxU
    1849   May 11 – June 21, 23 – 27,
           29 – July 13, 15 – Sept. 4, 6 –
           27, 29 – Dec. 31.
    1850   Jan. 1 – 6, 8 – 22.

EL GORRO FRIGIO. w.
  TxU
    1906   n.d. (2a. época, No. 1).

LOS GRACOS. sw. est. Apr. 9, 1834.
  DLC
    1834   Apr. 9 – May 31.
  NN
    1834   May 3, 17, 31.

EL GRAFICO. d. est. Apr. 1915.
  CU
    1929   July 6.
  DLC
    1915   May 6, 17.
  TxU
    1915   May 20.

LA GRAN PARADA.
  CU – B
    Micro (P)
    1885   May 4.

EL GRITO. w. est. Nov. 29, 1908.
  TxU
    1908   Nov. 29, Dec. 13 – 20.

EL GRITO sw.
  TxU
    1913   Jan. 31.

GRITO. w.
  CU
    1937   July 4.
    1938   June 30.

EL GRITO DE ALARMA. w. est. Jan. 16, 1910.
  TxU
    1910   Jan 16.

GRITO DEL PUEBLO. d. est. 1911.
  TxU
    1911   Aug. 27, 28, 30.

LA GUACAMAYA. w. est. 1902.
  TxU
    1902   July 21 – 28, Aug. 11 – Dec. 5.
    1903   Mar. 19, Apr. 6, June 12, July 2, 16, Aug. 6 – Sept. 1, 8 – 15, Nov. 12 – Dec. 31.
    1904   Jan. 14 – Apr. 28, May 5 – June 30, July 14 – 19, Aug. 1 – Sept. 15, 29 – Nov. 24, Dec. 8 – 26.
    1905   Jan. 9, 19, Feb. 9, Mar. 9 – May 11, 19 – 25, June 15 – July 13,

Aug. 3, Sept. 7 – Oct. 12, Nov. 23 – Dec. 31.
    1906   Jan. 1 – Mar. 25, Apr. 5 – July 4, 18 – Aug. 9, 23 – Oct. 11, 25 – Nov. 10.
    1907   Mar. 28 – Apr. 25, May 9 – 23, June 6, 20 – July 8, 22 – Oct. 22, 31 – Dec. 12.
    1908   Mar. 12, Apr. 2 – 16, 19 – June 25, July 23 – Oct. 4, Nov. 29.
    1909   Apr. 9.
    1911   Nov. 2.

LA GUERRA EUROPEA.
  See *Panorama mundial*.

EL GUERRERENSE. w.
  CU
    1915   July 25, Aug. 8 – Oct. 10, 24 – Nov. 7.

GUILLERMO TELL. 3w.
  NN
    1861   May 4.

LA GUILLOTINA. d. est. Oct. 19, 1917.
  DLC
    1917   Oct. 19 – 24.

EL HERALDO. 3w. est. Oct. 10, 1848.
  CU – B
    1848   Oct. 10 – Dec. 31.
    1849   Jan. 1 – Feb. 8, 27 – Mar. 10.

EL HERALDO, PERIODICO POLI-
TICO, INDUSTRIAL, AGRICOLA,
MERCANTIL, DE LITERATURA Y
ARTES.
  Note: Suspended publication May 11, 1858 – Jan. 10, 1861.
  CU – B
    Micro (P) & (N)
    1854   Mar. 1 – Dec. 31.
    1855 – 1857   Jan. 1 – Dec. 31.
    1858   Jan. 1 – 14, 23 – May 10.
    1861   Jan. 11 – Mar. 31, Apr. 2 – Dec. 31.
    1862   Jan. 1 – Dec. 31.
    1863   Jan. 1 – May 30.
  TxU
    1857   Nov. 10.

EL HERALDO. 3w.
  TxU
    1880   May 19 – 22, June 2 – 5.

EL HERALDO. irr. est. Sept. 15, 1883.
  CU – B
    Micro (P)
    1883   Sept. 15 – Nov. 4.

EL HERALDO; DIARIO CATOLICO. d.
  TxU
    1890   Jan. 1 – Sept. 27, Oct. 2, 8, 9,
            16, 21, Nov. 6, 8, 19, 21, 27, 28,
            30 – Dec. 2, 6, 12 – 14, 17, 23,
            31.
    1891   Jan. 3, 4, 9, 11.

EL HERALDO; PERIODICO DEL
  SIGLO XX. d. est. 1907.
  MWA
    1909   Extraordinario: July 10.
  TxU
    1907   July 15, 16, Sept. 5, 11, Oct. 8,
            23, Nov. 4, 23.
    1908   Jan. 8, 9, 15, 28, Feb. 4, 6, 14,
            17, 18, 20, 24, 25, Mar. 4, 7,
            11 – 13, 18, 20, 26 – 28, 30, Apr.
            6, 15, May 18, 19, 23, June 10,
            19, July 9, 25, Oct. 10, Dec. 10.
    1909   Feb. 4, Apr. 30, May 3 – 8, 12,
            19 – 21, 24, 25, 28, July 30, Aug.
            16, Oct. 2 – 4, Nov. 4, Dec. 6,
            17.
    1910   May 3, June 1.

EL HERALDO. d. est. Mar. 12, 1915.
  DLC
    1915   Mar. 12, 13, 16 – 19, 22, 23.
  TxU
    1915   Extraordinario: Mar. 16.

HERALDO; GACETA SEMANAL OR-
  GANO DE LA OFICIANA DE "IN-
  FORMACION MEXICANA." w. est.
  1918
    TxU
    1918   Oct. 31, Nov. 21 – Dec. 28.
    1919   Jan. 11 – May 3.

EL HERALDO COMERCIAL. sw. est.
  1881.

  TxU
    1881   Jan. 27, Feb. 13, Mar. 3,
            May 22.

EL HERALDO DE MEXICO. d. est.
  Apr. 27, 1919.
  CU
    1920   Sept. 15, Oct. 26, 28, 30, 31.
  DLC
    1919   Apr. 27 – Dec. 31.
    1920   Jan. 1 – July 31.
    1921   May 10 – Dec. 31.
    1922   Jan. 1 – June 9, July 13 – 17.
  TxU
    1919   May 3 – 5, 7 – 15, 18 – 25, June
            1 – Dec. 31.
    1920   Jan. 1 – Feb. 12, 14 – Mar. 17,
            20 – June 8, 10, 11, 13 – 17,
            19 – 28, 30 – Sept. 2, 4, 6 – Oct.
            1, 3 – Dec. 3.
    1921   Jan. 24.
    1925   Feb. 14.

EL HERALDO INDEPENDIENTE. d. est.
  Apr. 12, 1912.
  DLC
    1913   Jan. 18, 20.
            Extraordinario: Feb. 20.
  TxU
    1912   Apr. 29 – May 6, 10, 21, 22,
            30 – June 12, 14 – 18, 21, July 3,
            16, 18, 19, 25, 27, Aug. 2, 3, 8,
            9, 12 – Sept. 2, 5, 6, 9, 10, 13,
            23 – 25, 28, Oct. 3, 5, 9, 10, 12,
            14, 16, 17, 19 – 22, 24 – 29, 31 –
            Nov. 6, 9 – 11, 13, 22, 23, 26,
            28 – 30, Dec. 3, 10, 14.
    1913   Jan. 13, Feb. 20.

EL HERALDO MERCANTIL. w. est.
  Aug. 3, 1911.
  TxU
    1911   Aug. 3.

EL HERALDO MEXICANO. d. est.
  Oct. 1910.
  DLC
    1911   Extraordinario: May 17, 24.
  KHi
    1910   Nov. 12, 30.

1911 Feb. 18.
LNT—MA
  1911 [July 7—Dec. 31].
  1912 [Jan. 3—Feb. 7].
TxU
  1910 Nov. 9, 19—21, Dec. 6, 20,
        23—26, 28.
  1911 Jan. 5—7, 13—17, 21, 24—26,
        28, Feb. 4, 5, 8, 9, 14—17,
        20—25, 27, 28, Mar. 4, 8, 10,
        11, 15, 20—22, 24, 25, 27—Apr.
        2, 4—8, 10—15, 17—29, May
        1—6, 8—13, 15—27, 29—June
        17, 19—21, 23, 24, 26—July 1,
        3—Aug. 5, 7—12, 14—26, 28—
        Sept. 2, 4—15, 18—23, 25—30,
        Oct. 2—8, 30—Nov. 18, 20—
        Dec. 9, 11—16, 18—23, 26—30.
  1912 Jan. 1—6, 8—13, 15—19, 22—
        27, 29—Feb. 3, 5—17, 19—
        Mar. 2, 4—28.

EL HERALDO NACIONAL. d. est. Oct.
3, 1913.
  Note: Evening paper published by
  El Noticioso mexicano.
DLC
  1913 Extraordinario: Nov. 14.
TxU
  1913 Oct. 3, 10, 11, 15, 27, 28, 30.
  1914 Jan. 14.

EL HERMANO DEL PERICO QUE
CANTABA LA VICTORIA.
CtY
  1823 n.d. (Nos. 1, 4).

LA HESPERIA. sw. est. Mar. 15, 1840.
DLC
  1840 Mar. 15—May 2, 4—July 4,
        6—15, 31—Nov. 13, 15—Dec.
        26.
        Suplemento: Aug. 12, Sept. 12.
  1842 Mar. 16—Apr. 20, 27—May 4,
        11, 18—28, Aug. 9—Sept. 3,
        14—Oct. 22, 29—Dec. 31.
        Suplemento: May 28.
  1843 Jan. 4—21, Mar. 22, 25, Apr.
        5—29, May 6—20, 27—June

        10, 17, 21, 28—Aug. 16.
  1846 Mar. 4—Apr. 8.
MWA
  1842 Oct. 26.
  1844 Aug. 3—31.

EL HIJO DEL AHUIZOTE. w. est. Aug.
23, 1885.
  Note: Succeeded *El Ahuizote.* Suspended publication May 22—Sept.
  5, 1886; May 3, 1903—May 22,
  1913. *El Ahuizote jacobino* published during latter suspension.
CtY
  1885 Aug. 23—Dec. 27.
  1886 Jan. 3—May 22, Sept. 5—Dec.
        26.
  1887 Jan. 1—Dec. 25.
  1888 Jan. 1, May 6—Dec. 23.
  1889 Jan. 6—May 26, June 9—July
        14, Aug. 4—Sept. 8, Oct. 20.
  1890 July 13.
  1891 Mar. 1—Nov. 15, 29, Dec. 13—
        27.
  1892 Jan. 3—24, Feb. 7, 28, June
        26.
  1893 July 23, Aug. 18, Sept. 3.
  1897 Sept. 12, Nov. 21.
  1903 Jan. 4—May 3.
  1913 May 23—Dec. 27.
  1914 Jan. 3—Mar. 28.
LNT—MA
  1894 Jan. 1—Nov. 17, 19—Dec. 31.
  1897 Oct. 1—Dec. 31.
  1898 Jan. 1—Apr. 16, 18—Dec. 17,
        19, 31.
  1899 [Jan. 1—Dec. 31].
  1900 [Jan. 1—July 8].
  1901 [Jan. 1—Dec. 31].
  1902 [Jan. 12—Sept. 7, Nov. 24—
        Dec. 31].
  1903 [Jan. 1—Apr. 12].
TxU
  1885 Aug. 24—Dec. 31.
  1886—1888 Jan. 1—Dec. 31.
  1889 Feb. 3—Apr. 7, 21, May 26,
        June 9, 23—Nov. 10, 24—Dec.
        8.

1890   Feb. 2 — Dec. 28.
1891   Feb. 15 — Oct. 4, 18 — Dec. 31.
1892   Jan. 1 — Dec. 31.
1893   Jan. 1 — Oct. 15.
1894   Jan. 21 — Dec. 31.
1895   Jan. 1 — Nov. 3, Dec. 31.
1896 — 1899   Jan. 1 — Dec. 31.
1900   Jan. 1 — July 8.
1901   Jan. 20 — Dec. 31.
1902   Jan. 1 — Apr. 27, May 11,
          25, Sept. 28.
1903   Jan. 4 — Feb. 15.
1913   May 23, July 7 — Dec. 13.

EL HIJO DEL PUEBLO. est. Nov.
  30, 1914.
  DLC
    1914   Nov. 30.
  TxU
    1914   Nov. 30.

EL HIJO DEL TRABAJO. w.
  CU — B
    Micro (P)
    1877   June 10.
  TxU
    1879   July 27.
    1880   Jan. 4, 18, Mar. 28, June
              20 — Dec. 26.
    1881   Jan. 9 — Aug. 14, Sept. 11,
              Nov. 27.

HOGAR Y TALLER. bw. est. Oct.
  15, 1911.
  TxU
    1911   Oct. 15.

HOJA REPUBLICANA. d. est. Apr.
  29, 1911.
  TxU
    1911   Apr. 29, 30, May 3 — 5, 10,
              12, 14 — 20.

EL HOMBRE LIBRE: PERIODICO
  POLITICO. sw. est. Apr. 19, 1822.
    Note: Suspended publication May
    18, 1822 — Mar. 31, 1823; ceased
    publication Apr. 1, 1823.
  CU — B
    Micro (P) & (N)
    1822   Apr. 19 — May 10, 17.

CtY
  1822   May 10.
TxU
  1822   Apr. 19 — Dec. 31.
  1823   Jan. 1 — Apr. 1.

EL HOMBRE LIBRE; PERIODICO DE
  ACCION SOCIAL Y POLITICA. d.,
  sw., 3w. est. 1917.
    Note: Periodicity before Apr. 23,
    1918, daily; after Apr. 26, 1918, semi-
    weekly.
  CU
    1936   Jan. 3 — July 3.
  DLC
    1917   Dec. 27 — 29.
    1918   Jan. 2 — 26, 28 — May 15.
              Extraordinario: Jan. 14.
  LNT — MA
    1935   Aug. 7.
  NN
    Micro (P) & (N)
    1943   May 19, June 30, July 2 — 9,
              14 — Sept. 10, 22 — 24, 29 — Oct.
              31, Nov. 5 — Dec. 3, 10 — 24,
              29, 31.
    1944 — 1945   Jan. 1 — Dec. 31.
    1946   Jan. 1 — June 30.
    1947   Jan. 1 — Oct. 3.

EL HONOR. sw. est. June 8, 1850.
  CU — B
    Micro (N)
    1850   June 8 — 12.

HONOR NACIONAL.
  CtY
    1842   Vol. 1, No. 27; Vol. 2, Nos.
              1 — 3.

EL HONOR NACIONAL. d. est. Feb.
  1913.
  DLC
    1913   Feb. 17.

EL HOROSCOPO. d. est. 1857.
  NN
    1857   Apr. 10.

EL HUMO. w. est. 1905.
  TxU
    1905   Mar. 25, Apr. 30 — June 2.

EL HURACAN. sw. est. May 8, 1850.
  CU—B
    Micro (N)
    1850   May 8—Aug. 17.

EL HURACAN. w. est. July 16, 1910.
  TxU
    1910   July 16.

LA IBERIA. d.
  MoU
    Micro (N)
    1867   Sept. 18—Dec. 31.
    1868—1875   Jan. 1—Dec. 31.
    1876   Jan. 1—June. 29.

LA IDEA DEL SIGLO. sw.
  TxU
    1905   July 16.

IDEA LIBRE. 3w., d. est. Sept. 2, 1910.
  TxU
    1910   Prospecto: Aug. 23, 26.
        Sept. 2—7.

IDEA LIBRE. w. est. July 1914.
  DLC
    1914   Aug. 16.

IDEAL. w.
  TxU
    1907   Feb. 11, Mar. 11.

EL IDEAL DEMOCRATICO. 3w.
  TxU
    1912   May 24, 28—June 8, 12—23.

LA IGUALDAD. w. est. June 5, 1911.
  TxU
    1911   June 5.

LA ILUSTRACION. est. Nov. 24, 1901.
  LNT—MA
    1901   Nov. 24.

ILUSTRACION POPULAR. w.
  LNT—MA
    1911   Feb. 5, 12, July 2.

ILUSTRADOR EXTRAORDINARIO.
  NN
    1823   Apr. 20

EL ILUSTRADOR MEXICANO. bw.
  est. 1823.
  TxU
    1823   Prospecto. May 18.

EL IMPARCIAL;PERIODICO PO-
  LITICO, CIENTIFICO Y LITERARIO.
  sw. est. June 13, 1837.
    Note: Ceased publication Nov. 14,
    1837.
  CU—B
    Micro (N)
    1837   June 13—Nov. 14.
  CtY
    1837   July 14, 25—Aug. 1.
  DLC
    1837   June 13—Nov. 14.
        Alcance: July 11, Nov. 10.
        Suplemento: Oct. 3, 30.
  MWA
    1837   June 13—July 25, Aug. 1—Oct.
        10, 24—Nov. 14.

EL IMPARCIAL; PERIODICO HIS-
  PANO-MEJICANO, COMERCIAL,
  POLITICO, CIENTIFICO, ARTIS-
  TICO, ECONOMICO Y LITERARIO.
  3w. est. May 1844.
  DLC
    1844   May 21—29, 31—July 2.

EL IMPARCIAL. 3w. est. Sept. 5,
  1872.
  CU—B
    1872   Sept. 5—Nov. 12, 19.
    1873   Jan. 1—Feb. 2, 6—Mar. 2.

EL IMPARCIAL. d. est. May 15, 1880.
  CU—B
    Micro (P)
    1883   Jan. 14.
  TxU
    1880   May 15.

EL IMPARCIAL. d. est. Sept. 12, 1896.
    Note: Succeeded by *El Liberal*,
    Aug. 18, 1914. Ceased publication
    Aug. 17, 1914.
  CU
    1911   Nov. 16—Dec. 31.

1912   Mar. 1 – 31, Apr. 2 – June
         8, 10.
1913   Jan. 1 – Feb. 11, 20 – Apr.
         1, 3 – 9.

DLC
1910   June 10 – July 1, 3 – Aug. 26,
         Oct. 14 – 16, 19 – Dec. 31.
1911   Jan. 1 – July 17, 19 – Oct. 12.
1912   Jan. 12, Mar. 22.
1913   Feb. 2, 10 – 14, 20, 22, 24,
         25, 28 – Mar. 9, 12, 14 – 17,
         19 – 22, 24 – 29, 31, Apr. 1 – 5,
         7 – 13, 25 – Dec. 31.
         Extraordinario: Feb. 10, Apr. 1.
KHi
1914   Apr. 26, 27, May 14, June 20,
         25, 26, July 9.
LNT – MA
1907   July 30.
1910   Sept. 1 – 30, Oct. 10, Nov. 9.
1911   [July 12 – Dec. 31].
MWA
1901   June 5 – 7, 9.
1907   Nov. 21.

PU
1909   Oct. 1 – Dec. 31.
1910   Jan. 1 – May 31, July 1 – Dec.
         31.
1911 – 1912   Jan. 1 – Dec. 31.
1913   Jan. 1 – Mar. 31.
TxU
1896   Oct. 9, 28, 29, Nov. 1, 4, 5,
         7, 10 – 28, 30, Dec. 1 – 26, 28.
1897   Jan. 4 – Feb. 20, 22 – Apr. 14,
         17 – Dec. 31.
1898   Jan. 1 – Dec. 10, 12 – 31.
1899   Jan. 1 – 14, 16 – 28, 30 – Feb.
         18, 20 – 25, 27 – Mar. 4, 6 – 11,
         13 – 18, 20 – 30, Apr. 1, 3 – 15,
         17 – May 13, 15 – June 10, 13 –
         24, 26 – July 2, 4 – 8, 10 – 15,
         17 – 22, 24 – Aug. 5, 7 – 13,
         15 – Sept. 9, 11 – 30, Oct. 2 –
         31, Nov. 2 – 12, 14 – 22, 24,
         25, 27 – Dec. 2, 4 – 9, 12,
         13, 15, 16, 18 – 23, 25 – 31.

1900   Jan. 2 – 13, 16 – 20, 22 – Feb.
         2, 4 – 17, 19 – 24, 26 – Mar. 2,
         5 – 10, 12 – 16, 18, 20 – 24,
         26 – June 30, July 2 – 7, 10 –
         14, 16 – 18, 20, 21, 23 – 28, 30 –
         Aug. 11, 13 – 18, 20 – 25, 27 –
         Sept. 1, 3 – 6, 8, 10 – 14, 16,
         18 – 22, 24 – Oct. 2, 4 – 20,
         22 – Nov. 30, Dec. 3 – 31.
1901   Jan. 1 – Feb. 1, 3 – 25, 27 –
         Mar. 8, 10 – 27, 29 – July 5,
         7, 9 – 13, 15 – 20, 22, 23, 25 –
         Sept. 15, 17 – Oct. 5, 7 – 12,
         14 – 21, 23 – 26, 28 – Nov. 23,
         25 – Dec. 31.
1902   Jan. 1 – 4, 6 – 11, 13 – Feb.
         8, 10 – June 14, 16 – 21, 23 –
         28, 30 – Sept. 30, Oct. 2 – Dec.
         31.
1903   Jan. 1 – Mar. 15, 16 – 31, Apr.
         2 – 11, 13 – June 13, 15 – Dec.
         31.
1904   Jan. 1 – Mar. 11, 15 – 21, 23 –
         25, 27 – June 30, July 2 – 7, 9 –
         11, 13 – 16, 18 – 22, 24 – 31,
         Aug. 2 – 6, 8 – 24, 26 – Dec. 31.
1905   Jan. 1 – Feb. 14, 16 – 25, Mar.
         3, 27, Apr. 30, May 5, 16, 19,
         Sept. 14, 22, Oct. 2, 22, 24 –
         Nov. 8, 10 – 20, 22 – Dec. 10,
         12 – 22, 24, 26 – 31.
1906   Jan. 1 – 3, 6, 7, 9 – 12, 15,
         19, 25 – 27, 29, 31 – Mar. 5, 7 –
         10, 12, 14 – 17, 19 – Apr. 10,
         12, 14, 16, 17, 19 – 22, 24 – 30,
         May 2, 3, 5 – June 3, 5, 6, 9,
         11 – 13, 15, 16, 18 – Sept. 11,
         14, 16 – 18, 20 – 25, 27, 28, 30,
         Oct. 3, 4, 6 – 20, 22 – 25, 27, 31,
         Nov. 3 – 5, 7, 8, 10, 11, 14, 19 –
         28, 30, Dec. 3 – 7, 13 – 18, 21,
         22, 27 – 29, 31.

1907   Jan. 1 – 4, 7 – Feb. 5, 7 – 10,
         13 – May 4, 6 – 9, 11 – 13, 15 –
         18, 20 – June 29, July 1, 2, 4 –
         6, 8, 11, 13, 17, 19, 21, 23 – 25,
         27, 29 – Aug. 1, 3, 5 – 7, 9, 10,

12, 13, 16, 17, 19 – 24, 27 – 29,
31, Sept. 2 – 4, 6 – 10, 12 – 14,
16 – 19, 23 – 26, 28, Oct. 2 – 5,
7, 9 – 12, 14 – 18, 21, 22, 25 –
27, 29 – Nov. 1, 5, 6, 8, 11, 13,
15, 16, 18 – 20, 22, 24 – 30, Dec.
2, 4, 6, 9, 11 – 20, 23, 24, 26 –
28, 30, 31.

1908　Jan. 2 – 6, 11, 13, 14, 16 – 18,
20, 22, 23, 25, 27, 30, Feb. 4, 5,
7, 10 – 13, 15, 16, 19 – 21, 26,
29, Mar. 2, 6, 9, 10, 14, 16, 17,
19 – 21, 23, 24, 26 – 28, Apr.
1 – 4, 6, 8 – 16, 18, 19, 21 – 27,
30 – May 17, 20 – 22, 25 – 30,
June 1 – 3, 5, 6, 8 – 27, 29 –
July 4, 6 – 11, 13 – 29, 31 – Aug.
8, 10 – 21, 23 – 29, 31 – Sept.
16, 18 – 21, 23 – 26, 29 – Oct. 1,
3, 5, 7, 8, 12, 13, 15 – 26, 28 –
31, Nov. 2, 4 – 7, 9 – 26, 28 –
Dec. 2, 4 – 12, 14 – 17, 19 – 22.

1909　Jan. 1 – 12, 14 – 16, 19, 20 23 –
28, 30 – Feb. 6, 8 – Mar. 6, 8 –
Apr. 3, 5, 7 – 13, 15 – 18, 20,
22 – 24, 27, 28, 30, May 2 – 17,
19 – 26, 28 – June 26, 29 – July
10, 12 – 17, 19, 20, 22, 25 – 27,
30 – Aug. 3, 5, 7, 9 – 11, 14, 15,
18 – 24, 26 – 28, 30 – Sept. 11,
13 – 15, 17 – 26, Oct. 2, 10, 12,
19, Nov. 6 – 9, 12, 14, 16, 19,
25, 29, 30, Dec. 5, 7, 10, 12 – 14,
19, 20, 24, 25.

1910　Jan. 1 – 14, 16 – 18, 20 – Feb.
16, 18 – 24, 26, 27, Mar. 2 – 6,
10, 11, 22, 25, 26, 30, Apr.
1 – May 21, 23 – June 4, 6 – 17,
19 – 24, 26 – Aug. 26, 28 – Sept.
3, 6 – 10, 12 – 16, 19, 21, 23,
24, 28, 29, Oct. 1, 3 – Dec. 31.

1911　Jan. 1 – 12, 14.
1912　Jan. 1 – Dec. 31.
1913　Jan. 1 – Feb. 8, 10 – 14, 20 –
May 2, 4 – 30, June 1 – 17, 21 –
July 9, 16 – Aug. 17, 19 – 26,
28 – Dec. 31.
1914　Jan. 1 – Aug. 17.

EL IMPARCIAL. d. est. Sept. 8, 1915.
　DLC
　　1915　Sept. 8.

EL IMPARCIALITO. w.
　TxU
　　1903　Nov. 1/7.

IMPOLITICO. sw. est. June 6, 1866.
　MWA
　　1866　June 6 – 23.

EL IMPULSOR. sw. est. June 2, 1904.
　TxU
　　1904　June 2.

L'INDEPENDANT.
　　Note: In French.
　CU – B
　　Micro (N)
　　1834　July 23 – Aug. 23.

LA INDEPENDENCIA.
　NN
　　1861　May 8.

EL INDEPENDIENTE. sw. est. Mar.
　4, 1837.
　CtY
　　1837　Aug. 29.
　DLC
　　1837　Mar. 4 – May 30, June 1, 2, 4 –
　　　　　19, 21 – Aug. 5.
　　　　　Suplemento: Apr. 19.

EL INDEPENDIENTE; PERIODICO
POLITICO Y CIENTIFICO. sw. est.
Aug. 1839.
　DLC
　　1839　Sept. 25 – Oct. 4, 6 – Nov. 9.

EL INDEPENDIENTE. d. est. Apr. 8,
1912.
　TxU
　　1912　Apr. 8.

EL INDEPENDIENTE. d. est. Feb. 11,
1913.
　　Note: Ceased publication 1915.
　CU
　　1913　Mar. 2 – 15, 20 – 22, 24, 26 –
　　　　　Apr. 1, 13 – 22, June 14, 16 –

July 30, Aug. 1 – Oct. 16, 18 –
21, 23 – Nov. 29, Dec. 1 – 5, 7 –
18, 20 – 27, 29 – 31.
1914   Jan. 1 – 9, 11 – Apr. 19, 21,
May 30 – Aug. 10.
DLC
1913   Feb. 21, 22, 24, Mar. 2, 4,
8 – 10, 12, 15, 18, 24, 26 – 28,
30, 31, Apr. 2 – 4, 6, 9 – 12, 15,
Aug. 28, Sept. 12.
Broadside: Feb. 16.
Extraordinario: Feb. 11.
1914   Apr. 22, 23, 25 – 30, May 4 –
6, 8, 9, 11 – 14, 23, June 3, 7,
20, 21, July 8 – 10, 16, 17, 20 –
22, Aug. 5.
Extraordinario: Apr. 1, 22 – 30,
May 1, 2, 4 – 6, 8, 9, 11 – 14,
18 – 20.
PU
1913   [Mar. 2 – Dec. 31].
1914   [Jan. 1 – Mar. 31].
TxU
1913   Feb 11, 21, 22, 24, Mar. 6, 9 –
20, 22, 25 – May 18, 20 – 30,
June 1, 2, 4, 12 – 14, 16 – July
8, 10 – Aug. 26, 28, 30 – Sept.
14, 16 – 28, 30 – Oct. 31, Nov.
3 – 5, 7.
1914   Feb 6, Apr. 6, 11, 12, 16, 20 –
May 2, 4 – 7, 9, 10, 17, 20 – 26,
June 21 – 23, 27, 29, 30, Aug.
5, 6.

EL INDEPENDIENTE; SEMANARIO
POLITICO. w. est. Feb. 20, 1917.
Note: Title *Boletín del Club Potosino Ponciano Arriaga*, Feb. 20 – 28,
1917; *El Independiente*; *semanario
político*, after Mar. 1, 1917.
DLC
1917   Feb. 20, Mar. 1 – 8.

INDICATOR FEDERAL. d. est. Mar.
15, 1825.
CU – B
Micro (N)
1825   Mar. 15 – 21, 25 – Apr. 27,
29 – May 12, 15 – June 3, 5 – 7,
9 – 14, 16 – 28, July 1, 2.

INDOAMERICA.
LNT – MA
1938   Feb. 1 – May 31, July 1 – 31,
Sept. 1 – 30.

LA INDUSTRIA NACIONAL. sw. est.
1879.
TxU
1879   Sept. 7 – Oct. 5, 12, 23, 30,
Dec. 7 – 14, 21 – 28.
1880   Jan. 1 – Sept. 18, Oct. 23.

LA INFORMACION. d. est. Feb. 21,
1917.
DLC
1917   Feb. 21 – 26.

INFORMACIONES INALAMBRICAS. d
est. 1917.
DLC
1918   July 31, Aug. 16, 19, 20, 22.
TxU
1917   Feb. [16], 17.

EL INSURGENTE. sw. est. Jan. 2,
1908.
CLCM
1937   Mar. 31, July 31, Dec. 31.
1938   Sept. 1 – 30, Dec. 31.
1939   Mar. 9, May 18.
CU
1908   July 5.
LNT – MA
1909   [Jan. 24 – Aug. 15].
TxU
1908   Jan. 2, 12 – 16, 26, Feb. 9 –
20, 27, Mar. 8, 26, Apr. 5.
1909   June 13 – Sept. 2.

EL INTRANSIGENTE. d. est. 1906.
TxU
1906   July 2.

EL INTRANSIGENTE. w. est. Aug.
1, 1909.
TxU
1909   Aug. 1.

EL INTRANSIGENTE. d. est. 1912.
DLC
1913   Jan. 30, Feb. 5, 10.

TxU
1912 Apr. 18 – 27, 29 – May 4, 6,
8 – 11, 13 – June 12, 14 – 28,
July 1 – 3, 8 – 11, 18 – 27, Aug.
2 – Sept. 22, 24 – Oct. 2, 4 –
6, 8 – 10, 12, 13, 15 – 31, Nov.
1 – 11, 13, Dec. 12, 14, 30.

EL INTRANSIGENTE. sw. est. May
17, 1918.
DLC
1918 May 17 – July 2, 4 – Aug. 2, 4 –
17, 18 – 23, 25 – 28.

EL INTRUSO. sw.
CU – B
Micro (N)
1847 Jan. 26 – Feb. 25.

EL INVESTIGADOR MEXICANO. sw.
est. June 10, 1837.
Note: Ceased publication Aug. 2,
1837.
CU – B
Micro (N)
1837 June 10 – Aug. 2.
DLC
1837 June 10 – Aug. 2.

EL IRIS. sw. est. June 1, 1837.
DLC
1837 June 4 – Dec. 30.
Suplemento: Oct. 25, Nov. 29.
1838 May 2 – 4, 10 – Oct. 30, Nov.
1 – Dec. 14, 16 – 31.
1839 Jan. 1 – 25, 27 – Feb. 5, 7 –
Dec. 29.
1840 Jan. 3 – 23.

EL IRIS ESPAÑOL. sw. est. Oct. 3,
1846.
CU – B
1846 Oct. 3 – 14, 21 – Dec. 31.
1847 Jan. 1 – June 26, July 3 – 14.
NN
1847 Oct. 16, 23 – Nov. 27, Dec. 1,
8 – 31.
Suplemento: Nov. 27.
1848 Jan. 1 – 12, 19 – 26, Feb. 2, 9,
23 – 26.

IZQUIERDAS. w.
ICRL
1934 Aug. 21 – Dec. 31.
1935 – 1937 Jan. 1 – Dec. 31.
1938 Jan. 1 – Aug. 7.
TxU
1934 Aug. 21 – Dec. 31.
1935 Jan. 1 – July 29, Aug. 19 – Nov.
11, Dec. 1 – 31.
1936 Jan. 1 – Sept. 20, Oct. 12 – 20,
Nov. 9 – Dec. 31.
1937 Jan. 4, 25 – June 7, 21 – Sept.
13, Oct. 4 – Dec. 31.
1938 Jan. 1 – Feb. 14, May 28 – June
6, 20 – Aug. 7.

JOURNAL FRANÇAIS DU MEXIQUE. d.
Note: In French. Succeeded *Le
Courrier du Mexique*. Both the daily
and weekly editions of *Gaceta de la
guerra* (in Spanish) were originally
published as part of the *Journal
français du Mexique*; the weekly
edition began publishing separately
in [Nov.] 1940.
CSt
1934 July 14.
1937 May 13, June 22, 24, 26, 29,
July 1, 3, 6, 10, 13, 15, 20, Dec.
23, 28.
1938 Jan. 11, 13, 22, 25, 27, June
23, July 14.
1944 June 17, 18, 20 – July 2, 4 –
10, 12 – 17, 19 – Sept. 13, 15 –
Oct. 3, 5 – 13, 19 – Nov. 1,
3 – 29, Dec. 1 – 12, 14 – 31.
1945 Jan. 3 – 7, 9 – 12, 14 – Feb. 1,
3 – May 15, 17, 19, 21 – June 4.
DLC
1940 Aug. 1 – 3, 7 – 10, 31, Sept. 6.
1942 May 28, Oct. 13.
1943 July 14.

JUAN DIEGO. sw. est. July 7, 1872.
Note: Ceased publication Jan. 1,
1874.
CtY
1872 July 7 – Dec. 31.

1873   Jan. 3 – Dec. 27.
1874   Jan. 1.

JUAN PANDERO. w.
  LNT-MA
    1901   May 7.
  TxU
    1880   Sept. 2.
    1910   June 23, July 7, 21 – 28, Aug.
            21.
    1911   May 28.

EL JUEVES.
  CU – B
    Micro (P)
    1883   Oct. 4.

JUEVES DE "EL MUNDO." w.
  LNT – MA
    1902   Jan. 16 – Dec. 31.
  TxU
    1902   May 8.

JUEVES DE EXCELSIOR. w.
  TxU
    1922   Sept. 21, Nov. 2, 16 – Dec. 31.
    1923   Jan. 1 – Sept. 27.

LA JUSTICIA; ORGANO DEL PARTIDO
  CRITICO SOCIAL. w. est. June 11,
  1911.
  TxU
    1911   June 11 – 18.

JUVENTUD LIBERAL. w. est. Aug. 27,
  1911.
  TxU
    1911   Aug. 27, Sept. 10.

JUVENTUD ROJA.
  CU
    1935   Extraordinario: Jan. 3.

EL LATIGO. w. est. 1911.
  TxU
    1911   Sept. 10.

LEALTAD. est. Aug. 27, 1911.
  TxU
    1911   Aug. 27.

EL LIBERAL. w. est. June 19, 1904.
  TxU
    1904   June 19, July 18.

EL LIBERAL; DIARIO INDEPEN-
  DIENTE. d. est. 1914.
  TxU
    1914   July 11.

EL LIBERAL. d. est. Aug. 18, 1914.
    Note: Succeeded *El Imparcial*.
  DLC
    1914   Aug. 18 – Sept. 21, 26 – Oct.
            27, 29 – Nov. 19.
            Extraordinario: Aug. 19,
            Oct. 30, Nov. 11, 16, 19, 22, 23.
            Suplemento: Nov. 1.
    1920   Feb. 17, Mar. 15 – May 6.
  LNT – MA
    1914   [Aug. 19 – Nov. 22.]
  TxU
    1914   Aug. 18 – Nov. 23.

EL LIBERAL. THE DAILY LIBERAL.
  d. est. [1916].
    Note: In Spanish and English.
  MB
    1916   May 21.

EL LIBERAL YUCATECO. w.
  LNT – MA
    1918   Apr. 21, June 17.

LA LIBERTAD; PERIODICO LIBERAL-
  CONSERVADOR. d. est. Jan. 5, 1878.
    Note: Ceased publication Dec. 30,
    1900.
  CU – B
    Micro (P)
    1884   Dec. 7.
  DLC
    1880   Apr. 11.
  LNT – MA
    1880   Sept. 5.

  MWA
    1881   [Mar. 11 – Oct. 30.]
    1882   [May 11 – Dec. 31.]
    1883   [Jan. 1 – June 6,] Aug. 24,
            [Nov. 6 – Dec. 31.]
    1884   [Jan. 1 – July 22,] Nov. 11 – 28,
            Dec. 11 – 14.
  NcD
    1881   Apr. 3.

TxU
- 1878 June 30, Aug. 1, 4 — Dec. 31.
- 1879 Jan. 1 — Apr. 30, May 16, 21, June 14, 22, Nov. 6.
- 1880 Jan. 14 — Sept. 19.
- 1881 Mar. 1, 4, Apr. 10, 29, Aug. 27, Sept. 4, 11, Nov. 5, 13, 24, 26.
- 1882 July 5, Oct. 6, 7, 14.
- 1884 Apr. 24, May 4, June 3, 12, 21, July 24, Aug. 3, 9, 12, 21, Oct. 2, 3, 21, Nov. 2, 6.

LA LIBERTAD. sw.
TxU
- 1903 June 28, July 19.

LA LIBERTAD; ORGANO DE LA LIGA NACIONAL DE ESTUDIANTES CATOLICOS. w.
TxU
- 1912 May 19.

LIBERTAD. d. est. Nov. 15, 1912.
TxU
- 1912 Nov. 15, 18.

LA LIBERTAD. d. est. July 17, 1914.
DLC
- 1914 July 20 — 22.
TxU
- 1914 July 17 — Aug. 5.

LA LIBERTAD ELECTORAL. sw.
TxU
- 1880 Nov. 12 — 16, 23 — Dec. 7.

EL LIBERTADOR. d. est. Nov. 25, 1914.
DLC
- 1914 Nov. 25 — 29.
TxU
- 1914 Nov. 25.

EL LIBERTARIO. sw. est. May 1915.
DLC
- 1915 May 29, June 9, 16, July 7. Extraordinario: June 27, 30, July 3.
TxU
- 1915 June 9.

EL LIBRE SUFRAGIO. d. est. Nov. 15, 1879.
DLC
- 1879 Nov. 15 — Dec. 31.
- 1880 Jan. 1 — Aug. 19.
TxU
- 1879 Dec. 5.
- 1880 Jan. 25, Feb. 13, 18, 25, Mar. 9, 12 — July 3, 6 — Aug. 19.

LA LIMA. 3w., sw. est. Oct. 19, 1833.
Note: Title *La Lima de vulcano*, Oct. 19, 1833 — Mar. 27, 1839; *La Lima*, after Mar. 28, 1839. Periodicity Oct. 19, 1833 — May 30, 1837, three times a week; after June 2, 1837, semiweekly.
CU — B
Micro (N)
- 1833 Oct. 19 — 23.
- 1834 Mar. 19.
- 1835 Sept. 24.
CtY
- 1833 [Oct. 19 — Dec. 31].
- 1834 — 1838 [Jan. 1 — Dec. 31].
DLC
- 1835 Jan. 1 — July 6, 8 — Oct. 26, 28 — Dec. 31. Suplemento: Jan. 10, 24, Feb. 24, 26, Mar. 7, 17, July 11, 28, Sept. 3, 5, 19, 24, Oct. 29.
- 1836 Jan. 1 — Nov. 23, 25 — Dec. 28, 30, 31. Suplemento: Jan. 2, Mar. 19, Apr. 14, 16, July 7, 26, Aug. 25, Sept. 3, Oct. 15, 29, Nov. 10, Dec. 24.
- 1837 Jan. 1 — Feb. 28, Mar. 1 — 29, 31 — July 31, Aug. 2 — Dec. 31. Suplemento: May 5, 26, Sept. 8, Oct. 6, 17.
- 1838 Jan. 1 — 8, 10 — Dec. 31. Suplemento: July 7, 14, Aug. 4, Sept. 12, 15.
- 1839 Jan. 1 — Mar. 29, 31 — Oct. 19.

MWA
  1834   Mar. 12, 19, 26 – 29, Aug. 6,
          Sept. 9.
TxU
  1834   May 24 – 28, July 26 – 29,
          Aug. 4 – 17, Oct. 8 – Nov. 6,
          11 – Dec. 31.
  1835   Jan. 1 – 10, 15 – 20, 29 – Feb.
          28, Mar. 3 – Apr. 11, Oct. 10.
  1836   Apr. 9 – 12, 23 – 26, May 3 – 7,
          14, June 21, July 5 – 7, 16,
          Aug. 20, Sept. 3, 10, Nov. 29.
  1837   Jan. 19, Feb. 16, 23 – Mar. 4,
          9, 16.
  1838   Apr. 2, July 21, Dec. 22.

LA LINTERNA. w. est. [Apr.] 1877.
  CtY
  1877   Mar. 12, 26 – Dec. 2, 16 – 30.

LA LUCHA. sw. est. Aug. 24, 1911.
  TxU
  1911   Aug. 24.

LA LUCHA. est. June 16, 1913.
  TxU
  1913   June 16.

LA LUCHA. w. est. Nov. 8, 1916.
  DLC
  1916   Nov. 8.
  TxU
  1917   Sept. 30.

LUCHA OBRERA. sw. est. 1939.
  CSt
  1939   Apr. 19 – Oct. 29.
  1944   Apr. 1 – May 31, July 1 – 31,
          Sept. 1 – 30, Nov. 1 – 30.
  1945   Feb 1 – May 31, July 1 – Aug.
          31, Oct. 1 – Dec. 31.
  1946   Feb. 1 – July 31, Oct. 1 – Dec.
          31.
  1947   Jan. 1 – July 31.
  CU
  1939   Oct. 10.
  1941   June 1 – Aug. 21.

LUCHA PROLETARIA.
  CSt
  1934   Jan. 18.

LUCIFER.
  TxU
  1880   Oct. 31.

EL LUNES. w.
  TxU
  1881   Oct. 3 – 10, 24 – 31.
  1882   May 29, June 12, July 17 – Aug.
          14, 28 – Sept. 11, Oct. 1 – Nov.
          27, Dec. 11 – 25.
  1883   Jan. 1 – Feb. 19, Mar. 5 – 26.
  1884   Apr. 21.
  1887   Jan. 17.

LA LUZ. sw. est. Nov. 1835.
  DLC
  1835   Dec. 2 – 31.
  1836   Jan. 1 – Mar. 8, 10 – 15.
  TxU
  1836   Mar. 8.

LA LUZ. bw. est. Nov. 15, 1869.
  CU – B
  1869   Nov. 15 – Dec. 31.
  1870   Jan. 1 – Nov. 15, Dec. 30.
  1871   Jan. 31, Feb. 15, Apr. 30, May
          31.

¡LUZ! sw., w.
  TxU
  1917   June 16, 30.

LA LUZ DEL SABADO. w.
  CtY
  1889   Feb. 23 – Mar. 23.

MADERO. w. est. Aug. 9, 1914.
  DLC
  1914   Aug. 9 – 16.
  TxU
  1914   Aug. 9.

LA MADRE CELESTINA. sw. est.
  Oct. 16, 1861.
  CU – B
    Micro (N)
    1861   Oct. 16 – Dec. 21.
  NN
    1861   Dec. 7 – 11, 18.
    1862   Apr. 26 – May 1.

LA MADRE MATIANA. w. est. 1917.
DLC
   1917   Nov. 1.
TxU
   1917   Sept. 9.

EL MALCRIADO. w. est. Feb. 11, 1917.
DLC
   1917   Feb. 11.

LA MALIMCHE.
TxU
   1878   Dec. 8.

EL MANANA; PERIODICO POLITICO.
  sw., d. est. June 15, 1911.
    Note: Suspended publication Feb.
    11 — 18, 1913; ceased publication
    Feb. 28, 1913.
DLC
   1911   June 15 — Dec. 31.
   1912   Jan. 1 — Dec. 31.
   1913   Jan. 1 — Feb. 23.
LNT — MA
   1911   June 15 — Dec. 31.
   1912   Jan. 1 — Dec. 31.
   1913   Jan. 1 — Feb. 28.
MWA
   1912   Nov. 5.
TxU
   1911   June 15 — 22, July 2 — 9,
         Aug. 3 — 7, 21, Sept. 11, 18,
         25 — 29, Oct. 6 — 13, 20 — 28,
         Dec. 5 — 31.
   1912   Jan. 1 — 23, Feb. 2 — 9, 16 —
         June 14, 21 — Dec. 31.
   1913   Jan 1 — Feb. 28.

EL MAÑANA. w. est. Mar. 9, 1918.
DLC
   1919   Mar. 9 — May 21.

LA MARIMBA.
LNHT
   1832   June 27.

EL MARTILLO DE LOS CICLOPES.
  sw. est. Feb. 15, 1834.
    Note: Ceased publication Mar.
    15, 1834.

CU — B
  Micro (N)
   1834   Feb. 15 — Mar. 8, 15.

EL MASCARA. w. est. July 22, 1879.
CtY
   1879   July 22 — Dec. 31.
   1880   Jan. 8, 15.
LNT — MA
   1879   July 22 — Dec. 31.
   1880   Jan. 8, 15.

MEFISTOFÉLES. w. est. 1903.
TxU
   1903   Oct. 19, Nov. 11.

EL MEJICANO INDEPENDIENTE.
  bw. est. [1820].
NN
   1821   June 16.

MEMORIAL HISTORICO. d. est. Jan. 1,
  1846.
  CU — B
   1846   Jan. 1 — Feb. 28
  DLC
   1846   Jan. 1 — 14, 16, 19 — Feb. 10,
         12, 25 — 28.
         Suplemento: Jan. 21.

EL MENSAJERO. d., sw. est. Jan. 2,
  1871.
    Note: Periodicity Jan. 2, 1871 —
    July 30, 1880, daily; Aug. 1 — Dec.
    5, 1880, semiweekly. Ceased pub-
    lication Dec. 5, 1880.
  CU — B
   1871   Jan. 5 — Apr. 5, 20 — 26, 28 —
         June 11, 14 — 18, 20 — 27, 29 —
         July 30.
  Micro (P) & (N)
   1877   Dec. 23, 27 — 30.
   1878   Jan. 1 — 12, 15 — 17, 19, 20,
         24 — 31, Feb. 2, 5, 8 — 12, 17 —
         19, 21 — 23.
  MWA
   1878   Mar. 29, Apr. 6, 13, 14, 18,
         May 4,
   1880   Apr. 6 — June 15, July 28 —
         Nov. 7, 14, 21 — 25.
  LNT — MA
   1880   May 5, Aug. 1.

TxU
   1871   Jan. 2 – Sept. 30.
   1879   Apr. 13, May 17, 28, June
           19, 22, July 11, 15, 26, Aug.
           3, 5.
   1880   Apr. 7, 14, 29, May 1, 11 –
           16, 19 – Dec. 5.

MENSAJERO DE LA GUERRA. d. est.
   1914.
   TxU
      1914   Nov. 5 – 9.

MENSAJERO DE LA PAZ. sw. est. 1912.
   TxU
      1912   July 18, Aug. 1 – 11.

EL MENSAJERO DE LOS ESTADOS-
   UNIDOS MEXICANOS. sw. est. June
   5, 1850.
      Note: Ceased publication Nov.
      16, 1850.
   CU – B
      Micro (N)
      1850   June 5 – Nov. 16.

EL MENSAJERO ESPAÑOL. w. est.
   Jan. 7, 1860.
   CU – B
      1860   Jan. 7 – Dec. 31.

EL MENTIROSO MEXICANO. sw. est.
   Oct. 10, 1913.
   TxU
      1913   Oct. 10, 22 – 25.

EL MENTOR MEXICANO. w. est. Jan.
   7, 1811.
      Note: Succeeded *Semanario econó-
      mico de México.* Ceased publication
      Dec. 16, 1811.
   CtY
      1811   Jan. 7 – Dec. 16.
   TxU
      1811   Jan. 7 – Dec. 16.

EL MERIDIANO.
   DLC
      1916   Extraordinario: Dec. 8.

EL MERO PETRATERO. w. est. 1912.
   TxU
      1912   Aug. 25.

LA METRALLA. w. est. 1906.
   TxU
      1906   Feb. 3 – 18.

MEXICAN AMERICAN. w. est. May 31,
   1924.
      Note: In English.
   TxU
      1924   May 31 – Aug. 16, 30 – Dec.
              31.
      1925   Jan. 1 – [July 4].

MEXICAN COURIER.
      See *El Correo de México. Mexican
      Courier.*

MEXICAN DAILY NEWS. d. est. Feb.
   1920.
      Note: In English. Mimeographed.
   LNT – MA
      1928   Dec. 7, 20, 21, 24.
      1930   ₁Mar. 17 – June 30, Aug.
              27 – Sept. 24₁.
   TxU
      1930   Mar. 17, May 28, June 12,
              July 2, Aug. 19, 26, 27, Sept.
              2, 5, 6, 9 – 12, 16, 17, 19, 25.
   WU
      1930   ₁Mar. 17 – Apr. 26₁.

MEXICAN EXTRAORDINARY AND
   FOREIGN ADVERTISER. sw., 3w. est.
   May 1856.
      Note: In English. Title *Mexican
      Extraordinary*, May 1856 – 1861;
      *Mexican Extraordinary and Foreign
      Advertiser*, after 1861. Periodicity
      May 1856 – July 18, 1857, semi-
      weekly; after July 21, 1857, three
      times a week.
   CU – B
      Micro (N)
      1856   July 5 – 30.
      1857   Jan. 29 – Feb. 4, 10 – 14,
              19 – 25, Apr. 1 – 29, July 4 – 8,
              15 – Aug. 29, Sept. 5 – 9, 15 –
              Oct. 1, 10 – 14, 20 – 31.
   DLC
      1857   July 4 – Aug. 19, 21 – Dec.
              31.
      1858   Jan. 1 – May 28, 30 – July 23.

Suplemento: Jan. 2.
NN
 1861 May 25, Sept. 27.

THE MEXICAN FINANCIER.
 See *El Financiero mexicano. The Mexican Financier.*

THE MEXICAN GAZETTE.
 See *La Gaceta de México. The Mexican Gazette.*

THE MEXICAN GRAPHIC. w. est. Dec. 1, 1884.
 Note: In English.
 CU—B
 Micro (P)
 1884 Dec. 1, 29.

THE MEXICAN HERALD. d. est. Sept. 1, 1895.
 Note: Spanish and English editions. Succeeded *The Two Republics.* Published at Vera Cruz Apr. 25 — July 31, 1914. Suspended publication Feb. 16 — 18, 1913; Apr. 22 — 26, 1914; July 21 — Aug. 2, 1915; ceased publication Oct. 29, 1915.
 CLCM
 1901 July 12.
 CSt
 1913 Feb. 10, 14.
 1914 Nov. 20.
 CU
 1908 June 14 — Nov. 28, 30, Dec. 2 — 31.
 1909 — 1910 Jan. 1 — Dec. 31.
 1911 Jan. 1 — July 2, 4 — Dec. 2, 4 — 31.
 1912 Jan. 1 — Feb. 22, 24 — Aug. 17, 19 — [Oct. 22, 24 — Nov. 7].
 1913 Feb. 10, 14, 26 — Dec. 31.
 1914 Jan. 1 — Apr. 21, Aug. 7 — Sept. 22, 25 — Oct. 7, 9 — Nov. 20, Dec. 3 — 31.
 1915 Jan. 1 — 26, 29 — Mar. 3.
 DLC
 Micro (P) & (N)
 1895 Sept. 1 — Dec. 31.

1896 Jan. 1 — Dec. 31.
1897 Jan. 1 — Dec. 29, 31.
1898 Jan. 1 — July 9, 11 — Nov. 11, 13 — Dec. 31.
1899 Jan. 1 — May 11, 13 — Oct. 31.
1900 Jan. 1 — 29, 31 — Feb. 13, 16, 17, 19 — May 11, 13 — Dec. 20, 22 — 31.
1901 Jan. 1 — 23, 26 — 28, 31 — Feb. 7, 9 — Mar. 13, 15 — Dec. 24, 26 — 31.
1902 Jan. 1 — 14, 16 — 27, 29 — Dec. 31.
1903 Jan. 1 — Dec. 31.
1904 Jan. 1 — Feb. 12, 14 — July 30, Aug. 1 — Dec. 31.
1905 Jan. 1 — Oct. 11, 13 — Nov. 14, 16 — Dec. 31.
1906 — 1910 Jan. 1 — Dec. 31.
1911 Jan. 1 — Nov. 11, 13 — Dec. 31.
1912 — 1913 Jan. 1 — Dec. 31.
1914 Jan. 1 — May 23, 25 — June 1, 3 — 6, 9 — 11, 13 — 28, 30 — July 31, Aug. 7 — Dec. 31.
1915 Jan. 1 — July 20, Aug. 3 — Oct. 29.
IU
 Micro (N)
 1913 Mar. 1 — Dec. 31.
 1914 Jan. 1 — Aug. 1.
KHi
 1897 Apr. 13 — Dec. 31.
 1898 — 1905 Jan. 1 — Dec. 31.
 1906 Jan. 1 — July 19.
 1909 Oct. 1 — Dec. 31.
 1910 — 1914 Jan. 1 — Dec. 31.
 1915 Jan. 1 — Mar. 1.
LNT — MA
 1910 Sept. 16, Oct. 22.
 1911 July 13 — Dec. 31.
 1912 Jan. 1 — Feb. 29.
 1913 Feb. 10 — 15, 19, 20, 23.
 1915 June 3, July 15, Aug. 2.
MWA
 1909 May 2.
 1911 Oct. 26, 27.

1913   Feb. 19.
TxU
1902   Nov. 26, Dec. 1, 3.
1903   May 28, June 5, Nov. 1.
1904   Jan. 1 – 12, 21.
1905   Oct. 1.
1907   Jan. 26, May 1 – 25, 27, 29 –
        June 1, 3 – July 5, 7 – 11, 13 –
        30, Aug. 7 – 11, 13, 14.
1908   Jan. 1 – Feb. 14, 16 – 22,
        24 – June 19, 21 – 30.
1909   Jan. 21, 23, 25, 27 – 31,
        Feb. 2, 4, 6 – 10, 13, 14,
        Mar. 7, 10 – 12, 14, 15, 20,
        21, 23 – Apr. 1, 3 – 5, 7 – 9, 11,
        12, 15, 16, 20, May 2.
1910   Jan. 1 – Feb. 1, 3 – 15, 17,
        19, 21 – 24, 26, 28 – Mar. 5, 7 –
        19, 23 – 26, 28, 29, 31 – Apr.
        16, 18 – May 25, 27, 28, 30 –
        July 23, 25 – Aug. 16, 18 – Oct.
        22, 24 – Nov. 9, 11 – Dec. 31.
1911   Jan. 1 – Feb. 1, 3 – 10, 12, 14 –
        22, 24 – Mar. 10, 12 – 22, 24 –
        31, Apr. 2, 4 – 19, 21 – 23,
        25 – July 25, 27 – Aug. 11,
        13 – Dec. 31.
1912 – 1913   Jan. 1 – Dec. 31.
1914   Jan. 1 – July 31, Aug. 4 –
        Sept. 12, 14 – Nov. 20, Dec.
        3 – 31.
1915   Jan. 1 – 26, 29 – Feb. 28,
        Mar. 12 – Apr. 9, 11 – 30, May
        3 – July 21, Aug. 2 – Oct. 29.

THE MEXICAN POST. d. est. June 1,
1921.
    Note: In English.
    CU
    1921   July 10, 19 – 22, 29 – Oct.
            13, 15 – Dec. 31.
    1922   Jan. 1 – Mar. 1, 3 – 19, 21 –
            Apr. 29.
    DLC
    1921   June 1 – Dec. 31.
    1922   Jan. 1 – Apr. 30.
    MH
    1922   Jan. 22, 23, 25.

TxU
    1921   Oct. 19.

THE MEXICAN REPUBLIC.
    LNT – MA
    1901   Sept. 1.

THE MEXICAN TIMES. w., sw. est.
Sept. 16, 1865.
    Note: In English. Ceased publica-
    tion June 17, 1867.
    CU – B
    Micro (P)
    1865   Sept. 16 – Dec. 30.
    1866   Jan. 6 – Aug. 13, 27 – Oct.
            15, 29 – Nov. 19, Dec. 4 – 25.
    1867   Jan. 1 – Mar. 6, 13 – June
            17.

    DLC
    Micro (P) & (N)
    1865   Sept. 16 – Dec. 31.
    1866   Jan. 1 – Dec. 31.
    1867   Jan. 1 – June 17.
    LU
    1865   Sept. 16 – Dec. 31.
    1866   Jan. 1 – Oct. 15, 29 – Dec.
            31.
    1867   Jan. 1 – Mar. 3, 17 – June
            17.
    Micro (P)
    1865   Sept. 16 – Dec. 31.
    1866   Jan. 1 – Nov. 19, Dec. 4 – 31.
    1867   Jan. 1 – June 17.
    NHi
    1866   Feb. 17 – Mar. 31, Apr. 14 –
            July 23, Aug. 6 – 13, Oct. 1 –
            Nov. 19, Dec. 4.
    NN
    1865   Sept. 23.
MEXICAN WEEKLY NEWS. w. est.
[1926].
    Note: In English.
    CU
    1940   Aug. 24 – Sept. 28.
    DLC
    1941   Jan. 4 – Dec. 31.
    1942   Jan. 1 – 9, 11 – 17.

LNT—MA
  1938   Dec. 10, 17, 31.
  1939   Feb. 11, 18, Aug. 19.
NjP
  1941   July 19.
EL MEXICANO. sw., 3w. est. Jan. 1,
1839.
    Note: Periodicity Jan. 1—Mar. 11,
    1839, semiweekly; Mar. 14—Aug.
    10, 1839, three times a week.
  DLC
    1839   Prospecto.
            Jan. 1—24, 26—Aug. 10.
            Suplemento: Jan. 15, 22, June
            13, 20.
  MWA
    1839   Jan. 1—Aug. 10.
EL MEXICANO. 3w. est. Oct. 8, 1847.
  NN
    1847   Oct. 8—29, Nov. 6—Dec. 2,
            7—11, 18, 23—25, 30.
    1848   Jan. 8—13.

EL MEXICANO; PERIODICO BISE-
MANAL, DEDICADO AL PUEBLO.
sw. est. Jan. 7, 1866.
    Note: Ceased publication Dec.
    6, 1866.
  CU—B
    1866   Jan. 7—Apr. 8, 15—Dec. 6.
  CtY
    1866   Jan. 18—Feb. 11, 18, Mar.
            1—Dec. 6.
  LNHT
    1866   Jan. 7—Dec. 6.
  NHi
    1866   Aug. 12—19.
  TxU
    1866   Jan. 7—Dec. 6.

EL MEXICANO; PERIODICO POLI-
TICO Y DE INFORMACION. 3w., d.
est. July 8, 1910.
    Note: Periodicity July 8—31, 1910,
    three times a week; after Aug. 1,
    1910, daily.
  TxU
    1910   July 8—27, Aug. 1—4, 6,
            24, 26, 28, 30, 31, Sept. 2—
            Nov. 3, 5.

EL MEXICANO. d. est. Feb. 22, 1915.
  DLC
    1915   Feb. 22—Mar. 5.
            Extraordinario: Mar. 4, 6.
  TxU
    1915   Feb. 22, 23, 26, Mar. 1, 5, 6.

EL MEXICANO. d. est. July 16, 1915.
    Note: Suspended publication July
    18—Aug. 3, 1915.
  DLC
    1915   July 16—Oct. 31.
            Extraordinario: Aug. 12, Oct.
            9, 10.
            Suplemento: Sept. 16.
    1917   Jan. 2—13.
  TxU
    1915   July 16—Aug. 12, 14—Sept.
            25, 28—Oct. 28.

MEXICO. w. est. [1916].
  DLC
    1918   Alcance: Feb. 14—21.

MEXICO CITY COLLEGIAN. [bw.]
    Note: In English.
  TxU
    1949   May 25—June 30, July 27.
    1951   Apr. 12—26.

MEXICO CITY DAILY BULLETIN. d.
    Note: In English.
  DLC
    1953   Sept. 16.

THE MEXICO CITY POST. w. est.
1931.
    Note: In English.
  DLC
    1941   Aug. 9, Sept. 20, [Dec. 25].
    1942   Jan. 31, Feb. 7, Mar. 14,
            28, Apr. 4, 18, May 30.
    1943   Feb. 20.

THE MEXICO DAILY RECORD. d.
    Note: In English.
  DLC
    1910   July 4.
  TxU
    1909   July 30.

MEXICO EN LA CULTURA. w. est.
Feb. 6, 1949.
Note: Supplement to *Novedades*.
CLU
1965   Apr. 18 – Dec. 31.
1966   Jan. 1+.
CU
1957   Nov. 4.
1958   May 19 – Dec. 29.
1959   Jan. 1 – Dec. 31.
1960   Jan. 4 – 18, Feb. 1 – Dec.
31.
1961   Jan. 9 – Dec. 18.
1962   Jan. 1 – May 27.
IU
1957   Nov. 4.
1958   Jan. 8, 26, Feb. 16 – 23, Mar.
9 – 30, Apr. 13, May 5 – Aug.
25, Sept. 8 – Dec. 31.
WU
1949   Feb. 6 – Dec. 31.
1950   Jan. 1+.

MEXICO EVANGELICO. w.
TxU
1908   Jan. 28.

MEXICO GRAPHICO. w.
LNT – MA
1892   Jan. 1 – Dec. 31.
1893   Jan. 1 – Feb. 28.

MEXICO LIBRE. w., sw. est. 1913.
TxU
1913   Apr. 27.

MEXICO NEWS. w. est. [1950].
Note: In English.
LNT – MA
1958   [Sept. 1 – Dec. 31].
1959   [Jan. 12 – Oct. 17].
1960   Jan. 8, June 8, July 29, Oct.
23.
1961   Jan. 14.

MEXICO NEWS.
See *News from Mexico*.

MEXICO NUEVO. d. est. Jan. 1, 1909.
Note: Suspended publication [Mar.
7 – 29], June 14 – 19, 1910.

DLC
1919   Oct. 15 – Dec. 31.
1920   Jan. 1 – May 8.
TxU
1909   Feb. 10, 18, 20, Mar. 27, 30,
Apr. 9, 17, 23 – May 7, 10, 13,
14, 18, 20 – Sept. 1, 6 – 23,
25 – Oct. 2, 4, 5, 7 – 10, 18,
19, 26, 28 – 30, Nov. 1 – 4,
9, 12, 13, 19, 21, 23, 27 – Dec.
6, 8 – 30.
1910   Jan. 1 – Feb. 28, Mar. 4 – 6,
30 – Apr. 2, 4 – June 13, 20.

MEXICO OBRERO. bw. est. Sept.
1909
TxU
1909   Sept. 1/14.

MEXICO-PATRIA. d. est. Dec. 15,
1913.
TxU
1913   Número programa: Dec. 12.
Dec. 15, 30.

THE MEXICO TIMES. w. est. 1921.
Note: In English.
DLC
1921   Dec. 17 – 31.
1922   Jan. 1 – 13, 15 – 20, 22 – Mar. 3
5 – 31, Apr. 2 – May 27.

MEXICO TODAY. w. est. Dec. 24, 1938.
Note: In English.
CSt
1938   Dec. 24.
1939   Mar. 18, Apr. 22.
DLC
1938   Prospecto: Dec. 6.
Dec. 24 – 31.
1939   Jan. 1 – July 22.
LNT – MA
1939   Jan. 21, 28, Feb. 11, 25,
Mar. 11, July 22.

MI MUGER. 3w. est. Dec. 18, 1864.
CU – B
Micro (N)
1864   Dec. 18 – 25.

EL MICROBIO. d. est. Dec. 28, 1911.
　TxU
　　1911　Dec. 28.

EL MICROBIO. w. est. Mar. 1917.
　DLC
　　1917　Apr. 8 – 22.

LA MINERVA. d. est. Feb. 2, 1833.
　DLC
　　1833　Feb. 2 – 6, 8 – 28.

LA MINERVA. 3w. est. Mar. 15, 1845.
　　Note: Suspended publication June
　　10, 1845.
　CU – B
　　1845　Mar. 15 – June 10.
　DLC
　　1845　May 1, 6 – 17.

LA MINERVA MEXICANA. w. est.
　[Jan. 9], 1822.
　CtY
　　1822　n.d. (Nos. 1 – 4, 6).

MISCELANEA DE LITERATURA,
　CIENCIAS Y ARTES. w. est. Oct. 4,
　1828.
　CU – B
　　Micro (N)
　　1828　Oct. 4 – 25.

LA MISCELANEA DEL PUEBLO. bw.
　est. 1904.
　TxU
　　1904　Oct. 31.

EL MOMO. sw. est. Mar. 7, 1838.
　CtY
　　1838　Mar. 7 – Aug. 1.
　TxU
　　1838　Aug. 4 – Sept. 1.

EL MONITOR; PERIODICO DEL
　PUEBLO. d. est. Feb. 13, 1885.
　TxU
　　1885　Feb. 15 – May 31.

EL MONITOR. d.
　TxU
　　1903　Feb. 28, Apr. 26, July 19.

EL MONITOR. w. est. 1912.
　TxU
　　1912　Jan. 21.

EL MONITOR. d. est. Dec. 5, 1914.
　　Note: Suspended publication Jan.
　　28 – Mar. 20, 1915.
　DLC
　　1914　Dec. 5 – 31.
　　1915　Jan. 1 – 27, Mar. 21 – 27, 29,
　　　　　Apr. 3, 20, 30, May 5, 7, 10 –
　　　　　18, 20, 22 – June 6.
　TxU
　　1914　Dec. 5 – 31.
　　1915　Jan. 1 – June 6.

EL MONITOR CONSTITUCIONAL.
　See *El Monitor republicano.*

EL MONITOR CONSTITUCIONAL
INDEPENDIENTE.
　See *El Monitor republicano.*

EL MONITOR DEL PUEBLO. d.
　CLCM
　　1888　Jan. 17, Feb. 9.
　CtY
　　1887　Aug. 10, 21, Sept. 8, Nov.
　　　　　17.
　　1888　Jan. 1, Mar. 3, 8, 16, Sept.
　　　　　16.
　　1889　Jan. 1.
　TxU
　　1887　Aug. 10, 17, 21, Sept. 16,
　　　　　Nov. 8, 17.
　　1888　Jan. 1, 10, Mar. 8, 16, May
　　　　　8, Sept. 16.
　　1889　Jan. 1, May 19.

EL MONITOR DEL PUEBLO.
　TxU
　　1911　Apr. 10.

EL MONITOR LIBERAL. w. est. Jan.
　14, 1901.
　LNT – MA
　　1901　Jan. 14 – June 10.

EL MONITOR LIBERAL; ORGANO
DE LA CONFEDERACION CIVICA
INDEPENDIENTE. est. 1912.
　TxU
　　1913　Jan. 1.

EL MONITOR REPUBLICANO. d.
est. Dec. 21, 1844.
> Note: Title *El Monitor constitu-*
> *cional independiente*, 1845; *El*
> *Monitor constitucional*, Jan. 4—
> Feb. 13, 1846; *El Monitor repub-*
> *licano*, after Feb. 13, 1846. Sus-
> pended publication July 13—Sept.
> 26, 1847; 1858—1860; ceased
> publication Dec. 30, 1896.

CU—B
1845   Mar. 4—June 22.
1868   Oct. 1—3, 6—11, 14, 17—
        24, 28—Nov. 3, 6, 8—14,
        17, 18, 20, 22—26, 28—Dec.
        2, 4—22, 26—31.

1869   Jan. 1—Dec. 31.
1870   Jan. 1—Apr. 16, 19—30,
        May 3—7, 10, 11, 14, 15,
        18—27, 29, June 1—18, 22—
        July 19, 21—Oct. 2, 6—8,
        11—Nov. 6, 9—Dec. 30.

1871—1872   Jan. 1—Dec. 31.
1873   Jan. 1—Mar. 9, 12—July
        25, 27—Aug. 19, 21—Sept. 24,
        26—Dec. 31.

1874   Jan. 2—10, 13—23, 25—Mar.
        11, 13—28, 30—Apr. 1, 3—May
        2, 7—14, 16—27, 29—July 5,
        8—Aug. 30, Sept. 2—Oct. 16,
        18—Nov. 4, 6—25, 27, 28, Dec.
        1—16, 18—31.

1878   Sept. 1, Oct. 20.
1879   Nov. 22, Dec. 11.
1882   July 15, Oct. 14.
1883   July 15, Sept. 25, Oct. 16,
        21, Dec. 5.

1884   Jan. 9, 19, Nov. 16—18,
        20, 21, 27, 28, 30, Dec. 12,
        14, 30.

1885   Feb. 1, 8, 20, Apr. 30, May
        26, 27, 29, 30, June 2—July 3,
        5—Sept. 5, 8—Oct. 30.
1888   May 8, 29.
Micro (P)

1847   Sept. 28—Dec. 31.
1848—1852   Jan. 1—Dec. 31.
1853   Jan. 1—Apr. 30.
1861—1862   Jan. 1—Dec. 31.
1863   Jan. 1—May 30.
1889   Jan. 1—Dec. 31.
CtY
1845   Nos. 224—226, 232, 233, 235,
        236, 238.
1847   Dec. 1—6, 9, 10, 12—31.
1848   Jan. 1—5, 7—21, 23—Feb.
        4, 6—8, 12, 13.
1867   July 1—Dec. 31.
1891   Nov. 8.
DLC
1845   May 1—11, 20—25.
1846   Jan. 4—14, 16—Dec. 31.
        Suplemento: Feb. 21, May 22,
        Sept. 25, 26, Oct. 3, 5, 13, 17,
        24, 27, 31, Nov. 2, 23, 24, Dec.
        3, 4, 18, 19, 21, 23, 24, 26, 30,
        31.
1847   Jan. 1—Feb. 25, Mar. 2—8,
        10—May 27, 30—Oct. 22, 24—
        Dec. 10, 12—31.
        Suplemento: Jan. 11, Feb. 10,
        19, Apr. 28, June 2, Nov. 2.
1848   Jan. 1—Dec. 31.
        Suplemento: Jan. 6, 8, 29,
        Feb. 13, Apr. 9, May 1, 22,
        24, June 29, July 1, 5, 7,
        10, 21, Aug. 2, Sept. 21, 24,
        Oct. 15, Nov. 2, 11, Dec. 1, 30.
1849   Jan. 1—Dec. 31.
        Suplemento: Feb. 2, 3, 10,
        16, 18, 27, Mar. 22, 30, Apr.
        1, June 2, 14, 16, Oct. 3, 13,
        Nov. 1, 22, Dec. 7.
1850   Jan. 1—19, 21—Dec. 31.
        Alcance: May 10.
1851   Jan. 1—Dec. 31.
        Suplemento: May 21, June 14.
1873   May 18, 29, June 7, 17,
        29, July 17, 18, 20, 22—27,
        29—31, Aug. 12, 13, 31, Sept.
        3, 22, Oct. 2, 3, Nov. 18,
        26, Dec. 17.

1874 Jan. 6, 25, 27, Feb. 16, 24,
July 17, 18, Aug. 18, 20,
Sept. 26, 29, Oct. 20, 22, 28,
Nov. 6, 19.

1875 Jan. 2, 19, Feb. 13, 16, 19,
Mar. 24, 25, Apr. 4, 7, 9, 14,
15, 17, 24, Dec. 10, 11, 15,
18, 21, 22.

1877 Jan. 21 – Dec. 31.
Suplemento: Mar. 14, June
19, Oct. 16.

1878 Jan. 1 – May 12, 31, June
2, 4, 21, July 2, Aug. 2, 3,
13 – 15, 23, 31, Sept. 5, 17.

1882 July 19.

KHi

1889 Dec. 15.

MB

1848 Feb. 16 – 29, Mar. 1, 6, 8, 10 –
Apr. 23, July 30 – Aug. 1, 6 –
15.

1855 Dec. 22, 24, 27 – 29.

MWA

1845 Jan. 31, Mar. 15, Sept. 16 –
Dec. 31.

1846 Jan. 1 – Dec. 31.

1847 Jan. 1 – 25, Sept. 27 – Dec. 31.

1848 Jan. 1 – May 26, [Aug. 1 –
Dec. 31].

1849 Jan. 1 – Dec. 31.

1850 Jan. 1 – 31, [Feb. 1 – July 31].

1867 Nov. 17, 21, 22, 26 – 29,
Dec. 1.

1868 Feb. 25, 26, Mar. 1 – 3, 6,
8, 12, Apr. 3 – 5, Oct. 30, Nov.
11, 14, 18, 21, 28 – Dec. 3.
Supplement: Dec. 20 – 23,
26.

1869 Jan. 5 – 10, 16, 21, 22, 28,
30, Feb. 2.

1881 Apr. 1, 3, June 26, July
10, 17, Sept. 4 – 10, 17, 20,
22 – 23, 27 – 29, Oct. 13, 14.

1882 Jan. 4 – 7, 10, 11.

1883 Jan. 27.

1884 [Mar. 29 – Dec. 31].

1885 [Jan. 1 – Dec. 31].

1886 Jan. 17, 20, 22, 23.

MoU

Micro (N)

1868 Oct. 1 – 3, 6 – 11, 14, 17 – 24,
28, 29, Nov. 3, 6, 8 – 14, 17, 18,
20, 22 – 26, 28 – Dec. 2, 4 – 22,
26 – 31.

1869 Jan. 1 – Dec. 31.

1870 Jan. 1 – Apr. 16, 17 – 30,
May 3 – 7, 10, 14, 15, 18 – 27,
29, June 1 – 18, 22 – July 19,
21 – Oct. 2, 6 – 8, 11 – Nov. 6,
9 – Dec. 30.

1871 Jan. 1 – Mar. 10, 12, 16 – 31,
Apr. 6 – May 28, June 1 – Dec.
31.

1872 Apr. 2 – 27, 30 – June 19,
21 – July 31.

NHi

1882 Aug. 31.

NN

1847 Sept. 27 – Oct. 12, 14 – Nov.
23, 25 – Dec. 31.

1848 Jan. 1 – 18, 20 – Feb. 22,
24 – Mar. 4.

TxSjM

1847 Dec. 15, 16.

TxU

1847 Nov. 2.

1873 Jan. 1 – Dec. 31.

1874 Jan. 1 – Dec. 12, 15, 16,
18 – 20, 22 – 31.

1875 Jan. 1 – Dec. 31.

1876 Nov. 1 – Dec. 31.

1877 Jan. 1 – Dec. 30.

1878 – 1879 Jan. 1 – Dec. 31.

1880 Jan. 1 – Mar. 11, 14, Apr.
1 – May 6, 8 – Oct. 5, 7 – Dec.
31.

1881 Jan. 1 – Mar. 5, 8 – June 19,
22 – Aug. 28, 31 – Dec. 31.

1882 Jan. 1 – Feb. 28, Mar. 2 – Dec.
31.

1883 Jan. 1 – July 8, 11 – Dec. 31.

1884 – 1886 Jan. 1 – Dec. 31.

1887 Jan. 1 – Dec. 17, 25 – 31.

1888 Jan. 1 – June 15, Oct. 26 –
Dec. 2, 4.

1889 Mar. 7, Apr. 17, 27, May 10,

22, 25, 26, 29, 31, June 2,
4, 9, 11, 12, 18, 19, 21, 25 –
27, 29, 30, July 2 – 7, 9 – 13,
16 – 18, 20, Aug. 7, 9 – 11,
13, 15, 29, Sept. 3 – 5, Oct.
20, 22, Nov. 26, Dec. 27.
1890   Jan. 10, 24, Feb. 15, Mar.
18, May 10, June 20, 21.

EL MONITOR REPUBLICANO;
ORGANO DEL PARTIDO LIBERAL
CONSTITUCIONALISTA. est.
July 21, 1919.
DLC
1919   July 21 – Dec. 31.
1920   Jan. 1 – Apr. 14.
TxU
1920   Aug. 14.

EL MONITORCITO. est. Aug. 1892.
CtY
1892   n.d. (No. 1).

EL MONO. [sw.] est. Feb. 26, 1833.
CtY
1833   Feb. 26, Mar. 8, Apr. 2.

MONTE-CRISTO. 3w. est. June 20,
1850.
CU – B
Micro (N)
1850   June 20 – Aug. 1.

LA MORALIDAD. w. est. June 8, 1885.
CU – B
Micro (P)
1885   Prospecto: Apr.
June 8.
TxU
1885   Prospecto: June 1.
1888   Nov. 4.

EL MOSAICO MEXICO.
TxU
1839   Sept. 27.

EL MOSCON. w. est. Mar. 18, 1909.
TxU
1909   Mar. 18.
1911   Oct. 5 – 14, Nov. 12.

LA MOSQUITA. w., irr. est. Apr. 13,
1879.

CtY
1879   Apr. 13 – Oct. 27.

EL MOSQUITO. w. est. Aug. 13, 1911.
TxU
1911   Aug. 13, 27, Sept. 10, 19,
Oct. 15, 31, Nov. 23.

EL MOSQUITO MEXICANO. 3w., sw.
est. Mar. 14, 1834.
Note: Periodicity Mar. 14, 1834 – Apr.
13, 1838, three times a week; after
Apr. 17, 1838, semiweekly.
CU – B
Micro (P)
1835   Sept. 15.
1840   June 19.
CtY
1834   Mar. 14 – Dec. 30.
1835   Jan. 2 – Mar. 24.
1836   n.d. (Vol. 2, No. 101).
1838   Jan. 24, Feb. 5.
DLC
1838   Jan. 1 – Feb. 15, 17, 18, 20 –
Dec. 31.
Alcance: Aug. 24.
Suplemento: Mar. 5, 16, Apr.
27, June 8, Dec. 11.
1839   Jan. 1 – Dec. 30.
Alcance: Sept. 13.
Extraordinario: Oct. 18.
Suplemento: Jan. 25.
1840   Jan. 1 – Feb. 24, 26 – May
28, 30 – July 30, Aug. 1 – 17,
19 – Dec. 31.
Suplemento: Aug. 14, 28,
Sept. 11, 22, Oct. 9.
1841   Jan. 1 – Sept. 27, Oct. 9 – 29.
Suplemento: Feb. 16, May 21,
July 23.
1842   Jan. 4 – Nov. 10, 12 – Dec. 31.
Alcance: Mar. 11, Apr. 1,
May 27, July 22, Oct. 18, Nov.
1.
Extraordinario: Sept. 27.
Suplemento: Apr. 19, July
26, Aug. 23, Sept. 23.
1843   Jan. 1, 2, 4 – Mar. 6, 8 – June
15, 17 – Dec. 31.

Alcance: June 9.
Suplemento: Jan. 31, Dec. 12.
1844   Jan. 1 — Dec. 2, 4 — 6.
Alcance: Feb. 27.
Suplemento: Mar. 29.
1845   Apr. 2 — June 6, 8 — Aug. 16.
MWA
1842   Mar. 1 — May 24.
NN
1836   Suplemento.
TxSjM
1843   July 4.
TxU
1834   Mar. 14 — May 23, 30 — Aug.
19, 26 — 29, Sept. 4 — Oct. 7,
14 — Dec. 31.
1835   Jan. 23, 30 — Feb. 3, 10 —
Mar. 9, 13 — 20, 27 — Dec. 31.
1836 — 1842   Jan. 1 — Dec. 31.
1843   Jan. 1 — Dec. 29.

EL MOTIN. w. est. Oct. 18, 1914.
TxU
1914   Oct. 18 — Nov. 22.

EL MOVIMIENTO. d.
NN
1862   Dec. 6.
1863   Jan. 5.

LA MUELA DEL JUICIO. w. est. June
16, 1907.
TxU
1907   June 16, Oct. 27 — Nov. 3.

EL MUNDANO. w.
CU — B
Micro (P)
1883   Sept. 30, Oct. 14 — 28.

EL MUNDO. d.
LNT — MA
1889   Aug. 24, 28.
TxU
1889   Aug. 11, 22, Sept. 16, Nov. 4.
1890   June 2.

EL MUNDO; DIARIO DE NOTICIAS
UNIVERSALES, ECO DE LA OPIN-
ION Y RESUMEN DE LA PRENSA. d.

TxU
1892   Mar. 19, 23.

EL MUNDO; EDICION DIARIA. d.
TxU
1897   Nov. 16, 17.

EL MUNDO. d.
MWA
1906   Sept. 21, 22.

EL MUNDO; DIARIO DE LA TARDE.
d. est. Mar. 8, 1915.
DLC
1915   Mar. 8, Apr. 1, 8, 10 — 15.
Extraordinario: Mar. 10, 11,
Apr. 5, 13, 16.
TxU
1915   Mar. 8.
Extraordinario: Mar. 10 — 14.

EL MUNDO; DIARIO NOTICERO.
d. est. Apr. 1917.
DLC
1917   Apr. 21, 24.
TxU
1915   Apr. 10.

EL MUNDO. d. est. Aug. 6, 1917.
DLC
1917   Aug. 6 — 12.

EL MUNDO CRISTIANO.
TxU
1921   Apr. 1.

EL MUNICIPAL. 3w. est. Dec. 26,
1847.
CU — B
Micro (N)
1847   Dec. 26 — 31.
1848   Jan. 1 — Feb. 23.
CtY
1847   Dec. 26, 31.

MUNICIPAL MEXICANO. w. est. Feb.
6, 1836.
Note: Ceased publication Aug.
20, 1836.
CU — B
Micro (N)

1836   Feb. 6 – Aug. 20.
TxU
1836   Feb. 6 – Aug. 20.

EL MUNICIPIO LIBRE. sw., 3w., d.
est. [1877].
CU – B
1878   Apr. 6, 10, 13.
Micro (P)
1878   Apr. 6, 10, 13.
LNT – MA
1887 – 1888   [Jan. 1 – Dec. 31].
1889 – 1892   Jan. 1 – Dec. 31.
1893   [Jan. 1 – Dec. 31].
TxU
1878   Sept. 21.
1885   Dec. 19.
1890   Mar. 13, Oct. 18, Nov. 23,
28, Dec. 12, 17, 18.

LA NACION; PERIODICO GENERAL E
INDEPENDIENTE. est. Aug. 9, 1856.
CU – B
1856   Aug. 9 – Dec. 31.
1857   Jan. 1 – June 1.

LA NACION. d. est. Aug. 16, 1865.
CU – B
Micro (N)
1865   Aug. 16 – Dec. 31.
1866   Jan. 1 – Apr. 15.

LA NACION. d. est. 1873.
CU – B
1873   Nov. 11 – 26, 28 – Dec. 31.
1874   Jan. 1 – 6, 8 – Feb. 28.

LA NACION; ORGANO DEL PARTIDO
CATOLICO NACIONAL. est. 1912.
DLC
1913   Sept. 16.
TxU
1912   July 16, 20, 23, 24, 27, 28,
30, Aug. 17, 23 – 25, 27 – 31,
Sept. 2 – 6, 8, 10, 12 – 14,
16, 17, 19 – 21, 25, Oct. 3,
14, 19, 24.
1913   Feb. 26, July 31, Aug. 14,
19, Sept. 16, Oct. 11, 17,
Dec. 3 – 9, 12, 13, 15 – 22.
1914   Jan. 8, 14, July 27.

LA NACION. w. est. Oct. 18, 1941.
AzU
1944   Apr. 15 – Aug. 5, 19 – Dec. 31.
Dec. 31.
1945   Jan. 6 – Apr. 1, 14 – Dec.
29.
1946   Jan. 5 – Aug. 3, 17 – Dec.
28.
1947   Jan. 4 – Dec. 27.
1948   Jan. 3 – June 12, 26 – Aug. 1,
14 – Dec. 27.
1949   Jan. 3 – Dec. 5, 19 – 26.
1950   Jan. 2 – 16, 30 – Dec. 25.
1951   Jan. 1 – Aug. 6, 27 – Dec.
31.
1952   Jan. 7 – Dec. 28.
1953   Jan. 4 – Feb. 28, Apr. 12 –
Dec. 27.
1954   Jan. 3 – Dec. 26.
1955   Jan. 2 – Mar. 13, 27 – Dec. 25.
1956 – 1957   Jan. 1 – Dec. 31.
1958   Jan. 5 – Nov. 2, Dec. 7 – 28.
1959   Jan. 4 – Dec. 27.
1960   Jan. 3 – May 8, 15 – July 26,
Aug. 7 – Dec. 25.
1961   Jan. 1 – June 11, 25 – Aug.
27, Sept. 10, 17, Oct. 7, 22 –
Nov. 27, Dec. 10 – 31.
1962   Jan. 7 – July 22.
CSt
1941   Oct. 18 – Dec. 31.
1942 – 1948   Jan. 1 – Dec. 31.
1949   Jan. 1 – May 31.
1950   Jan. 1 – Nov. 30.
1951   Feb. 19, Aug. 27, Oct. 8.
1952   Feb. 4, May 12, 19, June
9, July 23, Sept 15, 22, Oct.
26, Nov. 2, 16, Dec. 14.
1953   Jan. 18, Feb. 1, 8, 15,
Mar. 15.
ICRL
1951   Feb. 1 – Dec. 31.
1952   Jan. 1 – Dec. 31.
1953   Jan. 1 – June 30.
LNT – MA
1944   Apr. 15 – Nov. 10, 12 – Dec.
31.
1945   Jan. 1 – Nov. 7, 9 – Dec. 31.

1946 [Jan. 1 – Dec. 31].
1947 – 1948 Jan. 1 – Dec. 31.
1949 – 1952 [Jan. 1 – Dec. 31].
1953 Jan. 1 – Oct. 3, 5 – Dec. 31.
1954 [Jan. 1 – June 6, Oct. 1 – Nov. 17].
1955 [Jan. 30 – Dec. 31].
1956 – 1959 [Jan. 1 – Dec. 31].
1960 Jan. 1 – Apr. 2, 4 – Dec. 31.
1961 [Jan. 1 – Dec. 31].
1962 [Jan. 1 – June 30].

EL NACIONAL; VERDAD, JUSTICIA, IMPARCIALIDAD. 3w. est. Sept. 1835.
Note: Ceased publication Nov. 30, 1844.
CtY
1844 Nov. 27 – 30.
DLC
1836 Jan. 1 – Mar. 17, 19 – 29, 31 – May 23.
NN
1836 June 17.
TxU
1835 Nov. 4, Dec. 23, 25.
1836 Apr. 8, 11.

EL NACIONAL. d. est. 1880.
CLCM
1887 Aug. 7, 9, 11, 13, 24, 25, 26, 28, Sept. 22, 25.
CU – B
Micro (N)
1882 Aug. 19 – 29.
1883 May 10 – 12, 16.
1884 Dec. 7.
1885 Jan. 8.
LNT – MA
1885 Nov. 8.
1886 Mar. 25.
1899 July 22.
MWA
1883 June 26, 27.
TxU
1880 Sept. 4, 11, 16, 28, Oct. 30.
1881 Jan. 29, Nov. 17, 26.
1884 Nov. 16.
1885 Nov. 10.

1886 June 15, 17, 24, July 18, Sept. 23, Dec. 19.
1887 Jan. 16, June 22, Aug. 23, Oct. 7.
1888 Dec. 9.
1889 Jan. 1, 29, Mar. 7, Sept. 11.
1890 Jan. 12, Feb. 1, Mar. 5 – 11, 13, 14, 16 – 18, 23 – 25, 29, 30, Apr. 3, 8, 10 – 16, 18 – 22, 24 – May 6, 8, 9, 11 – 15, 18 – 27, 30 – June 29, July 1 – 19, 22 – 26, 29 – Aug. 2, 5 – 14, 17 – Sept. 3, 5 – Dec. 31.
1892 Oct. 30.
1894 Dec. 25.

EL NACIONAL; DIARIO DE LA TARDE. d. est. Apr. 17, 1911.
TxU
1911 Apr. 17 – July 4, 6 – 10, 12 – 18, 20, 21, 24 – 29, Aug. 3, 5 – 7, 9 – 12, 18, 19, 26 – 29, Sept. 7, 13.

EL NACIONAL. 3w. est. Sept. 26, 1914.
TxU
1914 Sept. 26.

EL NACIONAL; DIARIO INDEPEN-DIENTE DE LA MAÑANA. d. est. Nov. 27, 1914.
Note: Ceased publication Dec. 1, 1914.
DLC
1914 Nov. 27 – Dec. 1.
LNT – MA
1914 Nov. 30.
TxU
1914 Nov. 27 – Dec. 1.

EL NACIONAL. d. est. May 8, 1916.
Note: Ceased publication 1917.
DLC
1916 May 10, 11, Nov. 7.
Extraordinario: July 31, Aug. 1, 2, Sept. 3.
1917 Mar. 28, Apr. 16, 18, 20, 21, 24, 26 – 28, 30 – May 3, 7.
Extraordinario: Mar. 2, 15, June 8.

TxU
  1916   Prospecto: Apr. 22.
         June 20, 27, July 31, Aug.
         3, 7, Nov. 15.
  1917   Oct. 17, Dec. 9.
  1919   Mar. 12.

EL NACIONAL. d. est. Feb. 19, 1929.
  Note: Title originally *El Nacional
  revolucionario*. Established *Suplemento dominical* in Apr. 1947.
  AU
  1945   Jan. 6, 8, 17 – 26, 28 – Feb.
         12, 14 – 18, 22 – 24, Mar. 19,
         20, Apr. 1, May 6.

  CSt
  1930   Apr. 1 – 30.
  1936   Sept. 2.
  1938   Aug. 26 – 31.
  1941   Apr. 1 – May 31, Aug. 1 –
         Dec. 31.
  1942 – 1946   Jan. 1 – Dec. 31.
  1947   Jan. 1 – Feb. 1, 10, Nov.
         2.
  1950   Jan. 15.
  1952   Mar. 30.

  CU
  1929   July 10.
  1930   Apr. 24.
  1936   Jan. 1 – 25, 27 – Feb. 7,
         9, 10, 15, 16, 18, 19, 22 –
         Dec. 31.
  1937 – 1947   ₍Jan. 1 – Dec. 31.₎
  1948 – 1949   Jan. 1 – Dec. 31.
  1950   Jan. 1 – 13, 15 – July 29.
  1954   June 9, 17 – 22, 24 – Oct.
         7, 9 – 11, 13 – Oct. 31, Nov.
         3 – Dec. 3.
  1956   Apr. 12 – Dec. 31.
  1957 – 1963   Jan. 1 – Dec. 31.
  1964   Jan. 2 – Aug. 28, 30 – Dec.
         31.

  DLC
  Micro (P)
  1943 – 1950   Jan. 1 – Dec. 31.
  Micro (P) & (N)
  1937   Nov. 1 – Dec. 25, 27 – 31.
  1938   Jan. 1 – Feb. 23, 25 – Dec. 31.

  1939   Jan. 1 – Apr. 9, May 1 –
         Dec. 31.
  1940   Jan. 1 – Sept. 19, 21 – Nov.
         20, 22 – Dec. 23, 25, 27 – 31.
  1941   Jan. 1 – June 20, July 1 – Dec.
         31.
  1942   Jan. 1 – 24, 26 – Dec. 31.
  1951   Jan. 1 – Mar. 7, 9 – May 25,
         28 – July 6, 8 – Aug. 15,
         17 – Nov. 25, 27 – Dec. 2,
         4 – 31.
  1952   Jan. 1 – Feb. 14, 17 – Sept. 15,
         17 – Nov. 19, 21 – Dec. 31.
  1953   Jan. 1 – Aug. 24, 26 – Nov. 18,
         20 – Dec. 31.
  1954   Jan. 1 – 21, 23 – Mar. 10, 12 –
         20, 22 – Aug. 3, 5 – 19, 21 –
         Sept. 8, 10 – Oct. 25, 27 – Nov.
         18, 21 – Dec. 30.
  1955   Jan. 1 – June 13, 15 – 24, 26 –
         Aug. 9, 11 – 18, 20 – Oct. 20,
         22, 24 – Nov. 17, 19, 21 – Dec.
         25, 27 – 31.
  1956   Jan. 1 – 16, 18 – Apr. 10,
         12, 14 – 28, 30 – Sept. 9, 11 –
         Oct. 28, 30 – Dec. 20, 22 – 31.
  1957   Jan. 1 – 24, 26 – 31, Feb. 2 –
         7, 9 – Apr. 16, 18 – May 15,
         17 – June 9, 11 – 27, 29 – Sept.
         11, 13 – Oct. 17, 19 – Dec. 1,
         3 – 12, 14 – 31.
  1958   Jan. 1 – Apr. 2, 4 – 19, 21 –
         24, 26 – May 14, 16 – June 13,
         15 – Nov. 18, 21 – 29, Dec. 1 –
         31.
  1959   Jan. 3 – Mar. 20, 22 – June 11,
         13 – Nov. 5, 7, 8, 10 – 19, 22 –
         Dec. 14, 16 – 31.
  1960   Jan. 2, 4 – 6, 8 – 28, 30 – Feb.
         28, Mar. 1 – 19, 21 – Aug. 18,
         20 – Sept. 15, 17 – Oct. 16,
         18 – Nov. 24, 26 – Dec. 31.
  1961   Jan. 1 – Apr. 3, 5 – May 11,
         13 – June 21, 24 – July 13, 15 –
         Aug. 17, 19 – Sept. 7, 9, 12 –
         Dec. 2, 4 – 10, 12 – 17, 19 –
         31.

1962 Jan. 1+.
DPU
Current (six months).
ICRL
1938 Aug. 26 – Oct. 13.
1941 Apr. 10 – Dec. 31.
1942 – 1947 Jan. 1 – Dec. 31.
1948 Jan. 1 – Oct. 8.
IEN
1941 Aug. 19 – Dec. 12.
1942 June 1 – Dec. 31.
1943 – 1946 Jan. 1 – Dec. 31.
1947 Jan. 1 – Feb. 10.
IU
Current (three months).
InU
1941 Apr. 1 – May 31, Aug. 1 – Dec.
31.
1942 – 1947 Jan. 1 – Dec. 31.
1948 Jan. 1 – Oct. 31.
LNT – MA
1930 June 27.
1931 Mar. 10, Aug. 19.
1933 Feb. 2, May 5.
1934 Aug. 10, 19, 25.
1938 [Aug. 26 – Oct. 13].
LU
1942 May 21 – Dec. 31.
1943 Jan. 1 – Dec. 31.
1944 Jan. 1 – Apr. 27, June 6 –
Nov. 22.
1945 July 13 – Dec. 31.
1946 Jan. 1 – Dec. 31.
1948 July 2 – Oct. 18.
1949 Apr. 24 – Nov. 30.
1950 Feb. 1 – June 30.
MiU
1934 Jan. 1 – Dec. 31.
1935 Jan. 1 – Oct. 31.
1936 Jan. 1 – Apr. 30, July 1 –
Aug. 31.
1937 Jan. 1 – Feb. 28, May 1 –
June 30.
1940 May 1 – June 30.
1941 Apr. 1 – May 31, Aug. 1 –
Dec. 31.
NN
Micro (P) & (N)

1941 Apr. 3, Sept. 1, 3 – 6.
1942 Jan. 2 – 11, 14 – 24, 26,
28 – 31, Feb. 3, 6 – 28, Mar.
1 – Apr. 18, 20 – May 1, 3 –
Aug. 15, 17 – Dec. 31.
1943 Jan. 1 – Dec. 30.
1944 Jan. 2 – Dec. 31.
1945 – 1946 Jan. 1 – Dec. 31.
1947 Jan. 1 – Feb. 28, Apr. 1 –
Dec. 31.
1948 – 1951 Jan. 1 – Dec. 31.
NcU
1945 May 1, 3 – 26, 28 – June 27,
29, July 1 – 15.
NjP
1942 Aug. 22.
OCl
1943 – 1947 Jan. 1 – Dec. 31.
1948 Jan. 1 – 7.
OU
Current (six months).
OrU
1938 Jan. 1 – July 31, Aug. 26 –
Oct. 13, Nov. 1 – Dec. 31.
1941 Jan. 1 – Mar. 30, Apr. 10 –
15, 17 – May 1, 3 – 6, June 1 –
Aug. 30, Sept. 1, 3 – 9, 11 –
16, 18 – 21, 23 – Oct. 1, 3, 4, 6 –
Nov. 19, 22 – Dec. 31.
1942 Jan. 1 – 10, 12 – Mar. 2, 4 –
Apr. 29, May 1, 3 – July 5,
7 – Sept. 16, 18, 19, 21 – Nov.
20, 22, Dec. 1, 9 – 25, 27 – 31.
1943 Jan. 1 – 31, Feb. 2 – 13,
15 – Mar. 25, 27, 29 – Apr.
5, 7 – May 1, 3 – Aug. 1, 3 –
Nov. 30, Dec. 2 – 5, 7 – 31.
1944 Jan. 1 – Feb. 5, 7 – 20, 22 –
Apr. 13, 15 – June 16, 18,
19, 21 – 23, 25 – Sept. 16, 18 –
Nov. 2, 4 – 20, 22 – 30, Dec.
2 – 31.
1945 Jan. 1 – 26, 28 – Aug. 25, 27 –
Sept. 16, 18 – Dec. 31.
1946 Jan. 1 – Mar. 2, 4 – 9, 11 – 21,
23 – 30, Apr. 1 – 6, 8 – 13, 15 –
May 2, 3 – 6, 8 – July 7, 8, 10 –
15, 18 – Sept. 14, 18 – 28, 30 –

Oct. 30, Nov. 1 – Dec. 31.
1947   Jan. 1 – 4, 6 – Feb. 5, 7 – 10,
Mar. 11 – May 22, 24, 25, 27 –
June 21, 23, 26 – 28, July 4,
7, 10 – 12, 16 – Aug. 1, 3, 5 –
Sept. 4, 7 – 14, 16 – Dec. 28,
30, 31.
1948   Jan. 1 – Mar. 5, 7 – 27, 29 –
Apr. 12, 15 – 30, May 2 – 6, 8 –
June 5, 7 – 26, 28 – Oct. 8.
PSt
Current (one month).
Suplemento dominical:
1947   Apr. 1+.
TxU
1938   Sept. 1 – 16, 18 – Oct. 10, 12,
13.
1940   Aug. 9 – Dec. 31.
1941   Jan. 1 – Nov. 20, 22 – Dec. 7,
9 – 31.
1942 – 1943   Jan. 1 – Dec. 31.
1944   Jan. 1 – July 15, 17 – Aug.
20, 22 – Sept. 15, 18 – Dec. 31.
1945   Jan. 1 – Mar. 2, 4 – May 1,
3 – Dec. 31.
1946 – 1955   Jan. 1 – Dec. 31.
1956   Jan. 1 – Nov. 30.
1958   Mar. 15 – 18, Apr. 26 – 30,
May 1, 10 – 16, 31, June 1 –
6, 14 – 28, July 5 – Nov. 19,
21, Dec. 24 – 31.
1959   Jan. 1+.
WaU
1945   Nov. 3, 4, 6, Dec. 3, 5, 7,
13.
1946   Jan. 19, Feb. 2, 3, 11, 12,
Mar. 25, Apr. 19, 22, 26, May
21 – 23, 26, June 1, 2, 15, 16,
27, Aug. 1, 8, 11, 15, 16, 23,
24, Sept. 2, 4, 6, 12, Oct. 8, Dec.
24 – 31.

EL NACIONALISTA. d. est. July 31, 1914.
DLC
1914   Aug. 3, 12, 14, 20, 21.
TxU
1914   Aug. 13 – 15, 18, 19, 22.

EL NACIONALISTA; DIARIO DE LA
TARDE. d. est. Sept. 10, 1917.

DLC
1917   Sept. 10 – 12, 14 – Oct. 30, Nov.
1, 3 – Dec. 31.
Extraordinario: Nov. 24.
Suplemento: Oct. 18.
1918   Jan. 2 – May 31, June 3 – 14.
LNT – MA
1918   Jan. 4.
TxU
1918   Mar. 12, 22.

EL NACUAL. w. est. 1880.
CtY
1880   n.d. (Nos. 1 – 5).

NEWS FROM MEXICO. w. est. May 31,
1941.
Note: Title *Mexico News*, May 31,
1941 – May 1945; *News from Mexico*,
May 1945 – Oct. 1, 1946. Ceased publication Oct. 1, 1946.
WU
1941   May 31 – Dec. 31.
1942 – 1945   Jan. 1 – Dec. 31.
1946   [Jan. 1 – Oct. 1].

EL NIETO DEL AHUIZOTE. d.
CU – B
Micro (P)
1886   Dec. 30.
1887   Jan. 3, 4.
TxU
1886   Nov. 19.

EL NIGROMANTE. w.
TxU
1906   May 7.

EL NORTE. d. est. Apr. 21, 1915.
DLC
1915   Apr. 21 – 23, 26 – 30, May 5 –
18, 21, 22, 25, 26, 31, June 1 –
5, July 6 – 9.
Extraordinario: May 14.
TxU
1915   May 19.

THE NORTH AMERICAN. EL NORTE
AMERICANO. sw., d. est. Sept.
29, 1847.
Note: In Spanish and English.
Ceased publication Mar. 31, 1848.

CLU
  Micro (P) & (N)
  1847   Sept. 29 – Dec. 31.
  1848   Jan. 1 – Mar. 31.
CU – B
  Micro (P) & (N)
  1847   Sept. 29 – Dec. 31.
  1848   Jan. 1 – Feb. 16, 18 – 29.
CtY
  1847   [Sept. 29 – Dec. 31].
  1848   [Jan. 1 – Mar. 31].
DLC
  1847   Oct. 12, 26, Nov. 30.
  1848   Jan. 19, 20, 24 – 26, Feb. 10,
         11.
  Micro (P)
  1847   Sept. 29 – Dec. 31.
  1848   Jan. 1 – Mar. 31.
MWA
  1847   Dec. 31.
NHi
  1848   Mar. 17, 18.
  Micro (P)
  1847   Sept. 29 – Dec. 31.
  1848   Jan. 1 – Mar. 31.
NN
  1847   Dec. 28.

NOSOTROS. bw.
  LNT – MA
  1941   Aug. 1, 15.

LAS NOTICIAS.
  LNT – MA
  1887   July 10.

LAS NOTICIAS. d. est. June 24, 1915.
  DLC
  1915   June 24, July 1.

LAS NOTICIAS; DIARIO DE LA
  TARDE. d. est. July 1, 1920.
  DLC
  1920   July 2, 14.
  NN
  1921   Extraordinario: Sept. 12.
  TxU
  1920   July 10, Nov. 3, 26.
  1921   Jan. 27, Feb. 1.
         Extraordinario: Jan. 27.

NOTICIAS SENSACIONALES.
  TxU
  1913   Extraordinario: Feb. 11, 12.

NOTICIERO DE LA C.T.A.L.
  See *C.T.A.L. News. Noticiero de la
  C.T.A.L.*

EL NOTICIERO INDEPENDIENTE.
  est. 1913.
  DLC
  1913   Feb. 18.
         Extraordinario: Feb. 19.

EL NOTICIOSO. d. est. Apr. 3, 1859.
  Note: Title *El Noticioso de la capital*, Apr. 3 – 13, 1859; *El Noticioso*,
  Apr. 14 – May 4, 1859. Ceased publication May 4, 1859.
  CtY
  1859   Apr. 3 – May 4.

EL NOTICIOSO; MOSAICO DE
  COMERCIO, FERROCARRILES,
  POLITICA, LITERATURA. w. est.
  1880.
  Note: In Spanish and English.
  CU – B
  Micro (P)
  1880   Nov. 29.
  1883   Oct. 21, Nov. 11.
  MWA
  1881   Mar. 13, June 27.
  TxU
  1880   Oct. 11.
  1881   Apr. 11, Nov. 28.

EL NOTICIOSO DE AMBOS MUNDOS.
  d. est. Mar. 25, 1861.
  CU – B
  Micro (N)
  1861   Mar. 25 – Apr. 29.

EL NOTICIOSO DE LA CAPITAL.
  See *El Noticioso*.

NOTICIOSO GENERAL. 3w., sw. est.
  July 24, 1815.
  Note: Succeeded by *El Redactor
  municipal*. Ceased publication
  Nov. 5, 1823.

CU—B
1815   July 24—Dec. 31.
1816—1820   Jan. 1—Dec. 31.
1821   Jan. 1—June 1.
1822   Nov. 22.
CtY
1815   Aug. 3, 4, 19—21, 22—25, 29—
        Sept. 1, Oct. 10—13, 14—16,
        Nov. 21—24, Dec. 2—11, 16—
        18.
1816   Jan. 5—Nov. 1, 8—11, 18—
        Dec. 30.
1817   [Jan. 1—Dec. 31].
1818   Jan. 2—Dec. 31.
1819   Jan. 1—Dec. 31.
1820   Jan. 5—Mar. 22, 27—29,
        Apr. 3, 7—26, May 3—10, 15,
        19—29, June 2—Dec. 25, 29.
1821   Jan. 1—Dec. 31.
1822   Jan. 2—Oct. 12.
1823   Jan. 1—Oct. 31.
LNT—MA
1820   Jan. 14—Dec. 31.
NN
1815   July 24—Aug. 25, Sept. 2, 5, 6,
        9—25, Nov. 25—Dec. 2.
        Suplemento: July 28, Sept. 3, 4.
        Extraordinario: Aug. 25, Sept.
        7, 8.
1817   Feb. 3, Apr. 25, June 6.
        Alcance: Mar. 20.
1818   Feb. 11, 15, Sept. 30.
        Alcance: May 6.
1819   July 14.
1820   Mar. 22, June 2, Sept. 22.
        Suplemento: Aug. 18, Sept. 22.
        Alcance: Sept. 22.
1821   Jan. 29, Sept. 21, Oct. 22,
        Nov. 14.
        Suplemento: Mar. 5, 28, Sept.
        14, Oct. 22.
1822   Apr. 10, 19, May 8.
        Suplemento: Apr. 19.
1823   May 9.
TxU
1817   Jan. 3, 8—Dec. 26, 31.
1821   Jan. 1—Dec. 31.
1822   Jan. 2—May 31, June 5—
        Dec. 30.

EL NOTICIOSO MEDICO.
TxU
1885   Aug. 1.

EL NOTICIOSO MEXICANO. d. est.
Oct. 1912.
DLC
1913   Jan. 27, Feb. 7, 10, 19, 21—
        24, 26, Mar. 3—19, 22—29,
        Apr. 1—15, 23, June 19, Aug.
        25, 27.
        Boletín: Jan. 15, Feb. 18.
        Extraordinario: Feb. 23, June 3.
TxU
1912   Nov. 5, 7.
1913   Jan. 11, 13, 16—18, 31, Feb.
        10, 20, Mar. 6—15, 18, 19, 24,
        26—May 3, 7—15, 17—24,
        27—30, June 2—11, 14—16, 18,
        20, 23—28, July 1, 2, 4, 19, 22,
        23, 25, 26, 29—31, Aug. 9, 19,
        21, Sept. 5, 10, 12, 15, 16, 22,
        24, Oct. 3, 7, 11, 13, 14, 27—
        29, Nov. 1.

LAS NOVEDADES. w. est. July 20, 1885.
CU—B
Micro (P)
1885   Oct. 12.
MWA
1885   Dec. 21.
TxU
1885   July 20—Aug. 3, 17, 31, Nov.
        2, 16, 30, Dec. 7, 21.
1887   Dec. 5.

NOVEDADES. d. est. 1935.
Note: Publishes weekly supplement *México en la cultura*. Suspended publication Nov. 20—Dec. 5,
1945.
CSt
1945   Aug. 2—Sept. 31.
1950   Aug. 6.
CU
1946   Aug. 18.
DLC
1941   Oct. 26.
1942   Mar. 25—Apr. 10, 12, 18, 21—

26, 28, 30, May 3 – 11, 14, 16 –
19, 21 – 24, 27 – 31, June 2, 3,
5 – 7, 9 – 13, 15 – Sept. 10, 14,
16 – 26, 28 – Oct. 25, 27 – Dec.
15, 17 – 31.
1943 Jan. 1 – 9, 11 – Feb. 6, 8 – 28,
Mar. 2 – May 5, 7 – 31, June
2 – July 1, 3, 5, 6, 15, 19, 29 –
Sept. 10, 12 – Oct. 11, 17, 23,
26, 27, 31, Nov. 2 – 7, 9 – 11,
13 – Dec. 1, 3 – 5, 7 – 11, 14,
15, 18 – 30.
1944 Jan. 1 – 24, 26, 28 – Feb. 29,
Mar. 2, 3, Apr. 3 – 5, 7 – 9, 11 –
13, 17 – 19, 21, 23, 24, 27 – 30,
May 3, 4, 7, 8, 10, 11, 15, 17,
24, 25, 27, 28, 30, 31, June 4, 10,
11 – 20, 22, 24, 27, 29 – July 8,
11, 13, 18, 21, 23, 24, 26,
28, 30, Aug. 1 – 3, 6 – Sept. 14,
16 – 24, 26 – Nov. 14, 16 – 23,
25 – Dec. 12, 14 – 16, 18 – 26,
29 – 31.
1945 Jan. 1 – 6, 8, 10 – 21, 23 – Feb.
24, 26 – Mar. 3, 6 – 20, 24 –
June 8, 12, 13, 15, 17, 21 –
27, 29 – July 14, 16 – 25, 27 –
Aug. 21, 24 – Sept. 12, 14 –
Nov. 3, 5 – 7, 9 – Dec. 20, 22 –
31.
1946 Jan. 1 – 15, 17 – 25, 27 – Feb.
13, 15 – Mar. 4, 6 – 8, 11, 13 –
15, 17 – 22, 24, 27, 29, Apr. 1,
3, 5, 8, 10, 12, 17, 19, 22, 24,
26, 29, May 4, 8 – 11, 17, 20 –
22, 24, 26, 27, 29, 31, June 2 –
5, 7, 10, 12, 15 – 19, 21, 23, 24,
26, 27, 30 – Sept. 2, 4 – Nov.
30, Dec. 2 – 31.
1947 Jan. 1 – 31, Mar. 1 – Apr.
5, 7 – Dec. 10, 12 – 31.
1948 Jan. 1 – 20, 22 – 31, Feb. 2 –
4, 6 – 10, 12 – Mar. 3, 5, 7 –
Apr. 2, 4 – 10, 12 – 15, 17 –
22, 24 – 29, June 1 – 11, 13,
15 – 17, 20 – Oct. 4, 6 – 12, 14 –
Nov. 24, 26 – Dec. 31.
1949 Jan. 1 – 25, 27 – Feb. 13, 16,

17, 19 – Mar. 24, 27 – 30, Apr.
1 – May 24, 26 – 28, 30 – July 4,
6 – Sept. 2, 4 – Dec. 8, 10 – 31.
FU
1961 Nov. 27 – Dec. 31.
1962 Jan. 1+.
InU
1957 Aug. 1 – Dec. 31.
1958 Jan. 1 – Feb. 28, May 1 – Dec.
31.
1959 Jan. 2 – Feb. 20, 22 – Mar. 20,
22 – Apr. 30, May 2, 3, 5 – 9,
11 – Sept. 15, 17 – Nov. 19,
21 – Dec. 24, 26 – 31.
1960 Jan. 2 – 17, Feb. 1 – Dec. 31.
1961 May 1 – Sept. 30, Nov. 1 – Dec.
31.
1962 Jan. 2 – Apr. 2 – 10, 14 – 30,
May 2 – Sept. 15, 17 – Oct. 1,
7 – Nov. 19, 21 – Dec. 24, 26 –
31.
1963 Jan. 1 – 15, Nov. 1 – Dec. 31.
1964 Jan. 2, 4 – Mar. 9, 21, 24 – Apr.
24, 26 – 30, May 2, 4, 6, 7, 9 –
16, 18 – 24, 26 – June 12, 14,
19 – 30, July 2 – 5, 7 – 18, 21 –
Aug. 16, 18 – Sept. 17, 19 –
Dec. 3, 5 – 24, 26 – 30.
1965 Jan. 2 – Mar. 20, 22 – Apr.
14, 16 – 23, 25 – 30, May 2 – 11,
13 – June 29, July 1 – 27, 29 –
Aug. 18, 20 – Sept. 1, 3, 5 – 15,
17 – 28, 30 – Oct. 3, 5 – 11, 13,
14, 26 – Nov. 2, 4 – 12, 14, 15,
Dec. 23, 24.
1966 Jan. 1+.
NjP
1942 Aug. 23.

EL 93. sw.
TxU
1893 Apr. 9.

LA NUEVA ERA. d. est. July 31, 1911.
CU
1911 Aug. 1 – Dec. 31.
1912 Jan. 1 – May 1, 8, 27, 31 – Oct.
7, 10.
1913 Jan. 1 – 12, 14 – 17, 19 – Feb. 9.

DLC
   1912   Extraordinario: Oct. 23.
   1913   Jan. 30, Feb. 9, 11.
LNT–MA
   1911   [Aug. 1–Dec. 31].
PU
   1911   Oct. 1–Dec. 31.
   1912   Jan. 1–Dec. 31.
TxU
   1911   July 31–Dec. 31.
   1912   Jan. 1–Dec. 31.
   1913   Jan. 1–Feb. 10.

LA NUEVA IBERIA. d.
TxU
   1887   Feb. 20.

NUEVA PATRIA. d. est. Sept. 26, 1914.
DLC
   1914   Sept. 26–Oct. 1, 3, 5–9, 11,
          17, 24, 27, 29, 31, Nov. 1.
          Extraordinario: Oct. 30.
TxU
   1914   Sept. 26–Oct. 28, 30–Nov. 1.

EL NUEVO DIA. w.
TxU
   1906   July 16.

NUEVO DIA; UN PERIODICO EN
BUSCA DE LA VERDAD. d. est.
1941.
DLC
   1941   Aug. 28.

NUEVO MUNDO. d. est. Feb. 2, 1918.
DLC
   1918   Feb. 2–Mar. 6.
TxU
   1918   Feb. 20.

NUEVO REGIMEN. w. est. Nov. 30, 1911.
TxU
   1911   Nov. 30.

NUEVO REGIMEN. 3w.
CU
   1934   Jan. 12–May 18, 23–June 30.
TxU
   1934   Jan. 24, 31–Feb. 9, 16, 21,
          Mar. 12, 16–26, 30–Apr. 23,

          28–30, May 16–26, June 1,
          6–25, 30.

EL OBRERO; ORGANO OFICIAL DE
LA SOCIEDAD MUTUA DEL RAMO
DE SOMBRERERIA.
CtY
   1872   Nov. 21.

EL OBRERO; ORGANO DEL "COMITE
LIBERAL CONSTITUCIONALISTA"
DEL 6° DISTRITO. est. 1917.
TxU
   1917   Nov. 30.

EL OBRERO LIBRE. w. est. [1913].
DLC
   1913   Extraordinario: Sept. 28.

EL OBRERO MEXICANO. w.
TxU
   1910   Jan. 28.

EL OBSERVADOR.
TxU
   1890   July 6.

EL OBSERVADOR DE LA REPUB-
LICA MEXICANA. w. est. June 6,
1827.
   Note: Ceased publication Oct.
   27, 1830.
CtY
   1827   June 6–Dec. 31.
   1828   Jan. 2.
   1830   Mar. 3–Oct. 27.
LNT–MA
   1827   Nov. 1–Dec. 31.
   1828   Jan. 9.

OMEGA. w., sw. est. Sept. 3, 1918.
   Note: Suspended publiction [June–
   July 15], 1919.
CU
   1919   July 18.
   1929   July 22.
   1936   Feb. 1, 13, 20–Dec. 26.
   1937   Jan. 1–Feb. 25, Mar. 6–25.
LNT–MA
   1918   Sept. 3, 17, 24, Oct. 1.
NN
   1921   Sept. 24.

TxU
  1919 Apr. 26, May 7, 21, 28, July
         22 – 25, Aug. 5 – 13, 20, 27 –
         Oct. 25, Nov. 15, 26, Dec. 3 –
         10, 17 – 31.
  1920 Jan. 1 – 28, Feb. 4 – 11.

EL OMNIBUS. 3w., d., sw. est. 1851.
  CU – B
  1851 Oct. 25 – Nov. 12, 19 – Dec. 31.
  1852 Jan. 3 – Dec. 4, 9 – 30.
  MoU
    Micro (P)
  1854 Oct. 4 – Dec. 22.
    Micro (P) & (N)
  1854 Dec. 23 – 30.
  1855 Jan. 1 – July 17, 19 – Sept. 3,
         5 – Dec. 3.
  1856 Jan. 2 – Nov. 5.
  NHi
  1853 May 21.
  1855 June 25.

LA OPINION; DIARIO POLITICO Y DE
  INFORMACION. d. est. 1911.
  TxU
  1911 Sept. 15, 19 – 23, 26 – Oct. 20.

LA OPINION. d. est. Dec. 6, 1914.
  DLC
  1914 Dec. 6 – 31.
         Extraordinario: Dec. 4, 5.
  1915 Jan. 1 – Feb. 6.
         Extraordinario: Jan. 27 – 29.
  TxU
  1914 Dec. 6 – 31.
         Extraordinario: Dec. 4, 5.
  1915 Jan. 1 – 9, 11, 12, 20, 27 – Feb.
         6.

LA OPINIÓN. sw. est. Feb. 24, 1918.
  TxU
  1918 June 23.

LA OPINION NACIONAL. d. est. Apr.
  1, 1868.
  Note: Ceased publication June 30,
  1870.
  TxU
  1868 Apr. 1 – Dec. 31.
  1869 Jan. 1 – Feb. 21, 23 – Mar. 1,

         3 – Dec. 31.
  1870 Jan. 1 – June 30.

LA OPOSICION. sw., 3w., d. est. July 2,
  1834.
  Note: Periodicity July 2 – Oct. 29,
  semiweekly; Nov. 1, 1834 – Mar. 24,
  1835, three times a week; after Mar.
  25, 1835, daily.
  CU – B
  1834 Sept. 10 – Nov. 11, 15 – 29,
         Dec. 6 – 9, 13.
  1835 Jan. 20, 24 – June 25.
  DLC
  1835 Jan. 13 – 23, 25 – Mar. 24, 29 –
         Apr. 5, 7 – May 15, 17 – June
         25.
         Suplemento: Jan. 13, 17, 20,
         31, Feb. 21, Mar. 18, 20, Apr.
         8, 25, May 7.
  MWA
  1834 Prospecto.
  NN
  1834 Aug. 13.

EL ORDEN. d. est. Aug. 1, 1852.
  Note: Ceased publication Mar. 29,
  1855.
  CU – B
    Micro (P) & (N)
  1852 Aug. 1 – Dec. 31.
  1853 – 1854 Jan. 1 – Dec. 31.
  1855 Jan. 1 – Mar. 29.
  DLC
  1854 July 1 – Dec. 31.

ORDEN. d.
  CLU
  1953 Nov. 1 – Dec. 31.
  1954 – 1955 Jan. 1 – Dec. 31.
  1956 Jan. – Aug.

EL ORIENTE; PERIODICO POLI-
  TICO Y LITERARIO. irr. est. Nov.
  24, 1841.
  DLC
  1841 Nov. 24 – Dec. 31.
  1842 Jan. 1 – 29, Feb. 19 – May 21,
         June 1 – Sept. 11, Oct. 22 –
         Nov. 5, 26.

MWA
    1841   Nov. 24 – Dec. 31.
    1842   Jan. 1 – 29.

ORIENTE. sw. est. 1916.
  DLC
    1917   Mar. 25.

LA ORQUESTA. sw. est. Mar. 1, 1861.
  Note: Suspended publication May
  28, 1863 – Dec. 3, 1864; July 17,
  1866 – June 26, 1867; July 3, 1875 –
  Mar. 1, 1877; ceased publication
  Sept. 29, 1877.
  CU – B
    1861   Prospecto.
           Mar. 20 – Dec. 31.
    1862   Jan. 1 – Dec. 31.
    1863   Jan. 1 – May 27.
    1864   Dec. 3 – 31.
    1865   Jan. 1 – Dec. 31.
    1866   Jan. 1 – Sept. 6.
    1867   June 26 – Dec. 31.
    1869 – 1873   Jan. 1 – Dec. 31.
    1874   Jan. 1 – Dec. 30.
  Micro (P) & (N)
    1861   Mar. 1 – Dec. 28.
    1862   Jan. 1 – Dec. 31.
    1863   Jan. 3 – May 27.
  CtY
    1861   May 8, Aug. 17.
    1862   Oct. 31, Nov. 12, Dec. 6 – 20.
    1863   Jan. 7, 14 – Feb. 11, 18 – 28,
           Mar. 11 – 14, 21 – 26, Apr. 1 –
           8, 15 – May 7, 16.
    1864   Dec. 3 – 31.
    1865   Jan. 4 – Dec. 30.
    1866   Jan. 3 – July 16.
    1867   June 26 – Dec. 28.
    1868   Jan. 2 – Oct. 10.
  TxU
    1861   Mar. 1 – Dec. 31.
    1862 – 1876   Jan. 1 – Dec. 31.
    1877   Jan. 1 – Sept. 29.

OTRO TIEMPO. 3w. est. Sept. 1, 1846.
  DLC
    1846   Sept. 1 – 10.

EL PABELLON ESPAÑOL. d.
  TxU
    1888   Oct. 14.

PABELLON NACIONAL. 3w. est. Oct.
  5, 1844.
  CU – B
    1844   Oct. 5 – Nov. 7, 12 – Dec. 5.
  DLC
    1844   Oct. 5 – 11, 13 – 29, 31 – Nov.
           28.

EL PABELLON NACIONAL. d.
  TxU
    1888   July 22.
    1889   Sept. 11.
    1890   Jan. 26.

EL PACTO FEDERAL. d. est. [1884].
  CU – B
    Micro (P)
    1885   June 12.

EL PADRE COBOS. bw., sw., w. est.
  Feb. 21, 1869.
  Note: Ceased publication 1880.
  CU – B
    Micro (P)
    1873   Jan. 5.
  CtY
    1871   Jan. 1 – Sept. 17.
    1873   July 20, 27, Aug. 7, 14 – 21,
           28 – Sept. 25, Oct. 2 – 29, 30 –
           Dec. 21, 28.
    1874   Jan. 1 – Feb. 12, Mar. 8 – 29,
           Apr. 9 – 23, 30, May 7.
  LNT – MA
    1871   [Jan. 9, Apr. 20 – Sept. 7].
    1873   [Jan. 1 – Dec. 31].
    1874   [Jan. 1 – June 30].
    1880   Jan. 1 – Mar. 6, 20 – 27, May 8,
           15, Oct. 23, 30.
  TxU
    1869   Feb. 21 – June 20.
    1871   Jan. 1 – Mar. 5.
    1873   July 31, Aug. 3, 10, Oct. 23,
           Nov. 16.
    1874   Jan. 1 – June 14, Aug. 23 – Dec.
           31.

1875   Jan. 1 – Dec. 26.
1876   Jan. 2 – July 9.

EL PADRE ETERNO. 3m. est. Jan. 10,
1908.
   Note: Succeeded by *El Padre*. Ceased
   publication Oct. 7, 1908.
   TxU
   1908   Jan. 10 – July 29, Aug. 26 –
          Sept. 9, 23 – Oct. 7.

EL PADRE PADILLA. w., sw. est. Oct.
21, 1908.
   Note: Succeeded *El Padre eterno*.
   DLC
   1916   May 7 – 14.
   TxU
   1908   Oct. 21 – Dec. 31.
   1909   Jan. 1 – Aug. 8.
   1916   May 22, June 6, 12, 19, Aug. 6.
   1917   Sept. 9.

LOS PADRES DEL AGUA FRIA. d.
   TxU
   1856   July 15 – Dec. 31.
   1857   Jan. 1 – 7.

EL PAIS. d. est. Jan. 1, 1899.
   Note: Ceased publication Aug. 1914.
   DLC
   1913   Jan. 27, 28, Feb. 5 – 7, 20, 22 –
          24, 28, Mar. 2 – 6, 8 – 11, 13 –
          15, 18 – 23, 25 – 29, 31 – Apr.
          15, June 10, 17, 19, 23, Aug.
          28, Sept. 15 – 17, 19, 20, 23,
          30 – Oct. 2, 4, 10, 11, 13, 17,
          24, 29, Nov. 2, 5.
          Extraordinario: Feb. 19.
   1914   Jan. 8, 27, Feb. 16, 17, Apr. 11,
          12, 16 – 18, 20 – May 6, 8, 9,
          11 – 16, 18, July 15, 16, 18,
          20 – 22, 27 – 30, Aug. 1 – 5, 7 –
          15, 17 – 23.
          Extraordinario: Apr. 21, 27,
          Aug. 1 – 5, 7, 8, 10 – 12, 14, 15,
          20.
   LNT – MA
   1901   May 30, July 1.
   1904   Aug. 16.
   1905   Sept. 18.

1906   June 11.
1911   July 12 – Dec. 31.
TxU
   1899 – 1901   Jan. 1 – Dec. 31.
   1902   Jan. 1 – Mar. 26, 31 – June 30.
   1903 – 1913   Jan. 1 – Dec. 31.

EL PAJARO VERDE. d. est. Jan. 5,
1861.
   Note: Suspended publication Feb.
   27 – Apr. 28, 1861; June 5, 1861 –
   July 16, 1863.
   CU – B
   1864   Nov. 9 – Dec. 3.
   1865   Jan. 4 – Dec. 30.
   1866   Jan. 1 – Dec. 31.
   1867   Jan. 2 – June 18.
   Micro (N)
   1861   Jan. 5 – Feb. 26, Apr. 29 –
          June 4.
   1863   July 17 – 31.
   1864   Jan. 1 – Dec. 3.
   1865   Jan. 4 – Mar. 26, 28 – Dec. 31.
   1866   Jan. 1 – June 30.
   CtY
   1863   July 17 – Oct. 30, Nov. 2 – Dec.
          31.
   1864   Jan. 1 – Feb. 3, 5 – July 5, 7 –
          30.
   1865   Jan. 4 – May 2, 4 – 30, June 1 –
          July 18, 20 – Dec. 30.
   1866   Jan. 1 – Mar. 28, 31 – Dec. 31.
   MWA
   1864   July 1 – Dec. 31.
   1865   Jan. 1 – Dec. 31.
   1866   Jan. 1 – June 30.
   TxU
   1861   Jan. 5 – Feb. 27, Apr. 30 – June
          4.
   1863   July 17 – Dec. 31.
   1864   Jan. 1 – Dec. 3.
   1865   Jan. 4 – Dec. 30.
   1866   Jan. 1 – Dec. 31.
   1875   July 6 – 13.

EL PALADIN. sw., d.
   CU – B
   Micro (P)
   1903   Feb. 19.

394

The Union List

1905   Aug. 6 – 10, Sept. 10.
DLC
1913   Extraordinario: Feb. 13, Nov.
        21.
1914   Extraordinario: Apr. 21, 29,
        May 1.
LNT – MA
1904   Nov. 10, 24.
1906   Jan. 18, Apr. 5.
TxU
1908   Aug. 6.
1909   Apr. 22.
1910   July 3, Sept. 4.
1911   June 1, 11, 25, Sept. 3, 21.
1912   May 5.
1913   May 26, Nov. 21, Dec. 28.

LA PALANCA. d., 3w. est. Sept. 1,
1848.
CU – B
Micro (P) & (N)
1848   Sept. 1 – Nov. 30.
1849   May 1 – Dec. 29.
1850   Jan. 1 – Nov. 16.
TxU
1904   Sept. 4 – Dec. 4, 18.
1905   Jan. 15.

LA PALANCA DEL OBRERO. w. est.
1905.
TxU
1905   Dec. 17.

EL PALO DE CIEGO. sw. est. Apr. 1,
1862.
Note: Ceased publication Mar. 14,
1863.
CU – B
1862   Apr. 1 – Dec. 31.
1863   Jan. 1 – Mar. 14.
MWA
1862   Apr. 1 – Oct. 7.
PU
1862   Apr. 1 – Dec. 31.
TxU
1862   Apr. 1 – Dec. 31.
1863   Jan. 1 – Mar. 14.

PALOS Y PEDRADAS. w. est. June 3,
1911.
TxU
1911   June 3.

PANORAMA MUNDIAL. w.
Note: Title *La Guerra europea*,
before Jan. 24, 1919; *Panorama
mundial*, after Jan. 24, 1919.
TxU
1915   Mar. 25 – Apr. 1, May 27 – June
        10, July 14, Aug. 30, Nov. 4,
        Dec. 16.
1916   Jan. 1 – Mar. 17, Apr. 14, June
        9, July 7, Aug. 18 – Sept. 1,
        15 – 29, Oct. 13 – Dec. 31.
1917   Jan. 1 – Apr. 27, May 11 –
        18, June 1 – July 27, Aug. 10,
        24 – Nov. 9, 23 – Dec. 31.
1918   Jan. 1 – Feb. 1, 15 – Nov. 8,
        22 – Dec. 31.
1919   Jan. 1 – Apr. 11, 25 – May 2,
        23.

PANTEON CARTEPERANO.
TxU
1885   Nov. 2.

PANTEON POLITICO Y COMERCIAL.
w.
KHi
1889   Nov. 1.

EL PAPAYO. w. est. July 17, 1904.
TxU
1904   July 17 – Sept. 11.

EL PARTIDO DEMOCRATICO. w. est.
1909.
LNT – MA
1909   Oct. 9, 24, 30.
TxU
1909   May 22, June 12 – Nov. 6.

EL PARTIDO LIBERAL; DIARIO DE
POLITICA, LITERATURA, CO-
MERCIO Y ANUNCIOS. d.
CU – B
Micro (P)
1886   June 1, Aug. 11, 13.

TxU
- 1886   July 22.
- 1887   May 19, Sept. 25, Nov. 13, 15.
- 1888   Mar. 25.
- 1889   Feb. 13, May 7, Sept. 11, Nov. 5.
- 1890   Feb. 26, 27, May 9, 19, Apr. 16, May 7, June 1, 29, Aug. 17, Nov. 9, 10, Dec. 3, 25.
- 1896   Feb. 4.

EL PARTIDO LIBERAL. w. est. Nov. 9, 1917.
DLC
- 1917   Nov. 9 – 23.
  Extraordinario: Dec. 1, 5.

PARTIDO POPULAR. w.
CSt
- 1947   Aug. 25, Sept. 8, 22, Oct. 13 – 27, Nov. 3 – 10, Dec. 15, 29.
- 1948   Jan. 19.

EL PARTIDO REPUBLICANO. d. est. Nov. 1, 1908.
TxU
- 1908   Nov. 1 – 9, 11, 14 – 25.

EL PARTIDO SOCIALISTA. w. est. Aug. 19, 1909.
TxU
- 1909   Aug. 19.

EL PASO DEL NORTE.
MB
- 1916   May 15, June 6.

LA PATA DE CABRA. d. est. Aug. 22, 1855.
Note: Ceased publication [Oct. 31], 1856.
CtY
- 1855   Aug. 22 – Nov. 19, Dec. 1 – 28, 31.
- 1856   Jan. 1 – Feb. 23, 26, 27, Apr. 1 – May 31, Sept. 16 – Oct. 31.
NN
- 1855   Oct. 26.

LA PATRIA. d.
CU – B
Micro (N)

1855   Aug. 17 – Dec. 31.
1856   Jan. 1 – July 26.

LA PATRIA. d. est. Sept. 20, 1866.
LNT – MA
- 1866   Sept. 20 – Dec. 31.
- 1867   Jan. 1 – 17.
TxU
- 1866   Sept. 20 – Dec. 31.
- 1867   Jan. 1 – Mar. 15.

PATRIA, PERIODICO LIBERAL E INDEPENDIENTE. w.
TxU
- 1908   Apr. 22, May 11.

LA PATRIA ILUSTRADA. w. est. 1883.
CtY
- 1889   Feb. 18, Aug. 12 – 19.
- 1894   Oct. 1.
- 1895   Aug. 19.
LNT – MA
- 1886   Jan. 1 – June 27, 29 – Aug. 31.
MWA
- 1884   Sept. 15.

LA PATRIA. d. est. Mar. 15, 1877.
Note: Title varies *La Patria de México*. Suspended publication Feb. 22 – Mar. 1, 3 – Apr. 30, 1911.
CU – B
Micro (P) & (N)
- 1882   June 18.
- 1883   Sept. 29, Oct. 6, 13, Nov. 25.
- 1886   June 2 – 12, 15, 17, 19 – July 7, 9 – 30.
- 1887   Apr. 15 – 17.
- 1891   Dec. 15.
- 1892   Jan. 19.
DLC
- 1878   Aug. 10, 19.
- 1913   Mar. 28.
  Extraordinario: Feb. 19, 20, Mar. 25, 26.
- 1914   Extraordinario: May 4, July 22, Aug. 25.
LNT – MA
- 1904   Sept. 18.
MWA
- 1878   Jan. 19.

1881   July 27, 31 – Aug. 6, 10, 12, 13,
        17, 19, 23, 24.
1883   Jan. 27, Aug. 9, Nov. 1 – 21.
1884   Nov. 26.
TxU
1877   May 13.
1878   Apr. 7.
1879   July 9, Dec. 4.
1880   Mar. 25 – May 9, 12 – Dec. 31.
1881   Jan. 1 – Dec. 27, 29 – 31.
1882   Jan. 1 – 17, Aug. 12.
1906   Apr. 12.
1909   July 29, Sept. 2.
1910   Apr. 2, 8, 28, June 28, 30 – July
        15, 18 – Aug. 6, 13, 16 – 26,
        29 – Sept. 10, 13, 17, 19, 21 –
        23, 28 – 30, Oct. 3, 4, 6, 10,
        11, 15 – 17, 21, 24 – Dec. 2, 4 –
        10, 12 – 23, 26 – 31.
1911   Jan. 1 – 5, 9 – 13, 16 – 18, 20 –
        Aug. 12, 17, Oct. 14, 17, 26.
1912   June 23, Sept. 12, 13.
1913   Feb. 20, Mar. 25.

LA PATRIA; DIARIO DE LA MAÑANA.
d.
TxU
1908   May 5.

EL PATRIOTA MEXICANA. sw. est.
Aug. 5, 1845.
DLC
1845   Aug. 5 – Sept. 11, 13 – Dec. 26.

LA PAZ. d. est. Jan. 1, 1858.
CU – B
1858   Jan. 1 – 14.

LA PAZ. d. est. Jan. 3, 1871.
CU – B
1871   Jan. 3 – Feb. 28, Apr. 7 – 21,
        24 – May 22, 24 – June 19, 21 –
        July 28.

LA PAZ. w.
TxU
1880   Mar. 2 – 9, Apr. 6 – July 13.

LA PAZ, PERIODICO DE ACTUA-
LIDAD.

TxU
1907   July 18.

EL PENDON REYISTA. w. est. July
19, 1909.
TxU
1909   July 19.

EL PENSADOR MEXICANO. w. est.
1812.
    Note: Ceased publication 1814.
CtY
    1812 – 1814   [Jan. 1 – Dec. 31].

EL PENSAMIENTO. d. est. Mar. 24,
1856.
CU – B
1856   Mar. 24 – May 15.

PENSAMIENTO EXTRAORDINARIO.
est. 1812.
CtY
1812   Nos. 1 – 5.

EL PENSAMIENTO NACIONAL. d.
est Nov. 13, 1855.
CU – B
1855   Nov. 13 – Dec. 31.
1856   Jan. 1 – 30, Feb. 3 – Mar. 21.

EL PERICO. w. est. Dec. 3, 1911.
TxU
1911   Dec. 3.

PERIODICO LIBRO.
CSt
1943   Oct. 28.

PERIODICO OFICIAL; ORGANO DE
LAS SOCIEDADES DE TRABAJA-
DORES DE LA REPUBLICA.
TxU
1880   Jan. 17, May 12 – 24, June 4,
        12 – July 8.

PERIODICO OFICIAL DEL IMPERIO
MEXICANO. 3w. est. July 21, 1863.
Note: French edition published
under title *Gazette officielle de l'Empire Mexicain*. Succeeded by *Diario
del imperio*. Ceased publication
Dec. 31, 1864.

CtY
1863 July 21 – Dec. 31.
1864 Jan. 2 – Dec. 31.
MBAt
1863 July 21 – Dec. 31.
1864 Jan. 1 – Dec. 31.
NHi
1864 Jan. 2, Oct. 1.

PERIODICO OFICIAL DEL SUPREMO GOBIERNO DE LOS ESTADOS-UNIDOS MEXICANOS. 3w. est. Feb. 28, 1849.
Note: Succeeded *El Correo nacional*; succeeded by *El Constitucional*. Ceased publication Sept. 15, 1851.
CU – B
Micro (P)
1849 Feb. 28 – Dec. 31.
1850 Jan. 1 – Dec. 31.
1851 Jan. 1 – Sept. 15.
CtY
1849 Feb. 28 – Dec. 29.
1850 Jan. 4 – Oct. 30.

PETIT JOURNAL POUR RIRE.
Note: In French.
TxU
1880 Sept. 23.

PICA-PICA. w. est. Sept. 4, 1913.
TxU
1913 Sept. 4.

LA PICOTA. w. est. Nov. 26, 1880.
TxU
1880 Nov. 26 – Dec. 3.

EL PILOTO DEL COMERCIO, INDUSTRIA Y ARTES. sw. est. Feb. 16, 1825.
CU – B
Micro (N)
1825 Feb. 16 – 19.

EL PINCHE. w. est. 1904.
TxU
1904 Apr. 28 – May 12, June 2 – July 21, Aug. 4, Dec. 1 – 18.
1906 Jan. 18 – Feb. 8.

EL PITO. w.
TxU
1917 Sept. 10.

EL PITO DE NOCHE BUENA.
TxU
1890 Dec. 25.

LA POLITICA. d. est. 1888.
CtY
1888 July 7.
LNT – MA
1888 June 15.

POLITICA DE LOS ESTADOS. w. est. 1906.
TxU
1906 Nov. 11.

LA POLITICA MEXICANA. w.
TxU
1913 June 9, July 27.

EL POPULAR. d., w. est. Jan. 1, 1897.
LNT – MA
1907 Sept. 17.
TxU
1897 Jan. 1 – Apr. 16, 21 – Sept. 17, 19 – Dec. 13, 15 – 25, 27 – 31.
1898 Jan. 1, 2, 4 – Apr. 8, 11 – May 9, 11 – Sept. 17, 19 – Dec. 13, 16 – 26, 28 – 31.
1899 Jan. 1, 2, 4 – Mar. 31, Apr. 3 – June 8, 10 – Sept. 7, 10 – 17, 20 – Dec. 13, 15 – 25, 27 – 31.
1900 Jan. 1, 3 – Apr. 12, 16 – Aug. 5, 7, 9 – Dec. 31.
1901 Jan. 1 – Apr. 5, 8 – July 20, 22 – Dec. 25, 27 – 31.
1902 Jan. 1 – Dec. 31.
1903 Jan. 1 – June 30, Oct. 21.
1908 Jan. 11, June 24.

EL POPULAR. w. est. Mar. 23, 1919.
DLC
1919 Mar. 23, Apr. 6 – July 6, 21 – Sept. 15, Oct. 15.
Extraordinario: June 3, 11, 17, 18, July 2, 24, Aug. 20.

TxU
  1919   Aug. 20, 22, June 15, July 3,
          Dec. 10.
EL POPULAR. d. est. June 1, 1938.
  CSt
  1938   June 2, 3, July 3.
  1942   July 5, 15.
  1943   Oct. 23, Nov. 14.
  1948   Sept. 2.
  CU
  1938   June 1 – Dec. 31.
  1939 – 1944   Jan. 1 – Dec. 31.
  1945   Jan. 1 – Mar. 3, 5 – Dec. 31.
  1946   Jan. 1 – May 15, 17 – Dec. 31.
  1947   Jan. 1 – Nov. 29, Dec. 1 – 31.
  1948   Jan. 1 – Dec. 31.
  1949   Jan. 1 – 21, 24 – Feb. 19, 21 –
          Mar. 10, 13 – 30, Apr. 1 – 11,
          13 – May 23, 25, 27 – June 2, 4,
          6 – 8, 10, 11, 13, 15 – 19, 21 –
          July 3, 5 – 12, 14, 16 – 20, 22 –
          23, 27, 28.

  DLC
  1941 – 1942   Jan. 1 – Dec. 31.
  1943   Jan. 1 – June 30, July 10, 13.
  1944   Jan. 1, 2, 4, 6, 11 – 14, 16 –
          19, 23, 24, 26, 28, 31 – Apr. 7,
          9, 21, 25 – May 24, 26, 28, 29,
          31 – July 11, 13 – 26, 28, 29,
          31 – Sept. 3, 5, 6, 8, 10, 12 –
          19, 22 – 24, 27, 29, 30, Oct. 6 –
          Nov. 4, 6 – 19, 21 – 27, 29 –
          Dec. 21, 23 – 29, 31.
  1945   Jan. 1 – 21, 23, 24, 26 – 28, Feb.
          3, 5, 7 – Mar. 17, 19 – 26, 28 –
          Apr. 8, 10 – May 11, 13, June
          2, 4, 6 – 21, 23, 24, 26, 28, July
          1 – 3, 5 – 16, 29, 30, Aug. 15,
          16, 18 – 23, 26 – 29, 31 – Sept.
          2, 4 – 7, 9 – Oct. 15, 20 – 26,
          29, 30, Nov. 1, 2, 5 – 7, 10 –
          16, 29 – Dec. 2, 4 – 10, 12 – 28,
          31.
  1946   Jan. 1 – 4, 6 – 12, 14 – 25, 27 –
          Feb. 5, 7, 15 – Mar. 1, 3 – 17,
          21 – 24, 26 – Apr. 16, 18 – Dec.
          31.
  1947 – 1948   Jan. 1 – Dec. 31.

  1949   Jan. 1 – Sept. 11, 13 – Dec. 3,
          5 – 8, 10, 11, 13, 16, 17, 19, 21,
          24 – 27, 29 – 31.
  1950   Jan. 1 – 29, 31 – June 10, 12 –
          Aug. 2, 4 – Oct. 15, 17 – Dec.
          31.
  1951   Jan. 1 – Feb. 18, 20 – Mar. 5,
          7 – May 15, 17 – June 11, 15, 16,
          21 – 29, July 1 – 27, 31 – Sept.
          12, 14, 15, 17 – Oct. 27, 29 –
          Nov. 9, 11 – Dec. 14, 16 – 31.
  1952   Jan. 1 – 16, 18 – 27, 29, 31 –
          Feb. 5, 7 – 10, 12 – Mar. 9, 11 –
          Apr. 24, 26 – May 8, 10 – June
          7, 9 – July 2, 4 – 19, 21 – Aug.
          6, 8 – Sept. 17, 19 – Nov. 30,
          Dec. 2 – 14, 16 – 31.
  1953   Jan. 1 – Feb. 20, 22 – 26, Mar.
          3 – Apr. 3, 5 – 9, 11, 12, 15, 16,
          21 – June 1, 3 – Sept. 1, 5 – 17,
          19 – Dec. 31.
  1954   Jan. 1 – 12, 16, 18 – 24, 26 –
          Mar. 7, 9 – 26, 29 – May 21,
          23 – 28, 30 – July 8, 10 – 16,
          18 – Aug. 23, 25 – 27, 29 – 31,
          Sept. 4 – 6, 9 – 13, 15, 17 – 20,
          22 – Oct. 3, 5 – 21, 23 – 25, 27 –
          Nov. 12, 15 – 29, Dec. 1 – 22,
          28 – 30.
  1955   Jan. 2, 4 – Feb. 12, 17, 18, 22 –
          Nov. 21, 23 – Dec. 19, 21 – 31.
  1956   Jan. 1 – July 21, 23 – Aug. 13,
          15 – Nov. 1, 3 – Dec. 31.
  1957   Jan. 1 – Feb. 7, 9 – 11, 13, 14,
          16, 18, 23 – July 11, 15 – Dec.
          31.
  1958   Jan. 1 – May 29, 31 – June 30,
          July 13, 15 – 18, 22 – 24, 26 –
          Aug. 8, 10 – Sept. 15, 17 – Oct.
          15, 17 – Nov. 14, 21 – 26, 28 –
          Dec. 28, 30, 31.
  1960   July 1 – 10, 12 – Nov. 24, 26 –
          Dec. 5, 7 – 31.
  1961   Jan. 2 – 18, 20 – Feb. 9, 13 –
          21, 23 – Apr. 15, 17 – May 15,
          17 – July 7, 9 – 11, 13 – Aug. 7,
          9 – 29, 31.

LNT−MA
  1943   May 25−31, June 1, 3.
NN
  Micro (P) & (N)
  1938 [Sept. 1−Dec. 31].
  1939−1948 [Jan. 1−Dec. 31].
NjP
  1941   July 19, 23, 28.
TxU
  1940   Jan. 1−4, 6−Dec. 31.
  1941−1942 Jan. 1−Dec. 31.
  1943   Jan. 1−9, 11−Feb. 8, 10−
          Mar. 23, 25, May 1, 3−June
          30, July 2−Aug. 26, 28−
          Sept. 16, 18−Oct. 3, 5−29,
          31−Nov. 20, 22−Dec. 25,
          27−31.
  1944   Jan. 1−Dec. 31.
  1945   Jan. 21−Apr. 30, May 3−
          June 8, 10−Sept. 16, 18−
          Nov. 20, 22−Dec. 25, 27−
          31.
  1946−1955 Jan. 1−Dec. 31.
  1956   Jan. 1−June 30.
  1958   Apr. 10−13, 15, 16, 18,
          May 18−22, June 14, 21−
          Dec. 15, 17−24, 26−31.
  1959−1960 Jan. 1−Dec. 31.
  1961   Jan. 1−Nov. 30.
ViU
  1950   July 16, Aug. 6.
  1952   Feb. 12−18, 20, 21, 23−25,
          27−Mar. 11, 13−15, 19, 20,
          22−29, 31−Apr. 6, 12, 13,
          17−24, 26−May 1, 3−18,
          20, 22, 24−29, June 1−5,
          7, 9−19, 22, 24, 26−July 2,
          6, 8, 10−15, 17−25, 28−30,
          Aug. 1, 3, 7−9, 13−17, 20−
          25, 27, 29, 31−Sept. 1, 3−
          22, 24−Oct. 5, 7−10, 12−
          17, 19−Nov. 2, 4−9, 11−14,
          17−19, 21−24, 26−Dec. 4,
          6−9, 11, 12, 14, 16, 18−21,
          23, 24, 27−31.
  1953   Jan. 1−6, 8, 11−19, 21−
          23, 26−Feb. 2, 4−8, 11−16,
          18−20, 22−Mar. 1, 4−20,

          22−26, 28−May 3, 5−26,
          28−31, June 2−11, 13−21,
          24−July 10, 12−Aug. 3, 5−
          10, 12−Sept. 2, 4, 12−15,
          17−Oct. 6, 8−18, 20, 21, 23,
          25, 26, 28−Nov. 14, 16−19,
          21−Dec. 7, 9, 10, 12−24, 26,
          29, 31.
  1954   Jan. 4−6, 8−22, 24−29,
          31−Feb. 12, 14−22, 24−27,
          Mar. 1−6, 9, 10, 12−20, 22−
          Apr. 3, 5−17, 19−May 16,
          18−29, 31−June 5, 7−11,
          13−19, 24, 26−28, 30−July
          9, 16, 18, 21, 24−29, 31−
          Aug. 3, 5−7, 9−11, 15−21,
          28, 29, 31−Sept. 4, 6−11,
          13, 14, 18−24, 26, 28−Oct.
          5, 9−12, 15, 18−20, 23−26,
          28−Nov. 1, 3, 4, 6, 8, 9, 11−
          19, 21−Dec. 2, 5, 6, 8, 10−
          21, 23, 24, 26, 28−31.
  1955   Jan. 1−Feb. 13, 15−19,
          22−Mar. 8, 10−20, 22, 23,
          26−Apr. 30, May 2−July 5,
          7−11, 22, 24, 25, 27−Aug. 3,
          6−8, 14, 16, 17, 19, 22, 23,
          26, 28, 30, Sept. 3, 5−11,
          13−15, 17−22, 25, 28, 30−
          Oct. 1, 4−9, 13, 15, 17, 19−
          22, 25−Nov. 1, 3−7, 9, 10,
          13−16, 19, 22, 24, 25, 27,
          Dec. 1−8, 11−13, 16, 21−
          24, 26−31.
  1956   Jan. 3−6, 12, 13, 16.

LA PORRA. w. est. Apr. 7, 1912.
  TxU
    1912   Apr. 7−May 2.

EL PORVENIR. irr., w., sw. est. Aug.
  8, 1846.
  CU−B
    Micro (N)
    1846   Aug. 8−Oct. 31, Nov. 14−
            Dec. 19.
  DLC
    1846   Aug. 8−Sept. 29, Oct. 1−
            Dec. 19.

EL PORVENIR; PERIODICO POLI-
TICO, CIENTIFICO Y LITERARIO.
TxU
    1874   Oct. 9.
    1875   June 30.

EL PORVENIR; DIARIO DEMO-
CRATICO. d. est. Aug. 25, 1911.
DLC
    1911   Aug. 26, 29, Sept. 9—15,
            18—27, 30.
LNT—MA
    1911   Sept. 13—15.
TxU
    1911   Aug. 30, Sept. 1, 13, 15, 18,
            22, 23, 27—30.

EL PORVENIR; SEMANARIO CATO-
LICO. w.
TxU
    1921   Mar. 6.

PORVENIR DE MEXICO. bw.
MWA
    1890   Aug. 19.

EL PRECURSOR; PERIODICO POLI-
TICO LITERARIO. sw. est. 1840.
DLC
    1841   Jan. 5—Aug. 31.
MWA
    1841   June 22, July 16, Aug. 3, 24.
TxU
    1840   Suplemento: Jan. 7.

EL PRECURSOR. w., bw. est. Oct. 7,
1874.
    Note: Periodicity Oct. 7, 1874—Aug.
    7, 1875, weekly; after Aug. 15, 1875,
    biweekly.
TxU
    1874   Oct. 7—Dec. 31.
    1875   Jan. 1—Dec. 22.

LA PRENSA. d. est. Feb. 15, 1861.
  CU—B
    Micro (N)
    1861   Feb. 15—June 1.

LA PRENSA; DIARIO POLITICO,
LITERARIA, CIENTIFICO Y
COMERCIAL. d.

CU—B
  Micro (P)
    1884   May 28, Dec. 1, 16.
    1885   May 2, 26.
            Suplemento: Apr. 4.
MWA
    1884   Sept. 15, [Dec. 25—31].
    1885   [Jan. 1—Mar. 11].
TxU
    1884   Dec. 1.

LA PRENSA. d. est. Dec. 12, 1911.
KHi
    1912   Feb. 17.
LNHT
    1911   Dec. 12—31.
    1912   Jan. 1—Feb. 21.
TxU
    1912   Jan. 14, 24, 27, 28, Feb. 1—3,
            5, 7—11, 13—29, Mar. 2—6,
            8, 10—13, 15—25, 27—Apr.
            6, 8—10, 12—May 8, 10—24,
            26—June 2, 4—23.

LA PRENSA. d. est. Feb. 7, 1915.
    Note: Ceased publication [Mar.
    9], 1915.
CtY
    1915   Feb. 16.
DLC
    1915   Feb. 7—24, 26—28, Mar. 1—
            7, 9.
TxU
    1915   Feb. 7—Mar. 9.

LA PRENSA; DIARIO ILUSTRADA DE
LA MAÑANA. d. est. Aug. 30, 1928.
CU
    1929   July 9, 11, 15—25, 27, 28.
    1936—1940   Jan. 1—Dec. 31.
    1941   Jan. 1—Apr. 13, 15—18, 21,
            23—June 15, 17—Aug. 10, 12—
            Dec. 31.
    1942   Jan. 1—Apr. 11.
DLC
    1941   July 29—Sept. 16, 18—Nov.
            13, 15, 16, 18—Dec. 31.
    1942   Jan. 1—Feb. 9.

LNT—MA
  1934   Sept. 12.
NjP
  1941   July 23, 30.

LA PRENSA ASOCIADA. est. May 1885.
  CU—B
  1885   May.

PRENSA LATINA. d.
  CSt—H
  1963   Oct. 10, 12, 15—17, 21—26,
           28—Nov. 1, 4—9, 11—16, 18,
           19, 21—23, 25—30, Dec. 2—7,
           4—14, 16—21, 23, 24, 26—28,
           30.
  1964   Jan. 1—4, 6—11, 13—Feb. 8,
           10—Mar. 26, 29—Apr. 11, 13—
           May 4, 6—9, 11—16, 18—23,
           26—30, June 1—6, 8, 9, 11—13,
           16—18, 20, 22, 24—27, 29—
           July 3, 7—11, 13—18, 20—25,
           27—Aug. 1, 3—8, 10—15, 17—
           22, 24, 25, 27—29, 31, Sept. 2—
           5, 7—12, 14, 17—19, 21—Oct.
           3, 5, 7, 9, 10, 13—31, Nov. 3—6,
           9—11, 24—27, 30, Dec. 2, 5—
           11, 14—23, 26—30.
  1965   Jan. 2—7, 9—16, 21, 23—Mar.
           30, Apr. 1—30, May 3—24,
           26—July 2, 6—Aug. 6, 10—23,
           25—Sept. 7, 9, 10, 13—Oct.
           12, 15—18, 20—Nov. 26, 30—
           Dec. 13, 15—31.
  1966   Jan. 1+.

¡PRENSA LIBRE! sw.
  TxU
  1911   Oct. 11.

EL PRESENTE; DIARIO DE LA
  MAÑANA. d.
  TxU
  1913   Mar. 19, 22.

EL PRESENTE; BISEMANARIO
  LIBRE. sw. est. June 9, 1918.
  TxU
  1918   June 9.

EL PROGRESISTA. d. est. Nov. 1,
  1864.

CU—B
  Micro (N)
  1864   Nov. 1—5.

EL PROGRESO. w.
  TxU
  1891   Sept. 7.

EL PROLETARIO. bw.
  CU—B
  Micro (P)
  1889   Dec. 15.

LA PROPIEDAD. w.
  CSt
  1946   June 1—Dec. 31.
  1947   Jan. 4—11.

LA PROTESTA. w. est. 1902.
  TxU
  1902   Dec. 14.

¡¡PSST...!! w. est. May 23, 1908.
  TxU
  1908   May 23, June 21.

EL PUEBLO. d. est. 1905.
  TxU
  1905   Aug. 24, 25, 29, Oct. 27.
  1906   Jan. 26.

EL PUEBLO. w. est. 1908.
  TxU
  1909   Jan. 31, Feb. 21.

EL PUEBLO. d. est. Oct. 1, 1914.
  Note: Removed to Vera Cruz Dec.
  1914; returned to Mexico City Oct.
  29, 1915.
  DLC
  1914   Oct. 1—3, 5, 22, 23, Nov. 1—
           7, 9—15.
           Extraordinario: Oct. 3, 30, Nov.
           14.
           Suplemento: Nov. 1, 8, 15.
  1915   Oct. 29—Dec. 31.
           Suplemento: Nov. 8, 22, 28,
           Dec. 13, 20.
  1916   Jan. 1—27, 29—Dec. 31.
           Extraordinario: May 31, Aug.
           10, Nov. 7, 8, Dec. 31.

Suplemento: Mar. 27, Apr. 3, 17.

1917   Jan. 1 – Dec. 31.
        Extraordinario: Feb. 3.
1918   Jan. 1 – June 28, 30 – July 5, 7 – Sept. 1, 3 – 21, 23 – Oct. 1, 3 – 7, 10 – Nov. 11, 13 – Dec. 10, 12 – 31.
1919   Jan. 1 – Feb. 12, 14 – May 15.
LNT – MA
1918   Jan. 28.
MB
1916   May 12, 14 – 21, 28, 29, June 17, 21, 22, 24, 27 – July 1, 4, 6, 7, 9, 10, 12, 13, 15, 18 – 22, 25, 30, Aug. 3 – 15, 17, 21, 23, 29 – Sept. 6, 8, 9, 12, 15, 17 – 23, 26, 28, 30 – Oct. 7, 13 – 17, 20 – 30, Nov. 1 – 3, 7, 15 – 18, 21, 22, 25, 28, Dec. 15, 16, 19, 21 – 23, 27 – 31.
1917   Jan. 1, 3, 5, 6, 8 – 17, 21 – 24, 27 – 30, Feb. 1, 2, 5 – 9, 12 – 16, 19, 21 – 23, 27, 28, Mar. 4, 6 – 10, 13, 15, 17 – 23, 27, 28, 30 – Apr. 1, 3, 5, 7, 25, 28, 29, May 1, 2, 4, 6 – 15, 17 – 24, 26 – 29, 31, June 1.
TxU
1914   Oct. 3 – Nov. 15.
1915   Jan. 6, 9, 11 – 17, 19 – 22, 25 – 28, Oct. 29, Nov. 1 – Dec. 31.
1916   Jan. 1 – Dec. 31.
1917   Jan. 1 – May 2, 4, 6 – Sept. 23, Oct. 1 – 30, Nov. 1 – Dec. 31.
1918   Jan. 1 – May 18, 21 – June 30, July 6 – Dec. 31.
1919   Jan. 1 – May 15.

¡PUEBLO LIBRE! d. est. 1909.
TxU
1909   Aug. 13, 14, 17 – 20.

EL PUEBLO SOBERANO.
CU – B
Micro (P)
1892   Jan. 11.

LA PULGA. sw. est. Nov. 1, 1861.
NN
1861   Nov. 1, 5.

PULGARCITO.
TxU
1916   Apr. 22.

¡PUM! w. est. Feb. 23, 1908.
TxU
1908   Feb. 23.

¡PUM! PERIODICO DECIDOR PARA EL PUEBLO.
Note: Ceased publication June 29, 1913.
TxU
1913   June 29.

EL PURITANO. 3w. est. Mar. 24, 1846.
DLC
1846   Mar. 24 – May 28.
        Suplemento: Apr. 14.
NN
1846   Mar. 24.

EL RADICAL. sw. est. 1911.
TxU
1911   July 8 – 16.

EL RADICAL; DIARIO POLITICO DE LA TARDE. d. est. July 20, 1914.
Note: Suspended publication Aug. 8 – 18; Oct. 9 – Dec. 9, 1914; Jan. 22, 23, 27 – Mar. 21; Apr. 1 – 12; May 4 – 6, 1915.
DLC
1914   July 29 – Aug. 22, 25, 27 – Sept. 4, 7 – 10, 12 – 21, 23 – 28, 30 – Oct. 3, Dec. 10, 15 – 31.
1915   Jan. 1 – 13, 15 – 26, Mar. 22, 26, May 1, 7 – 12, 14 – 20, 22 – June 3, 7.
LNT – MA
1914   Sept. 5, 11, 29.
1915   Jan. 14.
TxU
1914   July 20 – Dec. 31.
1915   Jan. 1 – Mar. 23, 25, 27 –

Apr. 17, 20, 21, 24 – 26,
28 – May 3, 7, 10 – 20, 24,
June 1 – 7.

EL RADICAL. sw. est. Feb. 20, 1917.
DLC
1917   Feb. 20, Mar. 9, 25, Apr. 29.
Extraordinario: Mar. 18.

EL RADICAL; PERIODICO POLI-
TICAL. w. est. Sept. 8, 1920.
NN
1920   Sept. 15.

THE RAILROADER AND BULLETIN
OF PUBLIC IMPROVEMENTS.
See *La República*.

LA RAZON. d. est. Dec. 23, 1857.
CU – B
1857   Dec. 23 – 31.
1858   Jan. 1 – 13.

LA RAZON; ORGANO DE ESTUDI-
ANTES. w. est. 1911.
TxU
1911   Sept. 14.

LA RAZON CATOLICA. bw. est. Apr.
22, 1870.
TxU
1870   Apr. 22 – Dec. 30.

LA RAZON DE LA SIN RAZON. bw.
TxU
1880   Nov. 1.

LA RAZON DE MEXICO. d. est. Oct. 16,
1864.
Note: Ceased publication Feb. 17,
1865.
CU – B
Micro (N)
1864   Oct. 16 – Dec. 31.
1865   Jan. 1 – Feb. 17.

LA RAZON DEL PUEBLO. w. est. 1905.
TxU
1905   Aug. 30.

EL RAZONADOR. sw. est. May 14, 1847.
CU – B
1847   May 14 – Dec. 31.
1848   Jan. 1 – Mar. 8.

NN
1847   Sept. 9, Oct. 13, 16 – Dec. 1,
15, 18 – 29.
1848   Jan. 5 – Feb. 26, Mar. 4.

EL REBELDE. w.
CU
1910   June 2 – 20.
1911   June 26, July 19 – 27.
TxU
1910   June 9.
1911   June 26.

RECONSTRUCCION. w. est. Mar. 18,
1915.
DLC
1915   Mar. 18, May 15, 22, June 12.
TxU
1915   Prospecto: Mar. 13.
May 29.

EL REDACTOR MEXICANO. irr est.
1814.
Note: Ceased publication June 16,
1815.
CtY
1814   Jan. 1 – Dec. 31.
1815   Jan. 1 – June 16.

REDACTOR MUNICIPAL. sw., 3w. est.
Nov. 3, 1823.
Note: Succeeded *Noticioso general*.
Ceased publication Dec. 29, 1824.
CtY
1823   Nov. 3 – Dec. 31.
NN
1824   Mar. 31.
TxU
1824   Jan. 2 – Dec. 29.

EL REDACTOR MUNICIPAL. irr. est.
Mar. 4, 1842.
Note: Ceased publication Mar. 20,
1842.
CU – B
Micro (N)
1842   Mar. 4 – 20.
CtY
1842   Mar. 4 – 20.

REDENCION. bw. est. Sept. 15, 1908.
TxU
   1908   Sept. 15.

REDENCION. w., d. est. 1909.
DLC
   1917   June 1 – 16, 21 – Dec. 31.
          Alcance: June 24.
          Extraordinario: June 13, July
          27, Sept. 25, Dec. 14, 19.
   1918   Jan. 1 – May 31.
   1919   Nov. 23.
          Extraordinario: Nov. 30.
LNT – MA
   1917   Dec. 18.
   1918   Jan. 1 – 31, Aug. 23.
TxU
   1909   June 13, Sept. 5, 19.
   1911   Nov. 26.
   1917   June 8, 9, 13, 18, 22, July 6, 9,
          12, 16 – 20, 23 – Aug. 15, 17,
          18, 21, 22, 24, 27 – Sept. 4, 6 –
          11, 13 – 18, 20, 22, 26 – 28, Oct.
          1 – 5, 8, 9, 11, 20 – 22, 24 – Nov.
          5, 8 – 13, 15, 20, 22, Dec. 1, 8 –
          10, 12, 22, 26, 31.
   1918   Jan. 11, Feb. 2, 8, 23, Mar. 1 –
          6, 25, Apr. 3, 13, 21, 22, 23, 25,
          28, May 3 – 5, 8.

EL REDENTOR. irr. est. Feb. 10, 1913.
DLC
   1913   Feb. 10 – 19.
          Extraordinario: Feb. 18.
TxU
   1913   Feb. 19.

EL REDONDEL.
CU
   1929   July 14.

LA REFORMA; PERIODICO CIENTI-
FICO, POLITICO, SEMINARIO. sw.
est. Nov. 23, 1839.
DLC
   1839   Prospecto.
          Nov. 23 – Dec. 20.
   1840   Jan. 12 – 22.
          Suplemento: Jan. 22.

LA REFORMA; DIARIO POLITICO. d.
est. Jan. 18, 1846.
   Note: Ceased publication Apr. 22,
   1846.
CU – B
   Micro (N)
   1846   Jan. 18 – Apr. 22.
DLC
   1846   Feb. 21, Mar. 3 – 11, 13, 16.

REFORMA SOCIAL. sw. est. Aug. 2,
1914.
DLC
   1914   Aug. 13, 20, 30.
TxU
   1914   Aug. 2 – Sept. 10.

EL REFORMADOR. sw. est. Jan. 1913.
DLC
   1913   Feb. 14, 17, 18.
TxU
   1913   Feb. 12, 15.

EL REFORMADOR. bw. est. Aug. 1,
1935.
CU
   1935   Aug. 1 – Feb. 15.

REGENERACION. d. est. Aug. 20,
1914.
   Note: Suspended publication Sept.
   1 – 4, 1914.
DLC
   1914   Aug. 24, Sept. 11.
TxU
   1914   Aug. 20, 21, 24, 26 – Sept. 5.

EL REGENERADOR. d. est. July 12, 1859.
   Note: Ceased publication July 20,
   1859.
CU – B
   Micro (N)
   1859   July 12 – 20.

REGISTRO OFICIAL DEL GOBIERNO
DE LOS ESTADOS UNIDOS MEXI-
CANOS. d. est. Jan. 22, 1830.
   Note: Succeeded by *El Telégrafo*.
   Ceased publication Jan. 10, 1833.
CU – B
   Micro (P)

1830   Jan. 22 – Dec. 31.
1831 – 1832   Jan. 1 – Dec. 31.
1833   Jan. 1 – 10.
CtY
1830   Jan. 22 – Dec. 31.
1831   May 1 – Aug. 18.
1832   Apr. 17, May 9 – June 30,
        July 7.
DLC
1830   [Jan. 22 – Dec. 31].
1831 – 1832   [Jan. 1 – Dec. 31].
1833   Jan. 1 – 10.
NN
1830   Suplemento.

LA REIVINDICACION. w. est. June 7,
1911.
TxU
1911   June 7.

REIVINDICACION. bw. est. Apr. 15,
1944.
LNT – MA
1944   Prospecto: Apr. 1.
        Apr. 15 – May 31, June 1,
        July 1 – Aug. 1.

EL RENACIMIENTO. w.
IU
1864   Jan. 1 – June 24.

EL RENACIMIENTO. w. est. Jan. 2,
1869.
IU
1869   Jan. 2 – Dec. 25.

EL RENOVADOR; PERIODICO CON-
STITUCIONALISTA. sw. est. Jan.
10, 1914.
DLC
1914   Mar. 15, Apr. 2, 22.
TxU
1914   Aug. 7 – 13.

EL RENOVADOR. d. est. June 16,
1915.
Note: Published in Cuernavaca July
10 – 21, 1915.
DLC
1915   June 16 – July 9, 22 – 31.
TxU
1915   June 16 – July 9, 22 – 31.

REPERTORIO MEXICANO. 3w. est.
June 2, 1827.
Note: Ceased publication Mar. 25,
1828.
CtY
1827   June 2 – 12, 16 – July 17, 21 –
        Dec. 29.
        Suplemento: June 2, 28, July
        28.
DLC
1827   June 2 – 12, 14 – July 3, Sept.
        1 – 4, 6 – Oct. 5, 7 – 30, Nov. 1,
        9 – 13, 15 – 23, 30 – Dec. 31.
1828   Jan. 1.
TxU
1827   Prospecto: June 2.
        July 28.
1828   Feb. 14 – 23, 28 – Mar. 4, 8 –
        18.
        Suplemento: Jan. 26, Mar. 11,
        15.

LA REPUBLICA. sw.
TxU
1849   Aug. 25 – Sept. 8.

LA REPUBLICA. d. est. Sept. 26, 1856.
Note: Ceased publication Nov. 9,
1856.
CU – B
Micro (N)
1856   Sept. 26 – Nov. 9.

LA REPUBLICA. d. est. Feb. 15, 1880.
CU – B
Micro (P)
1882   Aug. 19.
1883   Sept. 15, Nov. 7.
MWA
1881   Jan. 1, 6 – 8, 11 – 15, 18 – 22,
        25, 26.
        Suplemento: Jan. 15.
1882   [Jan. 7 – Aug. 2].
1883   [Aug. 1 – 31].
1884   Sept. 19.
TxU
1880   Feb. 15 – Sept. 12, 14 – Dec.
        31.
1881   Jan. 1 – Feb. 8, 10 – July 5, 7 –
        22, 24, Aug. 30, Sept. 1 – Nov.

4, 8 – Dec. 16, 20 – 31.
1882   Jan. 1 – Feb. 18, 20, Mar. 1 – 4,
        8, 22, Oct. 28.
1884   Aug. 2.
1885   Feb. 8 – Aug. 12, 15 – Dec. 6,
        10 – 31.

REPUBLICA; SEMANA LITERARIA. w.
MWA
    1882   Jan. 29 – Feb. 12, Mar. 5 – 12.

LA REPUBLICA. d. est. 1887.
    Note: Title *El Ferrocarrilero y
    boletín de mejores materiales. The
    Railroader and Bulletin of Public
    Improvements* (in Spanish and Eng-
    lish), 1887 – 1889; *La República*,
    after 1889.
    DLC
    1889   Feb. 22 – May 24.
    1890   Aug. 10 – Dec. 15, 17 – 31.

LA REPUBLICA. w. est. 1905.
    TxU
    1905   Oct. 1, Nov. 26, Dec. 17, 31.
    1906   Jan. 28, Feb. 18, Mar. 4 – 11,
            25, Apr. 8 – 15, May 6, 15 – 27,
            June 3 – 24, July 15, 29, Aug.
            5, 19, 26, Sept. 2, 16, 20, Nov.
            4 – Dec. 2, 16 – 23.
    1907   Jan. 20 – 27, Feb. 3 – Mar. 3,
            17 – 24, Apr. 28 – Sept. 8, 29 –
            Oct. 13, 27, Nov. 10, 24 – Dec.
            15, 29 – 31.
    1908   Jan. 1 – 9, Feb. 2 – 9, 23 – Mar.
            1, Apr. 5 – May 10, 24, June
            7 – 21, July 5 – Aug. 2, 16, 30 –
            Sept. 6, 20 – Oct. 4, 18 – Nov.
            1.
    1909   Jan. 28 – Mar. 11, Apr. 8, 29 –
            May 6, 20, June 3, July 29, Aug.
            19, Oct. 7, 21, Nov. 11, Dec.
            2 – 9, 30, 31.
    1910   Jan. 1 – 27.

LA REPUBLICA. w. est. Aug. 12, 1914.
    DLC
    1914   Aug. 12.

LA REPUBLICA. d. est. Feb. 28, 1917.
    DLC
    1917   Mar. 6.

TxU
    1917   Feb. 28 – Mar. 8.

LA REPUBLICA. d. est. Feb. 15, 1918.
    DLC
    1918   Feb. 15 – May 31, Aug. 1 – 15.

LA REPUBLICA. sw. est. May 31, 1919.
    CU
    1919   July 13.
    DLC
    1919   May 31 – Aug. 31.

LA REPUBLICA. d.
    TxU
    1919   Sept. 30, Oct. 21.

EL REPUBLICANO. d. est. Mar. 1,
1846.
    Note: Ceased publication [Dec.
    30, 1846].
    CU – B
    1846   Mar. 5 – 7, 12 – 16, 26 – Apr. 4,
            9 – June 30.
    DLC
    1846   Mar. 1 – 7, 11 – 14, 17 – May
            12, 14 – 27, 29 – 31.

EL REPUBLICANO. d. est. Jan. 2, 1879.
    DLC
    1879   Jan. 7 – Oct. 2.
    LNHT
    1879   Jan. 2 – Dec. 31.
    1880   Jan. 1 – Dec. 31.
    1881   Jan. 1 – 30.
    MWA
    1880   Oct. 15 – 19.
    TxU
    1879   Apr. 5, 8, 30 – June 29, July 4,
            16, 22 – 24, 27, 30, Aug. 2 – 5,
            Sept. 30, Oct. 2, 4, 11, Nov.
            14, 15, 23, Dec. 10, 11, 23.
    1880   Jan. 2, 6, 15, 18, 22, Feb. 5, 10,
            12, 13, 17, 18, 21 – 24, 27, Mar.
            2 – May 19, 25 – June 24, 26,
            27, 29 – Aug. 17, 19 – 22, 25, 26,
            28 – Sept. 10, 14 – 19, 21, 23 –
            Dec. 31.
    1881   Jan. 1 – 30.

EL REPUBLICANO. d. est. Sept. 1, 1885.
TxU
    1885   Sept. 1.

EL REPUBLICANO. w. est. Oct. 6, 1913.
TxU
    1913   Oct. 6 – 13.

EL REPUBLICANO. d. est. July 13, 1915.
DLC
    1915   July 13 – 20.
            Extraordinario: July 17, 22.

THE REPUBLICS.
    Note: In English.
NcD
    1881   Apr. 3.

RESTAURACIÓN. w.
TxU
    1911   June 30, July 15.

EL RESTAURADOR. est. June 20, 1846.
CU – B
    1846   June 20, Aug. 5 – Sept. 18.

EL RESTAURADOR MEXICANO. sw. est. Oct. 31, 1838.
CU – B
    Micro (N)
    1838   Oct. 31 – Dec. 31.
    1839   Jan. 1 – Apr. 10.
NN
    1838   Dec. 15, 22.
DLC
    1838   Oct. 31 – Nov. 2, 4 – Dec. 7, 30, 31.
    1839   Jan. 1 – Apr. 10.
TxU
    1838   Dec. 5, 27, 29 – 31.
    1839   Jan. 1 – Mar. 2, 13 – 30, Apr. 6.

EL RESUMEN. w. est. Jan. 1909.
LNHT
    1909   Feb. 1 – Dec. 31.

EL RESUMEN. d. est. Feb. 20, 1918.
DLC
    1918   Feb. 20, 21.

LA REVANCHA. w. est. May 25, 1913.
TxU
    1913   May 25, June 1.

REVISITA DE LOS ULTIMOS SUCESOS IN MEXICO. m.
NHi
    1864   Feb. 26, May 28, Apr. 28.

REVISTA DEL SABADO. w. est. Aug. 7, 1915.
DLC
    1915   Aug. 14.
TxU
    1915   Sept. 11.

REVISTA MILITAR DE LA QUINCENA. bw.
    Note: Separate Spanish and French editions.
NHi
    1865   Oct. 10, Nov. 2.
    1866   Apr. 18, May 2, June 3, 19, July 5, Sept. 29, Oct. 29.

REVISTA POLITICA DE LA QUINCENA. bw.
    Note: Separate Spanish and French editions.
    See also *Revue politique de la quinzaine.*
NHi
    1865   July 25, Sept. 11, Oct. 19, Nov. 2.
    1866   Apr. 18, June 3, 19, July 5, Sept. 29, Oct. 10, 29.

REVISTA UNIVERSAL. w.
CtY
    1867   Parte ilustrada: Oct. 13 – Dec. 29.

REVISTA UNIVERSAL DE POLITICA, LITERATURA, COMERCIO Y AVISOS. d.
LNT – MA
    1875   Aug. 2.
MWA
    1869   [Aug. 2 – Nov. 17].

1870   Jan. 31, Feb. 2, 4, 12, 14, July
        12−16, Aug. 22−29, Nov. 2,
        4−8, 10−19.
1871   Apr. 24−26, [June 24−July 8].
1872   Jan. 3, 10−11, 15.
TxU
1875   Apr. 16, July 9, Aug. 7.

LA REVOLUCION. sw. est. Jan. 15,
  1853.
  CU−B
    Micro (N)
    1853   Jan. 15−Mar. 19.

LA REVOLUCION; DIARIO POLI-
  TICO, LITERARIO COMERCIAL.
  d. est. Aug. 19, 1885.
  CU−B
    Micro (N)
    1885   Aug. 19−Dec. 4.
  TxU
    1885   Aug. 19.

LA REVOLUCION; DIARIO DE COM-
  BATE. d. est. Sept. 1, 1911.
  TxU
    1911   Sept. 1.

LA REVOLUCION. d. est. Aug. 14,
  1914.
  DLC
    1914   Aug. 14, 15, 17, 20, 21, 27,
            29.
            Extraordinario: Aug. 14.
  TxU
    1914   Aug. 14, 15, 17, 25−29.

LA REVOLUCION. sw., d. est. June 17,
  1915.
  DLC
    1915   June 17, Aug. 8, 13, Sept. 7−
            20.
            Extraordinario: July 13, 16,
            25−Aug. 1, 4, 5.

REVOLUCION; DIARIO DE MEDIO
  DIA. d. est. 1918.
    Note: Suspended publication June
    3−July 6, 1919.
  CU
    1919   July 11.

DLC
  1919   Jan. 1−Dec. 31.
  1920   Jan. 1−July 31.
LNT−MA
  1919   May 7−Aug. 5.
TxU
  1919   Jan. 16, 18, 21, 31−Feb. 5,
          10, 13, 15, 21, 24, 28, Mar. 1−
          17, 19, 20, 22, 26, 27, 29−Apr.
          1, 4−7, 9, 10, 14−17, 21−May
          1, 3−6, 12−15, 17−31, July
          10, 14−Aug. 6, 8−12, 14−25,
          27, 28, 30−Sept. 1, 4, 5, 8−
          10, 12, 15, 17−19, 23−26, 30−
          Oct. 4, 7, 8, 13−22, 24−Nov.
          1, 4−10, 12−22, 25−29, Dec.
          2−5, 9, 10, 12−24, 29−31.
  1920   Jan. 2−12, 14−23, 26, 27, 29,
          30, Feb. 2−4, 6, 7, 11, 12, 17−
          26, 28, Mar. 4−9, 11, 12, 15,
          17−27, 30, 31, May 14.
  1921   Mar. 27, Apr. 23−25, May 13.

REVUE DE LA QUINZAINE DE L'ES-
  TAFFETTE. bw.
    Note: In French.
  NHi
    1864   Feb. 27, Mar. 28, Apr. 29,
            May 11, June 29, July 11, 29,
            Aug. 29, Sept. 10, 28, Oct. 10.
    1866   Sept. 10, Oct. 10, 29.
  NN
    1865   June 29.

REVUE POLITIQUE DE LA QUIN-
  ZAINE. bw.
    Note: Separate Spanish and French
    editions.
    See also *Revista política de la
    quincena*.
  NHi
    1865   Sept. 11, Oct. 19, Nov. 2, 18.
    1866   Apr. 18, June 3, 19, July 5,
            Sept. 29, Oct. 10.

EL REY QUE RABIO. w.
  TxU
    1909   July 4.
    1911   Aug. 27−Sept. 3, 27−Oct. 6.

ROZONADOR. sw.
  MWA
    1847   Dec. 18—31.
    1848   Jan. 1—8, 22—26.

LA SABATINA UNIVERSAL. w. est.
  June 15, 1822.
    Note: Ceased publication Nov. 16,
    1822.
  TxU
    1822   June 15—Nov. 16.

EL SACRISTAN. w. est. Nov. 12, 1914.
  DLC
    1914   Nov. 12.

SAN LUNES. w. est. 1907.
  TxU
    1907   Nov. 4—Dec. 26.
    1909   Oct. 4—11.
    1910   Jan. 31—Feb. 21, May 2, 16.

SANCHO. d. est. May 23, 1919.
  DLC
    1919   Prospecto: May 16—18.
            May 23—July 2.
  TxU
    1919   May 29.

LA SATIRA. w. est. Nov. 19, 1910.
  CtY
    1911   June 25, July 16, 30—Aug. 27,
            Sept. 27—Oct. 15, 29, Nov.
            26—Dec. 31.
    1912   Jan. 14.
  TxU
    1910   Nov. 19—Dec. 31.
    1911   Jan. 1—Dec. 31.
    1912   Jan. 1—Feb. 18.

SATURNO. w. est. Jan. 2, 1909.
  TxU
    1909   Jan. 2.

LA SEMANA. w.
  CU
    1940   Nov. 7.

LA SEMANA EN EL HOGAR. w.
  TxU
    Prospecto.

SEMANA MERCANTIL. w.
  TxU
    1910   Nov. 14.

SEMANARIO ARTISTICO PARA LA
  EDUCACION Y PROGRESO DE LOS
  ARTESANOS. w. est. Feb. 9, 1844.
  CU—B
    Micro (N)
    1844   Feb. 9—Dec. 31.
    1845   Jan. 1—Dec. 31.
    1846   Jan. 1—10.

SEMANARIO CATOLICO. w. est.
  Feb. 20, 1869.
  LNHT
    1869   Feb. 20—Dec. 24.

SEMANARIO ECONOMICO DE ME-
  XICO. w. est. Dec. 1, 1808.
    Note: Title *Semanario económico
    de noticias curiosas y eruditas*,
    Dec. 1, 1808—Dec. 21, 1809; *Sema-
    nario económico de México*, Dec.
    27, 1809—Dec. 27, 1810. Succeeded
    by *Mentor mexicano*. Ceased pub-
    lication Dec. 27, 1810.
  CtY
    1808   Dec. 1—Dec. 29.
    1809   Jan. 5—Sept. 7, 21—Dec. 21.
    1810   Jan. 4—Dec. 27.

EL SEMANARIO ILUSTRADO. w. est.
  May 1, 1868.
  CU—B
    1868   May 1—Nov. 27.
  TxU
    1868   Oct. 30.

SEMANARIO POLITICO Y LITERARIO
  DE MEJICO. w., irr., w. est. July
  12, 1820.
    Note: Ceased publication Mar. 27,
    1822.
  CtY
    1820   Prospecto.
            July 12—Dec. 31.
    1821   Jan. 1—Nov. 7, 21—Dec. 31.
    1822   Jan. 1—Mar. 27.

SEMANARIO POLITICO Y LITERARIO
  1824. w. est. Mar. 29, 1837.
  CtY
    1837   Apr. 5.
  DLC
    1837   Mar. 29 – Apr. 19.
LOS SENTIMIENTOS DEL SIGLO.
  NN
    1860   Suplemento: Dec. 29.
SER.
  CSt
    1939   Nov. 1 – 30.
EL SIGLO.
  DLC
    1916   Extraordinario: Aug. 1.
EL SIGLO DIEZ Y NUEVE. d. est. Oct.
  8, 1841.
    Note: Suspended publication Jan.
    16 – Mar. 1, 1843; Jan. 1, 1846; May
    30, 1846; Sept. 13 – 30, 1856; Aug.
    1, 1858 – Jan. 14, 1861; May 15, 1863 –
    July 14, 1867; ceased publication
    Dec. 1896.
  CLCM
    1852   Nov. 6.
  CU – B
    1841   Oct. 8 – Nov. 7.
    1842   Apr. 1 – Sept. 30, Dec. 20.
            Suplemento: Mar. 31.
    1843   Mar. 1 – Dec. 31.
    1844   Apr. 1 – June 29.
    1845   Jan. 1 – 16, 18 – Mar. 30, Apr.
            1 – Dec. 31.
    1848   June 1 – Dec. 31.
    1849 – 1852   Jan. 1 – Dec. 31.
    1853   Jan. 1 – Feb. 21, 23 – June 21,
            23 – Nov. 8, 10 – Dec. 31.
    1855   Aug. 1 – 3, 7, 11 – Dec. 31.
    1856   Jan. 1 – Apr. 25, 27 – Dec. 31.
    1857 – 1861   Jan. 1 – Dec. 31.
    1862   Jan. 1 – June 30, Oct. 31.
    1873   Apr. 29.
    1878   Jan. 30.
    1879   Sept. 30.
    1880   Mar. 30.
    1883   Nov. 28.
    1884   Aug. 20, Dec. 1, 2, 8.
    1885   Jan. 19 – 23, Apr. 30, May 4.

    1886   Aug. 13.
  Micro (P) & (N)
    1841   Oct. 8 – Dec. 31.
    1842 – 1862   Jan. 1 – Dec. 31.
    1863   Jan. 1 – May 30.
    1867   July 15 – Dec. 31.
    1868   Jan. 1 – Feb. 8, 10 – 28, Mar.
            1 – May 26, 28 – Dec. 31.
    1869   Jan. 1 – Oct. 30, Nov. 1 – Dec.
            31.
    1870 – 1873   Jan. 1 – Dec. 31.
    1874   Jan. 1 – July 20, 22 – 25, 28 –
            Aug. 1, 3 – Dec. 30.
    1875   Jan. 1 – June 28, 30 – Dec. 31.
    1876   Jan. 1 – Dec. 30.
    1877   Jan. 1 – 8, 11 – May 12, 15 –
            June 16, 20 – 22, June 25 – Aug.
            25, 28 – Dec. 31.
    1878   Jan. 1 – Dec. 30.
    1879   Jan. 1 – 11, 13 – Dec. 31.
    1880   Jan. 1 – Feb. 19, 21 – Dec. 31.
    1881   Jan. 1 – Sept. 9, 12 – 16, 19 –
            Dec. 31.
    1882   Jan. 2 – Dec. 30.
    1883   Jan. 1 – July 27, 30 – Sept. 8,
            11 – Dec. 3, 5, 7 – 10, 15 – 18,
            22, 29.
    1884   Jan. 1 – Mar. 7, 10 – June 17,
            19 – Dec. 30.
    1885   Jan. 1 – June 30.
    1886   Jan. 1 – 14, 16 – Feb. 27, Mar.
            2 – Apr. 14, 16 – 30, May 3 – 7,
            10 – June 15, 17 – 25, 28 – July
            13, 15 – 21, 23 – 28, 30 – Aug.
            3, 5 – 7, 10 – 24, 27 – Sept. 14,
            16 – Oct. 6, 8 – Dec. 31.
    1887   Jan. 1 – Mar. 30, Apr. 1 – 30,
            May 3 – 7, 10 – June 10, 13 –
            22, 25 – 29, July 1 – 22, 25, 26,
            28 – Aug. 15, 17, 18, 20 – 22,
            24 – 27, 30, 31, Sept. 5, 7, 8, 10,
            13 – 17, 20 – 23, 26 – Oct. 3, 4,
            5 – 11, 13 – Dec. 31.
    1888   Jan. 2 – 17, 19 – May 5, 8 – Aug.
            4, 8 – Nov. 19, 21 – Dec. 1, 4 –
            31.
    1889   Apr. 19, July 1 – Aug. 16, 19 –
            Sept. 20, 23 – Dec. 30.

1890   Jan. 1 – Apr. 18, 21 – Aug. 27,
       29 – Dec. 31.
1891   Jan. 1 – Dec. 31.
1892   Jan. 1 – Dec. 30.
1893   Jan. 2 – Dec. 30.
1894   Jan. 2 – Oct. 17, 19 – Nov. 7,
       9 – Dec. 31.
1895   Jan. 2 – 5, 8 – Dec. 31.
1896   Jan. 2 – June 30.

CtY

1842   [Jan. 1 – Dec. 31].
1843   Jan. 1 – Dec. 31.
1845   [July 1 – Dec. 29].
1849   Oct. 3 – Dec. 31.
1861   June 15 – Dec. 31.

DLC

1841   Oct. 8 – Nov. 28, 30 – Dec. 6,
       8 – 31.
       Suplemento: Nov. 3.
1842   Jan. 1 – Apr. 1, 3 – 29, May 1 –
       11, 13 – June 26, 30, July 2, 3,
       7 – Oct. 24, 26 – Dec. 31.
       Suplemento: Jan. 2, 13, Feb.
       19, Mar. 2, 3, 31, Apr. 5, May
       10, June 16, Oct. 3, 21, Nov. 7,
       11, 14, 22, 30, Dec. 4, 13, 19,
       30, 31.
1843   Jan. 1 – 4.
1844   Jan. 2 – 25, 28 – 30, Feb. 2 –
       Mar. 31, Apr. 2 – 26, 28 – June
       30, Aug. 1 – Oct. 16, 18 – 29,
       31 – Dec. 4, 7 – 19, 21 – 31.
       Suplemento: Jan. 8, 11, Feb. 3,
       9, 12, 15, Mar. 14, 29, June 1,
       15, 28, Aug. 30, Sept. 6, 19, Oct.
       26, 29, Nov. 4, 6, 8, 12, 15, 18,
       20, 27, Dec. 6, 21.
1845   Jan. 1 – Dec. 31.
       Suplemento: Jan. 18, Feb. 21,
       24, 25, Mar. 7, 8, 12, 13, 15, 25,
       Apr. 5, 11, 15, June 5, 20, 21,
       July 12, 31, Aug. 25, Oct. 16,
       30, Nov. 26, Dec. 3, 5, 19, 23.
1851   Jan. 19.

ICN

1882   Feb. 13.
1885   Aug. 4.

LNT – MA

1877   Sept. 17.
1880   Aug. 17.
1881   July 20.
1889   Aug. 28 – Nov. 28, Dec. 17 – 26.
1891   May 12 – June 6, Sept. 2, Oct.
       8, 19 – Dec. 31.
1892   Jan. 4 – Mar. 10, June 6 – Oct.
       3, 14 – Dec. 2.
1894   Sept. 14.
1896   Aug. 29 – Sept. 2.

MB

1848   June 6, 8 – 11.
1856   Oct. 20.

MWA

1841   Oct. 8 – Dec. 31.
1842   Jan. 1 – Feb. 28, [Mar. 1 –
       Sept. 30], Oct. 1 – Dec. 31.
1843   Jan. 1 – 15.
1844   Jan. 1 – Dec. 1.
1845   Jan. 1 – Dec. 31.
1849   July 1 – Dec. 31.
1852   Apr. 1 – June 30, Nov. 1 – Dec.
       31.
1853   Jan. 1 – Apr. 31.
1854   Feb. 1 – Dec. 31.
1855   Aug. 1 – Sept. 30.
1869   Nov. 15.
1870   July 18, Sept. 11.
1871   Jan. 1 – June 30.
1878   Jan. 21, 30, Mar. 30.
1881   Mar. 10 – Dec. 31.
1882   Jan. 1 – June 2.

MoU

Micro (N)

1843   July 1 – Sept. 30.
1845   July 1 – Dec. 31.
1855   Aug. 1 – 3, 7, 11 – Dec. 31.
1856 – 1857   Jan. 1 – Dec. 31.
1858   Jan. 1 – July 31.
1862   Jan. 1 – Apr. 10, 12 – June 30,
       Oct. 31.
1883   Nov. 28.
1885   Jan. 19 – 23, Apr. 30, May 4.

NHi

1851   Dec. 28.
1853   Jan. 5.
1856   Sept. 5.

NN
　1845　Alcance: June 7.
TxFTC
　Micro (P)
　1841　Oct. 8 — Dec. 31.
　1842 — 1860　Jan. 1 — Dec. 31.
　1861　Jan. 1 — Feb. 28.
TxU
　1841　Oct. 8 — Dec. 31.
　1842 — 1845　Jan. 1 — Dec. 31.
　1848　June 1 — Dec. 31.
　1849 — 1854　Jan. 1 — Dec. 31.
　1855　Jan. 1 — June 30.
　1856 — 1857　Jan. 1 — Dec. 31.
　1858　Jan. 1 — June 31.
　1861 — 1862　Jan. 1 — Dec. 31.
　1863　Jan. 1 — May 30.
　1867　July 15 — Dec. 31.
　1868 — 1873　Jan. 1 — Dec. 31.
　1876　Jan. 1 — Oct. 15.
　1877　Jan. 30 — June 30.
　1878　Feb. 19.
　1879　Mar. 24.
　1880　Feb. 18, Mar. 2 — Dec. 31.
　1881 — 1883　Jan. 1 — Dec. 31.
　1884　Jan. 1 — Sept. 1.
　1885　May 7.
　1887　June 25.
　1888　Dec. 3.
　1890　Oct. 31 — Nov. 4, 6, 7, 11, 14,
　　　　21, 24, 26, 27, Dec. 2, 4, 5, 8 —
　　　　10, 15, 17, 19, 22 — 29.
　Micro (P)
　1841　Oct. 8 — Dec. 31.
　1842 — 1845　Jan. 1 — Dec. 31.
ViU
　1841　Oct. 8 — Dec. 31.
　1842　Jan. 1 — July 31, Aug. 1 — Dec.
　　　　31.
　1843 — 1862　Jan. 1 — Dec. 31.
　1863　Jan. 1 — May 30.
EL SINARQUISTA. w. est. Jan. 7, 1939.
　Note: Removed from León [Jan.
　1940]. Suspended publication May
　25 — June 3, 1942; ceased publica-
　tion June 1961.
　CLU
　1953 — 1960　Jan. 1 — Dec. 31.

　1961　Jan. 1 — June 30.
CSt
　1941　Dec. 1 — 31.
　1942　Jan. 1 — July 31.
　1943　June 24 — Dec. 31.
　1944　Jan. 1 — June 15.
　1945　Nov. 1 — 30.
DLC
　1941　Aug. 14 — 27, 29 — Sept. 3, 5 —
　　　　10, 12 — Nov. 19, 21 — Dec. 10,
　　　　12 — 25.
　1942　Jan. 1 — Nov. 19, 26 — Dec. 31.
　1943　Jan. 1 — Dec. 31.
　1944　Jan. 1 — June 15.
NjP
　1941　July 31 — Aug. 28.
　1942　Aug. 27.

LA SINCERIDAD. sw. est. Apr. 2, 1851.
　CU — B
　Micro (P)
　1851　Apr. 2 — July 30.

LA SISTEMA POSTAL DE LA RE-
PUBLICA MEXICANA. w. est. Nov.
9, 1877.

　CU — B
　1877　Nov. 9 — Dec. 31.
　1878　Jan. 1 — July 25, Aug. 5 — 22,
　　　　Sept. 6 — Dec. 31.
　1879 — 1880　Jan. 1 — Dec. 31.
　1881　Jan. 1 — Aug. 20.
　MWA
　1879　[Jan. 31 — Dec. 6].
　1880　[Jan. 17 — May 29].
　1881　Jan. 1, Feb. 5.
　TxU
　1880　June 12 — Dec. 31.
　1881　Jan. 1 — Aug. 20.

EL SOCIALISTA. w., sw.
　CU — B
　Micro (P)
　1874　Mar. 8.
　1883　Sept. 15.
　1884　Dec. 7.
　　　　Suplemento: Nov. 17, 18.
　1885　May 5.

LNT — MA
1883   June 30.
MWA
1884   Suplemento: Nov. 17, 20.
TxU
1880   Jan. 15, Mar. 16, May 28 — June 4.
1882   Dec. 8.
EL SOCIALISTA. w. est. Mar. 22, 1914.
TxU
1914   Mar. 22 — 29.
LA SOCIEDAD. d. est. Dec. 1, 1855.
Note: Suspended publication July 13, 1856 — Dec. 25, 1857; Jan. 17 — 21, 1858; Dec. 24, 1860 — June 9, 1863; June 12 — 20, 1863; July 14 — 30, 1866; ceased publication Nov. 31, 1867.
CU — B
Micro (P) & (N)
1855   Dec. 1 — 31.
1856   Jan. 1 — July 12.
1857   Dec. 27 — 31.
1858   Jan. 1 — 30, Feb. 1 — Dec. 31.
1859   Jan. 1 — Dec. 31.
1860   Jan. 1 — Dec. 23.
1863   June 10 — Dec. 31.
1864 — 1865   Jan. 1 — Dec. 31.
1866   Jan. 1 — June 30.
MWA
1859   Dec. 8.
NHi
1865   Suplemento: Aug. 30.
1866   May 11 — 14, 16 — 20, Oct. 11 — 28.
TxU
1855   Dec. 1 — 31.
1856   Jan. 1 — July 12.
1857   Dec. 26 — 31.
1858   Jan. 1 — 16, 22 — Apr. 1, 4 — Dec. 31.
1859   Jan. 1 — Dec. 31.
1860   Jan. 1 — Mar. 7, 9 — Apr. 6, 8 — Dec. 25.
1863   June 10, 11, 21 — Dec. 31.
1864   Jan. 1 — Dec. 31.
1865   Jan. 1 — Feb. 28, Mar. 2 — Apr. 28, 30 — Dec. 31.
1866   Jan. 1, 3 — Mar. 30, Apr. 1 —

Oct. 18, 20 — 29, 31 — Dec. 31.
1867   Jan. 1 — Mar. 31.
LA SOCIEDAD MERCANTIL. d. est. 1867.
CU — B
1867   Sept. 5 — 12, 14 — Oct. 30.
EL SOL. sw., d. est. Dec. 5, 1821.
Note: Periodicity Dec. 5, 1821 — June 11, 1823, semiweekly; June 15, 1823 — Dec. 29, 1832, daily. First series ended, June 11, 1823; second series, June 15, 1823 — Dec. 1, 1828; third series, July 1, 1829 — Dec. 29, 1832. Ceased publication Dec. 29, 1832.
CU — B
1823   Oct. 15.
1824   Feb. 11 — 20, 22 — 24, Oct. 13 — Nov. 30.
Suplemento: Dec. 11.
1825   Mar. 11, 12, Apr. 29 — May 1, 3, 4, 26, 27, 29 — June 8, 30 — July 2, Aug. 7, 8, 10, 21 — 24, Sept. 11 — 16, Oct. 9 — 11, Nov. 20 — 26.
Suplemento: Mar. 10.
1826   Mar. 16 — 18, May 7 — 13, June 22 — 24, Oct. 1 — 4, 12, 13.
1827   Jan. 21 — 24, July 3.
1828   Feb. 7 — 16, 24 — Mar. 1, Aug. 8, 9, Sept. 27.
1831   June 9.
Micro (P) & (N)
1821   Dec. 5 — 31.
1822   Jan. 1 — May 22.
1823   June 15 — Dec. 31.
1824 — 1827   Jan. 1 — Dec. 31.
1828   Jan. 1 — Dec. 1.
1829   July 1 — Dec. 31.
1830   Jan. 1 — June 30, July 2 — 13, 17, 18, 21 — Oct. 29, 31 — Nov. 20, 22 — Dec. 31.
1831   Jan. 1 — Mar. 12, 14 — June 13, 15 — Aug. 20, 22 — Dec. 31.
1832   Jan. 1 — Mar. 6, 8 — 31.
CtY
1823   June 15 — Sept. 14, Nov. 1 — Dec. 31.

1824 – 1828   Jan. 1 – Dec. 31.
1829   Sept. 29, Oct. 3.
        Suplemento: Nov. 14.
1832   June 15.
DLC
  1821   Prospecto.
          Dec. 5 – 31.
          Suplemento: Dec. 15.
  1822   Jan. 1 – May 22.
          Suplemento: Jan. 5, Feb. 23,
          Apr. 3, 13, 20, 27, May 4.
  1824   Apr. 25 – 27, May 2, Oct. 1 –
          Dec. 31.
          Extraordinario: Nov. 8.
          Suplemento: Oct. 23, Nov. 4,
          Dec. 11.
  1825   Jan. 1 – Dec. 31.
          Extraordinario: Jan. 22.
          Suplemento: Jan. 27, 31, Feb.
          4, 5, 10, Mar. 1, 10, 14, 15, 25,
          27, 29, Apr. 1, 6, 7, 12, 16, May
          6, 26, June 24, Aug. 3, 17, Nov.
          2, 7, 18.
  1826   Jan. 1 – Dec. 31.
          Suplemento: Jan. 31, Feb. 8, 9,
          11, 19, 24, 25, Mar. 6, 15, 23,
          30, May 6, 23, June 27, 29, July
          9, 13, 14, 23, 24, Aug. 6, 10,
          Sept. 1, 10, 21, 25, Oct. 10, 26,
          28, Nov. 2, 11, Dec. 9.
  1827   Jan. 1 – Apr. 7, 9 – May 18,
          20 – June 30.
          Suplemento: Jan. 6, 28, Feb.
          1, 14, 15, 24, 26, Mar. 1, 12, 22,
          26, 29, 30, May 17, 29.
  1828   Sept. 2 – 15, 17 – 20.
NN
  1826   Aug. 28.
TxU
  1821   Dec. 5 – 31.
  1822   Jan. 1 – May 22.
  1823   Prospecto: June 11.
          June 15 – Dec. 31.
  1825 – 1827   Jan. 1 – Dec. 31.
  1828   Jan. 1 – Dec. 1.
  Micro (P)
  1823   Oct. 15 – Dec. 31.
  1824   Jan. 1 – Feb. 14, May 1 – Oct.
          14.

1829   July 1 – Dec. 31.
1830   Jan. 1 – July 7, 9 – Dec. 31.
1831   Jan. 1 – Dec. 31.
1832   Jan. 1 – July 21, 23, Aug. 13,
        15 – Nov. 30, Dec. 2 – 8, 13 –
        20, 23 – 26, 29.
ViU
  1823   June 15 – Dec. 31.
  1824 – 1829   Jan. 1 – Dec. 31.
  1830   Jan. 1 – Mar. 31.

EL SOL. d. est. Feb. 1, 1835.
  Note: Ceased publication Sept. 16,
  1835.
CtY
  1835   Mar. 2, 3, 5, 8, 10 – 13, 17, 18,
          22 – 26, 30, Apr. 2, 4, 5, 7, 9,
          12, 13, 15, 17, 19 – 22, 28, May
          1, 5, 6, 9 – 12, 14, 15, 17, 19 –
          22, 26, 29, June 3, 4, 6 – 10, 15,
          16, 22, 23, 25, 27 – July 4, 8,
          11 – 20, 27 – Aug. 1, 20 – 24,
          26, 27, 30, Sept. 4, 6 – 9, 11 –
          13, 16.
DLC
  1835   Feb. 1 – 28, Apr. 2 – July 25,
          27 – Sept. 16.
          Suplemento: Feb. 24, Mar. 7,
          14, 28.
MWA
  1835   Feb. 1 – Mar. 3, 5 – 30, Apr. 6,
          23, May 9, 14 – 27, June 10 –
          12, 18, Sept. 16.
TxU
  1835   Feb. 1 – Sept. 16.
TxU
  Micro (P)
  1835   Feb. 1 – July 25, 27 – Sept. 16.

EL SOL. d. est. June 1, 1914.
  Note: Suspended publication Aug.
  26 – Nov. 8, 1914.
DLC
  1914   June 1, 5, 6, 8, 10 – 13, 15, 17,
          18, 21, 22, 25, 27 – July 1, 3, 6 –
          9, 11, 12, 14 – 18, 20 – 23, 27 –
          Nov. 13, 16, 17, 19 – 30, Dec.
          8 – 15, 17.
          Boletín: Aug. 5.

Extraordinario: July 15, Nov. 30.

Suplemento: Aug. 16.

1915   Jan. 2, 4, 5, 7–9, 11–15, 18–23, 25, 26, 30.

Extraordinario: Jan. 16, 27–29.

MWA

1914   June 23–July 4, 6–Aug. 21.

TxU

1914   June 1, 10, 14, July 13–16, 21–23, Aug. 5, 12, 16, 19, 23–Nov. 9, 11, 13, 16–21, 23–30, Dec. 8–26, 30.

1915   Jan. 2, 16–18, 26–30.

EL SOL DE MAYO. w. est. May 8, 1914.

TxU

1914   May 8.

LA SOMBRA. sw. est. Jan. 3, 1865.

CU–B

1865   Jan. 3–Dec. 31.

1866   Jan. 1–Nov. 23.

1867   Aug. 2–Oct. 29.

MoU

Micro (N)

1865   Jan. 3–Dec. 29.

1866   Jan. 3–Nov. 23.

1867   Aug. 2–Oct. 29.

TxU

1865   Jan. 6–Dec. 29.

LA SOMBRA DE GUERRERO. 3w.

TxU

1872   Dec. 8.

LA SOMBRA DE JARAUTA. sw. est. June 6, 1849.

CU–B

Micro (N)

1849   June 6–Aug. 31.

LA SOMBRA DE MIRAFUENTES.

TxU

1880   Oct. 30.

LA SOMBRA DE MOCTHEUZOMA XOCOYOTZIN.

CtY

1834   Nos. 1–12.

Suplemento: Nos. 1, 2.

EL SONORENSE. bw. est. Oct. 1, 1840.

Note: Ceased publication Apr. 5, 1841.

CU–B

Micro (N)

1840   Oct. 1–Dec. 31.

1841   Jan. 1–Mar. 13, 27–Apr. 5.

DLC

1840   Oct. 1–Nov. 17.

EL SORBETAZO DE MADERO w. est. Apr. 21, 1912.

TxU

1912   Apr. 21.

STAR FOR THE UNITED STATES. w. est. Mar. 27, 1848.

Note: In English.

NHi

1848   Mar. 27–Apr. 6.

DIE STIMME.

Note: In Hebrew.

CSt

1943   June 1–30.

LOS SUCESOS. d. est. 1904.

DLC

1914   June 12, 15, July 17, 29, 31, Aug. 6, 20, 24, 25.

Extraordinario: July 20.

1915   Jan. 4, 12, 14, 15, 18, 21.

Extraordinario: Jan. 7–9, 19, 20, 22.

1918   Aug. 1–31.

Extraordinario: Aug. 20, 25.

1919   Jan. 2–27.

TxU

1908   Mar. 21, 25, Apr. 2.

1914   June 10, July 16–18, 20–25, 27, 28, 30–Aug. 1, 3, 5, 17–19, 21, 22, Sept. 2, 7.

LOS SUCESOS NACIONALES.

DLC

1914   Extraordinario: Aug. 15.

EL SUFRAGIO LIBRE. w. est. 1903.

TxU

1903   Apr. 2.

1909   Jan. 22, Feb. 3.

1910   June 29—July 6.
1912   July 4.
1913   Feb. 27.
1914   Apr. 2.

SUPREMA LEY. w. est. 1913.
  TxU
    1913   Sept. 15, Oct. 10.

LA TARDE. d. est. 1914.
  TxU
    1914   May 16.

EL TECOLOTE. irr. est. Dec. 24, 1924.
  DLC
    1942   Nov. 20, Dec. 15.
    1943   Jan. 21, Mar. 24, Apr. 24,
            May 12.

EL TELEGRAFO; PERIODICO
OFICIAL. d. est. Jan. 11, 1833.
    Note: Succeeded *Registro oficial
    del gobierno de los Estados Unidos
    Mexicanos*; succeeded by *Diario
    del gobierno de la República Mej-
    icana*. Ceased publication Feb. 9,
    1835.
  CU—B
    Micro (P)
    1833   Jan. 11—Dec. 31.
    1834   Jan. 1—Dec. 31.
    1835   Jan. 1—Feb. 9.
  CtY
    1833   June 1, 4—Sept. 4, 6—24, 29,
            Oct. 1, 5, 7, 15—17, 19—Nov.
            27, 29—Dec. 3, 5—31.
    1834   Jan. 1—May 6, 8—28, 31—
            June 4, 6, 8, 9, 11—13, 21—
            23, 26—30, Aug. 1—8, 10—
            15, 18, 19, 21, 28, 29, 31.
  DLC
    1833   Jan. 11—Dec. 31.
            Alcance: Dec. 5.
            Extraordinario: Nov. 6, 15, 16,
            28, Dec. 18.
            Suplemento: June 28, July 21,
            22, 26.
    1834   Feb. 1—Dec. 28.
            Alcance: Mar. 25, 28.
            Suplemento: Apr. 5, Sept. 14.

1835   Jan. 1—Feb. 9.
LNHT
    1833   May 19, June 13—19, Dec. 26.
    1834   Feb. 20—25, Apr. 5, 8, May
            8—21.
MWA
    1833   Apr. 15, Oct. 1—6, 8—Nov.
            18, 20—Dec. 13, 15—31.
    1834   Jan. 15—17, Feb. 2, 22, 26,
            Mar. 10, June 16, 17, 25—27,
            29, 30, July 2, 5, 17, 30, 31,
            Aug. 2—8, 11, 13, 17, 30,
            Sept. 1, 19, 20, 27, Nov.
            1—8, 10—14, 19—30, Dec.
            17—31.
    1835   Jan. 1—Feb. 9.

EL TELEGRAFO; PERIODICO POLÍ-
TICO Y NOTICIOSO. sw. est.
[1846].
  CtY
    1846   May 5.

EL TELEGRAFO. sw.
  CU—B
    Micro (N)
    1852   Apr. 7—Oct. 9, 13—Dec. 31.
    1853   Jan. 1—Feb. 9, 16—Mar. 5,
            12, Apr. 13, 20, 27—29.

TELEGRAFO; DIARIO POLITICO Y
LITERARIO, COMERCIAL Y DE
AVISOS. d. est. Feb. 1881.
  MWA
    1881   Mar. 1, 2, 5—16, 30—Apr. 13,
            June 15.
  TxU
    1881   Mar. 1—4, 12, Apr. 13, 24,
            Sept. 4, 11, Oct. 2, 16, Nov.
            2—4, 16, 23—27.

TELEGRAFO AMERICANO. 3w. est.
Nov. 2, 1811.
    Note: Ceased publication [June 30],
    1812.
  CU—B
    Micro (N)
    1811   Nov. 4—Dec. 31.
    1812   Jan. 1—Mar. 8, May 7.

CtY
   1811   Nov. 2 – Dec. 30.
   1812   Jan. 2 – June 30.

EL TELEGRAMA. w.
  TxU
   1909   Sept. 5.

EL TELESCOPIO MEXICANO. d. est.
  Sept. 27, 1827.
  NN
   1827   Prospecto: Sept. 10.

EL TERCER IMPERIO. w. est. [1903].
  LNT – MA
   1904   July 30.
   1905   Dec. 16.
   1906   Jan. 1 – June 1, Aug. 5.

EL TIEMPO. d. est. July 3, 1834.
  CU – B
   1834   July 3 – Oct. 31.
  CtY
   1834   July 3 – Dec. 21.
  MWA
   1834   Sept. 24.

EL TIEMPO. d. est. Jan. 24, 1846.
  Note: Ceased publication June 7,
  1846.
  CU – B
   1846   Jan. 24 – June 7.
  CtY
   1846   Prospecto.
          Jan. 24 – June 7.
  TxU
   1846   Jan. 24 – June 7.

EL TIEMPO. d. est. Aug. 1, 1857.
  CU – B
   1857   Aug. 1 – Nov. 30.
EL TIEMPO; DIARIO CATOLICO. d.
  est. July 1, 1883.
  CLCM
   1887   Aug. 7, 9, 10, 11, 13, 14, 23,
          26, Dec. 11.
  CU
   Micro (P)
   1906   Jan. 3 – Oct. 4, 6 – Dec. 30.
   1907 – 1910   Jan. 1 – Dec. 31.
   1911   Jan. 2 – Oct. 19, 21 – 24, 26 –
          Dec. 30.

   1912   Jan. 1 – May 14, 16 – 30.
CU – B
  Micro (P)
   1883   July 1 – Dec. 31.
   1884 – 1905   Jan. 1 – Dec. 31.
LNHT
   1911   July 1 – Dec. 31.
MWA
   1884   [Nov. 15 – Dec. 30].
   1885   Jan. 3, 9, 11, 14, 16, Feb. 28,
          Mar. 1, Dec. 15, 19, 20.
   1886   Jan. 17, 20 – 23.
TxU
   1883   Prospecto: May 24.
          July 1 – Dec. 31.
   1884 – 1891   Jan. 1 – Dec. 31.
   1892   Jan. 1 – Apr. 13, 17 – 23, 26 –
          Dec. 31.
   1893 – 1895   Jan. 1 – Dec. 31.
   1896   Jan. 1 – May 2, 9, 31 – Dec. 31.
   1897 – 1911   Jan. 1 – Dec. 31.
   1912   Jan. 1 – Aug. 2.

EL TIEMPO ILUSTRADO.
  LNT – MA
   1906   Dec. 2.

TIERRA Y JUSTICIA. sw., d. est. Dec.
  20, 1914.
  DLC
   1914   Dec. 20 – 31.
   1915   Mar. 18 – 25, Apr. 1 – 25, May
          16 – 27, 29 – June 13.
          Extraordinario: Mar. 17, 29,
          Apr. 1, 13, 17, May 24.
  TxU
   1915   Mar. 18 – 28, Apr. 4, May 16,
          24 – 27.

TIERRA Y LIBERTAD. bw.
  CSt
   1944   Nov. 10.
   1945   Mar. 25, Sept. 10.
   1946   Apr. 10, June 10, Oct. 10,
          Nov. 10 – Dec. 10.
   1947   Jan. 10 – May 10, June 2 – July
          25, Aug. 25, Sept. 25 – Dec. 10.
   1948   Jan. 10, Feb. 10 – May 10,
          Apr. 10 – May 10, June 10,

Sept. 10, Oct. 10, Dec. 10–20.
1949   Jan. 20, Feb. 28, Mar. 25, Apr.
        10, June 25, July 10, Oct. 10.
1950   Jan. 10, Feb. 10, Mar. 10, May
        10, June 10– July 10, Aug. 10,
        Sept. 10, Oct. 10–25, Dec. 10.

EL TIGRE. w. est. Jan. 1, 1910.
  TxU
    1910   Jan. 1.

"TILIN TILIN." w., 3m.
  LNT–MA
    1910   July 31.
  TxU
    1904   Aug. 7.
    1908   Feb. 23, Mar. 27, Aug. 30.
    1910   May 27, June 9–Sept. 25.
    1911   Sept. 10, 30, Oct. 13.
            Edición ilustrada: Aug. 30–
            Oct. 15.
    1912   Apr. 28–May 19.

EL TIO JOB. d. est. Mar. 1, 1854.
  CU–B
    Micro (N)
    1854   Mar. 1–10.

EL TIO MONILLA. w. est. [1850].
  CtY
    1850   Oct. 30.
            Suplemento: Dec.

EL TITERE. d., 3w. est. 1861.
    Note: Before Nov. 20, 1861, daily;
    after Nov. 20, 1861, three times a
    week.
  NN
    1861   Nov. 7, 20, 30–Dec. 14.

LA TOS DE MI MAMA. sw. est. Dec. 4,
1864.
  CU–B
    Micro (N)
    1864   Dec. 4–31.
    1865   Jan. 1–Feb. 12.

EL TRABAJO.
  NN
    1929   Extraordinario: Nov. 19.

LE TRAIT D'UNION. d. est. May 5, 1849.
    Note: In French. Suspended publica-
    tion Jan. 24, 1858; during suspension,
    its editor successively established
    Le Courrier français; *journal univer-
    sal*; and *Les Deux Mondes*; *journal
    français universal*. *Le Trait d'union*
    resumed publication in Vera Cruz,
    Jan. 3, 1860 and in Mexico City Feb.
    4, 1860. Suspended publication a
    second time 1863–Jan. 31, 1868.
    Succeeded by *Le Courrier du Mex-
    ique et de L'Europe*.
  CU–B
    1861   Feb. 4–Apr. 7, 10–19, 22–
            Dec. 31.
    1862   Jan. 1–18, Apr. 12–May 3.
  Micro (N)
    1856   Jan. 5–Apr. 30.
  DLC
    1857   July 27, Aug. 2, 4–13, 16–
            Oct. 23, 25–Nov. 16.
    1875   Revue de quinzaine: June 15.
  LNT–MA
    1850   May 18.
    1851   Mar. 2, Aug. 28.
    1852   May 19, 29.
    1853   Nov. 19, 23, 30, Dec. 10, 14.
  TxU
    1868   Feb. 1–Dec. 31.
    1869   Jan. 1–Oct. 3, 5–Dec. 31.
    1870   Jan. 1, 4–Dec. 31.
    1871   Jan. 1–Aug. 15, 18–Dec. 31.
    1872–1873   Jan. 1–Dec. 31.
    1874   Jan. 1–May 31.
    1882   Aug. 12, Nov. 14.
    1884   Aug. 22, Oct. 1, 2.
    1885   May 24.
    1889   Sept. 11.

LA TRANCA. w.
  TxU
    1906   July 21, 22, Aug. 12.

LAS TRES GARANTIAS. sw. est. [June
15], 1841.
  NN
    1841   July 6.

TRIBUNA; PERIODICO POLITICO Y
LITERARIO. est. Jan. 1, 1874.
MWA
1874   Jan. 1–Feb. 27.

LA TRIBUNA. d. est. Sept. 2, 1879.
LNT–MA
1880   Sept. 16.
TxU
1879   Sept. 2–Dec. 31.
1880   Jan. 1–Dec. 31.
1881   Jan. 1–Feb. 25.

LA TRIBUNA. d.
TxU
1912   Mar. 14.

LA TRIBUNA. d. est. Oct. 1912.
DLC
1913   Feb. 6, 7, 22, Mar. 26, 27, Oct.
14, 22, 28.
Extraordinario: Oct. 22, 25.
1914   Apr. 9, 20–22, 24, 25, May 2, 6,
8, 19, 21, July 15–18, 21, 27,
Aug. 1, 12.
TxU
1912   Oct. 17, 19, 21–26, 28–Nov. 1,
4–9, 11–16, 18–22, 25–30,
Dec. 2–7, 9–14, 17, 19–21,
23, 24, 26–28, 30.
1913   Jan. 2–4, 6–11, 13–18, 20–
25, 27–Feb. 1, 3, 4, 6–8, 20–
22, 24–Mar. 1, 3–8, 10–15,
17–20, 22, 24–29, 31–Apr.
17, 19–May 4, 6–10, 13, 14,
16, 17, 20–24, 26, 28, 30, 31,
June 3–7, 9–11, 13–16, 19,
20, 23, 25–July 3, 5, 7–19, 21,
23, 25, 26, 28–Aug. 1, 4, 5, 22,
Sept. 1, 11, 13, 17, 22, 24, 25,
30, Oct. 1, 7, 8, 10, 11, 14, 18,
22, 23, 25, 27, 28, 30, Nov. 4, 10,
21, 22, 24, 25, 27, 28, Dec. 1, 5,
8, 9, 11, 15, 18, 19, 21, 22.
1914   Jan. 21, 26, Feb. 16, Mar. 23,
30, Apr. 8, 13, 20–25, 27, 29–
May 1, 4–6, 9, 29, June 8, 16,
July 11, 15, 16, 20–25, 27–
Aug. 1, 3–8, 10, 12, 14, 17, 24.

EL TRIBUNAL. w. est. 1913.
Note: Suspended publication Feb.
16–Mar. 9, 1913.
TxU
1913   Feb. 9, 23, Mar. 16.

EL TRIBUNAL. sw. est. June 21, 1916.
CU
1929   July 5.
DLC
1916   June 21.
Extraordinario: Aug. 2, Sept. 4.
MB
1916   July 14.

EL TRIBUNO DEL PUEBLO. 3w.
Note: Ceased publication Jan. 10,
1857.
CU–B
Micro (N)
1856   Aug. 19–Dec. 31.
1857   Jan. 1–10.

EL TRIUNFO DE LA REVOLUCION
DE 1913.
DLC
1913   Feb. 18.

EL TRUENO. sw. est. Feb. 12, 1847.
CU–B
Micro (N)
1847   Feb. 12–26.

THE TWO REPUBLICS. w., sw., d. est.
July 27, 1867.
Note: In English. Periodicity July 27–
Nov. 1, 1867, weekly; Nov. 2, 1867–
June 24, 1868, semiweekly; June 25,
1868–Jan. 26, 1869, weekly; Jan. 27–
May 12, 1869, semiweekly; May 13,
1869–Nov. 3, 1881, weekly; July 15,
1883–Nov. 30, 1900, daily. Suspended publication May 16–June 4,
1869. Superseded by *The Mexican
Herald.* Ceased publication Nov. 30,
1900. Additional edition published in
Monterey.
CLCM
1888   Dec. 12.
1889   Jan. 24.

CU–B
  Micro (P) & (N)
  1876   Jan. 5–Mar. 8, 22–Apr. 19,
         May 3–17, 31, June 28.
  1878   Jan. 5–12, 26–Feb. 2, 16–
         June 29, July 13–Sept. 28.
  1883   Oct. 4, 6, 7, 10, 11, 14, 21, Nov.
         27, Dec. 12, 23–25.
  1884   Jan. 6–8, Nov. 30, Dec. 7–9.
  1885   Mar. 22, July 5.
  1887   July 8.
  1888   Mar. 7, 9.
  1890   Jan. 5.
CtY
  1874   May 24–Dec. 31.
  1875–1879   Jan. 1–Dec. 31.
  1880   Jan. 1–Mar. 7.
DLC
  1867   July 27–Dec. 31.
  1868   Jan. 1–Dec. 31.
  1869   Jan. 1–Dec. 31.
         Supplement: Apr. 7.
  1870–1871   Jan. 1–Dec. 31.
  1872   Jan. 1–Dec. 31.
         Extra: Nov. 23, Dec. 14, 21.
  1873   Jan. 1–Dec. 31.
         Extra: Dec. 30.
  1874   Jan. 1–Dec. 31.
         Extra: Dec. 30.
  1875   Jan. 1–Dec. 31.
         Extra: Jan. 13, June 9.
  1876–1882   Jan. 1–Dec. 31.
  1883   Jan. 1–Oct. 15, 18–Dec. 17,
         19–31.
  1884   Jan. 1–Mar. 27, 29–Dec. 31.
  1885   Jan. 1–Apr. 20, 22–Nov. 20,
         22–Dec. 31.
  1886   Jan. 1–Dec. 31.
  1887   Jan. 1–Feb. 24, 26–Sept. 15,
         18–Nov. 3, 5–Dec. 31.
  1888–1889   Jan. 1–Dec. 31.
  1890   Jan. 1–Dec. 31.
         Supplement: Apr. 27–July 13.
  1891   Jan. 1–Dec. 31.
         Supplement: Jan. 4–Feb. 15,
         Apr. 5–June 28, July 19–Aug
         9, Sept. 13–Dec. 27.
  1892   Jan. 1–Dec. 31.

         Supplement: Jan. 3–Dec. 25.
  1893   Jan. 1–Dec. 31.
         Supplement: Jan. 1–May 28,
         June 11–Dec. 31.
  1894   Jan. 1–Dec. 31.
         Supplement: Jan. 7–Dec. 30.
  1895   Jan. 1–Dec. 31.
         Supplement: Jan. 6–Aug. 11,
         Sept. 1–Oct. 13, 27–Nov. 17.
  1896   Jan. 1–Apr. 9, 11–Dec. 31.
  1897   Jan. 1–Dec. 31.
  1898   Jan. 1–Oct. 5, 7–Dec. 31.
  1899   Jan. 1–Dec. 31.
  1900   Jan. 1–Feb. 10, 12–Mar. 31,
         Nov. 17.

KHi
  1883   Mar. 29.
  1890   Apr. 29–June 15.
  1896   Oct. 25–Dec. 31.
  1897   Jan. 1–Dec. 31.
  1898   Jan. 1–June 11.

MH
  1868   May 30–July 4.
  1869   Feb. 17–May 1, July 24–Aug.
         7, Sept. 25–Oct. 16, 30–Dec.
         25.
  1870   Jan. 1, 22–Dec. 3.
  1871   Jan. 7–Feb. 11.
  1872   Dec. 14, 21.
  1873   June 7.

MWA
  1867   Aug. 4, 24.
  1868   Feb. 26–Mar. 28, Aug. 22–
         Nov. 21.
  1869   July 3–Dec. 11.
  1870–1871   [Jan. 1–Feb. 18].
  1881   Mar. 6–13, Apr. 3–17, Oct. 2,
         16.
  1882   Oct. 29.
  1883   Aug. 9.
  1884   Jan. 22–27, 30, Feb. 2, 3, Dec.
         30.
  1885   Mar. 29–31.
  1892   Dec. 3.

ViU
  1898   Mar. 15.

ULTIMAS NOTICIAS. d.
  ICRL
    1942   [Sept. 24—Dec. 31].
    1943   [Jan. 1—Feb. 2].
  NjP
    1941   July 18, 19.

ULTIMAS NOTICIAS DE EXCELSIOR.
  d. est. 1935.
  DLC
    1941   July 24, 25, 28—31, Aug. 6.

LA UNIDAD CATOLICA. d. est. May 15,
  1861.
  CU—B
    Micro (P) & (N)
    1861   May 15—Dec. 31.
  TxU
    1861   Prospecto: May 1.
            May 15—Dec. 31.

LA UNION; PERIODICO POLITICO Y
  LITERARIO. sw. est. Nov. 11, 1840.
  DLC
    1840   Nov. 11—Dec. 31.
    1841   Jan. 1—Aug. 28.
            Suplemento: Jan. 16, Apr. 3.
  MWA
    1841   Jan. 2—Aug. 25.

LA UNION. d. est. Feb. 16, 1867.
  TxU
    1867   Feb. 16—June 9.

LA UNION; PERIODICO INDEPEN-
  DIENTE. est. July 10, 1870.
  MWA
    1870   July 10—Aug. 24.

LA UNION. 3w. est. Apr. 1880.
    Note: Ceased publication July 19,
    1880.
  TxU
    1880   May 12—July 19.

LA UNION LATINO-AMERICANA.
  DLC
    1914   Prospecto.

EL UNIVERSAL. est. Nov. 16, 1848.
    Note: Subtitle *periódico independi-
    ente*, Nov. 16, 1848—Mar. 1, 1854.

CU—B
    1849   June 1—Dec. 31.
    1850   Jan. 1—Dec. 31.
    1851   Jan. 1—31, Feb. 2—4, 6—July
            16, 18—Dec. 31.
    1852   Jan. 1—May 20, July 1—Oct.
            14, 16—Dec. 31.
    1853   Jan. 1—June 30.
  Micro (P) & (N)
    1848   Nov. 16—Dec. 31.
    1849—1854   Jan. 1—Dec. 31.
    1855   Jan. 1—Aug. 13.
  NHi
    1852   Jan. 7.
    1853   June 9.
  NN
    1851   Suplemento: June 3.

EL UNIVERSAL. d. est. [1888].
  LNT—MA
    1889   May 24, June 2—6, 8, 9, 16,
            July 24.
  MWA
    1895   Aug. 25.
  TxU
    1889   May 24.
    1890   Mar. 15, Nov. 8.
    1892   May 13.
    1893   May 12.
    1895   Oct. 29.

EL UNIVERSAL; PERIODICO INDE-
  PENDIENTE DE LA MAÑANA. d. est.
  Jan. 30, 1913.
    Note: Succeeded *El Imparcial*.
  DLC
    1913   Feb. 6, 11, 20, 22.
            Extraordinario: Feb. 19, 23.
  TxU
    1913   Jan. 30, Feb. 6, 10, 11, 21, Mar.
            3.

EL UNIVERSAL. d. est. Jan. 10, 1915.
  DLC
    1915   Jan. 10—16.

EL UNIVERSAL. d. est. Oct. 1, 1916.
    Note: Suspended publication Mar.
    30—Apr. 16, 1917.
  AzU
    1962   Jan. 1—Mar. 14, 16—23, 25—

Apr. 30, May 2 – June 7, 9 – 13,
15 – July 4, 6 – Aug. 6, 8 – Sept.
15, 17 – 29, Oct. 1 – 12, 14 –
Dec. 31.

1963   Jan. 1 – Apr. 30, May 2 – Aug.
2, 4 – Sept. 15, 17 – Nov. 19,
21 – Dec. 20, 22 – 31.

1964   Jan. 2, 4 – Mar. 16, 18 – Apr.
30. May 2 – Sept. 15, 17 – 23,
25 – Nov. 19, 21 – Dec. 3, 5 –
14, 16 – 24, 26 – 31.

1965   Jan. 2 – 14, 16 – 25, 27, 28, 30 –
Feb. 1, 3 – 28, Mar. 1 – 20, 22 –
Apr. 2, 4 – 22, 24 – May 3, 7 –
27, 29 – 31, June 2 – 7, Dec. 1 –
24, 26 – 31.

1966   Jan. 2 – Feb. 10, 12, 13+.

CLU

1942   June 1 – Dec. 31.
1943   Jan. 1 – Dec. 31.
1944   Feb. 1 – Dec. 31.
1945   Feb. 1 – Dec. 31.
1946   [Jan. 1 – Dec. 31].
1947   Jan. 1+.

CSt

1941   Aug. 1 – Sept. 31.
1945   Aug. 20 – 27.

CSt – H

1966   Jan. 14+.

CU

1917   Dec. 18, 20 – 31.
1918   Jan. 2 – Feb. 10, 12 – Apr. 14,
16 – May 2, 4 – Sept. 28.
1919   July 11, 13, 17 – Sept. 21, 23 –
27, 29 – Dec. 31.
1920   Jan. 1 – Apr. 23, 25 – May 6,
18 – 20, 22 – 31, June 2 – 9, 11,
13 – Aug. 6, 8 – 19, 21, 22, 24 –
30, Sept. 1 – Oct. 17, 19 – Nov.
22, 24 – Dec. 31.
1921   Jan. 1 – Apr. 12, 14 – May 1,
3 – June 25, 28 – July 19, 21 –
Aug. 10, 12 – 22, 25 – Sept. 16,
18 – Nov. 6, 8 – Dec. 18, 20 –
30.
1922   Jan. 1, 2, 4 – Mar. 11, 13 – 15,
17 – June 20.
1936   Jan. 30, Feb. 14.

1941   June 12, 13, July 28.
1945   May 27.

Micro (P)

1953   July 1 – Dec. 31.
1954 – 1955   Jan. 1 – Dec. 31.

DLC

1916   Oct. 1 – Dec. 31.
1917   Jan. 1 – Apr. 16, 18 – Dec. 31.
1918   Jan. 1 – June 30.
1919 – 1922   Jan. 1 – Dec. 31.
1923   Jan. 1 – Oct. 17, 19 – Dec. 1,
3 – 31.
1924   Jan. 1 – Apr. 6, 8 – 30, May 2 –
June 9, 11 – Dec. 31.
1925   Jan. 1 – Aug. 8, 11 – Dec. 29.
1926 – 1927   Jan. 1 – Dec. 31.
1928   Jan. 1 – Apr. 9, 11 – July 1, 3, 4,
6 – 9, 14 – Sept. 6, 9, 14 – 21,
23 – Dec. 31.
1929   Jan. 1 – Dec. 31.
1930   Jan. 1 – Sept. 30, Oct. 6 – 8, 12,
13, 17, 18, 22 – 28, Nov. 1 –
Dec. 31.
1931   Jan. 1 – Feb. 16, 18 – Dec. 31.

1932   Jan. 1 – 19, 21 – 31, Feb. 2, 3, 5,
6, 8, 9, 11, 13, 15 – 25, 29, Mar.
1, 4, 5, 8, 10, 11, 13, 15 – Apr. 3,
5, 7, 8, 10, 12, 14, 15, 17 – 19,
21 – 23, 25 – May 1, 5, 6, 8, 10 –
14, 17 – 21, 23 – 28, 30 – June 4,
7 – 11, 13, 14, 16 – 18, 20, 23 –
25, 27 – 30, July 2, 4, 5, 7, 8,
10 – 23, 25 – Aug. 6, 8, 9, 11 –
13, 15, 16, 18 – Sept. 10, 12 –
24, 26 – Oct. 1, 3 – 8, 11, 12, 14,
17 – Nov. 5, 8, 10, 11, 13 – 26,
28, Dec. 2, 3, 5, 6, 8, 9, 12, 14,
16, 19, 20, 22 – 24, 27 – 29, 31.

1933   Jan. 1 – 5, 7 – 9, 12, 13, 15 – 17,
19 – 23, 25 – Feb. 3, 5, 6, 8 –
17, 19, 20, 22 – 27, Mar. 1 – 11,
13 – 18, 20 – 25, 27, 28, 31 –
Apr. 4, 6, 8 – 15, 17 – 22, 24, 25,
27 – 29, May 3, 5 – 13, 15 – 21,
23, 24, 26 – 29, 31, June 2, 5, 6,
8 – 10, 12 – 14, 16 – 19, 22 –
July 18, 20 – Nov. 3, 5 – 8, 10 –
12, 14 – Dec. 8, 10 – 12, 14, 15,

17 – 21, 23 – 31.
1934   Jan. 1 – 10, 12 – Feb. 7, 9 – 13,
15, 16, 18, 20 – Mar. 14, 16 –
Apr. 28, 30 – May 9, 12 – 22,
24 – Nov. 16, 18 – 29, Dec. 1 –
31.
1935   Jan. 1 – 25, 28 – Mar. 9, 12 –
Apr. 25, 27, 29 – May 1, 3 –
Dec. 31.
1936   Jan. 1 – Mar. 14, 16 – 25, 27 –
29, 31 – July 18, 20 – 23, 25 –
Dec. 31.
1937   Jan. 1 – Dec. 31.
1938   Jan. 1 – Sept. 5, 7, 9 – Dec. 31.
1939   Jan. 1 – Sept. 1, 3 – 22, 24 –
Dec. 31.
1940   Jan. 1 – 14, 16 – Mar. 27, 29 –
May 29, 31 – June 14, 16 –
Aug. 25, 27 – Dec. 31.
1941   Jan. 1 – Dec. 31.
1942   Jan. 1 – Dec. 20, 22 – 31.
1943   Jan. 1 – July 26, 28 – Aug. 4,
6 – Sept. 25, 27 – Dec. 31.
1944   Jan. 1 – 16, 18 – Dec. 31.
1945   Jan. 1 – Dec. 31.
1946   Jan. 1 – Oct. 30, Nov. 1 – Dec.
31.
1947   Jan. 1 – 11, 13 – 22, 24 – Feb. 8,
11 – Oct. 4, 6 – 8, 10 – Nov. 10,
12 – Dec. 10, 12 – 31.
1948   Jan. 2 – Sept. 6, 8 – Dec. 17,
19 – 31.
Micro (P)
1949   Jan. 1+.
DPU
Current (six months).
Micro (P)
1938 – 1943   Jan. 1 – Dec. 31.
1946 – 1955   Jan. 1 – Dec. 31.
Micro (N)
1943   June 6 – Dec. 31.
1944 – 1945   Jan. 1 – Dec. 31.
ICRL
1928   Aug. 1 – Dec. 31.
1929 – 1932   Jan 1 – Dec. 31.
1933   Jan. 1 – June 30.
1835   Jan. 1 – June 30.
1941   Oct. 1 – Dec. 31.

1942 – 1949   Jan. 1 – Dec. 31.
1950   Jan. 1 – Mar. 31.
Micro (N)
1938 – 1955   Jan. 1 – Dec. 31.
(P) & (N)
1956   Jan. 1+.
IU
1950   Jan. 16 – Dec. 31.
1951 – 1954   Jan. 1 – Dec. 31.
1955   Jan. 1 – July 31.
InU
1945 – 1946   Jan. 1 – Dec. 31.
1947   Jan. 1 – June 30.
1966   Jan. 1+.
LNT – MA
1917   Sept. 3, Dec. 20 – 23.
1928   Jan. 18.
1932   Jan. 25, Oct. 18, 20.
1936   Dec. 3, 5.
1939   Aug. 5, 13.
1949 – 1952   [Jan. 1 – Dec. 31].
1953   Jan. 21, 22, 28, 29.
MB
1916   Oct. 13 – 17, 19 – 30, Nov. 1 –
3, 7, 15 – 18, 21, 22, Dec. 14, 15,
19, 21 – 23, 27 – 31.
1917   Jan. 1, 3 – 6, 8, 9, 11 – 17, 19,
21, 22, 24, 26, 27 – 30, Feb. 1, 2,
4, 7 – 19, 21, 23, 27, 28, Mar.
5 – 10, 13 – 15, 17 – 23, 27, 28,
Apr. 19 – 21, 23, 30, May 1, 3,
7 – 9, 11, 12, 14, 16, 19, 21, 22,
24, 28 – 31.
MH
1925   Jan. 25.
1928   July 12.
Micro (P)
1943   June 1 – Dec. 31.
1944 – 1955   Jan. 1 – Dec. 31.
MiEM
1965   Jan. 1+.
MoU
Micro (P)
1943   June 1 – Dec. 31.
1944 – 1964   Jan. 1 – Dec. 31.
1965   Jan. 1 – Nov. 30.
NBuU
Current (three months).

NN
- 1933   July 1 – Sept. 15, 17 – Dec. 9,
11, 12, 14 – 31.
- 1934   Jan. 1 – 10, 12 – Feb. 4, 6, 7,
9 – 13, 15, 16, 18, 20 – Mar. 11,
13, 14, 16 – Apr. 28, 30 – May 9,
11 – 22, 24 – 31, June 2, 3, 5, 6,
8 – 15, 17 – 21, 23 – July 3, 5 –
20, 22 – Aug. 8, 10 – 27, 29 –
Nov. 4, 6 – Dec. 31.
- 1935   Jan. 1 – May 1, 3 – Dec. 31.
- 1936   Jan. 1 – May 9, 11 – July 31,
Aug. 2 – Dec. 31.
- 1937   Jan. 1 – 19, 21 – May 22, 24 –
June 17, 19 – July 15, 17 – 21,
23 – Sept. 25, 27 – Dec. 31.
- 1938   Jan. 1 – 17, 19 – Aug. 18, 20 –
Dec. 6, 8 – 31.
- 1939   Jan.1 – Mar. 30, Apr. 1 – 29,
May 1 – July 7, 9 – Dec. 31.
- 1940   Jan. 1 – 26, 28 – Mar. 5, 7 –
Sept. 19, 21 – Dec. 31.
- 1941   Jan. 1 – Apr. 15, 17 – Nov. 9,
11, 13 – Dec. 15, 17 – 25, 27 –
31.
- 1942   Jan. 1 – Mar. 23, 25 – July 5,
7 – Nov. 30, Dec. 2 – 31.
- 1943   Jan. 1 – May 30, June 1 – Aug.
17, 19, 20, 22, 23, 25 – Nov. 30,
Dec. 2 – 9, 11 – 31.
- 1944   Jan. 1, 4 – 6, 8 – Mar. 25, 27 –
June 17, 19 – July 31, Aug. 2 –
Oct. 24, 26 – Nov. 20, 22 – Dec.
2, 4 – 15, 17 – 20, 22 – 31.
- 1945   Jan. 1 – Mar. 20, 22 – Apr. 15,
17 – May 5, 7, 9 – June 9, 11 –
13, 15 – 23, 26 – July 7, 9 –
13, 15 – Aug. 6, 8 – 28, 30 –
Sept. 2, 4 – 29, Oct. 1 – Nov.
10, 12 – 14, 16, 17, 19 – 24, 26 –
Dec. 16, 19, 21 – 23, 27 – 31.
- 1946   Jan. 1 – Feb. 19, 21 – Mar. 2,
4 – 8, 11 – 15, 17 – 19, 22 – Apr.
7, 9 – 24, 26, 27, 30 – May 11,
13 – June 22, 24 – 27, 30 – July
6, 8, 10 – 12, 17, 19, 22 – Aug. 3,
5 – 10, 12 – 17, 19, 21 – 23, 26 –
31, Sept. 2, 4 – 7, 9, 10, 12, 19,

20, 22 – 28, 30 – Oct. 4, 6 – 9,
11 – 18, 21 – 23, 25, 26, 28 –
30, Nov. 1 – Dec. 1, 3, 4, 6, 7, 9,
11, 13 – 24.
- 1947   Jan. 4, 7 – 11, 13 – 24, 27 – Feb.
1, 3 – 8, 10 – 12, 14, 16 – Mar.
1, 3 – 8, 10 – 12, 14, 15, 17 –
22, 24 – 28, 31 – Apr. 11, 14,
17, 18, 21, 23, 27 – May 9, 11 –
19, 21 – June 9, 11, 13, 15 – 28,
30 – July 15, 17 – 19, 21 – 24,
Aug. 1 – Oct. 16, 18 – 23, 25 –
30, Nov. 1 – 10, 12 – 14, 16 –
Dec. 1, 4, 5, 7 – 31.
- 1948   Jan. 1 – 17, 19 – Feb. 18, 20 –
Apr. 14, 16, 17, 19 – May 3, 8 –
June 14, 16 – July 20, 22 – Sept.
6, 8 – 15, 17 – Dec. 5, 7 – 28, 30,
31.
- 1949   Jan. 1 – Apr. 21, 23 – Dec. 12,
14 – 16, 18 – 31.
- 1950   Jan. 1 – Sept. 14, 17 – Oct. 14,
17 – Nov. 29, Dec. 1 – 10, 12 –
17, 19, 21 – 28, 30, 31.

Micro (P)
- 1951   Jan. 1+.

NSyU
- 1960   Jan. 15 – Dec. 31.
- 1961   Jan. 1+.

NcD
- 1927   Oct. 1, 4, 6, 8 – Dec. 14, 16 – 19,
24 – 31.
- 1928   Jan. 2 – Mar. 15, 18, 20 – Apr.
30, May 2 – Dec. 29, 31.
- 1929   Jan. 2 – 5, 7 – Apr. 30, May 2 –
Aug. 11, 13 – 31.
- 1930   Jan. 1 – 17, 19 – Apr. 30, May
2 – Dec. 31.
- 1931   Jan. 1 – Dec. 31.
- 1932   Jan. 1 – Feb. 6, 8 – 27, 29 – Apr.
23, 25 – May 1, 3 – 14, 16 – 21,
23 – June 4, 6 – 11, 13 – 18, 20,
22 – 25, 27 – 30, July 2, 4, 5, 7,
8, 10 – 23, 25 – Aug. 6, 8, 9,
11 – 13, 15, 16, 18 – Sept. 10,
12 – 24, 26 – Oct. 1, 4 – 8, 11,
12, 14, 17 – Nov. 5, 8, 10, 13 –
26, 28, Dec. 1 – 3, 5, 6, 8, 11, 12,

14, 16, 19, 22 – 24, 27 – 29, 31.
1933 – 1938   Jan. 1 – Dec. 31.
1939   Jan. 1 – June 1, 2, 4 – Dec. 31.
1940   Jan. 1 – Nov. 30.
1941 – 1942   Jan. 1 – Dec. 31.
1943   Jan. 1 – Feb. 29, Apr. 1 – 30,
    July 1 – Aug. 31, Oct. 1 – 31.
NjP
1941   Aug. 1, 3.
1942   Aug. 23.
NmU
1921   Feb. 23, 24, May 23 – Dec. 31.
1922   Jan. 1 – Dec. 31.
1923   Jan. 1 – Aug. 9.
Micro (N)
1934   Jan. 1 – Dec. 31.
1938   Jan. 1 – 31.
OCl
1954   Aug. 14 – Dec. 31.
1955   June 1+.
OkU
1952   May 2 – Dec. 31.
1953   Jan. 1+.
PSt
Current (one month).
PrU
Micro (P)
1961   Nov. 1 – 6, 8 – 19, 21 – Dec. 31.
1962   Jan. 2 – Feb. 2, 5, 6, Mar. 14,
    16 – 21, 23 – Apr. 30, May 2 –
    19, 21, 24 – June 15, 17 – Aug.
    2, 4 – Sept. 15, 17 – 27, 29 –
    Oct. 28, 30 – Nov. 19, 21, 23 –
    Dec. 24, 26 – 30.
1964   Jan. 2 – 15, 17 – 30, Feb. 1 –
    Apr. 7, 10, 12, 20 – 22, May 16,
    17, June 8, 12.
1965   Jan. 5, 6, 9 – Feb. 4, 6 – Mar. 20,
    22 – Apr. 18, 20 – 29, May 2 – 4,
    6 – 11, 13, 15 – 18, 20 – 25, 27,
    29 – June 15, 17, 19 – Sept. 14,
    17 – 27, 30 – Oct. 2, 4, 6, 9 – 11,
    21 – 30, Nov. 1 – 6, 8 – 19, 21 –
    Dec. 24, 26 – 31.
1966   Jan. 1+.
TxU
1916   Oct. 1 – Dec. 31.
1917   Jan. – 26, 28 – Dec. 31.

1918   Jan. 1 – Dec. 31.
1919   Jan. 1 – Nov. 25, 27 – Dec. 9,
    11 – 31.
1920   Jan. 2 – May 24, 26 – 31, June
    6, 7, 12 – 14, 16, 20, 27 – July
    1, 4, 5, 7, 11, 18, 25, Aug. 1,
    7 – 9, 15, 22, 29, Sept. 12, 25,
    Oct. 10, 13, 17, 24, Nov. 7, 8,
    15, 28, Dec. 4 – 10, 12.
1921   Mar. 27, Aug. 14.
1924   Jan. 1 – Mar. 1, 3 – Apr. 7, 9 –
    17, 19 – 30, May 2 – Nov. 14,
    16 – Dec. 31.
1925   Jan. 1 – Feb. 18, 20, 21, 23,
    25 – Mar. 3, 5 – Apr. 9, 11 – 21,
    23 – 25, 27 – 30, May 2 – 5, 8 –
    16, 18 – Dec. 31.
1926   Jan. 1 – 16, 18 – Feb. 15, 17 –
    Apr. 30, May 2 – June 25, 27 –
    Sept. 2, 4 – Oct. 13, 15 – Dec. 4,
    6 – 31.
1927   Jan. 1 – Apr. 1 – 30, May 3 –
    June 30, July 2 – Sept. 11, 13 –
    Dec. 31.
1928   Jan. 1 – Mar. 17, 19 – Apr. 1 –
    30, May 2 – Dec. 31.
1929   Jan. 1 – Apr. 1 – 30, May 2 –
    Oct. 7, 9 – Dec. 31.
1930   Jan. 1 – 30, Feb. 1 – Sept. 2,
    4 – Oct. 7, 9 – 18, 20 – Dec.
    17, 19 – 31.
1931   Jan. 1 – 24, 26 – Feb. 20, 22 –
    Oct. 27, 30 – Dec. 31.
1932   Jan. 11 – Feb. 88 – 13, 15 – 26,
    Mar. 1, 4 – 8, 10 – Apr. 3, 5, 8 –
    10, 12, 14, 15, 17 – 19, 21, 23 –
    June 4, 7 – 11, 13, 14, 16 – 18,
    20, 23 – 25 – Aug. 6, 8, 9, 11 –
    13, 15 – Sept. 10, 12 – 23, 26 –
    Dec. 31.
1936   Oct. 1 – Dec. 31.
1937   Jan. 1 – Feb. 28, June 14 – 16,
    20 – July 23.
1938   Feb. 2 – May 1, 3 – Dec. 31.
1939   Jan. 1 – Nov. 20, 22 – Dec. 25,
    28 – 31.
1940   Jan. 1 – Apr. 30, May 1 – Dec.
    30.

1941   Jan. 1 – Dec. 31.
1942   Jan. 1 – Apr. 15, 18 – June 27,
         29 – Dec. 31.
1943   Jan. 1 – Dec. 31.
1944   Jan. 18 – 24, 26 – Feb. 4, 6 –
         14, 16 – Apr. 2, 4 – 14, 16 – 27,
         29, May 1 – July 31, Aug. 2 –
         30, Sept. 1 – 16, 18 – Oct. 2,
         4 – 15, 17 – 25, 27 – Nov. 11,
         13 – 19, 22 – Dec. 2, 5 – 10, 12 –
         20, 22, 24, 27 – 31.
1945   Feb. 1 – Mar. 1, 3 – May 1, 3 –
         Dec. 30.
1946   Jan. 1 – 31, Apr. 1 – July 6, 8,
         10 – 12, 16, 17, 19, 20, 22 – 30,
         Aug. 1 – 3, 5 – 10, 12 – 17, 19,
         21 – 23, 25 – 31, Sept. 2, 4 – 7,
         9, 10, 12, 17, 19 – Oct. 4, 6 – 18,
         20 – 23, 25, 26, 28 – 30, Nov. 1,
         2, 4 – 7, 9, 11, 16 – 23, 25 – 29,
         Dec. 3, 4, 6 – 9, 11, 13 – 24.
1947   Jan. 8 – 11, 13 – 18, 21, 22, 24,
         27 – Feb. 12, 14, 16 – Mar. 1,
         3 – 24, 26 – Apr. 10, 12 – 17, 19,
         20, 22 – May 10, 12, 14 – June
         6, 8 – 13, 15 – July 7, 9 – Aug. 8,
         10 – Oct. 3, 5 – 17, 19 – Nov. 10,
         12, 13, 16 – Dec. 1, 3, 4, 6, 8 –
         31.
1948   Jan. 1 – Feb. 6, 8 – 26, 28 –
         Mar. 4, 6 – May 4, 6 – Sept. 25,
         27 – Dec. 31.
1949   Jan. 1 – July 14, 16 – Dec. 31.
1950 – 1952   Jan. 1 – Dec. 31.
ViU
1944   Jan. 3.
1949   Nov. 13.
1950   Jan. 22, Feb. 19, 26, Mar. 3,
         May 4, 28, June 11, 25, July 9,
         16, 30, Aug. 6, 13, 20, 26, Sept.
         1, 3, 10, 24, Oct. 1.
1952   Jan. 1 – Mar. 20, 22 – Apr. 30,
         May 2 – July 31, Aug. 2 – Sept.
         15, 17 – Oct. 13, 15, 16, 18 –
         27, 29 – Dec. 1, 3 – 11, 13, 14,
         16 – 21, 23, 24, 26 – 30.
1953   Jan. 1 – Mar. 20, 22 – Oct. 9,
         11 – 16, 18 – Nov. 19, 21 – Dec.

         24, 26 – 31.
1954   Jan. 1 – Apr. 30, May 2 – Sept.
         15, 17 – Nov. 19, 21 – Dec. 14,
         16 – 24, 26 – 31.
1955   Jan. 1 – 5, 7 – 9, 13 – Mar. 20,
         22 – Apr. 30, May 2 – Sept. 15,
         17 – Nov. 19, 21 – Dec. 24, 26 –
         31.
1956   Jan. 1 – Mar. 20, 22 – Sept. 13,
         15 – Dec. 31.
1957   Jan. 1 – 20.
WU
  Micro (P)
1949 – 1951   Jan. 1 – Dec. 31.
1952   Jan. 1 – Feb. 29.
WaU
1961   Nov. 17 – Dec. 31.
1962   Jan. 1+.

EL UNIVERSAL GRAFICO. d. est. Feb.
1, 1922.
CU
1929   July 8 – 13, 15 – 18, 20, 22.
DLC
1942   Dec. 1 – 31.
1943   Jan. 1 – Apr. 9, 11 – 16, 18, 20 –
         Dec. 31.
1944   Jan. 1 – 11, 13 – 26, 28 – Apr. 5,
         7 – 30, May 2, 4 – Dec. 31.
1945   Jan. 1 – Apr. 23, 25 – Aug. 30,
         Sept. 1 – Nov. 8, 10 – Dec. 19,
         21 – 31.
1946   Jan. 1 – Apr. 2, 4, 5, 7 – 12, 14 –
         17, 19 – 25, 27 – 30, May 3 – 10,
         12 – 21, 23, 25 – June 14, 16 –
         27, 29 – July 25, 27 – Nov. 6,
         8 – Dec. 25, 27 – 31.
1947   Jan. 1, 3, 5 – 22, 25 – Feb. 17,
         20 – Apr. 7, 9 – 27, 29, 30, May
         2 – Sept. 1, 3 – Nov. 7, 9 – 20,
         22 – Dec. 31.
1948   Jan. 1 – July 1, 3 – Aug. 10,
         12 – Oct. 29, 31 – Nov. 5, 7 –
         Dec. 5, 7 – 31.
1949   Jan. 1 – 31, Feb. 2 – 6, 8 – Mar.
         2, 4 – May 4, 6 – Oct. 11, 14 –
         Nov. 2, 4 – Dec. 31.
1950   Jan. 1 – 20, 22, 24 – Apr. 17,

19—Sept. 19, 21—Nov. 2, 4—
14, 16—Dec. 31.

1951   Jan. 1—Mar. 20, 22—May 22,
25—July 8, 10—18, 20—Aug.
31, Sept. 2—Oct. 18, 21—Dec.
31.

1952   Jan. 1—16, 19—Feb. 25, 27—
Mar. 27, 30—Apr. 13, 16, 17,
20, 21, 23—May 12, 14, 15,
17—June 1, 5—Aug. 31, Sept.
2, 3, 5—Oct. 1, 3—5, 7—Dec.
11, 13—31.

1953   Jan. 1—16, 18—23, 25—May 5,
7—July 7, 9—31, Aug. 2—
Sept. 7, 9—Oct. 14, 16—20,
22—Dec. 31.

1954   Jan. 1—June 18, 20—July 27,
29—Oct. 17, 19—Nov. 17, 19—
Dec. 22, 24—31.

1955   Jan. 1—25, 27—Mar. 27, 29—
Apr. 18, 20—22, 24, 25, 27,
29—May 15, 19—Aug. 9, 11—
Sept. 22, 24—28, 30—Nov. 11,
13—28, 30—Dec. 31.

1956   Jan. 1—3, 5—Mar. 28, 30—
Apr. 11, 13—June 26, 29—Aug.
22, 24—Oct. 21, 23—Nov. 1,
3—Dec. 31.

1957   Jan. 1—Mar. 20, 22—24, 26—
Apr. 9, 11—May 8, 10—23,
25—June 10, 12—July 4, 6—
24, 26—30, Aug. 1, 3—5, 7—28,
30—Sept. 15, 17—25, 27—Oct.
2, 4—10, 13—15, 18—Dec. 11,
13—31.

1958   Jan. 1—20, 22, 23, 25—Feb. 28,
Mar. 2, 4—31, Apr. 2—May 21,
23—27, 29—July 11, 13—Dec.
31.

1959   Jan. 1—Apr. 8, 10—Sept. 13,
15—Dec. 14, 16—31.

1960   Jan. 2—Mar. 2, 4—May 13, 15
—Oct. 12, 14—Nov. 10, 12, 13,
15—Dec. 31.

1961   Jan. 2—Mar. 31, Apr. 3—5, 7—
June 19, 21—Oct. 10, 12—Nov.
13, 15—27, 29—Dec. 14, 16—
30.

Micro (P) & (N)
1962   Jan. 1+.
LNT—MA
1930   Feb. 6.
NN
Micro (P) & (N)
1924   Mar. 1, 3—22, 26, 27, 29—Apr.
1, 3, 4, 8—17, 19, 21, 23, 25,
28—30.
NjP
1941   Aug. 20.
TxU
1924   Sept. 19, 25, 26, Oct. 6, 15.

EL UNIVERSAL ILUSTRADO.
TxU
1920   June 3.

EL UNIVERSO. w. est. Oct. 8, 1864.
CU—B
Micro (N)
1864   Oct. 8—Nov. 28.

UYUYUY. w. est. Aug. 24, 1914.
TxU
1914   Aug. 24.

EL VACILON. w. est. 1914.
TxU
1914   June 21.

EL VALECITO DEL PUEBLO Y PARA
EL PUEBLO. w. est. 1911.
TxU
1911   Apr. 6.

EL VALEDOR; PERIODICO JOCO-
SERIO, LADINO, CHISMOSO MEDI-
CO, LOCO Y DE TODO UN POCO. w.
est. Dec. 1, 1884.
TxU
1884   Dec. 1—31.
1885   Jan. 1—July 20, Aug. 24, Sept.
14, Oct. 26, Nov. 23.

EL VALEDOR. w. est. 1911.
TxU
1911   Oct. 17.

EL VALEPANCHITO. w. est. Sept. 3,
1911.
TxU
1911   Sept. 3—17, Oct. 1—29.

LA VANGUARDIA. d. est. Oct. 16, 1920.
  TxU
    1920   Oct. 16, Nov. 27.

EL VAPOR. d. est. Dec. 30, 1858.
    Note: Ceased publication Feb. 28,
    1859.
  CU–B
    Micro (N)
    1858   Dec. 30, 31.
    1859   Jan. 1–Feb. 28.

VERACRUZ. d. est. June 2, 1914.
  DLC
    1914   June 3, 5, 6, 9, 10, 12, 13, 15–
            19.
            Extraordinario: July 29.
  TxU
    1914   June 4, 5, 8.
            Extraordinario: July 27.

VERDA STELO.
    Note: In Spanish and Esperanto.
  TxU
    1908   Oct.

LA VERDAD. d. est. July 1, 1854.
    Note: Suspended publication Jan. 2–
    Aug. 14. 1855; ceased publication
    Jan. 1, 1856.
  CU–B
    Micro (N)
    1854   July 1–Dec. 31.
    1855   Jan. 1, Aug. 15–Dec. 31.
    1856   Jan. 1.

LA VERDAD; PERIODICO POLITICO
JUSTICIERO NOTICIOSO. 3w.
  NN
    1861   Dec. 14–17.

LA VERDAD; DIARIO SIN SUBVEN-
CION. d. est. Feb. 1, 1907.
  TxU
    1907   Feb. 1, 2, 6, 7, 9.

LA VERDAD. sw. est. [Feb. 24], 1912.
  TxU
    1912   Feb. 28–Mar. 23, 30–Apr. 4,
            13–17, 24–May 15, 22–25.

LA VERDAD. d. est. Apr. 5, 1915.
  DLC
    1915   Apr. 5, 7, 9, 19, May 1, 3, 7, 17
            –19, 21, 22, 25, 26, 28, 29,
            June 1, 3, 7–21, 28.
            Extraordinario: [Mar. 12], Apr.
            8, 17, 20–24, 26–28, 30, May
            4–6, 8, 10–14, June 22–26,
            29–July 3.
  TxU
    1915   Apr. 6, 20, May 21, June 8–11,
            14–16.

LA VERDAD. d., 3w. est. Nov. 29, 1917.
    Note: Periodicity Nov. 29, 1917–
    Sept. 6, 1918, daily; after Nov. 29,
    1918, three times a week.
  TxU
    1917   Nov. 30–Dec. 1, 4–7, 10, 11,
            13, 15–18, 20–29.
    1918   Jan. 2–9, 11–Feb. 6, 8–12,
            14, 15, 18, 19, 21–Mar. 18,
            21–Apr. 16, 18–27, 30–May
            3, 6–8, 10–13, 15–20, 22–
            July 8, 10–Aug. 9, 12, 13, 15–
            20, 22, 24–Sept. 24, 28–Oct.
            10, 24.

LA VERDAD AMARGA, PERO ES PRE-
CISO DECIRLA. est. 1820.
    Note: Ceased publication [Oct. 13],
    1821.
  CtY
    1820   n.d. (No. 1).
    1821   n.d.–Oct. 13 (Nos, 2, 4, 5).

VESPER. w., sw. est. 1901.
  LNT–MA
    1905   Feb. 1.
  TxU
    1909   Apr. 18.
    1910   May 8, 16, June 2, 15.
    1911   Oct. 29.

EL VESPERTINO. d. est. Sept. 26, 1917.
  DLC
    1917   Sept. 26–Oct. 5.

EL VIGILANTE. w.
  TxU
    1880   Apr. 25–May 15, June 4–27.

EL VIOLIN. sw. est. Nov. 20, 1862.
Note: Ceased publication [Nov. 30],
1862.
CU – B
Micro (N)
1862   Nov. 20 – 30.
CtY
1862   Nov. 23 – 30.

EL VOTO. w., sw. est. 1912.
DLC
1913   Apr. 21 – May 1.
1916   Dec. 26.
1917   Jan. 5, 14, Feb. 12, May 5.
TxU
1913   Apr. 3 – May 1.
Extraordinario: May 7.

EL VOTO NACIONAL. est. Dec. 11, 1837.
CU – B
Micro (P)
1838   Sept. 25.
CtY
1838   Sept. 11, 25 – 28.
Suplemento: Oct. 26.
NN
1838   Mar. 14, Sept. 11.
TxU
1838   Mar. 23.

LA VOZ COAHUILENSE. d. est. Apr.
1914.
DLC
1914   Apr. 24.

LA VOZ DE ESPAÑA MODERNA. d., 3w.
est. [1879].
Note: Title *La Voz de España*, 1879 –
Apr. 9, 1881; *La Voz de España moderna*, after Apr. 9, 1881.
LNT – MA
1881   Feb. 2.
MWA
1880   May 11.
1881   Mar. 31 – Apr. 9, 21 – 28, May
2 – 12, June 9 – 14, Aug. 6 – 9.
TxU
1885   Aug. 13, Sept. 3.

LA VOZ DE HIDALGO. w. est. Feb. 5,
1910.

TxU
1910   Feb. 5 – Mar. 28.

LA VOZ DE JUAREZ. sw., 3w., w. est.
1891.
Note: Established in San Antonio,
Texas; removed to Mexico City, Dec.
1901.
DLC
1913   Feb. 19, Apr. 10 – 30.
Extraordinario: Feb. 18, 19.
1914   Aug. 6 – 27.
Extraordinario: Aug. 9, 14,
Dec. 15.
TxU
1909   June 26 – 30.
1911   Aug. 13.
1913   Jan. 2, Feb. 19, Apr. 10 – 30.
1914   Aug. 6, 7, 20 – 27.

LA VOZ DE JUAREZ. w. est. Mar. 16,
1919.
DLC
1919   Mar. 16 – Apr. 8.

LA VOZ DE LERDO. est. May 21, 1919.
DLC
1919   May 21.

LA VOZ DE LA FRONTERA. est. 1880.
TxU
1880   Aug. 15 – Sept. 6.

LA VOZ DE LA NACION. est. [May]
1860.
CtY
1860   May 30.

VOZ DE LA PATRIA. irr. est. 1828.
Note: Ceased publication Oct. 14,
1831.
CtY
1828   [Mar. 1 – Dec. 31].
1829 – 1830   Jan. 1 – Dec. 31.
1831   Jan. 1 – Oct. 14.
LNHT
1828   [Mar. 1 – 31].
1829   Jan. 13, 28, Mar. 26, Apr. 1 –
Aug. 31.
1831   Aug. 18.

LA VOZ DE LA RELIGION. sw.
  CtY
    1848   July 19 – Dec. 30.
    1849   July 4 – Dec. 29.

LA VOZ DE MADERO. w. est. July 25,
  1914.
  DLC
    1914   July 25 – Sept. 27, Oct. 25.
  TxU
    1914   July 25 – Aug. 23, Sept. 6, 27.

LA VOZ DE MEXICO. d., w. est. Apr. 17,
  1870.
  CU – B
    1870   Apr. 17 – Dec. 31.
    1871 – 1873   Jan. 1 – Dec. 31.
    1874   Jan. 1 – June 28, July 1 –
            Dec. 31.
    1875 – 1881   Jan. 1 – Dec. 31.
    1882   Jan. 1 – [Dec. 31].
  NN
    Micro (P) & (N)
    1939   Mar. 23, 25 – 28, Apr. 1 – 28,
            30 – May 3, 5 – 14, 16 – June
            14, July 2 – Aug. 12, 14 – Oct.
            28, 30 – Nov. 3, 5 – Dec. 2, 4 –
            17.
    1940   Jan. 1 – 6, 8 – 13, 15 – May 4,
            6 – July 20, Aug. 4 – Dec. 31.
    1941   Jan. 1 – Dec. 31.
    1942   Jan. 1 – 3, 5 – 10, 12 – Oct. 10,
            12 – Dec. 31.
    1943   Jan. 1 – Dec. 31.
    1944   Jan. 1 – Feb. 27.
  NjP
    1942   Aug. 23.
  TxU
    1879   Jan. 5, May 18, June 26, July
            17, Nov. 16, 30.
    1880   Mar. 14, Sept. 16.
    1881   Feb. 1, Aug. 18.
    1884   July 11.
    1885   Oct. 20.
    1886   Jan. 1 – July 8, 10 – Sept. 1 –
            30, Oct. 2 – Dec. 31.
    1887   Jan. 1 – Oct. 1, 4 – Dec. 31.
    1888 – 1894   Jan. 1 – Dec. 31.
    1895   Jan. 1 – July 27, 30 – Dec. 31.

    1896   Jan. 1 – Aug. 15, 18 – Dec. 31.
    1897 – 1898   Jan. 1 – Dec. 31.
    1899   Jan. 1 – Dec. 12, 14 – 31.
    1900 – 1901   Jan. 1 – Dec. 31.
    1902   Jan. 1 – 30, Feb. 1 – Dec. 31.
    1903   Jan. 1 – Dec. 31.
    1904   Jan. 3 – Mar. 19, 22 – 31, Apr.
            15 – Dec. 31.
    1905 – 1907   Jan. 1 – Dec. 31.
    1908   Jan. 1 – Oct. 21, 23 – Dec. 1,
            3 – 9, 15 – 18, 20 – 31.
    1909   Jan. 1, 5 – 21, 29.

LA VOZ DEL NORTE. w. est. Feb. 24,
  1918.
  DLC
    1918   Feb. 24, Mar. 7.

LA VOZ DEL PACIFICO. [w].
  TxU
    1880   July 24, Aug. 21, Nov. 6 – 27.

LA VOZ DEL PAIS. d. est. Dec. 7, 1914.
  DLC
    1914   Dec. 7, 14.
            Extraordinario: Dec. 5.
  TxU
    1914   Dec. 7.
            Extraordinario: Dec. 5.

LA VOZ DEL PUEBLO. sw. est. Jan. 25,
  1845.
    Note: Ceased publication Dec. 31,
    1845.
  CU – B
    Micro (N)
    1845   Jan. 25 – Sept. 3.
  CtY
    1845   Tomo 2, Nos. 3, 5, 6, 21, 22.
  NN
    1845   July 9.
  TxU
    1845   Jan. 25 – Dec. 31.

LA VOZ DEL PUEBLO. sw. est. May 25,
  1913.
  TxU
    1913   May 25 – June 5, 12 – 22, July
            6, 13, 20 – 27, Aug. 24.

VOZ PATRONAL. w., irr.
  IU
    1947   Nov. 8 – Dec. 31.
    1948 – 1951   Jan. 1 – Dec. 31.
    1952   Jan. 1 – Feb. 2.

LA VOZ POPULAR. w. est. 1909.
  TxU
    1909   June 29.

VULCANO. w. est. Dec. 26, 1909.
  TxU
    1909   Dec. 26.

YANKEE DOODLE. w. est. Nov. 18,
  1847.
    Note: In Spanish and English.
  NN
    1847   Dec. 6.

EL YUNQUE. w. est. Jan. 13, 1910.
  TxU
    1910   Jan. 13 – 20.

ZAPATA. w. est. Oct. 1, 1912.
  TxU
    1912   Oct. 1.

EL ZURRIAGO DE LOS DE LA ACOR-
  DADA.
  NN
    1829   Aug. 22.

EL ZURRIAGO LITERARIO. w. est. Aug.
  27, 1839.
    Note: Ceased publication June 25,
    1840.
  TxU
    1839   Aug. 27 – Dec. 31.
    1840   Jan. 1 – 25.

Minatitlan

LA OPINION. d. est. 1934.
  DLC
    1941   Apr. 20 – Aug. 3, 5 – 23, 25 –
    Sept. 23.

Mocorito

VOZ DEL NORTE. w. est. 1891.
  TxU
    1912   Feb. 24.

Monclova

JUSTICIA. w. est. Aug. 13, 1911.
  TxU
    1911   Aug. 13.

Monterrey

THE AMERICAN PIONEER.
    Note: In English.
  MBAt
    1847   Apr. 19.
  TxU
    1847   May 20, 31.
  WaU
    1847   Feb. 22, Mar. 8, 29, Apr. 5, 20.

BOLETIN OFICIAL.
  CtY
    1840   No. 1.
    1846   Nos. 3, 6, 7.

EL CENTINELA DE NUEVO LEON.
  CtY
    1841   Vol. 3, Nos. 2 – 4.
  TxSjM
    1841   July 3, Aug. 14.
    1842   Jan. 22, Mar. 12, 26.

EL CUARTO PODER. w. est. 1911.
  TxU
    1911   Sept. 24.

LA DEMOCRACIA. sw. est. Aug. 27,
  1911.
  TxU
    1911   Aug. 27.

LA EPOCA. d. est. 1915.
  DLC
    1915   Apr. 11, 14, 17, 19.

EL ESPECTADOR. d. est. Oct. 1896.
  TxU
    1905   Mar. 2.

GACETA ESTRAORDINARIA DE
  NUEVO LEON.
  CtY
    1827   Mar. 14.

THE GAZETTE.
>   Note: In English.
>   CtY
>   1847 – 1848   Vol. 1, Nos. 17, 43.

EL HERALDO FERROCARRILERO.
>   est Jan. 1, 1912.
>   TxU
>   1912   Jan. 1.

LA LUZ. w. est. [1874].
>   CU – B
>   1877   Mar. 25, Apr. 1, 29, May 27,
>   June 3, 17 – July 8, 29, Aug.
>   26.
>   1878   Feb. 24, Aug. 25.

MERCURY. w. est. June 22, 1895.
>   CU – B
>   1895   June 22 – Dec. 31.
>   1896   Jan. 1 – Mar. 21.

MEXICAN-AMERICAN. d. est. Mar. 31,
1912.
>   Note: In English.
>   TxU
>   1912   Mar. 31.

THE MONTERREY NEWS. d. est. Apr.
23, 1892.
>   Note: English edition only until 1902;
>   English and Spanish editions, 1902 –
>   1911; after 1911, Spanish edition only.
>   DLC
>   1902   July 1 – 7, 10 – 23, 27 – Nov. 5,
>   8 – Dec. 31.
>   1903   Jan. 1 – Feb. 4, 6, 7, 9 – Dec.
>   31.
>   1904   Jan. 1 – Feb. 24, 26 – July 21,
>   23 – 28, 30 – Aug. 5, 7 – 14,
>   16 – 22, 24 – Sept. 23, 25, 27 –
>   Dec. 31.
>   1905 – 1908   Jan. 1 – Dec. 31.
>   1909   Jan. 6 – Aug. 27, 29 – Nov. 17,
>   19 – Dec. 31.
>   1910   Jan. 1 – Dec. 31.
>   1911   Jan. 1 – Mar. 18.
>   TxU
>   1906   Mar. 21.

MONTERREY TIMES-TRIBUNE. w.
>   Note: In English. Title *Monterrey
>   Times*, before 1930; *Monterrey Times-
>   Tribune*, after 1930. Absorbed the
>   *Tampico Tribune* 1930.
>   LNT – MA
>   1930   July 5.
>   1931   July 18 – Oct. 10.
>   1933   May 20 – June 16, Aug. 5,
>   Sept. 2.

MORNING STAR. w.
>   Note: In English.
>   MBAt
>   1864   Mar. 25.
>   NHi
>   1864   Mar. 25.

EL NIVEL.
>   CtY
>   1835   Tomo 1, No. 18.

EL NORTE. d. est. Sept. 15, 1938.
>   DLC
>   1941   Mar. 18, May 3, 5, 7, 9 – June 1,
>   3 – 6, 9 – 21, 25, 26, 28.
>   1942   June 1, 3 – 6, 9 – 11, 14 – 16, 18,
>   21 – 30, Aug. 4 – 10, 12, 13,
>   15 – 17, 19, 21 – 23, 26 – Sept.
>   8, 10 – 14, 16 – 26, 28 – Oct. 12,
>   14 – 19, 21 – 30, Nov. 1 – Dec.
>   5, 7 – 31.
>   1943   Jan. 1, 2, 4, 5, 7 – 12, 14 – 24,
>   26 – 28, 31 – Feb. 7, 9 – 15, 17
>   – 25, 27 – Mar. 7, 9 – 30, Apr.
>   1 – 3, 5 – 10, 12 – 20, 22 – 27,
>   29 – June 15, 17 – July 9, 11 –
>   Aug. 9, 11 – 17, 19 – 27, 29 –
>   Sept. 22, 24 – Oct. 26, 28 –
>   Nov. 9, 11 – Dec. 9, 11 – 31.
>   1944   Jan. 1 – 19, 23, 25, Feb. 1 – 8,
>   10, 11, 13 – 26, 28 – Mar. 10,
>   12 – 25, 27 – Apr. 6, 8 – 17,
>   21 – 26, 28 – 30, June 2 – 6, 17
>   – 20, 29 – July 9, 11 – 14, 16 –
>   29, 31 – Aug. 8, 10 – Sept. 2,
>   4 – 26, 28 – Oct. 17, 21, 22,
>   26 – Dec. 31.
>   1945   Jan. 1 – 12, 14 – 29, Feb. 1 – 3,
>   5 – 17, 19 – Apr. 12, 15 – 23,

25 – 27, 29, May 1 – July 15, 17
– Aug. 23, 25 – Sept. 8, 10 –
Dec. 6, 9 – 11, 16, 19 – 21, 23 –
31.
1946 Jan. 1 – 3, 6, 9 – Feb. 16, 18 –
22, 26 – Apr. 7, 9 – May 24,
26 – July 17, 19 – 21, 23 – Sept.
7, 9 – Oct. 23, 25 – Nov. 21,
23 – Dec. 6, 8, 11, 14 – 17, 20 –
23, 29 – 31.
1949 Nov. 1 – Dec. 14, 17 – 31.
1950 Jan. 1 – 19, 21 – July 20, 22 –
Oct. 2, 4 – 11, 13 – 17, 19 – 29,
Oct. 31 – Dec. 30.
1951 Jan. 2 – Feb. 4, 6 – May 4, 6 –
15, 17 – Aug. 4, 6 – Nov. 12,
14 – Dec. 31.
1952 Jan. 1 – Apr. 30, May 3 – 10,
12 – June 24, 26 – Aug. 2, 4 –
Sept. 8, 10 – Oct. 19, 21 – Nov.
2, 4 – 29, Dec. 1 – 20, 22 – 31.
1953 Jan. 1 – May 26, 28 – July 20,
22 – Aug. 23, 29 – Dec. 19, 21 –
31.
1954 Jan. 1, 2, 4 – 13, 15 – 17, 23 –
30, Feb. 1 – 3, 5 – 17, 19, 20,
22 – 24, 27, Mar. 1 – 29, 31 –
July 26, 28 – Dec. 31.
1955 Jan. 6 – July 17, 19 – Dec. 31.
1956 – 1958 Jan. 1 – Dec. 31.
1959 Jan. 1 – Oct. 18, 20 – Dec. 31.
1960 Jan. 1 – 16, 18 – Mar. 12, 14 –
Dec. 31.
1961 Jan. 1 – 8, 10 – 23, 25 – Mar. 4,
6 – May 4, 6, 7, 9 – Aug. 31,
Sept. 2 – 20, 22 – Dec. 11, 13 –
25, 27 – 31.
Micro (P) & (N)
1962 Jan. 1+.
FU
1962 May 22 – Dec. 31.
1963 – 1964 Jan. 1 – Dec. 31.
TxU
1949 Oct. 22.
1950 Nov. 22, 23, 26 – Dec. 31.
1951 Jan. 1 – 21, 23 – Feb. 26, 28 –
Apr. 12, 14 – May 6, 9 – 15, 17,
19 – Oct. 5.

EL NOTICIERO. d.
TxU
1925 Jan. 1, 2.

ORGANO OFICIAL DE NUEVO LEON.
w.
CtY
1848 Nos. 1 – 3, 5, 101, 164.

PERIODICO OFICIAL DEL GOBIERNO
CONSTITUCIONAL DE LA REPUB-
LICA MEXICANA. bw.
MBAt
1864 Apr. 10.

PERIODICO OFICIAL DEL GOBIERNO
DEL ESTADO DE NUEVO-LEON.
sw.
CU – B
Micro (P)
1874 May 6, 13.
1878 July 3, Aug. 21.
TxU
1880 July 10, 17, 24, 31, Aug. 7,
14 – 21, Sept. 25, Oct. 2, 9, 23,
30, Nov. 10 – 17, 24, Dec. 4,
11 – 25.
1881 Jan. 8 – 22, 29 – Mar. 2, 12 –
19, 26 – Apr. 6, 13 – 27, May
3 – June 1, 9 – 18, 25 – July 2,
9 – 30.
1884 June 4.

EL PORVENIR. d. est. Jan. 31, 1919.
CSt
1944 Apr. 1 – 30.
CSt – H
1964 June 1 – Dec. 31.
1965 Jan. 1+.
DLC
1941 Nov. 1 – 9, 11 – 20, 22 – 30,
Dec. 13, 15 – 25, 27, 29 – 31.
1942 Jan. 1 – 8, 10 – 17, 19 – 24, 26 –
28, 30, 31, Feb. 2 – 7, 9 – 14, 16
– 21, 23, 24, 26, 27, Mar. 3, 6,
12 – 15, 17 – 19, 21, 22, 24, 25,
27, 28, 31 – Apr. 6, 8 – 11, 13 –
16, 22 – 24, 27 – 30, May 5 –
9, 11 – 16, 18, 19, 21 – 23, 25,
26, 28, 29, June 1, 3, 5, 6, 8, 9,

11, 12, 15 — 19, 22 — 26, 29, 30,
Aug. 4 — 10, 12, 13, 15 — 17,
19 — 23, 26 — 30, Sept. 1 — 6, 8,
10, 13, 16, 19 — 29, Oct. 1 — 16,
18, 19, 21 — Nov. 20, 22 — Dec.
31.

1943   Jan. 1 — 5, 7 — 15, 17 — 25, 27 —
Feb. 7, 9 — 13, 15, 17 — 25, 27 —
Mar. 15, 18 — June 9, 11 — July
9, 11 — Aug. 27, 29 — Sept. 16,
18 — Oct. 2, 4 — Nov. 26, 28 —
Dec. 19, 22 — 31.

1944   Jan. 1 — 19, 21, 23 — 25, 31 —
Mar. 25, 27 — Apr. 1, 3 — 6, 8 —
17, 22, 24 — 26, 28 — May 31,
July 2 — 14, 17, 18, 20 — Aug. 7,
9 — 29, 31 — Dec. 24, 27 — 29, 31.

1945   Jan. 1 — 12, 14 — 20, 22 — Feb. 3,
5 — 25, 27 — Apr. 12, 15 — June
1, 3 — 26, 28 — July 16, 18 —
Sept. 16, 18 — 21, 23 — Dec. 21,
23 — 25, 27 — 29, 31.

1946   Jan. 1 — 4, 6 — 24, 26 — 29, Feb.
1 — 16, 18, 19, 26 — Mar. 2, 4 —
Apr. 30, May 3, 7 — 19, 21 —
July 16, 18 — 20, 22 — Sept. 16,
18 — Oct. 1, 3, 4, 6 — 14, 16, 17,
19, 20, 23 — 30, Nov. 2, 9 — 11,
13 — 15, 18 — Dec. 1, 3 — 6, 8 —
13, 15 — 23, 28 — 30.

1947   Sept. 1 — 18, 20 — Oct. 2, 5 —
Dec. 5, 8, 10 — 20, 22 — 27, 29 —
31.

1948   Jan. 1 — Feb. 8, 10 — 29, Mar.
2 — 10, 13 — June 30, July 2 — 6,
8 — 29, 31 — Aug. 3, 5 — Nov. 8,
10 — 19, 22 — 30, Dec. 2 — 10,
12 — 31.

1949   Jan. 1 — Mar. 31, Aug. 1 — Dec.
29, 31.

1950   Jan. 1 — July 25, 27 — Aug. 13,
15 — Sept. 27, 29 — Oct. 1, 3 —
17, 19 — Dec. 31.

1951   Jan. 1 — 31, Feb. 2, 3, 5 — 12,
14 — Mar. 26, 28 — May 8, 10 —
28, 30 — Sept. 4, 6 — Dec. 6, 8 —
31.

1952   Jan. 1 — Feb. 26, 28 — Mar. 26,

28 — Apr. 30, May 3 — June 10,
12 — Sept. 24, 26 — Oct. 10, 12 —
Nov. 24, 26 — 28, 30 — Dec. 31.

1953   Jan. 1 — Feb. 4, 6, 7, 9 — 13, 15 —
22, 24 — May 23, 25 — July 20,
22 — 28, 30 — Oct. 1, 3 — Nov. 7,
9 — Dec. 20, 22 — 24, 27 — 31.

1954   Jan. 1 — 17, 24 — Feb. 3, 5 —
July 27, 29 — Aug. 11, 13 — Oct.
1, 3 — Dec. 31.

1955 — 1958   Jan. 1 — Dec. 31.

1959   Jan. 1 — Apr. 17, 20 — May 2,
4 — Aug. 21, 23 — 27, 29 — Dec.
31.

1960   Jan. 1 — 16, 18 — Mar. 12, 14 —
Dec. 31.

1961   Jan. 1 — Mar. 2, 4, 7 — May 4,
6 — 20, 22 — June 27, 29 — July
15, 17 — Aug. 26, 28 — Sept. 18,
20 — 29, Oct. 1 — Nov. 21, 23 —
Dec. 31.

Micro (P) & (N)
1962   Jan 1+.

LNT — MA
1933   Jan. 31.
1940   Sept. 12 — Nov. 26.

TxU
1921   Sept. 25.
1924   Jan. 25, Sept. 21, 24 — 26, Oct.
1 — 18, 20 — 25, 27 — 30, Nov.
1 — 17, 19, 21 — 27, 29 — 30, Dec.
7, 9 — 11, 13, 18, 20 — 28.

1925   Jan. 1, 3, 5 — 13, 16, 17, 19 — 27,
Mar. 1, 2, 4 — Apr. 3, 9 — 29,
May 1 — Sept. 15, 17 — Oct. 4,
6 — 22, 24 — Dec. 10, 12, 13,
15 — 31.

1926   Jan. 1 — Dec. 18, 20 — 31.

1927   Jan. 1 — Mar. 9, 11 — Apr. 24,
27 — Oct. 22, 24 — Dec. 31.

1928   Jan. 1 — Oct. 3, 6 — 9.

PREVI. bw.
CU
1946   June 31 — Dec. 31.
1947 — 1948   Jan. 1 — Dec. 31.
1949   Jan. 15 — Nov. 15, Dec. 15 — 31.
1950   Jan. 15 — Feb. 15, Mar. 15 —

May 15, July 26, Aug. 26 —
Sept. 11.

EL PROGRESO. d.
Note: Established in Laredo, Texas;
removed to Monterrey 1914.
TxU
1919   May 21.

EL RELATOR.
TxSjM
1838   Mar. 26.

RENACIMIENTO. d. est. Aug. 15, 1911.
TxU
1911   Aug. 15.

EL REPUBLICANO. d. est. 1910.
TxU
1910   June 8.

REVISTA. d. est. 1880.
MWA
1881   Sept. 6 — 8.

SEMANARIO POLITICO DEL GOBIER-
NO DE NUEVO LEON. w. est. 1835.
CtY
1835   Nos. 4 — 6.
1837   [Jan. 19 — July 13].
1838   Dec. 27.
1839   [Jan. 4 — Nov. 7].
1840   [Feb. 6 — Dec. 17].
1841   [Jan. 1 — Apr. 15].
1842   [Jan. 13 — Dec. 29].
1843   [Jan. 5 — Dec. 28].
1844   [Jan. 2 — Dec. 25].
1846   [Jan. 15 — Aug. 27].
TxSjM
1843   Feb. 9, Apr. 6, 27, July 27, Aug.
3, 10.
Extraordinario: Feb. 9.
1844   Feb. 1, May 30, June 6, 13, 29,
July 11, 18, Aug. 15, 22, Sept.
5, Oct. 17, Dec. 5.
Extraordinario: May 23.
1845   Apr. 10.

EL SOL. d. est. Apr. 2, 1922.
Note: Suspended publication Apr.
15 — 20, 1957.

DLC
1941   Mar. 6, 22, 24, Apr. 19, May 9,
12 — 16, 19, 20, 22, 24, 26, 27,
29, 30, June 2, 4, 5, 9, 11 — 13,
16 — 20, 27.
1942   Aug. 3 — Sept. 11, 13 — 16, 18 —
27, 29 — Oct. 9, 11 — 19, 21 — 23,
25 — 30, Nov. 1 — 6, 8 — 19, 21 —
Dec. 11, 13 — 18, 20, 21, 23 — 31.
1943   Jan. 2 — Feb. 10, 12 — 14, 16 —
Mar. 12, 14 — Apr. 9, 11 — 13,
15 — May 2, 6 — 14, 16, 18 — 21,
23 — 25, 27, 28, 30, June 1 — 18,
20 — July 4, 6 — 9, 11 — 16, 18,
19, 21 — 23, 25 — 30, Aug. 1 — 9,
11 — 27, 29 — Sept. 1, 3 — 8, 10,
12 — 24, 26 — Oct. 2, 4 — 8, 10 —
22, 24 — 29, 31 — Nov. 4, 6 — 19,
21, 23, 25, 26, 28 — 30, Dec. 2 —
10, 12 — 16, 19 — 23, 25 — 31.
1950   July 1 — Aug. 20, 22 — 30, Sept.
1 — Oct. 1, 3 — 26, 28 — 30, Nov.
1 — Dec. 30.
1951   Sept. 1 — Nov. 25, 27 — Dec. 21,
23 — 31.
1952   Jan. 7 — 30, Feb. 1 — 18, 20 —
Mar. 17, 19 — 27, 29 — 31, Aug.
1, 2, 5 — 30, Sept. 1 — 17, 19 —
28, 30 — Dec. 2, 5 — 10, 13, 14,
16, 18 — 31.
1953   Jan. 2 — 12, 14 — Feb. 3, 5 —
Apr. 23, 25 — 30, May 2 — 6, 8 —
27, 29 — June 28, 30 — Aug. 20,
23 — Dec. 14, 16 — 31.
1954   Jan. 2 — Apr. 30, May 3 — 10,
12 — Aug. 6, 8 — 20, 22 — Sept. 3,
5, 8 — 10, 12 — 16, 18 — Nov. 23,
25 — Dec. 31.
1955   Jan. 1 — Apr. 30, May 2 — Dec.
31.
1956   Jan. 1 — Apr. 30, May 2 — Dec.
31.
1957   Jan. 1 — Apr. 14, 21 — 30, May
2 — July 16, 18 — Aug. 31, Sept.
2 — Dec. 31.
1958   Jan. 2 — Aug. 30, Sept. 1 — Dec.
31.
1959   Jan. 2 — Apr. 30, May 8 — July 3,
5 — Aug. 16, 18 — Sept. 11, 13 —

25, 27 — Oct. 9, 11 — 13, 15, 17 —
26, 28 — Nov. 1, 3 — 6, 8 — 10,
12 — 19, 22 — 27, 29 — Dec. 28,
30, 31.

1960 Jan. 1, 3, 4, 6 — 29, 31 — Mar. 11,
13, 15 — 18, 20 — 25, 27 — Apr. 8,
10 — 28, 30, May 2 — 4, 6, 8 — 27,
29, 31, June 2 — 10, 12 — 15,
19 — July 3, 5 — 8, 10 — 12, 14 —
19, 21, 22, 24 — Sept. 2, 4 — 14,
18 — 23, 25 — Oct. 4, 6 — Dec. 31.

1961 Jan. 3 — 16, 18 — 22, 24 — Feb.
21, 23 — Mar. 10, 12 — 26, May
1 — 7, 9 — 19, 21 — 26, 28 — June
30, July 2 — 4, 6 — 23, 25 — Aug.
3, 6 — 11, 13, 14, 16, 17, 19 —
Sept. 4, 6, 7, 9 — 12, 14 — 18,
21 — 29, Oct. 1, 3 — 6, 8 — 11,
15 — 24, 26 — Nov. 1, 3 — 8, 10 —
13, 15 — Dec. 4, 6 — 11, 13 — 15,
17, 18, 20 — 30.

Micro (P) & (N)
1962 Jan. 1+.
TxU
1924 Sept. 21, Oct. 9, 26, Dec. 16.
1925 Jan. 4, 11, Feb. 22, Mar. 6, 7.

EL TIEMPO. d. est. Aug. 5, 1936.
DLC
1941 May 13, 20, 21, 24, 26 — 29,
June 2, 7, 11, 14, 16 — 19, 28.
1942 Aug. 3, 4, 6 — 21, 23 — 28, 30 —
Sept. 1, 4, 6, 7, 9 — 11, 13, 18,
20 — 25, 27, 29, Oct. 2, 4, 7 — 19,
22 — 30, Nov. 1, 3 — 10, 12 — 16,
18 — 26, 28, 29, Dec. 1 — 7, 9,
12, 13, 16, 19 — 22, 24, 25, 28,
30, 31.
1943 Jan. 2, 3, 5, 6, 9 — 11, 13, 16 —
21, 23 — 25, 28, 30 — Feb. 3, 7, 9,
13 — 17, 19 — 21, 23, 24, 26, 28,
Mar. 1, 7, 14, 20, 21, 24, 25,
27 — Apr. 7, 10, 11, 13 — 15,
17 — 29, May 2 — 4, 6, 7, 9 — 28,
30, June 1 — 5, 7 — 12, 14 — 19,
21 — 26, 28, 29, July 1 — 3, 6 —
10, 12 — 17, 19, 21, 22, 24, 26 —
29, 31, Aug. 2, 3, 5 — 7, 9 — 12,
14, 16 — 21, 23 — 28, 30 — Sept.

4, 7, 8, 11, 13 — 15, 17, 18, 20 —
24, 27 — Oct. 1, 4 — 6, 8, 9, 11 —
16, 18 — 23, 25 — 30, Nov. 1 — 5,
8 — 13, 15, 16, 18, 19, 22 — 27,
30 — Dec. 8, 13, 16 — 18, 20,
22 — 25, 27 — 29, 31.

EL TRUEÑO. w.
TxU
1911 Aug. 27.

THE TWO REPUBLICS. d. est. July 27,
1867.
Note: In English. Main edition published in Mexico City.
DLC
1892 Aug. 15.

LA VOZ DE LA FRONTERA.
TxU
1859 Nov. 26, 28.

LA VOZ DE NUEVO LEON. w.
NN
1909 July 29.

Morelia

EL ASTRO MORELIANO. sw. est. Apr. 2,
1829.
Note: Ceased publication Mar. 29,
1830.
CtY
1829 Apr. 2 — Dec. 31.
1830 Jan. 4 — Mar. 29.
TxU
1829 Apr. 2 — Dec. 31.
1830 Jan. 1 — Mar. 29.

LA BANDERA IMPERIAL. w. est. Feb. 1,
1866.
Note: Ceased publication May 25,
1866.
TxU
1866 Feb. 1 — May 25.

LA BANDERA ROJA. sw. est. Jan. 10,
1859.
CU — B
Micro (N)
1859 Jan. 10 — Dec. 31.
1860 Jan. 1 — Dec. 31.

1861   Jan. 1 — June 19, 26 — Oct. 16, 26 — Nov. 1, 8 — Dec. 31.
1862   Jan. 1 — Feb. 21, 28 — Sept. 19, 30 — Nov. 14.

LA BRUJULA. irr. est. Mar. 2, 1867.
Note: Ceased publication Nov. 1, 1867.
TxU
1867   Mar. 2 — Nov. 1.

EL CINCO DE MAYO. w. est. Feb. 19, 1867.
Note: Ceased publication Apr. 9, 1868.
TxU
1867   Feb. 19 — Dec. 31.
1868   Jan. 1 — Apr. 9.

EL CLAMOR DE MICHOACAN. w. est. Oct. 11, 1868.
Note: Ceased publication Jan. 25, 1869.
TxU
1868   Oct. 11 — Dec. 31.
1869   Jan. 1 — 25.

EL CONSTITUCIONALISTA. 3w. est. Jan. 3, 1868.
TxSjM
1869   Nov. 18.
TxU
1868   Jan. 3 — Dec. 31.

EL ECO DE LA LIBERTAD.
LNT — MA
1833   Apr. 22.

EL ECO DE LA MONTAÑA. est. Dec. 27, 1868.
TxU
1868   Dec. 27 — 31.
1869   Jan. 1 — Apr. 3.

LA EPOCA. w. est. Aug. 25, 1866.
Note: Ceased publication Nov. 23, 1866.
TxU
1866   Aug. 25 — Nov. 23.

LA EPOCA. w.
TxU
1911   [July 30].

EL FEDERALISTA. bw. est. Sept. 6, 1846.
Note: Ceased publication Apr. 25, 1847.
TxU
1846   Sept. 6 — Dec. 31.
1847   Jan. 1 — Apr. 25.

GACETA OFICIAL DEL GOBIERNO DEL ESTADO DE MICHOACAN DE OCAMPO. sw. est. [1885].
MWA
1888   May 13.
1889   July 11 — Dec. 31.
1890 — 1891   Jan. 1 — Dec. 31.
1892   Jan. 1 — Aug. 28.
TxU
1888   Sept. 16.

EL GIRONDINO. w. est. May 16, 1912.
TxU
1912   May 16.

LA GUERRA. w. est. Dec. 20, 1861.
TxU
1861   Dec. 20 — 31.
1862   Jan. 1 — Feb. 7.

HOJA DOMINICAL. w. est. Feb. 18, 1912.
TxU
1912   Feb. 18.

IDEA LIBRE. w.
TxU
1912   May 26.

EL KASKABELITO. w. est. May 5, 1912.
TxU
1912   May 5.

LA LEALTAD. w. est. 1893.
TxU
1894   Jan. 23.

EL MICHOACANO. est. June 27, 1869.
TxU
1869   June 27 — July 7.

EL MONITOR COMERCIAL. w.
TxU
1911   Dec. 3.

EL MUNICIPAL. sw. est. Sept. 20, 1880.
TxU
  1880   Sept. 20 — Oct. 1.

EL MUNICIPIO. est. Aug. 6, 1869.
TxU
  1869   Aug. 6.

EL NACIONAL. bw. est. Feb. 16, 1863.
TxU
  1863   Feb. 16 — Apr. 6.

LAS NARICES. irr. est. Oct. 1, 1867.
TxU
  1867   Oct. 1 — Nov. 19.

EL NOTICIOSO. de. est. July 16, 1911.
TxU
  1911   July 16.

LA OPOSICION. w. est. Nov. 5, 1868.
TxU
  1868   Nov. 5 — Dec. 3.

EL ORDEN. w. est. Oct. 7, 1866.
TxU
  1866   Oct. 7 — Dec. 23.

LA PATRIA. 3w. est. Sept. 27, 1863.
TxU
  1863   Sept. 27 — Nov. 3.

PERIODICO OFICIAL DEL GOBIERNO
DEL ESTADO DE MICHOACAN DE
OCAMPO.
TxU
  1880   Aug. 3, 24, Sept. 7, 28, Oct. 5 —
          12, 26 — 29, Nov. 5, Dec. 10.

EL PROGRESISTA; PERIODICO OFI-
CIAL DEL GOBIERNO DEL ESTADO
DE MICHOACAN. sw. est. 1870.
  Note: Ceased publication 1876.
CU — B
  Micro (P)
  1874   Apr. 27.
TxU
  1876   Sept. 18.

LAS PULGAS. est. Dec. 24, 1868.
TxU
  1868   Dec. 24 — 31.
  1869   Jan. 1 — 6.

LA RAZON CATOLICA. bw. est. Dec. 13,
1863.
TxU
  1863   Dec. 13 — 31.
  1864   Jan. 1 — Mar. 27.

RENACIMIENTO. w. est. 1877.
MWA
  1881   June 5.

EL SANSCULOTE. sw. est. 1855.
NN
  1855   Dec. 28.

LA SOMBRA DE WASHINGTON. est.
July 18, 1833.
  Note: Ceased publication 1834.
TxU
  1833   July 18 — Dec. 19, 26 — 31.
  1834   Jan. 1 — May 22, 29 — June 2,
          9 — 19, July 3.

LOS TORREÑOS. w. est. Sept. 24, 1867.
  Note: Ceased publication Oct. 5,
  1867.
TxU
  1867   Sept. 24 — Oct. 5.

LA VOZ DE MICHOACAN. bw. est. Feb.
16, 1842.
  Note: Ceased publication Sept. 3,
  1846.
TxU
  1846   Jan. 8 — Sept. 3.

Mulege

LA CAMPAÑA. sw.
CU — B
  Micro (P)
  1878   June 20 — 27.

Navojoa

EL MAYO. sw. est. 1930.
LNT — MA
  1931   Apr. 23.

Nogales

ACCION. d. est. 1938.
DLC
  1941   Mar. 1 — May 18, 20 — June 13,

15 – 27, 29 – July 25, 27 – Aug.
8, 10 – Sept. 24, 27 – Oct. 13,
15 – 20, 22 – 29, 31 – Dec. 5,
7 – 16, 18 – 31.

1942   Jan. 1 – Mar. 31, Apr. 2 – Sept.
17, 19 – Oct. 5, 8, 10 – 23, 25 –
27, 29, 30, Nov. 1, 3 – 8, 13 –
25, 29, Dec. 1, 6, 8, 10, 12, 13,
20 – 22, 24 – 28.

1943   Feb. 1 – 4, 6 – 8, 10 – 15, 19 –
23, 25, Mar. 1 – Apr. 5, 9 – May
4, 8, 11 – 17, 20 – 28, June 1 – 4,
7 – 28, 30, July 2 – 6, 8, 9, 12,
Aug. 10 – 23, 25 – 27, 31, Sept.
6, 24 – 28, 30 – Oct. 13, 16, 19,
21 – 23, 26 – 30, Nov. 2 – 6, 11.

LA NACION. 3w.
   DLC
     1919   Oct. 21 – Nov. 6, 9, 15.

EL NOROESTE. d. est. 1926.
   DLC
     1941   Mar. 1 – Apr. 13, 18 – May 26,
28 – Oct. 8, 12 – 15, 18 – Nov. 2,
4, 6 – Dec. 12, 14 – 22, 24 – 31.
     1942   Jan. 1 – 14, 16 – 30, Feb. 1 –
Mar. 12, 15, 17 – Apr. 24, 26 –
28, May 2 – 21, 23, 24, 27, 28,
June 2, 4 – 7, 9, 10, 12, 14 – 19,
21, 23, 25, 27 – July 2, 5 – 8,
10 – 21, 23 – 31, Aug. 2 – 24,
26 – Sept. 11, 13 – 24, 26 – Oct.
1, 3 – 15, 17 – 29, 31, Nov. 2, 6,
8 – 11, 13, 15 – 18, 21, 22, 27 –
29, Dec. 6 – 14, 16, 17, 19 – 28.

Nuevo Laredo

EL BOLETIN FRONTERIZO COMER-
CIAL.
   LNHT
     1930   [July 15 – Dec. 31].
     1931   Jan. 1 – 8.

EL FRONTERIZO. w.
   LNT – MA
     1931   Dec. 19.
     1932   Jan. 9, 18.

LA TRIBUNA PUBLICA. w. est. Oct.
1919.
   DLC
     1919   Oct. 30.

VERBO LIBRE. sw. est. 1924.
   DLC
     1942   Dec. 12.

Oaxaca

EL BIEN PUBLICO. w., bw.
   TxU
     1906   Mar. 4, 21, June 3, Nov. 15.

BOLETIN LIBERAL.
   NN
     1860   Sept. 7.

CORREO AMERICANO DEL SUR. w.,
irr.
   CtY
     1813   Apr. 10 – May 13, June 17 –
July 19, 29, Aug. 12 – 17, Sept.
16, Oct. 13.

EL DIA. d.
   LNT – MA
     1914   Apr. 23.

EL ECO DE OAXACA. bw. est. 1887.
   LNT – MA
     1887   Dec. 1.

EL ECO DE OAXACA. w. est. 1912.
   TxU
     1912   Nov. 17.

EL ESTANDARTE. d. est. 1917.
   LNT – MA
     1918   Feb. 24.

EL IDEAL. w., irr.
   TxU
     1909   Jan. 1, 11, Aug. 9 – 15, 21, 29,
Sept. 5, 19 – Oct. 10, 21, Dec.
5 – 19.
     1910   Jan. 16, 30, Mar. 27, 10, 24,
May 1 – 15, June 6 – 26, July
10 – Aug. 7, 21 – Sept. 4, Oct.
16 – 30.
     1911   Jan. 8.

LA LEY.
  TxU
    1911   July 23.
MERCURIO. d.
  TxU
    1924   Oct. 25, Dec. 31.

EL MOMENTO.
  LNT—MA
    1941   June 4.

EL NOTICIADOR. est. Sept. 16, 1857.
  TxU
    1857   Sept. 16, 23.
            Alcance: Sept. 16.

EL OAJAQUEÑO CONSTITUCIONAL.
  sw. est. [1830].
  DLC
    1831   Jan. 30—Feb. 5, 7—9, 11—
            July 3.
            Suplemento: Feb. 20, Mar. 6.

EL OAJAQUEÑO FEDERALISTA.
  LNT—MA
    Micro (P)
    1831   Jan. 4.

OAXACA NUEVO. d. est. 1932.
  DLC
    1941   Sept. 20.
  LNT—MA
    1941   May 29.

PROVINCIA. d. est. [1947].
  LNT—MA
    1950   Aug. 6.

EL PUEBLO. est. 1874.
  TxU
    1874   Sept. 26.

EL REGENERADOR; PERIODICO DEL
GOBIERNO DEL DEPARTAMENTO
DE OAXACA. sw. est. 1834.
    Note: Ceased publication Apr. 15,
    1845.
  CU—B
    Micro (P)
    1840   June 29.
  CtY
    1843   Feb. 16.

LNHT
    1835   May 14.
  TxU
    1838   Dec. 12, 24.

EL REGENERADOR; ORGANO OFICI-
AL DEL GOBIERNO DEL ESTADO
DE OAXACA. sw.
  CU—B
    Micro (P)
    1875   Mar. 12.
  TxU
    1875   Sept. 21.

LA VICTORIA; PERIODICO DEL
GOBIERNO DE OAXACA. sw.
  TxU
    1861   Dec. 12.
    1863   Jan. 11, May 24—June 7, 18—
            21, July 2.
    1880   Apr. 2, Aug. 24.

LA VICTORIA; ORGANO OFICIAL DEL
GOBIERNO DEL ESTADO.
  CU—B
    Micro (P)
    1878   Sept. 10—13.
  TxU
    1878   Sept. 20.

LA VOZ DE LA VERDAD. w. est. 1896.
  CLCM
    1911   Apr. 13.

LA VOZ DE OAXACA. w.
  LNT—MA
    1949   [Jan. 1—Dec. 31].

EL ZAPOTECO. sw. est. 1832.
  DLC
    1833   Jan. 3—12, 14—16, 18—Feb. 2,
            4—Mar. 9, 11—Apr. 7.
            Suplemento: Jan. 6, 17, 20, 24,
            Mar. 28, 31.

Orizaba

BOLETIN DEL HOSPICIO DE ORIZA-
BA. w., sw.
    Note: Periodicity before July 1870,
    weekly.

MWA
1870   July 10−24, Oct. 16−20, 27−
        30.
1871   Apr. 27.

DESEO GENERAL. sw. est. Apr. 1871.
MWA
1871   Apr. 19−22, 29, July 12.

DESTINO DEL PUEBLO.
MWA
1861   Nov. 21.

ECO DE ORIZABA. w. est. 1868.
MWA
1868   Oct. 19−25.

LA EMULACION. est. 1881.
TxU
1881   July 15.

EPOCA. sw. est. 1870.
MWA
1871   Apr. 20, 30, July 13−16.
1872   Jan. 4−14.

FERRO CARRIL. sw. est. [1864].
MWA
1868   Mar. 25, Apr. 8.

EL GLADIADOR.
TxU
1880   May 19.

IRIS VERACRUZANO; PERIODICO
OFICIAL. 3w. est. May 1, 1881.
TxU
1881   May 1, 12−19, 24−28, June
        2−9, 14−July 9, 14−19, 23−
        Aug. 6, 20, Nov. 5.

LA LUCHA ELECTORAL. w. est. 1911.
TxU
1911   Aug. 13.

MENSAJERO. sw. est. Apr. 24, 1869.
MWA
1869   [Apr. 24−Nov. 14].

MEXICAN RAILWAY ERA.
    Note: In English.
TxU
1866   July 4.

EL ORIZAVEÑO. sw. est. 1848.
CU−B
    Micro (N)

1849   Mar. 18, Apr. 12−15.

PRO-PARIA. w.
NN
    Micro (P) & (N)
1939   Jan. 7−Dec. 30.
1940   Jan. 7−Dec. 28.
1941   Jan. 4−Dec. 27.
1946   Jan. 7−Dec. 28.

EL PUEBLO. w.
CU−B
    Micro (P)
1874   Feb. 15.

EL REPRODUCTOR. sw. est. [1877].
CU−B
    Micro (N)
1883   Mar. 13−18.
KHi
1883   Apr. 22.
MWA
1889   Dec. 5, 12, 19−22, 29.
TxU
1880   Aug. 12−29, Sept. 9−12, 26−
        30, Oct. 7, 14, 24, 31, Nov. 7−
        11, 25, Dec. 12, 23.

SIGLO QUE ACABA. w. est. Oct. 1888.
MWA
1889   Nov. 24, Dec. 29.
1890   Jan. 5.

30-30. sw.
DLC
1915   Oct. 14, 24.
1916   Apr. 30, May 14, June 5.

VOZ DE ORIZABA. sw. est. Jan. 1869.
MWA
1869   Feb. 11.

Pachuca

EL CHINACO. est. Mar. 1916.
DLC
1917   Feb. 5.

LA DEFENSA. bw. est. Dec. 24, 1911.
TxU
1911   Dec. 24.

EL DEMOCRATA. w. est. 1910.
TxU
1910   July 31.

EL GORRO FRIGIO. w. est. July 22, 1917.
DLC
1917   July 22, Oct. 10.

EL GRITO OBRERO. bw. est. Sept. 15,
1912.
TxU
1912   Sept. 15.

EL LIBERAL. bw. est. Dec. 1, 1911.
TxU
1911   Dec. 1.

PERIODICO OFICIAL DE HIDALGO.
TxU
1880   Sept. 28, Dec. 16.
1881   June 30.

EL PUCARO. w. est. 1880.
LNT – MA
1880   Aug. 22.

LA TRIBUNA. sw.
CU – B
Micro (P)
1874   Mar. 11.

Parral

EL CORREO DE PARRAL. 3w., d. est.
1922.
DLC
1942   Sept. 19.
LNT – MA
1930   Aug. 2.
TxU
1925   Mar. 3.
1928   Nov. 29, Dec. 5, 7.
1929   Jan. 26, 28 – 30, Feb. 1, 4, 6, 7,
13, 14, Mar. 6.

LA OPINION PUBLICA. d. est. Oct. 22,
1911.
TxU
1911   Oct. 22.

LA VOZ DE PARRAL.
TxU
1929   Feb. 7, 9 – 14, Mar. 5 – 7.

LA VOZ DEL OBRERO. d. est. Oct. 15,
1911.
TxU
1911   Oct. 15.

LA VOZ DEL PUEBLO. d. est. July 14,
1911.
TxU
1911   July 14.

Parras de la Fuente

EL POPULAR. w. est. 1935.
DLC
1942   Oct. 10.

Paso del Norte
See Ciudad Juarez.

Pénjamo

ALBA NUEVA. w. est. July 23, 1911.
TxU
1911   July 23.

Pichucalco

LA OPINION.
LNT – MA
1891   Oct. 11, Dec. 6.

Pinos

EL LATIGO. w. est. Nov. 26, 1911.
TxU
1911   Nov. 26.

Porfirio

EL PUEBLO LIBRE. w. est. June 25,
1911.
TxU
1911   June 25.

Puebla

LA ABEJA POBLANA. w. est. Nov. 30,
1820.
Note: Ceased publication Dec. 31,
1821.
CU – B
Micro (N)
1820   Nov. 30 – Dec. 31.

1821   Jan. 1 — Nov. 22.
CtY
   1821   Apr. 5.
      Suplemento: Sept. 5.
TxU
   Micro (P)
   1820   Prospecto: Nov. 29.
      Nov. 30 — Dec. 31.
   1821   Jan. 1 — Dec. 31.

AMERICAN STAR, NO. 2. sw. est. 1847.
   Note: In English.
   DLC
   1847   July 1, 8.

EL AMIGO DE LA VERDAD. sw. est.
   July 11, 1828.
   DLC
   1828   Prospecto.
      July 11 — Dec. 22.
      Suplemento: July 25, Aug. 1,
      15, Oct. 10, 24, Nov. 28.
   TxU
   1828   July 11 — Dec. 22.

EL AMIGO DEL PUEBLO. est. 1821.
   Note: Continuous pagination.
   CtY
   1821   n.d.
   NN
   1821   n.d. (No. 2).
   TxU
   1821   Aug. 18.
      Suplemento: Aug. 21.

EL ARGOS. sw. est. Feb. 25, 1827.
   DLC
   1827   July 8 — Dec. 8.
      Suplemento: Oct. 18, 31, Nov.
      4.

AVANTE. irr. est. Oct. 20, 1934.
   CU
   1934   Nov. 23 — Dec. 31.
   1935 — 1938   Jan. 1 — Dec. 31.
   1939   Jan. 1 — June 22.

EL BALUARTE.
   DLC
   1916   June 25.

LA BANDERA NACIONAL. irr. est. Feb.
   27, 1867.
   LNT — MA
   1867   Feb. 27 — Mar. 23.

BOLETIN.
   CtY
   1846   Nos. 9 — 14.
   1847   Nos. 1, 4 — 8, 12, 15.

BOLETIN MUNICIPAL.
   CU — B
   1840   No. 4.

BOLETIN OFICIAL.
   CU — B
   1845   Dec. 27.

EL CADUCEO. d. est. [1824].
   Note: Title *El Caduceo de Puebla,*
   before Dec. 31, 1824.
   CtY
   1824   Oct. 1 — Dec. 31.
   1825   Sept. 1.
   1926   Suplemento: Apr. 18.

EL CALAVERA. sw. est. Jan. 1, 1847.
   Note: Ceased publication June 18,
   1847.
   CtY
   1847   Jan. 1 — June 18.

EL CATOLICO. est. Aug. 5, 1820.
   CtY
   1820   Aug. 5.

EL CENTINELA.
   TxU
   1845   Alcance: July 18.

CHILTEPIN. w.
   TxU
   1912   Jan. 2.

EL CONSTITUCIONAL. d. est. 1915.
   DLC
   1916   June 24, 25.

EL CRESPUSCULO. bw. est. Jan. 11,
   1842.
   TxU
   1842   Jan. 11 — Dec. 24.

DIARIO DE PUEBLA. d. est. Apr. 1,
1912.
TxU
　　1912　Apr. 1.

DIARIO DE PUEBLA. d. est. 1935.
DLC
　　1942　Dec. 29.
　　1943　Apr. 30.

LA EGIDE DE LA LEY. d. est. Sept. 1,
1830.
DLC
　　1830　Prospecto: Aug. 25.
　　　　　Sept. 1 – Dec. 31.

EL FAROL. w. est. Oct. 28, 1821.
　　Note: Ceased publication Aug. 4,
　　1822.
CtY
　　1821　Prospecto: Oct. 4.
　　　　　Oct. 28 – Dec. 30.
　　1822　Jan. 6 – Aug. 4.
　　　　　Alcance: Mar. 10, June 30.
DLC
　　1821　Prospecto: Oct. 4.
　　　　　Oct. 28 – Dec. 31.
　　1822　Jan. 1 – Aug. 4.
　　　　　Alcance. Mar. 10.

FLAG OF FREEDOM. sw. est. Oct. 20,
1847.
　　Note: In English. Ceased publication
　　[Feb. 26], 1848.
CtY
　　1847　Oct. 20, Dec. 22.
DLC
　　1847　Oct. 27.
TxU
　　1847　Oct. 20 – Nov. 27, Dec. 4 – 31.
　　1848　Jan. 1 – Feb. 26.

FRAY PINGÜICA. w. est. Jan. 14, 1912.
TxU
　　1912　Jan. 14.

LA GACETA DE PUEBLA. sw. est. 1911.
TxU
　　1911　Oct. 12.

GACETA DEL GOBIERNO DE PUEBLA.
est. Jan. 22, 1830.

CU – B
　　1830　Jan. 22 – Mar. 19.

GIL BLAS. d. est. 1924.
　　Note: Ceased publication 1925.
TxU
　　1925　Jan. 9, 10, Feb. 21.

LA INSTRUCCION CATOLICA. w.
TxU
　　1911　May 22.

EL INVITADOR. 3w. est. June 2, 1826.
　　Note: Ceased publication July 1827.
DLC
　　1826　Prospecto: May 17.
　　　　　June 2 – Dec. 31.
　　　　　Suplemento: Aug. 4, 11, Sept.
　　　　　15, Oct. 1, 8, 15, Nov. 29, Dec.
　　　　　1.
　　1827　Jan. 3 – Feb. 26, 28 – Mar. 4.
　　　　　Suplemento: Jan. 7, Feb. 4,
　　　　　Mar. 4.

EL LIBERAL. d. est. 1916.
DLC
　　1917　June 23.

LA LIBERTAD. w. est. 1879.
　　Note: Ceased publication 1881.
TxU
　　1879　Nov. 28.
　　1880　Sept. 12.

EL MERCURIO POBLANO. w., sw. est.
June 27, 1843.
　　Note: Periodicity before July 19,
　　1845, weekly; after July 23, 1845,
　　semiweekly. Ceased publication
　　1845.
CtY
　　1845　Sept. 10, 13.
DLC
　　1845　Feb. 1 – 21, 23 – Mar. 21, Apr.
　　　　　13 – Aug. 2.
　　　　　Suplemento: Feb. 22.
TxU
　　1843　June 27 – Dec. 31.
　　1844　Jan. 1 – June 27, Aug. 3 – Dec.
　　　　　31.
　　1845　Jan. 1 – Dec. 27.

LA MINERVA. d. est. Nov. 12, 1828.
    Note: Ceased publication Dec. 24,
    1828.
    CtY
        1828   Nov. 12 – Dec. 24.
                Suplemento: Dec. 9, 12, 16, 22.

EL NACIONAL; PERIODICO OFICIAL
DEL ESTADO LIBRE Y SOBERANO
DE PUEBLA. est. 1847.
    CU – B
        1847   May 26, Aug. 7 – Dec. 31.
        1848   Jan. 1 – Apr. 29.

NOTICIAS CURIOSAS. est. 1821.
    CtY
        1821   n.d. (No. 1).

EL ORIENTAL.
    CtY
        1910   June 30.

LA PALABRA LIBRE. w.
    TxU
        1880   Sept. 9.

EL PATRICIO. w. est. 1846.
    DLC
        1846   June 27 – July 18.

EL PATRIOTA. sw. est. 1827.
    Note: Continuous pagination.
    NN
        1827   Oct. 14, 17.

PERIODICO DE LA CUARTILLA. w.
    est. Oct. 26, 1844.
    Note: Ceased publication Dec. 27,
    1845.
    TxU
        1844   Oct. 26 – Dec. 31.
        1845   Jan. 1 – Dec. 27.

PERIODICO OFICIAL DE PUEBLA DE
ZARAGOZA.
    TxU
        1880   Aug. 7 – 18, 28, Sept. 8, 15,
                Oct. 2 – 6, 23 – 27, Nov. 6, Dec.
                4, 22.

EL POBLANO. w. est. Feb. 25, 1827.
    DLC
        1827   Prospecto.

        Feb. 25 – Apr. 29.
        Suplemento: Mar. 11, 25.

EL PRESENTE. d. est. Nov. 13, 1890.
    TxU
        1891   Aug. 22, Dec. 29.
        1892   Jan. 1, 3, 6, 10, 16, 19 – 21, 23,
                25, 27, Feb. 2, 6, 9, 11, 14, 19,
                21, 25, Mar. 1, 2, 4 – 6, 8, 10 –
                13, 16, 18, 25.

EL PROCURADOR DEL PUEBLO. w.
    est. 1832.
    DLC
        1832   Aug. 4.

LA PROTESTA. bw. est. Jan. 13, 1846.
    Note: Ceased publication Jan. 30,
    1846.
    TxU
        1846   Jan. 13 – 30.

EL REBELDIA. w.
    CU
        1939   May 13, June 24 – July 8, 22 –
                Aug. 19, Sept. 9 – Dec. 30.
        1940   Jan. 6, 20 – Dec. 28.
        1941   Jan. 11 – Mar. 8, 22 – Apr. 12,
                26 – May 31, June 14 – 21, July
                12 – Dec. 6, 27.
        1942   Jan. 10, 24 – Feb. 7, 21, Mar.
                7 – Apr. 4, 18 – May 9, 23 –
                Dec. 26.
        1943   Jan. 2 – Apr. 17, May 1 – Aug.
                7, 21 – Nov. 13, 26 – Dec. 25.
        1944   Jan. 1 – Nov. 11, 25 – Dec. 9,
                23 – 30.
        1945   Jan. 6 – May 5, 19 – Oct. 13,
                27 – Dec. 29.
        1946   Jan. 12 – Feb. 2, 16 – Aug. 24,
                Sept. 7 – Dec. 14, 28.
        1947   Jan. 4 – Mar. 15, 29 – July 12,
                26 – Aug. 9, 23 – Dec. 27.

EL REGENERADOR REPUBLICANO.
    sw. est. Sept. 9, 1846.
    CU – B
        1846   Sept. 9 – Nov. 7, 14 – Dec. 31.
        1847   Jan. 1 – Apr. 21, 28.

EL REGULADOR. 3w. est. May 5, 1848.
CU—B
    1848   May 5—24, 30—June 17, 22—
            Dec. 31.
    1849   Jan. 1—Aug. 25, 30—Dec. 31.
    1850   Jan. 1—12, 19, 24—May 14,
            June 6—July 11, 16—Dec. 31.
    1851   Jan. 1—Dec. 31.
    1852   Jan. 1—Apr. 8.

LA REPUBLICA. w. est. Aug. 7, 1915.
DLC
    1915   Aug. 7, 15.

LA REVOLUCION. d. est. 1915.
    Note: Ceased publication 1915.
TxU
    1915   Aug. 8.

EL 606. w. est. Feb. 18, 1912.
TxU
    1912   Feb. 18.

LA TRINCHERA POBLANA. w. est.
Dec. 1846.
    Note: Ceased publication Mar. 19,
    1847.
CtY
    1846   [Dec. 1—31].
    1847   [Jan. 1—Mar. 19].

LA VERDAD. w. est. 1846.
CtY
    1846   Tomo 1, Nos. 1—3.

LA VERDAD. bw. est. Oct. 15, 1910.
TxU
    1910   Oct. 15.
    1911   Jan. 15.

Puerto de la Paz

See La Paz.

Puerto de Matamoros

See Matamoros.

Puerto México

EL ISTMO.
LNT—MA
    1925   Mar. 29.

EL OBSERVADOR. sw., 3w., irr.
    Note: Suspended publication Oct. 19,
    1934—Apr. 15, 1935.
CU
    1934   Mar. 16, 25—28, June 6—July
            12, 19—Oct. 19.
    1935   Apr. 15—May 3, 8—June 8, 14,
            July 14, 28—31, Aug. 2, 4, 10—
            17.

Querétaro

EL CONSTITUYENTE. sw. est. Dec.
1916.
DLC
    1917   Jan. 31.

LOS DEBATES. sw. est. Jan. 1, 1848.
CU—B
    Micro (N)
    1848   Jan. 1—June 3.
MWA
    1848   Apr. 13.

EL FEDERALISTA. w.
CtY
    1849   July 29—Dec. 30.
    1850   Jan. 3—Apr. 6.

EL MUNDO. w. est. Sept. 16, 1857.
DLC
    1857   Sept. 16.

EL PROGRESO. sw. est. Mar. 5, 1848.
CU—B
    Micro (N)
    1848   Mar. 5—Apr. 2.

LA SOMBRA DE ARTEAGA; PERIODI-
CO OFICIAL DEL ESTADO DE QUE-
RETARO. w.
CU—B
    Micro (P)
    1875   Mar. 28.
    1878   Sept. 6, Oct. 11.
TxU
    1880   Jan. 8—June 18, July 25—31,
            Aug. 15—28, Sept 15, Oct. 2,
            20—Dec. 21.

LA VERDAD. w.
KHi
    1883   Apr. 28.

Real del Castillo

EL FRONTERIZO. w. est. 1881.
  CU—B
    1881   Sept. 3.

Rosario

EL PROGRESISTA. w.
  CU—B
    Micro (P)
    1878   Nov. 21.

Saltillo

BOLETIN OFICIAL. est. 1840.
  CtY
    1840   No. 1.

EL CRONISTA DE COAHUILA.
  TxU
    1880   Oct. 15.

EL HERALDO DE COAHUILA. sw.
  DLC
    1941   Mar. 9.

EL INTRANSIGENTE. w.
  TxU
    1916   Jan. 15.

PERIODICO OFICIAL DEL GOBIERNO
  CONSTITUCIONAL DEL ESTADO
  DE COAHUILA DE ZARAGOZA. sw.
  CU—B
    Micro (P)
    1878   Sept. 3, 13.
  TxU
    1880   July 26, Sept. 1—Oct. 22, Dec.
            17.
    1881   Feb. 26.
            Alcance: Feb. 26.
    1884   Feb. 8.
    1885   Mar. 17—20.

PICKET GUARD. sw. est. Apr. 1847.
    Note: In English.
  DLC
    1847   May 3, 21.

EL PUEBLO. w. est. [1935].
  DLC
    1942   July 25, Sept. 16.

RENACIMIENTO. w. est. June 1, 1913.
  TxU
    1913   June 1.

EL REPUBLICANO. w.
  CU—B
    Micro (P)
    1845   Jan. 11—18, Feb. 1—15, Apr.
            5—12, 26, Aug. 2—23, Dec. 13.

EL REVOLUCIONARIO. w. est. 1932.
  CU
    1936   Nov. 20.
    1937   May 1, June 25, July 7, 21.
    1938   Feb. 5, Mar. 21.
  DLC
    1939   May 24.
    1941   Jan. 24, May 29, June 24, July
            1, 7, 14, 26, Aug. 1, 14, Sept. 3.
    1942   Jan. 10.
  TxU
    1942   Jan. 10.

SENTINEL. sw. est. 1848.
    Note: In English.
  CLCM
    1848   Apr. 17.
  DLC
    1848   Apr. 10.

LA UNION. est. 1853.
  CU—B
    Micro (P)
    1853   Oct. 8.

EL VOTO DE COAHUILA.
  CU—B
    1841   Sept. 25.
    1842   Jan. 1—8, 29, Feb. 26, Mar.
            19—26, Apr. 9—16, 30—July 9,
            30—Aug. 20, Sept. 3—17, Oct.
            1—8, 29—Nov. 5, Dec. 18—25.
    1843   Mar. 4—12, 25, Apr. 27—May
            6, July 29—Aug. 5, 26, Sept. 11,
            Oct. 2.
    1844   Feb. 19, Mar. 30—Apr. 20.
  CtY
    1841   Jan. 8.

Salvatierra

LA REFORMA.
  TxU
    1917   May 6.

San Cristóbal

ADELANTE. est. 1910.
    Note: Succeeded by *Más allá*.
  LNT—MA
    1910   Aug. 14.
EL ARTISTA. est. 1878.
  LNT—MA
    1886   Oct. 28.
AVISOS AL PUEBLO. sw. est. Aug. 1,
  1830.
  CtY
    1831   Feb. 15.
  LNT—MA
    1830   [Aug. 1—Dec. 19].
    1831   Jan. 2—Feb. 20.
BOLETIN DE NOTICIAS.
  LNT—MA
    1863   Sept. 12—30.
    1864   Feb. 13.
BOLETIN OFICIAL.
  LNHT
    1849   Nov. 6, 9, 12.
    1850   June 16.
    1851   June 2, 13, Aug. 16, 23, 30,
            Sept. 6, 13, 18, 27, Oct. 11, 18,
            Nov. 22.
    1875   Aug. 29, Sept. 10.
    1879   Sept. 24.
LA BRUJULA. w., bw., 3m., irr. est. Apr.
  23, 1869.
  LNT—MA
    1869   Apr. 23—Dec. 31.
    1870   Jan. 7—Dec. 30.
    1871   Jan. 6—Dec. 29.
    1872   [Jan. 12—Dec. 25].
    1873   Jan. 8, Aug. 1—Dec. 1.
    1874   Jan. 20, Feb. 10, Mar. 1, 20,
            Apr. 20, May 1.
EL CABO DE CUARTO. irr.
  LNT—MA
    1875   Sept. 2.

EL CAUDILLO. w. est. 1888.
  LNT—MA
    1888   Mar. 3, Apr. 2, 10, 15, 29, May
            5, 13, Aug. 12, Oct. 14.
    1889   May 12, Nov. 17.
EL CLUB POPULAR.
  LNT—MA
    1895   [May 26—Nov. 24].
LA CONCILIACION. w. est. Mar. 3,
  1877.
  LNT—MA
    1877   Mar. 3—June 9.
LA CRUZ DE CHIAPAS. w. est. Nov. 20,
  1904.
  LNT—MA
    1904   Nov. 20, 27.
LA DEFENSA. bw. est. Sept. 15, 1910.
  LNT—MA
    1910   Sept. 15—Oct. 30.
EL DEMOCRATA. 3w. est. Mar. 10, 1880.
  LNT—MA
    1880   Mar. 10—Nov. 1.
  TxU
    1880   Sept. 1, Oct. 10.
EL DIA. w. est. 1908.
  LNT—MA
    1908   Dec. 27.
EL DOS DE ABRIL. bw., m.
  LNT—MA
    1887   Nov. 26, Dec. 26, 31.
    1888   Feb. 27, Mar. 25, Apr. 2, May
            24, June 19.
EL DUENDE. w. est. 1862.
  LNT—MA
    1862   Oct. 10, 17.
EL ECO LIBERAL. 3m. est. Nov. 11,
  1878.
  LNT—MA
    1878   [Nov. 11—Dec. 31].
    1879   [Jan. 1—Dec. 21].
EL ESPIRITU DEL SIGLO. w.
  LNT—MA
    1861   [Feb. 16—Dec. 14].

1862 ₁Jan. 25 — Dec. 31₁.
1863 Feb. 21, 28, Mar. 21, 28, Apr. 4, 18, June 20, July 4.
1864 ₁Apr. 1 — Dec. 31₁.
1865 ₁Jan. 1 — Dec. 31₁.
1866 ₁Jan. 1 — Nov. 30₁.
1867 Jan. 19, 26, Mar. 30, Apr. 6, 20, 27, May 1 — June 30, Dec. 14.
1868 ₁Jan. 11 — Dec. 31₁.
1869 — 1871 ₁Jan. 1 — Dec. 31₁.
1872 ₁Jan. 1 — Oct. 31₁.
1873 ₁Jan. 1 — Mar. 31, May 1 — Dec. 31₁.
1874 ₁Jan. 1 — May 31, July 1 — Dec. 31₁.
1875 ₁Jan. 1 — July 31, Sept. 1 — Dec. 31₁.
1876 ₁Jan. 1 — Dec. 31₁.

EL ESTADO. w. est. 1912.
  LNT — MA
    1912 ₁Sept. 12 — Dec. 31₁.
    1913 Jan. 30.

LA EVOLUCION. m. est. Jan. 1, 1904.
  LNT — MA
    1904 Jan. 1, Feb. 5.

EL FENIX. irr.
  LNT — MA
    1910 May 5, Sept. 15, Nov. 2.

EL FESTIVAL DEL VOTO. w. est. May. 5, 1922.
  LNT — MA
    1922 May 5 — June 18.

EL FRONTERIZO CHIAPANECO. w.
  CU — B
    Micro (P)
    1878 June 19.
  LNT — MA
    1877 June 13 — Oct. 1, 3 — Dec. 31.
    1878 Jan. 1 — Mar. 5, 7 — Dec. 31.
    1879 Jan. 1 — Nov. 30.

GACETA MUNICIPAL.
  LNT — MA
    1892 Mar. 1 — June 15.

EL GAVILAN. w. est. 1911.
  LNT — MA

1911 Nov. 21 — Dec. 19.
1912 ₁Jan. 30, Mar. 12 — July 9₁.
1913 Apr. 15.

EL GUARDIA NACIONAL DE CHIAPAS.
  w. est. Aug. 24, 1848.
  LNT — MA
    1848 Aug. 24, Oct. 12.
    1849 ₁Mar. 22 — Oct. 18₁.
    1850 ₁Jan. 1 — July 7, Nov. 10 — Dec. 1₁.
    1851 Jan. 7, Mar. 13, July 15, Aug. 12.
  MWA
    1848 ₁Aug. 31 — Dec. 31.₁
    1849 ₁Jan. 1 — Dec. 20.₁
    1850 Jan. 17 — 24.

EL HIJO DEL PUEBLO. w. est. 1911.
  LNT — MA
    1911 Sept. 3 — Dec. 3.

LA IDEA CATOLICA. 3m.
  LNT — MA
    1885 May 1 — June 30.

EL IMPARCIAL. bw. est. Aug. 15, 1877.
  LNT — MA
    1877 Aug. 15 — Oct. 1, Nov. 1 — Dec. 31.
    1878 Jan. 15, Mar. 1 — Apr. 15.

EL IRIS. bw.
  LNT — MA
    1879 ₁Aug. 1 — Dec. 31₁.

LA JUVENTUD CHIAPANECA. bw.
  LNT — MA
    1877 ₁Aug. 15 — Dec. 31₁.
    1878 ₁Jan. 1 — Apr. 15₁.
    1888 Sept. 1, Oct. 15, Nov. 1, 15.
    1889 Jan. 1, Mar. 15, Oct. 1, 15.
    1890 Sept. 1.
    1891 Jan. 1.

LA JUVENTUD ESTUDIOSA. bw.
  LNT — MA
    1893 July 1, 18, Aug. 1, Sept. 1, 15, Oct. 15.
    1894 Feb. 25.

LA LIBERTAD DEL SUFRAGIO. w. est.
Apr. 20, 1911.
LNT—MA
1911 [Apr. 20—Dec. 31].
1912 [Jan. 1—June 11].

LA LUZ. w.
LNT—MA
1891 Oct. 1—Nov. 14, 16—Dec. 31.

LA LUZ DEL ALBA. w. est. 1907.
LNT—MA
1907 [May 12—Dec. 8].

MAS ALLA. w. est. Sept. 11, 1910.
Note: Succeeded *Adelante*.
LNT—MA
1910 [Sept. 11—Dec. 11].

EL NOTICIOSO CHIAPANECO. w. est.
Apr. 18, 1847.
LNT—MA
1847 June 13, Dec. 19.
TxU
1847 Apr. 18—May 9, 23—Aug. 31,
Oct. 31, Nov. 14.

EL OBRERO. w.
LNT—MA
1873 Sept. 6.

LA OPINION. est. 1950.
LNT—MA
1950 July 9.

LA OPINION POPULAR. w. est. June 1,
1887.
LNT—MA
1887 [June 1—July 1].

EL ORGANO DEL GOBIERNO. w.
CU—B
Micro (P)
1855 Sept. 1, 15.

EL PARA-RAYO. w. est. Oct. 3, 1827.
LNT—MA
1827 Oct. 3—Dec. 31.
1828 [Jan. 1—Dec. 31].
1829 [Feb. 12—Oct. 31].
1830 [Jan. 16—July 17].

EL PENSAMIENTO. bw. est. Oct. 15,
1884.
LNT—MA
1884 Oct. 15, Nov. 1.
TxU
1884 Oct. 15.
1885 Mar. 1.

EL PUEBLO LIBRE. w. est. 1879.
LNT—MA
1879—1883 [Jan. 1—Dec. 31].
TxU
1880 Aug. 4—11, Sept. 15, Oct. 27,
Nov. 3, Dec. 8.
1882 Sept. 13—20.
1883 Jan. 10—Feb. 21, June 27,
Aug. 1.

EL PUEBLO OBRERO. w. est. 1912.
LNT—MA
1912 Sept. 29.

LA RAZON. 3m. est. 1874.
LNT—MA
1874 Oct. 8.
1875 Feb. 28.

EL REGENERADOR; ORGANO DEL
GOBIERNO Y COMANDANCIA MILI-
TAR DEL ESTADO DE CHIAPAS. w.
est. Jan. 31, 1877.
LNT—MA
1877 Jan. 31—June 6.
TxU
1877 Jan. 31—May 2, 16—June 6.

REVISTA CHIAPANECA. w. est. [1909].
LNT—MA
1910 Apr. 10—Nov. 6.

EL SARNOSITO. est. Oct. 17, 1912.
LNT—MA
1921 Oct. 17.

EL SENTIMIENTO NACIONAL. 3m. est.
1883.
LNT—MA
1883 Dec. 14.
1884 Jan. 1—June 30.

EL SENTIMIENTO RELIGIOSO. est.
1875.
LNT — MA
1875   July 1.

LA SITUACION. w. est. 1872.
LNT — MA
1872   Oct. 19, Nov. 2, 16.
1873   Jan. 11, 18, 25.

EL TRABAJO. 3m.
LNHT
1885   Mar. 20 — Dec. 22.
1886   Jan. 15 — June 7.

EL TRIBUNO. bw. est. 1918.
LNT — MA
1918   Apr. 15.

LA UNION. w. est. 1891.
LNT — MA
1891   Jan. 25, Feb. 1 — Mar. 31, Apr.
5.

LA VERDAD. est. 1891.
LNT — MA
1891   Feb. 15, Oct. 11, 18, Nov. 15.

EL VOTO DE CHIAPAS. bw. est. June 1,
1895.
LNT — MA
1895   June 1 — Dec. 15.

LA VOZ DE CHIAPAS. w. est. Jan. 22,
1911.
LNT — MA
1911   Jan. 22 — Dec. 31.
1912   Jan. 1 — Dec. 31.
1913   Jan. 19 — 26.

LA VOZ DEL PUEBLO; PERIODICO
OFICIAL DE CHIAPAS. est. 1855.
LNT — MA
1855   Nov. 3, Dec. 1, 8.
1856 — 1857   [Jan. 1 — Dec. 31].
1858   Jan. 9.

LA VOZ DEL PUEBLO; PERIODICO
INDEPENDIENTE, DE LITERATURA
Y VARIEDADES. est. 1907.
LNT — MA
1907   May 2 — 5, June 9, July 14, Aug.
4.

VOZ JUVENIL. est. 1922.
LNT — MA
1922   June 15.

San Cristóbal Las Casas

See San Cristóbal.

San Juan Bautista
See Villahermosa.

San Juan del Río

EL HORIZONTE. w.
TxU
1873   Mar. 2 — 9.

San Luis Potosí

ACCION. d. est. 1917.
Note: Ceased publication 1942.
DLC
1941   Aug. 13.

LA BALANZA DE ASTREA. sw. est.
Sept. 4, 1834.
CtY
1834   Sept. 18, Nov. 20.
DLC
1834   Prospecto: Sept. 1.
Sept. 4 — Nov. 20.

LA BANDERA NEGRA. est. 1834.
CtY
1834   Mar. 25.

BOLETIN DEL EJERCITO FEDERAL.
CtY
1859   Sept. 1, 8.

BOLETIN OFICIAL. est. 1837.
CtY
1837   No. 8.
1842 — 1844   Nos. 1, 4 — 8, 10, 11, 30,
36, 38, 80, 115 — 124, 126 — 132,
134 — 136, 147.

BOLETIN OFICIAL. sw., irr. est. Aug.
1855.
Note: Ceased publication 1859.
CtY
1855   Aug. 20, 28 — Sept. 1, 10, 12, 19,

23, 25, 26, Oct. 3 – 19, 27, Nov.
3 – Dec. 26.
Suplemento: Aug. 20, 28, Sept.
12, 19, 23, 25, 26.

BOLETIN OFICIAL DEL EJERCITO
FEDERAL. irr. est. Apr. 28, 1860.
CtY
   1860   Apr. 28 – June 14, 20 – Aug. 2.
               Suplemento: June 21, 22.

BOLETIN OFICIAL DEL CUERPO DE
EJERCITO DEL CENTRO. est. 1862.
CtY
   1862   Feb. 15, 20, Mar. 1 – Apr. 1,
               21, 22, 29, May 3 – 15.
               Suplemento: Apr. 21.

EL COMERCIO MERCANTIL, POLITI-
CA, LITERARIO, DE INDUSTRIA,
ARTES, MEDICIANA.
TxU
   1874   Nov. 21 – 26.

EL CONSTITUCIONAL. w. est. 1877.
CU – B
   Micro (P)
   1878   Mar. 20.

CONTEMPORANEO. d. est. Jan. 6,
1896.
CtY
   1909   Nov. 5.

EL CORREO DE SAN LUIS. d., w. est.
Sept. 1882.
CtY
   1891   Feb. 12 – May 24.
   1895   Jan. 21 – Feb. 18.

EL CORREO POTOSINO. est. 1879.
CtY
   1879   Dec. 25.
   1880   May 5.

LA CRONICA; PERIODICO OFICIAL
DEL GOBIERNO DEL ESTADO DE
SAN LUIS POTOSI. sw. est. 1859.
CtY
   1860   Oct. 27, Nov. 3, 8, 17 – Dec. 5,
               12, 19, 29, 30.
               Suplemento: Nov. 6, 9, Dec. 24.
   1861   Feb. 3 – 7.

LA EPOCA; PERIODICO OFICIAL
DEL ESTADO DE S.L. POTOSI. sw., w.
est. 1846.
   Note: Ceased publication 1853.
CtY
   1849   Jan. 2 – Oct. 24, 31 – Dec. 12,
               19 – 29.
   1850   May 8.
   1851   Jan. 4 – Feb. 8, 22 – Oct. 1,
               18 – 25, Nov. 22.
   1852   July 3 – 17, 31 – Aug. 4, 11 –
               Sept. 4, 11 – Dec. 25.
   1853   Jan. 1 – 15.
               Suplemento: Jan. 21.

EL ESTANDARTE. sw., d. est. Jan. 18,
1885.
   Note: Periodicity Jan. 18, 1885 – Apr.
   7, 1890, semiweekly; after Apr. 8,
   1890, daily. Ceased publication 1911.
CtY
   1887   Suplemento: Apr. 21.
TxU
   1907   Feb. 15 – 24.
   1910   Feb. 24, Mar. 30.

EL ESTANDARTE DE LOS CHINA-
CATES. est. 1847.
CtY
   1847   July 11.

GACETA DEL GOBIERNO DE SAN
LUIS POTOSI. w. est. 1838.
   Note: Ceased publication 1842.
CtY
   1841   Nos. 162 – 177, 179, 180, 183 –
               187, 208, 221.
   1842   Nos 225 – 232, 235, 236, 238,
               240, 242, 244, 245.

GACETA DEL GOBIERNO DEL ES-
TADO LIBRE DE SAN LUIS POTOSI.
w., irr. est. 1831.
   Note: Ceased publication 1832.
CtY
   1831   Jan. 28 – Feb. 25, Mar, 4 – Apr.
               22, May 6 – 13, 27 – June 10,
               July 1, 15 – 22, Aug. 13 – 26,
               Sept. 23 – Dec. 3, 17 – 31.
   1832   June 9.

EL GARIBALDI; PERIODICO OFICIAL
DE GOBIERNO DEL ESTADO. sw. est.
1860.
  Note: Ceased publication 1863.
  CtY
    1861   Feb. 16 — Apr. 10, 24 — June 26,
            July 6 — 26, Aug. 17 — Dec. 21.
    1962   Jan. 11 — 25, Oct. 26 — Dec. 31.
            Suplemento: Jan. 10.
    1863   Jan. 3 — Feb. 18, 25.
  MWA
    1861   Feb. 20, Mar. 6, 13 — 23, Apr. 6,
            sup., 27, sup., May 11, sup.,
            26, 29, sup., Dec. 23.
    1862   Jan. 18.

LA IDEA LIBERAL. w. est. Dec. 19, 1860.
  Note: Title *La Idea*, Dec. 19, 1860 —
  1861; *La Idea liberal*, after 1861.
  CtY
    1860   Dec. 19 — 26.
    1861   Jan. 2 — 16, Aug. 25 — Sept. 19.

LA INDEPENDENCIA MEXICANA. d.
  est. June 15, 1863.
  CU — B
    Micro (N)
    1863   June 15 — Sept. 27, 29 — Nov.
            24, 26 — 28, 30, Dec. 2 — 5, 7 —
            21.

EL INDEPENDIENTE. est. 1847.
  CtY
    1847   Nov. 13.

LIBERAL; PERIODICO OFICIAL DE
GOBIERNO DEL ESTADO DE SAN
LUIS POTOSÍ. sw. est. 1857.
  Note: Ceased publication 1860.
  MWA
    1857   Feb. 24 — 27, Mar. 17, June 27,
            July 29, Aug. 12, Nov. 25.
    1859   July 30, Sept. 21, Oct. 1, 15.
    1860   May 19 — 26, June 16.

EL MEXICANO LIBRE POTOSINESE.
  sw. est. Feb. 24, 1828.
  Note: Ceased publication [Dec. 21,]
  1828.

CtY
    1828   Feb. 24 — Oct. 12, 23 — Dec. 21.
            Suplementos.

EL OBRERO POTOSINO. w.
  CtY
    1881   Feb. 10 — 24.

LA OPINION; PERIODICO OFICIAL
DEL GOBIERNO SUPERIOR DEL
DEPARTAMENTO DE SAN LUIS
POTOSÍ. w. est. 1834.
  Note: Ceased publication 1837.
  CtY
    1835   Nos. 23 — 25, 34 — 39, 45, 47, 48,
            52, 54 — 60, 62, 63, 65 — 68, 70,
            71, 73, 74, 77 — 83.
    1836   Nos. 115 — 117, 119 — 123, 130,
            131, 133, 134, 136 — 138, 140 —
            144, 153 — 168.
            Suplemento: Nos. 129, 139.
    1837   Nos. 169 — 173, 176, 177, 179.
            Suplemento: No. 174.
  TxSjM
    1836   Suplemento: Mar. 14.

LA PALABRA. irr.
  CtY
    1894   Mar. 8, Apr. 11 — 16, June 1 —
            13, 27 — Sept. 1.

PERIODICO OFICIAL DEL GOBIERNO
DEL ESTADO DE SAN LUIS POTOSI.
  est. Dec. 28, 1876.
  Note: Title *La Union democrática*,
  Dec. 28, 1876 — Apr. 7, 1885; *Periódi-
  co oficial del gobierno del estado de
  San Luis Potosí*, after Apr. 27, 1885.
  Succeeded *La Sombra de Zaragoza*.
  CU — B
    1879   Aug. 30.
    1881   Sept. 22.
    1883   Apr. 6.
  CtY
    1876   Dec. 28.
    1877   Jan. 3 — Dec. 31.
    1878   Jan. 4 — Mar. 14, Apr. 28 — Dec.
            19.
    1879   Jan. 5 — Dec. 27.
    1880   Jan. 3 — Dec. 30.
    1881   Jan. 3 — Dec. 30.

1882   Jan. 3 – Dec. 29.
1883   Jan. 2 – Dec. 25.
1884   Jan. 8 – Dec. 25.
1885   Jan. 6 – Dec. 28.
1886   Jan. 1 – Dec. 25.
1887   Jan. 1 – Dec. 31.
1888   Jan. 4 – Dec. 29.
1889   Jan. 2 – Dec. 29.
1890   Jan. 9 – Dec. 28.
TxU
1880   Oct. 27, Nov. 8 – 19, 27, Dec.
        15 – 19.

PERIQUILLO SARNIENTO. d. est. Sept.
1893.
CtY
1893   Sept. 9.

EL POTOSINO; PERIODICO OFICIAL
DEL GOBIERNO DEL ESTADO. sw.,
irr. est. 1862.
    Note: Ceased publication 1863.
CtY
1863   Mar. 7 – July 4, 15, 25 – Aug.
        15, 22, 29 – Sept. 5, 12 – 23,
        Oct. 7 – 17, 21, Nov. 25, Dec. 9.

EL POTOSINO; PERIODICO DE POL-
ITICA, LITERATURA, VARIEDADES
Y ANUNCIOS. est. Apr. 21, 1874.
CtY
1874   Apr. 26, July 8 – 17.

RECONQUISTA. w. est. 1911.
TxU
1911   June 1 – 30.

LA REFORMA; PERIODICO OFICIAL
DEL GOBIERNO DE SAN LUIS
POTOSI. sw. est. 1853.
    Note: Ceased publication 1861.
CU – B
    Micro (P)
1854   Dec. 27.
CtY
1853   Jan. 29 – Dec. 31.
1854   Jan. 1 – Dec. 20.
1855   Feb. 7 – Aug. 11.

LA RESTAURACION; PERIODICO OFI-
CIAL DEL DEPARTAMENTO. sw.,

3w., w. est. 1859.
    Note: Sub-title varies.
CtY
1859   Dec. 17 – 21.
1860   Jan. 4 – Apr. 18.
1864   Jan. 2 – 16, 23 – Feb. 18, 22 –
        Apr. 18, 27, May 21, 28 – June
        4, 12 – Dec. 29.
1865   Jan. 1 – 8, Jan. 22, Feb. 5 –
        Dec. 3, 17 – 24.

EL SOLDADO DE LA PATRIA.
CtY
1844   Tomo 1, No. 4.

LA SOMBRA DE ZARAGOZA; PERIO-
DICO OFICIAL DEL ESTADO. sw.
est. Jan. 5, 1867.
    Note: Succeeded by *Periódico oficial
    del gobierno del estado de San Luis
    Potosí*. Ceased publication 1876.
CtY
1867   Jan. 31 – Feb. 9, 23 – Mar. 6,
        Apr. 17, Mar. 18, June 1.
1868   Apr. 22.
1870   Feb. 16 – Dec. 30.
1871   Jan. 2 – Dec. 30.
1872   Jan. 4 – Dec. 29.
1873   Jan. 3 – Dec. 29.
1875   Jan. 3 – May 24, 29 – Dec. 29.

EL TELEGRAFO POTOSINENSE. sw.
est. Nov. 27, 1829.
CtY
1829   Nov. 27 – Dec. 29.
1830   Jan. 5 – Feb. 12, 19 – 23, Mar.
        2 – 9, Apr. 2, 13, 20 – 27, June
        4.

LA UNION DEMOCRATICA.
    See *Periódico oficial del gobierno del
    estado de San Luis Potosí*.

LA UNION DEMOCRATICA; PERIODI-
CO POLITICO, DE VARIEDADES Y
ANUNCIOS. w. est. 1873.
CtY
1873   Nov. 8 – 15, Dec. 6 – 27.
1874   Jan. 3 – Mar. 8, Apr. 6 – May
        15, June 15 – July 12, 26, Aug.

11 — Sept. 28, Oct. 27 — Dec.
30.

1875   Jan. 6 — Mar. 11, 18 — 25, Apr.
1 — 25, May 9 — July 6, 13 —
Aug. 12.

EL YUNQUE DE LA LIBERTAD. sw. est.
1832.
Note: Ceased publication 1834.
CtY
1832   Dec. 16, 23 — 30.
LNT — MA
1834   May 28, Apr. 2, 5, 9, 12, 16,
May 3, 10, 14.

San Pedro

EL COMBATE. w. est. July 9, 1911.
TxU
1911   July 9.

Santa Anna de Tamaulipas
See Tampico.

Sombrerete

ASILO DE LA LIBERTAD.
CU — B
Micro (P)
1831   Apr. 28.

Tacubaya

EL IDEAL DEMOCRATICA. 3w.
TxU
1912   May 24, 28 — June 8, 12 — 23.

EL LUCERO DE TACUBAYA. w., bw.,
sw. est. Jan. 11, 1844.
CU — B
Micro (N)
1844   Jan. 11 — Mar. 7, 21 — Apr. 27,
May 11 — Dec. 2.

LA OPINION. sw. est. Feb. 24, 1918.
DLC
1918   Feb. 26.

Tampico

ATALAYA.
TxSjM
1835   June 20.

EL BOLETIN. w.
CtY
1844   July 6, 13.
TxU
1844   July 13.

EL DESENGAÑO. bw.
TxSjM
1840   Alcance: Aug. 1.
TxU
1839   Alcance: Sept. 10.
1840   Nov. 8, Dec. 15.

EL COMERCIO DE SANTA ANNA DE
TAMAULIPAS. sw.
Note: Title *El Comercio de Tampico*,
1852; *El Comercio de Santa Anna de
Tamaulipas*, after 1853. Become official publication July 20, 1853.
TxU
1852   Apr. 3, May 1, June 30.
1853   Jan. 29, Feb. 5, May 4 — 18,
25 — Aug. 20, 31, Sept. 21 —
Nov. 30, Dec. 7, 14, 31.
1855   Jan. 6 — 20, 27 — 31, Feb. 7,
17 — Apr. 21, 28 — May 19,
26 — June 9, 16.

EL COMERCIO DE TAMPICO; PERI-
ODICO POLITICO, LITERARIO Y
MERCANTIL. 3w., sw.
TxU
1868   Mar. 7, Apr. 11 — 16, May 16,
23 — 27, Sept. 2, 28 — Oct. 1,
7 — 18, 25 — Nov. 25, Dec. 2 —
27.
1869   Jan. 2, 9, 17 — Feb. 7, 17 — 25,
Mar. 21, May 1, 9, 18, 25, 29,
June 3, 8, 10 — 26, Sept. 21, Oct.
22.
1870   June 17.

EL CORREO. d.
TxU
1824   Sept. 19, Oct. 26, Dec. 22, 31.
1825   Feb. 20, 21, 23.
LA ESPERANZA. sw., 3w. est. Feb. 5,
1845.
CtY
1846   Tomo 2, No. 48.

DLC
1845   Feb. 5 — Mar. 21, 23 — Apr. 30.
1846   July 28 — Aug. 5, 7 — 19, 21 —
         27.
TxU
1846   Jan. 10.

GACETA DE SANTA ANNA DE TAMAU-
LIPAS. sw., 3w., sw. est. 1831.
Note: Title varies *Gaceta de Tam-
pico* and *Gaceta de Tamaulipas*.
DLC
1836   Aug. 23, 30, Sept. 2, 9, 16, 20,
         Oct. 15 — 22.
TxU
1834   Mar. 10, Apr. 21 — 24, May 10,
         June 25 — 30, July 4, 9, 14 — 18,
         Aug. 4 — 18, 25 — Sept. 19.

GACETA DEL GOBIERNO DEL ESTA-
DO DE LAS TAMAULIPAS. est. 1840.
Note: Title *Gaceta de gobierno de
Tamaulipas* 1840 — May 9, 1844;
*Gaceta del gobierno del departmento
de Tamaulipas*, June 5 — Oct. 26,
1844; *Gaceta del gobierno constitucional de Tamaulipas*, Mar. 1,
1845 — May 24, 1846; *Gaceta del gobierno del estado de las Tamaulipas*,
after May 24, 1846.
CtY
1840   Nos. 2, 9, 10 — 16, 19 — 24, 41,
         42, 44, 45.
1841   Nos. 3, 5, 9, 12, 13, 15, 16, 19,
         21, 24, 26, 27, 31, 34 — 36, 39,
         40, 42 — 47, 49.
1842   Nos. 1 — 3, 8, 10, 11, 14, 15, 18,
         21, 23, 24, 29, 30, 34, 36, 37, 39,
         41, 47, 48, 51.
1843   Nos. 1, 5, 6, 9, 10, 19.
1844   Nos. 47, 49, 52, 56, 60 — 64,
         66 — 70, 72 — 75, 79 — 83.
1845   Nos. 3, 21, 22, 24, 26, 33, 36,
         42, 49.
1846   Nos. 51 — 57, 64, 66 — 70, 72 —
         83, 90, 132, 134, 135, 138, 139.
TxSjM
1844   July 3.

EL MUNDO. d. est. 1918.
DLC
1943   Mar. 14.
LNT — MA
1930   Jan. 20.
TxU
1924   Sept. 19, 26, 28, Oct. 26, 27,
         Dec. 27.
1925   Jan. 1, 9, 10, Feb. 21, Mar. 6.

LA OPINION. d.
TxU
1924   Oct. 26, 27.
1925   Jan. 10, Feb. 17, 20, Mar. 6, 8.

EL PORVENIR. w.
TxU
1839   June 30.
1893   Aug. 20.
1895   Jan. 13.
1897   July 4, 27.

EL PORVENIR DE TAMPICO. bw.
NN
1907   Mar. 1 — Aug. 15, Sept. 15 —
         Oct. 1, Nov. 1 — Dec. 15.
1908   Jan. 1 — Apr. 1, Sept. 1 — Dec.
         15.
1909   Jan. 1, Feb. 1 — May 1.

LA REPUBLICA. d. est. 1912.
Note: In English and Spanish.
DLC
1913   Dec. 11.
         Boletín: Dec. 12.

EL SEMANARIO. w.
TxU
1880   June 25, July 9 — 16, Aug. 6, 20,
         Oct. 8 — 15, 29 — Nov. 5.
1881   Feb. 4.

LA SOBERANIA DE TAMAULIPAS. w.
est. Sept. 23, 1866.
TxU
1866   Sept. 23, Oct. 17, Nov. 14 — 30.
1867   Jan. 5 — 16.

EL SOL. w. est. 1929.
LNT — MA
1929   Dec. 22 — 24.
1930   ₁Jan. 12, Feb. 5 — June 8₁.

EL TAMAULIPECO. sw.
  CU—B
    Micro (P)
    1852   Dec. 29.
        Suplemento: Dec. 29.

TAMPICO SENTINEL. w. est. 1847.
    Note: In English.
  CtY
    1847   Vol. 1.

TAMPICO TIMES. w. est. [1907].
    Note: In English.
  MWA
    1911   Apr. 15.

THE TAMPICO TRIBUNE. w. est.
  [1906].
    Note: In English. Ceased publica-
    tion July 11, 1931 and merged with
    the *Monterrey Times.*
  DLC
    1926   Aug. 7—Nov. 19, 28—Dec. 31.
    1927   Jan. 1—14, 16—Feb. 18, 20—
        Dec. 31.
    1928—1930   Jan. 1—Dec. 31.
    1931   Jan. 1—July 11.
  LNT—MA
    1920   Feb. 7.
    1929   Nov. 2.
    1930   Aug. 1—Dec. 31.
    1931   Jan. 1—July 11.
  TxU
    1923   Mar. 31—Apr. 7, 28—Oct. 6,
        20—Dec. 31.
    1924   Jan. 1—Sept. 13, 27—Nov. 22,
        Dec. 6—31.
    1925   Jan. 1—Mar. 14, 28—Dec. 31.
    1926—1930   Jan. 1—Dec. 31.
    1931   Jan. 1—7, 21—May 16, 30—
        July 11.

EL TELEGRAFO DE TAMPICO.
  TxU
    1839   Jan. 23.

LA TRIBUNA. d. est. 1933.
  DLC
    1943   Feb. 12, 13, Mar. 10, Apr. 19,
        30.

VIDA LIBRE. w. est. May, 1918.
  DLC
    1918   July 27.

Tapachula

LA LUCHA. sw. est. 1911.
  LNT—MA
    1911   Sept. 5.

EL PROGRESO. w.
  LNT—MA
    1911   Aug. 28.

EL SUR DE MEXICO. w. est. [1902].
  CU
    1937   Dec. 30.
    1938   Jan. 6, Feb. 3, Apr. 21.
  LNT—MA
    1904   Aug. 14.

Tarma

EL ECO DE SOCABAYA. est. 1838.
  DLC
    1838   Oct. 17.

Tecolotlan

LA VERDAD. w. est. Jan. 19, 1913.
  TxU
    1913   Jan. 19.

Tehuacan

LA EVOLUCION.
  TxU
    1910   Alcance: June 19.

Tepic

AURORA DEL TRABAJO. w. est. Aug.
  28, 1880.
  CU—B
    Micro (P)
    1882   May 26.
  TxU
    1880   Aug. 28, Sept. 4, 25, Oct. 19—
        26, Nov. 9—20, Dec. 14—21.

EL DESPERTADOR. w. est. Dec. 10,
  1911.
  TxU
    1911   Dec. 10.

PERIODICO OFICIAL DEL DISTRITO MILITAR DE TEPIC.
TxU
    1880   Nov. 5, Dec. 3.

PRENSA LIBRE. d.
CU
    1939   Dec. 2.
    1943   Aug. 12, Sept. 1–5, 7, Oct. 5–9, 12–19, 22–25, 28, Nov. 1–3, 6, 9, 10, 15–Dec. 6, 10–13, 15–18, 21–26, 28.
    1944   Jan. 5–14, 18–24, 26, 28, Feb. 1, 4, 7, 9, 11, 15, 16, 22–24, 26, 29, Mar. 1, 8, 10, 16, 21, 23–25, 28, 30, Apr. 12, July 22, 23, 25–27, 30, Aug. 1–7, 9–14, 18, 19, 21, 24, 25, 27–31, Sept. 4, 6, 9, 11–13, 19–21, 24, 27, 29, Oct. 4, 12, 19, 20, 23, 25–27, 31, Nov. 2, 5, 6, 8–12, 14, 15, 17, 19, 20, 23–25, 27–29, Dec. 1–3, 5, 8, 13–15, 17, 19–21, 26–28.
    1945   Jan. 1, 6, 7, 22, 28, 30, Feb. 1, 2, 5, 10, Apr. 6, 8, 23.
    1946   Jan. 29–Feb. 2, 6–10, 13, 21, 23, 26, 28, Mar. 2, 3, 9, 10, 14–22, 26, 30, Apr. 2, 4–7, 10, 11, 14, 25, May 3, 8, 9, 21, 25, 28, June 7, 9–14, 20, 22–26, 28, July 3–5, 10, 12, 13, 16, 19, 28, Aug. 2, 10, 13, 16, 19, 24, 28–30, Sept. 4, 26–28, Oct. 2, 4, 6, 18, 24, Nov. 2, 5, 8, 10, 12, 13, 15, 20, 23, 27–29, Dec. 5, 17, 28.
    1947   Jan. 3, 7, 14, 16, 17, 24, 29, 31, Feb. 4, 21, 23, 26–28, Mar. 1, 2, 7, 8, 20, Aug. 6–16, 20–Oct. 5, 8–17, 19–23, 25–Nov. 15, 18, 20–Dec. 9, 11, 13–15, 17–24, 27–31.
    1948   Jan. 1–Feb. 7, 10–12, 14–21, 23–Mar. 10, 12–16, 18–May 23, 26–28, June 1–July 8, 10–23, 27–Aug. 6, 8–17, 19–26, 28–Sept. 16, 19–Oct. 3, 6–23, 26–Nov. 3, 5–9,

11–28, Dec. 1, 3, 4, 7–10, 14, 16–18, 21–24, 28–31.
    1949   Jan. 1–15, 18–Feb. 8, 10–Apr. 13, 20–29, May 4, 6, 12, 13, 15, 17, 19–22, 24, 26, 27, 30–June 12, 14–July 7, 9–29, 31–Aug. 5, 7, 10–13, 16–20, 23–Sept. 2, 4–27, 29–Oct. 11, 13–22, 25–Dec. 30.

REVISTA COMERCIAL DE TEPIC. w. est. 1886.
CU–B
    Micro (P)
    1887   May 21, June 4.

VIGIA DEL PACIFICO. w. est. Jan. 13, 1846.
CU–B
    1846   Jan. 27–Apr. 7.

Teziutlan

ORIENTE. w.
CU
    1938   Dec. 4.
    1939   May 21–Dec. 31.
    1940   Jan. 1–Dec. 31.
    1941   Jan. 1–Dec. 28.

Ticul

EL CONSTITUCIONALISTA SUREÑO. w.
LNT–MA
    1917   n.d. (Oct.).

Tijuana

EL CONDOR. w. est. Feb. 8, 1938.
CU
    1943   Jan. 25, Feb. 1–8, Mar. 1–May 3, 12–Dec. 20.
    1944   Jan. 1, 18–24, Feb. 8, 21–Apr. 3, 17–June 19, July 4, 29, Aug. 9.

EL HERALDO DE LA BAJA CALIFORNIA. d. est. July 9, 1941.
CU
    1943   Dec. 28, 29, 31.
    1944   Jan. 1–31, Feb. 2–10, 14, 16, 18, 19, 22–24, 26, Mar. 8, 9, 13,

14, 17, 18, 24, 25, 28, Apr. 3 –
6, 15 – 17, 19 – 24, 26 – May 3,
5, 8, 9, 13, 16 – 19, 24 – June
1, 3 – 6, 8 – 10, 29, July 4 – 6,
22 – 25, 29, Aug. 7, 14 – 16,
18 – 22, 29, Sept. 26 – 30, Oct.
3 – 13, 16, 17, 19 – 26, 30, Nov.
2, 3, 6 – 8, 11, 14, 18, 22, 24,
27 – 29, Dec. 4 – 6, 14, 16 – 26,
29 – 30.
1945   Jan. 3 – 5, 8, 9, 13 – 15, 17 – 23,
26 – 31.
DLC
1942   Oct. 6, 7.

EL HISPANO AMERICANO. d., sw., w.,
sw., 3w. est. July 31, 1914.
Note: Removed to Tijuana from San
Diego, California, Mar. 28, 1928.
CU
1943   July 2 – 20, Aug. 10 – Dec. 9,
16 – 31.
1944   Jan. 1 – 13, 18 – Feb. 8, 12 – 17,
22 – Mar. 23, 28 – July 20, 25 –
Aug. 22, 31 – Sept. 2, 7 – Nov.
25, 30 – Dec. 18, 26 – 31.
1945   Jan. 1 – 6, 11 – Aug. 29, Sept.
13 – Dec. 31.
1946   Jan. 1 – Mar. 20, Apr. 1 – 9, 23,
June 12 – July 12, Aug. 10 –
Nov. 4, 26 – Dec. 31.
1947   Jan. 8 – 28, Feb. 11 – June 11,
July 2 – 23, Aug. 14 – 24, Sept.
12, 26, Oct. 10 – 22, Nov. 14,
27, Dec. 18.
1948   Jan. 9 – June 11.
DLC
1943   Apr. 30, May 7, 14, June 4, 29,
July 6, 9, 23, Aug. 14 – 20, Oct.
19, 21, 28 – Nov. 23, 30, Dec. 9,
16, 21, 31.
Extraordinario: Aug. 13 – 21.
1944   Jan. 6, 11, 13, 18 – Feb. 8, 12 –
19, 24, 29 – Mar. 4, 9 – 23, 30 –
Apr. 11, 15, 20, 25, 29, May 11,
17, 18, 25, 30 – June 3, 8 – 17,
29, July 6 – 20, 25 – Aug. 10,
15 – 22.

EL IMPARCIAL. w. est. July 8, 1938.
CU
1943   May 10 – June 16, 30, July 14 –
Aug. 11, 25 – Dec. 15, 30.
1944   Feb. 2, 16 – Mar. 22, Apr. 5 –
12, May 17 – June 7, Aug. 16 –
30.

LABOR. irr. est. Apr. 22, 1927.
CU
1943   July 2 – Dec. 31.
1944   Jan. 5 – Apr. 19, May 4 – Dec.
30.
1945   Jan. 1 – Dec. 31.
1946   Jan. 8 – Feb. 28, Mar. 22 – Aug.
15, Sept. 6, 20 – Dec. 14, 31.
1947 – 1948   Jan. 1 – Dec. 31.
1949   Jan. 1 – Oct. 31.

LA RAZON. w. est. 1937.
DLC
1937   Oct. 21.

Tlacotalpan

EL CORREO DE SOTAVENTO. sw.
TxU
1911   Apr. 27 – May 18, 25 – June 18,
25 – July 6, 13 – 16.

Tlalnepantla

LA SOMBRA DE MIRAFUENTES. est.
Oct. 30, 1880.
TxU
1880   Oct. 30.

Tlaxcala

LA ANTIGUA REPUBLICA.
TxU
1908   July 26.

LOS DERECHOS DEL PUEBLO. w. est.
Oct. 22, 1880.
TxU
1880   Oct. 22 – Nov. 20, 26 – Dec. 2,
18.

**EL ESTADO DE TLAXCALA; ORGANO
OFICIAL DEL GOBIERNO.** bw.
LNT – MA
1881   [Jan. 27 – Dec. 31].

1882   Jan. 1 – Dec. 31.
1883   [Jan. 1 – Dec. 31].
1884   Jan. 5, 14, [Mar. 1 – Dec. 31].
1885   [Jan. 1 – July 31].
TxU
1880   May 22, July 25 – Oct. 3, 29 –
        Dec. 27.

PERIODICO OFICIAL DEL GOBIERNO
DEL E.L.Y.S. DE TLAXCALA. w.
CU – B
    Micro (P)
    1874   Sept. 3.

SUFRAGIO EFECTIVO. w., sw. est. Aug.
6,1911.
TxU
    1911   Aug. 6.

Toluca

EL BIEN PUBLICO. w. est. 1880.
CtY
    1880   May 30, June 6, 13, 20, July 11,
            18, July 25, Aug. 8, 15.

BOLETIN DE NOTICIAS. irr. est. Aug.
24, 1847.
    Note: Ceased publication [Sept. 15],
    1847.
    CtY
    1847   Aug. 24 – 27, 29, Sept. 2 – 15.

EL CLARIN. w. est. Feb. 10, 1895.
LNT – MA
    1895   Feb. 10 – Sept. 1.

EL DEMOCRATA. w., sw. est. 1942.
CU
    1948   Dec. 12.
DLC
    1942   Aug. 14.

LA EMANCIPACION; PERIODICO
OFICIAL DEL GOBIERNO DEL
ESTADO LIBRE Y SOBERANO DE
MEXICO. est. Jan. 28, 1861.
CtY
    1861   Jan. 28 – May 6, 10, 15 – 17.

LA EVOLUCION ESCOLAR. bw.
TxU
    1917   May 31.

EL FANAL. 3w., irr., d., sw. est. 1832.
    Note: Ceased publication May 10,
    1833.
    CtY
    1832   Oct. 31 – Dec. 31.
    1833   Jan. 2 – Feb. 27, Mar. 1 – 31,
            Apr. 12 – May 10.

GERMINAL. sw. est. May 1915.
DLC
    1915   June 11.

LA LEY. sw.
    CU – B
    Micro (P)
    1871   June 20.

LA OLIVA DE LA PAZ; PERIODICO
OFICIAL. sw., 3w. est. Sept. 1834.
    Note: Ceased publication 1835.
    CtY
    1834   Sept. 27, Oct. 14.
    1835   Jan. 3 – 6, Mar. 31, May 5, 12,
            Sept. 29.
            Suplemento: Mar. 31.
    TxU
    1835   Oct. 1, 3, 15.

THE OUT-POST GUARD. sw. est. Mar.
1848.
    Note: In English.
    CtY
    1848   Mar. 11.

EL ORACULO SERAFICO. m. est. Nov.
8, 1908.
TxU
    1908   Nov. 8.

PORVENIR DEL ESTADO LIBRE Y
SOBERANO DE MEXICO; PERI-
ODICO OFICIAL. 3w. est. [1845].
MWA
    1848   May 20.

LA SOBERANIA DEL PUEBLO. w. est.
1880.
TxU
    1880   Aug. 26 – Sept. 16, Oct. 17 –
            Nov. 4, 21 – 25, Dec. 9 – 12.

EL TELEGRAFO. est. 1861.
CtY
  1861   Nov. 3.

LA VOZ DEL PUEBLO.
TxU
  1911   July 20.

Topolobampo

CREDIT FANCIER OF SINALOA. bw.
  Note: In English.
  CLCM
  1888   Oct. 15.
  1889   June 15.
  CU−B
  Micro (N)
  1890   Apr. 15.
  1891   Jan. 15, Feb. 15, Dec. 1.
  1892   Jan. 1.

Torreón

EL ATREVIDO. w.
TxU
  1912   Jan. 1.

EL DESPERTADOR. d.
TxU
  1912   May 8.

EL HERALDO DEPORTIVO. w. est.
  [1945].
  DLC
  1945   Mar. 26−Apr. 9, 24.

EL NOTICIOSO. d. est. May 12, 1912.
TxU
  1912   May 2.

NUEVO MUNDO. d.
CtY
  1907   Sept. 15.

LA OPINION. d. est. 1917.
  DLC
  1941   Apr. 2−15, 17−May 3, 5−
          10, 12−24, 26−June 14, 16−
          Aug. 30, Sept. 1−5, 7−Dec.
          31.
  1942   Jan. 1−31, Feb. 2−4, 6−28,
          Apr. 1−12, 14−29, May 1−6,
          8, 10−June 6, 8−July 4, 6−

          Sept. 27, 29, 30, Nov. 1−30,
          Dec. 2−6, 8−22, 25, 27−31.
  1943   Jan. 1−Feb. 13, 15−Mar. 13,
          15−Apr. 10, 12−17, 20−May
          12, 14−16, 18−25, 27−31,
          June 2−19, 21−July 21, 23−
          Aug. 8, 10−Oct. 2, 4, 6−Nov.
          14, 16−18, 20−22, 24, 26−
          Dec. 3, 6−11, 13−31.
  1944   Jan. 1−7, 10−18, 20−29, 31,
          Feb. 1, 3−5, 7−Mar. 18, 20−
          June 1, 3−July 3, 5−Aug. 9,
          11−26, 28−Nov. 25, 27−Dec.
          29, 31.
  1945   Jan. 1−Feb. 3, 5−May 1, 3−
          Nov. 20, 22−Dec. 25, 27−31.
  1946   Jan. 1−Apr. 5, 7−Dec. 31.
  1947   Jan. 1−24, 26−Mar. 16, 18−
          Aug. 9, 11−Dec. 31.
  1948   Jan. 1−Apr. 30, June 1−15,
          17−July 6, 8−25, 27−Dec. 31.
  1949   Jan. 1−May 19, 21−29, 31−
          Dec. 31.
  1950   Jan. 1−Dec. 31.
  1951   Jan. 1−July 6, 8−Dec. 31.
  1952   Jan. 1−June 5, 8−Oct. 18,
          20−29, 31−Dec. 18, 20−31.
  1953   Jan. 1−Mar. 8, 10−Apr. 30,
          May 3−22, 24−31.

EL SIGLO DE TORREON. d. est. 1922.
  DLC
  1941   Apr. 1−June 27, 29−Sept. 5,
          7−16, 18−Nov. 18, 20−Dec.
          26, 28−31.
  1942   Jan. 1−Feb. 28, Apr. 1−July
          28, 30−Aug. 21, 23, 25−Sept.
          30, Nov. 1−Dec. 31.
  1943   Jan. 1−Feb. 13, 15−Mar. 27,
          29−May 10, 12−23, 25−Nov.
          20, 23−Dec. 31.
  1944   Jan. 1−29, 31−Mar. 4, 6−18,
          20−Dec. 2, 4−25, 27−31.
  1945   Jan. 1−Feb. 3, 5−May 1, 3−
          Dec. 31.
  1946   Jan. 1−June 1, 3−Dec. 31.
  1947   Jan. 1−Feb. 14, 16−Aug. 9,
          11−Sept. 6, 8−Oct. 6, 8−Dec.
          31.

1948   Jan. 1 – 29, 31 – Mar. 31, Apr.
        2 – 30, June 1 – Sept. 9, 11 –
        Dec. 31.
1949   Jan. 1 – Apr. 22, 24 – May 5,
        7 – 19, 21 – 29, 31 – Dec. 31.
1950   Jan. 1 – May 12, 14 – Dec. 31.
1951   Jan. 1 – Dec. 31.
1952   Jan. 1 – May 6, 8 – July 2, 4 –
        Oct. 25, 27 – Nov. 22, 24 – Dec.
        31.
1953   Jan. 1 – 10, 12 – Feb. 3, 5 – Apr.
        13, 15 – May 31.
TxU
1924   Dec. 31.
1925   Jan. 8, 19 – Mar. 30, Apr. 1 –
        Sept. 9, 11 – 23, 25 – Dec. 31.
1926   Jan. 1 – Feb. 9, 11 – Apr. 30,
        May 2 – Dec. 31.
1927   Jan. 1 – May 1, 4 – June 5, 7 –
        30, July 3 – 6, 8 – Oct. 11, 13 –
        Nov. 26, 28 – Dec. 15, 17 – 31.
1928   Jan. 1 – 28, 30 – Feb. 22, 24 –
        June 30, July 2 – 16, 20 – Aug.
        11, 13 – 24, 26 – 28, Oct. 1 –
        Dec. 31.
1929   Jan. 1 – 12, 14 – Mar. 3, 5 – 12,
        15 – Apr. 30, May 2 – 31, June
        2 – Dec. 31.
1930 – 1931   Jan. 1 – Dec. 31.
1932   Jan. 1 – Apr. 23, 25 – 29, May 3,
        5 – 9, 11 – 15, 17 – June 11,
        13 – July 2, 4 – 11, 14 – 20, 22,
        23, 25 – Aug. 6, 10 – 13, 15 – 24,
        26 – Sept. 24, 26 – Oct. 8, 10 –
        24, 26 – 29, 31 – Nov. 7, 9 – 26,
        28 – Dec. 26 – 31.
1933   Jan. 1 – Feb. 3, 5 – Mar. 7, 10,
        11, 13 – 19, 21 – Apr. 8, 10, 11,
        13, May 1, 4, 6 – June 3, 5 –
        July 5, 7, 7 – 11, 13, 14, 16 –
        Aug. 27, 29.
1934   Jan. 3 – 10, 12 – Mar. 11, 13 –
        19, 22 – Apr. 1, 3 – 7, 9, 10,
        12 – 30, May 2 – June 2, 4 – 23,
        25 – July 1, 3 – 5, 7 – 15, 17 –
        25, 27 – Aug. 11, 15, 18 – Oct.
        1, 3 – 6, 8, 10 – 19, 22 – 27, 29,
        30, Nov. 1, 2, 4, 7 – 10, 16, 19,

        21, 22, 28, 30, Dec. 2, 8, 9, 13,
        15, 17 – 23, 25 – 31.
1935   Jan. 2 – 4, 6 – 12, 14 – Feb. 16,
        18 – Mar. 21, 23 – Apr. 19, 21 –
        May 2, 4, 7 – 25, 27 – June 1,
        3 – 8, 10, 11, 18, 19, 25 – 27,
        July 1, 4, 8 – 11, 13, 15 – 19, 21,
        22, 24 – 26, Aug. 1 – 3, 5 – 10,
        12, 13, 16, 17, 19 – 21, 24, 28 –
        30, Sept. 3, 5, 6, 8, 11 – 14, 18 –
        20, 26, 27, 30 – Oct. 2, 4 – 6,
        8 – 11, 16 – 18, 21, 23 – 26, 28 –
        Dec. 31.

Tula (*Hidalgo*)

EL CEFIRO. w. est. Nov. 11, 1888.
    Note: Suspended publication Jan.
    27 – Apr. 21, 1889; ceased publication
    [May 19, 1889].
CtY
    1888   Nov. 11 – Dec. 31.
    1889   Apr. 21 – May 19.

Tula (*Tamaulipas*)

EL DEFENSOR DE TAMAULIPAS. w.
    est. 1846.
    Note: Revmoved from Tula to
    Ciudad Victoria, Jan. 1848.
CtY
    1847   No. 41.
TxU
    1847   Feb. 1 – 15, Mar. 25 – Apr. 5,
            29 – June 10, July 1, 19 – Sept.
            9, 19, 30 – Oct. 13, Nov. 7,
            28 – Dec. 3, 23.

Tulancingo

EL TULANCINGUENSE. w. est. Dec.
    15, 1912.
TxU
    1912   Dec. 15.

Tuxtla Gutiérrez

LA BANDERA CONSTITUCIONAL;
    PERIODICO OFICIAL DEL GOBI-
    ERNO DE CHIAPAS. w.
LNT – MA
    1858   [Feb. 8 – Dec. 25].

1859   [Jan. 1 — Dec. 24].
1860   [Jan. 7 — Dec. 22].
1861   Jan. 1 — 31.
NN
1860   Sept. 22 — 29.

BOLETIN DE NOTICIAS.
LNT — MA
1863   July 28, Dec. 30.

CAMPAÑA CHIAPANECA. w. est. May 1, 1827.
LNT — MA
1827   [May 3 — Dec. 31].
1828   Jan. 12, Aug. 16 — Nov. 15.
1830   Jan. 9, Feb. 13.

EL CENTINELA. irr.
LNT — MA
1875   Jan. 28 — Mar. 4.

CHIAPAS NUEVO. sw. est. Oct. 1, 1916.
LNT — MA
1941   May 22.
TxU
1916   Oct. 1 — 19, 26 — 29, Nov. 9 — Dec. 31.
1917   Jan. 1 — 18, 25 — 28, Feb. 4 — Mar. 25, Apr. 1 — 8, 15 — May 6, 20 — 24, June 17 — July 1, 12 — 15.

EL COMETA. bw.
LNT — MA
1887   May 15, June 15, Aug. 15.

EL CONVENCIONALISTA. bw. est. Nov. 28, 1899.
LNT — MA
1899   Nov. 28 — Dec. 31.
1900   Jan. 1 — Mar. 1.

DIARIO DE CHIAPAS. d.
LNT — MA
1912   June 20, 25, 26, July 3, 5 — 7, 20, 21, Sept. 5, 29, Oct. 2, 11, 13, 15, 18, 19.

EL DUENDE. irr. est. Nov. 3, 1896.
LNT — MA
1896   Nov. 3.
1897   Jan. 1 — Aug. 12.

FRANCISCO CUSCATE. w. est. 1911.
LNT — MA
1911   Dec. 7, 14.

EL HERALDO. d.
LNT — MA
1950   June 23.

EL HERALDO DE CHIAPAS. w., bw., sw. est. July 10, 1906.
LNT — MA
1906   July 10, 17, 24, Aug. 7, Oct. 16, Dec. 4.
1907   [Jan. 15, Mar. 1 — Dec. 31].
1908   Jan. 1 — 31, Mar. 22 — Dec. 31.
1909   [Jan. 1 — Dec. 31].
1910   [Jan. 1 — Dec. 31].
1911   Jan. 8, 15, Feb. 5, 9, 12, 16, June 25, Aug. 28.
TxU
1910   June 12, 26 — 30, July 7, 21 — 28, Aug. 4 — 11, 18 — 25, Sept. 1 — 4, 11 — 15, 22, 29 — Oct. 9, 16 — Nov. 24, Dec. 1 — 4, 11.
1911   Jan. 1, 8 — 26, Feb. 2 — 16, 23, Mar. 5, 23 — Apr. 16, 23 — July 6.

LA IDEA DEMOCRATICA. 3m. est. May 5, 1909.
LNT — MA
1909   [May 5 — Nov. 15].

LA IGUALDAD. w.
DLC
1834   [May 1 — Oct. 31].

EL IRIS DE CHIAPAS.
CU — B
Micro (P)
1833   Dec. 9.
1834   Nov. 24.
LNT — MA
1834   Alcance: Apr. 11.

LA LUZ. w. est. 1892.
LNT — MA
1895   May 22.

EL OBSERVADOR. w. est. Feb. 13, 1898.
LNT — MA
1898   [Feb. 13 — Dec. 31].

1899   [Jan. 1 — Dec. 31].
TxU
   1898   Oct. 30.

LA OPINION PUBLICA. w. est. 1906.
   LNT — MA
   1906   June 9.

EL PANENQUE. sw. est. 1925.
   LNT — MA
   1925   Oct. 22, 25, Nov. 5.

LA PAZ. sw. est. Jan. 4, 1912.
   LNT — MA
   1912   Jan. 4.

PARA RAYO. w. est. 1827.
   DLC
   1827   Dec. 26 — 31.
          Suplemento: Feb. 2.
   1828   Jan. 1 — Feb. 12, 14 — 26, 28 —
          Aug. 11, 13 — Sept. 1, 3 — 15,
          19 — 31.
          Suplemento: May 6, 13.
   1829   Jan. 1 — 28, 30 — Mar. 4, 6 — 11,
          13 — 18, 20 — Apr. 15, 17 — May
          20, 22 — 27, 29 — July 8, 10 — 15,
          17 — 22, 24 — Nov. 25, 27 — Dec.
          30.
          Suplemento: June 18, Sept.
          17.
   1830   Apr. 26 — May 22.

PERIODICO OFICIAL.
   LNHT
   1883   Dec. 1 — 31.
   1884 — 1911   [Jan. 1 — Dec. 31].
   1912   Feb. 3.
   1914   July 23.

LA PROVINCIA. bw.
   CU
   1946   Oct. 13, Nov. 1.

EL REGENERADOR. sw. est. 1915.
   LNT — MA
   1915   Nov. 14 — Dec. 15.
   1916   Apr. 30 — May 18.
   TxU
   1916   Apr. 6 — Aug. 3, 10 — Sept. 14.

EL SUFRAGIO. est. 1903.
   LNT — MA
   1903   July 5 — 16.

30 — 30. w. est. 1911.
   LNT — MA
   1911   Nov. 18, Dec. 3, 10, 23.
   1912   Jan. 21.

LA VERDAD. w. est. 1877.
   LNT — MA
   1877   Apr. 8.

VERDAD Y JUSTICIA. d. est. [1913].
   LNT — MA
   1913   Jan. 21.

Ures

EL AMIGO DEL PUEBLO. w. est. 1874.
   CU — B
   Micro (P)
   1875   June 4 — 11, July 2, 16 — 30.
   1876   Feb. 28.

LA BALANZA POPULAR.
   CU — B
   Micro (P)
   1871   June 16.

BOLETIN OFICIAL. irr.
   CU — B
   Micro (P)
   1843   Oct. 26, Nov. 2 — 11, Dec. 7 —
          14.
          Suplemento: Nov. 28.
   1844   Feb. 1, 29, Mar. 14.

BOLETIN OFICIAL DEL GOBIERNO
   DEL ESTADO LIBRE Y SOBERANO
   DE SONORA. w.
   Note: Title varies. Published for
   a time in Guaymas.
   CU — B
   Micro (P)
   1876   Apr. 1 — Dec. 29.
   1877 — 1878   Jan. 1 — Dec. 31.
   1879   Jan. 3 — Mar. 14.

EL CALAVERA. irr.
   CU — B
   Micro (P)
   1863   Apr. 27, May 18, June 16.

Suplemento: May 4 — 14, June 9.

1864   Feb. 19.

EL CENTINELA DE SONORA. w. est. July 11, 1845.
   CU — B
     Micro (P)
     1845   July 11, Aug. 22, Sept. 26, Oct. 10.
          Suplemento: Aug. 16.
   DLC
     1845   July 11 — 17, 19 — Aug. 15.

LA CONSTITUCION. irr. est. 1879.
   CU — B
     Micro (P)
     1879   Mar. 28 — Apr. 30, May 13 — 16.

LA CRONICA JUDICIAL. irr.
   CU — B
     Micro (P)
     1862   May 15, June 28 — Aug. 12.
     1863   Apr. 15.

LA ESTRELLA DE OCCIDENTE; PERIODICO OFICIAL DEL GOBI- ERNO DEL ESTADO LIBRE Y SOBERANO DE SONORA. w. est. June 10, 1859.
   CU — B
     Micro (P) & (N)
     1859   June 10 — Dec. 30.
     1860 — 1862   Jan. 1 — Dec. 31.
     1871   Jan. 6 — 20, Feb. 3 — Dec. 29.
     1872   Jan. 5 — July 5, 19 — Oct. 18, Nov. 1 — Dec. 27.
     1873   Jan. 3 — Mar. 21, Apr. 4 — Dec. 12, 26.
     1874 — 1875   Jan. 1 — Dec. 31.
     1876   Jan. 21 — Mar. 10.

LA INTEGRIDAD NACIONAL. w. est. July 18, 1856.
   CU — B
     Micro (P)
     1856   July 18 — Aug. 1.

EL IRIS DE PAZ. w. est. 1845.
   CU — B

Micro (P)
1845   July 31, Aug. 21, Sept. 25 — Oct. 9.

EL MOCHUELO. irr. est. 1873.
   CU — B
     Micro (P)
     1873   Apr. 27, Aug. 15, 29, Sept. 30, Oct. 30.

EL MORTERO. irr. est. Apr. 8, 1842.
   CU — B
     Micro (P)
     1842   Prospecto.
          Apr. 8, May 22, Sept. 23.
     1843   Suplemento: May 30.

EL NACIONAL; PERIODICO DEL GOBIERNO DE SONORA. w. est. June 10, 1853.
   CU — B
     Micro (P) & (N)
     1853   June 10 — Dec. 30.
     1854   Jan. 1 — Dec. 31.
     1855   Jan. 26 — Feb. 16, Mar. 9 — 16, 30, Apr. 13, May 25, June 15, July 6, Aug. 3 — 31, Sept. 21.

PERIODICO OFICIAL DEL DEPARTA- MENTO DE SONORA. w.
   CU — B
     Micro (P)
     1865   Aug. 25, Nov. 3 — 10, Dec. 29.
     1866   Jan. 12 — 19, Feb. 9 — 23, Mar. 9 — 23, Apr. 20 — 27, May 18.

EL PUEBLO DE SONORA. w. est. Dec. 3, 1867.
   Note: Suspended publication Feb. 25, 1868.
   CU — B
     Micro (P)
     1867   Dec. 3 — 31.
     1868   Jan. 21 — Feb. 25.

EL PUEBLO INDEPENDIENTE. w. est. June 4, 1875.
   CU — B
     Micro (P)
     1875   June 4.

EL PUEBLO SONORENSE. w. est. Nov.
22, 1872.
CU – B
Micro (P)
1872   Nov. 22 – Dec. 27.
1873   Jan. 3.

LA SOMBRA DE TENA. w. est. 1871.
CU – B
Micro (P)
1871   June 18.

EL SONORENSE; PERIODICO OFI-
CIAL DEL GOBIERNO DEL ESTADO.
est. 1846.
CU – B
1846   May 29, June 26, July 24 – Aug.
21, Sept. 25, Oct. 9 – Nov. 13,
27 – Dec. 18.
1847   Jan. 1 – Apr. 9, 23.
1848   Jan. 1 – Dec. 31.
1849   Jan. 1 – May 2, 11 – June 29,
July 13 – Dec. 28.
1850   Jan. 4 – Mar. 29, Apr. 5, 19 –
June 14, July 5, 26 – Aug. 23,
Sept. 13 – Nov. 29, Dec. 27.
1851   Jan. 1 – Apr. 11, May 2 – Oct.
10, 17 – Dec. 26.
1852   Jan. 9, Mar. 5 – Apr. 2, 16 –
Aug. 6, 20 – Dec. 31.
1853   Jan. 14 – May 6, 20 – June 3.

UNO DE TANTOS. w. est. 1863.
CU – B
Micro (P)
1863   Mar. 26, Apr. 9, May 27, June
18.

EL VOTO DE SONORA; PERIODICO
OFICIAL DEL GOBIERNO. irr. est.
Dec. 20, 1841.
CU – B
Micro (P) & (N)
1841   Dec. 20.
1842   Jan. 1 – Apr. 15, July 15, Sept.
2, 21 – 28, Nov. 16 – Dec. 28.
Suplemento: [Aug. 12, Oct. 12].
1843   Jan. 26, Feb. 23, Mar. 9, May
18 – 25, July 6 – Aug. 17, 31,
Sept. 14 – 21.

Suplemento: Apr. 21, May 12,
June 1, 23.
1844   May 30 – Sept. 12, Oct. 10 –
24.
1845   Mar. 27, 8, June 26.
Suplemento: May 3.

EL VOTO LIBRE. w. est. 1871.
CU – B
Micro (P)
1871   Mar. 31, May 19, June 30.

LA VOZ DE SONORA; PERIODICO
DEL GOBIERNO DEL ESTADO. sw.,
w.
CU – B
Micro (P) & (N)
1855   Sept. 28 – Dec. 28.
1856   Jan. 4 – Apr. 18, May 2 – Dec.
26.
Suplemento: [Apr. 25.]
1857 – 1858   Jan. 1 – Dec. 31.
1859   Jan. 7 – June 3.
CtY
1856   Nov. 7.

LA VOZ DE URES. w. est. 1877.
CU – B
Micro (P)
1877   Apr. 13 – 20, May 11 – June 15.

LA VOZ DEL PUEBLO. w. est. July 23,
1851.
CU – B
Micro (P)
1851   July 23 – Oct. 8.
1852   Nov. 24.

Vera Cruz

THE AMERICAN EAGLE. sw., 3w. est.
Apr. 3, 1847.
Note: In English.
CtY
1847   Apr. 3, 6, 24, 27, May 8.
DLC
Micro (P)
1847   Apr. 3, 6.
MWA
1847   Apr. 3, 10, 26.
NN
1847   Apr. 6.

TxH-SJ
   1847   Extra: Apr. 26.
ViU
   1847   Apr. 3.

EL AMERICANO LIBRE.
See *The Free American. El Americano libre.*

EL ARCO IRIS. d. est. 1847.
Note: In Spanish and English beginning Nov. 1, 1847. A daily supplement, *El Crepúsculo*, was established Nov. 9, 1849.
CU – B
   1847   July 1 – Nov. 13, 15 – 28, Dec. 1 – 31.
   1848   Jan. 1 – Feb. 12, 14 – 16, 18 – Mar. 12.
DLC
   1847   Oct. 7.
   1849   July 1 – Aug. 9, 11 – Sept. 16, 18 – 25, 27 – Oct. 7, 9 – Nov. 23, 25 – Dec. 31.
         Suplemento (*El Crepúsculo*): Nov. 9, 24, Dec. 1, 8, 30.

EL CENSOR. d. est. Aug. 1828.
Note: Title *El Censor de Veracruz*, 1837 – 1838, 1843 – Sept. 30, 1844; *El Censor*, Aug. 1828 – 1837, 1839 – 1842, after Oct. 1, 1844.
CU – B
   1840   Sept. 12.
DLC
   1830   Jan. 1 – 16, 18 – 30, May 30 – June 12.
   1831   Jan. 30 – Feb. 26, Mar. 5 – Apr. 2, May 24, 29 – 31, June 5, 13, 14, 16, 17, 19 – 28, July 3, 10, 11, 14 – Aug. 1, 3 – 8, 10 – 15, 17 – Sept. 4, 6 – Oct. 5, 11, 13 – 15, 27 – Nov. 5, 10, 11.
         Suplemento: Feb. 4.
   1835   Mar. 19 – 31, Apr. 3 – 7, 10 – 16, 25 – 27, May 27, 29 – June 14, 16 – 22, 26 – July 6, 8 – 11, 17 – 27.
   1837   Mar. 1, 3, Apr. 10 – 12, May 1,

June 12.
   1838   Apr. 11 – 13, 16, 17.
   1839   July 1 – Aug. 12, 14 – Nov. 7, 10 – Dec. 2, 11 – 24.
   1841   Jan. 1, 3 – Mar. 18, 21 – June 19, 22 – Sept. 4, 6.
   1842   Jan. 2 – 14, 16 – 24, 26, 27.
   1843   Jan. 1 – 4, 9 – 31, Feb. 8 – 19, 21 – 23, 25, May 19 – 29, 31 – June 5, 9 – 17, 20 – July 7, 9 – 13, Aug. 5, 6, 8 – 11, 14, 15, 17 – 21, 23, 25, 26, 29 – Sept. 2, 5 – 7, 12 – 15, 17, 18, 22 – 25, 30, Oct. 3, 5 – 8, 10 – 13, 15 – Nov. 7, 9 – 17, 19 – 21, 23 – Dec. 5, 7 – 16, 18 – 31.
   1844   Jan. 1 – 6, 9, 12 – Feb. 15, 17 – Mar. 11, 15 – 29, Apr. 1 – 7, 12, 13, 15 – 18, 21 – 24, 26 – May 9, 11 – 28, 31 – June 11, 14 – July 21, 23 – Sept. 11, 13 – Oct. 24, 27 – Nov. 13, Dec. 4, 10, 11.
MB
   1844   Nov. 1 – Dec. 31.
NN
   1829   July 4.
TxU
   1831   Mar. 21 – 31, Apr. 10, 14 – 16.
   1832   Mar. 1 – 15.

EL CONSTITUCIONALISTA; PERIODICO OFICIAL DE LA FEDERACION. w., sw. est. Dec. 2, 1913.
Note: Ceased publication June 16, 1916.
CtY
   1914   Dec. 12 – 26.
   1915   Jan. 2 – Mar. 4, 9 – June 18.
DLC
   1915   Jan. 9.
MBAt
   1914   Dec. 12 – 31.
   1915   Jan. 1 – Oct. 1.

EL CREPUSCULO.
See *El Arco iris.*

EL DEMOCRATA. d. est. 1905.
Note: Removed from Mexico City, Dec. 8, 1914; returned to Mexico

City, Aug. 4, 1915.
DLC
  1914   Dec. 16 – 19, 23 – 31.
  1915   Jan. 1 – 9, 11 – 16, 20 – 30, Feb.
          3 – 9, 11 – 18, Mar. 2, 14, 17 –
          27, 29 – Apr. 2, 7, 8, 17, 20 –
          28, May 7, 17, 19 – 22, 25 – 28,
          31, June 2 – 4, 10, 11, 15, 23,
          28, 30, July 5, 8, 14, 19, 23, 26,
          27, 29, 30.

DIARIO COMERCIAL. d. est. 1880.
  LNT – MA
    1900   Mar. 17.
  MWA
    1883   Aug. 10.
  TxU
    1880   July 10, Sept. 19, Dec. 4.
    1881   Jan. 11, Apr. 13.

DIARIO DE VERACRUZ. d. est. 1844.
  DLC
    1845   Apr. 2, 3, 7 – 11, 17, 19, 20,
            22 – 27, 30, May 3, 5, 11, 13 –
            15, 25, June 4, 5, 9, 11, 13, 16,
            18, 27, 28, July 1, 2, 10, 11, 14,
            19, 20, 22 – 24.

DIARIO MERCANTIL DE VERACRUZ.
  d. est. 1807.
  CU – B
    1807   [Nov. 1 – 30].
  CtY
    1807   Dec. 7, 8.

EL DICTAMEN. d. est. Sept. 16, 1898.
  Note: Title *El Dictamen público*,
  Sept. 16, 1898 – Nov. 18, 1905; *El
  Dictamen*, after Nov. 19, 1905.
  Suspended publication June 25 –
  Sept. 7, 1930.
  CU
    1919   July 17.
    1937   Oct. 27 – 29.
  DLC
    1914   Dec. 18 – 26, 30, 31.
    1915   Jan. 1 – 16, 18, 20 – 29, 31 –
            Mar. 17, 19 – Apr. 28, 30, May
            3 – 6, 8, 10 – 12, 15 – 22, 26, 27,
            June 8, 9, 11 – 28, 30 – July 10,
            13 – 31, Aug. 3 – 7, 10 – 12,

15 – 21, Sept. 2, 3, 5 – 25, 27 –
29, Oct. 1, 2, Nov. 8, 9, 14, 16 –
18, 22 – 27, 30, Dec. 2, 3, 5, 7 –
11, 13 – 31.
  1916   Jan. 1 – 8, 10, 13 – 16, 18, 20 –
          22, 24 – 27, 30 – Feb. 7, 9 – 13,
          16, 17, 19 – 24, 26, 29, Mar.
          1 – 9.
  1938   Jan. 1, 3, 6 – 9, 12, 18, 29, Feb.
          1 – 4, 7, 8, 10 – 12, 14, 15, 18,
          20 – 22, 24, 25, Mar. 1, 4, 9, 11,
          14, 16, 20, 21, 23, 25, 27 – 29,
          Apr. 1, 2, 4 – 6, 8 – 13, 17, 18,
          24 – 27, 29, 30, May 2, 3, 5, 8,
          16, 22, 24, 27, 29, 30, June 6,
          10, 14, 22 – 28, July 2, 6, 9 – 11,
          13, 15, 17, 20, 22, 26, 28, 30 –
          Aug. 2, 4, 8 – 11, 14 – 18, 21, 22,
          24, 25, 27 – 30, Sept. 1, 2, 4, 8,
          9, 11 – 13, 16, 19, 21 – 24, 26,
          28.
  1939   Jan. 1 – 4, 8 – 10, 12 – 17, 19 –
          23, 25, 27 – 29, 31 – Feb. 7, 9,
          10, 13, 14, 16, 19, 22 – 25, 27,
          Mar. 1, 2, 4 – 6, 9, 12, 17, 19,
          20, 25 – Apr. 2, 6, 8, 10, 13, 15,
          16, 20, 21, 23, 24, 26, 28, May
          3 – 8, 10 – 12, 14 – 18, 21, 22,
          24, 25, 28 – 31.
  1948   Sept. 16.
LNT – MA
  1915   July 13.
  1917   Aug. 16.
  1918   Jan. 14.
  1930   Jan. 3, 19, Mar. 14, 21, 23, Apr.
          4.
  1935   July 3.
MWA
  1911   Apr. 14 – 16, 18, 19.
TxU
  1902   Apr. 2 – June 29.
  1904   Oct. 17 – Dec. 31.
  1905 – 1911   Jan. 1 – Dec. 31.
  1912   Jan. 1 – May 28.
  1913   Sept. 10.
  1924   Sept. 17, 18, 23, Oct. 22 –
          25, Nov. 21 – Dec. 31.
  1925   Jan. 1 – Mar. 4, 9 – Dec. 31.

1926 Jan. 1 – Feb. 25, 27 – Mar. 17,
      19 – Apr. 8, 10 – 30, May 2 – 9,
      11 – Dec. 31.
1927 Jan. 1 – Feb. 15, 17 – Mar. 24,
      26 – Apr. 7, 9 – May 27, 29 –
      July 7, 9 – Aug. 17, 19 – Dec.
      30, 31.
1928 Jan. 1 – Feb. 25, 27 – Apr. 1 –
      30, May 2 – June 24, 26 – July
      16, 18 – Sept. 16, 18 – Oct. 10,
      12 – Nov. 8, 10 – Dec. 31.
1929 Jan. 1 – Mar. 6, 8 – 17, 19 –
      Apr. 1 – 30, May 2 – 31, June
      2 – 10, 13 – 22, 24 – Dec. 31.
1930 Jan. 1 – Feb. 9, 12 – 20, 22 –
      Apr. 1 – 30, May 2 – 5, 7 – Sept.
      10, 12 – 15, 17, 19 – 28, 30 –
      Dec. 31.
1931 Jan. 1 – Nov. 9, 11 – Dec. 17,
      19 – 31.
1932 Jan. 2, 4 – Feb. 10, 12 – Mar.
      10, 12, 14 – 19, 21 – 24, 26 –
      Apr. 2, 4 – 20, 22, 23, 26 – 29,
      May 3 – 10, 12 – 15.

ECO DEL COMERCIO. d., 3w. est.
  1850.
  DLC
    1851 Feb. 19, 20, 22.
    1864 Jan. 5 – May 2, 8 – 14, 16 – Aug.
          29, Nov. 11 – Dec. 1.
  NHi
    1853 Feb. 13.

EL FERROCARRIL. d.
  CtY
    1880 Jan. 1 – Dec. 29.
  TxU
    1881 Apr. 13.

THE FREE AMERICAN. EL AMERI-
CANO LIBRE. d. est. Nov. 22, 1847.
  Note: In Spanish and English.
  CU – B
    1847 Nov. 22 – 27, Dec. 1 – 17, 20 –
          31.
    1848 Jan. 1 – Feb. 22, 24 – Mar. 12.
  DLC
    1848 Jan. 20.

EL GENIO DE LA LIBERTAD. sw. est.
  Apr. 24, 1832.
  DLC
    1832 Apr. 24 – Oct. 19.

GENIUS OF LIBERTY. EL GENIO DE
LA LIBERTAD. d. est. Sept. 25, 1847.
  Note: In Spanish and English.
  CU – B
    1847 Sept. 25 – Nov. 12.

GUILLERMO TELL. 3w. est. 1859.
  DLC
    1859 Dec. 16 – 31.
    1860 Jan. 1 – 12, 14 – 20.

EL INDICADOR. d. est. Jan. 1, 1846.
  DLC
    1846 Jan. 1 – 6, 8 – 11, 15 – Feb. 23,
          Mar. 1 – 3, 8, 9, 11, 12, 16, 21,
          22, Apr. 2, 12, 14 – 16, May 3,
          4, 12 – 14, 17 – 26, 29 – June
          18, 21 – July 7, 9 – Aug. 5, Sept.
          1 – 15, 19 – 25, 27 – Oct. 8, 12 –
          15, 18, 23 – 29, 31 – Nov. 2, 6 –
          11, 13, 15 – 25, 29 – Dec. 6, 8 –
          10, 12 – 17, 20, 22 – 31.

JORNAL ECONOMICO MERCANTIL
DE VERACRUZ. d.
  LNHT
    1806 Mar. 1 – July 31.

EL LIBERAL. d. est. July 22, 1912.
  TxU
    1912 July 22.

EL LOCOMOTOR. d. est. 1846.
  CtY
    1846 Nov. 15.
  DLC
    1846 Mar. 6, 11, 13, 23, 31, Apr. 2 –
          4, 17, 18, 20 – 22, 24, May 5, 6.

EL MONITOR. d. est. 1840.
  DLC
    1840 Dec. 3 – 23.

EL MONITOR VERACRUZANO. 3w.
  NHi
    1865 July 1 – Aug. 17, 21, 26, Sept.
          21 – Oct. 31, Nov. 14 – 21, Dec.

2 – 7, 12, 23 – 30.
1866   Jan. 2 – 6, 13 – Feb. 20, 24 –
Mar. 3, 8, 13 – May 1.

EL MOTIN. d. est. Aug. 1915.
DLC
1915   Aug. 10.

NOTICIAS SENSACIONALES.
DLC
1914   May 25.

EL NOTICIOSO. d. est. 1865.
NHi
1865   Oct. 3, 12 – 20.

NOTICIOSO COMERCIAL Y CIENTI-
FICO. d. est. 1827.
CtY
1827   June 10 – 16.
MWA
1828   Apr. 6.

NOVEDADES.
DLC
1914   Suplemento: [Apr. 24].

LA OPINION. d.
CU
1911   Nov. 11 – 26, 28 – Dec. 22,
24 – 31.
1912   Jan. 1 – Dec. 31.
1913   Jan. 1 – Oct. 20, 23 – 27, 30,
Nov. 1, 3, 4, 10, Dec. 18, 19.
1914   Jan. 3 – Apr. 20, May 29, 30,
June 1 – Dec. 31.
1915   Jan. 1 – 9.
DLC
1914   Apr. 29, May 6, Dec. 16 – 31.
1915   Jan. 1 – 8.
TxU
1911   Apr. 1 – 5, 10, 11, 13, 15 – 20,
22, 25 – 27, 29 – May 9, 12 – 19,
24, 27, 31, June 3, 9.
1913   Sept. 5, 9, Oct. 17.

PRECIOS CORRIENTES.
MWA
1828   Nov. 4.

EL PRESENTE. d. est. 1914.
CU
1914   Apr. 9 – 21.

EL PROGRESO. d.
CU – B
Micro (P)
1876   Mar. 16.

EL PROLETARIO. d.
TxU
1924   Dec. 25.

EL PUEBLO. d. est. Oct. 1, 1914.
Note: Removed from Mexico City,
Dec. 1914; suspended publication
Oct. 9 – 28, 1915; returned to
Mexico City Oct. 29, 1915.
CU
1915   May 10 – June 8, 10.
1916   July 8, 10 – 12.
DLC
1914   Dec. 17 – 31.
1915   Jan. 1 – 18, 20 – 29, 31 – Feb.
28, Mar. 2 – 17, 19 – 24, 26 –
Apr. 5, 8, 11 – May 23, 25 – 30,
June 1 – 23, 25 – 28, 30 – Oct.
9.
Suplemento: Feb. 7.

LA REFORMA SOCIAL. sw. est. 1859.
DLC
1859   Dec. 14 – 17, 24 – 31.
1860   Jan. 4 – 7.

LA REVISTA. 3w., d. est. 1864.
DLC
1864   Nov. 13 – 27.
NHi
1865   Apr. 30 – May 12, 15 – Aug. 27.

REVISTA MILITAR. w., sw. est. June 24,
1915.
DLC
1915   July 1 – 8, 22, Aug. 3, 10, 18.

REVISTA NACIONAL.
CU
1915   June 6.

EL SOL.
CLCM
1830   Jan. 30, 31.

SUN OF ANAHUAC. SOL DE ANA-
HUAC. d. est. 1847.
Note: In English and Spanish.
CU—B
1847   July 1, 3—Aug. 30, Sept. 1—
3, 7—20.

LE TRAIT D'UNION. 3w., d. est. 1849.
Note: In French. Removed from
Mexico City, Jan. 3, 1860; returned,
1862. Periodicity Jan. 3—Feb. 18,
1860, three times a week; Feb. 21,
1860—1862, daily. Suspended publication Mar. 15—30 and May 10—
Oct. 8, 1860.
DLC
1860   Jan. 3—Feb. 20, 27, Mar. 1—5,
9—Apr. 14, 16—24, 27, 29—
Oct. 8, 14, 17—19, 21—Nov.
6, 11, 13—Dec. 4, 9, 14—31.
MH
1860   Jan. 1, 3—24, 31, Feb. 7.

LA UNION.
NHi
1852   July 5, 8.
1853   Feb. 5, 9, 16.

EL VERACRUZANO. bw. est. Jan. 1,
1851.
Note: Ceased publication Aug. 16,
1851.
CU—B
Micro (N)
1851   Jan. 1—Aug. 16.

EL VERACRUZANO LIBRE. d.
CU—B
Micro (P)
1828   June 8—14.
CtY
1827   June 26, 29, 30, July 5—Aug.
25—27, Sept. 5, 9—29, Oct.
1—20, 26—29, 31, Nov. 4—
10, 18, 19—21, 24.
DLC
1845   Apr. 11, 12, 22, 29, 30, May 2,

3, Aug. 16, 18, 20, 22—24, 26,
28, 29, Sept. 16, 18—25, Nov.
3, 4, 6, 8, 10—12, 22—30, Dec.
3, 8—10, 12—15, 18—21, 23,
25, 27, 28.

LA VERDAD.
NHi
1866   Dec. 27.

Victoria
See Ciudad Victoria.

Victoria de Durango

ARISTARCO.
LNT—MA
1834   Feb. 5.

Villa de Hunucma

VOZ DEL PARTIDO. bw. est. [1883].
MWA
1884   Sept. 16.

Villahermosa

ACCION. w.
CU
1937   May 27—Apr. 10.

EL AMIGO DEL PUEBLO. w.
CU
1935   Jan. 5, Nov. 3—10, Dec. 8—
15, 22.
Extraordinario: Dec. 16, 18.
1936   Extraordinario: Jan. 8.

ANTI-REELECCIONISTA. d.
CU
1921   Aug. 19—22, 28—Sept. 1, 22.
Extraordinario: Aug. 23.
1922   Extraordinario: June 29.

EL ASTRO DE LA LIBERTAD; PERIO-
DICO OFICIAL DEL GOBIERNO
DEPARTMENTAL DE TABASCO.
NN
1845   Mar. 30.

BOLETIN DE PROGRESO. w.
CU
1918   Aug. 10—Sept. 7.

BOLETIN DEL EMPRESTITO. d.
CU
1917   Nov. 29–Dec. 20.
1918   Jan. 12–24.

BOLETIN DEL TABASCO.
CU
1916   Jan. 27.

BOLETIN MUNICIPAL. bw.
CU–B
1898   June 30, July 31, Aug. 31.
1901   Apr. 7–30, June 2–30, Nov. 24.

BOLETIN PATRIOTICO.
CU
1916   May 5.

BOLETIN TELEGRAFICO. d.
CU
1921   July 26.
        Extraordinario: Mar. 5.
1922   Mar. 10, June 30.
1924   Oct. 28.
LNT–MA
1924   Sept. 6, Oct. 7, Nov. 7.

BOLETIN TELEGRAFICO DE TABAS-
CO. d.
CU
1916   Jan. 13–19, 22–29.

EL CAMALEON. sw.
CU
1924   Apr. 24.

EL CENSOR. w. est. Jan. 5, 1941.
CU
1941   Jan. 5–Mar. 9.

EL CHAMUSCO. w.
CU
1939   May 21, July 30.

EL CHICHICASTE.
CU
1937   Apr. 11.

EL CHISME.
CU
1917   Feb. 17–27.

EL CORREO.
CU
1918   May 1.

CRISTO REY. w.
CU
1927   Oct. 9.

CUAUHTEMOC. w., bw., w.
CU
1917   Feb. 4–Mar. 22, Apr. 15, 22,
        May 6–20, 27–31, June 7,
        14–17, 24, July 1, 8–Sept.
        9, 20–Dec. 2.

DELTA.
CU
1938   May 1.

DEMOCRATA.
MWA
1863   June 13.

DIARIO DE TABASCO. d.
CU
Apr. 4.

EL DOMINGO. w.
CU
1928   June 17, Aug. 12.

EL ECO DE TABASCO. w.
CU–B
1905   May 14–Dec. 31.
1906–1910   Jan. 1–Dec. 31.

EJERCITO DE GLADIADORES.
CU
1926   Sept. 10.

EL EQUILIBRIO SOCIAL. d.
CU
1923   Nov. 18–Dec. 9, 11–28.
1924   Jan. 1–10.

EVOLUCION OBRERA. sw.
CU
1919   Oct. 26, Nov. 2, 16–30, Dec.
        28.

FRENTE POPULAR. w.
CU
1938   Feb. 27, Mar. 20, July 31.
1939   May 19.

FRENTE ROJO. w.
  CU
    1935   Aug. 22, Oct. 13, 27, Nov. 10,
            Dec. 8, 18.
            Extraordinario: Nov. 6.
    1938   Mar. 20, June 16, July 28.

EL GRIJALVA. sw.
  CU—B
    1858   July 10—Sept. 25.
    Micro (P)
    1857   Mar. 11—14.
  LNT—MA
    1856   Mar. 21.

EL HERALDO DE LA REVOLUCION. d.
  CU
    1924   Jan. 28, 29, Feb. 2, 7, 13, 16,
            18, 24, 27, 28, Mar. 9—11, 14,
            18, 27, 29, Apr. 4, 5, 16, 17,
            20—26, May 3, 5—8, 12, 13,
            16—20, 26, 28.

EL HERALDO DE TABASCO. d.
  CU
    1920   Feb. 6, 8—12, 15—18, 21, 22,
            25—27, 29, Mar. 4, 9, 16—20,
            25, Apr. 4, 8, 10—13, 17—21,
            23—25, 29, 30, May 3, 4, 7—
            25, 27, 29—31, June 2, 6, 18—
            July 2, 6—14, 16, 19—22, 24—
            29, 31—Aug. 2, 5, 6, 8, 13, 14,
            20, 21, 25—27, 29—31, Sept.
            3, 9—12, 14, 18—22, 25—Oct.
            3, 6—23, 26, 29, 30.
            Extraordinario: Apr. 28.

LA IDEA. sw.
  CU
    1918   Dec. 10—17, 24—31.
    1919   Jan. 4—Feb. 31.

EL INDEPENDIENTE. w.
  CU—B
    1877   Suplemento: July 29.
    1880   Oct. 10.
    1883   Mar. 11.
    1885   Aug. 13.
    1890   Nov. 21.
    1894   Sept. 16, Nov. 4—11, Dec. 9.

    Micro (P)
    1878   Sept. 8.

EL INDEPENDIENTE.
  CU
    1918   Aug. 28.

JUVENAL. d.
  CU
    1912   May 30, 31, June 4, 5, July 3,
            9, Aug. 21, Sept. 4, 30—Oct.
            10, 12—21, 24, 30, Nov. 5—12,
            18, 19, 23—26, Dec. 21.
    1913   Jan. 27—30, Feb. 1, 5, 17—20,
            24, Mar. 4, 5, 7, 8, 11—13, 28—
            Apr. 4, 8, 9, 14, 17, 18, 21—
            28, 30—May 5, 7—12, 14—20.

KAMARAZOS. w.
  CU
    1924   Mar. 23.

EL LIBERAL. w., sw.
  CU
    1917   Dec. 23—30.
    1918   Jan. 13, 27—Oct. 6, 24—Dec.
            29.
    1919   Jan. 1—26.

LA LINTERNA. w.
  CU
    1923   Aug. 12.

EL MAUSSER.
  CU
    1936   Aug. 9.

EL MOMENTO. w.
  CU
    1933   Apr. 20, May 4—June 1, July
            27—Aug. 17.

EL MONITOR TABASQUEÑO. w.
  CU
    1921   July 17, Nov. 6.
    1922   Mar. 5, Aug. 27—Sept. 3, 17.
            Extraordinario: Mar. 22, July
            6—11, Sept. 15, 19, Nov. 7.
    1924   Jan. 24, Mar. 9—23, Apr. 6.
            Extraordinario: Jan. 19.

NUEVA LUZ. w.
  CU
    1927   July 14.

OCTUBRE.
  CU
    1935   Oct. 8.
    1937   Oct. 9.

LA OPINION. bw.
  CU
    1923   Oct. 21.

LA OPINION PUBLICA. w.
  CU
    1935   Oct. 21, Nov. 11, 12, Dec. 6,
            16, 30.
            Extraordinario: Dec. 9, 10.
    1938   Jan. 23 – 30, Feb. 13, Mar. 20,
            May 15, June 26, July 31.

LA PALANCA. sw. est. 1829.
  DLC
    1829   May 6 – July 28, 30 – Sept. 22,
            24 – 28.
            Suplemento: Aug. 26, Sept. 19,
            Oct. 17, 21.
    1831   Apr. 9 – 23, May 14 – Aug. 10.
            Suplemento: Apr. 23.

PERIODICO OFICIAL.
  CU – B
    1884 – 1888   Jan. 1 – Dec. 31.
    1890 – 1896   Jan. 1 – Dec. 31.
    1898 – 1900   Jan. 1 – Dec. 31.
    Micro (P)
    1897   Jan. 1 – Dec. 31.
  LNT – MA
    1904   May 1 – 31.

PROTEO.
  CU
    1926   Sept. 9.

EL PUEBLO.
  CU
    1938   Extraordinario: Aug. 4.

EL QUETZAL TABASQUEÑO.
  CU
    1918   Mar. 2.

EL RADICAL. w., sw., w.
  CU
    1918   Feb. 10 – June 30, July 14 –
            Oct. 12, 27 – Dec. 29.
    1919   Jan. 5, 19 – Mar. 30, Apr. 27,
            May 4, Oct. 5 – Nov. 2, 16, 30 –
            Dec. 21.
    1920   Jan. 11 – Feb. 8, 22 – 29, Apr.
            4 – 18, Aug. 29 – Oct. 31, Nov.
            21 – Dec. 5.
    1924   May 8.
    1927   June 3.
    1928   Dec. 9.

EL RADIO. d.
  CU
    1924   Feb. 1 – Apr. 29.

REDENCION. d. est. 1924.
  CU
    1933   May 14, June 23, 24, 28 – 30,
            July 14, 19, 22, 25, 29, Aug. 1, 2,
            6, 7, 10, 13 – 15, 19 – 23, 26 –
            Sept. 5, 7, 8, 13 – Oct. 3, 17, 18,
            21 – 26, 31 – Nov. 4, 8, 10, 12 –
            17, 23 – 29, Dec. 1 – 7, 9, 12,
            13, 16 – 31.
    1934   Jan. 3 – 30, Feb. 16 – 23, 25 –
            28, Mar. 2, 3, 6 – 26, 28 – Apr.
            14, 17 – May 16.
  LNT – MA
    1924   Nov. 4 – 13.
    1925   Apr. 28 – Nov. 13.
    1926   Feb. 2 – Mar. 1.

LA REFORMA. sw.
  CU – B
    1879   Jan. 8, Feb. 8, 19 – 26, June
            4 – 18, Oct. 1 – 29, Dec. 3 – 31.
    1881   Nov. 19.
    1882   Suplemento: Dec. 11.
    Micro (P)
    1878   Aug. 9, 30.

REGENERACION. sw., irr.
  CU
    1914   Oct. 22 – Nov. 8, 19 – Dec. 26.
    1915   Jan. 1, Feb. 13, Mar. 6 – 26,
            31 – Apr. 12, 21 – May 1, 8, 15.

REGIONAL. w. est. 1912.
  TxU
    1912   Jan. 11.

EL RENACIMIENTO. w., d.
  CU
    1908   Aug. 13.
    1911   Mar. 9 – 16, Apr. 6, 20 – May
            11, June 8, Aug. 31 – Sept. 10,
            24, Oct. 26, Nov. 3, Dec. 4, 7 –
            12, 14.
    1912   Jan. 2, 15, Mar. 4, 20, Apr.
            19, Sept. 11, 25, 29, Oct. 1, 10,
            24, 25, Nov. 5, 11, 17.

LA REVISTA DE TABASCO. d.
  CU
    1922   July 28 – 31, Aug. 6 – 9, 11 –
            19, 21 – Sept. 7, 11 – 14, 18, 19,
            23, 27 – Oct. 7, 10, 12, 14 – 18,
            20, 23 – Nov. 3, 6 – 14, 16, 18 –
            24, 27, 29 – Dec. 1, 6 – 18, 20,
            21, 23, 27, 28, 30.
    1923   Jan. 1 – Feb. 17, 21 – Mar. 10,
            14 – 21, 23, 25, Apr. 1 – 12,
            14 – 17, May 5 – 11, 14 – 18,
            21 – June 4, 6, 7, 9, 12, 13, 15,
            16, 19 – 21, 25 – July 6, 10 –
            12, 14 – 24, 31, Oct. 16.

REVOLUCION.
  CU
    1939   Oct. 21.

LA SIMIENTE.
  CU
    1912   Mar. 17.

TABASCO. d.
  CU
    1915   Dec. 22 – 28, 31.
    1916   Jan. 1, 5, Feb. 3 – 5, 10 – Apr.
            1, 7 – May 2, 18 – July 30.

TABASCO GRAFICO.
  CU
    1916   Aug. 12.

TABASCO NUEVO. w., bw.
  CU
    1918   May 2, 16 – July 4, 18 – Aug.
            15.

    1935   July 25 – Aug. 11, Sept. 5 –
            12, 15 – 22, Nov. 7 – 10, Dec.
            5 – 19, 20.
    1936   Jan. 2 – 9.

EL TABASQUEÑO. sw.
  CU – B
    1847   Aug. 26.
    1849   Aug. 9.
    1851   Feb. 20.
    1852   July 29, Oct. 10.
  Micro (P)
    1852   July 15 – 18, Sept. 16.

EL TABASQUEÑO; REVISTA HEB-
  DOMADARIA DE CIENCIAS, ARTES,
  AGRICULTURA, COMERCIO, Y
  ANUNCIOS. w.
  TxU
    1881   Apr. 24, May 8 – June 12, 30.

EL TABASQUEÑO. sw.
  CU
    1912   May 6, 7, 9 – 11, 14 – 25, July
            2, 4, 15, Aug. 12, 19, 21, 31 –
            Sept. 3, 12 – 16, 23, 26 – Oct.
            1, 4, 5, 9, Nov. 7, 9.
    1913   Feb. 1.

EL TRABAJO. w.
  CU
    1938   Feb. 26, Mar. 19, Apr. 16 – 23,
            30, June 19 – July 2, 16, 30, Oct.
            6.
            Extraordinario: Apr. 25, Oct.
            11.

LA UNION LIBERAL.
  CU
    1910   Sept. 15 – Dec. 25.

LA VANGUARDIA.
  CU
    1929   Feb. 17.

VEDA NUEVA. w.
  CU
    1922   May 2, June 11, Sept. 3, Oct.
            1, 15 – 29, Nov. 19 – 26.
            Extraordinario: May 22.

LA VERDAD. w., sw.
  CU
    1919   Aug. 17, 31 – Oct. 2, 9,
            19 – 23.
    1922   Sept. 3.
    1929   Dec. 8.

LA VOZ DE LA CHONTALPA. w.
  CU
    1919   Dec. 20 – 28.
    1920   Jan. 1.

LA VOZ DE LA REVOLUCION. bw.
  CU
    1935   Nov. 20, Dec. 12.
    1936   Jan. 21.

LA VOZ DEL PUEBLO. w.
  CU
    1917   May 20 – 26.
    1926   Jan. 3, Feb. 7, June 27, July
            25.
    1937   Mar. 21.

        Xalapa-Enríquez
          See Jalapa.

        Yucatán
          See Mérida.

        Zacapoaxtla

LA IDEA LIBERAL. bw.
  TxU
    1866   Nov. 17.

        Zacatecas

ALBA ROJA. w. est. 1918.
  DLC
    1918   Aug. 10.

CENERRADA. est. 1872.
  CU – B
    Micro (P)
    1872   Dec. 5.

EL COMETA. w., sw. est. Jan. 9, 1832.
    Note: Periodicity Jan. 9 – 16, 1832,
    weekly; after Jan. 16, 1832, semi-
    weekly.
  DLC
    1832   Jan. 16, Feb. 14 – 22, 24 – Mar.

        7, 16 – Apr. 1, 17 – 25, 27, 29,
        May 1 – 10, 12 – 17, 19 – June
        20, July 3 – 11, 13 – 25, 27 –
        Aug. 8, 10 – 19, 21 – Sept. 2,
        7 – 26, 28 – Oct. 4, Dec. 3.
        Alcance: May 4.
        Extraordinario: Sept. 18.

CORREO DE ZACATECAS. w. est.
  June 29, 1902.
    Note: Ceased publication 1910.
  TxU
    1908   Aug. 9.

CRONICA MUNICIPAL. est. 1881.
    Note: Ceased publication 1903.
  TxU
    1881   Mar. 8.

EL DEFENSOR DE LA CONSTITU-
  CION; PERIODICO OFICIAL DEL
  ESTADO DE ZACATECAS. 3w., sw.
  est. 1876.
    Note: Ceased publication 1899.
  TxU
    1880   July 8 – 13, Aug. 5 – 10, Sept.
            30 – Oct. 5, 28 – Nov. 2, 11 –
            16, Dec. 2 – 21.
    1884   Mar. 22.

EL DEFENSOR DE LA REFORMA;
  PERIODICO OFICIAL DEL GO-
  BIERNO DEL ESTADO. 3w. est. Feb.
  16, 1860.
    Note: Suspended publication Oct.
    1, 1863 – Dec. 3, 1866; ceased
    publication 1870.
  CU – B
    1868   Jan. 2 – Dec. 31.
    1869   Jan. 1 – Dec. 31.
    1870   Jan. 1 – 27.
  TxU
    1864   Alcance: Jan. 15.

DIARIO OFICIAL; PERIODICO OFI-
  CIAL. sw., 3w., d. est. Feb. 9, 1870.
    Note: Ceased publication 1876.
  CU – B
    1870   Feb. 9 – Dec. 31.
    1871   Jan. 1 – Dec. 31.

1872   Jan. 1 – 30, Mar. 17 – Dec. 31.
1873   Jan. 1 – 4, 7 – Dec. 18, 20 –
        31.
1874   Jan. 1 – Dec. 31.
1875   Mar. 18.
1876   Mar. 7.
LNHT
1874   June 20, 21.
1875   Feb. 15 – Sept. 20.

LA EPOCA. w. est. 1889.
  CU – B
    Micro (P)
    1889   Mar. 23.

GACETA DEL GOBIERNO DE
  ZACATECAS. w.
    Note: A later paper bears the same
    title.
  CU – B
    Micro (P)
    1837   May 14.

GACETA DEL GOBIERNO DE
  ZACATECAS. w.
    Note: An earlier paper bears the same
    title.
  CU – B
    1841   Mar. 25.
    Micro (P)
    1840   July 5.

GAZETA DEL SUPREMO GOVIERNO
  DE ZACATECAS. 3w.
  CU – B
    1834   Jan. 2, 28.

EL INDEPENDIENTE. w. est. Mar. 7,
  1920.
  TxU
    1920   Mar. 21, Apr. 4 – 11, 25.

EL JOCOCON. w. est. 1906.
    Note: Ceased publication 1914.
  TxU
    1910   June 25 – July 2, 16, 30, Aug.
            13, 20 – Sept. 3, 24, Oct. 15,
            Nov. 19, Dec. 3 – 10, 24.
    1911   Jan. 7 – 14, Feb. 18 – 25, Mar.
            11, Apr. 8 – May 13, June 10,
            July 1 – 8.

EL OBSERVADOR ZACATECANO.
  sw. est. Mar. 20, 1833.
  DLC
    1833   Mar. 20 – May 14, 16 – June 4,
            13 – July 2, 4, 5, 7 – 30, Aug. 1,
            2, 4 – Dec. 21.

OBSERVADOR ZACATECANO;
  ORGANO OFICIAL. w. est. 1844.
    Note: Ceased publication 1845.
  CU – B
    Micro (P)
    1844   June 27.

REGENADOR; PERIODICO DEL
  GOBIERNO DEL ESTADO DE
  ZACATECAS. sw. est. Aug. 19, 1855.
    Note: Ceased publication 1856.
  CtY
    1856   Jan. 17 – June 26, July 6 – Oct.
            2, 12 – Nov. 27, Dec. 7 – 11.

LA UNION ZACATECANA. est. 1884.
  TxU
    1886   Feb. 7.

LA VERDAD. sw. est. May 4, 1917.
  TxU
    1917   May 4.

Zacatlán

EL ECO DE ZACATLAN. est. 1891.
  TxU
    1891   Nov. 1.

Zamora

DON BARBARITO. w.
  KHi
    1883   Feb. 18.
  TxU
    1880   Sept. 26.

NICARAGUA

Bluefields

THE AMERICAN.
    Note: In English.
  LNHT
    Micro (N)
    1905   [Mar. 7 – Dec. 31].
    1906 – 1917   [Jan. 1 – Dec. 31].

1930   ₍Nov. 1 – Dec. 31₎.
1931   ₍Jan. 1 – Aug. 29₎.

THE BLUEFIELDS MESSENGER. w.
   est. Jan. 1890.
   Note: In English.
   DLC
      1892   Oct. 28.

THE BLUEFIELDS SENTINEL. w. est.
   1892.
   Note: In English.
   DLC
      1892   Nov. 3, Dec. 29.

THE BLUEFIELDS WEEKLY. w.
   Note: In English.
   LNHT
      Micro (N)
      1928   ₍Apr. 28 – Dec. 31₎.
      1929   ₍Jan. 1 – Dec. 31₎.
      1930   ₍Jan. 1 – Feb. 15₎.

LA INFORMACION. est. 1917.
   FU
      Micro (N)
      1959   Dec. 23.
      1960   Dec. 23.
      1961   Dec. 22.
      1962   Sept. 14, Dec. 22.
      1963   Dec. 24 – 31.
      1964   Jan. 1 – Feb. 29, Mar. 14 –
             Nov. 17.

Granada

BOLETIN OFICIAL.
   CU – B
      1855   Sept. 1.

EL CANAL DE NICARAGUA. w. est.
   1847.
   NN
      1879   Aug. 31.

DIARIO DE GRANADA. d. est. Feb. 1,
   1907.
   DLC
      1907   Feb. 1 – Oct. 9, 11 – 16, 18 –
             Dec. 10, 12, 14 – 31.
      1908   Jan. 1 – 31.

EL DIARIO NICARAGÜENSE. d. est.
   Mar. 1, 1884.
   Note: Ceased publication [1959].
   CU – B
      Micro (P)
      1887   Jan. 23, Feb. 4, 16, 17.
      1889   Aug. 11, 23.
   DLC
      1927   Mar. 1 – 3, 5, 16, 18 – 20, 22 –
             26, Apr. 2 – 5, 10, 19, 21, 23,
             26 – 30, Mar. 5, 10, 17, 19 – 22,
             25, 28, 31, June 1, 5 – 9, 12, 15,
             16, 19 – 21, 24 – 27, 29, 30,
             July 3, 9, 13, 14, 17, 19 – 24,
             28, 30 – Aug. 1, 3 – 5, 7, 11,
             17 – 19, 23 – 25, 28, 29, Sept. 1,
             3, 6, 10 – 13, 18, 21, 27, 28, 30 –
             Oct. 1, 7 – 9, 12 – 15, 20, 25,
             28, Nov. 1, 6, 10, 12, 18, 20, 22,
             26, 28, Dec. 3, 5, 7, 8, 13, 15,
             20, 23, 25, 29, 31.
      1928   Feb. 5 – June 30, Aug. 1 – Nov.
             5, 7 – Dec. 31.
      1929   Jan. 1 – Feb. 8, 10, 12 – Mar.
             13, 15 – Apr. 22, 24 – 27, 29 –
             May 4, 6 – Aug. 13, 15 – 19, 21,
             22, 24, 26 – 30, Sept. 1 – 11,
             13 – Nov. 9, 11 – Dec. 16, 18 –
             31.
      1930   Jan. 1 – 5, 12 – 20, 22 – Feb. 12,
             14, 16 – Apr. 7, 23 – May 12,
             14 – June 2, 4 – Sept. 15, 22 –
             Dec. 1, 10 – 31.
      1931   Jan. 1 – Mar. 30, Apr. 13 – 25,
             May 4 – 25, 27, 29, 31 – Aug. 3,
             10 – 31, Sept. 6 – 28, Oct. 2, 5 –
             8, 10 – Dec. 7, 14 – 31.
      1932   Jan. 1 – June 26.
      1941   Jan. 29.
      1946   July 2 – 22, 24 – 29, 31, Aug.
             23 – 30, Sept. 9, 10, 12 – Oct. 4,
             7 – 18, 20 – 24, 26 – Nov. 15,
             17 – 20, 22, 23, 25 – 29, Dec.
             1 – 6, 8 – 14, 16 – 19, 22, 23,
             27 – 31.
      1947   Jan. 1 – 3, 5 – 10, 12, 13, 15 –
             17, 19 – 31, Feb. 2 – 7, 9 – 14,
             17 – 21, 23 – Mar. 21, 23 – Apr.

11, 13−29, May 3−June 19, 23,
25−28, 30−July 11, 13−15,
19−23, 25−Aug. 12, 14, 15.

1948   Aug. 1, 15.

1949   July 6−14.

LNT−MA

1929   July 3−7, Oct. 1−6, 15−27,
Nov. 5−17, Dec. 18−29.

1930   [Jan. 1−Dec. 31].

1931   Jan. 1−Mar. 31.

1940   Nov. 3, 5, 8.

Micro (N)

1925   Nov. 1−Dec. 31.

1926−1927   Jan. 1−Dec. 31.

1928   Jan. 1−Feb. 4.

EL ECO POPULAR. est. July 15, 1854.

CU−B

1854   July 15.

EL INDEPENDIENTE. d.

CU−B

Micro (P)

1887   Jan. 10.

INTEGRIDAD DE CENTRO-AMERICA.
w. est. Dec. 11, 1849.

CU−B

1849   Prospecto: Nov. 30.
Dec. 11−25.

1850   Jan. 1−8, 22−Feb. 5.

EL NICARAGÜENSE. w. est. Oct. 1855.

CU−B

1855   Oct. 27, Nov. 17.

1856   Jan. 5, 19−Feb. 23, May 31,
June 14, 28−Aug. 16.
Extraordinario: June 2.

EL PAIS. d.

TxU

1922   Sept. 9−Oct. 5.

EL REFLECTOR. d. est. Jan. 1926.

DLC

1926   Feb. 7−25, Mar. 24, 27, 28,
Apr. 6, 8−13, 17, 18, 21−24,
27, 28, May 1, 2.

LA SEMANA. w. est. 1925.

DLC

1926   Mar. 7−14, 28, Apr. 25−May
23.

TELEGRAFO SETENTIONAL. w. est.
Feb. 28, 1857.

CU−B

Micro (P)

1857   Feb. 28−Mar. 14, 28−June 13.

León

BOLETIN DE NOTICIAS.

CU−B

Micro (P)

1869   Aug. 31.

BOLETIN DEL GOBIERNO. irr.

CU−B

Micro (P)

1869   July 1−8, 30−Aug. 4, 19−
Sept. 4.

BOLETIN DEL PUEBLO. irr.

CU−B

Micro (P)

1865   June 22−Oct. 8, 24.

BOLETIN OFICIAL. irr., w. est. June 12,
1849.

CU−B

1849   June 12−July 12.

Micro (P)

1856   Apr. 9−16, May 29−Sept. 26,
Oct. 10−24, Nov. 7−21, Dec.
2−13, 29.

1857   Jan. 9−May 28.

BOLETIN OFICIAL NICARAGÜENSE.
irr.

CtY

1842   Feb. 19, Mar. 3, 4, 19, Apr. 30,
June 18, July 10, Sept. 28,
Oct. 5.
Suplemento: May 6.

EL CENTROAMERICANO. d. est. Oct. 7,
1917.

DLC

1928   July 3−Aug. 20, 27−Dec. 31.

1929   Jan. 1−May 7, 15−Dec. 16,
22−31.

1930   Jan. 1−9, 11−Feb. 21, 23−

29, Mar. 2 – Aug. 9, 11 – Sept.
8, 10 – 19, 21 – Oct. 3, 5 – 7,
10 – Nov. 8, 10 – 12, 14 – 24,
26 – Dec. 2, 4 – 16, 20 – 24.
1936   Oct. 4 – 10.
1941   Jan. 29, Feb. 1.
LNT – MA
1937   July 20 – Aug. 18, Oct. 12.
Micro (N)
1922 – 1931   Jan. 1 – Dec. 31.
1932   Jan. 1 – Apr. 30.
1933   May 1 – Dec. 31.

CORREO DEL ISTMO DE NICARAGUA.
bw., w. est. May 1, 1849.
CU – B
1849   May 1 – Dec. 16.
1850   Jan. 1 – July 11, Aug. 8 – Dec.
26.
1851   Jan. 2 – Feb. 20, Mar. 6 – Apr.
3, May 4, 22 – 29.
CtY
1850   Mar. 7, May 9.
Suplemento: Apr. 29.
NHi
1851   May 29.

LOS HECHOS. d. est. 1925.
DLC
1926   Jan. 26 – Feb. 6, 10 – 16, 19 –
21, 23, 24, Mar. 3 – 5, 9, 11, 12,
27, 28, Apr. 8 – 10, 15 – 18, May
8 – 15, 25, 29, June 12, 19,
July 3, 24, 25, 31, Aug. 1, 28,
Nov. 13, 17.

EL INDEPENDIENTE. d. est. 1896.
DLC
1926   Jan. 16, 22, 26, 27, 29 – 31, Feb.
4, 7 – 10, 13 – 17, 19 – 21, 24,
25, Mar. 14, 18, 23 – 28, Apr. 6,
7, 9, 10, 13, 14, 16 – 18, May
8 – 15, 22, 26, 27, 29, June 3, 9,
10, 17, 20, Aug. 29, Nov. 27.

EL NACIONAL. w. est. June 12, 1858.
Note: Suspended publication [Apr.
30], 1859 – Sept. 7, 1860.
CU – B
Micro (P) & (N)
1858   June 12 – Dec. 25.

1859   Jan. 1 – Apr. 30.
1860   Sept. 8 – Dec. 29.

NEW LIFE. NUEVA VIDA. sw. est [1912].
Note: In Spanish and English. Ceased
publication Oct. 24, 1912.
DLC
1912   Oct. 24.

EL NOTICIOSO. irr. est. Nov. 28, 1847.
CU – B
1847   Nov. 28 – Dec. 30.
1848   Jan. 8, 24 – Apr. 14.
CtY
1847   Dec. 6.
1848   Mar. 20.

NUEVA ERA DEL ESTADO DE NI-
CARAGUA EN LA AMERICA CEN-
TRAL. 3m., w. est. July 8, 1854.
CU – B
Micro (P)
1854   July 8 – Sept. 20, Oct. 10 – Dec.
2, 30.
1855   Jan. 13.

NUEVA VIDA.
See *New Life. Nueva vida.*

REJISTRO OFICIAL. w. est. Jan. 25,
1845.
Note: Removed from San Fernando to
León, Sept. 13, 1845; returned to San
Fernando, June 20, 1846; removed to
Managua, July 18, 1846; removed to
León, July 24, 1847. Ceased publication Dec. 4, 1847.
CU – B
1845   Sept. 13 – Dec. 31.
1846   Jan. 1 – June 13.
DLC
1845   Sept. 13 – Nov. 8, 22 – Dec. 31.
Alcance: Nov. 29.
1846   Jan. 1 – May 2, 16 – June 13.
1847   July 24 – Aug. 7, 28 – Nov. 6,
27 – Dec. 4.

LA VERDADERA UNION. w. est. 1861.
CtY
1862   Dec. 25.

Managua

BOLETIN OFICIAL.
  CtY
    1849   Extraordinario: July 5.

BOLETIN OFICIAL. w. est. Nov. 16, 1861.
    Note: Published during the suspen-
    sion of *La Gaceta*; *diario oficial*.
  CU−B
    Micro (P)
    1861   Nov. 16−Dec. 30.
    1862   Jan. 11−Nov. 15.
  DLC
    1861   Nov. 16−Dec. 31.
    1862   Jan. 1−Nov. 29.

EL COMERCIO. d. est. 1890.
  FU
    Micro (N)
    1929   Jan. 1−27, 29−Feb. 5, 7−23,
            25−27, Mar. 1−Apr. 1, 3−
            June 30.
  LNT−MA
    Micro (N)
    1918   July 1−Dec. 31.
    1919   Jan. 1−Oct. 31.
    1929   Jan. 1−31.
    1930   Dec. 1−31.

EL CORREO DE MANAGUA. d.
  DLC
    1911   Sept. 1−Dec. 31.
    1912   Jan. 1−Feb. 2, 4−Apr. 1, 3,
            5−7, 9−11, 13−June 17, 19−
            July 22, 24.

D. N. w. est. Sept. 12, 1944.
  LNT−MA
    1944   Sept. 12, Nov. 3−Dec. 29.
    1945   Jan. 6−Aug. 3.
  LU
    1944   Nov. 17, 24, Dec. 1, 8, 22, 29.
    1945   Jan. 6, 12, 19, 27.

EL DEBATE. d. est. Feb. 1928.
  DLC
    1928   Feb. 14, 17−19, 22−Mar. 2, 4,
            7, 8, 10, 13, 15, 18, 29−31, Apr.
            11.

DIARIO LATINO. d. est. [1935].
  LNT−MA
    1936   Feb. 17−21.

DIARIO MODERNO. d.
  TxU
    1924   Jan. 25, 26, 31−Feb. 3.

EL DIARITO. d. est. 1890.
  DLC
    1926   Apr. 15−18, 21, 23−May 2, 4,
            6, 7, 11−16, 25, 27, 30, June 1,
            6, Aug. 8.

LA ESTRELLA DE NICARAGUA. d. est.
    Jan. 1, 1940.
  DLC
    1947   Sept. 1, 3−21, 23−Oct. 25,
            27−Nov. 22, 25, 26, 28−Dec.
            7, 9, 11−25, 27, 28, 30, 31.
    1948   Jan. 1, 2, 4−16, 20−24, 27−
            31, Feb. 3−7, 10−13, 16−19,
            24−27. Mar. 1−7, 9−12, 16−
            20, 22−24, 30, 31, Mar. 1−4,
            6−21, 23−30, May 2−9, 11−
            16, 18−June 8, 10−Aug. 7,
            10−19, 21−Sept. 19, 21−Oct.
            17, 19−Dec. 31.
    1949   Jan. 1−Mar. 19, 22−Apr. 6,
            8−16, 18−24, 26−May 23,
            25−July 3, 5−Aug. 7, 9−Sept.
            3, 5−16, 18−Nov. 30.
  LNT−MA
    1940   Nov. 6−9.
  TxU
    1948   Nov. 21.

FLECHA. d. est. 1941.
    Note: Suspended publication July 1−
    Sept. 14, 1947; Apr. 1−June 15, 1948.
  DLC
    1946   Aug. 13−Sept. 4, 7−9, 11,
            14−16, 18−Oct. 25, 27−Dec.
            31.
    1947   Jan. 1−Feb. 21, 23−Mar. 9,
            11, 13, 14, 16, 18−21, 23−25,
            27−Apr. 10, 12−22, 24−29,
            May 3−15, 17−26, 28, 29, 31−
            Sept. 21, 23−Oct. 6, 8−Nov.
            23, 25−Dec. 5, 7, 8, 10, 12−17,
            19−28, 30, 31.
    1948   Jan. 1−18, 20−25, 27, 28, 30−
            Feb. 1, 3−8, 10−19, 21, 22,

24 – 27, 29 – Mar. 7, 9 – 12, 14,
16 – 24, 28, 30 – June 18, 20,
22 – 24, 26 – July 20, 22 – Aug.
8, 10 – Sept. 6, 8 – Oct. 17,
19 – Dec. 31.
1949   Jan. 1 – Mar. 18, 20, 22 – Apr.
3, 5 – 13, 17 – May 23, 25, 27 –
June 22, 26, 28, 30 – July 4, 6 –
Sept. 16, 18 – 20, 22 – Oct. 11,
13 – Nov. 30.
LNHT
Micro (N)
1944   Jan. 1 – Dec. 31.
TxU
1948   Nov. 21.
LA GACETA; DIARIO OFICIAL. w., irr.,
d. est. Nov. 22, 1851.
Note: Suspended publication 1854 –
1857; 1861 – 1862. *Boletín oficial*
published during latter suspension.
CU – B
Micro (P)
1852   Jan. 3.
1853   Apr. 2 – 23, May 28, Aug. 13 –
Sept. 10.
1854   Jan. 7, Feb. 11, 25 – Mar. 4.
1863   Jan. 3 – Mar. 28, Apr. 18, May
9 – June 27, Aug. 15 – 22, Sept.
5 – Dec. 26.
1864   Jan. 1 – Dec. 31.
1865   Jan. 7 – 14, Feb. 11 – 18, Mar.
4 – 11, 18 – 22, 29 – Apr. 1, 8 –
May 27, June 10 – July 1, 15,
29 – Aug. 26, Sept. 9 – 30, Oct.
14, Nov. 4 – Dec. 23.
1866   Jan. 1 – Dec. 31.
1867   Jan. 5 – 19, Feb. 2 – 16, Mar.
2 – Dec. 7, 21.
Extraordinario: Jan. 29.
1868   Jan. 1 – Dec. 31.
1869   Jan. 2 – Apr. 3, 17 – May 15,
29 – June 19, July 3 – Nov. 20,
Dec. 4 – 25.
1870   Jan. 1 – July 23, Aug. 6 – Dec.
31.
1871   Jan. 7 – 29, Feb. 11 – Mar. 18,
Apr. 1 – May 13, 27 – June 24,
July 8 – Dec. 30.

1872   Jan. 1 – Dec. 31.
1873   Jan. 11 – Dec. 27.
1874   Jan. 1 – Dec. 31.
1879   Oct. 9, 25 – Nov. 1, 27 – Dec.
27.
1880   Jan. 10.

DLC
1851   Nov. 22 – Dec. 31.
1852 – 1853   [Jan. 1 – Dec. 31].
1858 – 1860   [Jan. 1 – Dec. 31].
1863 – 1866   Jan. 1 – Dec. 31.
1867   [Jan. 1 – Dec. 31].
1868 – 1872   Jan. 1 – Dec. 31.
1873   [Jan. 1 – Dec. 31].
1874   Jan. 1 – Dec. 31.
1875   [Jan. 1 – Dec. 31].
1876 – 1878   Jan. 1 – Dec. 31.
1879   [Jan. 1 – Dec. 31].
1880 – 1883   Jan. 1 – Dec. 31.
1884 – 1885   [Jan. 1 – Dec. 31].
1886 – 1887   Jan. 1 – Dec. 31.
1889 – 1890   Jan. 1 – Dec. 31.
1892   Jan. 1 – Dec. 31.
1894   [Jan. 1 – Oct. 31].
1895   [Jan. 1 – Dec. 31].
1896   [Aug. 1 – Dec. 31].
1898   Jan. 1 – Dec. 31.
1899   [Jan. 1 – Dec. 31].
1900   Jan. 1 – Dec. 31.

GACETA DEL GOBIERNO SUPREMO
DEL ESTADO DE NICARAGUA. w.
est. June 1848.
Note: Also published in León.
CU – B
Micro (P)
1848   Sept. 16 – Dec. 30.
1849   Mar. 3 – Apr. 7.
CtY
1848   Oct. 28, Nov. 18, Dec. 9 – 16.
1849   Mar. 3 – 17.

EL HERALDO. d.
DLC
1947   July 3, 5, 7 – 11, 13 – 18, 20 –
25, 27 – 31, Aug. 2 – 8, 10 – 15,
17 – 22, 24 – 31.

EL IMPARCIAL. w.
  CU—B
    Micro (P)
    1887   Mar. 4.
JUVENTUD.
  LNT—MA
    1957   Jan. 9.
LA MAÑANA. d.
  DLC
    1926   Jan. 15, 19, 21, 27, 28, 30—Feb.
           4, 6—26, Mar. 14, 25, 26, 28,
           Apr. 6, 8—May 7, 11—16, 25—
           June 1, 11—16, 24—July 1, 3,
           4, 31, Aug. 1, 7—10, 22, 25,
           27—31, Sept. 2—11, 28—30,
           Oct. 7—9, Nov. 19—21, 28—
           Dec. 2, 8—12, 29, 30.
    1927   Jan. 1—6, 19—23.
EL MUNDO. d. est. [1948].
  DLC
    1948   May 31, June 7, 20, 21, 28,
           July 4, 5, 11, 12, 18, Aug. 1, 15,
           Nov. 2—Dec. 18, 20—31.
    1949   Jan. 1—May 21.
  TxU
    1948   Nov. 19, 20.
LA NOTICIA. d. est. July 15, 1915.
  DLC
    1926   Aug. 15—Sept. 17, 19, 20, 22,
           23, 26—Oct. 1, 4—9, 11, 14—
           16, 18, 20—Dec. 3, 5—11, 13,
           15—18, 20—31.
    1927   Jan. 1, 3—19, 21, 24—26, June
           8—July 2, 4—7, 11—22, 24—
           Aug. 1, 3—6, 8, 10—22, 24—
           29, 31—Sept. 2, 5, 7—9, 11—
           19, 28—Oct. 1, 3, 5—Nov. 21.
    1947   July 5, 7, 8, 10—16, 18, 19,
           21—24, 26—Aug. 1, 3—8, 10—
           19, 21, 22, 24—Oct. 25, 27—
           Nov. 3, 5—Dec. 5, 7—31.
    1948   Jan. 1—3, 5—12, 14—17, 19—
           24, 26—31, Feb. 2—7, 9—11,
           13, 14, 16—19, 21, 23—27, Mar.
           1—12, 15—20, June 17—19,
           21—26, 28—July 2, 4—10, 12—
           17, 19—Aug. 7, 9—Sept. 4, 6,
           8—18, 20—25, 27—30, Oct. 2,

           4—8, 10—Nov. 24, 26—Dec.
           31.
    1949   Jan. 2—29, 31—Apr. 4, 6—
           July 7, 9—Nov. 30.
    1950   July 1—Dec. 31.
    1960   Jan. 1—Oct. 25, 27—Dec. 31.
    1961   Jan. 1—Apr. 17, 19—30, May
           3—Nov. 21, 28—Dec. 6, 12—
           20, 27—31.
    Micro (P) & (N)
    1962   Jan. 1+.
  LNT—MA
    1934   Sept. 22.
    1937   July 16.
    1940   Nov. 8.
    Micro (N)
    1925   Jan. 7—Oct. 31.
    1928   Feb. 1—Sept. 30.

NOVEDADES. d. est. July 1, 1937.
  DLC
    1944   Nov. 10—Dec. 5.
    1945   Mar. 14—20, 22—Apr. 10,
           18—20, 24, 25, 27—29, May
           11—13, 16—18, 19, 20, 22—
           25, Sept. 5—7.
    1946   Jan. 23—Feb. 4, 24, Mar. 2—
           12, 23—30, Apr. 1—3, 23, 27—
           30, May 8—12, 14—June 6,
           8—11, 15—21, 25—July 3, 23,
           Sept. 10, 11, 17—24, 26—Oct.
           2, 4—7, 29—Nov. 4, Dec. 4—8.
    1947   Jan. 11, Feb. 5—20, 24—Mar.
           2, 4—6, June 7—10, 12, 13,
           July 3, 7—11, 13—27, 29—Aug.
           3, 5—Sept. 13, 15—30, Oct.
           2—25, 27—Nov. 23, 25—Dec.
           2, 4—16, 18—31.
    1948   Jan. 3—14, 16, 17, 19—24,
           26—31, Feb. 4—7, 10—19, 21,
           24—27, Mar. 1—12, 16—20,
           30—Apr. 4, 6—13, 15—30,
           May 3—Aug. 22, 24—28, 31,
           Oct. 1, 3—17, 19—31, Nov.
           3—Dec. 31.
    1949   Jan. 1—26, 28—Feb. 23, 25—
           Mar. 4, 6—20, 22—28, 30—
           Apr. 3, 5, 7—19, 21—Aug.

10, 12 – Sept. 17, 19 – Nov. 1,
3 – 30.

1955 Mar. 28 – Apr. 13, 15 – 26,
May 3, 5 – 12, 27 – July 2, 4 –
20, 22 – Sept. 30, Oct. 13 –
Dec. 4, 20 – 31.

1956 Jan. 1 – 14, 17 – 21, Feb.
7, Mar. 2, 3, 9, 10, 13, 19 – 28,
Apr. 3 – July 1, 3 – Nov. 7,
Dec. 3, 5 – 31.

1957 Jan. 1 – 20, 22 – Feb. 4, 6 –
13, Mar. 26 – 31, Apr. 4 – 12,
23, 24.

1960 July 11 – Nov. 2, 4 – Dec. 2,
4 – 12, 16 – 31.

1961 Jan. 1 – Feb. 10, May 13, 14,
24 – 27, 29, June 14 – 27, 30 –
Sept. 14, 17 – Oct. 3, 5 – Nov.
14, 16 – 18, 20 – Dec. 31.

Micro (P) & (N)
1962 Jan. 1+.

LNT – MA
1937 July 1 – Dec. 31.
1938 Jan. 1 – June 30, July 2, 3, 19 –
25, Aug. 28.
1939 Feb. 7 – 26.
1940 Nov. 7 – 9.
1949 June 6.
1956 Apr. 3, 4, May 24, June 6.

MH
1966 Jan. 1+.

LA NUEVA PRENSA. d. est. 1932.
Note: Spanish and English editions.
CU
1943 July 20 – 31, Aug. 4 – 12.
1944 Jan. 4 – 13, 15, 19 – 25, 27 – 30.
1947 Jan. 14 – 16, 19, 21 – 24, 26,
28 – Feb. 1, 5 – 11, 13, 14, 16,
19 – 23, 25 – Mar. 2, 5 – 9, 13 –
18, 20 – 26, 28, 29, Apr. 9, 10,
12, 13, 15 – 20, 23, 25, 26, 29,
May 3, 4, 6, 8, 9, 13, 14, 16 –
18, 20 – 24, 30, June 3 – 5, 8,
11, 13, 14, 17, 20 – 22, 25, 26,
July 3, 6 – 8, 10 – 13, 15 – 17,
20, 22, 23, 25, 26, 29 – Aug. 7,
10, 12 – 14, 16, 19 – 21, 23, 24,
27, 29, 30, Sept. 16 – 18, 20,

23, 24, 26 – 28, Oct. 2 – 5, 9,
15, Nov. 13, 18, 19, 21, 23, Dec.
10, 11, 16 – 20, 23, 25, 28, 30.

1948 Jan. 3, 4, 6 – 9, 13 – 17, 20, 21,
23 – 25, 27 – 31, Feb. 3 – 10,
12 – 19, 22 – 24, 26 – Mar. 2,
4 – 6, 9 – 16, 19 – 31, Apr. 9,
May 2, 7, June 25.

DLC
1945 Dec. 1 – 8, 13, 14, 16, 18 – 21,
28, 29.

1946 Jan. 8 – 12, 15 – 20, 22 – 26,
29 – Feb. 3, 5 – 10, 12 – 14, 16,
19 – 24, 28 – Mar. 3, 5 – 9,
12 – 15, 17, 19, 20, 22 – 24, 26,
28 – 31, Apr. 2 – 6, 9 – 13, 23 –
28, May 1 – 5, 7 – 11, 14 – 19,
21 – 25, 28 – June 2, 6 – 9, 11,
13 – 16, 18 – 23, 25, 27, 29,
July 3 – 7, 9 – 14, 16 – 21, 23 –
28, 30, Aug. 1, 3, 6 – 8, 14 – 17,
20 – 25, 27 – 31, Sept. 8, 10 –
14, 17 – 20, 24 – 29, Oct. 1, 2,
6, 8 – 11.

1947 Jan. 18, 19, 22, 24 – 26, 28, 30,
31, Feb. 5, 12 – 14, 25 – Mar.
1, 4 – 8, 11 – 14, 18, 20, 21,
25 – 27, Apr. 10, 11, 15 – 19,
22 – 27, 29, May 4, 6, 8, 9, 13 –
15, 17, 18, 20 – 25, 28 – June
1, 3 – 7, 11 – 15, 17 – 21, 24 –
29, July 1 – 5, 8 – 20, 22 – 27,
29 – Aug. 3, 5 – 10, 12 – 17,
19 – 24, 26 – 31, Sept. 2 – 7,
16 – 21, 23 – 28, 30 – Oct. 5,
7 – 12, 14 – 19, 21 – Nov. 7, 9,
11 – 16, 18 – 23, 25 – 30, Dec.
2 – 8, 10 – 13, 16 – 21, 23 – 28,
30, 31.

1948 Jan. 1 – 4, 6 – 11, 13 – 17, 20 –
24, 27 – 31, Feb. 3 – 7, 10 – 15,
17 – 19, 21, 24 – 26, Mar. 2 – 7,
9, 11, 12, 16 – 18, 20, 30 – Apr.
10, 13 – 18, 20 – 25, 27 – 30,
May 2, 4 – 9, 11 – 16, 18 – 23,
25 – 30, June 1 – 6, 8 – 13, 15 –
20, 22 – 27, 29 – July 4, 6 –
11, 13 – 18, 20 – 25, 27 – Aug.

1, 3 – 8, 10 – 15, 17 – 22, 24 –
29, 31, Sept. 1, 3 – 5, 7 – 12,
14 – 19, 22 – 26, 28 – Oct. 1, 3,
5 – 10, 12 – 17, 19 – 24, 26 –
31, Nov. 2 – 7, 9 – 14, 16 – 21,
23 – 28, 30 – Dec. 3, 5, 7 – 12,
14 – 19, 21 – 25, 28 – 31.
1949   Jan. 1, 4 – 9, 11 – 16, 18 – 23,
25 – 30, Feb. 1 – 6, 8 – 13,
15 – 20, 22 – 27, Mar. 1 – 6, 8 –
13, 15 – 19, 22 – 27, 29 – Apr.
3, 5 – 10, 12 – 17, 19 – 24, 26 –
May 1, 3 – 8, 10 – 15, 17 – 22,
24 – 29, 31 – June 5, 7 – 12,
14 – 19, 21 – 26, 28 – July 3,
5 – 10, 12 – 17, 19 – 24, 26 – 31,
Aug. 2 – 7, 9 – 14, 16 – 21, 23 –
28, 30 – Sept. 3, 6 – 15, 18,
20 – 25, 27 – Oct. 2, 4 – 9, 11 –
16, 18 – 23, 25 – 30, Nov. 1 –
6, 8 – 13, 15 – 20, 22 – 27, 29,
30.
LNT – MA
1937   June 16.
1940   Nov. 7, 8.

EL PACIFICO. d.
TxU
1922   June 23 – 27, July 4 – 6, 8, 9,
13, 29, 30, Aug. 18 – 24, 26 –
Sept. 6, 8 – 19, 22, 23, 26 – 28,
30 – Oct. 3, 5.

PORVENIR DE NICARAGUA. w. est.
1865.
MWA
1881   May 7.

LA PRENSA. d. est. Mar. 2, 1926.
Note: Suspended publication Apr.
8 – May 7, 1941.
CLU
1965   Jan. 1, 3 – 15, Mar. 1 – 15, Apr.
1 – 14, 20 – Dec. 31.
1965   Jan. 1+
CU
1943   Oct. 17, 20 – 24, Nov. 9 – 14,
17 – Dec. 5, 14 – 31.
1944   Jan. 1 – 4, 7 – 12, 15, 16, May
30 – June 25.

1947   Jan. 23, 28, 30 – Feb. 1, 4 – 16,
19 – Apr. 30, May 2 – 24, 28, 29.
1948   Feb. 4 – June 3, 12 – Oct. 10,
15 – 31, Nov. 3 – 19, 21 – Dec.
19, 22, 23, 25 – 30.
1949   Jan. 1 – 8, 11 – 14, 25 – Feb.
12, 15 – Apr. 2, 8 – 12, 19 –
June 18, 21 – 30, July 2 – Aug.
10, 13 – 21, 25 – 27, Sept. 1 – 9,
11 – 28, 30 – Oct. 6, 8 – 11,
13 – 28, 30 – Nov. 1, 3 – 13.
DLC
1933   Dec. 1 – 31.
1934 – 1940   Jan. 1 – Dec. 31.
1941   Jan. 1 – Apr. 7, 8 – Dec. 31.
1947   Jan. 28, 30 – Feb. 1, 4 – 13, 15,
16, 19 – 28, July 5, 7 – Sept. 8,
15 – 29, Oct. 1 – 25, 27 – Dec.
31.
1948   Jan. 1 – 17, 19 – 24, 26 – 31,
Feb. 2 – 7, 9 – 14, 16 – 19, 21,
23 – 27, Mar. 1 – 5, 7 – 12, 15 –
20, 22 – Apr. 30, May 2 – 10,
12 – 24, 26 – July 8, 10 – Sept.
18, 20 – Oct. 1, 3 – 28, 30 –
Dec. 31.
1949   Jan. 1 – Mar. 5, 7 – 19, 21 –
May 16, 19 – Sept. 3, 5 – 16,
18 – Nov. 5, 7 – 30.
1950   July 1 – Dec. 31.
1951 – 1955   Jan. 1 – Dec. 31.
Micro (P)
1956   Jan. 1+.
DPU
Current (six months).
FU
Micro (N)
1952   July 1 – Dec. 31.
1953   Jan. 1 – Apr. 28, 30 – Aug. 14,
16 – Sept. 29, Oct. 1 – 15.
ICRL
Micro (P) & (N)
1956   Jan. 1+.
LNT – MA
Micro (N)
1932   Feb. 1 – Dec. 31.
1933 – 1943   Jan. 1 – Dec. 31.
(P)

1956   Jan. 1+.
TxU
1941   June 19—Dec. 23, 27—31.
1942   Jan. 1—11, 14—22, 25—29,
       Feb. 1, 4—14, 20, 21, 25—Mar.
       26, 28, 31, Apr. 7—16, 18, 21,
       23, 25, 28, May 2, 7, 12, 14, 16,
       19, 21—June 2, 4, 6, 9, 11, 13,
       16, 20, 23, 25, July 1, 2, 5, 7—
       9, 12—23, 26—28, 31—Aug. 9,
       12, 15—18, 20—Sept. 3, 9—
       Oct. 30, Nov. 1—10, 15—19,
       22—Dec. 8, 10—25, 27—31.
1943   Jan. 3—6, 10—Feb. 2, 5, 6,
       10—16, 19—Mar. 4, 7—9, 12—
       18, 21—Apr. 14, 16—18, 27, 28.
1947   May 20—25, 28, 29, June 8.
1948   Mar. 10—18, Apr. 9—June 2,
       12—Oct. 11, 15—Nov. 19,
       21—Dec. 10, 12—14, 16—23,
       25—31.
1949   Jan. 1—8, 10—30.

LA RAZON. d. est. Oct. 1, 1930.
  DLC
    1930   Oct. 1—13.

REJISTRO OFICIAL. w. est. Jan. 25,
1845.
    Note: Removed from San Fernando
    to León, Sept. 13, 1845; returned to
    San Fernando, June 20, 1846; re-
    moved to Managua, July 18, 1846;
    removed to León, July 24, 1847.
    Ceased publication Dec. 4, 1847.
  CU—B
    1846   July 18—Dec. 31.
    1847   Jan. 1—30.
  DLC
    1846   July 18—Dec. 31.
           Alcance: Nov. 18.
    1847   Jan. 1—Apr. 24, May 8—June
           12, 26—July 17.

RENOVACION. d. est. Aug. 1931.
  DLC
    1931   Sept. 1—13.

SEMANAL NICARAGÜENSE. w. est.
May 30, 1872.

CU—B
  Micro (P)
    1872   May 30—Dec. 26.
    1873   Jan. 2—Dec. 27.

LA TRIBUNA. d. est. ₁1918₎.
  DLC
    1929   Jan. 1—Apr. 27, 29—May 25,
           27—29, June 1—Oct. 27.
  LNT—MA
    Micro (N)
    1928   ₁Sept. 1—Dec. 31₎.

ULTIMAS NOTICIAS. d. est. July 7,
1947.
  DLC
    1947   July 7—Sept. 18, 20, 21, 24—
           28, 30—Oct. 2, 4—8, 11, 12,
           17—24, 26, 27, 29—31.
    1948   June 27, July 4—6, 17—31,
           Aug. 9, 21.

LA UNION DE NICARAGUA. w. est.
Jan. 5, 1861.
  CU—B
    Micro (P)
    1861   Jan. 5—Nov. 2.
  CtY
    1862   Dec. 12.

Masaya

LOS ANALES. bw. est. 1872.
  CU—B
    Micro (P)
    1872   Aug. 1—Sept. 1, Oct. 15—
           Dec. 15.

Rivas

EL PORVENIR DE NICARAGUA. bw.
est. 1866.
    Note: Removed to Valle Gottel be-
    tween 1868 and 1871.
  CU—B
    Micro (P)
    1867   Oct. 15—Nov. 15, Dec. 15.
    1868   Feb. 1—15, May 9—16, June
           6—27, July 11—Aug. 8.

San Fernando

REJISTRO OFICIAL. w. est. Jan. 25, 1845.
> Note: Removed from San Fernando to León, Sept. 13, 1845; returned to San Fernando, June 20, 1846; removed to Managua, July 18, 1846; removed to León, July 24, 1847. Ceased publication Dec. 4, 1847.

CU – B
> 1845 Jan. 25 – Sept. 6.
> 1846 June 20 – July 11.

CtY
> 1845 Mar. 29.

DLC
> 1845 Feb. 7, 22 – Mar. 1, 29, June 14, 28 – Sept. 6.
> Alcance: June 16, 23.
> 1846 June 20 – July 11.

San Juan del Norte

CENTRAL AMERICAN. w., irr. est. Sept. 15, 1855.
> Note: In English. Ceased publication Oct. 27, 1855.

DLC
> 1855 Sept. 15 – Oct. 27.

NN
> 1855 Sept. 15.

Valle Gottel

EL PORVENIR. bw., w. est. 1866.
> Note: Title *El Porvenir de Nicaragua*, before 1872. Removed from Rivas to Valle Gottel between 1868 and 1871.

CU – B
> 1871 Oct. 1 – Dec. 24.
> 1872 Jan. 7 – 14, Feb. 11 – 25, Mar. 24 – 31, Apr. 28 – July 21, Aug. 4, 25 – Sept. 8, 29 – Oct. 6, 20 – Nov. 10, 24, Dec. 8 – 29.
> 1873 Jan. 5 – Feb. 2, 16 – Mar. 2, 16 – Oct. 12.

PANAMA
Aspinwall
See Colón.

Colón

ASPINWALL COURIER. sw. est. July 2, 1853.
> Note: In English and Spanish. Imprint "Aspinwall, New Granada." Ceased publication 1857.

DLC
> 1853 July 2, 6, 12, 19 – Aug. 1, 9 – 16, Oct. 18.
> 1854 Mar. 14, June 15.
> Suplemento: Mar. 18.

MWA
> 1855 Sept. 15.
> 1857 June 19.

NHi
> 1855 Oct. 9, 11, 16, 18.

NN
> 1856 Nov. 14.

COLON FREE PRESS. w.
> Note: In English.

MWA
> 1914 Mar. 15.

THE COLON STARLET. 3w. est. Nov. 3, 1898.
> Note: In English. Ceased publication [1914].

CU – B
> Micro (P)
> 1898 Nov. 3 – Dec. 31.
> 1899 Jan. 3 – Mar. 25, 30 – Dec. 30.
> 1900 Jan. 2 – Nov. 13, 17 – Dec. 13, 15, 20 – 29.
> 1901 Jan. 1 – 22, 26 – Dec. 31.
> 1903 Jan. 8 – 20, 24 – 27, 31 – Mar. 3, 7 – 14, 20 – Apr. 7, 14 – May 2, 7 – June 9, 13 – Aug. 1, 6 – Nov. 3, 7 – 17, 21 – Dec. 21, 31.
> 1904 Jan. 2 – Feb. 9, 13 – 16, 20 – Mar. 22, 26 – Apr. 16, 21 – July 12, 21 – Aug. 16, 20 – Sept. 8, 15 – 24, Oct. 4 – 6, 11 – 18, 22 – 29, Nov. 3 – 12, 19 – 22, 26 – Dec. 31.

DLC
> Micro (P)
> 1898 Nov. 3 – Dec. 31.

1899 – 1901   Jan. 1 – Dec. 31.
1903   Jan. 8 – Dec. 31.
1904   Jan. 2 – Dec. 31.
MWA
1913   Jan. 11.
1914   Mar. 17.
MoU
Micro (P)
1898   Nov. 3 – Dec. 31.
1899 – 1901   Jan. 1 – Dec. 31.
1903   Jan. 8 – Dec. 31.
NN
Micro (P)
1898   Nov. 3 – Dec. 31.
1899   Jan. 1 – Nov. 20, 23 – Dec. 31.
1901   Jan. 1 – Nov. 14, 16 – Dec. 31.
1903   [Jan. 8 – Dec. 31].
1904   [Jan. 1 – Dec. 31].

INDEPENDENT. 3w.
Note: In English.
MWA
1913   Jan. 10.
1914   Mar. 16.

THE ISTHMUS. sw., 3w. est. 1887.
Note: In Spanish, English, and
French.
CU – B
Micro (P)
1888   Mar. 18.
NN
1887   Mar. 20.

Fort Amador

JUNGLE MUDDER. w. est. [1940].
Note: In English.
ViU
1942   June 6, 20 – July 11, 25 – Aug.
8, 22, Sept. 19, 26.

Panama City

ACCION COMUNAL. w. est. Oct. 10,
1923.
Note: Ceased publication [1935].
DLC
1926   June 22.

LA ACTUALIDAD.
CU – B
Micro (P)
1884   Nov. 25.
1885   Jan. 8.

BOLETIN OFICIAL DEL ESTADO
SOBERANO DE PANAMA. irr. est.
1860.
CU – B
Micro (P)
1862   July 27, Sept. 6 – Oct. 1, 22 –
Dec. 11.
Extraordinario: Oct. 14.
1863   Mar. 8, Apr. 12, May 3 – July
31, Aug. 22 – Sept. 6, 13, Nov.
30.
1864   Feb. 20.
1865   Apr. 1 – 22, June 7 – July 25,
Sept. 11 – Dec. 6.
1866   Jan. 2 – Feb. 11, Nov. 1, Dec.
16.
Extraordinario: Apr. 15.
1867   Jan. 19 – Feb. 23, Mar. 22 –
June 1, 29 – Aug. 10, 24 – Sept.
28, Oct. 20 – Dec. 7, 27.
Extraordinario: Oct. 15.
1868   Jan. 8 – Feb. 1, 20 – Mar. 7,
21 – Apr. 23, May 2 – July
13, 30 – Sept. 19, Oct. 9, Nov.
14, Dec. 31.
Extraordinario: Apr. 30.
1869   Jan. 11, 27, Feb. 18 – Mar. 11,
Apr. 15 – July 1, 15 – Aug. 26,
Sept. 8, 17, Nov. 4 – 27, Dec.
15 – 20, 31.
1870   Jan. 20 – Feb. 10, Mar. 11, Apr.
9 – 16, June 2 – 25.

THE CANAL.
See *Panama Canal*.

COLONIA CHINA. d.
CLCM
1942   Dec. 24, 25.
1943   Jan. 4.

EL CONSTITUCIONAL DEL ISTMO.
w., 3m., bw. est. Nov. 30, 1831.
Note: Ceased publication [1837].

CU—B
1831 Dec. 21—28.
1832 Jan. 7—June 21, July 21, Nov. 7, 21, Dec. 28.
1833 Nov. 20.
1834 May 10—30, Oct. 30—Nov. 10, Dec. 10—20.
1836 Aug. 15—Sept. 15, Oct. 15.
1837 Apr. 30—May 15, June 15, July 30—Aug. 30.

EL CORREO DEL ISTMO. w. est. 1851.
CtY
1852 June 27—Dec. 25.
1853 Jan. 2—Mar. 27.

EL CORREO NACIONAL
CU
Micro (P)
1890 Sept. 22—Dec. 31.
1891 Jan. 1—June 12.
MoU
Micro (P)
1890 Sept. 22—Dec. 31.
1891 Jan. 1—June 12.

CRITICA. d. est. 1958.
CSt—H
1964 Apr. 21—25, 27—29, Oct. 1, 2, 5.

CRONICA ESCOLAR.
MWA
1883 July 24.

CRONICA MERCANTIL. sw. est. Sept. 15, 1864.
Note: See also *The Panama Mail.*
CU—B
Micro (N)
1864 Sept. 15.

LA CRONICA OFICIAL. w., bw. est. 1849.
CU—B
Micro (P) & (N)
1849 Oct. 23—Dec. 23.
1852 Jan. 1—29, Mar. 4, 25, May 2, July 25—Aug. 5, 22—Sept. 26, Oct. 10—31, Nov. 14.
1853 Jan. 19—Mar. 13, Apr. 8—May

4, June 4, July 4, Aug. 20— Oct. 4, 27—Dec. 4. Extraordinario: July 24, Oct. 16.
1854 Jan. 4, Feb. 8—Apr. 10, May 23.

EL CRONISTA. sw., 3w. est. Sept. 3, 1878.
Note: Ceased publication [1889].
CU—B
Micro (P) & (N)
1883 Jan. 6—20, 27—Feb. 24, Mar. 3—14, 31—Apr. 7, 18—May 12, 26—Oct. 3, 10, 17—Dec. 8, 15—29.
1884 Jan. 2—Feb. 2, Mar. 22, Apr. 2—5, 23—May 3, 10—14, June 18, July 9—19, 30—Aug. 20, 27, Oct. 15—29, Nov. 5—15, 22—29, Dec. 6, 13—31.
1885 Jan. 3—10, 17—31, Feb. 18, 25—Mar. 14, 28, Apr. 11, May 2.
1887 May 11—14, 21, 28, July 20, 27—Aug. 10, Sept. 7.
1888 Mar. 8, 15, 22, Apr. 3, Aug. 16, Sept. 1, 27, Oct. 6, Dec. 15.
1889 Feb. 26—Mar. 7.
MWA
1883 July 24.

THE DAILY ECHO. d. est. Jan. 5, 1852.
Note: In English. See also *The Weekly Echo.*
CU—B
Micro (P)
1852 Feb. 9.
DLC
1852 Feb. 28, Apr. 20, Oct. 16.

THE DAILY PANAMA STAR. w., irr. 3w., d. est. Feb. 24, 1849.
Note: In English. Title *Panama Star,* Feb. 24, 1849—Jan. 31, 1853; *The Daily Panama Star,* Feb. 1, 1853— May 1, 1854. Periodicity Feb. 24— June 1849, weekly; June 1849—Feb. Feb. 12, 1852, irregular; Feb. 13, 1852—

Jan. 31, 1853, three times a week; Feb. 1, 1853 — May 1, 1854, daily. Triweekly publication continued as a steamer edition. Suspended publication Dec. 5 — 15, 1850. Began publishing Spanish section (*La Estrella de Panamá*) Feb. 1, 1853. Merged with the *Panama Herald* to form the *Daily Panama Star and Herald*, May 2, 1854. See also the *Weekly Star*.

CU — B
  1850   Mar. 28.
  Micro (P)
  1849   Feb. 24 — Mar. 3, 17, Aug. 4, 18 — 27, Nov. 10.
  1850   Sept. 13 — Nov. 14, 29 — Dec. 5, 16 — 31.
  1851   Jan. 7 — May 13, June 3 — 24, July 1 — Aug. 1, 12 — Dec. 23.
  1852   Feb. 26, Apr. 17 — 20, July 17, 26, Nov. 2 — 13, 16 — 27, Dec. 4 — 30.
  1853   Jan. 1 — 11, 15 — Mar. 25, 27 — May 8, 10 — 27, 29 — July 1, 3, 6 — 10, 13 — Dec. 31.
  1854   Jan. 1 — 7, 10, 13 — Apr. 26, 28 — 30.

DLC
  1849   Feb. 24, Mar. 3.
  1850   Mar. 29.
  1851   Nov. 18.
  1852   Feb. 26, Apr. 17 — 20, June 17, 26, Nov. 2 — 27, Dec. 14, 16, 23 — 28.
  Micro (P)
  1849   Feb. 24 — Mar. 3, 17, Aug. 4, 18, 25, 27, Nov. 10.
  1850   Sept. 13 — Nov. 20, 23 — Dec. 31.
  1851   Jan. 1 — May 13, June 3 — 26, 28 — Aug. 4, 9 — Dec. 23.
  1852   Feb. 26, Apr. 17 — 20, June 17, 26, Nov. 2 — 27, Dec. 4 — 30.
  1853   Jan. 1 — 12, 14 — May 9, 13 — 27, June 1 — July 11, Dec. 31.
  1854   Jan. 1 — Apr. 30.

FU
  Micro (P)
  1849   Feb. 24 — Dec. 31.
  1850 — 1853   Jan. 1 — Dec. 31.
  1854   Jan. 1 — May 1.
LNHT
  Micro (P)
  1849   Feb. 24 — Dec. 31.
  1850 — 1853   Jan. 1 — Dec. 31.
  1854   Jan. 1 — May 1.
LU
  Micro (P)
  1849   Feb. 24, Mar. 3, 17, Aug. 4, 18, 25, 27, Nov. 10.
  1850   Sept. 13 — Dec. 31.
  1851 — 1853   Jan. 1 — Dec. 31.
  1854   Jan. 1 — Apr. 30.
MWA
  1849   Oct. 6.
  1854   Mar. 23.
MnU
  Micro (P)
  1849   Feb. 24 — Dec. 31.
  1850 — 1853   Jan. 1 — Dec. 31.
  1854   Jan. 1 — Apr. 30.
MoU
  Micro (P)
  1849   Feb. 24, Mar. 3, 17, Aug. 4, 18, 25, 27, Nov. 10.
  1850   Sept. 13 — Dec. 31.
  1851 — 1853   Jan. 1 — Dec. 31.
  1854   Jan. 1 — Apr. 30.
NHi
  1849   Mar. 17.
  1850   Jan. 4, Oct. 4.
  1851   June 3.
NN
  1850   Feb. 21.
          Supplement: Dec. 6.
  Micro (P)
  1849   Feb. 24 — Dec. 31.
  1850 — 1853   Jan. 1 — Dec. 31.
  1854   Jan. 1 — May 1.

THE DAILY PANAMA STAR. STEAMER EDITION.
DLC
  Micro (P)
  1851   Apr. 30.

1853 July 20.

THE DAILY PANAMA STAR AND HERALD.
See *Star & Herald.*

El DIA. d. est. 1947.
CSt—H
1964 Apr. 21—25, 28, 29, June 1—6,
8, 9, 11—13, 15—19, 22—27,
29, July 1—4, 13, 14, 21, 28,
Aug. 27, Oct. 1.

DIARIO DE PANAMA. PANAMA
JOURNAL. d. est. Dec. 5, 1904.
Note: In Spanish and English.
Ceased publication [1932].
DLC
1906 July 2—Dec. 31.
1907 Jan. 1—Dec. 3, 5—31.
1908 Jan. 1—June 13, 15—Nov. 27,
29—Dec. 11, 13—31.
1909 Jan. 2, 3, 5, 6, 8—14, 20—Feb.
3, 5—Mar. 22, 24—June 24,
26—July 11, 13—Aug. 1, 3—
22, 24—Oct. 22, 24—Nov. 19,
21—Dec. 31.
1910 Jan. 1—30, Feb. 1—11, 13—
15, 17—May 8, 11—15, 17—
July 5, 7—24, 26—Aug. 31.
1927 June 1—11, 13—July 2, 10—
22, 24—Aug. 4, 6—18, 20—
Sept. 3, 10—Oct. 1, 3—Dec.
11, 13—31.
1928 Jan. 1—18, 20—May 12, 14—
July 21, 23—Oct. 4, 6—Dec.
9, 17—31.
1929 Jan. 1—Mar. 19, 21—Apr. 3,
5—20, 22—30, May 2—11,
20—27, 29—Dec. 31.
1930 Jan. 1—Feb. 15, 24—Mar. 30,
Apr. 1—July 14, 16—Dec. 31.
1931 Jan. 1—Apr. 2, 4—June 14,
22—July 31, Aug. 2—Nov. 7,
10—30, Dec. 2—31.
1932 Jan. 1—4, 6—10, 12—Feb. 24,
26—Mar. 12, 14—Apr. 19,
21—28, 30—May 7, 16—June
4, 6—30.

FU
Micro (N)
1915 Jan. 1—7, 16, 18—21, 23—31,
Feb. 2—6, 9—11, 14—17, 19—
26, 28, Mar. 2, 4—6, 9, 10, 14—
Apr. 2, 4—15, 17—24, 26—
May 7, 9, 11—14, 16, 17, 19,
20, June 6, 7, 9—14, 17, 18,
20—July 11, 13—20, Aug. 1,
2, 4—6, 8, 10—15, 17—21, 23,
24, 26—Sept. 1, 3—Dec. 25,
28—31.
1916 Jan. 1—3, 5—14, 16—22, Feb.
8—Mar. 5, 8—Apr. 1, 3—8,
10—13, 17—20, 22, May 8—
13, 15—17, 19—21, July 2—
15, 17—21, 23, 24, 26—30,
Aug. 1—6, 8, 9, 19—21, 24—
26, 29—Sept. 1, 3—6, 8—18,
20, 21, 23, 25, 26, 28.
1917 May 4—8, 10—16, 18—20,
22—30, June 1—23, 25—July
7, 9—Aug. 4, 9—26, 28, 29, 31,
Sept. 1, 3—15, 17—22, 24—
27, 29, 30, Oct. 3, 5—7, 9—27,
29—31.

MWA
1910 Feb. 5.
1911 Jan. 23.
1913 Jan. 10.
1914 Feb. 26.
TxU
1926 June 1—16, 18—27, 29.

EL DIARIO NACIONAL. d. est. Apr. 7,
1920.
DLC
1921 Aug. 11.

DIGESTO LATINO AMERICANO. w.
est. 1933.
LNT—MA
1933 Nov. 1—Dec. 31.
1934 Jan. 1—June 18.

DOMINICAL. w. est. [1932].
DLC
1941 Apr. 6.

EL ELECTOR.
  CU – B
    Micro (P)
    1883   May 1, June 15.
LA ESTRELLA DE PANAMA. d. est.
  Feb. 1, 1853.
    Note: Began publishing as a Spanish
    section of *The Daily Panama Star*
    but became a separate edition of the
    Star & Herald, Sept. 3, 1951. Sus-
    pended publication July 7, 1855 – May
    12, 1857; Mar. 27 – May 29, 1886.
  CSt – H
    1963   Oct. 3, 28, 30, 31, Nov. 28.
    1964   Apr. 20 – 29, July 9, 12, Oct. 2.
  CU
    Micro (P)
    1939   Aug. 15.
    1953   Feb. 1, Nov. 3.
  CU – B
    Micro (P)
    1896   Feb. 24 – Dec. 31.
    1897   Jan. 1 – May 14, 16 – Dec. 31.
    1898   Jan. 1 – Apr. 30, May 3 –
           Dec. 31.
    1899   Jan. 1 – June 5, 7 – Dec. 31.
    1900   Jan. 4 – 19, 21 – Mar. 22, 24 –
           28, Apr. 1 – May 27, 29 – Oct.
           3, 5 – Nov. 19, 21 – Dec. 30.
    1901   Jan. 1 – June 29, Aug. 29 –
           Dec. 29.
    1902   Jan. 16 – Mar. 25, Apr. 1 –
           May 1, 3 – Aug. 3, 5 – Dec. 31.
    1903   Jan. 1 – Feb. 28, Mar. 3 – Nov.
           2, 6 – Dec. 31.
    1904   Jan. 3 – Feb. 28.
  DLC
    Micro (P)
    1876   Jan. 17 – Nov. 10.
    1877   Jan. 10 – Dec. 31.
    1878   Jan. 1 – May 10.
    1896   Feb. 24 – Dec. 31.
    1897 – 1914   Jan. 1 – Dec. 31.
    1919   Nov. 2 – Dec. 31.
    1920 – 1925   Jan. 1 – Dec. 31.
    1926   Jan. 1 – 5, 7 – Dec. 31.
    1927   Jan. 1 – Dec. 31.
    1928   Jan. 1 – Mar. 31, Apr. 2 – Nov.
           1, 3 – 28, 30 – Dec. 31.

    1929   Jan. 1 – 3, 5 – Feb. 22, 24 –
           Apr. 7, 9 – July 16, 18 – Dec.
           31.
    1930 – 1937   Jan. 1 – Dec. 31.
    1938   Jan. 1 – Nov. 3, 5 – Dec. 31.
    1939   Jan. 1 – Dec. 31.
    1940   Jan. 1 – Mar. 31, Apr. 2 – 5,
           7 – 12, 14 – 17, 19 – 24, 27,
           30 – May 3, 5, 6, 11, 14 – 18,
           June 16, 18, 20, 21, 25, 26, 30 –
           July 10, 13 – 18, 20 – Sept. 15,
           17 – Oct. 1, 3 – 11, 13 – 29,
           31 – Nov. 3, 6 – 10, 12, 13, 15 –
           Dec. 31.
    1941   Jan. 1 – Apr. 18, 20 – May 8,
           10 – 12, 17, 18, 20 – 22, 24 – 26,
           30 – July 11, 14 – Sept. 30,
           Oct. 2 – 31, Nov. 2 – 12, 14,
           16 – Dec. 10, 16 – 31.
    1942   Jan. 1 – Feb. 28, Mar. 2 – 9,
           11 – 19, 21 – 28, 31 – Apr. 14,
           19, 20, 24 – 28, 30 – Aug. 27,
           31 – Oct. 18, Nov. 1 – Dec. 31.
    1943   Jan. 1 – Dec. 31.
    1944   Jan. 1 – 16, 21 – Feb. 24, 28 –
           Mar. 2, 5 – Dec. 31.
    1945   Jan. 1 – May 31, June 3 – Dec.
           23, 25 – 31.
    1946   Jan. 1 – 31, Feb. 4 – Mar. 7,
           11 – May 19, 23 – Aug. 2, 4 –
           Dec. 31.
    1947   Jan. 1 – 19, 24 – Feb. 16, 18 –
           Dec. 31.
    1948   Jan. 1 – Apr. 27, 29 – Aug. 9,
           11 – Nov. 20, 22 – Dec. 31.
    1949 – 1951   Jan. 1 – Dec. 31.
    1952   Jan. 1 – Aug. 16, 19 – Sept. 1,
           3 – 12, 14, 16 – Oct. 15, 17, 19,
           21 – 26, 28 – Dec. 25.
    1953   Jan. 1 – Feb. 7, 9 – Mar. 1, 3 –
           Apr. 26, 28 – May 8, July 27,
           29 – Sept. 11, 15 – 23, 25 – Oct.
           8, 10 – 18, 20 – Nov. 5, 6, 8 – 13,
           15 – 22, 24 – Dec. 11, 13 – 31.
    1954   Jan. 1 – 9, 12, 13, 15, 20 – Feb.
           15, 17 – Mar. 30, Apr. 1 – 9,
           13 – 15, 19 – 23, 25, 26, 29 –
           May 3, 5 – 10, 12 – 16, 18, 21,
           23 – June 13, 15 – 17, 19 – 29,

July 1−5, 7−21, 23−27, 30,
Aug. 1−4, 6−18, 20, 21,
24, 29−31, Sept. 3, 4, 6−
10, 13−15, 17, 18, 20−22, 24,
25, 28, Oct. 1−6, 8−12, 15−
29, 31, Nov. 3−5, 8−13, 17−
Dec. 6, 8−10, 12−28, 30.
1955   Jan. 4−14, 16−Feb. 4, 12−
18, 20, 21, 25−Mar. 18, 20,
22−25, 28, Apr. 1, 2, 5−8, 10,
12, 14−17, 20, 24, 25, 27, 28,
30, May 1, 5, 6.
1956   Jan. 1+.

ICRL
   Micro (P) & (N)
   1956   Jan. 1+.

LU
   Micro (P)
   1939   Aug. 15.
   1953   Feb. 1, Nov. 3.

PrU
   1961   Mar. 21−27, Apr. 4−10, 15−
Sept. 1, 5−Oct. 30, Nov. 1−3,
5−9, 11−28, 30−Dec. 8, 10−
21, 23−25, 27−31.
   1962   Jan. 1−Feb. 21, 25−Oct. 30,
Nov. 1−Dec. 8, 10−25, 27−
31.
   1963   Jan. 1, 3−Mar. 1, 3−Apr. 3,
6−8, 15−22, 25−May 1, 3−
June 4, 6, 8−July 4, 6−Sept.
10, 12−Oct. 3, Nov. 1−3, 6−
10, 13−28, 30−Dec. 6, 8, 9,
12−25, 27−31.
   1964   Jan. 1, 3−13, 15−Feb. 11,
13−29, Mar. 1, 5−27, 29−
Apr. 20, 25−May 1, 3−22,
24−Oct. 1, 4−30, Nov. 6−9,
14−25, 27−Dec. 31.
   1965   Jan. 1, 3−Mar. 1, 4−June 6,
9−Aug. 31, Sept. 4−17, 21−
Oct. 30, Nov. 1−Dec. 31.
   1966   Jan. 1+.

TxU
   1881   Oct. 13.
   1921   Jan. 1−14, 16−Feb. 23, 25−
May 31.
   1923   Sept. 24−Oct. 9, 11−Nov. 4,

6−Dec. 31.
   1926   June 1−8, 11−30.
   1941   June 12−July 9, 12−30, Aug.
2−Oct. 8, 10−31, Nov. 2−14,
18−Dec. 31.
   1942   Jan. 1, 3−Feb. 17, 19−28,
Mar. 2−19, 21−28, 31−May
5, 9−June 11.
   1943   Jan. 1−Mar. 9, 11−May 27,
June 4−10, 14−July 1, 6−
Sept. 30, Oct. 2−Nov. 3, 5−
Dec. 31.
   1944   Jan. 1, 2, 4−Feb. 22, 24, 28−
Apr. 7, 9−July 4, 6−Nov. 3,
5−16, 23−Dec. 28.
   1945   Jan. 1, 3−May 10, 14−20,
24−June 11, 15−July 4, 6−
Aug. 2, 6−Oct. 21, 26−Nov.
4, 6−8, 12−25, 30−Dec. 31.
   1946   Jan. 1−May 31, June 3−July
18, 22−Dec. 25, 27−31.
   1947   Jan. 1−Dec. 12, 14−29, 31.
   1948−1952   Jan. 1−Dec. 31.

LA ESTRELLA DE PANAMA. STEAMER EDITION. est. 1858.

Note: Spanish edition of *Panama Star and Herald. Steamer Edition.*

DLC
   Micro (P)
   1858   Oct. 15−Dec. 31.
   1859−1864   Jan. 1−Dec. 31.
   1865   Jan. 1−Dec. 25.
   1868   Jan. 10−Dec. 31.
   1869−1875   Jan. 1−Dec. 31.

MoU
   Micro (P)
   1858   Oct. 15−Dec. 31.
   1859−1864   Jan. 1−Dec. 31.
   1865   Jan. 1−Dec. 25.
   1868   Jan. 10−Dec. 31.
   1869−1877   Jan. 1−Dec. 31.
   1878   Jan. 1−May 10.
   1896   Feb. 24−Dec. 31.
   1897−1903   Jan. 1−Dec. 31.
   1904   Jan. 1−Feb. 28.

NN
   Micro (P)

1858   Oct. 15 – Dec. 31.
1859 – 1864   Jan. 1 – Dec. 31.
1865   Jan. 1 – Dec. 25.
1868   Jan. 10 – Dec. 31.
1869 – 1877   Jan. 1 – Dec. 31.
1878   Jan. 1 – May 10.
1896   Feb. 24 – Dec. 31.
1897 – 1903   Jan. 1 – Dec. 31.
1904   Jan. 1 – Feb. 28.

LA ESTRELLA DE PANAMA. WEEKLY EDITION. est. May 8, 1854.

Note: Spanish edition of *Panama Star & Herald. Weekly Edition.* Suspended publication July 7, 1855 – May 11, 1857; Mar. 27 – May 29, 1886. *El Telegrama* published during latter suspension. Ceased publication Dec. 28, 1926.

CU – B
Micro (P)
1876   Jan. 17 – Nov. 10.
1877   Jan. 10 – May 10, 25 – Dec. 25.
1878   Jan. 1 – Dec. 31.
1879   Jan. 2 – Mar. 27, Apr. 10 – Aug. 14.
1880 – 1881   Jan. 1 – Dec. 31.
1882   Jan. 12 – Dec. 28.
1883 – 1885   Jan. 1 – Dec. 31.
1886   Jan. 2 – Feb. 6, 20 – Dec. 25.
1887 – 1892   Jan. 1 – Dec. 31.
1893   Jan. 5 – Aug. 10, 24 – Sept. 28, Oct. 12 – Dec. 28.
1894   Jan. 4 – Aug. 16, 30 – Dec. 27.
1895 – 1899   Jan. 1 – Dec. 31.
1900   Jan. 3 – July 25, Aug. 8 – Dec. 26.
1901 – 1903   Jan. 1 – Dec. 31.
1905   Jan. 2 – July 24, Aug. 7 – Dec. 25.
1906   Jan. 1 – Feb. 26.

CtY
1880   Apr. 29, May 6.
1883   Oct. 18.
1884   Feb. 7 – 14, Apr. 17 – 24, May 29.
1885   July 18, Aug. 1, 29, Sept. 12, 26 – Oct. 3, 31, Dec. 5 – 12.
1886   Feb. 27.

1887   Feb. 26, July 23 – Aug. 6, 20 – Sept. 10, 24 – Oct. 15, 29 – Nov. 5, Dec. 31.
1888   Jan. 21.

DLC
1885   July 18.
1888   Jan. 21.
1905   Feb. 4 – Dec. 31.
1906 – 1919   Jan. 1 – Dec. 31.
1920   Jan. 6 – Mar. 8.
Micro (P)
1878   May 17 – Dec. 31.
1879 – 1885   Jan. 1 – Dec. 31.
1886   Jan. 1 – Mar. 27, June 5 – Dec. 31.
1887 – 1902   Jan. 1 – Dec. 31.
1903   Jan. 1 – Aug. 19, Dec. 30.
1905 – 1909   Jan. 1 – Dec. 31.

MWA
1874   Apr. 25.
1875   Dec. 1.
1883   Oct. 18, Dec. 6.
1884   [Jan. 3 – May 29], Nov. 13.
1885   [June 13 – Dec. 12].
1886   Feb. 6, 27 – Mar. 13, Nov. 20 – Dec. 4, 25.
1887   Jan. 22, Feb. 26 – Mar. 5, 19, [July 23 – Dec. 31].
1888   Jan. 21, Feb. 4.
1891   Dec. 10 – 17.

MoU
Micro (P)
1878   May 17 – Dec. 31.
1879 – 1903   Jan. 1 – Dec. 31.
1905 – 1909   Jan. 1 – Dec. 31.

NN
Micro (P)
1878   May 17 – Dec. 31.
1879 – 1903   Jan. 1 – Dec. 31.
1905 – 1909   Jan. 1 – Dec. 31.

NcD
1883   Oct. 18.
1884   Feb. 14, Apr. 17, May 29.
1885   July 18, Aug. 29, Sept. 26, Oct. 3 – 31.
1886   Feb. 6, 27.
1887   July 23, Aug. 6, 20, Sept. 2, 10, 24 – Nov. 5, Dec. 31.

```
    1888    Jan. 21.
MB
    1903    Sept. 16 — Dec. 30.
    1904    Jan. 6 — June 13, 27 — Dec. 26.
    1905    Jan. 2 — 16.
TxU
    1920    Jan. 5 — 19, Feb. 9 — Mar. 1,
            15 — Apr. 5, 19 — May 10, 24 —
            Nov. 29, Dec. 13 — 27.
    1922    Jan. 1 — Feb. 27, Apr. 10 —
            Dec. 4, 18 — 31.
    1923    Jan. 1 — Sept. 17.
    1924    Jan. 7 — Feb. 18, Mar. 3 — 24,
            Apr. 7 — Sept. 14, 29 — Nov.
            24, Dec. 8 — 31.
    1925    Jan. 1 — Apr. 13.
    1926    Jan. 1 — Apr. 5, 19 — Dec. 20.
    1927    Jan. 1 — Feb. 6.
```

THE EVENING TELEGRAM. d. est.
Mar. 29, 1886.
    Note: In English. Published during
    the suspension of *The Panama Star
    & Herald.* Ceased publication May
    28, 1886. See also weekly edition
    and *El Telegrama.*
    CU — B
        Micro (P)
        1886   Mar. 29, 30, 31 — Apr. 1, 2 —
                May 28.
    DLC
        Micro (P)
        1886   Mar. 29 — May 29.
    FU
        Micro (P)
        1886   May 29 — May 29.
    MoU
        Micro (P)
        1886   Mar. 29 — May 28.
    NN
        Micro (P)
        1886   Mar. 29 — May 29.

THE EVENING TELEGRAM. WEEKLY
EDITION. w. est. Apr. 3, 1886.
    Note: In English. Published
    during suspension of *The
    Panama Star and Herald.* Ceased
    publication May 29, 1886.

CU — B
    Micro (P)
    1886   Apr. 3 — May 29.
DLC
    Micro (P)
    1886   Apr. 3 — May 29.
FU
    Micro (P)
    1886   Apr. 3 — May 29.
MoU
    Micro (P)
    1886   Apr. 3 — May 29.
NN
    Micro (P)
    1886   Apr. 3 — May 29.

GACETA DEL ESTADO. w., irr. est.
July 20, 1855.
    CU — B
        Micro (P)
        1855   July 20 — Dec. 15.
        1856   Jan. 5 — Feb. 9, 25, Mar. 24,
                Apr. 26 — May 27, June 14,
                Oct. 16, Nov. 13 — Dec. 18.
        1857   Jan. 1, 15 — June 20, July 21 —
                28, Aug. 19 — Dec. 23.
        1858   Jan. 9 — June 17.
        1859   Jan. 1 — Dec. 31.
        1860   Feb. 25 — May 16, Oct. 30,
                Dec. 23.
        1861   Jan. 1 — Dec. 31.
        1862   Feb. 26 — Mar. 8, Apr. 5 —
                May 10, July 2.
    CtY
        1855   July 20 — Dec. 29.
        1856   Jan. 1 — Dec. 18.
        1857   Jan. 8 — Dec. 23.

GACETA DEL ISTMO. 3m. est. July 10,
1841.
    CU — B
        Micro (P)
        1841   Sept. 20, Oct. 20.

GACETA DEL ISTMO DE PANAMA. w.
est. 1823.
    CtY
        1825   Mar. 27 — July 10, 24 — 31,
                Aug. 14.
        1826   Feb. 23 — Mar. 12, June 22.

MWA
   1826   July 16, 30.

GACETA OFICIAL. irr., w., d. est. July 28, 1870.
  CU — B
    Micro (P)
    1870   July 28 — Aug. 18, Sept. 15 — 22, Oct. 13 — Dec. 15.
    1871   Feb. 2 — 9, 23 — June 20, July 9 — Aug. 8, 19 — Oct. 7, 27 — Nov. 3, 18 — 23, Dec. 14.
    1872   Jan. 19 — June 28, July 13 — Aug. 10, 24, Sept. 13 — Nov. 20.
    1873   Jan. 4 — Apr. 29, June 7 — Dec. 23.
    1874   Jan. 17 — May 2, 16, 30, June 13, 27 — July 25, Aug. 7 — 29, Sept. 26, Oct. 31, Nov. 21.
    1875   Jan. 30 — Feb. 27, Mar. 13, Apr. 5 — May 15, 29 — June 5, July 24, Aug. 14 — 21, Sept. 4, 15, 25 — Oct. 16, 23, Nov. 3 — 17, 25 — Dec. 2, 16, 23, 29.
    1876   Jan. 1 — Dec. 31.
    1877   Jan. 7 — 14, Mar. 1 — 22, Apr. 19 — 26, May 24 — 31, June 30 — July 26, Aug. 4 — 9, 30, Sept. 20 — 28, Oct. 11, 26, Nov. 16.
    1878   Jan. 13, Feb. 17 — Mar. 10, 17 — 31, Apr. 7 — 14, 25, May 2, 9 — 16, 23 — June 9, 20 — July 11, 18 — Aug. 4, 15 — Dec. 29.
    1880   Jan. 1 — Dec. 31.
    1881   Jan. 9, 16 — 30, Feb. 6 — Mar. 24, May 1 — 29, June 5 — 21, Aug. 28 — Sept. 15, 22 — 25.
    1882   Jan. 28, Feb. 28, Mar. 7, Aug. 31.
    1883   June 30 — July 7.
    1884   July 10 — 16, Sept. 18, Nov. 1.
    1885   Jan. 20 — 27, Feb. 18 — 21, Mar. 14 — 18.
    Micro (N)
    1886   June 11, 19.
  DLC
    1876 — 1877   [Jan. 1 — Dec. 31].
    1880   Jan. 1 — Dec. 31.
    1882 — 1884   Jan. 1 — Dec. 31.

    1886   [Jan. 1 — Dec. 31].
    1887   [Jan. 1 — Nov. 9].
    1888 — 1896   Jan. 1 — Dec. 31.
  TxU
    1880   Aug. 12 — Dec. 16.

GRAFICO.
  CU
    Micro (P)
    1928   Nov. 3.
  LU
    Micro (P)
    1928   Nov. 3.

EL HERALDO. w. est. 1925.
  DLC
    1926   June 19.

HERALDO DEL ISTMO. bw. est. 1904.
  MWA
    1906   Feb. 15.

LA HORA. d. est. 1946.
  CLU
    1965   Feb. 3, 5, 8 — 12, 15 — 19, 23, Mar. 3, 4, 16 — Dec. 31.
    1966   Jan. 1+.
  CSt — H
    1965   Jan. 5 — Apr. 21.
  DLC
    1956   Dec. 15.

LA IDEA. w. est. Feb. 1, 1888.
  CU — B
    Micro (P)
    1888   Mar. 9.

EL ISTMEÑO.
  CU — B
    Micro (P)
    1884   May 24.

EL LATIGO INMORTAL. est. Aug. 9, 1885.
    Note: Title *El Látigo*, Aug. 9, 1885 — Apr. 1, 1889; *El Látigo inmortal*, after Apr. 7, 1889.
  TxU
    1885   Aug. 9 — Dec. 31.
    1886   Jan. 1 — Dec. 31.
    1887   Jan. 1 — June 19, July 10 — Dec. 31.

1888   Jan. 1—Dec. 31.
1889   Jan. 1—8, 22—Oct. 13, 27,
        Nov. 24, Dec. 15—31.
1890   Jan. 1—May 31, June 14—Aug.
        30, Sept. 13—Oct. 18, Nov.
        25—Dec. 27.

LATINOAMERICA. est. 1950.
  OrU
    1950   June 1.

THE MERCANTILE CHRONICLE.
  See *The Panama Mail*.

EL MOVIMIENTO. w. est. Nov. 10, 1844.
  CU—B
    1844   Nov. 10—Dec. 29.

MUNDO GRAFICO. w.
  MWA
    1937   Feb. 6.
  TxU
    1945   Jan. 27.

THE NATION. LA NACION. d. est.
  May 8, 1944.
    Note: In Spanish and English. English
    section established Aug. 17, 1948.
    Separate English and Spanish editions
    published beginning Jan. 1956.
  CU
    Micro (P)
    1953   Nov. 3.
  DLC
    1946   Aug. 17—25, 29, Sept. 1, 8, 9,
            12, 13, 15, 18, 22—Oct. 6, 8—
            20, 22—Dec. 31.
    1947   Jan. 1—Mar. 12, 14, 17—21,
            24—Apr. 9, 11, 14—May 21,
            23, 26—Aug. 31, Sept. 2—19,
            21, 22, 24—26, 28—Oct. 8,
            10—Nov. 7, 9—14, 16—Dec.
            23, 25—27, 29—31.
    1948   Jan. 2, 5—Feb. 9, 11, 14, 16—
            29, Mar. 4—22, Apr. 14—16,
            18—27, May 1—3, 6, 8—12,
            14—21, 23—June 1, 3—16,
            18—July 3, 6—27, 29, Oct. 1—
            Dec. 31.
    1949   Jan. 6—14, 16—23, 25—Mar.

        31, Apr. 2—May 1, 4—16, 18—
        July 5, 7—Aug. 31, Sept. 2—
        4, 6—Dec. 31.
    1950   Jan. 1—May 10, 12—14, June
            17—Dec. 31.
    1951   Jan. 2—18, 20—Feb. 24, 26—
            Apr. 24, 26—May 8, 10—12,
            14—19, 21—31, June 2—29,
            July 1—Aug. 1, 3—Sept. 4, 6—
            Nov. 3, 5—9, 12—Dec. 3, 5—
            21, 23—31.
    1952   Jan. 1—10, 12—Feb. 23, Mar.
            2—27, 29—Apr. 9, 13—May
            3, 5, 6, 8—11, 13—June 6, 8—
            12, 15—July 21, 24—Aug. 9,
            11—16, 18—28, 30—Sept. 8,
            10—Oct. 18, 20—31, Nov. 2—
            5, 8—12, 15—24, 26—Dec. 5,
            7—9, 11, 13—18, 20—31.
    1953   Jan. 2—Mar. 31, Apr. 1—May
            6, 8—June 10, 13—23, 25—
            July 3, 5—30, Aug. 1—24, 26,
            27, 29—Sept. 10, 12—19, 21—
            24, 26—Oct. 3, 5, 8—20, 22,
            23, 25—Nov. 13, 15—21, 23—
            28, Dec. 2—4, 6—10, 12—15,
            17—28, 31.
    1954   Jan. 3—9, 12—14, 20—22, 24,
            27—31, Feb. 2, 4, 6, 7, 10—
            12, 16, 18, 20, 21, 23, 25—28,
            Mar. 4—7, 12, 14, 16—19, 21,
            23, 25, 28, Apr. 2, 4, 7, 11, 13,
            14, 20—22, 25, 27—29, May 4,
            6—9, 11—14, 16, 18, 19, 21,
            23, 25—27, June 1, 5, 6, 8—
            10, 13, 15—17, 20, 22—24, 26,
            29, July 2, 3, 6—8, 11, 13, 15—
            18, 20, 22, 24, 25, 27—30, Aug.
            2—6, 8, 10, 12, 17, 28, 29,
            Sept. 1, 4, 5, 14, 18, 21, 23, 28,
            Oct. 2, 3, 5, 7, 9, 14, 22, 27, 28,
            Nov. 13, 14, 20, 26, 27, Dec. 4,
            7, 9, 12, 13, 15, 16, 18, 19, 21,
            24—26, 29, 30.
    1955   Jan. 7, 11, 13, 17, 18, 20, 23,
            24, Feb. 3, 16, 19—21, 23—
            Mar. 5, 7—26, 28—Apr. 7, 9—
            June 3, 5, 6, 8—20, 23, 26—

July 2, 4 – 16, 18 – 30, Aug. 1 –
8, 10 – 19, 21 – Sept. 12, 15 –
Oct. 8, 10 – 12, Nov. 30 – Dec.
7, 9 – 28, 31.

1956 English edition:
Jan. 4 – 25, Feb. 21 – 24, 26 –
Mar. 2, 4 – 23, 26 – Apr. 14,
16 – May 12, 14 – 22, 24 – June
9, 11 – 18, 24.
Spanish edition:
Jan. 4 – 20, Feb. 13, 14, 21, 22,
24 – June 9, 11 – 14, 16 – 19,
21, 23 – 30.

TxU
1946 Sept. 23, 25, 27, 28.
1951 May 9.

NUEVO DIARIO. d.
CU
Micro (P)
1939 Aug. 14.

EL OBSERVADOR. sw. est. May 16,
1890.
CLU
Micro (P)
1890 Mar. 26 – Dec. 31.
1891 Jan. 1 – Dec. 31.
1892 Jan. 1 – Mar. 16.
DLC
Micro (P)
1890 Mar. 26 – Dec. 31.
1891 Jan. 1 – Dec. 31.
1892 Jan. 1 – Mar. 16.

PACIFIC EXPRESS REGISTER.
Note: In English.
NHi
1856 Jan. 3.

EL PAIS. irr.
CU – B
Micro (P)
1883 Apr. 24 – May 19, June 14,
Sept. 21, Oct. 31.

THE PAN AMERICAN. EL PANAMA-
AMERICA. d. est. Oct. 7, 1925.
Note: In Spanish and English, Jan. 1,
1929 – Sept. 2, 1951; thereafter each
language edition published separately.

Absorbed *The Panama Times* and
published it as a weekly section,
Nov. 6, 1927 – Jan. 1, 1928.
CSt
1941 Aug. 1 – Dec. 31.
1942 Jan. 1 – Feb. 26, June 1 – Dec.
31.
1943 Jan. 1 – Dec. 31.
1944 Jan. 1 – Apr. 26, May 1 – Dec.
31.
1945 Jan. 1 – Dec. 31.
1946 Feb. 1 – Dec. 31.
1947 – 1948 Jan. 1 – Dec. 31.
1949 Jan. 1 – Aug. 7.
CSt – H
Spanish edition:
1963 Oct. 2 – 9, 11 – 15, 26 –
31, Nov.
1964 Apr. 20 – 25, 27 – 29, June 1,
3 – 29, July 1 – 5, 13, 16, 21,
27, Oct. 1, 2.

CU
1925 Nov. 20 – 25, Dec. 1 – 31.
1926 Jan. 1 – 7, 9 – 14, 16 – Feb. 14,
16 – 18, 20, 22 – 26, Mar. 1 –
10, 12 – 14, 16 – June 6, 8 –
13, 15, 17 – 19, 22, 25, 26.
1937 Oct. 21, 23 – 26.
Micro (P)
1939 Aug. 15.
1953 Nov. 2.
DLC
1925 Oct. 7 – Nov. 29, Dec. 1 – 31.
1926 Jan. 1 – Dec. 31.
1927 Jan. 1 – July 31, Aug. 3 – Nov.
30.
1928 – 1931 Jan. 1 – Dec. 31.
1932 Jan. 1 – July 28, 30 – Dec. 31.
1933 – 1935 Jan. 1 – Dec. 31.
1936 Jan. 1 – Feb. 25, 27 – Nov. 8,
10 – Dec. 25, 27 – 31.
1937 Jan. 1 – Nov. 3, 5 – 28, 30 –
Dec. 25, 27 – 31.
1938 Jan. 1 – Nov. 3, 5 – Dec. 25,
27 – 31.
1939 Jan. 1 – Dec. 31.
1940 Jan. 1 – Feb. 5, 8 – Apr. 13,
15 – June 13, 15 – July 12, 14 –

18, 20 — 23, 25 — 29, 31, Aug. 1,
3 — 5, 7, 8, 10 — 14, 16, 17, 19,
21 — 28, 30 — Sept. 7, 9, 10,
12 — 14, 17 — 24, 26, 31 — Oct.
4, 6 — 20, 22 — 24, 27 — Nov. 1,
3, 5 — 8, 10 — 20, 22 — 30, Dec.
2 — 10, 14 — 19, 21 — 31.

1941 Jan. 2 — 28, 30 — Feb. 8, 10 —
22, 24, 27 — Nov. 2, 4 — 9, 11 —
Dec. 4, 7 — 10, 13 — 20, 22 — 24,
26 — 31.

1942 Jan. 1 — Feb. 12, 14 — Mar. 17,
19 — Apr. 17, 20, 21, 23 — May
1, 3 — 9, 11 — June 19, 21 — 30,
July 6, 8 — Aug. 14, 16 — 24,
26 — Sept. 8, 11, 13 — Oct. 3,
5 — 11, 13 — 17, Nov. 1 — Dec.
31.

1943 Jan. 1 — May 3, 5 — Oct. 22,
24 — 28, 30 — Dec. 31.

1944 Jan. 1 — Mar. 4, 6 — 9, 11 — Apr.
5, 7 — Nov. 23, 25, 27 — Dec.
22, 24 — 31.

1945 Jan. 1 — 26, 28 — May 4, 6 —
June 24, 26 — July 3, 5 — 16,
18 — 20, 22, 24, 26 — 30, Aug.
1 — 5, 7, 9 — 12, 14 — Sept. 1,
3 — 5, 7 — 15, 17 — 20, 23, 25 —

27, 29 — Oct. 3, 6 — 12, 15 — 20,
22 — 25, 27 — Nov. 2, 4 — 28,
30 — Dec. 7, 9, 11 — 14, 16 —
22, 24, 27 — 29, 31.

1946 Jan. 1 — Feb. 16, 18 — Mar. 3,
6 — Apr. 8, 11 — 18, 20 — May
6, 8 — 15, 17 — 21, 23 — 28, 30 —
July 4, 6, 8 — Aug. 1, 3 — Nov.
2, 5 — Dec. 22, 24 — 31.

1947 Jan. 1 — Feb. 15, 17, 19 — 27,
29 — Apr. 3, 6 — 24, 26 — May 1,
3 — 21, 24 — Oct. 4, 7 — 18, 20 —
23, 26 — Dec. 31.

1948 Jan. 1 — 24, 26 — Feb. 5, 7 — 9,
11 — 13, 15 — 17, 19, 20, 23 —
Mar. 6, 8 — 10, 12 — 18, 20, 23,
Apr. 8, 9, 12 — 15, 19 — May 19,
21 — 26, 28 — June 3, 5, 7 — 9,

11, 12, 15, 17, 18, 22 — July 4,
6 — 10, 13 — 19, 21, 22, 24 —
Aug. 19, 21 — Sept. 13, 15, 17 —
Oct. 2, 4 — 9, 11 — 31, Nov. 2,
4 — 15, 17 — 27, 29 — Dec. 14,
16 — 31.

1949 Jan. 1 — Feb. 17, 19, 21 — 28,
Mar. 2 — Apr. 12, 14 — May 5,
7 — 21, 23 — June 2, 4, 5, 7 —
July 6, 8 — 20, 22 — 28, 30 — Aug.
7, 9 — 22, 24 — Oct. 8, 10 — 27,
29, 31 — Nov. 2, 4 — 22, 24 —
Dec. 24, 27 — 31.

1950 Jan. 1 — 28, 30 — Feb. 11, 13 —
20, 22 — Apr. 6, 8 — May 6, 8 —
July 1, 3 — Aug. 22, 25 — Sept.
2, 4 — 7, 9 — 31, Oct. 2 — 12, 14,
16 — Nov. 2, 4, 7, 9 — 14, 16 —
18, 20 — 30, Dec. 2, 3, 5 — 9,
11 — 23, 26 — 31.

1951 Jan. 1 — 13, 15 — June 28, 30,
July 3 — 9, 11, 12, 14 — 19, 22,
23, 25 — Sept. 3.
English edition:

1951 ₁Sept. 4 — Oct. 1, 3, 4, 6 — Nov.
2, 5 — Dec. 31₁.

1952 ₁Jan. 1 — 15, 17 — Feb. 9, 11 —
May 9, 11 — July 1, 3 — Aug. 9,
11 — Sept. 30,₁ Oct. 1 — 8, 10 —
28, 30 — Nov. 3, 5 — Dec. 9, 11 —
31.

1953 Jan. 1 — 3, 5 — Oct. 24, 26 — 31,
Nov. 2 — 20, 22 — 26, 28, 29,
Dec. 1 — 3, 5, 7 — 12, 14 — 31.

1954 Jan. 1 — Feb. 20, 22 — Mar. 6,
8 — 21, 23 — 28, Apr. 1, 3 — 10,
12 — 17, 19 — May 10, 12 — 15,
18, 19, 22, 23, 25 — 27, 29, 31,
June 2, 4, 5, 9 — 14, 16, 17, 21,
23, 25 — July 1, 3 — 5, 8 — 10,
12, 13, 15 — 17, 20 — 22, 26 —
Aug. 12, 14 — 19, 21 — Sept. 9,
14, 16 — 25, 29 — Oct. 2, 4 — 9,
12 — 14, 16 — 18, 20 — 23, 27 —
31, Nov. 4, 6, 9 — 11, 14 — 16,
18 — 20, 22, 25 — 28, Dec. 1 — 4,
6, 7, 9 — 18, 20 — 22, 27 — 31.

1955 Jan. 2, 4 — Feb. 4, 7 — 19, 21 —

Mar. 12, 14 – 17, 20 – Apr. 21,
23 – May 7, 9 – 12, 14 – June
15, 17 – 19, 22 – 29, July 1 – 4,
6 – 16, 20 – Aug. 4, 6 – 16, 19 –
27, 29, 30, Sept. 3, 5 – 10, 12 –
14, 18, 20 – 23, 25 – 29, Oct. 1,
3 – 8, 10 – 12, 14 – 17, 20 – 22,
24 – 29, 31, Nov. 1, 8 – 10, 14 –
19, 21 – 26, 29, 30, Dec. 16, 17,
19, 21 – 31.

1956　Jan. 1 – 16, 18 – 20, 22 – Feb.
2, 4 – 9, 13, 17 – 25, 27 – 29,
Mar. 2 – 4, 6 – 10, 12 – 15, 17 –
19, 21, 22, 24, 26 – 28, 31, Apr.
2 – 14, 16, 17, 22, 26, 27, May
2, 7 – 10, 12 – 15, 24 – 26, 29 –
June 2, 4 – 28, 30 – July 3, 5 –
11, 13, 14, 16 – 18, 21, 23 – 27,
Aug. 21 – Sept. 12 – 31, Nov.
4 – 10, 12 – 16, 19 – 28, 30, Dec.
7, 9, 11 – 18, 21, 22, 24, 26 –
28, 30, 31.

1957　Jan. 1 – 19, 21, 22, 24 – Feb. 3,
5 – 13, 15 – 18, 20 – Mar. 2, 7 –
10, 13, 14, 22, 23, 31 – Apr. 1 –
18, 23 – 29, May 2 – 7, 9 – June
6, 8 – 23, 25 – July 2, 6 – 14,
22, 25 – 27, 29 – Sept. 3, 5 – 7,
9 – 28, 30 – Oct. 5, 7 – 10, 14 –
24, 26 – Nov. 2, 5 – 10, 12 – 25,
28, 29, Dec. 1 – 8, 10 – 31.

1958　Jan. 1 – 8, 10, 12 – 15, 17 – 31,
Feb. 28 – Mar. 22, 24 – 29, 31 –
Apr. 3, 5, 7 – 29, May 3 – 16,
18 – 22, 24, 27 – June 4, 6 – 8,
10 – July 3, 5 – 12, 14 – 18, 20,
22 – Aug. 16, 19, 20, 22 – 30,
Sept. 1 – 13, 15 – 20, 22 – Oct.
4, 6 – 11, 13 – 25, 27 – Nov. 2,
4, 5, 7 – 11, 13, 14, 18 – 20,
26 – 29, Dec. 1 – 6, 9, 11 – 31.

1959　Jan. 2 – 6, 8 – Feb. 9, 11 – 14,
16 – 21, 23 – 26, Mar. 4 – 15,
17 – 20, 22 – 26, 28 – Apr. 19,
May 2, 3, 5 – 9, 11 – 26, 29 –
June 4, 6 – 13, 15 – 17, 20 – 25,
27, 29, 30, July 3, 4, 6 – 8, 13 –
29, Aug. 1 – 8, 11 – 31, Sept.
2 – 4, 6 – 11, 16 – Oct. 13, 17 –

Nov. 1, 5 – 25, 27, 29 – Dec.
16, 18, 22 – 31.

1960　Jan. 2 – 7, 9, 11 – 15, 27 – Feb.
9, 11 – 14, 19 – 25, 28 – Mar.
9, 14 – Apr. 6, 8 – 14, 16, 17,
19 – 26, 28, 29, May 1 – 6, 8 –
12, 14, 16 – 26, 29 – June 2, 7 –
9, 12, 13, 18 – 24, 26, 27.

Spanish edition:

1951　[Sept. 3 – Oct. 1, 3, 4, 6 – Nov.
2, 5 – Dec. 31].

1952　[Jan. 1 – 15, 17 – Feb. 9, 11 –
Apr. 30], May 1 – 9, 11 – June
2, 4 – 15, 17 – 30, July 2 – Sept.
30, Oct. 2 – Nov. 2, 5 – Dec. 31.

1953　Jan. 2 – 8, 10, 12 – Feb. 26,
Mar. 1 – Apr. 4, 6 – June 27,
29 – July 25, 27 – Aug. 1, 3 –
8, 10 – 26, 28 – Sept. 4, 6 – 18,
21, 22, 24 – Oct. 5, 7, 8, 10 –
13, 15, 16, 18 – 21, 23 – Nov. 7,
9 – 29, Dec. 1 – 31.

1954　Jan. 1 – 14, 18 – 30, Feb. 1,
3 – 18, Mar. 22, 24 – 29, Apr.
1, 3 – May 15, 17 – June 3,
5 – 20, 22 – July 4, 6 – 25, 29 –
Aug. 5, 7 – 10, 13, 14, 16 –
Sept. 9, 13 – 26, 28 – Oct. 4,
6 – 25, 27, 28, Nov. 4, 6 – 9, 11,
14, 16 – 28, 30 – Dec. 7, 9 –
16, 18 – 22, 24, 26 – 30.

Suplemento: Jan. 31.

1955　Jan. 3 – 21, 23 – Feb. 3, 11 –
21, 23 – 28, Mar. 2, 3, 24, 29,
30, Apr. 1 – 7, 10, 12, 13, 15 –
18, 21, 23 – 25.

1959　Oct. 2 – 7, 9 – 21, 26 – 29, Nov.
2 – 19, 25 – 27, 29 – Dec. 3, 5,
6, 9 – 13, 15, 18 – 20, 22 – 27.

1960　Jan. 2 – 7, 9 – 14, 16 – 18, 20 –
22, 24 – 31, Feb. 2 – 4, 6, 9 –
Mar. 2, 4, 5, 7 – 12, 14 – 27,
30 – Apr. 5, 7 – 14, 16 – 28, 30,
May 3, 5 – 7, 9 – 22, 24 – 27,
30 – June 5, 11 – 14, 19 – 21,
23 – 30, July 3, 4, 6, 8 – Aug.
14, 16 – 30, Sept. 1 – 3, 5 – 18,
21 – 30, Oct. 4 – 29, Nov. 1, 2,
4 – 14, 16, 17, 21 – 27, 29 – Dec.

7, 10 – 23, 25, 26, 29 – 31.
1961   Jan. 1, 3, 7, 8, 12 – 19, 21 – 25,
29, 31 – Feb. 12, 15, 19 – 28,
Mar. 2 – 4, 6 – 30, Apr. 2, 4,
6 – 8, 10 – 30, May 2 – 9, 11 –
June 11, 13 – 23, 26 – Aug. 7,
9 – 13, 15 – 20, 22 – 31, Sept.
2 – Oct. 6, 9 – 23, Nov. 7 – 9,
11 – 18, 20 – 25, 27, 29 – Dec.
2, 4 – 7, 9 – 14, 16 – 27.
LNT – MA
   1933   Feb. 17 – June 5.
LU
   Micro (P)
   1939   Aug. 15.
   1953   Nov. 2.
MWA
   1925   Oct. 8.
   1937   Feb. 11.
NN
   Micro (P) & (N)
   1925   Oct. 13, 26, 28, Nov. 20 –
Dec. 6, 8 – 17, 19 – 31.
   1926   Jan. 1 – Apr. 2, 9, 11 – 13, 18 –
27, 29 – May 4, 6 – Nov. 17,
Dec. 1 – 3, 5 – 13, 16, 17, 19 –
27, 29 – 31.
   1927   Jan. 1 – 8, 13, 16, 27 – 29, Feb.
4 – 7, 9 – 12, 15, 16, 18, 20,
23 – 25, 28 – Mar. 1, 3, 5, 7, 9 –
11, 14 – 18, 20 – 30, Apr. 1 –
Dec. 31.
   1928   Jan. 1 – Dec. 31.
   1929   Jan. 1 – Sept. 30.
   1942   Nov. 30 – Dec. 31.
   1943 – 1948   Jan. 1 – Dec. 31.
   1949   Jan. 1 – Mar. 31.
TxU
   1946   Sept. 22, 24, 26, Nov. 8 – 10,
22 – 24.

THE PANAMA AMERICAN. WEEKLY
EDITION.
   TxU
   1933   Sept. 4.

PANAMA CANAL. 3w., d. est. Apr. 2,
1881.
   Note: In Spanish, English and

French. Title *The Canal*, Apr. 2 –
June 28, 1881; *Panama Canal*, after
June 28, 1881. A weekly steamer
edition began publishing June 1,
1881 and changed title June 22, 1881.
CU – B
   Micro (P) & (N)
   1881   Apr. 5 – Nov. 3, 8 – Dec. 31.
   1882   July 7, 8, 11, 14, 18 – 20, 22 –
24, Aug. 5, 10, 15, 17, 28, Sept.
7, 9 – 12, 14, 16 – 18, 20, 22 –
25, 27, Oct. 2, 10 – 12, 14 –
16, 19, 20, 23, 24, 26, 31, Nov.
3, 10, 11, 18 – 22, 24, 27, Dec.
5, 6, 11, 16, 19 – 22.
   1883   Jan. 10, 13 – 23, 31, Feb. 2 –
13, 15 – 27, Mar. 1 – 6, 10, 13,
16 – 26, 28, 29, 31, Apr. 2, 6,
9, 10, 12 – 16, 19.
DLC
   Micro (P)
   1881   Apr. 5 – Nov. 4, 6 – Dec. 31.
NN
   Micro (P)
   1881   Apr. 5 – Nov. 4, 6 – Dec. 31.

PANAMA CANAL. STEAMER EDI-
TION.
   CU – B
   Micro (P) & (N)
   1881   June 1 – Dec. 28.
   1882   June 28, July 5, Sept. 13, Oct.
25, Nov. 15.
   1883   Jan. 17, Feb. 14, 28 – Mar. 7.
DLC
   Micro (P)
   1881   June 1 – Dec. 28.
FU
   Micro (P)
   1881   June 1 – Dec. 28.
MWA
   1882   Mar. 1 – 29, Apr. 19 – Aug. 30.
   1883   June 2.
MoU
   Micro (P)
   1881   June 1 – Dec. 28.
NN
   Micro (P)
   1881   June 1 – Dec. 28.

THE PANAMA ECHO. w. est. Nov. 1849.
    Note: In English.
  CtY
    1850   Mar. 9.
  NHi
    1849   Dec. 8 – 22.
    1850   Jan. 5, Apr. 27.
    1851   May 31.

PANAMA FREE PRESS. PRENSA
    LIBRE. w., sw. est. Feb. 24, 1940.
    Note: In English. Spanish section
    introduced Apr. 7, 1940. Periodicity
    Feb. 24 – [Mar. 30], 1940, weekly;
    after Apr. 7, 1940, semiweekly.
  DLC
    1940   June 5.

THE PANAMA HERALD. w., 3w. est.
    Apr. 14, 1851.
    Note: In English. Periodicity Apr.
    14, 1851 – May 25, 1853, weekly;
    May 26, 1853 – May 1, 1854,
    three times a week. Merged with
    The Daily Panama Star to form *The
    Daily Panama Star and Herald*,
    May 2, 1854.
  CU – B
    Micro (P)
    1851   Apr. 14 – Dec. 29.
    1852   Jan. 5 – May 1, 7, 18 – Dec. 28.
    1853   Jan. 4 – Dec. 31.
    1854   Jan. 5 – Apr. 27.
  CtY
    1853   July 2 – Dec. 24, 26 – 31.
    1854   Jan. 1 – Apr. 27.
  DLC
    1851   Apr. 14 – May 11, 20 – July 6,
            8 – Aug. 17, 19 – 31, Sept. 5 –
            14, 19 – Oct. 15, 17 – 26, 31 –
            Dec. 31.
    1852   Jan. 1 – Apr. 23, 28 – May 7,
            16 – June 3, July 10 – 15, Aug.
            4 – 9, Sept. 11 – 16, 18 – 23,
            Oct. 16 – 25, Nov. 10 – 18,
            Dec. 29 – 31.
    1853   Jan. 1 – 17, Mar. 30 – Apr. 7,
            9 – May 12, 14 – 27, July 31 –
            Aug. 16.

Micro (P)
    1851   Apr. 14 – Nov. 24, Dec. 1 – 31.
    1852   Jan. 1 – May 3, 18 – Dec. 31.
    1853   Jan. 1 – Dec. 31.
    1854   Jan. 1 – Apr. 27.
  FU
    Micro (P)
    1851   Apr. 14 – Dec. 31.
    1852 – 1853   Jan. 1 – Dec. 31.
    1854   Jan. 1 – Apr. 27.
  LU
    Micro (P)
    1851   Apr. 14 – Dec. 29.
    1852   Jan. 5 – Dec. 28.
    1853   Jan. 1 – Dec. 31.
    1854   Jan. 5 – Apr. 27.
  MnU
    Micro (P)
    1851   Apr. 14 – Dec. 31.
    1852 – 1853   Jan. 1 – Dec. 31.
    1854   Jan. 1 – Apr. 27.
  MoU
    Micro (P)
    1851   Apr. 14 – Nov. 24, Dec. 1 – 31.
    1852 – 1853   Jan. 1 – Dec. 31.
    1854   Jan. 1 – Apr. 27.
  NHi
    1851   May 26.
  NN
    Micro (P)
    1851   Apr. 14 – Dec. 31.
    1852 – 1853   Jan. 1 – Dec. 31.
    1854   Jan. 1 – Apr. 27.

PANAMA JOURNAL.
    See *Diario de Panamá. Panama
    Journal*.

THE PANAMA MAIL. 3w. est. Sept. 15,
    1864.
    Note: In English. Title *The Mercantile
    Chronicle*, Sept. 15, 1864 – Nov. 30,
    1866; *The Panama Mercantile Chron-
    icle*, Apr. 1 – 15, 1866; *Panama Mer-
    cantile Chronicle*, Apr. 18, 1866 –
    Aug. 16, 1869; *The Panama Mail*,
    after Aug. 18, 1869. See also *La
    Crónica mercantil*.

CU—B
  Micro (P) & (N)
  1865   Jan. 2—Dec. 31.
  1866—1867   Jan. 1—Dec. 31.
  1868   Jan. 1—Oct. 16, 19—Nov. 11,
          18—Dec. 30.
          Suplemento: Nov. 17.
  1869   Jan. 4—8, 13—Feb. 5, 10—
          Apr. 14, 19—23, May 3—19,
          24—June 2, 7—July 2, 7—14,
          19—26, Aug. 2—16, 18—Oct.
          29.
DLC
  Micro (P)
  1865   Jan. 2—Dec. 31.
  1866   Jan. 1—Dec. 30.
  1867   Jan. 2—Dec. 31.
  1868   Jan. 1—Oct. 16.
  1869   Mar. 12.
FU
  Micro (P)
  1865   Jan. 2—Dec. 31.
  1866—1867   Jan. 1—Dec. 31.
  1868   Jan. 1—Oct. 16.
LNHT
  Micro (P)
  1865   Jan. 2—Dec. 31.
  1866—1867   Jan. 1—Dec. 31.
  1868   Jan. 1—Oct. 16.
LU
  Micro (P)
  1865   Jan. 2—Dec. 31.
  1866—1867   Jan. 1—Dec. 31.
  1868   Jan. 1—Oct. 16.
MnU
  1865   Jan. 2—Dec. 31.
  1866—1867   Jan. 1—Dec. 31.
  1868   Jan. 1—Oct. 16.
MoU
  Micro (P)
  1865   Jan. 2—Dec. 31.
  1866—1867   Jan. 1—Dec. 31.
  1868   Jan. 1—Oct. 16.
NN
  Micro (P)
  1865   Jan. 2—Dec. 31.
  1866—1867   Jan. 1—Dec. 31.
  1868   Jan. 1—Oct. 16.

PANAMA MORNING JOURNAL. d.
  Note: In English.
  MWA
  1913   Jan. 12, Feb. 21.
  1914   Mar. 13, July 7.
  1915   June 2.

PANAMA STAR.
  See *The Daily Panama Star.*

PANAMA SUN. w.
  Note: In English.
  MWA
  1851   Jan. 22.

THE PANAMA TIMES. w. est. Mar. 21,
1925.
  Note: In English. Published as a
  section of *The Panama American,*
  Nov. 6, 1927—Jan. 1, 1928. Ceased
  publication Jan. 1, 1928.
  DLC
  1925   Mar. 21—Dec. 31.
  1926—1927   Jan. 1—Dec. 31.
  1928   Jan. 1.
  TxU
  1926   June 20.

THE PANAMA TRIBUNE. w. est. 1928.
  Note: In English.
  DLC
  1949   Jan. 2, 16, Feb. 13—Mar. 6,
          Apr. 17, May 1, 22, June 12,
          Sept. 11, Oct. 2, 16—30, Nov.
          13, 27, Dec. 11, 25.
  1950   Jan. 1, 22, Feb. 5, Mar. 12, Apr.
          2, May 28, Sept. 3, Oct. 29,
          Nov. 5, Dec. 10—24.
  1951   Jan. 21, Feb. 4, 11, 25, Sept.
          23, Dec. 23, 30.
  1952   Jan. 13—Aug. 23, 25—Dec. 31.
  1953   Jan. 1—Dec. 31.
  1954   Jan. 1—Mar. 20, 22—Apr. 10,
          12—June 5, 7—July 3, 5—Nov.
          6, 8—Dec. 31.
  1955   Jan. 1—May 7, 9—Dec. 31.
  1956   Jan. 1—Dec. 31.
  1957   Jan. 1—May 4, 6—Oct. 19,
          21—Dec. 31.
  1958   Jan. 1—Apr. 5, 7—June 21,

23 – July 12, 14 – Sept. 6, 8 –
27, 29 – Dec. 31.
1959   Jan. 1 – May 23, 25 – July 18,
20 – 25, 27 – Aug. 1, 3 – 8, 10 –
Dec. 23.
1960   Jan. 2 – 22, 24 – Feb. 5, 7 –
Apr. 15, 17 – Aug. 5, 7 – 19,
21 – Sept. 23, 25 – Dec. 23.
1961   Jan. 7 – June 30, July 2 – Dec.
31.
Micro (P) & (N)
1962   Jan. 1+.
LNT – MA
1949   Jan. 1+.

EL PANAMEÑISTA.
TxU
1946   Nov. 7.

EL PANAMEÑO. w. est. Jan. 1, 1849.
DLC
1849   Feb. 18 – Mar. 4.
Suplemento: Feb. 27.

LA PRENSA: DIARIO POLITICO Y
DE INFORMACION. d. est. 1908.
Note: Ceased publication [1917].
DLC
1912   Feb. 12.
MWA
1914   Mar. 14.

LA PRENSA. d.
CSt – H
1964   Apr. 24, 27, June 3, 8, 9, 12,
15, 16, 20 – 23, 30, July 14.

PRENSA LIBRE.
See *Panama Free Press. Prensa
libre.*

EL PUEBLO. est. 1858.
CU – B
Micro (N)
1858   Apr. 8.

EL PUEBLO. d. est. 1924.
DLC
1926   June 23.

RAZON. w.
MWA
1937   Jan. 24.

RELATOR. w.
MWA
1937   Jan. 30.

RUMBOS. bw. est. 1937.
LNT – MA
1937   Aug. 19.

EL SECCIONAL. est. 1883.
CU – B
Micro (P)
1883   July 8.

STAR & HERALD. d., 3w., d. est. May 2,
1854.
Note: In Spanish, English, and
French. French matter first appeared
Mar. 1, 1855 and a regular section,
La Étoile de Panamá, was published
Feb. 16, 1886 – Feb. 23, 1901. The
Spanish section, *La Estrella de
Panamá,* became a separate edition
Sept. 3, 1951. Formed by the merger
of *The Daily Panama Star* and *The
Panama Herald.* Title *The Daily
Panama Star* May 2 – Oct. 1, 1854;
The Panama Star and Herald, Oct. 3,
1854 – Sept. 17, 1855; *The Panama
Star & Herald,* Sept. 18, 1855 – Dec.
15, 1874; *Daily Panama Star &
Herald,* Dec. 16, 1874 – Feb. 23, 1901;
Star & Herald, after Feb. 24, 1901.
Periodicity May 2 – Oct. 1, 1854,
daily; Oct. 3, 1854 – Dec. 15, 1874,
three times a week; after Dec. 16,
1874, daily. Suspended publication
July 7, 1855 – May 12, 1857 (Spanish
section only); Mar. 27 – May 29,
1886. *The Evening Telegram* and
El Telegrama were published during the latter suspension.
CSt – H
1964   Sept. 11, Oct. 1 – 5, 7 – 17,
Nov. 3 – 6.
CU
Micro (P)
1939   Aug. 15.
1949   Feb. 24.
1953   Feb. 1.
CU – B
Micro (P)
1854   May 2 – Dec. 31.

1855   Jan. 1 – Apr. 7, 12 – Dec. 31.
1856   Jan. 1 – Oct. 25, 28 – Dec. 31.
1857   Jan. 1 – May 5, 9 – Dec. 31.
1858 – 1862   Jan. 1 – Dec. 31.
1863   Jan. 1 – Nov. 7, 12 – Dec. 31.
1864 – 1873   Jan. 1 – Dec. 31.
1874   Jan. 1 – Dec. 5, 10 – 31.
1875   Jan. 1 – Apr. 13, 15 – Dec. 31.
1876 – 1877   Jan. 1 – Dec. 31.
1878   Jan. 1 – Mar. 6, 8 – Dec. 31.
1879 – 1881   Jan. 1 – Dec. 31.
1882   Jan. 1 – Apr. 7, 10 – 25, 27 –
Nov. 16, 18 – 21, 23 – 25, 28,
30 – Dec. 2, 7, 9, 14, 16, 18.
1883   Jan. 1 – Apr. 26, 28 – Dec. 31.
1884   Jan. 1 – Dec. 31.
1885   Jan. 1 – 9, 12 – 16, 19 – 24,
26 – 28, Feb. 2 – 11, Mar. 6 –
11, 23, 31, Apr. 9 – 11, 22 –
29, May 4 – 6, July 1 – Aug. 8,
11 – Dec. 31.
1886   Jan. 1 – Dec. 31.
1887   Jan. 1 – Mar. 30, Apr. 2 – Dec.
31.
1888   Jan. 1 – Dec. 31.
1889   Jan. 1 – Feb. 2, 4 – Mar. 2, 4 –
Dec. 31.
1890   Jan. 1 – Nov. 10, 12 – Dec. 31.

CtY
1854   [May 2 – Dec. 31].
1855   [Jan. 1 – Apr. 28].
1858   [May 4 – Dec. 31].
1859   [Jan. 1 – May 7, 16 – Dec. 31].
1860   [Jan. 1 – Nov. 27].
1868   [Jan. 4 – Dec. 31].
1869   Jan. 2 – Dec. 31.
1870   Jan. 1 – 29.

DLC
1919   Nov. 2 – Dec. 31.
1920 – 1925   Jan. 1 – Dec. 31.
1926   Jan. 1 – 5, 7 – Dec. 31.
1927   Jan. 1 – Dec. 31.
1928   Jan. 1 – Mar. 31, Apr. 2 – Nov.
1, 3 – 28, 30 – Dec. 31.
1929   Jan. 1 – 3, 5 – Feb. 22, 24 –
Apr. 7, 9 – July 16, 18 – Dec.
31.

1930 – 1937   Jan. 1 – Dec. 31.
1938   Jan. 1 – Nov. 3, 5 – Dec. 31.
1939   Jan. 1 – Dec. 31.
1940   Jan. 1 – Mar. 31, Apr. 2 – 5,
7 – 12, 14 – 17, 19 – 24, 27,
30 – May 3, 5, 6, 11, 14 – 18,
21 – June 16, 18, 20, 21, 25,
26, 30 – July 10, 13 – 18, 20 –
Sept. 15, 17 – Oct. 1, 3 – 11,
13 – 29, 31 – Nov. 3, 6 – 10, 12,
13, 15 – Dec. 31.
1941   Jan. 1 – Apr. 18, May 10 – 12,
17, 18, 20 – 22, 24 – 26, 30 –
July 11, 14 – Sept. 30, Oct. 2 –
31, Nov. 2 – 12, 14 – Dec. 10,
16 – 31.
1942   Jan. 1 – Feb. 28, Mar. 2 – 9,
11 – 19, 21 – 28, 31 – Apr. 14,
19, 20, 24 – 28, 30 – Aug. 27,
31 – Oct. 18, Nov. 1 – Dec. 31.
1943   Jan. 1 – Dec. 31.
1944   Jan. 1 – 16, 21 – Feb. 24, 28 –
Mar. 2, 5 – Dec. 31.
1945   Jan. 1 – May 31, June 3 –
Dec. 23, 25 – 31.
1946   Jan. 1 – 31, Feb. 4 – Mar. 7,
11 – May 19, 23 – Aug. 2, 4 –
Dec. 31.
1947   Jan. 1 – 19, 24 – Feb. 16, 18 –
Dec. 31.
1948   Jan. 1 – Apr. 27, 29 – Aug. 9,
11 – Nov. 20, 22 – Dec. 31.
1949 – 1951   Jan. 1 – Dec. 31.
1952   Jan. 1 – July 6, 8 – Sept. 5, 7 –
21, 23 – Oct. 22, 24 – Dec. 18,
20 – 31.
1953   Jan. 1 – 23, 25 – Feb. 6, 8, 10 –
23, 25 – Mar. 1, 3 – Apr. 24,
26 – May 9, 11 – July 19, 21 –
28, 31 – Aug. 2, 4 – 14, 16 –
25, 27, 30 – Sept. 23, 25, 26,
28 – Oct. 13, 15 – 17, 19 – 31,
Nov. 2, 5 – 17, 19 – 30, Dec.
2 – 4, 6, 7, 9 – 11, 13 – 31.
1954   Jan. 2, 3, 6, 7, 9 – 11, 13, 14,
19 – Feb. 1, 3, 5 – Mar. 16, 18 –
Apr. 9, 11, 12, 15, 18 – 20, 22 –
25, 28, 30 – May 7, 10 – 13,

15 — 17, 19 — 23, 25 — 28, 31 —
June 3, 6 — 8, 11 — 18, 21, 23 —
July 5, 7, 9 — 18, 20, 21, 23 — 25,
27 — Aug. 4, 6 — 11, 13 — 15,
17 — 20, 23 — 25, 29, 31 — Sept.
3, 5, 7, 8, 15 — 17, 19, 20, 22 —
25, 27, 30, Oct. 2 — 11, 14 — 23,
27, 29, 31, Nov. 2, 3, 9, 10, 12,
15, 17 — 26, 28, Dec. 3, 4, 6, 7,
9 — 11, 18, 20, 24 — 29.
1955   Jan. 3, 4, 7, 9, 10, 17, 21, 22, 24,
25, 29 — 31, Feb. 2, 3, 12, 14,
16, 17, 20, 22 — 24, 26 — Mar. 1,
3 — 10, 12, 14 — 16, 18, 20, Apr.
6 — 8, 10, 11, 15 — 17, 23 — 25,
30, May 1, 3, 4, 6.
Micro (P)
1854   May 2 — Dec. 31.
1855 — 1884   Jan. 1 — Dec. 31.
1885   Jan. 1 — May 6, July 1 — Dec.
31.
1886   Jan. 1 — Mar. 27, May 29 — Dec.
31.
1887 — 1914   Jan. 1 — Dec. 31.
FU
Micro (P)
1854   May 2 — Dec. 31.
1855 — 1884   Jan. 1 — Dec. 31.
1885   Jan. 1 — May 6, July 1 — Dec. 31.
1886   Jan. 1 — Mar. 27, May 29 —
Dec. 31.
1887 — 1914   Jan. 1 — Dec. 31.
Micro (N)
1919   May 1 — Nov. 3, 5 — Dec. 31.
1920   Jan. 1 — Feb. 17, 19 — Mar. 1,
3 — Apr. 2, 4 — 8, 10, 13 — 16,
18, 22 — 24, 26, 27, 29, May 1 —
6, 8 — 12, 14 — June 20, 23 —
July 4, 6 — 20, 22 — Aug. 9, 11 —
Oct. 9, 11 — Nov. 11, 13 — Dec.
3, 5, 7, 9, 11, 13, 14, 17, 19,
20, 22 — 24, 26 — 28, 30, 31.
1921   Jan. 3, 5 — Feb. 8, 10 — May 29,
31 — July 4, 6 — Oct. 31.
1922   Jan. 1, 3 — 27, 29 — Feb. 28,
Mar. 2 — June 17, 19, 20, 22 —
July 4, 6 — Oct. 4, 6 — Nov. 3,
5 — 21, 23 — 25, 27 — Dec. 2, 4 —

31.
1923   Jan. 1, 3 — 14, 16 — Feb. 27,
Mar. 1 — 30, Apr. 1 — July 4,
6 — Aug. 10, 12, 14 — Nov. 4,
6, 7, 9 — Dec. 1, 3 — 14, 16 — 31.
1924   Jan. 1 — Feb. 12, 14, 15, 17 —
24, 26 — Mar. 4, 6 — Apr. 18,
20 — Dec. 31.
1925   Jan. 1 — Sept. 25, 30 — Oct. 24,
26 — Nov. 7, 9 — 13, 15 — Dec.
31.
1926   Jan. 1 — 25, 27 — June 5, 7 —
Oct. 27, 29 — Dec. 31.
1927   Jan. 1 — July 4, 6 — Dec. 15,
17 — 31.
1928   Jan. 1 — 17, 19 — Mar. 15, 17 —
29, 31, Apr. 2 — 14 15 — Aug.
5, 7 — Dec. 15, 17 — 31.
1929   Jan. 1 — Apr. 7, 9 — July 24,
26 — 31, Aug. 2 — Oct. 23, 25 —
Nov. 26, 28 — Dec. 30.
1930   Jan. 1 — 26, 28 — Feb. 5, 7, 8,
10 — 14, 17 — 19, 21, 22, 24 —
27, Mar. 3, 5 — June 3, 5 — 7,
9 — 14, 16 — Aug. 4, 6 — 14, 16 —
Sept. 26, 28 — Oct. 12, 14 —
Dec. 12, 14 — 31.
1931   Jan. 1 — Feb. 6, 8 — Mar. 30,
Apr. 1 — May 9, 12, 14, 15, 17 —
21, 24 — July 24, 26 — Nov. 3,
5 — Dec. 31.
1932   Jan. 1 — 13, 15 — Mar. 7, 9 —
Apr. 5, 7 — May 25, 27, 29, 30,
June 1 — Aug. 16, 18 — Sept.
6, 8 — 19, 22 — Dec. 5, 7, 9 —
13, 15 — 31.
1933   Jan. 1 — 25, 27 — Feb. 28, Mar.
3 — Apr. 17, 19 — May 17, 19 —
July 17, 19 — 26, 28 — Aug. 7,
9 — Nov. 7, 9 — Dec. 21, 23 — 31.
1934   Jan. 1 — 27, 30 — Feb. 3, 6 —
10, 13 — 17, 20 — Mar. 23, 25 —
Apr. 7, 9 — Dec. 31.
1935   Jan. 1 — 19, 22 — Mar. 8, 10, 11,
13 — 21, 23 — Apr. 6, 9 — 19,
22 — May 24, 26 — June 7, 9 —
26, 28 — July 5, 7 — 11, 13 — Aug.
6, 8 — 12, 14 — Oct. 2, 4, 5, 8,

10 – 12, 16, 19 – Nov. 13, 15, 16, 19 – 28, Dec. 1 – 31.

1936 Jan. 1 – 8, 10, 11, 14 – 24, 26 – Feb. 19, 21 – 25, Mar. 1 – 30, Apr. 2 – 6, 10 – 13, 16, 17, 21 – May 8, 10 – 15, 19, 20, 26, 28 – June 13, 16, 18 – 27, 30 – July 4, 6 – 14, 16 – 31, Aug. 2 – 16, 18 – 21, 23 – 27, Sept. 1, 2, 6 – 11, 13 – 16, 22, 23, 27 – 29, Oct. 3 – 16, 18, 19, 26 – Nov. 9, 14 – 16, 18 – 30, Dec. 2, 4, 6 – 14, 16 – 18, 22 – 31.

1937 Jan. 1 – 8, 10 – 15, 19, 22 – Feb. 8, 12 – 15, 19 – 22, 26 – Mar. 2, 4, 7 – 13, 16 – 19, 23 – 25, 27 – 29, 31, Apr. 1, 6 – 14, 18, 19, 21 – 23, 25, 26, 30 – May 7, 13 – 22, 27, 28, 20, 21, June 3 – 5, 11 – 14, 17, 19 – 21, 26 – 29, July 2 – 4, 7, 8, 10 – 14, 17 – 19, 22, 24 – 26, 29 – Aug. 5, 7 – 9, 14, 17 – 21, 24 – 30, Sept. 1 – Oct. 4, 6, 8, 9, 12, 14 – 16, 19 – 22, 24, 26, 28, 31, Nov. 1, 3, 5, 6, 9 – 11, 14 – 18, 23, 25, 30, Dec. 3, 4, 7, 14, 16, 17, 24 – 27.

1938 Jan. 1 – 3, 7 – 10, 13 – 15, 18 – 20, 25, 26, 28, Feb. 7, 10, 13, 14, 27, Mar. 6, 8, 9, 15, 16, 27, 29, 30, Apr. 9 – 13, 15 – 19, 21, 22, 24, 27 – 29, May 1 – 4, 5, 9 – 11, 16 – 20, 22, 26 – 28, 31 – June 18, 20 – 29, July 6 – 9, 12 – Aug. 2, 4 – 13, 16, 18 – Sept. 3, 5 – 7, 9, 17 – Oct. 7, 10 – 19, 22, 24, 25, 28, 30 – Nov. 2, 4 – 10, 12, 22 – Dec. 3, 5 – 10, 13 – 17, 19 – 25, 30, 31.

1939 Jan. 1 – 9, 12 – 14, 17, 19 – 26, 29 – Feb. 2, 4 – 6, 8, 9, 11 – 17, 19 – 25, 27 – May 21, 24 – June 7, 10, 13 – July 13, 15 – 26, 28 – Aug. 10, 12, 13, 17 – 25, 27, 29 – 31, Sept. 2 – 6, 9, 10, 12, 14 – 26, 28, 30 – Oct. 18, 21 – 26, 28 – Nov. 12, 16,

17, 21 – 24, 26 – Dec. 13, 16 – 31.

1940 Jan. 1 – 6, 9 – 12, 14 – 24, Feb. 1 – 5, 13 – Apr. 3, 6, 9 – 13, 16, 17, 19 – 27, 30 – May 8, 11 – 13, 16 – June 7, 15 – July 6, 9 – 18, 26 – Aug. 19, 22, 23, 25, 26, 29 – Sept. 8, 10 – 15, 17 – 26, Oct. 1 – 8, 10 – 15, 17 – 28, Nov. 3 – 10, 18 – Dec. 8, 13 – 31.

1941 Jan. 1 – Feb. 14, 28 – May 26, 28 – July 2, 4 – Oct. 24, Nov. 2 – 21, 23 – Dec. 12, 14 – 31.

1942 Jan. 1 – Feb. 28, Mar. 2 – 4, 8 – 16, 21 – 28, 31 – Apr. 7, 12 – 14, 24 – 28, 30 – May 11, 13 – June 5, 7 – 25, 27, 29 – July 23, 25, 30 – Aug. 27, Sept. 1 – Oct. 18, Nov. 2 – 8, 13 – Dec. 31.

1943 Jan. 5 – 31, Feb. 5 – Apr. 1, 9 – May 16, 21 – 27, 31 – June 20, 25 – July 1, 5 – 8, 12 – 15, 19 – Aug. 15, 23 – Sept. 12, 17 – Oct. 3, 20, 21, 25 – 31, Nov. 5 – 11, 13, 15 – 21, 26 – Dec. 23, 27 – 30.

1944 Jan. 1 – Feb. 10, 14 – Mar. 9, 13 – May 25, 29 – Nov. 12, 17 – Dec. 7, 11 – 31.

1945 Jan. 1 – 21, 23 – Feb. 26, 28, May 4 – 16, 19 – 22, 24, 28 – June 10, 17, July 1 – Aug. 16, 18, 20 – 23, 27 – 31, Nov. 2 – 15, 19 – Dec. 9, 14 – 30.

1946 Jan. 4, 6 – 31, Feb. 4 – 28, Mar. 4 – 18, 20, 21, 26 – 28, 30, Apr. 1 – 16, 18 – May 13, 15 – 20, 24 – June 13, 15, 23 – Aug. 1, 5 – Sept. 8, 11 – 22, 26, 30 – Oct. 10, 16 – Nov. 17, 22 – 29, Dec. 1 – 25.

1947 Jan. 1 – Feb. 16, 18 – 23, 28 – Mar. 9, 11 – 31, Apr. 2 – May 1, 3 – 22, 24 – Aug. 8, 10 – Sept. 2, 4 – 7, 9 – 18, 20, 21, 25 – Oct. 6, 8 – 16, 20 – 22,

24 — Nov. 2, 7 — 16, 24 — Dec.
7, 12 — 21, 29 — 31.
1948   Jan. 1 — 4, 9 — 29, Feb. 2 — June
3, 6 — 17, 19, 21 — 30.
1949   July 1 — 10, 15, 16, 18 — 22,
24 — Aug. 3, 5 — Sept. 30, Oct.
2 — Dec. 27, 29 — 31.
1950   Jan. 1 — Feb. 21, 23 — May 21,
26 — Sept. 30.
1951   Jan. 1 — 11, 13 — 15, 20 — Mar.
19.
IU
1940   May 2.
LNHT
1955   [Jan. 1 — Dec. 31].
Micro (P)
1854   May 2 — Dec. 31.
1855 — 1870   Jan. 1 — Dec. 31.
LU
Micro (P)
1854   May 2 — Oct. 1.
1855   Jan. 3 — Dec. 31.
1856 — 1869   Jan. 1 — Dec. 31.
1870   Jan. 1 — Dec. 25.
1939   Aug. 15.
1949   Feb. 24.
MWA
1871   Apr. 11 — 27.
1877   Feb. 5, 9, 21.
1913   Jan. 12, Feb. 21.
1914   Mar. 12.
1957   Dec. 26.
MnU
Micro (P)
1854   May 2 — Dec. 31.
1855 — 1870   Jan. 1 — Dec. 31.
MoU
Micro (P)
1854   May 2 — Dec. 31.
1855 — 1884   Jan. 1 — Dec. 31.
1885   Jan. 1 — May 6, July 1 — Dec.
31.
1886   Jan. 1 — Mar. 27, May 29 — Dec.
31.
1887 — 1914   Jan. 1 — Dec. 31.
NHi
1856   Jan. 3, 15, Apr. 19.
1907   Feb. 24.

NN
Micro (P)
1854   May 2 — Dec. 31.
1855 — 1884   Jan. 1 — Dec. 31.
1885   Jan. 1 — May 6, July 1 — Dec.
31.
1886   Jan. 1 — Mar. 27, May 29 — Dec.
31.
1887 — 1914   Jan. 1 — Dec. 31.
TxU
1881   Oct. 13.
1921   Jan. 1 — 14, 16 — Feb. 23, 25 —
May 31.
1923   Sept. 24 — Oct. 9, 11 — Nov. 4,
6 — Dec. 31.
1926   June 1 — 8, 11 — 30.
1941   June 12 — July 9, 12 — 30, Aug.
2 — Oct. 8, 10 — 31, Nov. 2 — 14,
18 — Dec. 31.
1942   Jan. 1, 3 — Feb. 17, 19 — 28,
Mar. 2 — 19, 21 — 28, 31 — May
5, 9 — June 11.
1943   Jan. 1 — Mar. 9, 11 — May 27,
June 4 — 10, 14 — July 1, 6 —
Sept. 30, Oct. 2 — Nov. 3, 5 —
Dec. 31.
1944   Jan. 1, 2, 4 — Feb. 22, 24, 28 —
Apr. 7, 9 — July 4, 6 — Nov. 3,
5 — 16, 23 — Dec. 28.
1945   Jan. 1, 3 — May 10, 14 — 20,
24 — June 11, 15 — July 4, 6 —
Aug. 2, 6 — Oct. 21, 26 — Nov.
4, 6 — 8, 12 — 25, 30 — Dec. 31.
1946   Jan. 1 — May 31, June 3 — July
18, 22 — Dec. 25, 27 — 31.
1947   Jan. 1 — Dec. 12, 14 — 29, 31.
1948 — 1952   Jan. 1 — Dec. 31.

PANAMA STAR & HERALD. STEAMER
EDITION. bw., irr., w. est. Jan. 3,
1856.
Note: In English. Steamer editions
replaced by *Weekly Panama Star &
Herald* May 17, 1878. See also *La
Estrella de Panamá.*
CU — B
Micro (P)
1856   Jan. 3 — Dec. 31.
1857 — 1875   Jan. 1 — Dec. 31.

1876   Jan. 1 – Dec. 1.
1877   July 6 – Oct. 21.
1878   May 17 – Sept. 12.
1879   Feb. 6 – Dec. 31.
1880   Jan. 1 – Dec. 30.
DLC
Edition for the United States:
1856   Mar. 5, 19, Apr. 3, May 5, 19,
        June 3, July 4, Aug. 4, Oct. 3,
        19, Nov. 19 – Dec. 19.
        Supplement: May 5.
1857   Jan. 19, Feb. 19, Mar. 19, Apr.
        19, May 19, June 19, Aug. 3, 19.
        Supplement: Jan. 19.
1867   Aug. 1, 12, Sept. 1, 12.
1868   July 28, Aug. 13, 20, 28, Sept.
        12 – 28, Oct. 28.
1871   Jan. 17, Mar. 4, 18, Apr. 1, 18,
        June 1, 19, July 2, 19, Aug. 2,
        19, Sept. 2, 18, Oct. 2, 19.
1872   Jan. 1, 21, Feb. 19, Mar. 5, 21,
        Apr. 3, 19, May 4, Aug. 2, 14,
        23, Sept. 13, 23, Oct. 14, 24,
        Nov. 16, 25, Dec. 4, 15, 28.
1873   Jan. 16, 25, Feb. 16, Mar. 8,
        18, Apr. 7.
1874   Apr. 1, July 18.
1875   Jan. 2, May 29, June 16, July
        1, 16, Aug. 1, 16, Sept. 1, 16,
        Oct. 1, 16, Nov. 1, 16, Dec. 1.
Edition for the United States, Europe
and the Antilles:
1867   July 23, Aug. 23, Sept. 23, Oct.
        23.
1868   Aug. 5, Sept. 5.
1869   Mar. 24.
1872   May 21, June 5, July 6, 21,
        Sept. 5, Oct. 6, Nov. 5.
1873   Feb. 5, Aug. 5, 21, Sept. 5, 21,
        Oct. 6, 21, Nov. 5, 21, Dec. 6,
        21.
1874   Jan. 5, 21, Feb. 5, 21, Mar. 7,
        21, May 6, July 6, Sept. 5, 21,
        Oct. 6, 21, Nov. 5, 21, Dec. 6,
        21.
Edition for Europe:
1857   Feb. 8.
1858   Apr. 24.

Edition for South and Central America:
1873   Apr. 25, May 1, 10, 25, June 1,
        10, 16, 25, July 1, 16, 25, Aug.
        1, 16, Oct. 25.
1874   Apr. 16, May 1, 16, 25, June
        10, 25, July 25, Aug. 1, 16, 25,
        Sept. 10.
1875   Jan. 16.
Supplements:
1872   Aug. 24.
1873   May 9, 15, 29, June 5, July 8.
1874   Mar. 3, Oct. 8, Nov. 7.
Micro (P)
1856   Jan. 3 – Dec. 31.
1857 – 1875   Jan. 1 – Dec. 31.
1876   Jan. 1 – Dec. 1.
1877   July 6 – Oct. 21.
FU
Micro (P)
1856 – 1875   Jan. 1 – Dec. 31.
1876   Jan. 1 – Dec. 1.
1877 – 1880   Jan. 1 – Dec. 31.
LU
Micro (P)
1856 – 1870   Jan. 1 – Dec. 31.
MWA
1857   Apr. 3.
1869   Mar. 24.
1874   Sept. 16.
MnU
Micro (P)
1856   Jan. 3 – Dec. 31.
1857 – 1869   Jan. 1 – Dec. 31.
1870   Jan. 1 – Dec. 25.
MoU
Micro (P)
1856 – 1875   Jan. 1 – Dec. 31.
1876   Jan. 1 – Dec. 1.
1877 – 1880   Jan. 1 – Dec. 31.
NN
Micro (P)
1856 – 1875   Jan. 1 – Dec. 31.
1876   Jan. 1 – Dec. 1.
1877 – 1880   Jan. 1 – Dec. 31.
NHi
1856   Jan. 19, Feb. 4, 20, Mar. 5, 18.

PANAMA STAR & HERALD. WEEKLY
EDITION.
>Note: In English. Formed by the
>merger of *The Weekly Star* and *The
>Panama Herald*, May 8, 1854. Title
>*The Weekly Panama Star and Herald*,
>May 8, 1854 – Apr. 30, 1855; *Panama
>Star & Herald*, [Jan. 2] – Feb. 25,
>1877; *Weekly Panama Star & Herald*,
>Mar. 2, 1877 – Feb. 20, 1901; *Panama
>Star & Herald* after Feb. 27, 1901.
>The weekly edition replaced all
>steamer editions May 17, 1878. See
>also *La Estrella de Panamá. Weekly
>Edition.*

CU – B
>Micro (P)
>1854 May 8 – Nov. 6, 20 – Dec. 25.
>1855 Jan. 1 – Mar. 12, 26 – Apr. 30.
>1877 Jan. 2 – May 10, 25 – Oct. 2,
>   17 – Dec. 25.
>1878 Jan. 2 – Feb. 25, Mar. 12 –
>   May 2, 10.
>1881 – 1904 Jan. 1 – Dec. 31.
>1905 Jan. 2 – July 31.

DLC
>1900 Jan. 3 – May 1, 3 – July 27,
>   Sept. 3 – Nov. 13, 15 – Dec. 31.
>1901 Jan. 1 – Oct. 22, 24 – Dec. 31.
>1902 Jan. 1 – Aug. 5, 7 – 26, 28 –
>   Sept. 24, Nov. 12, 19.
>1904 Jan. 6 – Dec. 26.
>1905 Feb. 4 – Dec. 31.
>1906 – 1915 Jan. 1 – Dec. 31.
>1916 Jan. 1 – Sept. 3, 5 – 17, 19 –
>   Dec. 31.
>1917 – 1919 Jan. 1 – Dec. 31.
>1920 Jan. 6 – 26, Feb. 23, Mar. 1.
>Micro (P)
>1854 May 8 – Nov. 12, 14 – Dec. 31.
>1855 Jan. 1 – Mar. 18, 20 – Apr. 30.
>1877 Jan. 2 – May 16, 18 – Oct. 9,
>   11 – Dec. 31.
>1878 Jan. 1 – Mar. 1, 3 – Sept. 12.
>1879 Feb. 6 – Dec. 31.
>1880 – 1909 Jan. 1 – Dec. 31.
>1910 Jan. 1 – Dec. 26.

FU
>Micro (P)

>1854 May 8 – Dec. 31.
>1855 Jan. 1 – Apr. 30.
>1877 Jan. 2 – Dec. 31.
>1878 Jan. 1 – May 8.
>1881 – 1910 Jan. 1 – Dec. 31.

LU
>Micro (P)
>1854 May 8 – Dec. 31.
>1855 Jan. 1 – Apr. 30.

MB
>1903 Sept. 9 – Dec. 30.
>1904 Jan. 6 – May 16, 30 – June 2,
>   27 – Dec. 26.
>1905 – 1908 Jan. 1 – Dec. 31.
>1909 Jan. 4 – June 28.
>1910 – 1915 Jan. 1 – Dec. 31.
>1916 Jan. 3 – Dec. 18.
>1917 Jan. 1 – Dec. 31.

MWA
>1885 Nov. 7.
>1891 Dec. 10 – 17.

MnU
>Micro (P)
>1854 May 8 – Dec. 31.
>1855 Jan. 1 – Apr. 30.

MoU
>Micro (P)
>1854 May 8 – Dec. 31.
>1855 Jan. 1 – Apr. 30.
>1877 Jan. 2 – Dec. 31.
>1878 Jan. 1 – May 8.
>1881 – 1910 Jan. 1 – Dec. 31.

TxU
>1920 Jan. 5 – 19, Feb. 9 – Mar. 1,
>   15 – Apr. 5, 19 – May 10, 24 –
>   Nov. 29, Dec. 13 – 27.
>1922 Jan. 1 – Feb. 27, Apr. 10 –
>   Dec. 4, 18 – 31.
>1923 Jan. 1 – Sept. 17.
>1924 Jan. 7 – Feb. 18, Mar. 3 – 24,
>   Apr. 7 – Sept. 14, 29 – Nov.
>   24, Dec. 8 – 31.
>1925 Jan. 1 – Apr. 13.
>1926 Jan. 1 – Apr. 5, 19 – Dec. 20.
>1927 Jan. 1 – Feb. 6.

THE SUN. EL SOL. 3w. est. Dec. 17,
1874.
>Note: In Spanish and English.

DLC
  Micro (P)
    1874   Dec. 17 – 24, 29 – 31.
    1875   Jan. 2 – 14, 21 – Apr. 27.

EL TELEGRAMA. w. est. Apr. 3, 1886.
    Note: Published during the suspen-
    sion of *La Estrella de Panamá.*
    Ceased publication May 29, 1886.
    See also *The Evening Telegram.*
  CU – B
    Micro (P)
      1886   Apr. 3 – May 29.
  DLC
    Micro (P)
      1886   Apr. 3 – May 29.
  MoU
    Micro (P)
      1886   Apr. 3 – May 29.
  NN
    Micro (P)
      1886   Apr. 3 – May 29.

EL TELEGRAMA. d. est. Oct. 13, 1886.
  CtY
    1886   Oct. 13 – Dec. 31.
    1887   Jan. 3 – Dec. 24.
    1888   Jan. 5 – Dec. 15.
    1889   Jan. 8 – Dec. 31.
    1890 – 1891   Jan. 1 – Dec. 31.
    1892   Jan. 1 – Dec. 30.

TIEMPO. d.
  MWA
    1937   Feb. 6.

THE TIMES. d. est. 1924.
    Note: In Spanish and English.
  DLC
    1926   June 22.
  TxU
    1926   June 22.

LA UNION LIBERAL. w. est. 1855.
  DLC
    1870   Apr. 10.

LA UNION REPUBLICANA. irr. est.
  Apr. 28, 1884.

CU – B
  Micro (P)
    1884   May 22 – June 21.

EL UNIVERSAL. sw. est. Nov. 3, 1884.
  CU – B
    Micro (P)
      1884   Nov. 24.
      1885   Mar. 17 – 20, May 1 – 5.

THE WEEKLY ECHO; A STEAMER
  PAPER. w. est. 1852.
    Note: In English. See also *The Daily
    Echo.*
  DLC
    1852   Apr. 25, May 2, 16, 30.

WEEKLY PANAMA STAR.
    See *Weekly Star.*

THE WEEKLY PANAMA STAR AND
  HERALD.
    See *Panama Star & Herald. Weekly
    Edition.*

WEEKLY STAR. w. est. Mar. 14, 1853.
    Note: In English. Title *Weekly
    Panama Star*, Mar. 14, 1853 – Jan.
    30, 1854: *Weekly Star*, Feb. 1 – May
    1, 1854. Merged with the weekly
    edition of the *Panama Herald* to
    form *The Weekly Panama Star and
    Herald*, May 8, 1854. See also *The
    Daily Panama Star.*
  CU – B
    Micro (P)
      1853   Mar. 14 – Dec. 31.
      1854   Jan. 1 – May 1.
  DLC
    Micro (P)
      1853   Mar. 14 – Dec. 31.
      1854   Jan. 1 – Feb. 6.
  FU
    Micro (P)
      1853   Mar. 14 – Dec. 31.
      1854   Jan. 1 – May 1.
  LU
    Micro (P)
      1853   Mar. 14 – Dec. 31.
      1854   Jan. 1 – May 1.

MnU
Micro (P)
1853 Mar. 14 – Dec. 31.
1854 Jan. 1 – May 1.
MoU
Micro (P)
1853 Mar. 14 – Dec. 31.
1854 Jan. 1 – 30, Feb. 6 – May 1.
NN
Micro (P)
1853 Mar. 14 – Dec. 31.
1854 Jan. 1 – May 1.

Penonomé

EL COCLESANO. bw. est. 1881.
CU – B
Micro (P)
1881 Aug. 5 – Sept. 5, Oct. 5 – 20.

Santiago

EL REPUBLICANO. bw. est. Jan. 1, 1879.
CU – B
Micro (P)
1879 Jan. 1 – Nov. 19.

PARAGUAY

Asunción

LA ACCION. d. est. [June 15], 1909.
DLC
1909 July 3 – 7, 9 – Aug. 1, 3 – 18, 20 – Sept. 20, 22 – Nov. 9, 11 – Dec. 6, 8, 9, 11 – 15, 17 – 31.

CABICHUI. w. est. 1867.
CU – B
Micro (N)
1867 [June 3 – Sept. 9].

LA CAPITAL. w., d. est. 1904.
Note: Periodicity before May 23, 1908, weekly; after June 1, 1908, daily.
DLC
1908 Jan. 4 – Aug. 28, 30 – Sept. 3, 5 – 25, 29 – Oct. 8, 10 – Nov. 24, 26 – Dec. 30.
1909 Jan. 1 – Feb. 25, 27, 28, Mar. 3 – 11, 13 – 15, 17 – 25, 27 –

31, Apr. 3 – 28, 30, May 2 – 5, 7 – 10, 12, 16, 18 – 29, 31 – June 3, 5 – 9, 11 – 15, 17 – 21, 23, 24, 27 – July 22, 24 – Oct. 18, 20 – Nov. 18, 20 – Dec. 31.

EL CIVICO. d. est. Sept. 2, 1895.
Note: Ceased publication [1908].
DLC
1907 May 2 – Aug. 24, 27 – Sept. 6, 8 – 10, 13 – Dec. 31.
Suplemento: Aug. 30, Sept. 14, 23, Oct. 17.
1908 Jan. 1 – June 30.
MWA
1896 Sept. 1 – Dec. 31.

CRITICA. d. est. 1929.
DLC
1933 Aug. 25.
1934 June 19.
1935 Mar. 20, June 13.

LA DEMOCRACIA. d. est. [1881].
DLC
1887 Sept. 20 – 27, 30, Oct. 3, 5 – Nov. 2, 4 – 6, 8 – 13, 15 – 18, 27, 28, 30 – Dec. 11, 14, 23, 27.
Suplemento: Dec. 6, 7.
1888 Jan. 6 – 8, 10 – 23, 25, Feb. 2, 7, 9 – 12, 15 – 20, 23, 25 – 27, Mar. 2 – 4, 11 – 14, 16, 21, 27, 28, Apr. 14 – 17, 19 – 30, May 2 – 4, 7, 8, 16 – 22, 24 – 26.
Suplemento: Jan. 19 – 21, 25, Feb. 10, 11, 16 – 18, 20, 23, 29, Mar. 2, 13, 14, 21, 27, Apr. 14.

DEUTSCHE WARTE. sw. est. [1932].
Note: In German. Title formerly *Deutsche Zeitung fur Paraguay*.
DLC
1941 Dec. 10, 13.
1942 Jan. 10 – 17.

EL DIARIO. d. est. June 1, 1904.
Note: Began publishing weekly supplement (*Edición dominical*) devoted to Chaco War with Bolivia Oct. 22, 1933.

DLC

1907 May 2–13, 16–Aug. 9, 11–
Sept. 10, 13–Dec. 31.

1908 Jan. 1–June 30, July 5, 8, 11–
Oct. 19, 21–Dec. 31.

1909 Jan. 1–May 19, 21–July 12,
16–22, 24–Aug. 6, 8, 9, 11–
24, 26–31, Sept. 2–Dec. 31.

1933 Aug. 9, Oct. 28, Dec. 2.
Edición dominical: Oct. 22–
Dec. 31.

1934 Jan. 10, Mar. 16, Aug. 18,
Sept. 8, 12, 15, 28, Oct. 1, 6–
8, 24, Nov. 15, 21, 26, Dec. 3,
5, 13, 21, 27, 28.
Edición dominical: Jan. 1–
Dec. 31.

1935 Jan. 2, 9, 12–14, Feb. 14,
Mar. 11, 12, 19, 22, 29, Apr. 1,
30, May 25, 31, June 19, 21,
25, July 18, Aug. 23, 28, 30,
Sept. 5, 18, Dec. 5, 10.
Edición dominical: Jan. 1–
13, Sept. 1, 15–Oct. 13, 27,
Nov. 24, Dec. 8, 22.

1936 Feb. 18–20, Mar. 26, Apr. 16,
18, 21, 22.
Edición dominical: Jan. 5, 12,
26, Mar. 29.

1939 Jan. 28–Feb. 1.

ENANITO. w. est. 1930.
DLC

1934 Dec. 8.
1935 Aug. 3.

EL ENANO. w., 3w. est. Nov. 10, 1901.
Note: Periodicity Nov. 10, 1901–
June 25, 1905, weekly; June 27–
Dec. 28, 1905, three times a week;
after Dec. 31, 1905, weekly. Sus-
pended publication Aug. 7, 1904–
Feb. 5, 1905; Feb. 19–June 4, 1905;
July 1–Oct. 7, 1906.
DLC

1901 Nov. 10–30, Dec. 9–31.
1902 Jan. 1–11, 20–Feb. 15, 17–
Apr. 19, 28–June 7, 9–Nov.
21, 23–Dec. 31.

Suplemento: Feb. 9, Mar. 23,
Aug. 3, 10, 24.

1903 Jan. 1–24, 26–Aug. 29, 31–
Sept. 5, 28–Dec. 31.

1904 Jan. 1–Apr. 9, 11–Dec. 31.

1905 Jan. 1–June 24, 26–Aug. 30,
Sept. 6–9, 11–18, 20–23,
25–27, 29–Oct. 2, 4–9, 16–
23, 27–30, Nov. 8–11, 17–
20, 22–29, Dec. 11–18, 22–
27.

1906 Jan. 1–Mar. 10, 12–17, 19–
24, 26–May 12, 14–June 16,
18–23, 25–30, July 2–Dec.
31.

1907 Jan. 1–5, 7–12, 14–19, 21–
26, 28–Feb. 2, 4–23, 25–
Mar. 2, 4–16, 18–Apr. 6, 8–
20, 22–28.

1908 Jan. 5–May 30, June 1–Aug.
9.

LA EVOLUCION. d. est. Feb. 28, 1909.
DLC

1909 Mar. 2–Apr. 1, 3–May 19,
21–25, 27–June 4, 6, 8–10,
12–Dec. 31.

1910 Jan. 1, 2, 4–Feb. 28.

GERMINAL. w. est. Aug. 2, 1908.
DLC

1908 Aug. 2–9, 23–Sept. 27.

EL GRITO DEL PUEBLO. 3w., w., sw.
est. May 3, 1903.
Note: Periodicity May 3–10, 1903,
three times a week; May 17–
June 21, 1903, weekly; after June 25,
1903, semiweekly.
DLC

1903 May 3–Sept. 22, 24–Oct. 3,
8–31, Nov. 2–Dec. 31.

1904 Jan. 1–19, 30–Feb. 2, 4–9,
11–15, 17–Apr. 29, May 1–
29, 31–Dec. 25, 27–31.

1905 Jan. 1–Feb. 4, 6–Mar. 4, 14–
May 20, 22–July 14, 16–Sept.
23, 25–Oct. 7, 9–21, 23–
Nov. 11, 13–18, 20–Dec. 17.

LA HORA.
DLC
 1936   Aug. 15.

HOY. w. est. 1935.
DLC
 1935   Mar. 24, 31, Apr. 28, May 12—
         26, June 9, 23, July 14, Aug. 4,
         Sept. 8—21, Oct. 13—27, Nov.
         24, Dec. 1, 22—29.
 1936   Jan. 5, 19, Feb. 2, 16.

LA IGUALDAD. w. est. [Nov. 17], 1905.
DLC
 1907   Sept. 1—22.
         Suplemento: Feb. 26.
 1908   Jan. 12—Feb. 22, Mar. 8.

EL INDEPENDIENTE. d. est. 1887.
DLC
 1887   Sept. 20—25, 27, 28, 30, Oct.
         2, 3, 5—17, 19—Nov. 6, 9—
         18, 27—Dec. 9, 11—27.
 1888   Jan. 5—15, 17, 18, 20—22, 24,
         25, Feb. 10—20, 22, 25, 26, 28,
         29, Mar. 10—13, 15, 17—19,
         21—28, Apr. 11, 14—May 8,
         15—26.
TxU
 1891   Mar. 2—Aug. 31.

INDUSTRIAS. w. est. Nov. 12, 1922.
DLC
 1924   Feb. 3—24, Mar. 9, 30—Apr.
         27.
 1925   Mar. 8, 22, 29, Apr. 19, 26,
         June 14, 28—July 12, Aug. 16,
         Sept. 3, 20, Oct. 4, Dec. 13—
         20.
 1926   Jan. 10, 24, Feb. 28—Mar. 28,
         Apr. 11—25, May 9, 23, June 6,
         13, 27—July 11, 25, Aug. 29,
         Sept. 5, Oct. 10—17.
 1927   May 29, July 17, Aug. 21.
 1933   Dec. 24.

INFORMACIONES. d. est. 1941.
NN
 1942   Jan. 8, Nov. 16—21, 23, 26, 27,
         Dec. 3, 4, 12, 13, 15, 21, 28, 29.
 1943   Jan. 11, 12, 16, 18—23, 25—

         30, Feb. 1, 2, 4—6, 8—12, 15,
         16, 18—20, 22—27, Mar. 2—6,
         10, 13, 15—18, 29, 30.

KAVICHU-I. w. est. 1941.
DLC
 1942   Jan. 17.

EL LATIGO INMORTAL. est. Aug. 9,
1885.
    Note: Title *El Látigo*, Aug. 9, 1885—
    Apr. 1, 1889; *El Látigo inmortal*,
    after Apr. 7, 1889.
TxU
 1885   Aug. 9—Dec. 31.
 1886   Jan. 1—Dec. 31.
 1887   Jan. 1—June 19, July 10—Dec.
         31.
 1888   Jan. 1—8, 22—Dec. 31.
 1889   Jan. 1—Oct. 13, 27—Nov. 24,
         Dec. 15—31.
 1890   Jan. 1—Dec. 31.
 1891   Jan. 1—May 31, June 14—Aug.
         30.
 1891   Jan. 1—May 31, June 14—Aug.
         30, Sept. 13—Oct. 18, Nov.
         25—Dec. 27.

LA LEY. d. est. Apr. 15, 1906.
DLC
 1907   May 2—Aug. 30, Sept. 1—15,
         17—Oct. 28.
         Suplemento: [Sept. 19.]
 1908   Jan. 1—Mar. 30, Apr. 1—May
         29, 31—June 17, 20—Oct. 7.

EL LIBERAL.
    See *Paraguay*.

LA LIBERTAD. d. est. 1936.
DLC
 1936   Mar. 11.

LA NACION. d. est. Sept. 12, 1908.
DLC
 1908   Sept. 12—17, 20—Nov. 7.

LA NACION. d. est. [1930].
DLC
 1936   Apr. 23.

EL NACIONAL. d.
MH
    1911   Aug. 1.
    1914   Oct. 19, 21.

OPINION. d. est. Dec. 7, 1894.
MWA
    1894   Dec. 7 – 31.
    1895   Jan. 1 – Dec. 31.

EL ORDEN.
    See *El País*.

EL PAIS. d. est. 1901.
DLC
    1903   Nov. 25.

EL PAIS. d. est. Oct. 12, 1923.
    Note: Title *El Orden*, Oct. 12, 1923 –
    Oct. 12, 1935; *El País* after Oct. 12,
    1935.
DLC
    1927   Apr.1 – 9, 11 – 30, May 2 – 16,
              18 – June 14, 20 – 27, 29 – July
              7, 9 – 23, 28 – Aug. 6, 8 – Sept.
              12, 14, 19 – 28, 30, Oct. 1, 5 –
              11, 14 – 29, 31, Nov. 2, 4 – 7,
              9 – 13, 15 – 23, 27 – 30, Dec.
              2 – 18, 20, 21, 27 – 31.
    1928   Jan. 1 – 8, 11 – 18, 20 – 29, Feb.
              1 – 29, Mar. 5, 7 – 11, 15 – 21,
              25 – Apr. 23, 25, 27 – June 19,
              21, 23 – Aug. 19, 21 – 24, 26 –
              Oct. 17, 19 – Dec. 23, 25 – 31.
    1929   Jan. 1, 2, 5, 6, 8 – Feb. 8, 10,
              14, 15, 17 – Apr. 14, 16 – 28,
               30 – May 14, 16 – July 12, 17 –
              Aug. 7, 9 – Sept. 2, 4 – 27, 29,
              31, Oct. 2 – Nov. 5, 9 – Dec.
              29, 31.
    1930   Jan. 1 – Feb. 7, 9 – 26, 28 –
              Apr. 29, May 1 – June 10, 14 –
              19, 22 – 24, 26, 27, 29 – July
              1, 3 – 8, 10 – 13, 15 – 22, 24 –
              30, Aug. 1, 6 – 19, 21 – 25, 28 –
              Oct. 1, 3 – Dec. 25, 27 – 31.
    1931   Jan. 1 – 7, 9 – 22, 24 – 27, 30 –
              Mar. 30, Apr. 5 – 9, 11 – 15,
              17 – May 25, 27 – June 5, 7 –

              Oct. 1, 3 – 21, Nov. 3 – Dec.
              31.
    1933   July 20, Aug. 3, 11, 21 – 23, 28,
              Sept. 16, 20, 22, Dec. 20, 26,
              29.
    1934   Jan. 2, Feb. 7, 15, 16, 26, 27,
              Mar. 16, 19, May 26, 31, June
              2 – 6, 29, July 11, 28 – 31, Aug.
              10, Sept. 12, 13, 15, 22, 26, 27,
              Oct. 2, 3, 8, 11 – 13, 17, 18, 20,
              24, 27, 31, Nov. 5, 9 – 12, 15,
              21 – 23, 29, Dec. 1 – 3, 12, 15,
              18, 21, 22, 29.
    1935   Jan. 3, 4, 5, 8 – 12, 15 – 21, 22,
              23, 26, 31 – Feb. 2, 5, 6, 13, 15,
              20, 23, 27 – Mar. 6, 9, 21, 22,
              28 – 30, Apr. 2, 8, 9, 15, 23,
              25 – 30, May 4 – 7, 13, 17, 21,
              22, 25, June 1, 8 – 12, 17, 20 –
              29, July 11, 12, 16, 18, 19, 31 –
              Aug. 3, 14 – 17, 21 – 24, 29, 31,
              Sept. 3, 7, 11, 13, 16, 18 – 21,
              Oct. 2, 3, 8, 9, 17, 25 – 30, Nov.
              9, 13 – 15, 23 – 26, 29, Dec. 16.
    1936   Jan. 8, 10, 11, 31, Feb. 10.
    1939   Jan. 17, 28, 30 – Feb. 1.
    1941   May 6, 7, 22 – 24, 26, 30, June
              2, 4, 6.
    1942   Feb. 9, 12, 19, 23, 28, Mar. 2,
              7, 9, 12, Aug. 24, Sept. 21 – 23.
    1943   Aug. 12 – 14, Nov. 4.
    1944   Aug. 1, 3 – 6, 8, 10, 12, 13, 15 –
              17, 19 – 30, Sept. 1 – 15, 17,
              18, 20, 22 – Nov. 3, 5 – Dec.
              5, 8 – 25, 27 – 31.
    1945   Jan. 1 – Apr. 27, 29 – May 3,
              5 – 8, 10 – July 31, Aug. 2 –
              Oct. 9, 11 – Dec. 31.
    1946 – 1950   Jan. 1 – Dec. 31.
    1951   Jan. 2 – June 30, July 2 – Dec.
              29.
    1952   Jan. 2 – Apr. 30, May 3 – Aug.
              30, Sept. 1 – Dec. 31.
    1953   Jan. 2 – Apr. 30, May 2 – Dec.
              31.
    1954   Jan. 4 – 7, 10, 11, 13 – May 3,
              8 – July 6, 8 – Sept. 8, 10 – Oct.
              11, 13 – Nov. 16, 18 – Dec. 7,

9−16, 18−31.
1955   Jan. 3−20, 22−May 2, 5−
        Aug. 14, 16−Oct. 20, 23−Dec.
        31.
1960   Jan. 2−Aug. 3, 5−9, 11−14,
        19−Sept. 28, Oct. 7−Dec. 31.
1961   Jan. 2−29, 31−Feb. 24, Mar.
        20−29, Apr. 2−Sept. 1, 14−
        Nov. 9, 17−Dec. 31.
NN
1942   July 1−Dec. 31.
1943   Jan. 1−31.
TxU
1934   Feb. 2, 6, 7, Mar. 8, 9, May 17,
        18, 21, 22, 24, 25, 28, 29, 31−
        June 1, 4, 7, 8, 11, 12, 15, Oct.
        29−Dec. 7, 10−22, 26−29.
1935   Jan. 2−24, 26−Feb. 6, 11, 12,
        14−20, Mar. 21−27.

PARAGUAY. d. est. Dec. 24, 1912.
    Note: Title *El Liberal* Dec. 24,
    1912−[Mar. 16], 1936; *Paraguay*
    after [Mar. 17], 1936.
DLC
1933   July 9, 23, Dec. 24.
1934   Apr. 29, May 20, July 20, Aug.
        7, Sept. 9, 16, 23, 29, Oct. 21,
        Nov. 11, 22, Dec. 8−11, 16,
        23, 28, 30.
1935   Jan. 6, 15, 20−22, 27, Feb. 2,
        3, 17, Mar. 1−3, 17, 31, Apr.
        23, 27−May 1, 12, June 2, 12−
        16, 23, 30, July 11, 21, Aug. 25,
        Sept. 1, 15, 22, 29−Oct. 1,
        Dec. 1.
1936   Jan. 5, 26, Feb. 2, 16, Mar. 25,
        Apr. 3, 15, 21.

EL PARAGUAYO. d. est. 1886.
DLC
1887   Sept. 7, 9, 21, 24−26, 28−Oct.
        2, 4, 7−Nov. 18, 25−27, Dec.
        1−13, 23.
1888   Jan. 5−14, 17−19, 21−26,
        Feb. 11, 16−18, 20, 22, 23,
        25−28, Mar. 11−13, 16, 22,
        28, Apr. 15−25, 28, 29, May
        1−9, 12, 13, 18−23, 25−27.

EL PARAGUAYO. d. est. Sept. 29, 1942.
    Note: Ceased publication Sept. 8,
    1946.
DLC
1942   Sept. 29−Dec. 31.
1943−1945   Jan. 1−Dec. 31.
1946   Jan. 1−Sept. 8.
NN
    Micro (P) & (N)
1943   Nov. 27, Dec. 19, 21, 22, 24,
        25, 28−31.
1944   Jan. 6, 8, 9, 11−23, 26−29,
        Feb. 3, 5, 6, 8, 9, 13, 15, 16,
        18−20, 22−26, Mar. 19, 21,
        22, 24−26, 28−Apr. 2, 4, 5,
        11, 13, 14, 27−29, May 5−7,
        9, 18−21, 28, 30−June 3, 11,
        14−21, 25−27, 29, July 1−5,
        7, 8, 14−16, 19, 20, 23, 30,
        Aug. 2−8.

EL PARAGUAYO INDEPENDIENTE.
    w., irr. est. Apr. 26, 1845.
    Note: Official gazette of Paraguay.
DLC
    Micro (P)
1845   Apr. 26−Dec. 31.
        Suplemento: Sept. 17.
1846−1851   Jan. 1−Dec. 31.
1852   Jan. 1−Sept. 18.
TxU
1850   Sept. 28.
WU
1845   Apr. 26−Dec. 31.
1846−1851   Jan. 1−Dec. 31.
1852   Jan. 1−Sept. 18.

LA PATRIA; DIARIO INDEPEN-
DIENTE. d.
    Note: Suspended publication Mar.
    14−May 1, 1908.
DLC
1902   Sept. 24, Dec. 29.
1907   May 2−12, 16, 18−28, 31−
        June 21, 23, 24, 26, 28−July
        19, 21−Aug. 21, 23−25, 27−
        29, Sept. 1, 5, 8−16, 18−22,
        24, 25, 28−Oct. 29, Nov. 3−7,
        9−11, 16−18, 20−Dec. 31.

1908   Jan. 1—July 1, 5—9, 11—Sept.
        20, 22—Oct. 7.

LA PATRIA; DIARIO COLORADO. d.
    est. [1932].
    Note: Suspended publication Feb.
    15, 1933—[1934].
    DLC
    1933   Feb. 14.

PATRIA. d. est. 1946.
    DLC
    Micro (P) & (N)
    1962   Jan. 1+.

PATRIA.
    See *Union.*

PREGON. d. est. 1938.
    DLC
    1942   Aug. 22.

LA PRENSA. d. est. 1934.
    DLC
    1934   Nov. 17, Dec. 7, 15, 19.
    1935   Jan. 7, 14, 16, Feb. 6, 21, Mar.
            30, Apr. 25, 26, May 22, 23,
            June 10, 11, 22, 27, July 10, 17,
            20, 27, Aug. 1, 3, 31, Sept. 4,
            Nov. 13.
    1936   Feb. 22, Mar. 9, 12, 14, Apr. 24.

LOS PRINCIPIOS. w. est. Sept. 5, 1908.
    DLC
    1908   Sept. 5—Dec. 11, 13—31.
    1909   Jan. 1—22, 24—Feb. 5, 7—
            12, 14—Mar. 26, Apr. 11—May
            28, 30—June 11, 13—26.

PUEBLO. d. est. Feb. 15, 1894.
    Note: Ceased publication [1896].
    MWA
    1894   Feb. 15—Dec. 31.
    1895   Jan. 1—Dec. 31.

LA RAZON. d. est. [1940].
    CSt
    1941   Jan. 10—12.

LA RAZON.
    See *La Unión.*

ROJO Y AZUL. w., 3m., sw. est. Dec. 31,
    1905.
    Note: Periodicity before Aug. 11,
    1907, weekly; Aug. 20—Oct. 20, 1907,
    three times a month; Oct. 27, 1907—
    Aug. 2, 1908, weekly; Aug. 6—Sept.
    27, 1908, semiweekly; after Oct. 4,
    1908, weekly. Suspended publication
    July 8—Oct. 7, 1906; Dec. 31, 1907—
    Feb. 9, 1908.
    DLC
    1906   Mar. 25—31, Apr. 2—28, 30—
            June 30, July 2—7, 9—Dec.
            22, 24—31.
    1907   Jan. 1—Feb. 9, 11—Dec. 31.
    1908   Jan. 1—Dec. 31.

LOS SUCESOS. d. est. 1906.
    DLC
    1907   May 2, 4—Apr. 14.

LA TARDE. d. est. [Mar. 25], 1903.
    DLC
    1904   May 3—July 12, 14—17, 19,
            21—28, 30—Aug. 1, 3—Oct.
            27, 29—Nov. 20, 22—24, 26—
            Dec. 31.
    1905   Jan. 1—8, 11—20, 22, 29, Feb.
            1, 2, 5—16, 18—27, Mar. 6, 13,
            20, 27, Apr. 3, 10, 17, 24, May
            1, 5, 6, 11, 14, 21, 28, June 4,
            11, 18, 25, July 2, 9—25, 30,
            Aug. 2, 3.

EL TIEMPO. d. est. 1912.
    Note: Ceased publication [1946].
    DLC
    1941   June 20, 21, 24—29, July 2, 3,
            Aug. 23, Nov. 1—12, 14—29,
            Dec. 3—7, 11—14, 17—21,
            23—25, 27, 28, 30, 31.
    1942   Jan. 1—13, 15—Feb. 13, 15—
            17, 19—Mar. 11, 13—24, 26—
            30, Apr. 1, 6—10, 12—25, 27—
            May 15, 17—June 9, 11—14,
            30—Nov. 4.

LA TRIBUNA. d. est. Dec. 31, 1925.
    CLU
    1965   Jan. 7—Mar. 3, 26—Apr. 7, 15,

18 – June 21, 23 – July 14,
22 – Aug. 12, 14 – Sept. 15, 23,
24, 26 – 28, Oct. 15 – 20, 28 –
Dec. 31.
1966   Jan. 1+.
DLC
1933   July 13, Aug. 3, 21, 22, Oct. 6.
1934   Jan. 29, Mar. 10, 17, June 26,
July 23, 26, Aug. 2, 27, Sept.
7, 13, 20, Nov. 19, Dec. 5, 18,
21.
1935   Jan. 10, 14, 18, Mar. 12, Apr.
25, 29, May 31, June 12 – 15,
Aug. 23, 30, Oct. 28, Nov. 28.
1939   Jan. 30 – Feb. 4.
1941   June 10, 13 – 23.
1942   Aug. 25.
1943   Nov. 2.
1944   Aug. 1 – 13, 16 – 22, 25 – Dec.
7, 10 – 31.
1945   Jan. 1 – Apr. 1, 3 – May 25,
27 – June 1, 3 – Sept. 3, 5 –
Dec. 31.
1946   Jan. 1 – Feb. 21, 23 – Apr. 27,
29 – Dec. 31.
1947 – 1948   Jan. 1 – Dec. 31.
1949   Jan. 1 – Feb. 5, 7 – Dec. 31.
1950   Jan. 1 – Dec. 31.
1951   Jan. 3 – Dec. 31.
1952   Jan. 3 – Aug. 3, 5 – Dec. 31.
1953   Jan. 3 – Dec. 31.
1954   Jan. 3 – 19, 21 – 27, 29 – Mar.
20, 25 – 28, 30 – Apr. 24, 29,
30, May 3, 7 – 22, 27 – June 9,
17 – July 3, 8 – Aug. 25, 27 –
Sept. 2, 4 – 12, 14 – 27, 29 –
Oct. 23, 25 – Dec. 18, 20 – 31.
1955   Jan. 3 – Feb. 2, 4 – June 10,
12 – Sept. 10, 12 – Oct. 10,
16 – 18, 20 – 22, Nov. 16, 17,
19 – 23, Dec. 1, 2, 4 – 7, 11, 12,
14.
Micro (P)
1956   July 1+.
DPU
Current (six months).
FU
Current (two years).

ICRL
Micro (P) & (N)
1956   Jan. 1+.
MH
1919   Dec. 3 – 31.
1920   Jan. 1.
NN
Micro (P) & (N)
1942   July 31, Aug. 5, 6, 16 – 19, 22,
25 – 29, Sept. 2, 15, 28, 30 –
Oct. 2, 15 – 17, 22 – 24, 27 –
31, Nov. 2 – 21, Dec. 3 – 5, 21,
22, 29.
1943   Jan. 12, 18 – 30, Feb. 1 – 27,
Mar. 2 – 6, 9 – 20, 25 – 27.

UNION. d. est. Apr. 19, 1894.
Note: Title *Patria*, Apr. 19 – June 10,
1894; *Unión*, after June 11, 1894.
MWA
1894   Apr. 19 – June 8, 11 – Nov. 30.

LA UNION. d. est. Sept. 10, 1946.
Note: Title *La Razón*, Sept. 10,
1946 – Dec. 15, 1948; *La Unión* after
Dec. 16, 1948. Suspended publication
May 2 – July 31, 1948.
DLC
1946   Sept. 10 – Dec. 31.
1947 – 1948   Jan. 1 – Dec. 31.
1949   Jan. 1 – Feb. 12, 15 – Dec. 7,
10 – 31.
1950   Jan. 3 – 6, 8 – Mar. 20, 22 –
May 17, 19 – 24, 26 – Sept. 13,
15 – Oct. 27, 30, 31, Nov. 3 –
Dec. 31.
1951   Jan. 3 – Mar. 17, 19 – May 24,
27 – Dec. 31.
1952   Jan. 3 – Aug. 31, Sept. 2 – Dec.
27, 29 – 31.
1953   Jan. 1 – June 11, 14 – Dec. 31.
1954   Jan. 1 – 6, 9 – 22, 24 – Feb. 7,
10 – 15, 17 – Mar. 12.

LA UNION LATINA. w. est. Feb. 5,
1905.
DLC
1906   Jan. 3 – 9, Dec. 27 – 31.
1907   Jan. 1, Apr. 25 – May 21, 23 –

28, 30 — Dec. 31.
1908   Jan. 1 — Sept. 8, 10 — 22, 24 —
       Oct. 14, 21 — Sept. 8, 10 — 22,
       Oct. 14, 22 — Dec. 31.
1909   Jan. 1 — 26, Feb. 4 — Mar. 2,
       4 — 23, 25 — Apr. 27, 29 — June
       23.

UNION NACIONAL. w. est. Nov. 1933.
  DLC
  1933   Dec. 3.

LA VERDAD. sw. est. June 18, 1908.
  DLC
  1908   June 18 — 28.

LA VERDAD. d. est. Sept. 14, 1908.
  DLC
  1908   Sept. 14 — 30, Oct. 2 — 16, 18 —
         23, 25 — Nov. 1, 3, 5 — 11, 15 —
         22, 27 — Dec. 6, 10 — 23, 25 —
         27, 29 — 31.
         Suplemento: n.d.
  1909   Jan. 3 — Feb. 4, 6 — Mar. 2, 4, 6,
         7, 9 — 16, 18 — Apr. 6, 11 — 20,
         23 — 25, 27, May 1, 2, 9, 11 —
         16, 18, 20 — 22, 24 — July 7, 9 —
         15, 17 — 22, 24 — Sept. 10, 12 —
         19, 21 — Oct. 1, 3 — 6, 8 — 10,
         12 — Nov. 11, 14 — Dec. 1, 3 —
         23, 26 — 31.
  1910   Jan. 1 — Mar. 7, 9 — 14.

VERDE OLIVO. d. est. Feb. 1936.
  DLC
  1936   Mar. 7, 16.

LA VOZ DEL PUEBLO. w. est. 1933.
  Note: In Spanish and Guaraní.
  DLC
  1934   May 7 — 14, June 4, Aug. 6, 27,
         Sept. 3, 24.
  1935   May 27.

Concepción

RESTAURACION. w. est. [Jan. 1942].
  DLC
  1942   Aug. 19.

Piribebui

ESTRELLA. sw. est. Feb. 24, 1869.

Note: Semi-official publication.
  DLC
  1869   Feb. 24 — July 10.
  NN
  1869   Feb. 24 — Mar. 24, 31 — Apr.
         17, May 1.

Villarrica

EL PUEBLO. d. est. [1938].
  DLC
  1942   Aug. 23.

EL SURCO. w. est. [1924].
  DLC
  1942   July 29.

PERU
Arequipa

AREQUIPA LIBRE. w. est. May 10, 1827.
  Note: Ceased publication Mar. 17,
  1830.
  CtY
  1827   June 14, 28.
  1828   Feb. 12, Mar. 18, Sept. 30,
         Dec. 2 — 16.
  1829   Jan. 13, Feb. 24, Mar. 10, 24,
         Apr. 7, 21.

ARIETE. w.
  MWA
  1909   Nov. 27.

BOLSA. irr., d. est. 1860.
  Note: Periodicity 1860 — Mar. 29,
  1901, irregular; after Mar. 30, 1901,
  daily.
  MWA
  1879   Aug. 1.
  1888   July 2.
  1892   June 25.
  1893   Jan. 20.
  1901   Mar. 29.
  1905   Oct. 2, Nov. 7, 8.
  1906   [Feb. 1 — June 21].

DEBER. d.
  MWA
  1891   Jan. 16, 23.

LA LUZ. 3m.
  MWA
    1913   July 10, Aug. 10.

EL MAESTRO DE ESCUELA. sw. est.
  Oct. 12, 1839.
  CtY
    1839   Oct. 12.

EL NACIONAL. sw. est. Oct. 30, 1844.
    Note: Ceased publication [Mar. 14],
    1845.
  CtY
    1844   Nov. 1 – 28.
    1845   Feb. 7 – Mar. 14.

NOTICIAS. d. est. Jan. 6, 1927.
  DLC
    1941   Sept. 3, 9, 10, 12 – 24, 26 – 29,
            Oct. 3 – 5, 8, 10, 11, 13.
    1942   Jan. 21, 28, Feb. 1, Apr. 3, 5, 6,
            10, 12, 14 – 16, 25, 26, Aug. 7 –
            10.
    1943   Jan. 17, 24, 30, 31, Feb. 9 –
            11, 13, 25, Apr. 16 – 26, 28 –
            May 2, 5 – 8, 10, 12, 13, 18,
            20 – June 3, 5 – 10, 17 – 19, 21,
            23 – 26, 28, 30 – July 12, 14,
            15, 18 – 23, 26, 30, Aug. 1, 4,
            5, 7, 9, 13, 15, 17 – 19, 23, 25 –
            Sept. 2, 4 – 11, 13, 14, 16 – 18,
            20, 22 – 27, Oct. 29 – Nov. 1,
            5 – 7, 10, 11, 13 – 15, 17, 20,
            22, 25 – 27, Dec. 1, 2, 4 – 9,
            12 – 19, 21 – 31.
    1944   Jan. 2 – 9, 11, 13 – 17, 21 – 31.
    1952   Jan. 6.

EL PENSADOR. irr. est. Oct. 7, 1834.
    Note: Ceased publication Dec. 10,
    1834.
  CtY
    1834   Nov. 22, Dec. 6 – 10.

PUEBLO. d.
  MWA
    1905   Nov. 3 – 9.

EL REPUBLICANO. w., sw. est. Nov.
  26, 1825.
  CtY
    1825   Prospecto.

    1828   Oct. 25.
    1829   Oct. 10.
    1831   Suplemento (No. 6).
    1832   Jan. 7 – Dec. 29.
    1835   Jan. 3.
  DLC
    1826   Aug. 5, Sept. 9, 16.
    1827   July 7.
    1828   Sept. 13.
            Suplemento: Sept. 12.
    1829   Mar. 7.
  MWA
    1826   Oct. 28.
    1837   Mar. 8.
    1845   Jan. 18 – 25.
    1852   Mar. 10.

EL REVISOR. w. est. Mar. 9, 1831.
    Note: Suspended publication Apr.
    28 – June 19, 1831; ceased publication
    Aug. 26, 1831.
  CtY
    1831   Prospecto: Mar. 2.
            Mar. 9 – June 19.

REVISTA DEL SUR. d. est. Jan. 8, 1886.
  MWA
    1889   Apr. 17, June 6 – 11, 14 – 22,
            Dec. 27.
    1890   Apr. 9.

SANCION. w.
  MWA
    1892   June 4.

VOZ DE LA VERDAD. w.
  MWA
    1885   July 25, Aug. 22.

Arica
See Chile. Arica.

Ayacucho

EL AYACUCHANO. w., irr. est. [May]
  1835.
  CtY
    1835   May 23 – Aug. 24, Sept. 13 –
            Nov. 12.

EL CADETE EN JEFE.
    See *El Supremo cadete en jefe.*

EL DEMOCRATA. irr. est. Nov. 28, 1850.
  Note: Ceased publication Feb. 1,
  1851.
  CtY
    1850   Nov. 28 – Dec. 20.
    1851   Jan. 21 – Feb. 1.

LA OLIVA DE AYACUCHO. irr. est. July
  1833.
  CtY
    1833   Dec. 23.
  DLC
    1833   Dec. 17.

RESTAURADOR DE AYACUCHO. irr.
  MWA
    1845   Jan. 4 – 15.

EL SUPREMO CADETE EN JEFE. d. est.
  Dec. 4, 1835.
    Note: Title varies *El Cadete en jefe*.
  CU – B
    Micro (N)
    1835   Dec. 4, 10 – 29.
    1836   Jan. 4.

VICTORIOSO. sw.
  MWA
    1835   Dec. 26.

Callao

EL CALLAO. d. est. Nov. 2, 1883.
  DLC
    1941   Apr. 27, June 18 – 22, 27 – 29,
            July 9, 10, 14, Aug. 9, 10, 12 –
            14, 20, 29, Sept. 1, 12.
    1942   Feb. 22, Apr. 25, 27, Aug. 23.
    1943   July 4, Aug. 17, Sept. 7, 23,
            Oct. 29, Nov. 2 – 6, 8 – Dec.
            21, 23 – 26, 28 – 30.
    1944   June 1 – 6, 9 – July 31, Aug.
            15 – Dec. 31.
    1945   Jan. 1 – 19, 21 – Mar. 18, 20,
            22 – Aug. 16, 18 – Dec. 31.
    1946   Jan. 1 – Aug. 24, 26 – Sept. 4,
            6, 7, 9 – Oct. 10, 12 – 30, Nov.
            1 – 14, 16 – Dec. 19, 21, 23 –
            31.
    1947   Jan. 1 – 3, 5 – 7, 10 – Mar. 16,
            18 – May 31, June 2, 14, 16 –

            Sept. 1, 3 – 6, 8, 9, 12 – 29,
            31 – Oct. 15, 17 – Dec. 31.
    1948   Jan. 1 – June 30.
    1949   Oct. 1, Nov. 18, 21, 22, 24 –
            26, 29, 30, Dec. 2 – 17, 20 –
            30.
    1950   Jan. 1 – 27, Feb. 1 – 6, 8 – 15,
            17 – Mar. 9, 11 – 15, 17 – Apr.
            28, May 2 – 17, 24, 25.
  MWA
    1889   June 12, Sept. 17 – 19.

EL COMERCIO. d. est. May 4, 1839.
  Note: Removed from Lima, Dec. 1,
  1881; returned to Lima, Oct. 23,
  1883.
  CtY
    1881   Dec. 1 – 31.
    1882   Jan. 1 – Dec. 31.
    1883   Jan. 1 – Oct. 22.
  NcD
    1881   Dec. 1 – 31.
    1882   Jan. 1 – Nov. 26, 28, 29, Dec.
            1 – 31.
    1883   Jan. 1 – June 30.

EL DEPOSITARIO. irr. est. 1821.
  Note: Established in Lima and removed to the interior (Yucay and
  Cuzco) in 1821; removed to Callao
  in 1823. Ceased publication ₁May 1₁,
  1825.
  CtY
    1824   Aug. 25 – Sept. 13, Nov. 9 –
            Dec. 17, 25.
    1825   Jan. 15 – Apr. 7, 24 – May 1.

EL DESENGAÑO. irr. est. Apr. 1, 1824.
  Note: Ceased publication Jan. 12,
  1825.
  CU – B
    Micro (N)
    1824   Apr. 15 – Sept. 27, Oct. 15 –
            29, Nov. 9, 21 – Dec. 30.
  CtY
    1824   Apr. 15 – June 17, July 1 –
            Sept. 27, Oct. 15 – 29, Nov. 9,
            21 – Dec. 30.

THE FOREIGN NEWS. w. est. 1854.
  Note: In English.
  DLC
    1855   Feb. 17.

LA FORTALEZA. w., sw. est. Feb. 6,
  1839.
  CU – B
    Micro (N)
    1839   Feb. 6 – Mar. 5.
  DLC
    1839   Feb. 23, Mar. 2.

EL INTRANSIGENTE. w. est. 1932.
  DLC
    1942   Feb. 1.
    1943   July 14.

EL PLAYERO. sw., w. est. Jan. 15, 1834.
  Note: Ceased publication Mar. 11,
  1834.
  CU – B
    Micro (N)
    1834   Jan. 15 – Feb. 5.

LA SANCION. w. est. 1913.
  DLC
    1941   Apr. 12, 26, June 22 – 29, Aug.
            9 – 16, Sept. 6 – 13, 27.
    1942   Jan. 17, Mar. 21 – 28, Apr. 4,
            25, May 16 – 24, June 6 – 13.

THE SOUTH PACIFIC TIMES. 3w., d.
  est. May 2, 1872.
  Note: In Spanish and English.
  CU – B
    Micro (N)
    1872   May 2 – Oct. 31.

Cerro de Pasco

MINERO. w.
  MWA
    1913   June 18.

RESTAURADOR; PERIODICO OFI-
  CIAL DE JUNIN. w.
  MWA
    1845   Jan. 18.

Chiclayo

ABEJA. w.
  MWA
    1913   June 29.

PROGRESO. d.
  MWA
    1913   June 24.

Cuzco

APU-RIMAC. irr.
  MWA
    1851   Jan. 25.

AURORA PERUANA.
  MWA
    1835   Sept. 5.

EL CAMPEON DE LA INDEPENDEN-
  CIA PERUANA. est. July 30, 1835.
  CtY
    1835   July 30.

EL CENSOR ECLESIASTICO. est. May
  5, 1825.
  CtY
    1825   Prospecto: Apr. 14.
            May 5.

EL COMERCIO. d. est. 1896.
  DLC
    1924   Dec. 27.
            Suplemento: Dec. 9.

EL DESPERTADOR POLITICO. irr. est.
  Oct. 22, 1835.
  CtY
    1835   Oct. 22.

DEMOCRATA AMERICANO. w.
  MWA
    1851   June 30.

EL ECO DE LA OPINION. est. Jan. 3,
  1841.
  CtY
    1841   Jan. 3 – 8.

EL ECO DE SOCABAYA. irr. est. [1837].
  Note: Ceased publication [June 1],
  1838.
  CtY
    1837   Nov. 25.
    1838   May 10 – June 1.

LA ESTRELLA FEDERAL. sw. est. 1836.
  Note: Ceased publication Jan. 1, 1839.
  CtY
    1838   May 30 — June 7.
  DLC
    1836 — 1837   [Jan. 1 — Dec. 31].

ESTADO SUD PERUANO.
  MWA
    1837   n.d.

FERROCARRIL. w.
  MWA
    1870   May 26.

JENIO DEL CUZCO. w. est. Sept. 18,
  1834.
  CtY
    1834   Sept. 18, Oct. 1 — 15.

LIBERTAD. w.
  MWA
    1888   May 2.

LA LIBERTAD RESTAURADA. irr. est.
  Jan. 1839.
  Note: Ceased publication [1841].
  CU — B
    Micro (N)
    1839   Dec. 21.
  CtY
    1839   May 25 — June 5.
            Extraordinario: June 11, 29.
    1840   Jan. 11 — Aug. 29, Sept. 12 —,
            Dec. 30.
    1841   Jan. 23 — Oct. 30.

MINERVA DEL CUZCO. w. est. Sept. 5,
  1829.
  Note: Ceased publication Mar. 29,
  1834.
  CtY
    1829   Sept. 5 — Dec. 26.
    1830   Jan. 2 — Aug. 14, 28 — Dec. 25.
    1831 — 1832   Jan. 1 — Dec. 31.
    1833   Jan. 5 — Aug. 31.

EL PABELLON NACIONAL. irr. est.
  Dec. 24, 1841.
  CtY
    1841   Dec. 24.
    1842   Jan. 1 — Mar. 17.

EL PACIFICADOR DEL PERU. sw., irr.
  est. Mar. 25, 1835.
  Note: Ceased publication July 31,
  1835.
  CtY
    1835   Mar. 25 — July 31.
            Extraordinarios.

EL REJENERADOR PERUANO. w. est.
  Jan. 6, 1841.
  CtY
    1841   Jan. 6 — 13.

EL RESTAURADOR. sw. est. Nov. 6,
  1841.
  CtY
    1841   Nov. 6 — Dec. 29.
    1842   Jan. 5 — Dec. 14.

EL SOL DEL CUZCO. w. est. Jan. 1,
  1825.
  Note: "Fulgente sole naturae tene-
  brae fugiunt" in place of title, Nov. 4,
  1826 — Mar. 21, 1827. Ceased publication Aug. 29, 1829.
  CtY
    1825   Jan. 1 — Dec. 30.
    1826   Jan. 7 — Nov. 25, Dec. 9 — 30.
    1827   Jan. 6 — Dec. 15.
  MWA
    1826   June 24, July 15, Sept. 2, Oct.
            21.
    1827   Mar. 31.
    1829   Apr. 25.

EL TIEMPO. w. est. Oct. 22, 1842.
  CtY
    1842   Oct. 22 — Nov. 2.

EL TRIUNFO DEL PUEBLO; PERIODI-
  CO OFICIAL. w., irr. est. Dec. 16,
  1843.
  Note: Ceased publication 1854.
  CtY
    1843   Dec. 16 — Apr. 6, 13 — Dec. 28.
    1845 — 1850   Jan. 1 — Dec. 31.
    1851   Jan. 4 — Oct. 11.
    1853   Jan. 1 — Oct. 22.
    1854   Jan. 1 — Oct. 12.

Huamachuco

CENTINELA EN CAMPAÑA. irr. est.
Apr. 22, 1824.
MWA
1824   Prospecto: Apr. 22.
May 4.

Huancavelica

OBRERO. bw.
MWA
1912   Sept. 30.
1913   Apr. 30 – May 15.

Huáncayo

LA PRENSA. d. est. 1932.
DLC
1941   May 17, June 9 – 11, 15, 16, 18,
23 – 25, Aug. 26, 29.

LA VOZ DE HUANCAYO.
MWA
1913   June 28, July 29.

Huánuco

EL ECO DE LA MONTAÑA. est. 1829.
DLC
1829   May 25.

HUALLAGA.
MWA
1912   Sept. 30.

IMPARCIAL. w.
MWA
1913   June 7 – 14.

SANCION.
MWA
1913   Jan. 25.

Huaura

REDACTOR.
MWA
1836   Extraordinario: Aug. 6.

Huarás

ACCION AUCASHINA. est. 1926.
DLC
1926   Sept. 17.

Ica

LA VOZ DE ICA. d. est. 1918.
CU
1957   July 1 – 11, 13 – 26, Aug. 1 –
Sept. 16, 19, 23 – 28, Oct. 1 –
26, 29 – Nov. 8, 11 – Dec. 2,
6 – 10, 13 – 16, 18, 19, 23 – 31.
1958   Jan. 2 – 20, 22 – 30, Feb. 1 – 25,
27 – Mar. 8, 11 – Apr. 22, 24 –
May 3, 6, 8, 9, 12 – 19, 21 – 26.

Iquitos

COMERCIO. d.
MWA
1913   Aug. 16, 22.

ORIENTE. d. est. Aug. 16, 1905.
MWA
1913   July 10, 12.

LA RAZON. d. est. [1915].
DLC
1941   Jan. 1.

LA SELVA. d. est. 1937.
DLC
1940   July 28.

Jauja

EL RAYO DE JUNIN. irr. est. Mar. 24,
1835.
CtY
1835   Mar. 24.

Lima

LA ABEJA REPUBLICANA. sw., w. est.
Aug. 4, 1822.
Note: Ceased publication June 7,
1823.
CtY
1822   Prospecto.
n.d. (Aug. 4) – Dec. 5, 14 – 28.
1823   Jan. 4 – June 7.

ADELANTE. d. est. Jan. 13, 1949.
TxU
1949   Jan. 13 – Mar. 18.

AHORA GRAFICA. w. est. Mar. 11, 1955.
TxU
1955   Mar. 11 – Dec. 31.

1956   Jan. 1 – June 27.

ALBUM. w. est. 1874.
  MWA
    1874   June 20 – July 11.

LA AMERICA. sw. est. Apr. 5, 1862.
    Note: Suspended publication Jan. 29,
    1863 – Apr. 30, 1864; ceased publica-
    tion Dec. 9, 1865.
  CtY
    1862   Apr. 5 – Dec. 31.
    1863   Jan. 7 – 28.
    1864   May 1 – June 30.

EL AMERICANO. est. July 10, 1821.
    Note: Published only three numbers.
    Succeeded by *Los Andes libres*.
    Ceased publication July 14, 1821.
  CtY
    1821   July 10.

EL AMIGO DEL PUEBLO. 3w. est. Mar.
  21, 1840.
    Note: Ceased publication Sept. 19,
    1840.
  DLC
    1840   Mar. 21 – Sept. 19.

ANDEAN AIR MAIL AND PERUVIAN
  TIMES. w. est. Sept. 22, 1961.
    Note: In English.
  CSt – H
    1963   Aug. 16, Sept. 7, 14 – Oct. 24,
            26 – Nov. 21, 23 – Dec. 19.
    1964   Jan. 1 – Feb. 21, Sept. 5 – 24,
            Oct. 29 – Nov. 12, 21 – Dec. 3,
            5 – 31.
    1965   Jan. 1+.
  CoDU
    1961   Sept. 22 – Dec. 31.
    1962 – 1963   Jan. 1 – Dec. 31.
    1964   Jan. 1 – Sept. 25, Oct. 9, 23 –
            Dec. 31.
    1965   Jan. 1 – Dec. 31.
    1966   Jan. 7 – Feb. 18, Mar. 11+.
  IU
    1963   Jan. 1+.
  RPB

1962   July 1 – Dec. 31.
1963   Jan. 1+.

LOS ANDES LIBRES. w. est. July 24,
  1821.
    Note: Succeeded *El Americano*; suc-
    ceeded by *Correo mercantil político
    y literario del Perú*. Ceased publica-
    tion Dec. 6, 1821.
  CtY
    1821   July 24 – Dec. 6.

ANHELOS. w. est. Feb. 26, 1949.
  TxU
    1949   Feb. 26 – Mar. 12.

ANTI-ARGOS. w., irr. est. Feb. 11, 1813.
    Note: Ceased publication Mar. 12,
    1813.
  CU – B
    Micro (N)
    1813   Feb. 11 – Mar. 12.
  CtY
    1813   Feb. 11 – Mar 12.

LA ANTORCHA. d. est. Oct. 1, 1834.
    Note: Ceased publication Oct. 11,
    1834.
  CtY
    1834   Prospecto: Sept. 23.
            Oct. 1 – 11.

LA ANTORCHA PERUANA. 3w. est.
  [Apr.] 1839.
  CtY
    1839   May 1.

ARGOS CONSTITUCIONAL DE LIMA.
  w. est. Feb. 7, 1813.
    Note: Ceased publication Mar. 21,
    1813.
  CU – B
    Micro (N)
    1813   Prospecto.
            Feb. 7 – Mar. 21.
  CtY
    1813   Feb. 7 – Mar. 21.

EL ARGOS DE LA LIBERTAD. d. est.
  Feb. 21, 1834.
    Note: Ceased publication Feb. 28,
    1834.

CtY
1834   Feb. 21 – 28.

LA AURORA PERUANA. sw. est. Oct.
6, 1838.
CU – B
Micro (N)
1838   Oct. 6 – Dec. 31.
1839   Jan. 1 – Feb. 3.
CtY
1838   Oct. 6 – Nov. 7.
DLC
1838   Oct. 31.

LA BALA ROJA. irr. est. Aug. 10, 1844.
CtY
1844   Aug. 10.

BANDERA POPULAR. est. July 16,
1948.
TxU
1948   July 16 – Aug. 27.

BANDERA ROJA. w.
CSt – H
1964   Aug. 29, Oct. 2.

EL BANQUILLO. w. est. Apr. 17, 1880.
CtY
1880   Apr. 17 – July 3.

BOLETIN INFORMATIVO DE LA
ALIANZA NATIONAL. w., bw. est.
Jan. 15, 1948.
NcD
1948   May 6 – Dec. 15.
TxU
1948   Jan. 15 – Nov. 1.

LA BOLSA. d. est. Jan. 11, 1841.
Note: Ceased publication 1878.
CtY
1841   Jan. 11 – Dec. 31.
1842   Jan. 3 – Mar. 18, 22 – June 23,
27, 30 – July 1, 4 – Aug. 31.
LNHT
1841   Oct. 1 – Dec. 31.

EL BOTAFUEGO. irr. est. Oct. 6, 1828.
CtY
1828   Oct. 6 – Dec. 13.
1829   Jan. 3 – May 16.

EL BUFALO. irr. est. 1961.
CU
1961   Nos. 1 – 3.

EL BUSCA-PIQUE. irr. est. Dec. 2, 1838.
Note: Ceased publication [Dec. 8,
1838].
CtY
1838   Dec. 2 – 8.

EL CALLAO EN REHENES. w. est. May
19, 1837.
DLC
1837   May 19 – 26.

EL CAÑON. d. est. Jan. 2, 1833.
Note: Ceased publication Jan. 31,
1833.
CtY
1832   Prospecto.
1833   Jan. 2 – 4, 7 – 28.
DLC
1833   Jan. 2 – 31.

CAPITAL. d.
MWA
1878   Nov. 20, 22.

EL CATOLICO CRISTIANO. [w.] est.
May 12, 1855.
CtY
1855   May 12 – 19.

EL CENSOR. irr. est. Mar 15, 1821.
Note: Ceased publication May 3,
1821.
CU – B
Micro (N)
1821   Mar. 15 – May 3.
CtY
1821   Mar. 15 – May 3.

EL CENSOR ECONOMICO. irr. est. Mar.
1821.
CU – B
Micro (N)
1821   Mar. 24 – May 28.
CtY
1821   Mar. 24 – May 28.

LA CENTELLA. irr. est. June 13, 1834.
CtY
1834   June 13 – Aug. 4.

EL CENTINELA DE LA LIBERTAD. sw.
est. Apr. 22, 1831.
  Note: Ceased publication June 23,
  1831.
  CtY
    1831   Apr. 22 — May 18, 25, June 4 —
            23.

EL CHICOTE. irr.
  CtY
    1834   Feb. 9 — Mar. 18.

EL COCO DE SANTA CRUZ. irr. est.
  Sept. 17, 1835.
    Note: Ceased publication Dec. 23,
    1835.
  CU — B
    Micro (N)
    1835   Sept. 17 — Dec. 23.
  CtY
    1835   Sept. 17 — Oct. 28.

EL COMERCIO. d. est. May 4, 1839.
    Note: Removed to Callao, Dec. 1,
    1881 — Oct. 22, 1883.
  CLU
    1965   Jan. 30 — Feb. 5, 13 — 28, Mar.
            1 — 13, 16 — Aug. 18, 21 — Oct.
            1, 9 — Dec. 31.
    1966   Jan. +.
  CLSU
    Micro (P)
    1954   Jan. 1 — Feb. 28.
  CU — B
    Micro (P) & (N)
    1839   May 4 — July 18, 20 — Dec. 31.
    1840   Jan. 1 — Dec. 31.
    1841   Jan. 4 — May 18, 21 — Dec. 31.
            Suplemento: Jan. 2.
    1842   Jan. 1 — Dec. 31.
    1843   Jan. 2 — Feb. 17, 20 — Aug. 29,
            Sept. 1 — Dec. 31.
    1844   Jan. 1 — Dec. 31.
    1845   Jan. 2 — Dec. 31.
    1846   Jan. 2 — Aug. 21, 24 — Oct. 27,
            29 — Dec. 31.
    1847   Jan. 1 — Dec. 31.
    1848   Jan. 2 — Aug. 31, Sept. 2 — 4,
            6 — Nov. 7, 9 — 28, 30 — Dec. 30.
    1849   Jan. 2 — Nov. 20.

    1851   Jan. 2 — July 9, 11 — Nov. 29,
            Dec. 2 — 31.
    1853   Jan. 4 — Dec. 7, 10 — 31.
    1854   Jan. 2 — July 14, Nov. 2 — Dec.
            31.
    1855   Jan. 2 — 30.
  Micro (N)
    1891   Sept. 3 — 23.
  CtY
    1839   Oct. 28 — Dec. 31.
    1840 — 1843   Jan. 1 — Dec. 31.
    1847 — 1854   Jan. 1 — Dec. 31.
    1856   Jan. 2 — Dec. 31.
    1857 — 1858   Jan. 1 — Dec. 31.
    1859   Jan. 1 — Dec. 29.
    1866   Jan. 2 — June 30.
    1867 — 1868   Jan. 1 — Dec. 31.
    1871   Jan. 2 — Dec. 31.
    1877   July 2 — Dec. 31.
    1878   Jan. 1 — Dec. 31.
    1884   July 1 — Dec. 31.
    1885 — 1888   Jan. 1 — Dec. 31.
    1889   Jan. 1 — July 31.
    1892   Jan. 2 — June 30.
    1897 — 1904   Jan. 1 — Dec. 31.
    1906 — 1908   Jan. 1 — Dec. 31.
    1909   Jan. 1 — June 30.
    1911   [Sept. 1 — Dec. 31].
    1912   Feb. 1 — May 31, Apr. 2, June
            1 — Nov. 3, 4, 6 — 8, 10 — 12.
    1913   Jan. 1 — Feb. 1, Mar. 1 — Dec.
            31.
    1925   Jan. 1 — Dec. 31.
    1926   Jan. 1 — Mar. 31, May 1 — Nov.
            31.
    1927 — 1928   Jan. 1 — Dec. 31.
    1929   Jan. 1 — June 4, July 1 — Dec.
            31.
    1930 — 1942   Jan. 1 — Dec. 31.
    1943 — 1944   [Jan. 1 — Dec. 31].
  Micro (P)
    1945 — 1958   Jan. 1 — Dec. 31.
    1959   Jan. 1 — Apr. 30, June 1 — Oct.
            31.
  DLC
    1839   May 4.
    1841   Nov. 18 — 20, 23, 25, 26, Dec.
            10 — 13, 15 — 22.

1859   Mar. 11, Apr. 10.
1860   Apr. 23, 24, Oct. 28.
1926   Jan. 16, 19, 21 — 24, 30, Feb.
        4 — 7, 10, 12, 14 — 20, 22, 23,
        Mar. 1 — 3, 4, 6 — 10, 12 — 19,
        21, 22, 26, 29, Apr. 4, 6, 9 — 12,
        14, 16 — 18, 20, 23, 27 — 30, May
        2, 3, 6, 7, 10, 11, 13 — 24, 31,
        June 1, 7 — 9, 15 — 17, 19, 21,
        22, 26, 28.

Micro (P)
1938   July 1 — Dec. 31.
1939 — 1943   Jan. 1 — Dec. 31.
1944   Jan. 1 — July 31.
1949   Jan. 16 — Dec. 31.
1950   Jan. 1+.

DPU
Current (six months).
Micro (P) & (N)
1938   July 9 — Dec. 31.
1939 — 1943   Jan. 1 — Dec. 31.
Micro (P)
1938   Jan. 1 — July 8.
1944 — 1946   Jan. 1 — Dec. 31.
1947   Jan. 16 — Dec. 31.
1948   Jan. 1 — Dec. 31.
1949   Jan. 16 — Dec. 31.
1950 — 1955   Jan. 1 — Dec. 31.

FU
Micro (N)
1945   May 1 — 9, 11 — 31.
ICRL
1940 — 1948   Jan. 1 — Dec. 31.
1949   Jan. 1 — May 9.
Micro (N)
1938   July 1 — Dec. 31.
1939 — 1955   Jan. 1 — Dec. 31.
        (P) & (N)
1956   Jan. 1+.

ICU
Micro (P)
1938   July 1 — Dec. 31.
1939 — 1955   Jan. 1 — Dec. 31.

IU
Micro (P)
1949 — 1954   Jan. 1 — Dec. 31.
1955   Jan. 1 — Aug. 15.

InU
1966   Jan. 1+.
MB
1861   Feb. 13 — Apr. 12.
MH
Micro (P)
1938   July 1 — Dec. 31.
1939 — 1941   Jan. 1 — Dec. 31.
1942   Jan. 1 — May 30, Aug. 1 — Dec.
        31.
1943   Feb. 20 — Dec. 31.
1944 — 1954   Jan. 1 — Dec. 31.
1955   Jan. 1 — Apr. 1.
1964   June 13 — 26, Nov. 1 — 13, 22 —
        30, Dec. 1 — 4, 19 — 30.
1965   Jan. 1 — 19, Feb. 13 — 19, Apr.
        2 — July 23.

MWA
1845   Jan. 3, 11, 14, 15, July 1 — 5.
1864   Nov. 28 — Dec. 31.
1865   Jan. 1 — 11.
1889   Sept. 18.
1890   Aug. 28, Sept. 5, Oct. 11, Dec.
        23.
1891   Dec. 23, 24, 26 — 29.
1893   Aug. 9, 11 — 14.
1901   Apr. 6, May 20, June 23, Aug.
        23, 24.

NNC
1965   June 12 — 18, Aug. 7 — Sept. 8,
        10 — Dec. 17, 25 — 31.
1966   Jan. 1 — 7.
NcD
1867   June 6.
1893   Jan. 1 — Mar. 11, 14 — June 23,
        25 — 28, 30 — Dec. 31.
1894   Jan. 2 — 13, 15 — 25, 27 — Feb.
        20, 22 — Mar. 17, 20 — 31, Apr.
        11 — June 28, 30, July 2 — 31,
        Aug. 2 — Sept. 29.
1895   Jan. 1 — June 6, 8, 9, 11, 14 —
        29.
1896   Apr. 1 — May 13, 17 — July 18,
        20 — Aug. 8, 10 — Sept. 7, 9 —
        Dec. 7, 9, 11 — 31.

NcU
1945   July 1 — 17, 19 — 31.
OrU
1965   Aug. 1 — Dec. 31.

1966   Jan. 1+.
PU
1908   ₁Jan. 1 – June 30₁.
1909   ₁Mar. 1 – Dec. 31₁.
1910 – 1911   ₁Jan. 1 – Dec. 31₁.
1912   ₁Jan. 1 – 31, July 1 – Dec. 31₁.
1913   ₁Jan. 1 – Nov. 30₁.
TxU
1941   July 1 – Dec. 31.
1942   Jan. 1 – Sept. 30, Oct. 14 – 27, Nov. 1 – Dec. 31.
1943   Jan. 1 – Apr. 30, July 1 – Oct. 31, Nov. 12 – Dec. 31.
1944   Jan. 1 – Dec. 31.
1945   Jan. 1 – June 23, 28 – Aug. 1 – 31, Oct. 1 – 31.
1947   Jan. 1 – Apr. 12, 14 – June 20, 22 – 28, 30 – July 19, 21 – Dec. 30.
1948   Jan. 1 – 6, 15 – Nov. 26, 29 – Dec. 31.
1949   Jan. 1 – 3, 5 – Apr. 23, 25 – 27, 29, May 2 – 31, June 2 – Dec. 31.
1950 – 1952   Jan. 1 – Dec. 31.

EL COMERCIO GRAFICO. d.
MH
1964   Nov. 1 – 12, 20 – 21, 26, 28, 30 – Dec. 4, 19, 21 – 31.
1965   Jan. 11 – 22, Feb. 12 – July 22.

EL COMETA.
CtY
1812   May 9.
1813   Oct. 15.

EL COMETA. bw. est. Aug. 17, 1822.
Note: Ceased publication Sept. 21, 1822.
CtY
1822   Aug. 17 – Sept. 21.

EL CONCILIADOR. sw. est. Jan. 9, 1830.
Note: Succeeded as official gazette by *El Redactor peruano*. Ceased publication Jan. 25, 1834.
CtY
1830   Jan. 9 – Dec. 29.
1831 – 1833   Jan. 1 – Dec. 31.

1834   Jan. 1 – 25.
DLC
1830   ₁Jan. 9 – Dec. 29₁.
1831 – 1833   ₁Jan. 1 – Dec. 31₁.
1834   Jan. 1 – 25.
MWA
1830   Jan. 9 – Dec. 31.
1832   Jan. 1 – Dec. 31.
1833   Jan. 1 – Dec. 28.
NcD
Micro (P)
1830   Jan. 9 – Dec. 31.
1831 – 1833   Jan. 1 – Dec. 31.
1834   Jan. 1 – 25.

EL CONSOLADOR. irr. est. July 19, 1821.
CtY
1821   Prospecto.
July 19 – 23, 31.

EL CONSTITUCIONAL. sw. est. Nov. 2, 1833.
Note: Ceased publication Oct. 29, 1834.
DLC
1833   Prospecto: Oct. 24.
Nov. 2 – 20, Dec. 11, 11 – 28.
1834   Feb. 15, 26.

EL CONSTITUCIONAL. d. est. Apr. 3, 1858.
Note: Ceased publication July 31, 1858.
CtY
1858   Apr. 3 – July 31.

EL CONSTITUCIONAL DE LIMA.
CtY
1844   June 1.

CONTRA ATAQUE. w., sw. est. Oct. 27, 1945.
Note: Periodicity Oct. 27, 1945 – Mar. 30, 1946, weekly; after Apr. 1, 1946, semiweekly.
CSt
1947   Sept. 13.
NcD
1945   Oct. 27 – Dec. 31.
1946   Jan. 1 – Dec. 31.

1947   Jan. 1 — Oct. 11.
TxU
  1945   Oct. 27 — Dec. 31.
  1946   Jan. 1 — Dec. 31.
  1947   Jan. 1 — Oct. 11.

EL CORACERO. bw. est. Aug. 29, 1835.
  Note: Ceased publication Oct. 7,
  1835.
  CU — B
  Micro (N)
  1835   Aug. 29 — Oct. 7.
  CtY
  1835   Aug. 29 — Oct. 7.

EL CORREO DEL PERU. w. est. Sept.
16, 1871.
  Note: Ceased publication May 19,
  1878.
  CtY
  1871   Sept. 16 — Dec. 30.
  1872 — 1876   Jan. 1 — Dec. 31.
  1877   Jan. 7 — Apr. 29, May 13 — Dec.
       23.
  1878   Jan. 6 — 20, Feb. 3 — 17, Mar.
       3 — Apr. 23, May 12 — 19.

CORREO MERCANTIL POLITICO Y
LITERARIO. irr. est. Dec. 19, 1921.
  Note: Succeeded *Los Andes libres*.
  Ceased publication Feb. 1824.
  CU — B
  Micro (N)
  1821   Dec. 19 — 28.
  1822   Jan. 3 — June 10, 20 — Sept. 10.
  1823   Feb. 7 — May 26, Sept. 3, 30 —
       Oct. 18, Nov. 21, 22, Dec. 10 —
       22.
  CtY
  1821   Prospecto.
       Dec. 19 — 28.
  1822   Jan. 3 — June 10, 20 — Sept. 10.
  1823   Feb. 7 — May 26, Sept. 3, 30 —
       Oct. 18, Nov. 21, 22, Dec. 10,
       13 — 22.

CORREO PERUANO. d. est. 1845.
  Note: Ceased publication 1847.
  CtY
  1845   July 22, 28.

MWA
  1845   May 15, July 4.
  1846   Dec. 29 — 31.
  1847   Jan. 1 — Apr. 30, May 11, 25 —
       27, July 29 — 31, Sept. 1, Oct.
       4 — 8, 12, Nov. 16 — Dec. 7, 10 —
       13, 23, 30.

LA COTORRA. w. est. July 14, 1882.
  CtY
  1822   July 14 — Oct. 27, n.d. (Nos.
       20 — 24).
  1823   n.d. (No. 25), Feb. 10, Mar. 5,
       22, Sept. 13, 20, Oct. 11 — 18.

LE COURRIER DE L'AMERIQUE DU
SUD. w.
  Note: In French.
  CU — B
  Micro (N)
  1891   Sept. 24 — Dec. 31.
  1892   Jan. 1 — July 14.

LE COURRIER DU PACIFIQUE. w. est.
1918.
  Note: In French.
  CU
  1919   Jan. 1.
  KHi
  1919   Oct. 30 — Dec. 31.
  1920   Jan. 1 — June 3.

LA CRITICA. w. est. [1917].
  CtY
  1918   Jan. 20, Feb. 10 — Apr. 7.

LA CRONICA. 3w. est. Jan. 4, 1861.
  Note: Ceased publication Mar. 16,
  1861.
  CtY
  1861   Jan. 4 — Mar. 16.

LA CRONICA; DIARIO ILUSTRADO
POLITICO. d. est. Apr. 7, 1912.
  CSt
  1941   Sept. 3, 18, Oct. 1 — Dec. 31.
  1942   Jan. 1 — Feb. 28, Apr. 1 — July
       31.
  CSt — H
  1964   June 15, 16, Nov. 19, 26.
  DLC
  1927   Aug. 2, 3, 5 — 7, 9 — 17, 19 — 22,

24 — Sept. 2, 4 — 31, Oct. 2 —
19, 21, 23 — Nov. 15, 17, 19 —
25, 28 — 30, Dec. 2, 3, 5 — 9,
11 — 14, 16 — 31.

1928   Jan. 1, 3 — 14, 16 — 19, 21 — 23,
25, 27 — Feb. 7, 9 — 13, 15, 17 —
20, 22 — Mar. 12, 14 — 18, 20 —
Apr. 2, 4 — 21, 23 — May 13,
15 — June 4, 12 — 24, 26 — 29,
July 1 — 7, 9 — 11, 13 — 20, 22 —
27, 30 — Aug. 22, 24 — 28, 30,
Sept. 6 — 9, 11 — 22, 24 — 28,
30 — Oct. 1, 3 — 19, 22, 28.

1935   Jan. 18.
1936   Jan. 1, 2.
1937   Apr. 7, Sept. 12.
1938   July 28, Dec. 9.
1939   Jan. 1, 26, July 28, Aug. 6, Oct.
29, Dec. 8.
1940   May 25, Oct. 12, 18 — 25.
1941   Feb. 17 — July 20, 22 — Dec. 31.
1942   Jan. 1 — Feb. 6, 8 — Mar. 10, 12,
13, 15 — 18, 20 — 23, 25 — 27,
29 — 31, Apr. 2, 3, 5 — 7, 9, 10,
12, 14, 15, 17 — 21, 26 — May 1,
3, 5 — 8, 10, 11, 13 — 15, 17 —
21, 23 — 27, 30, 31, June 4 — 9,
11 — 14, 16, July 4, Aug. 27 —
Sept. 3, 5 — 11.

1943   Apr. 3 — 5, 7 — 9, 12, 13, 17, 19,
May 15 — 18, 23, 24, 25, 27, 29,
June 1 — Sept. 12, 14 — Oct. 22,
24 — Nov. 4, 6 — 25, 27 — Dec.
31.
Extraordinario: Apr. 14.

1944   Jan. 1 — 15, 28 — Apr. 20, 22,
23, 25, 26, 28, 30 — July 3, 5 —
7, 9 — 15, 17 — 19, 21 — 24, 26 —
Aug. 16, 18 — 29, 31 — Dec. 31.
1945   Jan. 1 — Dec. 31.
1946   Jan. 1 — Aug. 31.
1947   Jan. 1, 3 — 14, 16 — Feb. 9, 11 —
19, 21 — 28, May 2 — June 30.
1948   Jan. 1 — June 30.
1949   Aug. 1 — 4, 6 — Sept. 30.
1950 — 1956   Jan. 1 — Dec. 31.
1957   Jan. 1 — May 17, 19 — Dec. 31.
1958   Jan. 1 — Dec. 31.

1959   Jan. 1 — 3, 5 — Dec. 5, 7 — 31.
1960 — 1961   Jan. 1 — Dec. 31.
Micro (P) & (N)
1962   Jan. 1+.
FU
1962   Apr. 23 — Dec. 31.
1963   Jan. 1+.
MWA
1915   Aug. 18.
1916   Jan. 23.
1923   Sept. 29.
OrU
1942   Jan. 16, Apr. 14, 16.

CRONICA POLITICA Y LITERARIA
DE LIMA. irr. est. June 4, 1827.
Note: Ceased publication Sept. 1827.
CtY
1827   June 4 — Sept. (No. 5).
MWA
1827   Sept. (No. 5).

DE FRENTE. 3w. est. Feb. 25, 1933.
TxU
1933   Feb. 25 — May 16.

EL DEPOSITARIO. irr. est. 1821.
Note: Removed from Lima to the
interior (Yucay and Cuzco); removed
to Callao in 1823. Ceased publication
[May 1] 1825.
CU — B
Micro (N)
1821   Apr. 25, June 26, July 2.
CtY
1821   Mar. 7, 24, Apr. 3, May 3,
June 20.
1823   May 6.

DIARIO. d.
MWA
1890   Feb. 8 — 11, Aug. 27, Sept. 1.

EL DIARIO. d. est. [1961].
DLC
1961   Nov. 2 — 16, 18 — Dec. 30.

EL DIARIO DE LA TARDE. d. est. Feb. 3,
1835.
CtY
1835   Prospecto: Jan. 31.
Feb. 3 — 21.

DIARIO DE LIMA. d. est. Oct. 1, 1789.
    Note: Ceased publication Sept.
    26, 1793.
  CtY
    1791   June 1 – Sept. 30.

DIARIO DE LIMA. d. est. Nov. 3, 1822.
    Note: Ceased publication Nov. 27,
    1822.
  CtY
    1822   Prospecto.
            Nov. 3 – 27.

EL DISCRETO. w. est. Feb. 24, 1827.
    Note: Ceased publication Apr. 28,
    1827.
  CtY
    1827   Feb. 24 – Apr. 28.

DOÑA MISERIA. w. est. Mar. 5, 1932.
  TxU
    1932   Mar. 5 – Dec. 31.
    1933   Jan. 1 – Feb. 10.

EL DUENDE. irr. est. Mar. 6, 1821.
  CtY
    1821   Mar. 6 – Apr. 12.

EL DUENDE REPUBLICANO. irr. est.
    Mar. 10, 1827.
    Note: Ceased publication June 24,
    1827.
  CtY
    1827   Mar. 10 – June 24.

EL ECO DE LA OPINION DEL PERU.
    sw. est. Aug. 6, 1827.
    Note: Ceased publication Sept. 18,
    1827.
  CtY
    1827   Aug. 6 – Sept. 13.
  DLC
    1827   Sept. 6.
  MWA
    1827   Aug. 12.

EL ECO DE PAUCARPATA. irr. est.
    Nov. 17, 1838.
    Note: Ceased publication [Jan. 15],
    1839.

CtY
    1838   Nov. 24 – Dec. 29.
    1839   Jan. 9 – 15.

EL ECO DEL NORTE. w., sw. est. Feb.
    18, 1837.
    Note: Periodicity Feb. 18 – 28, 1837,
    weekly; Mar. 1, 1837 – July 28, 1838,
    semiweekly. Ceased publication July
    28, 1838.
  CtY
    1837   Feb. 18 – Dec. 30.
    1838   Jan. 3 – Feb. 17, 24 – Mar. 28,
            Apr. 4, 14 – 25, May 2 – June
            30.
            Extraordinario: Apr. 13.
  DLC
    1837   Feb. 18 – Mar. 7, 9 – Apr. 14,
            16 – 25.
    1838   Jan. 1, 2, 21 – May 1, 3 – June
            12, 14 – July 7.
            Extraordinario: Apr. 13.
  MWA
    1837   Feb. 18 – Dec. 31.
    1838   Jan. 1 – July 28.
  NcD
    1837   Apr. 19, Oct. 21, Nov. 4, Dec.
            30.
    1838   June 27, July 4.

EL ECO DEL PROTECTORADO. sw. est.
    Aug. 20, 1836.
    Note: Established in Lima but re-
    moved to La Paz, Potosí, and Chu-
    quisaca, Aug. 24, 1837; removed to
    Cuzco, Aug. 8, 1838; returned to
    Lima, [Nov.] 1838. Ceased publication
    Jan. 28, 1839.
  CtY
    1836   Aug. 20 – Dec. 31.
    1837   Jan. 4 – Feb. 11, May 10 – June
            14, 21 – Aug. 23.
  DLC
    1837   Jan. 28, June 28, July 1, 5, 8.
  MWA
    1836   Aug. 20 – Dec. 31.
    1837   Jan. 1 – Feb. 11, Apr. 19 –
            Aug. 23, Nov. 22.
    1838   Nov. 14, 21 – Dec. 31.

1839   Jan. 1 – 23.

LA EPOCA. est. June 15, 1946.
  TxU
    1946   June 15 – 28.

EL ESPECTADOR. irr. est. Dec. 20,
  1832.
  CtY
    1832   Dec. 20.
    1833   Jan. 2 – 24.

EL ESPIA. irr. est. Feb. 27, 1834.
  Note: Ceased publication Mar. 13,
  1834.
  CtY
    1834   Feb. 27, Mar. 4 – 13.

LA ESTAFETA DEL PUEBLO. sw. est.
  Feb. 6, 1827.
  CU – B
  Micro (N)
    1827   May 22.
  CtY
    1827   Feb. 27, Mar. 6.

EL ESTANDARTE. sw. est. Nov. 8, 1836.
  Note: Ceased publication Nov. 29,
  1837.
  CtY
    1836   Nov. 8 – Dec. 30.
    1837   Jan. 3 – Nov. 29.

LA ESTRELLA. est. Apr. 16, 1947.
  Note: Suspended publication Nov. 7,
  1947 – Mar. 16, 1948.
  TxU
    1947   Apr. 16 – Dec. 31.
    1948   Jan. 1 – May 17.

EVENTUAL. irr. est. Oct. 1829.
  Note: Title *Periódico eventual*, Oct.
  1829 – Jan. 13, 1830; *Eventual*, Jan.
  14 – Apr. 15, 1830. Ceased publication
  Apr. 15, 1830.
  CtY
    1829   n.d. (Nos. 1 – 15).

EXPRESO. d. est. 1961.
  DLC
    1961   Oct. 25 – Nov. 20, 22 – Dec.
    31.

Micro (P) & (N)
    1962   Jan. 1+.
  NIC
  Micro (P)
    1962 – 1963   [Jan. 1 – Dec. 31].
    1964   Jan. 1 – Feb. 29, July 1 – Dec.
    31.
    1965   Jan. 1+.

EL FENIX. w. est. July 23, 1827.
  Note: Ceased publication Jan. 26,
  1828.
  DLC
    1827   July 23, Aug. 2.
  MWA
    1827   July 23 – Aug. 21, Sept. 15 –
    Dec. 31.
    1828   Jan. 1 – 26.

EL FISCAL. est. June 14, 1831.
  CtY
    1831   June 14.

LA FLORESTA. d. est. Mar. 1, 1831.
  Note: Succeeded *Diario de Lima*.
  Ceased publication Apr. 15, 1831.
  CtY
    1831   Prospecto: Feb. 21.
    Mar. 1 – 18, 22 – 28.

FOREIGN NEWS. w. est. 1854.
  Note: In English.
  MWA
    1854   Mar. 25.

EL FRAILE. est. [1821].
  CtY
    [1821]   n.d. (Nos. 1 – 3).

FRANCIA COMBATIENTE. w. est. 1941.
  DLC
    1943   Apr. 22.

GACETA DEL GOBIERNO. irr. est. Oct.
  13, 1810.
  Note: Title *Gaceta ministerial de
  Lima*, July 20 – Aug. 6, 1814. Ceased
  publication 1821.
  MWA
    1811   Sept. 6, Oct. 23.
    1813   Jan. 23, May 29, Oct. 27.
    1814   Feb. 16, Mar. 9, 23 – 26, Apr.

6 – 9, July 2, 20 – Aug. 20,
Sept. 3 – 17, 21 – Nov. 16.
1815   Extraordinario: June 19.
1816   Oct. 26.
1819   Extraordinario: Aug. 16, Oct. 4.

GACETA DEL GOBIERNO. w., sw., w.
est. July 16, 1821.
Note: Title *Gaceta del gobierno de
Lima independiente*, July 16 – Sept.
5, 1821; *Gaceta del gobierno*, Sept. 8,
1821 – 1826. Ceased publication
1826.
CtY
1821   July 16 – Dec. 29.
1822 – 1823   Jan. 1 – Dec. 31.
1824   Jan. 3 – 28, Feb. 21 – Dec. 22.
1825   Jan. 1 – Dec. 29.
1826   Jan. 4 – May 10.
DLC
1824   Dec. 22, 24.
1825   Jan. 1 – Dec. 31.
1826   Jan. 1 – May 31.
MWA
1825   Aug. 14 – 18, 25 – Sept. 1.
WU
1821   July 16 – Dec. 31.
1822   Jan. 1 – Dec. 31.

GACETA MERCANTIL. d.
NcD
1831   June 16 – Dec. 31.
1832 – 1834   Jan. 1 – Dec. 31.
1835   Jan. 1 – Apr. 29.

EL GENIO DEL RIMAC. d. est. Nov. 2,
1833.
Note: Ceased publication Feb. 25,
1835.
CtY
1833   Prospecto: Oct. 24.
Nov. 2 – Dec. 31.
1834   Jan. 2 – Dec. 31.
DLC
1833   Prospecto: Oct. 24.
Nov. 2 – 16, 19 – 22, 26, 28,
Dec. 3 – 7, 11, 13, 16 – 19, 21,
24 – 28, 31.
Suplemento: Dec. 30.
1834   Jan. 2, 3, Feb. 13 – 15, 21, 22,

26 – 28.
Suplemento: Mar. 11.

EL GLOBO. d. est. Feb. 1, 1833.
Note: Ceased publication Apr. 27,
1833.
CtY
1833   Apr. 18.

GRITOS CONTRA EL INVESTIGADOR
DON GUILLERMO DEL RIO, O
BEQUE.
MWA
1815   [Jan. 17.]

LA GUARDIA NACIONAL. sw. est. Jan.
19, 1844.
Note: Ceased publication June 1844.
CtY
1844   Jan. 19 – Feb. 6.

EL HERALDO. sw. est. 1933.
DLC
1933   Nov. 17.

EL HERALDO; VOCERO DE PRO-
PIEDAD PARTICULAR AL SERVI-
CIO DE PERU. w.
TxU
1945   June 15 – Sept. 29, Oct. 13 –
Dec. 31.
1946 – 1947   Jan. 1 – Dec. 31.
1948   Jan. 1 – June 20.

EL HERALDO DE LIMA. d. est. Feb. 15,
1854.
Note: Suspended publication Aug.
29, 1856 – July 27, 1870; ceased publication Dec. 31, 1870.
CU – B
Micro (P)
1855   Oct. 10.
DLC
1855   May 12, 13, 15 – 25, 30 – June
4, 6, 9 – 21, 23 – July 23, 25 –
29, 31 – Aug. 29, Sept. 1 – 5,
7 – 23, 26 – Oct. 10.

EL HIJO DE SU MADRE. sw. est. Feb.
10, 1827.
Note: Ceased publication May 12,
1827.

CtY
  1827   Feb. 10 – May 5.

HOGUERA. w. est. Dec. 22, 1945.
    Note: Suspended publication Dec. 1,
    1947 – Dec. 20, 1948.
  NcD
    1945   Dec. 22 – 31.
    1946   Jan. 1 – Dec. 31.
    1947   Jan. 1 – Nov. 30.
    1948   Dec. 20.
    1949   Jan. 11, Feb. 24, Mar. 14, 26,
            Apr. 9 – June 25, July 9 – 23,
            Aug. 6, 13.
    1950   May 20 – July 15.
    1952   May 24 – July 19, Aug. 2, 9.
    1953   Aug. 21 – Sept. 11.
  TxU
    1945   Dec. 22 – 29.
    1946   Jan. 1 – Dec. 31.
    1947   Jan. 1 – Nov. 3.
    1948   Dec. 20.
    1949   Jan. 1 – Dec. 31.
    1950   Jan. 1 – July 15.

IDEA LIBRE. w.
  MWA
    1901   Mar. 2.

LA ILLAPA. sw.
  CtY
    1833   May 1.

ILUSTRACION SUD AMERICANA. bw.
    Note: Title *Ilustración americana*
    prior to May 15, 1891; after [May 16,
    1891], *Ilustración sud americana.*
  MWA
    1891   May 15, Nov. 15.

EL IMPARCIAL. w. est. Nov. 2, 1822.
    Note: Ceased publication Nov. 30,
    1822.
  CtY
    1822   Prospecto.
            Nov. 2 – 30.

EL IMPARCIAL. sw. est. Nov. 21, 1838.
  CU – B
    Micro (N)
    1838   Nov. 21 – Dec. 8.

DLC
  1838   Nov. 21.

EL IMPERIO DE LA LEY. sw. est. Jan. 5,
    1836.
  CU – B
    Micro (N)
    1836   Jan. 5 – 28.
  CtY
    1836   Jan. 9 – 28.

INTEGRIDAD. w.
  MWA
    1891   May 23.
    1909   Nov. 27.

LOS INTERESES DEL PAIS. w., irr. est.
  July 4, 1848.
  CtY
    1848   July 4 – Dec. 31.
    1849 – 1850   Jan. 1 – Dec. 31.
    1851   Jan. 1 – Apr. 17.

EL INVESTIGADOR DEL PERU. d. est.
  July 1, 1813.
    Note: Title *El Investigador*, July 1 –
    Dec. 31, 1813; *El Investigador del
    Perú*, Jan. 1 – Dec. 31, 1814. Ceased
    publication Dec. 31, 1814.
  CU – B
    Micro (N)
    1813   July 1 – Oct. 31, Nov. 23, 24,
            26 – Dec. 6, 11 – 13, 15 – 17,
            20 – 24, 29 – 31.
    1814   Jan. 1 – Feb. 20, 22 – Apr. 16,
            20 – Nov. 1, 3 – Dec. 19, 21 –
            31.
  CtY
    1813   July 1 – Oct. 31, Nov. 23, 24,
            26 – Dec. 6, 11 – 13, 15 – 17,
            20 – 24, 29 – 31.
    1814   Jan. 1 – Dec. 31.
  MWA
    1814   [Jan. 5 – July 8, Oct. 3 – Nov.
            14].
  NN
    1814   Jan. 2 – 7, 12 – 21, 23, 24, 26 –
            Apr. 6, May 22, June 26, 27,
            30, July 2 – 7, 15 – 17, Aug. 30.

EL INVESTIGADOR RESUCITADO. d.,
   irr. est. Dec. 2, 1822.
      Note: Ceased publication Jan. 18,
      1823.
      CtY
      1822   Dec. 2 – 21, 24 – 31.
      1823   Jan. 3 – 18.

EL IRIS. irr. est. Nov. 1, 1834.
      Note: Published only three numbers.
      Ceased publication Nov. 11, 1834.
      CtY
      1834   Nov. 6.

EL IRIS. est. May 26, 1855.
      CtY
      1855   May 26 – June 30.

EL JUICIO NACIONAL. sw. est. Jan. 25,
   1836.
      Note: Ceased publication Apr. 2,
      1836.
      CU – B
      Micro (N)
      1836   Jan. 25 – Apr. 2.
      CtY
      1836   Jan. 25 – Apr. 2.
      DLC
      1836   Jan. 25.

LABOR. w. est. Jan. 5, 1946.
      Note: Suspended publication Feb.,
      Aug., Dec. 1947; Feb., Sept., 1948.
      NcD
      1946   Jan. 5 – Dec. 31.
      1947   Jan. 1 – Dec. 31.
      1948   Jan. 1 – Oct. 23.
      TxU
      1946   Jan. 5 – Dec. 31.
      1947   Jan. 1 – Dec. 31.
      1948   Jan. 1 – Oct. 23.

EL LIBERAL. irr. est. June 11, 1829.
      Note: Ceased publication Jan. 14,
      1830.
      CtY
      1829   Oct. 5, Nov. 29.

LIMA LIBRE. irr. est. July 2, 1842.
      CtY
      1842   July 2 – 11, Aug. 9 – 13.

EL LIMEÑO. 3w. est. Mar. 19, 1834.
      Note: Ceased publication Feb. 10,
      1835.
      CtY
      1834   Mar. 19 – Dec. 31.
      1835   Jan. 4 – Feb. 10.

EL LORO. w. est. Aug. 30, 1822.
      Note: Ceased publication Oct. 4,
      1822.
      CtY
      1822   Aug. 30 – Oct. 4.

M.C.I.; LA VOZ DEL MOVIMIENTO
   CIVICO INDEPENDIENTE. est. July
   20, 1948.
      TxU
      1948   July 20 – Sept. 10.

LA MADRE DE MONTONERO. irr. est.
   Dec. 1, 1834.
      CtY
      1834   Dec. 1 – 23.

MAN SHING PO.
      Note: [In Quechua.]
      CLCM
      1945   Dec. 22, 23.

EL MAPA POLITICO Y LITERARIO.
   irr. est. June 1, 1843.
      CtY
      1843   June 1 – Dec. 11.
      1844   Jan. 1 – Apr. 15.

MERCURIO. d. est. Nov. 17, 1862.
      MWA
      1864   Sept. 23 – Dec. 31.
      1865   Jan. 1 – 11.
      NcD
      1862   Nov. 17 – Dec. 31.
      1863   Jan. 1 – May 13, 15 – June 3,
              5 – 13. 15 – Dec. 31.

MERCURIO PERUANO. sw. est. 1791.
      Note: Ceased publication Aug. 28,
      1794.
      MWA
      1791   Sept. 1 – Dec. 31.
      1792   Jan. 1 – Apr.
      1793   Sept. 5 – Dec. 22.

TxU
1791 June 30.
1792 Sept. 2 – Dec. 31.
1793 Jan. 1 – Apr. 28, Aug. 15.
1794 Jan. 2 – Aug. 24.
MERCURIO PERUANO. d. est. Aug. 1,
1827.
Note: Suspended publication Mar. 9,
1834 – May 31, 1839; ceased publication Jan. 2, 1840.
CtY
1827 Prospecto: July 24.
Aug. 1 – Dec. 31.
1828 Jan. 2 – Oct. 17, 20 – Dec. 31.
1829 Jan. 2 – Dec. 31.
1830 Jan. 2 – June 28, 30 – Dec. 31.
1831 Jan. 4 – Dec. 31.
1832 – 1833 Jan. 2 – Dec. 31.
1834 Jan. 2 – 24, Mar. 3 – 8.
DLC
1827 Prospecto: July 24.
Aug. 1 – Oct. 21, 23 – Dec. 31.
1828 Jan. 1 – Dec. 31.
Alcance: Aug. 20, Nov. 6.
Extraordinario: Dec. 21.
Suplemento: Jan. 16, 18, 19,
23, 24, Feb. 4, 12, Apr. 10,
June 11, Sept. 1, 6, 17, 30,
Nov. 28.
1829 Jan. 1 – July 24, 26 – Aug. 24.
Alcance: n.d.
Extraordinario: June 22, July
26.
Suplemento: Jan. 15, 21, 30,
Feb. 11, 12, 18, 27, Mar. 14, 20,
Apr. 18, May 7, 9, 12, 21, 26,
30, June 13, July 4, 8, 23.
1830 Jan. 2 – Mar. 24, 27 – 31, Apr.
3, Sept. 1, Dec. 1 – 31.
Suplemento: Jan. 14, 26, 28,
Feb. 1, 11, 12, Dec. 10, 18.
1831 Jan. 3, 4, 7 – July 4, 6 – 12,
15 – Oct. 2, 5 – 24, 26, 27, 30,
31, Nov. 2, 4 – Dec. 9, 11 – 21,
25, 30, 31.
Suplemento: Jan. 15, Mar. 16,
Apr. 21, May 6, June 3, 4, 6 –
8, 14, Sept. 7, 12, 14, 16, 22,
27, Oct. 19, Nov. 11, 25.

1832 June 1 – 27.
Suplemento: June 2, 16.
1833 July 17, Aug. 7, 10 – 22, 24 –
31, Oct. 1 – 21, 23 – Nov. 4, 8,
9, 12 – 14, 16, 19 – 22, 25, 26,
28 – Dec. 13, 16 – 21, 24 – 28.
Suplemento: Aug. 13, 19.
1834 Mar. 1 – 4, 7.
Suplemento: Dec. 28.
MWA
1828 Oct. 8, 10, 13.
1829 Feb. 5, 6, 10, 16, May 9 – 18,
29, July 1, 2.
1831 Feb. 28.
1832 Suplemento: [Dec. 5].
NN
1829 Jan. 2 – Feb. 3, 5 – Mar. 18,
21 – Apr. 9, 11 – 30.

EL MERIDIANO. sw. est. June 3, 1833.
Note: Ceased publication Nov. 28,
1833.
DLC
1833 July 4.

MINERVA PERUANA. irr. est. [Mar.],
1805.
Note: Ceased publication [Oct. 8,
1810].
CtY
1807 Apr. 8 – 10, Aug. 31 – Sept.
5, Oct. 25 – Nov. 9, 19, 26 –
29, Dec. 5, 6.

MIRADOR. w. est. Jan. 25, 1946.
NcD
1946 Jan. 25 -- Apr. 5.

LA MISCELANEA. d. est. June 15, 1830.
Note: Ceased publication Dec. 31,
1833.
CU – B
Micro (N)
1832 Mar. 30.
CtY
1830 June 15 – 21, 23 – July 1, 3, 10,
13 – 19, 21 – 24, 27 – Aug. 9,
11 – Sept. 1, 3 – Oct. 2, 5, 6,
11, 12, 15, 16, 19, 20, 22 – Nov.
16, 18, 19, 22, 23, 25 – Dec. 1,

3−9, 11−20, 22−31.

1831   Jan. 3, 5, 8−13, 15−17, 19−
29, Feb. 1−26, Mar. 1, 4−9,
11, 14, 16, 17, 21, 23−26, 29,
Apr. 2−8, 11, 13−21, 23, 26,
28, 30, May 3, 4, 6−11, 21−
24, 26−June 23, 27−July 4,
6−9, 12−21, 23−29, Aug. 1,
12, 16−20, 23−25, 27−31,
Sept. 2−5, 7−9, 12, 13, 15−
17, 20, 22−30, Oct. 5−14,
17−21, 25, 27−31, Nov. 3, 5−
7, 9, 10, 12−14, 15−17, 19−
30, Dec. 2, 5, 6, 13, 14, 19, 21,
23−31.

1832   Jan. 2−5, 9−27, 30, Feb. 1,
3−Apr. 30, May 2−8, 11−
Aug. 29, Sept. 1−Oct. 12,
15−22, 24−Nov. 5, 7−12,
14−24, 29−31.

1833   Jan. 2, 5−11, 14−17, 19−21,
23, 24, 26−28, 30, Feb. 1−4,
6−20, 22, 23, 26−28, Mar. 4,
5, 7−Apr. 2, 16−19, 22−July
3, 5, 9−15, 18−22, Aug. 16,
Sept. 3, Nov. 2−16, 18−21.

MWA
1833   Feb. 1.

EL MONITOR PERUANO. sw. est. Feb.
23, 1831.
Note: Ceased publication Mar.
12, 1831.
CU−B
Micro (N)
1831   Feb. 23−Mar. 12.
CtY
1831   Feb. 23−Mar. 12.

MONITOR POPULAR. w. est. 1896.
WU
1896−1898   Jan. 1−Dec. 31.

MONOS Y MONADAS. w. est. Jan. 1,
1906.
TxU
1906   Jan. 1−Dec. 31.
1907   Jan. 1−Dec. 11.

LA MULATA. irr. est. Oct. 6, 1838.
CU−B
Micro (N)
1838   Oct. 6−Nov. 5.

LA NACION. d. est. Oct. 23, 1946.
TxU
1946   Oct. 23−Dec. 31.
1947   Jan. 1−Sept. 13.

LA NACION. d. est. July 28, 1953.
Note: Ceased publication July 31,
1956.
DLC
1953   July 28−Dec. 31.
1954   Jan. 1−June 30, Aug. 1−31,
Nov. 1−12, 14, 15, 17−Dec.
31.
1955   Jan. 1−Mar. 31, Apr. 1−June
28, 30−Oct. 31, Nov. 5, 6, 8−
17, 19−Dec. 31.
1956   Jan. 2−28, 30−July 11, 13−
31.

EL NACIONAL. w. est. July 25, 1835.
Note: Ceased publication Nov. 14,
1835.
CU−B
Micro (N)
1835   July 25−Nov. 14.
CtY
1835   July 25−Oct. 26, Nov. 14.

EL NACIONAL; PERIODICO POLI·
TICO Y LITERARIO. sw., irr. est.
Sept. 21, 1850.
Note: Ceased publication Mar. 9,
1851.
CtY
1850   Sept. 21−Dec. 25.
1851   Jan. 5−Mar. 9.

EL NACIONAL; POLITICO LITE-
RARIO Y COMERCIAL. est. Nov. 24,
1865.
Note: Ceased publication [1897].
DLC
1897   July 19, 31−Aug. 9, 16.
NcD
1867   June 11.
1877   May 9.
1878   Nov. 21.

THE NEW WEST COAST LEADER. w.
est. 1909.
    Note: In English; Spanish supplement
    published Sept. 3, 1929 — Jan. 7, 1930.
    Title *Peru Today*, 1909 — Dec. 27,
    1911; *The West Coast Leader*, Jan. 3,
    1912 — Nov. 10, 1925; *West Coast
    Leader*, Nov. 17, 1925 — Sept. 3,
    1929 — Dec. 27, 1932; *The New West
    Coast Leader*, Jan. 3, 1933 — June
    1940. Ceased publication June 1940.
CLCM
    1925   Feb. 1 — 28.
CU
    1916   July 20, Aug. 24 — 31.
    1917   Jan. 6 — Dec. 29.
    1918   Jan. 5 — Nov. 2, 16 — 30, Dec.
            14 — 28.
    1919   Jan. 4 — Nov. 27, Dec. 11 — 25.
    1920   Jan. 1 — 8, 22 — June 10, 26 —
            July 17, Aug. 7, 21 — Sept. 11,
            25 — Dec. 18.
    1921   Jan. 1 — 8, 22 — Mar. 19, Apr.
            9 — May 14, 28 — Dec. 28.
    1922   Jan. 4 — Dec. 27.
    1923   Jan. 3 — Dec. 25.
    1924   Jan. 1, 15 — July 15, 29 — Dec.
            30.
    1925   Jan. 6 — Dec. 29.
    1926   Jan. 1 — Dec. 31.
    1927   Jan. 4 — Dec. 6, 20 — 27.
    1928   Jan. 3 — Feb. 28, Mar. 13, 27,
            Apr. 17 — May 1, 15 — 22, June
            5 — Dec. 25.
    1929 — 1932   Jan. 1 — Dec. 31.
    1933   Jan. 3 — Feb. 7, Mar. 7 — Aug.
            29, Sept. 12 — Dec. 26.
    1934   Jan. 2 — Mar. 27.
    1939   Apr. 25 — Sept. 26, Oct. 10 —
            31, Nov. 28 — Dec. 26.
    1940   Jan. 2 — Feb. 27.
DLC
    1919   Jan. 5 — Dec. 31.
    1920 — 1926   Jan. 1 — Dec. 31.
    1927   Jan. 1 — Feb. 14, 16 — Dec. 31.
    1928 — 1929   Jan. 1 — Dec. 31.
    1930   Jan. 1 — 27, 29 — Dec. 31.
    1931   Jan. 1 — Dec. 31.

    1932   Jan. 1 — Dec. 27.
    1933   Jan. 3 — Feb. 6, 8 — Dec. 31.
    1934 — 1939   Jan. 1 — Dec. 31.
    1940   Jan. 1 — June 4.
KHi
    1919   Oct. 30 — Dec. 31.
    1920   Jan. 1 — June 3.
MWA
    1912   [Jan. 10 — Dec. 26].
    1919   [Jan. 11 — Dec. 25].
    1923   Aug. 14 — Sept. 11, Oct. 16 —
            23.
    1924   July 8 — 29, Aug. 12 — 19.
TxU
    1919   Feb. 8 — Mar. 15 — June 7, 21 —
            28, July 19 — Aug. 9, 23 — Sept.
            6, 20 — Oct. 4, 16 — Nov. 13,
            27 — Dec. 11, 25 — 31.
    1920   Jan. 1 — June 3, 19 — July 24,
            Aug. 7 — 28.

LA NOCHE. d. est. Oct. 28, 1930.
    Note: Established in Callao but re-
    moved to Lima in 1931. Suspended
    publication Dec. 8, 1931 — [June]
    1933.
CSt
    1935   Apr. 25, 26.
DLC
    1941   June 18, 19, 21, 28, July 9 —
            11, Aug. 12 — 14, Sept. 1.
    1944   Sept. 1 — Dec. 11, 13 — 15, 17 —
            31.
    1945   Jan. 1 — Apr. 12, 15 — 30.

NOTICIAS. w. est. June 27, 1913.
MWA
    1913   June 27 — Dec. 31.
    1914   Jan. 1 — Mar. 1.

NOTICIAS; SEMANARIO INFORMA-
TIVO AL SERVICIO DE LA PATRIA.
w. est. Dec. 16, 1948.
TxU
    1948   Dec. 16 — 23.

NUESTRA BANDERA. est. Nov. 8, 1947.
TxU
    1947   Nov. 8.

NUESTRA VOZ. w. est. Jan. 11, 1941.
  DLC
    1941   Jan. 11.

NUEVO MUNDO. est. 1941.
  DLC
    1943   July 26.

NUEVO TIEMPO. d. est. Dec. 17, 1948.
  NcD
    1948   Dec. 17−31.
    1949   Jan. 1−6.
  TxU
    1948   Dec. 17−31.
    1949   Jan. 1−6.

EL OBRERO. w. est. 1895.
  DLC
    1895   Oct. 5−Nov. 16.

EL OBRERO DE CONSTRUCCION
  CIVIL. est. Mar. 7, 1947.
  TxU
    1947   Mar. 7−Oct. 14.

EL OBSERVADOR DE LIMA. w. est.
  June 7, 1825.
    Note: Ceased publication Aug. 23,
    1825.
  CtY
    1825   Prospecto: June 2.
            June 7−Aug. 23.

EL OBSERVADOR IMPARCIAL. 3w.
  est. July 12, 1831.
    Note: Ceased publication Mar. 28,
    1833.
  CtY
    1831   July 14, Oct. 27.

OIGA. w. est. Nov. 8, 1948.
  TxU
    1948   Nov. 8−Dec. 4.

LA OPINION. w., irr. est. Nov. 14, 1838.
    Note: Ceased publication Jan. 23,
    1839.
  CU−B
    Micro (N)
    1838   Nov. 14−Dec. 31.
    1839   Jan. 1−13.

  CtY
    1838   Nov. 14−Dec. 28.
    1839   Jan. 10−23.
  DLC
    1838   Nov. 14.

LA OPINION DE LIMA. w. est. Apr. 4,
  1834.
  CtY
    1834   Apr. 4.

LA OPINION DE LOS PUEBLOS. est.
  1844.
  CtY
    1844   Prospecto: July 1.

LA OPINION NACIONAL. d. est. Dec.
  1, 1873.
  DLC
    1874   Aug. 25, 26, 28, Sept. 2, 5, 17.
    1875   Mar. 24, 25, May 10.
  MWA
    1875   Jan. 26.
    1888   Jan. 7, May 14, Nov. 16.
    1890   Sept. 2.
    1892   Dec. 22.
    1913   May 25.

EL ORDEN. d.
  NcD
    1861   Mar. 2−11, 13−18, 20−23,
            27−30, Apr. 1, 3−13, 17−
            May 6, 8−13, 15, 16, 18−Oct.
            5.
            Suplemento: Apr. 14.

EL PACIFICADOR DEL PERU. 3m. est.
  Apr. 10, 1821.
    Note: Originally published at Huara
    and Barranca. Ceased publication
    Sept. 1, 1821.
  CU−B
    Micro (N)
    1821   Apr. 10−Sept. 1.
  CtY
    1821   Apr. 10−Sept. 1.

LA PATRIA. d. est. July 28, 1871.
  CtY
    1871   July 28−Dec. 30.
    1872   Jan. 2−Dec. 31.
    1873   Jan. 2−June 30.

PATRIA. d. est. 1917.
  NcD
    1931   June 15 – Dec. 31.
    1932   Jan. 1 – 15.

LA PATRIA EN DUELO. irr. est. Apr. 8,
  1829.
    Note: A single issue entitled *La Patria
    sin duelo* published in Lima on June 7,
    1829, was written in answer to No. 6,
    May 12, 1829, of *La Patria en duelo*.
    Suspended publication June 8, 1829 –
    June 5, 1833.
  CtY
    1829   Apr. 8, 23 – May 12.
    1833   June 6.

EL PATRIOTA. est. July 8, 1844.
  CtY
    1844   July 8.

EL PENITENTE. d. est. Sept. 1, 1832.
    Note: Ceased publication Nov. 29,
    1834.
  CU – B
    Micro (N)
    1832   Dec. 28.
  CtY
    1832   Sept. 1 – Dec. 30.
    1833   Jan. 2 – Mar. 5, 7, 22, 23, 27,
            Apr. 1 – Oct. 28, 30 – Nov. 22,
            25 – 28, 30 – Dec. 31.
    1834   Mar. 1 – July 5.
  DLC
    1834   Feb. 14, 18 – 22, 25, 26.

PERIODICO EVENTUAL.
    See *Eventual.*

EL PERIODIQUITO. w. est. Sept. 1,
  1838.
  CtY
    1838   n.d. (No. 7).

PERU. d. est. June 18, 1864.
    Note: Ceased publication Nov. 26,
    1864.
  MWA
    1864   Sept. 26 – Nov. 26.

EL PERU-BOLIVIANO. irr. est. Mar.
  17, 1836.

    Note: Ceased publication May 6,
    1836.
  CtY
    1836   Mar. 17 – May 6.

PERU TODAY.
    See *The New West Coast Leader.*

EL PERUANO. sw. est. Sept. 6, 1811.
    Note: Succeeded by *El Peruano
    liberal.* Ceased publication June 9,
    1812.
  CU – B
    Micro (N)
    1811   Sept. 6 – Dec. 31.
    1812   Jan. 3 – June 9.

EL PERUANO. w., sw. est. Oct. 29, 1825.
    Note: Title *El Peruano independiente*,
    Oct. 29, 1825 – May 6, 1826; *El
    Peruano* (became official publication),
    May 13, 1826 – Dec. 11, 1827. Periodi-
    city Oct. 29, 1825 – June 24, 1826,
    weekly; June 28, 1826 – Dec. 11,
    1827, semiweekly. Ceased publication
    Dec. 11, 1827.
  CtY
    1826   May 13 – Dec. 31.
    1827   Jan. 1 – Dec. 11.
  DLC
    1826   May 13 – Dec. 31.
    1827   Jan. 1 – Dec. 11.
  MWA
    1826   Oct. 7 – 25.
    1827   Apr. 21 – May 2, June 16 –
            July 7, 28 – Aug. 4.

EL PERUANO; DIARIO OFICIAL. sw.,
  w., d. est. Aug. 25, 1838.
    Note: Subtitle varies. Publication
    suspended Apr. 21, 1851 – Jan. 3.
    1854. *Registro oficial* published
    during the suspension. Succeeded
    El Redactor peruano.
  CLU
    1880   July 17 – Dec. 31.
  CU – B
    Micro (N)
    1839   Apr. 24 – Dec. 31.
    1840 – 1848   Jan. 1 – Dec. 31.

1849   Jan. 1 – Dec. 29.
1854   July 6 – Dec. 31.
1855 – 1865   Jan. 1 – Dec. 31.
1866   Jan. 1 – Dec. 29.
1871   Jan. 1 – Dec. 31.
1872   Jan. 1 – Dec. 18.
CtY
1838   Aug. 25 – Dec. 6.
1839   Feb. 18 – Dec. 28.
1840   Jan. 1 – Dec. 26.
1841   Jan. 2 – Oct. 1, 6 – Dec. 29.
1842   Jan. 1 – Dec. 14, 21 – 31.
1843   Jan. 4 – Dec. 30.
1844   Jan. 3 – Mar. 27, 30 – Dec. 28.
1845   Jan. 1 – June 11, 18 – Dec. 31.
1846   Jan. 3 – Dec. 30.
1847   Jan. 2 – Feb. 20, 27 – May 1,
        8 – Aug. 18, 25 – Oct. 13, 20 –
        Dec. 29.
1848   Jan. 1 – Dec. 30.
1849   Jan. 3 – July 14, 18 – Oct. 10,
        17 – Nov. 1, 10, 14 – Dec. 5,
        12 – 19, 26 – 29.
1850   Jan. 2 – Dec. 28.
1851   Jan. 1 – Apr. 20.
1854   Jan. 4 – Dec. 25.
1855   Feb. 6 – Dec. 29.
1856   Jan. 2 – Oct. 20.
1857   Jan. 3 – Dec. 30.
1858   Jan. 9 – Aug. 28, Sept. 18 –
        Dec. 29.
1859   Jan. 1 – Dec. 31.
1860   Jan. 4 – Oct. 17, 26 – Dec. 29.
1861 – 1865   Jan. 1 – Dec. 31.
1866   Jan. 2 – Apr. 28, May 4 – Dec.
        29.
1867 – 1869   Jan. 1 – Dec. 31.
1870   Jan. 3 – May 17, 19 – Oct. 29,
        Nov. 2 – Dec. 24.
1871 – 1873   Jan. 1 – Dec. 31.
1874   Feb. 3 – Dec. 31.
1875 – 1879   Jan. 1 – Dec. 31.
1880   Jan. 2 – Mar. 23, 27 – Dec. 18.
1884   Jan. 5 – Dec. 27.
1886 – 1888   Jan. 1 – 15, 23 – Dec. 31.
1889   Jan. 4 – May 11, 15 – Dec. 31.
1890 – 1899   Jan. 1 – Dec. 31.
1900   Jan. 2 – Mar. 5, 9 – June 30.

DLC
1838   Aug. 25 – Dec. 31.
1839 – 1846   [Jan. 1 – Dec. 31].
1847   Jan. 1 – Sept. 30, Nov. 1 –
        Dec. 31.
1848   July 1 – Dec. 31.
1849 – 1850   [Jan. 1 – Dec. 31].
1851   Jan. 1 – Apr. 20.
1854   Jan. 4 – Dec. 25.
1855   Feb. 6 – Dec. 31.
1856 – 1859   Jan. 1 – Dec. 31.
1860   [Jan. 1 – Dec. 31].
1861 – 1868   Jan. 1 – Dec. 31.
1869   [Jan. 1 – Dec. 31].
1870 – 1900   Jan. 1 – Dec. 31.
MWA
1845   Jan. 8.
1863   Oct. 10.
1864   [Oct.] 8 – Dec. 24.
1884   Feb. 9, Mar. 22.

EL PERUANO LIBERAL. sw. est. Sept.
1813.
    Note: Succeeded *El Peruano*.
CU – B
    Micro (N)
    1813   Prospecto.
            Oct. 3 – Nov. 18, 25 – Dec. 12.
CtY
    1813   Prospecto.
            Oct. 3 – Nov. 18, 25 – Dec. 12.

EL PLAYERO. irr. est. Jan. 15, 1834.
    Note: Ceased publication Mar. 11,
    1834.
DLC
    1834   Feb. 24.

POLITICA. w. est. Apr. 17, 1948.
NcD
    1948   Apr. 17 – Oct. 2.

TxU
    1948   Apr. 17 – Oct. 2.

PORVENIR. bw.
MWA
    1915   June 20.

POUR LA FRANCE LIBRE. d.
Note: In French.
MH
1942 Aug. 6 – 20, Sept. 10 – Oct.
29, Nov. 19 – Dec. 10.

PRENSA. bw.
MWA
1889 Apr. 16.

LA PRENSA. d. est. Sept. 23, 1903.
Note: Suspended publication Feb.
17 – Mar. 7, 1956.
CLCM
1930 June 29 (Movie supplement
only).
CU
1912 Mar. 26 – May 7, 14 – Dec. 31.
1913 Jan. 1 – Mar. 20, 22 – Dec. 31.
1914 Jan. 1 – Feb. 28, Mar. 3 – Aug.
1, 3 – 24.
CSt – H
1964 Nov. 19, 26, 30, Dec. 3.
1965 Aug. 2 – Dec. 31.
1966 Jan. 1+.
DLC
1926 Jan. 14, 17 – 19, 21 – 26, Feb.
2, 4 – 9, 11 – 14, 18, 20 – 27,
Mar. 1 – 4, 7 – 12, 15 – 20, 22 –
24, 27, 29, 30, Apr. 4, 9, 10,
12 – 15, 17 – 19, 23 – 30, May
2, 5, 8 – 11, 14, 16, 18 – 22, 24,
27 – June 1, 8, 15, 20, 21, 24,
26, 28, 29, July 28, 31, Aug. 2,
4, 10.
1938 Dec. 9.
1939 July 28.
1941 Mar. 20, 21, 30, 31, Apr. 19,
25, 27 – May 2, 4 – 6, 8, 9, 11,
13 – 15, 17 – 23, 26, 28, 30,
June 1, 3 – 6, 8, 10, 13, 14, 16,
20, 22, 24, 25, 27, 29, 30, July
3 – 6, 12, 15, 17 – 19, 23, 25,
26, 29 – 31, Aug. 11, 18, 23, 25,
29, 31, Sept. 1, 5, 7 – 9, 11, 13,
22, 27 – 29, Oct. 1, 2, 4, 6 – 8,
12, 14, 16, 17, 20, 21, 23 – 26,
28, 29, 31 – Nov. 2, 5, 7 – 10,
12, 15, 16, 21 – 23, 28 – Dec. 1,

3, 6, 7, 9, 11, 13, 14, 16, 20,
22 – 28.
1942 Jan. 2, 3, 5, 8 – 11, 14, 17, 18,
22, 27, Feb. 3 – 5, 10, 11, 13,
17, 22 – 24, 26, Mar. 1 – 4, 6,
7, 10, 12, 13, 15 – 19, 22 – 26,
28, 29, 31, Apr. 1, 4 – 6, 8, 10 –
14, 16 – 20, 22, 24 – 28, May 1,
3, 5, 6, 9 – 11, 14, 16 – 18, 20 –
25, 27, 29 – 31, June 2 – 5, 7,
8, 10, 12 – 14, Aug. 22, 23, 26 –
31, Sept. 2 – 11.
1943 Jan. 20 – 24, 26 – 30, Feb. 1 –
4, 6 – 12, 14 – Apr. 11, 13 –
May 11, 14, 15, 17 – 29, June
1 – July 26, 28 – 31, Aug. 2 –
Oct. 26, 28 – Nov. 1, 3 – 5, 7 –
9, 12 – 25, 27 – Dec. 2, 4 – 11,
14 – 30.
1944 Jan. 1 – 8, 10 – 15, June 1 –
30, Oct. 1 – 12, 14 – Dec. 31.
1945 Jan. 1 – Mar. 17, 19 – July 17,
20 – 24, 26 – Dec. 31.
1946 Jan. 1 – Mar. 15, 17 – 20, 22 –
Apr. 26, 28 – Aug. 14, 16, 18 –
24, 26 – Sept. 12, 15, 17 – 26,
28 – Oct. 10, 13, 14, 16 – 18,
20 – 23, 26 – Nov. 11, 14 – 26,
28 – Dec. 5, 7 – 11, 13 – 19, 22,
24 – 26.
1947 Jan. 1 – Dec. 31.
1948 Jan. 1 – Apr. 23, 25 – Aug. 4,
6 – Dec. 31.
1949 Jan. 1 – July 2, 7 – 31, Aug. 2 –
Dec. 31.
1950 Jan. 1 – Feb. 28, Mar. 6 – 10,
18, 21, 23, 26 – 31, Apr. 2, 3,
6, 7, 9 – 12, 14 – 25, 27 – Dec.
31.
1951 – 1952 Jan. 1 – Dec. 31.
1953 Jan. 1 – Dec. 20, 22 – 31.
1954 – 1958 Jan. 1 – Dec. 31.
1959 Jan. 7 – Dec. 31.
1960 Jan. 1 – Mar. 9, 11 – Dec. 31.
1961 Jan. 1 – June 12, 14 – Dec. 31.
Micro (P) & (N)
1962 Jan. 1+.

FU
  Micro (N)
  1914   [Mar. 1 – Apr. 30].
  MWA
  1907   Extraordinario: July 28.
  1913   June 26.
  NIC
  Micro (P)
  1962 – 1964   Jan. 1 – Dec. 31.
  1965   Mar. 1 – Dec. 31.
  1966   Jan. 1+.
  NN
  1914   Oct. 15 – 19, Nov. 2, 22, Dec.
          9, 22 – 30.
  1915   Jan. 4 – Feb. 1, 3 – 7, 9, 11 – 17,
          19 – 21, 23, 25 – Mar. 2, 5 – 18,
          20 – Apr. 1, 4 – May 12, 14,
          16 – Aug. 21, 23 – Sept. 11, 13,
          14, 30 – Oct. 13, 16 – 23, 25 –
          Dec. 15, 17 – 19, 21, 22.
  1916   Jan. 1 – 10, 12 – 31, Feb. 18 –
          Mar. 8, 10 – May 3, 5 – 10, 12 –
          17, June 1 – 21, 29 – 30, July
          2 – 14, 16 – 19, 21 – 23, 25 –
          28, 30, Aug. 1 – 8, 10 – 17, 19 –
          27, 30 – Sept. 14, 16 – Oct. 15,
          17, 19 – Nov. 7, 9 – Dec. 31.
LA PRENSA PERUANA. 3w. est. Jan.
  29, 1828.
    Note: Ceased publication July 1,
    1829.
  CtY
  1828   Jan. 29 – Feb. 5, 9 – Mar. 8,
          15, 20 – Apr. 12, 18 – June 10,
          17 – 28, July 8, 17 – Aug. 19,
          28, Sept. 4, 13 – Oct. 7, 14 – 30,
          Nov. 6 – Dec. 30.
  DLC
  1828   Jan. 29 – Dec. 30.
  1829   Mar. 5, 10 – 17, 28 – Apr. 3,
          June 17.
          Alcance: Mar. 28, June 13.
EL PROGRESO. w. est. July 28, 1849.
    Note: Ceased publication Mar. 15,
    1851.
  CtY
  1849   July 28 – Aug. 18, 29 – Dec.
          29.

1850   Jan. 5 – Mar. 30.

EL PUEBLO. est. 1823.
    Note: Published only four numbers.
  CtY
  1823   n.d. (Nos. 1 – 4).

EL QUIPOS DEL CHIMU. w. est. Nov. 1,
  1832.
    Note: Ceased publication Dec. 1,
    1833.
  DLC
  1833   Jan. 19, 26.

EL REBENQUE. irr. est. Aug. 10, 1841.
    Note: Ceased publication Oct. 30,
    1841.
  CtY
  1841   Aug. 10 – Oct. 30.

EL REDACTOR ECLESIASTICO. sw.
  est. 1845.
  CtY
  1846   Jan. 28.

EL REDACTOR PERUANO. sw. est. Jan.
  16, 1834.
    Note: Title *El Redactor*, Jan. 16 –
    19, Feb. 12 – May 7, 1834; *El Redactor
    peruano*, Jan. 21 – Feb. 8, May 10,
    1834 – Aug. 20, 1838. Succeeded *El
    Conciliador* as the official gazette;
    succeeded by *El Peruano*; *diario
    oficial*. Ceased publication Aug. 20,
    1838.
  CtY
  1834   Jan. 16 – Dec. 31.
  1835   Jan. 3 – Feb. 21.
  1836   July 2 – Aug. 13.
  1838   July 31 – Aug. 20.
  DLC
  1834   Jan. 16 – Dec. 31.
  1835   Jan. 3 – Feb. 23.
  1836   Jan. 6 – Aug. 13.
  1838   July 31 – Aug. 20.
  MWA
  1834   June 9.
  1836   Mar. 16.

EL REJENERADOR. 3w. est. Apr. 26,
1835.
   Note: Ceased publication Dec. 25,
   1835.
   CU — B
   Micro (N)
   1835   July 31, Dec. 13.
   CtY
   1835   Apr. 26 — Dec. 25.
        Extraordinario: May 15 — Sept.
        25.
   MWA
   1835   Aug. 16.
        Suplemento: [Sept.]
REJISTRO OFICIAL. w. est. Apr. 30,
1851.
   Note: Published during suspension
   of *El Peruano*; *diario oficial*. Ceased
   publication Dec. 31, 1853.
   CtY
   1851   Apr. 30 — Dec. 31.
   1852 — 1853   Jan. 1 — Dec. 31.
   DLC
   1851   Apr. 30 — Dec. 31.
   1852 — 1853   Jan. 1 — Dec. 31.
EL REPERTORIO PERUANO. sw. est.
Jan. 18, 1843.
   Note: Ceased publication Mar. 15,
   1843.
   CtY
   1843   Jan. 18 — Mar. 15.
LA REPUBLICA. w., sw. est. Nov. 15,
1863.
   Note: Periodicity Nov. 15, 1863 — Apr.
   17, 1864, weekly; Apr. 20 — July 16,
   1864, semiweekly. Ceased publication
   July 16, 1864.
   CtY
   1863   Nov. 15 — Dec. 27.
   1864   Jan. 3 — June 4.
EL RESTAURADOR. 3w. est. Apr. 4,
1839.
   CtY
   1839   Apr. 4 — 6.
EL REVISOR. w. est. Feb. 23, 1827.
   Note: Suspended publication Apr.
   21 — May 29, 1827; ceased publication
   [May 30], 1827.

CtY
   1827   Feb. 23 — Apr. 20, May 30.

LA REVISTA. sw. est. Feb. 12, 1840.
   Note: Published only four numbers.
   Ceased publication Feb. 25, 1840.
   CtY
   1840   Prospecto: Feb. 12.
        Feb. 12 — 25.

REVISTA SOCIAL. w.
   MWA
   1887   May 24, July 16.

EL RIMAC. w. est. Mar. 16, 1850.
   Note: Ceased publication Feb. 1,
   1851.
   CtY
   1850   Mar. 16 — Nov. 2, Dec. 28.
   1851   Jan. 4 — 18.

EL RONDIN DE LA LIBERTAD. irr. est.
Dec. 31, 1835.
   Note: Ceased publication [Feb.] 1836.
   CU — B
   Micro (N)
   1835   Dec. 31.
   1836   Jan. 1 — Feb. 9.
   CtY
   1835   Dec. 31.
   1836   Jan. 2 — 25.

EL SEMANARIO. w. est. July 1, 1814.
   Note: Ceased publication Dec. 9,
   1814.
   CtY
   1814   July 1 — 15, Aug. 19, Sept. 2 —
        9, Oct. 14 — 21.

EL SEMANARIO DE LIMA. w. est. June
25, 1823.
   Note: Published only three numbers.
   Ceased publication July 9, 1823.
   CtY
   1823   June 25 — July 9.

SOL. w.
   MWA
   1826   Nov. 4 — 11.

SOL. sw.
  MWA
    1887   Jan. 5.

EL SOL DEL PERU. w., irr. est. Mar. 14,
  1822.
    Note: Ceased publication June 27,
    1822.
  CtY
    1822   Mar. 14 – June 27.

EL SOL DEL PERU. irr. est. Jan. 16,
  1823.
    Note: Published only two numbers.
    Ceased publication Jan. 30, 1823.
  CtY
    1823   Jan. 16, 30.
  DLC
    1823   Jan. 16.

EL SOLDADO DE LA PATRIA. w. est.
  Feb. 17, 1827.
    Note: Ceased publication July 28,
    1827.
  CtY
    1827   Feb. 17 – Apr. 14, May 12,
            June 9 – July 28.

SUCESOS DE LA SEMANA. w. est.
  Dec. 7, 1946.
  TxU
    1946   Dec. 7 – 31.
    1947   Jan. 1 – July 27.

LA TARDE. d. est. Aug. 5, 1948.
  TxU
    1948   Aug. 5 – Oct. 2.

EL TELEGRAFO DE LIMA. d. est. Apr.
  2, 1827.
    Note: Suspended publication Aug.
    30, 1829 – May 31, 1832; ceased pub-
    lication Jan. 31, 1839.
  CtY
    1829   Apr. 3, 6, 8 – 24, 27 – May 15,
            18 – 26, 29 – July 18, 21 – 27,
            29, 31 – Aug. 28.
    1833   July 5, 6.
    1837   May 23.
  DLC
    1827   Prospecto.
            Apr. 2 – May 1, 3 – 11, 14 – 21,

            31, June 5 – 16, 22 – July 4, 7 –
            18, 20, 21, 26, 30, Aug. 1, 3, 13.
    1828   Feb. 8, 9, Mar. 5, 6, 14 – 17.
            Suplemento: Feb. 5.
    1829   Jan. 2 – 27, 29 – Mar. 31.
            Suplemento: Feb. 2, 24.
    1832   Nov. 24.
    1833   Oct. 14, 16 – 22, 24, Dec. 2 – 5,
            7 – 12, 14 – 19, 21 – 23.
    1834   Feb. 15, 21, June 30 – Aug. 5,
            8 – 13, 16 – 18, 20, 22 – Sept.
            11, 13 – Oct. 29, 31 – Nov. 13,
            15 – Dec. 10, 13, 14, 16 – 31.
            Suplemento: Feb. 22, July 21.
    1835   Jan. 1 – Feb. 1, 4 – 20.
    1836   Mar. 21, 22, Dec. 30.
    1837   Jan. 2 – May 19, 22 – 31, Oct.
            27 – 31, Nov. 3 – 6, 8 – 11, 28 –
            Dec. 20, 22, 23.
            Suplemento: Apr. 24, 29, May
            17.
    1838   Jan. 13 – 22, 24 – 27, Feb. 13 –
            Mar. 1, 7 – 12, 24, 28 – Apr. 3,
            Nov. 19 – 28.
  MWA
    1827   May 1, 2, 4 – 8, 12, 18, 21, July
            18, 23, 24, Aug. 1, 3, 6, 13.

TIEMPO. d. est. July 1, 1864.
    Note: Ceased publication May 31,
    1865.
  MWA
    1864   Sept. 26, 27, Oct. 1 – Nov. 26.

TIEMPO. d. est. May 16, 1895.
    Note: Ceased publication ₍1907₎.
  MWA
    1905   July 31.

LA TRIBUNA. d. est. 1931.
    Note: Suspended publication ₍1934₎ –
    Sept. 26, 1945; Oct. 4, 1948 – July 2,
    1957.
  CSt
    1933   Nov. 12, 13, 27 – 30, Dec. 3 – 5.
    1948   Jan. 3, 6, 8, 10.
  CSt – H
    1965   Aug. 2 – Dec. 31.
    1966   Jan. 1+.

DLC
  1934 July 26.
  1945 Sept. 29 – Dec. 31.
  1946 Jan. 1 – Dec. 31.
  1947 Jan. 1 – Sept. 29, Oct. 1 – Dec. 31.
  1948 Jan. 1 – Oct. 3.
  1958 Jan. 1 – June 16, 18 – 30, July 2 – 25, 27 – Dec. 31.
  1959 Jan. 1 – 23, 25 – Feb. 8, 10 – July 29, 31 – Dec. 31.
  1960 Jan. 1 – Aug. 21, 23 – Nov. 5, 7 – 16, 18 – Dec. 31.
  1961 Jan. 1, 2, 4 – Feb. 26, 28 – Mar. 10, 12 – Dec. 31.
  Micro (P) & (N)
  1962 Jan. 1+.
FU
  1965 Jan. 1+.
  Micro (N)
  1957 July 3 – Dec. 31.
  1958 – 1964   Jan. 1 – Dec. 31.
NIC
  Micro (P)
  1962 Jan. 2 – Dec. 31.
  1963 Jan. 1+.
NcD
  1945 Sept. 27 – Dec. 31.
  1946 Jan. 1 – Dec. 31.
  1947 Jan. 1 – Oct. 3.
TxU
  1945 Sept. 29 – Dec. 31.
  1946 – 1947   Jan. 1 – Dec. 31.
  1948 Jan. 1 – Oct. 3.
  1957 July 3 – Sept. 10, 12 – Dec. 31.
  1958 – 1959   Jan. 1 – Dec. 31.
  1960 Jan. 1 – Mar. 8.

EL TRIBUNO DEL PUEBLO. sw., 3w.
  est. Sept. 1, 1838.
    Note: Ceased publication Dec. 27, 1839.
  CU – B
    Micro (P)
    1838 Sept. 1 – Nov. 8.
  CtY
    1838 Sept. 1, 12, 26, Oct. 11 – 25, 29 – Nov. 3.
    1839 Feb. 26, Mar. 12 – 16, Apr. 12,

23 – 25, June 7, 18, 25, July 2, 5, 23 – 26, Aug. 2 – Dec. 27.
  DLC
    1838 Sept. 1 – 12, 22 – 29, Oct. 4, 8, 13, 15, 27, 29.
      Extraordinario: Oct. 4.

EL TRIUNFO DE LA NACION. sw. est.
  Feb. 13, 1821.
    Note: Ceased publication June 26, 1821.
  CU – B
    Micro (N)
    1821 Feb. 16, 23 – 27, Mar. 6, 16, 30 – Apr. 20, 27, May 8, 22 – 29, June 5, 8 – 12.
  CtY
    1821 Feb. 16, 23 – 27, Mar. 6, 16, 30 – Apr. 20, 27, May 8, 22, 25, June 8 – 12.

EL TRIUNFO DE LA OPINION. irr.
  CU – B
    Micro (N)
    1836 Jan. 1 – 3.

TRIUNFO DEL CALLAO. irr., w. est.
  Mar. 1, 1824.
    Note: Ceased publication Jan. 5, 1825.
  CU – B
    Micro (N)
    1824 Mar. 1 – 24, Apr. 7 – June 16, July 28, Sept. 1 – 8, 22, Oct. 6 – 27, Nov. 10 – 24, Dec. 30.
  CtY
    1824 Mar. 1 – 24, Apr. 7 – June 16, July 28, Sept. 1 – 8, 22, Oct. 6 – 27, Nov. 10 – 24, Dec. 30.

ULTIMA HORA. d. est. Jan. 13, 1950.
  Note: Suspended publication Feb. 17 – Mar. 5, 1956.
  DLC
    1950 Jan. 16 – 24, 26, 27, 29, Feb. 1, 2, 5 – 15, 17 – 19, 23 – Mar. 9, 11 – May 17, 24, 25, Aug. 1 – 29, 31 – Dec. 31.
    1951 Jan. 1 – Aug. 29, Sept. 1 – Oct. 31, Nov. 2 – 26, 28 – Dec. 31.

1952   Jan. 1 – June 28, July 1 – 27, 31,
       Aug. 1 – 29, 31 – Sept. 23,
       25 – Oct. 22, 24, 26, 28, 30, 31,
       Nov. 2 – 26, 28 – Dec. 7, 9 – 31.
1953   Jan. 1 – 5, 7 – Feb. 15, 18 –
       Mar. 18, 20 – Apr. 1, 4 – 30,
       May 2 – 13, 15 – June 3, 5 – 23,
       25 – 28, 30 – Aug. 22, 25 – Nov.
       18, 20 – Dec. 31.
1954   Jan. 3 – Feb. 26, 28 – Mar. 25,
       27 – June 6, 8 – Aug. 12, 14, 15,
       17 – Sept. 3, 5 – 7, 9 – 14, 16 –
       Oct. 10, 13, 15 – 24, 26 – 31,
       Nov. 3 – Dec. 9, 11, 12, 14 – 31.
1955   Jan. 3 – 16, 18 – 27, 29 – Feb. 2,
       4 – Mar. 13, 15 – June 20, 22 –
       July 18, 20 – Oct. 1, 3 – 19, 21 –
       24, 26 – Nov. 9, 11 – 13, 15, 17
       – Dec. 15, 17 – 22, 24 – 31.
1956   Jan. 2 – 10, 13 – Feb. 9, 11, 12,
       15 – Mar. 5, 7 – 22, 24 – Apr. 2,
       4 – 22, 24 – June 8, 10 – 26,
       28 – July 12, 14 – 20, 22 – Sept.
       17, 19 – 29, Oct. 1 – 28, 30 –
       Nov. 11, 13 – 23, 25 – Dec. 31.
1957   Jan. 1 – 11, 13 – Mar. 29, Apr.
       1 – 3, 5 – May 8, 10, 12 – 29,
       June 2 – 6, 8 – 10, 12 – 19, 21 –
       27, July 1 – 27, Sept. 2, 4 – 14,
       17, 18, 20 – Oct. 8, 10 – 23, 26 –
       31, Nov. 2 – Dec. 12, 14 – 31.
1958   Jan. 1 – Mar. 9, 11 – Apr. 29,
       May 2, 4 – 6, 9 – 13, 16 – 27,
       29 – June 4, 6 – Aug. 8, 10 –
       19, 21 – Oct. 27, 29 – Dec. 4,
       6 – 19, 21 – 31.
1959   Jan. 2 – Feb. 6, 8 – Apr. 10,
       12 – 15, 18 – 24, 26 – May 17,
       19 – 22, 24 – 29, June 1, 3, 4,
       6 – Sept. 13, 15 – 30, Oct. 2 –
       Nov. 8, 10 – Dec. 31.
1960   Jan. 1 – May 6, 8 – June 23,
       25 – July 19, 21 – Sept. 29, Oct.
       1 – 9, 11 – Dec. 31.
1961   Jan. 2 – 4, 7 – 10, 12 – Feb. 23,
       25 – 27, Mar. 1 – 29, Apr. 1 –
       13, 15 – Aug. 20, 22, 23, 25 –
       Oct. 5, 7 – Nov. 17, 19 – Dec.

       30.
Micro (P) & (N)
1962   Jan. 1+.

UNIVERSAL. d. est. May 3, 1935.
  Note: Ceased publication July 7,
  1945.
  DLC
  1938   Dec. 9.
  1941   Mar. 20 – 22, 25, 30, 31, Apr.
         14, 23 – May 20, 22, 23, 25 –
         June 5, 7 – 12, 16, 17, 19 – July
         8, 10 – 18, 20 – 22, 24 – 28, 30 –
         Aug. 2, 4 – 12, 14, 16, 18, 22,
         24 – Sept. 11, 13 – 16, 18, 19,
         21, 23, 26 – Oct. 1, 3 – 9, 11, 12,
         15 – 17, 19 – Nov. 5, 7, 9, 10,
         12, 14, 15, 17, 18, 20 – 22, 24 –
         Dec. 3, 5 – 19, 21, 24 – 31.
  1942   Jan. 1 – 4, 6 – 14, 16 – 19, 21 –
         Feb. 7, 9 – 13, 15, 21 – 26, 28 –
         Apr. 14, 16 – May 5, 7 – June 1,
         3 – 14, 19, Aug. 12, 21, 23, 25 –
         Sept. 10.
  1943   Apr. 1, 2, 5 – 8, 12 – 16, 20, 22 –
         30, May 2, 3, 5, 6, 8 – 10, 13,
         15 – 26, 28 – June 4, 6 – 10, 12
         – Aug. 29, Sept. 1 – 6, 8 – Oct.
         26, 28, 29, Nov. 1 – 5, 7 – 22,
         24 – Dec. 2, 4, 6 – 25, 27 – 31.
  1944   Jan. 1 – 14, 16 – May 23, 25 –
         28, 30 – July 1, 3 – 5, 7 – Dec.
         31.
  1945   Jan. 1 – July 7.
  MH
  1939   Dec. 2.

VANGUARDIA. w. est. 1898.
  Note: Ceased publication 1899.
  MWA
  1898   Dec. 3.

VANGUARDIA; LA VOZ QUE DICE LO
QUE PUEBLO PIENSA. w., sw. est.
1945.
  Note: Periodicity 1945 – Apr. 5,
  1946, weekly; after Apr. 5, 1946,
  semiweekly. Suspended publication
  Aug. 21, 1948 – Jan. 6, 1949.

CSt
    1948   May 11.
NcD
    1945   Aug. 5 – Dec. 31.
    1946 – 1948   Jan. 1 – Dec. 31.
    1949   Jan. 1 – Mar. 11.
TxU
    1945   Aug. 28 – Dec. 31.
    1946   Jan. 1 – Apr. 23, 30 – Dec. 31.
    1947   Jan. 1 – Dec. 23.
    1948   Jan. 5 – Aug. 20.
    1949   Jan. 7 – Mar. 11.
    1957 – 1959   Jan. 1 – Dec. 31.
    1960   Jan. 1 – Mar. 5.

EL 29 JULIO. irr. est. July 31, 1838.
  CtY
    1838   July 31.

LA VERDAD. est. Dec. 5, 1832.
    Note: Ceased publication Oct. 14,
    1833.
  CtY
    1832   Dec. 5.

LA VERDAD. est. [1942].
  DLC
    1943   July 21.

EL VERDADERO PERUANO. w. est.
  Oct. 1, 1812.
    Note: Ceased publication 1813.
  CU – B
    Micro (N)
    1812   Prospecto.
            Oct. 1 – Dec. 31.
    1813   Jan. 7 – Apr. 1, July 1 – 8.
            Extraordinario: Apr. 13.
  CtY
    1812   Prospecto.
            Oct. 1 – Dec. 31.
    1813   Jan. 7 – Apr. 1, July 1 – 8.
            Extraordinario: Apr. 13.
  NHi
    1812   Prospecto.
            Oct. 1 – Dec. 31.
    1813   Jan. 1 – Aug. 26.

EL VETERANO. d. est. Oct. 15, 1834.
    Note: Ceased publication Jan. 31,

    1835.
  CtY
    1834   Oct. 15 – Dec. 31.
    1835   Jan. 2 – 31.

EL VETERANO DE GUIA. irr. est. Jan.
  1839.
    Note: Ceased publication Jan. 22,
    1839.
  CU – B
    Micro (N)
    1839   Jan. 10.
  CtY
    1839   Jan. 10 – 22.
  DLC
    1839   Jan. 10.

EL VINDICADOR. irr. est. Jan. 3, 1823.
    Note: Published only three numbers.
    Ceased publication Jan. 29, 1823.
  CtY
    1823   Jan. 3 – 29.

EL VOTO NACIONAL. d. est. Nov. 3,
  1834.
    Note: Ceased publication Mar. 20,
    1835.
  CU – B
    Micro (N)
    1834   Dec. 19 – 31.
    1835   Jan. 1 – Feb. 16.
  CtY
    1834   Prospecto.
            Nov. 3 – Dec. 31.
    1835   Jan. 2 – Mar. 20.

THE WEST COAST LEADER.
    See *The New West Coast Leader*.

LA ZAMACUECA POLITICA. sw. est.
  Jan. 1859.
  CtY
    1859   Jan. 29 – Feb. 5, 16 – 23, Mar.
            2, 30, Apr. 13 – May 4, 14, 18,
            June 18, 25 – July 6, 13 – 16,
            27 – Aug. 3.

Mendoza

See Argentina. Mendoza.

Mollendo

GACETA DEL PUERTO. sw.
  MWA
    1886   [Jan. 6 – May 26], Nov. 16, 23 –
           Dec. 4, 21 – 31.
    1887   Jan. 1.

PUERTO. w., sw. est. Sept. 3, 1893.
    Note: Periodicity Sept. 3, 1893 – Dec.
    31, 1897, weekly; after Jan. 1, 1898,
    semiweekly.
  MWA
    1901   Aug. 13.
    1905   July 5, Aug. 2.

Paita

ARTESANO. w.
  MWA
    1913   June 7, 21.
           Extraordinario: June 26.

Paz

EL ESTANDARTE. irr. est. Mar. 18, 1852.
  CtY
    1852   Mar. 18 – May 7, 16 – 23, June
           11 – 17, July 6 – Aug. 11, Sept.
           18 – Oct. 9.

Puno

ACTUALIDAD. w.
  MWA
    1879   Sept. 30.

BRISA. bw.
  MWA
    1878   Mar. 21.

EL CONSTITUCIONAL. w.
  CtY
    1851   Mar. 15 – May 10, Dec. 20.
  MWA
    1845   Sept. 6 – 13, Nov. 22.
    1846   Aug. 22, Dec. 12 – 31.
    1847   Jan. 1 – 9.
    1848   Jan. 22 – Feb. 12, Sept. 23.
    1849   June 9.
    1851   Jan. 4, Feb. 1, 22 – Apr. 19,
           May 3 – 10, 31, Aug. 30 – Nov.
           8, 29, Dec. 13, 27.
    1852   Jan. 17.

FEDERAL DE PUNO. w.
    Note: Title *Federal*, before June 10,
    1837; *Federal de Puno*, after June 11,
    1837.
  MWA
    1837   Jan. 14 – July 15, 29 – Aug. 12.

INANVARI. w.
  MWA
    1887   July 28.

LIBERTAD. sw. est. Apr. 12, 1891.
  MWA
    1891   Apr. 12 – 15, 26 – June 10, 17 –
           July 1, 15 – 22, Aug. 9 – 30,
           Sept. 9 – 16, 26.

PERUANO DEL SUD. w.
  MWA
    1829   Oct. 29.

TITICACA. w.
  MWA
    1851   July 19.

TRABAJO. bw. est. Jan. 1, 1876.
  MWA
    1876   Jan. 1.

Santiago de Chuco

EL CENTINELA EN CAMPAÑA. irr est.
    Apr. 22, 1824.
  CtY
    1824   Apr. 22.

Tacna

See Chile. Tacna.

Tarma

EL ECO DE SOCABAYA. est. 1838.
  DLC
    1838   Oct. 17.

EL TELEGRAFO. d. est. Nov. 1, 1861.
  CtY
    1861   Nov. 3.

Trujillo

LA CONCORDIA PERUANA. sw.
  CtY
    1836   July 13, 20, 27, Aug. 3, 10, 17,

24, 31, Sept. 7.
Suplemento: Sept. 7.

EL CONSTITUCIONAL PERUANO. irr.
est. Dec. 21, 1823.
Note: Ceased publication Mar. 6,
1824.
CtY
1823　Prospecto.
Dec. 21 – 29.
1824　Jan. 5 – Mar. 6.

INDUSTRIA. d. est. 1895.
MWA
1901　June 3.

LA NACION. d. est. 1932.
OrU
1936　May 6.

NUEVO DIA DEL PERU. w., irr. est.
July 1, 1824.
Note: Periodicity July 1 – Aug. 26,
1824, weekly; Sept. 2 – 25, irregular.
Ceased publication Sept. 25, 1824.
CtY
1824　July 1 – Sept. 25.

EL QUIPOS DEL CHIMU. w. est. 1833.
CtY
1833　May 18, 24, June 8, 22.
Suplemento: July 6.

EL REDACTOR DE TRUJILLO. w., sw.
est. Sept. 8, 1838.
Note: Official publication. Ceased
publication Apr. 24, 1841.
CtY
1838　Sept. 8.
Extraordinario: Sept. 10.
DLC
1839　Extraordinario: Jan. 14.

EL SEMANARIO. w. est. Jan. 6, 1842.
CtY
1842　Jan. 6 – Apr. 7.

PUERTO RICO

Aguadilla

EL JIBARO. w. est. May 1866.
Note: Ceased publication 1866.

CU – B
Micro (P)
1866　Aug. 18.

Arecibo

EL BALUARTE. w. est. Dec. 1, 1900.
DLC
1900　Dec. 1.

LA CAMPAÑA. d. est. Jan. 1911.
Note: Ceased publication 1915.
MWA
1913　Mar. 26.

LA DEMOCRACIA. w. est. Aug. 24, 1873.
CU – B
Micro (P)
1873　Aug. 24, Oct. 12, 26.

EL DUENDE. d., 3w. est. July 16, 1904.
Note: Succeeded by *El Demócrata*.
DLC
1908　Aug. 14, 20, 21, 25, Sept. 23.
MWA
1913　Mar. 18.

ECOS DE TANAMA. sw. est. Sept. 1902.
PrU
1903　July 2.

GAZETA DE PUERTO-RICO.
MWA
1808　Suplemento: Aug. 17.

EL PEQUEÑO DIARIO. d. est. Mar. 1895.
Note: Succeeded *La Voz de la montaña* (Utuado). Removed to Mayagüez [1898].
DLC
1895　Mar. 7, Aug. 11.
PrU
1895　Mar. 17, 19, 24, 25 – 28, Apr.
1, 2, 5, 6, 8, 10, 16, 18, 19, 20,
26, 27, May 23.

EL PUBLICISTA. w. est. May 1885.
Note: Ceased publication Nov. 1886.
PrU
1885　Oct. 17.

EL REGIONALISTA. d. est. 1914.
   Note: Ceased publication 1947.
   PrU
   1921   July 1 – Dec. 31.
   1922 – 1946   Jan. 1 – Dec. 31.
   1947   Jan. 1 – May 1.

LA REPUBLICA. sw. est. Jan. 19, 1893.
   Note: Ceased publication July 1893.
   PrU
   1893   Feb. 15, 18, 22, 25, Mar. 1, 4, 8,
             11, 15, 18, 22, 25, 29, Apr. 5, 8,
             12, 15, 19, 22, 26, 29, May 3, 6,
             13, 20, 24, 30, June 3, 7, 10, 14,
             17, 21, 24, 28, July 1, 5.

LA VOZ DEL NORTE. d. est. Aug. 7,
1895.
   Note: Removed to Manatí, Nov. 1895.
   Ceased publication Jan. 1896.
   DLC
   1895   Aug. 7.

Bayamón

EL BALUARTE REPUBLICANO. est.
Mar. 1913.
   MWA
   1913   Mar. 30.

EL PROGRESO. w. est. 1959.
   PrU
   1959   Aug. 20, Sept. 1 – Dec. 31.
   1960   Sept. 1, 8.
   1961   Oct. 3.

LA VOZ DE BAYAMON. irr. est. Oct. 29,
1965.
   PrU
   1965   Oct. 29, Nov. 12, Dec. 7, 30.
   1966   Feb. 1.

Cabo-Rojo

EL COCUYO. 3m. est. Sept. 1873.
   CU – B
   Micro (P)
   1873   Nov. 10 – 30.

EL PROGRESO. w. est. Apr. 1, 1906.
   DLC
   1906   Apr. 1.

Caguas

LA DEMOCRACIA. d. est. July 1, 1890.
   Note: Originally established in Ponce;
   removed to Caguas, Oct. 23, 1900;
   removed to San Juan, June 1, 1904.
   PrU
   1900   Oct. 23 – Dec. 31.
   1901 – 1903   Jan. 1 – Dec. 31.

Cayey

EL DEMOCRATA. w. est. Jan. 22, 1899.
   Note: Suspended publication Aug.
   1900.
   DLC
   1899   Jan. 22.
   PrU
   1900   Sept. 18.

Guánica

BRISAS DEL CARIBE. w. est. Nov. 21,
1915.
   Note: Removed to Yauco, 1923.
   PrU
   1921   July 25.

Juncos

EL ABANICO. w. est. July 1886.
   Note: Ceased publication Dec. 1886.
   PrU
   1886   Aug. 10.

Humacao

LA ABEJA. w. est. Dec. 1878.
   Note: Ceased publication Aug. 1881.
   CU – B
   Micro (P)
   1881   Jan. 2.
   PrU
   1879   Sept. 28.
   1880   May 23, Aug. 15, 22, Dec. 5.

LA JUVENTUD. 3m. est. July 1, 1880.
   CU – B
   Micro (P)
   1880   Dec. 20.

Lares

EL COMBATE. w. est. Mar. 24, 1928.
  Note: Ceased publication 1929.
  PrU
    1928   Mar. 24, May 5, June 2, July
        14, 28, Aug. 11, 18, Sept. 1, 8.

Manatí

LA VOZ DE NORTE. w. est. July 6, 1879.
  Note: Ceased publication Apr. 1880.
  PrU
    1879   July 20, Aug. 14, 15, 19.

Mayagüez

AMERICA. est. 1898.
  Note: In Spanish and English.
  DLC
    1898   Aug. 27.
  NN
    1898   Oct. 12, 13.

EL AVISADOR DEL COMERCIO. w.
  est. Feb. 12, 1863.
  CU−B
    Micro (P)
    1863   Nov. 5.

AYER Y HOY.
  See *Diario del oeste*.

LA BANDERA AMERICANA. d. est.
  1898.
    Note: Title *La Nueva bandera*, 1898−
    1906; *La Bandera americana*, after
    1906. Ceased publication 1921.
  DLC
    1899   June 6−Dec. 31.
    1900   Jan. 1−June 2.
    1908   Aug. 9.
  MWA
    1913   Apr. 3.
  NN
    1907   May 15, 19.
  PrU
    1919   Jan. 7.

BOLETIN INSTRUCTIVO Y MERCAN-
  TIL DE PUERTO RICO. sw. est. Mar.
  2, 1839.
    Note: Also published in San Juan.
    Ceased publication 1918.

CU−B
  Micro (P)
  1841   May 19, June 26.
  1844   Dec. 4.
  1846   Dec. 2.

LA BRUJA. w., d. est. Jan 9, 1898.
  Note: Succeeded by *Revista blanca*.
  Ceased publication Sept. 1917.
  PrU
    1898   Jan. 9−Dec. 31.

EL CENTINELA ESPAÑOL. 6m. est.
  Apr. 1871.
  PrU
    1872   Nov. 4.
    1873   Sept. 29.

EL COMPILADOR INDUSTRIAL. w. est.
  Sept. 1855.
  CU−B
    Micro (P)
    1863   Oct. 31.
  PrU
    1862   Sept. 20.

EL CORREO. d. est. Feb. 9, 1903.
  DLC
    1903   Feb. 9.

EL CREMATISTICO. d. est. Feb. 18,
  1896.
  DLC
    1896   Feb. 18.

EL CRITERIO ESPAÑOL. w. est. Mar.
  7, 1886.
    Note: Ceased publication June 1886.
  DLC
    1886   Mar. 7.

DIARIO DE MAYAGÜEZ. d. est. June 5,
  1891.
    Note: Suspended publication July
    1891.
  DLC
    1891   June 5, July 24.

DIARIO DEL OESTE. d. est. May 1910.
  Note: Title *Diario del oeste*, 1910−
  1920; *La Nueva era*, 1920−1932;
  Ayer y hoy, 1932−[1940]; *Diario del
  oeste*, after [1940].

DLC
  1940 Oct. 1 – Dec. 31.
  1941 Jan. 1 – 7.
MWA
  1913 Mar. 31.
PrU
  1931 Aug. 3, 5, 7, Sept. 19, Oct. 31,
        Nov. 17.
  1933 Oct. 10, 14, 17, 20, 21, 24.
  1936 Apr. 4, 6, 11.
  1940 Aug. 27 – Oct. 11, 14, 16, 17,
        22, 23, 25, 26, 28 – 31, Nov. 4,
        6 – 9, 12, 13, 16, 18, 20, 22, 23,
        26, 28, Dec. 3, 4, 12, 16, 17, 19.
  1941 Jan. 9 – 15, 17, May 19, 20,
        June 6, 12, 13, Dec. 1, 18.
  1942 Mar. 2, 19, 21, 23, Apr. 19, 23 –
        25, 27, May 14, 15, June 5, 6,
        15 – 20, 22, 23, 25, 29, 30, July
        1, 2, 3, 6 – 11, 13, 15 – 18, 20,
        22, 23, 28, 29, Aug. 3 – 8, 10 –
        15, 18 – 22, 27 – 29, 31, Sept.
        1, 2, 5, 8 – 12, 15, 16, 18, 19,
        21, 22, 25, 26, 28 – Oct. 3, 5 –
        10, 13 – 17, 19, 21 – 24, 26, 27,
        29 – 31, Nov. 2, 5, 6, 9, 12, 16,
        17, 24, 28, Dec. 2, 3, 5, 7, 9,
        12, 15, 16, 18, 19, 21, 24, 26,
        28, 29, 31.
  1943 Jan. 8, 9, 11, 12, 15, 16, 18 – 22,
        25, 26, 30, Feb. 1, 3, 5, 6, 8 –
        13, 15 – 18, 26, 27, June 17,
        21, 22, 26, July 6, 10, 12 – 14,
        15, 16.

EL ECO DE MAYAGÜEZ. 3w. est. June
18, 1891.
  DLC
  1891 June 18.

EL ECO DEL PUEBLO. w. est. Apr. 1871.
  Note: Ceased publication Feb. 1874.
  CU – B
  Micro (P)
  1874 Jan. 3 – 10.

LA EPOCA. w. est. July 1876.
  Note: Ceased publication Nov. 1878.
  PrU
  1878 Aug. 10.

EL IMPARCIAL. d. est. July 1885.
  Note: Ceased publication 1900.
  DLC
  1898 Aug. 2.
  1899 June 6 – Dec. 31.
  1900 Jan. 1 – June 1.
  PrU
  1887 Aug. 28.

EL LIBERAL. d. est. June 12, 1886.
  Note: Ceased publication Oct. 1887.
  DLC
  1886 June 12 – Dec. 30.
  PrU
  1887 Sept. 2.

LA NACION. w. est. Mar. 21, 1880.
  PrU
  1880 Mar. 28, June 12, Aug. 21, Sept.
        4, 11.

EL NACIONALISTA. 3w. est. Jan. 10,
1905.
  DLC
  1905 Jan. 10.

LA NUEVA BANDERA.
  See *La Bandera americana*.

LA NUEVA ERA.
  See *Diario del oeste*.

EL PEQUEÑO DIARIO.
  See Arecibo: *El Pequeño diario*.

THE PORTO RICO HERALD. est. Oct.
27, 1898.
  Note: In Spanish and English.
  DLC
  1898 Oct. 27.

EL PORVENIR DE BORINQUEN. sw.
est. Nov. 1898.
  Note: Ceased publication Oct. 1899.
  PrU
  1899 Mar. 1 – Sept. 30.

LA PRENSA. w. est. Mar. 4, 1875.
  Note: Ceased publication Nov. 1880.
  DLC
  1875 Mar. 4.
  PrU
  1876 June 1 – 30, Sept. 1 – 30.

1877   Jan. 1–Dec. 31.
1878   Mar. 1–31.
1879   May 1–31.
1880   Jan. 1–Mar. 31.

LA PROPAGANDA. d. est. Feb. 1883.
  Note: Ceased publication Dec. 1884.
  PrU
  1883   Mar. 22, May 1.

LA RAZON. w. est. Oct. 1870.
  Note: Ceased publication 1874.
  CU–B
  Micro (P)
  1873   Aug. 5, 15.

EL REPUBLICANO. 3w. est. June 27,
1899.
  DLC
  1899   June 27–July 8.

EL SEMANARIO MAYAGÜESANO. w.
est. Jan. 1850.
  CU–B
  Micro (P)
  1852   Aug. 11.

EL TIEMPO.
  See San Germán: *El Tiempo.*

LA UNIDAD NACIONAL. est. June 1887.
  Note: Ceased publication 1896.
  PrU
  1887   Dec. 26.

UNION OBRERA. w., d. est. Mar. 1902.
  Note: Established in Ponce as a weekly; removed to Mayagüez as a daily;
  second edition published in San
  Juan beginning in [1918]. Ceased publication [1932].
  DLC
  1908   June 15, 16, 18, July 2, 6–11,
          17, 18, 20, 22, 25, 29–Aug. 1,
          6, 11, 15, 20, 22.
  MWA
  1913   Apr. 2.

LA VOZ DE LA PATRIA. d. est. Dec. 14,
1901.
  Note: Ceased publication Aug. 5,
  1922.

DLC
  1901   Dec. 14.
  1908   Aug. 24, Sept. 4, 15, 22.
MWA
  1913   Mar. 17.

Ponce

EL AGUILA DE PUERTO RICO.
  See *The Puerto Rico Eagle. El Águi-
  la de Puerto Rico.*

EL AMIGO DEL PUEBLO. d. est. May
30, 1912.
  Note: Ceased publication July 1912.
  PrU
  1912   May 30.

EL ASIMILISTA. 3w. est. June 17, 1882.
  PrU
  1882   June 17, 20, Oct. 19.
  1883   Mar. 29, June 21, Oct. 20.
  1884   Jan. 12, Feb. 9, 28, Sept. 20,
          Dec. 17.

EL AVISADOR. w. est. Mar. 1874.
  PrU
  1874   Apr. 11, 25, May 16.

EL AVISADOR. w. est. May 21, 1874.
  Note: Succeeded by *La Crónica.*
  Ceased publication Apr. 1875.
  PrU
  1874   May 21, June 1, 18, 25, July 16,
          Aug. 13, 20, Oct. 15, 22, Nov.
          12, 16, 25, 26, Dec. 10.
  1875   Jan. 14, 21, 28, Feb. 4, 11, 18,
          25, Mar. 11, 18, 24, Apr. 1, 8,
          15.

LA BOMBA. 3w. est. Feb. 7, 1895.
  Note: Succeeded by *El Combate.* Suspended publication May 4, 1895–
  Sept. 21, 1898; Oct. 19–Dec. 31,
  1898; ceased publication Feb. 1899.
  PrU
  1895   Feb. 7, 23, Mar. 2, 13, 17, 24,
          28, 31, Apr. 4, 7, 14, 21, May 3.

EL CAUTIVO. 3w. est. Apr. 23, 1895.
  PrU
  1895   Apr. 23, 25, 27, 30, May 2, 4, 7,

9, 11, 14, 16, 18, 21, 28, June 1,
Aug. 8, 10, 13, 15, 17, 22, 31,
Sept. 3.

EL COMBATE. d. est. Feb. 25, 1899.
Note: Succeeded *La Bomba*. Suspended publication Feb. 28 — May
21, 1899.
PrU
1899   Feb. 27.

CORREO DE PUERTO RICO. d. est.
Aug. 1, 1898.
Note: See also English edition, *The
Porto Rico Mail*. Ceased publication
Apr. 1899.
DLC
1898   Aug. 1.
PrU
1898   Oct. 18, 25, 26, Nov. 17, Dec.
2, 6, 9, 10, 11, 13, 26, 27.
1899   Jan. 3, 5, 9, 10, 14, 18 — 22, 24,
27, 28, 31, Mar. 29, Apr. 10.

LA CRONICA. w., sw., 3w. est. May 1875.
Note: Succeeded *El Avisador*. Title
La Crónica de Ponce 1875 — 1879;
La Crónica, 1879 — 1881. Periodicity
1875 — 1879, weekly; 1879 — 1880,
semiweekly; 1880 — 1881, three times
a week. Succeeded by *El Pueblo*.
Ceased publication Oct. 1881.
CU — B
Micro (P)
1881   Jan. 11.
DLC
1879   July 22.
PrU
1877   May 3, July 12.
1878   June 14.
1879   Sept. 12, 19.
1880   June 19, Aug. 14.

EL CRONISTA. 3w. est. Dec. 1889.
Note: Ceased publication [1890].
DLC
1890   June 26.

EL DEBATE. d. est. Dec. 1899.
DLC
1899   Dec. 6.

EL DEBATE. w. est. Apr. 30, 1961.
Note: Ceased publication Aug. 29,
1965.
PrU
1961   Apr. 30 — Dec. 31.
1962 — 1964   Jan. 1 — Dec. 31.
1965   Jan. 1 — Aug. 29.

LA DEMOCRACIA. 3w., d. est. July 1,
1890.
Note: Periodicity July 1, 1890 — Apr.
30, 1893, three times a week; after
May 1, 1893, daily. Removed from
Ponce to Caguas, Oct. 23, 1900; removed to San Juan, June 1, 1904.
DLC
1890   July 1.
1898   Mar. 24.
1899   Feb. 1 — Dec. 27.
NN
1899   Apr. 26.
PrU
1890   July 1 — Dec. 31.
1891 — 1899   Jan. 1 — Dec. 31.
1900   Jan. 1 — Oct. 22.

EL DERECHO. 6m. est. Apr. 22, 1873.
Note: Ceased publication Oct. 22,
1873.
CU — B
Micro (P)
1873   Aug. 12 — 22.
PrU
1873   Apr. 27, May 7, 12, 17, 22, June
2, 7, 12, 17, 22, 27, July 2, 7, 12,
22, 27, Aug. 2, 7, 12, 17, Sept. 7,
Oct. 7, 12, 17, 22.

EL DERECHO POPULAR. sw. est. Jan.
1884.
PrU
1884   Jan. 7, Apr. 2, 8, 10, 15, 16,
June 4.

EL DIA. d. est. May 2, 1911.
Note: Succeeded *El Diario de Puerto Rico*.
DLC
1940   Oct. 23 — Dec. 31.
1941   Jan. 1 — 21, Oct. 25.

1943   Mar. 24 – 27, 29, 30.
LNT – MA
  1932   Sept. 28 – Dec. 31.
  1933   [Jan. 1 – July 31].
MWA
  1913   Apr. 3.
NcD
  1923   May 19, 22 – Oct. 4, 6 – Dec. 31.
  1924   Jan. 1 – Dec. 31.
  1925   Jan. 2 – 8, 12.
  1933   Aug. 25, 30.
PrU
  1919   Mar. 14, 19, 31 – Apr. 2, 5.
  1931   May 1, 2, 4, 6 – 11, 13 – 28, 30,
          June 1, 3 – 6, 9, 10, 12 – 15,
          17 – 23, 26 – 30, Oct. 5 – 13,
          15 – 20, 22, 26 – 31, Nov. 2 – 19,
          21, 25 – 28, Dec. 1 – 17, 21, 22,
          24 – 31.
  1932 – 1934   Jan. 1 – Dec. 31.
  1945   Jan. 1 – Mar. 31, Oct. 1 – 31.
  1946   Feb. 1 – 28.
  1947   June 1 – July 31.
  1948 – 1965   Jan. 1 – Dec. 31.
  1966   Jan. 1 – 31.

EL DIABLILLO-ROJO. w. est. Nov. 1873.
    Note: Ceased publication 1874.
  CU – B
    Micro (P)
    1873   Nov 9 – 16, 30.

EL DIARIO DE PONCE. d. est. Dec. 1, 1900.
    Note: Ceased publication July 13, 1903.
    PrU
    1902   May 14.

EL ECO DE PONCE. w. est. July 1880.
    Note: Ceased publication Nov. 1880.
    PrU
    1880   July 12.

EL ECO DE PUERTO RICO. 3w. est. June 2, 1905.
    Note: Ceased publication Oct. 1905.
    PrU
    1905   July 7, 8, 10, 13, 17, 18, 23, 27,
            29, Aug. 2, 5, 8, 10.

EL ECO DEL COMERCIO. w. est. June 1861.
    CU – B
      Micro (P)
      1863   Oct. 31.
    PrU
      1862   July 5.

LA ESTRELLA SOLITARIA.
    See *La Propaganda*.

EL FENIX. w. est. July 7, 1855.
    Note: Ceased publication 1860.
    DLC
      1855   Oct. 13 – 19.
      1856   Apr. 20 – May 2, 18 – 30, July
              6 – Aug. 15, 17 – Dec. 31.
      1857   Jan. 1 – 9, 11 – Feb. 6, 8 – Dec.
              31.
              Suplemento: Dec. 19.
      1858   Jan. 1 – 15, 17 – 29, 31 – May
              28, 30 – July 2, 4 – Nov. 5, 7 –
              Dec. 23.
    PrU
      1858   Sept. 5.
      1859   Jan. 22.

HERALDO DEL TRABAJO. w. est. May 16, 1877.
    Note: Ceased publication Oct. 1880.
    CU – B
      Micro (P)
      1880   Apr. 5, July 28.
    DLC
      1877   May 16.
    PrU
      1878   Jan. 1 – Feb. 28, Aug. 1 – 31,
              Nov. 1 – 30.
      1879   Sept. 1 – Nov. 30.
      1880   Apr. 1 – 30.

EL IDEAL CATOLICO. w. est. Aug. 15, 1899.
    Note: Ceased publication Mar. 1915.
    PrU
      1899   Aug. 15 – Dec. 31.
      1900 – 1910   Jan. 1 – Dec. 31.
      1911   June 3, Dec. 2, 9.
      1912 – 1914   Jan. 1 – Dec. 31.
      1915   Jan. 1 – Mar. 6.

EL IMPARCIAL. d. est. May 9, 1902.
DLC
1902   May 9.
PrU
1902   Prospecto: May 2.
        May 17.

THE JOURNAL. d. est. Nov. 5, 1898.
Note: In English.
DLC
1898   Nov. 5.

LA LIBERTAD. 3w., d. est. Feb. 18, 1894.
Note: Suspended publication June—
Dec. 16, 1894; Apr.—Aug. 7, 1895;
ceased publication July 18, 1897.
PrU
1894   Feb. 27, Mar. 1, 3, 8, 10, 15, 17.

EL NOTICIERO. d. est. Dec. 2, 1912.
Note: Ceased publication Sept. 1914.
DLC
1914   Feb. 24—Mar. 2.
MWA
1913   Apr. 3.

LA NUEVA ERA. d. est. July 1898.
Note: In Spanish and English until
Sept. 1898; after, in Spanish only.
Suspended publication Jan. 1899.
DLC
1898   Aug. 18, 19, Oct. 29, Nov. 25,
        26, 28, Dec. 21, 31.
1899   June 9, 10, 12, Aug. 4, 5, Sept.
        18, Oct. 19, 24, Nov. 21, 23,
        25, 28, Dec. 6, 7, 14—16, 21.
1900   Feb. 28.

EL PAIS. w. est. Aug. 8, 1866.
Note: Published in place of *El Propagador*. Ceased publication 1868.
PrU
1866   Sept. 21, Nov. 16.
1867   Feb. 1.

EL PAIS. w. est. Feb. 21, 1875.
PrU
1875   Feb. 21—Apr. 25.

LA PATRIA. d. est. Mar. 23, 1899.
DLC
1899   Mar. 23.

PrU
1899   Apr. 7, 12, 29, May 27.

LA PEQUEÑA ANTILLA.
See *La Propaganda*.

EL PITIRRE. d. est. Jan. 1899.
DLC
1901   Feb. 27.

EL PONCEÑO. w. est. July 1, 1852.
Note: Ceased publication July 1854.
CU—B
Micro (P)
1853   May 14.
DLC
1854   Mar. 25, Apr. 22, July 8.
PrU
1952   Aug. 28—Dec. 31.
1953   Jan. 1—June 30, Aug. 20—Dec.
        31.
1954   Jan. 1—June 30.

THE PORTO RICO AMERICAN. 3w. est.
Feb. 4, 1899.
Note: In English.
DLC
1899   Feb. 4.

THE PORTO RICO MAIL. d. est. Oct.
10, 1898.
Note: In English. See also Spanish
edition, *Correo de Puerto Rico*.
Ceased publication Apr. 1899.
DLC
1898   Oct. 22.
PrU
1898   Oct. 14.

EL PORVENIR. d. est. Feb. 3, 1902.
PrU
1902   Apr. 2, 29.

LA PROPAGANDA. 3w., d. est. Nov.
23, 1895.
Note: Title *La Pequeña antilla*,
Nov. 23, 1895—July 28, 1898; *La
Estrella solitaria*, July 28, 1898—
Sept. 1899; *La Propaganda*, after
Oct. 1899.
DLC
1898   May 14, Aug. 16.

1899   Nov. 10, 22, Dec. 9.
PrU
1896   Jan. 24, Apr. 29.

EL PUEBLO. 3w. est. Oct. 7, 1881.
Note: Ceased publication Oct. 6,
1887.
PrU
1881   Oct. 7.
1882   July 4.
1883   Mar. 29.
1884   July 8.
1885   May 14.

THE PUERTO RICO EAGLE. EL
AGUILA DE PUERTO RICO. d. est.
Jan. 8, 1902.
Note: In Spanish and English. Suspended publication July 3, 1931 –
Dec. 31, 1933. Ceased publication
Mar. 1934.
DLC
1905   Sept. 2 – Dec. 31.
1906 – 1912   Jan. 1 – Dec. 31.
1913   Jan. 1 – Feb. 20.
LNT – MA
1929   Oct. 1 – 15, Nov. 12 – 30, Dec.
1, 23 – 31.
1930   [Jan. 1 – Dec. 31].
1931   Jan. 1 – June 30.
MWA
1913   Apr. 5.
NcD
1923   Jan. 2 – 5, 7 – 21, 23 – June 25,
28 – July 2, 6 – Sept. 9, 13 – 24,
28 – Oct. 8, 12 – Nov. 8, 12 –
Dec. 6, 9 – 31.
1924   Jan. 2 – 17, 21 – Apr. 2, 8 –
17, 19 – 21, 24 – 27, May 2, 3,
6, 7, 9 – 21, 24 – June 15, 20 –
22, 26, 27, 30 – July 4, 6 – Aug.
28, 31 – Sept. 26, 28 – Oct. 16,
19 – Dec. 1, 4 – 15, 19 – 22.
1925   Jan. 2 – 5, 7 – 14, 18 – Feb. 23,
27 – Apr. 9, 12 – 27, 30 – Oct. 5,
8 – 12, 15 – Dec. 12, 15 – 31.
1926   Jan. 2 – 11, 19 – May 3, 6 – Nov.
4, 7, 9 – Dec. 31.
1927   Jan. 2 – May 23, 31 – Oct. 10,

18 – 30, Nov. 1 – Dec. 31.
1928   July 1, 3 – 8, 10, 11, 13 – 17,
19 – Sept. 3, 5 – 7, 9 – 13, 15 –
25, Oct. 2 – 22, 24 – Nov. 20,
27 – Dec. 3, 5 – 17, 26 – 31.
1929   Jan. 10 – Feb. 25, Mar. 5, 6,
8 – 25, 27 – Apr. 5, 7 – 29, May
7 – Dec. 31.
1930   Jan. 1 – 7, 11, 12, 14 – 20, Feb.
12 – 18, Mar. 1 – Apr. 21, 30 –
May 5, 14 – July 28, Aug. 5 –
31, Sept. 10 – 15, 23 – Oct. 6,
21 – Nov. 23, Dec. 16 – 31.
1931   Jan. 1 – June 30.
PrU
1902   Jan. 8 – Dec. 31.
1903   Jan. 1 – Dec. 31.
1913   Apr. 1 – Dec. 31.
1914   Jan. 1 – Dec. 31.
1915   Oct. 1 – Dec. 31.
1916   Apr. 1 – May 30.
1917   Apr. 1 – Dec. 31.
1918   Dec. 1 – 31.
1919   Jan. 1 – Feb. 28, Apr. 1 – 30.

LA VANGUARDIA. d. est. Oct. 29, 1899.
Note: Suspended publication 1900 –
1901. Ceased publication 1901.
DLC
1899   Nov. 21, 23, 28, Dec. 1, 2, 5,
11, 13, 15, 21.

Río Piedras

ACCION. w. est. Aug. 1948.
PrU
1948   Aug. 7, 28.

CIUDAD UNIVERSITARIA. w. est.
Nov. 1936.
PrU
1936   Dec. 13.
1937   Jan. 1 – Dec. 31.
1938   Jan. 1 – May 31, June 5, 19,
July 3, 10, 17, 24, Aug. 14, 21,
Sept. 4, 11, 18, Oct. 2, 16, 30,
Nov. 1 – Dec. 31.
1939   Jan. 1, 8, 29, Feb. 1 – 28, Mar.
19, 26, Apr. 1 – 30, May 14, 21,

28, June 1 – 30, July 2, 9, 16,
30.
1940   Feb. 12.

EL DIARIO DE RIO PIEDRAS. d. est.
Aug. 6, 1962.
PrU
1962   Aug. 6, 13, Sept. 15, 22.

HERALDO DE RIO PIEDRAS. est. Apr.
21, 1945.
PrU
1945   Apr. 21, May 5, June 2.

UNIVERSIDAD. irr.
CU
1948   Aug. 15 – Sept. 30, Oct. 20 –
Dec. 5.
1949   Jan. 17 – July 31, Sept. 30 –
Dec. 16.
1950   Feb. 20, Apr. 27 – Aug. 21.

San Germán

EL ECO DE LAS LOMAS. w. est. May
31, 1878.
Note: Ceased publication July 1878.
PrU
1878   July 13.

EL TIEMPO. w. est. Oct. 1874.
Note: Removed from Mayagüez,
May 1876.
PrU
1876   Oct. 8.

San Juan

EL AGENTE. 3w.
CU – B
Micro (P)
1880   Nov. 2 – 4.

EL AUTONOMISTA. w. est. May 2,
1895.
PrU
1895   May 2, 11, 25, June 1, 6, 8, 15,
22, 29, July 13, 20, 27, Aug. 3,
12, 19, Sept. 2, 9, 16, 23, 29.

LA BALANZA. w., 3w., d. est. Oct.
1887.
Note: Ceased publication Aug. 1897.

PrU
1893   Jan. 20, 29, Feb. 1, 3, 5, 8, 10,
12, 15, 17, 18, 22, 24, Mar. 1, 5,
8, 15, 17, 22, 24, 26, 29, Apr. 5,
7, 9, 12, 14, 16, 30, May 3, 7,
12, 14, 17, 19, 21, 24, 26, 28, 31,
June 4, 9, 11, 14, 16, 18, 21, 23,
25, 28, 30, July 2, 7, 13, 14, 16,
19, 21, 23, Aug. 2, 4, 9, 13, 20,
23.
1894   Jan. 13, 14, 17, 19, 21, 24, 26,
28, 31, Feb. 2, 4, 7, 9, 11, 14,
16, 18, 21, 25, 28, Mar. 2, 4, 9,
11, 14, 16, 18, 28, 30, Apr. 1,
4, 6, 8, 11, 13, 15, 18, 20, 22,
25, 27, 29, May 2, 4, 6, 9, 13, 16,
20, 23, 25, 27, 30, June 3, 6, 8.

EL BALUARTE. sw., w. est. Apr. 15,
1906.
Note: Ceased publication Nov. 8,
1906.
PrU
1906   Apr. 15, 19, 22, 26, 29, May 3, 6,
10, 13, 17, 20, 24, 27, 31, June 3,
7, 10, 14, 17, 21, 24, 28, July 1,
5, 8, 12, 15, 16, 19, 22, 26, 29,
Aug. 2, 9, 12, 15, 18, 23, 26, 30,
Sept. 6, 9, 13, 16, 20, 23, 27, 30,
Oct. 4, 7, 11, 14, 18, 21, 26, 27,
Nov. 1, 4, 8.

BOLETIN INSTRUCTIVO Y MER-
CANTIL DE PUERTO RICO. d. est.
Mar. 2, 1839.
Note: In Spanish and English. Title
Boletín mercantil de Puerto Rico,
1839 – 1916; *Boletín instructivo y
mercantil de Puerto Rico*, 1916 –
1918. Ceased publication 1918.
DLC
1857   May 16, Aug. 5.
Alcance: Aug. 1.
1864   Apr. 27.
1899   Aug. 1 – 3, 15 – 19, 21 – 24, 26,
28 – Sept. 2, 4, 5, 15, 16, 18 –
22, 25, Oct. 11, 12, 18, 31, Nov.
28, Dec. 13 – 16, 18 – 23.

1900   Jan. 11 – Dec. 31.
1901   Jan. 1 – June 28, July 1, 2, 5, 6,
        8 – 13, 15 – 20, 22 – 24, 26, 27,
        Aug. 13 – 17, 19 – 24, 26 – 31,
        Oct. 1 – Dec. 31.
1902   Jan. 2 – 4, 6, 8 – 11, 13 – 15, 17,
        18, 20, 24, 25, 27 – 31, Feb.
        12 – 15, 17, Mar. 1 – June 30,
        Sept. 2 – Dec. 31.
1903 – 1906   Jan. 1 – Dec. 31.
1907   Jan. 1 – Apr. 30, May 1 – 4.
1908   Mar. 30.
MWA
1843   May 24.
1913   Mar. 28.
PrU
1839   May 1 – Dec. 31.
1841 – 1842   Jan. 1 – Dec. 31.
1871 – 1872   Jan. 1 – Dec. 31.
1873   Jan. 1 – Feb. 28, Apr. 1 – 30,
        July 1 – 31, Nov. 1 – Dec. 31.
1874 – 1886   Jan. 1 – Dec. 31.
1887   Jan. 1 – June 30.
1888 – 1889   Jan. 1 – Dec. 31.
1890   Jan. 1 – June 30.
1891 – 1897   Jan. 1 – Dec. 31.
1898   Jan. 1 – July 31.
1899   Jan. 1 – June 30.
1900   Aug. 1 – Dec. 31.
1901   Jan. 1 – June 30.
1902   Jan. 1 – June, Nov. 1 – Dec. 31.
1904   July 1 – Dec. 31.
1905   Jan. 1 – June 30.
1906 – 1909   Jan. 1 – Dec. 31.
1910   Jan. 1 – Apr. 30, Sept. 1 – Dec.
        31.
1911   Jan. 1 – Dec. 31.
1918   Jan. 1 – May 30, Aug. 1 – 31.
ViU
1907   Feb. 5.

BRAZOS. w. est. 1945.
PrU
1945   Sept. 29, Nov. 17.

EL BUSCAPIE. w. est. Apr. 1, 1877.
    Note: Suspended publication June
    26, 1899 – Oct. 16, 1917; ceased pub-
    lication June 29, 1918.
PrU
1881   Feb. 13 – 27, Mar. 13 – Aug. 7,
        21, Sept. 1 – Nov. 20, Dec.
        11 – 25.
1882   Jan. 1 – Dec. 31.
1883   Jan. 1 – Mar. 11, 25 – Apr. 1,
        15 – 29, May 13 – June 3, 17,
        July 1, 8.
1887   Mar. 20, Apr. 10 – July 31, Aug.
        14, 21, Sept. 18, Oct. 9, 16, Dec.
        11, 18.
1888   Jan. 1 – 15, Feb. 12, 26, Mar. 4,
        25, Apr. 1 – 22, May 13, 27,
        June 3, 17, July 1, 22, Aug. 12,
        26, Sept. 9 – Dec. 31.
1889   Jan. 6. 20, 27, Feb. 17, 28, Mar.
        10 – Apr. 7, 21, May 12 – 21,
        June 22, Sept. 29, Oct. 5, Nov.
        17.
1890   Jan. 4, Apr. 13, May 11, Oct.
        12 – Nov. 23, Dec. 7 – 28.
1891   Jan. 1 – 3, 5 – Dec. 31.
1892   Jan. 1 – Dec. 31.
1893   Jan. 2 – Dec. 31.
1894   Dec. 1 – 31.
1895   Jan. 1 – June 30.
EL CLAMOR DEL PAIS. 3w. est. May
15, 1883.
    Note: Ceased publication 1894.
PrU
1885   Jan. 1 – Aug. 31.
1888 – 1889   Jan. 1 – Dec. 31.
1891 – 1893   Jan. 1 – Dec. 31.
1894   Jan. 1 – July 31.

EL CLAMOR DEL PAIS. d. est. Aug. 2,
1905.
DLC
1905   Aug. 2.
EL COMERCIO. 3w. est. 1878.
PrU
1879   Oct. 21.

CORREO DOMINICAL. w. est. July
1926.
NcD
1926   Aug. 15, Sept. 5, Oct. 31 – Nov.
        21, Dec. 5 -- 19.

1927   Jan. 2, 30, Feb. 13 — Dec. 4,
        18, 25.
1928   Jan. 1 — 3, Feb. 12 — Mar. 31,
        Apr. 15, 29, May 13 — 29, Aug.
        1 — Sept. 9, 23.
PrU
1926   Nov. 14 — 26.
1927   Jan. 2, Feb. 6 — Mar. 27.

LA CORRESPONDENCIA DE PUERTO
RICO. d. est. Dec. 18, 1890.
DLC
1892   Dec. 20.
1899   June 1 — Dec. 31.
1900 — 1903   Jan. 1 — Dec. 31.
1904   July 1 — Dec. 31.
1905 — 1917   Jan. 1 — Dec. 31.
1918   Jan. 1 — Nov. 11.
1919   Jan. 30 — Dec. 31.
1920 — 1942   Jan. 1 — Dec. 31.
1943   Jan. 1 — 7, 16 — 29, Feb. 5 — 11.

LNT — MA
1938   May 3.
MH
1904   July 27 — 30, Aug. 1 — 6, 8, 9.
MWA
1913   Apr. 4.
NcD
1911   July 1 — 22, 24 — Oct. 19, 21 —
        Nov. 8, 10 — Dec. 26, 28 — 31.
1912   Jan. 1 — Apr. 16, 18 — 20, 23,
        25 — June 27, 29 — Aug. 9, 11 —
        Dec. 31.
1913   Jan. 1 — June 14, 16 — Aug. 8,
        10 — 21, 23 — 26, 28 — Dec. 31.
1914   Jan. 1 — 6, 13 — 20, 28 — Feb. 11,
        13 — July 17, 20 — Dec. 31.
1915   Jan. 1 — Mar. 19, 21 — Apr. 4,
        6 — June 19, 23 — July 5, 7 —
        Aug. 1, 2, 4 — 10, 12 — 18, 20 —
        Sept. 1, 3 — 13, 15 — 27, 29 —
        Oct. 4, 6 — 18, 20 — 25, 27 — Nov.
        1, 3 — 6, 8 — 11, 13, 15 — 22, 24,
        25, 27 — Dec. 6, 8 — 27, 30, 31.
1916   Jan. 1 — 10, 13 — 15, 18, 21 — 25,
        28 — 31, Feb. 2 — 5, 8, 11 — 16,
        18 — 29, Mar. 2, 6, 8, 9, 11 — 20,
        22 — Apr. 5, 7, 8, 12, 14 — 22,

        25 — May 4, 8, 10 — 18, 20, 23,
        26, 29 — 31, June 5 — 24, 26 —
        July 24, 28 — 31, Aug. 5 — 7, 9 —
        19, 24 — Oct. 12, 14 — Nov. 11,
        14, 15, 18 — Dec. 11, 13 — 20,
        22 — 27, 29 — 31.
1917   Jan. 1 — 11, 13 — 22, 24 — Feb.
        1, 5 — 12, 14 — 19, 21 — 27, Mar.
        3 — 13, 21, 22, 27, Apr. 10, 17 —
        19, 21 — 23, 25, 27, May 1, 4, 7,
        9, 10, 12 — 21, 23 — 25, 30 — June
        2, 7, 9, 23 — 28, July 2 — 4, 10 —
        14, 18, 21 — 23, 26, Aug. 3 — 6,
        8 — 14, 16 — 22, 24 — 27, 29 —
        Sept. 4, 6 — 8, 11 — 13, 18 — 20,
        24, 25, 27, 29 — Oct. 2, 6 — 10,
        12 — 19, 22 — Nov. 6, 9 — 15,
        17 — 22, 26, 27, 30 — Dec. 3,
        10 — 12, 14, 15, 18, 26 — 29.
1918   Jan. 2, 7 — 11, 14, 16 — 25, 28 —
        Feb.4,8 — 14,16 — Mar.11,
        14 — 30, Apr. 1 — 25, 27 — 29,
        May 2, 3, 5 — 17, 19, 21, 29 —
        June 2, 5 — 9, 11 — 26, 28 — July
        15, 17 — 29, 31 — Aug. 1, 3 — 8,
        10, 11, 13, 14, 16, 22 — 25, 27 —
        29, Sept. 8 — 10, 13 — 15, 19,
        21 — 23, Oct. 3, 5 — 7, 10, 12, 13.
1919   Jan. 3 — 8, 10 — 14, 16 — 21, 24 —
        30, Feb. 1 — 13, 15 — 19, 21 — 24,
        26 — Mar. 20, 22 — 26, 28 — Apr.
        4, 7 — 29, May 2 — 19, 21 — 29,
        June 2, 3, 5 — 13, 17 — 25, 30,
        July 2, 5 — 7, 9 — 15, 17 — 19, 21,
        23, 25, 30 — Aug. 1, 4 — 6, 11, 12,
        14, 18 — 20, 22, 26, 29, 30, Sept.
        4, 8, 13, 16 — 19, 23, Oct. 6 — 8,
        10 — 13, 14, 17, 20 — 23, 30, Nov.
        1 — 4, 6, 7, 10 — 14, 17, 19, 21,
        24, 28, Dec. 1, 4 — 15, 17 — 20,
        24, 27 — 30.
1920   Jan. 3 — 5, 7 — 15, 19 — 21, 23,
        26, 27, 29, 30, Feb. 3, 4, 6, 10,
        12 — 23, 25, 26, Mar. 1, 3, 4, 6 —
        8, 10 — 20, 23, 24, 26 — 30, Apr.
        1, 6, 12, 13, 15 — 17, 19, 21, 23,
        24, 27, May 11, 12, 22, 28 — 31,
        June 2, 3, 7, 8, 10, 12, 15, 23,

25 – 28, 30, July 3, 10 – 12, 15,
16, 19, 21, 23, 28, 30, Aug. 2, 5,
9, 11, 13, 17, 20, 25 – 27, 30 –
Sept. 3, 7, 9, 13 – 16, 18 – 20,
22, 24, 27, 29, Oct. 1, 5.

1921   Jan. 3 – 11, 13 – Feb. 2, 4, 9,
10, 14, 24 – 26, Mar. 1, 2, 4, 7,
16 – 22, 24, 28 – Apr. 1, 3 – 5,
9 – 30, May 3, 4, 6 – 17, 20 – 24,
26 – June 23, 27 – Nov. 14, 23 –
Dec. 31.

1922   Jan. 1 – Aug. 2, 4 – Dec. 31.

1923   Jan. 1 – Feb. 20, Mar. 1 – 29,
31 – May 15, 17 – 29, 31 – Dec.
31.

1924   Jan. 1 – Nov. 3, 5 – Dec. 31.

1925   Jan. 2, 3, 5 – 7, 12, 15, 17 – Feb.
12, 14 – Mar. 25, 31, Apr. 2 – 9,
11 – June 6, 8 – 13, 16 – Sept. 6,
8 – 18, 20 – Dec. 31.

1926   Jan. 2 – 14, 16, 21 – Feb. 10,
12 – May 4, 6 – July 3, 6 – Aug.
11, 13 – Sept. 5, 7 – Dec. 31.

1927   Jan. 1 – Feb. 21, 23 – Mar. 24,
26 – Dec. 31.

1928 – 1931   Jan. 1 – Dec. 31.

1932   Jan. 1 – Mar. 30, Apr. 5 – 26,
28 – May 22, 24 – Oct. 12, 14 –
Dec. 31.

1933   Mar. 23 – 25, 27.

1934   Jan. 2, 3, 9 – 24, 26 – Feb. 20,
25, Mar. 1 – 22, 28 – July 3.

PrU

1891 – 1898   Jan. 1 – Dec. 31.
1902 – 1903   Jan. 1 – Dec. 31.
1912   July 1 – Aug. 31, Nov. 1 – 30.
1913   Apr. 1 – 30.
1914   Dec. 1 – 31.
1915   June 1 – 30.
1916   July 1 – Dec. 31.
1917   May 1 – June 30, Sept. 1 – Dec.
31.
1918   Jan. 1 – Mar. 31, July 1 – Dec.
31.
1919   Jan. 1 – Dec. 31.
1920   Jan. 1 – Apr. 30, July 1 – Dec.
31.
1921 – 1942   Jan. 1 – Dec. 31.
1943   Jan. 1 – 31.

LA DEMOCRACIA. 3w., d. est. July 1,
1890.

Note: Established in Ponce; removed
to Caguas Oct. 23, 1900; removed to
San Juan, June 1, 1904. Succeeded
by *Diario de Puerto Rico*. Ceased
publication Dec. 31, 1948.

DLC
Micro (P) & (N)
1905   Jan. 2 – Dec. 31.
1906 – 1947   Jan. 1 – Dec. 31.
1948   Jan. 1 – Oct. 9.

LA DEMOCRACIA. d. est. 1891.
MH
1904   Aug. 3 – 10.

NcD
1922   Jan. 1, 3 – 31, Feb. 2 – Mar. 1,
3 – June 8, 10, 12, 14 – Sept. 6,
8 – Dec. 30.

1923   Jan. 2 – Apr. 4, 6 – June 30,
July 2 – 8, 10 – 18, 21 – Dec. 1,
4 – 22, 26 – 29, 31.

1924   Jan. 1 – Dec. 31.

1925   Jan. 1 – 10, 13 – 20, 22 – Feb.
17, 19 – Mar. 4, 6 – 18, 20 –
Apr. 9, 11 – Dec. 9, 17 – 31.

1926   Jan. 1 – 13, 21 – Dec. 31.

1927   Jan. 1 – 5, 7 – Feb. 9, 17 – Apr.
14, 16 – May 31, June 2 – Sept.
7, 15 – 21, 28 – Dec. 21, 29 – 31.

1928   Jan. 1 – Nov. 5, 7 – Dec. 31.

1929 – 1930   Jan. 1 – Dec. 31.

1931   Jan. 1 – Mar. 3, 5 – 11, 13 – 31,
Apr. 2, 4 – Oct. 26, Nov. 1 –
Dec. 31.

1932   Jan. 1 – Apr. 20, May 1 – 19,
21 – Sept. 27, 30 – Dec. 31.

1933   Jan. 1 – May 8, 10 – June 30,
July 7, 9 – Aug. 30, Sept. 1 –
Dec. 31.

1934   Jan. 1 – July 3.

PrU
1904   June 1 – Dec. 31.
1905 – 1931   Jan. 1 – Dec. 31.
1932   Feb. 1 – 28, Sept. 1 – Oct. 31.
1933 – 1936   Jan. 1 – Dec. 31.
1937   Jan. 1 – June 30, Aug. 1 – Dec. 31.

1938 – 1948   Jan. 1 – Dec. 31.

EL DEMOCRATA. w. est. Jan. 23, 1937.
    PrU
        1937   Jan. 23.
        1938   Jan. 8, 22, Feb. 5, Mar. 12, 26,
                Apr. 23, May 14, June 11, 25,
                July 9, 23, Aug. 13, 27, Sept.
                24, Oct. 22, Nov. 26.
        1941   Nov. 29, Dec. 20.

EL DIARIO. d. est. Oct. 14, 1878.
        Note: Ceased publication Aug. 1879.
    PrU
        1879   Apr. 4.

EL DIARIO DE PUERTO RICO. d. est.
    July 6, 1893.
        DLC
        1893   Prospecto: June 27.
        1894   June 15.
        PrU
        1893   July 6 – Dec. 31.
        1894   Jan. 1 – June 30.

EL DIARIO DE PUERTO RICO. d. est.
    Sept. 1896.
        PrU
        1896   Oct. 22.

DIARIO DE PUERTO RICO. d. est. Jan.
    5, 1900.
        Note: In Spanish and English. Ceased
        publication Sept. 18, 1900.
        DLC
        1900   Jan. 5, Apr. 5 – 7, 9 – 11, 23.
        PRU
        1900   Jan. 5 – Sept. 18.

DIARIO DE PUERTO RICO. d. est. Oct.
    15, 1948.
        Note: Succeeded *La Democracia*.
        Ceased publication June 18, 1952.
        DLC
        1948   Oct. 15 – Dec. 31.
        1949 – 1951   Jan. 1 – Dec. 31.
        1952   Jan. 1 – June 18.
        PrU
        1949   Feb. 1 – Dec. 31.

1950 – 1951   Jan. 1 – Dec. 31.
1952   Jan. 1 – June 18.

DIARIO ECONOMICO DE PUERTO
    RICO. 3w. est. Mar. 14, 1814.
        Note: Ceased publication 1815.
        PrU
        1814   Mar. 18, 21, 23, 25, 28, May 2,
                4, 6, 9, 11, 12, 16, 18, 20, 25, 27,
                June 1, 3, 6, 8, 10, 13, 20, 22, 24,
                27, 29, July 1, 8, 11, 16, 23, 28,
                30, Aug. 3, 8, 11, 17, 19, 22, 26,
                29, Sept. 1, 12, 14, 19, 21, 24,
                27, 30, Oct. 3, 7, 12, 14, 18, 26,
                28, Nov. 2, 29, Dec. 2, 6, 15, 20,
                24, 30.
        1815   Jan. 7, 10, 14, 20.

DIARIO LIBERAL Y DE VARIEDADES.
    d. est. Dec. 16, 1821.
        Note: Ceased publication 1822.
        PrU
        1821   Dec. 20 – 31.
        1822   Jan. 1 – July 2.

DIARIO NOTICIOSO MERCANTIL.
    See *Noticioso mercantil de Puerto
    Rico.*

EL DOMINGO. d. est. June 1884.
    PrU
        1884   Oct. 12, 21, 25, 28, 31, Nov. 1,
                4, 6, 8, 13, 18, 20, 29.

DON DOMINGO. w. est. July 15, 1883.
        Note: Title *El Domingo* (published
        during suspension of *El Buscapié*),
        July 15 – Oct. 1, 1883; *Don Domingo*,
        after Oct. 7, 1883.
        PrU
        1883   July 22, Aug. 5 – Sept. 9, Oct.
                28, Nov. 4.

EL DUENDE. w. est. Feb. 22, 1866.
        Note: Ceased publication [1867].
        DLC
        1866   Oct. 7.

EL ECO. w. est. Sept. 1, 1822.
        Note: Ceased publication 1823.
        PrU
        1823   Jan. 1 – Apr. 30.

ECOS DE GALICIA. w. est. Nov. 6, 1892.
DLC
    1892   Nov. 6.

LA ESPAÑA RADICAL. sw. est. Dec.
1872.
PrU
    1873   June 10, 12, Nov. 21.

FLECHA. est. 1938.
LNT—MA
    1938   May 6.

EL FOMENTO DE PUERTO RICO. sw.,
3w., d. est. 1863.
    Note: Ceased publication Oct. 1866.
DLC
    1865   Oct. 6.
PrU
    1863   Aug. 1—Dec. 31.
    1864   Jan. 1—Dec. 31.

LA GACETA DE PUERTO RICO. sw., d.
est. [1806].
    Note: Official periodical. Period-
icity [1806]—1822, semiweekly; after
1823, daily.
CU—B
    1810   Nov. 28.
    1811   July 3—31.
    1812   June 3—27, Aug. 1—29.
           Extraordinario: June 1.
    1813   July 3—24, Aug. 4—25.
    1814   Feb. 2—Mar. 30, Apr. 27—30,
           May 7, 18—25, June 1—29,
           July 13—Aug. 13, Sept. 17—
           Oct. 22, 29—Dec. 10.
           Extraordinario: June 8.
    1815   Nov. 4.
    1816   Jan. 3—6, Feb. 1, Mar. 2, 15—
           18, Dec. 28.
    1817   Jan. 1, 8—15, Feb. 5—8, 15—
           19, Mar. 26—29, Apr. 5—12,
           19, May 17—21.
    1818   May 23—30, June 6—10, 20—
           July 1, Dec. 5.
CU—B
    1820   May 17—Dec. 30.
    1821   Jan. 3—10, 17—Dec. 26.
    1822   Jan. 2—Feb. 6, 13—27, May

           13—30, Apr. 20—Aug. 17, 24—
           Dec. 14, 21—28.
    1823   Jan. 4—15, 25, Mar. 12—19,
           Apr. 23—May 6, 21—June 18,
           Aug. 30—Sept. 13, 17—Oct. 9,
           29—Nov. 4, 6—8, 20—29.
    1826   Oct. 10, 31, Nov. 23, Dec. 7,
           13—19, 30.
    1827   Apr. 11, May 22, 23, June 5,
           July 10—12, 17, 19, 24, 25, Aug.
           11—15, 17, Sept. 8—17, Oct. 1,
           29—31, Dec. 1—28.
    1828   Jan. 29.
    1829   Mar. 10, 17, 26, 27, Apr. 22,
           June 26, July 29, Oct. 12, 16,
           19—23, Nov. 10—14, Dec. 5—
           9, 23—30.
DLC
    1836   [Jan. 1—Dec. 31].
    1841—1846   [Jan. 1—Dec. 31].
    1848—1851   [Jan. 1—Dec. 31].
    1853   [Jan. 1—Dec. 31].
    1855—1897   [Jan. 1—Dec. 31].
    1899   [Jan. 1—Dec. 31].
LNHT
    1847   [Mar. 1—Dec. 31].
    1848   [Jan. 1—Dec. 31].
    1849   [Jan. 1—Feb. 28].
NNC
Micro (N)
    1810   Nov. 28.
    1811   July 3—31.
    1812   June 1—27, Aug. 1—29.
    1813   July 3—10, 17—24, Aug. 4—
           28.
    1814   Feb. 2—Mar. 30, Apr. 27—30,
           May 7, 18, 25—June 29, July
           13—Aug. 31, Sept. 17—Oct.
           22, 29—Dec. 10.
    1815   Nov. 4.
    1816   Jan. 3—6, Feb. 1, May 15—
           18, Dec. 28.
    1817   Jan. 1, 8—15, Feb. 5—8, 15—
           19, Mar. 26—29, Apr. 5—12,
           19, May 17—21.
    1818   May 23—30, June 6—10, 20—
           July 1, Dec. 5.

PrU
  1808   Aug. 17, Sept. 7, Nov. 23.
  1809   Aug. 3.
  1810   May 26, 30.
  1812   Jan. 29.
  1817   Feb. 5, 15.
  1834   July 1 – 19, 29.
  1837 – 1844   Jan. 1 – Dec. 31.
  1847 – 1848   Jan. 1 – Dec. 31.
  1850   Jan. 1 – Dec. 31.
  1853   Jan. 1 – Dec. 31.
  1855 – 1856   Jan. 1 – Dec. 31.
  1867   May 1 – Dec. 31.
  1868 – 1900   Jan. 1 – Dec. 31.

EL GLOBO. d. est. Feb. 1924.
  PrU
  1924   Mar. 1 – 6, 8 – Apr. 10, 12, 13,
             15 – 23, 25 – May 31, July 1 –
             Dec. 31.
  1925   Jan. 1 – Feb. 3, 5 – 11, 13 – 18,
             20 – 22, 24 – Apr. 8, 10 – May 5,
             7, 9 – 22, 24 – 26, 28 – June 30,
             July 3 – Sept. 6, 8 – 17, 19, 20,
             23 – 26.

HERALDO ANTILLANO. est. Dec. 23,
  1949.
  PrU
  1949   Dec. 23.
  1950   Mar. 15, Aug. 31, Oct. 31.

EL HERALDO DE PUERTO RICO. d. est.
  Feb. 16, 1898.
    Note: Succeeded *La Integridad Naci-
    onal*. Ceased publication May 1898.
  DLC
  1898   Feb. 16.

HERALDO DE PUERTO RICO. d. est.
  Feb. 1924.
  PrU
  1924   Feb. 1 – Nov. 30.

HERALDO DOMINICAL. w. est.
  1936.
  PrU
  1939   Dec. 17, 24.
  1940   Jan. 7.

HERALDO ESPAÑOL. 3w., d. est.
  1894.

DLC
  1900   Jan. 30.
  1907   May 15.
MH
  1904   July 27 – Aug. 9.
MWA
  1913   Apr. 3.
PrU
  1907   Aug. 8.
  1909   Nov. 5.
  1913   Sept. 26.

HOY. w. est. Oct. 22, 1929.
  NcD
  1929   Nov. 16.

EL IMPARCIAL. d. est. Nov. 1, 1918.
    Note: In Spanish and English. Sus-
    pended publication Nov. 1932 – May
    21, 1933; Feb. 15 – Mar. 31, 1937.
  DLC
  1935   Apr. 20 – Dec. 31.
  1936 – 1941   Jan. 1 – Dec. 31.
  1942   Jan. 1 – Aug. 3.
  1945 – 1961   Jan. 1 – Dec. 31.
  Micro (P) & (N)
  1962   Jan. 1+.
  LNT – MA
  1938   May 4, 8, 11.
  NN
  Micro (P)
  1962   Jan. 1+.
  NcD
  1918   Dec. 1 – 10, 13 – 31.
  1921   Nov. 1.
  1922   Jan. 20 – 23, Feb. 3, 13, 14,
             Mar. 23, 30, Nov. 3, 6 – 30, Dec.
             2, 11, 13, 15 – 29.
  1923   Jan. 30, Feb. 1 – 16, 18 – 23,
             25 – 28, Mar. 2, 24, Apr. 18,
             25 – May 1, 9 – 16, 18 – July 3,
             11 – 17, 25 – 31, Aug. 13, 15,
             30 – Sept. 1, 5, 14 – 18, Oct.
             10 – 16, Dec. 12 – 18.
  1924   Jan. 10 – 29, 31 – Feb. 2, 6 –
             19, 28 – Mar. 4, 21 – 28, 30 –
             Apr. 7, 9 – 15, May 15 – 23,
             25 – 28, June 12, 13, 15 – July 2,
             10 – Aug. 27, Sept. 4 – Oct. 10,

12—15, 30—Nov. 5, 27—Dec.
9, 18—24.
1925   Feb. 5—27, Mar. 1—Apr. 15,
17—May 1, 3—27, June 4—11,
13—July 1, 9—Oct. 21, 29—
Nov. 25, Dec. 3—31.
1926   Jan. 2—13, 16, 17, 19, 21—Feb.
12, 16—Mar. 3, 11—Apr. 1,
3—May 9, 11—July 7, 21—28,
Aug. 5—11, 13—Dec. 21, 23—
31.
1927   Jan. 1—Apr. 3, 5—20, 22—
May 13, 15—June 16, 23, 25—
Aug. 22, 24—Sept. 21, 23—Oct.
12, 20—Dec. 21, 23—31.
1928   Jan. 1—Feb. 26, 28—Mar. 4,
6—Apr. 1, 3—5, 7—22, 24—
June 10, 12—July 1, 3—Sept.
6, 17, 28, Oct. 1—24, 26—Nov.
1, 2, 4, 5, 7—15, 17—21, 26—
Dec. 6, 8, 9, 11—13, 15—18,
20—31.
1929   Jan. 2—7, 9—24, 26—Mar. 7,
9—27, Apr. 5—15, 18—May 18,
20—June 26, July 3—6, 8—24,
Aug. 1—24, 26—Sept. 7, 9—
Oct. 2, 4—26, 28—30, Nov. 7—
Dec. 11, 19—31.
1930   Jan. 2—31, Feb. 2—5, 8, 13—
Mar. 19, 21—Apr. 8, 10, 12,
15—26, 28—30, May 6, 8—
June 14, 17—25, July 3—23,
Aug. 7—13, Sept. 5—Oct. 22,
30—Nov. 5, Dec. 4—17, 26—
31.
1931   Jan. 2—Feb. 4, 11—15, 19—21,
24, 25, 28—Apr. 2, 4—Sept. 2,
4—Nov. 27, 30, Dec. 26, 28—
31.
1932   Jan. 2—Feb. 20, 23—29, Mar.
9, 17—Apr. 1, 4—9, 18—Aug.
4, 6—19, 21—Sept. 16, 18—23,
25—Oct. 20, 22—25, 28—30,
Nov. 1, 2.
1933   June 21, Nov. 6, Dec. 1, 12.
OrU
1936   June 16.

PrU
1918   Nov. 1—18, 23, Dec. 2, 4, 9,
12—31.
1919—1931   Jan. 1—Dec. 31.
1932   Jan. 1—Nov. 30.
1933   May 1—Dec. 31.
1934—1935   Jan. 1—Dec. 31.
1936   May 1—31, Sept. 1—Dec. 31.
1937   Jan. 1—Feb. 28, Apr. 1—Dec.
31.
1938—1965   Jan. 1—Dec. 31.
1966   Jan. 1—31.

LA INFORMACION. d. est. Apr. 1905.
DLC
1905   Apr. 12.

LA INTEGRIDAD NACIONAL. d. est.
Oct. 1885.
    Note: Succeeded by *El Heraldo de
    Puerto Rico.*
PrU
1886   June 24.
1896   Aug. 17, 26.

EL INVESTIGADOR. 3w. est. June 19,
1820.
PrU
1820   June 19—Dec. 31.

THE ISLAND TIMES. w. est. Oct. 14,
1955.
    Note: In English. Ceased publication
    Apr. 1964.
DLC
1956   Apr. 27.
Micro (P) & (N)
1959   Sept. 4—Dec. 31.
1960—1963   Jan. 1—Dec. 31.
1964   Jan. 1—Mar. 31.
PrU
1955   Oct. 14—Dec. 31.
1956   Jan. 1—June 1, 22, July 1—
10, 24, Sept. 7, 14, 28—Dec. 31.
1957   Jan. 1—Sept. 13, 27, Oct. 11—
Nov. 8, Dec. 13—27.
1958   Jan. 3, 10, 24—Feb. 14, 28—
Apr. 11, 25, May 2, 23—Sept.
19, Oct. 10, 17, 31—Dec. 31.
1959   Jan. 9—23, Feb. 6, 20—Apr.
17, May 1, 8, 22—Dec. 31.

1960   Jan. 1 – Aug. 19, Sept. 2, 9,
        23 – Dec. 31.
1961   Jan. 1 – Oct. 20, Nov. 1 – 30,
        Dec. 8, 22, 29.
1962 – 1963   Jan. 1 – Dec. 31.
1964   Jan. 3, 10, 24, Feb. 7, Mar. 6 –
        20, Apr. 3.

EL LIBERAL. d. est. Jan. 10, 1898.
    Note: Ceased publication 1899.
  DLC
    1898   Nov. 22 – Dec. 31.
    1899   Jan. 1 – 31.
  PrU
    1898   Jan. 13, 15, 17, 18, 21, 22, 24 –
            30, Feb. 1 – 4, 7 – 28, Mar. 1 –
            30, Apr. 1 – 7, 9, 11 – 16, 18 –
            21, 23, 25 – 30, May 2 – 7, 9, 10,
            17, 18, 19, 21, 23, 24, 25, 27, 28,
            30 – June 4, 6 – 11, 13 – 18,
            20 – 25, 27 – 30.
    1899   Jan. 10.

EL MERCURIO. w. est. 1857.
    Note: Succeeded by *Diario de Puerto
    Rico*.
  PrU
    1858   Apr. 17.
    1859   May 17, 25, Aug. 4, Dec. 2.

EL MUNDO. d. est. Feb. 17, 1919.
    Note: Suspended publication Nov. 16,
    1965 – Jan. 10, 1966. See also *El
    Mundito*.
  CLU
    1964   Dec. 31.
    1965   Jan. 2, 4 – 31.
    1966   Jan. 1+.
  CSt – H
    1964   Nov. 2 – Dec. 31.
    1965   Jan. 1+.
  CU
    1943   Sept. 1 – Dec. 31.
    1944 – 1947   Jan. 1 – Dec. 31.
    1948   Jan. 2 – Aug. 14, 19, 21 – 24, 26,
            27, 31 – Sept. 3, 5 – 10, 12 – 17,
            20 – 29, Oct. 1 – 4, 6 – 10, 13,
            14, 18 – 20, 22 – Dec. 31.
    1949   Jan. 2 – Feb. 8, 10 – Mar. 4,
            6 – Apr.13,16 – May 10,12 –

            15,17,19 – July 26.
DLC
    1929   Jan. 2 – Dec. 31.
    1930 – 1941   Jan. 1 – Dec. 31.
    1942   Jan. 5 – 8, Apr. 13 – 16, May
            1 – Dec. 31.
    1944 – 1961   Jan. 1 – Dec. 31.
    Micro (P) & (N)
    1962   Jan. 1+.
FU
    Micro (N)
    1951   Jan. 8 – Nov. 15, 17 – Dec. 12,
            14 – 18, 20 – 31.
    1952 – 1956   Jan. 1 – Dec. 31.
    1957   Jan. 1 – Dec. 4, 6 – 25, 27 – 31.
    1958   Jan. 1 – 27, 29 – Feb. 9, 11 – 19,
            21 – 24, 26 – Dec. 31.
    1959   Jan. 1 – Nov. 17, 19, 20, 22,
            25 – Dec. 31.
    1960   Jan. 1 – Dec. 31.
    1961   Jan. 1 – May 8, 10 – June 19,
            21 – Sept. 30.
    Micro (P)
    1949   July 1 – Dec. 31.
    1950   Jan. 1+.
ICRL
    1948   Oct. 5 – Dec. 31.
    1949   Jan. 1 – Dec. 31.
    1950   Jan. 1 – 16.
LNT – MA
    1932   Sept. 29, 30.
    1938   Apr. 29, May 1, 6, 8, 9.
MB
    Current (one month).
MiEM
    1965   Jan. 1+.
NiC
    Micro (P)
    1951 – 1965   Jan. 8 – Nov. 15.
    1966   Jan. 11+.
NN
    Micro (P)
    1962   Jan. 1+.
NcD
    1922   Jan. 20, 21, 23, 25, Feb. 13, 14,
            May 17, 18, 20, Oct. 12.
    1923   May 2 – 5, 7 – 12, 14 – 19, 21 –
            26, 28 – June 2, 4 – 6, 8, 9, 11 –

16, 18−23, 25−30, July 2−7,
9−14, 16−21, 23−28, 30−
Aug. 4, 6−11, 13−18, 20−25,
27−Sept. 1, 3−8, 10−15, 17−
22, 24−29, Oct. 1−6, 8−13,
15−20, 22−27, 29−Nov. 4,
6−11, 14−18, 20−25, 27, 29−
Dec. 1, 3−8, 10−15, 17−22,
24−28.

1924 Jan. 1−5, 7−12, 14−19, 21−
26, 28−Feb. 2, 4−9, 11−16,
18, 19, 21, 23, 25−29, Mar. 1,
3−8, 10−15, 17−22, 24−29,
31−Apr. 5, 7−12, 19−24,
26−30, June 2−7, 9−14, 16−
21, 23−28, 30−July 5, 7−12,
14, 15, 23−26, 28−Aug. 2, 4−
9, 11−16, 18−23, 25−30,
Sept. 1−6, 8−13, 15−20, 22−
27, 29, 30, Oct. 2−4, 11, 15−
18, 20−25, 27−Nov. 1, 3−8,
10−15, 17−22, 24−29, Dec.
1−6, 8−13, 15−20, 22−27,
29−31.

1925 Jan. 1−3, 5−10, 12−17, 20−
24, 26−31, Feb. 2−4, 6, 7, 9−
14, 16−21, 23−28, Mar. 2−7,
9−14, 16−21, 23−28, 30−
Apr. 4, 6−11, 13−18, 20−25,
27−May 2, 4−9, 11−16, 18−
23, 25−30, June 1−6, 8−11,
13, 15−18, 19, 20, 22−27, 29−
July 3, 6−11, 13−19, 21−28,
Aug. 6−19, 21−Sept. 1, 23−
26, 28−Oct. 3, 5−10, 12−17,
19, 20, 28−31, Nov. 2−7, 9−
14, 16−21, 23−28, 30, Dec. 5,
7, 8, 10−12, 14−19, 21−24,
26, 28−31.

1926 Jan. 1, 2, 4−7, 9, 11−14, 19,
27−30, Feb. 1−4, 6, 8, 10−13,
15−20, 22−27, Mar. 1−6, 8, 9,
17−20, 22−27, 29−Apr. 1, 3,
5−10, 12−17, 19−24, 26, 27,
29−May 1, 3, 4, 12−15, 17−
22, 24−29, 31−June 3, 6−10,
12−17, 19−24, 26−July 3, 6−
10, 12−17, 19−24, 26−31,

Aug. 2−7, 9−14, 16, 18−21,
23−28, 30−Sept. 4, 7−11,
13−18, 20−25, 27−Oct. 2, 4−
9, 11, 13−16, 18−23, 25, 26,
28−30, Nov. 1−6, 8−13, 15−
20, 22−27, 29−Dec. 4, 6−11,
13−18, 20−24, 27−31.

1927 Jan. 3−8, 10−15, 17−22,
24−29, 31−Feb. 5, 7−12,
14−19, 21−26, 28−Mar. 5,
7−12, 14−19, 21−26, 28−
Apr. 2, 4−9, 11−14, 16, 18−
23, 25−30, May 2−7, 9, 10,
12−14, 16−21, 23−28, 30−
June 4, 6−11, 13−18, 20−22,
24, 25, 27−July 2, 4−9, 11−
16, 18−23, 25−30, Aug. 1−6,
8−13, 15−20, 22, 23, 25−27,
29−Sept. 3, 6−10, 12−Oct. 1,
5−8, 10−15, 17−22, 24−29,
31−Nov. 5, 7−12, 14−19,
21−26, 28−Dec. 3, 5−10,
12−17, 19−24, 27−31.

1928 Jan. 3−7, 10, 12−21, 23−28,
30−Feb. 1, 3, 4, 6, 8−11, 13−
18, 20−25, 27−Mar. 3, 5−10,
12−17, 19−24, 26−31, Apr.
2−5, 7, 9−14, 16−21, 23−28,
30−May 5, 7, 8, 16−19, 21−
26, 28−June 2, 4−9, 11−16,
18−23, 25−30, July 2, 3, 5−
7, 9−14, 16−Aug. 11, 13−17,
20, 21.

1931 May 14−July 3, 5−30, Aug.
2−Sept. 6, 8−Dec. 24, 26−31.

1932 Jan. 2−28, 30−Mar. 24, 26−
Apr. 4, 6−May 7, 9−13, 15−
29, 31−June 23, 25−July 10,
12−29, 31, Aug. 2−Sept. 4,
6−26, 29−Dec. 31.

1933 Jan. 1, 3−18, 20−May 20, 22−
July 3, 5−20, 22−Aug. 30,
Sept. 3, 7−Dec. 31.

1934 Jan. 1−Feb. 16, 18−22, 24−
Apr. 17, 19−May 31.

OCl

1961 July 12−Dec. 31.

1962 Jan. 1+.

PrU
  1919   Feb. 17 – Sept. 21,Oct. 1 – Dec.
          31.
  1920 – 1964   Jan. 1 – Dec. 31.
  1965   Jan. 1 – Nov. 15.
  1966   Jan. 11 – 31.

EL MUNDITO. d. est. Nov. 18, 1965.
  Note: Published during the suspen-
  sion of *El Mundo*. Ceased publication
  Dec. 18, 1965.
  PrU
  1965   Nov. 18 – 22, 24 – Dec. 7, 9,
          10 – 16, 18.

LA NACION. w. est. Dec. 12, 1931.
  PrU
  1931   Dec. 12 – 31.
  1932   Jan. 1 – 30.

LA NACION ESPAÑOLA. sw. est. Dec.
  1882.
  PrU
  1891   Feb. 19, 22, 25, Mar. 1 – Dec.
          31.
  1892   Jan. 1 – June 12.

LAS NOTICIAS. d., 3w. est. June 1894.
  Note: Periodicity June 1 – Dec. 31,
  1894, daily; after Jan. 1895, three
  times a week.
  DLC
  1894   Oct. 23.

LAS NOTICIAS DE PUERTO RICO. d.
  est. Nov. 16, 1894.
  DLC
  1894   Nov. 16.

LAS NOTICIAS DE PUERTO RICO.
  See *The Puerto Rico News. Las Noticias de Puerto Rico*.

NOTICIAS DEL TRABAJO. bw. est.
  1942.
  IU
  1943   June 30 – Dec. 31.
  1944 – 1948   Jan. 1 – Dec. 31.
  1949   Jan. 1 – Sept. 30.

EL NOTICIERO. d. est. Mar. 2, 1905.
  DLC
  1905   Mar. 2.

NOTICIOSO MERCANTIL DE PUERTO
  RICO. d. est. [1820].
  Note: Title varies *Diario noticioso
  mercantil*.
  CU – B
  Micro (P)
  1823   Sept. 29 – Oct. 1, 3 – 5.

LAS NOVEDADES. w. est. Sept. 30,
  1900.
  DLC
  1900   Sept. 30

EL PAIS. d. est. Aug. 7, 1895.
  Note: Ceased publication 1902.
  DLC
  1899   May 30 – Nov. 24.
  PrU
  1897   Aug. 23, 28, Sept. 1, 6, 8 – 11,
          13 – 17, 20 – 25, 28 – Oct. 2,
          4 – 9, 11 – 16, 18, 25 – 30, Nov.
          1 – 6, 10 – 13, 15, 16.
  1900   Jan. 1 – 6, 10, 11, 16 – 20, 22 –
          27, 29 – Feb. 3, 5 – 10, 12 – 17,
          19 – 24, 26 – Mar. 3, 5 – 10,
          12 – 17, 19 – 24, 26 – 31, Apr.
          2 – 7, 9 – 11, 17 – 21, 23 – 28,
          30, June 1, 2, 4 – 9, 11 – 16,
          18 – 23, 27 – 30, July 2 – 4, 6, 7,
          9 – 14, 16 – 21, 24 – 28, 30, 31,
          Aug. 2 – 4, 6 – 8, 10, 11, 13 –
          18, 20, 22 – 25, 27 – 29, 31.

EL PAIS. d. est. Sept. 1, 1932.
  Note: In Spanish and English. Suspended publication Feb. 28, 1938 –
  May 14, 1939.
  DLC
  1940   Oct. 1 – Dec. 31.
  1941   Jan. 1 – Dec. 19.
  NcD
  1932   Sept. 22 – Oct. 5, Nov. 3 – 14,
          16 – 20, Dec. 1 – 7, 15 – 31.
  1933   Jan. 3 – Mar. 15, 23 – May 2,
          4 – 16, Sept. 30 – Oct. 6, 8 –
          Nov. 2, 4 – 8, 15, 17, Dec. 8, 12
          – 31.
  1934   Jan. 1 – Feb. 5, 7, 15 – 22, 24 –
          Mar. 7, 15 – Apr. 17, 19 – May
          25, 27 – July 3.

PrU
1932   Sept. 2, 3.
1933   Jan. 2−4, 5−8, 10−22, 24−
Feb. 16, 18, 19, 21, 23−Mar. 5,
7, 20, 23−27, 29, 31−Apr. 7,
9−11, 13, 16, 18−May 8, 18−
30, June 1−Aug. 14, 16−29,
Sept. 1−3, 5−12, 14−26, 28,
29, Oct. 1−10, 12−31, Nov. 2,
3, 6−19, 22−24, 26−29, Dec.
1−4, 6−8, 10, 11, 13−15, 17,
19, 20, 22−24, 26−31.
1934   Jan. 2−5, 7−11, 13−19, 21,
22, 24, 26−28, Feb. 1, 4, 6−9,
11−15, 18−21, 23−27, Mar.
1−9, 11−21, 23, 25−28.
1935   Jan. 2−5, 8−15, 17, 18, 20−
29, 31, Feb. 3−13, 15−17, 19,
21−Mar. 7, 9−15, 17−21,
26−31, Oct. 2, 3, 6, 8−11, 13−
17, 19−23, 26−28, 30, 31.
1936   Jan. 1−5, 7−9, 11−Apr. 8,
11−29, May 1−22, 24−29,
June 1−30, Aug. 1−Sept. 6,
8−22, 26, 27, Oct. 1−14, 17−
29, Nov. 1, 4−30.
1937   Feb. 1−4, 6−28, Mar. 1−10,
12−24, 27−30, Apr. 1−16,
18−23, 25−30, May 22, June
1−3, 5−July 4, 6−Sept. 1,
3−5, 7−10, 12−30, Nov. 1−
18, 20−30.
1938   Jan. 2−5, 7−10, 12−19, 21−
Feb. 27.
1939   May 14, 15, 18, 19, 21−30,
June 1, 2, 4−6, 8−29, July
2−7, 9−20, 22−28, 30, Aug.
1−15, 18−23, 25−Sept. 1,
3−8, 10, 13−17, 19−29, Nov.
1−9, 11−Dec. 8, 10−14, 26−
31.
1940   Jan. 1−7, 9−16, 18, 20, 21, 23,
27, 28, 30, Feb. 1, 3−Mar. 21,
23−Apr. 14, 17, 18, 20−26,
28−May 2, 4−8, 10−20, 22−
31, June 2−30, July 2, 3, 5−10,
12−15, 17, 19−26, 28−31,
Aug. 2−7, 9−25, 27−30, Sept.

1−4, 30−Oct. 11, 13−31, Nov.
8, 12, 16, 18, 29, 30, Dec. 1−31.
1941   Jan. 3, 5, 7−11, 12, 14, 16−
18, 20, 22−31, Feb. 5, 10, 11,
22, 27−Mar. 9, 11−Apr. 10,
12−June 1, 3, 8−12, 15, 16,
18−22, 24, 30, July 1, 3, 5−7,
10−21, 23−27, 29−Aug. 29,
31, Nov. 15, 19, 21, 22.

LA PATRIA. d. est. July 1, 1898.
DLC
1898   July 1.

THE PORTO RICO HERALD. w. est.
Sept. 1, 1934.
Note: In English.
PrU
1934   Sept. 15−Dec. 31.
1935   Jan. 1−Dec. 31.
1936   Jan. 1−June 30, Aug. 15, Sept.
1, 15, 30−Dec. 31.
1937   Jan. 1−Dec. 31.
1938   Jan. 1−Apr. 30, Oct. 1−Dec.
31.
1939   Feb. 1−June 30, Aug. 1−Oct.
31.
1940   Jan. 1−Feb. 28, Apr. 1−30,
June 1−30, Aug. 1−Dec. 31.
1941   Feb. 1−May 31, Sept. 1−Oct.
31.
1942   Aug. 1−Dec. 31.
1943   Mar. 1−31.

THE PORTO RICO JOURNAL. d. est.
Dec. 23, 1903.
Note: In Spanish and English.
DLC
1903   Dec. 23, 26, 29.

PORTO RICO PROGRESS. w. est. Dec.
8, 1910.
Note: In English. Ceased publication
1933.
DLC
1928−1932   Jan. 1−Dec. 31.
1933   Jan. 1−Sept. 30.
LNT−MA
1922   Sept. 16, 23, 30, Oct. 28.
1924   Feb. 15, Nov. 1−Dec. 27.

1925   Jan. 1 – May 31, Oct. 24 – Dec. 26.
1926   Jan. 13 – July 7, Sept. 22, Nov. 10 – Dec. 29.
1927   Jan. 1 – Apr. 30.
PrU
1910   Dec. 8 – 31.
1911   Jan. 1 – May 31.
1913   Aug. 1 – Dec. 31.
1914   Jan. 1 – Dec. 31.
1915   Jan. 1 – July 31.
1916 – 1922   Jan. 1 – Dec. 31.
1923   Sept. 8, 15, Oct. 6, 13, 27, Nov. 24.
1924   Jan. 1 – Dec. 31.
1925   Apr. 18, Aug. 1.
1926   Jan. 1 – Dec. 31.
1927   Jan. 26, Feb. 16, Mar. 2, 9, 23, May 4, 11, 25, June 1, 15 – Dec. 31.
1928 – 1932   Jan. 1 – Dec. 31.
1933   Jan. 1 – Sept. 30, Oct. 5.

EL PREGONERO. d. est. Aug. 1898.
DLC
1898   Oct. 16, 18, 19.
PrU
1898   n.d. (Oct.).

LA PRENSA. w. est. June 3, 1960.
Note: Ceased publication Jan. 26, 1962.
PrU
1960   June 3 – Dec. 31.
1961   Jan. 1 – Dec. 31.
1962   Jan. 1 – 26.

PRIMERAS NOTICIAS. d. est. Oct. 1963.
PrU
1963   Oct. 29.

EL PROGRESO. 3w. est. Sept. 2, 1870.
Note: Ceased publication Feb. 4, 1874.
DLC
1872   Mar. 31.

EL PROPAGADOR. w. est. Nov. 4, 1865.
Note: Succeeded by *El País*. Ceased publication Apr. 1866.

PrU
1865   Nov. 11.
1866   Feb. 23, Mar. 23.

LA PROPAGANDA. d. est. 1893.
DLC
1893   Sept. 22.

LA PROVINCIA. w. est. Oct. 1871.
CU – B
Micro (P)
1871   Nov. 4 – 12, n.d.

PUERTO RICO. d. est. May 16, 1904.
DLC
1904   May 16.

THE PUERTO RICO NEWS. LAS NOTICIAS DE PUERTO RICO. d. est. 1903.
Note: In Spanish and English.
DLC
1903   Prospecto: Nov. 17.

THE PUERTO RICO SUN. d. est. Sept. 30, 1902.
Note: In Spanish and English. Suspended publication during 1903. Ceased publication 1905.
DLC
1902   Sept. 30.

THE PUERTO RICO TIMES. d. est. Oct. 17, 1902.
Note: In Spanish and English.
DLC
1902   Oct. 17.

PUERTO RICO WORLD JOURNAL. d. est. Mar. 8, 1940.
Note: In English. Suspended publication Aug. 1, 1945 – Apr. 1, 1956; ceased publication Jan. 19, 1957.
DLC
1940   Mar. 9, 10, 17, 24, 30 – Apr. 4, 6 – 8, 11, 12, 14, 15, 17 – Dec. 31.
1941 – 1944   Jan. 1 – Dec. 31.
1945   Jan. 1 – Apr. 28, June 1 – Aug. 1.
1956   Apr. 2 – Dec. 31.
1957   Jan. 1 – 19.

PrU
    1940   Mar. 8−21, 23−Apr. 12, 14−
            17, 19−23, 25−29, May 2−9,
            11−19, 22−28, Oct. 2−11,
            13−15, 17−Nov. 4, 6−19, 22,
            24, 26−Dec. 2, 4−6, 8, 9, 12,
            15, 19, 22, 23, 25−27, 29.
    1942   Jan. 10−17, 29−Mar. 16, 18−
            Apr. 2, 4−17, 19−May 13,
            16−27, 29−June 9, 13, 14,
            16−30, July 2−9, 11−26, 28,
            29, Aug. 1−3, 5−Sept. 6,
            8−Oct. 9, 11, Nov. 1, 3−18,
            20, 22−26, 28, 30−Dec. 6, 8−
            11, 13−16, 18−·23, 26−31.
    1943   Jan. 1−8, 10−20, 22−24, 26,
            29, Feb. 1−3, 5, 7, 8, 13−15,
            18, 19, 21−24, 26−Mar. 9,
            11−22, 24−28, 29−Apr. 2, 4−
            9, 11−22, 24−27, 29−31, May
            2−6, 9−17, 20, 23, June 2−7,
            20, 22−28, 30−July 4, 6−8,
            10−25, 28−Aug. 17, 19−23,
            25−Sept. 1, 3−8, 11−17, 19−
            27, 29−Oct. 5, 7−10, 12, 13,
            15−30, Nov. 1−25, 28−Dec.
            1, 3, 5−7, 9−15, 17−22,
            24−31.
    1944   Jan. 1−3, 5, 7−14, 16, 17,
            19−24, 26−Feb. 1, 3−20,
            22−Apr. 6, 8−20, 22−28,
            30−May 9, 11−July 16, 18−
            Sept. 11, 13, 14, 16−Oct. 31,
            Nov. 14, 15, 17, 23, Dec. 1−19,
            21, 22, 24−30.
    1945   Jan. 1−31, Feb. 2−Mar. 29,
            31, May 1−Aug. 31.
    1956   May 1−25, 27, 30, Apr. 24, 27,
            28, 30−Sept. 2, 4−Dec. 31.

THE SAN JUAN NEWS. d. est. Nov. 9,
1898.
    Note: In Spanish and English. Sus-
    pended publication Oct. 25, 27, 29−
    Nov. 9, 1903. Ceased publication
    May 20, 1905.
    DLC
    1898   Nov. 9.

    1899   Aug. 19, 20, 22−24, 27, 30−
            Sept. 3, 5, Oct. 11, 12, 31, Nov.
            1, Dec. 16, 19.
    1900   Jan. 3−Dec. 31.
    1901−1904   Jan. 1−Dec. 31.
    MiU
    1902   Apr. 1−Dec. 31.
    1903−1904   Jan. 1−Dec. 31.
    PrU
    1899   Nov. 8, 15, Dec. 3, 5, 7, 10, 12,
            16, 17, 20, 28, 31.
    1900   May 30, June 15, July 31, Aug.
            1−16, 18, 19, 22, 23, 26−Nov.
            7, 9−29, Dec. 1, 2, 5−7, 9,
            11−24, 27−31.
    1901   Jan. 3, 10−20, 22−27, 30−
            Feb. 1, 11−14, 17−22, 24−
            May 6, 13, 15−30, June 1, 3−
            24, 26−July 4, 6, 8−25, 27−
            Aug. 30, Dec. 20.
    1902   Jan. 1−Feb. 28, May 1−July
            31, Oct. 1−Nov. 5, 8−27, 29−
            Dec.
    1903   July 7, 8, Sept. 1−Oct. 2, 4, 5,
            8−10, 12−22, 24, Nov. 10, 15,
            18, 21, 22, Dec. 2, 4, 5, 7−11,
            13−24, 28.
    1904   Jan. 1, 8, 13, 14, 16, 26−Feb.
            2−4, 6, 8, 12, 13, 18, 21, 22,
            27−Mar. 1, 3−6, 9, 22, 25−
            27, 29, 31, Apr. 1, 8, 9, 12, 13,
            15, 22−24, 26, 28−May 2, 5−
            9, 11−30, June 1−9, 15−24,
            30, July 10, 13, 14, 16, 17, 21,
            Aug. 14, 16, 17, 19, 20, 21, 23−
            26, 28, 30, 31, Sept. 5, 7, 8, 9,
            21, 22, Oct. 8, Nov. 8.

THE SAN JUAN STAR. d. est. Nov. 2,
1959.
    Note: In English.
    CSt−H
    1964   Nov. 5−7, 9−14, 17−21, 23−
            28, 30−Dec. 5, 7−12, 14−19,
            21−26, 28−31.
    1965   Jan. 1−9, 11−30, Feb. 1−
            Mar. 20, 22, 24−May 1, 3−8,
            10−15, 17−29, 31−June 18,

20 — 26, 28 — July 3, 5 — 24, 26 —
Aug. 7, 9 — 21, 23 — Sept. 20,
22 — Nov. 6, 8 — Dec. 31.
1966   Jan. 1+.
DLC
1959   Nov. 2 — Dec. 31.
1960 — 1961   Jan. 1 — Dec. 31.
Micro (P) & (N)
1962   Jan. 1+.
FU
1964   Dec. 1 — 31.
1965   Jan. 1+
Micro (N)
1964   June 1, 2, 4 — 27, 29 — Oct. 3,
5 — 8, 10 — Nov. 30.
PrU
1959   Nov. 2 — Dec. 31.
1958 — 1965   Jan. 1 — Dec. 31.
1966   Jan. 1 — 31.

EL TELEGRAMA. d. est. July 3, 1895.
DLC
1895   July 3.
1896   Mar. 31.

EL TERRITORIO. d. est. Mar. 15, 1899.
Note: Ceased publication 1900.
DLC
1899   Mar. 15, May 30 — Dec. 31.
PrU
1899   July 4, Aug. 22.

EL TIEMPO. d. est. Jan. 1, 1907.
Note: In Spanish and English. Jan.
1, 1907 — 1930, with English section
titled *The Times*; after 1930, entirely
in Spanish with the title *El Tiempo*.
Ceased publication 1931.
DLC
1908   Jan. 8 — June 30.
1909   July 1 — Dec. 31.
1910 — 1928   Jan. 1 — Dec. 31.
1929   Jan. 1 — Dec. 21.
1930   Mar. 7 — Nov. 20.
1931   Apr. 15 — June 3.
MWA
1913   Mar. 1, 18, Apr. 9.
MiU
1926 — 1929   Jan. 1 — Dec. 31.

1930   Mar. 7 — Nov. 20.
NcD
1913   Jan. 1 — 9, 11 — 18, 21 — May 22,
24 — June 13, 15 — Dec. 22, 24 —
26, 29.
1914   Jan. 1 — Feb. 17, 25 — May 2,
5 — Dec. 30.
1915   Jan. 1 — May 15, 17 — Dec. 24,
28 — 31.
1916   Jan. 1 — Feb. 25, 28 — Oct. 14,
16 — Dec. 31.
1917   Jan. 1 — Feb. 12, 14 — Apr. 30,
July 1 — 19, 23 — Sept. 26, 28,
29, Oct. 1 — Nov. 20, 22 — Dec.
31.
1918   Jan. 1 — May 3, 6 — 27, 29 —
June 30, July 5, 8 — Aug. 15,
17 — Nov. 15, 17 — Dec. 31.
1919   Jan. 1 — Feb. 1, 3 — 12, 14 —
June 30, July 5, 8 — Aug. 15,
17 — Dec. 22, 24 — 31.
1920   Jan. 1 — Aug. 12, 14 — Nov. 3,
5 — Dec. 22, 24 — 31.
1921   Jan. 1 — Mar. 16, 18 — 21, 23 —
July 26, 28 — Dec. 5, 7 — 31.
1922   Jan. 1 — 22, 24 — Feb. 10, 12 —
Apr. 5, 7 — June 9, 11 — Dec. 31.
1923   Jan. 1 — Nov. 27, 29 — Dec. 31.
1925   Jan. 1 — 5, 7 — Mar. 22, 24 —
Dec. 31.
1926   Jan. 1 — Mar. 3, 5, 7 — Apr. 1,
3 — July 4, 6 — Sept. 20, 22 —
Dec. 31.
1927 — 1928   Jan. 1 — Dec. 31.
1929   Jan. 1 — May 31, June 2 — 28,
July 1 — Dec. 28.
1930   Mar. 2, 7 — May 20, 22 — June
25, 28 — July 13, 15 — Sept. 21,
23 — 29, Oct. 1 — Nov. 26, 30.
1931   Apr. 15 — 17, 20 — May 30, June
3.
PrU
1912   July 1 — Nov. 30.
1913 — 1919   Jan. 1 — Dec. 31.
1920   Jan. 1 — Oct. 31.
1921 — 1924   Jan. 1 — Dec. 31.
1925   Jan. 1 — July 31.
1926 — 1929   Jan. 1 — Dec. 31.

1930   Mar. 1 — Nov. 30.
1931   Apr. 1 — June 3.

LA TRIBUNA. d. est. Nov. 10, 1898.
    Note: Suspended publication 1899 —
    1907.
    DLC
    1898   Nov. 10 — Dec. 31.
    1899   Jan. 1 — 12.
    PrU
    1898   Nov. 10, 12, 15, 17, 19, Dec. 24,
            27, 29, 31.
    1899   Jan. 3, 5, 12.

EL TRIBUNAL. w. est. 1942.
    PrU
    1943   May 22, July 4, 20, Aug. 15,
            Oct. 12, Nov. 6, 12, Dec. 20, 31.
    1944   Jan. 31, Feb. 22, Mar. 15, Apr.
            1, Dec. 20.
    1945   Nov. 19, Dec. 20.
    1946   Jan. 30, Feb. 22, Mar. 12, Apr.
            20, May 12, June 9, July 4, Aug.
            3, 16, Sept. 14, Oct. 31, Nov. 19,
            Dec. 20, 30.
    1947   Feb. 22, Mar. 22.

LA UNION. d. est. Aug. 4, 1897.
    DLC
    1897   Aug. 4.

EL UNIVERSAL. d. est. Nov. 3, 1947.
    Note: Ceased publication June 2,
    1948.
    PrU
    1947   Nov. 3 — Dec. 31.
    1948   Feb. 1 — June 2.

LA VERDAD. w. est. Jan. 28, 1872.
    Note: Ceased publication 1879.
    PrU
    1873   July 13.
    1875   Jan. 24 — Feb. 7.
    1876   Feb. 20.

LA VOZ DEL OBRERO. w. est. May 5,
1903.
    DLC
    1908   Feb. 9.
    MWA
    1913   Mar. 30.

LA VOZ DEL PUEBLO. d. est. Jan. 2,
1901.
    DLC
    1901   Jan. 2.

San Sebastián

EL REGIONAL. w. est. Apr. 5, 1913.
    PrU
    1913   May 3.
    1914   Dec. 3.
    1915   Feb. 8.
    1916   May 15, Dec. 9.

Santurce

¡ACCION..! irr. est. Oct. 1960.
    Note: Ceased publication 1961.
    PrU
    1960   Oct. 12, 24, 26, Nov. 1, 7, 16,
            23 — 28, 30 — Dec. 12, 14 — 16,
            22, 23, 27 — 30.
    1961   Feb. 14, Mar. 8.

Utuado

LA VOZ DE LA MONTAÑA. d.
    Note: Succeeded by *El Pequeño*
    diario (Arecibo). Ceased publication
    Mar. 1895.
    DLC
    1894   May 27.

Yauco

LA ALIANZA. sw. est. 1924.
    Note: Ceased publication 1925.
    PrU
    1924   Oct. 29.

BRISAS DEL CARIBE. w., d. est. Nov.
21, 1915.
    Note: Removed from Guanica, 1923.
    PrU
    1938   Dec. 24.

EL ECO. sw. est. Nov. 3, 1895.
    Note: Succeeded by *El Éco de Yauco*.
    Ceased publication Nov. 1896.
    PrU
    1895   Nov. 3 — Dec. 31.
    1896   Jan. 1 — Nov. 30.

URUGUAY

Canelones

GACETA DE LA PROVINCIA ORIEN-
TAL. w., irr. est. Nov. 14, 1826.
Note: Ceased publication Feb. 23,
1827.
ICN
1826 Nov. 14—Dec. 31.
1827 Jan. 1—Feb. 23.
TxU
1826 Nov. 14—Dec. 31.
1827 Jan. 1—Feb. 23.
WU
1826 Nov. 14—Dec. 31.
1827 Jan. 1—Feb. 23.

Ciudad de Uruguay

LA JUVENTUD.
CSt
1915 Oct. 14.

Correos

EL SOL. w.
CSt
1944 May 1, 2.
1945 Jan. 1—4, Feb. 1, 2, 4, Mar. 2,
4, Apr. 1, 3—Oct. 31.

Durazno

TRIBUNA BLANCA. sw. est. [1939].
DLC
1943 Jan. 9—Apr. 2, 4—July 2, 4—
20, 22—Sept. 17, 19—28, 30—
Oct. 15, 17—22, 24—Nov. 2, 4,
5, 7—27.

Montevideo

ACCION. d. est. [1948].
DLC
1952 Apr. 24—Oct. 23, 25—Nov. 12,
14—Dec. 31.
1953 Jan. 2—6, 9—Dec. 30.
1956 Nov. 5—Dec. 31.
1957 Jan. 2—Feb. 19, 21—Apr. 20,
23—June 1, 3—17, 20—Nov.

16, 18—Dec. 31.
1958 Jan. 2—Feb. 27, Mar. 1—Oct.
30, Nov. 3—Dec. 31.
1959 Feb. 4—July 15, 17—20, 22—
Aug. 4, 6—9, 11—31, Sept. 3—
19, 22—Nov. 15, 17, 18, 20—
29, Dec. 1—31.
1960 Jan. 1—25, Apr. 2, 3, 5, 11—
May 1, 3—26, June 3—8, 10—
12, 14—18, 20—Aug. 14, 16—
Sept. 26, 29—Nov. 18, 20—
Dec. 31.
1961 Jan. 1—5, 7—29, 31—July 8,
10—Sept. 8, 11—19, 22—Dec.
31.
Micro (P) & (N)
1962 Jan. 1+.

EL AMIGO. w. est. Jan. 1, 1899.
DLC
1942 June 13—20.

EL BIEN PUBLICO. d. est. Nov. 1, 1878.
CLU
1965 May 12—14, 17, 18, 21, 24, 25,
29, 30, June 1—6, 9—18, 20—
July 17, 19—Aug. 6, 8—13, 15,
16, 18—24, 27—Sept. 20, 22—
Oct. 7, 9—11, 15, 17—20, 22,
23, Nov. 1, 6—Dec. 31.
1966 Jan. 1+.
CSt—H
1962 June 5—July 3, July 10—Dec.
4, 18, 25.
1963 Jan. 1—May 21, Oct. 22—Nov.
26, Dec. 10—31.
1964 Jan. 7—21.
DLC
1940 July 28, Nov. 24.
1941 Jan. 16, Apr. 25—Oct. 25, 27—
Dec. 31.
1942 Jan. 1—July 28, 30—Nov. 17,
22, 23, 30, Dec. 3—31.
1943 Jan. 1—June 23, 25—July 28,
31—Oct. 24, 26—29, 31—Dec.
31.
1944 Jan. 1—Feb. 7, 9—Mar. 3, 5—
8, 10—Dec. 31.

COMERCIO DEL PLATA. est. Oct. 1, 1845.

Note: Suspended publication Mar. 22 – June 1, 1848; 1857 – Sept. 30, 1859. Removed from Montevideo to Buenos Aires, Oct. 1, 1859. Ceased publication May 31, 1860.

TxU
- 1845   Oct. 1 – Dec. 31.
- 1846   Jan. 1 – 28, 30 – Dec. 31.
  Suplemento: Feb. 28.
- 1847 – 1848   Jan. 1 – Dec. 31.
- 1849   Jan. 1 – Dec. 31.
  Suplemento: Aug. 25.
- 1850   Jan. 1 – Dec. 31.
- 1851   Jan. 1 – June 16, 18, Oct. 22, 25 – Dec. 31.
  Suplemento: Feb. 16.
- 1852   Jan. 1 – Dec. 31.
  Suplemento: Oct. 4.
- 1853   Jan. 1 – Sept. 23, 25 – 29, Oct. 1 – Dec. 2, 7 – 31.
- 1854   Jan. 1 – July 31, Aug. 2 – 17, 19 – Dec. 31.
- 1855   Jan. 1 – Dec. 22.
  Suplemento: Nov. 13.
- 1856   June 30 – Aug. 21, 23 – Dec. 31.
- 1857   Jan. 1 – Feb. 20, 22 – Mar. 14, 16 – Apr. 3, 5 – 8, 10 – 15, 17 – Nov. 20, 22 – Dec. 10, 12 – 31.
- 1858   Jan. 1 – 30.

CORREIO DE PORTUGAL. w. est. [1880].

DLC
- 1885   July 12 – 26, Aug. 9 – 16.

CRITICA LIBRE. bw.

CSt
- 1945   May 3, 18, June 3, 23, Aug. 6.

EL DEBATE. d. est. June 29, 1931.

DLC
- 1941   Apr. 1 – 30.
- 1950   Sept. 1 – Oct. 6, 10 – 13, 15 – Dec. 31.
- 1951   Jan. 1 – Dec. 31.
- 1952   Jan. 2 – Apr. 7, 9 – Aug. 16, 18 – Sept. 8, 10, 12 – Oct. 24, 26 – Nov. 14, 16 – Dec. 9, 11, 13 – 31.

- 1953   Jan. 2 – Feb. 1, 5, 7 – 16, 18 – Apr. 30, May 2 – Oct. 11, 13 – Dec. 22, 24 – 31.
- 1954   Jan. 2 – 4, 6, 7, 10, 11, 13 – Apr. 26, 28 – July 26, 28 – Sept. 30, Oct. 2 – 4, 15 – 18, 20, 21, 23 – Dec. 31.
- 1955   Jan. 2 – Mar. 8, May 11 – 16, 18, 19, Sept. 2.
- 1956   Nov. 6 – Dec. 31.
- 1957   Jan. 3 – Mar. 10, 13 – Apr. 13, 15 – 27, 29 – Dec. 3, 5 – 9, 11 – 31.
- 1958   Jan. 2, 3, 5 – June 5, 7 – July 8, 11 – Sept. 12, 14 – Oct. 6, 8 – Dec. 10.
- 1959   Jan. 14 – 29, 31, Feb. 1, 3, 5, 7 – 27, Mar. 3 – 6, 8 – 12, 14 – Apr. 12, 14 – July 16, 19 – 21, 23 – Aug. 24, 27 – Sept. 19, 22, 24 – Oct. 3, 5 – Nov. 30, Dec. 2 – 31.
- 1960   Jan. 1 – 26, 28 – Mar. 17, 23 – May 11, 13 – Oct. 19, 21 – 25, 27 – Dec. 31.
- 1961   Jan. 2 – 5, 7 – 25, 27 – June 6, 8 – July 3, 5 – Aug. 5, 7 – 12, 14 – Dec. 31.

DEFENSOR DE LAS LEYES. d. est. Sept. 12, 1836.

Note: Ceased publication Feb. 15, 1838.

DLC
Micro (P)
- 1836   Sept. 12 – Dec. 31.
- 1837   Jan. 1 – Dec. 31.
- 1838   Jan. 1 – Feb. 15.

DEUTSCHE ZEITUNG. d. est. June 22, 1934.

Note: In Spanish and German.

DLC
- 1934   June 22.

EL DIA. d. est. June 16, 1886.

Note: Title *El Día noticioso*, May 12 – Sept. 4, 1897; *El Día* after Sept. 5, 1897. Suspended publication Sept. 5 – Dec. 31, 1897; Apr. 1 – June 30, 1900.

CLU
1943   Sept. 1 – Dec. 31.
1944   Jan. 1 – Apr. 30, June 1 – Dec. 31.
1945 – 1948   Jan. 1 – Dec. 31.
1949   Jan. 1 – Mar. 31.

DLC
Micro (P) & (N)
1890   Jan. 2 – Dec. 31.
1891 – 1896   Jan. 1 – Dec. 31.
1897   Jan. 1 – Sept. 4.
1898   Jan. 3 – Dec. 31.
1899   Jan. 1 – Dec. 31.
1900   Jan. 1 – Mar. 31, July 2 – Dec. 31.
1901 – 1927   Jan. 1 – Dec. 31.
1928   Jan. 1 – June 30.
1932   June 1 – Dec. 21.
1933 – 1959   Jan. 1 – Dec. 31.
1960   Jan. 2 – 30, Feb. 1 – Apr. 16, 19 – July 3, 5 – 11, 13 – Oct. 25, 27 – Nov. 10, 12 – 21, 23 – Dec. 31.
1961   Jan. 1 – 5, 7 – Aug. 19, 21 – Dec. 31.
1962   Jan. 1 – May 25, 27 – June 15, 17 – Dec. 31.
1963   Jan. 1+.

FMU
1928   July 1 – Dec. 31.
1929 – 1931   Jan. 1 – Dec. 31.
1932   Jan. 1 – June 30.
1941   May 1 – Dec. 31.
1942   Mar. 1 – Apr. 30, July 1 – Dec. 31.
1943   Mar. 1 – June 30, Sept. 1 – Dec. 31.
1944   Jan. 1 – Dec. 31.
1945   Jan. 1 – Apr. 30, July 1 – Oct. 31.
1946   Mar. 1 – Apr. 30, July 1 – Dec. 31.
1947 – 1959   Jan. 1 – Dec. 31.

FU
1952   Aug. 1 – Dec. 31.
1953   Jan 1+.

MH
1952   Nov. 19 – 22, 26 – Dec. 31.
1953 – 1955   Jan. 1 – Dec. 31.
1956   Jan. 1 – May 31, June 3 – 5, 10 – 30.
1958   June 13 – Sept. 20, 23 – Dec. 9, 14 – 30.
1959   Jan. 4 – Dec. 8.
1960   Apr. 28 – Dec. 31.
1961   Jan. 2 – Feb. 11, Mar. 1 – Dec. 31.
1962   Jan. 1 – Feb. 28, Apr. 8 – 10, 29 – June 2, 5 – 12, Aug. 8 – Oct. 7, 10, 11, 13 – 31, Nov. 1, 3, 7 – Dec. 18, 23, 24, 26 – 29.
1963   Jan. 2 – Feb. 15, 17 – 25, 27 – Apr. 10, 13 – 20, May 2, June 18, 20 – 28, 30, July 1 – 3, 5 – 13, 17, 19 – 23, 28, Aug. 24 – 31, Sept. 4 – 20, 23 – 30, Oct. 1 – 8, 18 – 29, Nov. 1 – 16, 20 – Dec. 31.
1964   Jan. 1 – 7, 12 – 21, 26 – Feb. 10, 12 – 17, 19 – Mar. 10, 15 – 18, Apr. 12 – 28, 20 – 25, 29 – July 5, 7 – 10, 15 – Aug. 8.

EL DIARIO. d. est. July 7, 1923.
DLC
1939   July 13.
1941   Apr. 24 – 30, May 6, 10.
1942   Jan. 25.
1951   Jan. 3 – 7, 9 – 24, 26, 27, 29 – Feb. 9, 11 – 14, 16 – Mar. 13, 17 – 20, 22 – 24, 26 – 28, 30, Apr. 1 – 4, 6 – 10, 12 – 14, 16 – May 27, 29 – June 4, 6 – 16, 20 – July 1, 3 – 18, 20 – Aug. 5, 7 – 19, 21, 25, 26, 28 – Sept. 18, 20, 21, 26 – Oct. 28, 30 – Nov. 6, 8 – 20, 22, 24 – Dec. 27, 29 – 31.
1952   Jan. 2 – 9, 11 – 16, 19, 21 – Feb. 1, 3 – 14, 16 – 18, 20.

DIARIO POPULAR. d. est. [1941].
DLC
1942   June 4 – 10, Dec. 8.

DIARIO RURAL. d.
CSt – H (Weekly edition only)

1963   Nov. 4.
1964   Jan. 13, 20, 27, Feb. 17, 24,
         Mar. 2, 9, 16.

EPOCA. d. est. 1918.
  CSt–H
    1965   Jan. 2–Dec. 31.
    1966   Jan. 1+.

LA ESTRELLA DEL SUR.
  See *The Southern Star. La Estrella
  del sur.*

GACETA DE MONTEVIDEO. w., irr. est.
  Oct. 13, 1810.
    Note: Ceased publication June 21,
    1814.
  CtY
    1810   Prospecto: Oct. 8.
           Oct. 13–Dec. 31.
    1811   Jan. 1--June 28.
  DLC
    1810   Prospecto: Oct. 8.
           Oct. 13–Dec. 31.
    1811   Jan. 1–June 28.
  TxU
    1810   Prospecto: Oct. 8.
           Oct. 13–Dec. 31.
    1811   Jan. 1–June 28.
  WU
    1810   Oct. 13–Dec. 31.
    1811   Jan. 1–June 28.

LA IDEA. d. est. [Apr. 3], 1874.
  MB
    1874   Apr. 7–July 31.

LA ILUSTRACION. w. est. Feb. 22, 1866.
  IU
    1866   Feb. 22–Dec. 31.
    1867   Jan. 1–Dec. 31.
    1868   Jan. 1–27.

LA ILUSTRACION SUD-AMERICANA.
  bw.
  CU–B
    Micro (N)
    1894   July 5–Dec. 31.
    1895   Jan. 1–Sept. 5.

ILUSTRACION URUGUAYA. bw. est.
  Aug. 15, 1883.

CU–B
  Micro (N)
  1883   Aug. 15–Dec. 31.
  1884   Jan. 1–Dec. 31.
  1885   Jan. 1–Nov. 30.

IMPARCIAL. d.
MWA
  1889   July 16.

JUSTICIA. w., d., w. est. 1919.
  Note: Succeeded by *El Popular.*
  Ceased publication Feb. 1, 1957.
  DLC
    1942   June 5.
    1945   Nov. 6, 9, 30–Dec. 21.
    1946   Jan. 4–18, June 7, 14, Sept.
           6–27, Nov. 1–Dec. 27.
    1947   Jan. 7, 10, 24, Feb. 14, Mar.
           7–May 30, June 13–Nov. 28,
           Dec. 12–26.
    1948   Jan. 2–Dec. 30.
    1949   Jan. 1–Mar. 3, 5–Apr. 14,
           16–June 23, 25–Dec. 31.
    1950   Jan. 1–5, 7–26, 28–Nov. 23,
           25–Dec. 31.
    1951   Jan. 1–4, 6–Feb. 8, 10–22,
           24–Mar. 8, 10–22, 24–Oct.
           18, 20–Nov. 22, 24–Dec. 28.
    1952   Jan. 2–Feb. 15, 29–Apr. 4,
           18–May 9, 23–Oct. 17, Dec.
           27.
    1953   Jan. 9, 16, 30, Apr. 2, May 7–
           12, 14, 18, 19, 21–27, July
           29–Aug. 24, 30–Oct. 15, 17–
           31, Nov. 3–10, 12–Dec. 9,
           11–26, 28–31.
    1954   Jan. 1–30, Feb. 1–24, 26–
           Apr. 1, 3–May 6, 11–June 14,
           16–29, July 2–5, 7–Sept. 4,
           6–Dec. 31.
    1955   Jan. 1–Dec. 30.
    1956   Jan. 2–Mar. 21, 23–Apr. 17,
           19–July 17, 19–Dec. 31.
    1957   Jan. 1–18.

LIBERTAD. d. est. May 31, 1941.
  DLC
    1941   May 31.

LA MAÑANA. d. est. 1917.
  CU
    1930   Feb. 19—Dec. 31.
    1931   Jan. 1—May 30, June 2—July
            31, Aug. 11—Nov. 1, 4—12,
            14—19, 21—Dec. 31.
    1932   Jan. 1—8, 10—15, 26—Mar. 1,
            3—Apr. 16, 19—May 9, 11—17,
            20—28, 30—June 17, 19—Aug.
            1, 3—6, 13, 15—22, 24—28, 30,
            Sept. 1—26, 28—Dec. 20, 22,
            24, 25, 28—30.
    1933   Jan. 2—10, 13—27, Feb. 4—6,
            8—10, 18—24.
  DLC
    1926   Jan. 3, 4, 6, 9—11, 14, 16, 18,
            19, 23—25, 27, 29, Feb. 1—3,
            5—10, 12—16, 19, 21, 22, 24,
            27, 29—Mar. 6, 8, 9, 11, 13,
            15—17, 19, 21—23, 25, 27—
            Apr. 1, 3—6, 8, 10—14, 16—
            19, 21, 22, 24—28, 30—May 3,
            6, 7, 9, 10, 12, 13, 15—18, 21,
            22, 24, 25, 28—31, June 2—18,
            20, 21, 24, 26—29, July 2, 4—7,
            10—12, 14—20, 25—27, 29—
            Aug. 2, 5—10, 13—23, 25, 26,
            28—Sept. 3, 18.
    1927   Feb. 2—Oct. 28, 30—Nov. 22,
            24—Dec. 31.
    1941   Mar. 31, Apr. 24—30, Sept. 9,
            Dec. 24, 29.
    1942   Feb. 8, 9, 15, 16, 22, 23, Mar.
            1, 5, 8, 12, 15, 17.
    1957   Jan. 2—Feb. 7, 9—Oct. 14,
            16—Nov. 1, 3—Dec. 31.
    1958   Jan. 2—27, 29—Feb. 9, Mar.
            8—11, 16—Apr. 14, 16—30,
            May 2—June 5, 7—15, 17—
            Oct. 11, 13—15, 17—Dec. 31.

MARCHA. w.
  CLU
    1939—1960   Jan. 1—Dec. 31.
    1961   Jan. 1—Aug. 31.
    1963   Jan. 11—Dec. 31.
    1964   Jan. 1+.
  CSt—H
    1965   Jan. 15—Dec. 31.

    1966   Jan. 1+.
  DPU
    Current (six months).
  IU
    1950   Jan. 1+.
  LNT—MA
    1953   May 9—Dec. 31.
    1954—1958   Jan. 1—Dec. 31.
  NNC
    1965   Jan. 15—Feb. 26, Mar. 12—
            Apr. 9, 23—Aug. 27.
  Micro (N)
    1958   Jan. 10—Mar. 7, 21—Dec. 26.
    1959   Jan. 16—Dec. 31.
    1960   Jan. 15—Dec. 29.
    1962   Jan. 12, 26, Feb. 9—Dec. 28.

MENSAJE. bw.
  CSt
    1944   Sept. 1, 12, Oct. 5, 31, Nov.
            15—30.
    1945   Jan. 1—15, Feb. 5, Apr. 15—28.

MERCANTIL DEL PLATA. d.
  MWA
    1868   Oct. 1—Dec. 31.
    1869   Jan. 1—Mar. 31.

THE MONTEVIDEAN. w. est. Oct. 11,
1951.
  Note: In English.
  DLC
    1951   Oct. 11.

THE MONTEVIDEO TIMES. d. est. 1888.
  Note: In English.
  DLC
    1899   Dec. 28—31.
    1900—1906   Jan. 1—Dec. 31.
    1907   Jan. 1—11, 20—Dec. 31.
    1908   Jan. 1—Sept. 19, 27—Dec. 31.
    1909   Jan. 1—July 3.

MUNDO URUGUAYO. w. est. 1918.
  IU
    1949   Sept. 1—Dec. 31.
    1950   Jan. 1—Aug. 31.
    1953   May 1—Dec. 31.
    1954—1958   Jan. 1—Dec. 31.

EL NACIONAL. w. est. Apr. 15, 1835.
  Note: Suspended publication July 23,

1836 – Nov. 10, 1838; ceased publication July 31, 1846.
CU – B
  Micro (N)
  1839   Aug. 22.

EL NACIONAL; DIARIO DEL PARTIDO
NACIONAL. d.
  MH
  1953   July 8 – Dec. 31.
  1954   Jan. 1 – May 26, 28 – June 30,
          July 8 – Aug. 3, 5 – Nov. 5, 7 –
          29.

EL PAIS. d. est. Sept. 14, 1918.
  DLC
  1939   June 6.
  1942   July 30.
  1946   Mar. 3, July 1, 3, 6 – 10, 20 –
          Aug. 1, 26 – Nov. 25, 27 – Dec.
          31.
  1947   Jan. 1 – May 20, 22 – Aug. 26,
          28 – Sept. 13, 15 – Nov. 5, 7 –
          Dec. 31.
  1948   Jan. 1 – Mar. 23, 25 – Dec. 31.
  1949   Jan. 1 – 17, 19 – 25, 28, 30 –
          Feb. 1, 3, 5 – 10, 12 – 18, 20 –
          24, Mar. 12 – 15, 19 – 22, 26 –
          Apr. 1, 7 – 12, 27, 28, May 24 –
          27, June 28, July 8 – 11, Aug.
          4 – 9, 19 – 26, Sept. 1, 9, Oct. 7,
          26, 28, Nov. 23 – 25, 27 – 29,
          Dec. 1 – 12, 14 – 31.
  1950   Jan. 1 – Feb. 6, 8 – Apr. 1, 3 –
          Dec. 4, 6 – 31.
  1951   Jan. 1 – Mar. 30, Apr. 1 – Nov.
          26, 28 – Dec. 31.
  1952   Jan. 1 – June 30, July 8, 10 –
          Aug. 20, 22 – Sept. 18, 22 – Oct.
          24, 26 – 30, Nov. 7 – 12, 19 –
          Dec. 31.
  1953   Jan. 1 – Dec. 31.
  1954   Jan. 1 – Apr. 26, 28 – Dec. 31.
  1955   Jan. 1 – Feb. 1, 3 – May 1, 3 –
          June 22, 24 – July 4, 8, 11 – 25,
          27 – 30, Aug. 1 – 28, 31 – Sept.
          9, 15, 18, 19, 22, 29, Oct. 14 –
          Nov. 4, 11 – 14, 19 – 21, 29 –
          Dec. 31.

  Micro (P)
  1956   Jan. 1+.
DPU
  Current (six months).
FU
  1951   [Jan. 1 – May 31].
ICRL
  Micro (P) & (N)
  1956   Jan. 1+.
TxU
  1948   Sept. 25, 26, 28 – Oct. 2, 4, 6 –
          12, 14.

EL PLATA. d. est. 1914.
  DLC
  1939   July 12.
  1951   Jan. 3, 4, 10 – 25, Feb. 1 – 18,
          20 – Mar. 8, 20, 24, 25, 27 –
          Apr. 16, 18, 19, 21 – 23, 25,
          27 – 29, May 1 – 3, 5 – 10, 12,
          19 – 24, 30 – June 4, 6 – 8, 10 –
          14, 16 – 28, 30 – July 2, 5 – 12,
          14, 17 – 19, 21, 23, 24, 29, 30,
          Aug. 2 – 11, 15 – 24, 26, 28 – 30,
          Sept. 21, 22, 24, 25, 29 – Oct. 2,
          4 – 11, 13, 18 – 20, 22, 24, 26 –
          Nov. 1, 3, 4, 6 – 11, 13 – 18,
          20 – 22, 25 – 27, 29 – Dec. 7, 9,
          11 – 15, 17 – 22, 24 – 27, 29 –
          31.
  1952   Jan. 2 – Feb. 1, 3 – 16, 18 – 23,
          25 – Apr. 24, 27 – 30, May 2 –
          7, 9 – 19, 22 – June 2, 4 – 12,
          14 – 27, 29 – Aug. 14, 16, 18 –
          23, 26 – 30, Sept. 1 – 16, 18 –
          Oct. 20, 22 – 31, Nov. 3 – 21,
          23 – Dec. 17, 19 – 31.
  1953   Jan. 2 – Mar. 29, 31 – Apr. 22,
          24 – 30, May 2 – June 18, 21 –
          July 15, 17 – Oct. 9, 11 – Nov.
          14, 16 – Dec. 23, 26 – 31.
  1954   Jan. 1 – 6, 8 – 21, 23 – Feb. 1,
          3 – Mar. 2, 4 – 20, 22 – June 28,
          30 – Aug. 15, 17 – 28, 30 – Sept.
          17, 23 – Oct. 7, 9 – 14, 16, 17,
          19 – 25, 28, Nov. 1, 4 – 6, 9 – 12,
          20 – 29, Dec. 2 – 4, 7, 9 – 16,
          18 – 23, 25 – 28, 30, 31.
  1955   Jan. 1 – 7, 9 – 17, 19 – 23, 25 –

29, Feb. 2 – 6, 9 – 21, 23 – 25,
Mar. 2 – 8, 10 – 14, 16 – 25,
Apr. 2 – 7, 9, 10, 12 – 19, 22 –
May 8, 10, 11, 13, 15 – 18, 20 –
26, 29 – June 1, 3 – 12, 14 – 16,
18, 20, 21, 23 – 26, 28 – July 2,
4 – 8, 10, 13 – 17, 19 – 26, 28 –
Aug. 11, 13 – 24, 27, 28, 30 –
Sept. 4, 8 – 14, 16, 20, 23 – 25,
Oct. 1, 3, 4, 6 – 10, 13, 15, 18 –
20, 22 – 28, 30 – Nov. 1, 3 – 6,
8, 10, 11, 13, 14, 16 – 18, 20,
22 – Dec. 1, 5, 7 – 11, 13 – 25,
27 – 31.

1956   Jan. 2, 3, 6 – 21, 23 – 30, Feb.
1 – 3, 5, 7 – 18, 20, 21, 23, 25,
26, 29, Mar. 2 – 7, 9 – 17, 19, 20,
22, 23, 25 – Apr. 4, 6 – 8, 10,
12, 15, 17 – 23, 25 – 28, May
3 – 5, 7 – 12, 16 – 19, 21, 24 –
26, 28, 29, June 2 – 4, 6, 7, 9,
13 – 16, 18, 23, 25, 27, 28, 30,
July 2, 3, 5, 7, 9 – 14, 19, 21,
23, 25 – 31, Aug. 2, 3, 5, 7 – 10,
17 – 22, 27, 31 – Sept. 2, 4 – 6,
8, 11 – 14, 19 – 22, 25 – 27, 29 –
Oct. 1, 5, 6, 11 – 13, 15 – 18,
20, 22, 23, 26, 27, Nov. 3 – 9,
11 – 22, 24 – 28, Dec. 1, 3, 7,
10 – 13, 24.

1957   Jan. 13 – 15, 17, 18, 20, 21, 31,
Feb. 1, 7, 14, Mar. 21, Apr. 11 –
30, May 2 – June 23, 25 – Aug.
8, 11 – 15, 17 – 20, 22, 31, Sept.
2 – Dec. 31.

1958   Jan. 2 – 6, 8 – 13, 15 – Aug. 3,
5 – 15, 17 – Oct. 1, 3, 5 – 21,
23 – Nov. 8, 10 – 19, 22, 25 – 27,
29, Dec. 1, 3 – 5, 7 – 28, 31.

1959   Jan. 1 – Mar. 3, 5 – 19, 21, 23,
25 – 30, Apr. 1 – 10, 12 – May
21, 23 – 30, June 1 – July 16,
19 – 30, Aug. 1 – 3, 5 – 15, 18 –
22, 24 – Sept. 5, 7 – 20, 22 –
Oct. 10, 13 – 17, 19 – Nov. 1,
3 – Dec. 2, 14 – 22, 24 – 31.

1960   Jan. 2 – Feb. 26, 28 – Mar. 6, 8,
9, 11 – 20, 22 – 29, 31 – Apr. 3,

5 – 26, 28 – June 23, 25 – Sept.
15, 17 – 20, 22 – 27, 29 – Oct.
15, 17 – Dec. 24, 29 – 31.

1961   Jan. 1 – 5, 7 – 21, 23, 25 – Feb.
11, 13, 15 – 25, 27 – Mar. 5, 7,
9 – Apr. 14, 16 – 26, 28 – 30,
May 2 – 22, 24 – 30, June 1 – 5,
7 – 13, 15, 16, 18, 20 – 23, 25,
27, 29 – July 26, 28, 29, 31 –
Aug. 7, 9 – 17, 19 – 26, 28 –
Sept. 1, 3 – 25, 27 – Oct. 5, 7, 9,
11 – 28, 31 – Nov. 4, 6 – 10,
12 – Dec. 7, 9 – 31.

1962   Jan. 1+.

TxU

1941   June 27 – Dec. 31.

1942   Jan. 2 – 4, 6 – 19, 21 – Feb. 15,
17 – Mar. 27, 29 – Apr. 2, 4 –
22, 24 – 27, 29, 30, May 2 – 16,
18 – June 4, 6 – 10, 12, 14, 16 –
22, 24, July 7 – 11, 14, 16 – 23,
25, 27 – Aug. 5, 7, 8, 10 – 15,
17, 19, 20, 25 – Sept. 6, 8, 30,
Oct. 1, 3, 5, 6, 10, 16, 19, 20, 22,
24, 26, 29 – 31, Nov. 3, 5 – 7, 9,
13, 14, 16, 17, Dec. 2 – 4, 6 –
12, 14 – 19, 21, 22, 24 – 26, 28 –
31.

1943   Jan. 1 – Apr. 30, May 2, 3, 5 –
13, 15 – June 23, 26, 27 – Aug.
7, 9, 11 – 15, 18 – 21, 24, 26 –
31, Sept. 2, 3, 5 – 9, 12 – 23,
26, 27, 29 – Oct. 2, 4 – 6, 8 – 11,
13, 15 – 18, 21 – 24, 26, 27 –
Dec. 1, 3, 5 – 12, 14 – 18, 21 –
26, 28 – 31.

1944   Jan. 2 – Feb. 29, Aug. 1 – Oct.
3, 5 – 8, 10 – Dec. 31.

1945   Jan. 1 – Apr. 15, 17 – May 8,
10 – June 7, 9 – 15, 17 – 20,
22 – Aug. 17, 19 – Nov. 3, 5 –
Dec. 10, 12 – 31.

1952   Jan. 2 – Feb. 16, 18 – 25, 27 –
Mar. 14, 16 – Apr. 4, 7 – 10,
12 – 31, May 2 – June 18, 20 –
July 17, 19 – Aug. 24, 27 – 30,
Sept. 2 – 7, 9, 10, 12 – 17, 22 –
Oct. 3, 5 – 11, 13 – Oct. 29,

31 – Dec. 23, 25 – 31.
1953 Jan. 3 – Feb. 16, 18 – 26, 28 –
Mar. 12, 14, 16 – 29, 31 – Apr.
2, 4 – 30, May 2 – June 18, 20 –
23, 25 – July 15, 17, 19 – Aug.
24, 26 – Sept. 10, 12 – 20, 22 –
Oct. 3, 5 – 11, 15 – Nov. 1, 3 –
Dec. 14, 16 – 24, 25 – 31.
1954 Jan. 2 – Feb. 4, 6 – Mar. 1, 3 –
11, 13 – Apr. 15, 17 – 30, May
2 – June 1, 3 – 18, 20 – 30, July
3, 14, 16, 17, 19 – 23, 25 – Aug.
2, 4 – 10, 12 – 16, 23, 24, 26 –
Sept. 19, 22 – 26, 29 – Nov. 23,
27 – Dec. 16, 18 – 24, 26 – 31.
1955 – 1956 Jan. 1 – Dec. 31.
1957 Nov. 19, 20, 23, 24, 27 – Dec. 5,
8.
1958 Jan. 21, 30, 31, Feb. 6, 7, May
10, Dec. 6.

EL POPULAR. d. est. Feb. 1, 1957.
Note: Succeeded *Justicia.*
CSt – H
1965 Jan. 2 – Dec. 31.
1966 Jan. 1+.
DLC
1957 Feb. 1 – Dec. 24, 26 – 31.
1958 Jan. 1 – 30, Feb. 1 – Dec. 10.
1959 Feb. 5 – Nov. 4, 6 – 16, 18 –
Dec. 31.
1960 Jan. 2 – Mar. 2, 4 – 18, 22 –
Apr. 26, 28 – Dec. 31.
1961 Jan. 1 – Apr. 30, May 3 – Nov.
15, 17 – Dec. 31.
Micro (P) & (N)
1962 Jan. 1+.

PUEBLO ARGENTINO. bw.
CSt
1944 Apr. 1 – Dec. 31.
1945 Jan. 1 – 31.
1946 Mar. 1 – 31.

LA RAZON. d. est. 1888.
DLC
1889 Oct. 2 – 4.
1925 Dec. 29 – 31.
1926 Jan. 1 – 13.

DLC
1942 Jan. 13, Feb. 4, 7, 9 – 16, 20 –
24, 28, Mar. 1, 2, 5, 8, 10, 15,
20, 22, 23, 26, 28 – Apr. 1, 7 –
9, 16, 20, 23 – 26, 28, 29, May 2,
8, 12, 14, 19, 22 – 24, 26, 28, 31,
June 4, 7, 11, 13, 14, July 7 – 9,
12, 13, 15, 16, 20, 21, 23, Aug. 2,
3, 5, 7, 8, 11, 16 – 18, 20, 22, 23,
25, 26, 31, Sept. 3 – 5, 7 – 9, 11,
12, 17, 18, 20, 22, 23, 25, 26,
29 – Oct. 1, 3, 5 – 11, 14 – 19,
21 – 26, 28 – 31, Nov. 2 – 4, 6 –
9, 11 – 17, Dec. 1 – 8, 10 – 15,
18, 20 – 27, 31.
1943 Jan. 2 – 9, 13 – 17, 24 – 29, 31,
Feb. 2, 7 – 9, 11, 13 – 16, 18,
20 – 22, 24 – 27, Mar. 1 – 8, 12,
13, 15 – 18, 20 – 22, 24 – 31,
Apr. 1 – 16, 18 – 22, 25, 29, May
3, 4, 8 – 14, 16, 18, 20, 22 – 24,
30, June 1, 4, 8, 9, 13, 18, 20,
22, 23, 28, July 6, 9, 10, 13, 25,
29, Aug. 4, 11, 13, 25, 26, Sept.
2, 13, 26, Oct. 3, 13, 15, 17, 18,
21, Nov. 6, 12, 14, 16, 17, 24.

REVISTA DEL PLATA. d.
CU – B
Micro (N)
1839 July 30.

EL SEMANA URUGUAYA. w. est. 1959.
LNHT
1959 Mar. 9, Apr. 13, 20, July 6.

EL SOL. d. est. [1925].
DLC
1942 June 4.

EL SOL; SEMANARIO SOCIALISTA. w.
CSt – H
1965 Jan. 22 – Dec. 31.
1966 Jan. 1+.
CU
1945 Jan. 1 – Dec. 31.
1946 Jan. 4 – Oct. 25.
1947 Nov. 27 – Dec. 24.
1948 Jan. 2 – May 28, June 18 – 25,
July 2 – 30, Aug. 13 – Dec. 31.
1949 Jan. 7 – Mar. 11, May 1 – 20,

June 3, 24 — July 8, 29, Aug.
5 — 12, Sept. 2 — 16.

THE SOUTHERN STAR. LA ESTRELLA
DEL SUR. w. est. May 23, 1807.
Note: In Spanish and English.
Ceased publication July 4, 1807.
IU
1807   Prospecto: May 9.
May 23 — July 4.
MWA
1807   Prospecto: May 9.
May 23 — July 4.
Extraordinario: July 11.
Suplemento: [July 4].
NN
1807   Prospecto: May 9.
May 23 — July 4.
TxU
1807   Prospecto: May 9.
May 23 — July 4.
Extraordinario: July 11.
WU
1807   Prospecto: May 9.
May 23 — July 4.
Extraordinario: July 11.

EL TELEGRAFO MARITIMO. d. est.
[1846].
DLC
1889   Oct. 7.

VOLUNTAD. m., irr. est. 1938.
DLC
1938   Aug. (two issues), Nov., Dec.
1939   Feb., Apr., June.

VOZ ARGENTINA. w. est. Oct. 1944.
CSt — H
1944   Oct. 1 — Dec. 31.
1945   Jan. 1 — June 30.
CU
1944   [Oct. 25 — Dec. 7, 15].

Paysandú

EL TELEGRAFO. d. est. 1910.
CSt — H
1964   July 6 — Oct. 1, Nov. 22, 24 —
Dec. 26, 28 — 31.
1965   Jan. 1+.

Salto

EL PUEBLO. d. est. Aug. 15, 1908.
DLC
1942   Oct. 14.

Sarandi Grande

SARANDI. d. est. [1924].
DLC
1942   Aug. 15.

VENEZUELA

Albarico

VOZ DEL DEBER.
MWA
1907   Feb. 2.

Altagracia de Orituco

IBIS.
MWA
1906   Apr. 19.

Angostura

See Ciudad Bolívar.

Aragua de Barcelona

ALBA LIRICA. w.
MWA
1908   Aug. 30.

Barcelona

UNIONISTA. w.
MWA
1911   Feb. 11.

VOTO POPULAR. bw.
MWA
1909   Dec. 8.

Barinas

UNION RESTAURADORA. 3m.
MWA
1907   Dec. 25.

Barquisimeto

ANUNCIADOR INDUSTRIAL. w.
MWA
   1911   Mar. 5.

AVISADOR. w.
MWA
   1911   Mar. 5.

CENTINELA. 3w.
MWA
   1911   Feb. 23.

ECO INDUSTRIAL. d.
MWA
   1909   July 23.
   1911   Mar. 1, 3.

LARENSE. d.
MWA
   1908   Nov. 14.
   1909   Mar. 9, Apr. 13.

SIMPATICO. w.
MWA
   1908   July 5 – 12, Aug. 23.

TELESCOPIO. d.
MWA
   1909   July 2, 17.

VOTO NACIONAL. sw.
MWA
   1909   July 17, Oct. 19.

VOZ DE LARA. d.
MWA
   1909   July 24.

Betijoque

PATRIA Y UNION. w.
MWA
   1911   Feb. 25.

Buenavista

RESURRECCION. w.
MWA
   1909   Aug. 20.

Cagua

PROPIO ESFUERZO. [w.]

MWA
   1908   Aug. 9.
   1911   Feb. 28.

Calabozo

PASATIEMPO. est. 1907.
MWA
   1907   June 3.

PATRIA Y CASTRO. d. est. 1904.
MWA
   1905   Nov. 6.

PATRIA Y UNION. w.
MWA
   1910   Nov. 4.
   1911   Feb. 21.

Caracas

AGENCIA MÜLLER. w.
MWA
   1908   Dec. 19.

AGENCIA PUMAR. irr.
MWA
   1908   Oct. 6, 23, Dec. 14.
   1909   June 28, July 7, 30.
   1911   Mar. 9.

EL AGRICULTOR. w. est. 1843.
NcD
   1844   Apr. 1 – May 1, 5, 8, 15, 22,
          June 1 – July 3, 17, 24, 31 –
          Nov. 30, Dec. 19.
   1845   Jan. 23, Feb. 1 – Apr. 30, June
          21.

AHORA. d. est. 1936.
CSt
   1941   Nov. 1 – Dec. 31.
   1942 – 1944   Jan. 1 – Dec. 31.
   1945   Jan. 1 – July 31, Sept. 1 – 31.
   1946   Aug. 1 – Sept. 31.
DLC
   1942   Feb. 1, 5, 8, 12, 15, 22, 26, Mar.
          1, 5, 8, 12, 15, 19.
   1943   Jan. 2 – May 31, June 2 – 13,
          15 – 17, 21, 27 – 30.

EL ALBA. irr. est. Jan. 1, 1829.
CtY
   1829   Jan. 1 – Mar. 16.

DLC
1829   Jan. 1−4, 19−24, Feb. 8,
24−Mar. 16.

AMIGO DEL PUEBLO. d. est. Jan. 3,
1909.
MWA
1909   Jan. 3, 6.

AMIGO DEL PUEBLO. sw.
MWA
1910   Jan. 28.

EL ANGLO-COLOMBIANO. irr. est.
Apr. 6, 1822.
DLC
1822   Apr. 6, 13, May 11, June 8, 15.
Suplemento: Apr. 6.

ANUNCIO. w.
MWA
1909   Oct. 7.

EL ASTRONOMO. est. Sept. 10, 1824.
MWA
1825   Sept. 30.

LAS AVISPAS. d. est. May 14, 1846.
NcD
1846   May 14−24, 28−31, June 2−5,
7−10, 13, 15−28, July 4, 22−
24, 28, Aug. 1.

LOS AYES DEL PUEBLO. est. Oct. 18,
1844.
NcD
1844   Oct. 18, 26, Nov. 10, 20.

LA BANDERA NACIONAL. w. est. Aug.
1, 1837.
CtY
1837   Aug. 1−Dec. 26.
1838   Jan. 2−July 16, 30−Aug. 27,
Sept. 10−24.

BOLETIN FUNERARIO. d.
MWA
1908   Dec. 15.

BOLETIN OFICIAL. est. Sept. 1846.
NcD
1846   Oct. 4, 6, 12, 16, 21, Nov. 6,
14, 28.

1848   May 11.
1849   Jan. 16, 18.

BOLETIN POPULAR.
MWA
1910   Jan. 9.

LA CALLE.
LNT−MA
1958   Jan. 23.

EL CANARIO.
NcD
1830   Aug. 15, 19.

CARACAS ARTISTICA. w.
MWA
1906   Oct. 27.

THE CARACAS JOURNAL.
See *The Daily Journal*.

CARATULA DEL REGISTRO LITER-
ARIO. w.
MWA
1884   Dec. 20.

CARIBE. d.
MWA
1911   Jan. 28, Feb. 4.

CATACLISMO. w.
MWA
1905   Aug. 2.

EL CENSOR. d. est. Feb. 10, 1836.
DLC
1836   Prospecto.
Feb. 10−12, 14−20, 23−26.
NcD
1836   Prospecto: Feb. 1.
Feb. 10−12.

CENTINELA. irr. est. Sept. 3, 1907.
MWA
1907   Sept. 3.

CICERON A CATILINA. irr. est. Nov.
22, 1845.
NcD
1845   Nov. 22−29, Dec. 6, 18.
1846   Jan. 19, 26, Feb. 5, 26, Mar.
13.

EL COJO ILUSTRADO. bw. est. Jan.
1, 1892.
    Note: Ceased publication Apr. 1,
    1915.
    LU
    1892—1893   Jan. 1—Dec. 31.
    WU
    1892—1905   Jan. 1—Dec. 31.

EL COLOMBIANO. w. est. May 3, 1823.
    Note: In Spanish and English. Ceased
    publication Nov. 29, 1826.
    CU—B
    Micro (P)
    1825   May 4.
    CtY
    1823   May 3—June 4, July 2—Nov.
            11, 26—Dec. 31.
    1824   Jan. 7—Dec. 29.
    1825   Jan. 1—Mar. 2, 16, Apr. 6—
            May 18, June 1—Dec. 28.
    1826   Jan. 4—Nov. 29.
    DLC
    1825   June 29.
    1826   May 3, 17—Oct. 11, 25—
            Nov. 29.
    MWA
    1826   Nov. 29.
    NcD
    1824   Aug. 18.
    1826   June 28, Oct. 4—Nov. 8, 22.

COMBATE. d.
    MWA
    1905   Sept. 5.

EL CONCISO. d. est. Feb. 7, 1832.
    Note: Published only during legis-
    lative sessions. Ceased publication
    Apr. 1, 1838.
    DLC
    1834   Jan. 20—Apr. 30, Mar. 2—May
            2, 4—17.
    1836   Jan. 21, 22, 24—May 17.
    1837   Jan. 20—May 2, 4—9.
    1838   Jan. 21—Apr. 1.
    NcD
    1836   Mar. 10.

CONSIGNA MILITAR. est. Aug. 9,
1909.

MWA
    1909   Aug. 9.

CONSTITUCIONAL. w. est. 1870.
    MWA
    1877   June 16.

CONSTITUCIONAL. d. est. 1889.
    MWA
    1906   May 23, June 18, Aug. 7, 8, Oct.
            9—11, 13, 16, Nov. 1, 26.
    1907   Aug. 2.
    1908   Jan. 28, July 21, 30, Sept. 1,
            Nov. 1, 16, Dec. 9, 10, 12.
    1909   Feb. 10—16, 24.

CORREO CONSTITUCIONAL DE
    CARACAS. irr. est. 1835.
    Note: Succeeded by *Correo de*
    Caracas.
    DLC
    1836   Jan. 16—Feb. 10.

CORREO DE CARACAS. w. est. Jan. 9,
1839.
    Note: Succeeded *Correo consti-*
    tucional de Caracas.
    CU—B
    Micro (P)
    1839   Oct. 1.
    DLC
    1839   June 4, Sept. 3.
    1840   Feb. 18—25, Mar. 10—Apr. 7,
            21, May 26, June 16, 30—July
            14, 28, Sept. 22—Oct. 13, Nov.
            3, 24, Dec. 22.
            Suplemento: Dec. 22.

CORREO DE CARACAS; REVISTA
    MERCANTIL. w. est. July 5, 1851.
    FU
    1851`   July 5—Dec. 31.
    1852   Jan. 1—June 26.
    NHi
    1851   July 5—Dec. 31.
    1852—1853   Jan. 1—Dec. 31.
    1854   Jan. 1—21.

CRITERIO. w.
    MWA
    1906   Dec. 8.

CRITERIO LIBERAL. d. est. Apr. 6, 1909.
MWA
1909   Apr. 6.

THE DAILY JOURNAL. w., sw., d. est. Feb. 17, 1945.
Note: In English. Title *The Caracas Journal*, Feb. 17, 1945 – 1956; *The Daily Journal*, after 1956.
CU
1946   Aug. 30 – Dec. 27.
1947   Jan. 3 – Apr. 4, 18 – May 2, 16 – Oct. 10, 24 – Dec. 26.
1948   Jan. 2 – June 25, July 9 – Dec. 27.
1949   Jan. 3 – 24, Feb. 7 – 21, Mar. 7 – 21, Apr. 4 – Dec. 26.
DLC
1945   Feb. 17 – Mar. 22, Apr. 6 – May 16, June 2 – July 5, 7 – 12, 14 – Oct. 25, 27 – Dec. 31.
1946 – 1947   Jan. 1 – Dec. 31.
1948   Jan. 1 – May 6, 8 – Nov. 28, 30 – Dec. 31.
1949   Jan. 1 – Dec. 26.
1950   Jan. 2 – Apr. 30, May 2 – July 16, 18 – Dec. 25.
1951   Jan. 1 – June 25, July 2 – Dec. 31.
1952   Jan. 7 – June 30, July 3 – Dec. 29.
1953   Jan. 2 – Feb. 1, 3 – June 29, July 2 – Dec. 30.
1954   Jan. 6 – Mar. 12, 14 – Apr. 30, May 2 – June 1, 3 – 8, 13 – 16, Dec. 18.
1955   Apr. 27, 30, May 7 – 21, 28, June 8.
1957   May 27, June 16, Aug. 3, 6 – 8, 14, 30, Sept. 22, 29, Oct. 7.
1958   Feb. 6, 7, July 10, Sept. 12, Oct. 13, Nov. 1, 13, 14, 16 – 18, 20, 22 – Dec. 15, 18, 31.
1959   Jan. 2 – 9, 14 – Feb. 6, 11 – 21, 23 – 26, Mar. 1, 2, 11, 13 – 19, Apr. 1 – 3, 5 – 9, 11 – 16, 19 – 27, 30 – May 4, 6, 9 – 12, 17 – 19, 21 – 27, 29 – June 7, 9 – 12,

15 – July 6, 22 – Aug. 7, 9 – 11, 13, 14, 19 – 25, Sept. 20, 27, 29 – Oct. 2, 4 – 7, 9 – 13, 15 – 20, 22 – 24, 26, Nov. 6 – 9, 24, 25, 27 – 30.
Micro (P) & (N)
1962   Jan. 1+.
LU
1945   Feb. 17 – Dec. 31.
1946 – 1949   Jan. 1 – Dec. 31.
1950   Jan. 1 – Feb. 6.
1958   June 30 – Aug. 15.

EL DESESTANQUERO. irr. est. Feb. 22, 1832.
NcD
1832   Mar. 19.

DIABLO ASMODEO. w.
MWA
1850   May 10 – 22, June 5 – 8, July 17.

DIARIO. d. est. Feb. 8, 1909.
MWA
1909   Feb. 8.

DIARIO DE AVISOS Y SEMANARIO DE LAS PROVINCIAS. est. Jan. 18, 1850. d. & sw.
Note: Published both daily and semi-weekly edition.
CtY
1857   Sept. 1 – Dec. 26.
DLC
1859   June 18.
MWA
1883   July 24.
NcD
Semiweekly edition:
1855   June 27, Aug. 8, 15, Sept. 2 – Dec. 31.
1856   Jan. 1 – May 31, June 4, 11 – Dec. 31.
Suplemento: June 7.
1857   Jan. 1 – 31, Feb. 4 – 21, 28, Mar. 1 – Apr. 4, 15 – 25, May 6 – 27, June 3, 5, 10 – 24, July 25, 29 – Dec. 31.
1858   Jan. 1 – Feb. 24, July 25, 29 – Dec. 31.
1859   Feb. 16 – Apr. 6, Nov. 9 – Dec.

3, 10—31.
1860   Jan. 4, 7, 14—Feb. 18, 29—
        Mar. 17, 31, Apr. 4, 11—21,
        28—Aug. 4.

DIARIO DE CARACAS. d.
NcD
1846   May 21, July 12, 18, Aug. 16,
        20, 22, 23, 25, Sept. 13.

DIARIO DE CARACAS. d. est. 1893.
DLC
1895   Mar. 11, 13, 14, Sept. 3, 7, 14,
        21, Oct. 2, 3, 8.

DIARIO DE LA TARDE. d. est. June 1,
    1846.
NcD
1846   Aug. 5, 18.

DIARIO NACIONAL. d.
MWA
1905   Apr. 6.

DIARIO OFICIAL.
See *Gaceta oficial*.

ECO RESTAURADOR. d.
MWA
1906   July 14.

ECO VENEZOLANO. d. est. Jan. 9,
    1911.
MWA
1911   Jan. 9, Apr. 5.

ECOS DE SAN BERNARDINO. w.
MWA
1908   Oct. 28, Dec. 21.
        Suplemento: n.d.

ELITE.
LNT—MA
1958   Feb. 1—29.

EPISTOLAS CATILINARIAS. est. 1835.
NcD
1835   July 8.

LA EPOCA. w. est. May 5, 1846.
    Note: Ceased publication June 28,
    1846.
NcD
1846   May 5—June 28.

EPOCA. 3w.
MWA
1908   Mar. 7.

EL ESCALPELO.
NcD
1844   July 17, 26.

LA ESFERA. d. est. 1927.
DLC
1934   Mar. 23.
1941   May 29.
1942   Sept. 7, Oct. 12, 16, 18.
1944   May 1—25, 28—June 28, 30—
        Aug. 6, Sept. 13—16, 18, 20—
        23, 25, 27—Nov. 1, 4—Dec.
        31.
1945   Jan. 2—Feb. 23, 25, 27—Mar.
        28, Apr. 1, 7, 8, 10—18, 20, May
        4, 5, 12—15.
1946   Jan. 2—Dec. 31.
1947   Jan. 1—June 30, Nov. 19—Dec.
        13, 16—31.
1948   Jan. 2—20, 24—May 14, 16—
        19, June 12—July 13, 15—Oct.
        31, Nov. 2—Dec. 2, 5—31.
1949   Jan. 1—Feb. 23, 25—May 5,
        7—27, 30—Oct. 29, 31—Dec.
        26, 29—31.
1950—1951   Jan. 1—Dec. 31.
1952   Jan. 1—22, 24—Mar. 26, 28—
        June 17, 19—July 10, 12—Sept.
        7, 9—Dec. 31.
1953   Jan. 2—27, 29—Dec. 31.
1954   Jan. 1—June 30.
1955   Jan. 2—Dec. 31.
1956   Apr. 21—26, 28, May 17, 31,
        June 7, 10, 11, 22, July 19, Aug.
        13.
1957   June 4, 7, 8, 10, 11, 21—27, 29,
        July 1—3, 5—11, 14, 15, 20, 21,
        23—26, 28—31, Aug. 2—4, 9,
        19, 20, 24—26, 29, 30, Sept. 4,
        8, 9, 14—17, 20, 22, 31, Oct. 1,
        6, 8, 12, 20, 21, Nov. 7, 24, Dec.
        17, 22.
1958   Jan. 6, 7, 12, 16, 19, 26, 29, 30,
        Feb. 1, 2, 4, 5, 7, 9—13, 18, 22,
        23, 25, 27, Mar. 2, 9, 23, 26,

Apr. 1 – July 2, 4 – 28, 30 –
Dec. 4, 6 – 31.

1959   Jan. 1 – Mar. 11, 13 – 15, 17 –
23, 25 – May 2, 4 – June 16,
18 – 21, 24, 26 – July 25, 27 –
Aug. 30, Sept. 1 – 12, 14, 16 –
19, 21 – 27, 29 – Oct. 6, 8 – 24,
27 – Nov. 6, 8 – 20, 25 – Dec.
10, 12 – 31.

1960   Jan. 2, 3, 5 – 29, 31 – Feb. 8, 10,
11, 13 – 18, 20 – Apr. 5, 10 – 13,
16 – May 31, June 6 – 10, 16, 17,
19 – 29, July 2 – Sept. 18, 20 –
Oct. 14, 16 – 21, 23, 24, 26 –
Nov. 4, 6 – 11, 13 – Dec. 16,
20 – 26.

1961   Jan. 3 – 13, 15 – 31, Feb. 2 –
Mar. 2, 4 – 29, Apr. 1 – 30, May
5, 10 – 23, 25 – Aug. 6, 8 – 19,
21 – 31.

Micro (P) & (N)
1962   Jan. 1+.
LNT – MA
1958   Jan. 23.
MB
Current (one month).
NBuU
Current (three months).

ESTUDIANTE. w. est. May 2, 1909.
MWA
1909   May 2.

¡EXTRA! d. est. Mar. 3, 1947.
DLC
1947   Mar. 3.

EL FANAL.
NcD
1830   Mar. 10.

EL FARO. est. 1848.
NcD
1848   Aug. 12, Sept. 1 – Dec. 1, 5, 11,
18, 29.
1849   Jan. 1 – 31, Feb. 10, 17, Mar.
12.

EL FEDERALISTA. d. est. July 30, 1863.
Note: Ceased publication [1869].

FU
1864   Jan. 2 – Dec. 31.
1865   Jan. 1 – June 30.

LA FRAGUA. d. est. Apr. 1, 1887.
FU
1887   Apr. 1 – 5.

FRATERNIZADOR. d.
MWA
1909   June 7.

FROU-FROU. w.
MWA
1909   May 23, June 20.

FUEGO LENTO.
MWA
1873   [June 5].
Suplemento: [Apr. 10].

GACETA CONSTITUCIONAL DE
CARACAS. est. June 7, 1831.
NcD
1831   Aug. 11, 20, 31, Sept. 6, Oct. 3,
Nov. 8, 19, 24, Dec. 3, 10, 23,
30.
1832   Jan. 6, Feb. 4.

GACETA DE CARACAS. w., sw. est.
Oct. 24, 1808.
Note: Several different editions
published Oct. 1810 – Dec. 1811.
Ceased publication Jan. 3, 1822.
CU – B
1808   Oct. 24 – Dec. 31.
1809   Jan. 1 – Dec. 31.
1810   Jan. 1 – Dec. 21.
1811   Jan. 1 – Dec. 31.
1812   Jan. 1 – Feb. 22, Oct. 12 – Dec.
31.
1813   Jan. 1 – 3, Aug. 26 – Dec. 31.
1814   Jan. 1 – June 20.
1815   Mar. 8 – Dec. 27.
1816   Feb. 21 – Dec. 31.
1817   Jan. 1 – Dec. 31.
1818   Jan. 1 – July 15.
Micro (P)
1818   Extraordinario: Sept. 26.
Micro (N)
1820   Dec. 31.
Suplemento: Aug 9.

CtY
1808 Oct. 24 – Dec. 20.
Extraordinario: Dec. 20.
1809 Jan. 3 – Sept. 1, 18 – 29, Nov.
24 – Dec. 1, 15 – 22.
Extraordinario: Sept. 18.
1810 Jan. 12 – 26, Feb. 12 – 25, Mar.
16 – Apr. 13, 27 – May 18, 25 –
June 8, 29 – July 6, 20, 27 –
Sept. 28, Oct. 12 – 19, Nov. 2 –
23, Dec. 7, 21.
Parallel series: Oct. 9 – 16,
30 – Nov. 6, 20 – Dec. 31, 18.
1811 Jan. 1 – 8, June 4 – 11, 25, July
9 – 30, Aug. 13, Sept. 24, Dec.
24 – 31.
Parallel series: Jan. 4, 13 – 24,
Apr. 5, June 7, 21 – July 26,
Aug. 16, Dec. 27.
1812 Nov. 8 – 15, Dec. 6 – 20.
1813 Jan. 3, Aug. 26 – Oct. 28, Nov.
1 – Dec. 30.
1814 Jan. 3 – June 20.
1815 Mar. 8 – May 10, 24 – July 26,
Sept. 23 – Dec. 27.
1816 Feb. 21 – Dec. 25.
1817 Jan. 1, Apr. 9, 30 – May 21,
Sept. 3 – 10, 17 – Dec. 17, 31.
1818 Feb. 4 – 25, Apr. 8 – 15, 29,
June 24 – July 15.
Extraordinario: Mar. 16, 27,
May 30.
DLC
1808 Oct. 24 – Dec. 31.
1809 Jan. 1 – Dec. 31.
1810 Jan. 1 – Dec. 21.
1811 Jan. 1 – Dec. 31.
1812 Jan. 1 – Feb. 22, Oct. 4 – Dec.
31.
1813 Jan. 1 – 3, Aug. 26 – Dec. 31.
1814 Jan. 1 – June 20.
1815 Mar. 8 – Dec. 27.
1816 Feb. 21 – Dec. 31.
1817 Jan. 1 – Dec. 31.
1818 Jan. 1 – July 15.
ICN
1808 Oct. 24 – Dec. 31.
1809 Jan. 1 – Sept. 1, 18 – 29, Nov.
24 – Dec. 3, 15 – 31.

Suplemento: Aug. 25.
1810 Jan. 1 – May 18, 25 – July 20,
27 – Sept. 28, Oct. 12 – 19,
Nov. 1 – 21.
Suplemento: Apr. 27, July 6.
Parallel series: Oct. 9 – Dec.
31.
Extraordinario: Dec. 18.
1811 Jan. 4, 15 – Oct. 4, 11 – Dec.
31.
Parallel series: Jan. 1 – Feb. 12,
26 – Apr. 2, 16 – Nov. 26, Dec.
10 – 31.
1812 Jan. 3 – Mar. 20, Apr. 25, May
2 – June 5.
Extraordinario: Jan. 4.
IU
1808 Oct. 24 – Dec. 31.
1809 Jan. 1 – Dec. 31.
1810 Jan. 1 – Dec. 21.
1811 Jan. 1 – Dec. 31.
1812 Jan. 1 – Feb. 22, Oct. 4 – Dec.
31.
1813 Jan. 1 – 3, Aug. 26 – Dec. 31.
1814 Jan. 1 – June 20.
1815 Mar. 8 – Dec. 27.
1816 Feb. 21 – Dec. 31.
1817 Jan. 1 – Dec. 31.
1818 Jan. 1 – July 15.
LNHT
1808 Oct. 24 – Dec. 31.
1809 Jan. 1 – Aug. 31, Sept. 1, 27,
Nov. 24, Dec. 1, 15, 22, 29.
1810 Jan. 1 – Dec. 31.
1811 Jan. 1 – Feb. 15.
MWA
1808 Oct. 24 – Dec. 31.
1809 Jan. 1 – Dec. 31.
1810 Jan. 1 – Dec. 21.
1811 Jan. 1 – 25, Apr. 5, June 4 –
11, 21 – 28, July 9 – 30, Aug.
13 – 16, Sept. 24, Dec. 24 – 31.
1812 Jan. 1 – 21, Feb. 19 – 22, Oct.
4, Nov. 8 – 15, Dec. 6, 20.
1813 Jan. 3, Aug. 26 – Dec. 31.
1814 Jan. 1 – June 20.
1815 Mar. 8 – May 10, 24 – July 26,
Sept. 23 – Dec. 27.
1816 Feb. 21 – Dec. 31.

1817   Jan. 1, Apr. 9, 30 – May 21,
        Sept. 3 – Dec. 17, 31.
1818   Feb. 4 – 25, Mar. 16, 27, Apr.
        8 – 15, 29, June 24 – July 15.
        Extraordinario: May 30.
NN
1808   Oct. 24 – Dec. 31.
1809 – 1817   Jan. 1 – Dec. 31.
1818   Jan. 1 – July 15.
NcD
1820   May 24.
1821   Dec. 6.
1822   Jan. 3.
PPAmP
1811   Jan. 8 – May 7.
TxU
1808   Oct. 24 – Dec. 31.
1809   Jan. 1 – Sept. 1, 18 – 29, Nov.
        24 – Dec. 3, 15 – 31.
        Suplemento: Aug. 25.
1810   Jan. 1 – May 18, 25 – Sept. 28,
        Oct. 12 – 19, Nov. 1 – 21, 23,
        Dec. 7, 21.
        Suplemento: Apr. 27, June 2,
        July 6.
        Parallel series: Oct. 9 – Dec.
        31.
        Extraordinario: Dec. 18.
1811   Jan. 4, 15 – Oct. 4, 11 – Dec.
        31.
        Parallel series: Jan. 1 – Feb.
        12, 26 – Apr. 2, 16 – Nov. 26,
        Dec. 10 – 31.
1812   Jan. 3 – Mar. 20, Apr. 25, May
        2 – June 5, Dec. 6 – 20.
        Suplemento: Jan. 4.
1813   Jan. 3, Aug. 26 – Dec. 31.
        Extraordinario: Oct. 14.
1814   Jan. 1 – Feb. 14, 21 – June 20.
1815   Mar. 8 – May 10, 24 – July 26,
        Sept. 23 – Dec. 31.
1816   Feb. 21 – Dec. 31.
        Suplemento: July 17.
1817   Jan. 1, Apr. 9, 30 – May 21,
        Sept. 3 – 10, 17 – Dec. 31.
1818   Feb. 4 – 25, Mar. 16, 27, Apr.
        8 – 15, 29, May 30, June 24 –
        July 1 – 15.

WU
1808   Oct. 24 – Dec. 31.
1809   Jan. 1 – Dec. 31.
1810   Jan. 1 – Dec. 21.
1811   Jan. 1 – Dec. 31.
1812   Jan. 1 – Feb. 22, Oct. 4 – Dec.
        31.
1813   Jan. 1 – 3, Aug. 26 – Dec. 31.
1814   Jan. 1 – June 20.
1815   Mar. 8 – Dec. 27.
1816   Feb. 21 – Dec. 31.
1817   Jan. 1 – Dec. 31.
1818   Jan. 1 – July 15.

GACETA DE CARACAS. irr. est. May 15,
    1854.
MWA
    1855   May 15 – Dec. 3.

GACETA OFICIAL. w., 3w., d. est.
    Sept. 15, 1827.
    Note: Title *Gaceta del gobierno*,
    Sept. 15, 1827 – Feb. 27, 1830;
    Gaceta de Venezuela, Jan. 9, 1831 –
    July 1959; *Diario oficial*, Aug. 17,
    1859 – Mar. 24, 1860; *Gaceta oficial*,
    June 15, 1860 – Aug. 1861; *Registro
    oficial*, Dec. 4, 1861 – Dec. 27, 1862;
    Recopilación oficial, Sept. 28, 1863 –
    Aug. 1868; *Gaceta federal*, Sept. 9,
    1868 – Nov. 1869; *Gaceta oficial*, after
    Oct. 11, 1871. Published in Valencia,
    Aug. 19, 1858 – Feb. 3, 1859.
CU – B
    1827   Sept. 15 – Dec. 31.
    1828 – 1829   [Jan. 1 – Dec. 31].
    1830   Jan. 9 – Feb. 27.
    1831 – 1853   [Jan. 1 – Dec. 31].
    1854   [Jan. 1 – June 30].
    1858   [Oct. 1 – Dec. 31].
    1859 – 1860   [Jan. 1 – Dec. 31].
    1861   [Jan. 1 – Aug. 31]., Dec. 4 – 31.
    1862   [Jan. 1 – Dec. 31].
    1863   Sept. 28 – Dec. 31.
    1864 – 1865   Jan. 1 – Dec. 31.
    1866   Jan. 1 – Feb. 14.
    1868   May 13, [Sept. 9 – Dec. 31].
    1869   [Jan. 1 – Nov. 30].
    Micro (N)

1831	Jan. 23 – Dec. 31.
1832 – 1842	Jan. 1 – Dec. 31.
1843	Jan. 1 – June 25.

CtY

1827	Nos. 1 – 31.
1828	Nos. 32 – 106, 108 – 118, 120 – 138.
1829	Nos. 139, 141 – 239.
1833	Jan. 19 – Dec. 28.
1834 – 1842	Jan. 1 – Dec. 31.
1843	Jan. 1 – June 25.
1844 – 1846	Jan. 1 – Dec. 31.
1847	Jan. 10 – June 27.
1850	July 14.
1858	Mar. 29.
1859	Feb. 4 – Dec. 31.
1860	Jan. 1 – Dec. 31.
1861	Jan. 5 – Aug. 24.
1875 – 1876	Jan. 1 – Dec. 31.
1877	Feb. 20 – Dec. 19, 21 – 29.
1878	Jan. 4 – Apr. 12, 23 – June 21.
1879	Mar. 1 – May 21, 23 – June 30.
1881	Jan. 3 – June 30.
1884 – 1892	Jan. 1 – Dec. 31.
1893	Jan. 1 – Feb. 4, 7 – Dec. 31.
1894 – 1897	Jan. 1 – Dec. 31.
1898	Jan. 3 – Mar. 18, 21 – June 27, 29 – July 4, 7 – Dec. 31.
1899	Jan. 1 – Dec. 31.
1900	Jan. 2 – June 5, 9, 18 – July 23, 26 – Aug. 22, 24 – 27, 29 – Sept. 1, 15 – Oct. 26, Nov. 1, 5 – Dec. 31.

DLC

1827	Sept. 15 – Dec. 31.
1828	Jan. 1 – Dec. 31.
1829	[Jan. 1 – Dec. 31].
1830	˙[Jan. 1 – Feb. 27].
1831	Jan. 9 – Dec. 31.
1832 – 1834	[Jan. 1 – Dec. 31].
1835 – 1838	Jan. 1 – Dec. 30.
1839	[Jan. 13 – Dec. 29].
1840 – 1842	Jan. 1 – Dec. 31.
1843 – 1844	[Jan. 1 – Dec. 31].
1845 – 1847	Jan. 1 – Dec. 31.
1848	Jan. 1 – June 11, July 2 – Dec. 31.
1849	Jan. 1 – Dec. 31.

1850 – 1853	[Jan. 1 – Dec. 31].
1854	July 16 – Dec. 31.
1855	Jan. 1 – Dec. 31.
1856 – 1859	[Jan. 1 – Dec. 31].
1860	Jan. 1 – Mar. 24, June 15 – Dec. 31.
1861 – 1862	[Jan. 1 – Dec. 31].
1865	Sept. 28 – Dec. 31.
1866 – 1867	Jan. 1 – Dec. 31.
1868	Jan. 1 – May 16, Sept. 9 – Dec. 31.
1869	Jan. 1 – Nov. 26.
1874	July 2 – Dec. 31.
1875 – 1876	[Jan. 1 – Dec. 31].
1877	[Jan. 2 – June 30].
1879	Mar. 1 – June 30, Oct. 1 – Dec. 31.
1880	Jan. 2 – Mar. 31.
1881	Jan. 3 – Dec. 31.
1882	[Jan. 1 – Dec. 31].
1883	Jan. 2 – June 30.
1884 – 1885	[Jan. 1 – Dec. 31].
1888	July 2 – Dec. 31.
1889 – 1896	Jan. 1 – Dec. 31.

IU

1861	Dec. 4 – 31.
1862	Jan. 1 – Dec. 31.
1863	Jan. 1 – June 17.

MWA

1843	May 28.
1848	July 2 – Dec. 31.
1849	Jan. 1 – June 17, Oct. 7.
1861	July 1 – Aug. 24, Dec. 4 – 31.
1862	Jan. 1 – Dec. 31.
1863	Jan. 1 – 28.
1869	Jan. 2 – Mar. 15.

NcD

1831	July 13 – Dec. 14.
1832	Mar. 14, 21, Apr. 4.
1834	Nov. 8, 29.
1835	July 25, 29, Aug. 1, 5, 15, 22, 26 – Nov. 30, Dec. 5, 12, 19.
1836	Jan. 2, 16, 23, Feb. 1 – 28, Mar. 5, 12, 19, Apr. 2, 30.
1837	June 10.
1841	Aug. 15.

1843   Jan. 22.
1847   Oct. 31, Nov. 7, 14.
1848   June 6, July 23, Sept. 3, 17, 29,
        Nov. 26.
1849   June 17, Aug. 27, Sept. 30, Oct.
        7, Nov. 11, 25, Dec. 9, 16.
1850   Jan. 6, 20, May 10, 19, 26, June
        2, 9, Sept. 1.
1851   Oct. 26.
1858   July 8, 15.
1860   June 15, 18, 20, 22, 25, 27, 29,
        July 2, 4, 6, 9, 11, 13, 16, 18, 23,
        25, Aug. 3, 8, 13, 24, 28, 31,
        Sept. 1, 3, 5, 8, 15, 22, 25, 28.

LA GAZZETTA. w. est. July 24, 1953.
    Note: In Italian.
    DLC
    1953   July 24 — Aug. 14.

GEDEON. irr.
    MWA
    1909   Mar. 14, Aug. 8.

EL GRAFICO. d. est. 1947.
    DLC
    1949   Oct. 1 — Nov. 18, 22, 23, 25 —
            Dec. 5, 7 — 31.
    1950   Jan. 1, 2, Mar. 1 — 31, Apr.
            14 — 17, 21, 23 — 29, May 2 —
            July 12, 14 — Dec. 31.
    1951   Jan. 1 — Apr. 30, May 2 — July
            9, 11 — 13.

GRAN BOLETIN. [w.]
    MWA
    1908   Dec. 20.
    1909   Jan. 1.
    1914   Mar. 19.

GRANUJA. d.
    MWA
    1909   Jan. 29, May 31.

GRITO DEL PUEBLO. d.
    MWA
    1907   Aug. 5.
    1909   Feb. 2, 3, 5, 9, 13, 24, Apr. 1,
            12, 13.

GUILLOTINA. bw.
    MWA
    1911   Feb. 15.

HERALDO DE CARACAS. sw.
    MWA
    1910   Jan. 8.

HERALDO CATOLICO. w. est. June 11,
1910.
    MWA
    1910   June 11, 25.
    1911   Feb. 4.
    1914   Mar. 14.

IMPARCIAL. d.
    MWA
    1909   Aug. 18.

EL INDEPENDIENTE. d. est. Apr. 9,
1860.
    Note: Ceased publication [1863].
    DLC
    1860   Apr. 9.

INDEPENDIENTE. d. est. Feb. 12, 1909.
    MWA
    1909   Feb. 12 — 14, 16, 18 — 24.

IRIS DE VENEZUELA. w. est. Jan. 14,
1822.
    Note: Ceased publication [Dec. 19,
    1832].
    CtY
    1822   Mar. 18 — 25, Apr. 22 — 29, May
            27.
    DLC
    1822   Jan. 21 — Feb. 10, 12 — 24, 26 —
            Mar. 3, 5 — 17, 19 — Apr. 7, 9 —
            28, 30 — May 5, June 18 — Aug.
            18, 20 — Oct. 24.
    NcD
    1822   Jan. 21, 28, Mar. 18, Apr. 15 —
            May 6, June 3, 10, July 8 — 22,
            Aug. 12 — Sept. 9, 23 — Dec. 31.
    1823   Jan. 2, 23 — Feb. 28, Mar. 6,
            May 22, 29, Sept. 19, Nov. 28,
            Dec. 19.

JEJEN. [3w.]
    MWA
    1868   Sept. 22 — 24.

JUICIO FINAL. w. est. Jan. 29, 1853.
    MWA
    1853   Jan. 29 — Feb. 12, Mar. 12 — 24,
            Apr. 29 — May 6.

JUSTICIA. d. est. Dec. 29, 1908.
MWA
1908   Dec. 29, 30.

EL LABERINTO. est. May 6, 1845.
NcD
1845   May 6.

LENGUA Y LATIGO. [w.]
MWA
1909   Apr. 7.

EL LIBERAL. w. est. May 28, 1836.
Note: Ceased publication [1847].
CU−B
Micro (N)
1841   Aug. 4, 10.
CtY
1844   Jan. 2−Dec. 30.
DLC
1836   May 28−Dec. 27.
1837   Jan. 3−Feb. 13, 15−May 1,
3−Sept. 25, 27−Dec. 31.
1838   Jan. 1−Nov. 26, 28−Dec. 25.
Extraordinario: Dec. 22.
1839   Jan. 8−May 13, 15−Dec. 31.
1840   Jan. 1−13, 15−Aug. 17, 19−
Sept. 1.
1845   Aug. 2−Oct. 3, 12−31, Nov.
2−28, 30−Dec. 20.
1846   Jan. 3−24, Apr. 18, 25, May 9,
16, June 6−Aug. 29, Oct. 3−
Nov. 14, Dec. 19.
1847   Jan. 23−30.
FU
1837   Jan. 10−Dec. 31.
1838   Jan. 1−Sept. 25.
MWA
1836   Nov. 22.
1837   May 23, Aug. 22, Dec. 12−19.
1843   Apr. 11−May 16.
1844   Jan. 2.

LIBERAL. d. est. Jan. 29, 1909.
MWA
1909   Jan. 29.

LIBERAL VENEZOLANO. d. est. June
7, 1909.
MWA
1909   June 7.

LIBERTAD Y ORDEN.
NcD
1844   July 17, Aug. 1.

LINTERNA MAGICA. d.
MWA
1902   Mar. 19.
1909   Apr. 6, 7, 12, 13.

MERCURIO DE CARACAS.
NcD
1844   June 12, 22, 29, July 27.

MERCURIO VENEZOLANO. m. est. Jan.
1, 1811.
WU
1811 Jan.−Mar.

MESA REVUELTA. sw. est. Sept. 7,
1906.
Note: Title *Miscelánea*, Sept. 7−
Oct. 10, 1906; *Mesa revuelta*, after
Oct. 10, 1906.
MWA
1906   Sept. 7−22, 29−Oct. 10, 31,
Nov. 7.

UN MILITAR RETIRADO.
NcD
1833   Feb. 20, Mar. 11.

MINERVA. w.
MWA
1909   Jan. 23.

MISCELANEA.
See *Mesa revuelta*.

EL MONITOR INDUSTRIAL. w., d. est.
June 22, 1858.
DLC
1858   June 22−July 21, Sept. 1−
Dec. 30.
Extraordinario: Sept. 6.
1859   Jan. 1−Feb. 5.

MONITOR REPUBLICANO. bw. est. Jan.
21, 1909.
MWA
1909   Jan. 21.

LA MOSCA LIBRE. irr. est. Sept. 7, 1820.
CtY
1820   Sept. 7−30, Oct. 10−31.

LA MOSCA LIBRE. est. Aug. 23, 1830.
  CtY
    1830   Aug. 23.

MOXA.
  NcD
    1844   July 18.

NACION. d.
  MWA
    1910   Oct. 5.
    1911   Feb. 24, Apr. 5.

LA NACION. sw. est. 1941.
  DLC
    1942   Aug. 15, 26, Sept. 12, 19, Nov.
            4, 7, Dec. 5.

EL NACIONAL. bw., 3m. est. Dec. 15,
1833.
  DLC
    1834   Jan. 10 – Feb. 21, Apr. 21.

EL NACIONAL. d. est. Aug. 3, 1943.
  CLU
    1964   Dec. 28 – 31.
    1965   Jan. 2 – 8, 10 – Feb. 21, Mar.
            1 – 7, 15 – 28, Apr. 12, 14, 17 –
            June 24, 28 – Aug. 29, Sept.
            7 – Oct. 10, 18 – 24, 25 – 31,
            Nov. 15 – Dec. 31.
    1966   Jan. 1+.
  CSt – H
    1964   Nov. 15, 16, 18 – 20, 24, 25,
            27 – Dec. 1, 3, 8, 12 – 14, 16 –
            31.
    1965   Jan. 1 – 22, 24 – 26, 28 – 31,
            Feb. 2 – 18, 20 – Apr. 24, 26 –
            June 27, 29 – July 10, 13 – 19,
            21 – Aug. 4, 6 – 24, 26 – Sept. 2,
            4 – 14, 26 – Nov. 30, Dec. 2 – 7,
            14 – 28, 30, 31.
    1966   Jan. 1+.
  DLC
    1945   Nov. 2, 4 – Dec. 9, 11 – 13,
            15 – 28, 30, 31.
    1946   Jan. 1 – 3, 5 – 23, 26 – Feb. 7,
            9 – 11, 13, 15 – Mar. 22, 24, 25,
            27 – Apr. 4, 6 – 12, 14 – 21,
            23 – 28, 30 – May 5, 7 – June
            15, July 1 – 14, 16 – 23, 25, 26,

            28 – Aug. 14, 16 – Nov. 2, 4 –
            Dec. 31.
    1947   Jan. 1 – Mar. 31, May 1 – 28,
            30 – June 24, 26 – July 7, Nov.
            19 – 30, Dec. 5 – 7, 9 – 13, 16 –
            31.
    1948   Jan. 1 – Apr. 28, 30 – Dec. 31.
    1949   Jan. 2 – Mar. 30, Apr. 1 – Dec.
            30.
    1950   Jan. 2 – Apr. 5, 8 – 21, May 1 –
            Aug. 27, 29 – Nov. 13, 15 – Dec.
            31.
    1951   Jan. 2 – Oct. 16, 18 – 25, 27 –
            Dec. 31.
    1952   Jan. 1 – Apr. 6, 8 – Oct. 24,
            26 – Dec. 31.
    1953   Jan. 1 – Feb. 13, 15 – Dec. 31.
    1954   Jan. 2 – Apr. 30, May 2 – June
            30.
    1955   Jan. 2 – Apr. 30, May 2 – Oct. 8,
            11 – 14, 17, 18, 22 – Nov. 4,
            11 – Dec. 31.
    1956   July 1 – 9, 18, 19, 21 – Aug. 17,
            19 – 25, 27, Sept. 6, 7, 11, 13 –
            Oct. 21, 23 – Dec. 31.
    1957   Jan. 2 – Mar. 7, 9 – Apr. 30,
            May 2 – Aug. 27, 29, 30, Sept.
            1 – Dec. 30.
    1960   June 8, 10, 12 – 15, 17 – Aug.
            31, Sept. 2 – 16, 18 – Oct. 14,
            16 – 21, 23, 24, 26 – Nov. 4, 6 –
            21, 24 – Dec. 12, 14 – 16, 18 –
            28, 30, 31.
    1961   Mar. 1 – Apr. 4, 8 – May 5, 7 –
            Dec. 31.
  Micro (P) & (N)
    1962   Jan. 1+.
  IU
    1965   Oct. 1 – Dec. 31.
    1966   Jan. 1+.
  KU
    Current (two months).
  LNT – MA
    1958   Jan. 23.
  NBuU
    Current (three months).
  NNC
    1965   Apr. 1 – 13, 17 – 23, 25 – 28,

30, 31, May 2 – June 12, 14 – 21,
23 – July 5, 8 – 28, 30 – Aug.
19, 23 – 28, Sept. 4 – 25, 27 –
Oct. 24, 26 – Nov. 6, 8 – 14.

OkU (Weekly edition only)
    1965   June 6 – Dec. 31.
    1966   Jan. 1+.
OrU
    1963   Nov. 22, 29.

LA NOCHE.
NcD
    1827   n.d. (No. 2).

LA NOCHE BUENA DE LA OLI-
GARCUIA. est. July 6, 1844.
NcD
    1844   July 6, 19, 25, Aug. 1, 16, 23.

NOTICIERO. d.
MWA
    1907   May 14, 15, Oct. 31.
    1908   Aug. 31, Dec. 14 – 16, 19 – 21,
           24 – 30.
    1909   Jan. 2, 26, Feb. 2.
    1914   Mar. 19.

NOVEDADES. d.
MH
    1942   Mar. 1 – Aug. 31, Nov. 15 –
           Dec. 31.
    1943   Jan. 15 – Sept. 30.

EL NUEVO DIARIO. d. est. Jan. 13,
1913.
DLC
    1931   Apr. 28 – Aug. 26, 28 – Oct. 23,
           25 – Nov. 16, 18 – Dec. 9, 11 –
           31.
    1932 – 1933   Jan. 1 – Dec. 31.
    1934   Jan. 1, 2, Aug. 26 – Sept. 1,
           9 – Dec. 29.
    1935   Jan. 6 – Feb. 16, 24 – June 24,
           26 – Aug. 15, 25 – Oct. 6, 8 –
           13, 15 – Dec. 14.
MWA
    1913   Aug. 2, 3.
    1914   Mar. 20.
    1932   Feb. 22, 23.
TxU
    1926   Aug. 8.

NUEVO TIEMPO. d. est. Jan. 18, 1909.
MWA
    1909   Jan. 18, 23 – 25, 27 – 30, Feb. 5,
           6, 19.

OBRERO. d.
MWA
    1883   July 10.

EL OBSERVADOR CARAQUEÑO. w.
est. Jan. 1, 1824.
    Note: Ceased publication Dec. 30,
    1824.
CtY
    1824   Jan. 1 – Dec. 30.

LA OLIVA. bw., 3m. est. Jan. 1, 1836.
    Note: Periodicity Jan. 1 – July 1,
    1836, biweekly; after July 10, 1836
    three times a month. Ceased pub-
    lication Oct. 1, 1836.
DLC
    1836   Apr. 1 – Sept. 10.
           Apéndice: Apr. 22.

LA OPINION NACIONAL. sw., d. est.
Nov. 14, 1868.
    Note: Ceased publication [Oct. 6,
    1892].
DLC
    1885   Sept. 19, Oct. 15, 19, 21, 22,
           Nov. 3 – 5, 7 – 9, 17 – 20.
MWA
    1883   July 4, Aug. 3 – 18.
    1884   [Oct. 17 – Dec. 31].
    1885   [Jan. 1 – Dec. 31]
    1886   [Jan. 1 – Oct. 2].
NN
    1888   Apr. 9.

LA OPOSICION. est. Feb. 28, 1844.
NcD
    1844   Mar. 14.

EL ORDEN. d. est. Apr. 17, 1865.
FU
    1865   Apr. 17 – July 24.

PAIS. [sw.]
MWA
    1908   Jan. 25.

EL PAIS. d. est. 1944.
  DLC
    1945   Nov. 4 – 6, 10, 11, 13, 16, 17,
            21 – 23, Dec. 1 – 3, 6 – 10, 12 –
            31.
    1946   Jan. 1 – 8, 10 – Apr. 16, 18 –
            May 27, 31, June 6, 8 – 10, 12,
            14, 18 – Dec. 31.
    1947   Jan. 1 – May 1, 3 – Aug. 3, 5 –
            12, 15 – 25, 27 – Sept. 1, 3, 5,
            14 – 22, Nov. 20 – Dec. 7, 9 –
            13, 16 – 31.
    1948   Mar. 19 – Dec. 9.

PATRIA. [w.]
  MWA
    1905   Mar. 15.
    1909   June 17.
    1911   Mar. 5.

EL PATRIOTA. w., irr. est. Mar. 23,
  1845.
    Note: Periodicity before Apr. 5, 1854,
    weekly; after Apr. 19, 1854, irregular.
    Suspended publication Feb. 9, 1850 –
    Oct. 27, 1851. Ceased publication
    [1854].
  DLC
    1846   Feb. 28 – Apr. 17, 19 – June 5,
            14 – July 17, 19 – Sept. 4, 13 –
            26.
            Extraordinario: July 28.
    1849   Jan. 27 – Apr. 13, 15 – Aug. 17,
            19 – Sept. 14, 16 – Oct. 5, Nov.
            4 – 16, Dec. 16 – 28.
    1850   Jan. 6 – Feb. 9.
    1851   Oct. 28 – Nov. 17, 19 – Dec. 31.
    1852   Jan. 1 – Apr. 9, 18 – 30, May
            2 – June 4, Aug. 18 – Sept. 6,
            8 – Dec. 31.
            Alcance: Mar. 20.
            Extraordinario: Feb. 4.
    1853   Jan. 1 – Dec. 31.
    1854   Jan. 1 – May 24, 26 – Oct. 27.
  MWA
    1845   Mar. 23 – Dec. 31.
    1846   Jan. 1 – Feb. 14, May 23.
    1849   July 15 – Mar. 10.
  NcD
    1845   Mar. 23 – July 31, Aug. 9, Sept.

            27, Oct. 1 – Dec. 31.
    1846   Jan. 1, 24.

PORVENIR. w., sw., d. est. Oct. 10,
  1863.
  FU
    1863   Oct. 10 – Dec. 31.
    1864 – 1867   Jan. 1 – Dec. 31.
    1868   Jan. 1 – Apr. 7.

PORVENIR DE LA REPUBLICA. est.
  May 6, 1858.
  MWA
    1858   May 6 – 14.

LA PRENSA. sw., w. est. Nov. 1, 1846.
    Note: Periodicity Nov. 1, 1846 – May
    1847, semiweekly; after July 1847,
    weekly. Suspended publication May –
    July 1847.
  DLC
    1846   Nov. 1 – Dec. 31.
    1847   Jan. 1 – May 4, July 12 – Dec.
            31.
            Suplemento: Mar. 16, 26, 30,
            Apr. 6, 9, 16.
    1848   Jan. 1 – 22.
            Suplemento: Jan. 15.
  NcD
    1846   Nov. 1, 7, 11, 14, 18, 21, 25, 29,
            Dec. 5, 9, 12, 16, 19, 23, 26, 30.
    1847   Jan. 2, 6, 13, 20, 23, 26, 27, 30,
            Feb. 2, 5, 9, 12, 19, 23, 26, Apr.
            1 – May 4, Nov. 6.

PROGRESISTA. d.
  MWA
    1909   Nov. 8.

PROGRESO. d.
  MWA
    1857   Nov. 10, 24.

PROGRESO. d.
  MWA
    1909   May 13.

PROMETEO. [w.]
  MWA
    1907   Sept. 5.

PROPAGANDA. est. May 14, 1904.
MWA
　1904　May 14.

RAZON. d.
MWA
　1885　Oct. 16, 21, 28.

REACCION. est. Dec. 26, 1908.
MWA
　1908　Dec. 26.

REACCION NACIONAL. d. est. Jan. 9,
1909.
MWA
　1909　Jan. 9, 12, 14.

RECEPCION OFICIAL.
MWA
　1911　July.

RECONCILIADOR. w. est. Mar. 1, 1827.
　Note: Imprint Colombia.
MWA
　1827　Apr. 3, 24 – 30.
NcD
　1827.　Mar. 27.

RECOPILACION OFICIAL.
　See *Gaceta oficial*.

EL REDACTOR GENERAL.
NcD
　1827　Aug. 4.

REGENERACION. w. est. May 26, 1856.
MWA
　1856　May 26, June 23.

REGISTRO LITERARIO. w.
MWA
　1884　Nov. 15.

REGISTRO OFICIAL.
　See *Gaceta oficial*.

LA RELIGION. d. est. July 17, 1890.
DLC
　1941　Dec. 16 – 21.
MWA
　1905　Aug. 21, 25.
　1907　Oct. 4.
　1914　Mar. 18.

REPERTORIO. w.
MWA
　1885　Feb. 8, Mar. 1.

REPUBLICA. d.
MWA
　1909　Jan. 12, 20, 28, Feb. 3, 8, 9, 13,
　　　　Apr. 7.

LA REPUBLICA. d.
CSt – H
　1964　Oct. 15 – Nov. 4, 6 – 17, 19 –
　　　　Dec. 2, 10 – 31.
　1965　Jan. 1 – 18, 20 – Feb. 4, 6, 7, 9,
　　　　11 – Aug. 3, 5 – Dec. 31.
　1966　Jan. 1+.
CU
　1963 – 1965　Jan. 1 – Dec. 31.

SANCHO PANZA. d.
MWA
　1909　Jan. 22, 25, 26, 28, 29, Feb. 3,
　　　　6, 9 – 13.

SANCION. w. est. June 19, 1909.
MWA
　1909　June 19.

SEMANARIO POLITICO. w.
NcD
　1832　Feb. 3.

EL SIGLO. d. est. Jan. 20, 1847.
NcD
　1847　Jan. 20, 26, Feb. 2, 9, 16.

SIGLO. d. est. July 1, 1881.
MWA
　1883　[July 27 – Dec. 31].
　1884　[Jan. 1 – Feb. 22, Aug. 25 –
　　　　Oct. 21], Dec. 15 – 31.
　1885　Jan. 1 – 21, [Feb. 19 – Sept. 23],
　　　　Oct. 14 – Dec. 31.
　1886　Jan. 1 – Mar. 31, May 15 – 29,
　　　　Sept. 4 – Nov. 27.
　1889　Mar. 8 – 31, Sept. 28 – Oct. 16,
　　　　21, Nov. 11.

EL TELEGRAFO.
NcD
　1846　Apr. 8.

EL TIEMPO.
  NcD
    1835   Oct. 23, 28.

TIEMPO. d.
  MWA
    1909   Jan. 9, 13 – 15, 20 – 21, 25, 26,
            29, July 31.
  NN
    1901   Jan. 2 – Dec. 31.
    1902   Jan. 1 – Feb. 28.

TIEMPO ECONOMICO. d.
  CSt – H
    1964   Sept. 3 – 17, Oct. 1, 15 – 22.

TIO CARCOMA. sw.
  MWA
    1908   Dec. 12.

TIO LAGARTO. w.
  MWA
    1907   Mar. 2.

TOREO. w., d.
  MWA
    1908   Dec. 19.
    1911   Feb. 4.

EL TRABUCO. est. Nov. 30, 1844.
  NcD
    1844   Dec. 19.
    1845   Jan. 4, Feb. 10.

TRECE. est. Jan. 1, 1909.
  MWA
    1909   Jan. 1.

LA TRIBUNA LIBERAL. d. est. May 26,
  1877.
  NN
    1877   May 26 – July 14, 16 – Dec. 28.
    1878   Jan. 2 – Mar. 1, 6 – June 28,
            July 2 – 4, 6 – Aug. 1, 3, 6, 12,
            Sept. 2 – Nov. 26, 28 – Dec. 2,
            6 – 13, 16 – 19, 21 – 27, 30.
    1879   Jan. 2 – 9, 11 – 13, 15 – 24, 27 –
            29, Feb. 1 – 5.

TRIBUNA POPULAR. w.
  DLC
    1959   Jan. 10 – July 9, 18 – Sept. 10,
            Oct. 10 – Dec. 31.
    1960   Jan. 8 – Nov. 29.

ULTIMAS NOTICIAS. d. est. 1941.
  DLC
    1943   May 8, 13 – 15, 20, 24, 25, 28 –
            31, June 22 – 25, 30.
    1945   Oct. 24 – Dec. 24, 26 – 31.
    1946   Jan. 1 – Feb. 28.
    1949   Jan. 16, 23.
    1950   June 15 – 28, 30, Aug. 4 – Sept.
            20, 22 – Dec. 15, 17 – 31.
    1951   Jan. 1 – Oct. 10, 12 – 26, 28 –
            Dec. 28, 30, 31.
    1952   Jan. 1 – 30, Feb. 1 – Apr. 1, 3 –
            9, 11 – 13, 15 – 17, 19 – June 4,
            7 – 12, 14 – 17, 19 – July 17,
            19 – Aug. 8, 11 – Sept. 8, 10 –
            20, 22 – Oct. 1, 3 – 10, 12 – 29,
            Nov. 1 – 4, 6 – 13, 15 – Dec. 2,
            6 – 25, 27 – 31.
    1953   Jan. 2 – 11, 13 – Feb. 15, 18, 19,
            21 – Mar. 6, 8 – Apr. 29, May
            2 – June 14, 16 – Oct. 6, 8 –
            Dec. 31.
    1954   Jan. 2 – 31.
  LNT – MA
    1958   Jan. 23, 24.

UNION OBRERA. w.
  MWA
    1909   Apr. 10.
    1910   Jan. 13.

EL UNIVERSAL. d. est. Apr. 1, 1909.
  CU
    1921   May 5 – 14, 24 – 31, June 28 –
            July 11.
  DLC
    1925   Apr. 1 – 24, May 3 – June 20,
            28 – July 3.
    1926   Jan. 2 – Oct. 20, 22 – Dec. 19,
            21 – 31.
    1927   Jan. 1 – Feb. 27, Mar. 2 – Dec.
            31.
    1928   Jan. 1 – Dec. 31.
    1929   Jan. 1 – 25, 27 – Dec. 20.
    1930   Jan. 1 – July 28, Aug. 1 – Dec.
            12, 17, 19 – 31.
    1931   Jan. 1 – June 13.
    1941   May 23, 25 – 28.
    1942   Feb. 1, 5, 8, 12, 15, 19, 22, 26,

Mar. 1, 5, 8, 12, 15, 19.
1944   Mar. 1 — Apr. 7, 9 — May 15,
        17 — 23, July 1 — Sept. 22, 24 —
        Dec. 15, 17 — 31.
1945   Jan. 1 — 19, 22 — Feb. 28, Apr.
        16 — 25, May 1 — June 30, July
        16 — Dec. 31.
1946   Jan. 1 — Mar. 2, 18, 20 — 31,
        Apr. 2 — 8, May 16 — June 15.
1948   Jan. 2 — 18, 25 — Feb. 18, 22 —
        27, Mar. 1 — 3, 6, 14 — June 5,
        7 — July 3, 11 — 31, Aug. 8 —
        Sept. 28, 30 — Oct. 31, Nov. 2 —
        5, 7 — Dec. 31.
1949   Jan. 2 — 8, 16 — Apr. 16, 19 —
        May 12, 14 — June 3, 5 — July 1,
        4 — 22, 24 — Oct. 19, 21 — Dec.
        31.
1950   Jan. 1 — 8, 10 — Dec. 31.
1951   Jan. 1 — Dec. 31.
1952   Jan. 1 — 3, 5 — Feb. 8, 11, 15, 17,
        24, 28, Mar. 1 — 26, 28 — Apr. 1,
        3 — 9, 12 — 16, 19, 21 — May 2,
        4 — 9, 11, 13 — 19, 21 — 28, 30 —
        June 4, 6 — 12, 14 — 30, July
        17 — 31, Aug. 2 — 28, 30 — Sept.
        1, 3 — 5, 7, 8, 11 — 19, 21 — Oct.
        1, 3, 4, 6, 8 — 10, 12 — 14, 16 —
        20, 23, 25 — 30, Nov. 1, 3, 4, 6 —
        10, 12 — Dec. 1, 7 — 9, 12, 13, 15,
        16, 18, 19, 22, 24 — 31.
1953   Jan. 6, 7, 9, 12, 13, 15 — 31, Feb.
        7 — 9, 12, 13, 18 — Mar. 20, 24 —
        Apr. 29, May 2 — 13, 20 — 26,
        29 — June 25, 27 — Aug. 21, 25 —
        Oct. 7, 9 — Dec. 31.
Micro (P) & (N)
1954 — 1955   Jan. 1 — Dec. 31.
Micro (P)
1956   Jan. 1+.
DPU
Current (six months)
Micro (P)
1944   Mar. 1 — Dec. 31.
1945 — 1954   Jan. 1 — Dec. 31.
1955   Jan. 1 — Dec. 5.
FU
1962   Nov. 9 — Dec. 31.
1963   Jan. 1+.

ICRL
Micro (P) & (N)
1956   Jan. 1+.
MWA
1909   Apr. 23, 24, May 18.
1910   Aug. 25.
1911   Apr. 5.
1914   Mar. 20.
OrU
1963   Nov. 15.
PrU
1963   Aug. 24 — 31, Sept. 2 — 19, 22 —
        Oct. 1, 5 — 30, Nov. 1 — 21, 26,
        Dec. 7 — 13.
1964   Jan. 2 — Feb. 28, Mar. 2 — 9,
        11 — 13, 17 — 25, 28 — Apr. 30,
        May 2 — 19, 23 — 28, June 1 — 29,
        July 1 — Oct. 30, Nov. 1 — Dec.
        31.
1965   Jan. 2 — Mar. 6, 9, 12, 16 — Apr.
        14, 17 — 26, 28 — 30, May 2 — 7,
        9 — 16, 18 — 30, June 1 — 22,
        24 — Aug. 9, 11, 12, 14 — 17,
        19 — Sept. 23, 25 — Oct. 2, 4 —
        17, 19 — 24, 26 — 30, Nov. 1 — 7,
        10 — 29, Dec. 1 — 31.
1966   Jan. 1+.
TxU
1922   Jan. 2 — Feb. 26, Mar. 1 — Aug.
        16, 18 — Nov. 12, 14 — 26, 28 —
        Dec. 31.
1923   Jan. 2 — Feb. 11, 15 — 23, 25 —
        Apr. 11, 14 — Dec. 31.
1924   Jan. 2 — Dec. 31.
1941   July 1 — Dec. 24.
1942   Jan. 2 — Feb. 15, 18 — Apr. 10,
        May 26 — Aug. 8, Sept. 1 — 8,
        16 — 30, Oct. 9 — Dec. 24.
1943   Jan. 1 — Mar. 31, Apr. 13 — 21,
        May 1 — Dec. 30.
1944   Jan. 3 — Feb. 20, 23 — Dec. 31.
1945   Jan. 3 — 10, 12 — Mar. 14, May
        1 — June 8, Aug. 1 — 7, 9 — 13,
        19 — 25, Sept. 2 — Oct. 6, 22, 23,
        25 — Nov. 3, 11 — Dec. 31.
1946 — 1947   Jan. 1 — Dec. 31.
1948   Jan. 1 — July 4, 10 — Aug. 1, 7 —
        Dec. 31.
1949   Jan. 1 — Apr. 16, 19 — July 2,

4 — Oct. 19, 21 — Dec. 31.

1950   Jan. 1 — Feb. 10, 12, 24, 27 —
Mar. 2, 5 — Apr. 1, 3 — 27, 29 —
May 11, 13 — June 2, 4 — 15,
24 — July 20, 23 — Aug. 3, 5 — 10,
13 — 18.

ViU
1945   Apr. 13.
1952   Oct. 5 — 30, Nov. 1 — 8, 10 — 15,
17 — 21, 24 — 29, Dec. 2, 3, 6,
8 — 14, 16 — 24, 26, 28, 30, 31.
1953   Jan. 2 — 8, 10 — 23, 25 — Feb. 7,
9 — 15, 18 — Apr. 1, 4 — 18, 20 —
22, 24 — 30, May 2 — June 13,
15 — 27, 29 — July 10, 12 — 29,
31 — Aug. 1, 3 — 15, 17 — 22, 24,
25, 27 — 29, 31 — Sept. 7, 9 —
Oct. 9, 11 — Nov. 28, 30 — Dec.
29.
1954   Jan. 1 — Feb. 28, Mar. 3, 5 — 8,
10 — 29, 31 — Apr. 14, 17 — 25,
27 — 30, May 2 — 31, July 1 —
Dec. 31.
1955   Jan. 2 — 17.

VANGUARDIA. d.
MWA
1909   Aug. 9.

23 DE MAYO. d.
MWA
1907   June 4.

EL VENEZOLANO. w. est. Apr. 6, 1822.
Note: Ceased publication May 1,
1824.
DLC
1822   Sept. 17, 30, Oct. 7, 21.

EL VENEZOLANO. w. est. Aug. 24, 1840.
FU
1840   Dec. 2.
1841   Sept. 6 — Dec. 31.
1842 — 1845   Jan. 1 — Dec. 31.
1846   Jan. 1 — Apr. 12.
MWA
1841   Feb. 15.
NN
1840   Aug. 24 — Dec. 28.
1841   Jan. 4 — Aug. 23, Sept. 6 — Dec.
17, 31.

1842   Jan. 4 — May 14, 28 — Dec. 27.
1843   Jan. 3, 17, 26 — Feb. 4, 14 —
Dec. 30.

THE VENEZUELAN HERALD. w. est.
1896.
Note: In Spanish and English.
DLC
1896   Sept. 5 — Dec. 26.
1898   July 15.
1900   Jan. 15 — Dec. 31.
1901 — 1903   Jan. 1 — Dec. 31.
1904   Jan. 1 — Nov. 5.
MiU
1897 — 1901   Jan. 1 — Dec. 31.
NN
1898   [Aug. 15 — Dec. 31].
1899 — 1903   [Jan. 1 — Dec. 31].
1904   [Jan. 1 — Nov. 5].

LA VOCE D' ITALIA. w. est. 1950.
Note: In Italian.
DLC
1955   Apr. 18.

VOZ DE PUEBLO. d.
MWA
1907   July 23, Aug. 5.

LA VOZ DEL ZULIA. irr. est. 1937.
CU
1937   Oct. 24.
1938   Jan. 15 — June 30, July 14 —
Aug. 6, 20 — Sept. 3, 24, Oct.
15 — Nov. 5, Dec. 24.
1939   Jan. 7, 24, Feb. 11 — 18, Mar.
25 — Apr. 22, May 6 — 13, 27 —
July 15, Sept. 2 — 30.
1940   Feb. 29 — June 13, July 31 —
Sept. 30, Oct. 29 — Dec. 31.
1941   Jan. 16 — Feb. 28.

YUNGUE. [w.]
MWA
1910   Apr. 14.

Carora

EL DIARIO. d. est. Sept. 1, 1919.
Note: Suspended publication Feb. 1,
1929 — Dec. 31, 1931.
DLC
1938   Feb. 1.

HAZ DE VIDA. bw.
　MWA
　　1911　Feb. 16.

LIBRE ALBEDRIO. 3m.
　MWA
　　1911　Feb. 23.

Carúpano

BOLETIN DE "EL RESTAURADOR."
　MWA
　　1905　Sept. 30.

ESTUDIANTE. w. est. June 7, 1907.
　MWA
　　1907　June 7.

MENSAJERO. w.
　MWA
　　1905　Dec. 30.

Ciudad Bolívar

EL CENTINELA.
　NcD
　　1846　May 10, 14, 23, June 3, 8.

EL CLARIN DEL TOTUMO. sw., d. est.
　Mar. 23, 1893.
　CtY
　　1893　Mar. 23 – Apr. 17.

CORREO DEL ORINOCO. w., irr. est.
　June 27, 1818.
　　Note: Suspended publication Nov.
　　28, 1818 – Jan. 29, 1819; Oct. 22 –
　　Nov. 24, 1820; Feb. 10 – Mar. 8, 1822;
　　ceased publication Mar. 23, 1822.
　CtY
　　1818　June 27 – Nov. 21.
　　1819　Jan. 30 – Dec. 18.
　　1820　Jan. 1 – Dec. 30.
　　1821　Jan. 20 – Dec. 29.
　　1822　Jan. 5 – Mar. 23.
　DLC
　　1818　Nov. 21.
　　1820　Mar. 25 – July 15, Aug. 12 –
　　　　　Sept. 23.
　IU
　　1818　June 27 – Dec. 31.
　　1819 – 1821　Jan. 1 – Dec. 31.

　MWA
　　1818　June 27 – Dec. 31.
　　1819 – 1821　Jan. 1 – Dec. 31.
　　1822　Jan. 1 – Mar. 23.
　TxU
　　1818　June 27 – Nov. 21.
　　1819　Jan. 30 – Dec. 18.
　　　　　Extraordinario: Sept. 19.
　　1820　Jan. 1 – Dec. 30.
　　1821　Jan. 30 – Dec. 29.
　　　　　Extraordinario: May 31, July
　　　　　12, 25, Oct. 30.
　　1822　Jan. 5 – Mar. 23.
　WU
　　1818　June 27 – Dec. 31.
　　1819 – 1821　Jan. 1 – Dec. 31.

CORREO EXTRAORDINARIO DEL
ORINOCO.
　　Note: In Spanish, English and French.
　NN
　　1821　July 25.

ECOS DE ANGOSTURA. w.
　MWA
　　1911　Feb. 15.

ECO DEL ORINOCO. d. est. Mar. 2,
1909.
　MWA
　　1909　Mar. 2.

HERALDO. w.
　MWA
　　1910　Jan. 21.

EL LUCHADOR. d. est. 1905.
　CSt – H
　　1964　Sept. 21, 22, 24 – Dec. 31.
　　1965　Jan. 1 – Mar. 15, 17, 18, 26 –
　　　　　Apr. 1, 9 – June 22, 24 – Dec.
　　　　　9, 17 – 31.
　　1966　Jan. 1+.
　DLC
　　1930　Feb. 17.
　MWA
　　1909　Feb. 6, Mar. 1 – 8, 10.
　　1910　Nov. 24.
　　1913　June 26, 27.

NUEVO REGIMEN. sw.
MWA
1909   Feb. 12, Mar. 16.

PUEBLO LIBRE. sw.
MWA
1909   Mar. 17.

EL REFORMADOR. d. est. Feb. 11, 1893.
CtY
1893   Feb. 11 – Mar. 10.

Colón del Táchira

CAMPAÑA DEL BOSQUE. bw.
MWA
1911   Feb. 9.

PRECURSOR. irr.
MWA
1911   Feb. 7.

Coro

CONCILIADOR. w. est. June 28, 1902.
MWA
1905   July 31, Nov. 20.
1911   Feb. 27.

DIARIO DE CORO. d. est. Mar. 6, 1911.
MWA
1911   Mar. 6.

PRENSA. w.
MWA
1911   Mar. 3.

UNION. bw.
MWA
1905   Dec. 13.

Cumaná

CORREO DE CUMANA.
NcD
1845   May 26.

LUCIFER. w.
MWA
1911   Feb. 25.

OBSERVADOR. irr.
MWA
1905   May 11.

PORVENIR. w.
MWA
1907   Nov. 16.

El Tocuyo

COSMOPOLITA. w.
MWA
1911   Feb. 26.

Guacara

SENDA LIRICA. bw.
MWA
1911   Feb. 28.

Guanara

VOZ DE PORTUGUESA. bw. est. Dec.
1, 1905.
MWA
1905   Dec. 1 – 15.

Guanarito

CAMPAÑA. bw.
MWA
1908   Nov. 30.

Guatiré

ESFUERZO. w.
MWA
1905   June 17.

La Guaira

EL COMERCIO. est. [1859].
FU
1860   Feb. 4 – Dec. 3.

DIARIO. d.
MWA
1909   Aug. 9.

DIARIO DE LA GUAIRA. d. est. 1867.
NN
1888   Apr. 10, 11.

LA ESTRELLA.
NcD
1846   Nov. 25.

HERALDO. 3w.
MWA
1908   Nov. 21.

La Pascua

NOTICIAS.
MWA
1907   Mar. 19.

PAMPA. bw.
MWA
1906   Nov. 22.

La Victoria

CASTRO UNICO. d.
MWA
1907   Oct. 7, 8.

COLMENA. bw. est. Oct. 15, 1909.
MWA
1909   Oct. 15, Dec. 15.

INDUSTRIAL. w.
MWA
1911   Mar. 7.

UNION. [w.]
MWA
1910   Jan. 29.

Libertad

ECOS DE ROJAS. bw.
MWA
1908   Aug. 15, Oct. 15.

Maracaibo

ARTESANO. w. est. 1910.
MWA
1911   Feb. 25.

EL ATALAYA. w. est. Nov. 22, 1830.
  Note: Ceased publication Feb. 20,
  1831.
CtY
1830   Dec. 5 — 26.
1831   Jan. 2 — Feb. 20.

BENEFACTOR. w.
MWA
1911   Mar. 3.

EL CORREO NACIONAL. w. est. May
  14, 1821.
  Note: Ceased publication Nov. 10,
  1821.

ICN
1821   June 23 — Aug. 18, Sept. 1, 15 —
       Oct. 6, 20, 27, Nov. 10.
IU
1821   [June 7 — Nov. 10].
MWA
1821   [June 7 — Nov. 10].
WU
1821   [May 14 — Nov. 10].

CRONICA. 3m.
MWA
1911   Feb. 11, 21 — 23, Mar. 4.

DIARIO DE OCCIDENTE. d. est. June
  23, 1949.
DLC
1949   June 24, 27 — July 1, 6, 7, 11,
       13 — 31, Aug. 2 — 5, 7 — Sept.
       23, 25 — Oct. 12, 14 — 26, 28 —
       Dec. 16, 18 — 31.
1950   Jan. 1 — 4, 6 — Apr. 30.
1951   July 1 — 15, 17 — 21, 23, 25 —
       Aug. 28, 30 — Sept. 2, 4, 6 — 14,
       16 — Oct. 3, 5, 7, 9 — 11, 13 —
       Nov. 3, 5 — 27, Dec. 1 — 19,
       21 — 31.
1952   Jan. 3 — 18, 20 — Feb. 24, 26 —
       29, Mar. 8 — Apr. 24, 26 — June
       8, 10 — 26, 28, 30 — July 2, 4 —
       17, 19 — Sept. 2, 4 — 14, 16 — 26,
       28 — 30.
1953   Jan. 3 — Feb. 1, 3 — Mar. 10,
       12 — 31.

ECOS DEL ZULIA. d.
MWA
1911   Mar. 1.

ESTRELLA DE LA MAÑANA. w. est.
  Dec. 1907.
MWA
1911   Feb. 14.

EL FONOGRAFO. d. est. Aug. 14, 1889.
  Note: Ceased publication 1917.
DLC
1899   Sept. 18, Oct. 7, 17.

GUTTENBERG. d. est. 1911.
MWA
1911   Feb. 11.

INFORMACION. d. est. Sept. 1923.
MWA
  1936   Dec. 23.

THE MARACAIBO HERALD. w., 3w.
  est. Sept. 22, 1928.
    Note: In English.
  DLC
    1931   Apr. 22, 25.
    1942   July 11.

LA MARIPOSA. irr. est. Apr. 12, 1840.
    Note: Ceased publication Sept. 25,
    1842.
  DLC
    1840   Apr. 12 – July 31, Sept. 1 – 30,
            Nov. 1 – Dec. 31.
    1841   Jan. 1 – June 30.
    1842   Apr. 1 – 15, May 1 – June 30,
            July 15 – Aug. 31, Sept. 24.

·OBRERO. d.
  MWA
    1911   Feb. 10.

EL PAIS. d. est. 1929.
    Note: Succeeded *El Nivel*.
  DLC
    1930   July 24.

PAN Y LETRAS. [sw.] est. 1906.
  MWA
    1908   Dec. 29.
    1909   Jan. 9.

EL PANORAMA. d. est. Dec. 1, 1914.
  DLC
    1941   June 1, 2, 4 – 20, 22 – July 11,
            13 – 18, 20 – 22, 24, 25, 27 –
            31, Aug. 26 – Sept. 1, 3, 4, 6 –
            12, 14 – Oct. 16, 18 – 23, 25 –
            Dec. 11, 13 – 15, 17 – 23, 25 –
            31.
    1942   Jan. 1, 2, 4 – 6, 8, 10 – 16, 18 –
            30, Feb. 1 – 21, 25 – 27, Mar.
            2 – 6, 8 – 14, 17 – 20, 22 – 27,
            29 – Apr. 1, 5, 7 – 17, 19 – 24,
            26 – May 1, 3 – 16, 18 – June
            3, 5 – 26, 28, 30 – July 2, 4 – 23,
            25 – 27, 29 – Aug. 7, 9 – 13, 16,
            17, 21, 23, 24, 26 – 28, 30 –

            Sept. 1, 4, 6 – 11, 13, 15 – 23,
            25 – 29, Nov. 1 – 6, 10 – 13, 20,
            22 – 27, 29, 30, Dec. 2 – 4, 6 –
            12, 14 – 16, 18, 21 – 25, 28 –
            31.
    1943   Jan. 1, 2, 4 – 9, 11 – 16, 18 – 20,
            22 – 29, Feb. 1 – 3, 5, 6, 9 – 13,
            15, 16, 18 – 20, 22 – Sept. 9,
            11 – 29, Oct. 3 – 18, 20 – Dec.
            31.
    1944 – 1945   Jan. 1 – Dec. 31.
    1946   Jan. 1 – Dec. 30.
    1947   Jan. 2 – Dec. 31.
    1948   Jan. 2 – 26, 28 – Feb. 12, 14 –
            Apr. 17, 19 – 24, 26 – 29, June
            1 – 8, 10 – 19, 22, 23, 25, 27 –
            July 9, 11 – 22, 24, 26 – Aug. 5,
            7, 9 – 26, 31, Sept. 1, 3, 4, 6 –
            10, 16, 17, 19, 20, 22 – 24, 26,
            29, 30, Oct. 25 – Nov. 8, 10 –
            17, 19 – 21, 23, 24, 26, 28 – 30,
            Dec. 3 – 10.
    1949   May 1, 2, 4 – 8, 10 – 28, 30 –
            July 22, 24 – Aug. 7, 9 – 16,
            19 – Nov. 15, 17 – 19, 21 – 30,
            Dec. 2 – 17, 20 – 24.
    1950   Mar. 1 – 12, 14 – 17, 19 – May
            6, 9 – 11, 13 – 19, 21 – 30, June
            1 – 3, 5 – 30.
  MWA
    1936   Dec. 15.

SIGLO. 3w. est. Oct. 1910.
    Note: Ceased publication 1927.
  MWA
    1911   Mar. 4.

SITUACION. 3w.
  MWA
    1911   Feb. 17.

EL TELEGRAFO DEL ZULIA. w. est.
  Jan. 8, 1827.
    Note: Succeeded *El Tribuno*.
  DLC
    1827   Mar. 18.

TRIBUNA. d. est. Apr. 13, 1940.
    Note: Ceased publication Oct. 6,
    1941.

DLC
    1941   June 4, 6, 9—11, 13, 14, 17—
            20, 25—27, 30, July 1, 15, 16,
            18—23, 25—Aug. 7, 9—23,
            26—Sept. 1, 5—18, 20—26,
            29—Oct. 2, 4—6.

LA UNIVERSIDAD DE ZULIA. w. est.
    1956.
    LNT—MA
        1898—1899   Jan. 1—Dec. 31.
        1956   Oct. 6, 12, Nov. 18, 24, Dec.
                15.
        1957   Jan. 1—Dec. 31.
        1958   May 6, 26, Nov. 3.

EL ZULIA ILUSTRADO. w. est. Oct.
    24, 1888.
        Note: Ceased publication Dec. 31,
        1891.
    CU—B
        Micro (N)
        1888   Oct. 24—Dec. 31.
        1889—1891   Jan. 1—Dec. 31.

Maracay

LEALTAD POLITICA. est. Mar. 23, 1907.
    MWA
        1907   Mar. 23.

Maturín

ORIENTAL. 3m.
    MWA
        1910   Jan. 12.

Mérida

CENTENARIO DE LA IMPRENTA EN
    VENEZUELA. bw. est. July 28, 1905.
    MWA
        1905   July 28.

CRONISTA.
    MWA
        1907   Dec. 20.

PALANCA. irr.
    MWA
        1905   Nov. 12.

PAZ. w.
    MWA
        1855   Mar. 8, 22, July 4.

PROGRESO. w.
    MWA
        1908   Dec. 2.

PUEBLO. w.
    MWA
        1910   Jan. 1.

Pampán

IRIS. bw.
    MWA
        1911   Feb. 16.

Petaré

RESTAURADOR. bw.
    MWA
        1905   Dec. 15.

Porlamar

SOL. bw.
    MWA
        1906   Dec. 23.
        1909   Jan. 10.

Puerto Cabello

BOLETIN DE NOTICIAS. d.
    MWA
        1909   July 30.
        1911   Mar. 13.

CENTENARIO. bw.
    MWA
        1911   Mar. 15.

CLAMOR DEL PUEBLO.
    MWA
        1909   July 31.

CLAMOR PUBLICO.
    MWA
        1909   July 21.

DEFENSOR.
    MWA
        1909   July 20.

ECO SOCIAL. bw.
    MWA
        1907   Dec. 31.

LETRAS Y NUMEROS. d.
MWA
   1909   July 30.
   1911   Mar. 10.

PROGRESO. 3m.
MWA
   1909   July 10 — 30.

REPORTER. sw.
MWA
   1911   Mar. 11.

Puerto Nutrias

PRIMERA PIEDRA. bw.
MWA
   1911   Feb. 11.

Quibor

PROEMIO. irr.
MWA
   1907   Dec. 1.

Sanaré

SAETA. irr.
MWA
   1911   Feb. 22.

San Cristóbal

ESTUDIANTE. w.
MWA
   1905   July 15.

HORIZONTES. d.
MWA
   1911   Jan. 30.

IDEA RESTAURADORA. w.
MWA
   1905   Feb. 17.

INFORMACIONES. 4w.
MWA
   1908   Oct. 29.

TUERCA Y TORNILLO. w.
MWA
   1911   Feb. 25.

UNION Y LEY. w.
MWA
   1910   Jan. 19 — 26.

VARIEDADES. w.
MWA
   1905   Jan. 7.

VANGUARDIA. d. est. [1937].
DLC
   1940   Aug. 1 — 3, 5, 17, 27, Sept. 7, 9,
           10, 12, 14, 17.

San Felípe

CIUDADANO. w.
MWA
   1910   Jan. 27.

ECOS DEL PUEBLO. bw.
MWA
   1907   Oct. 2, Nov. 22.

PARNASIDES.
MWA
   1908   Sept. 20.

RECORTES. w.
MWA
   1911   Feb. 24 — Mar. 3.

RESTAURACION LIBERAL. d.
MWA
   1907   Dec. 2.
   1908   Nov. 16.

UNION INDUSTRIAL. bw.
MWA
   1907   Dec. 1.

YARACUY. d.
MWA
   1909   Jan. 26.

Soledad

VOZ DEL DISTRITO. w.
MWA
   1909   Mar. 13.

Táriba

RIPIOS ANDINOS. bw.
MWA
   1908   June 6.

Trujillo

DEBER. w.
MWA
   1911   Feb. 25.

ESTADO.
MWA
1910 Jan. 22.

GLADIADOR. w. est. Oct. 4, 1904.
MWA
1905 Nov. 16.

Turmero

BROQUEL. w.
MWA
1909 Nov. 6.

MOTOR. w.
MWA
1907 Nov. 16.

Valencia

ALFABETO. d. est. Sept. 4, 1909.
MWA
1909 Sept. 4.

CARABOBO. d.
MWA
1911 Feb. 10, Mar. 2, 7.

CHERCHA. irr.
MWA
1905 Aug. 2.

5 DE JULIO. bw.
MWA
1911 Mar. 7.

CORREO DE CARABOBO. 3w.
MWA
1907 Oct. 24—26.

LA CORRESPONDENCIA. d. est. 1882.
DLC
1882 June 30, July 1, 10, 12, 31, Aug.
3, 17, 19—22, 24—26, Sept. 25,
Oct. 5, 7, 31, Nov. 3, 4, 6, 10,
11, 16, 20, 22—24, 27, Dec. 2,
5, 7, 16.

CRONISTA. d.
MWA
1908 Oct. 15.
1911 Mar. 4, 7.

DEMOFILO. est. Mar. 9, 1911.
MWA
1911 Mar. 9.

DIARIO DE NOTICIAS. d.
MWA
1908 Oct. 15.

DISCIPULO. d., w.
MWA
1908 Oct. 9.
1911 Mar. 8.
NcD
1911 Mar. 9.

DONTIMOTEO. d. est. 1895.
MWA
1908 Oct. 3, 15.
1910 Apr. 12, 15.

GACETA OFICIAL.
Note: Removed from Caracas to
Valencia, Aug. 19, 1858—Feb. 3,
1859.
CtY
1858 Aug. 19—Dec. 31.
1859 Jan. 1—Feb. 3.
NcD
1858 Oct. 10.

JUSTICIA. w.
MWA
1907 Aug. 10.

LUCHA. sw. est. 1906.
MWA
1909 July 28.
1911 Mar. 4.

RADICAL. d. est. 1909.
MWA
1909 Oct. 22.
1911 Mar. 4.

REVISTA. w.
MWA
1911 Mar. 4.

TRUENO. sw.
MWA
1909 Aug. 27.

LA VOZ PUBLICA. d. est. 1875.
    Note: Ceased publication 1892.
DLC
    1885   Nov. 6, 11.

Valera
REVISTA DEL CENTRO INDUSTRIAL.
    MWA
        1907   Nov. 17.

Valle de la Pascua
CANDIL.
    MWA
        1908   Aug. 23.

Villa de Cura
INDEPENDIENTE. w.
    MWA
        1908   Apr. 9.

PUNTOS Y COMAS. w.
    MWA
        1910   Dec. 26.
        1911   Mar. 4.

Zaraza
UNARE. d.
    MWA
        1911   Jan. 13.

SELECTED BIBLIOGRAPHY

GENERAL

Babcock, Charles Edwin. Newspaper files in the Pan American Union Library. *In* Hispanic-American Historical Review, vol. 6, no. 4, p. 288-303. Durham, N. C.: Duke University Press, 1926.

Doyle, Henry Grattan. A tentative bibliography of the belles-lettres of the republics of Central America. Cambridge, Mass.: Harvard University Press, 1935. 136 p.

Editor and Publisher, vol. 53. International Year Book. New York, 1921- . Annual.

Handbook of Latin American Studies, no. 1. Gainesville, Fla.: University of Florida Press, 1935- . Annual.

Hoole, William Stanley. Foreign newspapers in southeastern libraries. University, Ala.: University of Alabama Press, 1963. 64 p.

Ibero-American Red Book. (Anuario de la prensa ibero-americana.) New York: Pan-American News Service, 1930. Annual.

Inter-Continental Press Guide, vol. 1- . La Habana: R. Rayneri, 1944. Monthly.

International Bureau of the American Republics. Newspaper directory of Latin America, Bulletin no. 42 (January, 1892). Washington, D.C.: U.S. Gov't. Printing Office, 1892. 38 p.

La Plata. Biblioteca de la Universidad Nacional. Catálogo de periódicos sudamericanos existentes en la Biblioteca Pública de la Universidad (1791-1861). [Buenos Aires: Imprenta López], 1934. 231 p.

Louisiana State University and Agricultural and Mechanical College Library. Newspaper files. [Baton Rouge], 1953. 147 p.

Marchant, Alexander Nelson de Armand. Boundaries of the Latin American Republics; an annotated list of documents, 1493-1943. Washington, D.C.: U.S. Dept. of State Publication no. 2082, Inter-American Series no. 24, 1944. v, 386 p.

Pan American Union. Repertorio de publicaciones periódicas actuales latinoamericanas. (Directory of current Latin American periodicals. Répertoire des périodiques en cours publiés en Amérique latine.) Paris: UNESCO, Bibliographical Handbook no. 8, 1958. xxv, 266 p.

La Prensa Ibero-Americana. [Buenos Aires]: Edición de la Revista Americana de Buenos Aires, 1937. Annual.

U.S. Library of Congress. A guide to the official publications of the other American republics. Ed. James B. Childs and Henry V. Besso. Latin American Series nos. 9-11, 15, 17, 19, 22-25, 27, 29-31, 33-

37. Washington, D. C.: U. S. Gov't Printing Office [1945]-1948. 19 vols.

ARGENTINA

Anuario de la prensa argentina. Buenos Aires, 1896. 428 p.

Anuario prensa argentina y latino-americana, no. [1]. Buenos Aires: Agencia de recortes "Los Diarios," 1939-

Beltrán, Óscar Rafael. Historia del periodismo argentino, pensamiento y obra de los forjadores de la patria. Buenos Aires: Editorial Sopena Argentina [1943]. 359 p.

Buenos Aires (Province). Dirección General de Estadística. El periodismo en la provincia de Buenos Aires, año 1907. La Plata: Taller de Impresiones Oficiales, 1908. 60 p.

Castiglione, José Francisco Luis. El periodismo en Santiago del Estero. Santiago del Estero: Editorial Yussem, 1941.

Fernández, Juan Rómulo. Historia del periodismo argentino. Buenos Aires [Librería Perlado], 1943. 406 p.

Galván Moreno, C. El periodismo argentino, ámplia y documentada historia desde sus orígenes hasta el presente. Buenos Aires: Editorial Claridad [1944]. 520 p.

López, Antonio. Historia de las instituciones argentinas. Buenos Aires, 1962. 415 p.

Mantilla, Manuel Florencio. Bibliografía periodística de la provincia de Corrientes. Buenos Aires: Imprenta y Librería de Mayo, 1887. 167 p.

Méndez Paz, Emilio. Periódicos correntinos, 1825-1900. Buenos Aires, 1953. 123 p.

Orzali, Ignacio. La prensa argentina. Buenos Aires: Imprenta de J. Peuser, 1893. 218 p.

Peña, Enrique A. Estudio de los periódicos y revistas existentes en la "Biblioteca Enrique Peña." Buenos Aires: Imprenta Amorrortú, 1935. 632 p.

Pereyra, Miguel Carlos. Acción e influencia del periodismo argentino en la cultura popular. Rosario de Santa Fé: Fenner, 1918. 93 p.

BOLIVIA

Bolivia en el primer centenario de su independencia [New York: The University Society, 1925?] xvii, 1142 p.

Loza, Léon M. Bosquejo histórico del periodismo boliviano. 2d ed. La Paz, 1926. 48 p.

Mendoza L., Gunnar, et al. Contribución a la historia del periodismo en Bolivia. Sucre: Universidad de San Francisco Xavier, 1962. 77 p.

Moreno, Gabriel René. Ensayo de una bibliografía general de los periódicos de Bolivia, 1825-1905. Santiago de Chile, 1905. 344 p.

———— Suplemento de una bibliografía general de los periódicos de Bolivia, 1905-7. Santiago de Chile, 1908. 17 p.

BRAZIL

Bahia, Juarez. Três fases da imprensa brasileira. Santos: Editora Presença, 1960. 124 p.

Bahia, Brasil (State). Imprensa periódica. Bahia: Departamento Estadual de Estadística, 1947- .

Bellido, Remijio de. Catálogo dos jornães paraenses, 1822-1908. Pará: Imprensa Oficial, 1908. 163 p.

Bessa, Alberto. 100 annos de vida; a expensão da imprensa brasileira no primeiro seculo da sua existencia. Lisboa: Livraria Central de G. de Carvalho, 1929. 313 p.

Brasil. Departamento de Imprensa e Propaganda. Relação das publicações periódicas brasileiras anotadas na secretaria do Conselho Nacional de Imprensa. Rio de Janeiro [1945]. 257 p.

Carvalho, Alfredo de. Annaes da imprensa periódica pernambucana de 1821-1908. Recife: Tipografia do "Jornal do Recife," 1908. 640 p.

Fonseca, Gondin da. Biografia do jornalismo carioca (1808-1908). Rio de Janeiro: Livraria Quaresma, 1941. 416 p.

Instituto historico e geográfico brasileiro. Revista do Instituto historico e geografico brasileiro. vol. 1- . Tomo consagrado á exposicão commemorativa do primeiro centenario da imprensa periódica no Brasil, promovida pelo mesmo Instituto. Rio de Janeiro: Imprensa Nacional, 1908.

Nobre, José Freitas. História da imprensa de São Paulo. São Paulo: Edicões LEIA, 1950. 267 p.

Otero, Gustavo Adolfo. El periodismo en América, esquema de su historia a través de la cultura latino-americana (1492-1946). Lima [Editorial PTCM], 1946. 475 p.

Pontes, Eloy. The press in the intellectual formation of Brazil. Rio de Janeiro: Imprensa Nacional, 1943. 56 p.

The press of the state of São Paulo, Brazil, 1827-1904. São Paulo: Vanorden, 1904. 20 p.

Quesada, Ernesto. Discurso pronunciado en el banquete dado á los periodistas brasileños el sábado 27 de octubre de 1900. Buenos Aires: Bredahl, 1900.

Serra Sobrinho, Joaquim Maria. [Ignotus, *pseud.*] Sessenta annos de jornalismo: a imprensa no Maranhão, 1820-80. Rio de Janeiro; Faro e Lino, 1883. 153 p.

Studart, Guilherme. Catálogo dos jornães de pequeno e grande formato publicados em Ceará. Fortaleza: Tipografia Studart, 1896. 32 p.

———. Para a historia do jornalismo cearense, 1824-1924. Fortaleza: Tipografia Moderna do F. Carneiro, 1924. 228 p.

Timotheo, Pedro (ed.). Antologia do jornalismo brasileiro; seleção, preâmbulo e biografias. Rio [de Janeiro]: Z. Valverde, 1944- .

Vianna, Helio. Contribuição à história da imprensa brasileira, 1812-69. Rio de Janeiro: Imprensa Nacional, 1945. 664 p.

CHILE

Anrique Reyes, Nicolás. Bibliografía de las principales revistas y periódicos de Chile. (Anales, vol 115, p. [121]-62.) Santiago de Chile: Universidad de Chile, 1904.

Chacón del Campo, Julio. Reseña histórica de la prensa de Parral y relación de sus fiestas cincuentenarias. Parral: Imprenta "La Democracia," 1915. 84 p.

Edwards, Agustín. Elogio de don Eliodoro Yáñez y bosquejo panorámico de la prensa chilena. Santiago de Chile: Imprenta Universitaria, 1933. 166 p.

Hernández Cornejo, Roberto. Vistazo periodístico a los ochenta años. Valparaíso: Imprenta Victoria, 1958. 118 p.

Santiago de Chile. Biblioteca Nacional. Anuario de publicaciones periódicas chilenas. [Santiago de Chile.]

———. Semana retrospectiva de la prensa chilena. [Santiago de Chile]: Prensas de la Universidad de Chile, 1934. 90 p.

Silva, Jorge Gustavo. Los trabajadores del periodismo en Chile; memoria para optar a la calidad de profesor extraordinario de economía social y legislación obrera, en la Escuela de ciencias juridicas y sociales de la Universidad de Chile. Santiago de Chile: Imprenta Nacional, 1929. 139 p.

Silva Castro, Raúl. Prensa y periodismo en Chile, 1812-1956. [Santiago de Chile]: Ediciones de la Universidad de Chile, 1958. 413 p.

COLOMBIA

Arboleda, Gustavo. Apuntes sobre la imprenta y el periodismo en Popayán, 1813-99. Guayaquil: Talleres Poligráficos de "El Grito del Pueblo," 1905. iv, 56 p.

Bogotá. Biblioteca Nacional. Catálogo de todos los periódicos que existen desde su fundación hasta el año de 1915, inclusivo. Bogotá: Imprenta Nacional, 1917. 366 p.

———. Catálogo de todos los periódicos que existen desde su fundación hasta el año de 1935, inclusivo. Bogotá: Editorial "El Gráfico," 1936. 2 vol. 440 p., 481 p.

———. Catálogo de publicaciones del interior de Colombia. Bogotá. [n.d.].

Giraldo Jaramillo, Gabriel. Bibliografía de bibliografías colombianas. 2d ed.; Bogotá: Publicaciones del Instituto Caro y Cuervo, Serie bibliográfica 1, 1960. xvi, 204 p.

Martínez Delgado, Luis. El periodismo en la Nueva Granada, 1810-11. Bogotá: Editorial Kelly, 1960. 538 p.

Otero Muñoz, Gustavo. Don Manuel del Socorro Rodríguez; homenaje en el II centenario de su nacimiento. [Bogotá]: Banco de la República [1956]. 29 p.

———. Historia del periodismo en Colombia. [Bogotá: Editorial Minerva, 1936.] 140 p.

Periodismo colombiano, vol. 1 (May 1, 1962). Medellín: J. Olarte, 1962. Monthly.

Rodríguez, Marco Tulio. La gran prensa en Colombia. Bogotá: Editorial Minerva, 1963. 183 p.

Santos, Eduardo. La crisis de la democracia en Colombia y "El Tiempo." México: Gráfica Panamericana, 1955. 236 p.

Torre Revello, José. Ensayo de una biografía del bibliotecario y periodista don Manuel del Socorro Rodríguez. Bogotá: Instituto Caro y Cuervo, 1947. 35 p.

Vérez de Peraza, Elena Luisa. Directorio de revistas y periódicos de Medellín. Medellín: Ediciones Anuario Bibliográfico Cubano, 1962. 211.

COSTA RICA

Nuñez, Francisco María. La evolución del periodismo en Costa Rica. [vol. 1.] San José de Costa Rica: Imprenta Minerva, 1921. 86 p.

———. La evolución del periodismo en Costa Rica, 1833-1946; síntesis histórica escrita con motivo del cuarto Congreso Panamericano de Prensa. San José de Costa Rica, 1946. 15 p.

CUBA

Alcover y Beltrán, Antonio M. El periodismo en Sagua; sus manifestaciones. La Habana [Tipografía "La Australia"], 1901.

Alfonso Gonsé, Raoul, y Martí, Jorge Luis. En defensa de "El Mundo." La Habana, 1956. 347 p.

Aragonés Machado, Alberto. El periodismo en Las Villas. [Cienfuegos], 1953. 57 p.

Botifoll, Luis J. Golpe de estado en "El Mundo"; una página dolorosa del periodismo cubano. La Habana, 1955. 178 p.

Cepero Bonilla, Raúl. "El Siglo," 1862-68, un periódico en lucha contra la censura; conferencia pronunciada en el Lyceum y Lawn Tennis Club, el 19 de noviembre de 1957. La Habana, 1957. 85 p.

Cuesta Jiménez, Valentín Bernardo. Evolución del papel periódico en Güines; historia de la imprenta y del periodismo desde 1862 a 1899. [Güines: Biblioteca "Ideas"], 1956. 52 p.

Deschamps Chapeaux, Pedro. El negro en el periodismo cubano en el siglo XIX; ensayo bibliográfico. La Habana: Ediciones [Revolución], 1963. 110 p.

Directorio de revistas y periódicos de Cuba. La Habana: Anuario Bibliográfico Cubano, 1942. Annual.

Fina García, Francisco. Bibliografía de la prensa del término municipal de Santiago de las Vegas. Santiago de las Vegas: Asociación de corresponsales y prensa local, 1941. 4 p.

————. La prensa en Santiago de las Vegas. Santiago de las Vegas: Editorial "Antena," 1961. 15 p.

Guiral Moreno, Mario. "Cuba contemporánea," su origen, su existencia, y su significación. La Habana: Molina y Compañía, 1940. 36 p.

Llaverías Martínez, Joaquín. Contribución a la historia de la prensa periódica. (Publicaciones del Archivo Nacional de Cuba, nos. 47-48.) La Habana, 1957. 2 vols.

Martínez-Moles, Manuel. Periodismo y periódicos espirituanos. La Habana: Imprenta "El Siglo XX," 1930. 91 p.

Moliner, Israel M. Índice cronológico de la prensa en Matanzas. [Matanzas: Atenas de Cuba, 1955.] 18 p.

Peraza Sarausa, Fermín. Exhibición de la prensa cubana contemporánea. (Catálogo junio 7-11, 1943.) La Habana: Capitolio Nacional [1943]. 45 p.

Ponte Domínguez, Francisco José. El Cubana libre; una conferencia universitaria y un estudio adicional. La Habana: Editorial "Modas Magazine," 1957. 32 p.

Portell Vilá, Herminio. Medio siglo de "El Mundo"; historia de un gran periódico. La Habana [Editorial Lex], 1951. 172 p.

Portuondo, José Antonio. "La Aurora" y los comienzos de la prensa y de la organización obrera en Cuba. [La Habana]: Imprenta Nacional de Cuba, 1961. 115 p.

Roig de Leuchsenring, Emilio. El sesquicentenario del "Papel periódico de la Habana," primera de las publicaciones literarias de Cuba. La Habana: Molina y Compañía, 1941. 45 p.

Soto Paz, Rafael. Antología de periodistas cubanos; 35 biografías, 35 artículos. La Habana: Empresa Editora de Publicaciones, 1943. 256 p.

Dominican Republic

Amiama, Manuel A. El periodismo en la República Dominicana; notas para la historia crítico-narrativa del periodisma [sic] nacional, desde sus orígines [sic] hasta nuestros días. Santo Domingo: Talleres Tipográficos "La Nación," 1933. 95 p.

Boletín Bibliográfico Dominicano, año 1. Santo Domingo, julio-agosto-septiembre-diciembre, 1945.

Franco, Persio Celeste. Algunas ideas. Santiago de los Caballeros, 1926. 28 p.

Lugo Lovatón, Ramón. Periódicos dominicanos en el Archivo General de "La Nación." Santo Domingo: Editora Montalvo, 1953. 49 p.

Martínez, Julio César, y Ruíz Mejía, Rafael E. (eds.). El caso de "La Nación" ante la opinión pública. Santo Domingo: Editora del Caribe, 1962. 80 p.

Ecuador

Andrade Chiriboga, Alfonso. Hemeroteca azuaya. Cuenca: Editora "El Mercurio," 1950. 2 vols. 288 p., 246 p.

Andrade Coello, Alejandro. En torno de la prensa nacional. Quito: Imprenta "Ecuador," 1937. 143 p.

Anuario de la prensa ecuatoriana [año I]-III, 1892-94. Guayaquil: Biblioteca Municipal de Guayaquil, 1893-1895.

Árias Robalino, Augusto. El periodismo ecuatoriano. [Quito: Imprenta de la Universidad Central, 1938.]

[Casanova Loor, Neptali (ed.).] El Centenario; homenaje al centenario de la república . . . 1830-1930, cien años. Guayaquil: Imprenta "El Tiempo," 1930. 476 p.

Destruge, Camilo. Historia de la prensa de Guayaquil. (Memorias de la Academía Nacional de Historia, vols. 2-3) Quito: Tipografía y Encuadernación Salesianas, 1924-1925.

Ecuador. Biblioteca Nacional. Exposición del periodismo ecuatoriano — Quito, 13 de abril de 1941. [Quito]: Talleres gráficos del Ministerio de Educación, 1941. 119 p.

Jaramillo, Miguel Ángel. Índice bibliográfico de las revistas de la biblioteca "Jaramillo" de escritos nacionales. Cuenca [Editorial del Núcleo del Azuay de la Casa de la Cultura Ecuatoriana], 1953. 180 p.

Rodríguez, Máximo A. El periodismo lojano. Quito: Casa de la Cultura Ecuatoriana, 1948. 117 p.

Rolando, Carlos A. Cronología del periodismo ecuatoriano. Guayaquil: Imprenta Monteverde y Velarde, 1920. 166 p.

―――. Cronología del periodismo ecuatoriano. Guayaquil: Tipografía y Litografía de la Sociedad Filantrópica del Guayas, 1934. 87 p.

Vaca del Pozo, Telmo N. El periodismo y las leyes de imprenta. Guayaquil: Imprenta de la Universidad, 1941. 186 p.

EL SALVADOR

Gallegos Valdés, Luis. Panorama de la literatura salvadoreña. [2d. ed.] San Salvador: Ministerio de Educación, Dirección, General de Publicaciones [1962]. 238 p.

Lardé y Larín, Jorge. Orígenes del periodismo en El Salvador. [San Salvador: Ministerio de Cultura], 1950. 158 p.

San Salvador, Exposición Continental del Periódico Americano, celebrada en San Salvador, del 1° al 31 de julio de 1960. San Salvador: Ministerio de Cultura [1960]. 409 p.

GUATEMALA

Guatemala (City). Biblioteca Nacional. Catálogo. Ciudad de Guatemala, 1932. 257 p.

Villacorta Calderón, José Antonio. Bibliografía guatemalteca . . . Exposiciones abiertas en el Salón de historia y bellas-artes del Museo Nacional, en los meses de noviembre de 1939-42. Ciudad de Guatemala: Tipografía Nacional, 1944. 638 p.

HAITI

Bissainthe, Max. Dictionnaire de bibliographie haïtienne. Washington. D.C.: Scarecrow Press, 1951. x, 1051 p.

Cabon, Adolphe. Cabon's history of Haiti journalism. (Reprinted from the Proceedings of the American Antiquarian Society for April, 1939.) Worcester, Mass.: The Society, 1940. 87 p.

Vaval, Duraciné. Histoire de la littérature haïtienne; ou "L'âme noire." Port-au-Prince: Imprimerie Aug. A. Héraux, 1933. 506 p.

HONDURAS

Coello, Augusto C. La imprenta y el periódico oficial en Honduras. Tegucigalpa: Tipografía Nacional, 1929. 7 p.

Valle, Rafael H. El periodismo en Honduras; notas para su historia. [México, 1960?], 84 p.

MEXICO

Almada, Francisco R. La imprenta y el periodismo en Chihuahua. Publicación del gobierno del Estado de Chihuahua. México, 1943. 40 p.

Andrade, Vicente de Paula. Noticia de los periódicos que se publicaron durante el siglo XIX, dentro y fuera de la capital. México: Tipografía de "El Tiempo," 1901. 57 p.

Audit Bureau of Circulations. ABC Blue Book. (Newspaper publisher's statements.) [Chicago, 1940?]

Campeche, México (State). Centenario de "El espíritu público"; Biografía de un periódico. Campeche, 1957. 208 p.

Carrasco Puente, Rafael. Hemerografía de Zacatecas, 1825-1950; con datos biográficos de algunos periodistas zacatecanos. México: Secretaría de Relaciones Exteriores, Departamento de Información para el Extranjero, 1951. 203 p.

―――. La prensa en México; datos históricos. [México]: Universidad Nacional Autónoma de México, 1962. 300 p.

Cordero y Torres, Enrique. Historia del periodismo en Puebla, 1820-1946. [Puebla]: Editorial de Bohemia Poblana [1947]. 595 p.

Estrada Rousseau, Manuel. El cuarto poder en Sinaloa. [Culiacán?], 1943. 39 p.

González, Héctor. Bibliografía del Estado de Nuevo León de 1820 a 1946. [Monterrey, 1946.] 63 p.

Huitrón, Malaquías (ed.). Reseña histórica del periodismo y de la imprenta, en el Estado de México. Toluca [Escuela de Artes y Oficios], 1943. 127 p.

Ibarra de Anda, Fortino. El periodismo en México, lo que es y lo que debe ser; un estudio del periódico y del periodista mexicanos y de las posibilidades de ambos para el futuro. México: Imprenta Mundial, 1934-35. 2 vols. 183 p., 132 p.

Iguíniz, Juan Bautista. El periodismo en Guadalajara, 1809-1915. Guadalajara: Universidad de Guadalajara, 1955. 2 vols.

Lelevier, Armando I. Historia del periodismo y la imprenta en el territorio norte de la Baja California. México [Talleres Gráficos de "La Nación"], 1943. 29 p.

Lepidus, Henry. The history of Mexican journalism. (The University of Missouri Bulletin, vol. 29, no. 4, Journalism Series no. 49.) [Columbia, Mo.], 1928. 87 p.

McLean, Malcolm D. El contenido literario de "El Siglo diez y nueve." Washington, D.C.: Inter-American Bibliographical and Library Association, 1940. 75 p.

María y Campos, Armando de. Reseña histórica del periodismo español en México, 1821-1932. México: Compañía Editora, Distribuidora de Ediciones, 1960. 116 p.

Meade, Joaquín. Hemerografía potosina; historia del periodismo en San Luis Potosí, 1828-1956. San Luis Potosí: Bajo el Ángulo de Letras Potosinas, 1956. 199 p.

Mendoza López, Margarita. Catálogo de publicaciones periódicas mexicanas. México, 1959. xi, 262 p.

Menéndez, Carlos R. La evolución de la prensa en la península de Yucatán (Yucatán y Campeche) a través de los últimos cien años. Mérida: Talleres de la Compañía Tipográfica Yucateca, 1931. 136 p.

México. Oficina Técnica Postal. Lista general de publicaciones registradas como artículos de segunda clase, vigente hasta el 30 de noviembre de 1935. México [Multigrafos SCOP], 1936. 49 p.

México. Oficina Técnica Postal. Lista general de publicaciones registradas como artículo de segunda clase, vigente hasta el 31 de diciembre de 1943. México [Multigrafos SCOP], 1944. 32 p.

Moore, Ernest Richard. Notas bibliográficas sobre la prensa insurgente. Chihuahua, 1942. 114 p.

Ortega, Miguel F. La imprenta y el periodismo en el sur, en el siglo XIX. México [Editorial "Pluma y Lápiz" de México], 1943. 58 p.

Pérez Galaz, Juan de Dios. Reseña histórica del periodismo en Campeche. Campeche [Talleres Linotipográficos del Gobierno del Estado], 1943. 45 p.

Rodríguez Frausto, J. Jesús. Orígenes de la imprenta y el periodismo en Guanajuato. [Guanajuato]: Universidad de Guanajuato, Archivo Histórico, 1961. 107 p.

Romero Flores, Jesús. Apuntes para una bibliografía geográfica e histórica de Michoacán. (Monografías bibliográficas mexicanas, no. 25.) México [Imprenta de la Secretaría de Relaciones Exteriores], 1932. 325 p.

Ruíz Casteñeda, María del Carmen. El periodismo político de la reforma en la ciudad de México, 1854-61. México, 1950. 112 *l*.

Santamaría, Francisco Javier. Datos, materiales, y apuntes para la historia del periodismo en Tabasco (1825-1935). México: Ediciones Botas, 1936. 314 p.

Sierra, Carlos J. Periodismo mexicano ante la Intervención Francesa: hemerografía, 1861-63. (Congreso Nacional de Historia para el Estudio de la Guerra de Intervención, Colección 6.) México [Sociedad Mexicana de Geografía y Estadística, Sección de Historia], 1962. 173 p.

Tavera Alfaro, Xavier (ed.). El nacionalismo en la prensa mexicana del siglo XVIII. México: Club de Periodistas de México, 1963. lxxx, 189 p.

Torres, Teodoro. Periodismo. México: Ediciones Botas, 1937. 272 p.

Velasco Valdés, Miguel. Historia del periodismo mexicano; apuntes. México: Librería de Manuel Porrúa [1955]. 258 p.

NICARAGUA

Montalván, José H. Breves apuntes para la historia del periodismo nicaragüense. León: Universidad Nacional de Nicaragua, 1958.

Rivas y Solís, Ernesto. Periodismo. [Granada: Editorial "La Nueva Prensa," 1944.] 20 p.

PANAMA

Doyle, Henry Grattan. A tentative bibliography of the belles-lettres of Panamá. Cambridge, Mass.: Harvard University Press, 1934. 21 p.

[Recuero, María T.] Breve historia del periodismo en Panamá. [Panamá, 1935.] 196 p.

PARAGUAY

Centurión, Carlos R. Historia de las letras paraguayas. Buenos Aires: Editorial Ayacucho [1947-51]. 3 vols.

PERU

Leavitt, Sturgis Elleno. A bibliography of Peruvian literature (1821-1919). (Reprinted from The Romantic Review, vol. 13, no. 2, April-June, 1922, p. 151-194.)

[New York: Columbia University Press, 1922.]

Lima: Exposición de la prensa peruana. Primera Exposición, 1941. [Lima: Compañía Editora "El Universal," 1941.] [54 p.]

Magazine and newspaper publications in Perú. [n.p., 1941?] 68 l.

Medina, José Toribio. La imprenta en Arequipa, el Cuzco, Trujillo, y otros pueblos del Perú durante las campañas de la independencia (1820-25). Santiago de Chile: Imprenta Elzeviriana, 1904. 71 p.

———. La imprenta en Lima (1584-1824). Santiago de Chile: Impreso y grabado en casa del autor, 1904-7. 4 vols.

Paz Soldán, Mariano Felipe. Biblioteca peruana. Lima: Imprenta Liberal, 1879. 544 p.

Romero, Carlos Alberto. Los orígenes del periodismo en el Perú; de la relación al diario, 1594-1790. Lima: Gil, 1940. 71 p.

Winship, George Parker. Early South American newspapers. (Reprinted from the Proceedings of the American Antiquarian Society for October, 1908.) Worcester [Mass.: Davis Press], 1908. 11 p.

Zevallos Quiñes, Jorge. La imprenta en el norte del Perú; Trujillo, Piura, Huarás, Cajamarca, Chachapoyas, 1823-1900. Lima: Compañía de Impresiones y Publicidad, 1949. 84 p.

———. La imprenta en Lambayeque. Lima: Compañía de Impresiones y Publicidad, 1947. 79 p.

———. La imprenta en Lambayeque. (Adiciones.) Lima: Compañía de Impresiones y Publicidad, 1948. 25 p.

PUERTO RICO

Pedreira, Antonio Salvador. El periodismo en Puerto Rico, bosquejo histórico desde su iniciación hasta el 1930. La Habana: Imprenta Úcar, García y Compañía [1941]. 4 p.

URUGUAY

Lockhart, Washington. Historia del periodismo en Soriano. [Mercedes: Ediciones Revista Histórica de Soriano, 1963.] 82 p.

Montevideo. Biblioteca Nacional. Anales de la bibliografía uruguaya. Montevideo: Imprenta de "La Nación," 1896. 1 vol.

———. Catálogo de publicaciones periódicas de Montevideo. Montevideo [n.d.].

———. Memoria. 26 julio, 1880-diciembre, 1883. Montevideo, 1881-85. 3 vols.

Musso Ambrosi, Luis Alberto. Bibiografía de bibliografías uruguayas, con aportes a la historia del periodismo en el Uruguay. Montevideo, 1964. vii, 102 p.

Zinny, Antonio. Historia de la prensa periódica de la República Oriental del Uruguay, 1807-52. Buenos Aires: C. Casavalle, 1883. xxix, 504 p.

VENEZUELA

Biblioteca nacional. Anuario bibliográfico venezolano. Caracas: Tipografía Americana, 1942.

———. Alcance: Escritores venezolanos fallecidos entre 1942 y 1947. Caracas [n.d.].